HUTCHINS'

Small and Major Works
UK Building Costs Blackbook

2009 Edition

HUTCHINS'

Small and Major Works
UK Building Costs Blackbook

Compiled by
Franklin + Andrews Ltd
Construction Economists
Sea Containers House
20 Upper Ground
London SE1 9LZ

2009 Edition

Compiled and written
by Franklin + Andrews Ltd
Sea Containers House, Upper Ground, London, SE1 9LZ

© 2008 Franklin + Andrews Ltd

First Published
1945 – Hutchins' Small Works
1997 – Hutchins' Major Works

Printed in Great Britain by:
Antony Rowe
Bumper's Farm Industrial Estate
Chippenham, Wiltshire SN14 6LH

Typeset by: Spire Origination, Norwich

ISBN 978 1 901856 21 7

Contents

9th Edition

Franklin + Andrews Worldwide Offices

UK Offices

South East
London Head Office:
Franklin + Andrews
Sea Containers House
3rd Floor, 20 Upper Ground
London SE1 9LZ
Tel: +44 (0) 20 7633 9966
Fax: +44 (0) 20 7928 2471

Osprey Mott MacDonald Project
Management Ltd
10-11 Charterhouse Square
London EC1M 6EH
Tel: +44 (0) 20 7566 7900
Fax: +44 (0) 20 7566 7911

Norwich:
2nd Floor, East Wing
69-75 Thorpe Road
Norwich
NR1 1UA
Tel: +44 (0) 1603 226790
Fax: +44 (0) 1603 619365

Reading:
9th Floor
Thames Tower
37-45 Station Road
Reading
RG1 1LX
Tel: +44 (0) 1189 027800

Midlands
Birmingham:
Canterbury House
85 Newhall Street
Birmingham
B3 1LZ
Tel: +44 (0) 121 237 4250
Fax: +44 (0) 121 237 4251

North East
Leeds:
1st Floor Marshall Court
Marshall Street
Leeds
LS11 9YP
Tel: +44 (0) 113 394 6680
Fax: +44 (0) 113 394 6681

Sheffield:
Mott MacDonald House
111 St Mary's Road
Sheffield S2 4AP
Tel: +44 (0) 114 276 1242
Tel: +44 (0) 114 272 4699

North West
Chester:
No 10, Heritage Court
Lower Bridge Street
Chester CH1 1RD
Tel: +44 (0) 124 434 6261
Fax: +44 (0) 124 434 6008

Cumbria:
BNFL Sellafield
B537
Sellafield
Seascale
Cumbria
CA20 1PG

Manchester:
Spring Bank House
33 Stamford Street
Altrincham
Cheshire
WA14 1ES
Tel: +44 (0) 161 926 4000
Fax: +44 (0) 161 926 4100

Liverpool:
Merseyside Information Service
325 Royal Liver Building
Pier Head
Liverpool
Merseyside
L3 1JH
Tel: +44 (0) 151 236 4343
Fax: +44 (0) 151 236 2521

Western
Cardiff:
Fitzalan House
Fitzalan Road
Cardiff CF24 0EL
Tel: +44 (0) 292 046 7800
Fax: +44 (0) 292 046 7801

Colwyn Bay:
Ty Mott MacDonald
Woodland Road West
Colwyn Bay
LL29 7DH
Tel: +44 (0) 1492 534601
Fax: +44 (0) 1492 533063

Exeter:
31/32 Southernhay East
Exeter
Devon EX1 1NS
Tel: +44 (0) 139 220 7725
Fax: +44 (0) 139 220 7726

Scotland
Aberdeen:
16 Albert Street
Aberdeen
AB25 1XQ
Tel: +44 (0) 122 464 1348
Fax: +44 (0) 122 464 2640

Edinburgh:
Caledonian Exchange
3rd Floor
19A Canning Street
Edinburgh
EH3 8EG
Tel: +44 (0) 131 221 2300
Fax: +44 (0) 131 221 2399

Glasgow:
1 Atlantic Quay
Broomielaw
Glasgow
G2 8JB
Tel: +44 (0) 141 222 4500
Fax: +44 (0) 141 222 2048

Overseas Offices

Hong Kong:
7/F West Wing Office Building
New World Centre
20 Salisbury Road
Tsimshatsui
Kowloon
Hong Kong
Tel: +852 2828 5757
Fax: +852 2827 1823

Singapore:
Franklin + Andrews Pte Ltd
6 Raffles Quay
#17-02
Singapore
Tel: +65 6293 1900
Fax: +65 6293 1911

China:
HLSP China Office
A-1202 China International
Science & Tech Conference Centre
12 Yumin Road
Beijing 100029
China
Tel: +8610 8225 0257
Fax: +8610 8225 9779

Europe

Ireland:
Franklin + Andrews Ireland
4th Floor
South Block
Rockfield
Dundrum
Dublin 16 Ireland
Tel: +353 1 291 6750
Fax: +353 1 291 6760

Americas

Overseas Associations

Australia
Botswana
Ireland
Kuwait
Namibia
New Zealand
Portugal
South Africa
Thailand
Turkey
USA

Aberdeen
16 Albert Street
Aberdeen
AB25 1XQ
Tel: +44 (0) 1224 641348
Fax: +44 (0) 1224 642640

Abu Dhabi
PO Box 47094
Al Hashmi Tower
Airport Road
Abu Dhabi
Tel: +971 2 445 7470
Fax: +971 2 445 7490

Ankara
Milli Egitim Bankanligi (MEB)
Projeler Koordinasyon Merkezi
Besevler Kampsu
C-Blok,Kat Zemin 1-2
Teknikokullar
Ankara
Turkey

Bali
Jl Tukad Yeh Aye No 75x
Denpaser
Bali
Indonesia
Tel: +62 361 226401
Fax: +62 361 226401

Bangkok
5th Floor, Chamnan Phenjati Building
65/56-57, Rama 9 Road, Huay Kwang
Bangkok 10320, Thailand
Tel: +662 643 6848
Fax: +662 643 2514

Beijing
A-1202-China Int'l Science & Technology
Convention Centre
12 Yumin Road
Beijing
100029
China
Tel: +86 (0) 10 82250257
Fax: +86 (0) 10 8225 9779

Belfast
40 Linen Hall Street
Belfast
Northern Ireland
BT2 8BA
Tel: +44(0)28 9089 5850
Fax: +44(0)28 9023 5145

Birmingham
Canterbury House
85 Newhall Street
Birmingham
B3 1LZ
Tel: +44 (0) 121 2374000
Fax:+44 (0) 121 2374001

Brighton
John Proctor Travel Ltd
4 Church Street
Brighton
BN1 1UJ
Tel: +44 (0) 1273 811400
Fax: +44 (0) 1273 677380

Brighton
Victory House
Trafalgar Place
Brighton
BN1 4FY
Tel: +44 (0) 1273 365000
Fax:+44 (0) 1273 365100

Bristol
Prince House
43-51 Prince Street
Bristol
BS1 4PS
Tel: +44 (0) 117 9069500
Fax: +44 (0) 117 9221924

Bucharest
Iancu Capitanu Street No 15
District 2
21361 Bucharest
Romania
Tel: +40 (0) 21 252 2738
Fax: +40 (0) 21 252 2737

Cairo
Assiut Barrage Joint Venture Office
30 Haroun Street (First Floor)
Dokki
Giza
Greater Cairo
Egypt
Tel +202 336 4723
Fax: +202 749 2264

6th floor
Irrigation Improvement Dept
Fum el Ismailia Irrigation
Building, Shoubra El Mezalat
Cairo, Egypt
Tel: +202 444 1192
Fax: +202 444 1192

Cambridge
Demeter House
Station Road
Cambridge
CB1 2RS
Tel: +44 (0) 1223 463500
Fax: +44 (0) 1223 461007

Cardiff
Fitzalan House
Fitzalan Road
Cardiff
CF24 0EL
Tel: +44 (0) 29 2046 7800
Fax: +44 (0) 29 2046 7801

Colwyn Bay
Woodland Road West
Colwyn Bay
LL29 7DH
Tel: +44 (0) 1492 534601
Fax: +44 (0) 1492 533063

Croydon
St Anne House
20-26 Wellesley Road
Croydon
Surrey
CR9 2UL
Tel: +44 (0) 20 8774 2000
Fax: +44 (0) 20 8681 5706

Delhi NOIDA Premier
A20
Sector 2
NOIDA
201301
India
Tel: +91 (0) 120 254 3582
Fax: +91 (0) 120 254 3582

Derby- Profile House
Profile House
Sir Frank Whittle Road
Derby
DE21 4XE
Tel: 01332 378899
Fax: 01332 378890

Dhaka
HSLP Ltd
A1, Contessa
Plot 1/B
House 82
Road 123
Gulshan 1
Dhaka 1212
Bangladesh
Tel: +880 (0) 2 882 4026
Tel: +880 (0) 2 882 3393

Dubai
PO Box 11302
Emarat Atrium Building
Sheik Zayed Road
Dubai
239-246
United Arab Emirates
Tel: +971 (0) 4 3434 218
Fax: +971 (0) 4 3434 281

Durham
1 West Durham Office Park
St Johns Road
Meadowfield
Durham
DH7 8RD
Tel: +44 (0) 191 378 6700

Edinburgh
Caledonian Exchange
3rd Floor, 19A Canning Street
Edinburgh
EH3 8EG
Tel: +44 (0) 131 221 2300
Tel: +44 (0) 131 221 2399

Glasgow
1 Atlantic Quay
Broomielaw
Glasgow
G2 8JB
Tel: +44 (0) 141 222 4500
Fax:+44 (0) 141 221 2048

Inverness
Moray House
16-18 Bank Street
Inverness
Scotland
IV1 1QY
Tel: +44 (0) 1463 239323
Fax: +44 (0) 1463 224951

Jakarta
S Widjojo Centre, 4th Floor
Jalan Jenderal Sudirman Kav.71
Jakarta 12190
Indonesia
Tel: +62 21 252 6588
Fax: +62 21 252 6592

Kaohsiung MRT
Kaohsiung Rep. Office
No 1 Chung-An Road
KAOHSIUNG 806 Taiwan
Tel: +886 7 793 9339
Fax: +886 7 793 9246

Mott MacDonald Worldwide Offices

Karachi
MM Pakistan (Pvt) Ltd
Dolmen Estate, 1st Floor
18-C, Union Commercial Area
Shaheed-e-Millat Road
Karachi-75350
Sindh, Pakistan
Tel: +92 (0) 21 4543944
Fax: +92 (0) 21 4524819

Keynsham
Riverside
4th Floor North
Temple Street
Keynsham (nr Bristol)
BS31 1LA
Tel: +44 (0) 117 937 6070
Fax: +44 (0) 117 986 4513

**Kuala Lumpur - MM (Malaysia)
Sdn.Bhd**
Suite 11-5 Level 11
Wisma UOA 11
No 21, Jalan Pinang
50450 Kuala Lumpur
Tel: +603 2168 8316
Fax: +603 2168 8317

Lahore
MM Pakistan (Pvt) Ltd
17-A/1 Zafar Road
Lahore Cantt
Pakistan
Tel: +92 42 6662595
Fax: +92 42 6665049

Leeds
2nd Floor
Marshall Court
Marshall Street
Leeds
West Yorkshire
LS11 9YP
Tel:+44 (0) 113 394 6737
Fax:+44 (0) 113 394 6701

Strategic Projects Office
Seacroft Hospital
York Road
Leeds
LS14 6UH
Tel: 0113 206 2042
Fax: 0113 206 2043

Lerwick
Greenhead
Lerwick
Shetland
ZE1 0PY
Tel: +44 (0) 1595 695049
Fax:+44 (0) 1595 693404

Liverpool
Merseyside Information Service
325 Royal Liver Building
Pier Head
Liverpool
L3 1JH
Tel: +44 (0) 151 236 4343
Fax:+44 (0) 151 236 2521

London
HLSP Consulting
5-23 Old Street
London
EC1V 9HL
Tel: +44 (0) 20 7253 5064
Fax:+44 (0) 20 7251 4404

Osprey Mott MacDonald
10-11 Charterhouse Square
London
EC1M 6EH
Tel: +44 (0) 207 566 7900
Fax: +44 (0) 207 566 7911

London-Derbyshire House
Mott Parson Gibb
3rd Floor
Derbyshire House
St Chad's Street
London
WC1H 8DA

London-Kingsgate House
Bay 951
Kingsgate House
66-74 Victoria Street
London
SW1E 6SW

London-Parnell House
Transport for London
3rd Floor
Parnell House
25 Wilton Street
London
SW1V 1LW

London-St James Park
Devon House
12-15 Dartmouth Street
St James's Park
London
SW1H 9BL
Tel: +44 (0) 20 7340 2250
Fax: +44 (0) 20 7233 0574

London-Dft
Mott Parsons Gibb
c/o Department for Transport
Zone 1H18
Ashdown House
123 Victoria Street
London
SW1E 6DE
Tel: +44 (0) 20 7944 5900
Fax: +44 (0) 20 7944 5920

Manchester
Spring Bank House
33 Stamford Street
Altrincham
Cheshire
WA14 1ES
Tel: +44 (0) 161 926 4000
Fax: +44 (0) 161 926 4100

Manchester-Clarendon House
6th Floor
Clarendon House
22 Stamford New Road
Altrincham
Cheshire
WA14 1BY
Tel: 0161 927 8900
Fax: 0161 927 8901

Manchester-Royal Exchange Bld
c/o Bovis Lend Lease Ltd
Management Suite
Level 1, Royal Exchange Building
Exchange Street
Manchester
M2 7FE
Tel: +44 (0) 161 834 7768

Metronet Rail
Metronet Rail BCV Capital Projects
Floor 3
Templar House
81-87 High Holborn
London
WC1V 6NU
Tel: +44 (0) 20 7038 4000

Moscow Client Office

Office 11/03
33/13
ul B Yakimanka
Moscow
117997 Russia
Tel: +7 495 792 3523

Network Rail
Network Rail
8th Floor
111 Picadilly
Manchester

Newcastle
St Ann's Wharf
112 Quayside
Newcastle upon Tyne
NE1 3DX
Tel: +44 (0) 191 261 0866
Fax: +44 (0) 191 261 1100

Norwich
County Hall
Norwich
Norfolk
NR1 2US
Tel: +44 (0) 1603 767530
Fax:+44 (0) 1603 767463

2nd Floor, East Wing
69-75 Thorpe Road
Norwich
NR1 1UA
Tel: +44 (0) 1603 226790
Fax: +44 (0) 1603 619365

Philippines
7th Floor Room 709 Herrera Tower
VA Rufina Corner Valero sts
Salcedo Village
Makati City 1227
Philippines
Tel: +632 817 7782
Fax: +632 817 7770

Porton Down
Health Protection Agency/CAMR
Porton Down
Salisbury
Wiltshire
SP4 0JG

Prague
Mott MacDonald Praha
Narodni 984/15
110 00 Praha 1
CzechRepublic
Tel: +420 221 412 800
Fax:+420 221 412 810

Ruwi
PO Box 587
Al Barani Building - Wadi Kabir
Ruwi
112
Sultanate of Oman
Tel: +968 7712118
Fax: +968 7715850

Sheffield
Mott MacDonald House
111 St Mary's Road
Sheffield
S2 4AP
Tel: +44 (0) 114 2761242
Fax: +44 (0) 114 2724699

Strategic Rail Authority
James Forbes House
Floor 2 Block A
27 Great Suffolk Street
London
SE1 0NS
Tel: +44 (0) 2070233197

Singapore-MM Singapore Pte
6 Raffles Quay
#17-02
48580
Singapore

Surgut
Mott MacDonald
Surgut Municipal Services Project
37 Profsouzov Street
Surgut 628418
Khanty-Mansi Autonomous Area
Russian Federation
Tel:+7 3462 524216
Fax:+7 3462 524217

Taipei
Mott MacDonald Ltd
Taiwan Branch
5F No 92 Sec 2 Tun-Hua S Road
Taipei 106
Taiwan R.O.C
Tel :+886 2 2702 5389
Fax:+886 2 2702 5068

Tripoli
c/o National Consulting Bureau
14 Jamahiriya Street
PO Box 12795
Tripoli, Libya
Tel: 00 218 21 351 2192
Fax: 00 218 21 351 2192

Uganda
PO Box 22258
ROFRA House
Gaba Road
Kampala
Uganda
Tel: +256 (0) 78 2 532 241
Fax:+256 (41) 269602

Wembley-York House
Wembley National Stadium
6th Floor York House
Empire Way
Wembley
HA9 0PA

Site Offices:

Bahamas
89 Thompson Boulevard
PO Box CB-12882
Nassau, N.P.,
Bahamas
Tel: +1 242 356 5614
Fax: +1 242 356 5624

British Waterways - Leeds
British Waterways
Fearns Wharf
Neptune Street
Leeds
LS9 8PB

Carmarthenshire
Carmarthenshire CC
Technical Services Dept
Parc Myrddin
Richmond Terrace
Carmarthen
Carmarthenshire
SA31 1HQ
Tel: 01267 228 158

Didcot- Diamond Buidings Project
c/o Costain Limited
Diamond Buildings Project
Frome Road
Didcot
Oxon
OX11 0BW

Dundee - Bullion House
Scottish Water
Bullion House
Invergowrie
Dundee
DD2 5BB

Gravesend
The White House
Clifton Marine Parade
Imperial Business Park
Gravesend
Kent
DA11 0DY
Tel: 01474 333021
Fax: 01474 333371

Heathrow
Terminal 5 Project
Longford House
PO Box 620
West Drayton
Middlesex
UB7 0NX
Tel:+44 (0) 20 8745 2605

The team of dedicated surveyors responsible for this edition of Hutchins' combined Small and Major Works UK Building Costs Handbook has been instrumental in developing the publication into a leading reference work with comprehensive and unique pricing for the United Kingdom.

A special mention is due in particular to the senior editor, André Holden MACostE, and his editing team; James Fiske BSc, MQSi, MACostE, Karl Horton BSc (Hons), Nang Vo Kham Murng MRICS, MSc, BSc, Emma Will, Rachael Ogden, Aaron Wright and Jingxin Shen MSc, for their continued outstanding contributions to this publication. The editor extends his personal thanks to Philip Lesnik of Spire Origination whose assistance with the publication process has been invaluable.

Franklin + Andrews would also like to thank the many manufacturers, suppliers, merchants, contractors and specialist sub-contractors for their continued and valued assistance in the production of this publication.

Finally a special thanks to those readers who have taken the trouble to contact us with suggestions for new sections and content generally, much of which has been incorporated within the current publication. The editing team constantly review the content of this publication and welcome suggestions from readers for its improvement.

Franklin + Andrews Ltd

May 2008

As with the previous editions this latest publication combines both Hutchins' Small Works and Hutchins' Major Works into this one comprehensive volume, Hutchins' UK Building Costs Blackbook. The format of each section follows that of previous editions. Furthermore, for those seeking to fine tune the prices to a specific area, the publication has provided location factors for the various regions of the United Kingdom. Location factors have also, again, been included for international regions. The section on whole life costs, which was introduced a couple of years ago, has again been included, with adjustments to reflect the current climate. This enables the building owner to consider building life cycle costs and to budget for these operating costs in addition to the initial capital expenditure for the completed structure. To complete this latest publication benchmark elemental costs and facility construction costs per m^2 of gross floor area (GFA) have again been provided for a range of construction types in order to assist in the preparation of budget estimates. The approximate estimating section has been considerably extended in this latest edition, further composite items will be added in future editions of the publication.

To ensure prices always reflect the current economic climate, three quarterly updates, giving details of changes in the prices for materials, wage rates, plant hire costs and other relevant and significant items, will be issued periodically by post and e-mail free to subscribers upon registration.

Following the continuing success of the combined publication, this latest edition of Hutchins' UK Building Costs Blackbook retains this combined format. It continues to fully address the needs of the building industry in providing an accurate, comprehensive and up-to-date database of cost information. It preserves the specific format of each of the separate work sections as previous editions, Small Works being measured consistent with a trade based structured format and Major Works in accordance with the SMM7 measurement rules. This publication includes approximate estimating, location factors for the UK and for international settings and memoranda sections which were introduced within earlier editions. The rates have been updated to reflect the current climate within the building environment including all the new and available wage rates for the construction industry and any cost adjustments for both plant and material resources. The features within each section will prove invaluable to professionals checking or producing cost estimates. This is particularly so for all works measured under the latest SMM7 1998 edition measurement rules.

The approximate estimating sections include elementally analysed cost information for more than 40 facilities and cost data providing benchmarked costs per m^2 gross floor area (GFA) rates for approximately 100 construction types. The provision of this cost data will assist surveyors and estimators with feasibility and budget preparation. The list of location factors both for the UK and international locations will enable rapid cost adjustments to be made to both feasibility and tender predictions. The memoranda section detailing useful reference information in trade format has also been included in response to readers' requests.

Introduction to Small Works Section

Background

The edition for this year has retained the basic content as for previous years publications and maintains the additional enhancements to the format, introduced in previous works, in order to improve the value to the reader. These improvements will, hopefully, ensure that the production of estimates and cost appraisals is made easier and more effective than before.

The measured rates sections are, wherever possible, generally trade based ensuring that the task of locating prices is made more simple. These measured rates sections are presented with pricing information displayed at both Net and Gross cost levels. The Memoranda section provides general information relating to material statistics including required quantities for selected work elements, specification information generally and other useful data.

General Introduction

Labour Costs

Labour outputs used in this section remain unaltered and are derived from outputs used for previous editions

The wage rates agreed by the Building and Allied Trades Joint Industrial Council for the industry as of Monday 9th June 2008 and until Sunday 7th June 2009 are as follows:-

All areas

Advanced craftsman	£405.99 per 39 hour week	£10.41 per hour
Adult general operative	£301.47 per 39 hour week	£7.73 per hour

Computation of hourly cost	Advanced operative	Adult general operative
(a) Labour	£ p	£ p
Basic weekly wage	405.99	301.47
Overtime say 9 hours	93.69	69.57
Non-productive overtime, say 4.5 hours	46.85	34.79
Plus rate say 50%	273.27	202.92
	£819.80	£608.75
(b) Contributions and levies	£ p	£ p
Sickness and injury benefit	3.10	3.10
National insurance	93.41	66.40
CITB levy	4.10	3.04
Public Holidays	14.21	10.53
Holiday pay scheme	51.17	38.55
Retirement benefit	3.07	3.07
Death benefit	1.66	1.66
Trade supervision	39.95	33.43
Travel allowance, say	17.69	17.69
	£228.36	£177.47
(c) Computation of hourly cost	£ p	£ p
Operatives weekly rate as (a) above	819.80	608.75
Contributions etc as (b) above	228.36	177.47
	£1,048.16	£786.22
Inclement weather, say 2%	20.96	15.72
Redundancy reserve, say 2%	20.96	15.72
	£1,090.08	£817.66
Employers liability insurance @ 2%	21.80	16.35
	£1,111.88	£834.01
Site on-costs, say 6.75%	75.05	56.30
Overheads, say 13.25%	147.32	110.51
	£1,334.25	£1,000.82
Cost per hour	£27.80	£20.85

The wage rates agreed by the Joint Industry Board for Plumbing, Mechanical Engineering Services in England and Wales as from 7th January 2008 are as follows:-

All Areas

Trained Plumber	£389.63 per 37.5 hour week	£10.39 per hour
Advanced Plumber	£454.50 per 37.5 hour week	£12.12 per hour

Computation of hourly cost

	Trained Plumber	Advanced Plumber
(a) Labour	£ p	£ p
Basic weekly wage per 37.5 hours	389.63	454.50
Additional 1.5 hours	15.59	18.18
Overtime say 9 hours	140.27	163.62
Non-productive overtime say 4.5 hours	46.76	54.54
	£592.25	£690.84
Plus rate 50%	296.13	345.42
	£888.38	£1,036.26
(b) Contributions, levies and expenses	£ p	£ p
Public holidays	19.50	22.3
Welding supplement	39.33	39.33
Travel allowance, say	35.55	35.55
National insurance	116.44	136.52
Industry pension scheme	57.92	67.0
Holiday pay scheme	52.49	58.9
CITB levy	4.74	5.78
Trade supervision	46.39	51.88
	£372.36	£417.35
(c) Computation of hourly cost	£ p	£ p
Operative's weekly rate as (a) above	888.38	1,036.26
Contributions etc as (b) above	372.36	417.35
	£1,260.74	£1,453.61
Inclement weather, say 2%	25.21	29.07
Redundancy reserve, say 2%	25.21	29.07
	£1,311.16	£1,511.75
Employers liability insurance @ 2%	26.22	30.24
	£1,337.38	£1,541.99
Site on-costs, say 6.75%	90.27	104.08
Overheads, say 13.25%	177.20	204.31
	£1,604.85	£1,850.38
Cost per hour	£33.43	£38.55

Material costs

Material prices used in this publication have been supplied by manufacturers and merchants, they include delivery to site and are current at second quarter 2008. Considerable variation can occur in material prices arising from load size, geographic area and also the trading status of the builder. It is important, therefore, that before entering into contractual situations confirmation is obtained from local merchants of material costs relevant to the project. This advice would equally apply to the rising trading costs of metals recently recorded on the world markets in particular steel and copper products where recent price rises have been dramatic

Plant hire costs

Plant hire rates used in this publication reflect locally hired machines, with possible savings arising from long term hire rate reduction or situations where the contractor's own plant is used. Rates are current at second quarter 2008.

Plant and tool hire

The following products with rates are based on information provided by HSS Hire Service Group Ltd., 25 Willow Lane, Mitcham, Surrey CR4 4TS, www.hss.com, with over 400 branches nationwide.

The rates per week are the maximum charge for each 7-day period and exclude VAT and delivery charges.

	per week £
Access & support	
Alloy access towers:	
2.2m platform height	94.00
4.2m platform height	133.00
6.2m platform height	172.00
Lightweight staging:	
2.4m long	35.00
3.6m long	39.00
Steel trestles each	5.50
Scaffold board each	4.00
Decorators trestles	
1.8m high	20.00
2.4m high	24.00
Ladders, double section:	
lightweight, push-up	
3.5m closed, 6.3m extended	31.00
5.0m closed, 9.0m extended	44.00
Combination ladder 3.6m	56.00
Roof ladder 4.6m double	49.00
Steps, 6 tread	27.00
Steps, 8 tread	30.00
Steps, 10 tread	32.00

	per week £
General building	
Super Prop	20.00
Steel props – each:	
1.1m closed, 1.8m extended	4.00
1.8m closed, 3.0m extended	4.00
2.6m closed, 3.9m extended	4.00
Bolt croppers 19.00	
Wheelbarrow, tyred, heavy-duty	10.00
Paving mallet 10.00	
Tarpaulin, 5m x 4m	18.00
Concreting & compaction	
Surface scaler:	
heavy duty, petrol	204.00
light duty, petrol	204.00
Concrete floor grinder, electric	148.00
Indent roller	18.00
Needle gun for keying, air operated	46.00
Poker vibrator, 47mm head, electric	74.00
Poker vibrator, 50mm head, petrol	46.00
Beam screed, petrol, per unit	195.00
Cement mixers:	
diesel	68.00
electric	24.00
Vibrating plate, light	55.00
Vibrating plate, medium	58.00
Vibrating roller, 560mm wide	128.00
Rammer	94.00
Plumbing, pumping & drain clearing	
Pipe vice	27.00
Pipe cutters, 100mm	27.00
Clay pipe cutter, up to 150mm	33.00
Steel pipe bender, manual	78.00
Copper pipe bender	20.00
Drain clearer, power jet, petrol	366.00
Centrifugal pump, 50mm	64.00
Heating, cooling and drying	
Building dryers, portable, 10ltr	84.00
Building dryers, warm air, 17ltr	102.00
Welding, lighting & power	
Plasterers light	34.00
Telescopic floodlight, twin head	27.00

	per week £
Breaking & drilling	
Hydraulic breaker, medium duty	139.00
Breaker, medium duty	65.00
Fixing, carpentry & sanding	
Cartridge hammer	52.00
Floor edging sander	60.00
Floor sander	74.00
Sawing & cutting	
Chasing machine, light	78.00
Door trimming saw	55.00
Chain saw, petrol, safety kit	110.00
Chain saw, electric, safety kit	85.00
Painting & decorating	
Air compressor, 9cfm, electric	96.00
Air compressor, 15cfm, electric or petrol 140.00	
Tyrolean roughcast machine	27.00
Cleaning & floor maintenance	
Mini hot washer	174.00
Electric steam cleaner	62.00
Carpet cleaner	80.00
Carpet cleaner upholstery tool	5.00
Floor scrubber-dryer, single	215.00
Surface scaler, heavy duty	216.00
Floor tile stripper	106.00
Lifting & materials handling	
Compact excavator 1.5T	264.00
Compact excavator 3.0T	396.00
Skidsteer loader	309.00
Hi-Lift skip dumper, diesel	360.00
Rubbish chute	7.70
Rubbish chute hopper	11.40
Rubbish chute Y-section	12.60
Gardening	
Turf cutter	116.00
Petrol brush cutter	140.00
Rotary mower, 500mm, petrol	31.00
All-terrain mower, 660mm, petrol	202.00
Electric lawn raker	22.00
Brush cutter, petrol	57.00
Lawn scarifier, petrol	80.00

	per week £
Lawn aerator, petrol	134.00
Hedge trimmer, electric	24.00
Light duty tiller	50.00
Power digger	89.00
Cultivator	199.00
Post hole borer, manual	18.00
Post hole borer, one-man, petrol	95.00
Post hole borer, two-man, petrol	104.00
Post hole borer, hydraulic	184.00
Chain saw and safety kit, petrol	110.00
Chain saw and safety kit, electric	85.00
Logging saw	76.00
Stump grinder, petrol	214.00
Chipper/shredder, petrol	93.00
Leaf sucker/blower, petrol	54.00
Garden shredder, petrol	40.00

All costs displayed in this publication exclude VAT.

Explanatory Notes

Constants of labour

For the greater convenience of readers wishing to calculate bonus targets etc., a column headed 'Labour Hours' is included throughout this edition, indicating the man-hours required per unit. The time given is for all employees, irrespective of the ratio of craft and general operatives or the number of employees in a gang.

For example, in bricklaying the ratio varies according to the conditions of work or availability of labour. Ratio of bricklayer to general operative may be 1-1, 2-1, 3-1 or even 4-1. This means that if two hours per unit is given, the proportion of hours would be as follows:-

Ratio	Bricklayer(s)	General operative(s)	Hours per Unit
1-1	1.00 hour	1.00 hour	2 hours
2-1	1.33 hour	0.67 hour	2 hours
3-1	1.50 hour	0.50 hour	2 hours
4-1	1.60 hour	0.40 hour	2 hours

Taking another trade painting; on new work, a general operative's time is almost negligible, but on the other hand on repair or redecorating work involving washing down and preparatory work, one general operative may be required to service every four craft operatives. If the labour hours per unit for such an item were shown at 2.50 hours, this would mean four craft operatives and one general operative at 0.50 hours each.

Labour hours Conversion table for decimal hours to hours and minutes; figures along the top and down left-hand side of table represent decimal hours to two decimal places, other figures are minutes.

	0.00	0.01	0.02	0.03	0.04	0.05	0.06	0.07	0.08	0.09
0.00	-	1	2	2	3	3	4	5	5	6
0.10	6	7	7	8	9	9	10	11	11	12
0.20	12	12	13	13	15	15	16	17	17	18
0.30	18	19	19	20	21	21	22	23	23	24
0.40	24	25	25	26	27	28	28	29	29	30
0.50	30	31	31	32	33	34	34	35	35	36
0.60	36	37	37	38	38	39	40	41	41	42
0.70	42	43	43	44	44	45	46	47	47	48
0.80	48	49	49	50	50	51	52	52	53	54
0.90	54	55	55	56	56	57	58	58	59	60

Worked example 1

Labour hours column shows 0.75. To obtain equivalent minutes: read down the left hand column to 0.70, then across the line to the column headed 0.05.
Answer: 45 minutes.

Worked example 2
Labour Hours column shows 1.44
Read down the left hand column to 0.40, then across the line to the column headed 0.04 = 27 minutes. Add 1 hour:
  Answer: 1 hour 27 minutes.

Labour hours The time taken for the fixing of each of the items is expressed as a decimal portion of an hour, therefore 0.50 labour hours equals thirty minutes. The times are average and include for unloading distributing and subsequent fixing in position.

Labour hours Conversion table for hours and minutes to decimal hours, to two decimal places. Figures along the top and down the left side of table represent minutes.

Mins	0	1	2	3	4	5	6	7	8	9
0	-	0.02	0.03	0.05	0.07	0.08	0.10	0.12	0.13	0.15
10	0.17	0.18	0.20	0.22	0.23	0.25	0.27	0.28	0.30	0.32
20	0.33	0.35	0.37	0.38	0.40	0.42	0.43	0.45	0.47	0.48
30	0.50	0.52	0.53	0.55	0.57	0.58	0.60	0.62	0.63	0.65
40	0.67	0.68	0.70	0.72	0.73	0.75	0.77	0.78	0.80	0.82
50	0.83	0.85	0.87	0.88	0.90	0.92	0.93	0.95	0.97	0.98

Worked example 1
Man takes 45 minutes to complete a job. To obtain decimal hours: Read down the left hand column to 40, then across the line to column headed 5.
  Answer: 0.75 hours.

Worked example 2
Man takes 1 hour 27 minutes to complete a job. To obtain decimal hours; Read down the left hand column to 20 then across the line to column headed 7. = 0.45 hours. Add 1 hour:
  Answer: 1.45 hours.

Establishment charges & profit
20% has been included in the net cost of labour to cover site-on-costs, establishment charges, for both new; repairs and alteration work and is made up of:-

Site-on-costs	6.75%
Establishment charges (overheads)	13.25%

10% has been added to net cost of labour, plant and material to cover profit on both new and repair and alteration work.

It is considered that these percentages represent average overhead costs on competitive contracts of say £10,000 - £50,000, but they will necessarily vary according to the size and scope of the contract and the type of work involved.

The extra payments to which operatives are entitled under the Working Rule Agreement for executing certain types of work have been considered in the appropriate labour cost columns.

The following tables give the main items included in the assessment of the respective percentages.

Site on costs 6.75%
Setting out; cartage.
Protection and timekeeping.
Sanitary conveniences
Welfare arrangements and safety precautions.
Watching and lighting.
Sheds and site offices and record keeping.
Deterioration of non-chargeable plant.
Removal of debris and other cartage.
Site telephone; attendance; incidentals.
Gauge boxes; profiles; screeds; templates; samples; trial holes.
Replacements, making good and maintenance.

Establishment charges (overheads)

Third Party (about £0.4% on wages)	}	0.25%
Fire	}	
Bond fees (if any): Federation fees	}	
Estimating costs	}	
Rent, rates and taxes	}	13.00%
Lighting, heating, telephones	}	
Other office and overhead costs	}	
		13.25%

Cost of water

Cost of water is included in the materials columns. When water has to be separately priced in Bills of Quantities the rate is about £0.24% of contract figure, but district charges vary, and the rate can also vary with type of work.

Ratio-Labour: Material

	Percentage Labour	Material	Site on-costs Estab. charges
Excavation	75	5	20
Concrete and drainage	28	52	20
Brickwork	42	38	20
Woodwork	30	50	20
Plasterwork	57	23	20
Plumbing	24	56	20
Decorating	67	13	20
Glazing	17	63	20
Repair work	66	14	20
Roofing	27	53	20

In total, labour with materials, work out nearly equal but as certain trades (such as brickwork and woodwork) are disproportionate to other trades, it would be found that in average new work, the relative proportions will approximate to labour - 43%; material - 43%; with 'other items' - 14%.

Repairs & alterations section.

Important notes concerning establishment charges etc.

Most work of a repair and alteration nature is estimated on a specification only, or plan and specification without Bills of Quantities basis. The Schedules set out at the rear of each trade section therefore adhere in some cases to measurements and trade headings which are established and familiar; but where suitable standard measurement rules have been adopted.

Cost depends very much on size of job and distance from workshop (read remarks hereunder).

The repair sections of the publication are designed for the pricing of repair, adaptation and conversion work; and prices are based on the **average** conditions under which such work may be executed. Adjustments to prices should be made for exceptional working conditions of any work, **for a very small or large job**, simplicity or complexity of work, accessibility and weather conditions (season of year, especially in respect of external work). Circumstances necessitating adjustments as thus recommended will be apparent. For instance, if a tradesman has to travel especially to a job, such as re-hanging a door or repairing a burst pipe, it will obviously cost much more by comparison than if the tradesman was already on the site for other work.

Percentages where shown in the work section should be added for pricing work in occupied premises. This is for working in furnished rooms where the necessary extra care and protection retards speed of execution; but no allowance has been made for the removal and replacement of furniture, carpets etc.

It is possible for prices for many other items of repair work to be calculated from the items provided.

Unit prices have been built up as follows:

Labour including (a) site-on-costs and (b) establishment charges and material at cost, with allowances for waste and making good. Materials have been assessed on current prices as detailed in the preamble to each new work section, but with appropriate increases for small quantities and cost of cartage. Labour rates used are detailed under 'Labour costs wage rates'.

Removal of existing
All items of removal include for:-
The hiring of a skip; delivery to site; wheeling and loading debris into and the removal of skip when full; disposal of contents; payment of charges

A basis for the estimate without quantities
It is not usual practice for tenders for small jobbing or alteration work to be priced on a Bill of Quantities. The absence of measured details and contract rates may not be of great importance at the estimating stage (except perhaps on the occasion of making an application for a House Renovation Grant). Such matters can, however, become complicated at the final account stage, especially when, as so often happens, there is a long list of variation orders to be agreed with the quantity surveyor acting on behalf of the Local Authority or the building owner.

Contractors using these schedules as a basis for their estimating could save a great deal of time and expense when agreeing an estimate, or settling the final account, if the following simple procedure is adopted when submitting the estimate. The following or similar wording could be printed or written, as a footnote to the estimate:

Analysis of estimate

This estimate is based on Hutchin's Small Works section of the UK Building Costs Blackbook (2009 Edition), and rates and prices used are those contained in that edition, and the following percentage adjustments shall apply to this job only.

General building work	Add or Deduct* ...%
Specialist sub-contractors listed below	
Trade	Add or Deduct* ...%
Trade	Add or Deduct* ...%
Trade	Add or Deduct* ...%

* Delete whichever is not applicable.

The foregoing percentage adjustments are subject to the order to commence work being given within ..months from the date of this estimate. If the order to commence work is given after the expiry of the stated period, the Contractor reserves the right to revise the percentage adjustments. The foregoing adjustments do not preclude the Contractor from making any subsequent claim for increased cost arising from either national wage agreements, or agreed increases in the cost of materials occurring after the date of the estimate.

Advisory notes on the foregoing

Note 1: The number of months is left to individual contractors' discretion; six months is a reasonable interval, three or four months perhaps on small jobs.

Note 2: The percentage adjustment decisions are the absolute prerogative of the Contractor. This will depend on extra over payments, extra travel time, material costs, profit margin and a number of other factors.

Note 3: It is essential to enter the year of the edition of the price book used. The fact that a new edition might be published during the course of a contract, could cause misunderstanding if the edition year was not specified.

Note 4: Percentage adjustments stated are binding only to the contract to which they apply and are not obligatory on any succeeding contract.

Note 5: Percentage adjustments on specialist sub-contractors' work. rates included in the various sections are a general guide, quotations received from specialist firms may be substantially different from those quoted. It is, therefore, advisable to consider each specialist trade separately.

Note 6: Contractors must never lose sight of the fact that at some time they may, through no fault of their own, find that a contract may be the subject of dispute in a Court of Law. If the dispute revolved around the final account and/or the cost of building work, it is quite probable that both the judge and barristers will use the rates in the sections as a 'guiding light', it is understandable, therefore, that if the Contractor used certain percentage additions in the estimate and omitted to state the additions in writing he stands to forego what may have been a justifiable claim for extra cost, if, on the other hand, the percentage adjustments were written on the estimate, then such adjustments would have to be taken into consideration by all concerned. In this event the Contractor would not have to be subjected to a long and difficult cross-examination on estimating. This, in turn, would save litigation time and attendant costs, and could ensure a more generous settlement to the Contractor than might otherwise have been possible.

Dayworks advisory notes for use when there is no standard form of contract

From time to time building contractors may have the good fortune to have the opportunity to carry out either part or the whole of the contract on a daywork basis.

This may be due to extreme urgency (e.g. repair after fire, flood or storm damage), complexity of the work or the impatience of the owner, when of course, there is not sufficient time for an estimate to be prepared.

These notes are primarily intended for jobs in the £500–£25,000 range for private owners: too small to justify the services (and fees) of an architect and/or quantity surveyor, and any suggestion of a standard form of contract would be superfluous.

It is, however, essential that the contractors should ensure that there will be no misunderstanding about payment when the final account stage is reached. A letter to the owner on the following lines should suffice.

I/we confirm your written/verbal instructions to carrying out sundry repairs and reinstatement work. The cost of the work shall be based on an inclusive hourly rate of £... per hour for each operative engaged on the work. The cost of all materials shall be current local costs.

To the sum total of the foregoing wages and material costs shall be added ......% to cover overheads and profit. Unless we receive your instructions to the contrary it will be assumed that our terms and conditions are acceptable. End of letter.

If the total value of the work is expected to exceed £1,000 and/or more than one month's duration, add the following paragraph.

On the last day of each month a detailed account will be forwarded to you and payment shall be made within 15 days. In the event of any inadmissibility or otherwise of any charges the whole matter shall be referred to .....Esq., Quantity Surveyor, whose decision shall be final and binding.

The nomination of a quantity surveyor does not mean that the contractor has to pay the cost of a retaining fee for a quantity surveyor's services that may never be called on.

It does mean that, if necessary, there is a local quantity surveyor who would be prepared to examine all relevant documents for the contractor for an appropriate fee.

The hourly rate for operatives may be based on the cost to employ, that is standard wage rates, plus extra over rate, plus bonus, plus all employers' levies and contributions.

The percentage to be charged is a matter for individual firms. Taking into consideration the overall cost of wages and material is recoverable in full. Something between 120% and 150% should suffice.

Wage rates and percentage additions chargeable are the subject of a decision by the contractor and must be stated at the outset of the contract. The foregoing recommendations regarding hourly wage rates and percentage additions are not mandatory and may be varied from contract to contract.

How to prepare your own unit rate from the Schedules.
To help you to calculate your own Unit Price for each item, I have set out below, suggestions for adjusting the figures and costs in the columns to suit your particular requirements.

(a)   Unit column
      m^3 – means the measurement per cubic metre.
      m^2 – means the measurement per square metre.
      m – means the measurement per linear metre.
      Each – means the measurement per each or number.

(b)   Labour Hours column
      Labour hours for the time taken for the fixing of the item described, expressed as a decimal fraction of an hour. (e.g. 0.75 hours equals 45 minutes).

The times given are average and include for unloading, distribution and fixing.

(c)   Labour Net column
      Gives the total net labour cost by multiplying the labour hours by the all-in labour rate (inclusive of 6.75% site-on-costs and 13.25% overhead charges).

(d)   Plant Net column
      Provides the average net cost of the hire of plant per unit of measure.

(e)   Materials Net column
      Gives the discounted cost of materials plus an allowance for waste for materials used in each rate per unit of measure.

(f)   Unit Net column
      Shows the total net cost of the labour, plant and materials columns.

(g) Labour Gross column
Gives the gross labour cost by adding a profit of 10% to the net labour cost.

(h) Plant Gross column
Shows the gross plant cost by adding a profit of 10% to the net plant cost.

(i) Materials Gross column
Gives the gross material cost by adding a profit of 10% to the net material cost .

(j) Unit Price column
Gives the total gross cost of the labour, plant and materials columns.

A profit level of 10% of the total of the net labour, plant and material columns in both the new work and the repair and alterations sections is assessed as a reasonable return on expenditure.

Suggestions in adjusting labour costs taken from the work sections to suit your own requirements.

(a) To assess the percentage adjustment to be applied to the work section rates:-

$$\frac{\text{Your labour rate} - \text{Work section rate}}{\text{Schedule rate}} \times 100 = \% \text{ to add or deduct from the sections}$$

(b) Multiply the man hours given by your own labour rate.

(c) A Unit Cost example could be as follows:-
Description of item: Hutchins' ref. 310106A

Carcassing; sawn softwood; noggins; 38 mm x 50 mm – per m

Suggestion 1

Labour:
0.30 man hours x £28.00 per hour (Hutchins' craft rate)   £8.40
If your labour rate is £30.00, then

$$\frac{£30.00 - £28.00}{£28.00} \times 100\% = +7.14\%$$ £0.60

£9.00

Materials:
taken from the work section   + <u>£0.52</u>

£9.52

Profit:
given in the work section   +10%   <u>£0.95</u>

Therefore the **Unit Price** is   <u>**£10.47**</u>

Alt. Suggestion 2

Labour:
0.30 man hours x £30.00 (say your craft rate)   £9.00

Materials/Plant:
As above   + <u>£0.52</u>

£9.52

Profit:
Given in the work section   +10%   <u>£0.95</u>

Therefore the **Unit Price** is   <u>**£10.47**</u>

All costs displayed in this publication exclude VAT.

Introduction to Major Works Section

The complete content of the Major Works section has been compiled in accordance with the requirements of professional quantity and building surveyors, architects, property developers, building contractors and specialists in need of reliable and informative cost information.

The rates contained within this cost handbook have been derived from competitive estimates. It is intended that those using the prices within this price book will add an allowance for overheads and profit and for preliminaries. A suggested enhancement of 10% has been used for gross unit rate examples in both sections.

The rates do not include for other on-costs such as might be included under the preliminaries and general costs sections of bills of quantities. Sample preliminary build-ups are given in the publication to assist the reader in identifying these other costs for both Small and Major works and each provides a simple checklist for guidance.

Generally outputs used in the Major Works section of this publication are based on the assumption of reasonable quantities of repetitive work. In the event that small quantities exist, which can happen on even the largest of projects, suitable adjustment would be appropriate to reflect anticipated performance. Similarly where site conditions are poor, adjustments to outputs would also be necessary to reflect the likely loss of productivity.

Labour Costs

Labour rates used in the Major Works section are calculated on the basis that most builders and contractors pay in excess of the minimum national wage rate. In respect of larger scale construction sites supply and demand dictates labour costs more than wage agreements. Therefore, from our experience, we have used, for the Major Works section, a net cost labour rate for trade Craftsmen of £16.98 per hour and for General Operatives £12.70 per hour.

These rates are compiled generally in accordance with the Code of Estimating Practice published by the Chartered Institute of Building. Labour rates do not include for supervision.

Labour gangs used in the measured rates reflect modern working practice, e.g. a 2 and 1 bricklaying gang comprising two bricklayers and one labourer. The cost of the gang is recovered by adding together the total cost of the three members of the gang, the resultant total is then divided by the number of craftsmen using trowels in that gang, i.e. 2, this generates the hourly rate used in the measured rates section of this publication.

Labour costs do not include any allowance for travelling time to and from the place of work, this is more usually calculated and costed within the preliminary sections of the tender documents.

Plant Hire

Plant hire rates are typical of those being charged for the second quarter of 2008 and include for fuel in use and operators costs for plant normally hired with a plant operator. Travelling costs to and from site are not included and would normally be costed and included within the preliminary section of the tender documents. Small hand plant and tools are deemed included within the labour rates, being an essential part of a tradesman's tool bag on modern construction sites.

Materials

Material prices used within the Major Works section are at a National average level and are based on manufacturers' and merchants' price lists for the second quarter of 2008. They reflect average trade discounts for direct delivery loads and will generally, therefore, be at or near the lowest price available. Adjustment will be necessary to suit each specific project and location and we would, therefore, urge all to seek accurate quotations if submitting competitive tenders. Measured rates include an allowance for wastage in use and unloading costs.

VAT

Value Added Tax has not been included in the compilation of Net or Gross rates.

Pricing Guidelines

If the reader is unfamiliar with the use of price books it is suggested that a few moments are taken to study the introduction section of this publication to help understand the approach taken in compiling the cost information used prior to attempting to use the data.

Definition of Terms and Symbols Used

m = lineal metre

m^2 = square metre

m^3 = cubic metre

Nr = number

mm = millimetre

PC = Prime Cost

Labour Cost = Net cost of labour per unit of measure

Plant Cost = Net cost of plant hire per unit of measure

Material Cost = Net cost of material per unit of measure

Unit Cost = Total cost per unit of measure excluding overheads and profit

Unit Price = Total Unit Cost per unit of measure plus 10% for profit

Measured Unit Rates

This section identifies the build-up cost of labour, plant and material per unit of measure for an item of work. The Net unit rate column presents costs at an average value for the UK with no addition of a profit element. The Gross rate column shows rates inclusive of 10% for profit, this should be adjusted if an alternative mark-up for profit is required.

Location factors

This section identifies current location factors for the whole of the UK in accordance with the values prepared by Franklin + Andrews. The publication establishes rates at an average unit value for the Net rate column with application of an average location factor for the Gross rates columns, inclusive of a mark-up of 10% to cover profit.

In order to fully utilise the location factors provided in this publication, to generate a more locally appropriate rate specific to a region, it will be necessary to compare and adjust the value for the selected region with the location value given for that region within the United Kingdom and applying the differential accordingly. For example, the average location value for the United Kingdom has been established as 1.00, therefore a project situated in, say, East Midlands, which has a location value of 0.94, would give a location true adjustment factor of 94% of the unit price shown in the unit rates section.

Similarly, a development in Wales, location factor 0.91, would require adjustment against the rates of 91% in order to reflect the cost variance for Wales. Readers requiring to adjust rates for local authority areas within Scotland will need to adjust against the factor current for Scotland of 0.99.

The prices shown are for guidance only, in determining any adjustments to the Unit Cost values shown it will be necessary to consider other related factors, such as the actual location of the site in terms of the area infrastructure. Locations well served by roads would make for ease of delivery of materials but where a site is situated in an area of restricted access this would add to the costs for supplies to that site. Local project related issues may also impact on the cost of the project and due care should be exercised in using the guide prices shown in this publication.

Small Works Preliminaries

Generally

The measured rates contained within the Small Works section of this publication do not include for those costs referred to as Preliminaries.

Unlike the measured rates that are directly affected by quantity changes, certain costs are not so affected and require a different approach to recovery. Examples might be scaffolding hire or the provision of a telephone, neither of which are affected by small changes in work quantity. These costs are recovered by adding a sum in the Preliminaries section of the tender documents.

The following are examples of the range of items that may be included in the Preliminaries section. The list is not exhaustive but will identify those common items that, if not allowed for in the tender elsewhere, should be included under the Preliminaries section.

Conditions of Contract

Careful notice should be taken of the contract conditions in order to establish onerous obligations, restrictions or liabilities that may be imposed by the Employer. Particular care should be given to non-standard clauses. Many client bodies have developed contract forms for their own use. If presented with such contract forms the contractor should take legal advice on the significance of the conditions under which the works will be let.
Those items that should be evaluated with all contract forms may be considered under the following headings:

1) Access to and possession or use of the site
2) Limitations of working space
3) Limitations of working hours
4) The maintenance of existing services on, under or over the site
5) The carrying out of the work in any specific order
6) The requirement to provide Bonds
7) The requirement to provide Insurance cover

Building Contractors administrative arrangements

An assessment of the builders site management requirements will normally include allowances for the following:

1) Site supervision and administration
2) Safety, health and welfare of work people
3) Transport of work people

Plant Hire

A bar chart programme may be prepared in order to establish the quantity and type of plant required on site, as well as the hire periods involved. Items of plant required for general usage and not already included in the measured rates can be included under the following headings, together with an allowance for transport and maintenance costs.

1) Small plant and tools
2) Scaffolding
3) Cranes and lifting plant
4) Site transport
5) Plant required for specific trades

Employers Facilities

The contract may well require facilities to be provided by the contractor, these may include the following:

1) Temporary accommodation (e.g. offices)
2) Telephones
3) Programme or progress charts
4) Signboards

Contractors Facilities

The contractor should establish the extent of facilities required for his own operations and the cost of providing them against the following headings:

1) Office, compounds, mess-rooms
2) Hoardings and guard-rails
3) Temporary roads, hard-standings and crossings
4) Water for the works; temporary plumbing and distribution
5) Lighting and power for the works; temporary installations
6) Temporary telephones and the cost of calls

Temporary Works

Temporary works can best be considered under the following headings:

1) Traffic diversion
2) Access roads
3) Pumping and dewatering

Sundry Items

Items that do not fall easily under the above headings can be included under this heading, for example:

1) Testing of materials
2) Testing of the works
3) Protecting the works from inclement weather
4) Removing rubbish and cleaning
5) Maintenance of roads and services
6) Drying the works
7) Control of noise and pollution
8) Statutory requirements

Sample Preliminaries Example

Every Building Contractor will treat the requirement for Preliminaries differently depending upon a number of factors. In addition each project will have its own special requirements in respect of Preliminaries and should be carefully assessed.

Preliminary costs for a small building project of 12 weeks duration, for example the construction of a domestic extension, approximate value £175,000, might be priced as follows:

Supervision and administration	£2,300.00
Site accommodation	£490.00
Light and power	£130.00
Insurances	£740.00
Water for the works	£80.00
Scaffolding	£4,650.00
Small plant	£380.00
Transport and travelling costs	£465.00
Total Preliminaries	**£9,235.00**

This represents **5.28%** of the tender sum.

Project Overheads and Profit

Every building contractor will need to recover from his activities sufficient income to fund overheads. In addition the builder will look to receive a fair return (profit) on the capital invested in the project. Therefore, in addition to the measured rates net cost and the preliminaries mentioned before, a sum of money will need to be added to recover profit.

The recovery of overheads and profit can be achieved in a number of ways. Some contractors prefer to add a lump sum to the tender, others will prefer to apportion the value across the range of measured work items by means of a percentage adjustment to the rates.

The method adopted in these schedules is to add overheads and profit equally on each rate by the addition of a percentage amount to the rate shown. Net rates include an addition of 20% on labour for overheads, Gross rates include a further 10% addition on labour, plant and materials for profit.

Major Works Preliminaries and General Conditions

Generally

Items within the scope of the works required but which are not specifically priced under measured work element are normally included under the SMM7 section headed Preliminaries/General Conditions and are arranged as follows:

A10: Project particulars
States the name, nature and location of the Works and the names and addresses of the Employer and Consultants.

A11: Tender and Contract documents
Lists all documents that were used in the production of the bills of quantities.

A12: The site
Describes the site/existing buildings and any pertinent information in respect of boundaries, existing services, access and the like.

A13: Description of the work
Indicates the extent of the contract work involved with particular reference to physical shape and dimensions of each element where not indicated on the drawings and details of related work by others.

A20: The Contract/Sub-contract
Specifies the particular Form of Contract to be used with a schedule of clause headings of standard conditions and any special conditions or amendments to such. Points out the Employer's insurance responsibility and the need or otherwise for a performance guarantee bond.

A30: Employer's requirements: Tendering/Sub-letting/Supply
Describes the requirements and limitations laid down by the Employer and specifies any fixed or time related charges which may be requested in respect of the works.

A31: Employer's requirements: Provision, content and use of documents.
Describes the general requirements of the Employer in respect of the provision, content and use of all documents relating to the specific works.

A32: Employer's requirements: Management of the Works
Relates to the Employer's requirements for the administration of the Contract and proper conduct of the site activities.

A33: Employer's requirements: Quality standards/control
Sets out the expected degree of work standard and quality of materials utilised in the works.

A34: Employer's requirements: Security/Safety/Protection
Dictates the standard of provision of security of the Works and the extent of safety requirements that are to be provided. Any requirements in respect of maintaining adjacent structures, public and private roads and services and the like are specifically noted.

A35: Employer's requirements: Specific limitations on method/sequence/timing/use of site
Specifies the constraints relating to design of the Works and the method and sequence of the work .The access to the site and the use of the site during the Works are determined and the use or disposal of materials found on site are stated. The requirements in respect of working periods are also set out in this section, setting out daily working hours, specific start and finish times for the site staff.

A36: Employer's requirements: Facilities/Temporary works/Services
This item sets out the requirements in respect of all site accommodation that will be required to be provided by the contractor for the use of the Employer during the Works. It also sets out the needs in respect of all temporary services including toilet facilities, telephone and facsimile installation, fences, hoardings, screens and the like. The costs for heating, lighting, cleaning and maintenance will need to be included as required.

A37: Employer's requirements: Operation/Maintenance of the finished building
Draws attention to the requirements for the maintenance of the fabric of the structure and the engineering services during the work and following completion.

A40: Contractor's general cost items: Management and staff
This section allows for contractor's costs in respect of general site staff requirements, and costs of employment of such, specifically to control the Works and for support and supervision. It includes programming and production, quantity Surveying support staff and the like.

A41: Contractor's general cost items: Site accommodation
The costs for the contractor's own accommodation should be allowed for in respect of this item and to include offices, laboratories, cabins, stores, compounds, canteens, sanitary facilities and the like. Setting up or fixed costs and time related charges should all be considered in the build up of the total cost to be included.

A42: Contractor's general cost items: Services and facilities
Allowance can be included here for power, lighting, water, site telephone, safety, health and welfare, protection of the work, drying out, cleaning etc, small tools and plant, security and contractor specific costs in general respects. General attendance on nominated sub-contractors and the provision for use by such of contractor's own access equipment, hoists, lighting, power, plant and the like is deemed to be allowed for in this section.

A43: Contractor's general cost items: Mechanical plant
The cost for providing all heavy plant and equipment, transport and the like including bringing to site, maintaining and removing on completion should be allowed for in this item.

A44: Contractor's general cost items: Temporary works
Allowance can be included here for all items of temporary works required: roads, walkways, access and support scaffolding, hoardings, fencing and general compliance with all traffic regulations.

A50: Work/Products by/on behalf of the Employer
The extent of the works by others directly employed by the Employer are stated and detailed in this item, the attendance required on such and details of materials provided by the Employer are set out for consideration by the contractor.

A51: Nominated sub-contractors
Describes the work of the sub-contractors and allows for the main contractor's profit and special attendance on same when such sub-contract is given as a prime cost sum and has not been included within a measured work schedule. The provision of specific access and other requirements should be included.

A52: Nominated suppliers
Specifies the requirements for material provision by nominated suppliers including any costs for conveying the goods to site and details of special packing or similar, unloading, storing and hoisting of materials, placing in position and the return of packaging items to the supplier. Where a prime cost sum has been allowed the contractor would include an element of profit, the fixing of any item is allowed for within the measured work section.

A53: Work by statutory authorities/under takers
Work by statutory authorities includes that carried out by public companies responsible for statutory work during the execution of their statutory duty. A provisional sum is normally included to cover the cost of such work.

A54: Provisional work
Where work can be specifically detailed a provisional item is allowed for to cover unforeseen or unmeasurable work elements at pre-tender stage.

A55: Dayworks
Labour, materials and plant for works carried out under dayworks is allowed for under this section as a provisional sum.

Pricing

Each and every project will have its own unique requirements in respect of preliminaries and general conditions and these should be carefully considered and assessed.

As an example the following might be appropriate for, say, a new building project of traditional construction for an office structure with an expected contract period of nine months and carried out partially during winter months, the approximate value of the works being £1,500,000. Items are listed with their specific SMM7 reference code:

A20: Bond	£5,625.00
A40: Supervision and administration	£26,875.00
A41: Site accommodation	£5,450.00
A42: Heat, light and power	£3,625.00
A42: Insurances	£3,750.00
A42: Small plant	£3,125.00
A42: Water for the works	£3,500.00
A43: Transport and travelling costs	£6,500.00
A44: Winter working	£3,150.00
A44: Site dewatering	£7,000.00
A44: Scaffolding	£11,250.00
Total preliminaries	**£79,850.00**

This represents **5.32%** of the tender sum

The inclusion or otherwise of the above scheduled costs is often left to the adjudication pre-tender meeting for discussion and decision which may be affected by current workload and competitive demands.

Pricing of scaffolding

As a guide for pricing scaffolding and access equipment the following rates may be considered a guide to likely costs involved for hired equipment, erected and dismantled by a specialist company and for weekly hire of both putlog and independent scaffolds.

Guide prices per square metre of structure scaffold.

Erection, dismantling and initial 4-week period of hire for scaffolding up to 8 m above ground level:

Putlog scaffold	£9.95 m^2
Independent scaffold	£10.40 m^2
Chimney access	£250.00 Nr

Rental per additional week:

Putlog scaffold	£1.45 m^2
Independent scaffold	£1.60 m^2
Chimney access	£26.00 Nr

HUTCHINS' SMALL WORKS SECTION

EXCAVATION, EARTHWORK AND CONCRETE WORK

Small Works 2009		Unit	Labour Hours	Labour Net	Plant Net	Materials Net	Unit Net	Labour Gross	Plant Gross	Materials Gross	Unit Price
								(Gross rates include 10% profit)			
				£	£	£	£	£	£	£	£
101	**NEW WORK**										
10101	**SITE PREPARATION**										
1010101	**Form temporary site road; 150 mm hardcore; maintain during period of contract:**										
1010101A	3.00 m wide..............	m	2.70	56.29	–	12.14	68.43	61.92	–	13.35	75.27
1010102	**Break up and remove temporary site road 150 mm hardcore:**										
1010102A	3.00 m wide..............	m	2.25	46.91	–	–	46.91	51.60	–	–	51.60
1010103	**Temporarily enclose site; fencing up to twenty times used:**										
1010103A	1.35 m chestnut fencing ...	m	0.25	5.21	–	–	5.21	5.73	–	–	5.73
1010103B	2.70 m chainlink fencing ...	m	0.45	9.38	–	–	9.38	10.32	–	–	10.32
1010104	**Clear site of bushes, scrub and undergrowth; cut down small trees and grub up roots; burn or deposit in skip:**										
1010104A	average 1.50 m high.......	m²	0.30	6.26	–	–	6.26	6.89	–	–	6.89
1010105	**Cut down hedging and grub up roots; burn or deposit in skip; hedge height:**										
1010105A	600 mm.................	m	1.97	41.07	–	–	41.07	45.18	–	–	45.18
1010105B	900 mm.................	m	2.63	54.84	–	–	54.84	60.32	–	–	60.32
1010105C	1200 mm................	m	3.12	65.05	–	–	65.05	71.56	–	–	71.56
1010105D	1500 mm................	m	4.27	89.03	–	–	89.03	97.93	–	–	97.93
1010105E	1800 mm................	m	5.74	119.68	–	–	119.68	131.65	–	–	131.65

Excavation, Earthwork and Concrete Work

Small Works 2009		Unit	Labour Hours	Labour Net	Plant Net	Materials Net	Unit Net	Labour Gross	Plant Gross	Materials Gross	Unit Price
								(Gross rates include 10% profit)			
				£	£	£	£	£	£	£	£
101	**NEW WORK**										
10101	**SITE PREPARATION**										
1010106	**Cut down trees, lop off branches and grub up roots; burn or deposit in skip; fill hole with excavated material; girth and diameter:**										
1010106A	450 mm girth 140 mm diameter	Each	16.00	333.60	–	–	333.60	366.96	–	–	366.96
1010106B	900 mm girth 290 mm diameter	Each	28.00	583.80	–	–	583.80	642.18	–	–	642.18
1010106C	1350 mm girth 430 mm diameter	Each	42.00	875.70	–	–	875.70	963.27	–	–	963.27
1010106D	1800 mm girth 570 mm diameter	Each	56.00	1167.60	–	–	1167.60	1284.36	–	–	1284.36
1010106E	2250 mm girth 720 mm diameter	Each	69.00	1438.65	–	–	1438.65	1582.52	–	–	1582.52
1010106F	2700 mm girth 860 mm diameter	Each	81.00	1688.85	–	–	1688.85	1857.74	–	–	1857.74
1010106G	3150 mm girth 1000 mm diameter	Each	92.00	1918.20	–	–	1918.20	2110.02	–	–	2110.02
1010106H	3600 mm girth 1150 mm diameter	Each	102.00	2126.70	–	–	2126.70	2339.37	–	–	2339.37
1010107	**Excavate top soil to be preserved; by hand; average depth:**										
1010107A	150 mm	m²	0.64	13.34	–	–	13.34	14.67	–	–	14.67
1010107B	225 mm	m²	0.93	19.39	–	–	19.39	21.33	–	–	21.33
1010107C	300 mm	m²	1.26	26.27	–	–	26.27	28.90	–	–	28.90
1010108	**Excavate top soil to be preserved; by machine; average depth:**										
1010108A	150 mm	m²	–	–	0.29	–	0.29	–	0.32	–	0.32
1010108B	225 mm	m²	–	–	0.29	–	0.29	–	0.32	–	0.32
1010108C	300 mm	m²	–	–	0.29	–	0.29	–	0.32	–	0.32

Small Works 2009		Unit	Labour Hours	Labour Net	Plant Net	Materials Net	Unit Net	Labour Gross	Plant Gross	Materials Gross	Unit Price
								(Gross rates include 10% profit)			
				£	£	£	£	£	£	£	£
101	**NEW WORK**										
10102	**EXCAVATION BY HAND**										
1010201	**Excavate to reduce levels; maximum depth not exceeding 0.25 m:**										
1010201A	loose soil	m³	2.63	54.84	–	–	54.84	60.32	–	–	60.32
1010201B	firm soil; sand	m³	3.15	65.68	–	–	65.68	72.25	–	–	72.25
1010201C	light clay; compact soil;										
	gravel	m³	3.94	82.15	–	–	82.15	90.37	–	–	90.37
1010201D	stiff heavy clay	m³	5.25	109.46	–	–	109.46	120.41	–	–	120.41
1010201E	soft chalk	m³	7.88	164.30	–	–	164.30	180.73	–	–	180.73
1010202	**Excavate to reduce levels; maximum depth not exceeding 1.00 m:**										
1010202A	loose soil	m³	2.71	56.50	–	–	56.50	62.15	–	–	62.15
1010202B	firm soil; sand	m³	3.25	67.76	–	–	67.76	74.54	–	–	74.54
1010202C	light clay; compact soil;										
	gravel	m³	4.06	84.65	–	–	84.65	93.12	–	–	93.12
1010202D	stiff heavy clay	m³	5.42	113.01	–	–	113.01	124.31	–	–	124.31
1010202E	soft chalk	m³	8.13	169.51	–	–	169.51	186.46	–	–	186.46
1010203	**Excavate to reduce levels; maximum depth not exceeding 2.00 m:**										
1010203A	loose soil	m³	2.88	60.05	–	–	60.05	66.06	–	–	66.06
1010203B	firm soil; sand	m³	3.46	72.14	–	–	72.14	79.35	–	–	79.35
1010203C	light clay; compact soil;										
	gravel	m³	4.33	90.28	–	–	90.28	99.31	–	–	99.31
1010203D	stiff heavy clay	m³	5.77	120.30	–	–	120.30	132.33	–	–	132.33
1010203E	soft chalk	m³	8.65	180.35	–	–	180.35	198.39	–	–	198.39
1010205	**Excavate for basement; maximum depth not exceeding 0.25 m:**										
1010205A	loose soil	m³	2.63	54.84	–	–	54.84	60.32	–	–	60.32
1010205B	firm soil; sand	m³	3.15	65.68	–	–	65.68	72.25	–	–	72.25
1010205C	light clay; compact soil;										
	gravel;	m³	3.94	82.15	–	–	82.15	90.37	–	–	90.37
1010205D	stiff heavy clay;	m³	5.25	109.46	–	–	109.46	120.41	–	–	120.41
1010205E	soft chalk;	m³	7.88	164.30	–	–	164.30	180.73	–	–	180.73
1010206	**Excavate for basement; maximum depth not exceeding 1.00 m:**										
1010206A	loose soil	m³	2.71	56.50	–	–	56.50	62.15	–	–	62.15
1010206B	firm soil; sand	m³	3.25	67.76	–	–	67.76	74.54	–	–	74.54
1010206C	light clay; compact soil;										
	gravel	m³	4.06	84.65	–	–	84.65	93.12	–	–	93.12
1010206D	stiff heavy clay	m³	5.42	113.01	–	–	113.01	124.31	–	–	124.31
1010206E	soft chalk	m³	8.13	169.51	–	–	169.51	186.46	–	–	186.46
1010207	**Excavate for basement; maximum depth not exceeding 2.00 m:**										
1010207A	loose soil	m³	3.37	70.26	–	–	70.26	77.29	–	–	77.29
1010207B	firm soil; sand	m³	4.04	84.23	–	–	84.23	92.65	–	–	92.65
1010207C	light clay; compact soil;										
	gravel	m³	5.05	105.29	–	–	105.29	115.82	–	–	115.82
1010207D	stiff heavy clay	m³	6.73	140.32	–	–	140.32	154.35	–	–	154.35
1010207E	soft chalk	m³	10.10	210.59	–	–	210.59	231.65	–	–	231.65

Excavation, Earthwork and Concrete Work

Small Works 2009		Unit	Labour Hours	Labour Net	Plant Net	Materials Net	Unit Net	Labour Gross	Plant Gross	Materials Gross	Unit Price
								(Gross rates include 10% profit)			
				£	£	£	£	£	£	£	£
101	**NEW WORK**										
10102	**EXCAVATION BY HAND**										
1010209	**Excavate pit to receive bases of stanchions, isolated piers etc; maximum depth not exceeding 0.25 m:**										
1010209A	loose soil	m³	2.71	56.50	–	–	56.50	62.15	–	–	62.15
1010209B	firm soil; sand	m³	3.25	67.76	–	–	67.76	74.54	–	–	74.54
1010209C	light clay; compact soil;										
	gravel	m³	4.06	84.65	–	–	84.65	93.12	–	–	93.12
1010209D	stiff heavy clay	m³	5.42	113.01	–	–	113.01	124.31	–	–	124.31
1010209E	soft chalk	m³	8.13	169.51	–	–	169.51	186.46	–	–	186.46
1010210	**Excavate pit to receive bases of stanchions, isolated piers etc; maximum depth not exceeding 1.00 m:**										
1010210A	loose soil	m³	2.97	61.92	–	–	61.92	68.11	–	–	68.11
1010210B	firm soil; sand	m³	3.56	74.23	–	–	74.23	81.65	–	–	81.65
1010210C	light clay; compact soil;										
	gravel	m³	4.45	92.78	–	–	92.78	102.06	–	–	102.06
1010210D	stiff heavy clay	m³	5.93	123.64	–	–	123.64	136.00	–	–	136.00
1010210E	soft chalk	m³	8.90	185.57	–	–	185.57	204.13	–	–	204.13
1010211	**Excavate pit to receive bases of stanchions, isolated piers etc; maximum depth not exceeding 2.00 m:**										
1010211A	loose soil	m³	3.72	77.56	–	–	77.56	85.32	–	–	85.32
1010211B	firm soil; sand	m³	4.46	92.99	–	–	92.99	102.29	–	–	102.29
1010211C	light clay; compact soil;										
	gravel	m³	5.58	116.34	–	–	116.34	127.97	–	–	127.97
1010211D	stiff heavy clay	m³	7.43	154.92	–	–	154.92	170.41	–	–	170.41
1010211E	soft chalk	m³	11.15	232.48	–	–	232.48	255.73	–	–	255.73

Small Works 2009		Unit	Labour Hours	Labour Net	Plant Net	Materials Net	Unit Net	Labour Gross	Plant Gross	Materials Gross	Unit Price
								(Gross rates include 10% profit)			
				£	£	£	£	£	£	£	£
101	**NEW WORK**										
10102	**EXCAVATION BY HAND**										
1010213	**Excavate trenches to receive foundations; exceeding 0.30 m in width; maximum depth not exceeding 0.25 m:**										
1010213A	loose soil	m³	2.71	56.50	–	–	56.50	62.15	–	–	62.15
1010213B	firm soil; sand	m³	3.25	67.76	–	–	67.76	74.54	–	–	74.54
1010213C	light clay; compact soil; gravel	m³	4.06	84.65	–	–	84.65	93.12	–	–	93.12
1010213D	stiff heavy clay	m³	5.42	113.01	–	–	113.01	124.31	–	–	124.31
1010213E	soft chalk	m³	8.13	169.51	–	–	169.51	186.46	–	–	186.46
1010214	**Excavate trenches to receive foundations; exceeding 0.30 m in width; maximum depth not exceeding 1.00 m:**										
1010214A	loose soil	m³	2.97	61.92	–	–	61.92	68.11	–	–	68.11
1010214B	firm soil; sand	m³	3.56	74.23	–	–	74.23	81.65	–	–	81.65
1010214C	light clay; compact soil; gravel	m³	4.45	92.78	–	–	92.78	102.06	–	–	102.06
1010214D	stiff heavy clay	m³	5.93	123.64	–	–	123.64	136.00	–	–	136.00
1010214E	soft chalk	m³	8.90	185.57	–	–	185.57	204.13	–	–	204.13
1010215	**Excavate trenches to receive foundations; exceeding 0.30 m in width; maximum depth not exceeding 2.00 m:**										
1010215A	loose soil	m³	3.72	77.56	–	–	77.56	85.32	–	–	85.32
1010215B	firm soil; sand	m³	4.46	92.99	–	–	92.99	102.29	–	–	102.29
1010215C	light clay; compact soil; gravel	m³	5.58	116.34	–	–	116.34	127.97	–	–	127.97
1010215D	stiff heavy clay	m³	7.43	154.92	–	–	154.92	170.41	–	–	170.41
1010215E	soft chalk	m³	11.15	232.48	–	–	232.48	255.73	–	–	255.73

Excavation, Earthwork and Concrete Work

Small Works 2009		Unit	Labour Hours	Labour Net	Plant Net	Materials Net	Unit Net	Labour Gross	Plant Gross	Materials Gross	Unit Price
								(Gross rates include 10% profit)			
				£	£	£	£	£	£	£	£
101	**NEW WORK**										
10102	**EXCAVATION BY HAND**										
1010217	**Excavate trenches to receive foundations; not exceeding 0.30 m in width; maximum depth not exceeding 0.25 m:**										
1010217A	loose soil	m³	0.28	5.84	–	–	5.84	6.42	–	–	6.42
1010217B	firm soil; sand	m³	0.34	7.09	–	–	7.09	7.80	–	–	7.80
1010217C	light clay; compact soil; gravel	m³	0.43	8.97	–	–	8.97	9.87	–	–	9.87
1010217D	stiff heavy clay	m³	0.57	11.88	–	–	11.88	13.07	–	–	13.07
1010217E	soft chalk	m³	0.85	17.72	–	–	17.72	19.49	–	–	19.49
1010218	**Excavate trenches to receive foundations; not exceeding 0.30 m in width; maximum depth not exceeding 0.50 m:**										
1010218A	loose soil	m³	0.54	11.26	–	–	11.26	12.39	–	–	12.39
1010218B	firm soil; sand	m³	0.65	13.55	–	–	13.55	14.91	–	–	14.91
1010218C	light clay; compact soil; gravel	m³	0.81	16.89	–	–	16.89	18.58	–	–	18.58
1010218D	stiff heavy clay	m³	1.08	22.52	–	–	22.52	24.77	–	–	24.77
1010218E	soft chalk	m³	1.63	33.99	–	–	33.99	37.39	–	–	37.39
1010219	**Excavate trenches to receive foundations; not exceeding 0.30 m in width; maximum depth not exceeding 0.75 m:**										
1010219A	loose soil	m³	0.78	16.26	–	–	16.26	17.89	–	–	17.89
1010219B	firm soil; sand	m³	0.93	19.39	–	–	19.39	21.33	–	–	21.33
1010219C	light clay; compact soil; gravel	m³	1.16	24.19	–	–	24.19	26.61	–	–	26.61
1010219D	stiff heavy clay	m³	1.55	32.32	–	–	32.32	35.55	–	–	35.55
1010219E	soft chalk	m³	2.33	48.58	–	–	48.58	53.44	–	–	53.44
1010220	**Excavate trenches to receive foundations; not exceeding 0.30 m in width; maximum depth not exceeding 1.00 m:**										
1010220A	loose soil	m³	1.00	20.85	–	–	20.85	22.94	–	–	22.94
1010220B	firm soil; sand	m³	1.20	25.02	–	–	25.02	27.52	–	–	27.52
1010220C	light clay; compact soil; gravel	m³	1.50	31.28	–	–	31.28	34.41	–	–	34.41
1010220D	stiff heavy clay	m³	2.00	41.70	–	–	41.70	45.87	–	–	45.87
1010220E	soft chalk	m³	3.00	62.55	–	–	62.55	68.81	–	–	68.81

Small Works 2009		Unit	Labour Hours	Labour Net	Plant Net	Materials Net	Unit Net	Labour Gross	Plant Gross	Materials Gross	Unit Price
								(Gross rates include 10% profit)			
				£	£	£	£	£	£	£	£
101	**NEW WORK**										
10103	**EXCAVATION BY MACHINE**										
1010301	**Excavate to reduce levels; maximum depth not exceeding 0.25 m:**										
1010301A	loose soil	m³	–	–	4.82	–	4.82	–	5.30	–	5.30
1010301B	firm soil; sand	m³	–	–	5.99	–	5.99	–	6.59	–	6.59
1010301C	light clay; compact soil; gravel	m³	–	–	7.39	–	7.39	–	8.13	–	8.13
1010301D	stiff heavy clay	m³	–	–	9.96	–	9.96	–	10.96	–	10.96
1010301E	soft chalk	m³	–	–	15.07	–	15.07	–	16.58	–	16.58
1010302	**Excavate to reduce levels; maximum depth not exceeding 1.00 m:**										
1010302A	loose soil	m³	–	–	3.97	–	3.97	–	4.37	–	4.37
1010302B	firm soil; sand	m³	–	–	4.82	–	4.82	–	5.30	–	5.30
1010302C	light clay; compact soil; gravel	m³	–	–	5.99	–	5.99	–	6.59	–	6.59
1010302D	stiff heavy clay	m³	–	–	7.96	–	7.96	–	8.76	–	8.76
1010302E	soft chalk	m³	–	–	11.93	–	11.93	–	13.12	–	13.12
1010303	**Excavate to reduce levels; maximum depth not exceeding 2.00 m:**										
1010303A	loose soil	m³	–	–	4.82	–	4.82	–	5.30	–	5.30
1010303B	firm soil; sand	m³	–	–	5.99	–	5.99	–	6.59	–	6.59
1010303C	light clay; compact soil; gravel	m³	–	–	7.39	–	7.39	–	8.13	–	8.13
1010303D	stiff heavy clay	m³	–	–	9.96	–	9.96	–	10.96	–	10.96
1010303E	soft chalk	m³	–	–	15.07	–	15.07	–	16.58	–	16.58
1010305	**Excavate for basement; maximum depth not exceeding 0.25 m:**										
1010305A	loose soil	m³	–	–	5.68	–	5.68	–	6.25	–	6.25
1010305B	firm soil; sand	m³	–	–	6.82	–	6.82	–	7.50	–	7.50
1010305C	light clay; compact soil; gravel	m³	–	–	8.53	–	8.53	–	9.38	–	9.38
1010305D	stiff heavy clay	m³	–	–	11.39	–	11.39	–	12.53	–	12.53
1010305E	soft chalk	m³	–	–	17.35	–	17.35	–	19.09	–	19.09
1010306	**Excavate for basement; maximum depth not exceeding 1.00 m:**										
1010306A	loose soil	m³	–	–	5.39	–	5.39	–	5.93	–	5.93
1010306B	firm soil; sand	m³	–	–	6.53	–	6.53	–	7.18	–	7.18
1010306C	light clay; compact soil; gravel	m³	–	–	7.96	–	7.96	–	8.76	–	8.76
1010306D	stiff heavy clay	m³	–	–	10.50	–	10.50	–	11.55	–	11.55
1010306E	soft chalk	m³	–	–	15.92	–	15.92	–	17.51	–	17.51
1010307	**Excavate for basement; maximum depth not exceeding 2.00 m:**										
1010307A	loose soil	m³	–	–	5.68	–	5.68	–	6.25	–	6.25
1010307B	firm soil; sand	m³	–	–	6.82	–	6.82	–	7.50	–	7.50
1010307C	light clay; compact soil; gravel	m³	–	–	8.53	–	8.53	–	9.38	–	9.38
1010307D	stiff heavy clay	m³	–	–	11.39	–	11.39	–	12.53	–	12.53
1010307E	soft chalk	m³	–	–	17.35	–	17.35	–	19.09	–	19.09

Excavation, Earthwork and Concrete Work

Small Works 2009		Unit	Labour Hours	Labour Net	Plant Net	Materials Net	Unit Net	Labour Gross	Plant Gross	Materials Gross	Unit Price
								— (Gross rates include 10% profit) —			
				£	£	£	£	£	£	£	£
101	**NEW WORK**										
10103	**EXCAVATION BY MACHINE**										
1010309	**Excavate pit to receive bases of stanchions, isolated piers etc; maximum depth not exceeding 0.25 m:**										
1010309A	loose soil	m³	–	–	7.96	–	7.96	–	8.76	–	8.76
1010309B	firm soil; sand	m³	–	–	9.64	–	9.64	–	10.60	–	10.60
1010309C	light clay; compact soil; gravel	m³	–	–	11.93	–	11.93	–	13.12	–	13.12
1010309D	stiff heavy clay	m³	–	–	15.92	–	15.92	–	17.51	–	17.51
1010309E	soft chalk	m³	–	–	24.17	–	24.17	–	26.59	–	26.59
1010310	**Excavate pit to receive bases of stanchions, isolated piers etc; maximum depth not exceeding 1.00 m:**										
1010310A	loose soil	m³	–	–	6.25	–	6.25	–	6.88	–	6.88
1010310B	firm soil; sand	m³	–	–	7.68	–	7.68	–	8.45	–	8.45
1010310C	light clay; compact soil; gravel	m³	–	–	9.64	–	9.64	–	10.60	–	10.60
1010310D	stiff heavy clay	m³	–	–	12.78	–	12.78	–	14.06	–	14.06
1010310E	soft chalk	m³	–	–	19.35	–	19.35	–	21.29	–	21.29
1010311	**Excavate pit to receive bases of stanchions, isolated piers etc; maximum depth not exceeding 2.00 m:**										
1010311A	loose soil	m³	–	–	7.96	–	7.96	–	8.76	–	8.76
1010311B	firm soil; sand	m³	–	–	9.64	–	9.64	–	10.60	–	10.60
1010311C	light clay; compact soil; gravel	m³	–	–	11.93	–	11.93	–	13.12	–	13.12
1010311D	stiff heavy clay	m³	–	–	15.92	–	15.92	–	17.51	–	17.51
1010311E	soft chalk	m³	–	–	24.17	–	24.17	–	26.59	–	26.59
1010313	**Excavate trenches to receive foundations; exceeding 0.30 m in width; maximum depth not exceeding; 0.25m:**										
1010313A	loose soil	m³	–	–	4.82	–	4.82	–	5.30	–	5.30
1010313B	firm soil; sand	m³	–	–	5.99	–	5.99	–	6.59	–	6.59
1010313C	light clay; compact soil; gravel	m³	–	–	7.39	–	7.39	–	8.13	–	8.13
1010313D	stiff heavy clay	m³	–	–	9.96	–	9.96	–	10.96	–	10.96
1010313E	soft chalk	m³	–	–	15.07	–	15.07	–	16.58	–	16.58
1010314	**Excavate trenches to receive foundations; exceeding 0.30 m in width; maximum depth not exceeding; 1.00 m:**										
1010314A	loose soil	m³	–	–	3.97	–	3.97	–	4.37	–	4.37
1010314B	firm soil; sand	m³	–	–	4.82	–	4.82	–	5.30	–	5.30
1010314C	light clay; compact soil; gravel	m³	–	–	5.99	–	5.99	–	6.59	–	6.59
1010314D	stiff heavy clay	m³	–	–	7.96	–	7.96	–	8.76	–	8.76
1010314E	soft chalk	m³	–	–	11.93	–	11.93	–	13.12	–	13.12
1010315	**Excavate trenches to receive foundations; exceeding 0.30 m in width; maximum depth not exceeding; 2.00 m:**										
1010315A	loose soil	m³	–	–	4.82	–	4.82	–	5.30	–	5.30
1010315B	firm soil; sand	m³	–	–	5.99	–	5.99	–	6.59	–	6.59
1010315C	light clay; compact soil; gravel	m³	–	–	7.39	–	7.39	–	8.13	–	8.13
1010315D	stiff heavy clay	m³	–	–	15.92	–	15.92	–	17.51	–	17.51
1010315E	soft chalk	m³	–	–	24.17	–	24.17	–	26.59	–	26.59

Small Works 2009		Unit	Labour Hours	Labour Net	Plant Net	Materials Net	Unit Net	Labour Gross	Plant Gross	Materials Gross	Unit Price
								(Gross rates include 10% profit)			
				£	£	£	£	£	£	£	£
101	**NEW WORK**										
10103	**EXCAVATION BY MACHINE**										
1010317	**Excavate trenches to receive foundations; not exceeding 0.30 m in width; maximum depth not exceeding; 0.25 m:**										
1010317A	loose soil	m³	–	–	3.40	–	3.40	–	3.74	–	3.74
1010317B	firm soil; sand	m³	–	–	4.25	–	4.25	–	4.68	–	4.68
1010317C	light clay; compact soil;										
	gravel	m³	–	–	5.14	–	5.14	–	5.65	–	5.65
1010317D	stiff heavy clay	m³	–	–	6.82	–	6.82	–	7.50	–	7.50
1010317E	soft chalk	m³	–	–	10.24	–	10.24	–	11.26	–	11.26
1010318	**Excavate trenches to receive foundations; not exceeding 0.30 m in width; maximum depth not exceeding; 0.50 m:**										
1010318A	loose soil	m³	–	–	5.68	–	5.68	–	6.25	–	6.25
1010318B	firm soil; sand	m³	–	–	6.82	–	6.82	–	7.50	–	7.50
1010318C	light clay; compact soil;										
	gravel	m³	–	–	8.53	–	8.53	–	9.38	–	9.38
1010318D	stiff heavy clay	m³	–	–	11.39	–	11.39	–	12.53	–	12.53
1010318E	soft chalk	m³	–	–	17.35	–	17.35	–	19.09	–	19.09
1010319	**Excavate trenches to receive foundations; not exceeding 0.30 m in width; maximum depth not exceeding; 0.75 m:**										
1010319A	loose soil	m³	–	–	7.96	–	7.96	–	8.76	–	8.76
1010319B	firm soil; sand	m³	–	–	9.64	–	9.64	–	10.60	–	10.60
1010319C	light clay; compact soil;										
	gravel	m³	–	–	11.93	–	11.93	–	13.12	–	13.12
1010319D	stiff heavy clay	m³	–	–	15.92	–	15.92	–	17.51	–	17.51
1010319E	soft chalk	m³	–	–	24.17	–	24.17	–	26.59	–	26.59
1010320	**Excavate trenches to receive foundations; not exceeding 0.30 m in width; maximum depth not exceeding; 1.00 m:**										
1010320A	loose soil	m³	–	–	10.24	–	10.24	–	11.26	–	11.26
1010320B	firm soil; sand	m³	–	–	12.50	–	12.50	–	13.75	–	13.75
1010320C	light clay; compact soil;										
	gravel	m³	–	–	15.64	–	15.64	–	17.20	–	17.20
1010320D	stiff heavy clay	m³	–	–	20.77	–	20.77	–	22.85	–	22.85
1010320E	soft chalk	m³	–	–	30.99	–	30.99	–	34.09	–	34.09
10104	**BREAKING UP BY HAND**										
1010401	**Extra over excavation for breaking up:**										
1010401A	brickwork in lime mortar	m³	4.00	83.40	–	–	83.40	91.74	–	–	91.74
1010401B	brickwork in cement mortar	m³	5.33	111.13	–	–	111.13	122.24	–	–	122.24
1010401C	concrete	m³	8.00	166.80	–	–	166.80	183.48	–	–	183.48
1010401D	reinforced concrete	m³	10.00	208.50	–	–	208.50	229.35	–	–	229.35
1010401E	semi-hard rock (sandstone etc)	m³	7.50	156.38	–	–	156.38	172.02	–	–	172.02

Excavation, Earthwork and Concrete Work

Small Works 2009		Unit	Labour Hours	Labour Net	Plant Net	Materials Net	Unit Net	Labour Gross	Plant Gross	Materials Gross	Unit Price
								(Gross rates include 10% profit)			
				£	£	£	£	£	£	£	£
101	**NEW WORK**										
10105	**BREAKING UP BY MACHINE**										
1010501	**Extra over excavation for breaking up using compressed air equipment:**										
1010501A	concrete average thickness; 150 mm..................	m²	0.17	3.55	4.41	–	7.96	3.91	4.85	–	8.76
1010501B	concrete average thickness; 300 mm..................	m²	0.50	10.42	13.01	–	23.43	11.46	14.31	–	25.77
1010501C	reinforced concrete average thickness; 150 mm........	m²	0.25	5.22	6.50	–	11.72	5.74	7.15	–	12.89
1010501D	reinforced concrete average thickness; 300 mm.........	m²	0.75	15.64	19.51	–	35.15	17.20	21.46	–	38.67
1010501E	brickwork in lime mortar ...	m³	0.50	10.42	13.01	–	23.43	11.46	14.31	–	25.77
1010501F	brickwork in cement mortar	m³	0.67	13.97	17.42	–	31.39	15.37	19.16	–	34.53
1010501G	concrete.................	m³	3.35	69.85	87.18	–	157.03	76.84	95.90	–	172.73
1010501H	reinforced concrete	m³	5.00	104.25	130.11	–	234.36	114.68	143.12	–	257.80
1010501I	semi-hard rock (sandstone etc)....................	m³	2.60	54.21	67.67	–	121.88	59.63	74.44	–	134.07
10106	**EARTHWORK SUPPORT**										
1010601	**Earthwork support in firm ground to opposing faces not exceeding 2.00 m apart; maximum depth not exceeding:**										
1010601A	1.00 m..................	m²	0.64	13.34	–	2.08	15.42	14.67	–	2.29	16.96
1010601B	2.00 m..................	m²	0.70	14.60	–	2.30	16.90	16.06	–	2.53	18.59
1010602	**Earthwork support in loose ground to opposing faces not exceeding 2.00 m apart; maximum depth not exceeding:**										
1010602A	1.00 m..................	m²	4.98	103.83	–	16.49	120.32	114.21	–	18.14	132.35
1010602B	2.00 m..................	m²	4.98	103.83	–	16.49	120.32	114.21	–	18.14	132.35

Small Works 2009		Unit	Labour Hours	Labour Net	Plant Net	Materials Net	Unit Net	Labour Gross	Plant Gross	Materials Gross	Unit Price
								(Gross rates include 10% profit)			
				£	£	£	£	£	£	£	£
101	**NEW WORK**										
10107	**DISPOSAL OF EXCAVATED MATERIAL**										
1010701	**Fill barrows; deposit:**										
1010701A	wheel up to 20 m	m³	1.00	20.85	–	–	20.85	22.94	–	–	22.94
1010701B	add; wheel each additional 20 m	m³	0.45	9.38	–	–	9.38	10.32	–	–	10.32
1010702	**Excavated material moved by hand from spoil heap or side of excavations; deposit in skip ; average distance from spoil heap or excavation:**										
1010702A	25 m...................	m³	3.78	78.81	–	–	78.81	86.69	–	–	86.69
1010702B	50 m...................	m³	4.40	91.74	–	–	91.74	100.91	–	–	100.91
1010703	**Hand loading; transporting; depositing in spoil heaps; average distance from excavation:**										
1010703A	25 m...................	m³	3.78	78.81	–	–	78.81	86.69	–	–	86.69
1010703B	50 m...................	m³	4.40	91.74	–	–	91.74	100.91	–	–	100.91
1010704	**Hire of skip; delivery to site; removing when full; disposal of contents; payment of tipping charges; skip size:**										
1010704A	4.5 m³	m³	–	–	33.02	4.87	37.89	–	36.32	5.36	41.68
1010705	**Excavated material loaded from spoil heaps or side of excavation into lorry and cart to contractor's tip:**										
1010705A	by hand	m³	1.75	36.49	24.08	–	60.57	40.14	26.49	–	66.63
1010705B	by machine	m³	–	–	26.94	–	26.94	–	29.63	–	29.63

Excavation, Earthwork and Concrete Work

Small Works 2009		Unit	Labour Hours	Labour Net	Plant Net	Materials Net	Unit Net	Labour Gross	Plant Gross	Materials Gross	Unit Price
								(Gross rates include 10% profit)			
				£	£	£	£	£	£	£	£
101	**NEW WORK**										
10108	**FILLING**										
1010801	**Excavated material as filling to excavations; by hand; deposited; compacted:**										
1010801A	in 250 mm layers	m³	1.50	31.28	–	–	31.28	34.41	–	–	34.41
1010802	**Excavated material as filling in making up levels; by hand; wheeling average 25 m; deposited; compacted; thickness:**										
1010802A	over 250 mm.............	m³	2.20	45.87	–	–	45.87	50.46	–	–	50.46
1010802B	average 100 mm.........	m²	0.36	7.51	–	–	7.51	8.26	–	–	8.26
1010802C	average 150 mm.........	m²	0.46	9.59	–	–	9.59	10.55	–	–	10.55
1010802D	average 200 mm.........	m²	0.55	11.47	–	–	11.47	12.62	–	–	12.62
1010803	**Imported soil filling to make up levels by hand; wheel average 25 m; deposited; compacted; thickness:**										
1010803A	over 250 mm.............	m³	1.30	27.11	–	57.19	84.30	29.82	–	62.91	92.73
1010803B	average 100 mm.........	m²	0.17	3.55	–	5.74	9.29	3.91	–	6.31	10.22
1010803C	average 150 mm.........	m²	0.26	5.42	–	8.59	14.01	5.96	–	9.45	15.41
1010803D	average 200 mm.........	m²	0.35	7.30	–	11.44	18.74	8.03	–	12.58	20.61
1010804	**Imported hardcore filling to make up levels; by hand; wheel average 25 m; deposited; compacted; thickness:**										
1010804A	over 250 mm.............	m³	2.70	56.29	–	25.35	81.64	61.92	–	27.89	89.80
1010804B	average 75 mm...........	m²	0.27	5.63	–	1.91	7.54	6.19	–	2.10	8.29
1010804C	average 100 mm.........	m²	0.36	7.50	–	2.54	10.04	8.25	–	2.79	11.04
1010804D	average 150 mm.........	m²	0.54	11.26	–	3.81	15.07	12.39	–	4.19	16.58
1010804E	average 200 mm.........	m²	0.72	15.01	–	5.08	20.09	16.51	–	5.59	22.10
1010805	**Hand packing hardcore to form vertical or battering faces; thickness:**										
1010805A	over 250 mm.............	m²	1.26	26.27	–	–	26.27	28.90	–	–	28.90
1010805B	average 100 mm.........	m	0.20	4.17	–	–	4.17	4.59	–	–	4.59
1010805C	average 150 mm.........	m	0.30	6.26	–	–	6.26	6.89	–	–	6.89
1010805D	average 200 mm.........	m	0.34	7.09	–	–	7.09	7.80	–	–	7.80

Small Works 2009		Unit	Labour Hours	Labour Net	Plant Net	Materials Net	Unit Net	Labour Gross	Plant Gross	Materials Gross	Unit Price
								(Gross rates include 10% profit)			
				£	£	£	£	£	£	£	£
10109	**SURFACE TREATMENTS**										
1010901	**Level and compact:**										
1010901A	bottoms of excavation	m²	0.12	2.50	–	–	2.50	2.75	–	–	2.75
1010902	**Grade and compact bottom of excavation or surface of filling to:**										
1010902A	falls.	m²	0.15	3.13	–	–	3.13	3.44	–	–	3.44
1010902B	crossfalls.	m²	0.27	5.63	–	–	5.63	6.19	–	–	6.19
1010903	**Blind surfaces of soil or hardcore filling with sand; thickness:**										
1010903A	25 mm	m²	0.10	2.09	–	0.90	2.99	2.30	–	0.99	3.29
1010903B	50 mm	m²	0.14	2.92	–	1.80	4.72	3.21	–	1.98	5.19
1010904	**Blind surfaces of soil or hardcore filling with ash; thickness:**										
1010904A	25 mm	m²	0.12	2.50	–	1.18	3.68	2.75	–	1.30	4.05
1010904B	50 mm	m²	0.16	3.34	–	2.36	5.70	3.67	–	2.60	6.27

Excavation, Earthwork and Concrete Work

Small Works 2009		Unit	Labour Hours	Labour Net	Plant Net	Materials Net	Unit Net	Labour Gross	Plant Gross	Materials Gross	Unit Price
				£	£	£	£	£	£	£	£
								(Gross rates include 10% profit)			
101	**NEW WORK**										
10110	**CONCRETE WORK**										
1011001	**Concrete (1:3:6) in:**										
1011001A	foundation trench........	m³	4.50	93.82	–	99.00	192.82	103.20	–	108.90	212.10
1011001B	bed, spread over site and levelled 100 mm thick	m³	7.50	156.37	–	99.00	255.37	172.01	–	108.90	280.91
1011001C	bed, spread over site and levelled 150 mm thick	m³	7.00	145.95	–	99.00	244.95	160.55	–	108.90	269.45
1011001D	bed, spread over site and levelled 300 mm thick	m³	5.00	104.25	–	99.00	203.25	114.68	–	108.90	223.58
1011002	**Concrete (1:2:4) in:**										
1011002A	foundation trench........	m³	4.50	93.82	–	113.59	207.41	103.20	–	124.95	228.15
1011002B	treads, risers and landings (formwork measured separately)	m³	5.25	109.46	–	113.59	223.05	120.41	–	124.95	245.36
1011002C	isolated pier holes	m³	5.40	112.59	–	113.59	226.18	123.85	–	124.95	248.80
1011002D	small quantities to hearths (including formwork) 125 mm thick	m²	3.00	62.55	–	18.78	81.33	68.81	–	20.66	89.46
1011003	**Fill cavity with fine concrete:**										
1011003A	50 mm	m²	0.65	13.55	–	6.22	19.77	14.91	–	6.84	21.75
1011004	**Labour tamped finish surface of unset concrete to:**										
1011004A	levels	m²	0.15	3.13	–	–	3.13	3.44	–	–	3.44
1011004B	falls....................	m²	0.16	3.34	–	–	3.34	3.67	–	–	3.67
1011004C	crossfalls...............	m²	0.18	3.75	–	–	3.75	4.13	–	–	4.13
1011004D	cambers.................	m²	0.19	3.96	–	–	3.96	4.36	–	–	4.36
1011004E	slopes	m²	0.16	3.34	–	–	3.34	3.67	–	–	3.67
1011005	**Labour spade finish surface of unset concrete to:**										
1011005A	levels	m²	0.22	4.59	–	–	4.59	5.05	–	–	5.05
1011005B	falls....................	m²	0.25	5.21	–	–	5.21	5.73	–	–	5.73
1011005C	crossfalls...............	m²	0.29	6.05	–	–	6.05	6.66	–	–	6.66
1011005D	cambers.................	m²	0.32	6.67	–	–	6.67	7.34	–	–	7.34
1011005E	slopes	m²	0.25	5.21	–	–	5.21	5.73	–	–	5.73
1011006	**Labour trowelled finish surface of unset concrete to:**										
1011006A	levels	m²	0.29	6.05	–	–	6.05	6.66	–	–	6.66
1011006B	falls....................	m²	0.34	7.09	–	–	7.09	7.80	–	–	7.80
1011006C	crossfalls...............	m²	0.41	8.55	–	–	8.55	9.41	–	–	9.41
1011006D	cambers.................	m²	0.45	9.38	–	–	9.38	10.32	–	–	10.32
1011006E	slopes	m²	0.34	7.09	–	–	7.09	7.80	–	–	7.80
1011007	**Labour power floating finish surface of unset concrete to:**										
1011007A	levels	m²	0.24	5.01	1.21	–	6.22	5.51	1.33	–	6.84
1011007B	falls....................	m²	0.27	5.63	1.36	–	6.99	6.19	1.50	–	7.69
1011007C	crossfalls...............	m²	0.32	6.67	1.62	–	8.29	7.34	1.78	–	9.12
1011007D	cambers.................	m²	0.35	7.30	1.77	–	9.07	8.03	1.95	–	9.98
1011007E	slopes	m²	0.27	5.63	1.36	–	6.99	6.19	1.50	–	7.69
1011008	**Extra for working concrete around:**										
1011008A	pipes or cables	m²	0.20	4.17	–	–	4.17	4.59	–	–	4.59
1011010	**Carborundum non-slip grain surfacing to:**										
1011010A	concrete steps etc	m²	0.25	5.22	–	1.14	6.36	5.74	–	1.25	7.00

Small Works 2009		Unit	Labour Hours	Labour Net	Plant Net	Materials Net	Unit Net	Labour Gross	Plant Gross	Materials Gross	Unit Price
								(Gross rates include 10% profit)			
				£	£	£	£	£	£	£	£
101	**NEW WORK**										
10110	**CONCRETE WORK**										
1011011	**Sizalcraft building sheets and laying:**										
1011011A	under concrete floors......	m²	0.04	0.83	–	1.75	2.58	0.91	–	1.93	2.84
1011012	**Polythene building film and laying:**										
1011012A	under concrete floors......	m²	0.04	0.83	–	1.40	2.23	0.91	–	1.54	2.45
1011013	**Treat concrete floors with three applications of:**										
1011013A	silicate of soda solution....	m²	0.10	2.09	–	–	2.09	2.30	–	–	2.30
1011014	**Groove in concrete for and including galvanised iron water bar:**										
1011014A	25 mm × 6 mm........	m	0.75	15.64	–	9.31	24.95	17.20	–	10.24	27.45
1011015	**Groove including pinning lugs for:**										
1011015A	sliding door track (track fittings measured separately)	m	0.55	11.47	–	–	11.47	12.62	–	–	12.62
1011016	**Hack face of concrete for key:**										
1011016A	by hand	m²	0.50	10.43	–	–	10.43	11.47	–	–	11.47
1011016B	by machine	m²	0.25	5.21	0.83	–	6.04	5.73	0.91	–	6.64
1011017	**Bitumen expansion joint 9 mm:**										
1011017A	100 mm deep: seal top edge	m	0.50	10.43	–	3.29	13.72	11.47	–	3.62	15.09
1011018	**Form holes for pipes through 100 mm concrete and make good:**										
1011018A	small	Each	0.30	6.26	–	–	6.26	6.89	–	–	6.89
1011018B	large...................	Each	0.35	7.30	–	–	7.30	8.03	–	–	8.03
1011019	**Form hole for pipes through 150 mm concrete and make good:**										
1011019A	small	Each	0.35	7.30	–	–	7.30	8.03	–	–	8.03
1011019B	large...................	Each	0.38	7.92	–	–	7.92	8.71	–	–	8.71
1011020	**Form mortices in concrete for iron dowels and ragbolts and grout in:**										
1011020A	100 mm deep	Each	0.50	10.43	–	0.41	10.84	11.47	–	0.45	11.92
1011021	**Grouting in:**										
1011021A	foundation bolts and stanchion bases	Each	0.50	10.43	–	0.82	11.25	11.47	–	0.90	12.38

Excavation, Earthwork and Concrete Work

Small Works 2009		Unit	Labour Hours	Labour Net	Plant Net	Materials Net	Unit Net	Labour Gross	Plant Gross	Materials Gross	Unit Price
									(Gross rates include 10% profit)		
				£	£	£	£	£	£	£	£
101	**NEW WORK**										
10111	**READY-MIXED PLAIN CONCRETE**										
1011101	**Foundations:**										
1011101A	exceeding 300 mm thick ...	m³	3.00	62.55	–	156.19	218.74	68.81	–	171.81	240.61
1011101B	not exceeding 300 mm thick	m³	3.30	68.80	–	156.19	224.99	75.68	–	171.81	247.49
1011102	**Floors or oversite concrete:**										
1011102A	100 mm thick	m³	6.00	125.10	–	156.19	281.29	137.61	–	171.81	309.42
1011102B	150 mm thick	m³	5.50	114.67	–	156.19	270.86	126.14	–	171.81	297.95
1011102C	300 mm thick	m³	4.80	100.08	–	156.19	256.27	110.09	–	171.81	281.90
10112	**READY-MIXED REINFORCED CONCRETE (REINFORCEMENT AND FORMWORK MEASURED SEPARATELY)**										
1011201	**Foundations:**										
1011201A	exceeding 300 mm thick ...	m³	4.00	83.40	–	156.19	239.59	91.74	–	171.81	263.55
1011202	**Suspended floors or roofs:**										
1011202A	100 mm thick	m³	7.50	156.37	–	156.19	312.56	172.01	–	171.81	343.82
1011202B	150 mm thick	m³	7.00	145.95	–	156.19	302.14	160.55	–	171.81	332.35
1011202C	300 mm thick	m³	6.00	125.10	–	156.19	281.29	137.61	–	171.81	309.42
1011203	**Walls:**										
1011203A	100 mm thick	m³	8.00	166.80	–	156.19	322.99	183.48	–	171.81	355.29
1011203B	150 mm thick	m³	7.50	156.37	–	156.19	312.56	172.01	–	171.81	343.82
1011203C	300 mm thick	m³	6.50	135.52	–	156.19	291.71	149.07	–	171.81	320.88
1011204	**Columns; sectional area:**										
1011204A	not exceeding 0.05 sq.m ...	m³	10.00	208.50	–	156.19	364.69	229.35	–	171.81	401.16
1011204B	0.05 sq.m.-0.10 sq.m	m³	9.00	187.65	–	156.19	343.84	206.42	–	171.81	378.22
1011204C	exceeding 0.10 sq.m	m³	8.00	166.80	–	156.19	322.99	183.48	–	171.81	355.29
1011205	**Beams; sectional area:**										
1011205A	not exceeding 0.05 sq.m ...	m³	9.00	187.65	–	156.19	343.84	206.42	–	171.81	378.22
1011205B	0.05 sq.m-0.10 sq.m	m³	8.00	166.80	–	156.19	322.99	183.48	–	171.81	355.29
1011205C	exceeding 0.10 sq.m	m³	7.00	145.95	–	156.19	302.14	160.55	–	171.81	332.35

Small Works 2009		Unit	Labour Hours	Labour Net	Plant Net	Materials Net	Unit Net	Labour Gross	Plant Gross	Materials Gross	Unit Price
								(Gross rates include 10% profit)			
				£	£	£	£	£	£	£	£
101	**NEW WORK**										
10113	**SAWN SOFTWOOD FORMWORK**										
1011301	Horizontal soffit to floors, landings and the like:										
1011301A	first use	m²	2.70	75.06	–	9.79	84.85	82.57	–	10.77	93.34
1011301B	each subsequent use	m²	2.70	75.06	–	0.21	75.27	82.57	–	0.23	82.80
1011302	Sloping soffit of floors, roofs, staircases and the like:										
1011302A	first use	m²	3.60	100.08	–	9.79	109.87	110.09	–	10.77	120.86
1011302B	each subsequent use	m²	3.60	100.08	–	0.21	100.29	110.09	–	0.23	110.32
1011303	Vertical or battering sides of foundations, ground beams, large machine bases and the like:										
1011303A	first use	m²	3.45	95.91	–	3.26	99.17	105.50	–	3.59	109.09
1011303B	each subsequent use	m²	3.45	95.91	–	0.21	96.12	105.50	–	0.23	105.73
1011304	Vertical or battering sides of walls, solid balustrades and the like:										
1011304A	first use	m²	3.45	95.91	–	9.79	105.70	105.50	–	10.77	116.27
1011304B	each subsequent use	m²	3.45	95.91	–	0.21	96.12	105.50	–	0.23	105.73
1011305	Vertical or battering sides of stanchion casings, columns, piers, pilasters and the like:										
1011305A	first use	m²	3.60	100.08	–	9.45	109.53	110.09	–	10.40	120.48
1011305B	each subsequent use	m²	3.60	100.08	–	0.21	100.29	110.09	–	0.23	110.32
1011306	Sides and soffits of openings in walls, recesses in walls, projecting panels on walls and the like:										
1011306A	first use	m²	3.60	100.08	–	9.79	109.87	110.09	–	10.77	120.86
1011306B	each subsequent use	m²	3.60	100.08	–	0.21	100.29	110.09	–	0.23	110.32
1011308	Sides and soffits of horizontal beam casings, beams, lintels and the like:										
1011308A	first use	m²	3.90	108.42	–	9.79	118.21	119.26	–	10.77	130.03
1011308B	each subsequent use	m²	3.90	108.42	–	0.21	108.63	119.26	–	0.23	119.49
1011309	Sides and soffits of sloping beam casings, staircase strings and the like:										
1011309A	first use	m²	4.65	129.27	–	9.79	139.06	142.20	–	10.77	152.97
1011309B	each subsequent use	m²	4.65	129.27	–	0.21	129.48	142.20	–	0.23	142.43
1011310	Sloping upper surface of beam casings, beams, staircase strings and the like; exceeding 15 degrees from the horizontal:										
1011310A	first use	m²	3.90	108.42	–	9.79	118.21	119.26	–	10.77	130.03
1011310B	each subsequent use	m²	3.90	108.42	–	0.21	108.63	119.26	–	0.23	119.49
1011311	Isolated beam casings and isolated beams:										
1011311A	first use	m²	4.20	116.76	–	9.79	126.55	128.44	–	10.77	139.21
1011311B	each subsequent use	m²	4.20	116.76	–	0.21	116.97	128.44	–	0.23	128.67

Excavation, Earthwork and Concrete Work

Small Works 2009		Unit	Labour Hours	Labour Net	Plant Net	Materials Net	Unit Net	Labour Gross	Plant Gross	Materials Gross	Unit Price
								(Gross rates include 10% profit)			
				£	£	£	£	£	£	£	£
101	**NEW WORK**										
10113	**SAWN SOFTWOOD FORMWORK**										
1011312	**Edges or faces of beds and the like not exceeding 250 mm high:**										
1011312A	first use	m	0.38	10.56	–	0.79	11.35	11.62	–	0.87	12.49
1011312B	each subsequent use	m	0.38	10.57	–	0.05	10.62	11.63	–	0.06	11.68
1011313	**Edges of suspended floors, landings, roofs and the like not exceeding 250 mm wide:**										
1011313A	first use	m	0.75	20.85	–	2.48	23.33	22.94	–	2.73	25.66
1011313B	each subsequent use	m	0.75	20.85	–	0.10	20.95	22.94	–	0.11	23.05
1011314	**Sides of kerbs and upstands and the like not exceeding 250 mm high:**										
1011314A	first use	m	0.68	18.90	–	0.79	19.69	20.79	–	0.87	21.66
1011314B	each subsequent use	m	0.68	18.91	–	0.10	19.01	20.80	–	0.11	20.91
1011315	**Risers of steps and staircases not exceeding 250 mm wide:**										
1011315A	first use	m	0.60	16.68	–	2.48	19.16	18.35	–	2.73	21.08
1011315B	each subsequent use	m	0.60	16.68	–	0.10	16.78	18.35	–	0.11	18.46
1011316	**Edges and soffits of projecting eaves not exceeding 600 mm girth:**										
1011316A	first use	m	2.25	62.55	–	5.96	68.51	68.81	–	6.56	75.36
1011316B	each subsequent use	m	2.25	62.55	–	0.10	62.65	68.81	–	0.11	68.92
1011317	**Projecting or sunk cornices, bands and the like not exceeding 250 mm girth:**										
1011317A	first use	m	0.60	16.68	–	2.48	19.16	18.35	–	2.73	21.08
1011317B	each subsequent use	m	0.60	16.68	–	0.10	16.78	18.35	–	0.11	18.46
1011318	**Throats, grooves, chases, rebates, chamfers and the like not exceeding 100 mm wide:**										
1011318A	first use	m	0.20	5.56	–	1.01	6.57	6.12	–	1.11	7.23
1011318B	each subsequent use	m	0.20	5.56	–	0.11	5.67	6.12	–	0.12	6.24
1011319	**Labours on formwork:**										
1011319A	raking cutting	m	0.20	5.56	–	0.34	5.90	6.12	–	0.37	6.49
1011319B	curved cutting............	m	0.65	18.07	–	0.79	18.86	19.88	–	0.87	20.75

Small Works 2009		Unit	Labour Hours	Labour Net	Plant Net	Materials Net	Unit Net	Labour Gross	Plant Gross	Materials Gross	Unit Price
								(Gross rates include 10% profit)			
				£	£	£	£	£	£	£	£
101	**NEW WORK**										
10114	**PLYWOOD FORMWORK**										
1011401	**Horizontal soffit of floors, landings and the like:**										
1011401A	first use	m²	2.84	78.96	–	15.09	94.05	86.86	–	16.60	103.46
1011401B	each subsequent use	m²	2.84	78.95	–	0.41	79.36	86.85	–	0.45	87.30
1011402	**Sloping soffit of floors, roofs, staircases and the like:**										
1011402A	first use	m²	3.74	103.98	–	15.09	119.07	114.38	–	16.60	130.98
1011402B	each subsequent use	m²	3.74	103.97	–	0.41	104.38	114.37	–	0.45	114.82
1011403	**Vertical or battering sides of foundations, ground beams, large machine bases and the like:**										
1011403A	first use	m²	3.59	99.81	–	13.39	113.20	109.79	–	14.73	124.52
1011403B	each subsequent use	m²	2.39	66.44	–	0.41	66.85	73.08	–	0.45	73.54
1011404	**Vertical or battering sides of walls, solid balustrades and the like:**										
1011404A	first use	m²	3.59	99.81	–	13.39	113.20	109.79	–	14.73	124.52
1011404B	each subsequent use	m²	2.39	66.44	–	0.38	66.82	73.08	–	0.42	73.50
1011405	**Vertical or battering sides of stanchion casings, columns, piers, pilasters and the like:**										
1011405A	first use	m²	3.74	103.98	–	13.39	117.37	114.38	–	14.73	129.11
1011405B	each subsequent use	m²	2.54	70.62	–	0.26	70.88	77.68	–	0.29	77.97
1011406	**Sides and soffits of openings in walls, recesses in walls, projecting panels on walls and the like:**										
1011406A	first use	m²	3.74	103.97	–	13.71	117.68	114.37	–	15.08	129.45
1011406B	each subsequent use	m²	3.74	103.97	–	0.41	104.38	114.37	–	0.45	114.82
1011408	**Sides and soffits of horizontal beam casings, beams, lintels and the like:**										
1011408A	first use	m²	4.04	112.32	–	13.39	125.71	123.55	–	14.73	138.28
1011408B	each subsequent use	m²	2.84	78.95	–	0.41	79.36	86.85	–	0.45	87.30
1011409	**Sides and soffits of sloping beam casings, staircase strings and the like:**										
1011409A	first use	m²	4.79	133.17	–	13.39	146.56	146.49	–	14.73	161.22
1011409B	each subsequent use	m²	3.29	91.46	–	0.41	91.87	100.61	–	0.45	101.06

Excavation, Earthwork and Concrete Work

Small Works 2009		Unit	Labour Hours	Labour Net	Plant Net	Materials Net	Unit Net	Labour Gross	Plant Gross	Materials Gross	Unit Price
								(Gross rates include 10% profit)			
				£	£	£	£	£	£	£	£
101	**NEW WORK**										
10114	**PLYWOOD FORMWORK**										
1011410	**Sloping upper surface of beam casings, beams, staircase strings and the like, exceeding 15 degrees from the horizontal:**										
1011410A	first use	m²	4.04	112.32	–	13.39	125.71	123.55	–	14.73	138.28
1011410B	each subsequent use	m²	2.84	78.95	–	0.41	79.36	86.85	–	0.45	87.30
1011411	**Isolated beam casings and isolated beams:**										
1011411A	first use	m²	4.34	120.66	–	13.39	134.05	132.73	–	14.73	147.46
1011411B	each subsequent use	m²	3.14	87.29	–	0.41	87.70	96.02	–	0.45	96.47
1011412	**Edges or faces of beds and the like not exceeding 250 mm high:**										
1011412A	first use	m	0.38	10.56	–	2.85	13.41	11.62	–	3.14	14.75
1011412B	each subsequent use	m	0.38	10.56	–	0.11	10.67	11.62	–	0.12	11.74
1011413	**Edges of suspended floors, landings, roofs and the like not exceeding 250 mm wide:**										
1011413A	first use	m	0.75	20.85	–	3.43	24.28	22.94	–	3.77	26.71
1011413B	each subsequent use	m	0.75	20.85	–	0.12	20.97	22.94	–	0.13	23.07
1011414	**Sides of kerbs and upstands and the like not exceeding 250 mm high:**										
1011414A	first use	m	0.68	18.90	–	2.79	21.69	20.79	–	3.07	23.86
1011414B	each subsequent use	m	0.68	18.90	–	0.12	19.02	20.79	–	0.13	20.92
1011415	**Risers of steps and staircases not exceeding 250 mm wide:**										
1011415A	first use	m	0.60	16.68	–	3.67	20.35	18.35	–	4.04	22.39
1011415B	each subsequent use	m	0.60	16.68	–	0.12	16.80	18.35	–	0.13	18.48
1011416	**Edges and soffits of projecting eaves not exceeding 600 mm girth:**										
1011416A	first use	m	2.25	62.55	–	8.81	71.36	68.81	–	9.69	78.50
1011416B	each subsequent use	m	2.25	62.55	–	0.23	62.78	68.81	–	0.25	69.06
1011417	**Projecting or sunk cornices, bands and the like not exceeding 250 mm girth:**										
1011417A	first use	m	0.60	16.68	–	3.67	20.35	18.35	–	4.04	22.39
1011417B	each subsequent use	m	0.60	16.68	–	0.12	16.80	18.35	–	0.13	18.48
1011418	**Throats, grooves, chases, rebates, chamfers and the like not exceeding 100 mm wide:**										
1011418A	first use	m	0.20	5.56	–	1.36	6.92	6.12	–	1.50	7.61
1011418B	each subsequent use	m	0.20	5.56	–	0.06	5.62	6.12	–	0.07	6.18
1011419	**Labours on formwork:**										
1011419A	raking cutting	m	0.20	5.56	–	1.59	7.15	6.12	–	1.75	7.87
1011419B	curved cutting	m	0.65	18.07	–	3.19	21.26	19.88	–	3.51	23.39

Small Works 2009		Unit	Labour Hours	Labour Net	Plant Net	Materials Net	Unit Net	Labour Gross	Plant Gross	Materials Gross	Unit Price
								(Gross rates include 10% profit)			
				£	£	£	£	£	£	£	£
101	**NEW WORK**										
10115	**REINFORCEMENT**										
1011501	**Plain round mild steel bar reinforcement; BS 449; supplied, cut, bent, labelled and fixed including tying wire, distance blocks and ordinary spacers:**										
1011501A	6 mm	m	0.12	3.33	–	0.31	3.64	3.66	–	0.34	4.00
1011501B	8 mm	m	0.10	2.78	–	0.49	3.27	3.06	–	0.54	3.60
1011501C	10 mm	m	0.09	2.50	–	0.75	3.25	2.75	–	0.83	3.58
1011501D	12 mm	m	0.08	2.22	–	1.02	3.24	2.44	–	1.12	3.56
1011501E	16 mm	m	0.07	1.94	–	1.82	3.76	2.13	–	2.00	4.14
1011501F	20 mm	m	0.07	1.95	–	2.63	4.58	2.15	–	2.89	5.04
1011501G	25 mm	m	0.07	1.95	–	3.99	5.94	2.15	–	4.39	6.53
1011502	**Mild steel bar links, stirrups and binders; cut, bent, labelled and fixed including tying wire and special spacers:**										
1011502A	6 mm	m	0.14	3.89	–	0.31	4.20	4.28	–	0.34	4.62
1011502B	8 mm	m	0.12	3.34	–	0.49	3.83	3.67	–	0.54	4.21
1011503	**Fabric reinforcement; BS 4483; in slabs including tying wire and distance blocks, with allowance for 200 mm laps:**										
1011503A	A98	m²	0.14	3.89	–	2.02	5.91	4.28	–	2.22	6.50
1011503B	A142	m²	0.14	3.89	–	2.62	6.51	4.28	–	2.88	7.16
1011503C	A193	m²	0.14	3.89	–	3.54	7.43	4.28	–	3.89	8.17
1011503D	A252	m²	0.16	4.45	–	4.63	9.08	4.90	–	5.09	9.99
1011503E	A393	m²	0.18	5.01	–	7.37	12.38	5.51	–	8.11	13.62
1011503F	B283	m²	0.14	3.90	–	4.63	8.53	4.29	–	5.09	9.38
1011503G	B385	m²	0.16	4.45	–	5.57	10.02	4.90	–	6.13	11.02
1011503H	B503	m²	0.18	5.00	–	7.16	12.16	5.50	–	7.88	13.38
1011503I	B785	m²	0.20	5.56	–	9.19	14.75	6.12	–	10.11	16.23
1011503J	C283	m²	0.14	3.89	–	3.31	7.20	4.28	–	3.64	7.92
1011503K	C385	m²	0.14	3.90	–	4.23	8.13	4.29	–	4.65	8.94
1011503L	C503	m²	0.16	4.44	–	5.28	9.72	4.88	–	5.81	10.69
1011504	**Fabric reinforcement; BS 4483; in casings to steel columns and beams including bending tying wire and distance blocks, with allowance for 200 mm laps:**										
1011504A	D49	m²	0.30	8.34	–	0.88	9.22	9.17	–	0.97	10.14
1011504B	D98	m²	0.35	9.73	–	2.02	11.75	10.70	–	2.22	12.93

Excavation, Earthwork and Concrete Work

Small Works 2009		Unit	Labour Hours	Labour Net	Plant Net	Materials Net	Unit Net	Labour Gross	Plant Gross	Materials Gross	Unit Price
								(Gross rates include 10% profit)			
				£	£	£	£	£	£	£	£
101	**NEW WORK**										
10116	**PRECAST CONCRETE**										
1011601	**Copings; weathered and throated; bedded in gauged mortar; pointed:**										
1011601A	300 mm × 75 mm	m	1.00	24.43	–	19.84	44.27	26.87	–	21.82	48.70
1011601B	356 mm × 75 mm	m	1.70	41.53	–	24.13	65.66	45.68	–	26.54	72.23
1011602	**Jambs and heads; bedded in gauged mortar; pointed:**										
1011602A	100 mm × 75 mm	m	0.40	9.78	–	8.02	17.80	10.76	–	8.82	19.58
1011602B	225 mm × 75 mm	m	0.55	13.44	–	18.60	32.04	14.78	–	20.46	35.24
1011602C	350 mm × 75 mm	m	0.75	18.33	–	26.72	45.05	20.16	–	29.39	49.56
1011603	**Sills; weathered; throated; grooved; bedded in gauged mortar; pointed:**										
1011603A	225 mm × 75 mm	m	0.60	14.66	–	16.81	31.47	16.13	–	18.49	34.62
1011603B	275 mm × 100 mm	m	0.65	15.88	–	22.65	38.53	17.47	–	24.92	42.38
1011603C	275 mm × 150 mm	m	0.75	18.32	–	30.48	48.80	20.15	–	33.53	53.68
1011604	**Thresholds; weathered; bedded in gauged mortar; pointed:**										
1011604A	275 mm × 75 mm	m	0.55	13.43	–	16.67	30.10	14.77	–	18.34	33.11
1011605	**Duct covers; placed in floor rebates:**										
1011605A	300 mm × 50 mm	m	0.12	2.93	–	9.58	12.51	3.22	–	10.54	13.76
1011605B	300 mm × 63 mm	m	0.12	2.93	–	12.21	15.14	3.22	–	13.43	16.65
1011605C	300 mm × 75 mm	m	0.13	3.18	–	14.05	17.23	3.50	–	15.46	18.95
1011605D	300 mm × 100 mm	m	0.17	4.15	–	19.34	23.49	4.57	–	21.27	25.84
1011606	**Lintels; rectangular; purchased from manufacturer; reinforced; hoisted; bedded in gauged mortar: 100 mm × 65 mm length:**										
1011606A	450 mm	Each	0.10	2.44	–	5.10	7.54	2.68	–	5.61	8.29
1011606B	600 mm	Each	0.13	3.18	–	6.81	9.99	3.50	–	7.49	10.99
1011606C	750 mm	Each	0.17	4.15	–	8.51	12.66	4.57	–	9.36	13.93
1011606D	900 mm	Each	0.20	4.89	–	10.16	15.05	5.38	–	11.18	16.56
1011606E	1050 mm	Each	0.23	5.62	–	11.87	17.49	6.18	–	13.06	19.24
1011606F	1200 mm	Each	0.26	6.35	–	13.57	19.92	6.99	–	14.93	21.91
1011606G	1350 mm	Each	0.30	7.33	–	15.25	22.58	8.06	–	16.78	24.84
1011606H	1500 mm	Each	0.33	8.06	–	16.99	25.05	8.87	–	18.69	27.56
1011607	**Lintels; rectangular; purchased from manufacturer; reinforced; hoisted; bedded in gauged mortar; 100 mm × 150 m length:**										
1011607A	450 mm	Each	0.23	5.62	–	11.61	17.23	6.18	–	12.77	18.95
1011607B	600 mm	Each	0.30	7.33	–	15.49	22.82	8.06	–	17.04	25.10
1011607C	750 mm	Each	0.38	9.29	–	19.35	28.64	10.22	–	21.29	31.50
1011607D	900 mm	Each	0.45	10.99	–	23.24	34.23	12.09	–	25.56	37.65
1011607E	1050 mm	Each	0.53	12.95	–	27.11	40.06	14.25	–	29.82	44.07
1011607F	1200 mm	Each	0.60	14.65	–	30.99	45.64	16.12	–	34.09	50.20
1011607G	1350 mm	Each	0.68	16.61	–	34.86	51.47	18.27	–	38.35	56.62
1011607H	1500 mm	Each	0.75	18.32	–	38.73	57.05	20.15	–	42.60	62.76

Small Works 2009		Unit	Labour Hours	Labour Net	Plant Net	Materials Net	Unit Net	Labour Gross	Plant Gross	Materials Gross	Unit Price
								(Gross rates include 10% profit)			
				£	£	£	£	£	£	£	£
101	**NEW WORK**										
10116	**PRECAST CONCRETE**										
1011608	Lintels; rectangular; purchased from manufacturer; reinforced; hoisted; bedded in gauged mortar; 150 mm × 65 mm length:										
1011608A	450 mm	Each	0.15	3.67	–	7.21	10.88	4.04	–	7.93	11.97
1011608B	600 mm	Each	0.20	4.89	–	9.59	14.48	5.38	–	10.55	15.93
1011608C	750 mm	Each	0.25	6.10	–	12.01	18.11	6.71	–	13.21	19.92
1011608D	900 mm	Each	0.30	7.33	–	14.40	21.73	8.06	–	15.84	23.90
1011608E	1050 mm	Each	0.35	8.55	–	16.74	25.29	9.41	–	18.41	27.82
1011608F	1200 mm	Each	0.40	9.77	–	19.14	28.91	10.75	–	21.05	31.80
1011608G	1350 mm	Each	0.45	11.00	–	21.54	32.54	12.10	–	23.69	35.79
1011608H	1500 mm	Each	0.50	12.22	–	23.93	36.15	13.44	–	26.32	39.77
1011609	Lintels; rectangular; purchased from manufacturer; reinforced; hoisted; bedded in gauged mortar; 215 mm × 65 mm length:										
1011609A	450 mm	Each	0.21	5.13	–	10.42	15.55	5.64	–	11.46	17.11
1011609B	600 mm	Each	0.28	6.84	–	13.92	20.76	7.52	–	15.31	22.84
1011609C	750 mm	Each	0.35	8.55	–	17.39	25.94	9.41	–	19.13	28.53
1011609D	900 mm	Each	0.42	10.26	–	20.85	31.11	11.29	–	22.94	34.22
1011609E	1050 mm	Each	0.49	11.98	–	24.33	36.31	13.18	–	26.76	39.94
1011609F	1200 mm	Each	0.56	13.68	–	27.78	41.46	15.05	–	30.56	45.61
1011609G	1350 mm	Each	0.64	15.63	–	31.28	46.91	17.19	–	34.41	51.60
1011609H	1500 mm	Each	0.71	17.34	–	34.78	52.12	19.07	–	38.26	57.33
1011610	Lintels; rectangular; purchased from manufacturer; reinforced; hoisted; bedded in gauged mortar: 255 mm × 65 mm length:										
1011610A	450 mm	Each	0.25	6.11	–	12.26	18.37	6.72	–	13.49	20.21
1011610B	600 mm	Each	0.33	8.07	–	16.33	24.40	8.88	–	17.96	26.84
1011610C	750 mm	Each	0.41	10.02	–	20.39	30.41	11.02	–	22.43	33.45
1011610D	900 mm	Each	0.50	12.22	–	24.52	36.74	13.44	–	26.97	40.41
1011610E	1050 mm	Each	0.58	14.17	–	28.57	42.74	15.59	–	31.43	47.01
1011610F	1200 mm	Each	0.66	16.12	–	32.67	48.79	17.73	–	35.94	53.67
1011610G	1350 mm	Each	0.74	18.08	–	36.77	54.85	19.89	–	40.45	60.34
1011610H	1500 mm	Each	0.83	20.28	–	40.83	61.11	22.31	–	44.91	67.22
1011611	Lintels; rectangular; prepared on site by contractor: reinforcement; formwork; hoisted; in gauged mortar:										
1011611A	150 mm × 112 mm: 2 No.-10 mm rods.	m	0.45	10.99	–	4.97	15.96	12.09	–	5.47	17.56
1011611B	150 mm × 150 mm: 2 No.-12 mm rods.	m	0.55	13.43	–	6.60	20.03	14.77	–	7.26	22.03
1011611C	225 mm × 112 mm: 2 No.-12 mm rods.	m	0.65	15.88	–	7.52	23.40	17.47	–	8.27	25.74
1011611D	225 mm × 150 mm: 2 No.-19 mm rods.	m	0.85	20.76	–	11.05	31.81	22.84	–	12.16	34.99
1011611E	225 mm × 225 mm: 3 No.-19 mm rods.	m	1.10	26.87	–	16.12	42.99	29.56	–	17.73	47.29
1011612	Lintels; boot; prepared on site by contractor; reinforcement; formwork; hoisted; bedded in gauged mortar:										
1011612A	338 mm × 225 mm extreme; 3 No.-19 mm rods	m	1.70	41.53	–	19.77	61.30	45.68	–	21.75	67.43

Excavation, Earthwork and Concrete Work

Small Works 2009		Unit	Labour Hours	Labour Net	Plant Net	Materials Net	Unit Net	Labour Gross	Plant Gross	Materials Gross	Unit Price
								(Gross rates include 10% profit)			
				£	£	£	£	£	£	£	£
101	**NEW WORK**										
10116	**PRECAST CONCRETE**										
1011613	**Padstones; bedded in gauged mortar:**										
1011613A	225 mm × 225 mm × 150 mm	Each	0.60	14.65	–	3.81	18.46	16.12	–	4.19	20.31
1011613B	350 mm × 225 mm × 150 mm	Each	0.90	21.98	–	5.04	27.02	24.18	–	5.54	29.72
1011613C	450 mm × 225 mm × 150 mm	Each	1.20	29.31	–	7.08	36.39	32.24	–	7.79	40.03
1011613D	450 mm × 450 mm × 225 mm	Each	2.50	61.08	–	14.05	75.13	67.19	–	15.46	82.64
1011614	**Pier caps; bedded in gauged mortar:**										
1011614A	300 mm × 300 mm × 75 mm for 225 mm piers	Each	1.00	24.43	–	17.50	41.93	26.87	–	19.25	46.12
1011614B	400 mm × 400 mm × 75 mm for 337 mm piers	Each	1.30	31.76	–	24.75	56.51	34.94	–	27.23	62.16

Small Works 2009		Unit	Labour Hours	Labour Net	Plant Net	Materials Net	Unit Net	Labour Gross	Plant Gross	Materials Gross	Unit Price
								(Gross rates include 10% profit)			
				£	£	£	£	£	£	£	£
102	**REPAIRS AND ALTERATIONS**										
10201	**EXCAVATION**										
1020101	**Excavate by hand over site area; wheel 18 m; deposit in skip:**										
1020101A	average 300 mm deep	m²	1.86	38.78	–	–	38.78	42.66	–	–	42.66
1020102	**Excavate by hand for trenches to receive foundations; wheel 18 m; deposit in skip:**										
1020102A	not exceeding 1.0 m deep . .	m³	6.52	135.94	–	–	135.94	149.53	–	–	149.53
1020102B	exceeding 1.0 m deep and not exceeding 2.0 m deep . .	m³	8.02	167.22	–	–	167.22	183.94	–	–	183.94
1020103	**Excavate by hand for basement; wheel 18 m: deposit in skip:**										
1020103A	not exceeding 1.0 m deep . .	m³	6.00	125.10	–	–	125.10	137.61	–	–	137.61
1020103B	exceeding 1.0 m deep and not exceeding 2.0 m deep . .	m³	6.72	140.11	–	–	140.11	154.12	–	–	154.12
1020104	**Excavated material as filling to excavations deposited and compacted by hand in:**										
1020104A	250 mm layers	m³	2.00	41.70	–	–	41.70	45.87	–	–	45.87
1020105	**Extra over excavation for breaking up by hand brickwork in:**										
1020105A	old foundations	m³	7.09	147.83	–	–	147.83	162.61	–	–	162.61
1020106	**Hire of skip, delivery to site: removing when full, disposal of contents, payment of tipping charges skip size:**										
1020106A	4.5 m³	m³	–	–	49.56	–	49.56	–	54.52	–	54.52
1020107	**Earthwork support in firm ground to opposing faces not exceeding 2.00 m apart: maximum depth not exceeding:**										
1020107A	1.00 m	m²	0.85	17.72	–	2.08	19.80	19.49	–	2.29	21.78
1020107B	2.00 m	m²	0.93	19.39	–	2.30	21.69	21.33	–	2.53	23.86
1020108	**Earthwork support in loose ground to opposing faces not exceeding 2 m apart: maximum depth not exceeding:**										
1020108A	1.00 m	m²	6.62	138.03	–	16.49	154.52	151.83	–	18.14	169.97
1020108B	2.00 m	m²	6.62	138.03	–	16.49	154.52	151.83	–	18.14	169.97
1020109	**Imported hardcore compacted to receive concrete to finished thickness:**										
1020109A	100 mm	m²	0.48	10.01	–	2.54	12.55	11.01	–	2.79	13.81
1020109B	150 mm	m²	0.72	15.01	–	3.81	18.82	16.51	–	4.19	20.70
1020109C	225 mm	m²	1.08	22.52	–	5.72	28.24	24.77	–	6.29	31.06

Excavation, Earthwork and Concrete Work

Small Works 2009		Unit	Labour Hours	Labour Net	Plant Net	Materials Net	Unit Net	Labour Gross	Plant Gross	Materials Gross	Unit Price
				£	£	£	£	£	£	£	£
								(Gross rates include 10% profit)			
102	**REPAIRS AND ALTERATIONS**										
10202	**CONCRETE WORK**										
1020201	**Portland cement concrete in foundations**										
1020201A	1:2:4 mix	m³	6.00	125.10	–	124.95	250.05	137.61	–	137.45	275.06
1020201B	1:3:6 mix	m³	6.00	125.10	–	108.90	234.00	137.61	–	119.79	257.40
1020202	**Concrete (1:3:6) oversite; thickness:**										
1020202A	100 mm	m³	9.00	187.65	–	108.90	296.55	206.42	–	119.79	326.21
1020202B	150 mm	m³	8.50	177.22	–	108.90	286.12	194.94	–	119.79	314.73
1020203	**Concrete (1:3:6) oversite in patches not exceeding 4 sq.m in area including jointing to existing; thickness:**										
1020203A	100 mm	m³	14.00	291.90	–	108.90	400.80	321.09	–	119.79	440.88
1020203B	150 mm	m³	13.50	281.47	–	108.90	390.37	309.62	–	119.79	429.41
1020204	**Extra over site concrete for:**										
1020204A	preparing to receive asphalt, tiling etc including extra cement.	m²	0.45	9.38	–	3.59	12.97	10.32	–	3.95	14.27
1020204B	trowelling to smooth surface	m²	0.55	11.47	–	–	11.47	12.62	–	–	12.62
1020205	**Sprinkling surface of concrete with:**										
1020205A	coarse carborundum at 1 kg per sq.m and lightly trowelling	m²	0.55	11.47	–	1.20	12.67	12.62	–	1.32	13.94
1020206	**Clean existing concrete or rendered floors and treat with:**										
1020206A	application of silicate of soda solution	m²	0.30	6.25	–	0.34	6.59	6.88	–	0.37	7.25
1020207	**Reinforced concrete lintels cast in situ including reinforcement and formwork; size:**										
1020207A	113 mm × 150 mm	m	0.75	18.32	–	6.85	25.17	20.15	–	7.54	27.69
1020207B	113 mm × 225 mm	m	0.90	21.99	–	8.49	30.48	24.19	–	9.34	33.53
1020207C	225 mm × 150 mm	m	1.30	31.76	–	10.68	42.44	34.94	–	11.75	46.68
1020207D	225 mm × 225 mm	m	1.45	35.43	–	13.69	49.12	38.97	–	15.06	54.03
1020208	**Precast concrete lintels including reinforcement and formwork; size:**										
1020208A	113 mm × 150 mm	m	0.45	10.99	–	4.97	15.96	12.09	–	5.47	17.56
1020208B	113 mm × 225 mm	m	0.65	15.88	–	7.52	23.40	17.47	–	8.27	25.74
1020208C	225 mm × 150 mm	m	0.85	20.76	–	11.05	31.81	22.84	–	12.16	34.99
1020208D	225 mm × 225 mm	m	1.10	26.87	–	16.12	42.99	29.56	–	17.73	47.29
1020209	**Needle through 225 mm brickwork with 150mm × 100mm shore with one pair Acrow or other adjustable struts to every linear metre or part thereof (maximum span 2.70 m). Cut out and remove defective lintel and supply, hoist and build in precast reinforced concrete lintel and make good all brickwork and plaster disturbed; lintel size:**										
1020209A	225 mm × 150 mm	m	4.85	118.49	5.70	18.98	143.17	130.34	6.27	20.88	157.49
1020209B	225 mm × 225 mm	m	5.10	124.59	5.70	24.06	154.35	137.05	6.27	26.47	169.79

Small Works 2009		Unit	Labour Hours	Labour Net	Plant Net	Materials Net	Unit Net	Labour Gross	Plant Gross	Materials Gross	Unit Price
								—— (Gross rates include 10% profit) ——			
				£	£	£	£	£	£	£	£
102	**REPAIRS AND ALTERATIONS**										
10202	**CONCRETE WORK**										
1020210	Cut away triangular area of brickwork above lintel. Cut out and remove defective lintel and supply, hoist and build in precast reinforced concrete lintel, rebuild brickwork over including facing bricks to match existing and make good internal plaster; lintel size:										
1020210A	225 mm × 225 mm......	m	10.20	249.19	–	29.52	278.71	274.11	–	32.47	306.58
1020210B	225 mm × 338 mm......	m	14.50	354.23	–	41.80	396.03	389.65	–	45.98	435.63
1020211	Take out stone or concrete sill. Supply and build cast concrete sill including all making good; sill size:										
1020211A	225 mm × 75 mm.......	m	1.10	26.88	–	16.81	43.69	29.57	–	18.49	48.06
1020212	Pier caps:										
1020212A	300 mm × 300 mm × 75 mm for 225 mm piers...	Each	1.00	24.43	–	17.63	42.06	26.87	–	19.39	46.27
1020212B	400 mm × 400 mm × 75 mm for 338 mm piers...	Each	1.30	31.76	–	24.88	56.64	34.94	–	27.37	62.30
1020213	Break up and remove old concrete steps, form new steps in:										
1020213A	concrete 1:3:6, including wrought formwork to risers and ends, and surfaces of treads trowelled smooth...	m³	19.00	464.17	–	137.92	602.09	510.59	–	151.71	662.30
1020214	Break up and remove concrete floors, pavings etc, at ground level and load into skip:										
1020214A	not exceeding 150 mm....	m²	2.25	46.91	–	–	46.91	51.60	–	–	51.60
1020214B	150 mm-225 mm.........	m²	4.00	83.40	–	–	83.40	91.74	–	–	91.74
1020214C	225 mm-300 mm.........	m²	6.00	125.10	–	–	125.10	137.61	–	–	137.61
1020215	Break up and remove reinforced concrete floors, pavings, etc, at ground level and load into skip:										
1020215A	not exceeding 150 mm....	m²	3.40	70.89	–	–	70.89	77.98	–	–	77.98
1020215B	150 mm-225 mm.........	m²	6.00	125.10	–	–	125.10	137.61	–	–	137.61
1020215C	225 mm-300 mm.........	m²	9.00	187.65	–	–	187.65	206.42	–	–	206.42
1020216	Break up concrete paving 750 mm wide for new wall and remove. Excavate trench and part return, fill in and ram and remove remainder. Make good concrete paving. (Foundation concrete measured separately):										
1020216A	100 mm thick............	m	2.85	59.42	–	7.08	66.50	65.36	–	7.79	73.15

Excavation, Earthwork and Concrete Work

Small Works 2009		Unit	Labour Hours	Labour Net	Plant Net	Materials Net	Unit Net	Labour Gross	Plant Gross	Materials Gross	Unit Price
								(Gross rates include 10% profit)			
				£	£	£	£	£	£	£	£
102	**REPAIRS AND ALTERATIONS**										
10202	**CONCRETE WORK**										
1020217	**Hack up broken or sunken areas of concrete paving, spread and consolidate hardcore 150 mm, lay new concrete to falls, joint to existing including trowelling to form smooth surface:**										
1020217A	100 mm	m²	2.15	52.52	–	15.35	67.87	57.77	–	16.89	74.66
1020217B	150 mm	m²	2.45	59.85	–	20.77	80.62	65.84	–	22.85	88.68
1020218	**Hack surface of existing paving or floors and grout and render in:**										
1020218A	19 mm cement mortar (1:2.5)	m²	1.00	24.43	–	2.09	26.52	26.87	–	2.30	29.17
1020219	**Hack off defective cement rendering to steps (treads and risers) and make out in:**										
1020219A	25 mm cement and sand (1:3) trowelled including nosings and arrises	m²	2.50	61.07	–	3.27	64.34	67.18	–	3.60	70.77
1020220	**Clean and hack existing concrete surface to form key for:**										
1020220A	granolithic paving.	m²	0.40	8.34	–	–	8.34	9.17	–	–	9.17
1020221	**Roughen and grout edge of existing concrete paving to new:**										
1020221A	100 mm	m	0.40	8.34	–	–	8.34	9.17	–	–	9.17
1020221B	150 mm	m	0.50	10.43	–	–	10.43	11.47	–	–	11.47
1020222	**Breaking up reinforced concrete walls, columns, beams, suspended floors or roofs and loading into:**										
1020222A	skip.	m³	27.00	562.95	–	–	562.95	619.25	–	–	619.25
1020223	**Cutting holes through concrete for pipes, bars etc per 25 mm depth of cut and making good:**										
1020223A	area not exceeding 0.003 sq.m.	Each	0.20	4.17	–	0.22	4.39	4.59	–	0.24	4.83
1020223B	0.003-0.023 sq.m.	Each	0.40	8.34	–	0.22	8.56	9.17	–	0.24	9.42
1020224	**Cutting holes through reinforced concrete for pipes, bars, etc., per 25 mm depth of cut and making good:**										
1020224A	area not exceeding 0.003 sq.m.	Each	0.30	6.25	–	0.22	6.47	6.88	–	0.24	7.12
1020224B	0.003-0.023 sq.m.	Each	0.60	12.51	–	0.22	12.73	13.76	–	0.24	14.00
1020225	**Forming concrete (1:2:4) curbs and channels including all necessary formwork but excluding excavation:**										
1020225A	average 0.047 sq.m sectional area	m	1.00	24.43	–	7.49	31.92	26.87	–	8.24	35.11

BRICKWORK AND
BLOCKWORK

Small Works 2009		Unit	Labour Hours	Labour Net	Plant Net	Materials Net	Unit Net	Labour Gross	Plant Gross	Materials Gross	Unit Price
								(Gross rates include 10% profit)			
				£	£	£	£	£	£	£	£
201	**NEW WORK**										
20101	**CLASS B ENGINEERING BRICKWORK IN CEMENT MORTAR (1:3)**										
2010101	**Walls:**										
2010101A	half brick thick	m²	1.72	44.10	–	36.82	80.92	48.51	–	40.50	89.01
2010101B	one brick thick	m²	2.92	74.87	–	72.34	147.21	82.36	–	79.57	161.93
2010102	**Skins of hollow walls:**										
2010102A	half brick thick	m²	1.72	44.10	–	36.82	80.92	48.51	–	40.50	89.01
2010102B	one brick thick	m²	2.92	74.87	–	72.34	147.21	82.36	–	79.57	161.93
2010103	**Honeycomb sleeper walls:**										
2010103A	half brick thick	m²	1.32	33.84	–	27.94	61.78	37.22	–	30.73	67.96
2010104	**For every £10:00 per 1000 variation in the price of bricks, add or deduct as follows:**										
2010104A	half brick walls	m²	–	–	–	0.62	0.62	–	–	0.68	0.68
2010104B	one brick walls	m²	–	–	–	1.24	1.24	–	–	1.36	1.36
2010105	**Extra over Class B engineering brickwork in cement mortar (1:3) for fair face and flush pointing one side as the work proceeds:**										
2010105A	stretcher bond	m²	0.47	12.05	–	–	12.05	13.26	–	–	13.26
2010105B	Flemish bond	m²	0.50	12.82	–	–	12.82	14.10	–	–	14.10
2010105C	margins	m	0.11	2.82	–	–	2.82	3.10	–	–	3.10
20102	**COMMON BRICKWORK IN GAUGED MORTAR (1:1:6)**										
2010201	**Walls:**										
2010201A	half brick thick	m²	1.66	42.57	–	20.53	63.10	46.83	–	22.58	69.41
2010201B	one brick thick	m²	2.71	69.48	–	39.34	108.82	76.43	–	43.27	119.70
2010202	**Skins of hollow walls:**										
2010202A	half brick thick	m²	1.66	42.56	–	20.93	63.49	46.82	–	23.02	69.84
2010202B	one brick thick	m²	2.71	69.48	–	43.81	113.29	76.43	–	48.19	124.62
2010203	**Honeycomb sleeper walls:**										
2010203A	half brick wall	m²	1.28	32.82	–	16.44	49.26	36.10	–	18.08	54.19
2010204	**Projections of footings and chimney breasts:**										
2010204A	half brick thick	m²	1.86	47.69	–	20.93	68.62	52.46	–	23.02	75.48
2010204B	one brick thick	m²	3.05	78.20	–	43.81	122.01	86.02	–	48.19	134.21
2010204C	one and a half brick thick...	m²	3.65	93.58	–	66.45	160.03	102.94	–	73.10	176.03
2010205	**Isolated piers and chimney stacks:**										
2010205A	one brick thick	m²	3.38	86.66	–	43.81	130.47	95.33	–	48.19	143.52
2010205B	one and a half brick thick...	m²	4.04	103.58	–	66.45	170.03	113.94	–	73.10	187.03
2010205C	two bricks thick	m²	4.97	127.43	–	88.56	215.99	140.17	–	97.42	237.59

Brickwork and Blockwork

Small Works 2009		Unit	Labour Hours	Labour Net	Plant Net	Materials Net	Unit Net	Labour Gross	Plant Gross	Materials Gross	Unit Price
								(Gross rates include 10% profit)			
				£	£	£	£	£	£	£	£
20102	**COMMON BRICKWORK IN GAUGED MORTAR (1:1:6)**										
2010206	**Projection of attached piers, plinths, bands, oversailing courses and the like:**										
2010206A	215 mm × 102.5 mm	m	0.55	14.10	–	5.34	19.44	15.51	–	5.87	21.38
2010206B	215 mm × 215 mm	m	1.44	36.92	–	10.40	47.32	40.61	–	11.44	52.05
2010206C	327.5 mm × 102.5 mm...	m	0.79	20.25	–	7.59	27.84	22.28	–	8.35	30.62
2010206D	327.5 mm × 215 mm	m	2.17	55.64	–	15.87	71.51	61.20	–	17.46	78.66
2010207	**For every 10.00 per 1000 variation in the price of bricks, add or deduct as follows:**										
2010207A	half brick walls	m²	–	–	–	0.62	0.62	–	–	0.68	0.68
2010207B	one brick walls	m²	–	–	–	1.24	1.24	–	–	1.36	1.36
2010207C	one and a half brick walls ..	m²	–	–	–	1.86	1.86	–	–	2.05	2.05
2010207D	two brick walls	m²	–	–	–	2.48	2.48	–	–	2.73	2.73
2010208	**Extra over commons for:**										
2010208A	keyed bricks	m²	–	–	–	0.84	0.84	–	–	0.92	0.92
2010209	**Extra over common brickwork in gauged mortar (1:1:6) for fair face and flush pointing one side as the work proceeds:**										
2010209A	stretcher bond	m²	0.40	10.26	–	–	10.26	11.29	–	–	11.29
2010209B	Flemish bond	m²	0.44	11.28	–	–	11.28	12.41	–	–	12.41
2010209C	margins	m	0.10	2.56	–	–	2.56	2.82	–	–	2.82
20103	**FACING BRICKWORK, PC £325.00 PER 1000, IN GAUGED MORTAR (1:1:6)**										
2010301	**Walls:**										
2010301A	half brick thick; stretcher bond...................	m²	2.05	52.57	–	28.63	81.20	57.83	–	31.49	89.32
2010301B	one brick thick; double stretcher bond	m²	3.89	99.74	–	58.32	158.06	109.71	–	64.15	173.87
2010301C	one brick thick; English bond	m²	4.10	105.12	–	58.72	163.84	115.63	–	64.59	180.22
2010301D	one brick thick; English garden wall bond	m²	3.97	101.79	–	58.72	160.51	111.97	–	64.59	176.56
2010301E	one brick thick; English cross bond...................	m²	4.31	110.51	–	60.28	170.79	121.56	–	66.31	187.87
2010301F	one brick thick; Flemish bond	m²	4.23	108.45	–	58.59	167.04	119.30	–	64.45	183.74
2010301G	one brick thick; Flemish garden wall bond	m²	4.02	103.07	–	58.59	161.66	113.38	–	64.45	177.83
2010302	**Skins of hollow walls:**										
2010302A	half brick thick; stretcher bond...................	m²	2.05	52.56	–	28.50	81.06	57.82	–	31.35	89.17
2010302B	half brick thick; English bond (snapped headers)	m²	2.31	59.23	–	41.50	100.73	65.15	–	45.65	110.80
2010302C	half brick thick; Flemish bond (snapped headers)	m²	2.37	60.77	–	37.21	97.98	66.85	–	40.93	107.78
2010304	**For every 10:00 per 1000 variation in the price of bricks, add or deduct as follows:**										
2010304A	half brick walls; stretcher bond...................	m²	–	–	–	0.79	0.79	–	–	0.87	0.87
2010304B	half brick walls; Flemish bond	m²	–	–	–	1.07	1.07	–	–	1.18	1.18

Small Works 2009		Unit	Labour Hours	Labour Net	Plant Net	Materials Net	Unit Net	Labour Gross	Plant Gross	Materials Gross	Unit Price
								(Gross rates include 10% profit)			
				£	£	£	£	£	£	£	£
201	**NEW WORK**										
20104	**ARCHES AND COPINGS**										
2010401	**Extra over brickwork for flat arch, 112 mm soffit:**										
2010401A	commons: 112 mm high ...	m	0.60	15.39	–	0.28	15.67	16.93	–	0.31	17.24
2010401B	commons: 225 mm high ...	m	0.80	20.52	–	0.28	20.80	22.57	–	0.31	22.88
2010401C	facings: 112 mm high	m	0.75	19.23	–	–	19.23	21.15	–	–	21.15
2010401D	facings: 225 mm high	m	1.00	25.64	–	5.74	31.38	28.20	–	6.31	34.52
2010402	**Extra over brickwork for camber arch, 112 mm soffit:**										
2010402A	commons: 225 mm high ...	m	1.70	43.59	–	0.28	43.87	47.95	–	0.31	48.26
2010402B	facings: 225 mm high	m	1.80	46.15	–	5.74	51.89	50.77	–	6.31	57.08
2010403	**Extra over brickwork for segmental arch; 225 mm deep in two half brick rings:**										
2010403A	commons	m	1.90	48.71	–	0.57	49.28	53.58	–	0.63	54.21
2010403B	facings	m	2.10	53.84	–	5.74	59.58	59.22	–	6.31	65.54
2010404	**Extra over brickwork in rough relieving arches:**										
2010404A	commons: 112 mm high ...	m	0.30	7.70	–	0.28	7.98	8.47	–	0.31	8.78
2010404B	commons: 225 mm high ...	m	0.50	12.82	–	0.28	13.10	14.10	–	0.31	14.41
2010405	**Brick-on-edge coping to one brick wall; double tile creasing course; two small fillets; pointed all round:**										
2010405A	commons	m	2.40	61.54	–	12.60	74.14	67.69	–	13.86	81.55
2010405B	facings	m	2.50	64.10	–	14.20	78.30	70.51	–	15.62	86.13
20106	**SILLS AND STEPS**										
2010601	**Heatherbrown quarry tile sill rounded on one edge, bedded, jointed and pointed in cement mortar:**										
2010601B	194 mm × 194 mm × 12.5 mm	m	0.37	9.49	–	8.48	17.97	10.44	–	9.33	19.77
2010601C	150 mm × 150 mm × 12.5 mm	m	0.33	8.46	–	4.12	12.58	9.31	–	4.53	13.84
2010601D	150 mm × 150 mm × 19 mm	m	0.35	8.97	–	4.58	13.55	9.87	–	5.04	14.91
2010602	**Red quarry tile sill rounded on one edge, bedded, jointed and pointed in cement mortar:**										
2010602B	200 mm × 200 mm × 19 mm	m	0.38	9.74	–	11.33	21.07	10.71	–	12.46	23.18
2010602C	150 mm × 150 mm × 20 mm	m	0.35	8.98	–	6.62	15.60	9.88	–	7.28	17.16
2010602D	150 mm × 150 mm × 12.5 mm	m	0.33	8.46	–	6.03	14.49	9.31	–	6.63	15.94
2010603	**Two courses roofing tiles set sloping to form:**										
2010603A	external window sills; including pointing.........	m	1.35	34.62	–	8.39	43.01	38.08	–	9.23	47.31

Brickwork and Blockwork

Small Works 2009		Unit	Labour Hours	Labour Net	Plant Net	Materials Net	Unit Net	Labour Gross	Plant Gross	Materials Gross	Unit Price
								(Gross rates include 10% profit)			
				£	£	£	£	£	£	£	£
20106	**SILLS AND STEPS**										
2010604	**Brick-on-edge step in hard red paviors; bedded and pointed:**										
2010604A	225 mm wide	m	1.40	35.89	–	18.22	54.11	39.48	–	20.04	59.52
2010604B	338 mm wide	m	3.00	76.92	–	26.73	103.65	84.61	–	29.40	114.02
2010604C	Extra for bullnosed paviors .	m	–	–	–	32.26	32.26	–	–	35.49	35.49
2010605	**Brick-on-edge sill; bedded and pointed:**										
2010605A	225 mm in facing bricks . . .	m	1.30	33.33	–	6.38	39.71	36.66	–	7.02	43.68
2010605B	225 mm in single bullnosed engineering bricks	m	1.30	33.33	–	50.57	83.90	36.66	–	55.63	92.29
20108	**ARC CONBLOC DENSE AGGREGATE BLOCKS**										
2010801	**Blockwork in walls; partitions or skins of hollow walls:**										
2010801A	75 mm solid	m²	1.11	28.46	–	13.29	41.75	31.31	–	14.62	45.93
2010801B	100 mm solid	m²	1.31	33.59	–	16.87	50.46	36.95	–	18.56	55.51
2010801C	140 mm solid	m²	1.54	39.49	–	23.15	62.64	43.44	–	25.47	68.90
2010801D	140 mm hollow.	m²	1.64	42.05	–	20.51	62.56	46.26	–	22.56	68.82
2010801E	190 mm hollow.	m²	1.85	47.43	–	31.87	79.30	52.17	–	35.06	87.23
2010801F	215 mm hollow.	m²	2.04	52.30	–	30.82	83.12	57.53	–	33.90	91.43
2010801G	Extra for fair face and flush pointing blockwork as the work proceeds; any thickness; one face.	m²	0.13	3.33	–	0.53	3.86	3.66	–	0.58	4.25
2010801H	Extra for fair face and flush pointing blockwork as the work proceeds; any thickness; both faces	m²	0.34	8.71	–	0.53	9.24	9.58	–	0.58	10.16
20109	**CELCON/THERMALITE CONCRETE BLOCKS**										
2010901	**Standard blockwork in walls; partitions or skins of hollow walls:**										
2010901C	75 mm	m²	1.00	25.64	–	11.56	37.20	28.20	–	12.72	40.92
2010901E	100 mm	m²	1.20	30.77	–	14.94	45.71	33.85	–	16.43	50.28
2010901H	150 mm	m²	1.50	38.46	–	21.66	60.12	42.31	–	23.83	66.13
2010901K	215 mm	m²	1.90	48.72	–	31.31	80.03	53.59	–	34.44	88.03
2010901L	Extra for fair face and flush pointing blockwork as the work proceeds; any thickness; one face.	m²	0.13	3.34	–	1.05	4.39	3.67	–	1.16	4.83
2010901M	Extra for fair face and flush pointing blockwork as the work proceeds; any thickness; both faces	m²	0.34	8.72	–	1.05	9.77	9.59	–	1.16	10.75
2010902	**Solar/High insulation blockwork in walls; partitions or skins of hollow walls:**										
2010902A	115 mm	m²	1.51	38.72	–	17.59	56.31	42.59	–	19.35	61.94
2010902B	125 mm	m²	1.59	40.77	–	21.43	62.20	44.85	–	23.57	68.42
2010902E	150 mm	m²	1.80	46.15	–	25.41	71.56	50.77	–	27.95	78.72
2010902G	215 mm	m²	2.34	60.00	–	35.79	95.79	66.00	–	39.37	105.37
2010902H	Extra for fair face and flush pointing blockwork as the work proceeds; any thickness; one face.	m²	0.13	3.34	–	1.05	4.39	3.67	–	1.16	4.83
2010902I	Extra for fair face and flush pointing blockwork as the work proceeds; any thickness; both faces	m²	0.34	8.72	–	1.05	9.77	9.59	–	1.16	10.75

Small Works 2009		Unit	Labour Hours	Labour Net	Plant Net	Materials Net	Unit Net	Labour Gross	Plant Gross	Materials Gross	Unit Price
								(Gross rates include 10% profit)			
				£	£	£	£	£	£	£	£
201	**NEW WORK**										
20113	**DAMP PROOF COURSES**										
2011301	**Polythene; horizontal; bedded in gauged mortar (1:1:6):**										
2011301A	112.5 mm wide..........	m	0.04	1.03	–	0.36	1.39	1.13	–	0.40	1.53
2011301B	225 mm wide	m	0.08	2.05	–	0.88	2.93	2.26	–	0.97	3.22
2011301C	over 225 mm wide	m²	0.35	8.98	–	3.90	12.88	9.88	–	4.29	14.17
2011301D	over 225 mm wide; forming cavity gutter in hollow wall .	m²	0.56	14.36	–	3.90	18.26	15.80	–	4.29	20.09
2011302	**Polythene; vertical; bedded in gauged mortar (1:1:6):**										
2011302A	over 225 mm wide	m²	1.05	26.92	–	3.90	30.82	29.61	–	4.29	33.90
2011303	**Fibre based bitumen; horizontal; bedded in gauged mortar (1:1:6):**										
2011303A	112.5 mm wide...........	m	0.04	1.03	–	1.16	2.19	1.13	–	1.28	2.41
2011303B	225 mm wide	m	0.08	2.05	–	2.42	4.47	2.26	–	2.66	4.92
2011303C	over 225 mm wide	m²	0.35	8.98	–	12.27	21.25	9.88	–	13.50	23.38
2011303D	over 225 mm wide; forming cavity gutter in hollow wall .	m²	0.56	14.36	–	12.27	26.63	15.80	–	13.50	29.29
2011304	**Fibre based bitumen; vertical; bedded in gauged mortar (1:1:6):**										
2011304A	over 225 mm wide	m²	1.05	26.92	–	12.27	39.19	29.61	–	13.50	43.11
2011305	**Hessian based bitumen; horizontal; bedded in gauged mortar (1:1:6):**										
2011305A	112.5 mm wide..........	m	0.04	1.02	–	1.68	2.70	1.12	–	1.85	2.97
2011305B	225 mm wide	m	0.08	2.05	–	3.62	5.67	2.26	–	3.98	6.24
2011305C	over 225 mm wide	m²	0.35	8.97	–	17.38	26.35	9.87	–	19.12	28.99
2011305D	over 225 mm wide; forming cavity gutter in hollow wall .	m²	0.56	14.36	–	17.38	31.74	15.80	–	19.12	34.91
2011306	**Hessian based bitumen; vertical; bedded in gauged mortar (1:1:6):**										
2011306A	over 225 mm wide	m²	1.05	26.92	–	17.38	44.30	29.61	–	19.12	48.73
2011307	**Hyload pitch polymer; horizontal; 100 m laps sealed with Hyload contact adhesive; bedded in gauged mortar (1:1:6):**										
2011307A	112.5 mm wide..........	m	0.04	1.03	–	1.92	2.95	1.13	–	2.11	3.25
2011307B	225 mm wide	m	0.08	2.05	–	4.13	6.18	2.26	–	4.54	6.80
2011307C	over 225 mm wide	m²	0.35	8.97	–	19.84	28.81	9.87	–	21.82	31.69
2011307D	over 225 mm wide; forming cavity gutter in hollow wall .	m²	0.56	14.36	–	19.84	34.20	15.80	–	21.82	37.62
2011308	**Hyload pitch polymer; vertical; bedded in gauged mortar (1:1:6):**										
2011308A	over 225 mm wide	m²	1.05	26.92	–	19.84	46.76	29.61	–	21.82	51.44

Brickwork and Blockwork

		Unit	Labour Hours	Labour Net	Plant Net	Materials Net	Unit Net	Labour Gross	Plant Gross	Materials Gross	Unit Price
								(Gross rates include 10% profit)			
				£	£	£	£	£	£	£	£
201	**NEW WORK**										
20113	**DAMP PROOF COURSES**										
2011311	**Fibre based lead lined; horizontal; bedded in gauged mortar (1:1:6):**										
2011311A	112.5 mm wide..........	m	0.05	1.28	–	3.91	5.19	1.41	–	4.30	5.71
2011311B	225 mm wide	m	0.10	2.57	–	8.27	10.84	2.83	–	9.10	11.92
2011311C	over 225 mm wide	m²	0.46	11.79	–	39.63	51.42	12.97	–	43.59	56.56
2011311D	over 225 mm wide; forming cavity gutter in hollow wall .	m²	0.74	18.97	–	39.63	58.60	20.87	–	43.59	64.46
2011313	**Fibre based lead lined; vertical; bedded in gauged mortar (1:1:6):**										
2011313A	over 225 mm wide	m²	1.05	26.92	–	39.63	66.55	29.61	–	43.59	73.21
2011314	**Hessian based lead lined; horizontal; bedded in gauged mortar (1:1:6):**										
2011314A	112.5 mm wide...........	m	0.05	1.28	–	4.14	5.42	1.41	–	4.55	5.96
2011314B	225 mm wide	m	0.10	2.56	–	8.38	10.94	2.82	–	9.22	12.03
2011314C	over 225 mm wide	m²	0.46	11.79	–	41.92	53.71	12.97	–	46.11	59.08
2011314D	over 225 mm wide; forming cavity gutter in hollow wall .	m²	0.74	18.97	–	41.92	60.89	20.87	–	46.11	66.98
2011315	**Hessian based lead lined; vertical; bedded in gauged mortar (1:1:6):**										
2011315A	over 225 mm wide	m²	1.05	26.92	–	41.92	68.84	29.61	–	46.11	75.72
2011318	**Welsh slates; two courses; horizontal; bedded in cement mortar (1:3):**										
2011318A	over 225 mm wide	m²	2.06	52.82	–	721.37	774.19	58.10	–	793.51	851.61
2011319	**Welsh slates; two courses; vertical; bedded in cement mortar (1:3):**										
2011319A	over 225 mm wide	m²	3.15	80.76	–	721.37	802.13	88.84	–	793.51	882.34
2011320	**Synthaprufe; vertical membrane; three coats brushed on; final covering dusted with clean sharp sand:**										
2011320A	not exceeding 150 mm wide	m	0.11	2.82	–	1.09	3.91	3.10	–	1.20	4.30
2011320B	150 mm-300 mm wide.....	m	0.18	4.62	–	2.18	6.80	5.08	–	2.40	7.48
2011320C	over 300 mm wide	m²	0.39	10.00	–	7.22	17.22	11.00	–	7.94	18.94

Small Works 2009		Unit	Labour Hours	Labour Net	Plant Net	Materials Net	Unit Net	Labour Gross	Plant Gross	Materials Gross	Unit Price
								(Gross rates include 10% profit)			
				£	£	£	£	£	£	£	£
201	**NEW WORK**										
20115	**AIR BRICKS AND SOOT DOORS**										
2011501	**Air bricks; terracotta; building in:**										
2011501A	225 mm × 75 mm	each	0.22	5.64	–	3.65	9.29	6.20	–	4.02	10.22
2011501B	225 mm × 150 mm	each	0.30	7.69	–	5.56	13.25	8.46	–	6.12	14.58
2011501C	225 mm × 225 mm	each	0.33	8.46	–	13.41	21.87	9.31	–	14.75	24.06
2011502	**Air bricks; galvanised; building in:**										
2011502A	225 mm × 75 mm	each	0.22	5.64	–	7.10	12.74	6.20	–	7.81	14.01
2011502B	225 mm × 150 mm	each	0.30	7.69	–	13.17	20.86	8.46	–	14.49	22.95
2011502C	225 mm × 225 mm	each	0.33	8.46	–	19.25	27.71	9.31	–	21.18	30.48
2011503	**Louvred ventilators; aluminium; screw fixed:**										
2011503A	225 mm × 75 mm	each	0.22	5.64	–	2.83	8.47	6.20	–	3.11	9.32
2011503B	225 mm × 150 mm	each	0.30	7.69	–	3.43	11.12	8.46	–	3.77	12.23
2011503C	225 mm × 225 mm	each	0.33	8.46	–	4.79	13.25	9.31	–	5.27	14.58
2011504	**Air ventilators; plaster; flyproof; set in plastering:**										
2011504A	225 mm × 75 mm	each	0.22	5.64	–	2.14	7.78	6.20	–	2.35	8.56
2011504B	225 mm × 150 mm	each	0.30	7.70	–	3.29	10.99	8.47	–	3.62	12.09
2011504C	225 mm × 225 mm	each	0.33	8.46	–	4.48	12.94	9.31	–	4.93	14.23
2011505	**Air brick extension cavity liners; terracotta; 300 mm long; building in:**										
2011505A	225 mm × 75 mm	Each	0.30	7.69	–	5.94	13.63	8.46	–	6.53	14.99
2011505B	225 mm × 150 mm	Each	0.38	9.74	–	6.68	16.42	10.71	–	7.35	18.06
2011505C	225 mm × 225 mm	Each	0.55	14.11	–	16.57	30.68	15.52	–	18.23	33.75
2011506	**Soot doors; double cover; frame; cast iron; building in:**										
2011506A	225 mm × 150 mm	Each	0.40	10.25	–	26.13	36.38	11.28	–	28.74	40.02
2011506B	225 mm × 225 mm	Each	0.45	11.54	–	43.53	55.07	12.69	–	47.88	60.58

Brickwork and Blockwork

Small Works 2009		Unit	Labour Hours	Labour Net	Plant Net	Materials Net	Unit Net	Labour Gross	Plant Gross	Materials Gross	Unit Price
								(Gross rates include 10% profit)			
				£	£	£	£	£	£	£	£
201	**NEW WORK**										
20117	**CHIMNEY FLUE LININGS, BENDS, POTS ETC**										
2011701	**Parge and core flues:**										
2011701A	225 mm × 225 mm	m	1.00	25.64	–	1.74	27.38	28.20	–	1.91	30.12
2011702	**Clay flue linings; BS 1181; bedded and jointed in cement mortar (1:3):**										
2011702A	125 mm dia	m	0.50	12.82	–	25.60	38.42	14.10	–	28.16	42.26
2011702B	150 mm dia	m	0.55	14.10	–	25.11	39.21	15.51	–	27.62	43.13
2011702C	185 mm dia	m	0.60	15.38	–	32.47	47.85	16.92	–	35.72	52.64
2011702D	200 mm dia	m	0.60	15.39	–	45.02	60.41	16.93	–	49.52	66.45
2011702E	225 mm dia	m	0.62	15.90	–	53.65	69.55	17.49	–	59.02	76.51
2011702F	300 mm dia	m	0.70	17.95	–	128.58	146.53	19.75	–	141.44	161.18
2011702G	185 mm × 185 mm	m	0.60	15.39	–	37.35	52.74	16.93	–	41.09	58.01
2011702H	200 mm × 200 mm	m	0.60	15.38	–	52.13	67.51	16.92	–	57.34	74.26
2011702I	225 mm × 225 mm	m	0.62	15.90	–	53.53	69.43	17.49	–	58.88	76.37
2011704	**Clay flue bends; BS 1181; bedded and jointed in cement mortar (1:3):**										
2011704A	125 mm dia	Each	0.58	14.74	–	24.09	38.83	16.21	–	26.50	42.71
2011704B	150 mm dia	Each	0.63	16.02	–	24.84	40.86	17.62	–	27.32	44.95
2011704C	185 mm dia	Each	0.70	17.95	–	28.24	46.19	19.75	–	31.06	50.81
2011704D	200 mm dia	Each	0.73	18.72	–	48.13	66.85	20.59	–	52.94	73.54
2011704E	225 mm dia	Each	0.75	19.23	–	49.33	68.56	21.15	–	54.26	75.42
2011704F	300 mm dia	Each	1.00	25.64	–	111.12	136.76	28.20	–	122.23	150.44
2011704G	185 mm × 185 mm	Each	0.67	17.17	–	29.10	46.27	18.89	–	32.01	50.90
2011704H	200 mm × 200 mm	Each	0.70	17.95	–	47.14	65.09	19.75	–	51.85	71.60
2011704I	225 mm × 225 mm	Each	0.71	18.20	–	52.66	70.86	20.02	–	57.93	77.95
2011714	**Chimney pots; clay; roll top or cannon head; set and flaunched in cement mortar (1:3); height:**										
2011714A	300 mm	Each	1.15	29.49	–	31.81	61.30	32.44	–	34.99	67.43
2011714B	450 mm	Each	1.38	35.38	–	39.33	74.71	38.92	–	43.26	82.18
2011714C	600 mm	Each	1.63	41.79	–	56.11	97.90	45.97	–	61.72	107.69
2011714D	900 mm	Each	2.38	61.02	–	84.91	145.93	67.12	–	93.40	160.52
2011723	**Damp course to stacks (measured overall flues):**										
2011723A	double slate	m²	3.00	76.92	–	721.37	798.29	84.61	–	793.51	878.12

Small Works 2009		Unit	Labour Hours	Labour Net	Plant Net	Materials Net	Unit Net	Labour Gross	Plant Gross	Materials Gross	Unit Price
				£	£	£	£	£ (Gross rates include 10% profit)	£	£	£
201	**NEW WORK**										
20118	**FIREPLACES**										
2011801	**Building in only:**										
2011801A	continuous burning fire....	Each	3.60	92.31	–	9.26	101.57	101.54	–	10.19	111.73
2011801B	back boiler..............	Each	7.15	183.33	–	9.26	192.59	201.66	–	10.19	211.85
2011801C	underfloor draught fire	Each	8.00	205.12	–	9.26	214.38	225.63	–	10.19	235.82
2011801D	tiled surround and hearth including assembling, jointing and setting in cement mortar 1:3..............	Each	8.50	217.94	–	5.78	223.72	239.73	–	6.36	246.09
20120	**TURNING PIECES AND CENTERING**										
2012001	**Turning pieces to flat arches; 112 mm soffit:**										
2012001A	first use.................	m	0.45	11.54	–	1.80	13.34	12.69	–	1.98	14.67
2012001B	each subsequent use......	m	0.40	10.26	–	–	10.26	11.29	–	–	11.29
2012002	**Turning pieces to flat arches; 225 mm soffit:**										
2012002A	first use.................	m	0.55	14.10	–	5.29	19.39	15.51	–	5.82	21.33
2012002B	each subsequent use......	m	0.45	11.54	–	–	11.54	12.69	–	–	12.69
2012003	**Centering to segmental arches; 225 mm wide soffit:**										
2012003A	1.2 m span; first use.......	Each	1.25	32.05	–	11.59	43.64	35.26	–	12.75	48.00
2012003B	1.5 m span; first use.......	Each	1.30	33.33	–	14.51	47.84	36.66	–	15.96	52.62
2012003C	1.8 m span; first use.......	Each	1.45	37.18	–	17.44	54.62	40.90	–	19.18	60.08
2012003D	each subsequent use......	Each	0.40	10.26	–	–	10.26	11.29	–	–	11.29

Brickwork and Blockwork

Small Works 2009		Unit	Labour Hours	Labour Net	Plant Net	Materials Net	Unit Net	Labour Gross	Plant Gross	Materials Gross	Unit Price
								(Gross rates include 10% profit)			
				£	£	£	£	£	£	£	£
201	**NEW WORK**										
20122	**SUNDRIES**										
2012201	**Forming cavity not exceeding 100 mm between skins of hollow wall:**										
2012201A	no wall ties	m²	0.08	2.05	–	–	2.05	2.26	–	–	2.26
2012201B	butterfly ties; galvanised wire; 5 No. per sq.m.	m²	0.13	3.34	–	0.93	4.27	3.67	–	1.02	4.70
2012201C	twin triangular ties; galvanised wire; 5 No. per sq.m.	m²	0.13	3.33	–	2.47	5.80	3.66	–	2.72	6.38
2012201D	twisted ties; galvanised wire; 5 No. per sq.m	m²	0.13	3.34	–	0.93	4.27	3.67	–	1.02	4.70
2012201E	Catnic ties; stainless steel; 5 No. per sq.m	m²	0.13	3.33	–	3.19	6.52	3.66	–	3.51	7.17
2012202	**Close cavity not exceeding 100 mm between skins of hollow wall at ends, jambs or cills of openings:**										
2012202A	common brickwork half brick thick	m	0.36	9.23	–	2.25	11.48	10.15	–	2.48	12.63
2012202B	common brickwork half brick thick; bituminous felt	m	0.48	12.31	–	3.28	15.59	13.54	–	3.61	17.15
2012202C	common brickwork half brick thick; slate	m	0.60	15.38	–	34.88	50.26	16.92	–	38.37	55.29
2012202D	blockwork 100 mm thick . . .	m	0.30	7.69	–	4.67	12.36	8.46	–	5.14	13.60
2012202E	blockwork 100 mm thick; bituminous felt	m	0.36	9.24	–	5.70	14.94	10.16	–	6.27	16.43
2012202F	blockwork 100 mm thick; slate	m	0.48	12.31	–	74.59	86.90	13.54	–	82.05	95.59
2012202G	Thermabate 50; 50-60 mm cavity width	m	0.12	3.08	–	6.88	9.96	3.39	–	7.57	10.96
2012202H	Thermabate 65; 65-75 mm cavity width	m	0.15	3.85	–	7.56	11.41	4.24	–	8.32	12.55
2012202I	Thermabate 75; 75-85 mm cavity width	m	0.17	4.36	–	8.28	12.64	4.80	–	9.11	13.90
2012202J	Thermabate 85; 85-95 mm cavity width	m	0.20	5.12	–	9.02	14.14	5.63	–	9.92	15.55
2012202K	Thermabate 90; 90-100 mm cavity width	m	0.22	5.64	–	9.70	15.34	6.20	–	10.67	16.87
2012203	**Close cavity not exceeding 100 mm wide at top of hollow wall with single course of blocks laid flat in gauged mortar (1:1:6):**										
2012203A	75 mm	m	0.27	6.92	–	2.43	9.35	7.61	–	2.67	10.29
2012203B	100 mm	m	0.33	8.46	–	3.15	11.61	9.31	–	3.47	12.77
2012203C	150 mm	m	0.45	11.53	–	5.91	17.44	12.68	–	6.50	19.18
2012204	**Rake out joints of brickwork:**										
2012204A	to form key for plaster work	m²	0.50	12.82	–	–	12.82	14.10	–	–	14.10
2012204B	and point in cement mortar .	m²	1.20	30.76	–	0.53	31.29	33.84	–	0.58	34.42
2012205	**Prepare top of brick wall:**										
2012205A	for raising	m²	2.00	51.28	–	–	51.28	56.41	–	–	56.41
2012207	**Setting brickwork up to 50 mm forward or backward:**										
2012207A	raised or sunk panels	m²	0.65	16.67	–	–	16.67	18.34	–	–	18.34

Small Works 2009		Unit	Labour Hours	Labour Net	Plant Net	Materials Net	Unit Net	Labour Gross	Plant Gross	Materials Gross	Unit Price
								(Gross rates include 10% profit)			
				£	£	£	£	£	£	£	£
201	**NEW WORK**										
20122	**SUNDRIES**										
2012208	**Jablite expanded polystyrene board; cavity wall insulation; wedging in position between wall ties; fixing with insulation retaining discs:**										
2012208A	25 mm thick	m²	0.20	5.13	–	3.64	8.77	5.64	–	4.00	9.65
2012208B	50 mm thick	m²	0.20	5.13	–	4.94	10.07	5.64	–	5.43	11.08
2012208C	75 mm thick	m²	0.22	5.64	–	7.36	13.00	6.20	–	8.10	14.30
2012209	**Dritherm cavity wall insulation; wedging in position between wall ties:**										
2012209A	50 mm thick	m²	0.15	3.84	–	3.13	6.97	4.22	–	3.44	7.67
2012209B	75 mm thick	m²	0.17	4.36	–	3.77	8.13	4.80	–	4.15	8.94
2012210	**Rockwool cavity wall insulation; wedging in position between wall ties:**										
2012210A	50 mm thick	m²	0.15	3.84	–	5.56	9.40	4.22	–	6.12	10.34
2012210B	75 mm thick	m²	0.17	4.36	–	8.21	12.57	4.80	–	9.03	13.83
2012211	**Fill bottom of cavity wall with fine concrete; 50 mm cavity:**										
2012211A	300 mm high.............	m	0.13	3.33	–	1.84	5.17	3.66	–	2.02	5.69
2012212	**Double tile creasing course; nibless flat tiles; red; machine made; projecting 50 mm from wall face in cement mortar 1:3:**										
2012212A	half brick wall	m	0.95	24.36	–	9.56	33.92	26.80	–	10.52	37.31
2012212B	one brick wall	m	1.25	32.05	–	18.46	50.51	35.26	–	20.31	55.56
2012214	**Set one course of brickwork:**										
2012214A	forward or backward (strings).................	m	0.16	4.10	–	–	4.10	4.51	–	–	4.51
2012214B	dentil course up to 50 mm projection	m	0.33	8.46	–	–	8.46	9.31	–	–	9.31
2012214C	oversailing per course	m	0.20	5.13	–	–	5.13	5.64	–	–	5.64
2012214D	plinth course: per course to 50 mm projection.........	m	0.10	2.56	–	–	2.56	2.82	–	–	2.82
2012215	**Wedge and pin up brickwork to underside of existing construction with slates in cement mortar 1:3:**										
2012215A	half brick thick	m	0.42	10.77	–	4.31	15.08	11.85	–	4.74	16.59
2012215B	one brick thick	m	0.85	21.79	–	7.15	28.94	23.97	–	7.87	31.83
2012215C	one and a half brick thick...	m	1.30	33.33	–	10.26	43.59	36.66	–	11.29	47.95
2012216	**Bed wood frames and cills in mortar and point up:**										
2012216A	one side................	m	0.42	10.76	–	0.53	11.29	11.84	–	0.58	12.42
2012216B	both sides	m	0.66	16.92	–	0.92	17.84	18.61	–	1.01	19.62
2012217	**Pointing in gun-grade polysulphide based mastic sealant:**										
2012217A	one side................	m	0.23	5.89	–	2.22	8.11	6.48	–	2.44	8.92
2012217B	both sides	m	0.46	11.80	–	4.33	16.13	12.98	–	4.76	17.74
2012218	**Bed plate in:**										
2012218A	mortar	m	0.22	5.64	–	1.20	6.84	6.20	–	1.32	7.52

Brickwork and Blockwork

Small Works 2009		Unit	Labour Hours	Labour Net	Plant Net	Materials Net	Unit Net	Labour Gross	Plant Gross	Materials Gross	Unit Price
				£	£	£	£	(Gross rates include 10% profit)			
								£	£	£	£
201	**NEW WORK**										
20122	**SUNDRIES**										
2012222	**Beam filling to:**										
2012222A	one brick wall	m	0.66	16.92	–	–	16.92	18.61	–	–	18.61
2012223	**Cut chases in brickwork for:**										
2012223A	small pipe or conduit	m	0.90	23.08	–	–	23.08	25.39	–	–	25.39
2012224	**Cut groove in brick sill for:**										
2012224A	water bar	m	0.80	20.51	–	–	20.51	22.56	–	–	22.56
2012225	**Rake out joints in brickwork for:**										
2012225A	turn in of asphalt skirting or metal horizontal flashings . .	m	0.40	10.26	–	–	10.26	11.29	–	–	11.29
2012225B	turn in of asphalt skirting or metal stepped flashings. . . .	m	0.60	15.38	–	–	15.38	16.92	–	–	16.92
2012226	**Cut and bond ends of wall in engineering bricks to existing:**										
2012226A	half brick thick	m	0.48	12.31	–	1.07	13.38	13.54	–	1.18	14.72
2012226B	one brick thick	m	0.70	17.95	–	2.14	20.09	19.75	–	2.35	22.10
2012226C	one and a half brick thick. . .	m	1.03	26.41	–	3.21	29.62	29.05	–	3.53	32.58
2012227	**Cut and bond ends of wall in common bricks to existing:**										
2012227A	half brick thick	m	0.48	12.30	–	0.57	12.87	13.53	–	0.63	14.16
2012227B	one brick thick	m	0.70	17.95	–	1.13	19.08	19.75	–	1.24	20.99
2012227C	one and a half brick thick. . .	m	1.03	26.41	–	1.70	28.11	29.05	–	1.87	30.92
2012228	**Cut and bond ends of wall in facing bricks to existing:**										
2012228A	half brick thick	m	0.48	12.31	–	0.60	12.91	13.54	–	0.66	14.20
2012228B	one brick thick	m	0.70	17.95	–	1.20	19.15	19.75	–	1.32	21.07
2012228C	one and a half brick thick. . .	m	1.03	26.41	–	1.80	28.21	29.05	–	1.98	31.03
2012229	**Quoin up jambs in common bricks in gauged mortar 1:1:6:**										
2012229A	half brick	m	1.20	30.77	–	3.64	34.41	33.85	–	4.00	37.85
2012229B	one brick	m	1.80	46.15	–	6.87	53.02	50.77	–	7.56	58.32
2012229C	one and a half brick thick. . .	m	2.34	60.00	–	10.64	70.64	66.00	–	11.70	77.70
2012230	**Quoin up jambs in facing bricks in gauged mortar 1:1:6:**										
2012230A	half brick	m	1.50	38.46	–	4.82	43.28	42.31	–	5.30	47.61
2012230B	one brick	m	1.80	46.15	–	9.11	55.26	50.77	–	10.02	60.79
2012230C	one and a half brick thick. . .	m	2.76	70.76	–	14.06	84.82	77.84	–	15.47	93.30
2012232	**Mesh reinforcement in walls:**										
2012232A	65 mm wide.	m	0.26	6.66	–	0.83	7.49	7.33	–	0.91	8.24
2012232B	175 mm wide	m	0.34	8.72	–	2.21	10.93	9.59	–	2.43	12.02
2012233	**Angle fillets:**										
2012233A	cement mortar	m	0.40	10.25	–	0.44	10.69	11.28	–	0.48	11.76
2012234	**Raking and cutting:**										
2012234C	fair raking or splay cutting. .	m	0.33	8.46	–	3.30	11.76	9.31	–	3.63	12.94
2012234D	fair curved cutting	m	0.66	16.92	–	3.30	20.22	18.61	–	3.63	22.24
2012234E	fair squint or birdsmouth angle	m	0.33	8.46	–	4.20	12.66	9.31	–	4.62	13.93
2012234F	fair chamfered or round angle	m	0.45	11.54	–	3.30	14.84	12.69	–	3.63	16.32

Small Works 2009		Unit	Labour Hours	Labour Net	Plant Net	Materials Net	Unit Net	Labour Gross	Plant Gross	Materials Gross	Unit Price
								(Gross rates include 10% profit)			
				£	£	£	£	£	£	£	£
201	**NEW WORK**										
20122	**SUNDRIES**										
2012240	**Catnic stainless steel stronghold wall connector system; plugging to wall with plugs and coach screws provided; twist and sliding arms to 225 mm centres and building into joints of walls:**										
2012240A	60 mm-250 mm thick	m	0.31	7.95	–	8.14	16.09	8.75	–	8.95	17.70
2012244	**Unload; hoist; build in: metal windows; door frames; pinning lugs; to brickwork; pointing externally:**										
2012244A	not exceeding 0.5 sq.m	Each	1.10	28.20	–	0.33	28.53	31.02	–	0.36	31.38
2012244B	0.5-1.0 sq.m	Each	1.45	37.18	–	0.65	37.83	40.90	–	0.72	41.61
2012244C	1.0-1.5 sq.m	Each	2.00	51.28	–	1.09	52.37	56.41	–	1.20	57.61
2012244D	exceeding 1.5 sq.m	Each	2.25	57.69	–	1.42	59.11	63.46	–	1.56	65.02
2012245	**Hole for small pipe (not exceeding 55mm diameter) through walls and make good:**										
2012245A	half brick wall	Each	0.40	10.25	–	0.33	10.58	11.28	–	0.36	11.64
2012245B	one brick wall	Each	0.66	16.93	–	0.54	17.47	18.62	–	0.59	19.22
2012245C	one and a half brick wall . . .	Each	1.08	27.69	–	0.33	28.02	30.46	–	0.36	30.82
2012245D	blockwork 100 mm thick . . .	Each	0.36	9.23	–	0.22	9.45	10.15	–	0.24	10.40
2012246	**Hole for large pipe (55 mm-110 mm diameter) through walls and make good:**										
2012246A	half brick wall	Each	0.48	12.30	–	0.33	12.63	13.53	–	0.36	13.89
2012246B	one brick wall	Each	0.84	21.53	–	0.44	21.97	23.68	–	0.48	24.17
2012246C	one and half brick wall	Each	1.32	33.85	–	0.54	34.39	37.24	–	0.59	37.83
2012246D	blockwork 100 mm thick . . .	Each	0.42	10.77	–	0.33	11.10	11.85	–	0.36	12.21
2012247	**Hole for extra large pipe (exceeding 110 mm diameter) through walls and make good:**										
2012247A	half brick wall	Each	0.60	15.38	–	0.33	15.71	16.92	–	0.36	17.28
2012247B	one brick wall	Each	1.02	26.15	–	0.44	26.59	28.77	–	0.48	29.25
2012247C	one and half brick wall	Each	1.62	41.54	–	0.54	42.08	45.69	–	0.59	46.29
2012247D	blockwork 100 mm thick . . .	Each	0.54	13.84	–	0.33	14.17	15.22	–	0.36	15.59
2012250	**Cut mortices for iron bolts, stays etc in brickwork and grout in cement mortar**										
2012250A	per 25 mm depth of mortice	Each	0.08	2.05	–	0.11	2.16	2.26	–	0.12	2.38
2012252	**Cut and pin in brickwork:**										
2012252A	sink bearers, radiator brackets, holder bats etc . . .	Each	0.75	19.23	–	0.44	19.67	21.15	–	0.48	21.64
2012252B	end of steel joists; not exceeding 250 mm high . . .	Each	0.90	23.08	–	0.65	23.73	25.39	–	0.72	26.10
2012252C	end of steel joists; 250 mm-500 mm high.	Each	1.35	34.61	–	1.09	35.70	38.07	–	1.20	39.27
2012253	**Galvanised frame ties screwed to wood frame and built into brickwork:**										
2012253A	203 mm girth	Each	0.20	5.13	–	0.70	5.83	5.64	–	0.77	6.41
2012253B	254 mm girth	Each	0.22	5.64	–	0.74	6.38	6.20	–	0.81	7.02

Brickwork and Blockwork

		Unit	Labour Hours	Labour Net	Plant Net	Materials Net	Unit Net	Labour Gross	Plant Gross	Materials Gross	Unit Price
								(Gross rates include 10% profit)			
				£	£	£	£	£	£	£	£
202	**REPAIRS AND ALTERATIONS**										
20201	**DEMOLISHING BRICKWORK**										
2020101	**Demolish brickwork, any height, and set aside arisings:**										
2020101A	half brick walls	m²	0.75	15.64	–	–	15.64	17.20	–	–	17.20
2020101B	one brick walls	m²	1.35	28.15	–	–	28.15	30.97	–	–	30.97
2020101C	one and a half brick walls ..	m²	1.85	38.57	–	–	38.57	42.43	–	–	42.43
2020101D	two brick walls	m²	2.40	50.04	–	–	50.04	55.04	–	–	55.04
2020102	**Sort, clean and stack sound bricks for reuse; in:**										
2020102A	lime mortar	1000	14.00	291.90	–	–	291.90	321.09	–	–	321.09
2020102B	composite mortar.........	1000	17.00	354.45	–	–	354.45	389.90	–	–	389.90
2020102C	cement mortar	1000	22.00	458.70	–	–	458.70	504.57	–	–	504.57
2020103	**Hand load rubble to skip, cart away to tip:**										
2020103A	and pay all tipping fees	m³	2.00	41.70	33.02	4.87	79.59	45.87	36.32	5.36	87.55
20203	**CHIMNEY STACK REMOVAL**										
2020301	**Pulling down chimney stacks, clean sound whole bricks for reuse and remove remainder:**										
2020301A	up to 9 m high or two storeys; lime mortar..............	m³	28.00	717.92	–	–	717.92	789.71	–	–	789.71
2020301B	up to 9 m high or two storeys; cement mortar	m³	36.00	923.04	–	–	923.04	1015.34	–	–	1015.34
2020301C	Extra over for each additional 3 m or storey height; lime mortar	m³	7.00	179.48	–	–	179.48	197.43	–	–	197.43
2020301D	Extra over for each additional 3 m or storey height; cement mortar	m³	9.00	230.76	–	–	230.76	253.84	–	–	253.84
20205	**CHIMNEY STACK REBUILDING**										
2020501	**Rebuild single flue chimney in common bricks, in cement mortar 1:3, including building in 185 mm dia socketed and rebated clay flue liners, BS 1181; up to 9 m or two storeys high; overall plan dimensions:**										
2020501A	450 × 450 mm.........	m	6.00	153.84	–	72.99	226.83	169.22	–	80.29	249.51
2020501B	675 × 675 mm.........	m	9.66	247.69	–	100.93	348.62	272.46	–	111.02	383.48
2020502	**Rebuild double flue chimney in common bricks, in cement mortar 1:3, including building in 185 mm dia socketed and rebated clay flue liners, BS 1181; up to 9 m or two storeys high; overall plan dimensions:**										
2020502A	450 × 750 mm.........	m	5.20	133.33	–	104.06	237.39	146.66	–	114.47	261.13
2020502B	675 × 675 mm.........	m	8.70	223.07	–	133.54	356.61	245.38	–	146.89	392.27
2020503	**Take off loose chimney pot and reset including flaunching:**										
2020503A	up to two storeys or 9 m high	Each	2.00	51.28	–	0.76	52.04	56.41	–	0.84	57.24

Small Works 2009		Unit	Labour Hours	Labour Net	Plant Net	Materials Net	Unit Net	Labour Gross	Plant Gross	Materials Gross	Unit Price
								(Gross rates include 10% profit)			
				£	£	£	£	£	£	£	£
202	**REPAIRS AND ALTERATIONS**										
20205	**CHIMNEY STACK REBUILDING**										
2020504	**Take down and remove chimney pot, supply, set and flaunch new pot; up to two storeys or 9 m high:**										
2020504A	300 mm pot............	Each	2.50	64.10	–	30.29	94.39	70.51	–	33.32	103.83
2020504B	450 mm pot............	Each	2.60	66.67	–	37.80	104.47	73.34	–	41.58	114.92
2020504C	600 mm pot............	Each	2.70	69.23	–	54.58	123.81	76.15	–	60.04	136.19
2020504D	add for each additional storey or 3 m high; 300 mm pot...	Each	0.27	6.92	–	–	6.92	7.61	–	–	7.61
2020504E	add for each additional storey or 3 m high; 450 mm pot...	Each	0.38	9.74	–	–	9.74	10.71	–	–	10.71
2020504F	add for each additional storey or 3 m high; 600 mm pot...	Each	0.50	12.82	–	–	12.82	14.10	–	–	14.10
20206	**DAMP PROOFING**										
2020601	**Treating with silicone or similar damp-proofing liquid:**										
2020601A	external brick walls........	m²	0.22	5.64	–	0.90	6.54	6.20	–	0.99	7.19
20207	**BRICKWORK REPAIRS**										
2020701	**Cut out defective brickwork and reface with new facing bricks, PC 325:00 per 1000, in:**										
2020701A	cement mortar	m²	5.70	146.15	–	27.81	173.96	160.77	–	30.59	191.36
2020701B	lime mortar	m²	5.00	128.20	–	28.24	156.44	141.02	–	31.06	172.08
2020702	**Cut out single facing bricks and reface with new facing bricks, PC 325:00 per 1000, in:**										
2020702A	cement mortar	Each	0.50	12.82	–	0.50	13.32	14.10	–	0.55	14.65
2020702B	lime mortar	Each	0.35	8.98	–	0.52	9.50	9.88	–	0.57	10.45
2020703	**Rake out mortar and repoint:**										
2020703A	perished mortar	m²	0.86	22.05	–	0.53	22.58	24.26	–	0.58	24.84
2020703B	sound mortar	m²	2.15	55.12	–	0.53	55.65	60.63	–	0.58	61.22
2020704	**Cut out fractures in brickwork and lace in common bricks approximately 405 mm wide, 225 mm thick in:**										
2020704A	cement mortar	m	3.60	92.30	–	19.11	111.41	101.53	–	21.02	122.55
2020704B	lime mortar	m	2.40	61.54	–	19.47	81.01	67.69	–	21.42	89.11
2020705	**Cut out fractures in brickwork, and lace in facing bricks, PC 325:00 per 1000, approximately 405 mm wide, 225 mm thick in:**										
2020705A	cement mortar	m	3.95	101.28	–	25.77	127.05	111.41	–	28.35	139.76
2020705B	lime mortar	m	2.75	70.51	–	25.77	96.28	77.56	–	28.35	105.91
2020706	**Take down segmental arch and rebuild in facing bricks, PC 325:00 per 1000, 225 mm high on face, including centering:**										
2020706A	113 mm wide soffit........	m	6.00	153.84	–	6.51	160.35	169.22	–	7.16	176.39
2020706B	225 mm wide soffit........	m	7.80	199.99	–	12.23	212.22	219.99	–	13.45	233.44

Brickwork and Blockwork

Small Works 2009		Unit	Labour Hours	Labour Net	Plant Net	Materials Net	Unit Net	Labour Gross	Plant Gross	Materials Gross	Unit Price
								(Gross rates include 10% profit)			
				£	£	£	£	£	£	£	£
202	**REPAIRS AND ALTERATIONS**										
20209	**OPENINGS IN BRICK WALLS**										
2020901	**Cut opening through brickwork in cement mortar for doors, windows etc, including all necessary shoring and making good, in:**										
2020901A	half brick walls	m²	1.75	44.56	0.39	14.77	59.72	49.02	0.43	16.25	65.69
2020901B	one brick walls	m²	3.50	84.95	0.78	26.12	111.85	93.45	0.86	28.73	123.04
2020901C	one and a half brick walls ..	m²	5.25	127.42	1.07	37.58	166.07	140.16	1.18	41.34	182.68
2020901D	two brick walls	m²	6.50	159.47	1.41	48.65	209.53	175.42	1.55	53.52	230.48
2020903	**Infill openings in brickwork in common bricks, PC 250:00 per 1000, in gauged mortar; in small areas and bond to existing:**										
2020903A	half brick walls	m²	2.45	62.82	–	21.72	84.54	69.10	–	23.89	92.99
2020903B	one brick walls	m²	4.50	115.38	–	43.28	158.66	126.92	–	47.61	174.53
2020903C	one and a half brick walls ..	m²	6.75	173.07	–	65.00	238.07	190.38	–	71.50	261.88
20210	**DAMP PROOF COURSES**										
2021001	**Damp-proof course in short lengths in existing walls including cutting out brickwork and building in with new bricks:**										
2021001A	half brick wide; two course slate	m	1.85	47.44	–	124.58	172.02	52.18	–	137.04	189.22
2021001B	half brick wide; bitumen felt	m	1.55	39.74	–	1.67	41.41	43.71	–	1.84	45.55
2021001C	one brick wide and over; two course slate..............	m²	6.50	166.66	–	853.13	1019.79	183.33	–	938.44	1121.77
2021001D	one brick wide and over; bitumen felt..............	m²	5.30	135.89	–	39.76	175.65	149.48	–	43.74	193.22
20215	**FRAME REBEDDING**										
2021501	**Take out and rebed door or window frame including:**										
2021501A	point externally and make good internally	m	0.55	14.10	–	0.44	14.54	15.51	–	0.48	15.99
2021502	**Rake out defective pointing around door or window frame and repoint in:**										
2021502A	cement mortar	m	0.45	11.54	–	0.13	11.67	12.69	–	0.14	12.84
2021502B	mastic	m	0.60	15.39	–	0.77	16.16	16.93	–	0.85	17.78

Small Works 2009		Unit	Labour Hours	Labour Net	Plant Net	Materials Net	Unit Net	Labour Gross	Plant Gross	Materials Gross	Unit Price
								(Gross rates include 10% profit)			
				£	£	£	£	£	£	£	£
20216	**FIRE AND HEARTH REPAIRS**										
2021601	**Take out existing fireplace including surround and hearth:**										
2021601A	small iron...............	Each	4.00	102.56	–	–	102.56	112.82	–	–	112.82
2021601B	large tiled...............	Each	5.15	132.05	–	–	132.05	145.26	–	–	145.26
2021601C	free standing............	Each	3.20	82.05	–	–	82.05	90.26	–	–	90.26
2021602	**Take out and reset existing fireplace including surround and hearth:**										
2021602A	small iron...............	Each	10.00	256.40	–	11.55	267.95	282.04	–	12.71	294.75
2021602B	large tiled...............	Each	12.25	314.09	–	15.58	329.67	345.50	–	17.14	362.64
2021602C	free standing............	Each	8.20	210.25	–	4.58	214.83	231.28	–	5.04	236.31
20218	**VENTILATION**										
2021801	**Air ventilator: cut out and remove:**										
2021801A	plaster fly proof 225 mm × 75 mm..................	Each	0.30	7.69	–	–	7.69	8.46	–	–	8.46
2021801B	plaster fly proof 225 mm × 150 mm.................	Each	0.37	9.49	–	–	9.49	10.44	–	–	10.44
2021801C	terracotta 225 mm × 75 mm.................	Each	0.32	8.20	–	–	8.20	9.02	–	–	9.02
2021801D	terracotta 225 mm × 150 mm.................	Each	0.42	10.77	–	–	10.77	11.85	–	–	11.85
2021801E	galvanised iron 225 mm × 75 mm.................	Each	0.32	8.20	–	–	8.20	9.02	–	–	9.02
2021801F	galvanised iron 225 mm × 150 mm.................	Each	0.42	10.77	–	–	10.77	11.85	–	–	11.85
2021803	**Air ventilator: cut through brick wall (any thickness) build in and make good:**										
2021803A	plaster fly proof 225 mm × 75 mm..................	Each	0.48	12.31	–	2.21	14.52	13.54	–	2.43	15.97
2021803B	plaster fly proof 225 mm × 150 mm.................	Each	0.55	14.10	–	2.71	16.81	15.51	–	2.98	18.49
2021803C	terracotta 225 mm × 75 mm..................	Each	0.50	12.82	–	3.65	16.47	14.10	–	4.02	18.12
2021803D	terracotta 225 mm × 150 mm.................	Each	0.60	15.38	–	5.56	20.94	16.92	–	6.12	23.03
2021803E	galvanised iron 225 mm × 75 mm..................	Each	0.50	12.82	–	7.10	19.92	14.10	–	7.81	21.91
2021803F	galvanised iron 225 mm × 150 mm.................	Each	0.60	15.38	–	13.17	28.55	16.92	–	14.49	31.41

WOODWORK

Small Works 2009		Unit	Labour Hours	Labour Net	Plant Net	Materials Net	Unit Net	Labour Gross	Plant Gross	Materials Gross	Unit Price
								(Gross rates include 10% profit)			
				£	£	£	£	£	£	£	£
301	**NEW WORK**										
30101	**CARCASSING: SAWN SOFTWOOD**										
3010101	**Floors:**										
3010101A	50 mm × 100 mm	m	0.12	3.34	–	1.80	5.14	3.67	–	1.98	5.65
3010101B	50 mm × 125 mm	m	0.14	3.75	–	2.26	6.01	4.13	–	2.49	6.61
3010101C	50 mm × 150 mm	m	0.47	13.07	–	2.71	15.78	14.38	–	2.98	17.36
3010101D	50 mm × 175 mm	m	0.17	4.75	–	3.17	7.92	5.23	–	3.49	8.71
3010101E	50 mm × 200 mm	m	0.20	5.45	–	3.62	9.07	6.00	–	3.98	9.98
3010101F	50 mm × 225 mm	m	0.22	6.12	–	4.06	10.18	6.73	–	4.47	11.20
3010101G	63 mm × 125 mm	m	0.15	4.29	–	2.84	7.13	4.72	–	3.12	7.84
3010101H	63 mm × 150 mm	m	0.19	5.14	–	3.42	8.56	5.65	–	3.76	9.42
3010101I	63 mm × 175 mm	m	0.22	6.00	–	3.98	9.98	6.60	–	4.38	10.98
3010101J	63 mm × 200 mm	m	0.25	6.84	–	4.55	11.39	7.52	–	5.01	12.53
3010101K	63 mm × 225 mm	m	0.28	7.70	–	5.13	12.83	8.47	–	5.64	14.11
3010101L	75 mm × 125 mm	m	0.18	5.09	–	3.39	8.48	5.60	–	3.73	9.33
3010101M	75 mm × 150 mm	m	0.22	6.12	–	4.06	10.18	6.73	–	4.47	11.20
3010101N	75 mm × 175 mm	m	0.26	7.12	–	4.74	11.86	7.83	–	5.21	13.05
3010101O	75 mm × 200 mm	m	0.29	8.15	–	5.42	13.57	8.97	–	5.96	14.93
3010101P	75 mm × 225 mm	m	0.33	9.18	–	6.10	15.28	10.10	–	6.71	16.81
3010102	**Partitions:**										
3010102B	38 mm × 100 mm	m	0.21	5.83	–	1.38	7.21	6.41	–	1.52	7.93
3010102C	50 mm × 75 mm	m	0.22	6.11	–	1.35	7.46	6.72	–	1.49	8.21
3010102D	50 mm × 100 mm	m	0.27	7.51	–	1.80	9.31	8.26	–	1.98	10.24
3010103	**Flat roofs:**										
3010103A	50 mm × 150 mm	m	0.29	8.06	–	2.71	10.77	8.87	–	2.98	11.85
3010103B	50 mm × 175 mm	m	0.32	8.89	–	3.17	12.06	9.78	–	3.49	13.27
3010103C	50 mm × 200 mm	m	0.36	10.01	–	3.62	13.63	11.01	–	3.98	14.99
3010103D	75 mm × 100 mm	m	0.29	8.06	–	2.71	10.77	8.87	–	2.98	11.85
3010104	**Pitched roofs including ceiling joists:**										
3010104A	25 mm × 100 mm	m	0.12	3.33	–	0.91	4.24	3.66	–	1.00	4.66
3010104B	25 mm × 125 mm	m	0.14	3.89	–	1.14	5.03	4.28	–	1.25	5.53
3010104C	25 mm × 150 mm	m	0.14	3.89	–	1.35	5.24	4.28	–	1.49	5.76
3010104D	38 mm × 75 mm	m	0.14	3.89	–	1.03	4.92	4.28	–	1.13	5.41
3010104E	38 mm × 100 mm	m	0.14	3.89	–	1.38	5.27	4.28	–	1.52	5.80
3010104F	38 mm × 125 mm	m	0.14	3.89	–	1.72	5.61	4.28	–	1.89	6.17
3010104G	38 mm × 150 mm	m	0.15	4.17	–	2.06	6.23	4.59	–	2.27	6.85
3010104H	50 mm × 75 mm	m	0.14	3.89	–	1.35	5.24	4.28	–	1.49	5.76
3010104I	50 mm × 100 mm	m	0.15	4.17	–	1.80	5.97	4.59	–	1.98	6.57
3010104J	50 mm × 125 mm	m	0.15	4.17	–	2.26	6.43	4.59	–	2.49	7.07
3010104K	50 mm × 150 mm	m	0.15	4.17	–	2.71	6.88	4.59	–	2.98	7.57
3010104L	63 mm × 100 mm	m	0.15	4.17	–	2.27	6.44	4.59	–	2.50	7.08
3010104M	63 mm × 125 mm	m	0.15	4.17	–	2.84	7.01	4.59	–	3.12	7.71
3010104N	63 mm × 150 mm	m	0.16	4.45	–	3.42	7.87	4.90	–	3.76	8.66
3010104O	63 mm × 175 mm	m	0.16	4.45	–	3.98	8.43	4.90	–	4.38	9.27
3010104P	75 mm × 100 mm	m	0.15	4.17	–	2.71	6.88	4.59	–	2.98	7.57
3010104Q	75 mm × 125 mm	m	0.16	4.45	–	3.39	7.84	4.90	–	3.73	8.62
3010104R	75 mm × 150 mm	m	0.17	4.73	–	4.06	8.79	5.20	–	4.47	9.67
3010104S	75 mm × 175 mm	m	0.18	5.01	–	4.74	9.75	5.51	–	5.21	10.73
3010104T	100 mm × 150 mm	m	0.18	5.01	–	5.42	10.43	5.51	–	5.96	11.47
3010104U	100 mm × 175 mm	m	0.20	5.56	–	5.42	10.98	6.12	–	5.96	12.08
3010104V	100 mm × 200 mm	m	0.21	5.83	–	7.23	13.06	6.41	–	7.95	14.37
3010104W	100 mm × 225 mm	m	0.22	6.12	–	8.13	14.25	6.73	–	8.94	15.68
3010105	**Kerbs, bearers and the like:**										
3010105A	25 mm × 100 mm	m	0.20	5.56	–	6.33	11.89	6.12	–	6.96	13.08
3010105B	38 mm × 75 mm	m	0.05	1.39	–	1.03	2.42	1.53	–	1.13	2.66
3010105C	38 mm × 100 mm	m	0.07	1.94	–	1.38	3.32	2.13	–	1.52	3.65
3010105D	50 mm × 75 mm	m	0.07	1.94	–	1.35	3.29	2.13	–	1.49	3.62
3010105E	50 mm × 100 mm	m	0.09	2.51	–	1.80	4.31	2.76	–	1.98	4.74
3010105F	75 mm × 100 mm	m	0.14	3.89	–	2.71	6.60	4.28	–	2.98	7.26

Woodwork

Small Works 2009		Unit	Labour Hours	Labour Net	Plant Net	Materials Net	Unit Net	Labour Gross	Plant Gross	Materials Gross	Unit Price
								— (Gross rates include 10% profit) —			
				£	£	£	£	£	£	£	£
301	**NEW WORK**										
30101	**CARCASSING: SAWN SOFTWOOD**										
3010106	**Noggins:**										
3010106A	38 mm × 50 mm	m	0.30	8.34	–	0.63	8.97	9.17	–	0.69	9.87
3010106B	50 mm × 50 mm	m	0.35	9.73	–	0.83	10.56	10.70	–	0.91	11.62
3010106C	50 mm × 75 mm	m	0.40	11.12	–	1.23	12.35	12.23	–	1.35	13.59
3010107	**Herringbone strutting between joists (measured over joists):**										
3010107A	38 mm × 50 mm	m	0.45	12.51	–	0.63	13.14	13.76	–	0.69	14.45
3010107B	50 mm × 50 mm	m	0.50	13.90	–	0.83	14.73	15.29	–	0.91	16.20
3010109	**Solid strutting between joists (measured over joists):**										
3010109A	50 mm × 100 mm	m	0.35	9.73	–	1.64	11.37	10.70	–	1.80	12.51
3010109B	50 mm × 125 mm	m	0.40	11.12	–	2.06	13.18	12.23	–	2.27	14.50
3010109C	50 mm × 175 mm	m	0.50	13.90	–	2.87	16.77	15.29	–	3.16	18.45
3010110	**Sprocket pieces:**										
3010110A	50 mm × 50 mm × 200 mm	Each	0.17	4.72	–	0.17	4.89	5.19	–	0.19	5.38
3010110B	50 mm × 100 mm × 600 mm	Each	0.20	5.56	–	0.99	6.55	6.12	–	1.09	7.21
3010111	**Extra labour trimming to openings:**										
3010111A	500mm × 1000mm; joist 50mm × 100mm	Each	1.35	37.53	–	–	37.53	41.28	–	–	41.28
3010111B	750mm × 1000mm; joist 50mm × 100mm	Each	1.58	43.92	–	–	43.92	48.31	–	–	48.31
3010111C	600mm × 1200mm; joist 50mm × 175mm	Each	1.62	45.04	–	–	45.04	49.54	–	–	49.54
3010111D	900mm × 1800mm; joist 50mm × 175mm	Each	2.43	67.55	–	–	67.55	74.31	–	–	74.31
3010111E	600mm × 1200mm; joist 50mm × 200mm	Each	1.62	45.04	–	–	45.04	49.54	–	–	49.54
3010111F	900mm × 1500mm; joist 50mm × 200mm	Each	1.62	45.04	–	–	45.04	49.54	–	–	49.54
3010111G	600mm × 1200mm; joist 75mm × 175mm	Each	1.62	45.04	–	–	45.04	49.54	–	–	49.54
3010111H	1000mm × 2000mm; joist 75mm × 175mm	Each	2.70	75.06	–	–	75.06	82.57	–	–	82.57
3010112	**Trussed rafters; stress graded; sawn softwood; pressure impregnated; raised through two storeys; fixed in position; 450 mm eaves overhang: Fan truss 22.5 degree pitch; span over wall plates:**										
3010112A	5.00 m	Each	1.66	40.39	–	44.56	84.95	44.43	–	49.02	93.45
3010112B	6.00 m	Each	1.66	40.39	–	49.05	89.44	44.43	–	53.96	98.38
3010112C	7.00 m	Each	1.73	42.09	–	55.32	97.41	46.30	–	60.85	107.15
3010112D	8.00 m	Each	1.73	42.09	–	64.29	106.38	46.30	–	70.72	117.02
3010112E	9.00 m	Each	1.80	43.80	–	75.91	119.71	48.18	–	83.50	131.68
3010112F	10.00 m	Each	1.80	43.80	–	90.26	134.06	48.18	–	99.29	147.47

Small Works 2009		Unit	Labour Hours	Labour Net	Plant Net	Materials Net	Unit Net	Labour Gross	Plant Gross	Materials Gross	Unit Price
								(Gross rates include 10% profit)			
				£	£	£	£	£	£	£	£
301	**NEW WORK**										
30101	**CARCASSING: SAWN SOFTWOOD**										
3010113	**Trussed rafters; stress graded; sawn softwood; pressure impregnated; raised through two storeys; fixed in position; 450 mm eaves overhang: Fan truss 35 degree pitch; span over wall plates:**										
3010113A	5.00 m	Each	1.73	42.09	–	47.76	89.85	46.30	–	52.54	98.84
3010113B	6.00 m	Each	1.73	42.09	–	51.96	94.05	46.30	–	57.16	103.46
3010113C	7.00 m	Each	1.80	43.79	–	57.84	101.63	48.17	–	63.62	111.79
3010113D	8.00 m	Each	1.80	43.80	–	66.23	110.03	48.18	–	72.85	121.03
3010113E	9.00 m	Each	1.86	51.71	–	77.16	128.87	56.88	–	84.88	141.76
3010113F	10.00 m	Each	1.86	45.26	–	90.60	135.86	49.79	–	99.66	149.45
3010114	**Trussed rafters; stress graded; sawn softwood; pressure impregnated; raised through two storeys; fixed in position; 450 mm eaves overhang: Fink or W truss 22.5 degree pitch; span over wall plates:**										
3010114A	5.00 m	Each	1.66	40.39	–	59.11	99.50	44.43	–	65.02	109.45
3010114B	6.00 m	Each	1.66	40.38	–	72.75	113.13	44.42	–	80.03	124.44
3010114C	7.00 m	Each	1.73	42.09	–	83.34	125.43	46.30	–	91.67	137.97
3010114D	8.00 m	Each	1.73	42.09	–	101.49	143.58	46.30	–	111.64	157.94
3010114E	9.00 m	Each	1.80	43.79	–	133.31	177.10	48.17	–	146.64	194.81
3010114F	10.00 m	Each	1.80	43.79	–	162.04	205.83	48.17	–	178.24	226.41

Woodwork

Small Works 2009		Unit	Labour Hours	Labour Net	Plant Net	Materials Net	Unit Net	Labour Gross	Plant Gross	Materials Gross	Unit Price
				£	£	£	£	£	£	£	£
								(Gross rates include 10% profit)			
301	NEW WORK										
30101	CARCASSING: SAWN SOFTWOOD										
3010115	Trussed rafters; stress graded; sawn softwood; pressure impregnated; raised through two storeys; fixed in position; 450 mm eaves overhang: Fink or W truss 35 degree pitch; span over wall plates:										
3010115A	5.00 m	Each	1.73	42.09	–	69.69	111.78	46.30	–	76.66	122.96
3010115B	6.00 m	Each	1.73	42.09	–	81.80	123.89	46.30	–	89.98	136.28
3010115C	7.00 m	Each	1.80	43.80	–	89.38	133.18	48.18	–	98.32	146.50
3010115D	8.00 m	Each	1.80	43.79	–	122.66	166.45	48.17	–	134.93	183.10
3010115E	9.00 m	Each	1.86	45.25	–	148.42	193.67	49.78	–	163.26	213.04
3010115F	10.00 m	Each	1.86	45.25	–	171.11	216.36	49.78	–	188.22	238.00
30103	FIRST FIXINGS: CHIPBOARD										
3010301	Boarding to floors; butt joints; thickness:										
3010301A	18 mm	m²	0.35	9.73	–	4.38	14.11	10.70	–	4.82	15.52
3010301B	18 mm raking cutting	m	0.54	15.02	–	0.54	15.56	16.52	–	0.59	17.12
3010301C	18 mm curved cutting	m	0.93	25.86	–	1.25	27.11	28.45	–	1.38	29.82
3010301D	22 mm	m²	0.42	11.68	–	5.66	17.34	12.85	–	6.23	19.07
3010301E	22 mm raking cutting	m	0.60	16.68	–	0.70	17.38	18.35	–	0.77	19.12
3010301F	22 mm curved cutting	m	0.99	27.52	–	1.62	29.14	30.27	–	1.78	32.05
3010302	Boarding to floors; tongued and grooved joints; thickness:										
3010302A	18 mm	m²	0.44	12.23	–	4.61	16.84	13.45	–	5.07	18.52
3010302B	18 mm raking cutting	m	0.54	15.01	–	0.61	15.62	16.51	–	0.67	17.18
3010302C	18 mm curved cutting	m	0.93	25.86	–	1.36	27.22	28.45	–	1.50	29.94
3010302D	22 mm	m²	0.48	13.34	–	5.92	19.26	14.67	–	6.51	21.19
3010302E	22 mm raking cutting	m	0.60	16.68	–	0.79	17.47	18.35	–	0.87	19.22
3010302F	22 mm curved cutting	m	0.99	27.52	–	1.69	29.21	30.27	–	1.86	32.13

Woodwork

Small Works 2009		Unit	Labour Hours	Labour Net	Plant Net	Materials Net	Unit Net	Labour Gross	Plant Gross	Materials Gross	Unit Price
								(Gross rates include 10% profit)			
				£	£	£	£	£	£	£	£
30103	**FIRST FIXINGS: CHIPBOARD**										
3010303	**Boarding to floors; moisture resistant; butt joints; thickness:**										
3010303A	18 mm	m²	0.35	9.73	–	5.64	15.37	10.70	–	6.20	16.91
3010303B	18 mm raking cutting	m	0.54	15.01	–	0.75	15.76	16.51	–	0.83	17.34
3010303C	18 mm curved cutting	m	0.93	25.85	–	1.67	27.52	28.44	–	1.84	30.27
3010303D	22 mm	m²	0.42	11.68	–	7.01	18.69	12.85	–	7.71	20.56
3010303E	22 mm raking cutting	m	0.60	16.68	–	0.93	17.61	18.35	–	1.02	19.37
3010303F	22 mm curved cutting	m	0.99	27.53	–	2.00	29.53	30.28	–	2.20	32.48
3010304	**Boarding to floors; moisture resistant; tongued and grooved joints; thickness:**										
3010304A	18 mm	m²	0.44	12.23	–	7.21	19.44	13.45	–	7.93	21.38
3010304B	18 mm raking cutting	m	0.54	15.01	–	0.96	15.97	16.51	–	1.06	17.57
3010304C	18 mm curved cutting	m	0.93	25.85	–	2.06	27.91	28.44	–	2.27	30.70
3010304D	22 mm	m²	0.48	13.35	–	8.57	21.92	14.69	–	9.43	24.11
3010304E	22 mm raking cutting	m	0.60	16.68	–	1.14	17.82	18.35	–	1.25	19.60
3010304F	22 mm curved cutting	m	0.99	27.52	–	2.45	29.97	30.27	–	2.70	32.97
3010306	**Boarding to roofs; butt joints; thickness:**										
3010306A	12 mm	m²	0.33	9.17	–	4.01	13.18	10.09	–	4.41	14.50
3010306B	12 mm raking cutting	m	0.33	9.18	–	0.60	9.78	10.10	–	0.66	10.76
3010306C	12 mm curved cutting	m	0.73	20.30	–	1.20	21.50	22.33	–	1.32	23.65
3010306D	18 mm	m²	0.37	10.28	–	7.16	17.44	11.31	–	7.88	19.18
3010306E	18 mm raking cutting	m	0.54	15.02	–	1.07	16.09	16.52	–	1.18	17.70
3010306F	18 mm curved cutting	m	0.93	25.85	–	2.15	28.00	28.44	–	2.37	30.80
3010306G	25 mm	m²	0.49	13.62	–	5.66	19.28	14.98	–	6.23	21.21
3010306H	25 mm raking cutting	m	0.65	18.07	–	0.85	18.92	19.88	–	0.94	20.81
3010306I	25 mm curved cutting	m	1.04	28.91	–	1.70	30.61	31.80	–	1.87	33.67
3010307	**Boarding to roofs; sloping; butt joints; thickness:**										
3010307A	12 mm	m²	0.35	9.73	–	4.01	13.74	10.70	–	4.41	15.11
3010307B	12 mm raking cutting	m	0.33	9.18	–	0.60	9.78	10.10	–	0.66	10.76
3010307C	12 mm curved cutting	m	0.73	20.30	–	1.20	21.50	22.33	–	1.32	23.65
3010307D	18 mm	m²	0.46	12.79	–	7.16	19.95	14.07	–	7.88	21.95
3010307E	18 mm raking cutting	m	0.54	15.02	–	1.07	16.09	16.52	–	1.18	17.70
3010307F	18 mm curved cutting	m	0.93	25.85	–	2.15	28.00	28.44	–	2.37	30.80
3010307G	25 mm	m²	0.64	17.79	–	5.66	23.45	19.57	–	6.23	25.80
3010307H	25 mm raking cutting	m	0.65	18.07	–	0.85	18.92	19.88	–	0.94	20.81
3010307I	25 mm curved cutting	m	1.04	28.91	–	1.70	30.61	31.80	–	1.87	33.67
30105	**FIRST FIXINGS: STERLING BOARD**										
3010501	**Boarding to floors; butt joints; thickness:**										
3010501A	18 mm	m²	0.32	8.90	–	7.13	16.03	9.79	–	7.84	17.63
3010501B	18 mm raking cutting	m	0.49	13.62	–	1.07	14.69	14.98	–	1.18	16.16
3010501C	18 mm curved cutting	m	0.84	23.35	–	2.14	25.49	25.69	–	2.35	28.04
3010501D	11 mm	m²	0.27	7.50	–	4.29	11.79	8.25	–	4.72	12.97
3010501E	11 mm raking cutting	m	0.27	7.51	–	0.64	8.15	8.26	–	0.70	8.97
3010501F	11 mm curved cutting	m	0.63	17.51	–	1.29	18.80	19.26	–	1.42	20.68

Woodwork

	Unit	Labour Hours	Labour Net	Plant Net	Materials Net	Unit Net	Labour Gross	Plant Gross	Materials Gross	Unit Price
			£	£	£	£	£	£	£	£

(Gross rates include 10% profit)

301   **NEW WORK**

30106   **FIRST FIXINGS: PLYWOOD**

3010601   **Boarding to roofs; butt joints; thickness:**

	Unit	Labour Hours	Labour Net	Plant Net	Materials Net	Unit Net	Labour Gross	Plant Gross	Materials Gross	Unit Price
3010601A 18 mm	m²	0.44	12.24	–	16.25	28.49	13.46	–	17.88	31.34
3010601B 18 mm raking cutting	m	0.40	11.12	–	2.44	13.56	12.23	–	2.68	14.92
3010601C 18 mm curved cutting	m	1.06	29.47	–	4.88	34.35	32.42	–	5.37	37.79
3010601D 25 mm	m²	0.50	13.90	–	23.24	37.14	15.29	–	25.56	40.85
3010601E 25 mm raking cutting	m	0.43	11.95	–	3.49	15.44	13.15	–	3.84	16.98
3010601F 25 mm curved cutting	m	1.13	31.42	–	6.97	38.39	34.56	–	7.67	42.23

3010602   **Boarding to roofs; sloping; butt joints thickness:**

	Unit	Labour Hours	Labour Net	Plant Net	Materials Net	Unit Net	Labour Gross	Plant Gross	Materials Gross	Unit Price
3010602A 18 mm	m²	0.46	12.79	–	16.25	29.04	14.07	–	17.88	31.94
3010602B 18 mm raking cutting	m	0.40	11.12	–	2.44	13.56	12.23	–	2.68	14.92
3010602C 18 mm curved cutting	m	1.06	29.47	–	4.88	34.35	32.42	–	5.37	37.79
3010602D 25 mm	m²	0.52	14.46	–	23.24	37.70	15.91	–	25.56	41.47
3010602E 25 mm raking cutting	m	0.43	11.95	–	3.49	15.44	13.15	–	3.84	16.98
3010602F 25 mm curved cutting	m	1.13	31.42	–	6.97	38.39	34.56	–	7.67	42.23

3010605   **Boarding to dormers; tops or cheeks; butt joints; thickness:**

	Unit	Labour Hours	Labour Net	Plant Net	Materials Net	Unit Net	Labour Gross	Plant Gross	Materials Gross	Unit Price
3010605A 18 mm over 300 mm wide	m²	0.73	20.30	–	16.25	36.55	22.33	–	17.88	40.21
3010605B 18 mm not exceeding 150 mm wide	m	0.11	3.06	–	2.44	5.50	3.37	–	2.68	6.05
3010605C 18 mm 150 mm to 300 mm wide	m	0.22	6.11	–	4.88	10.99	6.72	–	5.37	12.09
3010605D 18 mm raking cutting	m	0.40	11.12	–	2.44	13.56	12.23	–	2.68	14.92
3010605E 18 mm curved cutting	m	1.06	29.47	–	4.88	34.35	32.42	–	5.37	37.79
3010605F 25 mm over 300 mm wide	m²	0.83	23.07	–	23.24	46.31	25.38	–	25.56	50.94
3010605G 25 mm not exceeding 150 mm wide	m	0.13	3.61	–	3.49	7.10	3.97	–	3.84	7.81
3010605H 25 mm 150 mm to 300 mm wide	m	0.25	6.95	–	6.97	13.92	7.65	–	7.67	15.31
3010605I 25 mm raking cutting	m	0.43	11.95	–	3.49	15.44	13.15	–	3.84	16.98
3010605J 25 mm curved cutting	m	1.13	31.42	–	6.97	38.39	34.56	–	7.67	42.23

3010606   **Boarding to gutters; bottoms or sides; butt joints; thickness:**

	Unit	Labour Hours	Labour Net	Plant Net	Materials Net	Unit Net	Labour Gross	Plant Gross	Materials Gross	Unit Price
3010606A 18 mm over 300 mm wide	m²	2.76	76.73	–	16.25	92.98	84.40	–	17.88	102.28
3010606B 18 mm not exceeding 150 mm wide	m	0.41	11.40	–	2.44	13.84	12.54	–	2.68	15.22
3010606C 18 mm 150 mm to 300 mm wide	m	0.83	23.07	–	4.88	27.95	25.38	–	5.37	30.75
3010606D 18 mm raking cutting	m	0.40	11.12	–	2.44	13.56	12.23	–	2.68	14.92
3010606E 18 mm curved cutting	m	1.06	29.47	–	4.88	34.35	32.42	–	5.37	37.79
3010606F 25 mm over 300 mm wide	m²	3.14	87.29	–	23.24	110.53	96.02	–	25.56	121.58
3010606G 25 mm not exceeding 150 mm wide	m	0.47	13.06	–	3.49	16.55	14.37	–	3.84	18.21
3010606H 25 mm 150 mm to 300 mm wide	m	0.94	26.14	–	6.97	33.11	28.75	–	7.67	36.42
3010606I 25 mm raking cutting	m	0.43	11.95	–	3.49	15.44	13.15	–	3.84	16.98
3010606J 25 mm curved cutting	m	1.13	31.42	–	6.97	38.39	34.56	–	7.67	42.23

Woodwork

Small Works 2009		Unit	Labour Hours	Labour Net	Plant Net	Materials Net	Unit Net	Labour Gross	Plant Gross	Materials Gross	Unit Price
								(Gross rates include 10% profit)			
				£	£	£	£	£	£	£	£
301	**NEW WORK**										
30106	**FIRST FIXINGS: PLYWOOD**										
3010607	**Boarding to eaves; verges; fascias and the like; butt joints; thickness:**										
3010607A	18 mm over 300 mm wide..	m²	1.52	42.26	–	16.25	58.51	46.49	–	17.88	64.36
3010607B	18 mm not exceeding 150 mm wide	m	0.23	6.39	–	2.44	8.83	7.03	–	2.68	9.71
3010607C	18 mm 150 mm to 300 mm wide	m	0.46	12.79	–	4.88	17.67	14.07	–	5.37	19.44
3010607D	18 mm raking cutting......	m	0.40	11.12	–	2.44	13.56	12.23	–	2.68	14.92
3010607E	18 mm curved cutting	m	1.06	29.47	–	4.88	34.35	32.42	–	5.37	37.79
3010607F	25 mm over 300 mm wide..	m²	1.66	46.15	–	23.24	69.39	50.77	–	25.56	76.33
3010607G	25 mm not exceeding 150 mm wide	m	0.25	6.95	–	3.49	10.44	7.65	–	3.84	11.48
3010607H	25 mm 150 mm to 300 mm wide	m	0.50	13.90	–	6.97	20.87	15.29	–	7.67	22.96
3010607I	25 mm raking cutting......	m	0.43	11.95	–	3.49	15.44	13.15	–	3.84	16.98
3010607J	25 mm curved cutting	m	1.13	31.42	–	6.97	38.39	34.56	–	7.67	42.23

Woodwork

Small Works 2009		Unit	Labour Hours	Labour Net	Plant Net	Materials Net	Unit Net	Labour Gross	Plant Gross	Materials Gross	Unit Price
								—— (Gross rates include 10% profit) ——			
				£	£	£	£	£	£	£	£
301	**NEW WORK**										
30108	**FIRST FIXINGS: SOFTWOOD**										
3010801	**Boarding to roofs; 150 mm wide boards; butt joints; thickness:**										
3010801A	19 mm	m²	0.70	19.46	–	19.77	39.23	21.41	–	21.75	43.15
3010801B	19 mm raking cutting	m	0.20	5.56	–	2.97	8.53	6.12	–	3.27	9.38
3010801C	19 mm curved cutting	m	0.60	16.68	–	5.93	22.61	18.35	–	6.52	24.87
3010801D	25 mm	m²	0.75	20.85	–	23.39	44.24	22.94	–	25.73	48.66
3010801E	25 mm raking cutting	m	0.20	5.56	–	3.51	9.07	6.12	–	3.86	9.98
3010801F	25 mm curved cutting	m	0.60	16.68	–	7.02	23.70	18.35	–	7.72	26.07
3010802	**Boarding to roofs; sloping; 150 mm wide boards; butt joints; thickness:**										
3010802A	19 mm	m²	1.05	29.19	–	19.77	48.96	32.11	–	21.75	53.86
3010802B	19 mm raking cutting	m	0.20	5.56	–	2.97	8.53	6.12	–	3.27	9.38
3010802C	19 mm curved cutting	m	0.60	16.68	–	5.93	22.61	18.35	–	6.52	24.87
3010802D	25 mm	m²	1.13	31.41	–	23.39	54.80	34.55	–	25.73	60.28
3010802E	25 mm raking cutting	m	0.20	5.56	–	3.51	9.07	6.12	–	3.86	9.98
3010802F	25 mm curved cutting	m	0.60	16.68	–	7.02	23.70	18.35	–	7.72	26.07
3010803	**Boarding to dormers; tops or cheeks; 150 mm wide boards; butt joints; thickness:**										
3010803A	19 mm	m²	0.99	27.52	–	19.77	47.29	30.27	–	21.75	52.02
3010803B	19 mm raking cutting	m	0.20	5.56	–	2.97	8.53	6.12	–	3.27	9.38
3010803C	19 mm curved cutting	m	0.60	16.68	–	5.93	22.61	18.35	–	6.52	24.87
3010803D	25 mm	m²	1.07	29.74	–	23.39	53.13	32.71	–	25.73	58.44
3010803E	25 mm raking cutting	m	0.20	5.56	–	3.51	9.07	6.12	–	3.86	9.98
3010803F	25 mm curved cutting	m	0.60	16.68	–	7.02	23.70	18.35	–	7.72	26.07
3010804	**Boarding to gutters; bottoms or sides; sloping; thickness:**										
3010804A	19 mm over 300 mm wide . .	m²	1.51	41.97	–	19.77	61.74	46.17	–	21.75	67.91
3010804B	19 mm not exceeding 150 mm wide	m	0.76	21.12	–	2.97	24.09	23.23	–	3.27	26.50
3010804C	19 mm 150 mm to 300 mm wide	m	0.98	27.25	–	5.93	33.18	29.98	–	6.52	36.50
3010804D	19 mm raking cutting	m	0.20	5.56	–	2.97	8.53	6.12	–	3.27	9.38
3010804E	19 mm curved cutting	m	0.60	16.68	–	5.93	22.61	18.35	–	6.52	24.87
3010804F	25 mm over 300 mm wide . .	m²	1.51	41.97	–	23.39	65.36	46.17	–	25.73	71.90
3010804G	25 mm not exceeding 150 mm wide	m	0.76	21.13	–	3.51	24.64	23.24	–	3.86	27.10
3010804H	25 mm 150 mm to 300 mm wide	m	0.98	27.24	–	7.02	34.26	29.96	–	7.72	37.69
3010804I	25 mm raking cutting	m	0.20	5.56	–	3.51	9.07	6.12	–	3.86	9.98
3010804J	25 mm curved cutting	m	0.60	16.68	–	7.02	23.70	18.35	–	7.72	26.07
3010805	**Boarding to verges; fascias; soffits, thickness:**										
3010805A	19 mm over 300 mm wide . .	m²	1.34	37.25	–	19.77	57.02	40.98	–	21.75	62.72
3010805B	19 mm not exceeding 150 mm wide	m	0.68	18.90	–	2.97	21.87	20.79	–	3.27	24.06
3010805C	19 mm 150 mm to 300 mm wide	m	0.87	24.19	–	5.93	30.12	26.61	–	6.52	33.13
3010805D	19 mm raking cutting	m	0.20	5.56	–	2.97	8.53	6.12	–	3.27	9.38
3010805E	19 mm curved cutting	m	0.60	16.68	–	5.93	22.61	18.35	–	6.52	24.87
3010805F	25 mm over 300 mm wide . .	m²	1.34	37.25	–	23.39	60.64	40.98	–	25.73	66.70
3010805G	25 mm not exceeding 150 mm wide	m	0.68	18.90	–	3.51	22.41	20.79	–	3.86	24.65
3010805H	25 mm 150 mm to 300 mm wide	m	0.60	16.68	–	7.02	23.70	18.35	–	7.72	26.07
3010805I	25 mm raking cutting	m	0.20	5.56	–	3.51	9.07	6.12	–	3.86	9.98
3010805J	25 mm curved cutting	m	0.60	16.68	–	7.02	23.70	18.35	–	7.72	26.07

Small Works 2009		Unit	Labour Hours	Labour Net	Plant Net	Materials Net	Unit Net	Labour Gross	Plant Gross	Materials Gross	Unit Price
								(Gross rates include 10% profit)			
				£	£	£	£	£	£	£	£
301	**NEW WORK**										
30108	**FIRST FIXINGS: SOFTWOOD**										
3010810	**Firrings; 50 mm wide; average depth:**										
3010810A	38 mm	m	0.15	4.17	–	1.04	5.21	4.59	–	1.14	5.73
3010810B	50 mm	m	0.15	4.17	–	0.80	4.97	4.59	–	0.88	5.47
3010810C	75 mm	m	0.17	4.73	–	1.59	6.32	5.20	–	1.75	6.95
3010811	**Bearers:**										
3010811A	25 mm × 50 mm	m	0.12	3.34	–	0.41	3.75	3.67	–	0.45	4.13
3010811B	38 mm × 50 mm	m	0.12	3.33	–	0.63	3.96	3.66	–	0.69	4.36
3010811C	50 mm × 50 mm	m	0.12	3.33	–	0.83	4.16	3.66	–	0.91	4.58
3010811D	50 mm × 75 mm	m	0.14	3.89	–	1.23	5.12	4.28	–	1.35	5.63
3010812	**Angle fillets:**										
3010812A	38 mm × 38 mm	m	0.13	3.62	–	0.53	4.15	3.98	–	0.58	4.57
3010812B	50 mm × 50 mm	m	0.13	3.61	–	0.67	4.28	3.97	–	0.74	4.71
3010812C	75 mm × 75 mm	m	0.15	4.17	–	1.36	5.53	4.59	–	1.50	6.08
3010813	**Tilting fillets:**										
3010813A	19 mm × 38 mm	m	0.12	3.34	–	0.24	3.58	3.67	–	0.26	3.94
3010813B	25 mm × 50 mm	m	0.12	3.34	–	0.41	3.75	3.67	–	0.45	4.13
3010813C	38 mm × 50 mm	m	0.12	3.33	–	0.63	3.96	3.66	–	0.69	4.36
3010813D	50 mm × 75 mm	m	0.14	3.89	–	1.23	5.12	4.28	–	1.35	5.63
3010813E	75 mm × 100 mm	m	0.16	4.45	–	2.47	6.92	4.90	–	2.72	7.61
3010814	**Grounds or battens:**										
3010814A	19 mm × 38 mm	m	0.07	1.95	–	0.24	2.19	2.15	–	0.26	2.41
3010814B	19 mm × 50 mm	m	0.07	1.94	–	0.31	2.25	2.13	–	0.34	2.48
3010814C	25 mm × 50 mm	m	0.07	1.95	–	0.41	2.36	2.15	–	0.45	2.60
3010815	**Framework to bath panel at 500 mm centres both ways:**										
3010815A	25 mm × 50 mm	m²	1.09	30.30	–	2.52	32.82	33.33	–	2.77	36.10

Woodwork

Small Works 2009		Unit	Labour Hours	Labour Net	Plant Net	Materials Net	Unit Net	Labour Gross	Plant Gross	Materials Gross	Unit Price
								(Gross rates include 10% profit)			
				£	£	£	£	£	£	£	£
301	**NEW WORK**										
30108	**FIRST FIXINGS: SOFTWOOD**										
3010818	**Framework to walls at 300 mm centres one way; 600 mm centres other way:**										
3010818A	25 mm × 50 mm	m²	1.54	42.81	–	2.07	44.88	47.09	–	2.28	49.37
3010818B	38 mm × 50 mm	m²	1.54	42.81	–	3.14	45.95	47.09	–	3.45	50.55
3010818C	50 mm × 50 mm	m²	1.54	42.81	–	4.14	46.95	47.09	–	4.55	51.65
3010818D	50 mm × 75 mm	m²	1.56	43.37	–	6.14	49.51	47.71	–	6.75	54.46
3010818E	75 mm × 75 mm	m²	1.58	43.92	–	9.22	53.14	48.31	–	10.14	58.45
3010819	**Framework as bracketing and cradling around steelwork:**										
3010819A	25 mm × 50 mm	m²	1.70	47.26	–	3.03	50.29	51.99	–	3.33	55.32
3010819B	50 mm × 50 mm	m²	1.80	50.04	–	6.06	56.10	55.04	–	6.67	61.71
3010819C	50 mm × 75 mm	m²	1.90	52.82	–	9.00	61.82	58.10	–	9.90	68.00
3010820	**Blockings wedged between flanges of steelwork:**										
3010820A	50 mm × 50 mm × 150 mm	Each	0.14	3.90	–	0.12	4.02	4.29	–	0.13	4.42
3010820B	50 mm × 75 mm × 225 mm	Each	0.15	4.17	–	0.28	4.45	4.59	–	0.31	4.90
3010820C	50 mm × 100 mm × 300 mm	Each	0.16	4.45	–	0.49	4.94	4.90	–	0.54	5.43
3010821	**Floors fillets fixed to floor clips:**										
3010821A	38 mm × 50 mm	m	0.12	3.34	–	1.98	5.32	3.67	–	2.18	5.85
3010821B	50 mm × 50 mm	m	0.12	3.34	–	2.18	5.52	3.67	–	2.40	6.07
3010822	**Floor fillets set in concrete:**										
3010822A	38 mm × 50 mm	m	0.14	3.89	–	0.63	4.52	4.28	–	0.69	4.97
3010822B	50 mm × 50 mm	m	0.14	3.89	–	0.83	4.72	4.28	–	0.91	5.19

Woodwork

Small Works 2009		Unit	Labour Hours	Labour Net	Plant Net	Materials Net	Unit Net	Labour Gross	Plant Gross	Materials Gross	Unit Price
								(Gross rates include 10% profit)			
				£	£	£	£	£	£	£	£
301	**NEW WORK**										
30109	**FIRST FIXINGS: SOFTWOOD BOARDING**										
3010901	**Boarding to floors; 100 mm wide boards; butt joints; thickness:**										
3010901A	19 mm	m²	0.60	16.68	–	27.93	44.61	18.35	–	30.72	49.07
3010901B	19 mm raking cutting.	m	0.20	5.56	–	4.19	9.75	6.12	–	4.61	10.73
3010901C	19 mm curved cutting	m	0.60	16.68	–	8.38	25.06	18.35	–	9.22	27.57
3010901D	25 mm	m²	0.60	16.68	–	33.04	49.72	18.35	–	36.34	54.69
3010901E	25 mm raking cutting.	m	0.20	5.56	–	4.96	10.52	6.12	–	5.46	11.57
3010901F	25 mm curved cutting	m	0.60	16.68	–	9.92	26.60	18.35	–	10.91	29.26
3010901G	32 mm	m²	0.66	18.35	–	37.74	56.09	20.19	–	41.51	61.70
3010901H	32 mm raking cutting.	m	0.22	6.12	–	5.66	11.78	6.73	–	6.23	12.96
3010901I	32 mm curved cutting	m	0.63	17.51	–	11.33	28.84	19.26	–	12.46	31.72
3010902	**Boarding to floors; 150 mm wide boards; butt joints; thickness:**										
3010902A	19 mm	m²	0.50	13.90	–	27.93	41.83	15.29	–	30.72	46.01
3010902B	19 mm raking cutting.	m	0.20	5.56	–	4.19	9.75	6.12	–	4.61	10.73
3010902C	19 mm curved cutting	m	0.60	16.68	–	8.38	25.06	18.35	–	9.22	27.57
3010902D	25 mm	m²	0.50	13.90	–	3.30	17.20	15.29	–	3.63	18.92
3010902E	25 mm raking cutting.	m	0.20	5.56	–	4.96	10.52	6.12	–	5.46	11.57
3010902F	25 mm curved cutting	m	0.60	16.68	–	9.92	26.60	18.35	–	10.91	29.26
3010902G	32 mm	m²	0.55	15.29	–	37.74	53.03	16.82	–	41.51	58.33
3010902H	32 mm raking cutting.	m	0.20	5.56	–	5.66	11.22	6.12	–	6.23	12.34
3010902I	32 mm curved cutting	m	0.60	16.68	–	11.33	28.01	18.35	–	12.46	30.81
3010903	**Boarding to floors; 125 mm wide boards; tongued and grooved joints, thickness:**										
3010903A	22 mm	m²	0.65	18.07	–	32.74	50.81	19.88	–	36.01	55.89
3010903B	22 mm raking cutting.	m	0.20	5.56	–	4.91	10.47	6.12	–	5.40	11.52
3010903C	22 mm curved cutting	m	0.60	16.68	–	9.82	26.50	18.35	–	10.80	29.15
3010903D	25 mm	m²	0.65	18.07	–	34.12	52.19	19.88	–	37.53	57.41
3010903E	25 mm raking cutting.	m	0.20	5.56	–	5.12	10.68	6.12	–	5.63	11.75
3010903F	25 mm curved cutting	m	0.60	16.68	–	10.24	26.92	18.35	–	11.26	29.61
3010904	**Boarding to floors; 150 mm wide boards; tongued and grooved joints; thickness:**										
3010904A	25 mm	m²	0.60	16.68	–	34.12	50.80	18.35	–	37.53	55.88
3010904B	25 mm raking cutting.	m	0.20	5.56	–	5.12	10.68	6.12	–	5.63	11.75
3010904C	25 mm curved cutting	m	0.60	16.68	–	10.24	26.92	18.35	–	11.26	29.61
3010905	**Mitred margin:**										
3010905A	25 mm × 75 mm	m	0.40	11.12	–	2.19	13.31	12.23	–	2.41	14.64

Woodwork

Small Works 2009	Unit	Labour Hours	Labour Net	Plant Net	Materials Net	Unit Net	Labour Gross	Plant Gross	Materials Gross	Unit Price
			£	£	£	£	(Gross rates include 10% profit)			
							£	£	£	£
301	**NEW WORK**									
30108	**FIRST FIXINGS: SOFTWOOD**									
3010906	**Boarding to integral walls; 125 mm wide boards; tongued and grooved and V jointed; thickness:**									
3010906A	19 mm	m²	0.91	25.29	–	31.43	56.72	27.82	–	34.57	62.39
3010906B	19 mm raking cutting	m	0.20	5.56	–	4.72	10.28	6.12	–	5.19	11.31
3010906C	19 mm curved cutting	m	0.60	16.68	–	9.43	26.11	18.35	–	10.37	28.72
3010906D	25 mm	m²	0.91	25.30	–	34.12	59.42	27.83	–	37.53	65.36
3010906E	25 mm raking cutting	m	0.20	5.56	–	5.12	10.68	6.12	–	5.63	11.75
3010906F	25 mm curved cutting	m	0.60	16.68	–	10.24	26.92	18.35	–	11.26	29.61
3010907	**Boarding to internal ceilings; 125 mm wide boards; tongued, grooved and V jointed; thickness:**									
3010907A	19 mm	m²	1.16	32.24	–	31.43	63.67	35.46	–	34.57	70.04
3010907B	19 mm raking cutting	m	0.20	5.56	–	4.72	10.28	6.12	–	5.19	11.31
3010907C	19 mm curved cutting	m	0.60	16.68	–	9.43	26.11	18.35	–	10.37	28.72
3010907D	25 mm	m²	1.16	32.25	–	34.12	66.37	35.48	–	37.53	73.01
3010907E	25 mm raking cutting	m	0.20	5.56	–	5.12	10.68	6.12	–	5.63	11.75
3010907F	25 mm curved cutting	m	0.60	16.68	–	10.24	26.92	18.35	–	11.26	29.61
3010908	**Boarding to internal walls; Knotty Pine; 100 mm wide boards; tongued and grooved; thickness:**									
3010908A	12 mm	m²	0.97	26.97	–	19.83	46.80	29.67	–	21.81	51.48
3010908B	12 mm raking cutting	m	0.20	5.56	–	2.98	8.54	6.12	–	3.28	9.39
3010908C	12 mm curved cutting	m	0.60	16.68	–	5.95	22.63	18.35	–	6.55	24.89
3010908D	16 mm	m²	0.97	26.97	–	26.47	53.44	29.67	–	29.12	58.78
3010908E	16 mm raking cutting	m	0.20	5.56	–	3.97	9.53	6.12	–	4.37	10.48
3010908F	16 mm curved cutting	m	0.60	16.68	–	7.94	24.62	18.35	–	8.73	27.08
3010908G	19 mm	m²	0.97	26.96	–	31.43	58.39	29.66	–	34.57	64.23
3010908H	19 mm raking cutting	m	0.20	5.56	–	4.72	10.28	6.12	–	5.19	11.31
3010908I	19 mm curved cutting	m	0.60	16.68	–	9.43	26.11	18.35	–	10.37	28.72
3010909	**Boarding to internal ceilings; Knotty Pine; 100 mm wide boards; tongued and grooved; thickness:**									
3010909A	12 mm	m²	1.21	33.64	–	19.83	53.47	37.00	–	21.81	58.82
3010909B	12 mm raking cutting	m	0.20	5.56	–	2.98	8.54	6.12	–	3.28	9.39
3010909C	12 mm curved cutting	m	0.60	16.68	–	5.95	22.63	18.35	–	6.55	24.89
3010909D	16 mm	m²	1.21	33.64	–	26.47	60.11	37.00	–	29.12	66.12
3010909E	16 mm raking cutting	m	0.20	5.56	–	3.97	9.53	6.12	–	4.37	10.48
3010909F	16 mm curved cutting	m	0.60	16.68	–	7.94	24.62	18.35	–	8.73	27.08
3010909G	19 mm	m²	1.21	33.63	–	31.43	65.06	36.99	–	34.57	71.57
3010909H	19 mm raking cutting	m	0.20	5.56	–	4.72	10.28	6.12	–	5.19	11.31
3010909I	19 mm curved cutting	m	0.60	16.68	–	9.43	26.11	18.35	–	10.37	28.72

Small Works 2009		Unit	Labour Hours	Labour Net	Plant Net	Materials Net	Unit Net	Labour Gross	Plant Gross	Materials Gross	Unit Price
								—— (Gross rates include 10% profit) ——			
				£	£	£	£	£	£	£	£
301	**NEW WORK**										
30110	**SECOND FIXINGS: SHEET LININGS**										
3011001	**3.2 mm Hardboard linings to walls:**										
3011001A	over 300 mm wide	m²	0.36	10.00	–	2.97	12.97	11.00	–	3.27	14.27
3011001B	not exceeding 300 mm wide	m	0.15	4.17	–	0.93	5.10	4.59	–	1.02	5.61
3011002	**3.2 mm Hardboard linings to ceilings:**										
3011002A	over 300 mm wide	m²	0.41	11.39	–	2.97	14.36	12.53	–	3.27	15.80
3011002B	not exceeding 300 mm wide	m	0.17	4.73	–	0.93	5.66	5.20	–	1.02	6.23
3011002C	raking cutting	m	0.16	4.45	–	0.15	4.60	4.90	–	0.17	5.06
3011002D	curved cutting.	m	0.53	14.73	–	0.30	15.03	16.20	–	0.33	16.53
3011003	**12 mm Chipboard lining to walls:**										
3011003A	over 300 mm wide	m²	0.46	12.78	–	3.01	15.79	14.06	–	3.31	17.37
3011003B	not exceeding 300 mm wide	m	0.19	5.29	–	0.94	6.23	5.82	–	1.03	6.85
3011004	**12 mm Chipboard lining to ceilings:**										
3011004A	over 300 mm wide	m²	0.53	14.73	–	3.01	17.74	16.20	–	3.31	19.51
3011004B	not exceeding 300 mm wide	m	0.22	6.11	–	0.94	7.05	6.72	–	1.03	7.76
3011004C	raking cutting	m	0.33	9.17	–	0.45	9.62	10.09	–	0.50	10.58
3011004D	curved cutting.	m	0.73	20.30	–	0.90	21.20	22.33	–	0.99	23.32
3011006	**12 mm Insulation board lining to walls:**										
3011006A	over 300 mm wide	m²	0.29	8.06	–	4.30	12.36	8.87	–	4.73	13.60
3011006B	not exceeding 300 mm wide	m	0.12	3.34	–	1.35	4.69	3.67	–	1.49	5.16
3011007	**12 mm Insulation board lining to ceilings:**										
3011007A	over 300 mm wide	m²	0.33	9.17	–	4.30	13.47	10.09	–	4.73	14.82
3011007B	not exceeding 300 mm wide	m	0.14	3.89	–	1.35	5.24	4.28	–	1.49	5.76
3011007C	raking cutting	m	0.14	3.89	–	0.65	4.54	4.28	–	0.72	4.99
3011007D	curved cutting.	m	0.40	11.12	–	1.29	12.41	12.23	–	1.42	13.65
3011008	**6 mm Sanded surface non-asbestos board lining to walls:**										
3011008A	over 300 mm wide	m²	0.40	11.12	–	14.38	25.50	12.23	–	15.82	28.05
3011008B	not exceeding 300 mm wide	m	0.16	4.45	–	4.52	8.97	4.90	–	4.97	9.87
3011009	**6 mm Sanded surface non-asbestos board lining to ceilings:**										
3011009A	over 300 mm wide	m²	0.46	12.79	–	14.38	27.17	14.07	–	15.82	29.89
3011009B	not exceeding 300 mm wide	m	0.18	5.01	–	4.52	9.53	5.51	–	4.97	10.48
3011009C	raking cutting	m	0.33	9.17	–	2.16	11.33	10.09	–	2.38	12.46
3011009D	curved cutting.	m	0.93	25.85	–	4.32	30.17	28.44	–	4.75	33.19

Woodwork

Small Works 2009		Unit	Labour Hours	Labour Net	Plant Net	Materials Net	Unit Net	Labour Gross	Plant Gross	Materials Gross	Unit Price
								(Gross rates include 10% profit)			
				£	£	£	£	£	£	£	£
301	**NEW WORK**										
30108	**FIRST FIXINGS: SOFTWOOD**										
3011010	**9 mm Sanded surface non-asbestos board lining to walls:**										
3011010A	over 300 mm wide	m²	0.43	11.95	–	21.85	33.80	13.15	–	24.04	37.18
3011010B	not exceeding 300 mm wide	m	0.18	5.01	–	6.87	11.88	5.51	–	7.56	13.07
3011011	**9 mm Sanded surface non-asbestos board lining to ceilings:**										
3011011A	over 300 mm wide	m²	0.50	13.90	–	21.85	35.75	15.29	–	24.04	39.33
3011011B	not exceeding 300 mm wide	m	0.21	5.84	–	6.87	12.71	6.42	–	7.56	13.98
3011011C	raking cutting	m	0.33	9.17	–	3.28	12.45	10.09	–	3.61	13.70
3011011D	curved cutting............	m	0.93	25.85	–	6.56	32.41	28.44	–	7.22	35.65
3011014	**4 mm Plywood WBP Birch faced lining to walls:**										
3011014A	over 300 mm wide	m²	0.44	12.23	–	8.84	21.07	13.45	–	9.72	23.18
3011014B	not exceeding 300 mm wide	m	0.18	5.00	–	2.78	7.78	5.50	–	3.06	8.56
3011016	**4 mm Plywood WBP Birch faced lining to ceilings:**										
3011016A	over 300 mm wide	m²	0.51	14.18	–	8.84	23.02	15.60	–	9.72	25.32
3011016B	not exceeding 300 mm wide	m	0.21	5.84	–	2.78	8.62	6.42	–	3.06	9.48
3011016C	raking cutting	m	0.27	7.50	–	1.33	8.83	8.25	–	1.46	9.71
3011016D	curved cutting............	m	0.60	16.68	–	2.65	19.33	18.35	–	2.92	21.26
3011018	**6.5 mm Plywood WBP Birch faced lining t walls:**										
3011018A	over 300 mm wide	m²	0.48	13.34	–	13.04	26.38	14.67	–	14.34	29.02
3011018B	not exceeding 300 mm wide	m	0.20	5.56	–	4.10	9.66	6.12	–	4.51	10.63
3011019	**6.5 mm Plywood WBP Birch faced lining t ceilings:**										
3011019A	over 300 mm wide	m²	0.55	15.29	–	13.04	28.33	16.82	–	14.34	31.16
3011019B	not exceeding 300 mm wide	m	0.23	6.39	–	4.10	10.49	7.03	–	4.51	11.54
3011019C	raking cutting	m	0.27	7.50	–	1.96	9.46	8.25	–	2.16	10.41
3011019D	curved cutting............	m	0.60	16.68	–	3.91	20.59	18.35	–	4.30	22.65
3011021	**12 mm Blockboard lining to walls:**										
3011021A	over 300 mm wide	m²	0.56	15.57	–	14.17	29.74	17.13	–	15.59	32.71
3011021B	not exceeding 300 mm wide	m	0.23	6.39	–	4.46	10.85	7.03	–	4.91	11.94
3011022	**12 mm Blockboard lining to ceilings:**										
3011022A	over 300 mm wide	m²	0.64	17.79	–	14.17	31.96	19.57	–	15.59	35.16
3011022B	not exceeding 300 mm wide	m	0.27	7.50	–	4.46	11.96	8.25	–	4.91	13.16
3011022C	raking cutting	m	0.33	9.17	–	2.13	11.30	10.09	–	2.34	12.43
3011022D	curved cutting............	m	0.73	20.30	–	4.25	24.55	22.33	–	4.68	27.01
3011024	**18 mm Blockboard lining to walls:**										
3011024A	over 300 mm wide	m²	0.60	16.68	–	13.93	30.61	18.35	–	15.32	33.67
3011024B	not exceeding 300 mm wide	m	0.25	6.95	–	4.38	11.33	7.65	–	4.82	12.46
3011025	**18 mm Blockboard lining to ceilings:**										
3011025A	over 300 mm wide	m²	0.69	19.18	–	13.93	33.11	21.10	–	15.32	36.42
3011025B	not exceeding 300 mm wide	m	0.29	8.06	–	4.38	12.44	8.87	–	4.82	13.68
3011025C	raking cutting	m	0.33	9.17	–	2.09	11.26	10.09	–	2.30	12.39
3011025D	curved cutting............	m	0.85	23.63	–	4.18	27.81	25.99	–	4.60	30.59

Small Works 2009		Unit	Labour Hours	Labour Net	Plant Net	Materials Net	Unit Net	Labour Gross	Plant Gross	Materials Gross	Unit Price
								(Gross rates include 10% profit)			
				£	£	£	£	£	£	£	£
301	**NEW WORK**										
30112	**SECOND FIXINGS: SHEET CASINGS**										
3011201	**Cupboards; 3.2 mm hardboard sides; softwood framing:**										
3011201A	25 mm × 25 mm	m²	6.45	179.31	–	11.25	190.56	197.24	–	12.38	209.62
3011201B	32 mm × 32 mm	m²	6.70	186.26	–	12.40	198.66	204.89	–	13.64	218.53
3011201C	38 mm × 38 mm	m²	6.70	186.26	–	13.83	200.09	204.89	–	15.21	220.10
3011202	**Cupboards; hardboard backs:**										
3011202A	3.2 mm	m²	0.40	11.12	–	2.97	14.09	12.23	–	3.27	15.50
3011204	**Cupboards; 3.2 mm hardboard doors; softwood framing:**										
3011204A	25 mm × 25 mm	m²	7.50	208.50	–	11.25	219.75	229.35	–	12.38	241.73
3011204B	32 mm × 32 mm	m²	7.80	216.84	–	12.40	229.24	238.52	–	13.64	252.16
3011204C	38 mm × 38 mm	m²	7.80	216.84	–	13.83	230.67	238.52	–	15.21	253.74
3011206	**Cupboards; 6.5 mm plywood sides; softwood framing:**										
3011206A	25 mm × 25 mm	m²	6.45	179.31	–	21.32	200.63	197.24	–	23.45	220.69
3011206B	32 mm × 32 mm	m²	6.70	186.26	–	22.47	208.73	204.89	–	24.72	229.60
3011206C	38 mm × 38 mm	m²	6.70	186.26	–	23.90	210.16	204.89	–	26.29	231.18
3011208	**Cupboards; plywood backs:**										
3011208A	6.5 mm	m²	0.50	13.90	–	10.52	24.42	15.29	–	11.57	26.86
3011209	**Cupboards; 6.5 mm plywood doors; softwood framing:**										
3011209A	25 mm × 25 mm	m²	7.50	208.50	–	18.81	227.31	229.35	–	20.69	250.04
3011209B	32 mm × 32 mm	m²	7.80	199.99	–	19.96	219.95	219.99	–	21.96	241.95
3011209C	38 mm × 38 mm	m²	7.80	216.84	–	21.39	238.23	238.52	–	23.53	262.05
3011212	**Boxed pipe casings; 300 mm girth; 19 mm × 25 mm sawn softwood framing; front fixed with brass screws and cups:**										
3011212A	3.2 mm hardboard front ...	m	1.15	31.97	–	1.51	33.48	35.17	–	1.66	36.83
3011212B	6.5 mm plywood front	m	1.30	36.14	–	3.89	40.03	39.75	–	4.28	44.03
3011212C	25 mm softwood front	m	1.40	38.92	–	24.36	63.28	42.81	–	26.80	69.61
3011213	**Pelmet casings 225 mm girth; 75 mm × 25 mm sawn softwood framing; 19 mm × 100 mm softwood top; 6.5 mm plywood front 125 mm deep:**										
3011213A	over 1.00 mm long	m	1.25	34.75	–	3.73	38.48	38.23	–	4.10	42.33
3011213B	short lengths; not exceeding 0.90 m long	Each	1.30	36.14	–	3.60	39.74	39.75	–	3.96	43.71
3011213C	short lengths; not exceeding 1.20 m long	Each	1.50	41.70	–	4.34	46.04	45.87	–	4.77	50.64
3011213D	extra for boxed ends	Each	0.45	12.51	–	0.20	12.71	13.76	–	0.22	13.98

Woodwork

Small Works 2009		Unit	Labour Hours	Labour Net	Plant Net	Materials Net	Unit Net	Labour Gross	Plant Gross	Materials Gross	Unit Price
								— (Gross rates include 10% profit) —			
				£	£	£	£	£	£	£	£
301	**NEW WORK**										
30112	**SECOND FIXINGS: SHEET CASINGS**										
3011214	**Pelmet casings 225 mm girth; 75 mm × 25 mm sawn softwood framing; part plugged and screwed to brick or concrete; 19 mm × 100 mm softwood top; 6.5 mm plywood front 125 mm deep:**										
3011214A	over 1.00 m long	m	1.50	41.70	–	3.73	45.43	45.87	–	4.10	49.97
3011214B	short lengths; not exceeding 0.90 m long	Each	1.60	44.48	–	3.60	48.08	48.93	–	3.96	52.89
3011214C	short lengths; not exceeding 1.20 m long	Each	1.80	50.04	–	4.34	54.38	55.04	–	4.77	59.82
3011214D	extra for boxed ends	Each	0.45	12.51	–	0.20	12.71	13.76	–	0.22	13.98
3011216	**Plastic curtain track including:**										
3011216A	brackets, gliders, stops and the like	m	0.65	18.07	–	10.84	28.91	19.88	–	11.92	31.80
30113	**SECOND FIXINGS: UPVC CLADDING**										
3011301	**Swish profiled cladding; fixed in accordance with manufacturers instructions; 38 × 25 mm sawn softwood framing at 450 mm centres:**										
3011301A	to walls over 300 mm wide .	m²	1.00	24.33	–	53.64	77.97	26.76	–	59.00	85.77
3011302	**Extra over cladding for:**										
3011302A	edge trim	m	0.23	5.47	–	2.19	7.66	6.02	–	2.41	8.43

Small Works 2009		Unit	Labour Hours	Labour Net	Plant Net	Materials Net	Unit Net	Labour Gross	Plant Gross	Materials Gross	Unit Price
								(Gross rates include 10% profit)			
				£	£	£	£	£	£	£	£
301	**NEW WORK**										
30116	**SECOND FIXINGS: WROUGHT SOFTWOOD**										
3011601	**Skirtings:**										
3011601A	19 mm × 100 mm chamfered or pencil rounded	m	0.12	3.33	–	3.89	7.22	3.66	–	4.28	7.94
3011601B	25 mm × 150 mm Torus-Ovolo; Torus- Ogee	m	0.14	3.89	–	7.17	11.06	4.28	–	7.89	12.17
3011601C	25 mm × 225 mm Torus	m	0.17	4.73	–	9.88	14.61	5.20	–	10.87	16.07
3011601D	returned ends	Each	0.19	5.28	–	–	5.28	5.81	–	–	5.81
3011601E	mitres	Each	0.12	3.34	–	–	3.34	3.67	–	–	3.67
3011602	**Picture rails:**										
3011602A	25 mm × 50 mm	m	0.12	3.33	–	3.01	6.34	3.66	–	3.31	6.97
3011603	**Dado rails:**										
3011603A	32 mm × 63 mm	m	0.19	5.28	–	3.74	9.02	5.81	–	4.11	9.92
3011604	**Architraves:**										
3011604A	19 mm × 50 mm chamfered and rounded	m	0.14	3.89	–	1.95	5.84	4.28	–	2.15	6.42
3011604B	19 mm × 63 mm chamfered and rounded	m	0.14	3.90	–	2.36	6.26	4.29	–	2.60	6.89
3011604C	19 mm × 75 mm chamfered and rounded	m	0.14	3.89	–	3.43	7.32	4.28	–	3.77	8.05
3011604D	19 mm × 50 mm Ogee	m	0.14	3.90	–	2.04	5.94	4.29	–	2.24	6.53
3011604E	19 mm × 63 mm Ogee	m	0.14	3.89	–	2.62	6.51	4.28	–	2.88	7.16
3011604F	19 mm × 50 mm Ovolo	m	0.14	3.90	–	2.36	6.26	4.29	–	2.60	6.89
3011604G	25 mm × 75 mm Torus	m	0.14	3.89	–	3.74	7.63	4.28	–	4.11	8.39
3011604H	38 mm × 150 mm Edwardian	m	0.14	3.89	–	16.27	20.16	4.28	–	17.90	22.18
3011604I	19 mm × 50 mm twice rounded	m	0.14	3.89	–	2.03	5.92	4.28	–	2.23	6.51
3011604J	returned ends	Each	0.19	5.28	–	–	5.28	5.81	–	–	5.81
3011604K	mitres	Each	0.12	3.34	–	–	3.34	3.67	–	–	3.67
3011606	**Stops:**										
3011606B	16 mm × 38 mm Ovolo	m	0.12	3.34	–	1.47	4.81	3.67	–	1.62	5.29
3011606C	16 mm × 50 mm Ovolo	m	0.12	3.34	–	1.91	5.25	3.67	–	2.10	5.78
3011606G	32 mm × 38 mm fire check	m	0.14	3.89	–	1.82	5.71	4.28	–	2.00	6.28
3011607	**Glazing beads:**										
3011607A	8 mm × 12 mm	m	0.06	1.67	–	0.57	2.24	1.84	–	0.63	2.46
3011607B	8 mm × 16 mm	m	0.06	1.67	–	0.57	2.24	1.84	–	0.63	2.46
3011607C	25 mm × 45 mm fire check	m	0.12	3.34	–	2.55	5.89	3.67	–	2.81	6.48
3011608	**Quadrants:**										
3011608A	12 mm	m	0.07	1.94	–	0.55	2.49	2.13	–	0.61	2.74
3011608B	16 mm	m	0.07	1.95	–	0.84	2.79	2.15	–	0.92	3.07
3011608C	19 mm	m	0.07	1.94	–	0.95	2.89	2.13	–	1.05	3.18
3011608E	25 mm	m	0.07	1.95	–	1.51	3.46	2.15	–	1.66	3.81
3011609	**Half rounds:**										
3011609A	19 mm	m	0.07	1.94	–	0.83	2.77	2.13	–	0.91	3.05
3011609B	25 mm	m	0.07	1.94	–	0.95	2.89	2.13	–	1.05	3.18
3011609C	12 mm × 25 mm	m	0.07	1.95	–	0.84	2.79	2.15	–	0.92	3.07

Woodwork

Small Works 2009		Unit	Labour Hours	Labour Net	Plant Net	Materials Net	Unit Net	Labour Gross	Plant Gross	Materials Gross	Unit Price
								(Gross rates include 10% profit)			
				£	£	£	£	£	£	£	£
301	**NEW WORK**										
30116	**SECOND FIXINGS: WROUGHT SOFTWOOD**										
3011611	**Scotia:**										
3011611A	19 mm	m	0.07	1.95	–	1.00	2.95	2.15	–	1.10	3.25
3011611B	25 mm	m	0.07	1.94	–	1.66	3.60	2.13	–	1.83	3.96
3011611D	38 mm	m	0.07	1.95	–	2.87	4.82	2.15	–	3.16	5.30
3011611E	50 mm	m	0.07	1.94	–	3.45	5.39	2.13	–	3.80	5.93
3011615	**Window boards:**										
3011615A	32 mm × 150 mm	m	0.24	6.68	–	8.57	15.25	7.35	–	9.43	16.78
3011615B	32 mm × 200 mm	m	0.27	7.51	–	11.46	18.97	8.26	–	12.61	20.87
3011615C	32 mm × 225 mm	m	0.32	8.89	–	13.13	22.02	9.78	–	14.44	24.22
3011617	**Shelves; worktops:**										
3011617A	19 mm × 150 mm	m	0.19	5.29	–	6.02	11.31	5.82	–	6.62	12.44
3011617B	19 mm × 175 mm	m	0.22	6.12	–	6.97	13.09	6.73	–	7.67	14.40
3011617C	25 mm × 150 mm	m	0.19	5.28	–	7.60	12.88	5.81	–	8.36	14.17
3011617D	25 mm × 200 mm	m	0.26	7.23	–	10.26	17.49	7.95	–	11.29	19.24
3011617E	32 mm × 150 mm	m	0.19	5.28	–	8.40	13.68	5.81	–	9.24	15.05
3011617F	32 mm × 175 mm	m	0.22	6.11	–	9.78	15.89	6.72	–	10.76	17.48
3011619	**Shelves; worktops; cross tongued joints:**										
3011619A	19 mm × 300 mm	m	0.33	9.17	–	12.57	21.74	10.09	–	13.83	23.91
3011619B	19 mm × 450 mm	m	0.40	11.12	–	18.91	30.03	12.23	–	20.80	33.03
3011619C	25 mm × 300 mm	m	0.33	9.18	–	15.85	25.03	10.10	–	17.44	27.53
3011619D	25 mm × 450 mm	m	0.40	11.12	–	26.32	37.44	12.23	–	28.95	41.18
3011619E	32 mm × 300 mm	m	0.33	9.17	–	17.59	26.76	10.09	–	19.35	29.44
3011619F	32 mm × 450 mm	m	0.40	11.12	–	26.32	37.44	12.23	–	28.95	41.18
3011621	**Shelves; worktops; slatted with 50 mm wide slats at 75 mm centres; thickness:**										
3011621A	19 mm	m²	1.56	43.37	–	19.05	62.42	47.71	–	20.96	68.66
3011621B	25 mm	m²	1.56	43.37	–	20.66	64.03	47.71	–	22.73	70.43
3011621C	32 mm	m²	1.56	43.37	–	23.33	66.70	47.71	–	25.66	73.37
3011623	**Bearers:**										
3011623A	19 mm × 38 mm	m	0.12	3.34	–	0.89	4.23	3.67	–	0.98	4.65
3011623B	25 mm × 50 mm	m	0.12	3.33	–	1.14	4.47	3.66	–	1.25	4.92
3011623C	50 mm × 50 mm	m	0.12	3.34	–	1.75	5.09	3.67	–	1.93	5.60
3011623D	50 mm × 75 mm	m	0.12	3.34	–	5.90	9.24	3.67	–	6.49	10.16
3011624	**Bearers; framed:**										
3011624A	19 mm × 38 mm	m	0.15	4.17	–	0.89	5.06	4.59	–	0.98	5.57
3011624B	25 mm × 50 mm	m	0.15	4.17	–	1.14	5.31	4.59	–	1.25	5.84
3011624C	50 mm × 50 mm	m	0.15	4.17	–	1.75	5.92	4.59	–	1.93	6.51
3011624D	50 mm × 75 mm	m	0.15	4.17	–	5.90	10.07	4.59	–	6.49	11.08
3011626	**Framing; framed:**										
3011626A	19 mm × 38 mm	m	0.19	5.29	–	0.89	6.18	5.82	–	0.98	6.80
3011626B	25 mm × 50 mm	m	0.19	5.28	–	1.14	6.42	5.81	–	1.25	7.06
3011626C	50 mm × 50 mm	m	0.19	5.28	–	1.75	7.03	5.81	–	1.93	7.73
3011626D	50 mm × 75 mm	m	0.19	5.29	–	5.90	11.19	5.82	–	6.49	12.31

Small Works 2009		Unit	Labour Hours	Labour Net	Plant Net	Materials Net	Unit Net	Labour Gross	Plant Gross	Materials Gross	Unit Price
								(Gross rates include 10% profit)			
				£	£	£	£	£	£	£	£
301	**NEW WORK**										
30116	**SECOND FIXINGS: WROUGHT SOFTWOOD**										
3011630	**Doors; wrought softwood 1.95 m × 0.75 m**										
3011630A	38 mm two panel square both sides	Each	5.25	145.95	–	32.40	178.35	160.55	–	35.64	196.19
3011630B	50 mm two panel moulded both sides	Each	6.20	172.36	–	47.25	219.61	189.60	–	51.98	241.57
3011630C	38 mm four panel square both sides	Each	7.00	194.60	–	48.06	242.66	214.06	–	52.87	266.93
3011630D	50 mm four panel moulded both sides	Each	8.00	222.40	–	122.72	345.12	244.64	–	134.99	379.63
3011630E	38 mm six panel square framed	Each	8.00	222.41	–	39.83	262.24	244.65	–	43.81	288.46
3011630F	50 mm six panel moulded both sides	Each	9.00	250.20	–	70.20	320.40	275.22	–	77.22	352.44
3011630G	50 mm half glazed	Each	8.00	222.41	–	29.02	251.43	244.65	–	31.92	276.57
3011630H	38 mm half glazed	Each	7.20	200.16	–	29.70	229.86	220.18	–	32.67	252.85
3011630I	38 mm skeleton flush......	Each	3.20	88.96	–	41.85	130.81	97.86	–	46.04	143.89
3011630J	38 mm solid flush........	Each	4.80	133.44	–	47.25	180.69	146.78	–	51.98	198.76
3011630K	ledged and braced with 100 mm × 25 mm ledging and bracing covered with matchboarding 19 mm	Each	3.30	91.74	–	49.87	141.61	100.91	–	54.86	155.77
3011630L	framed, ledged and braced with 100 mm × 50 mm framing and 100 mm × 32 mm ledging and bracing, covered with matchboarding 19 mm	Each	10.00	278.00	–	58.78	336.78	305.80	–	64.66	370.46
3011630M	50 mm casement divided into eight panes open for glass.................	Pair	16.20	450.36	–	56.70	507.06	495.40	–	62.37	557.77
3011630N	50 mm casement divided into eight panes open for glass.................	Each	8.70	241.86	–	28.35	270.21	266.05	–	31.19	297.23
3011630O	38 mm casement divided into eight panes open for glass.................	Pair	15.60	433.68	–	51.30	484.98	477.05	–	56.43	533.48
3011630P	38 mm casement divided into eight panes open for glass.................	Each	8.00	222.40	–	25.65	248.05	244.64	–	28.22	272.86

Woodwork

Small Works 2009		Unit	Labour Hours	Labour Net	Plant Net	Materials Net	Unit Net	Labour Gross	Plant Gross	Materials Gross	Unit Price
								(Gross rates include 10% profit)			
				£	£	£	£	£	£	£	£
301	**NEW WORK**										
30116	**SECOND FIXINGS: WROUGHT SOFTWOOD**										
3011631	**Garage door:**										
3011631A	1200 mm × 2100 mm high, with 125 mm × 50 mm framing, lined externally with 25 mm V jointed matchboarding to form solid front	Pair	17.50	486.50	–	162.14	648.64	535.15	–	178.35	713.50
3011640	**Frames; at jambs or heads:**										
3011640A	32 mm × 75 mm	m	0.25	6.95	–	4.46	11.41	7.65	–	4.91	12.55
3011640B	32 mm × 100 mm	m	0.25	6.95	–	5.77	12.72	7.65	–	6.35	13.99
3011640C	32 mm × 150 mm	m	0.25	6.95	–	8.36	15.31	7.65	–	9.20	16.84
3011640D	50 mm × 75 mm	m	0.28	7.79	–	5.82	13.61	8.57	–	6.40	14.97
3011640E	50 mm × 100 mm	m	0.28	7.79	–	7.57	15.36	8.57	–	8.33	16.90
3011640F	50 mm × 150 mm	m	0.28	7.78	–	11.46	19.24	8.56	–	12.61	21.16
3011641	**Frames; once rebated; at jambs or heads**										
3011641A	50 mm × 75 mm	m	0.28	7.78	–	6.37	14.15	8.56	–	7.01	15.57
3011641B	50 mm × 100 mm	m	0.28	7.78	–	8.11	15.89	8.56	–	8.92	17.48
3011641C	50 mm × 150 mm	m	0.31	8.62	–	11.95	20.57	9.48	–	13.15	22.63
3011641D	75 mm × 100 mm	m	0.35	9.73	–	12.41	22.14	10.70	–	13.65	24.35
3011641F	75 mm × 150 mm	m	0.35	9.73	–	17.42	27.15	10.70	–	19.16	29.87
3011642	**Frames; once rebated; once grooved; at jambs or heads:**										
3011642A	50 mm × 100 mm	m	0.28	7.79	–	8.64	16.43	8.57	–	9.50	18.07
3011642B	50 mm × 125 mm	m	0.28	7.78	–	10.70	18.48	8.56	–	11.77	20.33
3011642C	50 mm × 150 mm	m	0.31	8.62	–	12.51	21.13	9.48	–	13.76	23.24
3011642D	75 mm × 100 mm	m	0.35	9.73	–	12.96	22.69	10.70	–	14.26	24.96
3011642F	75 mm × 150 mm	m	0.35	9.73	–	17.95	27.68	10.70	–	19.75	30.45
3011643	**Frames; at mullions or transomes:**										
3011643A	32 mm × 75 mm	m	0.19	5.28	–	5.49	10.77	5.81	–	6.04	11.85
3011643B	32 mm × 100 mm	m	0.19	5.28	–	6.81	12.09	5.81	–	7.49	13.30
3011643C	32 mm × 150 mm	m	0.19	5.28	–	9.42	14.70	5.81	–	10.36	16.17

Small Works 2009		Unit	Labour Hours	Labour Net	Plant Net	Materials Net	Unit Net	Labour Gross	Plant Gross	Materials Gross	Unit Price
								(Gross rates include 10% profit)			
				£	£	£	£	£	£	£	£
301	**NEW WORK**										
30116	**SECOND FIXINGS: WROUGHT SOFTWOOD**										
3011644	**Frames; twice rebated; at mullions or transomes:**										
3011644A	38 mm × 100 mm	m	0.28	7.78	–	7.51	15.29	8.56	–	8.26	16.82
3011644B	38 mm × 150 mm	m	0.28	7.78	–	10.50	18.28	8.56	–	11.55	20.11
3011644C	50 mm × 100 mm	m	0.28	7.78	–	8.63	16.41	8.56	–	9.49	18.05
3011644D	75 mm × 100 mm	m	0.35	9.73	–	12.92	22.65	10.70	–	14.21	24.92
3011644E	75 mm × 150 mm	m	0.35	9.73	–	17.94	27.67	10.70	–	19.73	30.44
3011645	**Frames; once sunk weathered; once rebated; three times grooved; at cills:**										
3011645A	75 mm × 150 mm	m	0.35	9.73	–	22.24	31.97	10.70	–	24.46	35.17
3011645B	75 mm × 175 mm	m	0.35	9.73	–	28.37	38.10	10.70	–	31.21	41.91
3011646	**Linings; tongued at angles:**										
3011646A	25 mm × 75 mm	m	0.25	6.95	–	5.01	11.96	7.65	–	5.51	13.16
3011646B	25 mm × 100 mm	m	0.25	6.95	–	6.14	13.09	7.65	–	6.75	14.40
3011646C	25 mm × 125 mm	m	0.25	6.95	–	7.28	14.23	7.65	–	8.01	15.65
3011646D	25 mm × 150 mm	m	0.25	6.95	–	8.63	15.58	7.65	–	9.49	17.14
3011646E	32 mm × 100 mm	m	0.27	7.51	–	6.81	14.32	8.26	–	7.49	15.75
3011646F	32 mm × 125 mm	m	0.27	7.51	–	8.12	15.63	8.26	–	8.93	17.19
3011646G	32 mm × 150 mm	m	0.27	7.50	–	9.42	16.92	8.25	–	10.36	18.61
3011647	**Linings; once rebated; tongued at angles:**										
3011647A	38 mm × 100 mm	m	0.28	7.79	–	8.05	15.84	8.57	–	8.86	17.42
3011647B	38 mm × 150 mm	m	0.28	7.78	–	11.01	18.79	8.56	–	12.11	20.67

Woodwork

Small Works 2009		Unit	Labour Hours	Labour Net	Plant Net	Materials Net	Unit Net	Labour Gross	Plant Gross	Materials Gross	Unit Price
								(Gross rates include 10% profit)			
				£	£	£	£	£	£	£	£
301	**NEW WORK**										
30118	**SECOND FIXINGS: WROUGHT HARDWOOD**										
3011801	**Threshold:**										
3011801A	50 mm × 150 mm sunk, weathered and grooved....	m	0.40	11.12	–	22.05	33.17	12.23	–	24.26	36.49
30120	**WINDOWS: SOFTWOOD-PURPOSE MADE**										
3012001	**Casement window; side hung; rebated, moulded and grooved frame, mullions and transomes; 175 mm × 75 mm weathered, moulded and grooved cill; 45 mm sashes with 75 mm deep bottom rail:**										
3012001A	100 mm × 75 mm.......	m²	8.40	233.53	–	41.17	274.70	256.88	–	45.29	302.17
3012001B	sashes only-casement 45 mm without bars.......	m²	2.60	72.28	–	13.50	85.78	79.51	–	14.85	94.36
3012001C	sashes only-casement 45 mm with bars..........	m²	3.30	91.74	–	21.60	113.34	100.91	–	23.76	124.67
3012001D	frame only 100 mm × 75 mm	m	1.00	27.81	–	7.42	35.23	30.59	–	8.16	38.75
3012002	**Double hung sash window; 32 mm beaded inner lining; 25 mm outer lining; 32 mm pulley stile and bead; 25 mm back lining; 25 mm parting slip; all grooved tongued and blocked together and framed into hardwood sunk weathered, throated and check throated cill and fitted in with 50 mm rebated and moulded double hung sashes with splay rebated meeting rails hung on and including steel axle pulleys with brass plate and screws, sash lines and weights:**										
3012002A	175 mm × 100 mm......	m²	11.50	319.70	–	60.07	379.77	351.67	–	66.08	417.75
3012002B	175 mm × 100 mm sashes divided into small squares..	m²	12.25	340.55	–	62.10	402.65	374.61	–	68.31	442.92
3012003	**Frame for metal windows:**										
3012003A	75 mm × 50 mm	m	0.75	20.86	–	3.38	24.24	22.95	–	3.72	26.66

Small Works 2009	Unit	Labour Hours	Labour Net	Plant Net	Materials Net	Unit Net	Labour Gross	Plant Gross	Materials Gross	Unit Price
			£	£	£	£	£	£	£	£
								(Gross rates include 10% profit)		

301   NEW WORK

30122   SECOND FIXINGS: STANDARD DOORS

Small Works 2009	Unit	Labour Hours	Labour Net	Plant Net	Materials Net	Unit Net	Labour Gross	Plant Gross	Materials Gross	Unit Price
3012201 Flush door; internal quality; skeleton or cellular core; hardboard faced both sides:										
3012201A 35 mm thick; 1981 mm high; 686 mm wide	Each	1.54	42.82	–	40.28	83.10	47.10	–	44.31	91.41
3012201B 35 mm thick; 1981 mm high; 762 mm wide	Each	1.54	42.81	–	40.88	83.69	47.09	–	44.97	92.06
3012201C 35 mm thick; 1981 mm high; 838 mm wide	Each	1.54	42.82	–	43.04	85.86	47.10	–	47.34	94.45
3012201D 40 mm thick; 2040 mm high; 626 mm wide	Each	1.54	42.81	–	42.70	85.51	47.09	–	46.97	94.06
3012201E 40 mm thick; 2040 mm high; 726 mm wide	Each	1.54	42.81	–	43.54	86.35	47.09	–	47.89	94.99
3012201F 40 mm thick; 2040 mm high; 826 mm wide	Each	1.54	42.81	–	45.55	88.36	47.09	–	50.11	97.20
3012202 Flush door; internal quality; skeleton or cellular core; plywood faced both sides, lipped on two long edges:										
3012202A 35 mm thick; 1981 mm high; 686 mm wide	Each	1.54	42.81	–	54.09	96.90	47.09	–	59.50	106.59
3012202B 35 mm thick; 1981 mm high; 762 mm wide	Each	1.54	42.81	–	54.85	97.66	47.09	–	60.34	107.43
3012202C 35 mm thick; 1981 mm high; 838 mm wide	Each	1.54	42.81	–	57.01	99.82	47.09	–	62.71	109.80
3012202D 40 mm thick; 2040 mm high; 626 mm wide	Each	1.54	42.81	–	56.99	99.80	47.09	–	62.69	109.78
3012202E 40 mm thick; 2040 mm high; 726 mm wide	Each	1.54	42.81	–	58.22	101.03	47.09	–	64.04	111.13
3012202F 40 mm thick; 2040 mm high; 826 mm wide	Each	1.54	42.81	–	60.14	102.95	47.09	–	66.15	113.25
3012204 Flush door; half hour fire resisting (FD30); hardboard faced both sides:										
3012204B 44 mm thick; 1981 mm high; 762 mm wide	Each	2.15	59.77	–	90.58	150.35	65.75	–	99.64	165.39
3012204C 44 mm thick; 1981 mm high; 838 mm wide	Each	2.15	59.77	–	94.24	154.01	65.75	–	103.66	169.41
3012205 Flush door; half hour fire resisting; plywood faced both sides; lipped on two long edges:										
3012205A 44 mm thick; 2040 mm high; 726 mm wide	Each	2.15	59.77	–	95.06	154.83	65.75	–	104.57	170.31
3012205B 44 mm thick; 2040 mm high; 826 mm wide	Each	2.15	59.77	–	99.13	158.90	65.75	–	109.04	174.79
3012206 Flush door; external quality; skeleton or cellular core; plywood faced both sides:										
3012206A 44 mm thick; 1981 mm high; 762 mm wide	Each	1.82	50.59	–	95.01	145.60	55.65	–	104.51	160.16
3012206B 44 mm thick; 1981 mm high; 838 mm wide	Each	1.82	50.60	–	98.41	149.01	55.66	–	108.25	163.91
3012206C 44 mm thick; 1994 mm high; 806 mm wide	Each	1.82	50.60	–	98.41	149.01	55.66	–	108.25	163.91

Woodwork

Small Works 2009		Unit	Labour Hours	Labour Net	Plant Net	Materials Net	Unit Net	Labour Gross	Plant Gross	Materials Gross	Unit Price
								(Gross rates include 10% profit)			
				£	£	£	£	£	£	£	£
301	**NEW WORK**										
30122	**SECOND FIXINGS: STANDARD DOORS**										
3012207	**Flush door; external quality; skeleton or cellular core; plywood faced both sides; opening for glass:**										
3012207A	44 mm thick; 1981 mm high; 762 mm wide	Each	2.15	59.77	–	119.38	179.15	65.75	–	131.32	197.07
3012207B	44 mm thick; 1981 mm high; 838 mm wide	Each	2.15	59.77	–	122.49	182.26	65.75	–	134.74	200.49
3012208	**Flush door; external quality; half hour fire resisting; solid infill of flame retardant material; plywood faced both sides:**										
3012208A	44 mm thick; 1981 mm high; 762 mm wide	Each	2.43	67.55	–	90.58	158.13	74.31	–	99.64	173.94
3012208B	44 mm thick; 1981 mm high; 838 mm wide	Each	2.43	67.56	–	94.24	161.80	74.32	–	103.66	177.98
3012208C	44 mm thick; 1994 mm high; 806 mm wide	Each	2.43	67.56	–	94.24	161.80	74.32	–	103.66	177.98
3012209	**Panelled door; external quality; upper panel open for glass:**										
3012209A	44 mm thick; 1981 mm high; 762 mm wide	Each	2.15	59.77	–	385.51	445.28	65.75	–	424.06	489.81
3012209B	44 mm thick; 1981 mm high; 838 mm wide	Each	2.15	59.77	–	138.78	198.55	65.75	–	152.66	218.41
3012209C	44 mm thick; 1994 mm high; 806 mm wide	Each	2.15	59.77	–	145.33	205.10	65.75	–	159.86	225.61
3012210	**Panelled door; external quality; fully glazed; ten panels open for glass:**										
3012210A	44 mm thick; 1981 mm high; 762 mm wide	Each	2.15	59.77	–	113.39	173.16	65.75	–	124.73	190.48
3012210B	44 mm thick; 1981 mm high; 838 mm wide	Each	2.15	59.77	–	119.05	178.82	65.75	–	130.96	196.70
3012210C	44 mm thick; 1994 mm high; 806 mm wide	Each	2.15	59.77	–	119.05	178.82	65.75	–	130.96	196.70
3012211	**Matchboarded door; external quality; ledged and braced; 25 mm ledges and braces; 19 mm tongued, grooved and V jointed; one side vertical boarding:**										
3012211A	36 mm thick; 1981 mm high; 762 mm wide	Each	1.77	49.20	–	121.16	170.36	54.12	–	133.28	187.40
3012211B	36 mm thick; 1981 mm high; 838 mm wide	Each	1.77	49.20	–	121.15	170.35	54.12	–	133.27	187.39

Small Works 2009		Unit	Labour Hours	Labour Net	Plant Net	Materials Net	Unit Net	Labour Gross	Plant Gross	Materials Gross	Unit Price
								(Gross rates include 10% profit)			
				£	£	£	£	£	£	£	£
301	**NEW WORK**										
30122	**SECOND FIXINGS: STANDARD DOORS**										
3012212	Matchboarded door; external quality; framed, ledged and braced; 25 mm intermediate and bottom rails; 44 mm framing; 19 mm tongued, grooved and V jointed one side vertical boarding:										
3012212A	44 mm thick; 1981 mm high; 762 mm wide	Each	2.15	59.77	–	149.84	209.61	65.75	–	164.82	230.57
3012212B	44 mm thick; 1981 mm high; 838 mm wide	Each	2.15	59.77	–	149.84	209.61	65.75	–	164.82	230.57
3012213	Stable matchboarded door; external quality; framed, ledged and braced; 25 mm intermediate and bottom rails; 44 mm framing, 19 mm tongued, grooved and V jointed one side vertical boarding; in two leaves:										
3012213A	44 mm thick; 1981 mm high; 762 mm wide	Each	2.53	70.33	–	200.51	270.84	77.36	–	220.56	297.92
3012213B	44 mm thick; 1981 mm high; 838 mm wide	Each	2.53	70.34	–	204.37	274.71	77.37	–	224.81	302.18
30124	**SECOND FIXINGS: STANDARD DOOR FRAMES**										
3012401	External door frames; treated and primed; hardwood cills; opening inwards or outwards; to suit door:										
3012401A	806 mm × 1994 mm.....	Each	0.76	21.13	–	110.70	131.83	23.24	–	121.77	145.01
3012401B	838 mm × 1981 mm.....	Each	0.76	21.13	–	115.50	136.63	23.24	–	127.05	150.29
3012402	External door frames; firecheck; rebated; intumescent strip; hardwood cill; opening inwards or outwards; to suit door:										
3012402A	806 mm × 2100 mm.....	Each	0.76	21.13	–	151.90	173.03	23.24	–	167.09	190.33
3012402B	762 mm × 2047 mm.....	Each	0.76	21.13	–	151.04	172.17	23.24	–	166.14	189.39
3012402C	838 mm × 2047 mm.....	Each	0.76	21.13	–	149.79	170.92	23.24	–	164.77	188.01
3012403	Internal door frames; firecheck; rebated; intumescent strip; no cill; opening inwards or outwards; to suit door:										
3012403A	726 mm × 2040 mm.....	Each	0.63	17.52	–	134.65	152.17	19.27	–	148.12	167.39
3012403B	826 mm × 2040 mm.....	Each	0.63	17.51	–	137.33	154.84	19.26	–	151.06	170.32
3012403C	726 mm × 2017 mm.....	Each	0.63	17.51	–	127.28	144.79	19.26	–	140.01	159.27
3012403D	826 mm × 2017 mm.....	Each	0.63	17.51	–	128.13	145.64	19.26	–	140.94	160.20

Woodwork

	Unit	Labour Hours	Labour Net £	Plant Net £	Materials Net £	Unit Net £	Labour Gross £	Plant Gross £	Materials Gross £	Unit Price £
							(Gross rates include 10% profit)			
301 NEW WORK										
30126 SECOND FIXINGS: STANDARD WINDOWS										
3012601 Casement windows including frames; side hung; double glazed opening casements and ventilators; hung on rust proof hinges; fitted with aluminium anodised casement stays and fasteners; knot and primed before delivery:										
3012601A W107C: height 750 mm × 630 mm	Each	0.88	24.47	–	138.81	163.28	26.92	–	152.69	179.61
3012601B W109C: height 900 mm × 630 mm	Each	0.99	27.52	–	144.55	172.07	30.27	–	159.01	189.28
3012601C W110C: height 1050 mm × 630 mm	Each	1.15	31.97	–	145.17	177.14	35.17	–	159.69	194.85
3012601D W2N10CC: height 1050 mm × 915 mm	Each	1.25	34.75	–	210.44	245.19	38.23	–	231.48	269.71
3012601E W210C: height 1050 mm × 1200 mm	Each	1.50	41.70	–	184.83	226.53	45.87	–	203.31	249.18
3012601F W212C: height 1200 mm × 1200 mm	Each	1.50	41.70	–	186.07	227.77	45.87	–	204.68	250.55
3012601G W312CC: height 1200 mm × 1770 mm	Each	2.00	55.60	–	338.89	394.49	61.16	–	372.78	433.94
3012601H W310CC: height 1050 mm × 1770 mm	Each	1.55	43.09	–	327.95	371.04	47.40	–	360.75	408.14
3012601I W409CMC: height 900 mm × 2339 mm	Each	2.15	59.77	–	271.28	331.05	65.75	–	298.41	364.16
3012601J W410CMC: height 1050 mm × 2339 mm	Each	2.15	59.77	–	417.81	477.58	65.75	–	459.59	525.34
3012601K W412CMC: height 1200 mm × 2339 mm	Each	2.25	62.55	–	417.94	480.49	68.81	–	459.73	528.54
3012602 Velux roof windows; centre pivot; laminated Nordic red pine frame and sash; sealed unit double pre-glazing; 3 mm clear float glass; exterior aluminium cladding; natural brownish-grey finish; type EDZ flashings and soakers; for tiles and pantiles screwed to softwood (GGL); type:										
3012602A GGL C02: height 780 mm × 550 mm	Each	6.05	168.19	–	159.00	327.19	185.01	–	174.90	359.91
3012602B GGL C04: height 980 mm × 550 mm	Each	6.05	168.19	–	174.14	342.33	185.01	–	191.55	376.56
3012602C GGL F06: height 1180 mm × 660 mm	Each	7.26	201.83	–	211.66	413.49	222.01	–	232.83	454.84
3012602D GGL M04: height 980 mm × 780 mm	Each	6.65	184.87	–	193.47	378.34	203.36	–	212.82	416.17
3012602E GGL M08: height 1400 mm × 780 mm	Each	7.87	218.79	–	237.10	455.89	240.67	–	260.81	501.48
3012602F GGL P10: height 1600 mm × 940 mm	Each	7.87	218.78	–	282.77	501.55	240.66	–	311.05	551.71
3012602G GGL S06: height 1180 mm × 1140 mm	Each	8.47	235.47	–	263.43	498.90	259.02	–	289.77	548.79
3012602H GGL U04: height 980 mm × 1340 mm	Each	8.47	235.47	–	263.43	498.90	259.02	–	289.77	548.79
3012602I GGL U08: height 1400 mm × 1340 mm	Each	9.08	252.43	–	1581.22	1833.65	277.67	–	1739.34	2017.02

Small Works 2009		Unit	Labour Hours	Labour Net	Plant Net	Materials Net	Unit Net	Labour Gross	Plant Gross	Materials Gross	Unit Price
								(Gross rates include 10% profit)			
				£	£	£	£	£	£	£	£
301	**NEW WORK**										
30128	**SECOND FIXINGS: STANDARD KITCHEN UNITS**										
3012801	**Base units; depth 600 mm:**										
3012801A	500 mm wide × 900 mm high	Each	1.54	42.82	–	158.50	201.32	47.10	–	174.35	221.45
3012801B	600 mm wide × 900 mm high	Each	1.71	47.54	–	165.27	212.81	52.29	–	181.80	234.09
3012801C	1000 mm wide × 900 mm high	Each	1.98	55.04	–	273.98	329.02	60.54	–	301.38	361.92
3012802	**Sink units; depth 600 mm:**										
3012802A	1000 mm wide × 900 mm high	Each	2.00	55.60	–	246.26	301.86	61.16	–	270.89	332.05
3012802B	1200 mm wide × 900 mm high	Each	2.20	61.16	–	271.81	332.97	67.28	–	298.99	366.27
3012803	**Wall units; depth 300 mm:**										
3012803A	500 mm wide × 580 mm high	Each	1.54	42.81	–	100.13	142.94	47.09	–	110.14	157.23
3012803B	600 mm wide × 580 mm high	Each	1.71	47.54	–	110.13	157.67	52.29	–	121.14	173.44
3012803C	1000 mm wide × 580 mm high	Each	1.96	54.49	–	178.60	233.09	59.94	–	196.46	256.40
3012803D	500 mm wide × 780 mm high	Each	1.69	46.98	–	118.84	165.82	51.68	–	130.72	182.40
3012803E	600 mm wide × 780 mm high	Each	1.90	52.82	–	132.82	185.64	58.10	–	146.10	204.20
3012803F	1000 mm wide × 780 mm high	Each	2.20	61.16	–	205.68	266.84	67.28	–	226.25	293.52
3012804	**Store units; depth 600 mm:**										
3012804A	500 mm wide × 2056 mm high	Each	2.97	82.57	–	238.46	321.03	90.83	–	262.31	353.13
3012804B	600 mm wide × 2056 mm high	Each	3.14	87.29	–	255.81	343.10	96.02	–	281.39	377.41
3012805	**Laminated plastic worktop; cut to size; lipped all round; fixed to worktops of base units with adhesive:**										
3012805A	600 mm × 500 mm	Each	0.48	13.34	–	27.30	40.64	14.67	–	30.03	44.70
3012805B	600 mm × 600 mm	Each	0.55	15.29	–	32.77	48.06	16.82	–	36.05	52.87
3012805C	600 mm × 1200 mm	Each	0.85	23.63	–	54.61	78.24	25.99	–	60.07	86.06

Woodwork

Small Works 2009		Unit	Labour Hours	Labour Net	Plant Net	Materials Net	Unit Net	Labour Gross	Plant Gross	Materials Gross	Unit Price
								(Gross rates include 10% profit)			
				£	£	£	£	£	£	£	£
301	**NEW WORK**										
30142	**SOFTWOOD STAIRCASES: COMPONENTS**										
3014201	**Treads:**										
3014201A	25 mm nosed and risers 19 mm tongued	m²	5.40	150.13	–	24.97	175.10	165.14	–	27.47	192.61
3014201B	32 mm nosed and risers 25 mm tongued	m²	6.00	166.80	–	28.35	195.15	183.48	–	31.19	214.67
3014201C	Extra for bullnose step.....	Each	2.25	62.55	–	4.05	66.60	68.81	–	4.46	73.26
3014201D	Extra for double bullnose step	Each	4.00	111.21	–	8.78	119.99	122.33	–	9.66	131.99
3014202	**Winders:**										
3014202A	25 mm cross-tongued and risers 19 mm............	m²	7.50	208.50	–	33.75	242.25	229.35	–	37.13	266.48
3014202B	32 mm cross-tongued and risers 25 mm............	m²	8.00	222.41	–	37.13	259.54	244.65	–	40.84	285.49
3014203	**Landings:**										
3014203A	25 mm cross-tongued, including bearers	m²	5.30	147.34	–	33.08	180.42	162.07	–	36.39	198.46
3014203B	32 mm cross-tongued, including bearers	m²	5.30	147.34	–	36.45	183.79	162.07	–	40.10	202.17
3014205	**Strings:**										
3014205A	275 mm × 38 mm.......	m	0.75	20.86	–	10.13	30.99	22.95	–	11.14	34.09
3014205B	ends of string framed to newel	Each	0.65	18.07	–	–	18.07	19.88	–	–	19.88
3014206	**Handrails:**										
3014206A	50 mm mopstick..........	m	0.40	11.12	–	3.57	14.69	12.23	–	3.93	16.16
3014206B	75 mm × 50 mm	m	0.75	20.85	–	5.02	25.87	22.94	–	5.52	28.46
3014206C	75 mm × 50 mm hardwood	m	1.65	45.87	–	6.75	52.62	50.46	–	7.43	57.88
3014206D	Extra for ramps...........	Each	4.00	111.20	–	10.80	122.00	122.32	–	11.88	134.20
3014207	**Newels:**										
3014207A	100 mm × 100 mm framed	m	1.65	45.87	–	57.44	103.31	50.46	–	63.18	113.64
3014207B	half, 100 mm × 60 mm framed..................	m	1.10	30.58	–	6.08	36.66	33.64	–	6.69	40.33
3014207C	newel caps, splayed on four sides, 125 mm × 125 mm × 50 mm..............	Each	0.20	5.56	–	4.72	10.28	6.12	–	5.19	11.31
3014207D	newel caps, half splayed on three sides 125 mm × 63 mm × 50 mm	Each	0.20	5.56	–	4.05	9.61	6.12	–	4.46	10.57
3014208	**Framed spandrel:**										
3014208A	38 mm with plywood panelling	m²	6.50	180.70	–	21.60	202.30	198.77	–	23.76	222.53
3014209	**Balusters:**										
3014209A	38 mm × 38 mm	m	0.33	9.17	–	1.35	10.52	10.09	–	1.49	11.57
3014211	**Apron lining; chamfered and beaded:**										
3014211A	225 mm × 19 mm.......	m	0.45	12.51	–	4.72	17.23	13.76	–	5.19	18.95
3014211B	225 mm × 25 mm.......	m	0.50	13.90	–	6.75	20.65	15.29	–	7.43	22.72

Small Works 2009		Unit	Labour Hours	Labour Net	Plant Net	Materials Net	Unit Net	Labour Gross	Plant Gross	Materials Gross	Unit Price
								(Gross rates include 10% profit)			
				£	£	£	£	£	£	£	£
301	**NEW WORK**										
30144	**SOFTWOOD STAIRCASES: PURPOSE MADE UNITS**										
3014401	**Staircase comprising 25 mm treads, 19 mm risers, 38 mm strings, 100 mm × 100 mm newels, 75 mm × 63 mm handrail and 31 mm balusters and apron lining but excluding spandrel framing below stairs:**										
3014401A	900 mm wide × 2620 mm rise.....................	Each	73.00	2029.41	–	393.52	2422.93	2232.35	–	432.87	2665.22
3014401B	add for 25 mm quarter space landing and extra newel....	Each	5.50	152.91	–	56.03	208.94	168.20	–	61.63	229.83
3014401C	add for three winders and extra newel..............	Each	8.00	222.40	–	41.85	264.25	244.64	–	46.04	290.68
3014401D	deduct if stairs are built between enclosing walls with handrail fixed to one wall with brackets and without balusters, newel posts, or balustrade to upper floor...	Each	25.00	695.01	–	114.08	809.09	764.51	–	125.49	890.00
30146	**SOFTWOOD STAIRCASES: STANDARD UNITS**										
3014601	**Staircase with 25 mm treads and 19 mm risers, glued wedged and blocked with 25 mm wall string, 38 mm × 38 mm turned balusters, 32 mm × 63 mm grooved string capping, 13 mm × 38 mm distance pieces (type B10 balustrade) and 50 mm × 75 mm hardwood handrail between 75 mm × 75 mm newels, in one flight:**										
3014601A	855 mm wide × 2600 mm rise.....................	Each	18.00	500.40	–	692.59	1192.99	550.44	–	761.85	1312.29
3014602	**Closed tread, half straight flight; 864 mm wide; 1421 mm rise; balustrade fixed one side; fixing to walls with screws**										
3014602A	855 mm wide × 1421 mm rise.....................	Each	10.00	278.00	–	463.04	741.04	305.80	–	509.34	815.14
3014604	**Landing balustrade with 50 mm × 75 mm hardwood handrail, 38 mm × 38 mm turned Regency balusters, 32 mm × 140 mm baluster knee rails, 2 No. 32 mm × 50 mm stiffeners, one end joined to newel post, other end built into half newel:**										
3014604A	3 m long................	Each	12.00	333.60	–	177.46	511.06	366.96	–	195.21	562.17

Woodwork

		Unit	Labour Hours	Labour Net	Plant Net	Materials Net	Unit Net	Labour Gross	Plant Gross	Materials Gross	Unit Price
								(Gross rates include 10% profit)			
				£	£	£	£	£	£	£	£
301	**NEW WORK**										
30148	**SUNDRY ITEMS**										
3014802	**Trap door; 9 mm plywood panel; rebated softwood lining 35 mm × 107 mm:**										
3014802A	750 mm × 750 mm	Each	1.60	44.48	–	47.04	91.52	48.93	–	51.74	100.67
3014803	**Softwood weather mould, throated; screwed to door:**										
3014803A	50 mm × 75 mm	m	0.60	16.68	–	6.37	23.05	18.35	–	7.01	25.36
3014805	**Hat and coat rails, chamfered edges, plugged to brickwork:**										
3014805A	125 mm × 25 mm	m	0.34	9.46	–	3.53	12.99	10.41	–	3.88	14.29
3014805B	125 mm × 25 mm in short lengths.................	m	0.50	13.90	–	3.53	17.43	15.29	–	3.88	19.17
3014806	**Perforated zinc; safe or larder apertures:**										
3014806A	fixed with beads; in small areas	m^2	1.90	52.82	–	66.81	119.63	58.10	–	73.49	131.59
30150	**SUNDRY LABOURS**										
3015001	**Extra over fixing with nails for:**										
3015001A	steel screws	m	0.04	1.11	–	0.16	1.27	1.22	–	0.18	1.40
3015001B	steel screws; sinking; filling heads...................	m	0.07	1.94	–	0.16	2.10	2.13	–	0.18	2.31
3015001C	steel screws; sinking; pellating over	m	0.19	5.28	–	0.16	5.44	5.81	–	0.18	5.98
3015001D	brass cups and screws	m	0.12	3.33	–	0.59	3.92	3.66	–	0.65	4.31
3015002	**Plugging blockwork:**										
3015002A	300 mm centres; one way ..	m	0.08	2.22	–	0.05	2.27	2.44	–	0.06	2.50
3015002B	300 mm centres; both ways	m	0.14	3.89	–	0.14	4.03	4.28	–	0.15	4.43
3015003	**Plugging brickwork:**										
3015003A	300 mm centres; one way ..	m	0.12	3.33	–	0.05	3.38	3.66	–	0.06	3.72
3015003B	300 mm centres; both ways	m	0.24	6.67	–	0.14	6.81	7.34	–	0.15	7.49
3015004	**Plugging concrete:**										
3015004A	300 mm centres; one way ..	m	0.22	6.11	–	0.05	6.16	6.72	–	0.06	6.78
3015004B	300 mm centres; both ways	m	0.44	12.23	–	0.14	12.37	13.45	–	0.15	13.61
3015006	**Holes for pipes, bars etc; through softwood thickness:**										
3015006A	12 mm	Each	0.05	1.39	–	–	1.39	1.53	–	–	1.53
3015006B	25 mm	Each	0.08	2.22	–	–	2.22	2.44	–	–	2.44
3015006C	50 mm	Each	0.12	3.34	–	–	3.34	3.67	–	–	3.67
3015006D	75 mm	Each	0.16	4.45	–	–	4.45	4.90	–	–	4.90
3015006E	100 mm	Each	0.19	5.28	–	–	5.28	5.81	–	–	5.81

Small Works 2009		Unit	Labour Hours	Labour Net	Plant Net	Materials Net	Unit Net	Labour Gross	Plant Gross	Materials Gross	Unit Price
								(Gross rates include 10% profit)			
				£	£	£	£	£	£	£	£
301	**NEW WORK**										
30150	**SUNDRY LABOURS**										
3015007	**Head or nut in softwood:**										
3015007A	let in; flush..............	Each	0.07	1.95	–	–	1.95	2.15	–	–	2.15
3015009	**Head or nut in hardwood:**										
3015009A	let in; flush..............	Each	0.10	2.78	–	–	2.78	3.06	–	–	3.06
3015009B	let in; pellated	Each	0.24	6.67	–	–	6.67	7.34	–	–	7.34
3015010	**Mortice:**										
3015010A	for and including metal dowel	Each	0.11	3.06	–	–	3.06	3.37	–	–	3.37
3015011	**Notching and fitting:**										
3015011A	timber to steel............	Each	0.33	9.17	–	–	9.17	10.09	–	–	10.09
3015012	**Planing:**										
3015012A	by hand	m^2	0.40	11.12	–	–	11.12	12.23	–	–	12.23
3015014	**Hand labours on softwood:**										
3015014A	chamfers	m	0.19	5.28	–	–	5.28	5.81	–	–	5.81
3015014B	rounds	m	0.25	6.95	–	–	6.95	7.65	–	–	7.65
3015014C	grooves	m	0.36	10.01	–	–	10.01	11.01	–	–	11.01
3015014D	rebates	m	0.39	10.84	–	–	10.84	11.92	–	–	11.92
3015014E	throats	m	0.39	10.84	–	–	10.84	11.92	–	–	11.92
3015014F	mouldings per 25 mm girth.	m	1.13	31.41	–	–	31.41	34.55	–	–	34.55
3015014G	rebate in bottom of rail or door	m	0.30	8.34	–	–	8.34	9.17	–	–	9.17

Woodwork

Small Works 2009		Unit	Labour Hours	Labour Net	Plant Net	Materials Net	Unit Net	Labour Gross	Plant Gross	Materials Gross	Unit Price
								(Gross rates include 10% profit)			
				£	£	£	£	£	£	£	£
301	**NEW WORK**										
30151	**INSULATION AND VENTILATION**										
3015101	**13 mm glass fibre sound insulating quilt type PF:**										
3015101A	laid between joists	m²	0.15	4.17	–	5.10	9.27	4.59	–	5.61	10.20
3015101B	fixed vertically between softwood battens	m²	0.15	4.17	–	5.10	9.27	4.59	–	5.61	10.20
3015102	**Glass fibre thermal insulating quilt laid over ceiling joists:**										
3015102A	60 mm	m²	0.17	4.73	–	2.00	6.73	5.20	–	2.20	7.40
3015102B	80 mm	m²	0.17	4.73	–	2.39	7.12	5.20	–	2.63	7.83
3015102C	100 mm	m²	0.17	4.73	–	2.95	7.68	5.20	–	3.25	8.45
3015103	**Glass fibre thermal insulating quilt laid between joists:**										
3015103A	60 mm	m²	0.19	5.29	–	2.00	7.29	5.82	–	2.20	8.02
3015103B	80 mm	m²	0.19	5.28	–	2.39	7.67	5.81	–	2.63	8.44
3015103C	100 mm	m²	0.19	5.28	–	2.95	8.23	5.81	–	3.25	9.05
3015104	**Vermiculite granular loose fill insulation laid between joists:**										
3015104A	50 mm	m²	0.20	5.56	–	7.31	12.87	6.12	–	8.04	14.16
3015104B	75 mm	m²	0.30	8.34	–	10.99	19.33	9.17	–	12.09	21.26
3015104C	100 mm	m²	0.40	11.12	–	1.46	12.58	12.23	–	1.61	13.84
3015106	**Expanded polystyrene insulation board:**										
3015106A	53 mm	m²	0.38	10.56	–	18.77	29.33	11.62	–	20.65	32.26
3015106B	83 mm	m²	0.38	10.57	–	28.19	38.76	11.63	–	31.01	42.64
3015107	**Bitumen impregnated insulating board:**										
3015107A	13 mm	m²	0.25	6.95	–	3.50	10.45	7.65	–	3.85	11.50
3015107B	raking cutting	m	0.36	10.01	–	–	10.01	11.01	–	–	11.01
3015107C	curved cutting.	m	0.60	16.68	–	–	16.68	18.35	–	–	18.35
3015108	**UPVC push-in soffit ventilators, 70 m diameter, including cutting hole through timber soffit board and installing discs at:**										
3015108A	140 mm centres	m	1.20	33.36	–	10.40	43.76	36.70	–	11.44	48.14
3015109	**UPVC type C slotted soffit ventilator and screwing to:**										
3015109A	back of timber fascia	m	0.33	9.18	–	5.10	14.28	10.10	–	5.61	15.71

Small Works 2009		Unit	Labour Hours	Labour Net	Plant Net	Materials Net	Unit Net	Labour Gross	Plant Gross	Materials Gross	Unit Price
								(Gross rates include 10% profit)			
				£	£	£	£	£	£	£	£
301	**NEW WORK**										
30152	**METALWORK**										
3015201	**Galvanised steel water bars including grooves in timber:**										
3015201A	30 mm × 6 mm	m	0.30	8.34	–	10.06	18.40	9.17	–	11.07	20.24
3015201B	40 mm × 6 mm	m	0.32	8.90	–	11.99	20.89	9.79	–	13.19	22.98
3015202	**Black cup square carriage bolt with hexagon nut and washer:**										
3015202A	M10 × 50 mm	Each	0.12	3.33	–	0.32	3.65	3.66	–	0.35	4.02
3015202B	M10 × 75 mm	Each	0.14	3.89	–	0.37	4.26	4.28	–	0.41	4.69
3015202C	M10 × 100 mm	Each	0.14	3.89	–	0.56	4.45	4.28	–	0.62	4.90
3015202D	M10 × 150 mm	Each	0.16	4.45	–	1.17	5.62	4.90	–	1.29	6.18
3015202E	M12 × 50 mm	Each	0.14	3.89	–	1.34	5.23	4.28	–	1.47	5.75
3015202F	M12 × 75 mm	Each	0.14	3.89	–	1.68	5.57	4.28	–	1.85	6.13
3015202G	M12 × 100 mm	Each	0.15	4.17	–	0.71	4.88	4.59	–	0.78	5.37
3015202H	M12 × 150 mm	Each	0.17	4.73	–	1.27	6.00	5.20	–	1.40	6.60
3015204	**Galvanised mild steel joist restraint straps, twice bent, one end drilled and screwed to timber, other end built in:**										
3015204A	30 mm × 5 mm 700 mm girth bent at 75 mm	Each	0.40	11.12	–	3.23	14.35	12.23	–	3.55	15.79
3015204B	30 mm × 5 mm 800 mm girth bent at 100 mm	Each	0.48	13.35	–	3.71	17.06	14.69	–	4.08	18.77
3015204C	30 mm × 5 mm 1000 mm girth bent at 100 mm	Each	0.52	14.45	–	88.80	103.25	15.90	–	97.68	113.58
3015206	**Galvanised steel joist hangers built in:**										
3015206A	50 mm × 100 mm	Each	0.20	5.56	–	1.77	7.33	6.12	–	1.95	8.06
3015206B	50 mm × 125 mm	Each	0.21	5.84	–	1.77	7.61	6.42	–	1.95	8.37
3015206C	50 mm × 150 mm	Each	0.22	6.12	–	1.93	8.05	6.73	–	2.12	8.86
3015206D	50 mm × 175 mm	Each	0.23	6.40	–	1.93	8.33	7.04	–	2.12	9.16
3015206E	50 mm × 200 mm	Each	0.24	6.67	–	2.06	8.73	7.34	–	2.27	9.60
3015206H	75 mm × 100 mm	Each	0.27	7.50	–	2.14	9.64	8.25	–	2.35	10.60
3015206I	75 mm × 175 mm	Each	0.28	7.78	–	2.76	10.54	8.56	–	3.04	11.59
3015206J	75 mm × 200 mm	Each	0.29	8.06	–	2.76	10.82	8.87	–	3.04	11.90
3015207	**Double sided galvanised timber connectors:**										
3015207A	M12 × 50 mm	Each	0.05	1.39	–	0.48	1.87	1.53	–	0.53	2.06
3015207B	M12 × 64 mm	Each	0.06	1.67	–	90.69	92.36	1.84	–	99.76	101.60
3015208	**Bulldog single sided round tooth-plate timber connectors:**										
3015208A	63 mm	Each	0.07	1.95	–	0.86	2.81	2.15	–	0.95	3.09
3015209	**Bulldog double sided round toothed- plate timber connectors:**										
3015209A	50 mm	Each	0.05	1.39	–	0.59	1.98	1.53	–	0.65	2.18
3015209B	63 mm	Each	0.09	2.51	–	0.86	3.37	2.76	–	0.95	3.71
3015209C	75 mm	Each	0.11	3.06	–	1.13	4.19	3.37	–	1.24	4.61
3015210	**Floor clips inserted in concrete when green:**										
3015210A	50 mm	Each	0.05	1.39	–	0.41	1.80	1.53	–	0.45	1.98
3015211	**Gallows bracket; 50 mm × 50 mm mild steel angle; support width:**										
3015211A	350 mm	Each	1.04	28.91	–	46.33	75.24	31.80	–	50.96	82.76
3015211B	450 mm	Each	1.14	31.69	–	52.01	83.70	34.86	–	57.21	92.07
3015211C	600 mm	Each	1.24	34.47	–	56.54	91.01	37.92	–	62.19	100.11

Woodwork

Small Works 2009		Unit	Labour Hours	Labour Net	Plant Net	Materials Net	Unit Net	Labour Gross	Plant Gross	Materials Gross	Unit Price
								(Gross rates include 10% profit)			
				£	£	£	£	£	£	£	£
301	**NEW WORK**										
30154	**IRONMONGERY**										
3015401	**Light pattern pressed steel butts and labour hanging door:**										
3015401A	50 mm	Pair	0.58	16.12	–	1.26	17.38	17.73	–	1.39	19.12
3015401B	75 mm	Pair	1.17	32.52	–	1.13	33.65	35.77	–	1.24	37.02
3015401C	100 mm	Pair	1.42	39.47	–	1.85	41.32	43.42	–	2.04	45.45
3015401D	50 mm sheradised	Pair	0.58	16.13	–	1.72	17.85	17.74	–	1.89	19.64
3015401E	75 mm sheradised	Pair	1.17	32.52	–	2.65	35.17	35.77	–	2.92	38.69
3015401F	100 mm sheradised	Pair	1.42	39.48	–	4.48	43.96	43.43	–	4.93	48.36
3015404	**Strong pattern steel butts and labour hanging door:**										
3015404A	75 mm	Pair	1.17	32.52	–	3.45	35.97	35.77	–	3.80	39.57
3015404B	100 mm	Pair	1.42	39.48	–	5.15	44.63	43.43	–	5.67	49.09
3015404C	75 mm sheradised	Pair	1.17	32.53	–	4.54	37.07	35.78	–	4.99	40.78
3015404D	100 mm sheradised	Pair	1.42	39.48	–	6.54	46.02	43.43	–	7.19	50.62
3015406	**Steel rising butts and labour hanging doors:**										
3015406A	75 mm × 70 mm	Pair	1.45	40.31	–	4.66	44.97	44.34	–	5.13	49.47
3015406B	100 mm × 81 mm	Pair	1.70	47.26	–	6.37	53.63	51.99	–	7.01	58.99
3015406C	75 mm × 70 mm sheradised..............	Pair	1.45	40.31	–	6.12	46.43	44.34	–	6.73	51.07
3015406D	100 mm × 81 mm sheradised..............	Pair	1.70	47.26	–	8.91	56.17	51.99	–	9.80	61.79
3015409	**Steel washered brass butts and labour hanging door:**										
3015409A	76 mm	Pair	1.17	32.53	–	6.92	39.45	35.78	–	7.61	43.40
3015409B	102 mm	Pair	1.42	39.48	–	14.18	53.66	43.43	–	15.60	59.03
3015411	**Brass rising butts and labour hanging door:**										
3015411A	76 mm × 60 mm	Pair	1.45	40.31	–	10.34	50.65	44.34	–	11.37	55.72
3015411B	102 mm × 67 mm	Pair	1.70	47.26	–	19.67	66.93	51.99	–	21.64	73.62
3015412	**Hurlinge steel butts and labour hanging door:**										
3015412A	76 mm	Pair	0.33	9.17	–	3.49	12.66	10.09	–	3.84	13.93
3015412B	102 mm	Pair	0.42	11.67	–	5.27	16.94	12.84	–	5.80	18.63
3015412C	76 mm sheradised	Pair	0.33	9.17	–	4.28	13.45	10.09	–	4.71	14.80
3015412D	102 mm sheradised	Pair	0.42	11.67	–	6.44	18.11	12.84	–	7.08	19.92
3015415	**Steel tee hinges and labour hanging door:**										
3015415A	305 mm	Pair	0.83	23.07	–	4.99	28.06	25.38	–	5.49	30.87
3015415B	457 mm	Pair	0.92	25.57	–	8.31	33.88	28.13	–	9.14	37.27
3015416	**Steel light reversible hinges and labour hanging door:**										
3015416A	305 mm	Pair	1.05	29.19	–	13.80	42.99	32.11	–	15.18	47.29
3015416B	457 mm	Pair	1.15	31.97	–	19.59	51.56	35.17	–	21.55	56.72
3015418	**Steel heavy reversible hinges and labour hanging door:**										
3015418A	305 mm	Pair	1.33	36.97	–	17.91	54.88	40.67	–	19.70	60.37
3015418B	457 mm	Pair	1.50	41.70	–	24.69	66.39	45.87	–	27.16	73.03
3015418C	610 mm	Pair	1.67	46.42	–	36.47	82.89	51.06	–	40.12	91.18

Small Works 2009		Unit	Labour Hours	Labour Net	Plant Net	Materials Net	Unit Net	Labour Gross	Plant Gross	Materials Gross	Unit Price
								(Gross rates include 10% profit)			
				£	£	£	£	£	£	£	£
301	**NEW WORK**										
30154	**IRONMONGERY**										
3015419	**Interior straight sliding door gear; top track with wheel hangers; door guides; stops; finger pulls; steel pelmet and labour hanging:**										
3015419A	35 mm to 44 mm thick single softwood door	Each	3.50	97.30	–	56.50	153.80	107.03	–	62.15	169.18
3015420	**Locks and latches:**										
3015420A	rim lock and furniture	Each	1.25	34.75	–	43.57	78.32	38.23	–	47.93	86.15
3015420B	mortice lock and furniture..	Each	1.45	40.31	–	32.54	72.85	44.34	–	35.79	80.14
3015420C	mortice dead lock	Each	1.00	27.80	–	39.39	67.19	30.58	–	43.33	73.91
3015420D	cylinder rim night latch	Each	1.20	33.36	–	33.70	67.06	36.70	–	37.07	73.77
3015420E	Suffolk latch	Each	1.00	27.80	–	6.60	34.40	30.58	–	7.26	37.84
3015420F	escutcheon	Each	0.30	8.34	–	0.47	8.81	9.17	–	0.52	9.69
3015420G	Bales catch	Each	0.50	13.90	–	3.42	17.32	15.29	–	3.76	19.05
3015420H	cupboard catch	Each	0.30	8.34	–	6.35	14.69	9.17	–	6.99	16.16
3015420I	cupboard or drawer lock ...	Each	0.60	16.68	–	7.63	24.31	18.35	–	8.39	26.74
3015420J	cupboard button..........	Each	0.25	6.95	–	0.60	7.55	7.65	–	0.66	8.31
3015422	**Door closers:**										
3015422A	overhead door closer; surface fixing	Each	1.75	48.65	–	146.55	195.20	53.52	–	161.21	214.72
3015422B	Perko closer	Each	1.75	48.65	–	18.93	67.58	53.52	–	20.82	74.34
3015422C	coil gate spring	Each	0.40	11.12	–	10.89	22.01	12.23	–	11.98	24.21
3015424	**Bolts:**										
3015424A	150 mm barrel; straight	Each	0.45	12.51	–	4.15	16.66	13.76	–	4.57	18.33
3015424B	255 mm barrel; straight	Each	0.55	15.29	–	6.50	21.79	16.82	–	7.15	23.97
3015424C	150 mm tower; straight	Each	0.45	12.51	–	5.27	17.78	13.76	–	5.80	19.56
3015424D	255 mm tower; straight	Each	0.55	15.29	–	7.14	22.43	16.82	–	7.85	24.67
3015424E	455 mm monkey tail.......	Each	0.55	15.29	–	28.98	44.27	16.82	–	31.88	48.70
3015424F	225 mm flush	Each	0.85	23.63	–	23.63	47.26	25.99	–	25.99	51.99
3015424G	indicator	Each	1.20	33.36	–	15.84	49.20	36.70	–	17.42	54.12
3015424H	single door panic	Each	1.75	48.65	–	156.10	204.75	53.52	–	171.71	225.23
3015424I	double door panic........	Each	2.30	63.94	–	184.50	248.44	70.33	–	202.95	273.28
3015426	**Handles and pulls:**										
3015426A	door handle..............	Each	0.30	8.34	–	6.47	14.81	9.17	–	7.12	16.29
3015426B	drawer pull	Each	0.20	5.56	–	8.99	14.55	6.12	–	9.89	16.01
3015426C	cupboard knob	Each	0.20	5.56	–	11.19	16.75	6.12	–	12.31	18.43
3015428	**Plates:**										
3015428A	door push plate...........	Each	0.40	11.12	–	8.48	19.60	12.23	–	9.33	21.56
3015428B	letter plate and opening through door.............	Each	1.75	48.65	–	9.65	58.30	53.52	–	10.62	64.13
3015430	**Window fittings:**										
3015430A	casement stay; 305 mm; with two pins.................	Each	0.40	11.12	–	6.37	17.49	12.23	–	7.01	19.24
3015430B	casement fastener; wedge pattern..................	Each	0.50	13.90	–	5.26	19.16	15.29	–	5.79	21.08
3015430C	casement fastener; locking with keys	Each	0.55	15.29	–	11.53	26.82	16.82	–	12.68	29.50
3015430D	sliding sash fastener	Each	1.20	33.36	–	9.06	42.42	36.70	–	9.97	46.66
3015430E	sash lift	Each	0.30	8.34	–	4.21	12.55	9.17	–	4.63	13.81
3015430F	quadrant stay	Each	0.40	11.12	–	12.43	23.55	12.23	–	13.67	25.91

Woodwork

Small Works 2009		Unit	Labour Hours	Labour Net	Plant Net	Materials Net	Unit Net	Labour Gross	Plant Gross	Materials Gross	Unit Price
								(Gross rates include 10% profit)			
				£	£	£	£	£	£	£	£
301	**NEW WORK**										
30154	**IRONMONGERY**										
3015432	**Sundry items:**										
3015432A	hat and coat hooks........	Each	0.21	5.84	–	5.75	11.59	6.42	–	6.33	12.75
3015432B	cabin hook and eye........	Each	0.30	8.34	–	9.94	18.28	9.17	–	10.93	20.11
3015432C	padlock hasp and staple ...	Each	0.30	8.34	–	3.50	11.84	9.17	–	3.85	13.02
3015432D	swivel locking bar.........	Each	0.40	11.12	–	38.51	49.63	12.23	–	42.36	54.59
3015432E	rubber door stop	Each	0.20	5.56	–	0.30	5.86	6.12	–	0.33	6.45
3015432F	door buffer	Each	0.30	8.34	–	7.39	15.73	9.17	–	8.13	17.30
3015432G	shelf bracket	Each	0.40	11.12	–	3.80	14.92	12.23	–	4.18	16.41
3015432H	security door chain........	Each	0.30	8.34	–	5.45	13.79	9.17	–	6.00	15.17
3015432I	numerals; 75 mm high.....	Each	0.20	5.56	–	3.16	8.72	6.12	–	3.48	9.59

Small Works 2009		Unit	Labour Hours	Labour Net	Plant Net	Materials Net	Unit Net	Labour Gross	Plant Gross	Materials Gross	Unit Price
								(Gross rates include 10% profit)			
				£	£	£	£	£	£	£	£
302	**REPAIRS AND ALTERATIONS**										
30201	**REMOVE TIMBERS**										
3020101	**Roof timbers:**										
3020101A	complete including rafters, purlins, ceiling joists, plates and the like (measured flat on plan)	m²	0.37	7.71	–	–	7.71	8.48	–	–	8.48
3020102	**Floor construction:**										
3020102A	joists; softwood ; at ground level	m²	0.28	5.84	–	–	5.84	6.42	–	–	6.42
3020102B	joists; softwood; at first floor level	m²	0.55	11.47	–	–	11.47	12.62	–	–	12.62
3020102C	joists; softwood; at roof level	m²	0.77	16.05	–	–	16.05	17.66	–	–	17.66
3020102D	individual floor or roof members	m	0.30	6.26	–	–	6.26	6.89	–	–	6.89
3020102E	extra for cutting off end flush with wall	Each	0.50	10.43	–	–	10.43	11.47	–	–	11.47
3020102F	decayed or infected floor plates	m	0.40	8.34	–	–	8.34	9.17	–	–	9.17
3020102G	tilting fillet or roll	m	0.17	3.54	–	–	3.54	3.89	–	–	3.89
3020102H	fascia or barge board	m	0.65	13.55	–	–	13.55	14.91	–	–	14.91
3020103	**Boarding and flooring; softwood; including withdrawing nails; at:**										
3020103A	ground floor	m²	0.42	8.76	–	–	8.76	9.64	–	–	9.64
3020103B	first floor	m²	0.68	14.18	–	–	14.18	15.60	–	–	15.60
3020103C	roof, softwood	m²	0.80	16.68	–	–	16.68	18.35	–	–	18.35
3020103D	gutter, softwood	m²	0.88	18.35	–	–	18.35	20.19	–	–	20.19
3020103E	ground level; chipboard	m²	0.17	3.54	–	–	3.54	3.89	–	–	3.89
3020103F	first floor level; chipboard	m²	0.42	8.76	–	–	8.76	9.64	–	–	9.64
3020103G	ground level; plywood	m²	0.25	5.21	–	–	5.21	5.73	–	–	5.73
3020103H	first floor level; plywood	m²	0.48	10.01	–	–	10.01	11.01	–	–	11.01
3020104	**Stud partition; softwood; including finishings both sides:**										
3020104A	solid	m²	0.50	10.43	–	–	10.43	11.47	–	–	11.47
3020104B	glazed, including removal of glass	m²	0.67	13.97	–	–	13.97	15.37	–	–	15.37
3020105	**Wall linings; including battening behind:**										
3020105A	plain sheeting	m²	0.33	6.88	–	–	6.88	7.57	–	–	7.57
3020105B	matchboarding	m²	0.45	9.38	–	–	9.38	10.32	–	–	10.32

Woodwork

Small Works 2009		Unit	Labour Hours	Labour Net	Plant Net	Materials Net	Unit Net	Labour Gross	Plant Gross	Materials Gross	Unit Price
								— (Gross rates include 10% profit) —			
				£	£	£	£	£	£	£	£
302	REPAIRS AND ALTERATIONS										
30201	REMOVE TIMBERS										
3020106	Ceiling linings; including battening behind:										
3020106A	plain sheeting	m²	0.50	10.43	–	–	10.43	11.47	–	–	11.47
3020106B	matchboarding	m²	0.67	13.97	–	–	13.97	15.37	–	–	15.37
3020107	Skirtings etc:										
3020107A	skirtings, picture rails, dado rails architraves and the like	m	0.12	2.50	–	–	2.50	2.75	–	–	2.75
3020108	Shelves etc:										
3020108A	shelves, window boards and the like	m	0.35	7.30	–	–	7.30	8.03	–	–	8.03
3020109	Doors:										
3020109A	single	Each	0.45	9.38	–	–	9.38	10.32	–	–	10.32
3020109B	single with frame or lining . .	Each	0.88	18.35	–	–	18.35	20.19	–	–	20.19
3020109C	pair	Each	0.77	16.05	–	–	16.05	17.66	–	–	17.66
3020109D	pair with frame or lining	Each	1.32	27.52	–	–	27.52	30.27	–	–	30.27
3020109E	Extra for taking out spring box	Each	0.83	17.31	–	–	17.31	19.04	–	–	19.04
3020110	Windows:										
3020110A	casement; with frame	Each	1.32	27.52	–	–	27.52	30.27	–	–	30.27
3020110B	double hung sash; with frame	Each	1.77	36.90	–	–	36.90	40.59	–	–	40.59
3020110C	pair; french with frame	Pair	4.40	91.74	–	–	91.74	100.91	–	–	100.91
3020111	Staircase; balustrade:										
3020111A	single straight flight	Each	3.85	80.27	–	–	80.27	88.30	–	–	88.30
3020111B	dogleg flight	Each	5.50	114.68	–	–	114.68	126.15	–	–	126.15
3020111C	handrail and brackets	m	0.12	2.50	–	–	2.50	2.75	–	–	2.75
3020112	Bath panels:										
3020112A	including frame	Each	0.45	9.38	–	–	9.38	10.32	–	–	10.32
3020114	Kitchen fittings:										
3020114A	wall units	Each	0.50	10.43	–	–	10.43	11.47	–	–	11.47
3020114B	floor units	Each	0.33	6.88	–	–	6.88	7.57	–	–	7.57
3020114C	larder units	Each	0.45	9.38	–	–	9.38	10.32	–	–	10.32
3020114D	built in cupboards	Each	1.55	32.32	–	–	32.32	35.55	–	–	35.55
3020115	Casings:										
3020115A	for pipes	m	0.33	6.88	–	–	6.88	7.57	–	–	7.57
30202	ERECT TEMPORARY HOARDING										
3020201	Second-hand timber posts, rails and struts, cover with second-hand close boarding or corrugated iron sheets and dismantle on completion:										
3020201A	1.8 m high	m	2.75	66.91	–	9.33	76.24	73.60	–	10.26	83.86
3020201B	Extra for 0.75 m wide door .	Each	0.65	15.82	–	3.45	19.27	17.40	–	3.80	21.20
3020201C	Extra for pair of gates approx 2.4 m wide overall	Each	2.10	51.09	–	8.23	59.32	56.20	–	9.05	65.25
3020202	Enclose frontage to site with chestnut fencing with posts at 1.8 m intervals and dismantle on completion:										
3020202A	1.2 m high	m	0.28	6.81	–	6.37	13.18	7.49	–	7.01	14.50

Small Works 2009		Unit	Labour Hours	Labour Net	Plant Net	Materials Net	Unit Net	Labour Gross	Plant Gross	Materials Gross	Unit Price
				£	£	£	£	£	£	£	£
								(Gross rates include 10% profit)			
302	REPAIRS AND ALTERATIONS										
30204	REMOVE DEFECTIVE AND RENEW										
3020401	Take up defective gutter boards and bearers and supply and fix:										
3020401A	new.	m²	3.70	90.02	–	16.73	106.75	99.02	–	18.40	117.43
3020402	Take off defective rounded wood rolls to flats and supply and fix:										
3020402A	new.	m	0.22	5.36	–	1.52	6.88	5.90	–	1.67	7.57
3020403	Renew roof timbers:										
3020403A	100 mm × 50 mm	m	0.15	3.65	–	1.80	5.45	4.02	–	1.98	6.00
3020403B	125 mm × 50 mm	m	0.20	4.86	–	2.26	7.12	5.35	–	2.49	7.83
3020403C	150 mm × 50 mm	m	0.25	6.08	–	2.71	8.79	6.69	–	2.98	9.67
3020404	Take down defective hips and ridges and supply and fix new:										
3020404A	175 mm × 31 mm	m	0.40	9.73	–	2.03	11.76	10.70	–	2.23	12.94
3020405	Take down defective fascia and supply and fix new:										
3020405A	150 mm × 25 mm	m	0.40	9.73	–	3.98	13.71	10.70	–	4.38	15.08
3020406	Take down defective soffit and bearers and supply and fix new:										
3020406A	225 mm × 19 mm	m	0.60	14.60	–	4.56	19.16	16.06	–	5.02	21.08
3020407	Take off front gate, remove defective timber posts, grub up concrete, supply new post approximately 1.5 m long set in new concrete and rehang gate:										
3020407A	150 mm × 150 mm creosoted fir post	Each	3.00	72.99	–	25.41	98.40	80.29	–	27.95	108.24
3020407B	150 mm × 150 mm oak post	Each	3.25	79.07	–	92.31	171.38	86.98	–	101.54	188.52
3020408	Excavate for and bolt to wood gate post:										
3020408A	concrete or oak spur set in concrete.	Each	2.00	48.66	–	43.49	92.15	53.53	–	47.84	101.37

Woodwork

		Unit	Labour Hours	Labour Net	Plant Net	Materials Net	Unit Net	Labour Gross	Plant Gross	Materials Gross	Unit Price
								—	(Gross rates include 10% profit)	—	
				£	£	£	£	£	£	£	£
302	**REPAIRS AND ALTERATIONS**										
30204	**REMOVE DEFECTIVE AND RENEW**										
3020409	**Take down and remove all temporary weatherproofing together with all associated timber work to windows and doors and make good all existing joinery work including withdrawing all nails:**										
3020409A	polythene sheet, hardboard, chipboard and the like	m²	1.20	29.20	–	1.80	31.00	32.12	–	1.98	34.10
3020409B	galvanised iron sheet or corrugated asbestos covering including all timber backing and make good. . . .	m²	1.70	41.36	–	2.16	43.52	45.50	–	2.38	47.87
30206	**TEMPORARY SCREENS**										
3020601	**Temporary screen comprising:**										
3020601A	100 mm × 50 mm framing lined both side with building paper	m²	0.26	6.33	–	3.78	10.11	6.96	–	4.16	11.12
3020601B	100 mm × 50 mm framing lined one side with 19 mm matchboard.	m²	0.60	14.60	–	8.03	22.63	16.06	–	8.83	24.89
3020601C	50 mm × 50 mm framing lined one side with hardboard	m²	0.45	10.95	–	2.30	13.25	12.05	–	2.53	14.58
3020602	**Strut up ceiling and remove struts on completion:**										
3020602A	floor to ceiling average 2.6 m	m	1.10	26.76	–	1.02	27.78	29.44	–	1.12	30.56
3020603	**Strut and support window openings; area of window:**										
3020603A	1.0 sq.m	Each	0.45	10.95	–	1.20	12.15	12.05	–	1.32	13.37
3020603B	1.5 sq.m	Each	0.50	12.16	–	1.80	13.96	13.38	–	1.98	15.36
3020603C	2.0 sq.m	Each	0.55	13.38	–	1.80	15.18	14.72	–	1.98	16.70

Small Works 2009		Unit	Labour Hours	Labour Net	Plant Net	Materials Net	Unit Net	Labour Gross	Plant Gross	Materials Gross	Unit Price
								(Gross rates include 10% profit)			
				£	£	£	£	£	£	£	£
302	**REPAIRS AND ALTERATIONS**										
30208	**REPAIRS TO FLOORS**										
3020801	**Remove all grease and dirt from existing flooring, remove all projecting lino nails or tacks, punch down all floor brads, resecure any loose boards, plane off and leave smooth:**										
3020801A	generally	m²	0.85	20.68	–	–	20.68	22.75	–	–	22.75
3020801B	in small areas; less than 1 sq.m.	m²	1.10	26.76	–	–	26.76	29.44	–	–	29.44
3020801C	take up loose floor blocks and relay in mastic; single block	Each	0.35	8.51	–	0.20	8.71	9.36	–	0.22	9.58
3020801D	take up loose floor blocks and relay in mastic; in patches up to six blocks	Each	0.22	5.35	–	0.20	5.55	5.89	–	0.22	6.11
3020802	**Smooth hardwood floor with:**										
3020802A	electric sanding machine. . .	m²	1.00	24.33	–	–	24.33	26.76	–	–	26.76
3020803	**Take off existing skirting and refix:**										
3020803A	replug grounds	m	0.36	8.76	–	–	8.76	9.64	–	–	9.64
3020804	**Take off existing softwood skirting and supply and fix new:**										
3020804A	25 mm × 150 mm	m	0.50	12.17	–	7.17	19.34	13.39	–	7.89	21.27
3020806	**Take up existing shrunk or worn flooring, any thickness. Draw all nails, relay, cramp up, make up width or length with extra boarding of same thickness and clean off on completion; areas exceeding 0.5 sq.m:**										
3020806A	plain edge	m²	0.90	21.90	–	2.58	24.48	24.09	–	2.84	26.93
3020806B	tongued and grooved.	m²	1.10	26.76	–	2.77	29.53	29.44	–	3.05	32.48
3020807	**Remove damaged 25 mm softwood floor boards; clean joists and renew:**										
3020807A	plain edge	m²	0.85	20.68	–	21.60	42.28	22.75	–	23.76	46.51
3020807B	tongued and grooved.	m²	1.00	24.33	–	23.17	47.50	26.76	–	25.49	52.25
3020807C	plain edge; in small detached areas not exceeding 1.0 sq.m	m²	2.20	53.52	–	21.60	75.12	58.87	–	23.76	82.63
3020807D	tongued and grooved in small detached areas not exceeding 1.0 sq m	m²	2.70	65.69	–	23.17	88.86	72.26	–	25.49	97.75
3020807E	plain edge: exceeding 1.0 sq.m, not exceeding 2.5 sq.m	m²	2.00	48.66	–	21.60	70.26	53.53	–	23.76	77.29
3020807F	tongued and grooved: exceeding 1.0 sq.m, not exceeding 2.5 sq.m	m²	2.50	60.83	–	23.17	84.00	66.91	–	25.49	92.40

Woodwork

Small Works 2009		Unit	Labour Hours	Labour Net	Plant Net	Materials Net	Unit Net	Labour Gross	Plant Gross	Materials Gross	Unit Price
								(Gross rates include 10% profit)			
				£	£	£	£	£	£	£	£
302	**REPAIRS AND ALTERATIONS**										
30208	**REPAIRS TO FLOORS**										
3020809	**Renewing softwood joists and flooring including treating joists and underside of boards with creosote or other preservative:**										
3020809A	100 mm × 50 mm floor joists; 25 mm plain edge flooring	m²	1.00	27.80	–	32.82	60.62	30.58	–	36.10	66.68
3020810	**Oak strip flooring pinned and glued to existing softwood floor; clean off and wax polish:**										
3020810A	13 mm	m²	0.90	25.02	–	107.25	132.27	27.52	–	117.98	145.50
30210	**REPAIRS TO DOOR FRAMES, LININGS ETC**										
3021001	**Take down door:**										
3021001A	cut 13 mm off bottom edge and rehang	Each	1.60	44.48	–	–	44.48	48.93	–	–	48.93
3021002	**Cut down architraves (one side):**										
3021002A	reduce length by 13 mm and refix	Set	0.55	15.29	–	–	15.29	16.82	–	–	16.82
3021002B	reduce length by 13 mm without removal	Set	0.50	13.90	–	–	13.90	15.29	–	–	15.29
3021003	**Take off skirting:**										
3021003A	refix at higher level	m	0.30	8.34	–	–	8.34	9.17	–	–	9.17
3021004	**Hardwood border to hearth:**										
3021004A	mitred	Each	0.60	16.68	–	3.56	20.24	18.35	–	3.92	22.26
3021004B	Add if sheet metal inner lining	Each	0.40	11.12	–	4.79	15.91	12.23	–	5.27	17.50
3021006	**Take down door, take out lining or frame, realign and refix. Refix existing architraves and make good work disturbed:**										
3021006A	ease and adjust and rehang door	Each	5.00	139.00	–	–	139.00	152.90	–	–	152.90

Small Works 2009		Unit	Labour Hours	Labour Net	Plant Net	Materials Net	Unit Net	Labour Gross	Plant Gross	Materials Gross	Unit Price
								(Gross rates include 10% profit)			
				£	£	£	£	£	£	£	£
302	**REPAIRS AND ALTERATIONS**										
30210	**REPAIRS TO DOOR FRAMES, LININGS ETC**										
3021010	**Take down, ease and rehang:**										
3021010A	door	Each	1.80	50.04	–	–	50.04	55.04	–	–	55.04
3021010B	door on new butt hinges; remove lock and furniture and supply and fit new rim lock and furniture	Each	3.00	83.40	–	50.55	133.95	91.74	–	55.61	147.35
3021010C	door on new butt hinges; remove lock and furniture and supply and fit new mortice lock and furniture . .	Each	3.50	97.30	–	39.52	136.82	107.03	–	43.47	150.50
3021010D	door; take apart and fit new panel or rail	Each	4.80	133.44	–	5.36	138.80	146.78	–	5.90	152.68
3021010E	renew weatherboard to external softwood door	Each	1.00	27.80	–	5.29	33.09	30.58	–	5.82	36.40
3021010F	casement sash	Each	1.20	33.36	–	–	33.36	36.70	–	–	36.70
3021010G	defective staff and parting beads to double hung sash window and renew	Each	0.80	22.24	–	3.05	25.29	24.46	–	3.36	27.82
3021010H	double hung sashes; including new cords	Each	1.35	37.53	–	2.95	40.48	41.28	–	3.25	44.53
3021010I	cut out defective glazing bars to skylights, windows, doors or greenhouses and renew .	m	0.90	25.02	–	0.59	25.61	27.52	–	0.65	28.17
30212	**REPAIRS TO STAIRS AND HANDRAILS**										
3021201	**Strengthening handrail and balusters:**										
3021201A	including renewing defective balusters	m	1.25	34.75	–	6.69	41.44	38.23	–	7.36	45.58
3021202	**Cutting out defective or worn portion of tread:**										
3021202A	piecing in new	Each	0.80	22.24	–	2.70	24.94	24.46	–	2.97	27.43

Woodwork

Small Works 2009		Unit	Labour Hours	Labour Net	Plant Net	Materials Net	Unit Net	Labour Gross	Plant Gross	Materials Gross	Unit Price
								(Gross rates include 10% profit)			
				£	£	£	£	£	£	£	£
302	**REPAIRS AND ALTERATIONS**										
30213	**TAKE OFF AND RENEW IRONMONGERY**										
3021301	**Take off and renew ironmongery fixed to softwood:**										
3021301A	75 mm strong pattern steel butts....................	Pair	1.33	36.97	–	3.45	40.42	40.67	–	3.80	44.46
3021301B	100 mm strong pattern steel butts....................	Pair	1.58	43.93	–	5.15	49.08	48.32	–	5.67	53.99
3021301C	76 mm steel washered brass butts....................	Pair	1.33	36.98	–	6.92	43.90	40.68	–	7.61	48.29
3021301D	102 mm steel washered brass butts	Pair	1.58	43.93	–	14.18	58.11	48.32	–	15.60	63.92
3021301E	76 mm brass rising butts ..	Pair	1.61	44.76	–	10.34	55.10	49.24	–	11.37	60.61
3021301F	102 mm brass rising butts .	Pair	1.86	51.70	–	19.67	71.37	56.87	–	21.64	78.51
3021301G	305 mm steel tee hinges ...	Pair	1.13	31.41	–	17.91	49.32	34.55	–	19.70	54.25
3021301H	457 mm steel tee hinges ...	Pair	1.22	33.91	–	24.69	58.60	37.30	–	27.16	64.46
3021301I	rim lock and furniture	Each	1.58	43.92	–	43.57	87.49	48.31	–	47.93	96.24
3021301J	mortice lock and furniture..	Each	1.84	51.15	–	32.54	83.69	56.27	–	35.79	92.06
3021301K	Suffolk latch	Each	1.33	36.98	–	6.60	43.58	40.68	–	7.26	47.94
3021301L	150 mm bolt; straight; barrel	Each	0.68	18.90	–	5.33	24.23	20.79	–	5.86	26.65
3021301M	225 mm bolt; straight; barrel	Each	0.78	21.68	–	6.50	28.18	23.85	–	7.15	31.00
3021301N	250 mm casement stay with two pins................	Each	0.62	17.24	–	6.37	23.61	18.96	–	7.01	25.97
3021301O	casement fastener; wedge pattern	Each	0.72	20.01	–	6.12	26.13	22.01	–	6.73	28.74
3021301P	sliding sash fastener	Each	1.47	40.86	–	5.42	46.28	44.95	–	5.96	50.91
3021301Q	sash lift	Each	0.47	13.07	–	4.49	17.56	14.38	–	4.94	19.32

Small Works 2009		Unit	Labour Hours	Labour Net	Plant Net	Materials Net	Unit Net	Labour Gross	Plant Gross	Materials Gross	Unit Price
								(Gross rates include 10% profit)			
				£	£	£	£	£	£	£	£
302	**REPAIRS AND ALTERATIONS**										
30214	**TEMPORARY SHORING**										
3021401	**Erecting temporary dead shoring to form opening using three pairs 150 mm × 150 mm uprights and three 225 mm × 150 mm needles, braces and 225 mm base plates, holing brickwork for needles, all cartage, making good and removing on completion:**										
3021401A	cubic volume of timber 0.90 cu.m..................	Item	70.00	1703.10	–	116.07	1819.17	1873.41	–	127.68	2001.09
3021401B	add or deduct for every 0.3 cu.m more or less than 0.90 cu.m..................	Item	2.00	48.66	–	3.89	52.55	53.53	–	4.28	57.81
3021402	**Erecting temporary raking shoring including rakers, wall plates, needles, holing brickwork, cartage and making good on completion:**										
3021402A	cubic volume of timber 0.30 cu.m..................	Item	32.00	778.56	–	38.69	817.25	856.42	–	42.56	898.98
3021402B	add or deduct for every 0.03 cu.m more or less than 0.30 cu.m..................	Item	3.00	72.99	–	3.89	76.88	80.29	–	4.28	84.57
3021404	**Erecting temporary flying shoring including horizontal shores, struts, wall plates, posts, needles, holing brickwork, cartage and making good on completion:**										
3021404A	cubic volume of timber 0.60 cu.m..................	Item	80.00	1946.40	–	77.38	2023.78	2141.04	–	85.12	2226.16
3021404B	add or deduct for every 0.03 cu.m more or less than 0.60 cu.m..................	Item	4.00	97.32	–	3.89	101.21	107.05	–	4.28	111.33

Woodwork

		Unit	Labour Hours	Labour Net	Plant Net	Materials Net	Unit Net	Labour Gross	Plant Gross	Materials Gross	Unit Price
								(Gross rates include 10% profit)			
				£	£	£	£	£	£	£	£
302	**REPAIRS AND ALTERATIONS**										
30214	**TEMPORARY SHORING**										
3021406	**Erecting permanent raking shoring including horizontal shores, struts, wall plates, posts, needles, holing brickwork, cartage, left in position for an indefinite period:**										
3021406A	cubic volume of timber 0.30 cu.m..................	Item	20.00	486.60	–	83.52	570.12	535.26	–	91.87	627.13
3021406B	add or deduct for each 0.30 cu.m more or less than 0.30 cu.m..................	Item	2.00	48.66	–	8.40	57.06	53.53	–	9.24	62.77
3021407	**Erecting permanent flying shoring including horizontal shores, struts, wall plates, posts, needles, holing brickwork, cartage, left in position for an indefinite period:**										
3021407A	cubic volume of timber 0.60 cu.m..................	Item	54.00	1313.82	–	167.05	1480.87	1445.20	–	183.76	1628.96
3021407B	add or deduct for every 0.03 cu.m more or less 0.60 cu.m..................	Item	2.70	65.70	–	8.40	74.10	72.27	–	9.24	81.51

Small Works 2009		Unit	Labour Hours	Labour Net	Plant Net	Materials Net	Unit Net	Labour Gross	Plant Gross	Materials Gross	Unit Price
								(Gross rates include 10% profit)			
				£	£	£	£	£	£	£	£
401	**NEW WORK**										
40101	**CARLITE PLASTER**										
4010101	**Plaster; 8 mm bonding; 2 mm finish; steel trowelled; internal; 10 mm work; concrete or plasterboard base:**										
4010101A	over 300 mm wide to walls .	m²	0.52	12.70	–	2.22	14.92	13.97	–	2.44	16.41
4010101B	not exceeding 300 mm wide to walls	m²	0.78	19.05	–	2.22	21.27	20.96	–	2.44	23.40
4010101C	over 300 mm wide to ceilings	m²	0.65	15.88	–	2.22	18.10	17.47	–	2.44	19.91
4010101D	not exceeding 300 mm wide to ceilings	m²	0.97	23.69	–	2.22	25.91	26.06	–	2.44	28.50
4010102	**Plaster; 11 mm browning; 2 mm finish; steel trowelled; internal; 13 mm work; to brick or block base:**										
4010102A	over 300 mm wide to walls .	m²	0.53	12.95	–	2.54	15.49	14.25	–	2.79	17.04
4010102B	not exceeding 300 mm wide to ceilings	m²	0.79	19.30	–	2.54	21.84	21.23	–	2.79	24.02
4010104	**Plaster; 11 mm metal lathing undercoat; 2 mm finish; steel trowelled; internal; 13 mm work; metal lathing base:**										
4010104A	over 300 mm wide to walls .	m²	0.53	12.95	–	4.72	17.67	14.25	–	5.19	19.44
4010104B	not exceeding 300 mm wide to walls	m²	0.79	19.30	–	4.72	24.02	21.23	–	5.19	26.42
4010104C	over 300 mm wide to ceilings	m²	0.68	16.61	–	4.72	21.33	18.27	–	5.19	23.46
4010104D	not exceeding 300 mm wide to ceilings	m²	1.02	24.92	–	4.72	29.64	27.41	–	5.19	32.60

Woodwork

	Unit	Labour Hours	Labour Net	Plant Net	Materials Net	Unit Net	Labour Gross	Plant Gross	Materials Gross	Unit Price
			£	£	£	£	\(Gross rates include 10% profit\) £	£	£	£
401	**NEW WORK**									
40103	**THISTLE PLASTER**									
4010301	**Plaster; 11 mm renovating; 2 mm renovating finish; steel trowelled; internal; 13 mm work; to existing concrete, brick or block base:**									
4010301A	over 300 mm wide to walls .	m²	0.53	12.95	–	3.70	16.65	14.25	–	4.07	18.32
4010301B	not exceeding 300 mm wide to walls	m²	0.79	19.30	–	3.70	23.00	21.23	–	4.07	25.30
4010302	**Plaster; Universal one coat; steel trowelled; internal; 10 mm work; to concrete base:**									
4010302A	over 300 mm wide to walls .	m²	0.40	9.77	–	3.08	12.85	10.75	–	3.39	14.14
4010302B	not exceeding 300 mm wide to walls	m²	0.60	14.66	–	3.08	17.74	16.13	–	3.39	19.51
4010302C	over 300 mm wide to ceilings	m²	0.52	12.71	–	3.08	15.79	13.98	–	3.39	17.37
4010302D	not exceeding 300 mm wide to ceilings	m²	0.77	18.81	–	3.08	21.89	20.69	–	3.39	24.08
4010303	**Plaster; Universal one coat; steel trowelled; internal; 13 mm work; to brick or block base:**									
4010303A	over 300 mm wide to walls .	m²	0.42	10.26	–	3.64	13.90	11.29	–	4.00	15.29
4010303B	not exceeding 300 mm wide to walls	m²	0.62	15.15	–	3.64	18.79	16.67	–	4.00	20.67

Small Works 2009		Unit	Labour Hours	Labour Net	Plant Net	Materials Net	Unit Net	Labour Gross	Plant Gross	Materials Gross	Unit Price
								(Gross rates include 10% profit)			
				£	£	£	£	£	£	£	£
401	**NEW WORK**										
40103	**THISTLE PLASTER**										
4010304	**Plaster; Universal one coat; steel trowelled; internal; 5 mm work; to plasterboard base:**										
4010304A	over 300 mm wide to walls .	m²	0.37	9.04	–	1.40	10.44	9.94	–	1.54	11.48
4010304B	not exceeding 300 mm wide to walls	m²	0.57	13.93	–	1.40	15.33	15.32	–	1.54	16.86
4010304C	over 300 mm wide to ceilings	m²	0.49	11.97	–	1.40	13.37	13.17	–	1.54	14.71
4010304D	not exceeding 300 mm wide to ceilings	m²	0.74	18.08	–	1.40	19.48	19.89	–	1.54	21.43
4010305	**Plaster; Thistle; 3 mm one coat board finish; steel trowelled; internal; to plasterboard base:**										
4010305A	over 300 mm wide to walls .	m²	0.37	9.04	–	0.90	9.94	9.94	–	0.99	10.93
4010305B	not exceeding 300 mm wide to walls	m²	0.57	13.93	–	0.90	14.83	15.32	–	0.99	16.31
4010305C	over 300 mm wide to ceilings	m²	0.49	11.97	–	0.90	12.87	13.17	–	0.99	14.16
4010305D	not exceeding 300 mm wide to ceilings	m²	0.74	18.08	–	0.90	18.98	19.89	–	0.99	20.88
4010307	**Plaster; Thistle; 10 mm cement and sand (1:3); 3 mm finish; 13 mm work to concrete, brick or block base:**										
4010307A	over 300 mm wide to walls .	m²	0.55	13.44	–	2.21	15.65	14.78	–	2.43	17.22
4010307B	not exceeding 300 mm wide to walls	m²	0.83	20.28	–	2.21	22.49	22.31	–	2.43	24.74
4010307C	over 300 mm wide to ceilings	m²	0.72	17.59	–	2.21	19.80	19.35	–	2.43	21.78
4010307D	not exceeding 300 mm wide to ceilings	m²	1.07	26.14	–	2.21	28.35	28.75	–	2.43	31.19
40105	**LABOURS ON PLASTERING**										
4010501	**Rounded internal angle:**										
4010501A	not exceeding 10 mm radius	m	0.06	1.47	–	–	1.47	1.62	–	–	1.62
4010501B	over 10 mm radius	m	0.08	1.95	–	–	1.95	2.15	–	–	2.15
4010502	**Rounded external angle:**										
4010502A	not exceeding 10 mm radius	m	0.07	1.71	–	–	1.71	1.88	–	–	1.88
4010502B	over 10 mm radius	m	0.10	2.44	–	–	2.44	2.68	–	–	2.68
4010503	**Make good plaster around pipes, angles and the like:**										
4010503A	not exceeding 300 mm girth	Each	0.07	1.71	–	–	1.71	1.88	–	–	1.88
4010503B	over 300 mm girth	Each	0.08	1.95	–	–	1.95	2.15	–	–	2.15

Woodwork

Small Works 2009		Unit	Labour Hours	Labour Net	Plant Net	Materials Net	Unit Net	Labour Gross	Plant Gross	Materials Gross	Unit Price
								(Gross rates include 10% profit)			
				£	£	£	£	£	£	£	£
401	**NEW WORK**										
40106	**PLASTER BEADS AND THE LIKE**										
4010601	**Catnic galvanised steel beads; fixed with plaster dabs:**										
4010601A	standard angle bead	m	0.14	3.42	–	1.16	4.58	3.76	–	1.28	5.04
4010601B	Supasave angle bead	m	0.14	3.42	–	0.91	4.33	3.76	–	1.00	4.76
4010601C	micro mesh angle bead	m	0.14	3.42	–	1.02	4.44	3.76	–	1.12	4.88
4010601D	dry wall angle bead	m	0.14	3.42	–	1.10	4.52	3.76	–	1.21	4.97
4010601E	dry wall stop bead; 3 mm	m	0.14	3.42	–	1.66	5.08	3.76	–	1.83	5.59
4010601F	dry wall stop bead; 6 mm	m	0.14	3.42	–	1.66	5.08	3.76	–	1.83	5.59
4010601G	renderstop	m	0.14	3.42	–	1.56	4.98	3.76	–	1.72	5.48
4010601H	plaster stop; 12 mm	m	0.14	3.42	–	1.43	4.85	3.76	–	1.57	5.34
4010601I	plaster stop; 15 mm	m	0.14	3.42	–	1.43	4.85	3.76	–	1.57	5.34
4010601J	plaster stop; 18 mm	m	0.14	3.42	–	1.99	5.41	3.76	–	2.19	5.95
4010601K	plaster stop; 21 mm	m	0.14	3.42	–	1.99	5.41	3.76	–	2.19	5.95
4010601L	plasterboard edging bead; 9.5 mm	m	0.14	3.42	–	3.69	7.11	3.76	–	4.06	7.82
4010601M	plasterboard edging bead; 12.5 mm	m	0.14	3.42	–	3.69	7.11	3.76	–	4.06	7.82
4010601N	architrave bead; 10 mm	m	0.14	3.42	–	1.63	5.05	3.76	–	1.79	5.56
4010601O	movement bead; 12 mm	m	0.14	3.42	–	6.09	9.51	3.76	–	6.70	10.46

FLOOR, WALL AND CEILING FINISHES

Small Works 2009		Unit	Labour Hours	Labour Net	Plant Net	Materials Net	Unit Net	Labour Gross	Plant Gross	Materials Gross	Unit Price
								(Gross rates include 10% profit)			
				£	£	£	£	£	£	£	£
401	**NEW WORK**										
40108	**PORTLAND CEMENT FINISHES**										
4010801	**Render; cement and sand (1:3); 6 mm work; dubbing out; internal; to walls; brick or block base:**										
4010801A	over 300 mm wide	m²	0.29	7.09	–	0.65	7.74	7.80	–	0.72	8.51
4010801B	not exceeding 300 mm wide	m²	0.43	10.51	–	0.65	11.16	11.56	–	0.72	12.28
4010802	**Render; cement and sand (1:3); 13 mm work dubbing out; internal; to walls; brick or block base:**										
4010802A	over 300 mm wide	m²	0.42	10.27	–	1.63	11.90	11.30	–	1.79	13.09
4010802B	not exceeding 300 mm wide	m²	0.62	15.15	–	1.63	16.78	16.67	–	1.79	18.46
4010803	**Render; cement and sand (1:3); 19 mm work dubbing out; internal; to walls; brick or block base:**										
4010803A	over 300 mm wide	m²	0.53	12.95	–	2.29	15.24	14.25	–	2.52	16.76
4010803B	not exceeding 300 mm wide	m²	0.78	19.05	–	2.29	21.34	20.96	–	2.52	23:47
4010804	**Render; cement and sand (1:3); 25 mm work dubbing out; internal; to walls; brick or block base:**										
4010804A	over 300 mm wide	m²	0.60	14.66	–	3.05	17.71	16.13	–	3.36	19.48
4010804B	not exceeding 300 mm wide	m²	0.84	20.52	–	3.05	23.57	22.57	–	3.36	25.93
4010806	**Render; cement and sand (1:3); 13 mm on coat work to walls; wood floated; plain face; internal; to brick or block base:**										
4010806A	over 300 mm wide	m²	0.42	10.27	–	1.63	11.90	11.30	–	1.79	13.09
4010806B	not exceeding 300 mm wide	m²	0.62	15.15	–	1.63	16.78	16.67	–	1.79	18.46
4010807	**Render; cement and sand (1:3); 20 mm two coat work to walls; wood floated; plain face; internal; to brick or block base:**										
4010807A	over 300 mm wide	m²	0.60	14.66	–	2.40	17.06	16.13	–	2.64	18.77
4010807B	not exceeding 300 mm wide	m²	0.90	21.98	–	2.40	24.38	24.18	–	2.64	26.82
4010807C	curb to gulley	Each	0.85	20.76	–	1.42	22.18	22.84	–	1.56	24.40
4010807D	plinth at back of gulley	Each	0.40	9.77	–	0.87	10.64	10.75	–	0.96	11.70
4010808	**Render; cement and sand (1:3); rough cast face; wood floated; external; 20 mm two coat work to walls; brick or block base:**										
4010808A	over 300 mm wide	m²	0.90	21.98	–	2.40	24.38	24.18	–	2.64	26.82
4010808B	not exceeding 300 mm wide	m²	1.20	29.31	–	2.40	31.71	32.24	–	2.64	34.88
4010809	**Render; cement and sand (1:3); pebble dash finish; wood floated; external; 20 mm two coat work to walls; brick or block base:**										
4010809A	over 300 mm wide	m²	0.96	23.45	–	2.09	25.54	25.80	–	2.30	28.09
4010809B	not exceeding 300 mm wide	m²	1.26	30.78	–	2.09	32.87	33.86	–	2.30	36.16

Floor, Wall and Ceiling Finishes

Small Works 2009		Unit	Labour Hours	Labour Net	Plant Net	Materials Net	Unit Net	Labour Gross	Plant Gross	Materials Gross	Unit Price
								(Gross rates include 10% profit)			
				£	£	£	£	£	£	£	£
401	**NEW WORK**										
40108	**PORTLAND CEMENT FINISHES**										
4010811	**Render; cement-lime-sand (1:1:6); wood floated; plain face; external; 13 mm one coat work to walls; brick or block base:**										
4010811A	over 300 mm wide	m²	0.42	10.26	–	1.97	12.23	11.29	–	2.17	13.45
4010811B	not exceeding 300 mm wide	m²	0.62	15.15	–	1.97	17.12	16.67	–	2.17	18.83
4010812	**Render; cement-lime-sand (1:1:6); wood floated; plain face; external; 20 mm two coat work to walls; brick or block base:**										
4010812A	over 300 mm wide	m²	0.60	14.66	–	2.89	17.55	16.13	–	3.18	19.31
4010812B	not exceeding 300 mm wide	m²	0.90	21.99	–	2.89	24.88	24.19	–	3.18	27.37
4010813	**Render; cement-lime-sand (1:1:6); wood floated; rough cast face; external; 20 mm two coat work to walls; brick or block base:**										
4010813A	over 300 mm wide	m²	0.90	21.99	–	2.89	24.88	24.19	–	3.18	27.37
4010813B	not exceeding 300 mm wide	m²	1.20	29.32	–	2.89	32.21	32.25	–	3.18	35.43
4010814	**Render; cement-lime-sand (1:1:6); wood floated; pebbledash finish; external; 20 mm two coat work to walls; brick or block base:**										
4010814A	over 300 mm wide	m²	0.96	23.46	–	3.13	26.59	25.81	–	3.44	29.25
4010814B	not exceeding 300 mm wide	m²	1.26	30.78	–	3.13	33.91	33.86	–	3.44	37.30
4010815	**Render; cement-lime-sand (1:1:6); Snowcem; Cullamix Tyrolean finish; external; 16 mm one coat work to walls; brick or block base:**										
4010815A	over 300 mm wide	m²	0.78	19.05	–	5.97	25.02	20.96	–	6.57	27.52
4010815B	not exceeding 300 mm wide	m²	1.16	28.34	–	5.97	34.31	31.17	–	6.57	37.74

Small Works 2009		Unit	Labour Hours	Labour Net	Plant Net	Materials Net	Unit Net	Labour Gross	Plant Gross	Materials Gross	Unit Price
								(Gross rates include 10% profit)			
				£	£	£	£	£	£	£	£
401	**NEW WORK**										
40109	**LABOURS ON RENDERING**										
4010901	**Rounded internal angle:**										
4010901A	not exceeding 10 mm radius	m	0.08	1.95	–	–	1.95	2.15	–	–	2.15
4010901B	over 10 mm radius	m	0.11	2.69	–	–	2.69	2.96	–	–	2.96
4010902	**Rounded external angle:**										
4010902A	not exceeding 10 mm radius	m	0.10	2.44	–	–	2.44	2.68	–	–	2.68
4010902B	over 10 mm radius	m	0.12	2.93	–	–	2.93	3.22	–	–	3.22
4010903	**Make good rendering around pipes, angles and the like:**										
4010903A	not exceeding 300 mm girth	Each	0.07	1.71	–	–	1.71	1.88	–	–	1.88
4010903B	over 300 mm girth	Each	0.08	1.95	–	–	1.95	2.15	–	–	2.15
40110	**RENDER BEADS AND THE LIKE**										
4011001	**Expamet beads for external use; stainless steel:**										
4011001A	angle bead	m	0.14	3.42	–	4.47	7.89	3.76	–	4.92	8.68
4011001B	movement bead	m	0.14	3.42	–	10.04	13.46	3.76	–	11.04	14.81
4011001C	stop bead; 10 mm.	m	0.14	3.42	–	3.63	7.05	3.76	–	3.99	7.76
4011001D	stop bead; 13 mm.	m	0.14	3.42	–	3.63	7.05	3.76	–	3.99	7.76
4011001E	stop bead; 16 mm.	m	0.14	3.42	–	3.63	7.05	3.76	–	3.99	7.76
4011001F	stop bead; 19 mm.	m	0.14	3.42	–	3.94	7.36	3.76	–	4.33	8.10
4011001G	external render stop	m	0.14	3.42	–	3.63	7.05	3.76	–	3.99	7.76

Floor, Wall and Ceiling Finishes

Small Works 2009		Unit	Labour Hours	Labour Net	Plant Net	Materials Net	Unit Net	Labour Gross	Plant Gross	Materials Gross	Unit Price
								(Gross rates include 10% profit)			
				£	£	£	£	£	£	£	£
401	**NEW WORK**										
40111	**CEMENT SCREEDS**										
4011101	**Screed; cement and sand (1:3); steel trowelled smooth; floors; level and to falls:**										
4011101A	25 mm; over 300 mm wide	m²	0.90	21.99	–	3.27	25.26	24.19	–	3.60	27.79
4011101B	25 mm; not exceeding 300 mm wide	m²	1.80	43.97	–	3.27	47.24	48.37	–	3.60	51.96
4011101C	32 mm; over 300 mm wide	m²	1.00	24.43	–	4.03	28.46	26.87	–	4.43	31.31
4011101D	32 mm; not exceeding 300 mm wide	m²	2.00	48.86	–	4.03	52.89	53.75	–	4.43	58.18
4011101E	38 mm; over 300 mm wide	m²	1.10	26.88	–	4.90	31.78	29.57	–	5.39	34.96
4011101F	38 mm; not exceeding 300 mm wide	m²	2.20	53.75	–	4.90	58.65	59.13	–	5.39	64.52
4011101G	50 mm; over 300 mm wide	m²	1.30	31.76	–	6.32	38.08	34.94	–	6.95	41.89
4011101H	50 mm; not exceeding 300 mm wide	m²	2.60	63.52	–	6.32	69.84	69.87	–	6.95	76.82
4011102	**Skirtings; cement and sand (1:3); 150 m high; fair edge; ends and the like:**										
4011102A	straight	m	0.55	13.43	–	0.44	13.87	14.77	–	0.48	15.26
4011102B	curved	m	0.85	20.76	–	0.44	21.20	22.84	–	0.48	23.32
4011103	**Make good paving to:**										
4011103A	floor channel	m	0.25	6.11	–	–	6.11	6.72	–	–	6.72
4011103B	rainwater, soil and ventilation pipes	Each	0.40	9.77	–	–	9.77	10.75	–	–	10.75
4011103C	yard gulley	Each	0.50	12.22	–	–	12.22	13.44	–	–	13.44
4011103D	manhole cover frame	Each	1.00	24.43	–	–	24.43	26.87	–	–	26.87

Small Works 2009		Unit	Labour Hours	Labour Net	Plant Net	Materials Net	Unit Net	Labour Gross	Plant Gross	Materials Gross	Unit Price
								(Gross rates include 10% profit)			
				£	£	£	£	£	£	£	£
401	**NEW WORK**										
40112	**GRANOLITHIC**										
4011201	**Granolithic; cement and granite chippings (2:5); steel trowelled smooth floors; level and to falls:**										
4011201A	25 mm; over 300 mm wide .	m^2	0.46	11.23	–	6.54	17.77	12.35	–	7.19	19.55
4011201B	25 mm; not exceeding 300 mm wide	m^2	0.68	16.61	–	6.54	23.15	18.27	–	7.19	25.47
4011201C	32 mm; over 300 mm wide .	m^2	0.50	12.22	–	8.06	20.28	13.44	–	8.87	22.31
4011201D	32 mm; not exceeding 300 mm wide	m^2	0.76	18.57	–	8.06	26.63	20.43	–	8.87	29.29
4011201E	38 mm; over 300 mm wide .	m^2	0.54	13.20	–	9.80	23.00	14.52	–	10.78	25.30
4011201F	38 mm; not exceeding 300 mm wide	m^2	0.82	20.04	–	9.80	29.84	22.04	–	10.78	32.82
4011201G	50 mm; over 300 mm wide .	m^2	0.58	14.16	–	12.64	26.80	15.58	–	13.90	29.48
4011201H	50 mm; not exceeding 300 mm wide	m^2	0.86	21.00	–	12.64	33.64	23.10	–	13.90	37.00
4011202	**Lining to channels; to falls; rounded arrises; coved junction; ends, angles and the like; 150 mm girth:**										
4011202A	25 mm	m	0.52	12.70	–	0.87	13.57	13.97	–	0.96	14.93
4011202B	32 mm	m	0.55	13.44	–	1.09	14.53	14.78	–	1.20	15.98
4011202C	38 mm	m	0.91	22.23	–	1.31	23.54	24.45	–	1.44	25.89
4011202D	50 mm	m	0.96	23.46	–	1.74	25.20	25.81	–	1.91	27.72

Floor, Wall and Ceiling Finishes

Small Works 2009		Unit	Labour Hours	Labour Net	Plant Net	Materials Net	Unit Net	Labour Gross	Plant Gross	Materials Gross	Unit Price
								(Gross rates include 10% profit)			
				£	£	£	£	£	£	£	£
401	**NEW WORK**										
40112	**GRANOLITHIC**										
4011203	**Treads; rounded nosing; ends, angles and the like; 275 mm wide:**										
4011203A	25 mm	m	0.41	10.02	–	1.52	11.54	11.02	–	1.67	12.69
4011203B	32 mm	m	0.47	11.48	–	2.18	13.66	12.63	–	2.40	15.03
4011203C	38 mm	m	0.53	12.95	–	2.61	15.56	14.25	–	2.87	17.12
4011203D	50 mm	m	0.59	14.41	–	3.27	17.68	15.85	–	3.60	19.45
4011204	**Risers; coved junction to tread; undercut; 150 mm high:**										
4011204A	13 mm	m	0.32	7.81	–	0.44	8.25	8.59	–	0.48	9.08
4011204B	19 mm	m	0.37	9.04	–	0.65	9.69	9.94	–	0.72	10.66
4011205	**Strings or aprons; rounded top edge; ends, angles and the like; 275 mm wide:**										
4011205A	13 mm	m	0.59	14.42	–	0.87	15.29	15.86	–	0.96	16.82
4011205B	19 mm	m	0.78	19.05	–	1.31	20.36	20.96	–	1.44	22.40
4011206	**Skirtings; rounded top edge; coved junction to paving; ends, angles and the like; 150 mm high:**										
4011206A	13 mm	m	0.52	12.70	–	0.44	13.14	13.97	–	0.48	14.45
4011206B	19 mm	m	0.72	17.59	–	0.65	18.24	19.35	–	0.72	20.06
4011207	**Carborundum surface dressing:**										
4011207A	1 Kg per sq.m	m²	0.12	2.94	–	1.14	4.08	3.23	–	1.25	4.49
4011208	**Fair joint to flush edge:**										
4011208A	of existing finishes	m	0.14	3.42	–	–	3.42	3.76	–	–	3.76
4011209	**Making good around pipes and the like; not exceeding 300 mm girth:**										
4011209A	25 mm	Each	0.12	2.93	–	–	2.93	3.22	–	–	3.22
4011209B	32 mm	Each	0.12	2.93	–	–	2.93	3.22	–	–	3.22
4011209C	38 mm	Each	0.14	3.42	–	–	3.42	3.76	–	–	3.76
4011209D	50 mm	Each	0.14	3.42	–	–	3.42	3.76	–	–	3.76

Small Works 2009		Unit	Labour Hours	Labour Net	Plant Net	Materials Net	Unit Net	Labour Gross	Plant Gross	Materials Gross	Unit Price
								(Gross rates include 10% profit)			
				£	£	£	£	£	£	£	£
401	**NEW WORK**										
40114	**METAL LATHING**										
4011401	**Expamet; 9 mm galvanised expanded metal lathing; BB263; 0.500 mm thick; to walls:**										
4011401A	over 300 mm wide; fixed to softwood with galvanised nails	m²	0.20	4.88	–	7.27	12.15	5.37	–	8.00	13.37
4011401B	not exceeding 300 mm wide; fixed to softwood with galvanised nails	m²	0.31	7.57	–	7.27	14.84	8.33	–	8.00	16.32
4011401C	over 300 mm wide; fixed to steel with tying wire	m²	0.25	6.10	–	7.27	13.37	6.71	–	8.00	14.71
4011401D	not exceeding 300 mm wide; fixed to steel with tying wire	m²	0.36	8.79	–	7.27	16.06	9.67	–	8.00	17.67
4011402	**Expamet; 9 mm galvanised expanded metal lathing; BB263; 0.500 mm thick; to ceilings:**										
4011402A	over 300 mm wide; fixed to softwood with galvanised nails	m²	0.24	5.86	–	7.27	13.13	6.45	–	8.00	14.44
4011402B	not exceeding 300 mm wide; fixed to softwood with galvanised nails	m²	0.36	8.79	–	7.27	16.06	9.67	–	8.00	17.67
4011402C	over 300 mm wide; fixed to steel with tying wire	m²	0.29	7.08	–	7.27	14.35	7.79	–	8.00	15.79
4011402D	not exceeding 300 mm wide; fixed to steel with tying wire	m²	0.41	10.01	–	7.27	17.28	11.01	–	8.00	19.01
4011403	**Expamet; 9 mm galvanised expanded metal lathing; BB263; 0.500 mm thick; to beams, sides, soffits and tops:**										
4011403A	over 300 mm wide; fixed to steel with tying wire	m²	0.35	8.55	–	7.27	15.82	9.41	–	8.00	17.40
4011403B	not exceeding 300 mm wide; fixed to steel with tying wire	m²	0.50	12.21	–	7.27	19.48	13.43	–	8.00	21.43
4011403C	raking cutting	m	0.12	2.93	–	–	2.93	3.22	–	–	3.22
4011403D	curved cutting	m	0.18	4.40	–	–	4.40	4.84	–	–	4.84

Floor, Wall and Ceiling Finishes

Small Works 2009		Unit	Labour Hours	Labour Net	Plant Net	Materials Net	Unit Net	Labour Gross	Plant Gross	Materials Gross	Unit Price
								(Gross rates include 10% profit)			
				£	£	£	£	£	£	£	£
401	**NEW WORK**										
40114	**METAL LATHING**										
4011404	**Expamet; 9 mm galvanised expanded metal lathing; BB264; 0.725 mm thick; to walls:**										
4011404A	over 300 mm wide; fixed to softwood with galvanised nails	m²	0.23	5.62	–	8.45	14.07	6.18	–	9.30	15.48
4011404B	not exceeding 300 mm wide; fixed to softwood with galvanised nails	m²	0.34	8.31	–	8.45	16.76	9.14	–	9.30	18.44
4011404C	over 300 mm wide; fixed to steel with tying wire	m²	0.28	6.84	–	8.45	15.29	7.52	–	9.30	16.82
4011404D	not exceeding 300 mm wide; fixed to steel with tying wire	m²	0.39	9.53	–	8.45	17.98	10.48	–	9.30	19.78
4011405	**Expamet; 9 mm galvanised expanded metal lathing; BB264; 0.725 mm thick; to ceilings:**										
4011405A	over 300 mm wide; fixed to softwood with galvanised nails	m²	0.26	6.36	–	8.45	14.81	7.00	–	9.30	16.29
4011405B	not exceeding 300 mm wide; fixed to softwood with galvanised nails	m²	0.38	9.29	–	8.45	17.74	10.22	–	9.30	19.51
4011405C	over 300 mm wide; fixed to steel with tying wire	m²	0.31	7.58	–	8.45	16.03	8.34	–	9.30	17.63
4011405D	not exceeding 300 mm wide; fixed to steel with tying wire	m²	0.43	10.51	–	8.45	18.96	11.56	–	9.30	20.86
4011406	**Expamet; 9 mm galvanised expanded metal lathing; BB264; 0.725 mm thick; to beams, sides, soffits and tops:**										
4011406A	over 300 mm wide; fixed to steel with tying wire	m²	0.37	9.04	–	8.45	17.49	9.94	–	9.30	19.24
4011406B	not exceeding 300 mm wide; fixed to steel with tying wire	m²	0.53	12.95	–	8.45	21.40	14.25	–	9.30	23.54
4011406C	raking cutting	m	0.13	3.18	–	–	3.18	3.50	–	–	3.50
4011406D	curved cutting	m	0.19	4.64	–	–	4.64	5.10	–	–	5.10

Floor, Wall and Ceiling Finishes

Small Works 2009		Unit	Labour Hours	Labour Net	Plant Net	Materials Net	Unit Net	Labour Gross	Plant Gross	Materials Gross	Unit Price
				£	£	£	£	(Gross rates include 10% profit)			
								£	£	£	£
401	NEW WORK										
40116	DRY LININGS AND PARTITIONS										
4011601	Thistle baseboard; 9.5 mm work; fixed to timber base with galvanised nails; taped butt joints:										
4011601A	over 300 mm wide; to walls.	m²	0.31	7.57	–	3.75	11.32	8.33	–	4.13	12.45
4011601B	not exceeding 300 mm wide; to walls	m²	0.48	11.73	–	3.75	15.48	12.90	–	4.13	17.03
4011601C	over 300 mm wide; to ceilings	m²	0.37	9.04	–	3.75	12.79	9.94	–	4.13	14.07
4011601D	not exceeding 300 mm wide; to ceilings	m²	0.55	13.44	–	3.75	17.19	14.78	–	4.13	18.91
4011603	Gyproc square edge wallboard; 9.5 mm work; fixed to timber base with galvanised nails; taped butt joints:										
4011603A	over 300 mm wide; to walls.	m²	0.26	6.35	–	3.62	9.97	6.99	–	3.98	10.97
4011603B	not exceeding 300 mm wide; to walls	m²	0.40	9.77	–	3.62	13.39	10.75	–	3.98	14.73
4011603C	over 300 mm wide; to ceilings	m²	0.31	7.57	–	3.62	11.19	8.33	–	3.98	12.31
4011603D	not exceeding 300 mm wide; to ceilings	m²	0.47	11.48	–	3.62	15.10	12.63	–	3.98	16.61
4011604	Gyproc square edge wallboard; 12.5 mm work; fixed to timber base with galvanised nails; taped butt joints:										
4011604A	over 300 mm wide; to walls.	m²	0.31	7.57	–	4.30	11.87	8.33	–	4.73	13.06
4011604B	not exceeding 300 mm wide; to walls	m²	0.48	11.72	–	4.30	16.02	12.89	–	4.73	17.62
4011604C	over 300 mm wide; to ceilings	m²	0.37	9.04	–	4.30	13.34	9.94	–	4.73	14.67
4011604D	not exceeding 300 mm wide; to ceilings	m²	0.56	13.68	–	4.30	17.98	15.05	–	4.73	19.78
4011606	Gyproc taper edge thermal board; 25 mm work; fixed to timber base with galvanised nails; taped butt joints:										
4011606A	over 300 mm wide; to walls.	m²	0.37	9.04	–	9.62	18.66	9.94	–	10.58	20.53
4011606B	not exceeding 300 mm wide; to walls	m²	0.54	13.20	–	9.62	22.82	14.52	–	10.58	25.10
4011606C	over 300 mm wide; to ceilings	m²	0.43	10.51	–	9.62	20.13	11.56	–	10.58	22.14
4011606D	not exceeding 300 mm wide; to ceilings	m²	0.61	14.91	–	9.62	24.53	16.40	–	10.58	26.98

Floor, Wall and Ceiling Finishes

Small Works 2009		Unit	Labour Hours	Labour Net	Plant Net	Materials Net	Unit Net	Labour Gross	Plant Gross	Materials Gross	Unit Price
								(Gross rates include 10% profit)			
				£	£	£	£	£	£	£	£
401	**NEW WORK**										
40116	**DRY LININGS AND PARTITIONS**										
4011608	**Gyproc taper edge thermal board; 40 mm work; fixed to timber base with galvanised nails; taped butt joints:**										
4011608A	over 300 mm wide; to walls.	m²	0.43	10.50	–	13.50	24.00	11.55	–	14.85	26.40
4011608B	not exceeding 300 mm wide; to walls	m²	0.60	14.66	–	13.50	28.16	16.13	–	14.85	30.98
4011608C	over 300 mm wide; to ceilings	m²	0.49	11.97	–	13.50	25.47	13.17	–	14.85	28.02
4011608D	not exceeding 300 mm wide; to ceilings	m²	0.67	16.37	–	13.50	29.87	18.01	–	14.85	32.86
4011610	**Gyproc taper edge vapour check thermal board; 25 mm work; fixed to timber base with galvanised nails; taped butt joints:**										
4011610A	over 300 mm wide; to walls.	m²	0.37	9.04	–	10.65	19.69	9.94	–	11.72	21.66
4011610B	not exceeding 300 mm wide; to walls	m²	0.54	13.20	–	10.65	23.85	14.52	–	11.72	26.24
4011610C	over 300 mm wide; to ceilings	m²	0.43	10.51	–	10.65	21.16	11.56	–	11.72	23.28
4011610D	not exceeding 300 mm wide; to ceilings	m²	0.61	14.91	–	10.65	25.56	16.40	–	11.72	28.12
4011612	**Gyproc taper edge vapour check thermal board; 40 mm work; fixed to timber base with galvanised nails; taped butt joints:**										
4011612A	over 300 mm wide; to walls.	m²	0.43	10.50	–	14.49	24.99	11.55	–	15.94	27.49
4011612B	not exceeding 300 mm wide; to walls	m²	0.60	14.66	–	14.49	29.15	16.13	–	15.94	32.07
4011612C	over 300 mm wide; to ceilings	m²	0.49	11.97	–	14.49	26.46	13.17	–	15.94	29.11
4011612D	not exceeding 300 mm wide; to ceilings	m²	0.67	16.37	–	14.49	30.86	18.01	–	15.94	33.95

Small Works 2009		Unit	Labour Hours	Labour Net	Plant Net	Materials Net	Unit Net	Labour Gross	Plant Gross	Materials Gross	Unit Price
								(Gross rates include 10% profit)			
				£	£	£	£	£	£	£	£
401	**NEW WORK**										
40116	**DRY LININGS AND PARTITIONS**										
4011614	**Paramount dry partition; cardboard egg crate core; faced both sides with plasterboard; 30 mm × 37 mm vertical jointing battens; grey faced with square butt joints for plastering:**										
4011614C	57 mm; over 300 mm wide .	m²	0.85	20.77	–	14.69	35.46	22.85	–	16.16	39.01
4011614D	57 mm; not exceeding 300 mm wide	m²	1.28	31.27	–	14.69	45.96	34.40	–	16.16	50.56
4011614E	63 mm; over 300 mm wide .	m²	0.90	21.99	–	16.49	38.48	24.19	–	18.14	42.33
4011614F	63 mm; not exceeding 300 mm wide	m²	1.35	32.99	–	16.49	49.48	36.29	–	18.14	54.43
4011616	**Extra for taped joints:**										
4011616A	filled; one coat Gyproc drywall top coat to plasterboard; (both sides measured)	m²	0.18	4.39	–	1.12	5.51	4.83	–	1.23	6.06
4011620	**Perimeter fixing; battens for 57 mm or 63 mm partitions:**										
4011620A	37 mm × 19 mm	m	0.13	3.17	–	0.71	3.88	3.49	–	0.78	4.27
4011620B	37 mm × 19 mm; plugged to concrete o brickwork....	m	0.46	11.24	–	0.90	12.14	12.36	–	0.99	13.35
4011624	**Angle junction fixings; battens for 57 mm partitions:**										
4011624A	37 mm × 19 mm and 37 mm × 37 mm	m	0.43	10.51	–	0.72	11.23	11.56	–	0.79	12.35
4011626	**Angle junction fixings; battens for 63 mm partitions:**										
4011626A	37 mm × 19 mm and 37 mm × 37 mm	m	0.45	10.99	–	0.72	11.71	12.09	–	0.79	12.88
4011630	**Tee junction fixings; battens for 57 mm partitions:**										
4011630A	37 mm × 19 mm and 37 mm × 37 mm	m	0.34	8.31	–	0.72	9.03	9.14	–	0.79	9.93
4011632	**Tee junction fixings; battens for 63 mm partitions:**										
4011632A	37 mm × 19 mm and 37 mm × 37 mm	m	0.35	8.55	–	0.72	9.27	9.41	–	0.79	10.20
4011636	**Gyproc metal stud partition; 75 mm; comprising 50 mm metal stud framing, clad both sides with one layer of 12.5 mm Gyproc wallboard:**										
4011636A	over 300 mm wide	m²	1.30	31.75	–	15.75	47.50	34.93	–	17.33	52.25
4011636B	not exceeding 300 mm wide	m²	3.25	79.39	–	15.75	95.14	87.33	–	17.33	104.65

Floor, Wall and Ceiling Finishes

Small Works 2009		Unit	Labour Hours	Labour Net	Plant Net	Materials Net	Unit Net	Labour Gross	Plant Gross	Materials Gross	Unit Price
								(Gross rates include 10% profit)			
				£	£	£	£	£	£	£	£
401	**NEW WORK**										
40116	**DRY LININGS AND PARTITIONS**										
4011638	**Gyproc metal stud partition; 95 mm; comprising 70 mm metal stud framing clad both sides with one layer of 12.5 mm Gyproc wallboard:**										
4011638A	over 300 mm wide	m²	1.30	31.76	–	17.39	49.15	34.94	–	19.13	54.07
4011638B	not exceeding 300 mm wide	m²	3.25	79.40	–	17.39	96.79	87.34	–	19.13	106.47
4011639	**Tape and fill joints:**										
4011639A	with mechanical jointer	m	0.25	6.11	–	0.22	6.33	6.72	–	0.24	6.96
4011643	**Gyproc DriLyner system; Gyproc square edge wallboard; fixed with adhesive dab to masonry walls; taped butt joints; 9. mm work:**										
4011643A	over 300 mm wide	m²	0.41	10.02	–	4.95	14.97	11.02	–	5.45	16.47
4011643B	not exceeding 300 mm wide	m²	0.63	15.39	–	4.95	20.34	16.93	–	5.45	22.37
4011645	**Gyproc DriLyner system; Gyproc square edge wallboard; fixed with adhesive dab to masonry walls; taped butt joints; 12.5 mm work:**										
4011645A	over 300 mm wide	m²	0.49	11.97	–	5.46	17.43	13.17	–	6.01	19.17
4011645B	not exceeding 300 mm wide	m²	0.76	18.57	–	5.66	24.23	20.43	–	6.23	26.65
4011647	**Gyproc DriLyner system; taper edge thermal board; fixed with adhesive dabs to masonry walls; taped butt joints; 25 mm work:**										
4011647A	over 300 mm wide	m²	0.58	14.17	–	10.83	25.00	15.59	–	11.91	27.50
4011647B	not exceeding 300 mm wide	m²	0.85	20.76	–	11.29	32.05	22.84	–	12.42	35.26
4011649	**Gyproc DriLyner system; taper edge wallboard; fixed with adhesive dabs to masonry walls; taped butt joints; 40 mm work:**										
4011649A	over 300 mm wide	m²	0.68	16.61	–	14.67	31.28	18.27	–	16.14	34.41
4011649B	not exceeding 300 mm wide	m²	0.95	23.21	–	15.30	38.51	25.53	–	16.83	42.36

Small Works 2009		Unit	Labour Hours	Labour Net	Plant Net	Materials Net	Unit Net	Labour Gross	Plant Gross	Materials Gross	Unit Price
								(Gross rates include 10% profit)			
				£	£	£	£	£	£	£	£
401	**NEW WORK**										
40116	**DRY LININGS AND PARTITIONS**										
4011651	**Gyproc DriLyner system; 30 mm Tri-line laminate board; fixed with adhesive dab on masonry walls; taped butt joints:**										
4011651A	over 300 mm wide	m²	0.58	14.17	–	22.06	36.23	15.59	–	24.27	39.85
4011651B	not exceeding 300 mm wide	m²	0.85	20.77	–	23.05	43.82	22.85	–	25.36	48.20
4011653	**Gyproc DriLyner system; 40 mm Tri-line laminate board; fixed with adhesive dab masonry walls; taped butt joints:**										
4011653A	over 300 mm wide	m²	0.68	16.62	–	26.12	42.74	18.28	–	28.73	47.01
4011653B	not exceeding 300 mm wide	m²	0.95	23.21	–	27.31	50.52	25.53	–	30.04	55.57
4011655	**Gyproc DriLyner system; 50 mm Tri-line laminate board; fixed with adhesive dab to masonry walls; taped butt joints:**										
4011655A	over 300 mm wide	m²	0.85	20.76	–	31.23	51.99	22.84	–	34.35	57.19
4011655B	not exceeding 300 mm wide	m²	1.18	28.83	–	32.65	61.48	31.71	–	35.92	67.63
40118	**FIBROUS PLASTER**										
4011802	**Ventilator; louvred; fixing to plastered wall with adhesive:**										
4011802A	225 mm × 75 mm	Each	0.15	3.66	–	2.14	5.80	4.03	–	2.35	6.38
4011802B	225 mm × 150 mm	Each	0.20	4.89	–	3.29	8.18	5.38	–	3.62	9.00
4011802C	225 mm × 225 mm	Each	0.25	6.10	–	4.48	10.58	6.71	–	4.93	11.64
4011804	**Ventilator; louvred; perforated zinc flyscreen; fixing to plastered wall with adhesive:**										
4011804A	225 mm × 75 mm	Each	0.20	4.89	–	2.71	7.60	5.38	–	2.98	8.36
4011804B	225 mm × 150 mm	Each	0.25	6.11	–	3.47	9.58	6.72	–	3.82	10.54
4011804C	225 mm × 225 mm	Each	0.30	7.33	–	5.25	12.58	8.06	–	5.78	13.84
4011806	**Gyproc plaster core cornice cove; with mitres and ends; fixed with adhesive:**										
4011806A	100 mm girth	m	0.40	9.77	–	2.99	12.76	10.75	–	3.29	14.04
4011806B	127 mm girth	m	0.44	10.75	–	2.52	13.27	11.83	–	2.77	14.60

Floor, Wall and Ceiling Finishes

Small Works 2009	Unit	Labour Hours	Labour Net £	Plant Net £	Materials Net £	Unit Net £	Labour Gross £	Plant Gross £	Materials Gross £	Unit Price £
							(Gross rates include 10% profit)			
401 **NEW WORK**										
40120 **BEDS AND BACKINGS: PORTLAND CEMENT**										
4012001 Cement and sand (1:3); floated bed; laid level and to falls on concrete:										
4012001A 19 mm; over 300 mm wide	m²	0.60	14.66	–	2.70	17.36	16.13	–	2.97	19.10
4012001B 19 mm; not exceeding 300 mm wide	m²	1.20	29.31	–	2.70	32.01	32.24	–	2.97	35.21
4012001C 25 mm; over 300 mm wide	m²	0.70	17.10	–	3.68	20.78	18.81	–	4.05	22.86
4012001D 25 mm; not exceeding 300 mm wide	m²	1.40	34.20	–	4.54	38.74	37.62	–	4.99	42.61
4012001E 32 mm; over 300 mm wide	m²	0.80	19.54	–	4.54	24.08	21.49	–	4.99	26.49
4012001F 32 mm; not exceeding 300 mm wide	m²	1.60	39.09	–	5.52	44.61	43.00	–	6.07	49.07
4012001G 38 mm; over 300 mm wide	m²	0.90	21.99	–	5.52	27.51	24.19	–	6.07	30.26
4012001H 38 mm; not exceeding 300 mm wide	m²	1.80	43.97	–	5.52	49.49	48.37	–	6.07	54.44
4012001I 50 mm; over 300 mm wide	m²	1.10	26.88	–	7.11	33.99	29.57	–	7.82	37.39
4012001J 50 mm; not exceeding 300 mm wide	m²	2.20	53.75	–	7.11	60.86	59.13	–	7.82	66.95
4012002 Cement and sand (1:3) trowelled paving; laid level and to falls on concrete:										
4012002A 19 mm; over 300 mm wide	m²	0.80	19.54	–	2.70	22.24	21.49	–	2.97	24.46
4012002B 19 mm; not exceeding 300 mm wide	m²	1.60	39.09	–	2.70	41.79	43.00	–	2.97	45.97
4012002C 25 mm; over 300 mm wide	m²	0.90	21.99	–	3.68	25.67	24.19	–	4.05	28.24
4012002D 25 mm; not exceeding 300 mm wide	m²	1.80	43.97	–	3.68	47.65	48.37	–	4.05	52.42
4012002E 32 mm; over 300 mm wide	m²	1.00	24.43	–	4.54	28.97	26.87	–	4.99	31.87
4012002F 32 mm; not exceeding 300 mm wide	m²	2.00	48.86	–	4.54	53.40	53.75	–	4.99	58.74
4012002G 38 mm; over 300 mm wide	m²	1.10	26.87	–	5.52	32.39	29.56	–	6.07	35.63
4012002H 38 mm; not exceeding 300 mm wide	m²	2.20	53.74	–	5.52	59.26	59.11	–	6.07	65.19
4012002I 50 mm; over 300 mm wide	m²	1.30	31.76	–	7.11	38.87	34.94	–	7.82	42.76
4012002J 50 mm; not exceeding 300 mm wide	m²	2.60	63.52	–	7.11	70.63	69.87	–	7.82	77.69
4012006 Cement and sand (1:3); screeded backings; to walls:										
4012006A 13 mm work over 300 mm wide	m²	0.54	13.20	–	1.63	14.83	14.52	–	1.79	16.31
4012006B 13 mm work not exceeding 300 mm wide	m²	1.08	26.39	–	1.63	28.02	29.03	–	1.79	30.82
4012008 Cement and sand (1:3); trowelled backings; to walls:										
4012008A 13 mm work over 300 mm wide	m²	0.74	18.08	–	1.84	19.92	19.89	–	2.02	21.91
4012008B 13 mm work not exceeding 300 mm wide	m²	1.48	36.16	–	1.84	38.00	39.78	–	2.02	41.80

Small Works 2009		Unit	Labour Hours	Labour Net	Plant Net	Materials Net	Unit Net	Labour Gross	Plant Gross	Materials Gross	Unit Price
								(Gross rates include 10% profit)			
				£	£	£	£	£	£	£	£
401	**NEW WORK**										
40122	**LATEX SCREEDS**										
4012201	**Latex cement; screeded bed; laid level and to falls on existing concrete:**										
4012201A	3 mm; over 300 mm wide ..	m²	0.20	4.89	–	5.28	10.17	5.38	–	5.81	11.19
4012201B	3 mm; not exceeding 300 mm wide	m²	0.40	9.77	–	5.28	15.05	10.75	–	5.81	16.56
4012201C	5 mm; over 300 mm wide ..	m²	0.26	6.36	–	8.91	15.27	7.00	–	9.80	16.80
4012201D	5 mm; not exceeding 300 mm wide	m²	0.52	12.71	–	8.91	21.62	13.98	–	9.80	23.78
40124	**INSULATING SCREEDS**										
4012401	**Lightweight concrete screed; cement and vermiculite aggregate (1:8) on 13 mm cement and sand (1:4) screeded bed; laid level and to falls:**										
4012401A	25 mm; over 300 mm wide .	m²	0.25	6.10	–	4.17	10.27	6.71	–	4.59	11.30
4012401B	25 mm; not exceeding 300 mm wide	m²	0.50	12.21	–	4.17	16.38	13.43	–	4.59	18.02
4012401C	38 mm; over 300 mm wide .	m²	0.30	7.33	–	7.30	14.63	8.06	–	8.03	16.09
4012401D	38 mm; not exceeding 300 mm wide	m²	0.60	14.66	–	7.30	21.96	16.13	–	8.03	24.16
4012401E	50 mm; over 300 mm wide .	m²	0.35	8.55	–	9.84	18.39	9.41	–	10.82	20.23
4012401F	50 mm; not exceeding 300 mm wide	m²	0.70	17.10	–	9.84	26.94	18.81	–	10.82	29.63
4012401G	75 mm; over 300 mm wide .	m²	0.45	10.99	–	15.52	26.51	12.09	–	17.07	29.16
4012401H	75 mm; not exceeding 300 mm wide	m²	0.90	21.99	–	15.52	37.51	24.19	–	17.07	41.26
40126	**SCREED REINFORCEMENT**										
4012601	**Galvanised wire netting reinforcement; 150 mm laps; placing in floors:**										
4012601A	25 mm mesh; 20 gauge wire	m²	0.12	2.93	–	5.08	8.01	3.22	–	5.59	8.81
4012601B	38 mm mesh; 19 gauge wire	m²	0.12	2.94	–	4.23	7.17	3.23	–	4.65	7.89
4012601C	50 mm mesh; 19 gauge wire	m²	0.12	2.93	–	3.97	6.90	3.22	–	4.37	7.59

Floor, Wall and Ceiling Finishes

Small Works 2009		Unit	Labour Hours	Labour Net	Plant Net	Materials Net	Unit Net	Labour Gross	Plant Gross	Materials Gross	Unit Price
								(Gross rates include 10% profit)			
				£	£	£	£	£	£	£	£
401	**NEW WORK**										
40128	**GLAZED CERAMIC WALL TILING**										
4012801	**Glazed ceramic wall tiles; fixed with adhesive; butt joints; straight both ways; flush pointing with white grout; to plastered backings; to walls:**										
4012801A	102 mm × 102 mm × 6.5 mm (Group G); over 300 mm wide	m²	2.34	57.17	–	70.25	127.42	62.89	–	77.28	140.16
4012801B	102 mm × 102 mm × 6.5 mm (Group G); not exceeding 300 mm wide	m²	4.68	114.34	–	70.25	184.59	125.77	–	77.28	203.05
4012801C	152 mm × 152 mm × 5.5 mm (Group A); over 300 mm wide	m²	1.62	39.58	–	38.40	77.98	43.54	–	42.24	85.78
4012801D	152 mm × 152 mm × 5.5 mm (Group A); not exceeding 300 mm wide	m²	3.24	79.15	–	38.40	117.55	87.07	–	42.24	129.31
4012801E	152 mm × 152 mm × 5.5 mm (Group C); over 300 mm wide	m²	1.62	39.57	–	47.26	86.83	43.53	–	51.99	95.51
4012801F	152 mm × 152 mm × 5.5 mm (Group C); not exceeding 300 mm wide	m²	3.24	79.15	–	47.26	126.41	87.07	–	51.99	139.05
4012801G	200 mm × 100 mm × 6.5 mm (Group A); over 300 mm wide	m²	1.74	42.51	–	46.24	88.75	46.76	–	50.86	97.63
4012801H	200 mm × 100 mm × 6.5 mm (Group A); not exceeding 300 mm wide	m²	3.48	85.02	–	46.24	131.26	93.52	–	50.86	144.39
4012801I	straight cutting	m	0.06	1.47	–	–	1.47	1.62	–	–	1.62
4012801J	raking cutting	m	0.12	2.93	–	–	2.93	3.22	–	–	3.22
4012801K	curved cutting	m	0.24	5.86	–	–	5.86	6.45	–	–	6.45
4012801L	cut and fit tiling around small pipe	Each	0.22	5.37	–	–	5.37	5.91	–	–	5.91
4012801M	cut and fit tiling around large pipe	Each	0.35	8.55	–	–	8.55	9.41	–	–	9.41

Small Works 2009		Unit	Labour Hours	Labour Net	Plant Net	Materials Net	Unit Net	Labour Gross	Plant Gross	Materials Gross	Unit Price
								(Gross rates include 10% profit)			
				£	£	£	£	£	£	£	£
401	**NEW WORK**										
40132	**CLAY FLOOR TILING**										
4013203	**Heather brown tiles to BS 1286; bedded and jointed in cement mortar (1:3); but joints both ways; flush pointed with grout; to cement and sand backing:**										
4013203A	194 mm × 194 mm × 12.5 mm; to floors over 300 mm wide	m²	1.20	29.32	–	44.10	73.42	32.25	–	48.51	80.76
4013203B	194 mm × 194 mm × 12.5 mm; to floors not exceeding 300 mm wide ...	m²	2.40	58.63	–	43.91	102.54	64.49	–	48.30	112.79
4013203C	150 mm × 150 mm × 19 mm; to floors; over 300 mm wide	m²	1.56	38.11	–	30.57	68.68	41.92	–	33.63	75.55
4013203D	150 mm × 150 mm × 19 mm; to floors; not exceeding 300 mm wide	m²	3.12	76.22	–	30.57	106.79	83.84	–	33.63	117.47
4013204	**Coved skirtings; rounded top edge:**										
4013204A	194 mm × 112.5 mm × 12.5 mm	m	0.54	13.20	–	12.56	25.76	14.52	–	13.82	28.34
4013204B	150 mm × 150 mm × 12.5 mm	m	0.48	11.73	–	9.33	21.06	12.90	–	10.26	23.17
4013204C	150 mm × 112.5 mm × 12.5 mm	m	0.48	11.73	–	8.73	20.46	12.90	–	9.60	22.51
4013205	**Red tiles to BS 1286; bedded and jointed in cement mortar (1:3); butt joints both ways; flush pointed with grout; to cement and sand backing:**										
4013205A	200 mm × 200 mm × 19 mm; to floors; over 300 mm wide	m²	1.15	28.09	–	56.99	85.08	30.90	–	62.69	93.59
4013205B	200 mm × 200 mm × 19 mm; to floors; not exceeding 300 mm wide	m²	2.30	56.19	–	56.99	113.18	61.81	–	62.69	124.50
4013205C	150 mm × 150 mm × 20 mm; to floors; over 300 mm wide	m²	1.56	38.11	–	44.21	82.32	41.92	–	48.63	90.55
4013205D	150 mm × 150 mm × 20 mm; to floors; not exceeding 300 mm wide	m²	3.12	76.22	–	44.21	120.43	83.84	–	48.63	132.47

Floor, Wall and Ceiling Finishes

Small Works 2009		Unit	Labour Hours	Labour Net	Plant Net	Materials Net	Unit Net	Labour Gross	Plant Gross	Materials Gross	Unit Price
								(Gross rates include 10% profit)			
				£	£	£	£	£	£	£	£
401	**NEW WORK**										
40132	**CLAY FLOOR TILING**										
4013206	**Coved skirtings; rounded top edge:**										
4013206A	194 mm × 112.5 mm × 12.5 mm	m	0.54	13.20	–	12.56	25.76	14.52	–	13.82	28.34
4013206B	150 mm × 150 mm × 12.5 mm	m	0.48	11.72	–	9.28	21.00	12.89	–	10.21	23.10
4013206C	150 mm × 112.5 mm × 12.5 mm	m	0.48	11.73	–	8.67	20.40	12.90	–	9.54	22.44
4013210	**Labours on tiling:**										
4013210A	straight cutting	m	0.06	1.47	–	–	1.47	1.62	–	–	1.62
4013210B	raking cutting	m	0.16	3.91	–	–	3.91	4.30	–	–	4.30
4013210C	curved cutting	m	0.32	7.82	–	–	7.82	8.60	–	–	8.60
4013210D	cut and fit tiling around small pipe	Each	0.50	12.22	–	–	12.22	13.44	–	–	13.44
4013210E	cut and fit tiling around large pipe	Each	0.70	17.10	–	–	17.10	18.81	–	–	18.81
4013210F	cut and fit tiling around pedestal of W.C. or lavatory basin	Each	1.00	24.43	–	–	24.43	26.87	–	–	26.87

Small Works 2009		Unit	Labour Hours	Labour Net	Plant Net	Materials Net	Unit Net	Labour Gross	Plant Gross	Materials Gross	Unit Price
								— (Gross rates include 10% profit) —			
				£	£	£	£	£	£	£	£
401	**NEW WORK**										
40134	**HARDWOOD FLOORING BY SPECIALISTS**										
4013401	**Supplying and laying 25 mm × 75 mm nominal tongued and grooved and end matched flooring, kiln dried and secret nailed to joists or battens provided by contractor. Filled, sanded and sealed by either wax finish or lacquer and then polished:**										
4013401A	Prime Canadian Maple.....	m²	1.30	36.14	–	39.38	75.52	39.75	–	43.32	83.07
4013401B	Iroko....................	m²	1.25	34.75	–	33.60	68.35	38.23	–	36.96	75.19
4013401C	American White Oak Prime .	m²	1.35	37.53	–	40.95	78.48	41.28	–	45.05	86.33
4013401D	European Oak	m²	1.30	36.14	–	34.65	70.79	39.75	–	38.12	77.87
4013401E	Merbau	m²	1.20	33.36	–	28.35	61.71	36.70	–	31.19	67.88
4013402	**Supplying and laying 22 mm × 75 mm × 225 mm solid tongued and grooved hardwood blocks in mastic composition on cement floated level concrete surfacing provided by contractor and wax polishing or sealing on completion herring-bone pattern with two-block border:**										
4013402A	Merbau	m²	1.20	33.36	–	26.63	59.99	36.70	–	29.29	65.99
4013402B	Iroko...................	m²	1.30	36.14	–	25.29	61.43	39.75	–	27.82	67.57
4013402C	American Oak Prime	m²	1.40	38.92	–	37.40	76.32	42.81	–	41.14	83.95
4013402D	Rhodesian Teak	m²	1.35	37.53	–	27.23	64.76	41.28	–	29.95	71.24
4013402E	European Oak Prime 10 mm	m²	1.48	41.15	–	33.44	74.59	45.27	–	36.78	82.05
4013403	**8 mm felt backed mosaic flooring; laid basket pattern; sanded off, preparing and wax polishing or sealing on completion:**										
4013403A	Iroko...................	m²	0.85	23.63	–	13.80	37.43	25.99	–	15.18	41.17
4013403B	Merbau	m²	0.85	23.63	–	13.54	37.17	25.99	–	14.89	40.89
4013403C	Teak	m²	0.85	23.63	–	15.89	39.52	25.99	–	17.48	43.47
4013403D	European Oak Prime	m²	0.85	23.63	–	14.06	37.69	25.99	–	15.47	41.46
4013404	**8 mm paper faced mosaic flooring; laid basket pattern; sanded off, preparing and wax polishing or sealing on completion:**										
4013404A	Iroko...................	m²	0.85	23.63	–	13.27	36.90	25.99	–	14.60	40.59
4013404B	Jatoba	m²	0.85	23.63	–	13.27	36.90	25.99	–	14.60	40.59
4013404C	Teak	m²	0.85	23.63	–	14.85	38.48	25.99	–	16.34	42.33

Floor, Wall and Ceiling Finishes

Small Works 2009		Unit	Labour Hours	Labour Net	Plant Net	Materials Net	Unit Net	Labour Gross	Plant Gross	Materials Gross	Unit Price
								(Gross rates include 10% profit)			
				£	£	£	£	£	£	£	£
401	**NEW WORK**										
40136	**FLOOR TILING AND COVERINGS BY SPECIALISTS**										
4013601	**Econoflex tiles 300 mm × 300 mm × 2 mm:**										
4013601A	series 1/2	m²	0.25	7.00	–	7.18	14.18	7.70	–	7.90	15.60
4013601B	series 4	m²	0.25	7.01	–	7.01	14.02	7.71	–	7.71	15.42
4013602	**Marleyflex International Series 700/800 floor tiles:**										
4013602A	300 mm × 300 mm × 2 mm	m²	0.28	7.85	–	9.34	17.19	8.64	–	10.27	18.91
4013602B	300 mm × 300 mm × 2.5 mm	m²	0.31	8.69	–	11.28	19.97	9.56	–	12.41	21.97
4013603	**Travertine tiles:**										
4013603A	2.5 mm	m²	0.31	8.68	–	10.80	19.48	9.55	–	11.88	21.43
4013604	**Marley Vylon vinyl tiles:**										
4013604A	300 mm × 300 mm × 2 mm	m²	0.28	7.84	–	6.96	14.80	8.62	–	7.66	16.28
4013605	**Marley HD series 2 vinyl tiles:**										
4013605A	300 mm × 300 mm × 2 mm	m²	0.28	7.84	–	6.96	14.80	8.62	–	7.66	16.28
4013606	**Marley HD series 2 vinyl sheet:**										
4013606A	2 mm thick.	m²	0.28	7.85	–	8.15	16.00	8.64	–	8.97	17.60
4013607	**Marley HD Acoustic foam backed vinyl sheeting:**										
4013607A	3 mm thick.	m²	0.42	11.77	–	8.15	19.92	12.95	–	8.97	21.91
4013608	**Marley HD format extra contract quality vinyl sheet:**										
4013608A	2 mm thick.	m²	0.42	11.77	–	16.72	28.49	12.95	–	18.39	31.34
4013609	**Marley Vynatred vinyl sheeting:**										
4013609A	felt backed	m²	0.40	11.21	–	12.82	24.03	12.33	–	14.10	26.43
4013610	**Marley Safetred Universal:**										
4013610A	sheet	m²	0.40	11.21	–	13.65	24.86	12.33	–	15.02	27.35
4013611	**Marleytex heavy contract cord carpet:**										
4013611A	needleloom CT	m²	0.40	11.20	–	14.35	25.55	12.32	–	15.79	28.11
4013612	**Gradus PVC skirting:**										
4013612A	70 mm	m²	0.15	4.20	–	1.53	5.73	4.62	–	1.68	6.30
4013612B	100 mm	m²	0.12	3.36	–	3.95	7.31	3.70	–	4.35	8.04
4013612C	100 mm, set in	m²	0.23	6.44	–	2.63	9.07	7.08	–	2.89	9.98

Small Works 2009		Unit	Labour Hours	Labour Net	Plant Net	Materials Net	Unit Net	Labour Gross	Plant Gross	Materials Gross	Unit Price
								(Gross rates include 10% profit)			
				£	£	£	£	£	£	£	£
401	**NEW WORK**										
40138	**CARPETING**										
4013801	**Take up loose carpet; set aside:**										
4013801A	loose lay	m²	0.03	0.73	–	–	0.73	0.80	–	–	0.80
4013801B	gripper battens	m²	0.04	0.98	–	–	0.98	1.08	–	–	1.08
4013801C	stuck around edge	m²	0.05	1.22	–	–	1.22	1.34	–	–	1.34
4013801D	stuck direct	m²	0.10	2.44	–	–	2.44	2.68	–	–	2.68
4013802	**Lay only carpet:**										
4013802A	loose lay	m²	0.03	0.73	–	–	0.73	0.80	–	–	0.80
4013802B	gripper battens	m²	0.05	1.22	–	–	1.22	1.34	–	–	1.34
4013802C	stuck around edge	m²	0.07	1.71	–	0.08	1.79	1.88	–	0.09	1.97
4013802D	stuck direct	m²	0.13	3.18	–	1.16	4.34	3.50	–	1.28	4.77
4013804	**Fitted carpeting; domestic grade; to floors over 300 mm wide:**										
4013804A	loose lay	m²	0.30	7.33	–	62.55	69.88	8.06	–	68.81	76.87
4013804B	gripper battens	m²	0.35	8.55	–	62.55	71.10	9.41	–	68.81	78.21
4013804C	stuck around edge	m²	0.40	9.77	–	62.63	72.40	10.75	–	68.89	79.64
4013804D	stuck direct	m²	0.60	14.66	–	63.27	77.93	16.13	–	69.60	85.72
4013805	**Fitted carpeting; domestic grade; to floors not exceeding 300 mm wide:**										
4013805A	loose lay	m²	0.35	8.55	–	62.55	71.10	9.41	–	68.81	78.21
4013805B	gripper battens	m²	0.40	9.77	–	62.55	72.32	10.75	–	68.81	79.55
4013805C	stuck around edge	m²	0.45	10.99	–	62.63	73.62	12.09	–	68.89	80.98
4013805D	stuck direct	m²	0.65	15.88	–	62.61	78.49	17.47	–	68.87	86.34
4013806	**Fitted carpeting; domestic grade; to treads and risers over 300 mm wide:**										
4013806A	gripper battens	m²	1.40	34.20	–	62.55	96.75	37.62	–	68.81	106.43
4013808	**Underlay to carpeting; to floors:**										
4013808A	over 300 mm wide	m²	0.18	4.40	–	10.15	14.55	4.84	–	11.17	16.01
4013808B	not exceeding 300 mm wide	m²	0.20	4.89	–	10.15	15.04	5.38	–	11.17	16.54
4013809	**Tackless wood gripper; fixing carpet:**										
4013809A	to perimeter of floor	m	0.10	2.44	–	–	2.44	2.68	–	–	2.68
4013810	**Cutting carpet:**										
4013810A	raking cutting	m	0.10	2.44	–	–	2.44	2.68	–	–	2.68
4013810B	curved cutting............	m	0.15	3.66	–	–	3.66	4.03	–	–	4.03
4013812	**Aluminium cover strip:**										
4013812A	to openings	m	0.15	3.66	–	5.24	8.90	4.03	–	5.76	9.79

Floor, Wall and Ceiling Finishes

Small Works 2009		Unit	Labour Hours	Labour Net	Plant Net	Materials Net	Unit Net	Labour Gross	Plant Gross	Materials Gross	Unit Price
								(Gross rates include 10% profit)			
				£	£	£	£	£	£	£	£
402	**REPAIRS AND ALTERATIONS**										
40201	**REMOVE SURFACE FINISHES**										
4020101	**Floors:**										
4020101A	linoleum sheeting.........	m²	0.12	2.50	–	–	2.50	2.75	–	–	2.75
4020101B	carpet and underlay	m²	0.13	2.71	–	–	2.71	2.98	–	–	2.98
4020101C	screed	m²	0.50	10.43	–	–	10.43	11.47	–	–	11.47
4020101D	granolithic and screed	m²	0.67	13.97	–	–	13.97	15.37	–	–	15.37
4020101E	terrazzo or ceramic tiles; screed	m²	1.10	22.94	–	–	22.94	25.23	–	–	25.23
4020102	**Walls:**										
4020102A	plasterboard	m²	0.45	9.38	–	–	9.38	10.32	–	–	10.32
4020102B	plaster	m²	0.22	4.59	–	–	4.59	5.05	–	–	5.05
4020102C	cement rendering; pebbledashing	m²	0.45	9.38	–	–	9.38	10.32	–	–	10.32
4020102D	tiling and screed	m²	0.55	11.47	–	–	11.47	12.62	–	–	12.62
4020103	**Ceilings:**										
4020103A	plasterboard and skim including withdrawing nails	m²	0.33	6.88	–	–	6.88	7.57	–	–	7.57
4020103B	wood lath and plaster including withdrawing nails	m²	0.55	11.47	–	–	11.47	12.62	–	–	12.62
4020103C	suspended................	m²	0.83	17.31	–	–	17.31	19.04	–	–	19.04
4020103D	plaster moulded cornice; per 25 mm girth.............	m	0.17	3.54	–	–	3.54	3.89	–	–	3.89
40202	**PREPARE SURFACES**										
4020201	**Prepare surface to be sound and clean, apply Unibond universal pva adhesive an sealer to receive plaster or cement rendering:**										
4020201A	walls; existing cement and sand base over 300 mm wide	m²	0.30	7.33	–	0.81	8.14	8.06	–	0.89	8.95
4020201B	walls; existing glazed tile base over 300 mm wide....	m²	0.24	5.87	–	0.54	6.41	6.46	–	0.59	7.05
4020201C	walls; existing painted base over 300 mm wide	m²	0.28	6.84	–	0.63	7.47	7.52	–	0.69	8.22
4020201D	walls; existing concrete base over 300 mm wide	m²	0.30	7.33	–	0.68	8.01	8.06	–	0.75	8.81
4020201E	ceilings; existing cement and sand base over 300 mm wide	m²	0.37	9.04	–	0.81	9.85	9.94	–	0.89	10.84
4020201F	ceilings; existing painted base over 300 mm wide....	m²	0.34	8.31	–	0.63	8.94	9.14	–	0.69	9.83
4020201G	ceilings; existing concrete base over 300 mm wide....	m²	0.37	9.04	–	0.68	9.72	9.94	–	0.75	10.69
4020202	**Hack down defective ceiling plaster and laths:**										
4020202A	clean out old nails ready for new plaster	m²	0.85	20.77	–	–	20.77	22.85	–	–	22.85
4020204	**Take down temporary boarded linings and clean joists:**										
4020204A	to ceilings	m²	0.40	8.34	–	–	8.34	9.17	–	–	9.17

Small Works 2009		Unit	Labour Hours	Labour Net	Plant Net	Materials Net	Unit Net	Labour Gross	Plant Gross	Materials Gross	Unit Price
								(Gross rates include 10% profit)			
				£	£	£	£	£	£	£	£
402	**REPAIRS AND ALTERATIONS**										
40204	**CEILING REPAIRS**										
4020401	**Expanded metal lathing and 13 mm Carlite plaster to:**										
4020401A	ceiling joists	m²	1.70	41.53	–	11.94	53.47	45.68	–	13.13	58.82
4020403	**Thistle baseboard, scrim and 3 mm Thistle finish:**										
4020403A	to ceilings	m²	1.00	24.43	–	6.74	31.17	26.87	–	7.41	34.29
4020404	**Hack down defective ceiling plaster and fix Thistle baseboard, scrim and 3 mm Thistle finish including jointing to existing:**										
4020404A	area not exceeding 1 sq.m .	m²	2.00	48.86	–	6.74	55.60	53.75	–	7.41	61.16
4020404B	area 1-4 sq.m	m²	1.40	34.20	–	6.74	40.94	37.62	–	7.41	45.03
40206	**PLASTERWORK TO WALLS; REPAIRS**										
4020601	**Make good at intersection of wall and ceiling plaster after replastering:**										
4020601A	wall or ceiling	m	0.55	13.43	–	0.29	13.72	14.77	–	0.32	15.09
4020602	**Make good cracks in:**										
4020602A	ceiling plaster	m	0.45	10.99	–	0.29	11.28	12.09	–	0.32	12.41
4020603	**Hack brick, stone or concrete walls to form key for:**										
4020603A	plaster	m²	0.75	15.64	–	–	15.64	17.20	–	–	17.20
4020604	**Hack off wall plaster and rake out brick joints to form key for:**										
4020604A	new plaster	m²	0.75	15.64	–	–	15.64	17.20	–	–	17.20
4020605	**Rake out joints of brickwork to:**										
4020605A	form key	m²	0.40	8.34	–	–	8.34	9.17	–	–	9.17
4020606	**Dub out uneven walls to receive:**										
4020606A	new plaster	m²	0.40	9.77	–	2.00	11.77	10.75	–	2.20	12.95
4020607	**13 mm Thistle plaster on:**										
4020607A	brick or breeze walls	m²	0.85	20.77	–	3.08	23.85	22.85	–	3.39	26.24
4020610	**Hack down defective wall plaster in small quantities; apply 13 mm Thistle plaster including jointing to existing:**										
4020610A	area not exceeding 1 sq.m .	m²	1.75	42.75	–	3.08	45.83	47.03	–	3.39	50.41
4020610B	area 1-4 sq.m	m²	0.90	21.99	–	3.08	25.07	24.19	–	3.39	27.58

Floor, Wall and Ceiling Finishes

Small Works 2009		Unit	Labour Hours	Labour Net	Plant Net	Materials Net	Unit Net	Labour Gross	Plant Gross	Materials Gross	Unit Price
								(Gross rates include 10% profit)			
				£	£	£	£	£	£	£	£
402	**REPAIRS AND ALTERATIONS**										
40206	**PLASTERWORK TO WALLS; REPAIRS**										
4020611	**13 mm Thistle plaster to brick walls including:**										
4020611A	jointing new to old and a small quantity of dubbing out	m²	1.10	26.87	–	4.08	30.95	29.56	–	4.49	34.05
4020612	**Make good cracks in plaster:**										
4020612A	walls..................	m	0.45	10.99	–	0.26	11.25	12.09	–	0.29	12.38
4020612B	moulded cornice, per 25 mm girth of cornice...........	m	0.25	6.11	–	0.26	6.37	6.72	–	0.29	7.01
4020612C	around door and window frames and repoint........	m	0.40	9.77	–	0.26	10.03	10.75	–	0.29	11.03
4020613	**Hack down and re-run plaster cornices per 25 mm girth of cornice:**										
4020613A	coved.................	m	0.25	6.11	–	0.26	6.37	6.72	–	0.29	7.01
4020613B	moulded	m	0.33	8.06	–	0.26	8.32	8.87	–	0.29	9.15
4020614	**Make good plaster around pipes:**										
4020614A	small pipes	Each	0.30	7.33	–	0.26	7.59	8.06	–	0.29	8.35
4020614B	large pipes..............	Each	0.33	8.06	–	0.26	8.32	8.87	–	0.29	9.15

Small Works 2009		Unit	Labour Hours	Labour Net	Plant Net	Materials Net	Unit Net	Labour Gross	Plant Gross	Materials Gross	Unit Price
								(Gross rates include 10% profit)			
				£	£	£	£	£	£	£	£
402	**REPAIRS AND ALTERATIONS**										
40208	**CERAMIC TILING; REPAIRS**										
4020801	**Glazed ceramic wall tiles; fixed with adhesive, pointed in white cement grout in small quantities in repairs:**										
4020801A	102 mm × 102 mm × 6.5 mm; Group G	m²	4.68	114.33	–	66.95	181.28	125.76	–	73.65	199.41
4020801B	152 mm × 152 mm × 5.5 mm; Group B.............	m²	3.24	79.15	–	35.93	115.08	87.07	–	39.52	126.59
4020804	**Hack off glazed tiles to wall in:**										
4020804A	detached areas 2.0-5.0 sq.m	m²	1.00	20.85	–	–	20.85	22.94	–	–	22.94
4020804B	patches 0.5-2.0 sq.m......	Each	2.50	52.13	–	–	52.13	57.34	–	–	57.34
4020804C	single tiles in patches up to 0.5 sq.m	Each	0.30	6.26	–	–	6.26	6.89	–	–	6.89
4020805	**Take out broken angle beads horizontal or vertical and renew:**										
4020805A	150 mm × 25 mm	Each	0.18	4.40	–	0.35	4.75	4.84	–	0.39	5.23
4020805B	150 mm × 50 mm moulded cappings	Each	0.20	4.88	–	0.53	5.41	5.37	–	0.58	5.95
4020806	**Holes through wall tiling, any colour, and make good:**										
4020806A	for small pipes	Each	0.28	5.84	–	–	5.84	6.42	–	–	6.42
4020806B	for large pipes...........	Each	0.38	7.92	–	–	7.92	8.71	–	–	8.71
4020807	**Stripping loose tiles and cleaning:**										
4020807A	for reuse	m²	0.40	8.34	–	–	8.34	9.17	–	–	9.17
4020808	**Refixing only salvaged tiles:**										
4020808A	with adhesive	m²	2.25	54.97	–	1.91	56.88	60.47	–	2.10	62.57

Floor, Wall and Ceiling Finishes

Small Works 2009		Unit	Labour Hours	Labour Net	Plant Net	Materials Net	Unit Net	Labour Gross	Plant Gross	Materials Gross	Unit Price
								(Gross rates include 10% profit)			
				£	£	£	£	£	£	£	£
402	**REPAIRS AND ALTERATIONS**										
40209	**RENDERING; REPAIRS**										
4020901	**Hack off defective rendering to concreted areas; grout and render in cement mortar:**										
4020901A	19 mm thick	m²	1.00	24.43	–	2.28	26.71	26.87	–	2.51	29.38
4020902	**Hack off and renew cement rendered plinth:**										
4020902A	225 mm high including joints new to old	m	0.30	7.33	–	0.49	7.82	8.06	–	0.54	8.60
4020903	**Cut out cracks in Snowcrete or rough cast rendering:**										
4020903A	make good to existing	m	0.80	19.54	–	0.51	20.05	21.49	–	0.56	22.06
4020903B	make good to existing to match adjacent work around reset window and door frames	m	0.48	11.73	–	0.17	11.90	12.90	–	0.19	13.09
4020905	**Hack off defective rendering, prepare for and re-render in cement and sand (1:3); plain face:**										
4020905A	to walls	m²	1.00	24.43	–	2.38	26.81	26.87	–	2.62	29.49
4020907	**Hack off broken cement rendering and renew rendering to:**										
4020907A	three-sided curb to gulley ..	Each	0.90	21.99	–	2.29	24.28	24.19	–	2.52	26.71
4020908	**Hack off all loose rendering, hack back brick (or concrete) to form key and re-render with cement and sand (1:3), plain face including reproducing all profiles and ruled joints:**										
4020908A	to match existing	m²	2.00	48.86	–	2.38	51.24	53.75	–	2.62	56.36
4020908B	to match existing in patches not exceeding 1 sq.m......	Each	2.50	61.07	–	2.38	63.45	67.18	–	2.62	69.80

PLUMBING AND HEATING

Small Works 2009		Unit	Labour Hours	Labour Net	Plant Net	Materials Net	Unit Net	Labour Gross	Plant Gross	Materials Gross	Unit Price
								(Gross rates include 10% profit)			
				£	£	£	£	£	£	£	£
501	**NEW WORK**										
50120	**GUTTERWORK AND FITTINGS**										
5012001	**UPVC Osma Mini-Fit 3/2 System; fixing with standard brackets:**										
5012001A	75 mm	m	0.25	8.98	–	5.41	14.39	9.88	–	5.95	15.83
5012001B	Extra for stopend outlet	Each	0.15	5.39	–	6.13	11.52	5.93	–	6.74	12.67
5012001C	Extra for stopend; external .	Each	0.13	4.67	–	2.12	6.79	5.14	–	2.33	7.47
5012001D	Extra for running outlet	Each	0.25	8.98	–	6.23	15.21	9.88	–	6.85	16.73
5012001E	Extra for angle.	Each	0.25	8.98	–	6.13	15.11	9.88	–	6.74	16.62
5012002	**UPVC Osma Round Line 4 1/2 2 1/2 System; fixing with standard brackets:**										
5012002A	112 mm	m	0.27	9.70	–	6.46	16.16	10.67	–	7.11	17.78
5012002B	Extra for swivelock running outlet; straight	Each	0.27	9.70	–	6.78	16.48	10.67	–	7.46	18.13
5012002C	Extra for stopend; external .	Each	0.15	5.39	–	4.17	9.56	5.93	–	4.59	10.52
5012002D	Extra for angle.	Each	0.27	9.70	–	7.85	17.55	10.67	–	8.64	19.31
5012002F	Extra for connector to cast iron half round gutter.	Each	0.29	10.42	–	6.55	16.97	11.46	–	7.21	18.67
5012002G	Extra for connector to cast iron ogee gutter	Each	0.29	10.41	–	10.37	20.78	11.45	–	11.41	22.86
5012003	**UPVC Osma Super Line 5/2 1/2 System; fixing with standard brackets:**										
5012003A	125 mm	m	0.27	9.70	–	7.35	17.05	10.67	–	8.09	18.76
5012003B	Extra for stopend; external .	Each	0.15	5.39	–	4.69	10.08	5.93	–	5.16	11.09
5012003D	Extra for running outlet	Each	0.27	9.70	–	8.14	17.84	10.67	–	8.95	19.62
5012003E	Extra for angle.	Each	0.27	9.70	–	8.88	18.58	10.67	–	9.77	20.44
5012004	**UPVC Osma Roofline 6/4 System; fixing with standard brackets:**										
5012004A	150 mm	m	0.31	11.13	–	18.73	29.86	12.24	–	20.60	32.85
5012004B	Extra for stopend; external .	Each	0.17	6.10	–	10.09	16.19	6.71	–	11.10	17.81
5012004C	Extra for running outlet	Each	0.29	10.42	–	20.35	30.77	11.46	–	22.39	33.85
5012004D	Extra for angle.	Each	0.29	10.42	–	28.15	38.57	11.46	–	30.97	42.43
5012005	**UPVC Osma Squareline 4/2 1/4 System; fixing with standard brackets:**										
5012005A	100 mm	m	0.27	9.70	–	7.00	16.70	10.67	–	7.70	18.37
5012005B	Extra for stopend; external .	Each	0.15	5.38	–	2.42	7.80	5.92	–	2.66	8.58
5012005C	Extra for running outlet	Each	0.27	9.70	–	8.70	18.40	10.67	–	9.57	20.24
5012005D	Extra for angle.	Each	0.27	9.69	–	9.62	19.31	10.66	–	10.58	21.24

Plumbing and Heating

Small Works 2009		Unit	Labour Hours	Labour Net	Plant Net	Materials Net	Unit Net	Labour Gross	Plant Gross	Materials Gross	Unit Price
				£	£	£	£	£	£	£	£
								(Gross rates include 10% profit)			
501	**NEW WORK**										
50120	**GUTTERWORK AND FITTINGS**										
5012006	**Cast iron; half round; fixing with standard brackets:**										
5012006A	100 mm	m	0.36	12.93	–	21.15	34.08	14.22	–	23.27	37.49
5012006B	Extra for stopend	Each	0.19	6.83	–	4.13	10.96	7.51	–	4.54	12.06
5012006C	Extra for stopend outlet....	Each	0.21	7.54	–	9.01	16.55	8.29	–	9.91	18.21
5012006D	Extra for running outlet	Each	0.36	12.94	–	15.31	28.25	14.23	–	16.84	31.08
5012006E	Extra for angle...........	Each	0.36	12.93	–	15.65	28.58	14.22	–	17.22	31.44
5012007	**Cast iron; half round; fixing with standard brackets:**										
5012007A	115 mm	m	0.36	12.93	–	21.86	34.79	14.22	–	24.05	38.27
5012007B	Extra for stopend	Each	0.19	6.82	–	5.36	12.18	7.50	–	5.90	13.40
5012007C	Extra for stopend outlet....	Each	0.21	7.55	–	13.25	20.80	8.31	–	14.58	22.88
5012007D	Extra for running outlet	Each	0.36	12.93	–	16.41	29.34	14.22	–	18.05	32.27
5012007E	Extra for angle...........	Each	0.36	12.93	–	16.00	28.93	14.22	–	17.60	31.82
5012008	**Cast iron; half round; fixing with standard brackets:**										
5012008A	125 mm	m	0.41	14.73	–	25.01	39.74	16.20	–	27.51	43.71
5012008B	Extra for stopend	Each	0.24	8.62	–	8.70	17.32	9.48	–	9.57	19.05
5012008C	Extra for stopend outlet....	Each	0.26	9.34	–	16.64	25.98	10.27	–	18.30	28.58
5012008D	Extra for running outlet	Each	0.41	14.73	–	18.29	33.02	16.20	–	20.12	36.32
5012008E	Extra for angle...........	Each	0.41	14.73	–	18.29	33.02	16.20	–	20.12	36.32
5012009	**Cast iron; half round; fixing with standard brackets:**										
5012009A	150 mm	m	0.46	16.52	–	41.30	57.82	18.17	–	45.43	63.60
5012009B	Extra for stopend	Each	0.29	10.42	–	11.38	21.80	11.46	–	12.52	23.98
5012009C	Extra for stopend outlet....	Each	0.31	11.13	–	29.64	40.77	12.24	–	32.60	44.85
5012009D	Extra for running outlet	Each	0.46	16.52	–	30.07	46.59	18.17	–	33.08	51.25
5012009E	Extra for angle...........	Each	0.46	16.53	–	31.48	48.01	18.18	–	34.63	52.81
5012012	**Cast iron; ogee; fixing with standard brackets:**										
5012012A	100 mm	m	0.38	13.65	–	23.14	36.79	15.02	–	25.45	40.47
5012012B	Extra for stopend	Each	0.21	7.55	–	7.35	14.90	8.31	–	8.09	16.39
5012012C	Extra for stopend outlet....	Each	0.23	8.26	–	13.27	21.53	9.09	–	14.60	23.68
5012012D	Extra for running outlet	Each	0.38	13.65	–	16.26	29.91	15.02	–	17.89	32.90
5012012E	Extra for angle...........	Each	0.38	13.65	–	16.26	29.91	15.02	–	17.89	32.90
5012013	**Cast iron; ogee; fixing with standard brackets:**										
5012013A	115 mm	m	0.38	13.65	–	25.50	39.15	15.02	–	28.05	43.07
5012013B	Extra for stopend	Each	0.21	7.54	–	8.28	15.82	8.29	–	9.11	17.40
5012013C	Extra for stopend outlet....	Each	0.23	8.26	–	13.13	21.39	9.09	–	14.44	23.53
5012013D	Extra for running outlet	Each	0.38	13.65	–	17.24	30.89	15.02	–	18.96	33.98
5012013E	Extra for angle...........	Each	0.38	13.65	–	17.24	30.89	15.02	–	18.96	33.98
5012014	**Cast iron; ogee; fixing with standard brackets:**										
5012014A	125 mm	m	0.43	15.44	–	27.08	42.52	16.98	–	29.79	46.77
5012014B	Extra for stopend	Each	0.26	9.33	–	9.15	18.48	10.26	–	10.07	20.33
5012014C	Extra for stopend outlet....	Each	0.28	10.06	–	15.80	25.86	11.07	–	17.38	28.45
5012014D	Extra for running outlet	Each	0.43	15.44	–	19.39	34.83	16.98	–	21.33	38.31
5012014E	Extra for angle...........	Each	0.43	15.44	–	19.39	34.83	16.98	–	21.33	38.31

Small Works 2009		Unit	Labour Hours	Labour Net	Plant Net	Materials Net	Unit Net	Labour Gross	Plant Gross	Materials Gross	Unit Price
								(Gross rates include 10% profit)			
				£	£	£	£	£	£	£	£
501	**NEW WORK**										
50122	**RAINWATER PIPEWORK**										
5012201	**UPVC; Osma Mini-Fit 3:2 System; fixing with standard brackets:**										
5012201A	55 mm	m	0.21	7.54	–	8.34	15.88	8.29	–	9.17	17.47
5012201B	Extra for offset bend.	Each	0.15	5.39	–	3.74	9.13	5.93	–	4.11	10.04
5012201C	Extra for bend	Each	0.15	5.39	–	5.05	10.44	5.93	–	5.56	11.48
5012201E	hopper head adaptor	Each	0.13	4.67	–	5.06	9.73	5.14	–	5.57	10.70
5012201F	hopper head	Each	0.55	19.76	–	15.21	34.97	21.74	–	16.73	38.47
5012201G	connection to back inlet gulley; cement mortar (1:3)	Each	0.15	5.38	–	0.33	5.71	5.92	–	0.36	6.28
5012202	**UPVC; Osma RoundLine 4.5:2.5 System; fixing with standard brackets:**										
5012202A	68 mm	m	0.26	9.34	–	6.31	15.65	10.27	–	6.94	17.22
5012202B	Extra for offset bend.	Each	0.16	5.74	–	3.87	9.61	6.31	–	4.26	10.57
5012202D	Extra for shoe	Each	0.31	11.14	–	4.07	15.21	12.25	–	4.48	16.73
5012202E	Extra for branch	Each	0.21	7.54	–	12.30	19.84	8.29	–	13.53	21.82
5012202F	Extra for access pipe; bolted access door.	Each	0.21	7.55	–	18.30	25.85	8.31	–	20.13	28.44
5012202G	hopper head	Each	0.46	16.52	–	15.62	32.14	18.17	–	17.18	35.35
5012202H	connection to back inlet gulley; cement mortar (1:3)	Each	0.16	5.74	–	0.33	6.07	6.31	–	0.36	6.68
5012202I	connector; to 63 mm cast iron.	Each	0.19	6.83	–	6.18	13.01	7.51	–	6.80	14.31
5012202J	connector; to 82 mm pvc drain socket.	Each	0.11	3.95	–	8.64	12.59	4.35	–	9.50	13.85
5012202K	universal connector to 110 mm pvc drain.	Each	0.11	3.95	–	6.36	10.31	4.35	–	7.00	11.34
5012203	**UPVC; Osma SquareLine 4:2.25 System; fixing with standard brackets:**										
5012203A	61 mm	m	0.26	9.34	–	6.55	15.89	10.27	–	7.21	17.48
5012203B	Extra for offset bend.	Each	0.16	5.74	–	4.06	9.80	6.31	–	4.47	10.78
5012203D	Extra for shoe	Each	0.31	11.13	–	5.69	16.82	12.24	–	6.26	18.50
5012203E	Extra for branch	Each	0.21	7.55	–	13.76	21.31	8.31	–	15.14	23.44
5012203F	adaptor; square to round. . .	Each	0.11	3.96	–	5.44	9.40	4.36	–	5.98	10.34
5012203G	hopper head	Each	0.41	14.72	–	17.34	32.06	16.19	–	19.07	35.27
5012203H	connection to back inlet gulley; cement mortar (1:3)	Each	0.16	5.74	–	0.33	6.07	6.31	–	0.36	6.68
5012203I	connector; to 82 mm pvc drain socket.	Each	0.21	7.54	–	8.64	16.18	8.29	–	9.50	17.80
5012203J	universal connector to 110 mm pvc drain.	Each	0.21	7.55	–	5.30	12.85	8.31	–	5.83	14.14
5012203K	Access pipe: bolted access door	Each	0.21	7.55	–	18.86	26.41	8.31	–	20.75	29.05

Plumbing and Heating

		Unit	Labour Hours	Labour Net	Plant Net	Materials Net	Unit Net	Labour Gross	Plant Gross	Materials Gross	Unit Price
								(Gross rates include 10% profit)			
				£	£	£	£	£	£	£	£
501	**NEW WORK**										
50122	**RAINWATER PIPEWORK**										
5012205	**Cast iron; round; fixing with standard holder bats:**										
5012205A	65 mm	m	0.29	10.42	–	45.61	56.03	11.46	–	50.17	61.63
5012205B	Extra for bend	Each	0.19	6.83	–	17.13	23.96	7.51	–	18.84	26.36
5012205C	Extra for branch	Each	0.24	8.62	–	36.44	45.06	9.48	–	40.08	49.57
5012205F	Extra for offset; 150 mm projection	Each	0.24	8.62	–	26.23	34.85	9.48	–	28.85	38.34
5012205G	Extra for offset; 230 mm projection	Each	0.24	8.62	–	30.55	39.17	9.48	–	33.61	43.09
5012205H	Extra for shoe	Each	0.34	12.21	–	28.00	40.21	13.43	–	30.80	44.23
5012205J	hopper head; flat back	Each	0.41	14.73	–	15.10	29.83	16.20	–	16.61	32.81
5012205L	connection to back inlet gulley; cement mortar (1:3)	Each	0.16	5.74	–	0.33	6.07	6.31	–	0.36	6.68
5012206	**Cast iron; round; fixing with standard holder bats:**										
5012206A	75 mm	m	0.36	12.93	–	45.61	58.54	14.22	–	50.17	64.39
5012206B	Extra for bend	Each	0.26	9.34	–	18.91	28.25	10.27	–	20.80	31.08
5012206C	Extra for branch	Each	0.31	11.14	–	36.44	47.58	12.25	–	40.08	52.34
5012206F	Extra for offset; 150 mm projection	Each	0.31	11.13	–	26.23	37.36	12.24	–	28.85	41.10
5012206G	Extra for offset; 230 mm projection	Each	0.31	11.14	–	30.55	41.69	12.25	–	33.61	45.86
5012206H	Extra for shoe	Each	0.41	14.73	–	24.27	39.00	16.20	–	26.70	42.90
5012206J	hopper head; flat back	Each	0.41	14.72	–	21.87	36.59	16.19	–	24.06	40.25
5012206L	connection to back inlet gulley; cement mortar (1:3)	Each	0.18	6.46	–	0.33	6.79	7.11	–	0.36	7.47
5012207	**Cast iron; round; fixing with standard holder bats:**										
5012207A	100 mm	m	0.41	14.72	–	62.08	76.80	16.19	–	68.29	84.48
5012207B	Extra for bend	Each	0.31	11.13	–	29.40	40.53	12.24	–	32.34	44.58
5012207C	Extra for branch	Each	0.36	12.93	–	43.30	56.23	14.22	–	47.63	61.85
5012207F	Extra for offset; 150 mm projection	Each	0.36	12.93	–	49.48	62.41	14.22	–	54.43	68.65
5012207G	Extra for offset; 230 mm projection	Each	0.36	12.93	–	59.94	72.87	14.22	–	65.93	80.16
5012207H	Extra for shoe	Each	0.46	16.52	–	32.73	49.25	18.17	–	36.00	54.18
5012207J	hopper head; flat back	Each	0.41	14.73	–	55.06	69.79	16.20	–	60.57	76.77
5012207L	connection to back inlet gulley; cement mortar (1:3)	Each	0.21	7.55	–	0.54	8.09	8.31	–	0.59	8.90
50124	**RAINWATER ANCILLARIES**										
5012402	**Balloon guards; plastic coated wire:**										
5012402A	50 mm	Each	0.14	5.03	–	3.00	8.03	5.53	–	3.30	8.83
5012402B	65 mm	Each	0.16	5.75	–	3.00	8.75	6.33	–	3.30	9.63
5012402C	75 mm	Each	0.18	6.47	–	3.09	9.56	7.12	–	3.40	10.52
5012402D	100 mm	Each	0.21	7.54	–	3.28	10.82	8.29	–	3.61	11.90
5012402E	150 mm	Each	0.24	8.62	–	7.72	16.34	9.48	–	8.49	17.97

Small Works 2009		Unit	Labour Hours	Labour Net	Plant Net	Materials Net	Unit Net	Labour Gross	Plant Gross	Materials Gross	Unit Price
								(Gross rates include 10% profit)			
				£	£	£	£	£	£	£	£
501	**NEW WORK**										
50126	**SOIL AND VENT PIPEWORK**										
5012601	**UPVC; OsmaSoil ring seal; fixing with standard brackets:**										
5012601A	82 mm	m	0.34	12.21	–	16.05	28.26	13.43	–	17.66	31.09
5012601B	Extra for bend	Each	0.31	11.14	–	17.60	28.74	12.25	–	19.36	31.61
5012601C	Extra for offset bend.	Each	0.31	11.13	–	13.69	24.82	12.24	–	15.06	27.30
5012601D	Extra for branch	Each	0.36	12.93	–	25.35	38.28	14.22	–	27.89	42.11
5012601E	Extra for bossed pipe	Each	0.26	9.34	–	12.57	21.91	10.27	–	13.83	24.10
5012601F	Extra for access pipe; bolted access door.	Each	0.36	12.93	–	29.18	42.11	14.22	–	32.10	46.32
5012601G	connection to drain; connector ring	Each	0.26	9.34	–	0.44	9.78	10.27	–	0.48	10.76
5012602	**UPVC; OsmaSoil ring seal; fixing with standard brackets:**										
5012602A	110 mm	m	0.38	13.65	–	15.09	28.74	15.02	–	16.60	31.61
5012602B	Extra for bend	Each	0.35	12.58	–	17.60	30.18	13.84	–	19.36	33.20
5012602C	Extra for offset bend.	Each	0.35	12.57	–	19.63	32.20	13.83	–	21.59	35.42
5012602D	Extra for branch	Each	0.40	14.37	–	25.90	40.27	15.81	–	28.49	44.30
5012602E	Extra for bossed pipe	Each	0.35	12.57	–	15.32	27.89	13.83	–	16.85	30.68
5012602F	Extra for access pipe; bossed; screwed	Each	0.35	12.58	–	28.73	41.31	13.84	–	31.60	45.44
5012602G	Extra for w.c. connecting bend.	Each	0.30	10.78	–	15.25	26.03	11.86	–	16.78	28.63
5012602H	w.c. connector	Each	0.30	10.77	–	12.99	23.76	11.85	–	14.29	26.14
5012602I	connection to drain; connector ring	Each	0.30	10.78	–	9.51	20.29	11.86	–	10.46	22.32
5012603	**Cast iron; Timesaver System; flexible joints; fixing with holderbats:**										
5012603A	50 mm	m	0.41	14.73	–	31.68	46.41	16.20	–	34.85	51.05
5012603B	Extra for bend	Each	0.31	11.14	–	18.16	29.30	12.25	–	19.98	32.23
5012603C	Extra for access bend.	Each	0.31	11.13	–	44.75	55.88	12.24	–	49.23	61.47
5012603D	Extra for branch; single	Each	0.36	12.93	–	27.31	40.24	14.22	–	30.04	44.26
5012603F	Extra for access pipe; oval door	Each	0.31	11.14	–	43.69	54.83	12.25	–	48.06	60.31
5012603J	roof connector; for asphalt .	Each	0.41	14.73	–	82.46	97.19	16.20	–	90.71	106.91
5012603M	connection to stoneware drain; cement mortar (1:3) joint	Each	0.16	5.74	–	0.33	6.07	6.31	–	0.36	6.68

Plumbing and Heating

<table>

Small Works 2009		Unit	Labour Hours	Labour Net	Plant Net	Materials Net	Unit Net	Labour Gross	Plant Gross	Materials Gross	Unit Price
								(Gross rates include 10% profit)			
				£	£	£	£	£	£	£	£
501	**NEW WORK**										
50126	**SOIL AND VENT PIPEWORK**										
5012604	**Cast iron; Timesaver System; flexible joints; fixing with holderbats:**										
5012604A	75 mm	m	0.46	16.53	–	31.65	48.18	18.18	–	34.82	53.00
5012604B	Extra for bend	Each	0.36	12.94	–	18.16	31.10	14.23	–	19.98	34.21
5012604C	Extra for access bend.	Each	0.36	12.93	–	44.75	57.68	14.22	–	49.23	63.45
5012604D	Extra for branch; single	Each	0.41	14.73	–	27.31	42.04	16.20	–	30.04	46.24
5012604E	Extra for branch; double . . .	Each	0.46	16.52	–	45.97	62.49	18.17	–	50.57	68.74
5012604F	Extra for access pipe; round door	Each	0.36	12.93	–	43.69	56.62	14.22	–	48.06	62.28
5012604H	Extra for offset; 150 mm projection	Each	0.41	14.73	–	22.37	37.10	16.20	–	24.61	40.81
5012604I	Extra for offset; 300 mm projection	Each	0.46	16.53	–	22.37	38.90	18.18	–	24.61	42.79
5012604K	roof connector; for asphalt .	Each	0.46	16.52	–	49.75	66.27	18.17	–	54.73	72.90
5012604M	roof outlet; circular; flat grate	Each	0.51	18.32	–	119.87	138.19	20.15	–	131.86	152.01
5012604N	connection to stoneware drain; cement mortar (1:3) joint	Each	0.18	6.46	–	0.44	6.90	7.11	–	0.48	7.59
5012605	**Cast iron; Timesaver System; flexible joints; fixing with holderbats:**										
5012605A	100 mm	m	0.56	20.12	–	37.62	57.74	22.13	–	41.38	63.51
5012605B	Extra for bend	Each	0.46	16.53	–	25.13	41.66	18.18	–	27.64	45.83
5012605C	Extra for access bend.	Each	0.46	16.52	–	53.16	69.68	18.17	–	58.48	76.65
5012605D	Extra for branch; single	Each	0.51	18.32	–	38.86	57.18	20.15	–	42.75	62.90
5012605E	Extra for branch; double . . .	Each	0.56	20.11	–	48.07	68.18	22.12	–	52.88	75.00
5012605F	Extra for access pipe; round door	Each	0.46	16.52	–	45.97	62.49	18.17	–	50.57	68.74
5012605H	Extra for offset; 150 mm projection	Each	0.51	18.32	–	31.51	49.83	20.15	–	34.66	54.81
5012605I	Extra for offset; 300 mm projection	Each	0.56	20.11	–	40.72	60.83	22.12	–	44.79	66.91
5012605K	w.c. connecting pipe	Each	0.51	18.32	–	27.35	45.67	20.15	–	30.09	50.24
5012605L	roof connector; for asphalt .	Each	0.56	20.11	–	43.85	63.96	22.12	–	48.24	70.36
5012605M	roof connector; for felt.	Each	0.56	20.12	–	137.54	157.66	22.13	–	151.29	173.43
5012605N	roof outlet; circular; flat grate	Each	0.61	21.92	–	144.80	166.72	24.11	–	159.28	183.39
5012605O	connection to stoneware drain; cement mortar (1:3) joint	Each	0.21	7.55	–	0.54	8.09	8.31	–	0.59	8.90

</table>

Small Works 2009		Unit	Labour Hours	Labour Net	Plant Net	Materials Net	Unit Net	Labour Gross	Plant Gross	Materials Gross	Unit Price
				£	£	£	£	£	£	£	£
								(Gross rates include 10% profit)			
501	**NEW WORK**										
50128	**WASTE PIPEWORK**										
5012801	**ABS; OsmaWeld System; solvent welded joints; fixing with clips or brackets:**										
5012801A	32 mm	m	0.25	8.98	–	2.93	11.91	9.88	–	3.22	13.10
5012801C	bend	Each	0.23	8.26	–	4.54	12.80	9.09	–	4.99	14.08
5012801F	tee	Each	0.26	9.34	–	2.85	12.19	10.27	–	3.14	13.41
5012801H	straight tank connector	Each	0.25	8.98	–	3.59	12.57	9.88	–	3.95	13.83
5012801I	bottle trap; 38 mm seal	Each	0.26	9.34	–	5.95	15.29	10.27	–	6.55	16.82
5012801J	bottle trap; 76 mm seal	Each	0.26	9.33	–	7.42	16.75	10.26	–	8.16	18.43
5012801K	tubular P trap; 76 mm seal	Each	0.28	10.06	–	5.62	15.68	11.07	–	6.18	17.25
5012801L	tubular S trap; 76 mm seal	Each	0.28	10.06	–	6.88	16.94	11.07	–	7.57	18.63
5012802	**ABS; OsmaWeld System; solvent welded joints; fixing with clips or brackets:**										
5012802A	40 mm	m	0.28	10.06	–	3.46	13.52	11.07	–	3.81	14.87
5012802C	bend	Each	0.25	8.98	–	2.14	11.12	9.88	–	2.35	12.23
5012802F	tee	Each	0.29	10.41	–	3.12	13.53	11.45	–	3.43	14.88
5012802H	straight tank connector	Each	0.27	9.70	–	3.94	13.64	10.67	–	4.33	15.00
5012802I	bottle trap; 38 mm seal	Each	0.31	11.13	–	7.29	18.42	12.24	–	8.02	20.26
5012802J	bottle trap; 76 mm seal	Each	0.31	11.14	–	9.08	20.22	12.25	–	9.99	22.24
5012802K	tubular P trap; 76 mm seal	Each	0.33	11.86	–	6.74	18.60	13.05	–	7.41	20.46
5012802L	tubular S trap; 76 mm seal	Each	0.33	11.85	–	9.26	21.11	13.04	–	10.19	23.22
5012802N	bath trap; 76 mm seal	Each	0.34	12.21	–	9.57	21.78	13.43	–	10.53	23.96
5012802P	washing machine half trap; 76 mm seal	Each	0.41	14.73	–	10.21	24.94	16.20	–	11.23	27.43
5012803	**ABS; OsmaWeld System; solvent welded joints; fixing with clips or brackets:**										
5012803A	50 mm	m	0.31	11.13	–	8.57	19.70	12.24	–	9.43	21.67
5012803B	bend	Each	0.27	9.70	–	3.27	12.97	10.67	–	3.60	14.27
5012803E	tee	Each	0.31	11.14	–	4.50	15.64	12.25	–	4.95	17.20
5012804	**Polypropylene; Osma ClearBore System; ring seal socket joints; fixing with clips or brackets:**										
5012804A	32 mm	m	0.22	7.90	–	2.11	10.01	8.69	–	2.32	11.01
5012804C	bend	Each	0.20	7.18	–	2.62	9.80	7.90	–	2.88	10.78
5012804E	tee	Each	0.23	8.26	–	3.75	12.01	9.09	–	4.13	13.21
5012804F	straight tank connector	Each	0.26	9.34	–	3.74	13.08	10.27	–	4.11	14.39
5012804G	bottle trap; 38 mm seal	Each	0.26	9.34	–	4.90	14.24	10.27	–	5.39	15.66
5012804H	bottle trap; 76 mm seal	Each	0.26	9.34	–	5.65	14.99	10.27	–	6.22	16.49
5012804I	tubular P trap; 76 mm seal	Each	0.28	10.06	–	5.20	15.26	11.07	–	5.72	16.79
5012804J	tubular S trap; 76 mm seal	Each	0.28	10.05	–	6.25	16.30	11.06	–	6.88	17.93

Plumbing and Heating

Small Works 2009		Unit	Labour Hours	Labour Net	Plant Net	Materials Net	Unit Net	Labour Gross	Plant Gross	Materials Gross	Unit Price
								(Gross rates include 10% profit)			
				£	£	£	£	£	£	£	£
501	**NEW WORK**										
50128	**WASTE PIPEWORK**										
5012805	**Polypropylene; Osma ClearBore System; ring seal socket joints; fixing with clips or brackets:**										
5012805A	40 mm	m	0.25	8.98	–	2.63	11.61	9.88	–	2.89	12.77
5012805D	bend....................	Each	0.22	7.90	–	2.94	10.84	8.69	–	3.23	11.92
5012805E	tee	Each	0.26	9.34	–	4.35	13.69	10.27	–	4.79	15.06
5012805F	straight tank connector	Each	0.30	10.78	–	4.07	14.85	11.86	–	4.48	16.34
5012805G	bottle trap; 38 mm seal	Each	0.31	11.14	–	6.05	17.19	12.25	–	6.66	18.91
5012805H	bottle trap; 76 mm seal	Each	0.31	11.14	–	6.70	17.84	12.25	–	7.37	19.62
5012805I	tubular P trap; 76 mm seal .	Each	0.33	11.85	–	6.27	18.12	13.04	–	6.90	19.93
5012805J	tubular S trap; 76 mm seal .	Each	0.33	11.85	–	7.58	19.43	13.04	–	8.34	21.37
5012805L	bath trap; 76 mm seal	Each	0.34	12.21	–	7.05	19.26	13.43	–	7.76	21.19
5012805N	washing machine half trap; 76 mm seal	Each	0.41	14.73	–	11.42	26.15	16.20	–	12.56	28.77
5012806	**Polypropylene; Osma ClearBore System; ring seal socket joints; fixing with clips or brackets:**										
5012806A	50 mm	m	0.28	10.06	–	3.51	13.57	11.07	–	3.86	14.93
5012806B	bend....................	Each	0.24	8.63	–	5.16	13.79	9.49	–	5.68	15.17
5012806D	tee	Each	0.28	10.05	–	6.35	16.40	11.06	–	6.99	18.04
50130	**OVERFLOW PIPEWORK**										
5013001	**ABS; OsmaWeld System; solvent welded joints; fixing with clips or brackets:**										
5013001A	19 mm	m	0.20	7.19	–	1.50	8.69	7.91	–	1.65	9.56
5013001B	bend....................	Each	0.18	6.46	–	1.26	7.72	7.11	–	1.39	8.49
5013001C	tee	Each	0.21	7.54	–	1.36	8.90	8.29	–	1.50	9.79
5013001D	tank connector; straight ...	Each	0.21	7.54	–	1.63	9.17	8.29	–	1.79	10.09
5013001E	tank connector; bent	Each	0.21	7.55	–	1.84	9.39	8.31	–	2.02	10.33
5013002	**Polypropylene; Osma ClearBore System; ring seal socket joints; fixing with clips or brackets:**										
5013002A	19 mm	m	0.20	7.19	–	1.22	8.41	7.91	–	1.34	9.25
5013002B	bend....................	Each	0.18	6.46	–	1.26	7.72	7.11	–	1.39	8.49
5013002C	tee	Each	0.21	7.54	–	1.36	8.90	8.29	–	1.50	9.79
5013002D	tank connector; bent	Each	0.21	7.54	–	1.76	9.30	8.29	–	1.94	10.23

Small Works 2009		Unit	Labour Hours	Labour Net	Plant Net	Materials Net	Unit Net	Labour Gross	Plant Gross	Materials Gross	Unit Price
								(Gross rates include 10% profit)			
				£	£	£	£	£	£	£	£
501	**NEW WORK**										
50132	**WATER MAINS**										
5013201	**Form stopcock pit with 100 mm concrete base and with one length 102 mm clayware pipe set vertically and surrounded with concrete with 125 mm × 125 mm × 100 mm cast iron stopcock box with flanged hinged lid provide stopcock key:**										
5013201A	650 mm deep	Each	2.00	56.02	–	24.01	80.03	61.62	–	26.41	88.03
5013201B	650 mm deep with half brick sides.	Each	3.00	84.03	–	36.54	120.57	92.43	–	40.19	132.63
5013202	**Stopcock, jointing to MDPE pipe:**										
5013202A	20 mm	Each	0.23	8.26	–	11.45	19.71	9.09	–	12.60	21.68
5013202B	25 mm	Each	0.26	9.34	–	19.96	29.30	10.27	–	21.96	32.23
5013203	**Excavate trench 750 mm deep for and supply and lay Blue MDPE pressure water service pipe with push fit joints; refill and consolidate trench:**										
5013203A	20 mm	m	3.08	86.27	–	8.97	95.24	94.90	–	9.87	104.76
5013203B	25 mm	m	3.10	86.83	–	9.37	96.20	95.51	–	10.31	105.82

Plumbing and Heating

Small Works 2009		Unit	Labour Hours	Labour Net	Plant Net	Materials Net	Unit Net	Labour Gross	Plant Gross	Materials Gross	Unit Price
								(Gross rates include 10% profit)			
				£	£	£	£	£	£	£	£
501	**NEW WORK**										
50134	**SERVICE PIPEWORK: COPPER**										
5013401	**Pipes; Table Y; laid in trench:**										
5013401A	15 mm	m	0.15	5.39	–	6.54	11.93	5.93	–	7.19	13.12
5013401B	22 mm	m	0.16	5.75	–	11.61	17.36	6.33	–	12.77	19.10
5013402	**Pipes; Table X; fixing with pipe clips plugged and screwed to walls:**										
5013402A	15 mm	m	0.30	10.77	–	3.30	14.07	11.85	–	3.63	15.48
5013402B	15 mm in short lengths	m	0.32	11.49	–	3.30	14.79	12.64	–	3.63	16.27
5013402C	22 mm	m	0.31	11.14	–	6.44	17.58	12.25	–	7.08	19.34
5013402D	22 mm in short lengths	m	0.33	11.86	–	6.44	18.30	13.05	–	7.08	20.13
5013402E	28 mm	m	0.35	12.57	–	9.15	21.72	13.83	–	10.07	23.89
5013403	**Made bends:**										
5013403A	15 mm	Each	0.18	6.47	–	–	6.47	7.12	–	–	7.12
5013403B	22 mm	Each	0.24	8.62	–	–	8.62	9.48	–	–	9.48
5013403C	28 mm	Each	0.30	10.78	–	–	10.78	11.86	–	–	11.86
5013404	**Made offsets:**										
5013404A	15 mm	Each	0.48	17.24	–	–	17.24	18.96	–	–	18.96
5013404B	22 mm	Each	0.54	19.40	–	–	19.40	21.34	–	–	21.34
5013404C	28 mm	Each	0.60	21.55	–	–	21.55	23.71	–	–	23.71
5013405	**Pipes; Table Z; fixing with pipe clips plugged and screwed to walls:**										
5013405A	15 mm	m	0.30	10.78	–	3.35	14.13	11.86	–	3.69	15.54
5013405B	15 mm in short lengths	m	0.32	11.49	–	3.37	14.86	12.64	–	3.71	16.35
5013405C	22 mm	m	0.31	11.14	–	6.24	17.38	12.25	–	6.86	19.12
5013405D	22 mm in short lengths	m	0.33	11.86	–	6.24	18.10	13.05	–	6.86	19.91
5013405E	28 mm	m	0.35	12.58	–	8.34	20.92	13.84	–	9.17	23.01
5013406	**Capillary fittings; straight union couplings:**										
5013406A	15 mm	Each	0.20	7.18	–	0.42	7.60	7.90	–	0.46	8.36
5013406B	22 mm	Each	0.26	9.34	–	0.93	10.27	10.27	–	1.02	11.30
5013406C	28 mm	Each	0.34	12.21	–	1.97	14.18	13.43	–	2.17	15.60
5013408	**Capillary fittings; elbows:**										
5013408A	15 mm	Each	0.20	7.18	–	0.93	8.11	7.90	–	1.02	8.92
5013408B	22 mm	Each	0.26	9.34	–	1.93	11.27	10.27	–	2.12	12.40
5013408C	28 mm	Each	0.34	12.21	–	3.65	15.86	13.43	–	4.02	17.45
5013409	**Capillary fittings; equal tees:**										
5013409A	15 mm	Each	0.30	10.78	–	1.78	12.56	11.86	–	1.96	13.82
5013409B	22 mm	Each	0.40	14.37	–	3.74	18.11	15.81	–	4.11	19.92
5013409C	28 mm	Each	0.49	17.60	–	8.47	26.07	19.36	–	9.32	28.68

Small Works 2009		Unit	Labour Hours	Labour Net	Plant Net	Materials Net	Unit Net	Labour Gross	Plant Gross	Materials Gross	Unit Price
								(Gross rates include 10% profit)			
				£	£	£	£	£	£	£	£
501	**NEW WORK**										
50134	**SERVICE PIPEWORK: COPPER**										
5013410	**Capillary fittings; straight tap connectors:**										
5013410A	15 mm	Each	0.16	5.75	–	2.99	8.74	6.33	–	3.29	9.61
5013410B	22 mm	Each	0.20	7.18	–	15.42	22.60	7.90	–	16.96	24.86
5013411	**Capillary fittings; straight tank connectors; backnut:**										
5013411A	15 mm	Each	0.30	10.77	–	7.38	18.15	11.85	–	8.12	19.97
5013411B	22 mm	Each	0.40	14.36	–	10.93	25.29	15.80	–	12.02	27.82
5013411C	28 mm	Each	0.49	17.60	–	12.80	30.40	19.36	–	14.08	33.44
5013414	**Compression fittings; straight couplings:**										
5013414A	15 mm	Each	0.18	6.47	–	2.21	8.68	7.12	–	2.43	9.55
5013414B	22 mm	Each	0.24	8.62	–	3.70	12.32	9.48	–	4.07	13.55
5013414C	28 mm	Each	0.30	10.77	–	9.06	19.83	11.85	–	9.97	21.81
5013415	**Compression fittings; elbows:**										
5013415A	15 mm	Each	0.18	6.47	–	2.62	9.09	7.12	–	2.88	10.00
5013415B	22 mm	Each	0.24	8.62	–	4.48	13.10	9.48	–	4.93	14.41
5013415C	28 mm	Each	0.30	10.77	–	11.21	21.98	11.85	–	12.33	24.18
5013416	**Compression fittings; equal tees:**										
5013416A	15 mm	Each	0.26	9.34	–	3.60	12.94	10.27	–	3.96	14.23
5013416B	22 mm	Each	0.36	12.93	–	6.23	19.16	14.22	–	6.85	21.08
5013416C	28 mm	Each	0.44	15.80	–	19.21	35.01	17.38	–	21.13	38.51
5013418	**Compression fittings; straight swivel tap adaptors:**										
5013418A	15 mm	Each	0.14	5.03	–	4.48	9.51	5.53	–	4.93	10.46
5013418B	22 mm	Each	0.19	6.82	–	8.64	15.46	7.50	–	9.50	17.01
5013420	**Compression fittings; tank couplings; flange and locknut:**										
5013420A	15 mm	Each	0.26	9.34	–	4.54	13.88	10.27	–	4.99	15.27
5013420B	22 mm	Each	0.36	12.93	–	4.54	17.47	14.22	–	4.99	19.22
5013420C	28 mm	Each	0.44	15.80	–	12.80	28.60	17.38	–	14.08	31.46

Plumbing and Heating

Small Works 2009		Unit	Labour Hours	Labour Net	Plant Net	Materials Net	Unit Net	Labour Gross	Plant Gross	Materials Gross	Unit Price
								(Gross rates include 10% profit)			
				£	£	£	£	£	£	£	£
501	**NEW WORK**										
50136	**SERVICE PIPEWORK: GALVANISED STEEL**										
5013601	**Pipes; medium grade; screwed and socketed joints; fixing with galvanised steel clips plugged and screwed to walls:**										
5013601A	15 mm	m	0.36	12.93	–	6.33	19.26	14.22	–	6.96	21.19
5013601B	20 mm	m	0.38	13.65	–	7.89	21.54	15.02	–	8.68	23.69
5013601C	25 mm	m	0.43	15.44	–	11.30	26.74	16.98	–	12.43	29.41
5013601D	32 mm	m	0.50	17.96	–	14.28	32.24	19.76	–	15.71	35.46
5013602	**Pipes; heavy grade; screwed and socketed joints; laying in trench:**										
5013602A	15 mm	m	0.18	6.46	–	7.23	13.69	7.11	–	7.95	15.06
5013602B	20 mm	m	0.19	6.82	–	8.79	15.61	7.50	–	9.67	17.17
5013602C	25 mm	m	0.22	7.91	–	12.55	20.46	8.70	–	13.81	22.51
5013604	**Fittings; elbows:**										
5013604A	15 mm	Each	0.30	10.78	–	3.33	14.11	11.86	–	3.66	15.52
5013604B	20 mm	Each	0.40	14.36	–	4.24	18.60	15.80	–	4.66	20.46
5013604C	25 mm	Each	0.50	17.96	–	6.64	24.60	19.76	–	7.30	27.06
5013604D	32 mm	Each	0.60	21.55	–	10.67	32.22	23.71	–	11.74	35.44
5013605	**Fittings; bends:**										
5013605A	15 mm	Each	0.30	10.77	–	4.90	15.67	11.85	–	5.39	17.24
5013605B	20 mm	Each	0.40	14.37	–	6.82	21.19	15.81	–	7.50	23.31
5013605C	25 mm	Each	0.50	17.96	–	9.69	27.65	19.76	–	10.66	30.42
5013605D	32 mm	Each	0.60	21.56	–	13.67	35.23	23.72	–	15.04	38.75
5013606	**Fittings; equal tees:**										
5013606A	15 mm	Each	0.44	15.81	–	4.26	20.07	17.39	–	4.69	22.08
5013606B	20 mm	Each	0.56	20.11	–	5.79	25.90	22.12	–	6.37	28.49
5013606C	25 mm	Each	0.68	24.43	–	7.87	32.30	26.87	–	8.66	35.53
5013606D	32 mm	Each	0.80	28.74	–	12.53	41.27	31.61	–	13.78	45.40
5013607	**Fittings; longscrews complete with backut:**										
5013607A	15 mm	Each	0.44	15.81	–	9.37	25.18	17.39	–	10.31	27.70
5013607B	20 mm	Each	0.56	20.12	–	10.77	30.89	22.13	–	11.85	33.98
5013607C	25 mm	Each	0.68	24.42	–	15.38	39.80	26.86	–	16.92	43.78
5013607D	32 mm	Each	0.80	28.74	–	19.05	47.79	31.61	–	20.96	52.57

Plumbing and Heating

Small Works 2009		Unit	Labour Hours	Labour Net	Plant Net	Materials Net	Unit Net	Labour Gross	Plant Gross	Materials Gross	Unit Price
								\multicolumn — (Gross rates include 10% profit) —			
				£	£	£	£	£	£	£	£
501	**NEW WORK**										
50138	**SERVICE PIPEWORK: POLYTHENE**										
5013802	**Pipes; medium density; black; fixing with galvanised clips plugged and screwed to walls:**										
5013802A	20 mm	m	0.30	10.77	–	2.97	13.74	11.85	–	3.27	15.11
5013802B	20 mm in short lengths	m	0.32	11.50	–	3.65	15.15	12.65	–	4.02	16.67
5013802C	25 mm	m	0.34	12.21	–	3.90	16.11	13.43	–	4.29	17.72
5013802D	25 mm in short lengths	m	0.36	12.93	–	4.72	17.65	14.22	–	5.19	19.42
5013802E	32 mm	m	0.38	13.65	–	7.05	20.70	15.02	–	7.76	22.77
5013804	**Compression fittings; straight couplings:**										
5013804A	20 mm	Each	0.24	8.62	–	5.72	14.34	9.48	–	6.29	15.77
5013804B	25 mm	Each	0.30	10.77	–	6.86	17.63	11.85	–	7.55	19.39
5013804C	32 mm	Each	0.36	12.93	–	15.56	28.49	14.22	–	17.12	31.34
5013805	**Compression fittings; elbows:**										
5013805A	20 mm	Each	0.24	8.62	–	7.47	16.09	9.48	–	8.22	17.70
5013805B	25 mm	Each	0.30	10.78	–	11.00	21.78	11.86	–	12.10	23.96
5013805C	32 mm	Each	0.36	12.93	–	18.85	31.78	14.22	–	20.74	34.96
5013806	**Compression fittings; equal tees:**										
5013806A	20 mm	Each	0.36	12.94	–	10.82	23.76	14.23	–	11.90	26.14
5013806B	25 mm	Each	0.44	15.81	–	16.38	32.19	17.39	–	18.02	35.41
5013806C	32 mm	Each	0.50	17.96	–	23.35	41.31	19.76	–	25.69	45.44

Plumbing and Heating

		Unit	Labour Hours	Labour Net	Plant Net	Materials Net	Unit Net	Labour Gross	Plant Gross	Materials Gross	Unit Price
								(Gross rates include 10% profit)			
				£	£	£	£	£	£	£	£
501	**NEW WORK**										
50140	**ANCILLARIES, SCREWED JOINTS AND FITTING**										
5014001	**Bib tap; brass:**										
5014001A	13 mm	Each	0.18	6.47	–	14.59	21.06	7.12	–	16.05	23.17
5014001B	19 mm	Each	0.24	8.62	–	19.53	28.15	9.48	–	21.48	30.97
5014002	**Bib tap; chromium plated; cross top:**										
5014002A	13 mm	Each	0.31	11.13	–	27.44	38.57	12.24	–	30.18	42.43
5014002B	19 mm	Each	0.36	12.93	–	41.71	54.64	14.22	–	45.88	60.10
5014003	**Bib tap; brass; hose union:**										
5014003A	13 mm	Each	0.18	6.46	–	16.63	23.09	7.11	–	18.29	25.40
5014003B	19 mm	Each	0.24	8.62	–	28.40	37.02	9.48	–	31.24	40.72
5014004	**Pillar tap; basin and bath; chromium plated; cross top:**										
5014004A	13 mm	Each	0.31	11.13	–	27.95	39.08	12.24	–	30.75	42.99
5014004B	19 mm	Each	0.36	12.93	–	37.37	50.30	14.22	–	41.11	55.33
5014005	**Mixer tap; sink; chromium plated; deck pattern; swivel spout:**										
5014005A	13 mm	Each	0.40	14.36	–	88.37	102.73	15.80	–	97.21	113.00
5014006	**Mixer tap; basin; chromium plated; monobloc pop-up waste; fixed spout:**										
5014006A	13 mm	Each	0.50	17.96	–	107.45	125.41	19.76	–	118.20	137.95
5014007	**Mixer tap; bath; chromium plated; deck pattern; hose and handspray; fixed spout:**										
5014007A	19 mm	Each	0.70	25.15	–	95.50	120.65	27.67	–	105.05	132.72

Small Works 2009		Unit	Labour Hours	Labour Net	Plant Net	Materials Net	Unit Net	Labour Gross	Plant Gross	Materials Gross	Unit Price
								(Gross rates include 10% profit)			
				£	£	£	£	£	£	£	£
501	**NEW WORK**										
50140	**ANCILLARIES, SCREWED JOINTS AND FITTING**										
5014008	**Servicing valve; brass; compression joint for copper:**										
5014008A	13 mm	Each	0.22	7.91	–	5.67	13.58	8.70	–	6.24	14.94
5014008B	19 mm	Each	0.29	10.42	–	24.84	35.26	11.46	–	27.32	38.79
5014009	**Drain cock; brass:**										
5014009A	13 mm	Each	0.12	4.31	–	6.42	10.73	4.74	–	7.06	11.80
5014010	**Spring safety valve; brass:**										
5014010A	13 mm	Each	0.31	11.13	–	8.12	19.25	12.24	–	8.93	21.18
5014010B	19 mm	Each	0.36	12.93	–	8.87	21.80	14.22	–	9.76	23.98
5014011	**Main gas cock; brass:**										
5014011A	13 mm	Each	0.20	7.19	–	19.84	27.03	7.91	–	21.82	29.73
5014011B	19 mm	Each	0.25	8.98	–	26.53	35.51	9.88	–	29.18	39.06
5014012	**High pressure ball valve; brass; with plastic float:**										
5014012A	13 mm	Each	0.30	10.77	–	12.01	22.78	11.85	–	13.21	25.06
5014012B	19 mm	Each	0.36	12.93	–	19.50	32.43	14.22	–	21.45	35.67
5014012C	25 mm	Each	0.42	15.09	–	40.51	55.60	16.60	–	44.56	61.16
5014013	**Gate valve; brass; wheelhead:**										
5014013A	13 mm	Each	0.22	7.90	–	10.52	18.42	8.69	–	11.57	20.26
5014013B	19 mm	Each	0.29	10.41	–	12.71	23.12	11.45	–	13.98	25.43
5014013C	25 mm	Each	0.36	12.93	–	18.42	31.35	14.22	–	20.26	34.49
5014014	**Gunmetal stopcock:**										
5014014A	15 mm	Each	0.24	8.62	–	8.69	17.31	9.48	–	9.56	19.04
5014014B	22 mm	Each	0.32	11.49	–	15.19	26.68	12.64	–	16.71	29.35
5014014C	28 mm	Each	0.41	14.72	–	38.43	53.15	16.19	–	42.27	58.47

Plumbing and Heating

Small Works 2009		Unit	Labour Hours	Labour Net	Plant Net	Materials Net	Unit Net	Labour Gross	Plant Gross	Materials Gross	Unit Price
								(Gross rates include 10% profit)			
				£	£	£	£	£	£	£	£
501	**NEW WORK**										
50142	**EQUIPMENT**										
5014201	**Plastic water storage cistern; 13 mm ball valve; holes for pipes; hoisting and placing in position; complete with lid; capacity:**										
5014201A	18 litre	Each	1.15	41.31	–	23.96	65.27	45.44	–	26.36	71.80
5014201B	114 litre	Each	1.28	45.98	–	95.55	141.53	50.58	–	105.11	155.68
5014201C	227 litre	Each	1.55	55.68	–	179.95	235.63	61.25	–	197.95	259.19
5014202	**Galvanised steel open top water storage cistern; 13 mm ball valve; holes for pipes; hoisting and placing in position; capacity:**										
5014202A	227 litre	Each	1.79	64.30	–	209.22	273.52	70.73	–	230.14	300.87
5014202B	327 litre	Each	1.87	67.17	–	245.34	312.51	73.89	–	269.87	343.76
5014203	**Galvanised steel hot water tank; Grade A; bolted hand hole cover; holes for pipes; hoisting and placing in position; capacity:**										
5014203A	95 litre	Each	1.42	51.00	–	261.82	312.82	56.10	–	288.00	344.10
5014203B	123 litre	Each	1.75	62.86	–	279.61	342.47	69.15	–	307.57	376.72
5014204	**Galvanised steel; direct cylinder; Grade A with five screwed bosses; immersion heater boss; hoisting and placing in position; capacity:**										
5014204A	100 litre	Each	1.05	37.71	–	445.23	482.94	41.48	–	489.75	531.23
5014204B	136 litre	Each	1.31	47.06	–	477.89	524.95	51.77	–	525.68	577.45
5014205	**Galvanised steel indirect cylinder; Grade B; with five screwed bosses; immersion heater boss; hoisting and placing in position; capacity:**										
5014205A	109 litre	Each	1.05	37.72	–	665.10	702.82	41.49	–	731.61	773.10
5014205B	136 litre	Each	1.31	47.06	–	708.50	755.56	51.77	–	779.35	831.12
5014206	**Copper direct cylinder; Grade 3; with four bosses; immersion heater boss; hoisting and placing in position; capacity:**										
5014206A	96 litre	Each	1.10	39.51	–	196.78	236.29	43.46	–	216.46	259.92
5014206B	120 litre	Each	1.15	41.30	–	231.75	273.05	45.43	–	254.93	300.36
5014206C	166 litre	Each	1.42	51.01	–	275.22	326.23	56.11	–	302.74	358.85
5014207	**Copper indirect cylinder; Grade 3; with four bosses; immersion heater boss; hoisting and placing in position; capacity:**										
5014207A	114 litre	Each	1.15	41.30	–	252.28	293.58	45.43	–	277.51	322.94
5014207B	140 litre	Each	1.28	45.98	–	281.90	327.88	50.58	–	310.09	360.67
5014207C	162 litre	Each	1.42	51.01	–	360.05	411.06	56.11	–	396.06	452.17

Small Works 2009		Unit	Labour Hours	Labour Net	Plant Net	Materials Net	Unit Net	Labour Gross	Plant Gross	Materials Gross	Unit Price
								(Gross rates include 10% profit)			
				£	£	£	£	£	£	£	£
501	**NEW WORK**										
50142	**EQUIPMENT**										
5014208	Copper combination hot water storage units; direct pattern; insulation; four connections; immersion heater boss; drain boss; hoisting and placing in position; capacity:										
5014208A	115 litre hot; 25 litre cold...	Each	1.50	53.88	–	331.98	385.86	59.27	–	365.18	424.45
5014208B	115 litre hot; 45 litre cold...	Each	1.56	56.03	–	353.43	409.46	61.63	–	388.77	450.41
5014208C	115 litre hot; 115 litre cold .	Each	1.62	58.19	–	535.69	593.88	64.01	–	589.26	653.27
5014209	Copper combination hot water storage units; indirect pattern; insulation; four connections; immersion heater boss drain boss; hoisting and placing in position; capacity:										
5014209A	115 litre hot; 25 litre cold...	Each	1.50	53.88	–	411.63	465.51	59.27	–	452.79	512.06
5014209B	115 litre hot; 45 litre cold...	Each	1.56	56.04	–	432.76	488.80	61.64	–	476.04	537.68
5014209C	115 litre hot; 115 litre cold .	Each	1.62	58.19	–	596.05	654.24	64.01	–	655.66	719.66
5014213	Solid fuel boiler for domestic central heating and indirect hot water; white stove enamelled casing; thermostat; conventional flue; placing in position; capacity:										
5014213A	45000 Btu/h	Each	6.60	237.07	–	2234.97	2472.04	260.78	–	2458.47	2719.24
5014213B	60000 Btu/h	Each	6.60	237.08	–	2600.88	2837.96	260.79	–	2860.97	3121.76
5014214	Oil fired boiler for domestic central heating and indirect hot water; white stove enamelled casing; fully automatic; conventional flue; placing in position; capacity:										
5014214A	70000 Btu/h	Each	5.28	189.65	–	1792.62	1982.27	208.62	–	1971.88	2180.50
5014214B	90000 Btu/h	Each	5.28	189.66	–	2098.39	2288.05	208.63	–	2308.23	2516.86
5014216	Gas fired boiler for domestic central heating and indirect hot water; white stove enamelled casing; floor standing; conventional flue; placing in position; capacity:										
5014216A	output 30-40000 Btu/h	Each	4.62	165.95	–	961.03	1126.98	182.55	–	1057.13	1239.68
5014216B	output 45-60000 Btu/h	Each	4.62	165.95	–	1070.08	1236.03	182.55	–	1177.09	1359.63
5014217	Gas fired boiler for domestic central heating and indirect hot water; white stove enamelled casing; floor standing; balanced flue; placing in position; capacity:										
5014217A	output 40-50000 Btu/h	Each	5.62	201.87	–	1232.26	1434.13	222.06	–	1355.49	1577.54
5014217B	output 45-60000 Btu/h	Each	5.62	201.87	–	1388.32	1590.19	222.06	–	1527.15	1749.21
5014218	Circulator pump; domestic type:										
5014218A	all connections	Each	1.19	42.75	–	236.35	279.10	47.03	–	259.99	307.01
5014219 5014219A	**Programming control:** domestic type; combined heating and hot water system; all connections....	Each	1.32	47.42	–	124.87	172.29	52.16	–	137.36	189.52

Plumbing and Heating

Small Works 2009		Unit	Labour Hours	Labour Net	Plant Net	Materials Net	Unit Net	Labour Gross	Plant Gross	Materials Gross	Unit Price
								(Gross rates include 10% profit)			
				£	£	£	£	£	£	£	£
501	**NEW WORK**										
50142	**EQUIPMENT**										
5014220	**Oil storage tank 12 gauge mild steel; rectangular; primed finish; fill and vent holes; screwed sockets for fill, vent, sludge and draw-off; capacity:**										
5014220A	1364 litre	Each	1.52	54.60	–	364.44	419.04	60.06	–	400.88	460.94
5014220B	1818 litre	Each	1.79	64.29	–	416.90	481.19	70.72	–	458.59	529.31
5014220C	2727 litre	Each	2.05	73.64	–	521.85	595.49	81.00	–	574.04	655.04
50143	**RADIATORS**										
5014301	**Radiators; steel single panel: 600 mm high; 3 mm chromium plated air valve; 15 mm chromium plated easy clean straight valve with union; 15 mm chromium plated lockshield valve with union; concealed brackets plugged and screwed to wall: length:**										
5014301A	640 mm	Each	2.50	89.80	–	103.90	193.70	98.78	–	114.29	213.07
5014301B	800 mm	Each	2.50	89.80	–	117.58	207.38	98.78	–	129.34	228.12
5014301C	1280 mm	Each	2.75	98.78	–	158.24	257.02	108.66	–	174.06	282.72
5014301D	1760 mm	Each	2.75	98.78	–	197.11	295.89	108.66	–	216.82	325.48
50144	**SANITARY FITTINGS**										
5014401	**Sink; stainless steel; waste; overflow with chain and plastic plug; fixing to top of standard sink unit (excluding taps and trap):**										
5014401A	single bowl with single drainer; 1000 mm × 500 mm (PC 115:00)	Each	3.70	132.90	–	160.17	293.07	146.19	–	176.19	322.38
5014401B	single bowl with double drainer; 1500 mm × 500 mm (PC 135:00)	Each	3.96	142.24	–	179.90	322.14	156.46	–	197.89	354.35
5014402	**Sink; fireclay; Belfast pattern; white glazed; waste; chain and plastic plug; wall mounted on pair brackets screwed t wall (excluding taps and trap):**										
5014402A	610 mm × 455 mm × 255 mm (PC 175:00)	Each	3.23	116.02	–	249.64	365.66	127.62	–	274.60	402.23
5014402B	760 mm × 455 mm × 255 mm (PC 245:00)	Each	3.23	116.03	–	348.27	464.30	127.63	–	383.10	510.73
5014403	**Bath; white reinforced acrylic; rectangular; with cradle feet; waste; overflow with chain and plastic plug (excluding taps and trap):**										
5014403A	1700 mm long (PC 165:00)	Each	4.30	154.45	–	215.34	369.79	169.90	–	236.87	406.77

Small Works 2009		Unit	Labour Hours	Labour Net	Plant Net	Materials Net	Unit Net	Labour Gross	Plant Gross	Materials Gross	Unit Price
								(Gross rates include 10% profit)			
				£	£	£	£	£	£	£	£
501	**NEW WORK**										
50144	**SANITARY FITTINGS**										
5014404	**Bath; cast iron; white porcelain enamelled; rectangular; with cradle feet; waste; overflow with chain and plastic plug (excluding taps or trap):**										
5014404A	1700 mm long (PC 325:00).	Each	4.96	178.16	–	398.98	577.14	195.98	–	438.88	634.85
5014405	**Bath panel; enamelled hardboard; cutting to required size; fixed with chromium plated dome headed screws to timber frame:**										
5014405A	end panel................	Each	0.46	16.52	–	16.30	32.82	18.17	–	17.93	36.10
5014405B	side panel	Each	0.73	26.22	–	32.07	58.29	28.84	–	35.28	64.12
5014406	**Bath panel angle strip; polished aluminium; cut to length:**										
5014406A	fixing with chromium plated dome headed screws......	Each	0.26	9.34	–	7.02	16.36	10.27	–	7.72	18.00
5014407	**Basin; white vitreous china; 560 mm × 405 mm; waste; overflow with chain and plastic plug:**										
5014407A	wall mounted on pair of brackets screwed to wall, (excluding taps or traps) (PC 85:00)	Each	3.43	123.21	–	140.34	263.55	135.53	–	154.37	289.91
5014407B	bowl screwed to wall and bedded in mastic on pedestal mounting screwed to floor, (excluding taps or trap) (PC 120:00)	Each	4.16	149.43	–	178.87	328.30	164.37	–	196.76	361.13
5014408	**W.C. suite; white vitreous china; trapped pan screwed to floor; plastic seat and cover; plastic cistern with brackets screwed to wall; ball valve and fittings; connection to cistern and pan:**										
5014408A	high level; plastic flush pipe with clips to wall; (PC 145:00)	Each	4.26	153.02	–	212.65	365.67	168.32	–	233.92	402.24
5014408B	low level; flush bend connected (PC 115:00)	Each	4.40	158.05	–	161.29	319.34	173.86	–	177.42	351.27
5014408C	close-coupled; washdown; flush bend (PC 200:00)	Each	3.16	113.51	–	280.50	394.01	124.86	–	308.55	433.41
5014408D	close-coupled; syphonic; flush bend (PC 325:00)	Each	3.30	118.53	–	455.81	574.34	130.38	–	501.39	631.77
5014409	**Urinal; white vitreous china; white vitreous chine automatic cistern on wall hangers screwed to wall; stainless steel flush pipe with spreader; domed outlet grating:**										
5014409A	single bowl (PC 255:00) ...	Each	2.96	106.32	–	350.63	456.95	116.95	–	385.69	502.65
5014409B	single stall 610 mm × 1065 mm high (PC 515:00).	Each	5.02	180.32	–	701.24	881.56	198.35	–	771.36	969.72

Plumbing and Heating

Small Works 2009		Unit	Labour Hours	Labour Net	Plant Net	Materials Net	Unit Net	Labour Gross	Plant Gross	Materials Gross	Unit Price
								(Gross rates include 10% profit)			
				£	£	£	£	£	£	£	£
501	**NEW WORK**										
50146	**INSULATION**										
5014601	**Hardboard casing comprising; 3 mm hardboard sides; bottom and loose lid; on and including 50 mm × 38 mm softwood framing; 50 mm space packed with Micafil; to cold water storage tank:**										
5014601A	182 litre	Each	2.20	61.63	–	29.70	91.33	67.79	–	32.67	100.46
5014601B	273 litre	Each	2.80	78.43	–	37.58	116.01	86.27	–	41.34	127.61
5014601C	455 litre	Each	3.30	92.43	–	48.00	140.43	101.67	–	52.80	154.47
5014602	**Matchboard casing comprising; 19 mm matchboard sides; bottom and loose lid; on and including 50 mm × 38 mm softwood framing; 50 mm space packed with Micafil; to cold water storage tank:**										
5014602A	182 litre	Each	4.00	112.04	–	82.90	194.94	123.24	–	91.19	214.43
5014602B	273 litre	Each	4.50	126.04	–	105.98	232.02	138.64	–	116.58	255.22
5014602C	455 litre	Each	5.00	140.05	–	141.80	281.85	154.06	–	155.98	310.04
5014603	**50 mm fibreglass jacket in one piece; fixed complete with hoop iron bands; to enclose tank:**										
5014603A	182 litre	Each	0.75	21.01	–	17.60	38.61	23.11	–	19.36	42.47
5014603B	273 litre	Each	1.00	28.01	–	19.03	47.04	30.81	–	20.93	51.74
5014603C	455 litre	Each	1.25	35.01	–	22.83	57.84	38.51	–	25.11	63.62
5014604	**Hair felt pipe sheath around pipes; external diameter:**										
5014604A	13 mm	m	0.20	5.61	–	0.49	6.10	6.17	–	0.54	6.71
5014604B	19 mm	m	0.22	6.17	–	0.49	6.66	6.79	–	0.54	7.33
5014604C	25 mm	m	0.25	7.01	–	0.49	7.50	7.71	–	0.54	8.25
5014604D	38 mm	m	0.33	9.25	–	0.49	9.74	10.18	–	0.54	10.71
5014605	**Flexible foam pipe lagging around pipes; external diameter:**										
5014605A	13 mm	m	0.10	2.80	–	0.99	3.79	3.08	–	1.09	4.17
5014605B	19 mm	m	0.12	3.36	–	1.30	4.66	3.70	–	1.43	5.13
5014605C	25 mm	m	0.14	3.92	–	1.90	5.82	4.31	–	2.09	6.40
5014605D	38 mm	m	0.17	4.76	–	3.19	7.95	5.24	–	3.51	8.75

Small Works 2009		Unit	Labour Hours	Labour Net	Plant Net	Materials Net	Unit Net	Labour Gross	Plant Gross	Materials Gross	Unit Price
								—— (Gross rates include 10% profit) ——			
				£	£	£	£	£	£	£	£
501	**NEW WORK**										
50156	**BUILDERS WORK**										
5015601	**Cut holes for pipes or the like; not exceeding 55 mm diameter; make good:**										
5015601A	100 mm concrete	Each	0.60	16.80	–	0.33	17.13	18.48	–	0.36	18.84
5015601B	150 mm concrete	Each	1.00	28.01	–	0.33	28.34	30.81	–	0.36	31.17
5015601C	100 mm reinforced concrete	Each	0.80	22.40	–	0.33	22.73	24.64	–	0.36	25.00
5015601D	150 mm reinforced concrete	Each	1.05	29.41	–	0.33	29.74	32.35	–	0.36	32.71
5015601E	75 mm blockwork.	Each	0.33	9.24	–	0.33	9.57	10.16	–	0.36	10.53
5015601F	100 mm blockwork	Each	0.33	9.24	–	0.33	9.57	10.16	–	0.36	10.53
5015601G	102 mm brickwork	Each	0.45	12.60	–	0.33	12.93	13.86	–	0.36	14.22
5015601H	215 mm brickwork	Each	0.80	22.40	–	0.33	22.73	24.64	–	0.36	25.00
5015601I	softwood floor boarding . . .	Each	0.15	4.20	–	–	4.20	4.62	–	–	4.62
5015601J	softwood floor boarding and plaster board soffit under . .	Each	0.35	9.80	–	0.46	10.26	10.78	–	0.51	11.29
5015602	**Cut holes for pipes or the like; 55 mm 110 mm diameter; make good:**										
5015602A	100 mm concrete	Each	0.85	23.81	–	0.54	24.35	26.19	–	0.59	26.79
5015602B	150 mm concrete	Each	1.25	35.02	–	0.54	35.56	38.52	–	0.59	39.12
5015602C	100 mm reinforced concrete	Each	1.00	28.01	–	0.54	28.55	30.81	–	0.59	31.41
5015602D	150 mm reinforced concrete	Each	1.40	39.22	–	0.54	39.76	43.14	–	0.59	43.74
5015602E	75 mm blockwork.	Each	0.45	12.61	–	0.54	13.15	13.87	–	0.59	14.47
5015602F	100 mm blockwork	Each	0.45	12.61	–	0.54	13.15	13.87	–	0.59	14.47
5015602G	102 mm brickwork	Each	0.60	16.81	–	0.54	17.35	18.49	–	0.59	19.09
5015602H	215 mm brickwork	Each	1.10	30.82	–	0.54	31.36	33.90	–	0.59	34.50
5015602I	softwood floor boarding . . .	Each	0.20	5.60	–	–	5.60	6.16	–	–	6.16
5015602J	softwood floor boarding and plaster board soffit under . .	Each	0.50	14.01	–	0.56	14.57	15.41	–	0.62	16.03
5015603	**Framing; sawn softwood; 38 mm × 50 mm; for bath panel:**										
5015603A	end panel.	Each	0.36	10.09	–	5.66	15.75	11.10	–	6.23	17.33
5015603B	side panel	Each	0.72	20.17	–	11.12	31.29	22.19	–	12.23	34.42
5015604	**Take up existing softwood floor boarding; 25 mm thick; one board wide; cut holes or notches for pipes and refix boards:**										
5015604A	service cables	m	0.90	25.21	–	–	25.21	27.73	–	–	27.73
5015604B	pipes not exceeding 55 mm diameter	m	1.10	30.81	–	–	30.81	33.89	–	–	33.89
5015604C	pipes 55 mm-110 mm diameter	m	1.30	36.41	–	–	36.41	40.05	–	–	40.05
5015605	**Tank bearers nailed to ceiling joists:**										
5015605A	75 mm × 50 mm	m	0.12	3.36	–	1.35	4.71	3.70	–	1.49	5.18
5015605B	100 mm × 50 mm	m	0.16	4.48	–	1.80	6.28	4.93	–	1.98	6.91
5015606	**Boarded platform; softwood nailed to bearers:**										
5015606A	for tank or cistern	m²	1.55	43.42	–	23.17	66.59	47.76	–	25.49	73.25

Plumbing and Heating

Small Works 2009		Unit	Labour Hours	Labour Net	Plant Net	Materials Net	Unit Net	Labour Gross	Plant Gross	Materials Gross	Unit Price
								(Gross rates include 10% profit)			
				£	£	£	£	£	£	£	£
502	**REPAIRS AND ALTERATIONS**										
50201	**REMOVE GUTTERWORK AND PIPEWORK**										
5020101	**Gutterwork and supports:**										
5020101A	asbestos-free cement	m	0.35	12.57	–	–	12.57	13.83	–	–	13.83
5020101B	upvc	m	0.38	13.65	–	–	13.65	15.02	–	–	15.02
5020101C	cast iron	m	0.45	16.16	–	–	16.16	17.78	–	–	17.78
5020102	**Rainwater pipework and supports:**										
5020102A	asbestos-free cement	m	0.30	10.78	–	–	10.78	11.86	–	–	11.86
5020102B	upvc	m	0.33	11.85	–	–	11.85	13.04	–	–	13.04
5020102C	cast iron	m	0.40	14.37	–	–	14.37	15.81	–	–	15.81
5020103	**Rainwater shoe:**										
5020103A	upvc	Each	0.07	2.51	–	–	2.51	2.76	–	–	2.76
5020103B	cast iron	Each	0.10	3.59	–	–	3.59	3.95	–	–	3.95
5020104	**Rainwater head and support:**										
5020104A	upvc	Each	0.37	13.29	–	–	13.29	14.62	–	–	14.62
5020104B	cast iron	Each	0.45	16.16	–	–	16.16	17.78	–	–	17.78
5020105	**Soil and ventilation pipework and supports:**										
5020105A	upvc	m	0.60	21.55	–	–	21.55	23.71	–	–	23.71
5020105B	cast iron	m	0.67	24.07	–	–	24.07	26.48	–	–	26.48
5020105C	lead	m	0.75	26.94	–	–	26.94	29.63	–	–	29.63
5020106	**Service, waste and overflow pipework and supports:**										
5020106A	upvc	m	0.13	4.67	–	–	4.67	5.14	–	–	5.14
5020106B	copper	m	0.17	6.11	–	–	6.11	6.72	–	–	6.72
5020106C	lead	m	0.17	6.11	–	–	6.11	6.72	–	–	6.72
5020106D	galvanised steel	m	0.17	6.11	–	–	6.11	6.72	–	–	6.72

Small Works 2009		Unit	Labour Hours	Labour Net	Plant Net	Materials Net	Unit Net	Labour Gross	Plant Gross	Materials Gross	Unit Price
								——— (Gross rates include 10% profit) ———			
				£	£	£	£	£	£	£	£
502	**REPAIRS AND ALTERATIONS**										
50201	**REMOVE GUTTERWORK AND PIPEWORK**										
5020107	**Remove sanitary fittings including taps and trap:**										
5020107A	w.c. suite	Each	0.42	15.09	–	–	15.09	16.60	–	–	16.60
5020107B	wash hand basin	Each	0.37	13.29	–	–	13.29	14.62	–	–	14.62
5020107C	bath	Each	0.52	18.68	–	–	18.68	20.55	–	–	20.55
5020107D	sink unit	Each	0.37	13.29	–	–	13.29	14.62	–	–	14.62
5020107E	shower	Each	0.15	5.39	–	–	5.39	5.93	–	–	5.93
5020108	**Remove sanitary fittings including taps, trap and service and waste pipes not exceeding 3.00 m girth:**										
5020108A	w.c. suite	Each	0.52	18.68	–	–	18.68	20.55	–	–	20.55
5020108B	wash hand basin	Each	0.42	15.09	–	–	15.09	16.60	–	–	16.60
5020108C	bath	Each	0.62	22.27	–	–	22.27	24.50	–	–	24.50
5020108D	sink unit	Each	0.42	15.09	–	–	15.09	16.60	–	–	16.60
5020108E	shower	Each	0.22	7.90	–	–	7.90	8.69	–	–	8.69
5020109	**Remove bathroom toilet fittings:**										
5020109A	toilet roll holder	Each	0.05	1.80	–	–	1.80	1.98	–	–	1.98
5020109B	soap dispenser	Each	0.05	1.80	–	–	1.80	1.98	–	–	1.98
5020109C	towel rail	Each	0.08	2.87	–	–	2.87	3.16	–	–	3.16
5020109D	towel holder	Each	0.17	6.11	–	–	6.11	6.72	–	–	6.72
5020109E	mirror	Each	0.17	6.11	–	–	6.11	6.72	–	–	6.72
5020110	**Remove equipment; excluding any necessary draining down of system:**										
5020110A	cold water tank	Each	2.65	95.19	–	–	95.19	104.71	–	–	104.71
5020110B	hot water cylinder	Each	1.33	47.77	–	–	47.77	52.55	–	–	52.55
5020110C	gas water heater	Each	4.40	158.05	–	–	158.05	173.86	–	–	173.86
5020110D	gas fire	Each	2.20	79.02	–	–	79.02	86.92	–	–	86.92
5020110E	expansion tank	Each	2.00	71.84	–	–	71.84	79.02	–	–	79.02

Plumbing and Heating

Small Works 2009		Unit	Labour Hours	Labour Net	Plant Net	Materials Net	Unit Net	Labour Gross	Plant Gross	Materials Gross	Unit Price
								—— (Gross rates include 10% profit) ——			
				£	£	£	£	£	£	£	£
502	**REPAIRS AND ALTERATIONS**										
50202	**REPAIRS TO PIPEWORK AND GUTTERWORK**										
5020201	**Cleaning out eaves or parapet gutters, removing rubbish:**										
5020201A	any height or position	m	0.13	4.67	–	–	4.67	5.14	–	–	5.14
5020202	**Cleaning out rainwater pipes, stack pipes etc, removing rubbish:**										
5020202A	any height or position	m	0.13	4.67	–	–	4.67	5.14	–	–	5.14
5020203	**Take down existing gutters, clean and refix to fascia or on brackets:**										
5020203A	seal joints with red lead putty and set to proper falls	m	0.70	25.14	–	0.43	25.57	27.65	–	0.47	28.13
5020204	**Take down and remove existing 100 mm iron gutters and provide and fix new gutters:**										
5020204A	half-round	m	1.10	39.51	–	21.15	60.66	43.46	–	23.27	66.73
5020204B	ogee	m	1.10	39.51	–	23.14	62.65	43.46	–	25.45	68.92
5020205	**Take down existing rainwater pipes and refix to walls:**										
5020205A	50 mm, 63 mm, or 75 mm .	m	0.75	26.94	–	–	26.94	29.63	–	–	29.63
5020206	**Take down and remove existing iron rain water pipes and provide and fix new:**										
5020206A	63 mm and 75 mm pipes...	m	1.10	39.51	–	36.08	75.59	43.46	–	39.69	83.15
5020206B	rainwater shoe (not extra over)...................	Each	0.50	17.96	–	27.74	45.70	19.76	–	30.51	50.27
5020207	**Cut out and reform caulked lead joints in cast-iron soil, vent or waste pipes:**										
5020207A	50 mm	Each	0.70	25.14	–	–	25.14	27.65	–	–	27.65
5020207B	75 mm	Each	0.80	28.74	–	–	28.74	31.61	–	–	31.61
5020207C	100 mm	Each	1.15	41.31	–	–	41.31	45.44	–	–	45.44
5020208	**Cut and adapt existing 100 mm iron soil pipe for a new w.c. by inserting branch and bend (or long junction), connect to pan trap and make good to:**										
5020208A	wall....................	Each	4.80	172.42	–	91.34	263.76	189.66	–	100.47	290.14
5020208B	Extra for access door	Each	–	–	–	45.97	45.97	–	–	50.57	50.57

Small Works 2009		Unit	Labour Hours	Labour Net	Plant Net	Materials Net	Unit Net	Labour Gross	Plant Gross	Materials Gross	Unit Price
								(Gross rates include 10% profit)			
				£	£	£	£	£	£	£	£
502	**REPAIRS AND ALTERATIONS**										
50206	**REPAIRS TO PIPEWORK AND PLUMBING**										
5020601	**Renew broken stopcock box with hinged lid:**										
5020601A	127 mm × 127 mm × 76 mm	Each	0.50	17.96	–	13.06	31.02	19.76	–	14.37	34.12
5020601B	152 mm × 152 mm × 76 mm	Each	0.55	19.75	–	14.39	34.14	21.73	–	15.83	37.55
5020604	**Cutting existing iron pipe and inserting new tees:**										
5020604A	15 mm	Each	0.70	25.15	–	4.26	29.41	27.67	–	4.69	32.35
5020604B	20 mm	Each	0.85	30.53	–	5.79	36.32	33.58	–	6.37	39.95
5020604C	25 mm	Each	1.00	35.92	–	7.87	43.79	39.51	–	8.66	48.17
5020607	**Cutting existing copper pipes and inserting new capillary tees:**										
5020607A	15 mm	Each	1.00	35.92	–	1.78	37.70	39.51	–	1.96	41.47
5020607B	22 mm	Each	1.20	43.10	–	3.74	46.84	47.41	–	4.11	51.52
5020607C	28 mm	Each	1.50	53.88	–	8.47	62.35	59.27	–	9.32	68.59
5020609	**Cutting existing polythene pipes and inserting new compression tees:**										
5020609A	20 mm	Each	1.50	53.88	–	10.82	64.70	59.27	–	11.90	71.17
5020609B	25 mm	Each	1.70	61.07	–	16.38	77.45	67.18	–	18.02	85.20
5020609C	32 mm	Each	2.00	71.84	–	23.35	95.19	79.02	–	25.69	104.71
5020610	**Covering iron or copper pipes with hair felt and twine in any position:**										
5020610A	up to 25 mm diameter	m	0.70	25.15	–	0.49	25.64	27.67	–	0.54	28.20

Plumbing and Heating

Small Works 2009		Unit	Labour Hours	Labour Net	Plant Net	Materials Net	Unit Net	Labour Gross	Plant Gross	Materials Gross	Unit Price
								(Gross rates include 10% profit)			
				£	£	£	£	£	£	£	£
502	**REPAIRS AND ALTERATIONS**										
50206	**REPAIRS TO PIPEWORK AND PLUMBING**										
5020612	**Take off existing bib valves and prepare iron or copper pipes and provide and fix new bib valve:**										
5020612A	13 mm	Each	1.00	35.92	–	14.59	50.51	39.51	–	16.05	55.56
5020612B	19 mm	Each	1.20	43.10	–	19.53	62.63	47.41	–	21.48	68.89
5020614	**Cut into iron or copper pipes and fit new stopcock:**										
5020614A	13 mm	Each	1.30	46.70	–	8.28	54.98	51.37	–	9.11	60.48
5020614B	19 mm	Each	1.50	53.88	–	13.13	67.01	59.27	–	14.44	73.71
5020616	**Rewasher ball valve, tap or indoor stopcock:**										
5020616A	13 mm	Each	0.50	17.96	–	0.36	18.32	19.76	–	0.40	20.15
5020616B	19 mm	Each	0.60	21.55	–	0.36	21.91	23.71	–	0.40	24.10
5020618	**Take off existing copper trap to bath, basin or sink and provide and fit new plastic trap:**										
5020618A	32 mm	Each	1.20	43.11	–	3.56	46.67	47.42	–	3.92	51.34
5020618B	38 mm	Each	1.30	46.70	–	8.93	55.63	51.37	–	9.82	61.19
5020620	**Take off stopcock to iron or copper pipe both ends and provide and fit new stopcock:**										
5020620A	13 mm	Each	0.65	23.35	–	8.28	31.63	25.69	–	9.11	34.79
5020620B	19 mm	Each	0.85	30.53	–	13.13	43.66	33.58	–	14.44	48.03
5020620C	25 mm	Each	1.05	37.72	–	33.63	71.35	41.49	–	36.99	78.49
5020622	**Take off ball valve to iron or copper pipes and provide and fit new ball valve and ball float complete:**										
5020622A	13 mm	Each	0.50	17.96	–	12.01	29.97	19.76	–	13.21	32.97
5020622C	19 mm	Each	0.65	23.35	–	19.50	42.85	25.69	–	21.45	47.14

Small Works 2009		Unit	Labour Hours	Labour Net	Plant Net	Materials Net	Unit Net	Labour Gross	Plant Gross	Materials Gross	Unit Price
								(Gross rates include 10% profit)			
				£	£	£	£	£	£	£	£
502	**REPAIRS AND ALTERATIONS**										
50208	**REPAIRS TO SANITARYWARE AND FITTINGS**										
5020801	**Supply w.c. suite complete and connect to existing services:**										
5020801A	copper or iron	Each	5.80	208.33	–	210.38	418.71	229.16	–	231.42	460.58
5020802	**Supply low level w.c. suite (complete and connect to existing services:**										
5020802A	copper or iron	Each	6.30	226.30	–	161.29	387.59	248.93	–	177.42	426.35
5020803	**Remove defective w.c. pan and fix new; make good all connections:**										
5020803A	white	Each	3.90	140.09	–	105.18	245.27	154.10	–	115.70	269.80
5020804	**Take off defective seat to pedestal pan and supply and fix new plastic seat:**										
5020804A	single	Each	0.75	26.94	–	19.18	46.12	29.63	–	21.10	50.73
5020804B	double	Each	0.90	32.33	–	26.85	59.18	35.56	–	29.54	65.10
5020805	**Take off w.c. seat, renew joints to flush pipe including closet and outlet connection and pan:**										
5020805A	refix seat	Each	1.15	41.31	–	2.59	43.90	45.44	–	2.85	48.29

Plumbing and Heating

Small Works 2009		Unit	Labour Hours	Labour Net	Plant Net	Materials Net	Unit Net	Labour Gross	Plant Gross	Materials Gross	Unit Price
								(Gross rates include 10% profit)			
				£	£	£	£	£	£	£	£
502	**REPAIRS AND ALTERATIONS**										
50208	**REPAIRS TO SANITARYWARE AND FITTINGS**										
5020806	**Disconnect and remove 9 litres of water waste preventer, supply and fix new complete with ball valve and brackets and joint to existing overflow and service pipe:**										
5020806A	copper or iron	Each	3.20	114.94	–	122.65	237.59	126.43	–	134.92	261.35
5020807	**Disconnect ball valve to water waste preventer or storage tank:**										
5020807A	re-washer and clean out . . .	Each	1.45	52.08	–	0.36	52.44	57.29	–	0.40	57.68
5020807B	unscrew ball valve and supply and fit new ball	Each	0.30	10.77	–	4.38	15.15	11.85	–	4.82	16.67
5020808	**Supply and fix flat back basin including taps, traps and wall brackets, connect to existing services:**										
5020808A	iron or copper	Each	5.80	208.34	–	119.21	327.55	229.17	–	131.13	360.31
5020809	**Supply and fix pedestal basin including taps, traps and wall brackets, connect to existing services:**										
5020809A	iron or copper	Each	5.80	208.33	–	168.30	376.63	229.16	–	185.13	414.29

Small Works 2009		Unit	Labour Hours	Labour Net	Plant Net	Materials Net	Unit Net	Labour Gross	Plant Gross	Materials Gross	Unit Price
								(Gross rates include 10% profit)			
				£	£	£	£	£	£	£	£
502	**REPAIRS AND ALTERATIONS**										
50208	**REPAIRS TO SANITARYWARE AND FITTINGS**										
5020812	**Supply and fix cast iron; white porcelain enamelled; rectangular; 1700 mm long bath complete with taps and trap, connect to existing services:**										
5020812A	iron or copper	Each	5.80	208.33	–	503.88	712.21	229.16	–	554.27	783.43
5020814	**Clear blockage and flush out; to:**										
5020814A	w.c. pans and traps	Each	1.25	44.90	–	–	44.90	49.39	–	–	49.39
5020814B	traps and waste pipes of baths, sinks, lavatory basins etc	Each	1.00	35.92	–	–	35.92	39.51	–	–	39.51
5020816	**Disconnect all pipework, take out and remove galvanised steel hot water tank, provide and install copper indirect cylinder, allow for cutting holes, tank connectors, make up and connections to existing pipework:**										
5020816A	114 litre	Each	3.00	107.76	–	279.29	387.05	118.54	–	307.22	425.76
5020818	**Empty water storage system and disconnect back boiler and supply and connect:**										
5020818A	new back boiler and test . . .	Each	4.00	143.68	–	194.25	337.93	158.05	–	213.68	371.72
5020819	**Clean and scale back boiler and ends of pipe:**										
5020819A	reconnect and recirculate water	Each	7.00	251.44	–	–	251.44	276.58	–	–	276.58
5020820	**Turn off water supply, disconnect all pipework, take out and remove galvanised steel cold water storage tank, provide and install plastic tank complete with ball valve, lid and insulation and allow for cutting holes, tank connectors, make up and connections to existing pipework:**										
5020820A	182 litre	Each	6.30	226.30	–	179.11	405.41	248.93	–	197.02	445.95
5020821	**Cleaning and scouring out open-top storage tanks:**										
5020821A	generally	Each	7.40	265.81	–	–	265.81	292.39	–	–	292.39

GLAZING, PAINTING AND DECORATING

Small Works 2009		Unit	Labour Hours	Labour Net	Plant Net	Materials Net	Unit Net	Labour Gross	Plant Gross	Materials Gross	Unit Price
								(Gross rates include 10% profit)			
				£	£	£	£	£	£	£	£
601	**NEW WORK**										
60101	**GLASS IN OPENINGS**										
6010101	**2 mm Clear sheet glass and glazing to wood with putty; in panes:**										
6010101A	not exceeding 0.10 sq.m ...	m²	1.20	33.61	–	34.67	68.28	36.97	–	38.14	75.11
6010101B	0.10-0.50 sq.m	m²	0.90	25.21	–	33.93	59.14	27.73	–	37.32	65.05
6010101C	0.50-1.0 sq.m	m²	0.45	12.61	–	33.93	46.54	13.87	–	37.32	51.19
6010102	**3 mm Clear sheet glass and glazing to wood with putty; in panes:**										
6010102A	not exceeding 0.10 sq.m ...	m²	1.20	33.61	–	42.31	75.92	36.97	–	46.54	83.51
6010102B	0.10-0.50 sq.m	m²	0.90	25.20	–	42.31	67.51	27.72	–	46.54	74.26
6010102C	0.50-1.0 sq.m	m²	0.45	12.60	–	42.31	54.91	13.86	–	46.54	60.40
6010102D	exceeding 1.0 sq.m	m²	0.35	9.80	–	42.31	52.11	10.78	–	46.54	57.32
6010103	**4 mm Clear sheet glass and glazing to wood with putty; in panes:**										
6010103A	0.10-0.50 sq.m	m²	1.00	28.01	–	47.89	75.90	30.81	–	52.68	83.49
6010103B	0.50-1.0 sq.m	m²	0.50	14.01	–	48.62	62.63	15.41	–	53.48	68.89
6010103C	exceeding 1.0 sq.m	m²	0.40	11.21	–	48.62	59.83	12.33	–	53.48	65.81
6010104	**2 mm Clear sheet glass and glazing to metal with putty; in panes:**										
6010104A	not exceeding 0.10 sq.m ...	m²	1.75	49.02	–	36.21	85.23	53.92	–	39.83	93.75
6010104B	0.10-0.50 sq.m	m²	1.35	37.81	–	35.48	73.29	41.59	–	39.03	80.62
6010104C	0.50-1.0 sq.m	m²	0.70	19.60	–	34.67	54.27	21.56	–	38.14	59.70
6010105	**3 mm Clear sheet glass and glazing to metal with putty; in panes:**										
6010105A	not exceeding 0.10 sq.m ...	m²	1.75	49.02	–	43.85	92.87	53.92	–	48.24	102.16
6010105B	0.10-0.50 sq.m	m²	1.35	37.81	–	43.04	80.85	41.59	–	47.34	88.94
6010105C	0.50-1.0 sq.m	m²	0.70	19.60	–	42.31	61.91	21.56	–	46.54	68.10
6010105D	exceeding 1.0 sq.m	m²	0.55	15.40	–	42.31	57.71	16.94	–	46.54	63.48
6010106	**4 mm Clear sheet glass and glazing to metal with putty; in panes:**										
6010106A	0.10-0.50 sq.m	m²	1.50	42.02	–	48.62	90.64	46.22	–	53.48	99.70
6010106B	0.50-1.0 sq.m	m²	0.80	22.41	–	47.89	70.30	24.65	–	52.68	77.33
6010106C	exceeding 1.0 sq.m	m²	0.65	18.21	–	47.89	66.10	20.03	–	52.68	72.71
6010107	**Figured, Rolled or Cathedral glass and glazing to wood with putty; in panes:**										
6010107A	not exceeding 0.10 sq.m ...	m²	1.20	33.61	–	98.87	132.48	36.97	–	108.76	145.73
6010107B	0.10-0.50 sq.m	m²	0.90	25.21	–	98.87	124.08	27.73	–	108.76	136.49
6010107C	0.50-1.0 sq.m	m²	0.45	12.60	–	99.68	112.28	13.86	–	109.65	123.51
6010107D	exceeding 1.0 sq.m	m²	0.35	9.81	–	98.13	107.94	10.79	–	107.94	118.73

Glazing, Painting and Decorating

Small Works 2009		Unit	Labour Hours	Labour Net	Plant Net	Materials Net	Unit Net	Labour Gross	Plant Gross	Materials Gross	Unit Price
								(Gross rates include 10% profit)			
				£	£	£	£	£	£	£	£
601	**NEW WORK**										
60101	**GLASS IN OPENINGS**										
6010108	**Figured, Rolled or Cathedral glass and glazing to metal with putty; in panes:**										
6010108A	not exceeding 0.10 sq.m...	m²	1.75	49.02	–	100.41	149.43	53.92	–	110.45	164.37
6010108B	0.10-0.50 sq.m..........	m²	1.35	37.81	–	98.87	136.68	41.59	–	108.76	150.35
6010108C	0.50-1.0 sq.m...........	m²	0.70	19.61	–	98.13	117.74	21.57	–	107.94	129.51
6010108D	exceeding 1.0 sq.m	m²	0.50	14.00	–	98.87	112.87	15.40	–	108.76	124.16
6010109	**6 mm Wired cast glass and glazing to wood with putty; in panes:**										
6010109A	not exceeding 0.10 sq.m...	m²	1.40	39.21	–	47.19	86.40	43.13	–	51.91	95.04
6010109B	0.10-0.50 sq.m..........	m²	1.20	33.62	–	46.45	80.07	36.98	–	51.10	88.08
6010109C	0.50-1.0 sq.m...........	m²	0.60	16.81	–	44.91	61.72	18.49	–	49.40	67.89
6010109D	exceeding 1.0 sq.m	m²	0.50	14.00	–	45.65	59.65	15.40	–	50.22	65.62
6010110	**6 mm Wired cast glass and glazing to metal with putty; in panes:**										
6010110A	not exceeding 0.10 sq.m...	m²	2.10	58.82	–	45.65	104.47	64.70	–	50.22	114.92
6010110B	0.10-0.50 sq.m..........	m²	1.65	46.22	–	47.19	93.41	50.84	–	51.91	102.75
6010110C	0.50-1.0 sq.m...........	m²	0.85	23.80	–	45.65	69.45	26.18	–	50.22	76.40
6010110D	exceeding 1.0 sq.m	m²	0.75	21.01	–	44.91	65.92	23.11	–	49.40	72.51
6010111	**6 mm Wired glass and glazing to wood with putty, roof lights, lantern lights, skylights etc; in panes:**										
6010111A	0.10-0.50 sq.m..........	m²	2.20	61.62	–	45.65	107.27	67.78	–	50.22	118.00
6010111B	0.50-1.0 sq.m...........	m²	1.10	30.81	–	44.91	75.72	33.89	–	49.40	83.29
6010111C	exceeding 1.0 sq.m	m²	0.90	25.20	–	45.65	70.85	27.72	–	50.22	77.94
6010112	**6 mm Wired glass glazing to metal with putty; in panes:**										
6010112A	0.10-0.50 sq.m..........	m²	3.00	84.03	–	44.91	128.94	92.43	–	49.40	141.83
6010112B	0.50-1.0 sq.m...........	m²	1.70	47.61	–	45.65	93.26	52.37	–	50.22	102.59
6010112C	exceeding 1.0 sq.m	m²	1.50	42.01	–	46.09	88.10	46.21	–	50.70	96.91
6010113	**6 mm Single glaze quality float glass, bedding in wash-leather and beads, both measured separately; in panes:**										
6010113A	not exceeding 4.0 sq.m	m²	3.30	92.43	–	70.07	162.50	101.67	–	77.08	178.75
6010114	**Bed edges of glass in:**										
6010114A	wash leather	m	0.07	1.97	–	0.89	2.86	2.17	–	0.98	3.15
6010114B	velvet	m	0.06	1.68	–	0.25	1.93	1.85	–	0.28	2.12
6010114C	fix only beads	m	0.07	1.96	–	–	1.96	2.16	–	–	2.16
6010114D	fix only beads (if screwed) .	m	0.09	2.52	–	–	2.52	2.77	–	–	2.77
6010115	**Curved cutting, including risk, on the following:**										
6010115A	sheet glass	m	0.25	7.00	–	–	7.00	7.70	–	–	7.70
6010115B	obscure glass	m	0.33	9.24	–	–	9.24	10.16	–	–	10.16
6010115C	wire cast glass	m	0.60	16.81	–	–	16.81	18.49	–	–	18.49
6010115D	6 mm single glaze quality float glass	m	0.40	11.20	–	–	11.20	12.32	–	–	12.32

Small Works 2009		Unit	Labour Hours	Labour Net	Plant Net	Materials Net	Unit Net	Labour Gross	Plant Gross	Materials Gross	Unit Price
								(Gross rates include 10% profit)			
				£	£	£	£	£	£	£	£
601	**NEW WORK**										
60103	**DOUBLE GLAZING UNITS**										
6010301	**Hermetically sealed in two panes of 4 mm clear float glass to wood or metal with non-setting compound and screwed or clipped beads:**										
6010301B	1.00-2.00 sq.m...........	m²	2.00	56.02	–	39.18	95.20	61.62	–	43.10	104.72
6010301C	0.75-1.00 sq.m...........	m²	2.50	70.03	–	46.10	116.13	77.03	–	50.71	127.74
6010301D	0.50-0.75 sq.m...........	m²	3.00	84.03	–	56.00	140.03	92.43	–	61.60	154.03
6010301E	0.35-0.50 sq.m...........	m²	3.50	98.04	–	64.86	162.90	107.84	–	71.35	179.19
6010301F	0.25-0.35 sq.m...........	m²	4.00	112.04	–	85.79	197.83	123.24	–	94.37	217.61
6010301G	not exceeding 0.25 sq.m...	m²	4.50	126.04	–	85.79	211.83	138.64	–	94.37	233.01
6010302	**Hermetically sealed one pane of 4 mm clear float glass and one pane of 4 mm white patterned glass with non-setting compound and screwed or clipped beads**										
6010302B	1.00-2.00 sq.m...........	m²	2.00	56.02	–	44.56	100.58	61.62	–	49.02	110.64
6010302C	0.75-1.00 sq.m...........	m²	2.50	70.03	–	51.49	121.52	77.03	–	56.64	133.67
6010302D	0.50-0.75 sq.m...........	m²	3.00	84.03	–	61.37	145.40	92.43	–	67.51	159.94
6010302E	0.35-0.50 sq.m...........	m²	3.50	98.04	–	70.27	168.31	107.84	–	77.30	185.14
6010302F	0.25-0.35 sq.m...........	m²	4.00	112.04	–	91.18	203.22	123.24	–	100.30	223.54
6010302G	not exceeding 0.25 sq.m...	m²	4.50	126.04	–	91.18	217.22	138.64	–	100.30	238.94
60106	**PAINTING AND DECORATING INTERNALLY**										
6010601	**Limewhite:**										
6010601A	one coat brick walls	m²	0.15	4.20	–	0.17	4.37	4.62	–	0.19	4.81
6010601B	two coat brick walls	m²	0.25	7.01	–	0.30	7.31	7.71	–	0.33	8.04
6010601C	two coat plaster walls	m²	0.20	5.60	–	0.06	5.66	6.16	–	0.07	6.23
6010601D	two coat plaster ceilings ...	m²	0.22	6.16	–	0.06	6.22	6.78	–	0.07	6.84
6010602	**Primer, two coats matt or silk emulsion paint:**										
6010602A	concrete walls...........	m²	0.41	11.48	–	2.85	14.33	12.63	–	3.14	15.76
6010602B	concrete walls to stairwell..	m²	0.50	14.01	–	2.85	16.86	15.41	–	3.14	18.55
6010602C	concrete ceilings	m²	0.53	14.85	–	2.85	17.70	16.34	–	3.14	19.47
6010602D	concrete ceilings to stairwell	m²	0.59	16.53	–	2.85	19.38	18.18	–	3.14	21.32
6010602E	brick walls...............	m²	0.50	14.00	–	3.66	17.66	15.40	–	4.03	19.43
6010602F	brick walls to stairwell	m²	0.56	15.69	–	3.66	19.35	17.26	–	4.03	21.29
6010602G	block walls...............	m²	0.62	17.37	–	3.66	21.03	19.11	–	4.03	23.13
6010602H	block walls to stairwell.....	m²	0.68	19.05	–	3.66	22.71	20.96	–	4.03	24.98
6010602I	plastered walls...........	m²	0.38	10.64	–	2.47	13.11	11.70	–	2.72	14.42
6010602J	plastered walls to stairwell .	m²	0.44	12.32	–	2.47	14.79	13.55	–	2.72	16.27
6010602K	plastered ceilings	m²	0.50	14.00	–	2.47	16.47	15.40	–	2.72	18.12
6010602L	plastered ceilings to stairwell	m²	0.53	14.84	–	2.47	17.31	16.32	–	2.72	19.04
6010602M	embossed papered or textured walls	m²	0.41	11.48	–	2.85	14.33	12.63	–	3.14	15.76
6010602N	embossed papered or textured walls to stairwell ..	m²	0.50	14.01	–	2.85	16.86	15.41	–	3.14	18.55
6010602O	embossed papered or textured ceilings...........	m²	0.53	14.85	–	2.85	17.70	16.34	–	3.14	19.47
6010602P	embossed papered or textured ceilings to stairwell	m²	0.59	16.53	–	2.85	19.38	18.18	–	3.14	21.32

Small Works 2009		Unit	Labour Hours	Labour Net	Plant Net	Materials Net	Unit Net	Labour Gross	Plant Gross	Materials Gross	Unit Price
								(Gross rates include 10% profit)			
				£	£	£	£	£	£	£	£
601	**NEW WORK**										
60106	**PAINTING AND DECORATING INTERNALLY**										
6010603	**Primer, two coats eggshell paint:**										
6010603A	concrete walls............	m²	0.46	12.88	–	3.36	16.24	14.17	–	3.70	17.86
6010603B	concrete walls to stairwell..	m²	0.55	15.40	–	3.36	18.76	16.94	–	3.70	20.64
6010603C	concrete ceilings	m²	0.58	16.25	–	3.36	19.61	17.88	–	3.70	21.57
6010603D	concrete ceilings to stairwell	m²	0.64	17.93	–	3.36	21.29	19.72	–	3.70	23.42
6010603E	brick walls..............	m²	0.54	15.12	–	3.86	18.98	16.63	–	4.25	20.88
6010603F	brick walls to stairwell.....	m²	0.60	16.80	–	3.86	20.66	18.48	–	4.25	22.73
6010603G	block walls..............	m²	0.66	18.49	–	4.81	23.30	20.34	–	5.29	25.63
6010603H	block walls to stairwell.....	m²	0.72	20.17	–	4.81	24.98	22.19	–	5.29	27.48
6010603I	plastered walls	m²	0.43	12.04	–	2.91	14.95	13.24	–	3.20	16.45
6010603J	plastered walls to stairwell .	m²	0.50	14.00	–	2.91	16.91	15.40	–	3.20	18.60
6010603K	plastered ceilings	m²	0.55	15.40	–	2.91	18.31	16.94	–	3.20	20.14
6010603L	plastered ceilings to stairwell	m²	0.59	16.52	–	2.91	19.43	18.17	–	3.20	21.37
6010603M	embossed papered or textured walls	m²	0.47	13.16	–	3.36	16.52	14.48	–	3.70	18.17
6010603N	embossed papered or textured walls to stairwell ..	m²	0.56	15.68	–	3.36	19.04	17.25	–	3.70	20.94
6010603O	embossed papered or textured ceiling	m²	0.59	16.53	–	3.36	19.89	18.18	–	3.70	21.88
6010603P	embossed papered or textured ceilings to stairwell	m²	0.66	18.49	–	3.36	21.85	20.34	–	3.70	24.04
6010604	**Primer, one undercoat, one coat gloss finishing paint:**										
6010604A	concrete walls............	m²	0.46	12.88	–	3.23	16.11	14.17	–	3.55	17.72
6010604B	concrete walls to stairwell..	m²	0.55	15.41	–	3.23	18.64	16.95	–	3.55	20.50
6010604C	concrete ceilings	m²	0.58	16.25	–	3.23	19.48	17.88	–	3.55	21.43
6010604D	concrete ceilings to stairwell	m²	0.64	17.93	–	3.23	21.16	19.72	–	3.55	23.28
6010604E	brick walls..............	m²	0.54	15.12	–	4.23	19.35	16.63	–	4.65	21.29
6010604F	brick walls to stairwell.....	m²	0.60	16.80	–	4.23	21.03	18.48	–	4.65	23.13
6010604G	block walls..............	m²	0.66	18.49	–	4.92	23.41	20.34	–	5.41	25.75
6010604H	block walls to stairwell.....	m²	0.72	20.17	–	4.92	25.09	22.19	–	5.41	27.60
6010604I	plastered walls	m²	0.43	12.04	–	3.23	15.27	13.24	–	3.55	16.80
6010604J	plastered walls to stairwell .	m²	0.50	14.00	–	3.23	17.23	15.40	–	3.55	18.95
6010604K	plastered ceilings	m²	0.55	15.41	–	3.23	18.64	16.95	–	3.55	20.50
6010604L	plastered ceilings to stairwell	m²	0.59	16.53	–	3.23	19.76	18.18	–	3.55	21.74
6010604M	embossed papered or textured walls	m²	0.47	13.16	–	3.23	16.39	14.48	–	3.55	18.03
6010604N	embossed papered or textured walls to stairwell ..	m²	0.56	15.69	–	3.23	18.92	17.26	–	3.55	20.81
6010604O	embossed papered or textured ceilings	m²	0.59	16.53	–	3.23	19.76	18.18	–	3.55	21.74
6010604P	embossed papered or textured ceilings to stairwell	m²	0.66	18.49	–	3.23	21.72	20.34	–	3.55	23.89
6010604Q	dado line 25 mm wide including cutting in both edges	m	0.30	8.41	–	0.15	8.56	9.25	–	0.17	9.42

Small Works 2009		Unit	Labour Hours	Labour Net	Plant Net	Materials Net	Unit Net	Labour Gross	Plant Gross	Materials Gross	Unit Price
								(Gross rates include 10% profit)			
				£	£	£	£	£	£	£	£
601	**NEW WORK**										
60106	**PAINTING AND DECORATING INTERNALLY**										
6010605	**Primer, two undercoats, one coat gloss finishing paint:**										
6010605A	concrete walls...........	m²	0.58	16.24	–	5.38	21.62	17.86	–	5.92	23.78
6010605B	concrete walls to stairwell..	m²	0.70	19.60	–	5.38	24.98	21.56	–	5.92	27.48
6010605C	concrete ceilings	m²	0.74	20.72	–	5.38	26.10	22.79	–	5.92	28.71
6010605D	concrete ceilings to stairwell	m²	0.82	22.96	–	5.38	28.34	25.26	–	5.92	31.17
6010605E	brick walls..............	m²	0.69	19.33	–	5.18	24.51	21.26	–	5.70	26.96
6010605F	brick walls to stairwell	m²	0.77	21.57	–	5.18	26.75	23.73	–	5.70	29.43
6010605G	block walls..............	m²	0.85	23.81	–	6.37	30.18	26.19	–	7.01	33.20
6010605H	block walls to stairwell.....	m²	0.93	26.05	–	6.37	32.42	28.66	–	7.01	35.66
6010605I	plastered walls	m²	0.54	15.12	–	3.73	18.85	16.63	–	4.10	20.74
6010605J	plastered walls to stairwell .	m²	0.63	17.65	–	3.73	21.38	19.42	–	4.10	23.52
6010605K	plastered ceilings	m²	0.70	19.61	–	3.73	23.34	21.57	–	4.10	25.67
6010605L	plastered ceilings to stairwell	m²	0.75	21.01	–	3.73	24.74	23.11	–	4.10	27.21
6010605M	embossed papered or textured walls	m²	0.59	16.53	–	4.18	20.71	18.18	–	4.60	22.78
6010605N	embossed papered or textured walls to stairwell ..	m²	0.71	19.89	–	4.18	24.07	21.88	–	4.60	26.48
6010605O	embossed papered or textured ceilings	m²	0.75	21.01	–	4.18	25.19	23.11	–	4.60	27.71
6010605P	embossed papered or textured ceilings to stairwell	m²	0.84	23.53	–	4.18	27.71	25.88	–	4.60	30.48
6010605Q	dado line 25 mm wide included cutting in both edges..................	m	0.40	11.20	–	0.20	11.40	12.32	–	0.22	12.54
6010606	**Knot, stop, prime, one undercoat, one gloss finishing coat oil paint on woodwork:**										
6010606A	general surfaces not exceeding 150 mm girth ...	m	0.32	8.96	–	0.31	9.27	9.86	–	0.34	10.20
6010606B	general surfaces 150-300 mm girth	m	0.41	11.49	–	0.70	12.19	12.64	–	0.77	13.41
6010606C	general surfaces over 300 mm girth	m²	0.75	21.01	–	2.45	23.46	23.11	–	2.70	25.81
6010606G	windows, glazed doors, screens in small panes	m²	1.66	46.50	–	2.01	48.51	51.15	–	2.21	53.36
6010606H	windows, glazed doors, screens in medium panes ..	m²	1.45	40.61	–	1.75	42.36	44.67	–	1.93	46.60
6010606I	windows, glazed doors, screens in large panes.....	m²	1.23	34.45	–	1.58	36.03	37.90	–	1.74	39.63
6010606J	windows, glazed doors, screens in extra large panes	m²	1.01	28.29	–	1.22	29.51	31.12	–	1.34	32.46
6010606K	frames and sashes (measure over glass)..............	m²	1.11	31.09	–	1.58	32.67	34.20	–	1.74	35.94
6010606L	open balustrade to staircase (measured flat both sides overall)..................	m²	0.78	21.84	–	2.19	24.03	24.02	–	2.41	26.43

Glazing, Painting and Decorating

Small Works 2009		Unit	Labour Hours	Labour Net	Plant Net	Materials Net	Unit Net	Labour Gross	Plant Gross	Materials Gross	Unit Price
								(Gross rates include 10% profit)			
				£	£	£	£	£	£	£	£
601	**NEW WORK**										
60106	**PAINTING AND DECORATING INTERNALLY**										
6010608	**Knot, stop, prime, two undercoats, one finishing coat gloss oil paint on woodwork:**										
6010608A	general surfaces not exceeding 150 mm girth ...	m	0.41	11.49	–	0.44	11.93	12.64	–	0.48	13.12
6010608B	general surfaces 150-300 mm girth	m	0.52	14.57	–	0.97	15.54	16.03	–	1.07	17.09
6010608C	general surfaces over 300 mm girth	m²	0.97	27.17	–	3.22	30.39	29.89	–	3.54	33.43
6010608G	windows, glazed doors, screens in small panes	m²	2.16	60.50	–	2.65	63.15	66.55	–	2.92	69.47
6010608H	windows, glazed doors, screens in medium panes ..	m²	1.88	52.66	–	2.25	54.91	57.93	–	2.48	60.40
6010608I	windows, glazed doors, screens in large panes.....	m²	1.60	44.82	–	1.98	46.80	49.30	–	2.18	51.48
6010608J	windows, glazed doors, screens in extra large panes	m²	1.31	36.69	–	1.63	38.32	40.36	–	1.79	42.15
6010608K	frames and sashes (measure over glass)..............	m²	1.44	40.34	–	1.98	42.32	44.37	–	2.18	46.55
6010608L	open balustrade to staircase (measured flat both sides overall).................	m²	1.02	28.57	–	2.91	31.48	31.43	–	3.20	34.63
6010609	**Primer, one undercoat, one finishing coat gloss oil paint on metalwork:**										
6010609A	general surfaces not exceeding 150 mm girth ...	m	0.30	8.41	–	0.37	8.78	9.25	–	0.41	9.66
6010609B	general surfaces 150-300 mm girth	m	0.39	10.92	–	0.84	11.76	12.01	–	0.92	12.94
6010609C	general surfaces over 300 mm girth	m²	0.69	19.33	–	2.95	22.28	21.26	–	3.25	24.51
6010609D	windows, glazed doors, screens in small panes	m²	1.66	46.50	–	2.42	48.92	51.15	–	2.66	53.81
6010609E	windows, glazed doors, screens in medium panes ..	m²	1.45	40.61	–	2.12	42.73	44.67	–	2.33	47.00
6010609F	windows, glazed doors, screens in large panes.....	m²	1.23	34.45	–	1.90	36.35	37.90	–	2.09	39.99
6010609G	windows, glazed doors, screens in extra large panes	m²	1.01	28.29	–	1.50	29.79	31.12	–	1.65	32.77
6010609H	corrugated surfaces over 300 mm girth	m²	0.75	21.01	–	3.33	24.34	23.11	–	3.66	26.77
6010609I	structural steelwork over 300 mm girth	m²	0.84	23.53	–	2.95	26.48	25.88	–	3.25	29.13
6010609J	radiators over 300 mm girth	m²	0.69	19.33	–	2.95	22.28	21.26	–	3.25	24.51
6010609K	pipes, ducts etc. not exceeding 150 mm girth ...	m	0.25	7.01	–	0.37	7.38	7.71	–	0.41	8.12
6010609L	pipes, ducts etc. 150-300 mm girth	m	0.35	9.80	–	0.84	10.64	10.78	–	0.92	11.70
6010609M	pipes, ducts etc. over 300 mm girth	m²	0.68	19.05	–	2.95	22.00	20.96	–	3.25	24.20
6010609O	sundry fittings-casement stays etc	Each	0.15	4.20	–	0.22	4.42	4.62	–	0.24	4.86

Small Works 2009		Unit	Labour Hours	Labour Net	Plant Net	Materials Net	Unit Net	Labour Gross	Plant Gross	Materials Gross	Unit Price
								(Gross rates include 10% profit)			
				£	£	£	£	£	£	£	£
601	**NEW WORK**										
60106	**PAINTING AND DECORATING INTERNALLY**										
6010610	**Primer, two undercoats, one finishing coat gloss oil paint on metalwork:**										
6010610A	general surfaces not exceeding 150 mm girth ...	m	0.38	10.64	–	0.51	11.15	11.70	–	0.56	12.27
6010610B	general surfaces 150-300 mm girth	m	0.50	14.01	–	1.11	15.12	15.41	–	1.22	16.63
6010610C	general surfaces over 300 mm girth	m²	0.90	25.20	–	3.73	28.93	27.72	–	4.10	31.82
6010610D	windows, glazed doors, screens in small panes	m²	2.16	60.50	–	3.06	63.56	66.55	–	3.37	69.92
6010610E	windows, glazed doors, screens in medium panes ..	m²	1.88	52.66	–	2.61	55.27	57.93	–	2.87	60.80
6010610F	windows, glazed doors, screens in large panes	m²	1.60	44.82	–	2.30	47.12	49.30	–	2.53	51.83
6010610G	windows, glazed doors, screens in extra large panes	m²	1.31	36.70	–	1.90	38.60	40.37	–	2.09	42.46
6010610H	corrugated surfaces over 300 mm girth	m²	0.98	27.45	–	4.19	31.64	30.20	–	4.61	34.80
6010610I	structural steelwork over 300 mm girth	m²	1.10	30.81	–	3.73	34.54	33.89	–	4.10	37.99
6010610J	radiators over 300 mm girth	m²	0.90	25.20	–	3.73	28.93	27.72	–	4.10	31.82
6010610K	pipes, ducts etc. not exceeding 150 mm girth ...	m	0.33	9.24	–	0.51	9.75	10.16	–	0.56	10.73
6010610L	pipes, ducts etc. 150 mm-300 mm girth	m	0.46	12.89	–	1.11	14.00	14.18	–	1.22	15.40
6010610M	pipes, ducts etc. over 300 mm girth	m²	0.89	24.92	–	3.73	28.65	27.41	–	4.10	31.52
6010610O	sundry fittings-casement stays etc	Each	0.20	5.60	–	0.31	5.91	6.16	–	0.34	6.50

Glazing, Painting and Decorating

Small Works 2009		Unit	Labour Hours	Labour Net	Plant Net	Materials Net	Unit Net	Labour Gross	Plant Gross	Materials Gross	Unit Price
								(Gross rates include 10% profit)			
				£	£	£	£	£	£	£	£
601	**NEW WORK**										
60106	**PAINTING AND DECORATING INTERNALLY**										
6010620	**One coat Cuprinol clear preserver on wrought timber:**										
6010620A	General surfaces not exceeding 150 mm girth ...	m	0.09	2.52	–	0.06	2.58	2.77	–	0.07	2.84
6010620B	General surfaces 150 mm–300 mm girth	m	0.14	3.92	–	0.14	4.06	4.31	–	0.15	4.47
6010620C	General surfaces over 300 mm girth	m²	0.19	5.32	–	0.45	5.77	5.85	–	0.50	6.35
6010621	**Two coats Cuprinol clear preserver on wrought timber:**										
6010621A	General surfaces not exceeding 150 mm girth ...	m	0.18	5.04	–	0.14	5.18	5.54	–	0.15	5.70
6010621B	General surfaces 150 mm–300 mm girth	m	0.25	7.00	–	0.28	7.28	7.70	–	0.31	8.01
6010621C	General surfaces over 300 mm girth	m²	0.37	10.37	–	0.92	11.29	11.41	–	1.01	12.42
6010622	**One coat Cuprinol oak preserver on wrought timber:**										
6010622A	General surfaces not exceeding 150 mm girth ...	m	0.08	2.24	–	0.06	2.30	2.46	–	0.07	2.53
6010622B	General surfaces 150 mm–300 mm girth	m	0.12	3.36	–	0.14	3.50	3.70	–	0.15	3.85
6010622C	General surfaces over 300 mm girth	m²	0.18	5.04	–	0.48	5.52	5.54	–	0.53	6.07
6010623	**Two coats Cuprinol oak preserver wrought timber:**										
6010623A	General surfaces not exceeding 150 mm girth ...	m	0.16	4.48	–	0.14	4.62	4.93	–	0.15	5.08
6010623B	General surfaces 150 mm–300 mm girth	m	0.23	6.44	–	0.28	6.72	7.08	–	0.31	7.39
6010623C	General surfaces over 300 mm girth	m²	0.36	10.09	–	0.92	11.01	11.10	–	1.01	12.11

Glazing, Painting and Decorating

Small Works 2009		Unit	Labour Hours	Labour Net	Plant Net	Materials Net	Unit Net	Labour Gross	Plant Gross	Materials Gross	Unit Price
								(Gross rates include 10% profit)			
				£	£	£	£	£	£	£	£
601	**NEW WORK**										
60106	**PAINTING AND DECORATING INTERNALLY**										
6010624	**Two coats clear polyurethane on woodwork:**										
6010624A	General surfaces not exceeding 150 mm girth ...	m	0.16	4.48	–	0.26	4.74	4.93	–	0.29	5.21
6010624B	General surfaces 150 mm-300 mm girth	m	0.24	6.72	–	0.52	7.24	7.39	–	0.57	7.96
6010624C	General surfaces over 300 mm girth	m²	0.36	10.08	–	1.71	11.79	11.09	–	1.88	12.97
6010624G	windows, glazed doors, screens in small panes	m²	0.80	22.41	–	1.35	23.76	24.65	–	1.49	26.14
6010624H	windows, glazed doors, screens in medium panes ..	m²	0.72	20.17	–	1.19	21.36	22.19	–	1.31	23.50
6010624I	windows, glazed doors, screens in large panes.....	m²	0.64	17.93	–	1.03	18.96	19.72	–	1.13	20.86
6010624J	windows, glazed doors, screens in extra large panes	m²	0.56	15.69	–	0.87	16.56	17.26	–	0.96	18.22
6010625	**Three coats clear polyurethane on woodwork:**										
6010625A	General surfaces not exceeding 150 mm girth ...	m	0.26	7.28	–	0.39	7.67	8.01	–	0.43	8.44
6010625B	General surfaces 150 mm-300 mm girth	m	0.32	8.97	–	0.77	9.74	9.87	–	0.85	10.71
6010625C	General surfaces over 300 mm girth	m²	0.54	15.13	–	2.58	17.71	16.64	–	2.84	19.48
6010625G	windows, glazed doors, screens in small panes	m²	1.10	30.82	–	2.06	32.88	33.90	–	2.27	36.17
6010625H	windows, glazed doors, screens in medium panes ..	m²	1.02	28.57	–	1.81	30.38	31.43	–	1.99	33.42
6010625I	windows, glazed doors, screens in large panes.....	m²	0.94	26.33	–	1.55	27.88	28.96	–	1.71	30.67
6010625J	windows, glazed doors, screens in extra large panes	m²	0.86	24.09	–	1.29	25.38	26.50	–	1.42	27.92
6010626	**Two coats coloured polyurethane on woodwork:**										
6010626A	General surfaces not exceeding 150 mm girth ...	m	0.16	4.48	–	0.67	5.15	4.93	–	0.74	5.67
6010626B	General surfaces 150 mm-300 mm girth	m	0.24	6.72	–	1.34	8.06	7.39	–	1.47	8.87
6010626C	General surfaces over 300 mm girth	m²	0.36	10.08	–	4.45	14.53	11.09	–	4.90	15.98
6010626G	windows, glazed doors, screens in small panes	m²	0.80	22.41	–	3.52	25.93	24.65	–	3.87	28.52
6010626H	windows, glazed doors, screens in medium panes ..	m²	0.72	20.17	–	3.10	23.27	22.19	–	3.41	25.60
6010626I	windows, glazed doors, screens in large panes.....	m²	0.64	17.93	–	2.68	20.61	19.72	–	2.95	22.67
6010626J	windows, glazed doors, screens in extra large panes	m²	0.56	15.69	–	2.26	17.95	17.26	–	2.49	19.75

Small Works 2009		Unit	Labour Hours	Labour Net	Plant Net	Materials Net	Unit Net	Labour Gross	Plant Gross	Materials Gross	Unit Price
								\multicolumn{3}{c}{(Gross rates include 10% profit)}	
				£	£	£	£	£	£	£	£
601	**NEW WORK**										
60106	**PAINTING AND DECORATING INTERNALLY**										
6010627	**Three coats coloured polyurethane on woodwork:**										
6010627A	General surfaces not exceeding 150 mm girth ...	m	0.26	7.28	–	1.01	8.29	8.01	–	1.11	9.12
6010627B	General surfaces 150 mm-300 mm girth	m	0.32	8.97	–	2.01	10.98	9.87	–	2.21	12.08
6010627C	General surfaces over 300 mm girth	m²	0.54	15.12	–	6.71	21.83	16.63	–	7.38	24.01
6010627G	windows, glazed doors, screens in small panes	m²	1.10	30.81	–	5.37	36.18	33.89	–	5.91	39.80
6010627H	windows, glazed doors, screens in medium panes ..	m²	1.02	28.57	–	4.70	33.27	31.43	–	5.17	36.60
6010627I	windows, glazed doors, screens in large panes.....	m²	0.94	26.33	–	4.03	30.36	28.96	–	4.43	33.40
6010627J	windows, glazed doors, screens in extra large panes	m²	0.86	24.09	–	3.35	27.44	26.50	–	3.69	30.18
6010628	**Two coats raw or boiled linseed oil on woodwork:**										
6010628A	General surfaces not exceeding 150 mm girth ...	m	0.12	3.37	–	0.19	3.56	3.71	–	0.21	3.92
6010628B	General surfaces 150 mm-300 mm girth	m	0.16	4.48	–	0.36	4.84	4.93	–	0.40	5.32
6010628C	General surfaces over 300 mm girth	m²	0.30	8.40	–	1.23	9.63	9.24	–	1.35	10.59
6010630	**Seal and wax polish woodwork:**										
6010630A	General surfaces not exceeding 150 mm girth ...	m	0.09	2.52	–	0.24	2.76	2.77	–	0.26	3.04
6010630B	General surfaces 150 mm-300 mm girth	m	0.13	3.64	–	0.51	4.15	4.00	–	0.56	4.57
6010630C	General surfaces over 300 mm girth	m²	0.20	5.61	–	1.87	7.48	6.17	–	2.06	8.23
6010630G	windows, glazed doors, screens in small panes	m²	0.60	16.81	–	1.40	18.21	18.49	–	1.54	20.03
6010630H	windows, glazed doors, screens in medium panes ..	m²	0.50	14.00	–	1.15	15.15	15.40	–	1.27	16.67
6010630I	windows, glazed doors, screens in large panes.....	m²	0.40	11.21	–	0.94	12.15	12.33	–	1.03	13.37
6010630J	windows, glazed doors, screens in extra large panes	m²	0.30	8.40	–	0.56	8.96	9.24	–	0.62	9.86
6010640	**One coat Artex sealer, one coat Artex standard compound with stipple finish:**										
6010640A	Concrete walls	m²	0.42	11.76	–	1.45	13.21	12.94	–	1.60	14.53
6010640B	Concrete walls to stairwell..	m²	0.44	12.32	–	1.45	13.77	13.55	–	1.60	15.15
6010640C	Brick walls...............	m²	0.42	11.76	–	1.68	13.44	12.94	–	1.85	14.78
6010640D	Brick walls to stairwell.....	m²	0.44	12.32	–	1.68	14.00	13.55	–	1.85	15.40
6010640E	Block walls	m²	0.42	11.77	–	1.90	13.67	12.95	–	2.09	15.04
6010640F	Block walls to stairwell	m²	0.44	12.33	–	1.90	14.23	13.56	–	2.09	15.65
6010640G	Plastered walls	m²	0.37	10.36	–	1.45	11.81	11.40	–	1.60	12.99
6010640H	Plastered walls to stairwell .	m²	0.39	10.92	–	1.45	12.37	12.01	–	1.60	13.61
6010640I	Plastered ceilings........	m²	0.41	11.48	–	1.45	12.93	12.63	–	1.60	14.22
6010640J	Plastered ceilings to stairwell	m²	0.43	12.04	–	1.45	13.49	13.24	–	1.60	14.84
6010640K	Plasterboard walls	m²	0.37	10.36	–	1.45	11.81	11.40	–	1.60	12.99
6010640L	Plasterboard walls to stairwell.................	m²	0.39	10.92	–	1.45	12.37	12.01	–	1.60	13.61
6010640M	Plasterboard ceiling	m²	0.41	11.48	–	1.45	12.93	12.63	–	1.60	14.22
6010640N	Plasterboard ceiling to stairwell.................	m²	0.43	12.04	–	1.45	13.49	13.24	–	1.60	14.84

Small Works 2009		Unit	Labour Hours	Labour Net	Plant Net	Materials Net	Unit Net	Labour Gross	Plant Gross	Materials Gross	Unit Price
								(Gross rates include 10% profit)			
				£	£	£	£	£	£	£	£
601	**NEW WORK**										
60108	**PAINTING AND DECORATING EXTERNALLY**										
6010802	**Two coats Snowcem on walls:**										
6010802A	Concrete	m²	0.45	12.61	–	0.54	13.15	13.87	–	0.59	14.47
6010802B	Brick.	m²	0.48	13.45	–	0.54	13.99	14.80	–	0.59	15.39
6010802C	Block	m²	0.54	15.13	–	0.54	15.67	16.64	–	0.59	17.24
6010802D	Cement rendered	m²	0.42	11.77	–	0.54	12.31	12.95	–	0.59	13.54
6010802E	Rough cast	m²	0.57	15.97	–	1.58	17.55	17.57	–	1.74	19.31
6010803	**Stabilising solution, two coats Sandtex matt on walls:**										
6010803A	Concrete	m²	0.57	15.97	–	4.66	20.63	17.57	–	5.13	22.69
6010803B	Brick.	m²	0.60	16.81	–	5.47	22.28	18.49	–	6.02	24.51
6010803C	Block	m²	0.66	18.48	–	6.74	25.22	20.33	–	7.41	27.74
6010803D	Cement rendered	m²	0.54	15.13	–	4.66	19.79	16.64	–	5.13	21.77
6010803E	Rough cast	m²	0.69	19.32	–	9.76	29.08	21.25	–	10.74	31.99
6010804	**Two coats Weathershield masonry paint on walls:**										
6010804A	Concrete	m²	0.50	14.01	–	2.53	16.54	15.41	–	2.78	18.19
6010804B	Brick.	m²	0.61	17.08	–	3.00	20.08	18.79	–	3.30	22.09
6010804C	Block	m²	0.69	19.33	–	3.59	22.92	21.26	–	3.95	25.21
6010804D	Cement rendered	m²	0.53	14.84	–	3.00	17.84	16.32	–	3.30	19.62
6010804E	Rough cast	m²	0.72	20.16	–	4.48	24.64	22.18	–	4.93	27.10
6010810	**Prime only woodwork:**										
6010810A	General surfaces not exceeding 150 mm girth . . .	m	0.13	3.64	–	0.12	3.76	4.00	–	0.13	4.14
6010810B	General surfaces 150 mm–300 mm girth	m	0.17	4.76	–	0.25	5.01	5.24	–	0.28	5.51
6010810C	General surfaces over 300 mm girth	m²	0.26	7.28	–	0.91	8.19	8.01	–	1.00	9.01
6010810G	Windows, glazed doors, screens in small panes	m²	0.66	18.49	–	0.74	19.23	20.34	–	0.81	21.15
6010810H	Windows, glazed doors, screens in medium panes . .	m²	0.58	16.24	–	0.66	16.90	17.86	–	0.73	18.59
6010810I	Windows, glazed doors, screens in large panes	m²	0.50	14.00	–	0.58	14.58	15.40	–	0.64	16.04
6010810J	Windows, glazed doors, screens in extra large panes	m²	0.42	11.77	–	0.49	12.26	12.95	–	0.54	13.49
6010810K	Frames and sashes (measured over glass).	m²	0.44	12.32	–	0.58	12.90	13.55	–	0.64	14.19
6010820	**Knot, stop, prime, one undercoat one gloss finishing coat oil paint on woodwork:**										
6010820A	General surfaces not exceeding 150 mm girth . . .	m	0.39	10.92	–	0.31	11.23	12.01	–	0.34	12.35
6010820B	General surfaces 150 mm–300 mm girth	m	0.51	14.29	–	0.70	14.99	15.72	–	0.77	16.49
6010820C	General surfaces over 300 mm girth	m²	0.78	21.85	–	2.45	24.30	24.04	–	2.70	26.73
6010820G	Windows, glazed doors, screens in small panes	m²	1.98	55.46	–	2.01	57.47	61.01	–	2.21	63.22
6010820H	Windows, glazed doors, screens in medium panes . .	m²	1.74	48.74	–	1.75	50.49	53.61	–	1.93	55.54
6010820I	Windows, glazed doors, screens in large panes	m²	1.50	42.01	–	1.58	43.59	46.21	–	1.74	47.95
6010820J	Windows, glazed doors, screens in extra large panes	m²	1.20	33.61	–	1.22	34.83	36.97	–	1.34	38.31
6010820K	Frames and sashes (measured over glass).	m²	1.32	36.97	–	1.58	38.55	40.67	–	1.74	42.41
6010820L	Open balustrade to staircase (measured flat both sides) .	m²	0.87	24.36	–	2.19	26.55	26.80	–	2.41	29.21

Small Works 2009		Unit	Labour Hours	Labour Net	Plant Net	Materials Net	Unit Net	Labour Gross	Plant Gross	Materials Gross	Unit Price
								(Gross rates include 10% profit)			
				£	£	£	£	£	£	£	£
601	**NEW WORK**										
60108	**PAINTING AND DECORATING EXTERNALLY**										
6010821	**Knot, stop, prime, two undercoats, one gloss finishing coat oil paint on woodwork:**										
6010821A	General surfaces not exceeding 150 mm girth ...	m	0.52	14.57	–	0.44	15.01	16.03	–	0.48	16.51
6010821B	General surfaces 150 mm–300 mm girth	m	0.68	19.05	–	0.97	20.02	20.96	–	1.07	22.02
6010821C	General surfaces over 300 mm girth	m²	1.04	29.13	–	3.22	32.35	32.04	–	3.54	35.59
6010821G	Windows, glazed doors, screens in small panes	m²	2.64	73.94	–	2.65	76.59	81.33	–	2.92	84.25
6010821H	Windows, glazed doors, screens in medium panes ..	m²	2.32	64.98	–	2.25	67.23	71.48	–	2.48	73.95
6010821I	Windows, glazed doors, screens in large panes	m²	2.00	56.02	–	1.98	58.00	61.62	–	2.18	63.80
6010821J	Windows, glazed doors, screens in extra large panes	m²	1.60	44.82	–	1.63	46.45	49.30	–	1.79	51.10
6010821K	Frames and sashes (measured over glass).....	m²	1.76	49.30	–	1.98	51.28	54.23	–	2.18	56.41
6010821L	Open balustrade to staircase (measured flat both sides) .	m²	1.16	32.49	–	3.64	36.13	35.74	–	4.00	39.74
6010830	**Prime only metalwork:**										
6010830A	General surfaces not exceeding 150 mm girth ...	m	0.13	3.64	–	0.19	3.83	4.00	–	0.21	4.21
6010830B	General surfaces 150 mm–300 mm girth	m	0.17	4.77	–	0.38	5.15	5.25	–	0.42	5.67
6010830C	General surfaces over 300 mm girth	m²	0.26	7.28	–	1.41	8.69	8.01	–	1.55	9.56
6010830D	Windows, glazed doors, screens in small panes	m²	0.66	18.49	–	1.15	19.64	20.34	–	1.27	21.60
6010830E	Windows, glazed doors, screens in medium panes ..	m²	0.58	16.24	–	1.03	17.27	17.86	–	1.13	19.00
6010830F	Windows, glazed doors, screens in large panes	m²	0.50	14.00	–	0.90	14.90	15.40	–	0.99	16.39
6010830G	Windows, glazed doors, screens in extra large panes	m²	0.42	11.76	–	0.77	12.53	12.94	–	0.85	13.78
6010830H	Stairs (measured overall) ..	m²	0.28	7.84	–	1.22	9.06	8.62	–	1.34	9.97
6010830I	Corrugated surfaces over 300 mm girt.............	m²	0.29	8.13	–	1.60	9.73	8.94	–	1.76	10.70
6010830J	Structural steelwork over 300 mm girth	m²	0.32	8.96	–	1.41	10.37	9.86	–	1.55	11.41
6010830K	Railings, balustrades (measured flat both sides overall).................	m²	0.29	8.12	–	1.22	9.34	8.93	–	1.34	10.27
6010830L	Eaves gutters inside and out not exceeding 150 mm girth	m	0.15	4.20	–	0.19	4.39	4.62	–	0.21	4.83
6010830M	Eaves gutters inside and out 150 mm–300 mm girth.....	m	0.17	4.77	–	0.38	5.15	5.25	–	0.42	5.67
6010830N	Eaves gutters inside and out over 300 mm girth	m²	0.27	7.56	–	1.41	8.97	8.32	–	1.55	9.87
6010830O	Pipes, ducts etc not exceeding 150 m girth	m	0.15	4.20	–	0.19	4.39	4.62	–	0.21	4.83
6010830P	Pipes, ducts etc 150 mm–300 mm girth	m	0.19	5.33	–	0.38	5.71	5.86	–	0.42	6.28
6010830Q	Pipes, ducts etc over 300 mm girth	m²	0.26	7.28	–	1.41	8.69	8.01	–	1.55	9.56
6010830R	Rainwater heads inside and out	Each	0.08	2.24	–	0.19	2.43	2.46	–	0.21	2.67

Small Works 2009		Unit	Labour Hours	Labour Net	Plant Net	Materials Net	Unit Net	Labour Gross	Plant Gross	Materials Gross	Unit Price
								(Gross rates include 10% profit)			
				£	£	£	£	£	£	£	£
601	**NEW WORK**										
60108	**PAINTING AND DECORATING EXTERNALLY**										
6010831	**Primer, one undercoat, one gloss finishing coat oil paint on metalwork:**										
6010831A	General surfaces not exceeding 150 mm girth ...	m	0.39	10.93	–	0.37	11.30	12.02	–	0.41	12.43
6010831B	General surfaces 150 mm-300 mm girth	m	0.51	14.28	–	0.84	15.12	15.71	–	0.92	16.63
6010831C	General surfaces over 300 mm girth	m²	0.78	21.85	–	2.95	24.80	24.04	–	3.25	27.28
6010831D	Windows, glazed doors, screens in small panes	m²	1.98	55.46	–	2.42	57.88	61.01	–	2.66	63.67
6010831E	Windows, glazed doors, screens in medium panes ..	m²	1.74	48.73	–	2.12	50.85	53.60	–	2.33	55.94
6010831F	Windows, glazed doors, screens in large panes.....	m²	1.50	42.01	–	1.90	43.91	46.21	–	2.09	48.30
6010831G	Windows, glazed doors, screens in extra large panes	m²	1.20	33.61	–	1.50	35.11	36.97	–	1.65	38.62
6010831H	Stairs (measured overall) ..	m²	0.84	23.53	–	2.58	26.11	25.88	–	2.84	28.72
6010831I	Corrugated surfaces over 300 mm girt.............	m²	0.87	24.37	–	3.33	27.70	26.81	–	3.66	30.47
6010831J	Structural steelwork over 300 mm girth	m²	0.96	26.89	–	2.95	29.84	29.58	–	3.25	32.82
6010831K	Railings, balustrades (measured flat both sides overall).................	m²	0.87	24.37	–	2.31	26.68	26.81	–	2.54	29.35
6010831L	Eaves gutters inside and out not exceeding 150 mm girth	m	0.45	12.61	–	0.37	12.98	13.87	–	0.41	14.28
6010831M	Eaves gutters inside and out 150 mm-300 mm girth.....	m	0.51	14.28	–	0.84	15.12	15.71	–	0.92	16.63
6010831N	Eaves gutters inside and out over 300 mm girth	m²	0.81	22.69	–	2.95	25.64	24.96	–	3.25	28.20
6010831O	Pipes, ducts etc not exceeding 150 m girth	m	0.45	12.61	–	0.37	12.98	13.87	–	0.41	14.28
6010831P	Pipes, ducts etc 150 mm-300 mm girth	m	0.51	14.28	–	0.84	15.12	15.71	–	0.92	16.63
6010831Q	Pipes, ducts etc. over 300 mm girth	m²	0.78	21.85	–	2.95	24.80	24.04	–	3.25	27.28
6010831R	Rainwater heads inside and out	Each	0.24	6.73	–	0.37	7.10	7.40	–	0.41	7.81

Glazing, Painting and Decorating

Small Works 2009		Unit	Labour Hours	Labour Net	Plant Net	Materials Net	Unit Net	Labour Gross	Plant Gross	Materials Gross	Unit Price
								(Gross rates include 10% profit)			
				£	£	£	£	£	£	£	£
601	**NEW WORK**										
60108	**PAINTING AND DECORATING EXTERNALLY**										
6010832	**Primer, two undercoats, one gloss coat oil finishing paint on metalwork:**										
6010832A	General surfaces not exceeding 150 mm girth ...	m	0.52	14.57	–	0.51	15.08	16.03	–	0.56	16.59
6010832B	General surfaces 150 mm-300 mm girth	m	0.68	19.05	–	1.11	20.16	20.96	–	1.22	22.18
6010832C	General surfaces over 300 mm girth	m²	1.04	29.13	–	3.73	32.86	32.04	–	4.10	36.15
6010832D	Windows, glazed doors, screens in small panes	m²	2.64	73.95	–	3.06	77.01	81.35	–	3.37	84.71
6010832E	Windows, glazed doors, screens in medium panes ..	m²	2.32	64.99	–	2.61	67.60	71.49	–	2.87	74.36
6010832F	Windows, glazed doors, screens in large panes	m²	2.00	56.02	–	2.30	58.32	61.62	–	2.53	64.15
6010832G	Windows, glazed doors, screens in extra large panes	m²	1.60	44.82	–	1.90	46.72	49.30	–	2.09	51.39
6010832H	Stairs (measured overall) ..	m²	1.12	31.37	–	3.22	34.59	34.51	–	3.54	38.05
6010832I	Corrugated surfaces over 300 mm girt.	m²	1.16	32.49	–	4.19	36.68	35.74	–	4.61	40.35
6010832J	Structural steelwork over 300 mm girth	m²	1.28	35.85	–	3.73	39.58	39.44	–	4.10	43.54
6010832K	Railings, balustrades (measured flat both sides overall).................	m²	1.16	32.49	–	2.81	35.30	35.74	–	3.09	38.83

Small Works 2009		Unit	Labour Hours	Labour Net	Plant Net	Materials Net	Unit Net	Labour Gross	Plant Gross	Materials Gross	Unit Price
									(Gross rates include 10% profit)		
				£	£	£	£	£	£	£	£
601	**NEW WORK**										
60108	**PAINTING AND DECORATING EXTERNALLY**										
6010832	**Primer, two undercoats, one gloss coat oil finishing paint on metalwork:**										
6010832L	Eaves gutters inside and out not exceeding 150 mm girth	m	0.60	16.81	–	0.51	17.32	18.49	–	0.56	19.05
6010832M	Eaves gutters inside and out 150 mm-300 mm girth.....	m	0.68	19.05	–	1.11	20.16	20.96	–	1.22	22.18
6010832N	Eaves gutters inside and out over 300 mm girth	m²	1.08	30.25	–	3.73	33.98	33.28	–	4.10	37.38
6010832O	Pipes, ducts etc not exceeding 150 m girth	m	0.60	16.81	–	0.51	17.32	18.49	–	0.56	19.05
6010832P	Pipes, ducts etc 150 mm-300 mm girth	m	0.68	19.05	–	1.11	20.16	20.96	–	1.22	22.18
6010832Q	Pipes, ducts etc over 300 mm girth	m²	1.04	29.13	–	3.73	32.86	32.04	–	4.10	36.15
6010832R	Rainwater heads inside and out	Each	0.32	8.96	–	0.51	9.47	9.86	–	0.56	10.42
6010840	**One coat bituminous paint on metalwork:**										
6010840A	Water storage cistern, tanks, inside and out	m²	0.40	11.20	–	0.49	11.69	12.32	–	0.54	12.86
6010840B	Gutters (inside surfaces)...	m	0.10	2.80	–	0.18	2.98	3.08	–	0.20	3.28
6010841	**Two coat bituminous paint on metalwork:**										
6010841A	Water storage cistern, tanks, inside and out	m²	0.80	22.41	–	1.03	23.44	24.65	–	1.13	25.78
6010841B	Corrugated surfaces over 300 mm girt.	m²	1.00	28.01	–	1.03	29.04	30.81	–	1.13	31.94
6010841C	Gutters (inside surfaces)...	m	0.18	5.05	–	0.30	5.35	5.56	–	0.33	5.89
6010841D	Pipes not exceeding 150 mm girth	m	0.13	3.64	–	0.18	3.82	4.00	–	0.20	4.20
6010841E	Pipes 150 mm-300 mm girth	m	0.24	6.73	–	0.30	7.03	7.40	–	0.33	7.73
6010841F	Pipes over 300 mm girth ...	m²	0.34	9.53	–	1.03	10.56	10.48	–	1.13	11.62

Glazing, Painting and Decorating

Small Works 2009		Unit	Labour Hours	Labour Net	Plant Net	Materials Net	Unit Net	Labour Gross	Plant Gross	Materials Gross	Unit Price
								(Gross rates include 10% profit)			
				£	£	£	£	£	£	£	£
601	**NEW WORK**										
60108	**PAINTING AND DECORATING EXTERNALLY**										
6010842	**Two coats timber preserver on wrought timber:**										
6010842A	General surfaces not exceeding 150 m girth	m	0.20	5.60	–	0.05	5.65	6.16	–	0.06	6.22
6010842B	General surfaces 150 mm–300 mm girth	m	0.26	7.28	–	0.10	7.38	8.01	–	0.11	8.12
6010842C	General surfaces over 300 mm girth	m²	0.38	10.64	–	0.34	10.98	11.70	–	0.37	12.08
6010843	**Two coats timber preserver on sawn timber:**										
6010843A	General surfaces not exceeding 150 m girth	m	0.21	5.88	–	0.10	5.98	6.47	–	0.11	6.58
6010843B	General surfaces 150 mm–300 mm girth	m	0.27	7.57	–	0.18	7.75	8.33	–	0.20	8.53
6010843C	General surfaces over 300 mm girth	m²	0.40	11.21	–	0.43	11.64	12.33	–	0.47	12.80
6010850	**Two coats Solignum on wrought timber:**										
6010850A	General surfaces not exceeding 150 m girth	m	0.19	5.32	–	0.21	5.53	5.85	–	0.23	6.08
6010850B	General surfaces 150 mm–300 mm girth	m	0.25	7.00	–	0.42	7.42	7.70	–	0.46	8.16
6010850C	General surfaces over 300 mm girth	m²	0.36	10.08	–	1.36	11.44	11.09	–	1.50	12.58

Glazing, Painting and Decorating

Small Works 2009		Unit	Labour Hours	Labour Net	Plant Net	Materials Net	Unit Net	Labour Gross	Plant Gross	Materials Gross	Unit Price
								(Gross rates include 10% profit)			
				£	£	£	£	£	£	£	£
601	NEW WORK										
60108	PAINTING AND DECORATING EXTERNALLY										
6010851	Two coats Solignum on sawn timber:										
6010851A	General surfaces not exceeding 150 m girth	m	0.20	5.60	–	0.28	5.88	6.16	–	0.31	6.47
6010851B	General surfaces 150 mm-300 mm girth	m	0.26	7.28	–	0.63	7.91	8.01	–	0.69	8.70
6010851C	General surfaces over 300 mm girth	m²	0.38	10.64	–	2.02	12.66	11.70	–	2.22	13.93
6010855	Two coats Cuprinol preserver on wrought timber (green):										
6010855A	General surfaces not exceeding 150 m girth	m	0.20	5.61	–	0.22	5.83	6.17	–	0.24	6.41
6010855B	General surfaces 150 mm-300 mm girth	m	0.26	7.28	–	0.45	7.73	8.01	–	0.50	8.50
6010855C	General surfaces over 300 mm girth	m²	0.38	10.65	–	1.48	12.13	11.72	–	1.63	13.34
6010856	Two coats Cuprinol preserver on sawn timber (green):										
6010856A	General surfaces not exceeding 150 m girth	m	0.21	5.88	–	0.31	6.19	6.47	–	0.34	6.81
6010856B	General surfaces 150 mm-300 mm girth	m	0.27	7.56	–	0.59	8.15	8.32	–	0.65	8.97
6010856C	General surfaces over 300 mm girth	m²	0.40	11.20	–	1.99	13.19	12.32	–	2.19	14.51
6010857	Two coats Cuprinol preserver on wrought timber (clear):										
6010857A	General surfaces not exceeding 150 m girth	m	0.20	5.61	–	0.22	5.83	6.17	–	0.24	6.41
6010857B	General surfaces 150 mm-300 mm girth	m	0.26	7.28	–	0.45	7.73	8.01	–	0.50	8.50
6010857C	General surfaces over 300 mm girth	m²	0.38	10.65	–	1.48	12.13	11.72	–	1.63	13.34
6010858	Two coats Cuprinol preserver on sawn timber (clear):										
6010858A	General surfaces not exceeding 150 m girth	m	0.21	5.88	–	0.31	6.19	6.47	–	0.34	6.81
6010858B	General surfaces 150 mm-300 mm girth	m	0.27	7.56	–	0.59	8.15	8.32	–	0.65	8.97
6010858C	General surfaces over 300 mm girth	m²	0.40	11.20	–	1.99	13.19	12.32	–	2.19	14.51
6010859	Two coats raw or boiled linseed oil on woodwork:										
6010859A	General surfaces not exceeding 150 m girth	m	0.14	3.93	–	0.43	4.36	4.32	–	0.47	4.80
6010859B	General surfaces 150 mm-300 mm girth	m	0.18	5.05	–	0.85	5.90	5.56	–	0.94	6.49
6010859C	General surfaces over 300 mm girth	m²	0.32	8.97	–	2.86	11.83	9.87	–	3.15	13.01

Glazing, Painting and Decorating

Small Works 2009		Unit	Labour Hours	Labour Net	Plant Net	Materials Net	Unit Net	Labour Gross	Plant Gross	Materials Gross	Unit Price
								(Gross rates include 10% profit)			
				£	£	£	£	£	£	£	£
601	**NEW WORK**										
60108	**PAINTING AND DECORATING EXTERNALLY**										
6010860	**Two coats clear polyurethane on woodwork:**										
6010860A	General surfaces not exceeding 150 m girth	m	0.20	5.60	–	0.26	5.86	6.16	–	0.29	6.45
6010860B	General surfaces 150 mm-300 mm girth	m	0.26	7.28	–	0.55	7.83	8.01	–	0.61	8.61
6010860C	General surfaces over 300 mm girth	m²	0.38	10.64	–	1.81	12.45	11.70	–	1.99	13.70
6010860G	Windows, glazed doors, screens in small panes	m²	0.84	23.53	–	1.35	24.88	25.88	–	1.49	27.37
6010860H	Windows, glazed doors, screens medium panes	m²	0.76	21.29	–	1.16	22.45	23.42	–	1.28	24.70
6010860I	Windows, glazed doors, screens large panes	m²	0.68	19.04	–	0.94	19.98	20.94	–	1.03	21.98
6010860J	Windows, glazed doors, screens extra large panes ..	m²	0.60	16.80	–	0.55	17.35	18.48	–	0.61	19.09
6010861	**Three coats clear polyurethane on woodwork:**										
6010861A	General surfaces not exceeding 150 m girth	m	0.28	7.84	–	0.42	8.26	8.62	–	0.46	9.09
6010861B	General surfaces 150 mm-300 mm girth	m	0.34	9.52	–	0.81	10.33	10.47	–	0.89	11.36
6010861C	General surfaces over 300 mm girth	m²	0.56	15.69	–	2.74	18.43	17.26	–	3.01	20.27
6010861G	Windows, glazed doors, screens in small panes	m²	1.14	31.94	–	2.06	34.00	35.13	–	2.27	37.40
6010861H	Windows, glazed doors, screens medium panes	m²	1.06	29.69	–	1.74	31.43	32.66	–	1.91	34.57
6010861I	Windows, glazed doors, screens large panes	m²	0.98	27.45	–	1.35	28.80	30.20	–	1.49	31.68
6010861J	Windows, glazed doors, screens extra large panes ..	m²	0.90	25.21	–	0.81	26.02	27.73	–	0.89	28.62

Glazing, Painting and Decorating

Small Works 2009		Unit	Labour Hours	Labour Net	Plant Net	Materials Net	Unit Net	Labour Gross	Plant Gross	Materials Gross	Unit Price
								(Gross rates include 10% profit)			
				£	£	£	£	£	£	£	£
601	**NEW WORK**										
60109	**SIGNWRITING**										
6010901	**Gloss oil paint, per coat, per 25 mm high:**										
6010901A	Capital letters	Each	0.14	3.92	–	0.11	4.03	4.31	–	0.12	4.43
6010901B	Lower case letters	Each	0.16	4.49	–	0.05	4.54	4.94	–	0.06	4.99
6010901C	Numerals	Each	0.16	4.48	–	0.11	4.59	4.93	–	0.12	5.05
6010901D	Stops, commas and hyphens	Each	0.05	1.41	–	0.05	1.46	1.55	–	0.06	1.61
6010902	**Gilt or gold leaf, per 25 mm high:**										
6010902A	Capital letters	Each	0.16	4.48	–	0.39	4.87	4.93	–	0.43	5.36
6010902B	Lower case letters	Each	0.14	3.92	–	0.29	4.21	4.31	–	0.32	4.63
6010902C	Numerals	Each	0.16	4.48	–	0.39	4.87	4.93	–	0.43	5.36
60110	**PRESSURE SPRAY PAINTING**										
6011001	**One coat emulsion paint:**										
6011001A	Brick	m²	0.13	3.33	–	0.81	4.14	3.66	–	0.89	4.55
6011001B	Block	m²	0.16	4.10	–	1.04	5.14	4.51	–	1.14	5.65
6011001C	Concrete	m²	0.10	2.56	–	0.81	3.37	2.82	–	0.89	3.71
6011001D	Plaster	m²	0.10	2.57	–	0.69	3.26	2.83	–	0.76	3.59
6011002	**One coat oil colour:**										
6011002B	Brick	m²	0.18	4.62	–	0.95	5.57	5.08	–	1.05	6.13
6011002C	Block	m²	0.23	5.89	–	1.23	7.12	6.48	–	1.35	7.83
6011002D	Concrete	m²	0.23	5.90	–	0.95	6.85	6.49	–	1.05	7.54
6011002E	Plaster	m²	0.15	3.84	–	0.82	4.66	4.22	–	0.90	5.13
6011003	**One base coat by brush; one coat multicolour:**										
6011003A	Brick	m²	0.34	8.72	–	5.38	14.10	9.59	–	5.92	15.51
6011003C	Block	m²	0.34	8.72	–	5.38	14.10	9.59	–	5.92	15.51
6011003D	Concrete	m²	0.34	8.72	–	5.38	14.10	9.59	–	5.92	15.51
6011003E	Plaster	m²	0.30	7.69	–	5.38	13.07	8.46	–	5.92	14.38

Glazing, Painting and Decorating

Small Works 2009		Unit	Labour Hours	Labour Net	Plant Net	Materials Net	Unit Net	Labour Gross	Plant Gross	Materials Gross	Unit Price
								(Gross rates include 10% profit)			
				£	£	£	£	£	£	£	£
601	**NEW WORK**										
60111	**PAPERHANGING**										
6011101	**Strip off one layer woodchip paper, stop cracks and rub down:**										
6011101A	Walls	m²	0.18	5.04	–	0.07	5.11	5.54	–	0.08	5.62
6011101B	Walls to stairwell	m²	0.20	5.60	–	0.07	5.67	6.16	–	0.08	6.24
6011101C	Ceilings	m²	0.22	6.16	–	0.07	6.23	6.78	–	0.08	6.85
6011101D	Ceilings to stairwell	m²	0.24	6.72	–	0.07	6.79	7.39	–	0.08	7.47
6011102	**Strip off one layer of standard patterned or ready pasted paper, stop cracks and rub down:**										
6011102A	Walls	m²	0.21	5.88	–	0.07	5.95	6.47	–	0.08	6.55
6011102B	Walls to stairwell	m²	0.23	6.44	–	0.07	6.51	7.08	–	0.08	7.16
6011102C	Ceilings	m²	0.25	7.00	–	0.07	7.07	7.70	–	0.08	7.78
6011102D	Ceilings to stairwell	m²	0.27	7.56	–	0.07	7.63	8.32	–	0.08	8.39
6011103	**Strip off one layer of vinyl paper, stop cracks and rub down:**										
6011103A	Walls	m²	0.23	6.44	–	0.07	6.51	7.08	–	0.08	7.16
6011103B	Walls to stairwell	m²	0.25	7.00	–	0.07	7.07	7.70	–	0.08	7.78
6011103C	Ceilings	m²	0.27	7.56	–	0.07	7.63	8.32	–	0.08	8.39
6011103D	Ceilings to stairwell	m²	0.29	8.12	–	0.07	8.19	8.93	–	0.08	9.01
6011104	**Strip off one layer of embossed paper, stop cracks and rub down:**										
6011104A	Walls	m²	0.23	6.44	–	0.07	6.51	7.08	–	0.08	7.16
6011104B	Walls to stairwell	m²	0.25	7.00	–	0.07	7.07	7.70	–	0.08	7.78
6011104C	Ceilings	m²	0.27	7.56	–	0.07	7.63	8.32	–	0.08	8.39
6011104D	Ceilings to stairwell	m²	0.29	8.12	–	0.07	8.19	8.93	–	0.08	9.01

Small Works 2009		Unit	Labour Hours	Labour Net	Plant Net	Materials Net	Unit Net	Labour Gross	Plant Gross	Materials Gross	Unit Price
								—— (Gross rates include 10% profit) ——			
				£	£	£	£	£	£	£	£
601	**NEW WORK**										
60111	**PAPERHANGING**										
6011105	**Strip off one layer of lincrusta or anaglypta paper, stop cracks and rub down:**										
6011105A	Walls	m^2	0.28	7.84	–	0.07	7.91	8.62	–	0.08	8.70
6011105B	Walls to stairwell	m^2	0.30	8.40	–	0.07	8.47	9.24	–	0.08	9.32
6011105C	Ceilings	m^2	0.33	9.24	–	0.07	9.31	10.16	–	0.08	10.24
6011105D	Ceilings to stairwell	m^2	0.38	10.65	–	0.07	10.72	11.72	–	0.08	11.79
6011106	**Strip off two layers of woodchip paper, stop cracks and rub down:**										
6011106A	Walls	m^2	0.28	7.84	–	0.07	7.91	8.62	–	0.08	8.70
6011106B	Walls to stairwell	m^2	0.30	8.40	–	0.07	8.47	9.24	–	0.08	9.32
6011106C	Ceilings	m^2	0.35	9.81	–	0.07	9.88	10.79	–	0.08	10.87
6011106D	Ceilings to stairwell	m^2	0.38	10.65	–	0.07	10.72	11.72	–	0.08	11.79
6011107	**Strip off two layers of standard patterned or ready pasted paper, stop cracks and rub down:**										
6011107A	Walls	m^2	0.32	8.96	–	0.07	9.03	9.86	–	0.08	9.93
6011107B	Walls to stairwell	m^2	0.35	9.81	–	0.07	9.88	10.79	–	0.08	10.87
6011107C	Ceilings	m^2	0.38	10.65	–	0.07	10.72	11.72	–	0.08	11.79
6011107D	Ceilings to stairwell	m^2	0.42	11.77	–	0.07	11.84	12.95	–	0.08	13.02
6011108	**Strip off two layers of vinyl paper, stop cracks and rub down:**										
6011108A	Walls	m^2	0.35	9.81	–	0.07	9.88	10.79	–	0.08	10.87
6011108B	Walls to stairwell	m^2	0.38	10.65	–	0.07	10.72	11.72	–	0.08	11.79
6011108C	Ceilings	m^2	0.40	11.21	–	0.07	11.28	12.33	–	0.08	12.41
6011108D	Ceilings to stairwell	m^2	0.45	12.61	–	0.07	12.68	13.87	–	0.08	13.95

Glazing, Painting and Decorating

Small Works 2009		Unit	Labour Hours	Labour Net	Plant Net	Materials Net	Unit Net	Labour Gross	Plant Gross	Materials Gross	Unit Price
								(Gross rates include 10% profit)			
				£	£	£	£	£	£	£	£
601	**NEW WORK**										
60111	**PAPERHANGING**										
6011109	**Strip off two layers of embossed paper, stop cracks and rub down:**										
6011109A	Walls	m²	0.34	9.52	–	0.07	9.59	10.47	–	0.08	10.55
6011109B	Walls to stairwell	m²	0.37	10.37	–	0.07	10.44	11.41	–	0.08	11.48
6011109C	Ceilings	m²	0.42	11.77	–	0.07	11.84	12.95	–	0.08	13.02
6011109D	Ceilings to stairwell	m²	0.54	15.13	–	0.07	15.20	16.64	–	0.08	16.72
6011110	**Strip off two layers of lincrusta or anaglypta paper, stop cracks and rub down:**										
6011110A	Walls	m²	0.38	10.65	–	0.07	10.72	11.72	–	0.08	11.79
6011110B	Walls to stairwell	m²	0.42	11.77	–	0.07	11.84	12.95	–	0.08	13.02
6011110C	Ceilings	m²	0.50	14.01	–	0.07	14.08	15.41	–	0.08	15.49
6011110D	Ceilings to stairwell	m²	0.53	14.85	–	0.07	14.92	16.34	–	0.08	16.41
6011111	**Prepare and hang lining paper:**										
6011111A	Walls	m²	0.25	7.00	–	0.41	7.41	7.70	–	0.45	8.15
6011111B	Walls to stairwell	m²	0.28	7.84	–	0.41	8.25	8.62	–	0.45	9.08
6011111C	Ceilings	m²	0.30	8.40	–	0.41	8.81	9.24	–	0.45	9.69
6011111D	Ceilings to stairwell	m²	0.32	8.96	–	0.41	9.37	9.86	–	0.45	10.31
6011112	**Prepare and hang woodchip paper:**										
6011112A	Walls	m²	0.26	7.28	–	0.51	7.79	8.01	–	0.56	8.57
6011112B	Walls to stairwell	m²	0.29	8.12	–	0.51	8.63	8.93	–	0.56	9.49
6011112C	Ceilings	m²	0.31	8.68	–	0.51	9.19	9.55	–	0.56	10.11
6011112D	Ceilings to stairwell	m²	0.33	9.24	–	0.51	9.75	10.16	–	0.56	10.73
6011113	**Prepare and hang ready pasted paper:**										
6011113A	Walls	m²	0.26	7.28	–	2.50	9.78	8.01	–	2.75	10.76
6011113B	Walls to stairwell	m²	0.29	8.12	–	2.50	10.62	8.93	–	2.75	11.68
6011113C	Ceilings	m²	0.31	8.68	–	2.50	11.18	9.55	–	2.75	12.30
6011113D	Ceilings to stairwell	m²	0.33	9.24	–	2.50	11.74	10.16	–	2.75	12.91

Glazing, Painting and Decorating

Small Works 2009		Unit	Labour Hours	Labour Net	Plant Net	Materials Net	Unit Net	Labour Gross	Plant Gross	Materials Gross	Unit Price
				£	£	£	£	£	£	£	£
								(Gross rates include 10% profit)			
601	**NEW WORK**										
60111	**PAPERHANGING**										
6011114	**Prepare and hang standard patterned paper:**										
6011114A	Walls	m²	0.26	7.28	–	2.78	10.06	8.01	–	3.06	11.07
6011114B	Walls to stairwell	m²	0.29	8.12	–	2.78	10.90	8.93	–	3.06	11.99
6011114C	Ceilings	m²	0.31	8.68	–	2.78	11.46	9.55	–	3.06	12.61
6011114D	Ceilings to stairwell	m²	0.33	9.24	–	2.78	12.02	10.16	–	3.06	13.22
6011115	**Prepare and hang vinyl surface paper:**										
6011115A	Walls	m²	0.26	7.28	–	2.83	10.11	8.01	–	3.11	11.12
6011115B	Walls to stairwell	m²	0.29	8.12	–	2.83	10.95	8.93	–	3.11	12.05
6011115C	Ceilings	m²	0.31	8.68	–	2.83	11.51	9.55	–	3.11	12.66
6011115D	Ceilings to stairwell	m²	0.33	9.24	–	2.83	12.07	10.16	–	3.11	13.28
6011116	**Prepare and hang anaglypta paper:**										
6011116A	Walls	m²	0.27	7.56	–	0.93	8.49	8.32	–	1.02	9.34
6011116B	Walls to stairwell	m²	0.30	8.40	–	0.93	9.33	9.24	–	1.02	10.26
6011116C	Ceilings	m²	0.32	8.96	–	0.93	9.89	9.86	–	1.02	10.88
6011116D	Ceilings to stairwell	m²	0.33	9.24	–	0.93	10.17	10.16	–	1.02	11.19
6011117	**Prepare and hang flock paper:**										
6011117A	Walls	m²	0.27	7.57	–	3.76	11.33	8.33	–	4.14	12.46
6011117B	Walls to stairwell	m²	0.30	8.41	–	3.76	12.17	9.25	–	4.14	13.39
6011117C	Ceilings	m²	0.32	8.97	–	3.76	12.73	9.87	–	4.14	14.00
6011117D	Ceilings to stairwell	m²	0.33	9.25	–	3.76	13.01	10.18	–	4.14	14.31
6011118	**Cut and hang standard border strip:**										
6011118A	75 mm-150 mm wide	m	0.09	2.52	–	0.20	2.72	2.77	–	0.22	2.99

Glazing, Painting and Decorating

Small Works 2009		Unit				Specialist Net	Unit Net			Specialist Gross	Unit Price
									(Gross rates include 10% profit)		
				£	£	£	£	£	£	£	£
601	**NEW WORK**										
60112	**POLISHING BY SPECIALIST**										
6011201	**Body in and polish:**										
6011201A	General surfaces..........	m²	–	–	–	31.16	31.16	–	–	34.28	34.28
6011201B	General surfaces in narrow widths; not exceeding										
	150 mm..................	m	–	–	–	7.75	7.75	–	–	8.53	8.53
6011201C	General surfaces in narrow widths; 150 mm-300 mm ...	m	–	–	–	10.23	10.23	–	–	11.25	11.25
6011202	**Seal and wax polish:**										
6011202A	General surfaces..........	m²	–	–	–	14.57	14.57	–	–	16.03	16.03
6011202B	General surfaces in narrow widths; not exceeding										
	150 mm..................	m	–	–	–	3.72	3.72	–	–	4.09	4.09
6011202C	General surfaces in narrow widths; 150 mm-300 mm ...	m	–	–	–	4.81	4.81	–	–	5.29	5.29
6011203	**Body in and wax polish:**										
6011203A	General surfaces..........	m²	–	–	–	21.23	21.24	–	–	23.35	23.36
6011203B	General surfaces in narrow widths; not exceeding										
	150 mm..................	m	–	–	–	5.27	5.27	–	–	5.80	5.80
6011203C	General surfaces in narrow widths; 150 mm-300 mm ...	m	–	–	–	6.97	6.98	–	–	7.67	7.68
6011204	**Set and dry shine:**										
6011204A	General surfaces..........	m²	–	–	–	16.74	16.74	–	–	18.41	18.41
6011204B	General surfaces in narrow widths; not exceeding										
	150 mm..................	m	–	–	–	4.18	4.19	–	–	4.60	4.61
6011204C	General surfaces in narrow widths; 150 mm-300 mm ...	m	–	–	–	5.58	5.58	–	–	6.14	6.14
6011205	**Body in with polish and two coats yacht varnish:**										
6011205A	General surfaces..........	m²	–	–	–	152.83	152.83	–	–	168.11	168.11
6011205B	General surfaces in narrow widths; not exceeding										
	150 mm..................	m	–	–	–	8.21	8.22	–	–	9.03	9.04
6011205C	General surfaces in narrow widths; 150 mm-300 mm ...	m	–	–	–	10.85	10.85	–	–	11.94	11.94
6011206	**Grain fill, body in and spirit off piano type finish:**										
6011206A	General surfaces..........	m²	–	–	–	91.30	91.31	–	–	100.43	100.44
6011206B	General surfaces in narrow widths; not exceeding										
	150 mm..................	m	–	–	–	22.79	22.80	–	–	25.07	25.08
6011206C	General surfaces in narrow widths; 150 mm-300 mm ...	m	–	–	–	30.23	30.24	–	–	33.25	33.26

Small Works 2009		Unit				Specialist Net	Unit Net			Specialist Gross	Unit Price
									(Gross rates include 10% profit)		
			£	£	£	£	£	£	£	£	£
601	**NEW WORK**										
60113	**FIRE RETARDANT CLEAR FINISHES**										
6011301	**Quelfire:**										
6011301A	Class 1	m²	–	–	–	36.65	36.65	–	–	40.32	40.32
6011301B	Class 0	m²	–	–	–	44.70	44.70	–	–	49.17	49.17
6011302	**Nullifire:**										
6011302A	Class 1	m²	–	–	–	42.61	42.61	–	–	46.87	46.87
6011302B	Class 0	m²	–	–	–	50.51	50.51	–	–	55.56	55.56
6011303	**Albi:**										
6011303A	Class 1	m²	–	–	–	29.95	29.95	–	–	32.95	32.95
6011304	**Envirograf:**										
6011304A	Class 0	m²	–	–	–	40.08	40.08	–	–	44.09	44.09
6011304B	Class 1	m²	–	–	–	32.03	32.04	–	–	35.23	35.24
60114	**LACQUERS AND POLYURETHANE BY SPECIALIST**										
6011401	**Prepare and seal:**										
6011401A	General surfaces	m²	–	–	–	7.75	7.75	–	–	8.53	8.53
6011401B	General surfaces in narrow widths; not exceeding 150 mm girth	m	–	–	–	1.94	1.94	–	–	2.13	2.13
6011401C	General surfaces in narrow widths; 150 mm-300 mm girth	m	–	–	–	2.53	2.53	–	–	2.78	2.78
6011402	**Each additional coat of lacquer:**										
6011402A	General surfaces	m²	–	–	–	7.00	7.00	–	–	7.70	7.70
6011402B	General surfaces in narrow widths; not exceeding 150 mm girth	m	–	–	–	1.79	1.79	–	–	1.97	1.97
6011402C	General surfaces in narrow widths; 150 mm-300 mm girth	m	–	–	–	2.23	2.24	–	–	2.45	2.46
6011403	**Wire wool and burnish with wax:**										
6011403A	General surfaces	m²	–	–	–	18.03	18.03	–	–	19.83	19.83
6011403B	General surfaces in narrow widths; not exceeding 150 mm girth	m	–	–	–	4.62	4.62	–	–	5.08	5.08
6011403C	General surfaces in narrow widths; 150 mm-300 mm girth	m	–	–	–	6.11	6.11	–	–	6.72	6.72

Glazing, Painting and Decorating

Small Works 2009		Unit				Specialist Net	Unit Net			Specialist Gross	Unit Price
								(Gross rates include 10% profit)			
			£	£	£	£	£	£	£	£	£
601	**NEW WORK**										
60115	**PREPARE EXISTING WORK BY SPECIALIST**										
6011501	**Wash down to degrease and repolish:**										
6011501A	General surfaces..........	m²	–	–	–	19.65	19.65	–	–	21.62	21.62
6011501B	General surfaces in narrow widths; not exceeding 150 mm girth	m	–	–	–	4.65	4.65	–	–	5.12	5.12
6011501C	General surfaces in narrow widths; 150 mm-300 mm girth	m	–	–	–	6.15	6.15	–	–	6.77	6.77
6011502	**Wash down, degrease and clean to revive**										
6011502A	General surfaces..........	m²	–	–	–	15.00	15.00	–	–	16.50	16.50
6011502B	General surfaces in narrow widths; not exceeding 150 mm girth	m	–	–	–	3.75	3.75	–	–	4.13	4.13
6011502C	General surfaces in narrow widths; 150 mm-300 mm girth	m	–	–	–	4.95	4.95	–	–	5.45	5.45
6011503	**Wash down to degrease and rewax:**										
6011503A	General surfaces..........	m²	–	–	–	15.00	15.00	–	–	16.50	16.50
6011503B	General surfaces in narrow widths; not exceeding 150 mm girth	m	–	–	–	3.75	3.75	–	–	4.13	4.13
6011503C	General surfaces in narrow widths; 150 mm-300 mm girth	m	–	–	–	4.95	4.95	–	–	5.45	5.45
6011504	**Strip off chemically, standard bleach and neutralise:**										
6011504A	General surfaces..........	m²	–	–	–	22.65	22.65	–	–	24.92	24.92
6011504B	General surfaces in narrow widths; not exceeding 150 mm girth	m	–	–	–	5.70	5.70	–	–	6.27	6.27
6011504C	General surfaces in narrow widths; 150 mm-300 mm girth	m	–	–	–	7.50	7.50	–	–	8.25	8.25

Small Works 2009		Unit	Labour Hours	Labour Net	Plant Net	Materials Net	Unit Net	Labour Gross	Plant Gross	Materials Gross	Unit Price
								(Gross rates include 10% profit)			
				£	£	£	£	£	£	£	£
602	**REPAIRS AND ALTERATIONS**										
60201	**GLAZING**										
6020101	**Hack out:**										
6020101A	broken glass other than plate	m²	2.34	65.54	–	–	65.54	72.09	–	–	72.09
6020101B	plate glass	m²	3.55	99.44	–	–	99.44	109.38	–	–	109.38
6020102	**Carefully take out:**										
6020102A	all types of glass other than plate and set aside for re-use	m²	3.23	90.47	–	–	90.47	99.52	–	–	99.52
6020102B	plate glass and set aside for re-use..................	m²	4.68	131.09	–	–	131.09	144.20	–	–	144.20
6020103	**Remove old putty:**										
6020103A	paint rebate one coat oil colour ready to receive new glass...................	m	0.16	4.48	–	0.50	4.98	4.93	–	0.55	5.48
6020104	**Glaze, sprig and putty to wood:**										
6020104A	sashes; average 0.40 sq.m 3 mm sheet..............	m²	1.10	30.81	–	42.31	73.12	33.89	–	46.54	80.43
6020104B	sashes; average 0.40 sq.m obscured...............	m²	1.10	30.82	–	47.75	78.57	33.90	–	52.53	86.43
6020104C	sashes; average 0.40 sq.m wired cast..............	m²	1.20	33.61	–	44.91	78.52	36.97	–	49.40	86.37
6020105	**Glaze, putty and sprig to metal:**										
6020105A	sashes extra over foregoing	m²	0.40	11.20	–	–	11.20	12.32	–	–	12.32
6020106	**Wired cast glass in rooflights:**										
6020106A	panes up to 0.70 sq.m	m²	0.90	25.21	–	44.91	70.12	27.73	–	49.40	77.13
6020106B	panes exceeding 0.70 sq.m	m²	1.00	28.01	–	44.91	72.92	30.81	–	49.40	80.21
6020107	**S.G. quality float glass:**										
6020107A	6mm....................	m²	3.50	98.03	–	67.79	165.82	107.83	–	74.57	182.40
6020108	**Bed edge of glass:**										
6020108A	in chamois leather	m	0.23	6.45	–	0.89	7.34	7.10	–	0.98	8.07
6020108B	in velvet	m	0.17	4.77	–	0.25	5.02	5.25	–	0.28	5.52
6020109	**Remove temporary coverings to sashes:**										
6020109A	stopping up nail holes etc...	m²	1.10	30.81	–	–	30.81	33.89	–	–	33.89

Glazing, Painting and Decorating

Small Works 2009		Unit	Labour Hours	Labour Net	Plant Net	Materials Net	Unit Net	Labour Gross	Plant Gross	Materials Gross	Unit Price
								(Gross rates include 10% profit)			
				£	£	£	£	£	£	£	£
602	**REPAIRS AND ALTERATIONS**										
60202	**INTERNAL DECORATING**										
6020201	**Brush down and apply two coats lime white on brick walls, plaster walls and ceilings:**										
6020201A	new work	m²	0.33	9.24	–	0.22	9.46	10.16	–	0.24	10.41
6020201B	old work	m²	0.38	10.64	–	0.22	10.86	11.70	–	0.24	11.95
6020202	**Brush down and apply two coats emulsion to plaster:**										
6020202A	new work	m²	0.46	12.88	–	1.39	14.27	14.17	–	1.53	15.70
6020202B	old work	m²	0.51	14.28	–	1.39	15.67	15.71	–	1.53	17.24
6020203	**Brush down and apply two coats emulsion paint on brick walls**										
6020203A	new work	m²	0.58	16.25	–	2.58	18.83	17.88	–	2.84	20.71
6020203B	old work	m²	0.63	17.65	–	2.58	20.23	19.42	–	2.84	22.25
6020204	**Wash down plaster surfaces, fill cracks nail holes etc with filler:**										
6020204A	bring forward for new decoration	m²	0.20	5.60	–	0.31	5.91	6.16	–	0.34	6.50
6020205	**Prepare and apply oil colour on plaster ceilings:**										
6020205A	one coat	m²	0.27	7.56	–	0.82	8.38	8.32	–	0.90	9.22
6020205B	two coats	m²	0.55	15.41	–	1.63	17.04	16.95	–	1.79	18.74
6020206	**Prepare and apply oil colour on walls:**										
6020206A	plaster walls; one coat	m²	0.21	5.88	–	0.82	6.70	6.47	–	0.90	7.37
6020206B	plaster walls; two coats	m²	0.43	12.05	–	1.63	13.68	13.26	–	1.79	15.05
6020206C	brick walls; one coat	m²	0.27	7.57	–	1.63	9.20	8.33	–	1.79	10.12
6020206D	brick walls; two coats	m²	0.54	15.12	–	3.27	18.39	16.63	–	3.60	20.23
6020207	**Wash down, touch up and two coats oil:**										
6020207A	general surfaces of wood	m²	0.65	18.21	–	1.13	19.34	20.03	–	1.24	21.27
6020207B	add for each extra coat applied or deduct for one coat	m²	0.24	6.72	–	0.59	7.31	7.39	–	0.65	8.04
6020207C	general surfaces of windows frames and sashes (measured over glass)	m²	1.00	28.01	–	1.73	29.74	30.81	–	1.90	32.71
6020207D	add for each extra coat applied or deduct for one coat	m²	0.40	11.21	–	0.86	12.07	12.33	–	0.95	13.28
6020207E	on surfaces exceeding 150 mm girth	m	0.14	3.92	–	0.23	4.15	4.31	–	0.25	4.57
6020207F	on surfaces 150 mm- 300 mm girth	m	0.24	6.72	–	0.50	7.22	7.39	–	0.55	7.94
6020207G	add for each extra coat applied or deduct for one coat, not exceeding 150 mm girth	m	0.07	1.96	–	0.14	2.10	2.16	–	0.15	2.31
6020207H	add for extra coat applied or deduct for one coat, 150 mm-300 mm girth	m	0.11	3.08	–	0.23	3.31	3.39	–	0.25	3.64

Small Works 2009		Unit	Labour Hours	Labour Net	Plant Net	Materials Net	Unit Net	Labour Gross	Plant Gross	Materials Gross	Unit Price
								(Gross rates include 10% profit)			
				£	£	£	£	£	£	£	£
602	**REPAIRS AND ALTERATIONS**										
60202	**INTERNAL DECORATING**										
6020208	**Clean down and apply two coats oil colour to metal frames and sashes, bring forward bare patches:**										
6020208A	measured over glass	m²	1.11	31.09	–	1.73	32.82	34.20	–	1.90	36.10
6020208B	general surfaces over 300 mm girth	m²	0.69	19.33	–	1.63	20.96	21.26	–	1.79	23.06
6020208C	general surfaces not exceeding 150 m girth	m	0.30	8.41	–	0.45	8.86	9.25	–	0.50	9.75
6020208D	general surfaces 150 mm-300 mm girth	m	0.39	10.93	–	0.86	11.79	12.02	–	0.95	12.97
6020209	**Clean down and one coat gloss oil paint**										
6020209A	to fireplace jambs, stoves, mantel registers and the like	Each	1.00	28.01	–	1.23	29.24	30.81	–	1.35	32.16
6020210	**Prepare and two coats oil paint:**										
6020210A	to water waste preventer and backboard	Each	0.55	15.40	–	0.50	15.90	16.94	–	0.55	17.49
6020210B	add to last if including overflow pipes	Each	0.45	12.60	–	0.32	12.92	13.86	–	0.35	14.21
6020211	**Clean and apply one coat gloss paint:**										
6020211A	on casement stays, fasteners, bolts, rimlocks and sundry fittings	Each	0.20	5.60	–	0.14	5.74	6.16	–	0.15	6.31
6020212	**Prepare and repolish existing wood surfaces:**										
6020212A	general surfaces	m²	2.10	58.82	–	0.77	59.59	64.70	–	0.85	65.55
6020212B	handrails	m	0.60	16.80	–	0.30	17.10	18.48	–	0.33	18.81

Glazing, Painting and Decorating

Small Works 2009		Unit	Labour Hours	Labour Net	Plant Net	Materials Net	Unit Net	Labour Gross	Plant Gross	Materials Gross	Unit Price
								——— (Gross rates include 10% profit) ———			
				£	£	£	£	£	£	£	£
602	**REPAIRS AND ALTERATIONS**										
60202	**INTERNAL DECORATING**										
6020213	**Strip, body in and repolish wood surfaces:**										
6020213A	general surfaces	m²	4.70	131.64	–	1.05	132.69	144.80	–	1.16	145.96
6020213B	handrails	m	1.10	30.81	–	0.31	31.12	33.89	–	0.34	34.23
6020214	**Prepare and wax polish floors:**										
6020214A	general surfaces	m²	0.50	14.00	–	0.83	14.83	15.40	–	0.91	16.31
6020216	**Strip paper from walls or ceilings:**										
6020216A	stop, size ready for new paper; first layer	m²	0.30	8.40	–	0.16	8.56	9.24	–	0.18	9.42
6020216B	add for each extra layer stripped	m²	0.12	3.36	–	–	3.36	3.70	–	–	3.70
6020217	**Strip varnished paper from walls or ceilings:**										
6020217A	stop, size ready for new paper; first layer	m²	0.60	16.81	–	0.16	16.97	18.49	–	0.18	18.67
6020217B	add for each extra layer stripped	m²	0.22	6.16	–	–	6.16	6.78	–	–	6.78
6020218	**Cut, trim and hang paper to walls:**										
6020218A	woodchip.	m²	0.26	7.28	–	0.64	7.92	8.01	–	0.70	8.71
6020218B	standard	m²	0.26	7.29	–	2.90	10.19	8.02	–	3.19	11.21
6020219	**Cut, trim and hang paper to ceilings:**										
6020219A	lining	m²	0.30	8.41	–	0.53	8.94	9.25	–	0.58	9.83

Small Works 2009		Unit	Labour Hours	Labour Net	Plant Net	Materials Net	Unit Net	Labour Gross	Plant Gross	Materials Gross	Unit Price
								(Gross rates include 10% profit)			
				£	£	£	£	£	£	£	£
602	**REPAIRS AND ALTERATIONS**										
60203	**EXTERNAL DECORATING**										
6020301	**Wash down and apply two coats of masonry paint on:**										
6020301A	rendered walls	m²	0.53	14.84	–	2.79	17.63	16.32	–	3.07	19.39
6020302	**Wash down and apply two coats Sandtex Matt masonry paint on:**										
6020302A	rendered walls	m²	0.54	15.12	–	2.82	17.94	16.63	–	3.10	19.73
6020303	**Wash down and apply two coats Snowcem masonry paint on:**										
6020303A	rendered walls	m²	0.42	11.76	–	0.94	12.70	12.94	–	1.03	13.97
6020305	**Wash down, touch up and two coats oil:**										
6020305A	General surfaces wood	m²	0.68	19.05	–	1.63	20.68	20.96	–	1.79	22.75
6020305B	Add for each extra coat applied.................	m²	0.27	7.56	–	0.82	8.38	8.32	–	0.90	9.22
6020305C	Window frames and sashes (over glass..............	m²	1.21	33.89	–	1.73	35.62	37.28	–	1.90	39.18
6020305D	Add for each extra coat applied.................	m²	0.43	12.05	–	0.86	12.91	13.26	–	0.95	14.20
6020306	**Burn off paint to woodwork general surfaces:**										
6020306A	and prepare for priming....	m²	0.80	22.41	–	–	22.41	24.65	–	–	24.65
6020307	**Strip paint to wood with paint remover:**										
6020307A	and prepare for priming....	m²	0.50	14.00	–	0.19	14.19	15.40	–	0.21	15.61
6020308	**Prime and two coats oil paint to putties**										
6020308A	after reglazing............	m	0.18	5.04	–	0.14	5.18	5.54	–	0.15	5.70

Glazing, Painting and Decorating

Small Works 2009		Unit	Labour Hours	Labour Net	Plant Net	Materials Net	Unit Net	Labour Gross	Plant Gross	Materials Gross	Unit Price
								(Gross rates include 10% profit)			
				£	£	£	£	£	£	£	£
602	**REPAIRS AND ALTERATIONS**										
60203	**EXTERNAL DECORATING**										
6020313	**Clean down wire brush metal surfaces an bring forward bare patches and apply oil colour on previously painted surfaces;**										
6020313A	general surfaces; over 300 mm girth	m²	0.78	21.84	–	1.23	23.07	24.02	–	1.35	25.38
6020313B	general surfaces; not exceeding 150 mm girth ...	m	0.39	10.93	–	0.36	11.29	12.02	–	0.40	12.42
6020313C	general surfaces 150 mm- 300 mm girth	m	0.51	14.29	–	0.77	15.06	15.72	–	0.85	16.57
6020313D	corrugated iron surfaces; (measured flat)	m²	0.87	24.37	–	1.36	25.73	26.81	–	1.50	28.30
6020313E	structural steelwork	m²	0.96	26.89	–	1.23	28.12	29.58	–	1.35	30.93
6020313G	railings, balustrades; (measured flat overall).....	m²	0.87	24.37	–	1.04	25.41	26.81	–	1.14	27.95
6020313I	stairs; (measured overall) ..	m²	0.84	23.53	–	0.86	24.39	25.88	–	0.95	26.83
6020313J	windows, glazed doors in small panes.............	m²	1.98	55.46	–	0.86	56.32	61.01	–	0.95	61.95
6020313K	windows, glazed doors in medium pane	m²	1.74	48.74	–	0.77	49.51	53.61	–	0.85	54.46
6020313L	windows, glazed doors in large panes.............	m²	1.50	42.02	–	0.68	42.70	46.22	–	0.75	46.97
6020313M	eaves gutters (inside and outside)	m	0.51	14.29	–	0.45	14.74	15.72	–	0.50	16.21
6020313N	rainwater pipes, soil pipes etc	m	0.51	14.29	–	0.18	14.47	15.72	–	0.20	15.92
6020313O	pipes, bars, straps, etc up to 150 mm girth	m	0.45	12.61	–	0.18	12.79	13.87	–	0.20	14.07
60204	**WOOD PRESERVATIVES**										
6020401	**Two coats timber preserver:**										
6020401A	sawn surfaces...........	m²	0.40	11.21	–	0.43	11.64	12.33	–	0.47	12.80
6020401B	wrought surfaces	m²	0.38	10.64	–	0.34	10.98	11.70	–	0.37	12.08
6020402	**Two coats Cuprinol clear preserver:**										
6020402A	sawn surfaces...........	m²	0.40	11.21	–	1.48	12.69	12.33	–	1.63	13.96
6020402B	wrought surfaces	m²	0.38	10.65	–	1.17	11.82	11.72	–	1.29	13.00
6020403	**Two coats Solignum:**										
6020403A	sawn surfaces...........	m²	0.38	10.64	–	1.85	12.49	11.70	–	2.04	13.74
6020403B	wrought surfaces	m²	0.36	10.09	–	1.46	11.55	11.10	–	1.61	12.71

MASONRY

Small Works 2009		Unit			Specialist Net			Unit Net		Specialist Gross		Unit Price
							(Gross rates include 10% profit)					
			£	£	£	£	£		£	£	£	£
701	**NEW WORK**											
70101	**RECONSTRUCTED STONE BY SPECIALIST**											
7010101	**Plain cladding:**											
7010101A	50 mm	m²	–		–	–	177.62	177.62		–	–	195.38	195.38
7010101B	75 mm	m²	–		–	–	213.25	213.25		–	–	234.58	234.58
7010102	**Plain face ashlar:**											
7010102A	100 mm	m²	–		–	–	226.30	226.30		–	–	248.93	248.93
7010103	**Plain string:**											
7010103A	100 mm × 300 mm.......	m	–		–	–	66.78	66.78		–	–	73.46	73.46
7010104	**Plain sills, jambs and heads:**											
7010104A	150 mm × 75 mm........	m	–		–	–	39.03	39.03		–	–	42.93	42.93
7010104B	200 mm × 75 mm........	m	–		–	–	45.56	45.56		–	–	50.12	50.12
7010104C	280 mm × 100 mm.......	m	–		–	–	68.41	68.41		–	–	75.25	75.25
7010105	**Coping:**											
7010105A	300 mm × 75 mm........	m	–		–	–	63.51	63.51		–	–	69.86	69.86
7010105B	325 mm × 100 mm.......	m	–		–	–	73.30	73.30		–	–	80.63	80.63
7010105C	400 mm × 125 mm.......	m	–		–	–	112.34	112.34		–	–	123.57	123.57
7010106	**Chimney cap; weathered and throated all round:**											
7010106A	940 mm × 600 mm × 100 mm holed for two 225 mm × 225 mm flues ..	Each	–		–	–	127.02	127.02		–	–	139.72	139.72
7010107	**Pier cap; weathered and throated all round:**											
7010107A	525 mm × 100 mm.......	Each	–		–	–	61.88	61.88		–	–	68.07	68.07
7010108	**Boot lintel:**											
7010108A	325 mm × 150 mm consisting of 225 mm × 100 mm reinforced concrete main section with 100 mm × 75 mm projecting toe in reconstructed stone........	m	–		–	–	110.70	110.70		–	–	121.77	121.77

Masonry

Small Works 2009		Unit			Specialist Net	Unit Net			Specialist Gross	Unit Price
			£	£	£	£	£	£	£	£

(Gross rates include 10% profit)

Code	Description	Unit			Specialist Net £	Unit Net £			Specialist Gross £	Unit Price £
701	**NEW WORK**									
70102	**SOFT STONE BY SPECIALIST**									
7010201	Cut out to a depth of approximately 25 mm, properly key, dowel and reinforce as necessary with non-ferrous metal and make good in plastic artificial stone to match existing:									
7010201A	ashlar	m²	–	–	630.09	630.09	–	–	693.10	693.10
7010201B	moulding 75 mm girth	m	–	–	196.93	196.93	–	–	216.62	216.62
7010201C	moulding 75 mm girth increasing per 25 mm of girth	m	–	–	65.14	65.14	–	–	71.65	71.65
7010201D	plain or weathered coping, 300 mm wide	m	–	–	262.07	262.07	–	–	288.28	288.28
7010201E	plain or weathered coping 300 mm wide increasing per 25 mm of width	m	–	–	65.14	65.14	–	–	71.65	71.65
7010201F	tracery	m²	–	–	1035.50	1035.50	–	–	1139.05	1139.05
7010201G	mullion front from glazing, 150 mm wide	m	–	–	278.39	278.39	–	–	306.23	306.23
7010201H	circular labels or hoods to 225 mm girth	m	–	–	393.99	393.99	–	–	433.39	433.39
7010201I	circular columns, plain	m	–	–	657.70	657.70	–	–	723.47	723.47
7010201J	circular columns, fluted	m	–	–	1035.50	1035.50	–	–	1139.05	1139.05
7010201K	stooling to jambs or mullions, moulded	Each	–	–	146.47	146.47	–	–	161.12	161.12
7010201L	stooling to jambs or mullions, plain	Each	–	–	86.36	86.36	–	–	95.00	95.00
70103	**PORTLAND STONE BY SPECIALIST**									
7010301	Cut out to a depth of approximately 25 mm, properly key, dowel and reinforce as necessary with non-ferrous metal and make good in plastic artificial stone to match existing:									
7010301A	ashlar	m²	–	–	755.44	755.44	–	–	830.98	830.98
7010301B	moulding 75 mm girth	m	–	–	236.02	236.02	–	–	259.62	259.62
7010301C	moulding 75 mm girth increasing per 25 mm of girth	m	–	–	78.14	78.14	–	–	85.95	85.95
7010301D	plain or weathered coping 300 mm wide	m	–	–	314.29	314.29	–	–	345.72	345.72
7010301E	plain or weathered coping 300 mm wide per 25 mm of width	m	–	–	78.14	78.14	–	–	85.95	85.95
7010301F	tracery	m²	–	–	1242.25	1242.25	–	–	1366.48	1366.48
7010301G	mullion front from glazing, 150 mm wide	m	–	–	335.41	335.41	–	–	368.95	368.95
7010301H	circular labels or hoods to 225 mm girth	m	–	–	472.16	472.16	–	–	519.38	519.38
7010301I	circular columns, plain	m	–	–	788.04	788.04	–	–	866.84	866.84
7010301J	circular columns, fluted	m	–	–	1242.25	1242.25	–	–	1366.48	1366.48
7010301K	stooling to jambs or mullions, moulded	Each	–	–	177.41	177.41	–	–	195.15	195.15
7010301L	stooling to jambs or mullions, plain	Each	–	–	104.15	104.15	–	–	114.57	114.57

Small Works 2009		Unit				Specialist Net	Unit Net			Specialist Gross	Unit Price
									(Gross rates include 10% profit)		
				£	£	£	£	£	£	£	£
701	**NEW WORK**										
70104	**YORK STONE BY SPECIALIST**										
7010401	**Cut out to a depth of approximately 25 mm, properly key, dowel and reinforce as necessary with non-ferrous metal and make good in plastic artificial stone to match existing:**										
7010401A	ashlar..................	m^2	–	–	–	832.00	832.00	–	–	915.20	915.20
7010401B	moulding 75 mm girth......	m	–	–	–	258.98	258.98	–	–	284.88	284.88
7010401C	moulding 75 mm girth increasing per 25 mm of girth	m		–	–	86.33	86.33	–	–	94.96	94.96
7010401D	plain or weathered coping 300 mm wide	m	–	–	–	346.76	346.76	–	–	381.44	381.44
7010401E	plain or weathered coping 300 mm wide increasing per 25 mm of width...........	m	–	–	–	86.33	86.33	–	–	94.96	94.96
7010401F	tracery..................	m^2	–	–	–	1365.94	1365.94	–	–	1502.53	1502.53
7010401G	mullion front from glazing, 150 mm wide	m		–	–	367.88	367.88	–	–	404.67	404.67
7010401H	circular labels or hoods to 225 mm girth	m	–	–	–	519.42	519.42	–	–	571.36	571.36
7010401I	circular columns, plain	m	–	–	–	867.77	867.77	–	–	954.55	954.55
7010401J	circular columns, fluted.....	m	–	–	–	1365.94	1365.94	–	–	1502.53	1502.53
7010401K	stooling to jambs or mullions, moulded	Each	–	–	–	193.78	193.78	–	–	213.16	213.16
7010401L	stooling to jambs or mullions, plain....................	Each	–	–	–	112.33	112.33	–	–	123.56	123.56
70105	**CLEANING STONEWORK OR BRICKWORK BY SPECIALIST**										
7010501	**Cleaning by nebulous cold water:**										
7010501A	spray process assisted by suitable graded brushes	m^2	–	–	–	23.40	23.40	–	–	25.74	25.74
7010502	**Dry cleaning:**										
7010502A	by the use of silica free abrasive grit under regulated air pressure...............	m^2	–	–	–	20.10	20.10	–	–	22.11	22.11
7010502B	by the use of spinning carborundum pads.........	m^2	–	–	–	35.10	35.10	–	–	38.61	38.61
7010503	**Cleaning by chemicals:**										
7010503A	and high pressure water process	m^2	–	–	–	16.65	16.65	–	–	18.32	18.32

Masonry

Small Works 2009		Unit	Labour Hours	Labour Net	Plant Net	Materials Net	Unit Net	Labour Gross	Plant Gross	Materials Gross	Unit Price
								(Gross rates include 10% profit)			
				£	£	£	£	£	£	£	£
701	**NEW WORK**										
70106	**REPOINTING BY SPECIALIST**										
7010601	**Rake out and repoint:**										
7010601A	rubble walling	m²	2.00	51.28	–	1.65	52.93	56.41	–	1.82	58.22
7010601B	flint walling	m²	6.75	173.07	–	2.76	175.83	190.38	–	3.04	193.41
7010601C	ashlar walling	m²	1.50	38.46	–	0.97	39.43	42.31	–	1.07	43.37
70107	**STONE FIXING BY SPECIALIST**										
7010701	**Labours on stonework:**										
7010701A	fixing only natural or reconstructed stonework ..	m³	120.00	3076.80	–	3.45	3080.25	3384.48	–	3.80	3388.28
7010701B	cutting out and piecing into existing work............	m³	375.00	9615.00	–	1.65	9616.65	10576.50	–	1.82	10578.32
7010701C	fixing only rubble walling average 125 mm thick faced one side only	m²	12.25	314.09	–	1.79	315.88	345.50	–	1.97	347.47
7010701D	fixing only flint walling	m²	28.75	737.15	–	1.79	738.94	810.87	–	1.97	812.83
7010701E	laying paving stones	m²	3.60	92.30	–	0.69	92.99	101.53	–	0.76	102.29
70110	**BRADSTONE CAST STONEWORK**										
7011001	**Walling blocks 100 mm thick in Cotswold limestone colour in gauged mortar 1:1:6 flush pointed on exposed faces as the work proceeds; walls and skins of hollow walls:**										
7011001A	tooled finish	m²	4.10	105.12	–	45.13	150.25	115.63	–	49.64	165.28
7011001B	rough hewn finish.........	m²	4.10	105.13	–	46.01	151.14	115.64	–	50.61	166.25
7011001C	squared course rubble finish	m²	4.10	105.13	–	46.44	151.57	115.64	–	51.08	166.73
7011001D	masonry finish	m²	4.10	105.13	–	46.01	151.14	115.64	–	50.61	166.25
7011002	**Extra for quoin blocks:**										
7011002A	masonry finish	m	1.65	42.31	–	66.38	108.69	46.54	–	73.02	119.56
7011002B	tooled finish	m	1.65	42.31	–	66.38	108.69	46.54	–	73.02	119.56
7011003	**Fair returns 100 mm wide:**										
7011003A	masonry finish; masonry ends....................	m	0.52	13.33	–	–	13.33	14.66	–	–	14.66
7011003B	masonry finish; dressed ends....................	m	0.52	13.33	–	3.46	16.79	14.66	–	3.81	18.47
7011003C	squared course rubble finish	m	1.04	26.67	–	–	26.67	29.34	–	–	29.34
7011003D	rough hewn finish........	m	1.13	28.97	–	–	28.97	31.87	–	–	31.87
7011004	**Lintel dressings in Cotswold limestone colour; bedded, jointed and pointed in cement mortar (1:6); in stock lengths:**										
7011004A	102 mm × 152 mm; 762 mm-1219 mm	m	0.80	20.51	–	12.94	33.45	22.56	–	14.23	36.80
7011004B	102 mm × 152 mm; 1373 mm-1676 mm	m	1.00	25.64	–	18.05	43.69	28.20	–	19.86	48.06
7011004C	102 mm × 152 mm; 1829 mm-1981 mm	m	1.40	35.90	–	21.56	57.46	39.49	–	23.72	63.21
7011004D	102 mm × 229 mm; 914 mm-1524 mm	m	1.20	30.77	–	20.33	51.10	33.85	–	22.36	56.21
7011004E	102 mm × 229 mm; 1676 mm-1981 mm	m	1.40	35.90	–	26.66	62.56	39.49	–	29.33	68.82
7011004F	102 mm × 229 mm; 2134 mm-2438 mm	m	1.60	41.03	–	32.66	73.69	45.13	–	35.93	81.06
7011004G	102 mm × 229 mm; 2591 mm-2896 mm	m	1.80	46.16	–	38.66	84.82	50.78	–	42.53	93.30

Small Works 2009		Unit	Labour Hours	Labour Net	Plant Net	Materials Net	Unit Net	Labour Gross	Plant Gross	Materials Gross	Unit Price
								(Gross rates include 10% profit)			
				£	£	£	£	£	£	£	£
701	**NEW WORK**										
70110	**BRADSTONE CAST STONEWORK**										
7011005	**Sill dressings including stooling in Cotswold limestone colour; bedded, jointed and pointed in cement mortar 1:6; in stock lengths:**										
7011005A	197 mm × 67 mm; 673 mm-2623 mm	m	0.60	15.39	–	22.24	37.63	16.93	–	24.46	41.39
7011006	**Coping dressings in Cotswold limestone colour; bedded, jointed and pointed in cement mortar 1:6:**										
7011006A	178 mm × 64 mm × 38 mm; twice weathered and rebated.	m	0.40	10.25	–	13.15	23.40	11.28	–	14.47	25.74
7011006B	191 mm × 76 mm × 63 mm; once weathered	m	0.50	12.82	–	13.84	26.66	14.10	–	15.22	29.33
7011006C	305 mm × 76 mm × 51 mm; twice weathered.	m	0.70	17.94	–	22.20	40.14	19.73	–	24.42	44.15
7011007	**Traditional window surround components for non-standard windows:**										
7011007A	146 mm × 143 mm; head.	m	0.80	20.51	–	32.32	52.83	22.56	–	35.55	58.11
7011007B	146 mm × 143 mm; continuous jamb.	m	0.80	20.51	–	34.73	55.24	22.56	–	38.20	60.76
7011007C	146 mm × 143 mm; sill . .	m	0.80	20.52	–	31.98	52.50	22.57	–	35.18	57.75
7011007D	146 mm × 108 mm; mullion.	m	0.80	20.51	–	44.93	65.44	22.56	–	49.42	71.98
7011007E	162 mm × 102 mm; label mould.	m	0.80	20.52	–	29.46	49.98	22.57	–	32.41	54.98
7011007F	162 mm × 102 mm; kneeler	Each	0.30	7.70	–	17.04	24.74	8.47	–	18.74	27.21
7011008	**Traditional door surround; continuous jambs; to suit 839 mm × 1982 mm door in 102 mm × 63 mm frame:**										
7011008A	without label mould	Each	3.00	76.92	–	432.87	509.79	84.61	–	476.16	560.77
7011008B	with label mould	Each	3.30	84.61	–	440.87	525.48	93.07	–	484.96	578.03

Masonry

Small Works 2009		Unit	Labour Hours	Labour Net	Plant Net	Materials Net	Unit Net	Labour Gross	Plant Gross	Materials Gross	Unit Price
								(Gross rates include 10% profit)			
				£	£	£	£	£	£	£	£
701	**NEW WORK**										
70112	**NATURAL STONE RUBBLE WORK**										
7011201	**Random walling in Yorkshire limestone (PC 275:00 per m³); in mortar; unfaced; average thickness:**										
7011201A	300 mm	m²	3.50	89.74	–	123.08	212.82	98.71	–	135.39	234.10
7011201B	450 mm	m²	5.25	134.61	–	185.40	320.01	148.07	–	203.94	352.01
7011201C	600 mm	m²	7.00	179.48	–	246.15	425.63	197.43	–	270.77	468.19
7011201D	Extra for one fair face	m²	1.00	25.64	–	–	25.64	28.20	–	–	28.20
7011201E	Extra for two fair faces	m²	1.90	48.72	–	–	48.72	53.59	–	–	53.59
7011202	**Square rubble walling in Yorkshire limestone (PC 275:00 per m³); average thickness:**										
7011202A	300 mm	m²	5.00	128.20	–	121.76	249.96	141.02	–	133.94	274.96
7011202B	450 mm	m²	7.60	194.86	–	182.51	377.37	214.35	–	200.76	415.11
7011202C	600 mm	m²	10.00	256.40	–	243.39	499.79	282.04	–	267.73	549.79
7011202D	Extra for one fair face	m²	1.00	25.64	–	–	25.64	28.20	–	–	28.20
7011202E	Extra for two fair faces	m²	1.90	48.72	–	–	48.72	53.59	–	–	53.59
70120	**NATURAL FLINTWORK**										
7012010	**Random flintwork; in cement/ lime mortar (1:2:9); face pointed one side; to backing blockwork (measured separately) thickness:**										
7012010A	100 mm	m²	2.75	70.51	–	47.07	117.58	77.56	–	51.78	129.34
7012010B	215 mm	m²	5.25	134.61	–	85.93	220.54	148.07	–	94.52	242.59

Small Works 2009		Unit	Labour Hours	Labour Net	Plant Net	Materials Net	Unit Net	Labour Gross	Plant Gross	Materials Gross	Unit Price
								(Gross rates include 10% profit)			
				£	£	£	£	£	£	£	£
702	**REPAIRS AND ALTERATIONS**										
70201	**LABOURS**										
7020101	**Take down masonry, clean and set aside:**										
7020101A	ashlar walling	m²	3.00	76.92	–	–	76.92	84.61	–	–	84.61
7020101B	cornices etc.	m	1.20	30.77	–	–	30.77	33.85	–	–	33.85
7020101C	arches	Each	0.80	20.51	–	–	20.51	22.56	–	–	22.56
7020101D	steps, sills etc.	m	1.50	38.46	–	–	38.46	42.31	–	–	42.31
7020102	**Take down masonry, clean and reset:**										
7020102A	ashlar walling	m²	7.75	198.71	–	11.84	210.55	218.58	–	13.02	231.61
7020102B	cornices etc.	m	3.30	84.61	–	2.76	87.37	93.07	–	3.04	96.11
7020102C	arches	Each	2.20	56.40	–	4.87	61.27	62.04	–	5.36	67.40
7020102D	steps, sills etc.	m	2.00	51.28	–	3.55	54.83	56.41	–	3.91	60.31
7020103	**Cut out decayed Portland (or similar) stone in:**										
7020103A	facings of wall built in lime mortar in adjacent stones. Prepare for and supply and fix new stones, average 50 mm thick, point and clean down on completion	m²	3.00	76.92	–	148.69	225.61	84.61	–	163.56	248.17
7020103B	facings of wall built in lime mortar in separate stones. Prepare for and supply and fix new stones, average 50 mm thick, point and clean down on completion	m²	3.60	92.30	–	155.66	247.96	101.53	–	171.23	272.76
7020104	**Rake out joints of:**										
7020104A	ashlar stonework and repoint	m²	1.40	35.90	–	0.92	36.82	39.49	–	1.01	40.50
7020104B	squared rubble and repoint.	m²	1.60	41.02	–	0.92	41.94	45.12	–	1.01	46.13
7020105	**Redress face of walling where decayed:**										
7020105A	with picked face and repoint	m²	8.00	205.12	–	0.53	205.65	225.63	–	0.58	226.22
7020106	**Take up and reset 50 mm thick York stone slabs, any size, in landings, hearths, cover stones, pavings etc in:**										
7020106A	lime mortar	m²	2.00	51.28	–	3.55	54.83	56.41	–	3.91	60.31
7020106B	cement mortar	m²	2.40	61.54	–	2.94	64.48	67.69	–	3.23	70.93
7020107	**Cut and form toothing in old masonry for:**										
7020107A	new brick or stone	m²	2.00	51.28	–	–	51.28	56.41	–	–	56.41
7020108	**Take down and reset blocking courses, cornices, strings, plinths, apexes, kneelers etc in:**										
7020108A	lime mortar	m	1.20	30.76	–	0.53	31.29	33.84	–	0.58	34.42
7020108B	cement mortar	m	1.40	35.89	–	0.44	36.33	39.48	–	0.48	39.96
7020109	**Take down and reset window sills, steps etc including cutting away and making good:**										
7020109A	lime mortar	m	2.00	51.28	–	0.26	51.54	56.41	–	0.29	56.69
7020109B	cement mortar	m	2.20	56.41	–	0.22	56.63	62.05	–	0.24	62.29
7020110	**Repair with 'granite chippings' concrete, including cutting out to a depth of at least 19 mm, finish concrete fair and flush with original surface:**										
7020110A	treads	m²	2.60	66.67	–	6.58	73.25	73.34	–	7.24	80.58
7020110B	landing	m²	1.60	41.03	–	6.58	47.61	45.13	–	7.24	52.37

CITADEL OFFICE, MOOR HOUSE, LONDON

MAKING YOUR BUSINESS OUR PRIORITY

In today's constantly shifting global business climate our customers' operations are constantly expanding and diversifying into new services and markets. Combine this with the ever growing complexity of projects and the application of expert project management becomes vital.

It's not only the quality of personnel that is vital for delivering an excellent service, it is just as important that they're supported by advanced systems, reliable and accurate data and innovative management techniques.

Mott MacDonald fully understands the ever-changing commercial environment of our clients and develops and delivers solutions that best meet the needs of their business and culture.

To find out more please contact Charles Blane:

T   +44 (0)20 7593 9700

E   charles.blane@mottmac.com

www.mottmac.com

ROOFING

Small Works 2009		Unit	Labour Hours	Labour Net	Plant Net	Materials Net	Unit Net	Labour Gross	Plant Gross	Materials Gross	Unit Price
				£	£	£	£	£	£	£	£
								(Gross rates include 10% profit)			
801	**SLATE ROOFING**										
80101	**WELSH SLATES**										
8010101	**Welsh slates; size 610 mm × 305 mm; 75 mm lap; 50 × 25 mm treated sawn softwood battens; reinforced slaters underlining felt type 1F:**										
8010101A	sloping..................	m²	0.35	8.97	–	853.78	862.75	9.87	–	939.16	949.03
8010101B	vertical or mansard	m²	0.55	14.10	–	853.78	867.88	15.51	–	939.16	954.67
8010101C	Extra for double eaves course	m	0.40	10.26	–	116.88	127.14	11.29	–	128.57	139.85
8010101D	Extra for mitred hips; both sides measured	m	2.40	61.54	–	172.24	233.78	67.69	–	189.46	257.16
8010101E	Extra for cutting to valleys; both sides measured	m	1.45	37.17	–	141.49	178.66	40.89	–	155.64	196.53
8010101F	hole for small pipe	Each	0.60	15.38	–	–	15.38	16.92	–	–	16.92
8010101G	hole for large pipe........	Each	0.80	20.51	–	–	20.51	22.56	–	–	22.56
8010101H	fix only lead soakers......	Each	0.05	1.28	–	–	1.28	1.41	–	–	1.41
8010101I	fix only hip irons	Each	0.25	6.41	–	–	6.41	7.05	–	–	7.05
8010102	**Welsh slates; size 510 mm × 255 mm; 75 mm lap; 50 mm × 25 mm treated sawn softwood battens; reinforced slaters underlining felt type 1F:**										
8010102A	sloping..................	m²	0.50	12.82	–	685.41	698.23	14.10	–	753.95	768.05
8010102B	vertical or mansard	m²	0.80	20.51	–	685.41	705.92	22.56	–	753.95	776.51
8010102C	Extra for double eaves course	m	0.45	11.54	–	73.34	84.88	12.69	–	80.67	93.37
8010102D	Extra for mitred hips; both sides measured	m	2.70	69.22	–	113.35	182.57	76.14	–	124.69	200.83
8010102E	Extra for cutting to valleys; both sides measured	m	1.75	44.87	–	97.89	142.76	49.36	–	107.68	157.04
8010102F	hole for small pipe	Each	0.60	15.38	–	–	15.38	16.92	–	–	16.92
8010102G	hole for large pipe........	Each	0.80	20.51	–	–	20.51	22.56	–	–	22.56
8010102H	fix only lead soakers......	Each	0.05	1.28	–	–	1.28	1.41	–	–	1.41
8010102I	fix only hip irons	Each	0.25	6.41	–	–	6.41	7.05	–	–	7.05
8010103	**Welsh slates; size 405 mm × 205 mm; 75 mm lap; 50 mm × 25 mm treated sawn softwood battens; reinforced slaters underlining felt type 1F:**										
8010103A	sloping..................	m²	0.85	21.79	–	779.87	801.66	23.97	–	857.86	881.83
8010103B	vertical or mansard	m²	1.25	32.05	–	779.87	811.92	35.26	–	857.86	893.11
8010103C	Extra for double eaves course	m	0.60	15.38	–	65.26	80.64	16.92	–	71.79	88.70
8010103D	Extra for mitred hips; both sides measured	m	3.50	89.74	–	97.89	187.63	98.71	–	107.68	206.39
8010103E	Extra for cutting to valleys; both sides measured	m	2.00	51.28	–	74.58	125.86	56.41	–	82.04	138.45
8010103F	hole for small pipe	Each	0.60	15.38	–	–	15.38	16.92	–	–	16.92
8010103G	hole for large pipe........	Each	0.80	20.51	–	–	20.51	22.56	–	–	22.56
8010103H	fix only lead soakers......	Each	0.05	1.28	–	–	1.28	1.41	–	–	1.41
8010103I	fix only hip irons	Each	0.25	6.41	–	–	6.41	7.05	–	–	7.05

Roofing

Small Works 2009		Unit	Labour Hours	Labour Net	Plant Net	Materials Net	Unit Net	Labour Gross	Plant Gross	Materials Gross	Unit Price
								(Gross rates include 10% profit)			
				£	£	£	£	£	£	£	£
801	SLATE ROOFING										
80102	ARTIFICIAL SLATES										
8010201	Asbestos-free artificial slates; blue/black; Eternit 2000 or the like; size 600 mm × 300 mm; 75 mm lap; 50 mm × 25 mm treated sawn softwood battens; reinforced slaters underlining felt type 1F:										
8010201A	sloping.................	m²	0.50	12.82	–	24.27	37.09	14.10	–	26.70	40.80
8010201B	vertical or mansard	m²	0.65	16.66	–	24.27	40.93	18.33	–	26.70	45.02
8010201C	Extra for double eaves course	m	0.40	10.26	–	4.16	14.42	11.29	–	4.58	15.86
8010201D	Extra for mitred hips or cutting to valleys; both sides measured	m	1.45	37.18	–	4.16	41.34	40.90	–	4.58	45.47
80103	HARDROW SLATES										
8010301	Hardrow slates; size 457 × 305 mm; 75 mm lap; 38 × 25 mm treated softwood battens; reinforced slaters underlining felt type 1F:										
8010301A	sloping.................	m²	0.50	12.82	–	29.37	42.19	14.10	–	32.31	46.41
8010301B	vertical or mansard	m²	0.65	16.66	–	30.04	46.70	18.33	–	33.04	51.37
8010301C	Extra for eaves course	m	0.20	5.13	–	3.80	8.93	5.64	–	4.18	9.82
8010301D	Extra for ridge slates	m	0.30	7.69	–	20.24	27.93	8.46	–	22.26	30.72
8010301E	Extra for mitred hips or cutting to valleys; both sides measured	m	1.45	37.18	–	6.33	43.51	40.90	–	6.96	47.86

Small Works 2009	Unit	Labour Hours	Labour Net	Plant Net	Materials Net	Unit Net	Labour Gross	Plant Gross	Materials Gross	Unit Price
			£	£	£	£	£	£	£	£
							(Gross rates include 10% profit)			
802 **TILE ROOFING**										
80201 **PLAIN TILES**										
8020101 Clay plain tiles; machine made; smooth red; size 265 mm × 165 mm; 64 mm lap; 19 mm × 38 mm treated sawn softwood battens; reinforced slaters felt type 1F:										
8020101A sloping..................	m²	1.40	35.90	–	51.35	87.25	39.49	–	56.49	95.98
8020101B vertical or mansard	m²	1.60	41.02	–	51.35	92.37	45.12	–	56.49	101.61
8020101C Extra for verges	m	0.20	5.13	–	1.31	6.44	5.64	–	1.44	7.08
8020101D Extra for double eaves course	m	0.20	5.12	–	3.96	9.08	5.63	–	4.36	9.99
8020101E Extra for half round ridge tiles	m	0.85	21.79	–	21.37	43.16	23.97	–	23.51	47.48
8020101F Extra for half round hip tiles; cutting both sides.........	m	1.00	25.64	–	24.51	50.15	28.20	–	26.96	55.17
8020101G Extra for angle ridge tiles...	m	0.85	21.79	–	21.37	43.16	23.97	–	23.51	47.48
8020101H Extra for bonnet hip tiles; cutting both sides.........	m	1.00	25.64	–	75.15	100.79	28.20	–	82.67	110.87
8020101I Extra for valley tiles; cutting both sides	m	1.00	25.64	–	75.15	100.79	28.20	–	82.67	110.87
8020101J Extra for intersection of ridge and hip.................	Each	0.70	17.95	–	–	17.95	19.75	–	–	19.75
8020103 Clay plain tiles; hand made; sand faced size 265 mm × 165 mm; 64 mm lap; 19 mm × 38 mm treated sawn softwood battens; reinforced slaters underlining felt type 1F:										
8020103A sloping..................	m²	1.40	35.89	–	112.14	148.03	39.48	–	123.35	162.83
8020103B vertical or mansard	m²	1.60	41.02	–	112.14	153.16	45.12	–	123.35	168.48
8020103C Extra for verges	m	0.20	5.13	–	1.31	6.44	5.64	–	1.44	7.08
8020103D Extra for double eaves course	m	0.20	5.13	–	11.06	16.19	5.64	–	12.17	17.81
8020103E Extra for half round ridge tiles	m	0.85	21.80	–	26.17	47.97	23.98	–	28.79	52.77
8020103F Extra for hip tiles; cutting both sides	m	1.00	25.64	–	30.68	56.32	28.20	–	33.75	61.95
8020103G Extra for angle ridge tiles...	m	0.85	21.80	–	26.17	47.97	23.98	–	28.79	52.77
8020103H Extra for bonnet hip tiles; cutting both sides.........	m	1.00	25.64	–	93.99	119.63	28.20	–	103.39	131.59
8020103I Extra for valley tiles; cutting both sides	m	1.00	25.64	–	93.99	119.63	28.20	–	103.39	131.59
8020103J Extra for intersection of ridge and hip.................	Each	0.70	17.95	–	–	17.95	19.75	–	–	19.75
8020105 Concrete plain tiles; BS473 and 550 group A; size 265 mm × 165 mm; 64 mm lap; 19 mm × 38 mm treated sawn softwood battens; reinforced slaters felt type 1F:										
8020105A sloping..................	m²	1.40	35.90	–	50.88	86.78	39.49	–	55.97	95.46
8020105B vertical or mansard	m²	1.60	41.03	–	50.88	91.91	45.13	–	55.97	101.10
8020105C Extra for verges	m	0.17	4.36	–	1.31	5.67	4.80	–	1.44	6.24
8020105D Extra for double eaves course	m	0.20	5.13	–	3.91	9.04	5.64	–	4.30	9.94
8020105E Extra for segmental ridge tiles....................	m	0.85	21.79	–	10.82	32.61	23.97	–	11.90	35.87
8020105F Extra for segmental hip tiles; cutting both sides.........	m	1.00	25.64	–	13.43	39.07	28.20	–	14.77	42.98
8020105G Extra for bonnet hip tiles; cutting both sides.........	m	1.00	25.64	–	38.62	64.26	28.20	–	42.48	70.69
8020105H Extra for valley tiles; cutting both sides	m	1.00	25.64	–	38.62	64.26	28.20	–	42.48	70.69
8020105I Extra for intersection of ridge and hip.................	Each	0.70	17.95	–	–	17.95	19.75	–	–	19.75

Roofing

Small Works 2009		Unit	Labour Hours	Labour Net	Plant Net	Materials Net	Unit Net	Labour Gross	Plant Gross	Materials Gross	Unit Price
								(Gross rates include 10% profit)			
				£	£	£	£	£	£	£	£
802	**TILE ROOFING**										
80202	**INTERLOCKING TILES**										
8020201	**Concrete interlocking tiles; smooth finish; size 381 mm × 229 mm; 75 mm lap 22 mm × 38 mm treated sawn softwood battens; reinforced underlining felt type 1F:**										
8020201A	sloping..................	m²	0.33	8.46	–	19.91	28.37	9.31	–	21.90	31.21
8020201B	vertical or mansard	m²	0.45	11.54	–	19.91	31.45	12.69	–	21.90	34.60
8020201C	Extra for verges; 150 mm fibre reinforced cement strip undercloak	m	0.35	8.97	–	4.34	13.31	9.87	–	4.77	14.64
8020201D	Extra for ridge tiles........	m	0.64	16.41	–	10.82	27.23	18.05	–	11.90	29.95
8020201E	Extra for hip tiles; cutting both sides	m	0.83	21.28	–	13.43	34.71	23.41	–	14.77	38.18
8020201F	Extra for valley trough tiles; cutting both sides........	m	0.69	17.70	–	94.22	111.92	19.47	–	103.64	123.11
8020203	**Concrete interlocking tiles; granular finish; granular finish; size 418 mm × 330 mm; 75 mm lap; 22 mm × 38 mm treated sawn softwood battens; reinforced slaters underlining felt type 1F:**										
8020203A	sloping.................	m²	0.22	5.64	–	20.41	26.05	6.20	–	22.45	28.66
8020203B	vertical or mansard	m²	0.30	7.69	–	20.41	28.10	8.46	–	22.45	30.91
8020203C	Extra for verges; 150 mm fibre reinforced cement strip undercloak	m	0.35	8.97	–	4.34	13.31	9.87	–	4.77	14.64
8020203D	Extra for ridge tiles........	m	0.64	16.41	–	10.82	27.23	18.05	–	11.90	29.95
8020203E	Extra for hip tiles; cutting both sides	m	0.83	21.28	–	13.43	34.71	23.41	–	14.77	38.18
8020203F	Extra for valley trough tiles; cutting both sides........	m	0.69	17.69	–	84.45	102.14	19.46	–	92.90	112.35

Small Works 2009		Unit	Labour Hours	Labour Net	Plant Net	Materials Net	Unit Net	Labour Gross	Plant Gross	Materials Gross	Unit Price
								(Gross rates include 10% profit)			
				£	£	£	£	£	£	£	£
803	**COUNTER-BATTENS AND UNDERFELT**										
80301	**COUNTER-BATTENS**										
8030101	**Treated sawn softwood counter-battens; fixed with galvanised nails to softwood**										
8030101A	19 mm × 38 mm; 450 mm centres..................	m²	0.08	2.05	–	1.10	3.15	2.26	–	1.21	3.47
8030101B	19 mm × 38 mm; 600 mm centres..................	m²	0.07	1.79	–	0.83	2.62	1.97	–	0.91	2.88
8030101C	19 mm × 38 mm; 750 mm centres..................	m²	0.06	1.54	–	0.66	2.20	1.69	–	0.73	2.42
8030101D	25 mm × 38 mm; 450 mm centres..................	m²	0.10	2.56	–	0.82	3.38	2.82	–	0.90	3.72
8030101E	25 mm × 38 mm; 600 mm centres..................	m²	0.09	2.30	–	0.62	2.92	2.53	–	0.68	3.21
8030101F	25 mm × 38 mm; 750 mm centres..................	m²	0.08	2.05	–	0.49	2.54	2.26	–	0.54	2.79
8030101G	38 mm × 38 mm; 450 mm centres..................	m²	0.14	3.59	–	1.19	4.78	3.95	–	1.31	5.26
8030101H	38 mm × 38 mm; 600 mm centres..................	m²	0.12	3.08	–	0.89	3.97	3.39	–	0.98	4.37
8030101I	38 mm × 38 mm; 750 mm centres..................	m²	0.10	2.56	–	0.71	3.27	2.82	–	0.78	3.60
8030101J	38 mm × 50 mm; 450 mm centres..................	m²	0.16	4.10	–	1.58	5.68	4.51	–	1.74	6.25
8030101K	38 mm × 50 mm; 600 mm centres..................	m²	0.13	3.33	–	1.19	4.52	3.66	–	1.31	4.97
8030101L	38 mm × 50 mm; 750 mm centres..................	m²	0.11	2.82	–	0.95	3.77	3.10	–	1.05	4.15
80303	**UNDERFELT**										
8030301	**Reinforced slaters underlining felt; BS747; type 1F; 150 mm laps; secured with galvanised felt nails:**										
8030301A	standard	m²	0.07	1.80	–	2.81	4.61	1.98	–	3.09	5.07
8030301B	aluminium foil faced.......	m²	0.07	1.80	–	3.90	5.70	1.98	–	4.29	6.27

Roofing

Small Works 2009		Unit	Labour Hours	Labour Net	Plant Net	Materials Net	Unit Net	Labour Gross	Plant Gross	Materials Gross	Unit Price
								(Gross rates include 10% profit)			
				£	£	£	£	£	£	£	£
804	**ASPHALT : BITUMEN FELT**										
80401	**MASTIC ASPHALT TO BS 988**										
8040101	**20 mm two coat coverings; felt isolating membrane:**										
8040101A	over 300 mm wide	m²	0.80	20.52	1.64	16.06	38.22	22.57	1.80	17.67	42.04
8040101B	not exceeding 150 mm wide	m	0.29	7.43	1.07	2.42	10.92	8.17	1.18	2.66	12.01
8040101C	150 mm-300 mm wide.....	m	0.38	9.75	1.78	4.82	16.35	10.73	1.96	5.30	17.99
8040102	**Extra over two coat coverings for:**										
8040102A	turning nibs into grooves ..	m	0.21	5.49	–	–	5.49	6.04	–	–	6.04
8040102B	working to metal flashings .	m	0.29	7.49	–	–	7.49	8.24	–	–	8.24
8040102C	working into outlets	Each	2.03	52.07	–	–	52.07	57.28	–	–	57.28
8040103	**13 mm two coat skirtings; internal angle fillet; top edge turned into groove:**										
8040103A	150 mm high.............	m	0.77	19.74	1.43	1.41	22.58	21.71	1.57	1.55	24.84
8040103B	250 mm high.............	m	0.95	24.36	1.14	2.35	27.85	26.80	1.25	2.59	30.64
8040104	**13 mm two coat aprons; undercut drip edge and rounded arris; including angles:**										
8040104A	75 mm high.............	m	0.70	17.95	1.14	0.71	19.80	19.75	1.25	0.78	21.78
8040104B	100 mm high.............	m	0.90	23.08	0.50	0.94	24.52	25.39	0.55	1.03	26.97
8040105	**13 mm two coat linings to gutter; two rounded arrises; two internal angle fillets; including angles and intersections:**										
8040105A	300 mm	m	1.95	49.99	1.28	2.65	53.92	54.99	1.41	2.92	59.31
8040105B	Extra for ends	Each	0.73	18.59	–	–	18.59	20.45	–	–	20.45
8040105C	Extra for outlets	Each	2.00	51.28	–	–	51.28	56.41	–	–	56.41
8040107	**13 mm two coat collar; 100 mm high; internal angle fillet at junction with covering; fair edge and arris:**										
8040107A	small pipes and the like	Each	0.93	23.71	1.07	0.49	25.27	26.08	1.18	0.54	27.80
8040107B	large pipes and the like	Each	1.38	35.25	1.78	0.89	37.92	38.78	1.96	0.98	41.71
8040108	**Accessories for asphalt roofing:**										
8040108A	aluminium edge trims; 50 mm × 65 mm; including butt straps and working asphalt to trim...........	m	0.50	12.82	–	8.40	21.22	14.10	–	9.24	23.34
8040108B	Extra for right angle corner pieces...................	Each	0.85	21.79	–	6.76	28.55	23.97	–	7.44	31.41
8040108C	aluminium edge trims; 75 mm × 65 mm; including butt straps and working asphalt to trim...........	m	0.50	12.82	–	13.13	25.95	14.10	–	14.44	28.55
8040108D	Extra for right angle corner pieces.................	Each	0.85	21.80	–	9.25	31.05	23.98	–	10.18	34.16
8040108E	aluminium pressure release ventilators including asphalt collars	Each	1.20	30.77	–	20.00	50.77	33.85	–	22.00	55.85

Roofing

Small Works 2009		Unit	Labour Hours	Labour Net	Plant Net	Materials Net	Unit Net	Labour Gross	Plant Gross	Materials Gross	Unit Price
								(Gross rates include 10% profit)			
				£	£	£	£	£	£	£	£
804	**ASPHALT : BITUMEN FELT**										
80402	**BITUMEN FELT ROOFING TO BS 747**										
8040201	**Glassfibre felt coverings; stone chippings surfacing:**										
8040201A	two layer; flat coverings; over 300 mm wide	m²	0.60	15.38	–	10.36	25.74	16.92	–	11.40	28.31
8040201B	Extra for working into outlets	Each	1.00	25.64	–	–	25.64	28.20	–	–	28.20
8040201C	three layer; flat coverings; over 300 mm wide	m²	0.80	20.52	–	15.37	35.89	22.57	–	16.91	39.48
8040201D	Extra for working into outlets	Each	1.00	25.64	–	–	25.64	28.20	–	–	28.20
8040203	**Asbex' glassfibre felt mineral surface coverings:**										
8040203A	two layer; sloping coverings; over 300 mm wide	m²	0.80	20.51	–	7.89	28.40	22.56	–	8.68	31.24
8040203B	Extra for working into outlets	Each	1.00	25.64	–	–	25.64	28.20	–	–	28.20
8040203C	three layer; sloping coverings; over 300 mm wide	m²	1.00	25.64	–	11.83	37.47	28.20	–	13.01	41.22
8040203D	Extra for working into outlets	Each	1.00	25.64	–	–	25.64	28.20	–	–	28.20
8040203E	75 mm wide aprons; fair drip edge at eaves or verges	m	0.37	9.48	–	0.30	9.78	10.43	–	0.33	10.76
8040203F	150 mm wide aprons; fair drip edge at eaves or verges	m	0.54	13.90	–	0.59	14.49	15.29	–	0.65	15.94
8040203G	150 mm girth skirtings; dressed over angle fillet....	m	0.43	10.95	–	0.59	11.54	12.05	–	0.65	12.69
8040203H	300 mm girth skirtings; dressed over angle fillet....	m	0.55	13.98	–	1.31	15.29	15.38	–	1.44	16.82
8040203I	200 mm three coat linings to gutters dressed over two angle fillets	m	0.41	10.41	–	2.37	12.78	11.45	–	2.61	14.06
8040203J	Extra for ends	Each	0.76	19.44	–	–	19.44	21.38	–	–	21.38
8040203K	Extra for outlets	Each	1.00	25.64	–	–	25.64	28.20	–	–	28.20
8040203L	300 mm three coat linings to gutters dressed over two angle fillets	m	0.61	15.56	–	3.55	19.11	17.12	–	3.91	21.02
8040203M	Extra for ends	Each	0.75	19.23	–	–	19.23	21.15	–	–	21.15
8040203N	Extra for outlets	Each	1.00	25.64	–	–	25.64	28.20	–	–	28.20
8040203O	collars around small pipes .	Each	1.50	38.46	–	–	38.46	42.31	–	–	42.31
8040203P	collars around large pipes ..	Each	2.00	51.28	–	–	51.28	56.41	–	–	56.41

Roofing

Small Works 2009		Unit	Labour Hours	Labour Net	Plant Net	Materials Net	Unit Net	Labour Gross	Plant Gross	Materials Gross	Unit Price
								(Gross rates include 10% profit)			
				£	£	£	£	£	£	£	£
804	**ASPHALT : BITUMEN FELT**										
80402	**BITUMEN FELT ROOFING TO BS 747**										
8040204	**Fibre insulation board; bedded in hot bitumen:**										
8040204A	19 mm thick	m²	0.46	11.80	–	4.55	16.35	12.98	–	5.01	17.99
8040204B	Extra for forming holes for pipes	Each	0.29	7.44	–	–	7.44	8.18	–	–	8.18
8040205	**Resin bonded glassfibre slabs; bedded in hot bitumen:**										
8040205A	25 mm thick	m²	1.14	29.31	–	20.64	49.95	32.24	–	22.70	54.95
8040205B	Extra for forming holes for pipes	Each	0.29	7.54	–	–	7.54	8.29	–	–	8.29
8040206	**Vapour barrier; bedded in hot bitumen:**										
8040206A	felt	m²	0.45	11.54	–	2.79	14.33	12.69	–	3.07	15.76
8040208	**Accessories for felt roofing:**										
8040208A	aluminium edge trims; 40 mm × 65 mm; including butt straps; working feltwork to trim	m	0.34	8.72	–	7.09	15.81	9.59	–	7.80	17.39
8040208B	Extra for right angle corner pieces..................	Each	0.65	16.54	–	5.90	22.44	18.19	–	6.49	24.68
8040208C	aluminium edge trims; 75 mm × 65 mm; including butt straps; working feltwork to trim	m	0.20	5.21	–	12.50	17.71	5.73	–	13.75	19.48
8040208D	Extra for right angle corner pieces..................	Each	0.60	15.39	–	9.25	24.64	16.93	–	10.18	27.10

Small Works 2009		Unit	Labour Hours	Labour Net	Plant Net	Materials Net	Unit Net	Labour Gross	Plant Gross	Materials Gross	Unit Price
								(Gross rates include 10% profit)			
				£	£	£	£	£	£	£	£
805	**CORRUGATED SHEETING**										
80501	**REINFORCED CEMENT**										
8050101	**Coverings; horizontal; 750 mm nominal width; 76 mm corrugations; 100 mm side and 152 mm end laps; straight cutting and waste:**										
8050101A	fixed to wood with galvanised drive screws and washers..	m²	0.50	12.82	–	40.17	52.99	14.10	–	44.19	58.29
8050101B	fixed to steel purlins with hook bolts	m²	0.70	17.95	–	40.08	58.03	19.75	–	44.09	63.83
8050102	**Coverings; mansard and vertical; 750 mm nominal width; 76 mm corrugations; 100 mm side and 152 mm end laps; straight cutting and waste:**										
8050102A	fixed to wood with galvanised drive screws and washers..	m²	0.70	17.94	–	40.93	58.87	19.73	–	45.02	64.76
8050102B	fixed to steel framing with hook bolts	m²	1.00	25.64	–	40.81	66.45	28.20	–	44.89	73.10
8050103	**Extra over cement sheets for vinyl translucent sheets:**										
8050103A	762 mm wide	m²	–	–	–	-7.74	-7.74	–	–	-8.51	-8.51
8050104	**Sundry labours and finishings:**										
8050104A	raking cutting	m	0.35	8.97	–	–	8.97	9.87	–	–	9.87
8050104B	barge boards.	m	0.35	8.97	–	22.17	31.14	9.87	–	24.39	34.25
8050104C	two piece close fitting ridge	m	0.55	14.10	–	25.20	39.30	15.51	–	27.72	43.23
8050104D	ridge finials	Each	1.10	28.21	–	22.29	50.50	31.03	–	24.52	55.55
8050104E	eaves filler pieces	m	0.35	8.97	–	16.90	25.87	9.87	–	18.59	28.46
8050104F	apron flashings.	m	0.35	8.97	–	16.43	25.40	9.87	–	18.07	27.94

Roofing

Small Works 2009		Unit	Labour Hours	Labour Net	Plant Net	Materials Net	Unit Net	Labour Gross	Plant Gross	Materials Gross	Unit Price
								(Gross rates include 10% profit)			
				£	£	£	£	£	£	£	£
805	**CORRUGATED SHEETING**										
80502	**GALVANISED STEEL**										
8050201	**22 gauge galvanised corrugated steel sheeting; including one corrugation side lap and 150 mm end lap:**										
8050201A	to wood purlins with drive screws and washers	m²	0.35	8.97	–	35.50	44.47	9.87	–	39.05	48.92
8050201B	to steel purlins with hook bolts....................	m²	0.50	12.82	–	35.41	48.23	14.10	–	38.95	53.05
8050202	**Sundry labours and finishings:**										
8050202A	raking cutting	m	0.70	17.95	–	–	17.95	19.75	–	–	19.75
8050202B	26 gauge corrugated steel ridge; 375 mm girth	m	0.30	7.70	–	6.86	14.56	8.47	–	7.55	16.02
806	**NURALITE : THATCH**										
80601	**NURALITE SHEET; D12C JOINTING STRIP SYSTEM**										
8060102	**Nuralite FX roof coverings:**										
8060102A	flat	m²	0.45	11.53	–	31.43	42.96	12.68	–	34.57	47.26
8060102B	sloping.................	m²	0.60	15.38	–	31.43	46.81	16.92	–	34.57	51.49
8060102C	dormer cheeks	m²	0.55	14.10	–	31.43	45.53	15.51	–	34.57	50.08
8060102D	gutters	m²	0.80	20.51	–	31.43	51.94	22.56	–	34.57	57.13
8060102E	flashings; wedging into groove	m	0.70	17.95	–	5.06	23.01	19.75	–	5.57	25.31
8060102F	stepped flashings; wedging into groove	m	0.75	19.23	–	6.17	25.40	21.15	–	6.79	27.94
8060102G	raking cutting	m	0.17	4.36	–	–	4.36	4.80	–	–	4.80
8060102H	curved cutting...........	m	0.20	5.13	–	–	5.13	5.64	–	–	5.64

Roofing

Small Works 2009		Unit				Specialist Net	Unit Net			Specialist Gross	Unit Price
									(Gross rates include 10% profit)		
			£	£	£	£	£	£	£	£
806	**NURALITE : THATCH**										
80602	**THATCHING BY SPECIALIST**										
8060201	**Thatching to a thickness of about 300 mm fixed with iron hooks and finished with a block cut and patterned and saddled ridge:**										
8060201A	best quality water reed	m²	–	–	–	150.00	150.00	–	–	165.00	165.00
8060201B	best quality combed wheat straw	m²	–	–	–	135.00	135.00	–	–	148.50	148.50
8060201C	best quality long straw	m²	–	–	–	120.00	120.00	–	–	132.00	132.00
8060202	**Ridge:**										
8060202A	block cut, patterned and saddled	m	–	–	–	270.00	270.00	–	–	297.00	297.00
8060202B	flush	m	–	–	–	150.00	150.00	–	–	165.00	165.00
8060203	**Wiring over to thatch with netting:**										
8060203A	1200 mm × 19 mm × 20G galvanised netting	m²	–	–	–	10.00	10.00	–	–	11.50	11.50
8060210	**Firestopping:**										
8060210A	Magma TAS Firestop	m²	–	–	–	9.60	9.60	–	–	10.56	10.56
8060210B	IMW 435	m²	–	–	–	4.80	4.80	–	–	5.28	5.28

Roofing

Small Works 2009		Unit	Labour Hours	Labour Net	Plant Net	Materials Net	Unit Net	Labour Gross	Plant Gross	Materials Gross	Unit Price
								(Gross rates include 10% profit)			
				£	£	£	£	£	£	£	£
808	**SHEET METAL : ROOF DECKING**										
80801	**COVERINGS (CODE 4) LEAD 1.80 mm**										
8080101	**Coverings:**										
8080101A	flat roof	m²	4.40	112.82	–	40.36	153.18	124.10	–	44.40	168.50
8080101B	gutters, valleys, dormer roofs and cheeks	m²	5.50	141.02	–	40.36	181.38	155.12	–	44.40	199.52
8080101C	aprons; cappings to ridges or hips	m²	5.70	146.15	–	40.36	186.51	160.77	–	44.40	205.16
8080101D	damp proof course	m²	2.20	56.41	–	40.36	96.77	62.05	–	44.40	106.45
8080102	**Flashings; wedging into groove:**										
8080102A	150 mm girth	m	0.44	11.28	–	6.06	17.34	12.41	–	6.67	19.07
8080102B	200 mm girth	m	0.60	15.38	–	8.09	23.47	16.92	–	8.90	25.82
8080102C	300 mm girth	m	0.88	22.57	–	12.11	34.68	24.83	–	13.32	38.15
8080103	**Stepped flashings; wedging into groove:**										
8080103A	150 mm girth	m	0.55	14.10	–	6.06	20.16	15.51	–	6.67	22.18
8080103B	200 mm girth	m	0.94	24.10	–	8.09	32.19	26.51	–	8.90	35.41
8080103C	300 mm girth	m	1.16	29.74	–	12.11	41.85	32.71	–	13.32	46.04
8080104	**Soakers and hand to roofer:**										
8080104A	200 mm × 200 mm	Each	0.33	8.46	–	1.63	10.09	9.31	–	1.79	11.10
8080104B	300 mm × 300 mm	Each	0.38	9.74	–	3.63	13.37	10.71	–	3.99	14.71
8080105	**Slate; 400 mm × 400 mm with collar 200 mm high around pipe:**										
8080105A	100 mm diameter	Each	1.65	42.31	–	9.32	51.63	46.54	–	10.25	56.79
8080105B	150 mm diameter	Each	1.67	42.82	–	10.48	53.30	47.10	–	11.53	58.63
8080106	**Slate; dressed through 225 mm wall into rainwater head:**										
8080106A	600 mm × 450 mm	Each	2.50	64.10	–	11.31	75.41	70.51	–	12.44	82.95
80802	**COVERINGS (CODE 5) LEAD 2.24 mm**										
8080201	**Coverings:**										
8080201A	flat roof	m²	4.62	118.46	–	50.46	168.92	130.31	–	55.51	185.81
8080201B	gutters, valleys, dormer roofs and cheeks	m²	5.78	148.20	–	50.46	198.66	163.02	–	55.51	218.53
8080201C	aprons; cappings to ridges or hips	m²	5.98	153.33	–	50.46	203.79	168.66	–	55.51	224.17
8080201D	damp proof course	m²	2.31	59.23	–	50.46	109.69	65.15	–	55.51	120.66
8080202	**Flashings; wedging into groove:**										
8080202A	150 mm girth	m	0.49	12.56	–	7.57	20.13	13.82	–	8.33	22.14
8080202B	200 mm girth	m	0.66	16.92	–	10.11	27.03	18.61	–	11.12	29.73
8080202C	300 mm girth	m	0.91	23.33	–	15.14	38.47	25.66	–	16.65	42.32
8080203	**Stepped flashings; wedging into groove:**										
8080203A	150 mm girth	m	0.61	15.64	–	7.57	23.21	17.20	–	8.33	25.53
8080203B	200 mm girth	m	0.99	25.38	–	10.11	35.49	27.92	–	11.12	39.04
8080203C	300 mm girth	m	1.21	31.03	–	15.14	46.17	34.13	–	16.65	50.79

Small Works 2009		Unit	Labour Hours	Labour Net	Plant Net	Materials Net	Unit Net	Labour Gross	Plant Gross	Materials Gross	Unit Price
								(Gross rates include 10% profit)			
				£	£	£	£	£	£	£	£
808	**SHEET METAL : ROOF DECKING**										
80802	**COVERINGS (CODE 5) LEAD 2.24 mm**										
8080204	**Soakers and hand to roofer:**										
8080204A	200 mm × 200 mm......	Each	0.43	11.03	–	20.17	31.20	12.13	–	22.19	34.32
8080204B	300 mm × 300 mm......	Each	0.48	12.31	–	4.53	16.84	13.54	–	4.98	18.52
8080205	**Slate; 400 mm × 400 mm with collar 200 mm high around pipe:**										
8080205A	100 mm diameter........	Each	1.76	45.13	–	11.65	56.78	49.64	–	12.82	62.46
8080205B	200 mm diameter........	Each	1.98	50.77	–	13.10	63.87	55.85	–	14.41	70.26
8080206	**Slate; dressed through 225 mm wall into rainwater head:**										
8080206A	600 mm × 450 mm......	Each	2.60	66.67	–	14.14	80.81	73.34	–	15.55	88.89
80803	**SUNDRIES LEAD SHEET COVERINGS**										
8080301	**Coverings:**										
8080301A	beaded edges	m	0.60	15.38	–	–	15.38	16.92	–	–	16.92
8080301B	soldered seam	m	3.00	76.92	–	7.93	84.85	84.61	–	8.72	93.34
8080301C	soldered dots with brass screws	Each	1.00	25.64	–	0.10	25.74	28.20	–	0.11	28.31
8080301D	bossed ends to rolls.......	Each	1.20	30.77	–	–	30.77	33.85	–	–	33.85
8080301E	bossed angles to rolls	Each	1.50	38.46	–	–	38.46	42.31	–	–	42.31
8080301F	bossed intersections to rolls	Each	1.75	44.87	–	–	44.87	49.36	–	–	49.36
80804	**COPPER SHEET COVERINGS (24 SWG) 0.55 mm**										
8080401	**Coverings:**										
8080401A	flat roof covering; rolls and laps.....................	m²	3.52	90.25	–	49.19	139.44	99.28	–	54.11	153.38
8080401B	gutters, valleys, dormer roofs and cheeks	m²	4.40	112.82	–	49.19	162.01	124.10	–	54.11	178.21
8080401C	aprons; cappings to ridges or hips	m²	4.60	117.94	–	49.19	167.13	129.73	–	54.11	183.84
8080402	**Flashings; wedging into groove:**										
8080402A	150 mm girth	m	0.55	14.10	–	7.38	21.48	15.51	–	8.12	23.63
8080402B	200 mm girth	m	0.66	16.92	–	9.86	26.78	18.61	–	10.85	29.46
8080402C	300 mm girth	m	0.99	25.39	–	14.76	40.15	27.93	–	16.24	44.17
8080403	**Stepped flashings; wedging into groove:**										
8080403A	150 mm girth	m	0.66	16.92	–	7.38	24.30	18.61	–	8.12	26.73
8080403B	200 mm girth	m	0.77	19.74	–	9.86	29.60	21.71	–	10.85	32.56
8080403C	300 mm girth	m	1.10	28.21	–	14.76	42.97	31.03	–	16.24	47.27

Roofing

Small Works 2009		Unit	Labour Hours	Labour Net	Plant Net	Materials Net	Unit Net	Labour Gross	Plant Gross	Materials Gross	Unit Price
								(Gross rates include 10% profit)			
				£	£	£	£	£	£	£	£
808	**SHEET METAL : ROOF DECKING**										
80805	**ZINC SHEET COVERINGS (12.G) 0.64 mm**										
8080501	**Coverings:**										
8080501A	flat roof covering; rolls and laps....................	m²	3.30	84.61	–	33.00	117.61	93.07	–	36.30	129.37
8080501B	gutters, valleys, dormer roofs and cheeks	m²	4.13	105.90	–	33.00	138.90	116.49	–	36.30	152.79
8080501C	aprons; cappings to ridges or hips	m²	4.33	111.02	–	33.00	144.02	122.12	–	36.30	158.42
8080502	**Flashings; wedging to groove:**										
8080502A	150 mm girth	m	0.44	11.28	–	4.95	16.23	12.41	–	5.45	17.85
8080502B	200 mm girth	m	0.55	14.10	–	6.61	20.71	15.51	–	7.27	22.78
8080502C	300 mm girth	m	0.88	22.57	–	9.90	32.47	24.83	–	10.89	35.72
8080503	**Stepped flashings; wedging into groove:**										
8080503A	150 mm girth	m	0.55	14.10	–	4.95	19.05	15.51	–	5.45	20.96
8080503B	200 mm girth	m	0.66	16.92	–	6.61	23.53	18.61	–	7.27	25.88
8080503C	300 mm girth	m	0.99	25.39	–	9.90	35.29	27.93	–	10.89	38.82
80806	**ZINC SHEET COVERINGS (14.G) 0.79 mm**										
8080601	**Coverings:**										
8080601A	flat roof covering; rolls and laps....................	m²	3.30	84.61	–	40.56	125.17	93.07	–	44.62	137.69
8080601B	gutters, valleys, dormer roofs and cheeks	m²	4.13	105.90	–	40.56	146.46	116.49	–	44.62	161.11
8080601C	aprons; cappings to ridges or hips	m²	4.33	111.02	–	40.56	151.58	122.12	–	44.62	166.74
8080602	**Flashings; wedging to groove:**										
8080602A	150 mm girth	m	0.44	11.28	–	6.09	17.37	12.41	–	6.70	19.11
8080602B	200 mm girth	m	0.55	14.10	–	8.13	22.23	15.51	–	8.94	24.45
8080602C	300 mm girth	m	0.88	22.57	–	12.17	34.74	24.83	–	13.39	38.21
8080603	**Stepped flashings; wedging into groove:**										
8080603A	150 mm girth	m	0.55	14.10	–	6.09	20.19	15.51	–	6.70	22.21
8080603B	200 mm girth	m	0.66	16.92	–	8.13	25.05	18.61	–	8.94	27.56
8080603C	300 mm girth	m	0.99	25.39	–	12.17	37.56	27.93	–	13.39	41.32

Small Works 2009		Unit	Labour Hours	Labour Net	Plant Net	Materials Net	Unit Net	Labour Gross	Plant Gross	Materials Gross	Unit Price
								(Gross rates include 10% profit)			
				£	£	£	£	£	£	£	£
808	**SHEET METAL : ROOF DECKING**										
80808	**ALUMINIUM SHEET COVERINGS (21.G) 0.99 mm: COMMERCIAL GRADE**										
8080801	**Coverings:**										
8080801A	flat roof covering; rolls and laps	m²	3.52	90.25	–	11.45	101.70	99.28	–	12.60	111.87
8080801B	gutters, valleys, dormer roofs and cheeks	m²	4.40	112.81	–	11.45	124.26	124.09	–	12.60	136.69
8080801C	aprons; cappings to ridges or hips	m²	4.60	117.94	–	11.45	129.39	129.73	–	12.60	142.33
8080802	**Flashings; wedging to groove:**										
8080802A	150 mm girth	m	0.55	14.10	–	1.72	15.82	15.51	–	1.89	17.40
8080802B	200 mm girth	m	0.66	16.93	–	2.29	19.22	18.62	–	2.52	21.14
8080802C	300 mm girth	m	0.99	25.39	–	3.43	28.82	27.93	–	3.77	31.70
8080803	**Stepped flashings; wedging into groove:**										
8080803A	150 mm girth	m	0.66	16.92	–	1.72	18.64	18.61	–	1.89	20.50
8080803B	200 mm girth	m	0.77	19.75	–	2.29	22.04	21.73	–	2.52	24.24
8080803C	300 mm girth	m	1.10	28.21	–	3.43	31.64	31.03	–	3.77	34.80
80809	**ROOF DECKING**										
8080901	**Woodwool unreinforced slabs; BS 1105; type SB; fixing to timber with galvanised nails:**										
8080901A	50 mm	m²	0.48	12.31	–	12.26	24.57	13.54	–	13.49	27.03
8080901B	75 mm	m²	0.54	13.84	–	15.55	29.39	15.22	–	17.11	32.33
8080901C	100 mm	m²	0.60	15.39	–	20.46	35.85	16.93	–	22.51	39.44
8080903	**Mineral fibre insulating decking slabs:**										
8080903A	50 mm	m²	0.38	9.74	–	30.20	39.94	10.71	–	33.22	43.93
8080905	**Laminated polyurethane insulation standard roof boarding:**										
8080905A	26 mm	m²	0.25	6.41	–	12.74	19.15	7.05	–	14.01	21.07
8080905B	35 mm	m²	0.25	6.41	–	13.25	19.66	7.05	–	14.58	21.63
8080905C	50 mm	m²	0.38	9.75	–	17.32	27.07	10.73	–	19.05	29.78
8080907	**Purldek combined deck insulation board:**										
8080907A	50 mm; fixing to timber with galvanised nails	m²	0.68	17.43	–	51.37	68.80	19.17	–	56.51	75.68
8080907B	raking cutting	m	0.36	9.23	–	–	9.23	10.15	–	–	10.15
8080907C	curved cutting	m	0.60	15.38	–	–	15.38	16.92	–	–	16.92

Roofing

Small Works 2009		Unit	Labour Hours	Labour Net	Plant Net	Materials Net	Unit Net	Labour Gross	Plant Gross	Materials Gross	Unit Price
								(Gross rates include 10% profit)			
				£	£	£	£	£	£	£	£
809	**REPAIRS AND ALTERATIONS**										
80901	**REMOVE COVERINGS AND LOAD INTO SKIP**										
8090101	**Roof coverings:**										
8090101A	slates	m²	0.55	11.47	–	–	11.47	12.62	–	–	12.62
8090101B	nibbed tiles	m²	0.45	9.38	–	–	9.38	10.32	–	–	10.32
8090101C	corrugated metal sheeting	m²	0.45	9.38	–	–	9.38	10.32	–	–	10.32
8090101D	underfelt and nails	m²	0.07	1.46	–	–	1.46	1.61	–	–	1.61
8090101E	three layers felt	m²	0.28	5.84	–	–	5.84	6.42	–	–	6.42
8090101F	sheet metal	m²	0.55	11.47	–	–	11.47	12.62	–	–	12.62
8090102	**Metal finishings:**										
8090102A	horizontal	m	0.22	4.59	–	–	4.59	5.05	–	–	5.05
8090102B	stepped	m	0.28	5.84	–	–	5.84	6.42	–	–	6.42
8090103	**Battens including withdrawing nails:**										
8090103A	tile or slate	m²	0.10	2.09	–	–	2.09	2.30	–	–	2.30
8090104	**Remove coverings, carefully handling and disposing of by an approved method toxic or other special waste:**										
8090104A	asbestos cement sheeting	m²	2.20	56.41	–	1.25	57.66	62.05	–	1.38	63.43
8090105	**Stripping, cleaning and setting aside sound slates or tiles for re-use:**										
8090105A	slates	m²	0.40	8.34	–	–	8.34	9.17	–	–	9.17
8090105B	tiles	m²	0.30	6.26	–	–	6.26	6.89	–	–	6.89
8090105C	cement slates	m²	0.40	8.34	–	–	8.34	9.17	–	–	9.17
8090106	**Stripping, cleaning and setting aside for removal:**										
8090106A	slates	m²	0.30	6.26	–	–	6.26	6.89	–	–	6.89
8090106B	tiles	m²	0.24	5.00	–	–	5.00	5.50	–	–	5.50
8090106C	cement slates	m²	0.30	6.26	–	–	6.26	6.89	–	–	6.89

Small Works 2009		Unit	Labour Hours	Labour Net	Plant Net	Materials Net	Unit Net	Labour Gross	Plant Gross	Materials Gross	Unit Price
								(Gross rates include 10% profit)			
				£	£	£	£	£	£	£	£
809	**REPAIRS AND ALTERATIONS**										
80902	**RENEWALS**										
8090201	**Tile battens to 100 mm gauge:**										
8090201A	area not exceeding 8.5 sq.m	m²	0.34	8.72	–	4.09	12.81	9.59	–	4.50	14.09
8090201B	area exceeding 8.5 sq.m ...	m²	0.26	6.67	–	4.09	10.76	7.34	–	4.50	11.84
8090202	**Slate battens to 205 mm gauge:**										
8090202A	area not exceeding 8.5 sq.m	m²	0.26	6.66	–	2.35	9.01	7.33	–	2.59	9.91
8090202B	area exceeding 8.5 sq.m ...	m²	0.17	4.36	–	2.35	6.71	4.80	–	2.59	7.38
8090203	**Roofing felt:**										
8090203A	per sq.m	m²	0.14	3.59	–	2.94	6.53	3.95	–	3.23	7.18
8090204	**Single slates with clips, including taking off; first slate:**										
8090204A	405 mm × 205 mm......	Each	0.53	13.59	–	1.56	15.15	14.95	–	1.72	16.67
8090204B	510 mm × 255 mm......	Each	0.56	14.36	–	3.24	17.60	15.80	–	3.56	19.36
8090204C	610 mm × 305 mm......	Each	0.58	14.88	–	5.58	20.46	16.37	–	6.14	22.51
8090205	**Single slates with clips, including taking off; second and subsequent slate up to 30 no:**										
8090205A	405 mm × 205 mm......	Each	0.22	5.64	–	1.56	7.20	6.20	–	1.72	7.92
8090205B	510 mm × 255 mm......	Each	0.23	5.90	–	3.24	9.14	6.49	–	3.56	10.05
8090205C	610 mm × 305 mm......	Each	0.24	6.16	–	5.58	11.74	6.78	–	6.14	12.91
8090206	**Single tiles, including taking off; first tile:**										
8090206A	clay............	Each	0.36	9.23	–	0.66	9.89	10.15	–	0.73	10.88
8090206B	concrete..........	Each	0.36	9.23	–	0.65	9.88	10.15	–	0.72	10.87
8090207	**Single tiles, including taking off; second and subsequent tiles up to 50 no**										
8090207A	clay..............	Each	0.22	5.64	–	0.66	6.30	6.20	–	0.73	6.93
8090207B	concrete..........	Each	0.22	5.64	–	0.65	6.29	6.20	–	0.72	6.92
8090208	**Single blue asbestos slates, including taking off; first slate:**										
8090208A	610 mm × 305 mm......	Each	0.37	9.49	–	2.26	11.75	10.44	–	2.49	12.93
8090209	**Single blue asbestos slates, second and subsequent slates up to 30 no:**										
8090209A	610 mm × 305 mm......	Each	0.22	5.65	–	2.26	7.91	6.22	–	2.49	8.70
8090210	**Cement mortar (1:3) angle fillet to slate, tile or asbestos roof at abutment to:**										
8090210A	walls or chimney stacks ...	m	0.40	10.25	–	0.33	10.58	11.28	–	0.36	11.64
8090211	**Strip roof slating, sort slates and reslate roof using 50% salvaged slates:**										
8090211A	405 mm × 205 mm......	m²	1.15	29.49	–	23.45	52.94	32.44	–	25.80	58.23
8090211B	510 mm × 255 mm......	m²	0.80	20.51	–	30.03	50.54	22.56	–	33.03	55.59
8090211C	610 mm × 305 mm......	m²	0.50	12.82	–	35.03	47.85	14.10	–	38.53	52.64
8090212	**Strip 267 mm × 165 mm plain roof tiles and retile using 50% salvaged tiles:**										
8090212A	clay............	m²	1.70	43.59	–	21.76	65.35	47.95	–	23.94	71.89
8090212B	concrete..........	m²	1.70	43.59	–	21.53	65.12	47.95	–	23.68	71.63

Roofing

Small Works 2009		Unit	Labour Hours	Labour Net	Plant Net	Materials Net	Unit Net	Labour Gross	Plant Gross	Materials Gross	Unit Price
								(Gross rates include 10% profit)			
				£	£	£	£	£	£	£	£
809	**REPAIRS AND ALTERATIONS**										
80903	**REPAIRS TO SHEET METAL**										
8090301	**Take up old lead; any position or weight:**										
8090301A	and set aside............	m²	0.40	10.26	–	–	10.26	11.29	–	–	11.29
8090301B	and relay to boarded flats including dressing over rolls and drips, with new bossed ends etc.	m²	4.30	110.25	–	–	110.25	121.28	–	–	121.28
8090302	**Redress lead flashings:**										
8090302A	and rewedge and repoint...	m	0.80	20.51	–	–	20.51	22.56	–	–	22.56
8090303	**Take up old zinc; in any position:**										
8090303A	and remove from site......	m²	1.00	25.64	–	–	25.64	28.20	–	–	28.20
8090304	**Take up existing zinc and supply and lay new zinc including rolls, laps etc:**										
8090304A	0.50 mm thick............	m²	4.00	102.56	–	18.00	120.56	112.82	–	19.80	132.62
8090304B	0.65 mm thick............	m²	4.50	115.38	–	33.00	148.38	126.92	–	36.30	163.22
8090304C	0.80 mm thick............	m²	5.00	128.20	–	40.56	168.76	141.02	–	44.62	185.64
8090305	**Prepare zinc roofs and supply and lay bitumenised fabric:**										
8090305A	bedded in bitumen, apply two coats o bitumen emulsion..	m²	1.90	48.71	–	1.96	50.67	53.58	–	2.16	55.74
8090306	**Seal crack in holes in zinc or asphalt flats:**										
8090306A	and apply two coats of bitumen waterproofer	m²	0.90	23.08	–	1.22	24.30	25.39	–	1.34	26.73
8090307	**Clean and treat defective sheet zinc with:**										
8090307A	Rito', 'Matex' or similar compound..............	m²	1.10	28.21	–	1.81	30.02	31.03	–	1.99	33.02
8090308	**Remove slates, take out defective box gutter linings or valleys and:**										
8090308A	renew wood linings and line with 12G zinc and replace slates	m²	8.00	205.12	–	395.81	600.93	225.63	–	435.39	661.02

Roofing

Small Works 2009		Unit	Labour Hours	Labour Net	Plant Net	Materials Net	Unit Net	Labour Gross	Plant Gross	Materials Gross	Unit Price
								(Gross rates include 10% profit)			
				£	£	£	£	£	£	£	£
809	**REPAIRS AND ALTERATIONS**										
80904	**PROVISION OF LADDERS**										
8090401	**Labour and transport up to 5 miles each way and setting up and removing ladders up to:**										
8090401A	two storeys high.........	Each	4.99	97.02	6.13	–	103.15	106.72	6.74	–	113.47
8090401B	four storeys high	Each	2.83	52.13	6.13	–	58.26	57.34	6.74	–	64.09
8090401C	extra over last two items if access is difficult e.g. one house in a terrace where there is no side entrance ...	Each	2.33	41.70	6.13	–	47.83	45.87	6.74	–	52.61
80905	**REMOVAL OF ASPHALT**										
8090501	**Remove waterproofing finishes and load into skip:**										
8090501A	asphalt paving...........	m²	0.67	13.97	2.75	–	16.72	15.37	3.03	–	18.39
8090501B	asphalt roofing	m²	1.10	22.93	1.89	–	24.82	25.22	2.08	–	27.30
8090501C	asphalt skirting	m	0.17	3.55	0.43	–	3.98	3.91	0.47	–	4.38
80906	**ROOF TREATMENTS BY SPECIALISTS**										
8090601	**Clean, prepare and apply 'DC500' flexible roofing compound:**										
8090601A	to sound surfaces; asbestos, asphalt, concrete, felt, slate or tile	m²	0.55	11.47	–	6.26	17.73	12.62	–	6.89	19.50
8090601B	and fungicide solution to surfaces likely to support fungal or algae growth; asbestos, asphalt, concrete, felt, slate or tile	m²	0.60	12.51	–	7.26	19.77	13.76	–	7.99	21.75

SUNDRIES

Small Works 2009		Unit	Labour Hours	Labour Net	Plant Net	Materials Net	Unit Net	Labour Gross	Plant Gross	Materials Gross	Unit Price
								(Gross rates include 10% profit)			
				£	£	£	£	£	£	£	£
901	**STEELWORK AND METALWORK**										
90101	**UNFRAMED STEELWORK**										
9010101	**Rolled joist beams:**										
9010101A	127 mm × 76 mm × 13 kg	m	0.30	7.32	–	15.12	22.44	8.05	–	16.63	24.68
9010101B	152 mm × 89 mm × 18 kg	m	0.41	10.02	–	20.15	30.17	11.02	–	22.17	33.19
9010101C	178 mm × 102 mm × 21 kg	m	0.48	11.73	–	25.75	37.48	12.90	–	28.33	41.23
9010101D	203 mm × 102 mm × 25 kg	m	0.58	14.17	–	29.22	43.39	15.59	–	32.14	47.73
9010102	**Universal beams:**										
9010102A	203 mm × 133 mm × 25 kg	m	0.58	14.17	–	36.74	50.91	15.59	–	40.41	56.00
9010102B	203 mm × 133 mm × 30 kg	m	0.69	16.86	–	33.25	50.11	18.55	–	36.58	55.12
9010102C	254 mm × 146 mm × 31 kg	m	0.71	17.34	–	47.48	64.82	19.07	–	52.23	71.30
9010102D	254 mm × 146 mm × 37 kg	m	0.85	20.76	–	55.62	76.38	22.84	–	61.18	84.02
9010102E	254 mm × 146 mm × 43 kg	m	0.99	24.19	–	50.16	74.35	26.61	–	55.18	81.79
9010102F	305 mm × 165 mm × 40 kg	m	0.92	22.48	–	61.04	83.52	24.73	–	67.14	91.87
9010102G	305 mm × 165 mm × 46 kg	m	1.06	25.90	–	69.18	95.08	28.49	–	76.10	104.59
9010102H	305 mm × 165 mm × 54 kg	m	1.24	30.29	–	62.70	92.99	33.32	–	68.97	102.29
9010102I	254 mm × 102 mm × 25 kg	m	0.58	14.17	–	44.17	58.34	15.59	–	48.59	64.17
9010102J	305 mm × 102 mm × 33 kg	m	0.76	18.57	–	52.37	70.94	20.43	–	57.61	78.03
9010102K	356 mm × 171 mm × 51 kg	m	1.17	28.59	–	79.00	107.59	31.45	–	86.90	118.35
90102	**METALWORK**										
9010201	**Mild steel flats and plates:**										
9010201A	50 mm × 6 mm	m	0.28	6.84	–	6.46	13.30	7.52	–	7.11	14.63
9010201B	80 mm × 6 mm	m	0.40	9.77	–	9.31	19.08	10.75	–	10.24	20.99
9010201C	80 mm × 12 mm	m	0.40	9.77	–	17.63	27.40	10.75	–	19.39	30.14
9010201D	100 mm × 6 mm	m	0.48	11.72	–	12.13	23.85	12.89	–	13.34	26.24
9010201E	100 mm × 12 mm	m	0.48	11.72	–	23.15	34.87	12.89	–	25.47	38.36
9010201F	125 mm × 6 mm	m	0.58	14.17	–	14.81	28.98	15.59	–	16.29	31.88
9010201G	150 mm × 6 mm	m	0.68	16.61	–	17.63	34.24	18.27	–	19.39	37.66
9010201H	150 mm × 12 mm	m	0.68	16.62	–	34.28	50.90	18.28	–	37.71	55.99
9010201I	200 mm × 6 mm	m	0.88	21.49	–	23.15	44.64	23.64	–	25.47	49.10
9010201J	254 mm × 6 mm	m	1.10	26.88	–	28.74	55.62	29.57	–	31.61	61.18
9010201K	254 mm × 12 mm	m	1.10	26.87	–	56.43	83.30	29.56	–	62.07	91.63
90103	**CATNIC; GALVANISED STEEL LINTELS**										
9010301	**CN7; combined lintel; for standard 50 mm cavity wall; 143 mm high; length:**										
9010301A	750 mm	Each	0.36	9.23	–	44.18	53.41	10.15	–	48.60	58.75
9010301B	900 mm	Each	0.38	9.75	–	53.18	62.93	10.73	–	58.50	69.22
9010301C	1050 mm	Each	0.40	10.25	–	61.91	72.16	11.28	–	68.10	79.38
9010301D	1200 mm	Each	0.42	10.77	–	70.62	81.39	11.85	–	77.68	89.53
9010301E	1350 mm	Each	0.44	11.28	–	79.45	90.73	12.41	–	87.40	99.80

Sundries

Small Works 2009		Unit	Labour Hours	Labour Net	Plant Net	Materials Net	Unit Net	Labour Gross	Plant Gross	Materials Gross	Unit Price
								(Gross rates include 10% profit)			
				£	£	£	£	£	£	£	£
901	**STEELWORK AND METALWORK**										
90103	**CATNIC; GALVANISED STEEL LINTELS**										
9010302	**CN7; combined lintel; for standard 50 mm cavity wall; 143 mm high; length:**										
9010302A	1500 mm	Each	0.46	11.80	–	91.76	103.56	12.98	–	100.94	113.92
9010302B	1650 mm	Each	0.48	12.31	–	103.17	115.48	13.54	–	113.49	127.03
9010302C	1800 mm	Each	0.50	12.82	–	112.36	125.18	14.10	–	123.60	137.70
9010302E	1950 mm	Each	0.52	13.34	–	122.96	136.30	14.67	–	135.26	149.93
9010302F	2100 mm	Each	0.54	13.85	–	130.99	144.84	15.24	–	144.09	159.32
9010302G	2250 mm	Each	0.56	14.35	–	148.79	163.14	15.79	–	163.67	179.45
9010302H	2400 mm	Each	0.58	14.87	–	158.68	173.55	16.36	–	174.55	190.91
9010302I	2550 mm	Each	0.60	15.38	–	165.40	180.78	16.92	–	181.94	198.86
9010302J	2700 mm	Each	0.62	15.90	–	175.04	190.94	17.49	–	192.54	210.03
9010303	**CN8; combined lintel; for standard 50 mm cavity wall; 219 mm high; length:**										
9010303A	2250 mm	Each	0.56	14.35	–	160.95	175.30	15.79	–	177.05	192.83
9010303B	2400 mm	Each	0.58	14.88	–	172.95	187.83	16.37	–	190.25	206.61
9010303C	2550 mm	Each	0.60	15.38	–	185.22	200.60	16.92	–	203.74	220.66
9010303D	2700 mm	Each	0.62	15.90	–	195.15	211.05	17.49	–	214.67	232.16
9010303E	2850 mm	Each	0.64	16.41	–	224.15	240.56	18.05	–	246.57	264.62
9010303F	3000 mm	Each	0.66	16.92	–	237.98	254.90	18.61	–	261.78	280.39
9010303G	3300 mm	Each	0.68	17.43	–	264.92	282.35	19.17	–	291.41	310.59
9010303H	3600 mm	Each	0.70	17.95	–	290.08	308.03	19.75	–	319.09	338.83
9010303I	3900 mm	Each	0.72	18.47	–	386.34	404.81	20.32	–	424.97	445.29
9010303J	4200 mm	Each	0.74	18.97	–	415.87	434.84	20.87	–	457.46	478.32
9010303K	4575 mm	Each	0.76	19.49	–	483.87	503.36	21.44	–	532.26	553.70
9010303L	4800 mm	Each	0.78	19.99	–	509.86	529.85	21.99	–	560.85	582.84
9010304	**CN71; single lintel for external solid walls; 143 mm high; length:**										
9010304A	750 mm	Each	0.34	8.72	–	45.93	54.65	9.59	–	50.52	60.12
9010304B	900 mm	Each	0.36	9.23	–	55.22	64.45	10.15	–	60.74	70.90
9010304C	1050 mm	Each	0.38	9.74	–	64.39	74.13	10.71	–	70.83	81.54
9010304D	1200 mm	Each	0.40	10.26	–	73.52	83.78	11.29	–	80.87	92.16
9010304E	1350 mm	Each	0.42	10.77	–	82.72	93.49	11.85	–	90.99	102.84
9010304F	1500 mm	Each	0.44	11.28	–	97.72	109.00	12.41	–	107.49	119.90
9010304G	1650 mm	Each	0.46	11.79	–	107.41	119.20	12.97	–	118.15	131.12
9010304H	1800 mm	Each	0.48	12.31	–	117.01	129.32	13.54	–	128.71	142.25
9010304I	1950 mm	Each	0.50	12.82	–	126.93	139.75	14.10	–	139.62	153.73
9010304J	2100 mm	Each	0.52	13.33	–	137.39	150.72	14.66	–	151.13	165.79
9010304K	2250 mm	Each	0.54	13.85	–	155.55	169.40	15.24	–	171.11	186.34
9010304L	2400 mm	Each	0.56	14.36	–	165.93	180.29	15.80	–	182.52	198.32
9010304M	2550 mm	Each	0.58	14.88	–	176.32	191.20	16.37	–	193.95	210.32
9010304N	2700 mm	Each	0.60	15.39	–	186.69	202.08	16.93	–	205.36	222.29
9010305	**CN92; single lintel; for 75 mm internal partitions and non-loadbearing walls; 23 mm high; length:**										
9010305A	900 mm	Each	0.38	9.74	–	7.24	16.98	10.71	–	7.96	18.68
9010305B	1050 mm	Each	0.40	10.25	–	8.26	18.51	11.28	–	9.09	20.36
9010305C	1200 mm	Each	0.42	10.77	–	9.34	20.11	11.85	–	10.27	22.12
9010306	**CN102; single lintel; for 100 mm internal partitions and non-loadbearing walls; 25 mm high; length:**										
9010306A	900 mm	Each	0.38	9.75	–	8.90	18.65	10.73	–	9.79	20.52
9010306B	1050 mm	Each	0.40	10.26	–	10.43	20.69	11.29	–	11.47	22.76
9010306C	1200 mm	Each	0.42	10.77	–	11.50	22.27	11.85	–	12.65	24.50

Small Works 2009		Unit	Labour Hours	Labour Net	Plant Net	Materials Net	Unit Net	Labour Gross	Plant Gross	Materials Gross	Unit Price
								——— (Gross rates include 10% profit) ———			
				£	£	£	£	£	£	£	£
901	**STEELWORK AND METALWORK**										
90104	**STRUCTURAL STEELWORK BY SPECIALISTS**										
9010401	**Portal framework where members are in the range of:**										
9010401A	18-30 kg per linear metre ..	Tonne	29.00	708.47	–	1227.62	1936.09	779.32	–	1350.38	2129.70
9010401B	30-45 kg per linear metre ..	Tonne	25.25	616.86	–	1227.62	1844.48	678.55	–	1350.38	2028.93
9010401C	45-70 kg per linear metre ..	Tonne	23.75	580.21	–	1318.57	1898.78	638.23	–	1450.43	2088.66
9010401D	70-100 kg per linear metre .	Tonne	22.50	549.67	–	1364.03	1913.70	604.64	–	1500.43	2105.07
9010401E	exceeding 100 kg per linear metre	Tonne	21.25	519.13	–	1409.50	1928.63	571.04	–	1550.45	2121.49
9010401F	purlins	Tonne	27.00	659.61	–	1205.64	1865.25	725.57	–	1326.20	2051.78
9010402	**Beam and post work with rigid connection where members are in the range of:**										
9010402A	18-30 kg per linear metre ..	Tonne	27.50	671.83	–	1227.62	1899.45	739.01	–	1350.38	2089.40
9010402B	30-45 kg per linear metre ..	Tonne	26.00	635.18	–	1273.10	1908.28	698.70	–	1400.41	2099.11
9010402C	45-70 kg per linear metre ..	Tonne	25.00	610.75	–	1318.57	1929.32	671.83	–	1450.43	2122.25
9010402D	70-100 kg per linear metre .	Tonne	22.00	537.46	–	1364.03	1901.49	591.21	–	1500.43	2091.64
9010402E	exceeding 100 kg per linear metre	Tonne	19.00	464.17	–	1409.50	1873.67	510.59	–	1550.45	2061.04
9010403	**Beam and post work with simple web cleated connections where members are in the range of:**										
9010403A	18-30 kg per linear metre ..	Tonne	25.25	616.86	–	1227.62	1844.48	678.55	–	1350.38	2028.93
9010403B	30-45 kg per linear metre ..	Tonne	25.77	629.47	–	1273.10	1902.57	692.42	–	1400.41	2092.83
9010403C	45-70 kg per linear metre ..	Tonne	20.00	488.60	–	1318.57	1807.17	537.46	–	1450.43	1987.89
9010403D	70-100 kg per linear metre .	Tonne	19.00	464.17	–	1364.03	1828.20	510.59	–	1500.43	2011.02
9010403E	exceeding 100 kg per linear metre	Tonne	17.00	415.31	–	1409.50	1824.81	456.84	–	1550.45	2007.29
9010404	**Staircase, catwalks, parapets and the like in:**										
9010404A	steel	Tonne	35.00	855.05	–	2150.00	3005.05	940.56	–	2365.00	3305.56
9010406	**Tubular constructions:**										
9010406A	light	Tonne	23.75	580.21	–	1800.00	2380.21	638.23	–	1980.00	2618.23
9010406B	heavy	Tonne	22.25	543.57	–	1475.00	2018.57	597.93	–	1622.50	2220.43

Sundries

Small Works 2009		Unit	Labour Hours	Labour Net	Plant Net	Materials Net	Unit Net	Labour Gross	Plant Gross	Materials Gross	Unit Price
								(Gross rates include 10% profit)			
				£	£	£	£	£	£	£	£
902	**METAL WINDOWS AND DOORS**										
90201	**STANDARD GALVANISED STEEL WINDOWS**										
9020101 9020101A	**Type NG1:** 508 mm × 292 mm......	Each	0.73	18.72	–	69.96	88.68	20.59	–	76.96	97.55
9020102 9020102A	**Type NH1:** 508 mm × 457 mm......	Each	0.89	22.82	–	82.34	105.16	25.10	–	90.57	115.68
9020103 9020103A	**Type NE6F:** 279 mm × 628 mm......	Each	1.03	26.41	–	76.14	102.55	29.05	–	83.75	112.81
9020104 9020104A	**Type NE5:** 508 mm × 628 mm......	Each	1.03	26.41	–	33.36	59.77	29.05	–	36.70	65.75
9020105 9020105A	**Type NES1:** 508 mm × 628 mm......	Each	1.03	26.41	–	95.41	121.82	29.05	–	104.95	134.00
9020106 9020106A	**Type NC6F:** 279 mm × 923 mm......	Each	1.18	30.26	–	80.96	111.22	33.29	–	89.06	122.34
9020107 9020107A	**Type NC5:** 508 mm × 923 mm......	Each	1.18	30.26	–	38.83	69.09	33.29	–	42.71	76.00
9020108 9020108A	**Type NC1:** 508 mm × 923 mm......	Each	1.18	30.26	–	103.17	133.43	33.29	–	113.49	146.77
9020109 9020109A	**Type NC5F:** 508 mm × 923 mm......	Each	1.18	30.25	–	90.06	120.31	33.28	–	99.07	132.34
9020110 9020110A	**Type NC05:** 508 mm × 1067 mm.....	Each	1.32	33.84	–	43.29	77.13	37.22	–	47.62	84.84
9020111 9020111A	**Type NC01:** 508 mm × 1067 mm.....	Each	1.32	33.85	–	109.16	143.01	37.24	–	120.08	157.31
9020112 9020112A	**Type NC05F:** 508 mm × 1067 mm.....	Each	1.32	33.84	–	92.82	126.66	37.22	–	102.10	139.33
9020113 9020113A	**Type ND5:** 508 mm × 1218 mm.....	Each	1.48	37.95	–	44.34	82.29	41.75	–	48.77	90.52
9020114 9020114A	**Type ND1:** 508 mm × 1218 mm.....	Each	1.48	37.94	–	117.41	155.35	41.73	–	129.15	170.89
9020115 9020115A	**Type ND5F:** 508 mm × 1218 mm.....	Each	1.48	37.95	–	95.77	133.72	41.75	–	105.35	147.09
90202	**STANDARD GALVANISED STEEL DOORS**										
9020201 9020201A	**Type NA15:** 761 mm × 2056 mm.....	Each	3.84	98.46	–	724.99	823.45	108.31	–	797.49	905.80
9020202 9020202A	**Type NA2:** 997 mm × 2056 mm.....	Each	4.14	106.15	–	1088.84	1194.99	116.77	–	1197.72	1314.49
9020203 9020203A	**Type NA25:** 1143 mm × 2056 mm....	Each	4.38	112.31	–	1110.35	1222.66	123.54	–	1221.39	1344.93

Small Works 2009		Unit	Labour Hours	Labour Net	Plant Net	Materials Net	Unit Net	Labour Gross	Plant Gross	Materials Gross	Unit Price
								(Gross rates include 10% profit)			
				£	£	£	£	£	£	£	£
902	METAL WINDOWS AND DOORS										
90203	STANDARD GALVANISED STEEL WINDOWS; WHITE POLYESTER POWDER COATING FINISH										
9020301 9020301A	Type NG1: 508 mm × 292 mm......	Each	0.73	18.72	–	114.54	133.26	20.59	–	125.99	146.59
9020302 9020302A	Type NH1: 508 mm × 457 mm......	Each	0.89	22.82	–	135.61	158.43	25.10	–	149.17	174.27
9020303 9020303A	Type NE6F: 279 mm × 628 mm.......	Each	1.03	26.41	–	130.05	156.46	29.05	–	143.06	172.11
9020304 9020304A	Type NE5: 502 mm × 628 mm......	Each	1.03	26.41	–	61.02	87.43	29.05	–	67.12	96.17
9020305 9020305A	Type NES1: 508 mm × 628 mm......	Each	1.03	26.41	–	156.48	182.89	29.05	–	172.13	201.18
9020306 9020306A	Type NC6F: 279 mm × 923 mm......	Each	1.18	30.25	–	139.53	169.78	33.28	–	153.48	186.76
9020307 9020307A	Type NC5: 508 mm × 923 mm......	Each	1.18	30.25	–	71.30	101.55	33.28	–	78.43	111.71
9020308 9020308A	Type NC1: 508 mm × 923 mm......	Each	1.18	30.25	–	169.93	200.18	33.28	–	186.92	220.20
9020309 9020309A	Type NC5F: 508 mm × 923 mm......	Each	1.18	30.26	–	159.85	190.11	33.29	–	175.84	209.12
9020310 9020310A	Type NC05: 508 mm × 1067 mm......	Each	1.32	33.84	–	79.87	113.71	37.22	–	87.86	125.08
9020311 9020311A	Type NC01: 508 mm × 1067 mm......	Each	1.32	33.85	–	182.12	215.97	37.24	–	200.33	237.57
9020312 9020312A	Type NC05F: 508 mm × 1067 mm......	Each	1.32	33.85	–	164.81	198.66	37.24	–	181.29	218.53
9020313 9020313A	Type ND5: 508 mm × 1218 mm......	Each	1.48	37.94	–	81.83	119.77	41.73	–	90.01	131.75
9020314 9020314A	Type ND1: 508 mm × 1218 mm......	Each	1.48	37.95	–	194.18	232.13	41.75	–	213.60	255.34
9020315 9020315A	Type ND5F: 508 mm × 1218 mm......	Each	1.48	37.95	–	170.83	208.78	41.75	–	187.91	229.66

Sundries

		Unit	Labour Hours	Labour Net	Plant Net	Materials Net	Unit Net	Labour Gross	Plant Gross	Materials Gross	Unit Price
								(Gross rates include 10% profit)			
				£	£	£	£	£	£	£	£
902	**METAL WINDOWS AND DOORS**										
90204	**STANDARD GALVANISED STEEL DOORS; WHITE POLYESTER POWDER COATING FINISH**										
9020401 9020401A	**Type NA15:** 761 mm × 2056 mm.....	Each	3.84	98.46	–	1115.52	1213.98	108.31	–	1227.07	1335.38
9020402 9020402A	**Type NA2:** 997 mm × 2056 mm.....	Each	4.14	106.15	–	1690.72	1796.87	116.77	–	1859.79	1976.56
9020403 9020403A	**Type NA25:** 1143 mm × 2056 mm....	Each	4.38	112.31	–	1723.71	1836.02	123.54	–	1896.08	2019.62
90205	**STANDARD GALVANISED STEEL SIDELIGHTS**										
9020501 9020501A	**Type NA6:** 279 mm × 2056 mm.....	Each	1.68	43.08	–	135.67	178.75	47.39	–	149.24	196.63
9020502 9020502A	**Type NA5:** 508 mm × 2056 mm.....	Each	2.04	52.31	–	164.91	217.22	57.54	–	181.40	238.94
9020503 9020503A	**Type NA13F:** 997 mm × 2056 mm.....	Each	2.40	61.53	–	282.08	343.61	67.68	–	310.29	377.97
90206	**STANDARD GALVANISED STEEL SIDELIGHTS; WHITE POLYESTER POWDER COATING FINISH**										
9020601 9020601A	**Type NA6:** 279 mm × 2056 mm.....	Each	1.68	43.08	–	222.04	265.12	47.39	–	244.24	291.63
9020602 9020602A	**Type NA5:** 508 mm × 2056 mm.....	Each	2.04	52.31	–	264.65	316.96	57.54	–	291.12	348.66
9020603 9020603A	**Type NA13F:** 997 mm × 2056 mm.....	Each	2.40	61.54	–	470.74	532.28	67.69	–	517.81	585.51

Small Works 2009		Unit	Labour Hours	Labour Net	Plant Net	Materials Net	Unit Net	Labour Gross	Plant Gross	Materials Gross	Unit Price
								(Gross rates include 10% profit)			
				£	£	£	£	£	£	£	£
903	**ASPHALT WORK**										
90301	**MASTIC ASPHALT TANKING; BS6925**										
9030101	**13 mm One coat horizontal covering on concrete:**										
9030101A	over 300 mm wide	m^2	0.65	16.69	1.53	8.00	26.22	18.36	1.68	8.80	28.84
9030101B	not exceeding 150 mm wide	m	0.23	5.98	0.57	1.20	7.75	6.58	0.63	1.32	8.53
9030101C	150 mm-300 mm wide.	m	0.33	8.51	0.75	2.40	11.66	9.36	0.83	2.64	12.83
9030102	**20 mm Two coat horizontal covering on concrete:**										
9030102A	over 300 mm wide	m^2	0.72	18.46	1.64	12.32	32.42	20.31	1.80	13.55	35.66
9030102B	not exceeding 150 mm wide	m	0.28	7.08	0.71	1.85	9.64	7.79	0.78	2.04	10.60
9030102C	150 mm-300 mm wide.	m	0.38	9.80	0.93	3.69	14.42	10.78	1.02	4.06	15.86
9030103	**30 mm Three coat horizontal covering on concrete:**										
9030103A	over 300 mm wide	m^2	1.31	33.59	3.30	18.47	55.36	36.95	3.63	20.32	60.90
9030103B	not exceeding 150 mm wide	m	0.48	12.31	1.18	2.77	16.26	13.54	1.30	3.05	17.89
9030103C	150 mm-300 mm wide.	m	0.69	17.70	1.64	5.54	24.88	19.47	1.80	6.09	27.37
9030104	**13 mm Two coat vertical covering on brickwork:**										
9030104A	over 300 mm wide	m^2	2.37	60.77	5.71	8.00	74.48	66.85	6.28	8.80	81.93
9030104B	not exceeding 150 mm wide	m	0.71	18.21	1.78	1.20	21.19	20.03	1.96	1.32	23.31
9030104C	150 mm-300 mm wide.	m	1.07	27.44	2.78	2.40	32.62	30.18	3.06	2.64	35.88
9030105	**20 mm Three coat vertical covering on brickwork:**										
9030105A	over 300 mm wide	m^2	3.05	78.20	7.85	12.32	98.37	86.02	8.64	13.55	108.21
9030105B	not exceeding 150 mm wide	m	0.93	23.85	2.43	1.85	28.13	26.24	2.67	2.04	30.94
9030105C	150 mm-300 mm wide.	m	1.39	35.64	3.57	3.69	42.90	39.20	3.93	4.06	47.19
9030106	**Labours:**										
9030106A	internal angle fillets	m	0.41	10.56	–	–	10.56	11.62	–	–	11.62
9030106B	turning nibs into grooves . .	m	0.23	5.97	–	–	5.97	6.57	–	–	6.57
9030106C	working into outlets	Each	2.45	62.87	–	–	62.87	69.16	–	–	69.16
9030106D	collars and internal angle fillets around small pipes. . .	Each	1.99	51.10	–	–	51.10	56.21	–	–	56.21
9030106E	collars and internal angle fillets around large pipes . . .	Each	2.91	74.61	–	–	74.61	82.07	–	–	82.07

Sundries

		Unit	Labour Hours	Labour Net	Plant Net	Materials Net	Unit Net	Labour Gross	Plant Gross	Materials Gross	Unit Price
								(Gross rates include 10% profit)			
				£	£	£	£	£	£	£	£
903	**ASPHALT WORK**										
90302	**MASTIC ASPHALT TANKING; BS6577**										
9030201	**13 mm One coat horizontal covering on concrete:**										
9030201A	over 300 mm wide	m²	1.12	28.72	2.85	9.40	40.97	31.59	3.14	10.34	45.07
9030201B	not exceeding 150 mm wide	m	0.38	9.74	0.86	1.41	12.01	10.71	0.95	1.55	13.21
9030201C	150 mm-300 mm wide.....	m	0.55	14.11	1.28	2.82	18.21	15.52	1.41	3.10	20.03
9030202	**20 mm Two coat horizontal covering on concrete:**										
9030202A	over 300 mm wide	m²	1.27	32.46	3.14	14.46	50.06	35.71	3.45	15.91	55.07
9030202B	not exceeding 150 mm wide	m	0.44	11.28	1.07	2.17	14.52	12.41	1.18	2.39	15.97
9030202C	150 mm-300 mm wide.....	m	0.63	16.15	1.57	4.34	22.06	17.77	1.73	4.77	24.27
9030203	**30 mm Three coat horizontal covering on concrete:**										
9030203A	over 300 mm wide	m²	2.15	55.12	5.50	21.68	82.30	60.63	6.05	23.85	90.53
9030203B	not exceeding 150 mm wide	m	0.65	16.67	1.64	3.25	21.56	18.34	1.80	3.58	23.72
9030203C	150 mm-300 mm wide.....	m	1.06	27.25	2.71	6.50	36.46	29.98	2.98	7.15	40.11

Small Works 2009		Unit	Labour Hours	Labour Net	Plant Net	Materials Net	Unit Net	Labour Gross	Plant Gross	Materials Gross	Unit Price
								(Gross rates include 10% profit)			
				£	£	£	£	£	£	£	£
903	**ASPHALT WORK**										
90302	**MASTIC ASPHALT TANKING; BS6577**										
9030204	**13 mm Two coat vertical covering on brickwork:**										
9030204A	over 300 mm wide	m²	2.95	75.64	7.64	9.40	92.68	83.20	8.40	10.34	101.95
9030204B	not exceeding 150 mm wide	m	0.89	22.82	2.28	1.41	26.51	25.10	2.51	1.55	29.16
9030204C	150 mm–300 mm wide.	m	1.33	34.18	3.46	2.82	40.46	37.60	3.81	3.10	44.51
9030205	**20 mm Three coat vertical covering on brickwork:**										
9030205A	over 300 mm wide	m²	3.81	97.69	9.92	14.45	122.06	107.46	10.91	15.90	134.27
9030205B	not exceeding 150 mm wide	m	1.17	30.00	3.03	2.17	35.20	33.00	3.33	2.39	38.72
9030205C	150 mm–300 mm wide.	m	1.74	44.61	4.53	4.34	53.48	49.07	4.98	4.77	58.83
9030206	**Labours:**										
9030206A	internal angle fillets	m	0.41	10.59	–	–	10.59	11.65	–	–	11.65
9030206B	turning nibs into grooves . .	m	0.23	5.97	–	–	5.97	6.57	–	–	6.57
9030206C	working into outlets	Each	2.45	62.87	–	–	62.87	69.16	–	–	69.16
9030206D	collars and internal angle fillets around small pipes. . .	Each	1.99	51.13	–	–	51.13	56.24	–	–	56.24
9030206E	collars and internal angle fillets around large pipes . . .	Each	2.91	74.61	–	–	74.61	82.07	–	–	82.07
90303	**MASTIC ASPHALT FLOORING; BS6925**										
9030301	**15 mm One coat light duty flooring on and including isolating membrane:**										
9030301A	over 300 mm wide	m²	0.80	20.51	1.64	10.85	33.00	22.56	1.80	11.94	36.30
9030301B	not exceeding 150 mm wide	m	0.29	7.38	0.68	1.63	9.69	8.12	0.75	1.79	10.66
9030301C	150 mm–300 mm wide.	m	0.40	10.25	1.14	3.26	14.65	11.28	1.25	3.59	16.12
9030302	**20 mm One coat medium duty flooring on and including isolating membrane:**										
9030302A	over 300 mm wide	m²	0.80	20.51	1.64	13.92	36.07	22.56	1.80	15.31	39.68
9030302B	not exceeding 150 mm wide	m	0.29	7.44	1.07	2.33	10.84	8.18	1.18	2.56	11.92
9030302C	150 mm–300 mm wide.	m	0.38	9.74	1.78	4.18	15.70	10.71	1.96	4.60	17.27
9030303	**30 mm One coat medium duty flooring on and including isolating membrane:**										
9030303A	over 300 mm wide	m²	1.00	25.64	1.86	20.08	47.58	28.20	2.05	22.09	52.34
9030303B	not exceeding 150 mm wide	m	0.37	9.35	1.96	3.01	14.32	10.29	2.16	3.31	15.75
9030303C	150 mm–300 mm wide.	m	0.50	12.69	2.12	6.02	20.83	13.96	2.33	6.62	22.91
9030304	**Labours:**										
9030304A	working against metal frames	m	0.11	2.82	–	–	2.82	3.10	–	–	3.10
9030304B	Extra for working into recessed covers; not exceeding 1.00 m²	Each	0.90	23.08	–	–	23.08	25.39	–	–	25.39
9030305	**Skirtings; 13 mm two coat; fair edge, angles, coved angle fillet and nib turned into groove:**										
9030305A	150 mm high.	m	0.77	19.74	1.43	1.20	22.37	21.71	1.57	1.32	24.61

Sundries

Small Works 2009		Unit	Labour Hours	Labour Net	Plant Net	Materials Net	Unit Net	Labour Gross	Plant Gross	Materials Gross	Unit Price
								(Gross rates include 10% profit)			
				£	£	£	£	£	£	£	£
903	**ASPHALT WORK**										
90304	**COLOURED MASTIC ASPHALT FLOORING; BS692**										
9030401	**15 mm One coat light duty brown flooring on and including isolating membrane:**										
9030401A	over 300 mm wide	m^2	1.02	26.02	2.36	12.05	40.43	28.62	2.60	13.26	44.47
9030401B	not exceeding 150 mm wide	m	0.35	8.97	0.89	1.81	11.67	9.87	0.98	1.99	12.84
9030401C	150 mm-300 mm wide.....	m	0.50	12.82	1.28	3.62	17.72	14.10	1.41	3.98	19.49
9030402	**Labours:**										
9030402A	working against metal frames	m	0.11	2.82	–	–	2.82	3.10	–	–	3.10
9030402B	Extra for working into recessed covers; not exceeding 1.00 m^2	Each	0.90	23.08	–	–	23.08	25.39	–	–	25.39
9030403	**Skirtings; 13 mm two coat; brown with fair edge, angles, coved angle fillet and nib turned into groove:**										
9030403A	150 mm high.............	m	0.83	21.15	1.78	1.36	24.29	23.27	1.96	1.50	26.72

904 ELECTRICAL WORK

90401 LIGHTING POINTS

	Unit	£	£	£	Specialist Net £	Unit Net £	£	£	Specialist Gross £	Unit Price £
							(Gross rates include 10% profit)			
9040101 P.V.C. insulated and sheathed cables in houses or flats, installed in floor cavities or roof voids, protected by steel or P.V.C. channel in walls:										
9040101A lighting point controlled by 1 switch	Each	–	–	–	51.03	51.03	–	–	56.13	56.13
9040101B lighting point controlled by 2 switches	Each	–	–	–	70.07	70.07	–	–	77.08	77.08
9040101C lighting point controlled by 3 switches	Each	–	–	–	87.48	87.48	–	–	96.23	96.23
9040101D 2 lighting points controlled by 1 switch	Each	–	–	–	62.10	62.10	–	–	68.31	68.31
9040102 P.V.C. insulated cables contained in black enamelled screwed, welded conduit in commercial property:										
9040102A lighting point controlled by 1 switch	Each	–	–	–	71.55	71.55	–	–	78.71	78.71
9040102B lighting point controlled by 2 switches	Each	–	–	–	92.34	92.34	–	–	101.57	101.57
9040102C lighting point controlled by 3 switches	Each	–	–	–	113.13	113.13	–	–	124.44	124.44
9040102D 2 lighting points controlled by 1 switch	Each	–	–	–	87.48	87.48	–	–	96.23	96.23
9040103 P.V.C. insulated cables contained in galvanised screwed, welded conduit in industrial property:										
9040103A lighting point controlled by 1 switch	Each	–	–	–	87.48	87.48	–	–	96.23	96.23
9040103B lighting point controlled by 2 switches	Each	–	–	–	114.61	114.62	–	–	126.07	126.08
9040103C lighting point controlled by 3 switches	Each	–	–	–	138.51	138.51	–	–	152.36	152.36
9040103D 2 lighting points controlled by 1 switch	Each	–	–	–	109.76	109.77	–	–	120.74	120.75
9040104 M.I.C.S. cables in commercial property:										
9040104A lighting point controlled by 1 switch	Each	–	–	–	62.10	62.10	–	–	68.31	68.31
9040104B lighting point controlled by 2 switches	Each	–	–	–	93.96	93.96	–	–	103.36	103.36
9040104C lighting point controlled by 3 switches	Each	–	–	–	117.72	117.72	–	–	129.49	129.49
9040104D 2 lighting points controlled by 3 switches	Each	–	–	–	148.10	148.11	–	–	162.91	162.92
9040105 M.I.C.S. cables in industrial property:										
9040105A lighting point controlled by 1 switch	Each	–	–	–	74.93	74.94	–	–	82.42	82.43
9040105B lighting point controlled by 2 switches	Each	–	–	–	111.38	111.39	–	–	122.52	122.53
9040105C lighting point controlled by 3 switches	Each	–	–	–	135.27	135.27	–	–	148.80	148.80
9040105D 2 lighting points controlled by 1 switch	Each	–	–	–	92.34	92.34	–	–	101.57	101.57

Sundries

Small Works 2009		Unit			Specialist Net	Unit Net			Specialist Gross	Unit Price
								(Gross rates include 10% profit)		
			£	£	£	£	£	£	£	£
904	**ELECTRICAL WORK**									
90402	**SWITCHED SOCKET OUTLETS**									
9040201	**P.V.C. insulated and sheathed cable in houses or flats, installed:**									
9040201A	13 amp single switch socket outlet	Each	–	–	–	55.75	55.76	–	–	61.33	61.34
9040201B	1-13 amp dual switch socket outlet	Each	–	–	–	60.48	60.48	–	–	66.53	66.53
9040202	**P.V.C. insulated cables contained in black enamelled screwed welded conduit in commercial property:**									
9040202A	1-13 amp single switch socket outlet	Each	–	–	–	70.07	70.07	–	–	77.08	77.08
9040202B	13 amp dual switch socket outlet	Each	–	–	–	74.93	74.94	–	–	82.42	82.43
9040203	**P.V.C. insulated cables contained in galvanised screwed welded conduit in industrial property:**									
9040203A	1-13 amp single switch socket outlet	Each	–	–	–	84.38	84.39	–	–	92.82	92.83
9040203B	1-13 amp dual switch socket outlet	Each	–	–	–	92.34	92.34	–	–	101.57	101.57
9040204	**M.I.C.S. cables in commercial property:**									
9040204A	1-13 amp single switch socket outlet	Each	–	–	–	65.34	65.34	–	–	71.87	71.87
9040204B	1-13 amp dual switch socket outlet	Each	–	–	–	71.55	71.55	–	–	78.71	78.71
90404	**COOKER POINTS**									
9040401	**P.V.C. insulated and sheathed cable in houses or flats, installed:**									
9040401A	cooker point 30 amp with cooker panel	Each	–	–	–	97.20	97.20	–	–	106.92	106.92
9040401B	cooker point 45 amp with cooker panel	Each	–	–	–	105.17	105.17	–	–	115.69	115.69
9040402	**P.V.C. insulated cables contained in enamelled screwed welded conduit in commercial property:**									
9040402A	cooker point 30 amp with cooker panel	Each	–	–	–	132.16	132.17	–	–	145.38	145.39
9040402B	cooker point 45 amp with cooker panel	Each	–	–	–	138.51	138.51	–	–	152.36	152.36
9040403	**M.I.C.S. cables in commercial properties:**									
9040403A	cooker point 30 amp with cooker panel	Each	–	–	–	135.27	135.27	–	–	148.80	148.80
9040403B	cooker point 45 amp with cooker panel	Each	–	–	–	141.62	141.63	–	–	155.78	155.79

Small Works 2009		Unit			Specialist Net	Unit Net			Specialist Gross	Unit Price
								(Gross rates include 10% profit)		
			£	£	£	£	£	£	£	£
904	**ELECTRICAL WORK**									
90406	**IMMERSION HEATER POINTS**									
9040601	**Immersion heater point with control switch (excluding heater):**									
9040601A	P.V.C. insulated cables in P.V.C. conduit (domestic) . . .	Each	–	–	–	73.31	73.32	–	–	80.64	80.65
9040601B	in enamelled steel welded conduit etc.	Each	–	–	–	87.48	87.48	–	–	96.23	96.23
9040602	**M.I.C.S. cables in commercial property:**									
9040602A	immersion heater point with control switch (excluding heater)	Each	–	–	–	90.72	90.72	–	–	99.79	99.79
9040602B	supply and connect 3 kw immersion heater complete with fixed thermostat to new cylinder	Each	–	–	–	59.00	59.00	–	–	64.90	64.90
90408	**INFRA RED HEATER POINTS**									
9040801	**P.V.C. insulated and sheathed cables installed in houses and flats:**									
9040801A	infra red heater with control switch (excluding heater and earth bonding)	Each	–	–	–	63.59	63.60	–	–	69.95	69.96
9040802	**P.V.C. insulated cables in black enamelled screwed conduit in commercial property:**									
9040802A	infra red heater point with control switch (excluding heater and earth bonding) . . .	Each	–	–	–	78.03	78.03	–	–	85.83	85.83
9040803	**M.I.C.S. cables in commercial property:**									
9040803A	infra red heater point with control switch (excluding heater and earth bonding) . . .	Each	–	–	–	78.03	78.03	–	–	85.83	85.83
9040803B	supply and fix 750 w infra red heater	Each	–	–	–	55.75	55.76	–	–	61.33	61.34
9040803C	supply and fix 1000 w infra red heater	Each	–	–	–	59.00	59.00	–	–	64.90	64.90

Sundries

Small Works 2009		Unit			Specialist Net	Unit Net			Specialist Gross	Unit Price
							——— (Gross rates include 10% profit) ———			
			£	£	£	£	£	£	£	£
904	**ELECTRICAL WORK**									
90409	**BELL INSTALLATIONS**									
9040901	**P.V.C. insulated cable in houses or flats:**									
9040901A	bell controlled by front door push including transformer .	Each	–	–	–	81.27	81.27	–	–	89.40	89.40
9040901B	bell and buzzer controlled by front door push and back door push including transformer .	Each	–	–	–	92.34	92.34	–	–	101.57	101.57
9040901C	Hi-Low chimes controlled by front door push and back door push including transformer .	Each	–	–	–	108.27	108.27	–	–	119.10	119.10
9040902	**P.V.C. insulated cables contained in black enamelled screwed welded conduit in commercial property:**									
9040902A	bell controlled by front door push including transformer .	Each	–	–	–	111.38	111.39	–	–	122.52	122.53
9040902B	bell and buzzer controlled by front door push and back door push including transformer .	Each	–	–	–	135.27	135.27	–	–	148.80	148.80
9040902C	Hi-Low chimes controlled by front door push and back door push including transformer .	Each	–	–	–	150.26	150.27	–	–	165.29	165.30
9040903	**M.I.C.S. cables in commercial property:**									
9040903A	bell controlled by front door push including transformer .	Each	–	–	–	109.76	109.77	–	–	120.74	120.75
9040903B	bell and buzzer controlled by front door push and back door push including transformer .	Each	–	–	–	133.65	133.65	–	–	147.02	147.02
9040903C	Hi-Low chimes controlled by front door push and back door push including transformer .	Each	–	–	–	148.10	148.11	–	–	162.91	162.92

Small Works 2009		Unit			Specialist Net	Unit Net		Specialist Gross	Unit Price
							——— (Gross rates include 10% profit) ———		
			£	£	£	£	£	£	£
904	**ELECTRICAL WORK**								
90410	**T.V. OUTLETS**								
9041001	**Low loss coaxial cable in houses or flats protected by P.V.C. conduit in walls, terminating with a single T.V. outlet and allowing 3 metres of cable in roof void:**								
9041001A	for connection to aerial by others....................	Each	–	–	–	57.38	57.39	–	–	63.12	63.13
90412	**ELECTRICAL SHAVER POINT**								
9041201	**P.V.C. insulated and sheathed cable in houses and flats:**								
9041201A	dual voltage type, isolated for bathrooms etc.............	Each	–	–	–	79.52	79.53	–	–	87.47	87.48
9041202	**P.V.C. insulated cables contained in black enamelled screwed and welded conduit in commercial property:**								
9041202A	dual voltage type, isolated for bathrooms etc.............	Each	–	–	–	89.24	89.24	–	–	98.16	98.16

Sundries

Small Works 2009		Unit				Specialist Net	Unit Net			Specialist Gross	Unit Price
								(Gross rates include 10% profit)			
			£	£	£	£	£	£	£	£	£
904	**ELECTRICAL WORK**										
90414	**STORAGE HEATING**										
9041401	**P.V.C. insulated and sheathed cable in houses and flats:**										
9041401A	3 kw heater point controlled by switch adjacent to heater position (from independent fuse).....................	Each	–	–	–	66.96	66.96	–	–	73.66	73.66
9041402	**P.V.C. insulated cables contained in black enamelled screwed and welded conduit in commercial property:**										
9041402A	3 kw heater point controlled by switch adjacent to heater position (from independent fuse).....................	Each	–	–	–	87.48	87.48	–	–	96.23	96.23
90416	**LIGHTING FITTINGS**										
9041602	**Fluorescent fitting, single, complete with tube, ceiling mounted:**										
9041602A	609 mm..................	Each	–	–	–	36.72	36.72	–	–	40.39	40.39
9041602B	1219 mm.................	Each	–	–	–	43.07	43.07	–	–	47.38	47.38
9041602C	1524 mm.................	Each	–	–	–	47.79	47.79	–	–	52.57	52.57
9041602D	1828 mm.................	Each	–	–	–	55.75	55.76	–	–	61.33	61.34
9041602E	2438 mm.................	Each	–	–	–	71.55	71.55	–	–	78.71	78.71
9041603	**Fluorescent fitting, single, opal diffuser, complete with tube, ceiling mounted:**										
9041603A	609 mm..................	Each	–	–	–	55.75	55.76	–	–	61.33	61.34
9041603B	1219 mm.................	Each	–	–	–	62.10	62.10	–	–	68.31	68.31
9041603C	1524 mm.................	Each	–	–	–	70.07	70.07	–	–	77.08	77.08
9041603D	1828 mm.................	Each	–	–	–	78.03	78.03	–	–	85.83	85.83
9041603E	2438 mm.................	Each	–	–	–	109.76	109.77	–	–	120.74	120.75
90418	**REWIRING**										
9041801	**To an average dwelling house containing:**										
9041801A	15 no. 13 amp twin power points and 14 no. 5 amp lighting points, 3 no. two-way lighting points complete with switches, lamp holders, all in two circuits and immersion heater and cooker feed complete and 1 no. outside light including consumer unit with MCBs...............	Each	–	–	–	2009.20	2009.21	–	–	2210.12	2210.13

Small Works 2009		Unit	Labour Hours	Labour Net	Plant Net	Materials Net	Unit Net	Labour Gross	Plant Gross	Materials Gross	Unit Price
								(Gross rates include 10% profit)			
			£	£	£	£	£	£	£	£	£
905	**DAMP-PROOFING**										
90501	**GENERALLY**										
9050101	**Chase out mortar joint in brickwork with mechanical saw, insert flexible membrane of lead, zinc, copper, bituminous material or low density polythene and force in new mortar (material cost of membrane not included):**										
9050101A	to half brick walls	m	2.06	40.00	2.28	0.13	42.41	44.00	2.51	0.14	46.65
9050101B	to one brick walls	m	4.12	79.99	4.56	0.26	84.81	87.99	5.02	0.29	93.29
9050101C	to one and a half brick walls	m	6.18	119.99	6.84	0.39	127.22	131.99	7.52	0.43	139.94
9050101D	Extra over last for material cost of membrane in one brick wall in 26SWG (0.45 mm) copper	m	–	–	–	8.63	8.63	–	–	9.49	9.49
9050101E	Extra over for material cost of membrane in one brick wall in 26SWG Code 4 (1.80 mm) lead.	m	–	–	–	10.47	10.47	–	–	11.52	11.52
9050101F	Extra over for 2000 gauge low density polythene	m	–	–	–	3.62	3.62	–	–	3.98	3.98
9050102	**Drill brickwork and provide Vandex damp proof course to:**										
9050102A	half brick walls	m	0.23	5.77	–	1.42	7.19	6.35	–	1.56	7.91
9050102B	one brick walls	m	0.43	10.90	–	2.36	13.26	11.99	–	2.60	14.59
9050102C	one and half brick wall	m	0.60	15.38	–	3.87	19.25	16.92	–	4.26	21.18
9050103	**Drill brickwork and provide chemical damp-proof course injected under pressure to:**										
9050103A	half brick wall	m	0.20	5.20	–	4.05	9.25	5.72	–	4.46	10.18
9050103B	one brick wall	m	0.38	9.82	–	8.10	17.92	10.80	–	8.91	19.71
9050103C	one and a half brick wall	m	0.55	14.20	–	12.15	26.35	15.62	–	13.37	28.99
9050104	**Hack off existing plastering or rendering to a height of one metre above the damp-proof course and later replace with:**										
9050104A	two coats of Premix DR5 and a setting coat.	m²	1.40	31.51	–	3.05	34.56	34.66	–	3.36	38.02
9050105	**Cerinol tanking:**										
9050105A	five coat	m²	1.50	31.28	–	12.60	43.88	34.41	–	13.86	48.27
9050106	**Clean, prepare and apply DC500 flexible roofing compound to:**										
9050106A	sound surfaces, asbestos, asphalt, concrete, felt, slate or tile	m²	0.55	11.47	–	6.26	17.73	12.62	–	6.89	19.50
9050107	**Clean, prepare and apply DC500 flexible roofing compound and fungicide solution to:**										
9050107A	surfaces likely to support fungal or algae growth, asbestos, asphalt, concrete, felt, slate or tile	m²	0.60	12.51	–	6.70	19.21	13.76	–	7.37	21.13

Sundries

Small Works 2009		Unit	Labour Hours	Labour Net	Plant Net	Materials Net	Unit Net	Labour Gross	Plant Gross	Materials Gross	Unit Price
								(Gross rates include 10% profit)			
				£	£	£	£	£	£	£	£
906	**UNDERPINNING**										
90601	**GENERALLY**										
9060101	**Break up concrete paving and hardcore under, level and ram hardcore on completion, 150 mm concrete paving with screeded finish:**										
9060101A	150 mm concrete paving ...	m²	2.60	54.21	–	19.05	73.26	59.63	–	20.96	80.59
9060102	**Excavate for access trench, part backfill:**										
9060102A	dispose of surplus in skip ..	m³	7.00	145.95	–	–	145.95	160.55	–	–	160.55
9060103	**Excavate under existing wall or foundation:**										
9060103A	and get out	m³	5.40	112.59	–	–	112.59	123.85	–	–	123.85
9060104	**Hire of skip; delivery to site; removing when full; dispose of contents; payment of tipping charges:**										
9060104A	skip size; 4.5 m³	m³	–	–	33.02	4.87	37.89	–	36.32	5.36	41.68
9060106	**Break out existing foundations in short lengths and get out:**										
9060106A	concrete.................	m³	32.00	667.20	–	–	667.20	733.92	–	–	733.92
9060106B	brickwork	m³	27.00	562.95	–	–	562.95	619.25	–	–	619.25
9060107	**Concrete underpinning in short lengths including necessary formwork; mix:**										
9060107A	1:2:4...................	m³	13.00	271.05	–	155.01	426.06	298.16	–	170.51	468.67
9060107B	1:3:6...................	m³	13.00	271.05	–	124.01	395.06	298.16	–	136.41	434.57
9060108	**Concrete in projecting pier bases including necessary formwork; mix:**										
9060108A	1:2:4...................	m³	15.50	323.17	–	155.01	478.18	355.49	–	170.51	526.00
9060108B	1:3:6...................	m³	15.50	323.17	–	124.01	447.18	355.49	–	136.41	491.90
9060109	**Reinforced concrete in ground beams including one 13 mm mild steel bar for each 0.02 sq.m sectional area of beam; including necessary formwork; mix:**										
9060109A	1:2:4...................	m³	14.70	376.91	–	211.18	588.09	414.60	–	232.30	646.90
9060110	**Brickwork one brick thick in short lengths in underpinning:**										
9060110A	engineering bricks	m²	8.00	205.12	–	75.09	280.21	225.63	–	82.60	308.23
9060110B	common bricks...........	m²	8.00	205.12	–	42.14	247.26	225.63	–	46.35	271.99
9060111	**Wedge and pin up new brickwork to underside of existing with slates; thickness:**										
9060111A	215 mm.................	m	1.00	25.64	–	12.08	37.72	28.20	–	13.29	41.49
9060111B	327 mm.................	m	1.40	35.90	–	18.05	53.95	39.49	–	19.86	59.35
9060112	**Timber in dwarf, dead and sundry shoring:**										
9060112A	generally	m³	80.00	2051.20	–	106.24	2157.44	2256.32	–	116.86	2373.18

HOUSE RENOVATION GRANTS, REPAIRS AND ALTERATIONS

House Renovation Grants, Repairs and Alterations

Small Works 2009		Unit	Labour Hours	Labour Net	Plant Net	Materials Net	Unit Net	Labour Gross	Plant Gross	Materials Gross	Unit Price
				£	£	£	£	£	£	£	£
								(Gross rates include 10% profit)			

A01 GRANTWORK

A0101 HOUSE RENOVATION

A010101 Take up old wood flooring in basement including joists and plates, excavate for, breaking up any obstructions, lay 150 mm hardcore and 100 mm concrete and thermoplastic tile floor on screed base

A010101A	take up flooring and excavate to required depth	m²	6.00	125.10	–	–	125.10	137.61	–	–	137.61
A010101B	lay 150 mm hardcore	m²	0.30	6.25	–	3.90	10.15	6.88	–	4.29	11.17
A010101C	lay 100 mm concrete	m²	1.00	20.85	–	10.55	31.40	22.94	–	11.61	34.54
A010101D	lay screed for tiles	m²	0.60	16.81	–	2.85	19.66	18.49	–	3.14	21.63
A010101E	inclusive cost for preparing.	m²	7.90	169.01	–	16.62	185.63	185.91	–	18.28	204.19
A010101F	tile flooring	m²	0.37	6.06	–	7.74	13.80	6.67	–	8.51	15.18
A010101G	total cost	m²	8.27	175.07	–	24.36	199.43	192.58	–	26.79	219.37

A010102 Break up existing concrete area paving; excavate over site 150 mm deep, prepare subsoil and lay new concrete paving:

A010102A	break up concrete paving	m²	2.25	46.91	–	–	46.91	51.60	–	–	51.60
A010102B	excavate over site	m²	0.42	8.76	–	–	8.76	9.64	–	–	9.64
A010102C	lay 100 mm concrete	m²	1.00	20.85	–	10.55	31.40	22.94	–	11.61	34.54
A010102D	total cost	m²	3.67	76.52	–	10.55	87.07	84.17	–	11.61	95.78

A010103 Build concrete block and cavity lining to existing external and party walls including plastering and two coats emulsion paint:

A010103A	100 mm concrete block walling with four ties per sq.m.	m²	1.20	30.77	–	14.04	44.81	33.85	–	15.44	49.29
A010103B	render and set walls	m²	0.85	20.77	–	2.27	23.04	22.85	–	2.50	25.34
A010103C	emulsion paint:	m²	0.32	8.97	–	1.46	10.43	9.87	–	1.61	11.47
A010103D	total cost	m²	2.37	60.49	–	17.78	78.27	66.54	–	19.56	86.10

A010104 Rake out existing brickwork joints to form key, plaster walls and emulsion paint:

A010104A	rake out brickwork	m²	0.40	10.26	–	–	10.26	11.29	–	–	11.29
A010104B	render and set walls	m²	0.85	20.77	–	2.27	23.04	22.85	–	2.50	25.34
A010104C	emulsion paint	m²	0.32	8.97	–	1.46	10.43	9.87	–	1.61	11.47
A010104D	total cost	m²	1.57	39.99	–	3.73	43.72	43.99	–	4.10	48.09

A010105 Build 100 mm concrete block partition walls off site concrete, plastered and emulsion painted both sides, including tying into existing walls and pinning to soffit:

A010105A	100 mm concrete block walling including tying in	m²	1.20	30.77	–	17.04	47.81	33.85	–	18.74	52.59
A010105B	render and set both sides	m²	1.70	41.53	–	2.27	43.80	45.68	–	2.50	48.18
A010105C	emulsion paint both sides	m²	0.84	23.53	–	2.93	26.46	25.88	–	3.22	29.11
A010105D	total cost	m²	3.74	95.82	–	22.24	118.06	105.40	–	24.46	129.87

House Renovation Grants, Repairs and Alterations

Small Works 2009		Unit	Labour Hours	Labour Net	Plant Net	Materials Net	Unit Net	Labour Gross	Plant Gross	Materials Gross	Unit Price
								(Gross rates include 10% profit)			
				£	£	£	£	£	£	£	£
A01	**GRANTWORK**										
A0101	**HOUSE RENOVATION**										
A010106	**Take out and remove kitchen range and mantel-shelf; build up half brick thick wall across opening flush with existing walls and render and set:**										
A010106A	take out range and remove .	Each	6.00	125.10	–	–	125.10	137.61	–	–	137.61
A010106B	take out and remove mantel-shelf	Each	0.80	16.68	–	–	16.68	18.35	–	–	18.35
A010106C	half-brick wall including tying (3 sq.m)	Each	7.00	179.48	–	84.98	264.46	197.43	–	93.48	290.91
A010106D	render and set including jointing to existing (3 sq.m)	Each	3.00	73.29	–	7.28	80.57	80.62	–	8.01	88.63
A010106E	total cost	Each	16.80	394.55	–	92.26	486.81	434.01	–	101.49	535.49
A010108	**Take out existing window frame, size 1.2 m × 1.0 m. Cut away stone sill and one brick apron below, about 1.2 m × 0.45 m. Reform brick jambs and build in brick-on-edge sill. Provide and fix new standard casement window size 1.2 m × 1.35 m. Glaze, paint both sides and make good all plaster. No alteration work to lintel or arch over:**										
A010108A	take out window sill	Each	1.60	33.36	–	–	33.36	36.70	–	–	36.70
A010108B	cut away brickwork (0.5 sq.m)	Each	1.90	39.62	–	–	39.62	43.58	–	–	43.58
A010108C	reform jambs (1 lin.m).....	Each	2.50	64.10	–	5.96	70.06	70.51	–	6.56	77.07
A010108D	brick sill (1 lin.m)	Each	1.30	33.33	–	7.56	40.89	36.66	–	8.32	44.98
A010108E	window casement	Each	1.80	46.15	–	103.95	150.10	50.77	–	114.35	165.11
A010108F	glazing (1.5 sq.m)	Each	1.65	46.22	–	101.31	147.53	50.84	–	111.44	162.28
A010108G	paint window casement (3.5 sq.m)	Each	3.50	98.04	–	3.45	101.49	107.84	–	3.80	111.64
A010108H	make good plaster	Each	0.90	21.99	–	1.00	22.99	24.19	–	1.10	25.29
A010108I	total cost	Each	15.15	382.80	–	223.10	605.90	421.08	–	245.41	666.49
A010109	**Take out old door frame and wing light 1.8 m × 2.0 m (extreme). Build up one brick wall in old door opening up to sill level, take out old stone sill and build up new brick sill. Provide and fix new purpose made window frame 1.8 m × 1.0 m. Glaze, paint both sides and make good all plaster:**										
A010109A	take out existing frame	Each	1.85	38.57	–	–	38.57	42.43	–	–	42.43
A010109B	take out old sill	Each	0.40	8.34	–	–	8.34	9.17	–	–	9.17
A010109C	build up one-brick wall in old opening 0.75 m × 0.9 m ..	Each	3.75	96.15	–	42.02	138.17	105.77	–	46.22	151.99
A010109D	build new brick sill (2 lin.m):	Each	2.60	66.67	–	18.60	85.27	73.34	–	20.46	93.80
A010109E	window frame and sashes..	Each	11.00	282.04	–	71.55	353.59	310.24	–	78.71	388.95
A010109F	glass in window frame and sashes (1.6 sq.m)	Each	5.20	145.65	–	108.36	254.01	160.22	–	119.20	279.41
A010109G	painting window frame and sashes (4.0 sq.m)	Each	5.20	145.66	–	2.81	148.47	160.23	–	3.09	163.32
A010109H	make good wall plaster	Each	0.90	21.99	–	2.00	23.99	24.19	–	2.20	26.39
A010109I	total cost	Each	30.90	805.06	–	245.09	1050.15	885.57	–	269.60	1155.17

Small Works 2009		Unit	Labour Hours	Labour Net	Plant Net	Materials Net	Unit Net	Labour Gross	Plant Gross	Materials Gross	Unit Price
								——— (Gross rates include 10% profit) ———			
				£	£	£	£	£	£	£	£
A01	**GRANTWORK**										
A0101	**HOUSE RENOVATION**										
A010110	**Make and fix cupboard front and return end to form linen cupboard, internal size 750 mm × 750 mm, full height floor to ceiling 2.40 m. Return wall and over door wall to be 75 mm × 50 mm fir stud covered both sides with expanded metal lathing and plastered. Hardboard flush door hung on 75 mm light steel hinges, fitted with bow handle and Bales catch. Standard door lining with 50 mm × 18 mm architrave outside. Four open slat shelves, comprising 50 mm × 25 mm in softwood slats spaced 25 mm apart and including bearers full width and depth of cupboard. New wall plaster and existing plaster inside cupboard to be painted in two coats emulsion. Door, lining and architrave to be primed and painted two coats of oil colour:**										
A010110A	stud partition wall with expanded metal lathing and plaster both sides 3 sq.m:..	Each	10.00	278.00	–	93.30	371.30	305.80	–	102.63	408.43
A010110B	shelving 2.5 sq.m including bearers:.................	Each	5.00	139.00	–	51.08	190.08	152.90	–	56.19	209.09
A010110C	door lining:	Each	0.75	20.85	–	22.25	43.10	22.94	–	24.48	47.41
A010110D	door:	Each	0.75	20.85	–	40.28	61.13	22.94	–	44.31	67.24
A010110E	architrave 5 lin.m:........	Each	0.75	20.85	–	7.73	28.58	22.94	–	8.50	31.44
A010110F	hinges:.................	Each	0.45	12.51	–	3.39	15.90	13.76	–	3.73	17.49
A010110G	handle:.................	Each	0.30	8.34	–	6.47	14.81	9.17	–	7.12	16.29
A010110H	catch:..................	Each	0.60	16.68	–	3.42	20.10	18.35	–	3.76	22.11
A010110I	emulsion paint 8 sq.m:	Each	2.60	72.83	–	9.51	82.34	80.11	–	10.46	90.57
A010110J	painting 4 sq.m:	Each	2.75	77.03	–	6.08	83.11	84.73	–	6.69	91.42
A010110K	total cost:...............	Each	23.95	666.93	–	243.53	910.46	733.62	–	267.88	1001.51

House Renovation Grants, Repairs and Alterations

Small Works 2009		Unit	Labour Hours	Labour Net	Plant Net	Materials Net	Unit Net	Labour Gross	Plant Gross	Materials Gross	Unit Price
								(Gross rates include 10% profit)			
				£	£	£	£	£	£	£	£
A01	**GRANTWORK**										
A0101	**HOUSE RENOVATION**										
A010112	**Take out old door frame, provide and fix new 50 mm standard softwood entrance door and frame, including cylinder night latch and letter plate, and decorate:**										
A010112A	take out door and frame: ...	Each	1.50	31.28	–	–	31.28	34.41	–	–	34.41
A010112B	new door and frame:	Each	3.00	83.41	–	155.93	239.34	91.75	–	171.52	263.27
A010112C	cylinder latch:	Each	1.60	44.48	–	33.70	78.18	48.93	–	37.07	86.00
A010112D	letter plate:	Each	1.75	48.65	–	9.65	58.30	53.52	–	10.62	64.13
A010112E	painting 3.5 sq.m:	Each	3.00	84.03	–	3.72	87.75	92.43	–	4.09	96.53
A010112F	total cost:..............	Each	10.85	291.83	–	203.00	494.83	321.01	–	223.30	544.31
A010113	**Take down old timber stair flight and remove, fill over stair opening with 150 mm × 50 mm joists and board over to form extension to upper floor. Plaster baseboard and set soffit and emulsion paint. Make good wall plaster of spandrel and emulsion paint on wall:**										
A010113A	take out stairs:	Each	9.40	195.99	–	–	195.99	215.59	–	–	215.59
A010113B	floor joists and boarding over 2.25 sq.m:.............	Each	3.25	90.35	–	106.74	197.09	99.39	–	117.41	216.80
A010113C	ceiling plaster 2.6 sq.m	Each	2.40	58.63	–	4.06	62.69	64.49	–	4.47	68.96
A010113D	emulsion paint 2.6 sq.m:...	Each	1.05	29.41	–	1.35	30.76	32.35	–	1.49	33.84
A010113E	wall plaster 3.5 sq.m:......	Each	3.40	83.06	–	8.82	91.88	91.37	–	9.70	101.07
A010113F	emulsion paint 3.5 sq.m:...	Each	1.12	31.37	–	5.20	36.57	34.51	–	5.72	40.23
A010113G	total cost:..............	Each	20.62	488.82	–	126.17	614.99	537.70	–	138.79	676.49

Small Works 2009		Unit	Labour Hours	Labour Net	Plant Net	Materials Net	Unit Net	Labour Gross	Plant Gross	Materials Gross	Unit Price
								(Gross rates include 10% profit)			
				£	£	£	£	£	£	£	£
A01	**GRANTWORK**										
A0101	**HOUSE RENOVATION**										
A010114	**Take down existing door and lining and set aside and fix in new partition wall including architraves both sides. Oil and adjust lock and decorate woodwork:**										
A010114A	take out door and lining: ...	Each	1.50	31.28	–	–	31.28	34.41	–	–	34.41
A010114B	reset door and lining in new opening:.................	Each	3.75	104.25	–	–	104.25	114.68	–	–	114.68
A010114C	architrave 10 lin.m:	Each	1.80	50.04	–	8.75	58.79	55.04	–	9.63	64.67
A010114D	painting 3.5 sq.m:	Each	3.30	92.43	–	5.54	97.97	101.67	–	6.09	107.77
A010114E	oil and adjust lock:	Each	0.25	6.95	–	–	6.95	7.65	–	–	7.65
A010114F	total cost:...............	Each	10.60	284.95	–	14.29	299.24	313.45	–	15.72	329.16
A010115	**Excavate over site 225 mm deep to annexe building for bathroom and WC or kitchen and deposit soil over adjacent garden:**										
A010115A	excavate and deposit soil: ..	m²	1.00	20.85	–	–	20.85	22.94	–	–	22.94
A010116	**Excavate foundation trench 450 mm × 600 mm deep. Lay concrete foundation 450 mm × 300 mm thick. New 275 mm cavity brickwork 450 mm high up to and including dampcourse:**										
A010116A	trench excavation:	m	1.20	25.02	–	–	25.02	27.52	–	–	27.52
A010116B	foundation concrete:	m	1.00	20.85	–	14.76	35.61	22.94	–	16.24	39.17
A010116C	brickwork:...............	m	1.70	43.59	–	19.65	63.24	47.95	–	21.62	69.56
A010116D	slate dampcourse:	m	0.23	5.90	–	11.37	17.27	6.49	–	12.51	19.00
A010116E	total cost:...............	m	4.13	95.36	–	45.78	141.14	104.90	–	50.36	155.25
A010118	**Lay 100 mm hardcore and 100 mm concrete over site and wood flooring on and including 150 mm × 50 mm joists (no sleeper walls):**										
A010118A	hardcore:................	m²	0.25	5.22	–	2.59	7.81	5.74	–	2.85	8.59
A010118B	concrete:	m²	1.00	20.85	–	10.93	31.78	22.94	–	12.02	34.96
A010118C	flooring and joists:	m²	1.10	30.58	–	41.33	71.91	33.64	–	45.46	79.10
A010118D	total cost:...............	m²	2.35	56.64	–	54.85	111.49	62.30	–	60.34	122.64
A010119	**Build 275 mm cavity brick wall in common bricks with fletton facings externally, plastered and emulsion paint internally:**										
A010119A	cavity wall:..............	m²	4.25	108.97	–	49.04	158.01	119.87	–	53.94	173.81
A010119B	wall plaster:.............	m²	0.85	20.77	–	2.27	23.04	22.85	–	2.50	25.34
A010119C	emulsion paint:...........	m²	0.32	8.96	–	1.35	10.31	9.86	–	1.49	11.34
A010119D	total cost:...............	m²	5.42	138.70	–	52.65	191.35	152.57	–	57.92	210.49

House Renovation Grants, Repairs and Alterations

Small Works 2009		Unit	Labour Hours	Labour Net	Plant Net	Materials Net	Unit Net	Labour Gross	Plant Gross	Materials Gross	Unit Price
								—— (Gross rates include 10% profit) ——			
				£	£	£	£	£	£	£	£
A01	**GRANTWORK**										
A0101	**HOUSE RENOVATION**										
A010120	**Form lean-to roof of concrete tiles on battens including felt, 125 mm × 50 mm rafters and 100 mm × 75 mm plate:**										
A010120A	plates and rafters:.........	m²	0.80	22.24	–	11.15	33.39	24.46	–	12.27	36.73
A010120B	battens and tiles:	m²	1.40	35.90	–	17.46	53.36	39.49	–	19.21	58.70
A010120C	felt:.....................	m²	0.13	3.33	–	2.94	6.27	3.66	–	3.23	6.90
A010120D	total cost:...............	m²	2.33	61.47	–	31.55	93.02	67.62	–	34.71	102.32
A010121	**150 mm × 25 mm fascia and painting and uPVC half round gutter:**										
A010121A	fascia board:.............	m	0.25	6.95	–	4.07	11.02	7.65	–	4.48	12.12
A010121B	paint fascia boards:	m	0.30	8.40	–	0.48	8.88	9.24	–	0.53	9.77
A010121C	uPVC gutter including stop ends and outlets:	m	0.50	17.96	–	9.53	27.49	19.76	–	10.48	30.24
A010121D	total cost:...............	m	1.05	33.31	–	14.08	47.39	36.64	–	15.49	52.13
A010122	**UPVC downpipe including swanneck and shoe:**										
A010122A	63 mm uPVC downpipe 3 lin.m:	Each	1.50	53.88	–	28.05	81.93	59.27	–	30.86	90.12
A010122B	swanneck comprising two bends:	Each	0.50	17.96	–	8.12	26.08	19.76	–	8.93	28.69
A010122C	shoe:	Each	0.33	11.86	–	4.27	16.13	13.05	–	4.70	17.74
A010122D	total cost:...............	Each	2.33	83.70	–	40.44	124.14	92.07	–	44.48	136.55
A010123	**Renew ceiling joists and plasterboard and emulsion paint ceiling:**										
A010123A	joists 100 mm × 50 mm: .	m²	0.20	5.56	–	4.51	10.07	6.12	–	4.96	11.08
A010123B	plasterboard and set ceiling:	m²	0.90	21.99	–	5.09	27.08	24.19	–	5.60	29.79
A010123C	emulsion paint plasterboard and ceiling:	m²	0.40	11.20	–	1.58	12.78	12.32	–	1.74	14.06
A010123D	total cost:...............	m²	1.50	38.75	–	11.18	49.93	42.63	–	12.30	54.92
A010124	**Provide and fix standard casement window size 630 mm × 1050 mm including lintel, brick sill, glazing and painting:**										
A010124A	steel lintel for external solid wall 143 mm high, 1050 mm long	Each	0.85	17.72	–	52.49	70.21	19.49	–	57.74	77.23
A010124B	brick sill:	Each	1.30	33.33	–	5.74	39.07	36.66	–	6.31	42.98
A010124C	casement window:........	Each	1.20	33.36	–	145.80	179.16	36.70	–	160.38	197.08
A010124D	glazing 0.6 sq.m	Each	0.80	22.40	–	40.51	62.91	24.64	–	44.56	69.20
A010124E	paint both sides 1.3 sq.m:..	Each	2.00	56.02	–	1.54	57.56	61.62	–	1.69	63.32
A010124F	total cost:...............	Each	6.15	162.84	–	245.95	408.79	179.12	–	270.55	449.67

Small Works 2009		Unit	Labour Hours	Labour Net	Plant Net	Materials Net	Unit Net	Labour Gross	Plant Gross	Materials Gross	Unit Price
								(Gross rates include 10% profit)			
				£	£	£	£	£	£	£	£
A01	**GRANTWORK**										
A0101	**HOUSE RENOVATION**										
A010125	**Cut through one brick external wall for new door opening including lintel over. Provide and fix new door and frame size 825 mm × 2025 mm overall:**										
A010125A	cut opening through one brick wall 2 sq.m:	Each	7.50	156.38	–	–	156.38	172.02	–	–	172.02
A010125B	steel lintel for external solid wall 143 mm high, 1200 mm long	Each	1.00	20.85	–	74.57	95.42	22.94	–	82.03	104.96
A010125C	door frame:	Each	1.10	30.58	–	145.80	176.38	33.64	–	160.38	194.02
A010125D	door 762 mm × 1981 mm including lock hinges etc.:	Each	4.00	111.20	–	191.40	302.60	122.32	–	210.54	332.86
A010125E	paint door and frame overall both sides 4 sq.m:	Each	3.60	100.83	–	7.63	108.46	110.91	–	8.39	119.31
A010125F	make good wall plaster:	Each	1.00	24.43	–	4.54	28.97	26.87	–	4.99	31.87
A010125G	total cost:	Each	18.20	444.27	–	349.01	793.28	488.70	–	383.91	872.61
A010126	**Break up concrete paving, excavate drain trench, average 0.60 m deep. Lay 3.0 lin.m of 100 mm clayware pipe including hole through existing manhole and make good. Drain bend and vertical pipe set in concrete floor to receive W.C. pan. Trench refilled and paving reinstated on completion:**										
A010126A	break up concrete paving 0.60m wide 3 lin.m long:	Each	3.00	62.55	–	–	62.55	68.81	–	–	68.81
A010126B	excavate trench 3 lin.m:	Each	2.80	58.38	–	–	58.38	64.22	–	–	64.22
A010126C	drain 100 mm 3 lin.m long:	Each	1.65	34.40	–	18.23	52.63	37.84	–	20.05	57.89
A010126D	reinstate concrete paving 3 lin.m:	Each	3.60	75.06	–	26.71	101.77	82.57	–	29.38	111.95
A010126E	end of drain into side of manhole and reform channel benching:	Each	1.80	50.04	–	17.46	67.50	55.04	–	19.21	74.25
A010126F	drain bend and vertical pipe:	Each	3.60	75.06	–	49.81	124.87	82.57	–	54.79	137.36
A010126G	total cost:	Each	16.45	355.49	–	112.21	467.70	391.04	–	123.43	514.47

House Renovation Grants, Repairs and Alterations

Small Works 2009		Unit	Labour Hours	Labour Net	Plant Net	Materials Net	Unit Net	Labour Gross	Plant Gross	Materials Gross	Unit Price
								(Gross rates include 10% profit)			
				£	£	£	£	£	£	£	£
A01	**GRANTWORK**										
A0101	**HOUSE RENOVATION**										
A010128	**Break up concrete paving, excavate drain trench, average 0.60 m deep. Lay 3.0 lin.m of 100 mm clayware pipe including hole through existing manhole and make good. Drain for surface and/or disposal waste pipes, 100 mm clayware gully trap in paving with gully surround:**										
A010128A	break up concrete paving 0.60 wide, 3 lin.m long:	Each	3.00	62.55	–	–	62.55	68.81	–	–	68.81
A010128B	excavate trench 3 lin.m long:	Each	2.80	58.38	–	–	58.38	64.22	–	–	64.22
A010128C	drain 100 mm 3 lin.m long:.	Each	1.65	34.40	–	18.23	52.63	37.84	–	20.05	57.89
A010128D	reinstate concrete paving 3 lin.m:	Each	3.60	75.06	–	26.71	101.77	82.57	–	29.38	111.95
A010128E	end of drain into side of manhole and reform channel benching:................	Each	1.80	50.04	–	17.46	67.50	55.04	–	19.21	74.25
A010128F	clayware gully and curb: ...	Each	1.10	22.94	–	54.18	77.12	25.23	–	59.60	84.83
A010128G	total cost:...............	Each	13.95	303.37	–	116.58	419.95	333.71	–	128.24	461.95
A010130	**Take down existing partition wall 2.4 m high (brick, clinker concrete or stud) and clear away. Make good ceiling plaster along top of wall and make good wood flooring at base of wall:**										
A010130A	take down and clear away wall:	m	0.70	14.60	–	–	14.60	16.06	–	–	16.06
A010130B	make good ceiling plaster and emulsion paint 0.3 m wide:	m	0.50	12.22	–	0.46	12.68	13.44	–	0.51	13.95
A010130C	make good wood flooring and emulsion paint 0.3 m wide:	m	0.65	18.07	–	7.12	25.19	19.88	–	7.83	27.71
A010130D	total cost:...............	m	1.85	44.88	–	7.58	52.46	49.37	–	8.34	57.71

Small Works 2009	Unit	Labour Hours	Labour Net	Plant Net	Materials Net	Unit Net	Labour Gross	Plant Gross	Materials Gross	Unit Price
							(Gross rates include 10% profit)			
			£	£	£	£	£	£	£	£
A01 **GRANTWORK**										
A0101 **HOUSE RENOVATION**										
A010132 **Make good existing wall plaster 2.4 m high after removal of partition wall. Piece in skirting and picture rail and paint:**										
A010132A make good wall plaster 450 mm wide and joint to existing 3 lin.m:	Each	1.90	46.41	–	3.81	50.22	51.05	–	4.19	55.24
A010132B piece in 200 mm wood skirting about 300 mm long and paint:	Each	1.10	30.58	–	0.72	31.30	33.64	–	0.79	34.43
A010132C piece in wood picture rail about 300 mm long and paint:	Each	0.50	13.90	–	0.57	14.47	15.29	–	0.63	15.92
A010132D total cost:	Each	3.50	90.90	–	5.00	95.90	99.99	–	5.50	105.49
A010133 **Build half brick partition 2.4 m high, both sides plastered and emulsion painted. Fix 150 mm softwood skirting and decorate both sides:**										
A010133A half brick wall 2.4 m high:	m	6.00	153.84	–	52.77	206.61	169.22	–	58.05	227.27
A010133B plaster both sides half brick wall 2.4 m high:	m	4.25	103.83	–	13.03	116.86	114.21	–	14.33	128.55
A010133C emulsion paint both sides:	m	1.53	42.85	–	6.05	48.90	47.14	–	6.66	53.79
A010133D skirting both sides:	m	0.70	19.46	–	8.95	28.41	21.41	–	9.85	31.25
A010133E paint skirting both sides:	m	0.40	11.20	–	2.19	13.39	12.32	–	2.41	14.73
A010133F total cost:	m	12.88	331.18	–	82.99	414.17	364.30	–	91.29	455.59
A010134 **Build 100 mm concrete block wall 2.4 m high, both sides plastered and emulsion painted. Fix 150 mm softwood skirting both sides and paint:**										
A010134A concrete block wall 100 mm:	m	3.00	76.92	–	36.83	113.75	84.61	–	40.51	125.13
A010134B plaster both sides:	m	4.25	103.83	–	13.03	116.86	114.21	–	14.33	128.55
A010134C emulsion paint both sides:	m	1.53	42.85	–	6.05	48.90	47.14	–	6.66	53.79
A010134D skirting both sides:	m	0.70	19.46	–	8.95	28.41	21.41	–	9.85	31.25
A010134E paint both sides:	m	0.40	11.20	–	2.19	13.39	12.32	–	2.41	14.73
A010134F total cost:	m	9.88	254.27	–	67.04	321.31	279.70	–	73.74	353.44
A010135 **Construct stud partition 2.4 m high of 100 mm × 50 mm studs clad both sides with plasterboard set in plaster and emulsion painted. Fix 150 mm wood skirting both sides and paint:**										
A010135A stud partition 100 mm × 50 mm-2.4 m high:	m	1.00	24.33	–	17.21	41.54	26.76	–	18.93	45.69
A010135B plasterboard and set both sides:	m	4.35	106.27	–	23.28	129.55	116.90	–	25.61	142.51
A010135C emulsion paint both sides:	m	1.53	42.85	–	6.05	48.90	47.14	–	6.66	53.79
A010135D skirting both sides:	m	0.70	19.46	–	8.95	28.41	21.41	–	9.85	31.25
A010135E paint both sides:	m	0.40	11.20	–	2.19	13.39	12.32	–	2.41	14.73
A010135F total cost:	m	7.98	204.12	–	56.80	260.92	224.53	–	62.48	287.01

House Renovation Grants, Repairs and Alterations

Small Works 2009		Unit	Labour Hours	Labour Net	Plant Net	Materials Net	Unit Net	Labour Gross	Plant Gross	Materials Gross	Unit Price
								(Gross rates include 10% profit)			
				£	£	£	£	£	£	£	£
A01	**GRANTWORK**										
A0101	**HOUSE RENOVATION**										
A010138	**Take down door and frame and set aside. Fill opening with half brick walling and plaster both sides, including jointing to existing. Emulsion paint both sides. Fix 150 mm skirting both sides and paint:**										
A010138A	take down door and frame: .	Each	1.50	31.28	–	–	31.28	34.41	–	–	34.41
A010138B	half brick wall (2 sq.m):....	Each	4.80	123.07	–	42.68	165.75	135.38	–	46.95	182.33
A010138C	plaster both sides (4 sq.m):	Each	4.25	103.83	–	5.54	109.37	114.21	–	6.09	120.31
A010138D	emulsion paint both sides (4 sq.m):	Each	1.28	35.85	–	5.01	40.86	39.44	–	5.51	44.95
A010138E	skirting (2 lin.m):	Each	0.70	19.46	–	8.95	28.41	21.41	–	9.85	31.25
A010138F	paint (2 lin.m):	Each	0.40	11.20	–	2.19	13.39	12.32	–	2.41	14.73
A010138G	total cost:..............	Each	12.93	324.69	–	64.37	389.06	357.16	–	70.81	427.97
A010140	**Take down door and frame and set aside. Fill opening with 50 mm × 100 mm studs clad both sides with plaster baseboard and set in plaster, including making good to existing, emulsion paint both sides. Fix 150 mm skirting both sides and paint:**										
A010140A	stud partition in opening (2 sq.m)	Each	2.00	55.60	–	18.77	74.37	61.16	–	20.65	81.81
A010140B	plaster baseboard and set both sides (4 sq.m)	Each	3.40	83.06	–	22.48	105.54	91.37	–	24.73	116.09
A010140C	emulsion paint both sides (4 sq.m)	Each	1.28	35.85	–	5.01	40.86	39.44	–	5.51	44.95
A010140D	take down door and frame..	Each	1.50	31.28	–	–	31.28	34.41	–	–	34.41
A010140E	skirting (2 lin.m)..........	Each	0.70	19.46	–	8.95	28.41	21.41	–	9.85	31.25
A010140F	paint (2 lin.m)...........	Each	0.40	11.20	–	2.19	13.39	12.32	–	2.41	14.73
A010140G	total cost	Each	9.28	236.45	–	57.40	293.85	260.10	–	63.14	323.24

Small Works 2009		Unit	Labour Hours	Labour Net	Plant Net	Materials Net	Unit Net	Labour Gross	Plant Gross	Materials Gross	Unit Price
								(Gross rates include 10% profit)			
				£	£	£	£	£	£	£	£
A01	**GRANTWORK**										
A0101	**HOUSE RENOVATION**										
A010142	**Existing door frame and door re-used in door opening in new partition. Fix new architraves both sides. Paint door frame and architrave both sides:**										
A010142A	Fix existing door frame in new opening	Each	1.20	33.36	–	–	33.36	36.70	–	–	36.70
A010142B	architraves (10 lin.m):	Each	1.50	41.70	–	21.10	62.80	45.87	–	23.21	69.08
A010142C	rehang door:	Each	0.50	13.90	–	–	13.90	15.29	–	–	15.29
A010142D	paint door and frame overall sides (4 sq.m):	Each	3.75	105.03	–	7.63	112.66	115.53	–	8.39	123.93
A010142E	total cost:	Each	6.95	194.00	–	28.73	222.73	213.40	–	31.60	245.00
A010143	**Provide and hang 762 mm × 1981 mm × 35 mm standard hardboard flush door and lining with new architraves both sides in new door opening. Door to be hung on 75 mm butt hinges and fitted with mortice lock, all to be primed and painted two coats oil colour:**										
A010143A	door lining:	Each	0.68	18.91	–	28.74	47.65	20.80	–	31.61	52.42
A010143B	door:	Each	0.75	20.85	–	40.88	61.73	22.94	–	44.97	67.90
A010143C	architraves (10 lin.m):	Each	1.50	41.70	–	21.10	62.80	45.87	–	23.21	69.08
A010143D	butt hinges 75 mm:	Each	0.80	22.24	–	2.15	24.39	24.46	–	2.37	26.83
A010143E	mortice lock and furniture:	Each	2.00	55.60	–	32.54	88.14	61.16	–	35.79	96.95
A010143F	painting (4 sq.m):	Each	3.75	105.03	–	7.63	112.66	115.53	–	8.39	123.93
A010143G	total cost:	Each	9.48	264.33	–	133.04	397.37	290.76	–	146.34	437.11

House Renovation Grants, Repairs and Alterations

Small Works 2009		Unit	Labour Hours	Labour Net	Plant Net	Materials Net	Unit Net	Labour Gross	Plant Gross	Materials Gross	Unit Price
								(Gross rates include 10% profit)			
				£	£	£	£	£	£	£	£
A01	**GRANTWORK**										
A0101	**HOUSE RENOVATION**										
A010144	**Cut opening through one brick wall for window frame, 1200 mm × 1200 mm. Build in steel lintel and roofing tile sill and reform brick jambs. Provide and fix new casement window and frame. Glaze an paint both sides. Plaster reveals inside and make good internal wall plaster. Fix 100 mm softwood window board and paint:**										
A010144A	cut opening through one-brick wall for window 1200 mm × 1200 mm and lintel over (1.5 sq.m):......	Each	7.20	150.12	–	–	150.12	165.13	–	–	165.13
A010144B	steel lintel for solid wall 143 mm high 1500 mm long	Each	1.50	31.28	–	100.71	131.99	34.41	–	110.78	145.19
A010144C	roofing tile sill 1.5 m long:...	Each	0.90	18.77	–	11.49	30.26	20.65	–	12.64	33.29
A010144D	reform brick jambs to opening (3 lin.m):........	Each	7.50	208.50	–	12.88	221.38	229.35	–	14.17	243.52
A010144E	casement window and frame:	Each	1.80	50.04	–	205.88	255.92	55.04	–	226.47	281.51
A010144F	glazing window and frame (1 sq.m) small squares:....	Each	1.20	33.61	–	67.38	100.99	36.97	–	74.12	111.09
A010144G	painting window sashes and both side (3.5 sq.m):	Each	4.50	126.05	–	5.31	131.36	138.66	–	5.84	144.50
A010144H	plaster reveals and make good around opening:.....	Each	0.40	9.77	–	3.81	13.58	10.75	–	4.19	14.94
A010144I	window board 1.2 m long including painting:........	Each	0.50	13.90	–	10.74	24.64	15.29	–	11.81	27.10
A010144J	total cost:...............	Each	25.50	640.83	–	418.32	1059.15	704.91	–	460.15	1165.07
A010146	**Take off tiles or slates and form opening in roof size 1200 mm × 1200 mm for dormer window size 1200 mm × 900 mm frame and board dormer flat and cheeks. Provide and fix standard window and glaze and paint. Internally plasterboard and set to soffit and dormer cheeks and make good existing plaster:**										
A010146A	strip tiles or slates and battens (1.7 sq.m):.......	Each	1.30	27.11	–	–	27.11	29.82	–	–	29.82
A010146B	trim opening:	Each	0.45	12.51	–	28.79	41.30	13.76	–	31.67	45.43
A010146C	carcassing timber 100 mm × 50 mm to sides and roof of dormer (1.5 lin.m):	Each	3.60	100.08	–	25.29	125.37	110.09	–	27.82	137.91
A010146D	boarding to cheeks and roof of dormer (2.5 sq.m):	Each	4.35	120.93	–	55.17	176.10	133.02	–	60.69	193.71
A010146E	2.27kg lead covering to roof and cheeks (3 sq.m):......	Each	17.10	614.23	–	144.17	758.40	675.65	–	158.59	834.24
A010146F	casement window and frame:	Each	1.55	43.09	–	177.53	220.62	47.40	–	195.28	242.68
A010146G	glazing window and frame, 1 sq.m (medium squares): .	Each	1.10	30.81	–	67.35	98.16	33.89	–	74.09	107.98
A010146H	painting window sashes and frame both sides (3.5 sq.m):	Each	4.50	126.04	–	0.73	126.77	138.64	–	0.80	139.45
A010146I	plasterboard and set to soffit and cheeks (3.5 sq.m):	Each	3.40	83.06	–	17.60	100.66	91.37	–	19.36	110.73
A010146J	make good new plaster to existing:.................	Each	0.50	12.21	–	1.74	13.95	13.43	–	1.91	15.35
A010146K	emulsion paint new plastering (3.5 sq.m):	Each	1.13	31.65	–	5.43	37.08	34.82	–	5.97	40.79
A010146L	total cost:...............	Each	38.98	1200.32	–	523.79	1724.11	1320.35	–	576.17	1896.52

Small Works 2009		Unit	Labour Hours	Labour Net	Plant Net	Materials Net	Unit Net	Labour Gross	Plant Gross	Materials Gross	Unit Price
								(Gross rates include 10% profit)			
				£	£	£	£	£	£	£	£
A01	**GRANTWORK**										
A0101	**HOUSE RENOVATION**										
A010147	**Take down length of stair handrail and balustrade to stair flights 3 m long × 2.4 m high. Fill in triangular stair spandrel between stair tread and soffit with stud partition, covered with expanded metal lathing and plastered both sides. 25 mm × 225 mm cut wall string to be fitted over tread risers 63 mm. Mopstick hand rail to be fixed full length of wall.**										
A010147A	Take down and remove handrail and balustrade	Each	3.50	72.98	–	–	72.98	80.28	–	–	80.28
A010147B	triangular stud spandrel wall with expanded metal lathing and plaster both sides (average 4 sq. m)	Each	14.40	350.35	–	92.14	442.49	385.39	–	101.35	486.74
A010147C	emulsion paint wall both sides (8 sq. m)	Each	2.56	71.71	–	5.93	77.64	78.88	–	6.52	85.40
A010147D	225 mm × 25 mm cut wall string planted on (3.6 lin. m) and painting	Each	4.30	119.54	–	23.70	143.24	131.49	–	26.07	157.56
A010147E	mopstick handrail (3.6 lin. m)	Each	2.60	72.28	–	28.41	100.69	79.51	–	31.25	110.76
A010147F	total cost	Each	27.36	686.85	–	150.18	837.03	755.54	–	165.20	920.73
A010148	**Take down length of stair handrail and balustrade to stair flights 3 m long × 2.4 m high. Fill in triangular stair spandrel between stair tread and soffit with stud partition, covered with expanded metal lathing and plastered both sides. 25 mm × 225 mm cut wall string to be fitted over tread risers. 63 mm mopstick hand rail to be fixed full length of wall.**										
A010148A	take down handrail and balustrade	Each	3.50	72.98	–	–	72.98	80.28	–	–	80.28
A010148B	spandrel wall as last described but with parallel raking sides (7.5 sq. m)....	Each	28.20	783.96	–	173.28	957.24	862.36	–	190.61	1052.96
A010148C	emulsion paint wall both sides (15 sq. m)	Each	4.80	134.45	–	11.09	145.54	147.90	–	12.20	160.09
A010148D	225 mm × 25 mm cut wall string planted on (3.6 lin. m) and painting	Each	4.30	119.54	–	23.70	143.24	131.49	–	26.07	157.56
A010148E	mopstick handrail (3.5 lin. m)	Each	3.10	86.18	–	28.41	114.59	94.80	–	31.25	126.05
A010148F	total cost	Each	43.90	1197.10	–	236.48	1433.58	1316.81	–	260.13	1576.94

Small Works 2009		Unit	Labour Hours	Labour Net	Plant Net	Materials Net	Unit Net	Labour Gross	Plant Gross	Materials Gross	Unit Price
								(Gross rates include 10% profit)			
				£	£	£	£	£	£	£	£
A01	**GRANTWORK**										
A0101	**HOUSE RENOVATION**										
A010149	**Take down and remove handrail and balustrade to landing. Form new wall 2.4 m high in studwork covered with metal lath and plastered both sides. Provide and fix 25 mm × 150 mm skirting one side, decorate wall and skirting.**										
A010149A	take down handrail and balustrade..............	m	1.00	20.85	–	–	20.85	22.94	–	–	22.94
A010149B	stud partition wall as described...............	m	7.85	218.23	–	77.19	295.42	240.05	–	84.91	324.96
A010149C	emulsion paint wall both sides...................	m	1.53	42.86	–	3.31	46.17	47.15	–	3.64	50.79
A010149D	skirting one side 150 mm × 25 mm.................	m	0.35	9.73	–	4.47	14.20	10.70	–	4.92	15.62
A010149E	painting skirting one side 150 mm × 25 mm.......	m	0.20	5.60	–	0.73	6.33	6.16	–	0.80	6.96
A010149F	total cost	m	10.93	297.27	–	85.70	382.97	327.00	–	94.27	421.27
A010150	**Make and fix cupboard front in 38 mm softwood framing and plywood panelling including 750 mm × 1950 mm door across recess 1.2 m × 2.4 m high to form food store. Supply and fit three shelves 200 mm × 25 mm and one shelf 300 mm × 25 mm. Cut hole in back wall and fit two 225 mm × 225 mm air bricks with perforated zinc panels inside.**										
A010150A	cupboard front 38 mm 1.2 m × 2.4 mm	Each	20.00	556.00	–	90.06	646.06	611.60	–	99.07	710.67
A010150B	Extra over for hanging door on 75 mm butt hinges with bales catch and bow handle	Each	2.00	55.60	–	12.05	67.65	61.16	–	13.26	74.42
A010150C	set of three 200 mm × 25 mm shelves and one 300 mm × 25 mm shelf ..	Each	3.20	88.96	–	42.38	131.34	97.86	–	46.62	144.47
A010150D	cut hole in wall for two 225 mm × 225 mm air bricks and build in	Each	1.25	32.05	–	27.08	59.13	35.26	–	29.79	65.04
A010150E	two perforated zinc panels .	Each	0.30	8.34	–	7.75	16.09	9.17	–	8.53	17.70
A010150F	painting cupboard front both sides 5.75 sq.m	Each	4.60	128.85	–	9.44	138.29	141.74	–	10.38	152.12
A010150G	total cost	Each	31.35	869.80	–	188.76	1058.56	956.78	–	207.64	1164.42
A010152	**Stainless steel sink complete with single drainer fixed complete on brackets built into wall. Waste trap fitted and connected to waste pipe and discharging into external hopper head or gully. Mixer tap with swivel spout, service pipes measured separately:**										
A010152A	steel sink and drainer (PC 115.00) and fixing	Each	4.10	147.27	–	151.24	298.51	162.00	–	166.36	328.36
A010152B	plastic waste trap 40 mm ..	Each	0.90	32.33	–	9.26	41.59	35.56	–	10.19	45.75
A010152C	plastic waste pipe 40 mm (2.7 lin. m) long	Each	1.50	53.88	–	9.26	63.14	59.27	–	10.19	69.45
A010152D	hole through wall for plastic waste pipe 40 mm (2.7 lin. m) long and make good.......	Each	0.70	19.60	–	0.33	19.93	21.56	–	0.36	21.92
A010152E	mixer tap: swivel spout	Each	0.40	14.36	–	42.34	56.70	15.80	–	46.57	62.37
A010152F	total cost	Each	7.60	267.46	–	203.86	471.32	294.21	–	224.25	518.45

Small Works 2009		Unit	Labour Hours	Labour Net	Plant Net	Materials Net	Unit Net	Labour Gross	Plant Gross	Materials Gross	Unit Price
								(Gross rates include 10% profit)			
				£	£	£	£	£	£	£	£
A01	**GRANTWORK**										
A0101	**HOUSE RENOVATION**										
A010157	**1.7 m enamelled iron panelled bath complete with mixer tap, fixed spout, plug and chain, side panel and fixing. Waste trap fitted and connected, waste pipe discharging into external hopper head or gully. Service pipes measured separately:**										
A010157A	bath (PC 325.00) and fixing	Each	6.40	229.89	–	394.01	623.90	252.88	–	433.41	686.29
A010157B	plastic waste trap 40 mm ..	Each	0.90	32.33	–	9.26	41.59	35.56	–	10.19	45.75
A010157C	plastic waste pipe 40 mm dia × 2.7 m long............	Each	1.50	53.88	–	9.26	63.14	59.27	–	10.19	69.45
A010157D	hole through wall for plastic waste pipe 40 mm dia × 2.7 m long and make good .	Each	0.70	19.60	–	0.33	19.93	21.56	–	0.36	21.92
A010157E	plastic overflow pipe 19 mm dia × 0.6 m long	Each	0.65	23.35	–	1.49	24.84	25.69	–	1.64	27.32
A010157F	hole through wall for plastic overflow pipe 19 mm dia × 0.6 m long and make good .	Each	0.70	19.60	–	0.33	19.93	21.56	–	0.36	21.92
A010157G	total cost	Each	10.85	378.66	–	451.44	830.10	416.53	–	496.58	913.11
A010158	**550 mm × 400 mm white vitreous china lavatory basin complete with pair of taps, plug and chain. Waste trap fitted and connected to waste pipe discharging into external hopper-head or gully. Service pipes measured separately:**										
A010158A	lavatory basin (PC 85:00) and fixing	Each	4.80	172.42	–	126.22	298.64	189.66	–	138.84	328.50
A010158B	plastic waste trap 32 mm ..	Each	0.65	23.35	–	6.88	30.23	25.69	–	7.57	33.25
A010158C	plastic waste pipe 32 mm dia × 2.7 m long............	Each	1.25	44.90	–	7.87	52.77	49.39	–	8.66	58.05
A010158D	hole through wall for plastic waste pipe 32 mm dia × 2.7 m long and make good .	Each	0.70	19.60	–	0.33	19.93	21.56	–	0.36	21.92
A010158E	total cost	Each	7.40	260.27	–	185.33	445.60	286.30	–	203.86	490.16
A010159	**Extra over waste pipe in last three items for cutting and fitting end of waste pipe into existing 100 mm cast iron soil stack pipe, including cutting in and jointing 100 mm cast iron boss pipe connector:**										
A010159A	labour and material	Each	5.40	193.97	–	40.18	234.15	213.37	–	44.20	257.57

House Renovation Grants, Repairs and Alterations

Small Works 2009		Unit	Labour Hours	Labour Net	Plant Net	Materials Net	Unit Net	Labour Gross	Plant Gross	Materials Gross	Unit Price
								(Gross rates include 10% profit)			
				£	£	£	£	£	£	£	£
A01	**GRANTWORK**										
A0101	**HOUSE RENOVATION**										
A010160	**W.C. suite low level complete and fixing at upper floor level including 100 mm cast-iron bend, long arm and junction t existing stack pipe. Service pipes measured separately:**										
A010160A	W.C. suite complete (PC 115:00) and fixing	Each	5.40	193.96	–	170.26	364.22	213.36	–	187.29	400.64
A010160B	cast-iron bend 100 mm	Each	1.00	35.92	–	25.13	61.05	39.51	–	27.64	67.16
A010160C	cast-iron bend junction 100 mm	Each	2.00	71.84	–	38.86	110.70	79.02	–	42.75	121.77
A010160D	cut 100 mm cast-iron soil pipe to receive cast-iron bend junction	Each	3.40	122.13	–	–	122.13	134.34	–	–	134.34
A010160E	cut hole through one brick wall for 100 mm pipe and make good	Each	1.10	30.81	–	0.65	31.46	33.89	–	0.72	34.61
A010160F	plastic overflow pipe 19 mm (1 lin. m) long	Each	0.75	26.94	–	2.34	29.28	29.63	–	2.57	32.21
A010160G	cut hole through one brick wall for small pipe and make good	Each	0.70	19.60	–	0.33	19.93	21.56	–	0.36	21.92
A010160H	total cost	Each	14.35	501.21	–	237.68	738.89	551.33	–	261.45	812.78
A010161	**W.C. suite low level complete and fixing at ground level including jointing to clayware drain bend (measured separately). Service pipes measured separately:**										
A010161A	W.C. suite complete (PC 115:00) and fixing	Each	5.40	193.96	–	175.13	369.09	213.36	–	192.64	406.00
A010161B	plastic overflow pipe 19 mm dia × 1. m long	Each	0.75	26.94	–	2.34	29.28	29.63	–	2.57	32.21
A010161C	cut hole through one brick wall for small pipe and make good	Each	0.70	19.60	–	0.33	19.93	21.56	–	0.36	21.92
A010161D	total cost	Each	6.85	240.52	–	172.92	413.44	264.57	–	190.21	454.78
A010162	**227 litre plastic cold water cistern in loft space, including 13 mm ball valve 19 mm overflow pipe, tank bearers and hardboard tank casing. Service pipes measured separately:**										
A010162A	cistern 227 litre ball valve and float	Each	3.45	123.93	–	167.94	291.87	136.32	–	184.73	321.06
A010162B	plastic overflow pipe 19 mm dia × average 3.0 m long	Each	2.25	80.82	–	7.02	87.84	88.90	–	7.72	96.62
A010162C	cut hole through wall for plastic overflow pipe 19 mm dia × average 3.0 m long and make good	Each	0.70	19.60	–	0.33	19.93	21.56	–	0.36	21.92
A010162D	pair tank bearers 100 mm × 50 mm each 1.8 m long	Each	0.12	3.34	–	5.63	8.97	3.67	–	6.19	9.87
A010162E	hardboard tank casing	Each	2.15	59.77	–	18.71	78.48	65.75	–	20.58	86.33
A010162F	total cost	Each	8.67	287.46	–	199.63	487.09	316.21	–	219.59	535.80

Small Works 2009		Unit	Labour Hours	Labour Net	Plant Net	Materials Net	Unit Net	Labour Gross	Plant Gross	Materials Gross	Unit Price
								(Gross rates include 10% profit)			
				£	£	£	£	£	£	£	£
A01	**GRANTWORK**										
A0101	**HOUSE RENOVATION**										
A010163	**Cut through existing ceiling and trim joists to form opening for 750 mm × 750 mm trap door. Softwood lining with planted stop and architraves. Trap door comprises plywood face on 75 mm × 25 mm framed backing, hinged to lining and fitted with bow handle. All exposed woodwork painted:**										
A010163A	cut opening and trim joists .	Each	0.60	16.68	–	15.06	31.74	18.35	–	16.57	34.91
A010163B	trap door and lining 150 mm × 25 mm × 3.0 m long ..	Each	2.00	55.60	–	24.21	79.81	61.16	–	26.63	87.79
A010163C	architrave × 3.5 m.......	Each	0.45	12.51	–	6.41	18.92	13.76	–	7.05	20.81
A010163D	bow handle	Each	0.25	6.95	–	6.47	13.42	7.65	–	7.12	14.76
A010163E	painting (0.85 m^2)	Each	0.80	22.40	–	1.82	24.22	24.64	–	2.00	26.64
A010163F	make good plaster	Each	0.35	8.55	–	0.68	9.23	9.41	–	0.75	10.15
A010163G	total cost	Each	4.45	122.70	–	54.64	177.34	134.97	–	60.10	195.07
A010166	**The following rates for water service pipes including bends, sockets and an average allowance of one tee (or junction) for every four linear metres of pipe. Holes through walls for pipes and making good plaster included, one hole for every four linear metres of pipe:**										
A010166A	galvanised steel water pipe 15 mm diameter including extra cost of tees and holes and through partition walls etc, all as described	m	1.10	39.52	–	9.04	48.56	43.47	–	9.94	53.42
A010166B	galvanised steel water pipe 20 mm diameter including extra cost of tees and holes and through partition walls etc, all as described	m	1.20	43.10	–	11.45	54.55	47.41	–	12.60	60.01
A010166C	copper water pipe 15 mm diameter including extra cost of tees and holes and through partition walls etc, all as described................	m	0.90	32.33	–	7.89	40.22	35.56	–	8.68	44.24
A010166D	copper water pipe 22 mm diameter including extra cost of tees and holes and through partition walls etc, all as described................	m	0.95	34.12	–	8.29	42.41	37.53	–	9.12	46.65
A010166E	polythene normal gauge water pipe 20 mm diameter including extra cost of tees and holes through partition walls etc, all as described ..	m	1.25	44.90	–	6.99	51.89	49.39	–	7.69	57.08
A010166F	polythene normal gauge water pipe 25 mm diameter including extra cost of tees and holes through partition walls etc, all as described ..	m	1.60	57.47	–	10.34	67.81	63.22	–	11.37	74.59

House Renovation Grants, Repairs and Alterations

Small Works 2009		Unit	Labour Hours	Labour Net	Plant Net	Materials Net	Unit Net	Labour Gross	Plant Gross	Materials Gross	Unit Price
								(Gross rates include 10% profit)			
				£	£	£	£	£	£	£	£
A02	**REPAIRS AND ALTERATIONS**										
A0201	**EXCAVATION**										
A020101	**Excavate by hand over site area, wheel 18 m, deposit in skip:**										
A020101A	average 300 mm deep	m²	1.86	38.78	–	–	38.78	42.66	–	–	42.66
A020102	**Excavate by hand for trenches to receive foundations, wheel 18 m, deposit in skip:**										
A020102A	not exceeding 1.0 m deep . .	m³	6.52	135.94	–	–	135.94	149.53	–	–	149.53
A020102B	exceeding 1.0 m deep and not exceeding 2.0 deep	m³	8.02	167.22	–	–	167.22	183.94	–	–	183.94
A020103	**Excavate by hand for basement, wheel 18 m, deposit in skip:**										
A020103A	not exceeding 1.0 m deep . .	m³	6.00	125.10	–	–	125.10	137.61	–	–	137.61
A020103B	exceeding 1.0 m deep and not exceeding 2.0 deep	m³	6.72	140.11	–	–	140.11	154.12	–	–	154.12
A020104	**Excavated material as filling to excavations, deposited and compacted by hand:**										
A020104A	in 250 mm layers	m³	2.00	41.70	–	–	41.70	45.87	–	–	45.87
A020105	**Extra over excavation for breaking up brickwork by hand:**										
A020105A	in old foundations.	m³	7.09	147.83	–	–	147.83	162.61	–	–	162.61
A020106	**Hire of skip, delivery to site, removing when full, disposal of contents, payment of tipping charges:**										
A020106A	size 4.5 m³.	m³	–	–	33.02	4.87	37.89	–	36.32	5.36	41.68
A0202	**EARTHWORK SUPPORT AND HARDCORE**										
A020201	**In firm ground to opposing faces not exceeding 2.00 m apart; maximum depth not exceeding:**										
A020201A	1.00 m	m²	0.85	17.72	–	2.61	20.33	19.49	–	2.87	22.36
A020201B	2.00 m	m²	0.93	19.39	–	2.88	22.27	21.33	–	3.17	24.50
A020202	**In loose ground to opposing faces not exceeding 2.00 m apart; maximum depth not exceeding:**										
A020202A	1.00 m	m²	6.62	138.02	–	20.61	158.63	151.82	–	22.67	174.49
A020202B	2.00 m	m²	6.62	138.02	–	20.61	158.63	151.82	–	22.67	174.49
A020203	**Imported hardcore compacted to receive concrete to finished thickness:**										
A020203A	100 mm	m²	0.48	10.00	1.11	2.54	13.65	11.00	1.22	2.79	15.02
A020203B	150 mm	m²	0.72	15.01	1.33	3.90	20.24	16.51	1.46	4.29	22.26
A020203C	225 mm	m²	1.08	22.52	1.55	5.85	29.92	24.77	1.71	6.44	32.91

Small Works 2009		Unit	Labour Hours	Labour Net	Plant Net	Materials Net	Unit Net	Labour Gross	Plant Gross	Materials Gross	Unit Price
								(Gross rates include 10% profit)			
				£	£	£	£	£	£	£	£
A02	**REPAIRS AND ALTERATIONS**										
A0203	**CONCRETE**										
A020301	**Portland cement concrete in foundations:**										
A020301A	1:2:4 mix	m³	6.00	125.10	–	124.95	250.05	137.61	–	137.45	275.06
A020301B	1:3:6 mix	m³	6.00	125.10	–	108.90	234.00	137.61	–	119.79	257.40
A020302	**Concrete 1:3:6 oversite; thickness:**										
A020302A	100 mm	m³	9.00	187.65	–	108.90	296.55	206.42	–	119.79	326.21
A020302B	150 mm	m³	8.50	177.22	–	108.90	286.12	194.94	–	119.79	314.73
A020303	**Concrete 1:3:6 oversite; in patches not exceeding 4 sq.m in area, including jointing to existing, thickness:**										
A020303A	100 mm	m³	14.00	291.90	–	108.90	400.80	321.09	–	119.79	440.88
A020303B	150 mm	m³	13.50	281.47	–	108.90	390.37	309.62	–	119.79	429.41
A020304	**Extra over site concrete for:**										
A020304A	preparing to receive asphalt, tiling etc including extra cement.................	m²	0.45	9.38	–	2.18	11.56	10.32	–	2.40	12.72
A020304B	trowelling to smooth surface	m²	0.55	11.47	–	–	11.47	12.62	–	–	12.62
A020305	**Sprinkling surface with coarse carborundum at:**										
A020305A	1 kg per sq. m and lightly trowelling	m²	0.55	11.47	–	1.20	12.67	12.62	–	1.32	13.94
A020306	**Clean existing concrete or rendered floors:**										
A020306A	treat with application of silicate of soda solution	m²	0.30	6.25	–	0.34	6.59	6.88	–	0.37	7.25

House Renovation Grants, Repairs and Alterations

Small Works 2009		Unit	Labour Hours	Labour Net	Plant Net	Materials Net	Unit Net	Labour Gross	Plant Gross	Materials Gross	Unit Price
								(Gross rates include 10% profit)			
				£	£	£	£	£	£	£	£
A02	**REPAIRS AND ALTERATIONS**										
A0204	**PRECAST CONCRETE**										
A020401	**Reinforced concrete lintels cast in situ including reinforcement and formwork:**										
A020401A	113 mm × 150 mm......	m	0.75	19.23	–	6.82	26.05	21.15	–	7.50	28.66
A020401B	113 mm × 225 mm......	m	0.90	23.07	–	8.18	31.25	25.38	–	9.00	34.38
A020401C	225 mm × 150 mm......	m	1.30	33.33	–	11.45	44.78	36.66	–	12.60	49.26
A020401D	225 mm × 225 mm......	m	1.45	37.18	–	14.17	51.35	40.90	–	15.59	56.49
A020402	**Precast concrete lintels including bedding:**										
A020402A	113 mm × 150 mm......	m	0.45	11.53	–	11.77	23.30	12.68	–	12.95	25.63
A020402B	113 mm × 225 mm......	m	0.65	16.67	–	17.64	34.31	18.34	–	19.40	37.74
A020402C	225 mm × 150 mm......	m	0.85	21.79	–	25.30	47.09	23.97	–	27.83	51.80
A020402D	225 mm × 225 mm......	m	1.10	28.20	–	39.72	67.92	31.02	–	43.69	74.71
A020403	**Needle through 225 mm brickwork with 150 mm × 100 mm shore with one pair Acrow or other adjustable struts to every linear metre or part thereof (maximum span 2.70 m). Cut out and remove defective lintel. Supply, hoist and build in precast reinforced concrete lintel and make good all brickwork and plaster disturbed:**										
A020403A	225 mm × 150 mm lintel .	m	4.85	124.35	5.18	25.30	154.83	136.79	5.70	27.83	170.31
A020403B	225 mm × 225 mm lintel .	m	5.10	130.77	5.18	39.72	175.67	143.85	5.70	43.69	193.24
A020404	**Cut away triangular area of brickwork above lintel. Cut out and remove defective lintel. Supply, hoist and build in precast reinforced concrete lintel, rebuild brickwork over, including facing bricks to match existing, and make good internal plaster:**										
A020404A	225 mm × 225 mm lintel .	m	10.20	261.53	–	28.60	290.13	287.68	–	31.46	319.14
A020404B	225 mm × 338 mm lintel .	m	14.50	371.78	–	38.49	410.27	408.96	–	42.34	451.30
A020405	**Take out stone or concrete sill. Supply and build in cast concrete sill including all making good:**										
A020405A	225 mm × 75 mm	m	1.10	28.21	–	17.73	45.94	31.03	–	19.50	50.53
A020406	**Pier caps:**										
A020406A	300 mm × 300 mm × 75 mm for 225 mm piers...	Each	1.00	25.64	–	19.34	44.98	28.20	–	21.27	49.48
A020406B	400 mm × 400 mm × 75 mm for 338 mm piers...	Each	1.30	33.34	–	27.77	61.11	36.67	–	30.55	67.22

Small Works 2009		Unit	Labour Hours	Labour Net	Plant Net	Materials Net	Unit Net	Labour Gross	Plant Gross	Materials Gross	Unit Price
								(Gross rates include 10% profit)			
				£	£	£	£	£	£	£	£
A02	**REPAIRS AND ALTERATIONS**										
A0205	**BREAKING UP CONCRETE STEPS AND FLOORS**										
A020501	**Break up and remove old concrete steps:**										
A020501A	form new steps in concrete 1:3:6 including wrought formwork to risers and ends, surfaces of treads trowelled smooth	m³	19.00	396.15	–	148.00	544.15	435.77	–	162.80	598.57
A020502	**Break up and remove concrete floors, paving etc at ground level and load into skip:**										
A020502A	not exceeding 150 mm	m²	2.25	46.91	–	–	46.91	51.60	–	–	51.60
A020502B	150 mm-225 mm	m²	4.00	83.40	–	–	83.40	91.74	–	–	91.74
A020502C	225 mm-300 mm	m²	6.00	125.10	–	–	125.10	137.61	–	–	137.61
A020503	**Break up and remove reinforced concrete floors, pavings etc at ground level and load into skip:**										
A020503A	not exceeding 150 mm	m²	3.40	70.89	–	–	70.89	77.98	–	–	77.98
A020503B	150 mm-225 mm	m²	6.00	125.10	–	–	125.10	137.61	–	–	137.61
A020503C	225 mm-300 mm	m²	9.00	187.65	–	–	187.65	206.42	–	–	206.42
A020504	**Break up concrete paving 750 mm wide and 100 mm thick for new wall and remove. Excavate trench and part return, fill in and ram and remove remainder:**										
A020504A	Make good concrete paving. (Foundation concrete measured separately.)	m	2.85	59.42	–	9.58	69.00	65.36	–	10.54	75.90
A020505	**Hack up broken or sunken areas of concrete paving, spread and consolidate hardcore 150 mm, lay new concrete to falls, joint to existing including trowelling to form smooth surface:**										
A020505A	100 mm	m²	2.15	44.83	–	17.71	62.54	49.31	–	19.48	68.79
A020505B	150 mm	m²	2.45	51.08	–	24.03	75.11	56.19	–	26.43	82.62
A0206	**PAVINGS**										
A020601	**Hack surface of existing paving of floors and grout and render in:**										
A020601A	19 mm cement mortar 1:2.5	m²	1.00	24.43	–	3.15	27.58	26.87	–	3.47	30.34
A020602	**Hack off defective cement rendering to steps (treads and risers) and make out in:**										
A020602A	25 mm cement and sand 1:3 trowelled including nosings and arises	m²	2.50	61.07	–	3.27	64.34	67.18	–	3.60	70.77
A020603	**Clean and hack existing concrete surface to form key for:**										
A020603A	granolithic paving	m²	0.40	8.34	–	–	8.34	9.17	–	–	9.17
A020604	**Roughen and grout edge of existing concrete paving to new:**										
A020604A	100 mm	m	0.40	8.34	–	–	8.34	9.17	–	–	9.17
A020604B	150 mm	m	0.50	10.43	–	–	10.43	11.47	–	–	11.47

House Renovation Grants, Repairs and Alterations

Small Works 2009		Unit	Labour Hours	Labour Net	Plant Net	Materials Net	Unit Net	Labour Gross	Plant Gross	Materials Gross	Unit Price
								(Gross rates include 10% profit)			
				£	£	£	£	£	£	£	£
A02	**REPAIRS AND ALTERATIONS**										
A0207	**BREAKING OUT REINFORCED CONCRETE**										
A020701	**Breaking up reinforced concrete:**										
A020701A	walls, columns, beams, suspended floors or roofs and loading into skip	m³	27.00	562.95	–	–	562.95	619.25	–	–	619.25
A020702	**Cutting holes through concrete for pipes, bars etc, per 25 mm depth of cut and making good:**										
A020702A	area not exceeding 0.003 sq.m..................	Each	0.20	4.17	–	0.65	4.82	4.59	–	0.72	5.30
A020702B	0.003–0.023 sq.m.........	Each	0.40	8.34	–	0.87	9.21	9.17	–	0.96	10.13
A020703	**Cutting holes through reinforced concrete for pipes, bars etc, per 25 mm depth of cut and making good:**										
A020703A	area not exceeding 0.003 sq.m..................	Each	0.30	6.26	–	0.65	6.91	6.89	–	0.72	7.60
A020703B	0.003–0.023 sq.m.........	Each	0.60	12.51	–	0.87	13.38	13.76	–	0.96	14.72
A0208	**CONCRETE CURBS AND CHANNELS**										
A020801	**Forming concrete 1:2:4 curbs and channels including all necessary formwork but excluding excavation:**										
A020801A	average 0.047 sq.m sectional area	m	1.00	24.43	–	5.89	30.32	26.87	–	6.48	33.35
A0209	**WORKS TO CHIMNEYS**										
A020901	**Demolishing brickwork, any height, cleaning sound whole bricks to:**										
A020901A	reuse and remove remainder	m³	9.50	243.58	–	–	243.58	267.94	–	–	267.94
A020902	**Collect, clean and stack bricks for reuse:**										
A020902A	lime mortar	1000	14.00	358.96	–	–	358.96	394.86	–	–	394.86
A020902B	compo mortar...........	1000	17.00	435.88	–	–	435.88	479.47	–	–	479.47
A020902C	cement mortar	1000	22.00	564.08	–	–	564.08	620.49	–	–	620.49
A020903	**Pulling down chimney stacks, clean sound whole bricks for reuse and remove; up to 9 m high or two storeys:**										
A020903A	lime mortar	m³	28.00	717.92	–	–	717.92	789.71	–	–	789.71
A020903B	cement mortar	m³	36.00	923.04	–	–	923.04	1015.34	–	–	1015.34
A020904	**Extra over last for each additional 3 m or storey height:**										
A020904A	lime mortar	m³	7.00	179.48	–	–	179.48	197.43	–	–	197.43
A020904B	cement mortar	m³	9.00	230.76	–	–	230.76	253.84	–	–	253.84

Small Works 2009		Unit	Labour Hours	Labour Net	Plant Net	Materials Net	Unit Net	Labour Gross	Plant Gross	Materials Gross	Unit Price
								(Gross rates include 10% profit)			
				£	£	£	£	£	£	£	£
A02	**REPAIRS AND ALTERATIONS**										
A0209	**WORKS TO CHIMNEYS**										
A020905	Rebuild single flue chimney in common bricks, PC £250:00 per 1000, in cement mortar 1:3, including building in 185 m dia socketed and rebated clay flue liners, BS 1181; up to 9 m or two storeys high; overall plan dimensions:										
A020905A	450 × 450 mm..........	m	2.84	72.82	–	60.82	133.64	80.10	–	66.90	147.00
A020905B	675 × 675 mm..........	m	7.07	181.27	–	114.20	295.47	199.40	–	125.62	325.02
A020907	Rebuild double flue chimney in common bricks, PC 250:00 per 1000, in cement mortar 1:3, including building in 185 m dia socketed and rebated clay flue liners, BS 1181; up to 9 m or two storeys high; overall plan dimensions:										
A020907A	450 × 750 mm..........	m	5.05	129.48	–	114.10	243.58	142.43	–	125.51	267.94
A020907B	675 × 975 mm..........	m	10.34	265.07	–	181.78	446.85	291.58	–	199.96	491.54
A020909	Take off loose chimney pot and reset including flaunching:										
A020909A	up to two storeys or 9 m high	Each	2.00	51.28	–	0.66	51.94	56.41	–	0.73	57.13
A020910	Take down and remove chimney pot, supply, set and flaunch new pot; up to two storeys or 9 m high:										
A020910A	300 mm pot..............	Each	2.50	64.10	–	30.18	94.28	70.51	–	33.20	103.71
A020910B	450 mm pot..............	Each	2.60	66.66	–	37.70	104.36	73.33	–	41.47	114.80
A020910C	600 mm pot..............	Each	2.70	69.22	–	54.48	123.70	76.14	–	59.93	136.07
A020911	Add to the foregoing for each additional storey or 3 m high:										
A020911A	300 mm pot..............	Each	0.27	6.92	–	–	6.92	7.61	–	–	7.61
A020911B	450 mm pot..............	Each	0.38	9.74	–	–	9.74	10.71	–	–	10.71
A020911C	600 mm pot..............	Each	0.50	12.82	–	–	12.82	14.10	–	–	14.10

House Renovation Grants, Repairs and Alterations

Small Works 2009		Unit	Labour Hours	Labour Net	Plant Net	Materials Net	Unit Net	Labour Gross	Plant Gross	Materials Gross	Unit Price
								(Gross rates include 10% profit)			
				£	£	£	£	£	£	£	£
A02	**REPAIRS AND ALTERATIONS**										
A0212	**BRICKWORK REPAIRS: DPCs: SUNDRIES**										
A021201	**Treating brick walls with silicone, or similar, damp-proof liquid:**										
A021201A	external	m²	0.22	5.64	–	0.90	6.54	6.20	–	0.99	7.19
A021202	**Cut out defective brickwork and reface with new facing bricks (PC 325.00 per 1000):**										
A021202A	cement mortar	m²	5.70	146.14	–	27.93	174.07	160.75	–	30.72	191.48
A021202B	lime mortar	m²	5.00	128.20	–	28.77	156.97	141.02	–	31.65	172.67
A021203	**Cut out defective brickwork and reface with single facing bricks (PC 325.00 per 1000):**										
A021203A	cement mortar	Each	0.50	12.82	–	0.52	13.34	14.10	–	0.57	14.67
A021203B	lime mortar	Each	0.35	8.98	–	0.52	9.50	9.88	–	0.57	10.45
A021204	**Rake out mortar and repoint:**										
A021204A	perished mortar	m²	0.86	22.05	–	0.53	22.58	24.26	–	0.58	24.84
A021204B	sound mortar	m²	2.15	55.12	–	0.53	55.65	60.63	–	0.58	61.22
A021205	**Cut out fractures in brickwork and build in new brickwork approximately 405 mm wide, 225 thick:**										
A021205A	cement mortar	m	3.60	92.30	–	17.04	109.34	101.53	–	18.74	120.27
A021205B	lime mortar	m	2.35	60.26	–	17.10	77.36	66.29	–	18.81	85.10
A021206	**Take down segmental arch and rebuild in facings (PC 325.00 per 1000) 225 mm high on face including centering:**										
A021206A	113 mm wide soffit.	m	6.00	153.84	–	11.94	165.78	169.22	–	13.13	182.36
A021206B	225 mm wide soffit.	m	7.80	199.99	–	13.54	213.53	219.99	–	14.89	234.88
A021207	**Cut opening through brick walls in cement mortar for doors, windows etc including all necessary shoring and making good:**										
A021207A	half brick walls	m²	1.75	42.47	0.39	14.77	57.63	46.72	0.43	16.25	63.39
A021207B	one brick walls	m²	3.50	84.95	0.78	26.12	111.85	93.45	0.86	28.73	123.04
A021207C	one and a half brick walls . .	m²	5.25	127.42	1.07	37.58	166.07	140.16	1.18	41.34	182.68
A021207D	two brick walls	m²	7.00	169.90	1.41	48.65	219.96	186.89	1.55	53.52	241.96
A021208	**Brickwork in common bricks (PC 250:00 per 1000) in gauged mortar in small areas, bonding to existing:**										
A021208A	half brick	m²	2.45	62.82	–	22.64	85.46	69.10	–	24.90	94.01
A021208B	one brick	m²	4.50	115.38	–	45.91	161.29	126.92	–	50.50	177.42
A021208C	one and a half brick	m²	6.75	173.07	–	69.60	242.67	190.38	–	76.56	266.94

Small Works 2009		Unit	Labour Hours	Labour Net	Plant Net	Materials Net	Unit Net	Labour Gross	Plant Gross	Materials Gross	Unit Price
									(Gross rates include 10% profit)		
				£	£	£	£	£	£	£	£
A02	**REPAIRS AND ALTERATIONS**										
A0212	**BRICKWORK REPAIRS: DPCs: SUNDRIES**										
A021209	**Damp-proof course in short lengths in existing walls including cutting out brickwork and building in with new bricks:**										
A021209A	half brick wide-two course slate	m	1.85	47.44	–	9.78	57.22	52.18	–	10.76	62.94
A021209B	half brick wide-bitumen felt.	m	1.55	39.74	–	5.69	45.43	43.71	–	6.26	49.97
A021209C	one brick wide and over-two course slate	m²	6.50	166.66	–	99.26	265.92	183.33	–	109.19	292.51
A021209D	one brick wide and over-bitumen felt	m²	5.30	135.89	–	54.05	189.94	149.48	–	59.46	208.93
A021210	**Cut, tooth and bond new brickwork to existing:**										
A021210A	half brick	m	0.55	14.10	–	2.38	16.48	15.51	–	2.62	18.13
A021210B	one brick	m	1.00	25.64	–	4.91	30.55	28.20	–	5.40	33.61
A021210C	one and a half brick	m	1.40	35.90	–	7.28	43.18	39.49	–	8.01	47.50
A021211	**Cut hole for pipes, brackets, fittings etc, through clinker concrete walls per 25 mm in depth of cut and make good:**										
A021211A	area n.e. 0.003 sq.m	Each	0.12	3.07	–	0.22	3.29	3.38	–	0.24	3.62
A021211B	exceeding 0.003 sq.m, n.e. 0.03 sq.m	Each	0.18	4.61	–	0.33	4.94	5.07	–	0.36	5.43
A021211C	exceeding 0.03 sq.m, n.e. 0.06 sq.m	Each	0.25	6.41	–	0.44	6.85	7.05	–	0.48	7.54
A021212	**Cut hole for pipes, brackets, fittings etc, through brickwork in lime mortar and make good:**										
A021212A	area n.e. 0.003 sq.m	Each	0.20	5.13	–	0.26	5.39	5.64	–	0.29	5.93
A021212B	exceeding 0.003 sq.m, n.e. 0.03 sq.m	Each	0.30	7.70	–	0.39	8.09	8.47	–	0.43	8.90
A021212C	exceeding 0.03 sq.m, n.e. 0.06 sq.m	Each	0.40	10.25	–	0.53	10.78	11.28	–	0.58	11.86
A021213	**Cut hole for pipes, brackets, fittings etc, through brickwork in cement mortar and make good:**										
A021213A	area n.e. 0.003 sq.m	Each	0.28	7.18	–	0.22	7.40	7.90	–	0.24	8.14
A021213B	exceeding 0.003 sq.m, n.e. 0.03 sq.m	Each	0.48	12.30	–	0.33	12.63	13.53	–	0.36	13.89
A021213C	exceeding 0.03 sq.m, n.e. 0.06 sq.m	Each	0.63	16.15	–	0.44	16.59	17.77	–	0.48	18.25

House Renovation Grants, Repairs and Alterations

Small Works 2009		Unit	Labour Hours	Labour Net	Plant Net	Materials Net	Unit Net	Labour Gross	Plant Gross	Materials Gross	Unit Price
								(Gross rates include 10% profit)			
				£	£	£	£	£	£	£	£
A02	**REPAIRS AND ALTERATIONS**										
A0212	**BRICKWORK REPAIRS: DPCs: SUNDRIES**										
A021214	**Cut horizontal chase in brickwork 112 mm deep for concrete floor or landing; chase width:**										
A021214A	100 mm	m	2.00	51.28	–	–	51.28	56.41	–	–	56.41
A021214B	125 mm	m	2.20	56.41	–	–	56.41	62.05	–	–	62.05
A021214C	150 mm	m	2.50	64.10	–	–	64.10	70.51	–	–	70.51
A021214D	200 mm	m	3.00	76.92	–	–	76.92	84.61	–	–	84.61
A021215	**Cut horizontal chase in fair faced brickwork 112 mm deep for concrete floor or landing; chase width:**										
A021215A	100 mm	m	3.00	76.92	–	–	76.92	84.61	–	–	84.61
A021215B	125 mm	m	3.30	84.61	–	–	84.61	93.07	–	–	93.07
A021215C	150 mm	m	3.75	96.15	–	–	96.15	105.77	–	–	105.77
A021215D	200 mm	m	4.50	115.38	–	–	115.38	126.92	–	–	126.92
A021216	**Reform brick jambs after cutting new opening in existing brickwork, in common bricks (PC 250:00 per 1000):**										
A021216A	half brick	m	2.00	51.28	–	2.70	53.98	56.41	–	2.97	59.38
A021216B	one brick	m	2.50	64.10	–	5.40	69.50	70.51	–	5.94	76.45
A021216C	one and a half brick	m	3.00	76.92	–	8.32	85.24	84.61	–	9.15	93.76

Small Works 2009		Unit	Labour Hours	Labour Net	Plant Net	Materials Net	Unit Net	Labour Gross	Plant Gross	Materials Gross	Unit Price
								(Gross rates include 10% profit)			
				£	£	£	£	£	£	£	£
A02	**REPAIRS AND ALTERATIONS**										
A0212	**BRICKWORK REPAIRS: DPCs: SUNDRIES**										
A021217	**Reform brick jambs after cutting new opening in existing brickwork, in facing bricks (PC 325.00 per 1000):**										
A021217A	half brick	m	2.70	69.22	–	3.65	72.87	76.14	–	4.02	80.16
A021217B	one brick	m	3.10	79.49	–	7.29	86.78	87.44	–	8.02	95.46
A021217C	one and a half brick	m	3.50	89.74	–	11.20	100.94	98.71	–	12.32	111.03
A021219	**Take out and rebed door or window frame:**										
A021219A	point externally and make good internally	m	0.55	14.11	–	0.39	14.50	15.52	–	0.43	15.95
A021220	**Rake out defective pointing around door or window frame and repoint in:**										
A021220A	cement mortar	m	0.45	11.54	–	0.39	11.93	12.69	–	0.43	13.12
A021220B	cement mortar but using mastic	m	0.60	15.38	–	0.67	16.05	16.92	–	0.74	17.66
A021222	**Take out existing fireplace including surround and hearth:**										
A021222A	small iron	Each	4.00	102.56	–	–	102.56	112.82	–	–	112.82
A021222B	large tiled	Each	5.15	132.05	–	–	132.05	145.26	–	–	145.26
A021222C	free standing	Each	3.20	82.05	–	–	82.05	90.26	–	–	90.26
A021223	**Take out and reset existing fireplace including surround and hearth:**										
A021223A	small iron	Each	10.00	256.40	–	3.16	259.56	282.04	–	3.48	285.52
A021223B	large tiled	Each	12.25	314.09	–	4.47	318.56	345.50	–	4.92	350.42
A021223C	free standing	Each	8.20	210.25	–	1.20	211.45	231.28	–	1.32	232.60
A021224	**Fix only new fireplace including surround and hearth:**										
A021224A	small iron	Each	8.50	217.94	–	3.16	221.10	239.73	–	3.48	243.21
A021224B	large tiled	Each	10.65	273.06	–	4.47	277.53	300.37	–	4.92	305.28
A021224C	free standing	Each	4.70	120.51	–	1.20	121.71	132.56	–	1.32	133.88
A021225	**Take out existing fireplace and fix only solid brick back with fine concrete behind:**										
A021225A	fix tiled surround and tiled hearth (cost of interior, surround, hearth tiles and fret NOT included)	Each	13.00	333.32	–	2.94	336.26	366.65	–	3.23	369.89

House Renovation Grants, Repairs and Alterations

Small Works 2009		Unit	Labour Hours	Labour Net	Plant Net	Materials Net	Unit Net	Labour Gross	Plant Gross	Materials Gross	Unit Price
								(Gross rates include 10% profit)			
				£	£	£	£	£	£	£	£
A02	**REPAIRS AND ALTERATIONS**										
A0212	**BRICKWORK REPAIRS: DPCs: SUNDRIES**										
A021226	**Remove small kitchen range, adapt opening for and supply and set:**										
A021226A	400 mm fire back and basket fire and fret, fill in and point.	Each	9.00	230.76	–	100.74	331.50	253.84	–	110.81	364.65
A021227	**Remove existing basket or other low fire and supply and fix to hearth:**										
A021227A	new 400 mm Allnight basket fire with enamelled front. Seal edges and make good all round	Each	8.00	205.12	–	100.47	305.59	225.63	–	110.52	336.15
A021228	**Galvanised iron air bricks built into wall as work proceeds:**										
A021228A	225 mm × 75 mm	Each	0.22	5.64	–	7.10	12.74	6.20	–	7.81	14.01
A021228B	225 mm × 150 mm	Each	0.30	7.69	–	13.17	20.86	8.46	–	14.49	22.95
A021229	**Terracotta air bricks built into wall as work proceeds:**										
A021229A	225 mm × 75 mm	Each	0.22	5.64	–	3.65	9.29	6.20	–	4.02	10.22
A021229B	225 mm × 150 mm	Each	0.30	7.69	–	5.56	13.25	8.46	–	6.12	14.58
A021229C	225 mm × 225 mm	Each	0.33	8.46	–	13.41	21.87	9.31	–	14.75	24.06
A021230	**Plaster louvre type air bricks into wall as work proceeds:**										
A021230A	225 mm × 75 mm	Each	0.20	5.13	–	2.71	7.84	5.64	–	2.98	8.62
A021230B	225 mm × 150 mm	Each	0.25	6.41	–	3.47	9.88	7.05	–	3.82	10.87
A021230C	225 mm × 225 mm	Each	0.30	7.70	–	5.25	12.95	8.47	–	5.78	14.25
A021231	**Add to the foregoing air brick items for cutting through existing brick wall (any thickness), building in and make good:**										
A021231A	225 mm × 75 mm	Each	0.28	7.18	–	0.39	7.57	7.90	–	0.43	8.33
A021231B	225 mm × 150 mm	Each	0.30	7.69	–	0.53	8.22	8.46	–	0.58	9.04
A021231C	225 mm × 225 mm	Each	0.35	8.97	–	0.66	9.63	9.87	–	0.73	10.59
A021232	**Add to the foregoing for cutting out and removing existing:**										
A021232A	225 mm × 75 mm	Each	0.10	2.56	–	–	2.56	2.82	–	–	2.82
A021232B	225 mm × 150 mm	Each	0.12	3.08	–	–	3.08	3.39	–	–	3.39
A021232C	225 mm × 225 mm	Each	0.15	3.85	–	–	3.85	4.24	–	–	4.24
A0214	**DENSE AGGREGATE CONCRETE BLOCK WALLS**										
A021401	**Dense aggregate concrete blocks in walls etc in composition mortar:**										
A021401A	rough both sides 100 mm slabs...................	m²	1.25	32.05	–	15.75	47.80	35.26	–	17.33	52.58
A021401B	fair face one side.........	m²	1.85	47.43	–	15.75	63.18	52.17	–	17.33	69.50
A021401C	fair face both sides........	m²	2.00	51.28	–	15.75	67.03	56.41	–	17.33	73.73

House Renovation Grants, Repairs and Alterations

Small Works 2009		Unit	Labour Hours	Labour Net	Plant Net	Materials Net	Unit Net	Labour Gross	Plant Gross	Materials Gross	Unit Price
								(Gross rates include 10% profit)			
				£	£	£	£	£	£	£	£
A02	**REPAIRS AND ALTERATIONS**										
A0216	**WOODWORK REPAIRS AND REMOVALS**										
A021601	**Remove timber and load into skip:**										
A021601A	roof timbers complete, including rafters, purlins, ceiling joists, plates and the like (measured flat on plan).	m²	0.37	7.71	–	–	7.71	8.48	–	–	8.48
A021601B	floor construction; ground floor level...............	m²	0.28	5.84	–	–	5.84	6.42	–	–	6.42
A021601C	floor construction; first floor level...................	m²	0.55	11.47	–	–	11.47	12.62	–	–	12.62
A021601D	floor construction; roof level	m²	0.77	16.05	–	–	16.05	17.66	–	–	17.66
A021601E	individual floor or roof members...............	m	0.30	6.26	–	–	6.26	6.89	–	–	6.89
A021601F	Extra for cutting off ends flush with wall...........	Each	0.50	10.43	–	–	10.43	11.47	–	–	11.47
A021601G	decayed or infected floor plates.................	m	0.40	8.34	–	–	8.34	9.17	–	–	9.17
A021601H	tilting fillet or roll.........	m	0.17	3.54	–	–	3.54	3.89	–	–	3.89
A021601I	fascia or barge board......	m	0.65	13.55	–	–	13.55	14.91	–	–	14.91
A021602	**Remove boarding, including withdrawing nails, and load into skip:**										
A021602A	softwood flooring; at ground floor level...............	m²	0.42	8.76	–	–	8.76	9.64	–	–	9.64
A021602B	softwood flooring; at first floor level...............	m²	0.68	14.18	–	–	14.18	15.60	–	–	15.60
A021602C	softwood flooring; at roof level...................	m²	0.80	16.68	–	–	16.68	18.35	–	–	18.35
A021602D	softwood flooring; at gutter level...................	m²	0.88	18.35	–	–	18.35	20.19	–	–	20.19
A021602E	chipboard flooring; at ground floor level...............	m²	0.17	3.54	–	–	3.54	3.89	–	–	3.89
A021602F	chipboard flooring; at first floor level...............	m²	0.42	8.76	–	–	8.76	9.64	–	–	9.64
A021602G	plywood flooring; at ground level...................	m²	0.25	5.21	–	–	5.21	5.73	–	–	5.73
A021602H	plywood flooring; at first floor level...............	m²	0.48	10.01	–	–	10.01	11.01	–	–	11.01
A021603	**Remove stud partition, softwood, including finishings both sides, and load into skip:**										
A021603A	solid...................	m²	0.50	10.43	–	–	10.43	11.47	–	–	11.47
A021603B	glazed, including removal of glass..................	m²	0.67	13.97	–	–	13.97	15.37	–	–	15.37
A021604	**Remove wall linings, including battening behind, and load into skip:**										
A021604A	plain sheeting...........	m²	0.33	6.88	–	–	6.88	7.57	–	–	7.57
A021604B	matchboarding..........	m²	0.45	9.38	–	–	9.38	10.32	–	–	10.32
A021605	**Remove ceiling linings, including battening behind, and load into skip:**										
A021605A	plain sheeting...........	m²	0.50	10.43	–	–	10.43	11.47	–	–	11.47
A021605B	matchboarding..........	m²	0.67	13.97	–	–	13.97	15.37	–	–	15.37

House Renovation Grants, Repairs and Alterations

Small Works 2009		Unit	Labour Hours	Labour Net	Plant Net	Materials Net	Unit Net	Labour Gross	Plant Gross	Materials Gross	Unit Price
								(Gross rates include 10% profit)			
				£	£	£	£	£	£	£	£
A02	**REPAIRS AND ALTERATIONS**										
A0216	**WOODWORK REPAIRS AND REMOVALS**										
A021606	**Remove mouldings and load into skip:**										
A021606A	skirtings, picture rails, dado rails, architraves and the like	m	0.12	2.50	–	–	2.50	2.75	–	–	2.75
A021606B	shelves, window boards and the like	m	0.35	7.30	–	–	7.30	8.03	–	–	8.03
A021607	**Remove door and load into skip:**										
A021607A	single	Each	0.45	9.38	–	–	9.38	10.32	–	–	10.32
A021607B	single with frame or lining..	Each	0.88	18.35	–	–	18.35	20.19	–	–	20.19
A021607C	pair.......................	Each	0.77	16.05	–	–	16.05	17.66	–	–	17.66
A021607D	pair with frame or lining....	Each	1.32	27.52	–	–	27.52	30.27	–	–	30.27
A021607E	Extra for taking out spring box	Each	0.83	17.31	–	–	17.31	19.04	–	–	19.04
A021608	**Remove window and load into skip:**										
A021608A	casement; with frame	Each	1.32	27.52	–	–	27.52	30.27	–	–	30.27
A021608B	double hung sash; with frame	Each	1.77	36.90	–	–	36.90	40.59	–	–	40.59
A021608C	pair; french with frame.....	Pair	4.40	91.74	–	–	91.74	100.91	–	–	100.91
A021609	**Remove staircase balustrade and load into skip:**										
A021609A	single straight flight	Each	3.85	80.27	–	–	80.27	88.30	–	–	88.30
A021609B	dogleg flight	Each	5.50	114.68	–	–	114.68	126.15	–	–	126.15
A021609C	handrail and brackets......	m	0.12	2.50	–	–	2.50	2.75	–	–	2.75
A021610	**Remove bath panels and load into skip:**										
A021610A	frame	Each	0.45	9.38	–	–	9.38	10.32	–	–	10.32
A021611	**Remove kitchen fittings and load into skip:**										
A021611A	wall units	Each	0.50	10.43	–	–	10.43	11.47	–	–	11.47
A021611B	floor units	Each	0.33	6.88	–	–	6.88	7.57	–	–	7.57
A021611C	larder units	Each	0.45	9.38	–	–	9.38	10.32	–	–	10.32
A021611D	built-in cupboards	Each	1.55	32.32	–	–	32.32	35.55	–	–	35.55
A021611E	pipe casings	m	0.33	6.88	–	–	6.88	7.57	–	–	7.57

Small Works 2009		Unit	Labour Hours	Labour Net	Plant Net	Materials Net	Unit Net	Labour Gross	Plant Gross	Materials Gross	Unit Price
								— (Gross rates include 10% profit) —			
				£	£	£	£	£	£	£	£
A02	**REPAIRS AND ALTERATIONS**										
A0216	**WOODWORK REPAIRS AND REMOVALS**										
A021613	**Erect temporary hoarding comprising second-hand timber posts, rails and struts and covered with second-hand close boarding or corrugated iron sheets and dismantle on completion:**										
A021613A	1.8 m high	m	2.75	66.90	–	12.36	79.26	73.59	–	13.60	87.19
A021613B	Extra for 0.75 m wide door .	Each	0.65	15.82	–	1.55	17.37	17.40	–	1.71	19.11
A021613C	Extra for pair of gates approximately 2.4 m wide overall	Each	2.10	51.10	–	4.62	55.72	56.21	–	5.08	61.29
A021614	**Enclose frontage to site with chestnut fencing with posts at 1.8 m intervals and dismantle on completion:**										
A021614A	1.2 m high	m	0.28	6.81	–	5.70	12.51	7.49	–	6.27	13.76
A021616	**Take up defective gutter boards and bearers, supply and fix:**										
A021616A	new.....................	m²	3.70	90.02	–	23.51	113.53	99.02	–	25.86	124.88
A021617	**Take off defective rounded wood rolls to flats, supply and fix:**										
A021617A	new.....................	m	0.22	5.35	–	2.08	7.43	5.89	–	2.29	8.17
A021618	**Renew roof timbers:**										
A021618A	100 mm × 50 mm	m	0.15	3.64	–	1.85	5.49	4.00	–	2.04	6.04
A021618B	125 mm × 50 mm	m	0.20	4.87	–	2.31	7.18	5.36	–	2.54	7.90
A021618C	150 mm × 50 mm	m	0.25	6.09	–	2.77	8.86	6.70	–	3.05	9.75

House Renovation Grants, Repairs and Alterations

Small Works 2009		Unit	Labour Hours	Labour Net	Plant Net	Materials Net	Unit Net	Labour Gross	Plant Gross	Materials Gross	Unit Price
								——— (Gross rates include 10% profit) ———			
				£	£	£	£	£	£	£	£
A02	**REPAIRS AND ALTERATIONS**										
A0216	**WOODWORK REPAIRS AND REMOVALS**										
A021619	**Take down defective timber, supply and fix new:**										
A021619A	175 mm × 31 mm hips and ridges..................	m	0.40	9.73	–	2.08	11.81	10.70	–	2.29	12.99
A021619B	150 mm × 25 mm fascia .	m	0.40	9.74	–	4.07	13.81	10.71	–	4.48	15.19
A021619C	225 mm × 19 mm soffit and bearers.................	m	0.60	14.59	–	5.96	20.55	16.05	–	6.56	22.61
A021620	**Take off front gate, remove defective 150 mm × 150 mm timber posts; grub up concrete, supply new post approximately 1.5 m long, set in new concrete and rehang gate:**										
A021620A	creosoted fir post.........	Each	3.00	72.99	–	24.61	97.60	80.29	–	27.07	107.36
A021620B	oak post................	Each	3.25	79.07	–	91.39	170.46	86.98	–	100.53	187.51
A021621	**Excavate for and bolt to wood gate post:**										
A021621A	a concrete or oak spur set in concrete................	Each	2.00	48.66	–	43.48	92.14	53.53	–	47.83	101.35
A021623	**Take down and remove all temporary weatherproofing, e.g. polythene sheet, hardboard, chipboard and the like, together with all associated timber work to windows and doors:**										
A021623A	make good all existing joinery work including withdrawing all nails	m²	1.20	29.20	–	–	29.20	32.12	–	–	32.12
A021624	**Take down and remove all galvanised iron sheet (or corrugated asbestos) covering:**										
A021624A	including all timber backings and make good..........	m²	1.70	41.36	–	–	41.36	45.50	–	–	45.50
A021626	**Temporary screens comprising:**										
A021626A	100 mm × 50 mm framing lined both sides with building paper	m²	0.26	6.32	–	6.64	12.96	6.95	–	7.30	14.26
A021626B	100 mm × 50 mm framing lined one side with 19 mm matchboard..............	m²	0.60	14.60	–	30.48	45.08	16.06	–	33.53	49.59
A021626C	50 mm × 50 mm framing lined one side with hardboard	m²	0.45	10.95	–	5.65	16.60	12.05	–	6.22	18.26
A021628	**Strut up ceiling floor to ceiling and remove struts on completion:**										
A021628A	average 2.6 m...........	m	1.10	26.76	2.59	–	29.35	29.44	2.85	–	32.29
A021630	**Strut and support window openings; area of window:**										
A021630A	1.0 sq.m	Each	0.45	10.95	–	1.29	12.24	12.05	–	1.42	13.46
A021630B	1.5 sq.m	Each	0.50	12.16	–	1.51	13.67	13.38	–	1.66	15.04
A021630C	2.0 sq.m	Each	0.55	13.38	–	1.68	15.06	14.72	–	1.85	16.57

Small Works 2009		Unit	Labour Hours	Labour Net	Plant Net	Materials Net	Unit Net	Labour Gross	Plant Gross	Materials Gross	Unit Price
								(Gross rates include 10% profit)			
				£	£	£	£	£	£	£	£
A02	**REPAIRS AND ALTERATIONS**										
A0216	**WOODWORK REPAIRS AND REMOVALS**										
A021631	**Remove all grease and dirt from existing flooring, remove all projecting lino nails or tacks, punch down all floor brads, resecure any loose boards, plane off and leave smooth:**										
A021631A	generally	m²	0.85	20.68	–	–	20.68	22.75	–	–	22.75
A021631B	in areas less than 1 sq.m . . .	m²	1.10	26.76	–	–	26.76	29.44	–	–	29.44
A021632	**Take up loose floor blocks and relay in mastic:**										
A021632A	single block	Each	0.35	8.51	–	0.20	8.71	9.36	–	0.22	9.58
A021632B	in patches up to six blocks .	Each	0.22	5.35	–	0.41	5.76	5.89	–	0.45	6.34
A021633	**Smooth hardwood floor:**										
A021633A	with electric sanding machine	m²	1.00	24.33	–	–	24.33	26.76	–	–	26.76
A021634	**Take off existing skirting:**										
A021634A	replug grounds and refix skirting	m	0.36	8.76	–	–	8.76	9.64	–	–	9.64
A021635	**Take off existing softwood skirting, supply and fix new:**										
A021635A	25 mm × 150 mm	m	0.50	12.16	–	7.34	19.50	13.38	–	8.07	21.45
A021639	**Take up existing shrunk or worn flooring, any thickness, drawing all nails, relaying, cramping up, making up width or length with extra boarding of same thickness and cleaning off on completion. Areas exceeding 0.5 sq.m:**										
A021639A	plain edge	m²	0.90	21.90	–	2.27	24.17	24.09	–	2.50	26.59
A021639B	tongued and grooved	m²	1.10	26.76	–	2.44	29.20	29.44	–	2.68	32.12
A021640	**Remove damaged 25 mm softwood floor boards; clean joists and renew:**										
A021640A	plain edge	m²	0.85	20.68	–	24.50	45.18	22.75	–	26.95	49.70
A021640B	tongued and grooved	m²	1.00	24.33	–	25.26	49.59	26.76	–	27.79	54.55
A021640C	plain edge in small detached areas not exceeding 1.0 sq.m	m²	2.20	53.53	–	24.50	78.03	58.88	–	26.95	85.83
A021640D	tongued and grooved in detached area not exceeding 1.0 sq.m	m²	2.70	65.69	–	25.26	90.95	72.26	–	27.79	100.05
A021640E	plain edge exceeding 1.0 sq.m, not exceeding 2.5 sq.m	m²	2.00	48.66	–	24.50	73.16	53.53	–	26.95	80.48
A021640F	tongued and grooved exceeding 1.0 sq.m, not exceeding 2.5 sq.m	m²	2.50	60.82	–	25.26	86.08	66.90	–	27.79	94.69

House Renovation Grants, Repairs and Alterations

Small Works 2009		Unit	Labour Hours	Labour Net	Plant Net	Materials Net	Unit Net	Labour Gross	Plant Gross	Materials Gross	Unit Price
									(Gross rates include 10% profit)		
				£	£	£	£	£	£	£	£
A02	**REPAIRS AND ALTERATIONS**										
A0216	**WOODWORK REPAIRS AND REMOVALS**										
A021642	**New joists and softwood floor boarding, treating joists and underside of boards with creosote or other preservative:**										
A021642A	100 mm × 50 mm floor joists and 25 mm plain edge flooring	m²	1.00	27.80	–	28.84	56.64	30.58	–	31.72	62.30
A021644	**Oak strip flooring pinned and glued to existing softwood floor; clean off and wax polish:**										
A021644A	13 mm	m²	0.90	25.02	–	110.46	135.48	27.52	–	121.51	149.03
A021646	**Take down door, cut 13 mm off bottom edge and rehang:**										
A021646A	rehang	Each	1.60	39.09	–	–	39.09	43.00	–	–	43.00
A021647	**Take down architraves and reduce length by 13 mm and refix:**										
A021647A	one side	Set	0.55	13.44	–	–	13.44	14.78	–	–	14.78
A021647B	reduce length without removal	Set	0.50	12.22	–	–	12.22	13.44	–	–	13.44
A021648	**Take off skirting and refix:**										
A021648A	at higher level	m	0.30	7.33	–	–	7.33	8.06	–	–	8.06
A021649	**Hardwood border to hearth:**										
A021649A	mitred	Each	0.60	14.66	–	3.64	18.30	16.13	–	4.00	20.13
A021649B	add if sheet metal inner lining	Each	0.40	9.78	–	4.90	14.68	10.76	–	5.39	16.15
A021650	**Take down door, take out lining or frame, realign and refix:**										
A021650A	ease, adjust and rehang door; refix existing architraves and make good work disturbed .	Each	5.00	122.15	–	–	122.15	134.37	–	–	134.37
A021652	**Take down door:**										
A021652A	ease and rehang	Each	1.80	43.97	–	–	43.97	48.37	–	–	48.37
A021653	**Take down door, ease and rehang on new butt hinges; remove lock and furniture, supply and fit new lock and furniture:**										
A021653A	rim lock	Each	3.00	73.29	–	43.57	116.86	80.62	–	47.93	128.55
A021653B	mortice lock	Each	3.50	85.50	–	32.54	118.04	94.05	–	35.79	129.84
A021654	**Take down door, take apart and fit new panel or rail:**										
A021654A	rehang	Each	4.80	117.27	–	5.31	122.58	129.00	–	5.84	134.84
A021655	**Renew weatherboard:**										
A021655A	to external softwood door ..	Each	1.00	24.43	–	5.42	29.85	26.87	–	5.96	32.84

Small Works 2009		Unit	Labour Hours	Labour Net	Plant Net	Materials Net	Unit Net	Labour Gross	Plant Gross	Materials Gross	Unit Price
								(Gross rates include 10% profit)			
				£	£	£	£	£	£	£	£
A02	**REPAIRS AND ALTERATIONS**										
A0216	**WOODWORK REPAIRS AND REMOVALS**										
A021656	**Take down, ease and adjust and rehang:**										
A021656A	casement sash	Each	1.20	29.32	–	–	29.32	32.25	–	–	32.25
A021657	**Take off defective staff and parting beads:**										
A021657A	to double hung sash window and renew	Each	0.80	19.55	–	2.95	22.50	21.51	–	3.25	24.75
A021658	**Take out double hung sashes:**										
A021658A	ease, adjust and rehang, including new cords	Each	1.35	32.98	–	2.58	35.56	36.28	–	2.84	39.12
A021659	**Cut out defective glazing bars to skylights, windows, doors or greenhouses:**										
A021659A	renew.................	m	0.90	21.99	–	0.60	22.59	24.19	–	0.66	24.85
A021660	**Strengthening handrail and balusters including:**										
A021660A	renewing defective balusters	m	1.25	30.53	–	6.66	37.19	33.58	–	7.33	40.91
A021661	**Cutting out defective and worn portion of tread:**										
A021661A	piecing in new............	Each	0.80	19.55	–	1.31	20.86	21.51	–	1.44	22.95
A021662	**Take off and renew ironmongery fixed to softwood:**										
A021662A	strong pattern steel butts 75 mm	Pair	1.33	32.49	–	2.95	35.44	35.74	–	3.25	38.98
A021662B	strong pattern steel butts 100 mm.................	Pair	1.58	38.59	–	4.66	43.25	42.45	–	5.13	47.58
A021662C	steel washered brass butts 76 mm	Pair	1.33	32.50	–	6.42	38.92	35.75	–	7.06	42.81
A021662D	steel washered brass butts 102 mm.................	Pair	1.58	38.60	–	13.69	52.29	42.46	–	15.06	57.52
A021662E	brass rising butts 76 mm ..	Pair	1.61	39.33	–	9.85	49.18	43.26	–	10.84	54.10
A021662F	brass rising butts 102 mm .	Pair	1.86	45.44	–	19.17	64.61	49.98	–	21.09	71.07
A021662G	steel tee hinges 305 mm ...	Pair	1.13	27.61	–	6.13	33.74	30.37	–	6.74	37.11
A021662H	steel tee hinges 457 mm ...	Pair	1.22	29.80	–	13.75	43.55	32.78	–	15.13	47.91
A021662I	rim lock and furniture	Each	1.58	38.60	–	43.57	82.17	42.46	–	47.93	90.39
A021662J	mortice lock and furniture..	Each	1.84	44.95	–	32.54	77.49	49.45	–	35.79	85.24
A021662K	suffolk latch.............	Each	1.33	32.49	–	6.60	39.09	35.74	–	7.26	43.00
A021662L	bolt; straight; barrel 150 mm	Each	0.68	16.61	–	5.33	21.94	18.27	–	5.86	24.13
A021662M	bolt; straight; barrel 225 mm	Each	0.78	19.06	–	6.50	25.56	20.97	–	7.15	28.12
A021662N	casement stay with two pins 250 mm.................	Each	0.62	15.15	–	6.37	21.52	16.67	–	7.01	23.67
A021662O	casement fastener; wedge pattern..................	Each	0.72	17.59	–	6.12	23.71	19.35	–	6.73	26.08
A021662P	sliding sash fastener	Each	1.47	35.91	–	5.42	41.33	39.50	–	5.96	45.46
A021662Q	sash lift	Each	0.47	11.48	–	4.49	15.97	12.63	–	4.94	17.57

House Renovation Grants, Repairs and Alterations

Small Works 2009		Unit	Labour Hours	Labour Net	Plant Net	Materials Net	Unit Net	Labour Gross	Plant Gross	Materials Gross	Unit Price
								(Gross rates include 10% profit)			
				£	£	£	£	£	£	£	£
A02	**REPAIRS AND ALTERATIONS**										
A0217	**SHORING**										
A021701	**Erecting temporary DEAD shoring to form opening using three pairs 150 mm × 150 mm uprights and three 225 mm × 150 mm needles, braces and 225 mm × 225 mm base plates, holing brickwork for needles, all cartage, making good and removing on completion:**										
A021701A	assumed cubic volume of timber-0.09 cu. m.........	Item	70.00	1703.10	–	76.89	1779.99	1873.41	–	84.58	1957.99
A021701B	add to or deduct for every 0.03 cu. m more or less than 0.09 cu. m..............	Item	2.00	48.66	–	2.80	51.46	53.53	–	3.08	56.61
A021702	**Erecting temporary RAKING shoring including rakers, wall plate, needles, holing brickwork, cartage and making good on completion:**										
A021702A	assumed cubic volume of timber 0.30 cu. m.........	Item	32.00	778.56	–	25.16	803.72	856.42	–	27.68	884.09
A021702B	add to or deduct for every 0.03 cu. m..............	Item	3.00	72.99	–	2.80	75.79	80.29	–	3.08	83.37
A021703	**Erecting temporary FLYING shoring including horizontal shores, struts, wall plates, posts, needles, holing brickwork, cartage and making good on completion:**										
A021703A	assumed cubic volume of timber 0.60 cu. m.........	Item	80.00	1946.40	–	50.33	1996.73	2141.04	–	55.36	2196.40
A021703B	add to or deduct for every 0.03 cu. m more or less than 0.60 cu. m..............	Item	4.00	97.32	–	53.12	150.44	107.05	–	58.43	165.48
A021704	**Erecting permanent RAKING shoring as described above but left in position for an indefinite period:**										
A021704A	0.30 1 cu. m	Item	20.00	486.60	•–	53.12	539.72	535.26	–	58.43	593.69
A021704B	add to or deduct for each 0.03 cu. m or timber more or less than 0.30 cu. m..........	Item	2.00	48.66	–	5.59	54.25	53.53	–	6.15	59.68
A021705	**Erecting permanent FLYING shoring as described above but left in position for an indefinite period:**										
A021705A	0.60 cu. m..............	Item	54.00	1313.82	–	107.65	1421.47	1445.20	–	118.42	1563.62
A021705B	add to or deduct for every 0.03 cu. m more or less than 0.60 cu. m..............	Item	2.70	65.70	–	10.48	76.18	72.27	–	11.53	83.80

Small Works 2009		Unit	Labour Hours	Labour Net	Plant Net	Materials Net	Unit Net	Labour Gross	Plant Gross	Materials Gross	Unit Price
								(Gross rates include 10% profit)			
				£	£	£	£	£	£	£	£
A02	**REPAIRS AND ALTERATIONS**										
A0219	**FINISHES, REPAIRS AND RENEWALS**										
A021901	**Remove surface finishes. Floor:**										
A021901A	carpet and underlay	m²	0.13	2.71	–	–	2.71	2.98	–	–	2.98
A021901B	linoleum sheeting.........	m²	0.12	2.50	–	–	2.50	2.75	–	–	2.75
A021901C	screed	m²	0.50	10.43	–	–	10.43	11.47	–	–	11.47
A021901D	granolithic and screed	m²	0.67	13.97	–	–	13.97	15.37	–	–	15.37
A021901E	terrazzo or ceramic tiles; screed	m²	1.10	22.94	–	–	22.94	25.23	–	–	25.23
A021902	**Remove surface finishes. Wall:**										
A021902A	plasterboard	m²	0.45	9.38	–	–	9.38	10.32	–	–	10.32
A021902B	plaster	m²	0.22	4.59	–	–	4.59	5.05	–	–	5.05
A021902C	cement rendering; pebbledashing	m²	0.45	9.38	–	–	9.38	10.32	–	–	10.32
A021902D	tiling and screed	m²	0.55	11.47	–	–	11.47	12.62	–	–	12.62
A021903	**Remove surface finishes. Ceiling:**										
A021903A	plasterboard and skim including withdrawing nails	m²	0.33	6.88	–	–	6.88	7.57	–	–	7.57
A021903B	wood lath and plaster including withdrawing nails	m²	0.55	11.47	–	–	11.47	12.62	–	–	12.62
A021903C	suspended...............	m²	0.83	17.31	–	–	17.31	19.04	–	–	19.04
A021903D	plaster moulded cornice; per 25 mm girth..............	m	0.17	3.54	–	–	3.54	3.89	–	–	3.89
A021904	**Prepare surface to be sound and clean; apply two coats Unibond universal pva adhesive and sealer to receive plaster or cement rendering:**										
A021904A	walls; existing cement and sand base over 300 mm wide	m²	0.30	7.33	–	1.13	8.46	8.06	–	1.24	9.31
A021904B	walls; existing glazed tile base over 300 mm wide....	m²	0.24	5.86	–	0.77	6.63	6.45	–	0.85	7.29
A021904C	walls; existing painted base over 300 mm wide	m²	0.28	6.84	–	0.86	7.70	7.52	–	0.95	8.47
A021904D	walls; existing concrete base over 300 mm wide	m²	0.30	7.33	–	0.95	8.28	8.06	–	1.05	9.11
A021904E	ceilings; existing cement and sand base over 300 mm wide	m²	0.37	9.04	–	1.13	10.17	9.94	–	1.24	11.19
A021904F	ceilings; existing painted base over 300 mm wide....	m²	0.34	8.30	–	0.86	9.16	9.13	–	0.95	10.08
A021904G	ceilings; existing concrete base over 300 mm wide....	m²	0.37	9.04	–	0.95	9.99	9.94	–	1.05	10.99
A021905	**Hack down defective ceiling plaster and laths. Clean out old nails ready for:**										
A021905A	new laths or plasterboard ..	m²	0.85	20.77	–	–	20.77	22.85	–	–	22.85

House Renovation Grants, Repairs and Alterations

Small Works 2009		Unit	Labour Hours	Labour Net	Plant Net	Materials Net	Unit Net	Labour Gross	Plant Gross	Materials Gross	Unit Price
								(Gross rates include 10% profit)			
				£	£	£	£	£	£	£	£
A02	**REPAIRS AND ALTERATIONS**										
A0219	**FINISHES, REPAIRS AND RENEWALS**										
A021906	**Hack down defective ceiling plaster and clean laths ready for:**										
A021906A	new plaster	m^2	0.60	14.66	–	–	14.66	16.13	–	–	16.13
A021907	**Take down temporary boarded linings to ceilings:**										
A021907A	clean joists	m^2	0.40	8.34	–	–	8.34	9.17	–	–	9.17
A021908	**Expanded metal lathing to ceiling joists and render:**										
A021908A	float and set.	m^2	1.70	41.53	–	12.16	53.69	45.68	–	13.38	59.06
A021909	**Plaster and set on:**										
A021909A	existing laths.	m^2	1.25	30.53	–	4.55	35.08	33.58	–	5.01	38.59
A021910	**Plaster baseboard, scrim and set ceilings with:**										
A021910A	patent plaster	m^2	1.00	24.43	–	4.89	29.32	26.87	–	5.38	32.25
A021912	**Hack down defective ceiling plaster and fix plaster baseboard, scrim and set with patent plaster including jointing to existing:**										
A021912A	area n.e. 1 sq.m	m^2	2.00	48.86	–	4.89	53.75	53.75	–	5.38	59.13
A021912B	area 1-4 sq.m	m^2	1.40	34.20	–	4.89	39.09	37.62	–	5.38	43.00
A021913	**Make good at intersection of wall and ceiling plaster after replastering:**										
A021913A	wall or ceiling	m	0.55	13.43	–	0.23	13.66	14.77	–	0.25	15.03
A021913B	make good cracks in ceiling plaster	m	0.45	10.99	–	0.23	11.22	12.09	–	0.25	12.34
A021914	**Hack brick, stone or concrete walls to form key:**										
A021914A	for plaster	m^2	0.75	15.64	–	–	15.64	17.20	–	–	17.20
A021916	**Hack off wall plaster and rake out brick joints to form key:**										
A021916A	for new plaster	m^2	0.75	15.64	–	–	15.64	17.20	–	–	17.20

Small Works 2009		Unit	Labour Hours	Labour Net	Plant Net	Materials Net	Unit Net	Labour Gross	Plant Gross	Materials Gross	Unit Price
								(Gross rates include 10% profit)			
				£	£	£	£	£	£	£	£
A02	**REPAIRS AND ALTERATIONS**										
A0219	**FINISHES, REPAIRS AND RENEWALS**										
A021918	**Rake out joints of brickwork:**										
A021918A	to form key	m²	0.40	8.34	–	–	8.34	9.17	–	–	9.17
A021919	**Dub out uneven walls to receive:**										
A021919A	new plaster	m²	0.40	9.77	–	1.52	11.29	10.75	–	1.67	12.42
A021920	**Render and set:**										
A021920A	brick or block walls	m²	0.85	20.76	–	3.36	24.12	22.84	–	3.70	26.53
A021921	**Hack down defective wall plaster in small quantities; plaster and set including jointing to existing:**										
A021921A	area n.e. 1 sq.m	m²	1.75	42.75	–	4.67	47.42	47.03	–	5.14	52.16
A021921B	area 1-4 sq.m	m²	0.90	21.99	–	4.67	26.66	24.19	–	5.14	29.33
A021924	**Render and set brick walls:**										
A021924A	including jointing new to old and a small quantity of dubbing out.............	m²	1.10	26.87	–	6.00	32.87	29.56	–	6.60	36.16
A021926	**Make good cracks:**										
A021926A	in wall plaster	m	0.45	10.99	–	0.23	11.22	12.09	–	0.25	12.34
A021926B	in moulded cornice, per 25 mm girth of cornice	m	0.25	6.11	–	0.45	6.56	6.72	–	0.50	7.22
A021926C	around door and window frames and repoint........	m	0.40	9.77	–	0.23	10.00	10.75	–	0.25	11.00

House Renovation Grants, Repairs and Alterations

Small Works 2009		Unit	Labour Hours	Labour Net	Plant Net	Materials Net	Unit Net	Labour Gross	Plant Gross	Materials Gross	Unit Price
								(Gross rates include 10% profit)			
				£	£	£	£	£	£	£	£
A02	**REPAIRS AND ALTERATIONS**										
A0219	**FINISHES, REPAIRS AND RENEWALS**										
A021928	**Hack down and re-run plaster cornices per 25 mm girth of cornice:**										
A021928A	coved	m	0.25	6.11	–	0.45	6.56	6.72	–	0.50	7.22
A021928B	moulded	m	0.33	8.07	–	0.27	8.34	8.88	–	0.30	9.17
A021930	**Make good plaster around pipes:**										
A021930A	small pipes	Each	0.30	7.33	–	0.45	7.78	8.06	–	0.50	8.56
A021930B	large pipes..............	Each	0.33	8.06	–	0.45	8.51	8.87	–	0.50	9.36
A021932	**White glazed wall tiles fixed with adhesive, pointed in white cement grout to wall in small quantities in repairs:**										
A021932A	108 mm × 108 mm × 4 mm	m²	2.75	67.18	–	70.51	137.69	73.90	–	77.56	151.46
A021932B	152 mm × 152 mm × 5.5 mm	m²	2.38	58.14	–	47.67	105.81	63.95	–	52.44	116.39
A021934	**White glazed wall tiles bedded in cement mortar, pointed in white cement in small quantities in repairs:**										
A021934A	108 mm × 108 mm × 4 mm	m²	5.63	137.55	–	71.30	208.85	151.31	–	78.43	229.74
A021934B	152 mm × 152 mm × 5.5 mm	m²	5.00	122.15	–	48.47	170.62	134.37	–	53.32	187.68
A021936	**Coloured glazed wall tiles fixed with adhesive, pointed in white cement grout to wall in small quantities in repairs:**										
A021936A	108 mm × 108 mm × 4 mm	m²	2.75	67.18	–	38.82	106.00	73.90	–	42.70	116.60
A021936B	152 mm × 152 mm × 5.5 mm	m²	2.38	58.14	–	46.66	104.80	63.95	–	51.33	115.28
A021938	**Hack off glazed tiles to wall:**										
A021938A	in detached areas 2-5 sq.m.	m²	1.00	20.85	–	–	20.85	22.94	–	–	22.94
A021938B	in patches 0.5-2 sq.m	Each	2.50	52.13	–	–	52.13	57.34	–	–	57.34
A021938C	in single tiles in patches up to 0.5 sq.m	Each	0.30	6.26	–	–	6.26	6.89	–	–	6.89
A021940	**Take out broken cappings horizontal or vertical and renew:**										
A021940A	12 mm × 150 mm × 75 mm angle.............	Each	0.18	4.40	–	4.27	8.67	4.84	–	4.70	9.54
A021941	**Take out broken moulded cappings and renew:**										
A021941A	12 mm × 150 mm × 75 mm	Each	0.20	4.89	–	0.87	5.76	5.38	–	0.96	6.34

Small Works 2009		Unit	Labour Hours	Labour Net	Plant Net	Materials Net	Unit Net	Labour Gross	Plant Gross	Materials Gross	Unit Price
								(Gross rates include 10% profit)			
				£	£	£	£	£	£	£	£
A02	**REPAIRS AND ALTERATIONS**										
A0219	**FINISHES, REPAIRS AND RENEWALS**										
A021942	**Holes through wall tiling, any colour, for pipes, brackets etc and make good:**										
A021942A	small pipe	Each	0.28	5.84	–	–	5.84	6.42	–	–	6.42
A021942B	large pipe...............	Each	0.38	7.92	–	–	7.92	8.71	–	–	8.71
A021944	**Stripping loose tiles and cleaning:**										
A021944A	for reuse	m²	0.40	8.34	–	–	8.34	9.17	–	–	9.17
A021945	**Refixing only salvaged tiles with:**										
A021945A	adhesive	m²	2.25	54.96	–	1.93	56.89	60.46	–	2.12	62.58
A021948	**Provide and fix wall tiles with adhesive:**										
A021948A	150 mm × 150 mm × 6 mm	m²	2.25	54.97	–	48.00	102.97	60.47	–	52.80	113.27
A021949	**Hack off defective rendering to concreted areas; grout and render in cement mortar:**										
A021949A	19 mm thick	m²	1.00	24.43	–	0.19	24.62	26.87	–	0.21	27.08
A021950	**Hack off and renew cement rendered plinth including joints new to old:**										
A021950A	225 mm high............	m	0.30	7.32	–	0.67	7.99	8.05	–	0.74	8.79
A021952	**Cut out cracks in rendering and make good to existing:**										
A021952A	Snowcrete or rough cast...	m	0.80	19.54	–	0.63	20.17	21.49	–	0.69	22.19
A021952B	make good to Snowcrete or rough cast to match adjacent work around reset window and door frames	m	0.48	11.73	–	0.43	12.16	12.90	–	0.47	13.38
A021954	**Hack off defective rendering to walls, prepare for and cement render:**										
A021954A	two coats (plain face)......	m²	1.00	24.43	–	2.57	27.00	26.87	–	2.83	29.70
A021956	**Cement wash walls:**										
A021956A	one coat.................	m²	0.30	7.33	–	0.63	7.96	8.06	–	0.69	8.76
A021956B	two coats...............	m²	0.54	13.20	–	0.82	14.02	14.52	–	0.90	15.42
A021958	**Hack off broken cement rendering and renew rendering to:**										
A021958A	three-sided curb to gully ...	Each	0.90	21.98	–	0.48	22.46	24.18	–	0.53	24.71
A021960	**Hack off all loose stucco rendering, hack back brick or concrete to form key and render with cement mortar, trowelled smooth including reproducing all profiles and ruled joints:**										
A021960A	to match existing	m²	2.00	48.86	–	2.28	51.14	53.75	–	2.51	56.25
A021960B	in patches not exceeding 1 sq.m...................	m²	2.50	61.08	–	2.28	63.36	67.19	–	2.51	69.70

House Renovation Grants, Repairs and Alterations

Small Works 2009		Unit	Labour Hours	Labour Net	Plant Net	Materials Net	Unit Net	Labour Gross	Plant Gross	Materials Gross	Unit Price
								(Gross rates include 10% profit)			
				£	£	£	£	£	£	£	£
A02	**REPAIRS AND ALTERATIONS**										
A0229	**PLUMBING REPAIRS AND RENEWALS**										
A022901	**Remove gutterwork and pipework; gutterwork and supports:**										
A022901A	asbestos-free cement	m	0.35	12.57	–	–	12.57	13.83	–	–	13.83
A022901B	uPVC	m	0.38	13.65	–	–	13.65	15.02	–	–	15.02
A022901C	cast iron................	m	0.45	16.16	–	–	16.16	17.78	–	–	17.78
A022902	**Remove gutterwork and pipework; rainwater pipework and supports:**										
A022902A	asbestos-free cement	m	0.30	10.78	–	–	10.78	11.86	–	–	11.86
A022902B	uPVC	m	0.33	11.85	–	–	11.85	13.04	–	–	13.04
A022902C	cast iron................	m	0.40	14.37	–	–	14.37	15.81	–	–	15.81
A022903	**Remove gutterwork and pipework; rainwater shoe:**										
A022903A	uPVC	Each	0.07	2.51	–	–	2.51	2.76	–	–	2.76
A022903B	cast iron................	Each	0.10	3.59	–	–	3.59	3.95	–	–	3.95
A022904	**Remove gutterwork and pipework; rainwater head and support:**										
A022904A	uPVC	Each	0.37	13.29	–	–	13.29	14.62	–	–	14.62
A022904B	cast iron................	Each	0.45	16.16	–	–	16.16	17.78	–	–	17.78
A022905	**Remove gutterwork and pipework; soil and ventilation pipework and supports:**										
A022905A	uPVC	m	0.60	21.55	–	–	21.55	23.71	–	–	23.71
A022905B	cast iron................	m	0.67	24.07	–	–	24.07	26.48	–	–	26.48
A022905C	lead....................	m	0.75	26.94	–	–	26.94	29.63	–	–	29.63
A022906	**Remove gutterwork and pipework; service, waste and overflow pipework and supports:**										
A022906A	uPVC	m	0.13	4.67	–	–	4.67	5.14	–	–	5.14
A022906B	copper	m	0.17	6.11	–	–	6.11	6.72	–	–	6.72
A022906C	lead....................	m	0.17	6.11	–	–	6.11	6.72	–	–	6.72
A022906D	galvanised steel	m	0.17	6.11	–	–	6.11	6.72	–	–	6.72
A022908	**Remove sanitary fittings including taps and trap:**										
A022908A	W.C. suite	Each	0.42	15.09	–	–	15.09	16.60	–	–	16.60
A022908B	wash hand basin..........	Each	0.37	13.29	–	–	13.29	14.62	–	–	14.62
A022908C	bath	Each	0.52	18.68	–	–	18.68	20.55	–	–	20.55
A022908D	sink unit................	Each	0.37	13.29	–	–	13.29	14.62	–	–	14.62
A022908E	shower.................	Each	0.15	5.39	–	–	5.39	5.93	–	–	5.93

House Renovation Grants, Repairs and Alterations

Small Works 2009		Unit	Labour Hours	Labour Net	Plant Net	Materials Net	Unit Net	Labour Gross	Plant Gross	Materials Gross	Unit Price
								(Gross rates include 10% profit)			
				£	£	£	£	£	£	£	£
A02	**REPAIRS AND ALTERATIONS**										
A0229	**PLUMBING REPAIRS AND RENEWALS**										
A022910	**Remove sanitary fittings including taps, trap and service and waste pipes not exceeding 3.00 m girth:**										
A022910A	W.C. suite	Each	0.52	18.68	–	–	18.68	20.55	–	–	20.55
A022910B	wash hand basin.	Each	0.42	15.09	–	–	15.09	16.60	–	–	16.60
A022910C	bath	Each	0.62	22.27	–	–	22.27	24.50	–	–	24.50
A022910D	sink unit.	Each	0.42	15.09	–	–	15.09	16.60	–	–	16.60
A022910E	shower.	Each	0.22	7.90	–	–	7.90	8.69	–	–	8.69
A022911	**Remove bathroom toilet fittings:**										
A022911A	toilet roll holder.	Each	0.05	1.80	–	–	1.80	1.98	–	–	1.98
A022911B	soap dispenser	Each	0.05	1.80	–	–	1.80	1.98	–	–	1.98
A022911C	towel rail	Each	0.08	2.87	–	–	2.87	3.16	–	–	3.16
A022911D	towel holder	Each	0.17	6.11	–	–	6.11	6.72	–	–	6.72
A022911E	mirror.	Each	0.17	6.11	–	–	6.11	6.72	–	–	6.72
A022912	**Remove equipment: excluding any necessary draining down of system:**										
A022912A	cold water tank	Each	2.65	95.19	–	–	95.19	104.71	–	–	104.71
A022912B	hot water cylinder.	Each	1.33	47.77	–	–	47.77	52.55	–	–	52.55
A022912C	gas water heater	Each	4.40	158.05	–	–	158.05	173.86	–	–	173.86
A022912D	gas fire.	Each	2.20	79.02	–	–	79.02	86.92	–	–	86.92
A022912E	expansion tank	Each	2.00	71.84	–	–	71.84	79.02	–	–	79.02
A022914	**Cleaning out eaves and parapet gutters, removing rubbish:**										
A022914A	any height or position	m	0.13	4.67	–	–	4.67	5.14	–	–	5.14
A022916	**Cleaning out rain-water pipes, stack pipes, etc:**										
A022916A	any height or position	m	0.13	4.67	–	–	4.67	5.14	–	–	5.14
A022917	**Take down existing gutters, clean and refix to fascia or on brackets, seal joints with red lead putty:**										
A022917A	set to proper falls	m	0.70	25.14	–	3.66	28.80	27.65	–	4.03	31.68
A022918	**Take down and remove existing 100 mm cast iron gutters, provide and fix new gutters:**										
A022918A	half-round	m	1.10	39.51	–	24.69	64.20	43.46	–	27.16	70.62
A022918B	ogee	m	1.10	39.51	–	26.64	66.15	43.46	–	29.30	72.77
A022919	**Take down existing rainwater pipes and refix to walls:**										
A022919A	50 mm, 63 mm, or 75 mm .	m	0.75	26.94	–	0.22	27.16	29.63	–	0.24	29.88
A022920	**Take down and remove existing cast iron rain-water pipes and provide and fix new pipes:**										
A022920A	63 mm and 75 mm	m	1.10	39.51	–	46.25	85.76	43.46	–	50.88	94.34
A022920B	rainwater shoe (not extra over).	Each	0.50	17.96	–	28.00	45.96	19.76	–	30.80	50.56
A022922	**Cut out and reform caulked lead joints in cast-iron soil, vent or waste pipes:**										
A022922A	50 mm	Each	0.70	25.15	–	3.61	28.76	27.67	–	3.97	31.64
A022922B	75 mm	Each	0.80	28.74	–	5.41	34.15	31.61	–	5.95	37.57
A022922C	100 mm	Each	1.15	41.30	–	6.57	47.87	45.43	–	7.23	52.66

House Renovation Grants, Repairs and Alterations

Small Works 2009		Unit	Labour Hours	Labour Net	Plant Net	Materials Net	Unit Net	Labour Gross	Plant Gross	Materials Gross	Unit Price
								(Gross rates include 10% profit)			
				£	£	£	£	£	£	£	£
A02	**REPAIRS AND ALTERATIONS**										
A0229	**PLUMBING REPAIRS AND RENEWALS**										
A022924	**Cut and adapt existing iron soil pipe for a new W.C. by inserting a branch and bend or long junction, connect to pan trap and make good to wall:**										
A022924A	100 mm	Each	4.80	172.42	–	63.99	236.41	189.66	–	70.39	260.05
A022924B	Extra for access door	Each	–	–	–	41.98	41.98	–	–	46.18	46.18
A022942	**Renew broken stopcock box with hinged lid:**										
A022942A	127 mm × 127 mm × 76 mm	Each	0.50	17.96	–	10.77	28.73	19.76	–	11.85	31.60
A022942B	152 mm × 152 mm × 76 mm	Each	0.55	19.76	–	11.88	31.64	21.74	–	13.07	34.80
A022944	**Galvanised water tube including bends, sockets etc (tees excepted), in repairs to existing work; heavy weight:**										
A022944A	15 mm	m	0.66	23.71	–	7.22	30.93	26.08	–	7.94	34.02
A022944B	20 mm	m	0.75	26.94	–	8.64	35.58	29.63	–	9.50	39.14
A022944C	25 mm	m	0.80	28.74	–	12.55	41.29	31.61	–	13.81	45.42
A022946	**Galvanised water tube including bends, sockets etc (tees excepted), in repairs to existing work; medium weight:**										
A022946A	15 mm	m	0.66	23.71	–	6.22	29.93	26.08	–	6.84	32.92
A022946B	20 mm	m	0.75	26.94	–	7.36	34.30	29.63	–	8.10	37.73
A022946C	25 mm	m	0.80	28.73	–	10.55	39.28	31.60	–	11.61	43.21
A022948	**Cutting existing iron pipe for and inserting new tees:**										
A022948A	15 mm	Each	0.70	25.15	–	4.26	29.41	27.67	–	4.69	32.35
A022948B	20 mm	Each	0.85	30.53	–	5.79	36.32	33.58	–	6.37	39.95
A022948C	25 mm	Each	1.00	35.92	–	7.87	43.79	39.51	–	8.66	48.17
A022950	**Copper tubing including capillary bends etc (tees excepted), in repairs to existing work:**										
A022950A	15 mm	m	0.60	21.56	–	3.31	24.87	23.72	–	3.64	27.36
A022950B	22 mm	m	0.70	25.14	–	6.67	31.81	27.65	–	7.34	34.99
A022950C	28 mm	m	0.80	28.74	–	9.61	38.35	31.61	–	10.57	42.19
A022952	**Cutting existing copper pipes and inserting new capillary tees:**										
A022952A	15 mm	Each	1.00	35.92	–	1.78	37.70	39.51	–	1.96	41.47
A022952B	22 mm	Each	1.20	43.10	–	3.74	46.84	47.41	–	4.11	51.52
A022952C	28 mm	Each	1.50	53.88	–	8.47	62.35	59.27	–	9.32	68.59
A022954	**Polythene tubing including compression bends etc (tees excepted), in repairs t existing work:**										
A022954A	20 mm	m	1.20	43.10	–	4.09	47.19	47.41	–	4.50	51.91
A022954B	25 mm	m	1.40	50.29	–	5.85	56.14	55.32	–	6.44	61.75
A022954C	32 mm	m	1.70	61.07	–	9.76	70.83	67.18	–	10.74	77.91

Small Works 2009		Unit	Labour Hours	Labour Net	Plant Net	Materials Net	Unit Net	Labour Gross	Plant Gross	Materials Gross	Unit Price
								(Gross rates include 10% profit)			
				£	£	£	£	£	£	£	£
A02	**REPAIRS AND ALTERATIONS**										
A0229	**PLUMBING REPAIRS AND RENEWALS**										
A022956	**Cutting existing polythene pipes and inserting new compression tees:**										
A022956A	20 mm	Each	1.50	53.88	–	10.82	64.70	59.27	–	11.90	71.17
A022956B	25 mm	Each	1.70	61.07	–	16.38	77.45	67.18	–	18.02	85.20
A022956C	32 mm	Each	2.00	71.84	–	23.35	95.19	79.02	–	25.69	104.71
A022958	**Covering iron or copper pipes with hair felt and twine; in any position:**										
A022958A	up to 25 mm diameter	m	0.70	25.15	–	0.49	25.64	27.67	–	0.54	28.20
A022960	**Take off existing bib valve, prepare iron or copper pipes and provide and fit new bib valve:**										
A022960A	13 mm	Each	1.00	35.92	–	14.59	50.51	39.51	–	16.05	55.56
A022960B	19 mm	Each	1.20	43.10	–	19.53	62.63	47.41	–	21.48	68.89
A022961	**Cut into iron or copper pipes and fit new stopcock:**										
A022961A	13 mm	Each	1.30	46.70	–	8.28	54.98	51.37	–	9.11	60.48
A022961B	19 mm	Each	1.50	53.88	–	13.13	67.01	59.27	–	14.44	73.71
A022962	**Rewasher ball valve, tap or indoor stopcock:**										
A022962A	13 mm	Each	0.50	17.96	–	0.37	18.33	19.76	–	0.41	20.16
A022962B	19 mm	Each	0.60	21.56	–	0.37	21.93	23.72	–	0.41	24.12
A022964	**Take off existing copper trap to bath, basin or sink and provide and fit new plastic trap:**										
A022964A	32 mm	Each	1.20	43.10	–	7.42	50.52	47.41	–	8.16	55.57
A022964B	38 mm	Each	1.30	46.70	–	9.08	55.78	51.37	–	9.99	61.36
A022966	**Take off stopcock to iron or copper pipes both ends and provide and fit new stopcock:**										
A022966A	13 mm	Each	0.65	23.35	–	8.28	31.63	25.69	–	9.11	34.79
A022966B	19 mm	Each	0.85	30.53	–	13.13	43.66	33.58	–	14.44	48.03
A022966C	25 mm	Each	1.05	37.72	–	33.63	71.35	41.49	–	36.99	78.49
A022968	**Take off ball valve to iron or copper pipes and provide and fit new ball valve and ball float complete:**										
A022968A	13 mm	Each	0.50	17.96	–	12.01	29.97	19.76	–	13.21	32.97
A022968B	19 mm	Each	0.65	23.35	–	19.50	42.85	25.69	–	21.45	47.14
A022970	**Supply W.C. suite complete (PC £200:00) and connect to existing services:**										
A022970A	copper or iron	Each	5.80	208.34	–	280.50	488.84	229.17	–	308.55	537.72
A022971	**Supply low level W.C. suite (PC £115:00) and connect to existing services:**										
A022971A	copper or iron	Each	6.30	226.30	–	161.29	387.59	248.93	–	177.42	426.35

House Renovation Grants, Repairs and Alterations

Small Works 2009		Unit	Labour Hours	Labour Net	Plant Net	Materials Net	Unit Net	Labour Gross	Plant Gross	Materials Gross	Unit Price
								(Gross rates include 10% profit)			
				£	£	£	£	£	£	£	£
A02	**REPAIRS AND ALTERATIONS**										
A0229	**PLUMBING REPAIRS AND RENEWALS**										
A022972	**Remove defective W.C. pan and fix new (PC 60:00):**										
A022972A	make good all connections .	Each	3.90	140.09	–	60.00	200.09	154.10	–	66.00	220.10
A022974	**Take off defective seat to pedestal pan and supply and fix new plastic seat:**										
A022974A	single	Each	0.75	26.94	–	18.10	45.04	29.63	–	19.91	49.54
A022974B	double	Each	0.90	32.33	–	25.33	57.66	35.56	–	27.86	63.43
A022976	**Take off W.C. seat, renew joints to flush pipe including closet and outlet connection and pan:**										
A022976A	refix seat	Each	1.15	41.31	–	2.59	43.90	45.44	–	2.85	48.29
A022978	**Disconnect and remove 9 litre water waste preventer. Supply and fix new complete with ball valve and brackets (PC 70:00) and joint to existing overflow and service pipes:**										
A022978A	copper or iron	Each	3.20	114.95	–	105.18	220.13	126.45	–	115.70	242.14
A022980	**Disconnect ball valve to water waste preventer or storage tank:**										
A022980A	re-washer and clean out . . .	Each	1.45	52.09	–	0.37	52.46	57.30	–	0.41	57.71
A022981	**Unscrew ball to valve, supply and fit:**										
A022981A	new ball	Each	0.30	10.77	–	4.38	15.15	11.85	–	4.82	16.67
A022982	**Supply and fix flat back basin (PC 85:00) including taps, traps and wall brackets, connect to existing services:**										
A022982A	iron or copper	Each	5.80	208.34	–	119.21	327.55	229.17	–	131.13	360.31
A022984	**Supply and fix pedestal basin (PC 110:00) including taps, traps and wall brackets, connecting to existing services:**										
A022984A	iron or copper	Each	5.80	208.33	–	168.30	376.63	229.16	–	185.13	414.29
A022986	**Supply and fix cast iron white porcelain enamelled, rectangular 1700 mm long bat (PC 325:00) complete with taps and trap; connect to existing services:**										
A022986A	iron or copper	Each	5.80	208.34	–	394.01	602.35	229.17	–	433.41	662.59
A022988	**Clear blockage; flush out to:**										
A022988A	W.C. pans and traps	Each	1.25	44.90	–	–	44.90	49.39	–	–	49.39
A022988B	traps and waste pipes of baths, sinks, lavatory basins etc	Each	1.00	35.92	–	–	35.92	39.51	–	–	39.51

Small Works 2009		Unit	Labour Hours	Labour Net	Plant Net	Materials Net	Unit Net	Labour Gross	Plant Gross	Materials Gross	Unit Price
								——— (Gross rates include 10% profit) ———			
				£	£	£	£	£	£	£	£
A02	**REPAIRS AND ALTERATIONS**										
A0229	**PLUMBING REPAIRS AND RENEWALS**										
A022990	**Disconnect all pipework; take out and remove galvanised steel hot water tank; provide and install 114 litre copper indirect cylinder allow for cutting holes; tank connectors; make up and connections to existing pipework:**										
A022990A	complete	Each	3.00	107.76	–	285.48	393.24	118.54	–	314.03	432.56
A022992	**Empty water storage system and disconnect back boiler, supply and connect new boiler and test:**										
A022992A	back boiler (PC 150:00)	Each	4.00	143.68	–	194.25	337.93	158.05	–	213.68	371.72
A022994	**Clean and scale back boiler and ends of pipe:**										
A022994A	reconnect and recirculate water	Each	7.00	251.44	–	–	251.44	276.58	–	–	276.58
A022996	**Turn off water supply, disconnect all pipework, take out and remove galvanised steel cold water storage tank, provide and install plastic tank complete with ball valve, lid and insulation and allow for cutting holes, tank connectors, making up and all connections to existing pipework:**										
A022996A	182 litre	Each	6.30	226.30	–	195.20	421.50	248.93	–	214.72	463.65
A022998	**Cleaning and scouring out open-top storage tanks:**										
A022998A	any size and position	Each	7.40	265.81	–	–	265.81	292.39	–	–	292.39

House Renovation Grants, Repairs and Alterations

Small Works 2009		Unit	Labour Hours	Labour Net	Plant Net	Materials Net	Unit Net	Labour Gross	Plant Gross	Materials Gross	Unit Price
								—— (Gross rates include 10% profit) ——			
				£	£	£	£	£	£	£	£
A02	**REPAIRS AND ALTERATIONS**										
A0239	**GLAZING REPAIRS AND RENEWALS**										
A023901	**Hack out all types of broken glass:**										
A023901A	except plate glass.........	m²	2.34	65.54	–	–	65.54	72.09	–	–	72.09
A023901B	plate glass..............	m²	3.55	99.44	–	–	99.44	109.38	–	–	109.38
A023902	**Carefully take out all types of glass and set aside for re-use:**										
A023902A	except plate glass.........	m²	3.23	90.47	–	–	90.47	99.52	–	–	99.52
A023902B	plate glass..............	m²	4.68	131.09	–	–	131.09	144.20	–	–	144.20
A023904	**Remove old putty, paint rebate one coat oil colour ready to receive:**										
A023904A	new glass	m	0.16	4.48	–	0.18	4.66	4.93	–	0.20	5.13
A023905	**Glaze, sprig and putty to wood sashes; average 0.40 sq.m:**										
A023905A	sheet	m²	1.10	30.81	–	41.72	72.53	33.89	–	45.89	79.78
A023905B	obscured...............	m²	1.10	30.81	–	47.17	77.98	33.89	–	51.89	85.78
A023905C	wired cast	m²	1.20	33.61	–	44.32	77.93	36.97	–	48.75	85.72
A023905D	add for glazing to metal sashes	m²	0.40	11.20	–	0.15	11.35	12.32	–	0.17	12.49
A023908	**Wired cast glass in roof lights in panes:**										
A023908A	up to 0.70 sq.m...........	m²	0.90	25.21	–	44.32	69.53	27.73	–	48.75	76.48
A023908B	exceeding 0.70 sq.m	m²	1.00	28.01	–	44.32	72.33	30.81	–	48.75	79.56
A023910	**S.g. quality Float glass:**										
A023910A	6 mm	m²	3.50	98.04	–	67.20	165.24	107.84	–	73.92	181.76
A023911	**Bed edge of glass in:**										
A023911A	chamois leather	m	0.23	6.45	–	0.89	7.34	7.10	–	0.98	8.07
A023911B	velvet	m	0.17	4.77	–	0.25	5.02	5.25	–	0.28	5.52
A023912	**Remove temporary coverings to sashes:**										
A023912A	stopping nail holes etc.....	m²	1.10	30.81	–	–	30.81	33.89	–	–	33.89

Small Works 2009		Unit	Labour Hours	Labour Net	Plant Net	Materials Net	Unit Net	Labour Gross	Plant Gross	Materials Gross	Unit Price
								(Gross rates include 10% profit)			
				£	£	£	£	£	£	£	£
A02	**REPAIRS AND ALTERATIONS**										
A0241	**PAINTING AND DECORATING**										
A024101	**Brush down brick walls, plaster walls, or ceilings and apply two coats lime white on brick walls:**										
A024101A	new work...............	m²	0.33	9.24	–	0.22	9.46	10.16	–	0.24	10.41
A024101B	old work...............	m²	0.38	10.64	–	0.22	10.86	11.70	–	0.24	11.95
A024102	**Brush down brick walls, plaster walls, or ceilings and apply two coats emulsion paint on plaster:**										
A024102A	new work...............	m²	0.46	12.88	–	1.39	14.27	14.17	–	1.53	15.70
A024102B	old work................	m²	0.51	14.28	–	1.39	15.67	15.71	–	1.53	17.24
A024103	**Brush down brick walls, plaster walls, or ceiling and apply two coats emulsion paint on brick walls:**										
A024103A	new work...............	m²	0.58	16.25	–	2.08	18.33	17.88	–	2.29	20.16
A024103B	old work................	m²	0.63	17.65	–	2.08	19.73	19.42	–	2.29	21.70
A024104	**Wash down plaster surfaces, fill in minor cracks, nail holes etc with filler, bring forward paint as necessary ready for:**										
A024104A	new decoration..........	m²	0.20	5.60	–	0.31	5.91	6.16	–	0.34	6.50
A024106	**Prepare and apply oil colour on ceilings:**										
A024106A	one coat................	m²	0.27	7.56	–	0.64	8.20	8.32	–	0.70	9.02
A024106B	two coats...............	m²	0.55	15.40	–	1.32	16.72	16.94	–	1.45	18.39
A024108	**Prepare and apply oil colour on plaster walls:**										
A024108A	one coat................	m²	0.21	5.88	–	0.64	6.52	6.47	–	0.70	7.17
A024108B	two coats...............	m²	0.43	12.04	–	1.32	13.36	13.24	–	1.45	14.70
A024110	**Prepare and apply oil colour on brick walls:**										
A024110A	one coat................	m²	0.27	7.56	–	1.00	8.56	8.32	–	1.10	9.42
A024110B	two coats...............	m²	0.54	15.13	–	2.04	17.17	16.64	–	2.24	18.89

House Renovation Grants, Repairs and Alterations

Small Works 2009		Unit	Labour Hours	Labour Net	Plant Net	Materials Net	Unit Net	Labour Gross	Plant Gross	Materials Gross	Unit Price
								(Gross rates include 10% profit)			
				£	£	£	£	£	£	£	£
A02	**REPAIRS AND ALTERATIONS**										
A0241	**PAINTING AND DECORATING**										
A024111	**Wash down, touch up and apply two coats of oil colour to:**										
A024111A	general wood surfaces.....	m²	0.65	18.21	–	1.54	19.75	20.03	–	1.69	21.73
A024111B	add for each extra coat applied or deduct for one coat	m²	0.24	6.72	–	0.77	7.49	7.39	–	0.85	8.24
A024111C	window frames and sashes (measured over glass).....	m²	1.00	28.01	–	1.09	29.10	30.81	–	1.20	32.01
A024111D	add for each extra coat applied or deduct for one coat on window frames and sashes	m²	0.40	11.21	–	0.54	11.75	12.33	–	0.59	12.93
A024114	**Wash down, touch up and apply two coats of oil colour on surfaces:**										
A024114A	n.e. 150 mm girth.........	m	0.14	3.92	–	0.18	4.10	4.31	–	0.20	4.51
A024114B	150 mm-300 mm girth.....	m	0.24	6.73	–	0.45	7.18	7.40	–	0.50	7.90
A024114C	add for each extra cost applied or deduct for one coat n.e. 150 mm girt..........	m	0.07	1.96	–	0.09	2.05	2.16	–	0.10	2.26
A024114D	add for each extra cost applied or deduct for one coat 150 mm-300 mm girth.....	m	0.11	3.08	–	0.23	3.31	3.39	–	0.25	3.64

Small Works 2009		Unit	Labour Hours	Labour Net	Plant Net	Materials Net	Unit Net	Labour Gross	Plant Gross	Materials Gross	Unit Price
								(Gross rates include 10% profit)			
				£	£	£	£	£	£	£	£
A02	**REPAIRS AND ALTERATIONS**										
A0241	**PAINTING AND DECORATING**										
A024116	**Clean down and bring forward all bare patches and apply oil colour to metal:**										
A024116A	frames and sashes (measured over glass)	m²	1.11	31.09	–	1.54	32.63	34.20	–	1.69	35.89
A024116B	general surfaces over 300 mm girth	m²	0.69	19.33	–	1.09	20.42	21.26	–	1.20	22.46
A024116C	not exceeding 150 mm girth	m	0.30	8.40	–	0.18	8.58	9.24	–	0.20	9.44
A024116D	150 mm-300 mm girth	m	0.39	10.93	–	0.45	11.38	12.02	–	0.50	12.52
A024118	**Clean down and apply gloss oil to fireplace jambs, stoves, mantel registers and similar:**										
A024118A	one coat	Each	1.00	28.01	–	2.91	30.92	30.81	–	3.20	34.01
A024120	**Prepare and apply oil colour on water waste preventer and backboard:**										
A024120A	two coats	Each	0.55	15.40	–	0.50	15.90	16.94	–	0.55	17.49
A024120B	add if including overflow pipes	Each	0.45	12.60	–	0.50	13.10	13.86	–	0.55	14.41
A024122	**Clean and apply gloss oil on casement stays, fasteners, bolts, rim locks and sundry similar fittings:**										
A024122A	one coat	Each	0.20	5.60	–	0.09	5.69	6.16	–	0.10	6.26
A024124	**Prepare polished wood surfaces and repolish:**										
A024124A	existing	m²	2.10	58.82	–	0.77	59.59	64.70	–	0.85	65.55
A024124B	handrails	m	0.60	16.81	–	0.25	17.06	18.49	–	0.28	18.77
A024126	**Strip, body in and repolish:**										
A024126A	wood surfaces	m²	4.70	131.65	–	1.28	132.93	144.82	–	1.41	146.22
A024126B	handrail	m	1.10	30.81	–	0.32	31.13	33.89	–	0.35	34.24
A024128	**Prepare and wax polish:**										
A024128A	flooring	m²	0.50	14.00	–	0.77	14.77	15.40	–	0.85	16.25
A024132	**Strip paper from walls or ceilings, stop, size ready for new paper:**										
A024132A	first layer	m²	0.30	8.40	–	0.07	8.47	9.24	–	0.08	9.32
A024132B	each extra layer	m²	0.12	3.36	–	0.07	3.43	3.70	–	0.08	3.77
A024132C	first layer varnished paper	m²	0.60	16.80	–	0.07	16.87	18.48	–	0.08	18.56
A024132D	each extra layer varnished paper	m²	0.22	6.16	–	0.07	6.23	6.78	–	0.08	6.85
A024134	**Cut, trim and hang paper to:**										
A024134A	walls; woodchip	m²	0.26	7.28	–	0.66	7.94	8.01	–	0.73	8.73
A024134B	walls; standard	m²	0.26	7.28	–	3.15	10.43	8.01	–	3.47	11.47
A024134C	ceilings; lining	m²	0.30	8.40	–	0.46	8.86	9.24	–	0.51	9.75
A024136	**Wash down and apply masonry paint on external rendered walls:**										
A024136A	two coats	m²	0.53	14.85	–	1.35	16.20	16.34	–	1.49	17.82

House Renovation Grants, Repairs and Alterations

Small Works 2009		Unit	Labour Hours	Labour Net	Plant Net	Materials Net	Unit Net	Labour Gross	Plant Gross	Materials Gross	Unit Price
								——— (Gross rates include 10% profit) ———			
				£	£	£	£	£	£	£	£
A02	**REPAIRS AND ALTERATIONS**										
A0241	**PAINTING AND DECORATING**										
A024138	**Wash down and apply two coats of masonry paint on external rendered walls:**										
A024138A	Sandtex Matt............	m²	0.54	15.13	–	4.22	19.35	16.64	–	4.64	21.29
A024138B	Snowcem Matt	m²	0.42	11.77	–	0.54	12.31	12.95	–	0.59	13.54
A024144	**Wash down, touch up and apply oil colour externally to general wood surfaces:**										
A024144A	two coats external	m²	0.68	19.04	–	1.73	20.77	20.94	–	1.90	22.85
A024144B	add for each extra coat applied external	m²	0.27	7.57	–	0.86	8.43	8.33	–	0.95	9.27
A024146	**Wash down, touch up and apply oil colour on window frames and sashes (measured over glass):**										
A024146A	two coats external	m²	1.21	33.89	–	1.09	34.98	37.28	–	1.20	38.48
A024146B	add for each extra coat applied.................	m²	0.43	12.05	–	0.54	12.59	13.26	–	0.59	13.85
A024150	**Burn off paint to woodwork and prepare for priming:**										
A024150A	general surfaces	m²	0.80	22.41	–	–	22.41	24.65	–	–	24.65
A024151	**Strip paint with:**										
A024151A	paint remover	m²	0.50	14.01	–	0.16	14.17	15.41	–	0.18	15.59
A024152	**Prime and apply oil colour to putties after reglazing:**										
A024152A	two coats................	m	0.18	5.04	–	0.23	5.27	5.54	–	0.25	5.80

Small Works 2009	Unit	Labour Hours	Labour Net	Plant Net	Materials Net	Unit Net	Labour Gross	Plant Gross	Materials Gross	Unit Price
			£	£	£	£	£	£	£	£
A02 **REPAIRS AND ALTERATIONS**										
A0241 **PAINTING AND DECORATING**										
A024162 **Clean down, wire brush and bring forward all bare patches and apply oil colour on previously painted metalwork:**										
A024162A general surfaces; over 300 mm girth	m²	0.78	21.84	–	1.73	23.57	24.02	–	1.90	25.93
A024162B general surfaces; n.e. 150 mm girth	m	0.39	10.93	–	0.27	11.20	12.02	–	0.30	12.32
A024162C general surfaces; 150 mm- 300 mm girth	m	0.51	14.29	–	0.54	14.83	15.72	–	0.59	16.31
A024162D corrugated surfaces (measured flat)...........	m²	0.87	24.37	–	2.00	26.37	26.81	–	2.20	29.01
A024162E structural steelwork	m²	0.96	26.88	–	1.73	28.61	29.57	–	1.90	31.47
A024162F railings, balusters etc (measured flat overall).....	m²	0.87	24.36	–	1.73	26.09	26.80	–	1.90	28.70
A024162G stairs (measured overall) ..	m²	0.84	23.52	–	1.73	25.25	25.87	–	1.90	27.78
A024162H windows glazed doors in small panes.............	m²	1.98	55.46	–	1.18	56.64	61.01	–	1.30	62.30
A024162I windows glazed doors in medium panes	m²	1.74	48.74	–	1.09	49.83	53.61	–	1.20	54.81
A024162J windows glazed doors in large panes	m²	1.50	42.01	–	0.91	42.92	46.21	–	1.00	47.21
A024162K eaves gutters (inside and outside)................	m	0.51	14.29	–	1.18	15.47	15.72	–	1.30	17.02
A024162L rainwater pipes, soil pipes etc	m	0.51	14.28	–	0.64	14.92	15.71	–	0.70	16.41
A024162M pipes bars, straps etc, up to 150 mm girth	m	0.45	12.61	–	0.27	12.88	13.87	–	0.30	14.17
A024166 **Treating wood surfaces with two coats preservative:**										
A024166A sawn surfaces; creosote ...	m²	0.40	11.20	–	0.31	11.51	12.32	–	0.34	12.66
A024166B wrought surfaces; creosote	m²	0.38	10.64	–	0.21	10.85	11.70	–	0.23	11.94
A024166C sawn surfaces; Cuprinol clear....................	m²	0.40	11.21	–	1.48	12.69	12.33	–	1.63	13.96
A024166D wrought surfaces; Cuprinol clear....................	m²	0.38	10.64	–	0.98	11.62	11.70	–	1.08	12.78
A024166E sawn surfaces; Solignum ..	m²	0.38	10.64	–	1.85	12.49	11.70	–	2.04	13.74
A024166F wrought surfaces; Solignum	m²	0.36	10.08	–	1.22	11.30	11.09			

(Gross rates include 10% profit)

Small Works 2009		Unit	Labour Hours	Labour Net	Plant Net	Materials Net	Unit Net	Labour Gross	Plant Gross	Materials Gross	Unit Price
								(Gross rates include 10% profit)			
				£	£	£	£	£	£	£	£
A02	**REPAIRS AND ALTERATIONS**										
A0244	**MASONRY REPAIRS AND RENEWALS**										
A024401	**Take down masonry, clean and set aside:**										
A024401A	ashlar walling	m²	3.00	76.92	–	–	76.92	84.61	–	–	84.61
A024401B	cornices etc.	m	1.20	30.77	–	–	30.77	33.85	–	–	33.85
A024401C	arches	Each	0.80	20.51	–	–	20.51	22.56	–	–	22.56
A024401D	steps, sills etc	m	1.50	38.46	–	–	38.46	42.31	–	–	42.31
A024402	**Take down masonry, clean and reset:**										
A024402A	ashlar walling	m²	7.75	198.71	–	11.18	209.89	218.58	–	12.30	230.88
A024402B	cornices etc.	m	3.30	84.61	–	2.90	87.51	93.07	–	3.19	96.26
A024402C	arches	Each	2.20	56.41	–	5.10	61.51	62.05	–	5.61	67.66
A024402D	steps, sills etc	m	2.00	51.28	–	4.14	55.42	56.41	–	4.55	60.96
A024403	**Cut out decayed Portland (or similar) stone in facings of wall built in lime mortar in adjacent stones. Prepare for, supply and fix new stones:**										
A024403A	average 50 mm thick, point and clean down on completion	m²	3.00	76.92	–	153.36	230.28	84.61	–	168.70	253.31
A024403B	in separate stones	m²	3.60	92.31	–	169.53	261.84	101.54	–	186.48	288.02
A024404	**Rake out joints and repoint:**										
A024404A	ashlar stonework	m²	1.40	35.90	–	0.69	36.59	39.49	–	0.76	40.25
A024404B	squared rubble	m²	1.60	41.02	–	0.69	41.71	45.12	–	0.76	45.88
A024405	**Redress face of walling, where decayed, with picked face and repoint:**										
A024405A	generally	m²	8.00	205.12	–	0.97	206.09	225.63	–	1.07	226.70
A024408	**Take up and reset 50 mm thick York stone slabs, any size, in landings, hearths, cover stones, paving, etc:**										
A024408A	in lime mortar	m²	2.00	51.28	–	3.55	54.83	56.41	–	3.91	60.31
A024408B	in cement mortar	m²	2.40	61.54	–	2.94	64.48	67.69	–	3.23	70.93
A024410	**Cut and form toothing in old masonry for:**										
A024410A	new brick or stone	m²	2.00	51.28	–	–	51.28	56.41	–	–	56.41
A024411	**Take down and reset blocking courses, cornices, strings, plinths, apexes, kneelers etc:**										
A024411A	in lime mortar	m	1.20	30.77	–	0.66	31.43	33.85	–	0.73	34.57
A024411B	in cement mortar	m	1.40	35.90	–	0.54	36.44	39.49	–	0.59	40.08
A024414	**Take down and reset window sills, steps etc including cutting away and making good:**										
A024414A	in lime mortar	m	2.00	51.28	–	0.39	51.67	56.41	–	0.43	56.84
A024414B	in cement mortar	m	2.20	56.40	–	0.33	56.73	62.04	–	0.36	62.40
A024415	**Repair with 'granite chipping' concrete including cutting out to depth of at least 19 mm finish concrete fair and flush with original surface:**										
A024415A	treads.	m²	2.60	66.66	–	6.31	72.97	73.33	–	6.94	80.27
A024415B	landings.	m²	1.60	41.02	–	6.31	47.33	45.12	–	6.94	52.06

Small Works 2009		Unit	Labour Hours	Labour Net	Plant Net	Materials Net	Unit Net	Labour Gross	Plant Gross	Materials Gross	Unit Price
								(Gross rates include 10% profit)			
				£	£	£	£	£	£	£	£
A02	**REPAIRS AND ALTERATIONS**										
A0246	**ROOFING REPAIRS AND RENEWALS**										
A024601	**Remove coverings and load into skip; roof coverings:**										
A024601A	slates	m²	0.55	11.47	–	–	11.47	12.62	–	–	12.62
A024601B	nibbed tiles	m²	0.45	9.38	–	–	9.38	10.32	–	–	10.32
A024601C	corrugated metal sheeting .	m²	0.45	9.38	–	–	9.38	10.32	–	–	10.32
A024601D	underfelt and nails	m²	0.07	1.46	–	–	1.46	1.61	–	–	1.61
A024601E	three layers felt	m²	0.28	5.84	–	–	5.84	6.42	–	–	6.42
A024601F	sheet metal	m²	0.55	11.47	–	–	11.47	12.62	–	–	12.62
A024601G	metal flashings; horizontal .	m	0.22	4.59	–	–	4.59	5.05	–	–	5.05
A024601H	metal flashings; stepped . . .	m	0.28	5.84	–	–	5.84	6.42	–	–	6.42
A024601I	tile or slate battens, including withdrawing nails	m²	0.10	2.09	–	–	2.09	2.30	–	–	2.30
A024602	**Remove coverings, carefully handling and disposing by an approved method toxic or other special waste:**										
A024602A	asbestos cement sheeting . .	m²	2.20	56.41	–	–	56.41	62.05	–	–	62.05
A024603	**Stripping, cleaning and setting aside sound slates or tiles for re-use:**										
A024603A	slates	m²	0.40	8.34	–	–	8.34	9.17	–	–	9.17
A024603B	tiles.	m²	0.30	6.26	–	–	6.26	6.89	–	–	6.89
A024603C	cement slates	m²	0.40	8.34	–	–	8.34	9.17	–	–	9.17
A024604	**Stripping, cleaning and setting aside for removal:**										
A024604A	slates	m²	0.30	6.26	–	–	6.26	6.89	–	–	6.89
A024604B	tiles.	m²	0.24	5.00	–	–	5.00	5.50	–	–	5.50
A024604C	cement slates	m²	0.30	6.26	–	–	6.26	6.89	–	–	6.89
A024606	**Renew tile battens to 100 mm gauge:**										
A024606A	area n.e. 8.5 sq.m	m²	0.34	8.72	–	4.84	13.56	9.59	–	5.32	14.92
A024606B	exceeding 8.5 sq.m	m²	0.26	6.67	–	4.84	11.51	7.34	–	5.32	12.66
A024608	**Renew slate battens to 205 mm gauge:**										
A024608A	area n.e. 8.5 sq.m	m²	0.26	6.67	–	2.62	9.29	7.34	–	2.88	10.22
A024608B	exceeding 8.5 sq.m	m²	0.17	4.36	–	2.62	6.98	4.80	–	2.88	7.68
A024610	**Renew roofing felt:**										
A024610A	generally	m²	0.14	3.59	–	1.40	4.99	3.95	–	1.54	5.49
A024612	**Taking off and renewing single slates including clips; first slate:**										
A024612A	405 mm × 205 mm	Each	0.53	13.59	–	25.64	39.23	14.95	–	28.20	43.15
A024612B	510 mm × 255 mm	Each	0.56	14.36	–	36.67	51.03	15.80	–	40.34	56.13
A024612C	610 mm × 305 mm	Each	0.58	14.87	–	67.67	82.54	16.36	–	74.44	90.79
A024614	**Taking off and renewing second and subsequent slates; up to 30 no:**										
A024614A	405 mm × 205 mm	Each	0.22	5.64	–	25.64	31.28	6.20	–	28.20	34.41
A024614B	510 mm × 255 mm	Each	0.23	5.90	–	36.67	42.57	6.49	–	40.34	46.83
A024614C	610 mm × 305 mm	Each	0.24	6.15	–	67.67	73.82	6.77	–	74.44	81.20
A024616	**Taking off and renewing single tiles; first tile:**										
A024616A	clay.	Each	0.36	9.23	–	0.66	9.89	10.15	–	0.73	10.88
A024616B	concrete.	Each	0.36	9.23	–	0.65	9.88	10.15	–	0.72	10.87

House Renovation Grants, Repairs and Alterations

Small Works 2009		Unit	Labour Hours	Labour Net	Plant Net	Materials Net	Unit Net	Labour Gross	Plant Gross	Materials Gross	Unit Price
								(Gross rates include 10% profit)			
				£	£	£	£	£	£	£	£
A02	**REPAIRS AND ALTERATIONS**										
A0246	**ROOFING REPAIRS AND RENEWALS**										
A024618	**Taking off and renewing second and subsequent tiles; up to 50 no:**										
A024618A	clay.....................	Each	0.22	5.64	–	0.66	6.30	6.20	–	0.73	6.93
A024618B	concrete................	Each	0.22	5.64	–	0.65	6.29	6.20	–	0.72	6.92
A024619	**Taking off and renewing single blue asbestos slates; first slate:**										
A024619A	610 mm × 305 mm......	Each	0.37	9.49	–	2.26	11.75	10.44	–	2.49	12.93
A024620	**Taking off and renewing second and subsequent slates; up to 30 no:**										
A024620A	610 mm × 305 mm......	Each	0.22	5.64	–	0.21	5.85	6.20	–	0.23	6.44
A024621	**Cement mortar angle fillet to slate, tile or asbestos roof at abutment to walls or chimney stacks:**										
A024621A	1-3 no	m	0.40	10.25	–	0.33	10.58	11.28	–	0.36	11.64
A024622	**Strip roof slating, sort slates and reslate roof using 50% existing slates:**										
A024622A	405 mm × 205 mm......	m²	1.15	29.49	–	386.90	416.39	32.44	–	425.59	458.03
A024622B	510 mm × 255 mm......	m²	0.80	20.51	–	340.04	360.55	22.56	–	374.04	396.61
A024622C	610 mm × 305 mm......	m²	0.50	12.82	–	424.46	437.28	14.10	–	466.91	481.01
A024624	**Strip 267 mm × 165 mm plain roof tiles and retile using 50% existing tiles:**										
A024624A	clay.....................	m²	1.70	43.59	–	23.08	66.67	47.95	–	25.39	73.34
A024624B	concrete................	m²	1.70	43.59	–	22.83	66.42	47.95	–	25.11	73.06
A024626	**Take up old lead, any position or weight:**										
A024626A	set aside	m²	0.40	14.37	–	–	14.37	15.81	–	–	15.81
A024628	**Take up and relay lead to boarded flats:**										
A024628A	including dressing over rolls and drips with new bossed ends etc................	m²	4.30	154.46	–	–	154.46	169.91	–	–	169.91
A024629	**Redress lead flashings:**										
A024629A	rewedge and repoint	m	0.80	28.74	–	–	28.74	31.61	–	–	31.61
A024630	**Take up old zinc and remove from site:**										
A024630A	in any position	m²	1.00	35.92	–	–	35.92	39.51	–	–	39.51

Small Works 2009		Unit	Labour Hours	Labour Net	Plant Net	Materials Net	Unit Net	Labour Gross	Plant Gross	Materials Gross	Unit Price
								—— (Gross rates include 10% profit) ——			
				£	£	£	£	£	£	£	£
A02	**REPAIRS AND ALTERATIONS**										
A0246	**ROOFING REPAIRS AND RENEWALS**										
A024632	**Take up existing zinc and supply and lay new zinc including rolls, laps etc:**										
A024632A	0.50 mm thick............	m²	4.00	143.68	–	18.00	161.68	158.05	–	19.80	177.85
A024632B	0.65 mm thick............	m²	4.50	161.64	–	33.00	194.64	177.80	–	36.30	214.10
A024632C	0.80 mm thick............	m²	5.00	179.60	–	40.56	220.16	197.56	–	44.62	242.18
A024634	**Prepare zinc roofs for and supply and lay bituminised fabric bedded in bitumen and apply bitumen emulsion:**										
A024634A	two coats...............	m²	1.90	48.72	–	1.67	50.39	53.59	–	1.84	55.43
A024636	**Seal crack in holes in zinc or asphalt flats and apply bitumen waterproofer:**										
A024636A	two coats...............	m²	0.90	23.08	–	0.45	23.53	25.39	–	0.50	25.88
A024638	**Clean and treat defective sheet zinc:**										
A024638A	Rito, Matex or similar compound...............	m²	1.10	28.21	–	2.00	30.21	31.03	–	2.20	33.23
A024639	**Remove slates, take out defective box gutter linings or valleys and renew wood linings and line with zinc and replace slates:**										
A024639A	12G.....................	m²	8.00	287.36	–	59.02	346.38	316.10	–	64.92	381.02
A024640	**Labour and transport up to 5 miles each way, setting up and removing ladders:**										
A024640A	up to two storeys high.....	Job	2.36	41.70	6.61	–	48.31	45.87	7.27	–	53.14
A024640B	up to four storeys high.....	Job	2.86	52.13	6.61	–	58.74	57.34	7.27	–	64.61
A024640C	Extra over last two items if access is difficult e.g. one house in a terrace where there is no side entrance ...	Job	2.36	41.70	6.61	–	48.31	45.87	7.27	–	53.14
A024642	**Remove waterproofing finishes and load into skip:**										
A024642A	asphalt paving...........	m²	0.67	13.97	–	–	13.97	15.37	–	–	15.37
A024642B	asphalt roofing	m²	1.10	22.94	–	–	22.94	25.23	–	–	25.23
A024642C	asphalt skirting..........	m	0.17	3.54	–	–	3.54	3.89	–	–	3.89
A0250	**ROOFING REPAIRS BY SPECIALISTS**										
A025001	**Clean, prepare and apply DC500 roofing compound to:**										
A025001A	sound surfaces, asbestos, asphalt, concrete, felt, slate or tile	m²	0.55	11.47	–	6.26	17.73	12.62	–	6.89	19.50
A025002	**Clean, prepare and apply DC500 flexible roofing compound and fungicide solution**										
A025002A	to surfaces likely to support fungal or algae growth, asbestos, asphalt, concrete, felt, slate or tile	m²	0.60	12.51	–	6.70	19.21	13.76	–	7.37	21.13

House Renovation Grants, Repairs and Alterations

Small Works 2009		Unit	Labour Hours	Labour Net	Plant Net	Materials Net	Unit Net	Labour Gross	Plant Gross	Materials Gross	Unit Price
								(Gross rates include 10% profit)			
				£	£	£	£	£	£	£	£
A02	**REPAIRS AND ALTERATIONS**										
A0252	**DRAINAGE REPAIRS AND RENEWALS**										
A025201	**Break up 100 mm concrete paving and hardcore for excavation drain trench:**										
A025201A	not exceeding 600 mm wide	m	1.10	22.94	–	–	22.94	25.23	–	–	25.23
A025202	**Hand excavate trench for 100 mm drain including backfilling and carting away remainder including necessary earthwork support:**										
A025202A	average 0.5 m deep	m	1.44	30.02	–	–	30.02	33.02	–	–	33.02
A025202B	average 1.0 m deep	m	2.90	60.47	–	–	60.47	66.52	–	–	66.52
A025202C	average 1.5 m deep	m	5.16	107.59	–	–	107.59	118.35	–	–	118.35
A025203	**100 mm concrete bed and haunch to:**										
A025203A	pipe	m	1.10	22.93	–	17.75	40.68	25.22	–	19.53	44.75
A025204	**HepSeal clayware pipes, laid and jointed in short lengths:**										
A025204A	100 mm	m	0.50	12.21	–	6.08	18.29	13.43	–	6.69	20.12
A025205	**Make good 100 mm concrete paving and hardcore under, after drainwork:**										
A025205A	average 600 mm wide	m	1.30	27.10	–	6.54	33.64	29.81	–	7.19	37.00
A025206	**Cutting into brick side of exposed manhole and concrete benching for new branch drain and three quarter section channel, make good brickwork and benching:**										
A025206A	100 mm	Each	3.00	73.29	–	35.22	108.51	80.62	–	38.74	119.36
A025207	**Glazed clayware gully and grid 150 mm × 150 mm × 100 mm with 100 mm outlet join to drain:**										
A025207A	including necessary excavation and concrete bed	Each	2.40	58.63	–	45.55	104.18	64.49	–	50.11	114.60
A025208	**Concrete curb 100 mm outlet joint to drain:**										
A025208A	including necessary formwork	Each	1.25	30.54	–	6.97	37.51	33.59	–	7.67	41.26
A025209	**Demolish curb, disconnect and remove gully, supply and connect new gully and grid including work to concrete bed, new grid, rendering three sides and remake connection after rodding:**										
A025209A	150 mm × 150 mm × 100 mm	Each	6.00	146.58	–	55.63	202.21	161.24	–	61.19	222.43

Small Works 2009		Unit	Labour Hours	Labour Net	Plant Net	Materials Net	Unit Net	Labour Gross	Plant Gross	Materials Gross	Unit Price
								(Gross rates include 10% profit)			
				£	£	£	£	£	£	£	£
A02	**REPAIRS AND ALTERATIONS**										
A0252	**DRAINAGE REPAIRS AND RENEWALS**										
A025210	**Break up defective curb-surround to manhole and reform in:**										
A025210A	fine concrete splayed and rendered	Each	1.55	37.86	–	3.16	41.02	41.65	–	3.48	45.12
A025212	**Cut through external 225 mm brick wall and 150 mm concrete floor and connect to trap of pan at one end and existing pipe at the other end:**										
A025212A	102 mm bend	Each	7.50	183.22	–	38.78	222.00	201.54	–	42.66	244.20
A025214	**Form new manhole on line of existing drain with 150 mm concrete base, 225 mm brick walls, cover and frame. Cut away existing drain within manhole to form channel, provide and set two three quarter section channels and form concrete benching and cement render walls:**										
A025214A	0.9 m deep.	Each	36.00	879.48	–	238.54	1118.02	967.43	–	262.39	1229.82
A025214B	add for every extra 300 mm depth in excess of 0.9 m . . .	Each	9.00	219.87	–	56.92	276.79	241.86	–	62.61	304.47
A025215	**Take up existing manhole cover and frame and provide, bed and seal new cover and frame 610 mm × 457 mm:**										
A025215A	25 kg	Each	1.10	26.87	–	77.71	104.58	29.56	–	85.48	115.04
A025215B	38 kg	Each	1.30	31.76	–	71.04	102.80	34.94	–	78.14	113.08
A025216	**Excavate for stoppage in 100 mm drain, cut out and renew two lengths of pipe, fill in and test. Reform paving:**										
A025216A	assumed depth 0.9 m	Each	10.00	244.30	–	39.35	283.65	268.73	–	43.29	312.02
A025218	**Unstop gullies:**										
A025218A	remove silt, clean and flush with disinfectant	Each	1.15	28.09	–	–	28.09	30.90	–	–	30.90
A025220	**Clear soil drains, rod and flush in sections:**										
A025220A	average length 25 m.	Each	5.75	140.47	–	–	140.47	154.52	–	–	154.52
A025221	**Unstop and smoke test:**										
A025221A	cast iron soil pipe	Each	4.20	102.61	–	–	102.61	112.87	–	–	112.87
A025222	**Take up manhole cover, clean and sand out and rebed in grease:**										
A025222A	frame channels	Each	1.10	26.87	–	–	26.87	29.56	–	–	29.56
A025224	**Clayware channel to gully set in concrete with brick curb rendered in cement mortar:**										
A025224A	450 mm long.	Each	2.00	48.86	–	11.03	59.89	53.75	–	12.13	65.88
A025224B	supply and fit new gully grid	Each	0.25	6.11	–	4.96	11.07	6.72	–	5.46	12.18

House Renovation Grants, Repairs and Alterations

Small Works 2009		Unit	Labour Hours	Labour Net	Plant Net	Materials Net	Unit Net	Labour Gross	Plant Gross	Materials Gross	Unit Price
								(Gross rates include 10% profit)			
				£	£	£	£	£	£	£	£
A02	REPAIRS AND ALTERATIONS										
A0252	DRAINAGE REPAIRS AND RENEWALS										
A025226	Open up manhole, break out brickwork and benching to main channel, provide for and insert one three quarter channel bend and join to existing channel, reform benching, make good all work disturbed and refix manhole cover:										
A025226A	100 mm	Each	10.00	244.30	–	21.58	265.88	268.73	–	23.74	292.47
A025228	Open up manhole 0.9 m × 0.9 m inside on plan and 1.27 m deep. Break out all channels and branches. Break out one brick side of manhole at one end and extend manhole:										
A025228A	by 150 mm × 0.9 m inside with 150 mm concrete at bottom, one brick side in stock bricks and 150 mm concrete cover. Build in two pipes 150 mm and one pipe 100 mm, provide and insert straight main channel 150 mm and six half branch channel bends 100 mm and reform benching. Make good all work disturbed and refix manhole cover	Each	24.00	586.32	–	280.36	866.68	644.95	–	308.40	953.35
A025228B	Extra over excavation for breaking out brick manhole 0.8 m × 0.7 m inside on plan and 0.9 m deep to invert	Each	3.00	73.29	–	–	73.29	80.62	–	–	80.62
A025228C	add or deduct for every 300 mm more or less than 0.9 m deep to invert	Each	1.00	24.43	–	–	24.43	26.87	–	–	26.87
A025230	Seal open ends of disused clayware pipes with concrete plugs 300 mm long:										
A025230A	100 mm diameter	Each	0.60	14.65	–	0.33	14.98	16.12	–	0.36	16.48
A025230B	150 mm diameter	Each	0.80	19.55	–	0.76	20.31	21.51	–	0.84	22.34
A025230C	225 mm diameter	Each	1.10	26.88	–	2.61	29.49	29.57	–	2.87	32.44

312

DRAINAGE, SEWERAGE AND PUBLIC WORKS

Small Works 2009		Unit	Labour Hours	Labour Net	Plant Net	Materials Net	Unit Net	Labour Gross	Plant Gross	Materials Gross	Unit Price
								(Gross rates include 10% profit)			
			£	£	£	£	£	£	£	£
B01	**DRAINAGE AND SEWERAGE**										
B0101	**EXCAVATING TRENCHES**										
B010101	Excavate trenches in firm clay; 450 mm wide; earthwork support; grade bottom; backfill; compact; dispose of surplus; hand labour; average depth:										
B010101A	0.50 m	m	1.31	27.32	–	0.33	27.65	30.05	–	0.36	30.42
B010101B	0.75 m	m	1.97	41.08	–	0.46	41.54	45.19	–	0.51	45.69
B010101C	1.00 m	m	2.63	54.83	–	0.60	55.43	60.31	–	0.66	60.97
B010101D	1.25 m	m	3.92	81.73	–	0.75	82.48	89.90	–	0.83	90.73
B010101E	1.50 m	m	4.69	97.79	–	0.93	98.72	107.57	–	1.02	108.59
B010101F	1.75 m	m	5.48	114.26	–	1.06	115.32	125.69	–	1.17	126.85
B010101G	2.00 m	m	6.26	130.52	–	1.20	131.72	143.57	–	1.32	144.89
B010101H	2.25 m	m	8.52	177.64	–	1.33	178.97	195.40	–	1.46	196.87
B010101I	2.50 m	m	9.46	197.24	–	1.55	198.79	216.96	–	1.71	218.67
B010101J	2.75 m	m	10.42	217.26	–	1.66	218.92	238.99	–	1.83	240.81
B010101K	3.00 m	m	11.35	236.65	–	1.77	238.42	260.32	–	1.95	262.26
B010102	Excavate trenches in firm soil; 600 mm wide earthwork support; grade bottom; compact; dispose of surplus; hand labour; average depth:										
B010102A	0.50 m	m	1.75	36.48	–	0.38	36.86	40.13	–	0.42	40.55
B010102B	0.75 m	m	2.63	54.83	–	0.60	55.43	60.31	–	0.66	60.97
B010102C	1.00 m	m	3.50	72.97	–	0.80	73.77	80.27	–	0.88	81.15
B010102D	1.25 m	m	5.22	108.83	–	1.02	109.85	119.71	–	1.12	120.84
B010102E	1.50 m	m	6.26	130.52	–	1.20	131.72	143.57	–	1.32	144.89
B010102F	1.75 m	m	7.30	152.21	–	1.39	153.60	167.43	–	1.53	168.96
B010102G	2.00 m	m	8.34	173.89	–	1.59	175.48	191.28	–	1.75	193.03
B010102H	2.25 m	m	11.35	236.65	–	1.77	238.42	260.32	–	1.95	262.26
B010102I	2.50 m	m	12.62	263.13	–	1.99	265.12	289.44	–	2.19	291.63
B010102J	2.75 m	m	13.88	289.40	–	2.19	291.59	318.34	–	2.41	320.75
B010102K	3.00 m	m	15.14	315.67	–	2.41	318.08	347.24	–	2.65	349.89
B010103	Excavate trenches in firm soil; 750 mm wide earthwork support; grade bottom; compact; dispose of surplus; hand labour; average depth:										
B010103A	0.50 m	m	2.18	45.45	–	0.53	45.98	50.00	–	0.58	50.58
B010103B	0.75 m	m	3.29	68.60	–	0.75	69.35	75.46	–	0.83	76.29
B010103C	1.00 m	m	4.37	91.11	–	1.02	92.13	100.22	–	1.12	101.34
B010103D	1.25 m	m	6.54	136.36	–	1.28	137.64	150.00	–	1.41	151.40
B010103E	1.50 m	m	7.82	163.05	–	1.55	164.60	179.36	–	1.71	181.06
B010103F	1.75 m	m	9.13	190.36	–	1.73	192.09	209.40	–	1.90	211.30
B010103G	2.00 m	m	10.44	217.68	–	1.99	219.67	239.45	–	2.19	241.64
B010103H	2.25 m	m	14.21	296.28	–	2.26	298.54	325.91	–	2.49	328.39
B010103I	2.50 m	m	15.78	329.02	–	2.52	331.54	361.92	–	2.77	364.69
B010103J	2.75 m	m	17.35	361.75	–	2.72	364.47	397.93	–	2.99	400.92
B010103K	3.00 m	m	18.94	394.90	–	2.99	397.89	434.39	–	3.29	437.68

Drainage, Sewerage and Public Works

Small Works 2009		Unit	Labour Hours	Labour Net	Plant Net	Materials Net	Unit Net	Labour Gross	Plant Gross	Materials Gross	Unit Price
								(Gross rates include 10% profit)			
				£	£	£	£	£	£	£	£
B01	**DRAINAGE AND SEWERAGE**										
B0101	**EXCAVATING TRENCHES**										
B010104	Excavate trenches in firm soil; 450 mm wide earthwork support; grade bottom; compact; dispose of surplus; machine excavation; average depth:										
B010104A	0.50 m	m	0.17	3.54	4.82	0.24	8.60	3.89	5.30	0.26	9.46
B010104B	0.75 m	m	0.24	5.01	6.82	0.64	12.47	5.51	7.50	0.70	13.72
B010104C	1.00 m	m	0.34	7.09	9.64	0.43	17.16	7.80	10.60	0.47	18.88
B010104D	1.25 m	m	0.47	9.80	13.35	0.24	23.39	10.78	14.69	0.26	25.73
B010104E	1.50 m	m	0.55	11.47	15.64	0.49	27.60	12.62	17.20	0.54	30.36
B010104F	1.75 m	m	0.65	13.56	18.49	0.33	32.38	14.92	20.34	0.36	35.62
B010104G	2.00 m	m	0.74	15.43	21.03	0.30	36.76	16.97	23.13	0.33	40.44
B010104H	2.25 m	m	0.97	20.22	24.74	0.60	45.56	22.24	27.21	0.66	50.12
B010104I	2.50 m	m	1.07	22.30	28.42	0.46	51.18	24.53	31.26	0.51	56.30
B010104J	2.75 m	m	1.18	24.61	30.70	0.62	55.93	27.07	33.77	0.68	61.52
B010104K	3.00 m	m	1.28	26.69	33.56	0.45	60.70	29.36	36.92	0.50	66.77
B010105	Excavate trenches in firm soil; 600 mm wide earthwork support; grade bottom; compact; dispose of surplus; machine excavation; average depth:										
B010105A	0.50 m	m	0.23	4.79	6.53	0.23	11.55	5.27	7.18	0.25	12.71
B010105B	0.75 m	m	0.34	7.09	9.64	0.43	17.16	7.80	10.60	0.47	18.88
B010105C	1.00 m	m	0.44	9.18	12.50	0.86	22.54	10.10	13.75	0.95	24.79
B010105D	1.25 m	m	0.62	12.93	17.63	0.30	30.86	14.22	19.39	0.33	33.95
B010105E	1.50 m	m	0.74	15.43	21.03	0.30	36.76	16.97	23.13	0.33	40.44
B010105F	1.75 m	m	0.88	18.35	23.60	0.89	42.84	20.19	25.96	0.98	47.12
B010105G	2.00 m	m	1.00	20.85	27.02	0.91	48.78	22.94	29.72	1.00	53.66
B010105H	2.25 m	m	1.28	26.69	33.56	0.45	60.70	29.36	36.92	0.50	66.77
B010105I	2.50 m	m	1.43	29.82	37.81	0.46	68.09	32.80	41.59	0.51	74.90
B010105J	2.75 m	m	1.57	32.73	41.23	0.49	74.45	36.00	45.35	0.54	81.90
B010105K	3.00 m	m	1.70	35.44	45.48	0.46	81.38	38.98	50.03	0.51	89.52
B010106	Excavate trenches in firm soil; 750 mm wide earthwork support; grade bottom; compact; dispose of surplus; machine excavation; average depth:										
B010106A	0.50 m	m	0.26	5.42	7.39	0.32	13.13	5.96	8.13	0.35	14.44
B010106B	0.75 m	m	0.40	8.34	11.39	0.53	20.26	9.17	12.53	0.58	22.29
B010106C	1.00 m	m	0.53	11.05	15.07	0.95	27.07	12.16	16.58	1.05	29.78
B010106D	1.25 m	m	0.74	15.43	21.03	0.41	36.87	16.97	23.13	0.45	40.56
B010106E	1.50 m	m	0.90	18.77	25.60	0.25	44.62	20.65	28.16	0.28	49.08
B010106F	1.75 m	m	1.04	21.68	29.56	0.91	52.15	23.85	32.52	1.00	57.37
B010106G	2.00 m	m	1.19	24.81	33.81	0.97	59.59	27.29	37.19	1.07	65.55
B010106H	2.25 m	m	1.55	32.31	41.23	0.55	74.09	35.54	45.35	0.61	81.50
B010106I	2.50 m	m	1.72	35.86	45.48	0.60	81.94	39.45	50.03	0.66	90.13
B010106J	2.75 m	m	1.88	39.20	49.77	1.10	90.07	43.12	54.75	1.21	99.08
B010106K	3.00 m	m	2.05	42.74	55.44	0.24	98.42	47.01	60.98	0.26	108.26

Small Works 2009		Unit	Labour Hours	Labour Net	Plant Net	Materials Net	Unit Net	Labour Gross	Plant Gross	Materials Gross	Unit Price
								(Gross rates include 10% profit)			
				£	£	£	£	£	£	£	£
B01	**DRAINAGE AND SEWERAGE**										
B0102	**PIPE BEDS AND COVERINGS**										
B010201	**Sand; 50 mm beds; width:**										
B010201A	450 mm	m	0.11	2.29	–	1.18	3.47	2.52	–	1.30	3.82
B010201B	525 mm	m	0.12	2.50	–	1.49	3.99	2.75	–	1.64	4.39
B010201C	600 mm	m	0.12	2.50	–	1.49	3.99	2.75	–	1.64	4.39
B010201D	750 mm	m	0.17	3.55	–	2.08	5.63	3.91	–	2.29	6.19
B010202	**Granular material; DTp grade 1; 50 mm beds; width:**										
B010202A	450 mm	m	0.11	2.30	–	0.59	2.89	2.53	–	0.65	3.18
B010202B	525 mm	m	0.12	2.50	–	0.91	3.41	2.75	–	1.00	3.75
B010202C	600 mm	m	0.12	2.50	–	0.91	3.41	2.75	–	1.00	3.75
B010202D	750 mm	m	0.17	3.54	–	1.19	4.73	3.89	–	1.31	5.20
B010203	**Granular material; DTp grade 1; 100 mm beds; width:**										
B010203A	450 mm	m	0.20	4.17	–	1.50	5.67	4.59	–	1.65	6.24
B010203B	525 mm	m	0.24	5.00	–	1.50	6.50	5.50	–	1.65	7.15
B010203C	600 mm	m	0.28	5.84	–	1.81	7.65	6.42	–	1.99	8.42
B010203D	750 mm	m	0.35	7.29	–	2.41	9.70	8.02	–	2.65	10.67
B010204	**Granular material; DTp grade 1; 150 mm beds; width:**										
B010204A	450 mm	m	0.31	6.46	–	2.10	8.56	7.11	–	2.31	9.42
B010204B	525 mm	m	0.36	7.50	–	2.41	9.91	8.25	–	2.65	10.90
B010204C	600 mm	m	0.42	8.76	–	2.69	11.45	9.64	–	2.96	12.60
B010204D	750 mm	m	0.53	11.05	–	3.31	14.36	12.16	–	3.64	15.80
B010205	**Granular material; DTp grade 1; 100 mm beds; filling to half height of pipe; width:**										
B010205A	450 mm to 100 mm pipe	m	0.32	6.67	–	1.81	8.48	7.34	–	1.99	9.33
B010205B	525 mm to 150 mm pipe	m	0.42	8.75	–	2.41	11.16	9.63	–	2.65	12.28
B010205C	600 mm to 225 mm pipe	m	0.53	11.05	–	3.00	14.05	12.16	–	3.30	15.46
B010205D	750 mm to 300 mm pipe	m	0.73	15.22	–	4.19	19.41	16.74	–	4.61	21.35
B010206	**Granular material; DTp grade 1; 150 mm beds; filling to half height of pipe; width:**										
B010206A	450 mm to 100 mm pipe	m	0.43	8.97	–	2.69	11.66	9.87	–	2.96	12.83
B010206B	525 mm to 150 mm pipe	m	0.54	11.26	–	3.31	14.57	12.39	–	3.64	16.03
B010206C	600 mm to 225mm pipe	m	0.66	13.76	–	3.91	17.67	15.14	–	4.30	19.44
B010206D	750 mm to 300 mm pipe	m	0.91	18.97	–	5.41	24.38	20.87	–	5.95	26.82
B010207	**Granular material; DTp grade 1; bed and covering; thickness:**										
B010207A	450 mm × 350 mm thick to 100 mm pipe	m	0.70	14.60	–	4.50	19.10	16.06	–	4.95	21.01
B010207B	450 mm × 450 mm thick to 100 mm pipe	m	0.90	18.77	–	6.00	24.77	20.65	–	6.60	27.25
B010207C	525 mm × 400 mm thick to 150 mm pipe	m	0.89	18.56	–	6.00	24.56	20.42	–	6.60	27.02
B010207D	525 mm × 500 mm thick to 150 mm pipe	m	1.14	23.77	–	7.50	31.27	26.15	–	8.25	34.40
B010207E	600 mm × 475 mm thick to 225 mm pipe	m	1.14	23.77	–	7.50	31.27	26.15	–	8.25	34.40
B010207F	600 mm × 575 mm thick to 225 mm pipe	m	1.42	29.60	–	9.32	38.92	32.56	–	10.25	42.81
B010207G	750 mm × 550 mm thick to 300 mm pipe	m	1.58	32.94	–	10.51	43.45	36.23	–	11.56	47.80
B010207H	750 mm × 650 mm thick to 300 mm pipe	m	1.91	39.83	–	12.60	52.43	43.81	–	13.86	57.67

Drainage, Sewerage and Public Works

		Unit	Labour Hours	Labour Net	Plant Net	Materials Net	Unit Net	Labour Gross	Plant Gross	Materials Gross	Unit Price
								(Gross rates include 10% profit)			
				£	£	£	£	£	£	£	£
B01	**DRAINAGE AND SEWERAGE**										
B0102	**PIPE BEDS AND COVERINGS**										
B010209	**Plain concrete mix 1:3:6- 40 mm aggregate; 100 mm beds; width:**										
B010209A	450 mm	m	0.29	6.05	–	5.77	11.82	6.66	–	6.35	13.00
B010209B	525 mm	m	0.34	7.09	–	6.64	13.73	7.80	–	7.30	15.10
B010209C	600 mm	m	0.38	7.92	–	7.62	15.54	8.71	–	8.38	17.09
B010209D	750 mm	m	0.48	10.01	–	9.58	19.59	11.01	–	10.54	21.55
B010210	**Plain concrete mix 1:3:6- 40 mm aggregate; 150 mm beds; width:**										
B010210A	450 mm	m	0.43	8.97	–	8.49	17.46	9.87	–	9.34	19.21
B010210B	525 mm	m	0.50	10.42	–	10.02	20.44	11.46	–	11.02	22.48
B010210C	600 mm	m	0.58	12.09	–	11.43	23.52	13.30	–	12.57	25.87
B010210D	750 mm	m	0.72	15.01	–	14.26	29.27	16.51	–	15.69	32.20
B010211	**Plain concrete mix 1:3:6- 40 mm aggregate; 100 mm beds; filling to half height of pipe; width:**										
B010211A	450 mm to 100 mm pipe ...	m	0.44	9.18	–	8.49	17.67	10.10	–	9.34	19.44
B010211B	525 mm to 150 mm pipe ...	m	0.56	11.67	–	11.00	22.67	12.84	–	12.10	24.94
B010211C	600 mm to 225 mm pipe ...	m	0.72	15.01	–	11.00	26.01	16.51	–	12.10	28.61
B010211D	750 mm to 300 mm pipe ...	m	1.01	21.06	–	14.05	35.11	23.17	–	15.46	38.62
B010212	**Plain concrete mix 1:3:6- 40 mm aggregate; 150 mm beds; filling to half height of pipe; width:**										
B010212A	450 mm to 100 mm pipe ...	m	0.59	12.30	–	9.04	21.34	13.53	–	9.94	23.47
B010212B	525 mm to 150 mm pipe ...	m	0.74	15.43	–	10.67	26.10	16.97	–	11.74	28.71
B010212C	600 mm to 225 mm pipe ...	m	0.91	18.97	–	14.70	33.67	20.87	–	16.17	37.04
B010212D	750 mm to 300 mm pipe ...	m	1.25	26.06	–	19.27	45.33	28.67	–	21.20	49.86
B010213	**Plain concrete mix 1:3:6- 40 mm aggregate; bed and covering; 450 mm wide:**										
B010213A	350 mm thick to 100 mm pipe	m	0.96	20.02	–	19.92	39.94	22.02	–	21.91	43.93
B010213B	450 mm thick to 100 mm pipe	m	1.24	25.86	–	25.69	51.55	28.45	–	28.26	56.71
B010214	**Plain concrete mix 1:3:6- 40 mm aggregate; bed and covering; 525 mm wide:**										
B010214A	400 mm thick to 150 mm pipe	m	1.22	25.43	–	26.57	52.00	27.97	–	29.23	57.20
B010214B	500 mm thick to 150 mm pipe	m	1.56	32.52	–	33.32	65.84	35.77	–	36.65	72.42
B010215	**Plain concrete mix 1:3:6- 40 mm aggregate; bed and covering; 600 mm wide:**										
B010215A	475 mm thick to 225 mm pipe	m	1.56	32.53	–	33.42	65.95	35.78	–	36.76	72.55
B010215B	575 mm thick to 225 mm pipe	m	1.94	40.45	–	41.59	82.04	44.50	–	45.75	90.24
B010216	**Plain concrete mix 1:3:6- 40 mm aggregate; bed and covering; 750 mm wide:**										
B010216A	550 mm thick to 300 mm pipe	m	2.17	45.25	–	47.36	92.61	49.78	–	52.10	101.87
B010216B	650 mm thick to 300 mm pipe	m	2.62	54.62	–	56.51	111.13	60.08	–	62.16	122.24

Small Works 2009		Unit	Labour Hours	Labour Net	Plant Net	Materials Net	Unit Net	Labour Gross	Plant Gross	Materials Gross	Unit Price
								(Gross rates include 10% profit)			
				£	£	£	£	£	£	£	£
B01	**DRAINAGE AND SEWERAGE**										
B0104	**BREAKING UP PAVED SURFACES**										
B010401	**Break up paving with compressed air equipment for trenches 600 mm wide; average thickness:**										
B010401A	75 mm tarmacadam	m	0.43	8.96	1.68	–	10.64	9.86	1.85	–	11.70
B010401B	150 mm plain concrete	m	1.35	28.15	5.19	–	33.34	30.97	5.71	–	36.67
B010401C	150 mm reinforced concrete	m	1.83	38.15	10.30	–	48.45	41.97	11.33	–	53.30
B0105	**REINSTATE PAVED SURFACES**										
B010501	**Reinstate paving; average 600 mm wide; 100 mm hardcore bed; paving average thickness:**										
B010501A	75 mm tarmacadam	m²	0.42	8.76	–	6.47	15.23	9.64	–	7.12	16.75
B010501B	150 mm concrete	m²	0.85	17.72	–	32.17	49.89	19.49	–	35.39	54.88
B0106	**SUPERSLEVE DRAIN PIPES AND FITTINGS**										
B010601	**Push-fit polypropylene flexible couplings; for underground drainage; in trenches; 100 mm nominal size pipes:**										
B010601A	in runs exceeding 3.00 m long	m	0.22	5.37	–	6.08	11.45	5.91	–	6.69	12.60
B010601B	in runs not exceeding 3.00 m long	m	0.28	6.84	–	6.08	12.92	7.52	–	6.69	14.21
B010601C	Extra for; bend	Each	0.30	7.32	–	12.05	19.37	8.05	–	13.26	21.31
B010601E	Extra for; junction	Each	0.25	6.11	–	25.67	31.78	6.72	–	28.24	34.96
B010602	**Push-fit polypropylene flexible couplings; for underground drainage; in trenches; 150 mm nominal size pipes:**										
B010602A	in runs exceeding 3.00 m long	m	0.28	6.84	–	12.29	19.13	7.52	–	13.52	21.04
B010602B	in runs not exceeding 3.00 m long	m	0.38	9.28	–	12.29	21.57	10.21	–	13.52	23.73
B010602C	Extra for; bend	Each	0.33	8.06	–	16.09	24.15	8.87	–	17.70	26.57
B010602E	Extra for; junction	Each	0.30	7.33	–	21.52	28.85	8.06	–	23.67	31.74

Drainage, Sewerage and Public Works

Small Works 2009		Unit	Labour Hours	Labour Net	Plant Net	Materials Net	Unit Net	Labour Gross	Plant Gross	Materials Gross	Unit Price
								(Gross rates include 10% profit)			
				£	£	£	£	£	£	£	£
B01	**DRAINAGE AND SEWERAGE**										
B0107	**SUPERSLEVE ACCESSORIES**										
B010701	**Jointing to drains; excavation and concrete surrounds:**										
B010701A	square gulley; trapped; square grid; 100 mm outlet.	Each	1.50	36.65	–	58.49	95.14	40.32	–	64.34	104.65
B010701B	square gulley; trapped; horizontal back inlet to small waste pipe; square grid; 100 mm outlet.	Each	1.80	43.97	–	49.81	93.78	48.37	–	54.79	103.16
B010701C	square gulley; trapped; horizontal back inlet to large waste pipe; square grid; 100 mm outlet.	Each	1.80	43.97	–	34.28	78.25	48.37	–	37.71	86.08
B010701D	square hopper; integral vertical back inlet; trapped; square sealing plate; 100 mm outlet.	Each	1.80	43.97	–	49.81	93.78	48.37	–	54.79	103.16
B010701E	square hopper; integral vertical back inlet; untrapped; square sealing plate; 100 mm outlet	Each	1.80	43.97	–	53.32	97.29	48.37	–	58.65	107.02
B010701F	access gulley; integral vertical back inlet; rodding eye; stopper; plastic grid; hinged grate and frame	Each	1.80	43.97	–	53.32	97.29	48.37	–	58.65	107.02
B010701G	inspection chamber; vitrified clay; 225 mm diameter; 600 mm deep; comprising straight through base with junction for 100 mm pipes; raising piece with cover and frame; couplings to sleeve and pipes	Each	2.00	48.86	–	191.02	239.88	53.75	–	210.12	263.87
B010701H	inspection chamber; PPIC polypropylene; 475 mm diameter; 585 mm deep; five 100 mm stoppered inlets; base; ductile iron cover and frame	Each	2.00	48.86	–	246.05	294.91	53.75	–	270.66	324.40
B010701I	inspection chamber; PICC polypropylene; 930 mm deep; five 100 mm inlets; base; Ductile iron cover and frame	Each	2.00	48.86	–	343.77	392.63	53.75	–	378.15	431.89
B010701J	inspection chamber; PPIC polypropylene; 930 mm deep; three 150 mm inlets (two stoppered); base; ductile iron cover and frame	Each	2.20	53.74	–	343.77	397.51	59.11	–	378.15	437.26

Small Works 2009		Unit	Labour Hours	Labour Net	Plant Net	Materials Net	Unit Net	Labour Gross	Plant Gross	Materials Gross	Unit Price
								(Gross rates include 10% profit)			
				£	£	£	£	£	£	£	£
B01	**DRAINAGE AND SEWERAGE**										
B0108	**HEPSEAL DRAIN PIPES AND FITTINGS**										
B010801	**Push-fit flexible socket joints; for drainage; in trenches; 100 mm nominal size pipes:**										
B010801A	in runs exceeding 3.00 m long	m	0.25	6.10	–	6.08	12.18	6.71	–	6.69	13.40
B010801B	in runs not exceeding 3.00 m long	m	0.33	8.06	–	6.08	14.14	8.87	–	6.69	15.55
B010801C	Extra for; bend	Each	0.30	7.33	–	8.20	15.53	8.06	–	9.02	17.08
B010801E	Extra for; junction	Each	0.25	6.11	–	17.39	23.50	6.72	–	19.13	25.85
B010802	**Push-fit flexible socket joints; for drainage; in trenches; 150 mm nominal size pipes:**										
B010802A	in runs exceeding 3.00 m long	m	0.35	8.55	–	12.29	20.84	9.41	–	13.52	22.92
B010802B	in runs not exceeding 3.00 m long	m	0.45	10.99	–	12.29	23.28	12.09	–	13.52	25.61
B010802C	Extra for; bend	Each	0.47	11.48	–	38.49	49.97	12.63	–	42.34	54.97
B010802E	Extra for; junction	Each	0.30	7.33	–	44.56	51.89	8.06	–	49.02	57.08
B010803	**Push-fit flexible socket joints; for drainage; in trenches; 225 mm nominal size pipes:**										
B010803A	in runs exceeding 3.00 m long	m	0.40	9.78	–	31.37	41.15	10.76	–	34.51	45.27
B010803B	in runs not exceeding 3.00 m long	m	0.50	12.22	–	31.37	43.59	13.44	–	34.51	47.95
B010803C	Extra for; bend	Each	0.50	12.22	–	90.21	102.43	13.44	–	99.23	112.67
B010803E	Extra for; junction	Each	0.44	10.74	–	125.92	136.66	11.81	–	138.51	150.33
B010804	**Push-fit flexible socket joints; for drainage; in trenches; 300 mm nominal size pipes:**										
B010804A	in runs exceeding 3.00 m long	m	0.62	15.14	–	66.93	82.07	16.65	–	73.62	90.28
B010804B	in runs not exceeding 3.00 m long	m	0.78	19.05	–	66.93	85.98	20.96	–	73.62	94.58
B010804C	Extra for; bend	Each	0.78	19.06	–	155.78	174.84	20.97	–	171.36	192.32
B010804E	Extra for; junction	Each	0.74	18.08	–	245.18	263.26	19.89	–	269.70	289.59

Drainage, Sewerage and Public Works

Small Works 2009		Unit	Labour Hours	Labour Net	Plant Net	Materials Net	Unit Net	Labour Gross	Plant Gross	Materials Gross	Unit Price
								(Gross rates include 10% profit)			
				£	£	£	£	£	£	£	£
B01	**DRAINAGE AND SEWERAGE**										
B0110	**PLASTIDRAIN UPVC UNDERGROUND DRAINAGE PIPES AND FITTINGS**										
B011001	**Seal ring jointing; in trenches; 110 mm nominal size pipes:**										
B011001A	in runs exceeding 3.00 m long	m	0.24	5.87	–	7.45	13.32	6.46	–	8.20	14.65
B011001B	in runs not exceeding 3.00 m long	m	0.28	6.84	–	7.45	14.29	7.52	–	8.20	15.72
B011001C	Extra for; bend	Each	0.28	6.84	–	18.72	25.56	7.52	–	20.59	28.12
B011001E	Extra for; junction	Each	0.24	5.87	–	26.44	32.31	6.46	–	29.08	35.54
B011002	**Seal ring jointing; in trenches; 160 mm nominal size pipe:**										
B011002A	in runs exceeding 3.00 m long	m	0.29	7.08	–	17.15	24.23	7.79	–	18.87	26.65
B011002B	in runs not exceeding 3.00 m long	m	0.33	8.06	–	17.15	25.21	8.87	–	18.87	27.73
B011002C	Extra for; short radius bend	Each	0.35	8.55	–	47.79	56.34	9.41	–	52.57	61.97
B011002E	Extra for; junction	Each	0.33	8.06	–	86.32	94.38	8.87	–	94.95	103.82
B011003	**Plastidrain uPVC accessories; jointing to drains; excavation and concrete surrounds:**										
B011003A	Rodding eye; sealed; 110 mm rodding point	Each	0.72	17.59	–	58.96	76.55	19.35	–	64.86	84.21
B011003C	Access gulley; round; sealing rings; grid and access plug; 110 mm outlet	Each	1.20	29.32	–	39.62	68.94	32.25	–	43.58	75.83
B011003D	Inspection chamber; 315 mm diameter; 600 mm deep; concrete cover and plastic frame; stoppered inlets; lifting handle; 110 mm outlet	Each	2.07	50.57	–	245.20	295.77	55.63	–	269.72	325.35

Small Works 2009		Unit	Labour Hours	Labour Net	Plant Net	Materials Net	Unit Net	Labour Gross	Plant Gross	Materials Gross	Unit Price
								(Gross rates include 10% profit)			
				£	£	£	£	£	£	£	£
B01	**DRAINAGE AND SEWERAGE**										
B0112	**CAST IRON DRAIN PIPES AND FITTINGS**										
B011201	**Spigot and socket caulked lead joints; in trenches; 100 mm pipes:**										
B011201A	laid straight	m	0.92	33.04	–	48.79	81.83	36.34	–	53.67	90.01
B011201B	in runs not exceeding 3.00 m long	m	1.25	44.90	–	48.52	93.42	49.39	–	53.37	102.76
B011201C	Extra for; bend; short radius	Each	0.92	33.04	–	32.57	65.61	36.34	–	35.83	72.17
B011201D	Extra for; bend; long radius .	Each	0.92	33.05	–	48.67	81.72	36.36	–	53.54	89.89
B011201E	Extra for; branch; single . . .	Each	1.25	44.90	–	46.75	91.65	49.39	–	51.43	100.82
B011201F	Extra for; branch; double . . .	Each	1.55	55.68	–	62.84	118.52	61.25	–	69.12	130.37
B011201G	Extra for; drain connector; large socket for clayware; 305 mm long	Each	0.92	33.04	–	30.85	63.89	36.34	–	33.94	70.28
B011201H	Extra for; drain connector; large socket for WC; 300 mm long	Each	0.69	24.78	–	28.29	53.07	27.26	–	31.12	58.38
B011202	**Spigot and socket caulked lead joints; in trenches; 150 mm pipes:**										
B011202A	laid straight	m	1.15	41.30	–	88.67	129.97	45.43	–	97.54	142.97
B011202B	in runs not exceeding 3.00 m long	m	1.55	55.67	–	88.67	144.34	61.24	–	97.54	158.77
B011202C	Extra for; bend; short radius	Each	1.15	41.31	–	112.76	154.07	45.44	–	124.04	169.48
B011202D	Extra for; bend; long radius .	Each	1.15	41.30	–	143.79	185.09	45.43	–	158.17	203.60
B011202E	Extra for; branch; single . . .	Each	1.55	55.68	–	104.15	159.83	61.25	–	114.57	175.81
B011202F	Extra for; branch; double . . .	Each	1.95	70.04	–	159.68	229.72	77.04	–	175.65	252.69
B011202G	Extra for; drain connector; large socket for clayware; 305 mm long	Each	1.15	41.31	–	54.06	95.37	45.44	–	59.47	104.91
B011203	**Rainwater shoes; horizontal or vertical inlet; setting on and bedding in site mixed concrete 1:3:6:**										
B011203A	100 mm	Each	0.86	30.90	–	49.57	80.47	33.99	–	54.53	88.52
B011203B	150 mm	Each	0.98	35.20	–	88.43	123.63	38.72	–	97.27	135.99
B011204	**Yard gulley; bedding on and setting in site mixed concrete 1:3:6:**										
B011204A	Deans; trapped; galvanised sediment pan; 267 mm round heavy grating; 100 mm outlet	Each	3.70	132.90	–	419.07	551.97	146.19	–	460.98	607.17
B011204B	Garage; trapless; galvanised sediment pan; 267 mm round heavy grating; 100 mm outlet	Each	3.45	123.93	–	852.79	976.72	136.32	–	938.07	1074.39
B011204C	Garage; trapped; rodding eye; galvanised perforated sediment pan; stopper; 267 mm round heavy grating; 100 mm outlet	Each	4.60	165.23	–	900.68	1065.91	181.75	–	990.75	1172.50
B011204D	Square top; trapped; galvanised sediment pan; 255 × 255 mm square grating; 100 mm outlet	Each	4.55	163.44	–	353.21	516.65	179.78	–	388.53	568.32

Drainage, Sewerage and Public Works

Small Works 2009		Unit	Labour Hours	Labour Net	Plant Net	Materials Net	Unit Net	Labour Gross	Plant Gross	Materials Gross	Unit Price
								(Gross rates include 10% profit)			
				£	£	£	£	£	£	£	£
B01	**DRAINAGE AND SEWERAGE**										
B0114	**CAST IRON TIMESAVER PIPES AND FITTINGS**										
B011401	**Drainage Castings Timesaver System; mechanical coupling joints; in trenches; 100 mm pipes:**										
B011401A	laid straight	m	0.58	20.83	–	48.63	69.46	22.91	–	53.49	76.41
B011401B	in runs not exceeding 3.00 m long	m	0.78	28.02	–	48.63	76.65	30.82	–	53.49	84.32
B011401C	Extra for; bend; medium radius	Each	0.69	24.79	–	46.72	71.51	27.27	–	51.39	78.66
B011401D	Extra for; bend; long radius.	Each	0.69	24.79	–	46.72	71.51	27.27	–	51.39	78.66
B011401E	Extra for; branch; single-plain 100 × 100 mm	Each	0.86	30.89	–	68.85	99.74	33.98	–	75.74	109.71
B011401G	Extra for; branch double-plain 100 × 100 mm	Each	1.10	39.51	–	102.73	142.24	43.46	–	113.00	156.46
B011401I	Extra for; transitional pipe; socket for WC	Each	0.58	20.83	–	30.85	51.68	22.91	–	33.94	56.85
B011401J	Extra for; transitional pipe; socket for clayware	Each	0.40	14.37	–	10.19	24.56	15.81	–	11.21	27.02
B011402	**Drainage Castings Timesaver System; mechanical coupling joints; in trenches 150 mm pipes:**										
B011402A	laid straight	m	0.69	24.79	–	79.75	104.54	27.27	–	87.73	114.99
B011402B	in runs not exceeding 3.00 m long	m	0.94	33.77	–	79.75	113.52	37.15	–	87.73	124.87
B011402C	Extra for; bend; medium radius	Each	0.81	29.09	–	84.07	113.16	32.00	–	92.48	124.48
B011402D	Extra for; bend; long radius.	Each	0.81	29.10	–	79.75	108.85	32.01	–	87.73	119.74
B011402E	Extra for; branch; single . . .	Each	0.98	35.20	–	109.56	144.76	38.72	–	120.52	159.24
B011402H	Extra for; transitional pipe; socket for clayware	Each	0.92	33.05	–	43.08	76.13	36.36	–	47.39	83.74
B011402I	Extra for; isolated Timesaver joint	Each	0.48	17.24	–	10.19	27.43	18.96	–	11.21	30.17
B011403	**Rainwater shoes; horizontal or vertical inlet; setting on and bedding in site mixed concrete 1:3:6:**										
B011403A	100 mm	Each	0.58	20.84	–	45.79	66.63	22.92	–	50.37	73.29
B011403B	150 mm	Each	0.98	35.20	–	97.27	132.47	38.72	–	107.00	145.72

Small Works 2009		Unit	Labour Hours	Labour Net	Plant Net	Materials Net	Unit Net	Labour Gross	Plant Gross	Materials Gross	Unit Price
								(Gross rates include 10% profit)			
				£	£	£	£	£	£	£	£
B01	**DRAINAGE AND SEWERAGE**										
B0114	**CAST IRON TIMESAVER PIPES AND FITTINGS**										
B011404	**Yard gulley; bedding on and setting in site mixed concrete 1:3:6:**										
B011404A	Deans; trapped; galvanised sediment pan; 267 mm round heavy grating; 100 mm outlet...........	Each	3.35	120.34	–	411.36	531.70	132.37	–	452.50	584.87
B011404B	Garage; trapless; galvanised sediment pan; 267 mm round heavy grating; 100 mm outlet...........	Each	3.10	111.35	–	845.09	956.44	122.49	–	929.60	1052.08
B011404C	Garage; trapped; rodding eye; galvanised perforated sediment pan; stopper; 267 mm round heavy grating; 100 mm outlet	Each	3.45	123.92	–	896.57	1020.49	136.31	–	986.23	1122.54
B011404D	Square top; trapped; galvanised sediment pan; 255 × 255 mm square grating; 100 mm outlet	Each	3.40	122.13	–	345.51	467.64	134.34	–	380.06	514.40
B011405	**Inspection chambers; bolted flat cover; bedding in cement mortar 1:3:**										
B011405A	100 × 100 mm; one branch either side	Each	1.20	43.10	–	211.43	254.53	47.41	–	232.57	279.98
B011405B	100 × 100 mm; one branch each side	Each	1.20	43.10	–	211.43	254.53	47.41	–	232.57	279.98
B011405C	100 × 100 mm; two branches either side.......	Each	1.95	70.05	–	414.71	484.76	77.06	–	456.18	533.24
B011405D	150 × 100 mm; one branch either side	Each	1.65	59.26	–	273.92	333.18	65.19	–	301.31	366.50
B011405E	150 × 100 mm; one branch each side	Each	1.65	59.27	–	552.68	611.95	65.20	–	607.95	673.15
B011405F	150 × 100 mm; two branches either side.......	Each	2.55	91.60	–	417.37	508.97	100.76	–	459.11	559.87

Drainage, Sewerage and Public Works

Small Works 2009		Unit	Labour Hours	Labour Net	Plant Net	Materials Net	Unit Net	Labour Gross	Plant Gross	Materials Gross	Unit Price
								(Gross rates include 10% profit)			
				£	£	£	£	£	£	£	£
B01	**DRAINAGE AND SEWERAGE**										
B0116	**HEPWORTH DRAIN PIPES AND FITTINGS**										
B011601	**Butt jointed; in trenches; 75 mm nominal size pipes:**										
B011601A	in runs exceeding 3.00 m long	m	0.25	5.22	–	17.64	22.86	5.74	–	19.40	25.15
B011601B	in runs not exceeding 3.00 m long	m	0.30	6.26	–	17.64	23.90	6.89	–	19.40	26.29
B011601C	Extra for; junction	Each	0.23	4.80	–	15.96	20.76	5.28	–	17.56	22.84
B011602	**Butt jointed; in trenches; 100 mm nominal size pipes:**										
B011602A	in runs exceeding 3.00 m long	m	0.29	6.04	–	6.08	12.12	6.64	–	6.69	13.33
B011602B	in runs not exceeding 3.00 m long	m	0.34	7.09	–	6.08	13.17	7.80	–	6.69	14.49
B011602C	Extra for; junction	Each	0.24	5.01	–	21.19	26.20	5.51	–	23.31	28.82
B011603	**Butt jointed; in trenches; 150 mm nominal size pipes:**										
B011603A	in runs exceeding 3.00 m long	m	0.37	7.71	–	12.29	20.00	8.48	–	13.52	22.00
B011603B	in runs not exceeding 3.00 m long	m	0.42	8.75	–	12.29	21.04	9.63	–	13.52	23.14
B011603C	Extra for; junction	Each	0.29	6.05	–	26.09	32.14	6.66	–	28.70	35.35
B011604	**Butt jointed; in trenches; 225 mm nominal size pipes:**										
B011604A	in runs exceeding 3.00 m long	m	0.57	11.89	–	31.37	43.26	13.08	–	34.51	47.59
B011604B	in runs not exceeding 3.00 m long	m	0.62	12.93	–	31.37	44.30	14.22	–	34.51	48.73
B011604C	Extra for; junction	Each	0.43	8.96	–	26.09	35.05	9.86	–	28.70	38.56

Small Works 2009	Unit	Labour Hours	Labour Net	Plant Net	Materials Net	Unit Net	Labour Gross	Plant Gross	Materials Gross	Unit Price
			£	£	£	£	£	£	£	£
B01 **DRAINAGE AND SEWERAGE**										
B0118 **HEPLINE PERFORATED PIPES AND FITTINGS**										
B011801 Dry push-fit flexible integral polyethylene sleeve joints; in trenches 100 mm nominal size pipes:										
B011801A in runs exceeding 3.00 m long	m	0.21	4.38	–	10.19	14.57	4.82	–	11.21	16.03
B011801B in runs not exceeding 3.00 m long	m	0.26	5.42	–	10.19	15.61	5.96	–	11.21	17.17
B011801C Extra for; bends	Each	0.29	6.04	–	12.05	18.09	6.64	–	13.26	19.90
B011801D Extra for; junctions	Each	0.24	5.00	–	25.39	30.39	5.50	–	27.93	33.43
B011802 Dry push-fit flexible integral polyethylene sleeve joints; in trenches 150 mm nominal size pipes:										
B011802A in runs exceeding 3.00 m long	m	0.28	5.84	–	18.51	24.35	6.42	–	20.36	26.79
B011802B in runs not exceeding 3.00 m long	m	0.38	7.92	–	18.51	26.43	8.71	–	20.36	29.07
B011802C Extra for; bends	Each	0.32	6.67	–	16.09	22.76	7.34	–	17.70	25.04
B011802D Extra for; junctions	Each	0.29	6.05	–	50.32	56.37	6.66	–	55.35	62.01
B011803 Dry push-fit flexible integral polyethylene sleeve joints; in trenches 225 mm nominal size pipes:										
B011803A in runs exceeding 3.00 m long	m	0.45	9.38	–	37.32	46.70	10.32	–	41.05	51.37
B011803B in runs not exceeding 3.00 m long	m	0.51	10.63	–	37.32	47.95	11.69	–	41.05	52.75
B011803C Extra for; bends	Each	0.50	10.43	–	110.19	120.62	11.47	–	121.21	132.68
B011803D Extra for; junctions	Each	0.40	8.34	–	125.92	134.26	9.17	–	138.51	147.69
B0120 **UPVC PERFORATED FLEXIBLE CORRUGATED DRAIN PIPES AND FITTINGS**										
B012002 Polythene joints; in trenches; 82 mm nominal size pipes:										
B012002A in runs exceeding 3.00 m long	m	0.15	3.13	–	4.46	7.59	3.44	–	4.91	8.35
B012002B in runs not exceeding 3.00 m long	m	0.20	4.17	–	4.46	8.63	4.59	–	4.91	9.49
B012002C Extra for; end cap	Each	0.10	2.08	–	0.73	2.81	2.29	–	0.80	3.09
B012002D Extra for; junction	Each	0.18	3.75	–	30.52	34.27	4.13	–	33.57	37.70
B012003 Polythene joints; in trenches; 110 mm nominal size pipes:										
B012003A in runs exceeding 3.00 m long	m	0.20	4.17	–	5.61	9.78	4.59	–	6.17	10.76
B012003B in runs not exceeding 3.00 m long	m	0.25	5.21	–	5.61	10.82	5.73	–	6.17	11.90
B012003C Extra for; end cap	Each	0.10	2.09	–	2.40	4.49	2.30	–	2.64	4.94
B012003D Extra for; junction	Each	0.22	4.59	–	26.44	31.03	5.05	–	29.08	34.13

Drainage, Sewerage and Public Works

Small Works 2009		Unit	Labour Hours	Labour Net	Plant Net	Materials Net	Unit Net	Labour Gross	Plant Gross	Materials Gross	Unit Price
								(Gross rates include 10% profit)			
				£	£	£	£	£	£	£	£
B01	**DRAINAGE AND SEWERAGE**										
B0122	**POROUS CONCRETE DRAIN PIPES**										
B012202	**Ogee joints; in trenches; 150 mm nominal size pipes:**										
B012202A	in runs exceeding 3.00 m long	m	0.53	11.05	–	9.20	20.25	12.16	–	10.12	22.28
B012202B	in runs not exceeding 3.00 m long	m	0.56	11.68	–	9.20	20.88	12.85	–	10.12	22.97
B012203	**Ogee joints; in trenches; 225 mm nominal size pipes:**										
B012203A	in runs exceeding 3.00 m long	m	0.80	16.68	–	14.00	30.68	18.35	–	15.40	33.75
B012203B	in runs not exceeding 3.00 m long	m	0.83	17.30	–	14.00	31.30	19.03	–	15.40	34.43
B0124	**MANHOLES ETC**										
B012401	**Excavate for manholes and soakaways; dispose of surplus; hand labour; maximum depth not exceeding:**										
B012401A	1.00 m	m³	5.45	113.63	–	–	113.63	124.99	–	–	124.99
B012401B	2.00 m	m³	6.58	137.19	–	–	137.19	150.91	–	–	150.91
B012402	**Excavated material; part backfill:**										
B012402A	remainder wheel and deposit	m³	2.50	52.13	–	–	52.13	57.34	–	–	57.34
B012403	**Fill hardcore:**										
B012403A	into soakaways	m³	0.50	10.43	–	20.47	30.90	11.47	–	22.52	33.99
B012404	**Earthwork support to sides of excavation:**										
B012404A	firm ground; depth n.e. 1.00 m	m²	0.64	13.34	–	2.08	15.42	14.67	–	2.29	16.96
B012404B	firm ground; depth n.e. 2.00 m	m²	0.70	14.60	–	2.32	16.92	16.06	–	2.55	18.61
B012404C	loose ground; depth n.e. 1.00 m	m²	4.98	103.83	–	16.49	120.32	114.21	–	18.14	132.35
B012404D	loose ground; depth n.e. 2.00 m	m²	4.98	103.83	–	16.49	120.32	114.21	–	18.14	132.35
B012405	**Hire of skip; delivery to site; removing when full; disposal of contents; payment of tipping charges; size of skip:**										
B012405A	4.5 m³	m³	–	–	33.02	4.87	37.89	–	36.32	5.36	41.68
B012406	**Base; concrete 1:3:6:**										
B012406A	100 mm thick	m³	0.75	15.64	–	126.95	142.59	17.20	–	139.65	156.85
B012406B	150 mm thick	m³	1.15	23.98	–	126.95	150.93	26.38	–	139.65	166.02

Small Works 2009		Unit	Labour Hours	Labour Net	Plant Net	Materials Net	Unit Net	Labour Gross	Plant Gross	Materials Gross	Unit Price
								(Gross rates include 10% profit)			
				£	£	£	£	£	£	£	£
B01	**DRAINAGE AND SEWERAGE**										
B0124	**MANHOLES ETC**										
B012407	**Benching; concrete 1:3:6 to steep slopes to channels and branches; finished with 13 mm cement mortar 1:3 trowelled smooth; average thickness:**										
B012407A	225 mm	m²	2.65	55.25	–	26.57	81.82	60.78	–	29.23	90.00
B012407B	300 mm	m²	3.31	69.02	–	35.82	104.84	75.92	–	39.40	115.32
B012408	**Fine concrete splayed curb around manhole frame:**										
B012408A	600 mm × 450 mm	Each	1.40	29.19	–	2.29	31.48	32.11	–	2.52	34.63
B012409	**Reinforced suspended cover slab; including fabric reinforcement:**										
B012409A	100 mm-150 mm thick	m³	7.76	161.80	–	130.45	292.25	177.98	–	143.50	321.48
B012410	**Common bricks in cement mortar 1:3 manhole walls:**										
B012410A	half brick	m²	1.99	48.61	–	21.20	69.81	53.47	–	23.32	76.79
B012410B	one brick	m²	3.25	79.40	–	43.31	122.71	87.34	–	47.64	134.98
B012411	**Extra over common brickwork for fair face and flush pointing as the work proceeds:**										
B012411A	stretcher bond	m²	0.56	13.68	–	–	13.68	15.05	–	–	15.05
B012411B	Flemish bond	m²	0.60	14.66	–	–	14.66	16.13	–	–	16.13
B012412	**Oversail common brickwork at top of manhole:**										
B012412A	one course.	m	0.40	9.77	–	–	9.77	10.75	–	–	10.75
B012412B	two courses.	m	0.80	19.54	–	–	19.54	21.49	–	–	21.49
B012412C	three courses	m	1.20	29.32	–	–	29.32	32.25	–	–	32.25
B012413	**Building in end of pipe to half brick wall; common bricks:**										
B012413A	100 mm pipe.	Each	0.17	4.15	–	–	4.15	4.57	–	–	4.57
B012413B	150 mm pipe.	Each	0.20	4.89	–	–	4.89	5.38	–	–	5.38
B012413C	225 mm pipe.	Each	0.22	5.37	–	–	5.37	5.91	–	–	5.91

Drainage, Sewerage and Public Works

Small Works 2009		Unit	Labour Hours	Labour Net	Plant Net	Materials Net	Unit Net	Labour Gross	Plant Gross	Materials Gross	Unit Price
								(Gross rates include 10% profit)			
				£	£	£	£	£	£	£	£
B01	**DRAINAGE AND SEWERAGE**										
B0124	**MANHOLES ETC**										
B012415	**Building in end of pipe to one brick wall; common bricks:**										
B012415A	100 mm pipe............	Each	0.29	7.44	–	–	7.44	8.18	–	–	8.18
B012415B	150 mm pipe............	Each	0.35	8.97	–	–	8.97	9.87	–	–	9.87
B012415C	225 mm pipe............	Each	0.38	9.74	–	–	9.74	10.71	–	–	10.71
B012416	**Class B engineering bricks in cement mortar 1:3 manhole walls:**										
B012416A	half brick	m²	2.06	50.33	–	37.36	87.69	55.36	–	41.10	96.46
B012416B	one brick	m²	3.50	85.51	–	75.28	160.79	94.06	–	82.81	176.87
B012417	**Extra over engineering brickwork for fair face and flush pointing as the work proceeds:**										
B012417A	stretcher bond	m²	0.56	13.68	–	–	13.68	15.05	–	–	15.05
B012417B	Flemish bond	m²	0.60	14.66	–	–	14.66	16.13	–	–	16.13
B012418	**Oversail engineering brickwork at top of manhole:**										
B012418A	one course.............	m	0.40	9.77	–	–	9.77	10.75	–	–	10.75
B012418B	two courses............	m	0.80	19.54	–	–	19.54	21.49	–	–	21.49
B012418C	three courses	m	1.20	29.32	–	–	29.32	32.25	–	–	32.25
B012419	**Building in end of pipe to half brick wall; engineering bricks:**										
B012419A	100 mm pipe............	Each	0.20	4.89	–	–	4.89	5.38	–	–	5.38
B012419B	150 mm pipe............	Each	0.23	5.62	–	–	5.62	6.18	–	–	6.18
B012419C	225 mm pipe............	Each	0.24	5.86	–	–	5.86	6.45	–	–	6.45
B012420	**Building in end of pipe to one brick wall; engineering bricks:**										
B012420A	100 mm pipe............	Each	0.31	7.57	–	–	7.57	8.33	–	–	8.33
B012420B	150 mm pipe............	Each	0.37	9.04	–	–	9.04	9.94	–	–	9.94
B012420C	225 mm pipe............	Each	0.42	10.26	–	–	10.26	11.29	–	–	11.29
B012421	**Step irons; galvanised general purpose pattern; building into brickwork:**										
B012421A	115 mm tails	Each	0.11	2.69	–	8.42	11.11	2.96	–	9.26	12.22
B012421B	230 mm tails	Each	0.13	3.17	–	10.14	13.31	3.49	–	11.15	14.64

Small Works 2009		Unit	Labour Hours	Labour Net	Plant Net	Materials Net	Unit Net	Labour Gross	Plant Gross	Materials Gross	Unit Price
								(Gross rates include 10% profit)			
				£	£	£	£	£	£	£	£
B01	**DRAINAGE AND SEWERAGE**										
B0124	**MANHOLES ETC**										
B012422	**Vitrified clay channel; set and jointed in cement mortar 1:3:**										
B012422A	100 mm half round straight main channel 600 mm long.	Each	0.40	9.77	–	6.48	16.25	10.75	–	7.13	17.88
B012422B	150 mm half round straight main channel 600 mm long.	Each	0.55	13.44	–	10.59	24.03	14.78	–	11.65	26.43
B012422C	100 mm half round main channel bend.............	Each	0.42	10.26	–	7.88	18.14	11.29	–	8.67	19.95
B012422D	150 mm half round main channel bend.............	Each	0.60	14.66	–	13.24	27.90	16.13	–	14.56	30.69
B012422E	150 mm-100 mm half round straight taper main channel	Each	0.60	14.66	–	32.40	47.06	16.13	–	35.64	51.77
B012422F	150 mm-100 mm half round taper main channel bend ...	Each	0.60	14.65	–	53.01	67.66	16.12	–	58.31	74.43
B012422G	100 mm half section branch channel bend.............	Each	0.42	10.26	–	17.23	27.49	11.29	–	18.95	30.24
B012422H	150 mm half section branch channel bend.............	Each	0.58	14.17	–	27.99	42.16	15.59	–	30.79	46.38
B012422I	100 mm three quarter section branch channel bend	Each	0.42	10.26	–	18.86	29.12	11.29	–	20.75	32.03
B012422J	150 mm three quarter section branch channel bend	Each	0.58	14.17	–	31.35	45.52	15.59	–	34.49	50.07
B012423	**Covers and frames; bedded and flaunched in cement mortar 1:3; cover sealed in grease and sand:**										
B012423A	Grade B class 2; 600 mm × 450 mm................	Each	1.13	27.61	–	212.67	240.28	30.37	–	233.94	264.31
B012423B	Grade C double seal; 600 mm × 450 mm......	Each	0.66	16.13	–	35.39	51.52	17.74	–	38.93	56.67
B012424	**Intercepting trap; vitrified clay; with stopper; cement joints to channel and pipe; bedding and surrounding with 150 mm concrete 1:3:6:**										
B012424A	100 mm................	Each	1.06	25.90	–	90.96	116.86	28.49	–	100.06	128.55
B012424B	150 mm................	Each	1.45	35.42	–	129.19	164.61	38.96	–	142.11	181.07
B012424C	225 mm................	Each	2.00	48.86	–	321.22	370.08	53.75	–	353.34	407.09
B012425	**Sewer connection; hand excavation; searching for existing 225 mm vitrified clay live sewer pipe; breaking into; inserting and connecting new 100 mm vitrified clay saddle junction; make good; backfill; consolidate; depth:**										
B012425A	2.00 m................	Each	21.53	525.98	–	16.56	542.54	578.58	–	18.22	596.79
B012425B	3.00 m................	Each	26.83	655.46	–	16.56	672.02	721.01	–	18.22	739.22

Drainage, Sewerage and Public Works

Small Works 2009		Unit	Labour Hours	Labour Net	Plant Net	Materials Net	Unit Net	Labour Gross	Plant Gross	Materials Gross	Unit Price
								(Gross rates include 10% profit)			
				£	£	£	£	£	£	£	£
B01	**DRAINAGE AND SEWERAGE**										
B0124	**MANHOLES ETC**										
B012426	**Inspection chamber; 0.60 m × 0.45 m × 0.90 m deep. All excavation work; concrete base 150 mm; one brick walls in common bricks in cement mortar, rendered internally; one straight channel and two branch channels with concrete benching; building in ends of 100 mm drain pipes; manhole cover and frame:**										
B012426A	0.60 m × 0.45 m × 38 kg	Each	29.00	708.47	–	249.62	958.09	779.32	–	274.58	1053.90
B012426B	Extra; Class B engineering bricks in lieu of commons ..	Each	0.90	21.99	–	90.55	112.54	24.19	–	99.61	123.79
B012426C	add or deduct for each 150 mm depth in excess of or less than 0.9 m in the foregoing inspection chamber if built in common bricks...................	Each	3.50	85.51	–	40.82	126.33	94.06	–	44.90	138.96
B012426D	add or deduct for each 150 mm depth in excess of or less than 0.9 m in the foregoing inspection chamber if built in class B engineering bricks	Each	4.00	97.72	–	70.25	167.97	107.49	–	77.28	184.77
B012427	**Rendering; 13 mm cement and sand:**										
B012427A	to brick walls; internally	m²	0.80	19.55	–	1.74	21.29	21.51	–	1.91	23.42
B012428	**Interceptor chamber; 0.75 m × 0.60 m × 1.20 m deep. All excavation work; concrete base 150 mm; one brick walls in common bricks in cement mortar, rendered internally; one straight channel and concrete benching; 100 mm interceptor trap and one end of 100 mm drain pipe built in; brickwork at top corbelled over for, and fitted with, manhole cover and frame:**										
B012428A	0.60 m × 0.45 m × 38 kg	Each	44.00	1074.92	–	351.75	1426.67	1182.41	–	386.93	1569.34
B012428B	Extra; Class B engineering bricks in lieu of commons ..	Each	1.50	36.65	–	142.87	179.52	40.32	–	157.16	197.47
B012428C	add or deduct for each 150 mm depth in excess of or less than 1.20 m in the foregoing interceptor chamber built in common bricks...................	Each	4.20	102.61	–	48.80	151.41	112.87	–	53.68	166.55
B012428D	add or deduct for each 150 mm depth in excess of or less than 1.20 m in the foregoing interceptor chamber built in class B engineering bricks	Each	4.80	117.26	–	84.52	201.78	128.99	–	92.97	221.96

Small Works 2009		Unit	Labour Hours	Labour Net	Plant Net	Materials Net	Unit Net	Labour Gross	Plant Gross	Materials Gross	Unit Price
								(Gross rates include 10% profit)			
				£	£	£	£	£	£	£	£
B01	**DRAINAGE AND SEWERAGE**										
B0126	**INSPECTION CHAMBERS**										
B012601	**Shallow inspection chamber; 250 mm diameter; placing in excavation; invert depth:**										
B012601A	600 mm	Each	1.66	40.56	–	104.63	145.19	44.62	–	115.09	159.71
B012602	**Single seal circular cast iron cover and frame:**										
B012602A	Grade C	Each	0.58	14.17	–	71.21	85.38	15.59	–	78.33	93.92
B012603	**Universal inspection chamber; 450 mm diameter; placing in excavation; invert depth:**										
B012603A	500 mm	Each	1.75	42.76	–	185.51	228.27	47.04	–	204.06	251.10
B012603B	730 mm	Each	2.08	50.82	–	268.18	319.00	55.90	–	295.00	350.90
B012603C	960 mm	Each	2.40	58.63	–	283.23	341.86	64.49	–	311.55	376.05
B012604	**Single seal circular cast iron cover and frame:**										
B012604A	Grade C	Each	0.66	16.12	–	71.21	87.33	17.73	–	78.33	96.06
B012610	**Inspection chamber; bolted flat cover; bedding in cement mortar 1:3:**										
B012610A	100 × 100 mm; one branch either side	Each	1.90	68.25	–	209.14	277.39	75.08	–	230.05	305.13
B012610B	150 × 100 mm; one branch either side	Each	2.20	79.03	–	270.97	350.00	86.93	–	298.07	385.00
B012610C	150 × 150 mm; one branch either side	Each	2.30	82.62	–	550.39	633.01	90.88	–	605.43	696.31

Drainage, Sewerage and Public Works

Small Works 2009		Unit	Labour Hours	Labour Net	Plant Net	Materials Net	Unit Net	Labour Gross	Plant Gross	Materials Gross	Unit Price
								(Gross rates include 10% profit)			
				£	£	£	£	£	£	£	£
B01	**DRAINAGE AND SEWERAGE**										
B0128	**PIPE TRENCHES IN SOFT SOIL**										
B012801	**Excavate trenches; by machine; grade bottoms; backfill; compact; dispose of surplus excavated material; earthwork support measured separately:**										
B012801A	0.60 m width × 0.90 m depth	m	1.45	30.24	2.85	–	33.09	33.26	3.14	–	36.40
B012801B	0.60 m width × 1.20 m depth	m	1.80	37.53	3.71	–	41.24	41.28	4.08	–	45.36
B012801C	0.60 m width × 1.50 m depth	m	2.30	47.95	4.57	–	52.52	52.75	5.03	–	57.77
B012801D	0.75 m width × 0.90 m depth	m	1.65	34.40	3.40	–	37.80	37.84	3.74	–	41.58
B012801E	0.75 m width × 1.20 m depth	m	2.30	47.95	4.57	–	52.52	52.75	5.03	–	57.77
B012801F	0.75 m width × 1.50 m depth	m	2.70	56.29	5.68	–	61.97	61.92	6.25	–	68.17
B012801G	0.75 m width × 1.80 m depth	m	3.50	72.97	6.82	–	79.79	80.27	7.50	–	87.77
B012801H	0.75 m width × 2.10 m depth	m	3.65	76.10	8.25	–	84.35	83.71	9.08	–	92.79
B012801I	0.75 m width × 2.40 m depth	m	4.40	91.74	9.10	–	100.84	100.91	10.01	–	110.92
B012801J	0.75 m width × 2.70 m depth	m	5.00	104.25	11.07	–	115.32	114.68	12.18	–	126.85
B012801K	0.75 m width × 3.00 m depth	m	5.90	123.02	11.07	–	134.09	135.32	12.18	–	147.50
B012801L	0.90 m width × 1.80 m depth	m	3.65	76.10	8.25	–	84.35	83.71	9.08	–	92.79
B012801M	0.90 m width × 2.10 m depth	m	4.00	83.40	9.64	–	93.04	91.74	10.60	–	102.34
B012801N	0.90 m width × 2.40 m depth	m	5.00	104.25	11.07	–	115.32	114.68	12.18	–	126.85
B012801O	0.90 m width × 2.70 m depth	m	5.40	112.59	12.24	–	124.83	123.85	13.46	–	137.31
B012801P	0.90 m width × 3.00 m depth	m	6.70	139.69	13.64	–	153.33	153.66	15.00	–	168.66

Small Works 2009		Unit	Labour Hours	Labour Net	Plant Net	Materials Net	Unit Net	Labour Gross	Plant Gross	Materials Gross	Unit Price
				£	£	£	£	(Gross rates include 10% profit)			£
								£	£	£	
B01	**DRAINAGE AND SEWERAGE**										
B0129	**PIPE TRENCHES IN CLAY OR COMPACT GRAVEL**										
B012901	Excavate trenches; by machine; grade bottoms; backfill; compact; dispose of surplus excavated material; earthwork support measured separately:										
B012901A	0.60 m width × 0.90 m depth	m	1.55	32.31	3.40	–	35.71	35.54	3.74	–	39.28
B012901B	0.60 m width × 1.20 m depth	m	1.90	39.61	4.57	–	44.18	43.57	5.03	–	48.60
B012901C	0.60 m width × 1.50 m depth	m	2.40	50.04	5.68	–	55.72	55.04	6.25	–	61.29
B012901D	0.75 m width × 0.90 m depth	m	1.75	36.49	3.71	–	40.20	40.14	4.08	–	44.22
B012901E	0.75 m width × 1.20 m depth	m	2.40	50.04	5.39	–	55.43	55.04	5.93	–	60.97
B012901F	0.75 m width × 1.50 m depth	m	2.80	58.38	6.82	–	65.20	64.22	7.50	–	71.72
B012901G	0.75 m width × 1.80 m depth	m	3.40	70.89	8.25	–	79.14	77.98	9.08	–	87.05
B012901H	0.75 m width × 2.10 m depth	m	3.80	79.23	9.64	–	88.87	87.15	10.60	–	97.76
B012901I	0.75 m width × 2.40 m depth	m	4.60	95.91	11.07	–	106.98	105.50	12.18	–	117.68
B012901J	0.75 m width × 2.70 m depth	m	5.30	110.51	12.24	–	122.75	121.56	13.46	–	135.03
B012901K	0.75 m width × 3.00 m depth	m	6.50	135.53	13.35	–	148.88	149.08	14.69	–	163.77
B012901L	0.90 m width × 1.80 m depth	m	3.80	79.23	9.64	–	88.87	87.15	10.60	–	97.76
B012901M	0.90 m width × 2.10 m depth	m	4.15	86.53	11.67	–	98.20	95.18	12.84	–	108.02
B012901N	0.90 m width × 2.40 m depth	m	5.30	110.50	13.10	–	123.60	121.55	14.41	–	135.96
B012901O	0.90 m width × 2.70 m depth	m	5.60	116.76	14.78	–	131.54	128.44	16.26	–	144.69
B012901P	0.90 m width × 3.00 m depth	m	7.25	151.17	16.49	–	167.66	166.29	18.14	–	184.43

Drainage, Sewerage and Public Works

Small Works 2009		Unit	Labour Hours	Labour Net	Plant Net	Materials Net	Unit Net	Labour Gross	Plant Gross	Materials Gross	Unit Price
								(Gross rates include 10% profit)			
				£	£	£	£	£	£	£	£
B01	**DRAINAGE AND SEWERAGE**										
B0130	**PIPE TRENCHES IN CHALK**										
B013001	**Excavate trenches; by machine; grade bottoms; backfill; compact; dispose of surplus excavated material; earthwork support measured separately:**										
B013001A	0.60 m width × 0.90 m depth	m	1.80	37.53	3.97	–	41.50	41.28	4.37	–	45.65
B013001B	0.60 m width × 1.20 m depth	m	2.75	57.33	5.14	–	62.47	63.06	5.65	–	68.72
B013001C	0.60 m width × 1.50 m depth	m	3.20	66.72	6.53	–	73.25	73.39	7.18	–	80.58
B013001D	0.75 m width × 0.90 m depth	m	2.10	43.79	4.82	–	48.61	48.17	5.30	–	53.47
B013001E	0.75 m width × 1.20 m depth	m	3.20	66.72	6.53	–	73.25	73.39	7.18	–	80.58
B013001F	0.75 m width × 1.50 m depth	m	4.35	90.69	7.68	–	98.37	99.76	8.45	–	108.21
B013001G	0.75 m width × 1.80 m depth	m	4.80	100.08	9.64	–	109.72	110.09	10.60	–	120.69
B013001H	0.75 m width × 2.10 m depth	m	5.10	106.33	11.39	–	117.72	116.96	12.53	–	129.49
B013001I	0.75 m width × 2.40 m depth	m	5.90	123.02	12.78	–	135.80	135.32	14.06	–	149.38
B013001J	0.75 m width × 2.70 m depth	m	7.00	145.95	14.21	–	160.16	160.55	15.63	–	176.18
B013001K	0.75 m width × 3.00 m depth	m	8.70	181.39	15.64	–	197.03	199.53	17.20	–	216.73
B013001L	0.90 m width × 1.80 m depth	m	5.10	106.33	11.39	–	117.72	116.96	12.53	–	129.49
B013001M	0.90 m width × 2.10 m depth	m	5.90	123.01	13.64	–	136.65	135.31	15.00	–	150.32
B013001N	0.90 m width × 2.40 m depth	m	7.00	145.95	15.35	–	161.30	160.55	16.89	–	177.43
B013001O	0.90 m width × 2.70 m depth	m	7.75	161.59	17.06	–	178.65	177.75	18.77	–	196.52
B013001P	0.90 m width × 3.00 m depth	m	9.00	187.65	19.03	–	206.68	206.42	20.93	–	227.35
B0132	**BREAK UP PAVED SURFACES**										
B013201	**Extra over trench excavation for breaking up with compressed air equipment:**										
B013201A	75 mm tarmacadam	m²	0.43	8.97	–	–	8.97	9.87	–	–	9.87
B013201B	150 mm plain concrete	m²	1.35	28.15	5.19	–	33.34	30.97	5.71	–	36.67
B013201C	150 mm reinforced concrete	m²	1.83	38.16	7.02	–	45.18	41.98	7.72	–	49.70

Small Works 2009		Unit	Labour Hours	Labour Net	Plant Net	Materials Net	Unit Net	Labour Gross	Plant Gross	Materials Gross	Unit Price
								(Gross rates include 10% profit)			
				£	£	£	£	£	£	£	£
B01	**DRAINAGE AND SEWERAGE**										
B0133	**REINSTATE PAVED SURFACES**										
B013301	**Reinstate paving; 100 mm hardcore bed:**										
B013301A	75 mm tarmacadam	m²	0.42	8.75	–	25.18	33.93	9.63	–	27.70	37.32
B013302	**Reinstate paving; 150 mm hardcore bed:**										
B013302A	150 mm plain concrete	m²	0.85	17.73	–	21.95	39.68	19.50	–	24.15	43.65
B0134	**OPEN EARTHWORK SUPPORT**										
B013401	**Both sides of trench measured; average depth of trench:**										
B013401A	0.90 m	m	0.22	4.59	–	2.48	7.07	5.05	–	2.73	7.78
B013401B	1.20 m	m	0.30	6.25	–	3.17	9.42	6.88	–	3.49	10.36
B013401C	1.50 m	m	0.40	8.34	–	3.92	12.26	9.17	–	4.31	13.49
B013401D	1.80 m	m	0.45	9.39	–	4.60	13.99	10.33	–	5.06	15.39
B013401E	2.10 m	m	0.55	11.47	–	5.69	17.16	12.62	–	6.26	18.88
B013401F	2.40 m	m	0.70	14.59	–	6.42	21.01	16.05	–	7.06	23.11
B013401G	2.70 m	m	0.85	17.73	–	7.08	24.81	19.50	–	7.79	27.29
B013401H	3.00 m	m	1.00	20.85	–	7.81	28.66	22.94	–	8.59	31.53
B0136	**CLOSE EARTHWORK SUPPORT**										
B013601	**Both sides of trench measured; average depth of trench:**										
B013601A	0.90 m	m	1.65	34.41	–	7.41	41.82	37.85	–	8.15	46.00
B013601B	1.20 m	m	2.20	45.87	–	9.58	55.45	50.46	–	10.54	61.00
B013601C	1.50 m	m	2.90	60.46	–	11.69	72.15	66.51	–	12.86	79.37
B013601D	1.80 m	m	3.50	72.98	–	13.85	86.83	80.28	–	15.24	95.51
B013601E	2.10 m	m	4.10	85.49	–	17.06	102.55	94.04	–	18.77	112.81
B013601F	2.40 m	m	5.20	108.42	–	19.79	128.21	119.26	–	21.77	141.03
B013601G	2.70 m	m	6.20	129.27	–	21.31	150.58	142.20	–	23.44	165.64
B013601H	3.00 m	m	7.25	151.16	–	23.37	174.53	166.28	–	25.71	191.98

Small Works 2009		Unit	Labour Hours	Labour Net	Plant Net	Materials Net	Unit Net	Labour Gross	Plant Gross	Materials Gross	Unit Price
				£	£	£	£	£	£	£	£
								(Gross rates include 10% profit)			
B01	**DRAINAGE AND SEWERAGE**										
B0138	**PIPE BEDS AND COVERINGS**										
B013801	**Plain concrete mix 1:3:6; 150 mm bed; width:**										
B013801A	400 mm	m	0.43	8.96	–	6.26	15.22	9.86	–	6.89	16.74
B013801B	450 mm	m	0.50	10.42	–	8.17	18.59	11.46	–	8.99	20.45
B013801C	525 mm	m	0.58	12.09	–	9.58	21.67	13.30	–	10.54	23.84
B013801D	600 mm	m	0.72	15.01	–	10.89	25.90	16.51	–	11.98	28.49
B013801E	675 mm	m	0.85	17.73	–	12.19	29.92	19.50	–	13.41	32.91
B013801F	750 mm	m	1.00	20.85	–	13.61	34.46	22.94	–	14.97	37.91
B013801G	825 mm	m	1.14	23.77	–	15.02	38.79	26.15	–	16.52	42.67
B013801H	900 mm	m	1.28	26.69	–	16.44	43.13	29.36	–	18.08	47.44
B013802	**Plain concrete mix 1:3:6; 150 mm bed and filling to half height of pipe; width:**										
B013802A	400 mm to 100 mm pipe	m	0.59	12.30	–	9.15	21.45	13.53	–	10.07	23.60
B013802B	450 mm to 150 mm pipe	m	0.74	15.42	–	11.11	26.53	16.96	–	12.22	29.18
B013802C	525 mm to 225 mm pipe	m	0.91	18.98	–	13.17	32.15	20.88	–	14.49	35.37
B013802D	600 mm to 300 mm pipe	m	1.25	26.06	–	16.77	42.83	28.67	–	18.45	47.11
B013802E	675 mm to 375 mm pipe	m	1.37	28.56	–	19.82	48.38	31.42	–	21.80	53.22
B013802F	750 mm to 450 mm pipe	m	1.63	33.99	–	23.08	57.07	37.39	–	25.39	62.78
B013802G	825 mm to 525 mm pipe	m	1.90	39.62	–	26.67	66.29	43.58	–	29.34	72.92
B013802H	900 mm to 600 mm pipe	m	2.06	42.95	–	30.16	73.11	47.25	–	33.18	80.42
B013804	**Plain concrete mix 1:3:6; 150 mm bed and covering; width:**										
B013804A	400 mm to 100 mm pipe	m	1.24	25.86	–	18.07	43.93	28.45	–	19.88	48.32
B013804B	450 mm to 150 mm pipe	m	1.56	32.53	–	21.99	54.52	35.78	–	24.19	59.97
B013804C	525 mm to 225 mm pipe	m	1.94	40.45	–	26.24	66.69	44.50	–	28.86	73.36
B013804D	600 mm to 300 mm pipe	m	2.62	54.62	–	33.32	87.94	60.08	–	36.65	96.73
B013804E	675 mm to 375 mm pipe	m	3.44	71.72	–	39.63	111.35	78.89	–	43.59	122.49
B013804F	750 mm to 450 mm pipe	m	5.00	104.25	–	46.16	150.41	114.68	–	50.78	165.45
B013804G	825 mm to 525 mm pipe	m	7.58	158.04	–	53.46	211.50	173.84	–	58.81	232.65
B013804H	900 mm to 600 mm pipe	m	9.77	203.70	–	60.10	263.80	224.07	–	66.11	290.18
B0140	**SOLID WALL CONCENTRIC EXTERNAL RIB REINFORCED UPVC**										
B014001	**For sewers; in trenches; 150 mm nominal size pipes:**										
B014001A	in runs exceeding 3.00 m long	m	0.25	5.21	–	9.08	14.29	5.73	–	9.99	15.72
B014001B	Extra for; bends	Each	0.22	4.59	–	21.32	25.91	5.05	–	23.45	28.50
B014001C	Extra for; junctions	Each	0.29	6.05	–	43.91	49.96	6.66	–	48.30	54.96
B014001D	Extra for; adaptor to clay	Each	0.13	2.71	–	83.30	86.01	2.98	–	91.63	94.61
B014002	**For sewers; in trenches; 225 mm nominal size pipes:**										
B014002A	in runs exceeding 3.00 m long	m	0.29	6.05	–	22.50	28.55	6.66	–	24.75	31.41
B014002B	Extra for; bends	Each	0.26	5.42	–	90.92	96.34	5.96	–	100.01	105.97
B014002C	Extra for; junctions	Each	0.35	7.30	–	119.57	126.87	8.03	–	131.53	139.56
B014002D	Extra for; adaptor to clay	Each	0.17	3.55	–	103.78	107.33	3.91	–	114.16	118.06
B014003	**For sewers; in trenches; 300 mm nominal size pipes:**										
B014003A	in runs exceeding 3.00 m long	m	0.42	8.76	–	34.66	43.42	9.64	–	38.13	47.76
B014003B	Extra for; bends	Each	0.37	7.72	–	181.60	189.32	8.49	–	199.76	208.25
B014003C	Extra for; junctions	Each	0.48	10.01	–	244.40	254.41	11.01	–	268.84	279.85
B014003D	Extra for; adaptor to clay	Each	0.18	3.76	–	272.98	276.74	4.14	–	300.28	304.41

Small Works 2009		Unit	Labour Hours	Labour Net	Plant Net	Materials Net	Unit Net	Labour Gross	Plant Gross	Materials Gross	Unit Price
								(Gross rates include 10% profit)			
				£	£	£	£	£	£	£	£
B01	**DRAINAGE AND SEWERAGE**										
B0142	**HEPSEAL DRAIN PIPES AND FITTINGS**										
B014201	**Push-fit flexible socket joints; for sewerage; in trenches; 100 mm nominal size pipes:**										
B014201A	in runs exceeding 3.00 m long	m	0.25	6.10	–	6.08	12.18	6.71	–	6.69	13.40
B014201B	in runs not exceeding 3.00 m long	m	0.33	8.06	–	6.08	14.14	8.87	–	6.69	15.55
B014201C	Extra for; bend	Each	0.30	7.33	–	8.20	15.53	8.06	–	9.02	17.08
B014201E	Extra for; junction	Each	0.25	6.11	–	17.39	23.50	6.72	–	19.13	25.85
B014202	**Push-fit flexible socket joints; for sewerage; in trenches; 150 mm nominal size pipes:**										
B014202A	in runs exceeding 3.00 m long	m	0.35	8.55	–	12.29	20.84	9.41	–	13.52	22.92
B014202B	in runs not exceeding 3.00 m long	m	0.45	10.99	–	12.29	23.28	12.09	–	13.52	25.61
B014202C	Extra for; bend	Each	0.47	11.48	–	38.49	49.97	12.63	–	42.34	54.97
B014202E	Extra for; junction	Each	0.30	7.33	–	44.56	51.89	8.06	–	49.02	57.08
B014203	**Push-fit flexible socket joints; for sewerage; in trenches; 225 mm nominal size pipes:**										
B014203A	in runs exceeding 3.00 m long	m	0.40	9.78	–	31.37	41.15	10.76	–	34.51	45.27
B014203B	in runs not exceeding 3.00 m long	m	0.50	12.22	–	31.37	43.59	13.44	–	34.51	47.95
B014203C	Extra for; bend	Each	0.50	12.22	–	90.21	102.43	13.44	–	99.23	112.67
B014203E	Extra for; junction	Each	0.44	10.74	–	125.92	136.66	11.81	–	138.51	150.33
B014204	**Push-fit flexible socket joints; for sewerage; in trenches; 300 mm nominal size pipes:**										
B014204A	in runs exceeding 3.00 m long	m	0.62	15.14	–	66.93	82.07	16.65	–	73.62	90.28
B014204B	in runs not exceeding 3.00 m long	m	0.78	19.05	–	66.93	85.98	20.96	–	73.62	94.58
B014204C	Extra for; bend	each	0.78	19.06	–	155.78	174.84	20.97	–	171.36	192.32
B014204E	Extra for; junction	each	0.74	18.08	–	245.18	263.26	19.89	–	269.70	289.59
B014205	**Push-fit flexible socket joints; for sewerage; in trenches; 400 mm nominal size pipes:**										
B014205A	in runs exceeding 3.00 m long	m	0.74	18.07	–	155.24	173.31	19.88	–	170.76	190.64
B014205B	in runs not exceeding 3.00 m long	m	0.85	20.76	–	156.79	177.55	22.84	–	172.47	195.31
B014205C	Extra for; bend	each	0.34	8.30	–	525.76	534.06	9.13	–	578.34	587.47
B014205D	Extra for; junction	each	0.23	5.61	–	525.76	531.37	6.17	–	578.34	584.51
B014206	**Push-fit flexible socket joints; for sewerage; in trenches; 450 mm nominal size pipes:**										
B014206A	in runs exceeding 3.00 m long	m	0.84	20.52	–	203.65	224.17	22.57	–	224.02	246.59
B014206B	in runs not exceeding 3.00 m long	m	0.96	23.46	–	203.65	227.11	25.81	–	224.02	249.82
B014206C	Extra for; bend	each	0.40	9.77	–	527.75	537.52	10.75	–	580.53	591.27
B014206D	Extra for; junction	each	0.26	6.35	–	525.76	532.11	6.99	–	578.34	585.32

Drainage, Sewerage and Public Works

Small Works 2009		Unit	Labour Hours	Labour Net	Plant Net	Materials Net	Unit Net	Labour Gross	Plant Gross	Materials Gross	Unit Price
								(Gross rates include 10% profit)			
				£	£	£	£	£	£	£	£
B01	**DRAINAGE AND SEWERAGE**										
B0142	**HEPSEAL DRAIN PIPES AND FITTINGS**										
B014207	**Push-fit flexible socket joints; for sewerage; in trenches; 500 mm nominal size pipes:**										
B014207A	in runs exceeding 3.00 m long	m	0.93	22.72	–	226.97	249.69	24.99	–	249.67	274.66
B014207B	in runs not exceeding 3.00 m long	m	1.06	25.90	–	226.97	252.87	28.49	–	249.67	278.16
B014207C	Extra for; bend	each	0.45	10.99	–	655.16	666.15	12.09	–	720.68	732.77
B014207D	Extra for; junction	each	0.29	7.09	–	6.79	13.88	7.80	–	7.47	15.27
B0144	**CONCRETE CYLINDRICAL CLASS L DRAIN PIPES AND FITTINGS**										
B014401	**Flexible joints; for drainage and sewerage; in trenches; 150 mm nominal size pipes:**										
B014401A	in runs exceeding 3.00 m long	m	0.50	12.21	–	7.72	19.93	13.43	–	8.49	21.92
B014401B	in runs not exceeding 3.00 m long	m	0.62	15.15	–	7.72	22.87	16.67	–	8.49	25.16
B014401C	Extra for; bend	each	0.25	6.11	–	73.46	79.57	6.72	–	80.81	87.53
B014401D	Extra for; junction 150 mm .	each	0.17	4.15	–	51.43	55.58	4.57	–	56.57	61.14
B014402	**Flexible joints; for drainage and sewerage; in trenches; 225 mm nominal size pipes:**										
B014402A	in runs exceeding 3.00 m long	m	0.75	18.32	–	11.57	29.89	20.15	–	12.73	32.88
B014402B	in runs not exceeding 3.00 m long	m	0.99	24.18	–	11.57	35.75	26.60	–	12.73	39.33
B014402C	Extra for; bend	each	0.33	8.07	–	110.19	118.26	8.88	–	121.21	130.09
B014402D	Extra for; junction 150 mm .	each	0.21	5.13	–	77.13	82.26	5.64	–	84.84	90.49
B014403	**Flexible joints; for drainage and sewerage; in trenches; 300 mm nominal size pipes:**										
B014403A	in runs exceeding 3.00 m long	m	0.88	21.49	–	15.43	36.92	23.64	–	16.97	40.61
B014403B	in runs not exceeding 3.00 m long	m	1.10	26.87	–	15.43	42.30	29.56	–	16.97	46.53
B014403C	Extra for; bend	each	0.42	10.26	–	146.92	157.18	11.29	–	161.61	172.90
B014403D	Extra for; junction 150 mm .	each	0.21	5.13	–	102.84	107.97	5.64	–	113.12	118.77
B014404	**Flexible joints; for drainage and sewerage; in trenches; 375 mm nominal size pipes:**										
B014404A	in runs exceeding 3.00 m long	m	1.05	25.65	–	19.03	44.68	28.22	–	20.93	49.15
B014404B	in runs not exceeding 3.00 m long	m	1.24	30.30	–	19.03	49.33	33.33	–	20.93	54.26
B014404C	Extra for; bend	each	0.46	11.24	–	181.26	192.50	12.36	–	199.39	211.75
B014404D	Extra for; junction 150 mm .	each	0.21	5.13	–	126.88	132.01	5.64	–	139.57	145.21
B014405	**Flexible joints; for drainage and sewerage; in trenches; 450 mm nominal size pipes:**										
B014405A	in runs exceeding 3.00 m long	m	1.33	32.49	–	22.95	55.44	35.74	–	25.25	60.98
B014405B	in runs not exceeding 3.00 m long	m	1.50	36.64	–	22.95	59.59	40.30	–	25.25	65.55
B014405C	Extra for; bend	each	0.77	18.81	–	218.47	237.28	20.69	–	240.32	261.01
B014405D	Extra for; junction 150 mm .	each	0.21	5.13	–	152.93	158.06	5.64	–	168.22	173.87

Small Works 2009		Unit	Labour Hours	Labour Net	Plant Net	Materials Net	Unit Net	Labour Gross	Plant Gross	Materials Gross	Unit Price
								(Gross rates include 10% profit)			
				£	£	£	£	£	£	£	£
B01	**DRAINAGE AND SEWERAGE**										
B0142	**HEPSEAL DRAIN PIPES AND FITTINGS**										
B014406	**Flexible joints; for drainage and sewerage; in trenches; 525 mm nominal size pipes:**										
B014406A	in runs exceeding 3.00 m long	m	1.50	36.64	–	29.25	65.89	40.30	–	32.18	72.48
B014406B	in runs not exceeding 3.00 m long	m	1.70	41.53	–	29.25	70.78	45.68	–	32.18	77.86
B014406C	Extra for; bend	each	0.83	20.27	–	278.57	298.84	22.30	–	306.43	328.72
B014406D	Extra for; junction 150 mm .	each	0.21	5.13	–	195.00	200.13	5.64	–	214.50	220.14
B014407	**Flexible joints; for drainage and sewerage; in trenches; 600 mm nominal size pipes:**										
B014407A	in runs exceeding 3.00 m long	m	1.66	40.56	–	37.06	77.62	44.62	–	40.77	85.38
B014407B	in runs not exceeding 3.00 m long	m	1.88	45.93	–	37.06	82.99	50.52	–	40.77	91.29
B014407C	Extra for; bend	each	0.97	23.70	–	352.98	376.68	26.07	–	388.28	414.35
B014407D	Extra for; junction 150 mm .	each	0.21	5.13	–	247.09	252.22	5.64	–	271.80	277.44

Drainage, Sewerage and Public Works

Small Works 2009		Unit	Labour Hours	Labour Net	Plant Net	Materials Net	Unit Net	Labour Gross	Plant Gross	Materials Gross	Unit Price
								(Gross rates include 10% profit)			
				£	£	£	£	£	£	£	£
B01	DRAINAGE AND SEWERAGE										
B0148	HEPWORTH PRECAST CONCRETE CIRCULAR MANHOLE RINGS AND ACCESSORIES										
B014801	Bedding, jointing and pointing in cement mortar (1:3) on prepared bed; ring diameter:										
B014801B	900 mm	m	8.00	195.44	–	42.99	238.43	214.98	–	47.29	262.27
B014801C	1050 mm	m	10.75	262.62	–	45.44	308.06	288.88	–	49.98	338.87
B014801D	1200 mm	m	13.50	329.81	–	55.66	385.47	362.79	–	61.23	424.02
B014802	Cover slabs; heavy duty; reinforced; 600 mm access opening; ring diameter:										
B014802B	900 mm	each	3.10	75.73	–	45.13	120.86	83.30	–	49.64	132.95
B014802C	1050 mm	each	3.60	87.94	–	48.39	136.33	96.73	–	53.23	149.96
B014802D	1200 mm	each	4.10	100.16	–	60.24	160.40	110.18	–	66.26	176.44
B014803	Reducing slab; heavy duty; reinforced:										
B014803A	1200-900 mm diameter	each	1.25	30.54	–	212.18	242.72	33.59	–	233.40	266.99

Small Works 2009		Unit	Labour Hours	Labour Net	Plant Net	Materials Net	Unit Net	Labour Gross	Plant Gross	Materials Gross	Unit Price
								(Gross rates include 10% profit)			
				£	£	£	£	£	£	£	£
B01	**DRAINAGE AND SEWERAGE**										
B0150	**ROAD GULLIES, GRATINGS, COVERS AND FRAMES**										
B015001	**Vitrified clay road gullies including excavation, 150 mm concrete bed and surround and jointing to drain:**										
B015001A	300 mm × 600 mm deep; 100 mm outlet...........	each	4.35	106.27	–	143.19	249.46	116.90	–	157.51	274.41
B015001B	450 mm × 900 mm deep; 150 mm outlet...........	each	8.60	210.10	–	237.32	447.42	231.11	–	261.05	492.16
B015002	**Cast iron hinged roadway gratings and frames; bedding on one course of brickwork built brick-on-edge:**										
B015002A	400 mm × 350 mm × 58 kg......................	each	2.10	51.31	–	200.77	252.08	56.44	–	220.85	277.29
B015002B	500 mm × 350 mm × 66 kg....................	each	2.20	53.74	–	211.96	265.70	59.11	–	233.16	292.27
B015003	**Access cover and frame; Grade B; medium duty; circular single seal solid top; bedding frame in cement and sand 1:3 and the cover in grease and sand:**										
B015003A	600 mm diameter........	each	2.50	61.08	–	134.41	195.49	67.19	–	147.85	215.04
B015004	**Access cover and frame; grade A; heavy duty; double triangular solid top; bedding frame in cement and sand 1:3 an the cover in grease and sand:**										
B015004A	600 mm × 600 mm......	each	2.50	61.07	–	198.98	260.05	67.18	–	218.88	286.06

Drainage, Sewerage and Public Works

Small Works 2009		Unit	Labour Hours	Labour Net	Plant Net	Materials Net	Unit Net	Labour Gross	Plant Gross	Materials Gross	Unit Price
								(Gross rates include 10% profit)			
				£	£	£	£	£	£	£	£
B02	**DRAINAGE AND SEWERAGE REPAIRS AND ALTERATIONS**										
B0201	**REPAIRS**										
B020101	**Break up concrete paving and hardcore under 600 mm wide for excavation drain trench:**										
B020101A	100 mm thick	m	1.10	22.94	–	–	22.94	25.23	–	–	25.23
B020102	**Hand excavate trench for 100 mm drain including backfilling, carting away remainder, including necessary earthwork support:**										
B020102A	average 0.5 m deep	m	1.44	30.02	–	3.43	33.45	33.02	–	3.77	36.80
B020102B	average 1.0 m deep	m	2.90	60.47	–	6.86	67.33	66.52	–	7.55	74.06
B020102C	average 1.5 m deep	m	5.16	107.59	–	10.29	117.88	118.35	–	11.32	129.67
B020102D	100 mm concrete bed and haunch to pipe	m	1.10	22.93	–	9.04	31.97	25.22	–	9.94	35.17
B020104	**HepSeal clayware pipes, laid and jointed in short lengths:**										
B020104A	100 mm	m	0.50	12.21	–	6.08	18.29	13.43	–	6.69	20.12
B020105	**Make good 100 mm concrete paving and hardcore under, after drainwork:**										
B020105A	average 600 mm wide	m	1.30	27.11	–	7.62	34.73	29.82	–	8.38	38.20
B020106	**Cutting into brick side of exposed manhole and concrete benching for new branch drain and three quarter section channel, make good brickwork and benching:**										
B020106A	100 mm	each	3.00	73.29	–	39.80	113.09	80.62	–	43.78	124.40
B020108	**Glazed clayware gully and grid with 100 mm outlet joint to drain, including necessary excavation and concrete bed:**										
B020108A	150 mm × 150 mm × 100 mm	each	2.40	58.63	–	50.54	109.17	64.49	–	55.59	120.09
B020109	**Concrete curb around glazed clayware gully including necessary formwork:**										
B020109A	100 mm	each	1.25	30.54	–	6.31	36.85	33.59	–	6.94	40.54
B020110	**Demolish curb, disconnect and remove gully, supply and connect new gully and grid including work to concrete bed, new curb, rendering three sides and remake connection after rodding:**										
B020110A	150 mm × 150 mm × 100 mm	each	6.00	146.58	–	54.92	201.50	161.24	–	60.41	221.65

Small Works 2009		Unit	Labour Hours	Labour Net	Plant Net	Materials Net	Unit Net	Labour Gross	Plant Gross	Materials Gross	Unit Price
								(Gross rates include 10% profit)			
				£	£	£	£	£	£	£	£
B02	**DRAINAGE AND SEWERAGE REPAIRS AND ALTERATIONS**										
B0201	**REPAIRS**										
B020111	**Break up defective curb surround to manhole and reform in:**										
B020111A	fine concrete splayed and rendered	each	1.55	37.86	–	7.19	45.05	41.65	–	7.91	49.56
B020112	**Cut through external brick wall and 150 mm concrete floor and connect 102 mm bend to trap of pan at one end and existing pipe at the other end:**										
B020112A	225 mm brick wall	each	7.50	183.23	–	20.08	203.31	201.55	–	22.09	223.64
B020114	**Form new manhole on line of existing drain with 150 mm concrete base, 225 mm brick walls, cover and frame. Cut away existing drain within manhole to form channel, provide and set 2 no. three quarter section channels, form concrete benching and cement render walls:**										
B020114A	0.9 m deep...............	each	36.00	879.48	–	239.38	1118.86	967.43	–	263.32	1230.75
B020114B	add for every extra 300 mm depth in excess depth in excess of 0.9 m..........	each	9.00	219.87	–	35.47	255.34	241.86	–	39.02	280.87
B020116	**Take up existing manhole cover and frame and provide, bed and seal new cover and frame 610 mm × 457 mm:**										
B020116A	25 kg	each	1.10	26.88	–	78.03	104.91	29.57	–	85.83	115.40
B020116B	38 kg	each	1.30	31.76	–	85.58	117.34	34.94	–	94.14	129.07

Drainage, Sewerage and Public Works

Small Works 2009		Unit	Labour Hours	Labour Net	Plant Net	Materials Net	Unit Net	Labour Gross	Plant Gross	Materials Gross	Unit Price
								(Gross rates include 10% profit)			
				£	£	£	£	£	£	£	£
B02	**DRAINAGE AND SEWERAGE REPAIRS AND ALTERATIONS**										
B0201	**REPAIRS**										
B020118	**Excavate for stoppage in 100 mm drain, cut out and renew two lengths of pipe, fill in and test. Reform paving:**										
B020118A	assumed depth 0.9 m	each	10.00	244.30	–	29.47	273.77	268.73	–	32.42	301.15
B020119	**Unstop gullies, remove silt:**										
B020119A	clean and flush with disinfectant	each	1.15	28.09	–	–	28.09	30.90	–	–	30.90
B020121	**Clear drains, rod and flush in sections**										
B020121A	average length 25 m.......	each	5.75	140.47	–	–	140.47	154.52	–	–	154.52
B020122	**Unstop and smoke test soil pipe:**										
B020122A	cast iron.................	each	4.20	102.61	–	–	102.61	112.87	–	–	112.87
B020123	**Take up manhole cover, clean and sand out frame channels:**										
B020123A	rebed in grease	each	1.10	26.87	–	–	26.87	29.56	–	–	29.56
B020124	**Clayware channel to gully set in concrete with brick curb rendered in cement mortar:**										
B020124A	450 mm long.............	each	2.00	48.86	–	10.21	59.07	53.75	–	11.23	64.98
B020124B	supply and fit new gully grid	each	0.25	6.11	–	4.96	11.07	6.72	–	5.46	12.18

Small Works 2009		Unit	Labour Hours	Labour Net	Plant Net	Materials Net	Unit Net	Labour Gross	Plant Gross	Materials Gross	Unit Price
								(Gross rates include 10% profit)			
				£	£	£	£	£	£	£	£
B02	**DRAINAGE AND SEWERAGE REPAIRS AND ALTERATIONS**										
B0201	**REPAIRS**										
B020126	**Open up manhole, break out brickwork and benching to main channel, provide for and insert one three quarter channel bend 100 mm and join to existing channel, reform benching:**										
B020126A	make good all work disturbed and refix manhole cover ...	each	10.00	244.30	–	26.70	271.00	268.73	–	29.37	298.10
B020128	**Open up manhole, 0.9 m × 0.9 m inside on plan. Break out all channels and branches. Break out one brick side of manhole at one end and extend manhole by 150 mm × 0.9 m inside with 150 mm concrete at bottom, one brick side in stock bricks and 150 mm concrete cover. Build in two pipes 150 mm and one pipe 100 mm provide and insert straight main channel 150 mm and six half branch channel bends 100 mm and reform benching. Make good all work disturbed and refix manhole cover:**										
B020128A	1.27 m deep	each	24.00	586.32	–	280.36	866.68	644.95	–	308.40	953.35
B020128B	Extra over excavation for breaking out brick manhole 0.8 m × 0.7 m inside on plan and 0.9 m deep to invert	each	3.00	73.29	–	–	73.29	80.62	–	–	80.62
B020128C	add or deduct for every 300 mm more or less than 0.9 m deep to invert	each	1.00	24.43	–	–	24.43	26.87	–	–	26.87
B020130	**Seal open ends of disused clayware pipes with concrete plugs 300 mm long:**										
B020130A	100 mm diameter.........	each	0.60	14.65	–	0.33	14.98	16.12	–	0.36	16.48
B020130B	150 mm diameter.........	each	0.80	19.55	–	0.76	20.31	21.51	–	0.84	22.34
B020130C	225 mm diameter.........	each	1.10	26.88	–	2.61	29.49	29.57	–	2.87	32.44

Drainage, Sewerage and Public Works

Small Works 2009		Unit	Labour Hours	Labour Net	Plant Net	Materials Net	Unit Net	Labour Gross	Plant Gross	Materials Gross	Unit Price
									(Gross rates include 10% profit)		
				£	£	£	£	£	£	£	£
B03	**ROADS AND FOOTWAYS, KERBS ETC: WATER MAINS: CABLE LAYING: PILING**										
B0301	**ROADS**										
B030101	**Cut up turves, wheel away and stack:**										
B030101A	not exceeding 100 mm	m²	0.40	8.34	–	–	8.34	9.17	–	–	9.17
B030102	**Take turves off stack, re-lay, level an well roll:**										
B030102A	not exceeding 100 m	m²	0.55	11.47	–	–	11.47	12.62	–	–	12.62
B030103	**Excavate over site average 150 mm deep and wheel and deposit:**										
B030103A	by hand	m²	0.38	7.92	–	–	7.92	8.71	–	–	8.71
B030103B	by machine	m²	–	–	0.57	–	0.57	–	0.63	–	0.63
B030104	**Hand excavation to reduce levels average 150 mm deep; remove excavated material by dumper 100 m; spread and level:**										
B030104A	loose soil...............	m²	0.55	11.47	0.27	–	11.74	12.62	0.30	–	12.91
B030104B	firm soil; sand...........	m²	0.66	13.76	0.27	–	14.03	15.14	0.30	–	15.43
B030104C	light clay; compact soil; gravel..................	m²	0.69	14.39	0.27	–	14.66	15.83	0.30	–	16.13
B030104D	stiff heavy clay	m²	0.92	19.18	0.27	–	19.45	21.10	0.30	–	21.40
B030104E	soft chalk...............	m²	1.38	28.77	0.27	–	29.04	31.65	0.30	–	31.94
B030105	**Hand excavation to reduce levels average 225 mm deep; remove excavated material by dumper 100 m; and deposit:**										
B030105A	loose soil..............	m²	0.65	13.55	0.45	–	14.00	14.91	0.50	–	15.40
B030105B	firm soil; sand...........	m²	0.78	16.26	0.45	–	16.71	17.89	0.50	–	18.38
B030105C	light clay; compact soil; gravel..................	m²	0.81	16.89	0.45	–	17.34	18.58	0.50	–	19.07
B030105D	stiff heavy clay	m²	1.08	22.52	0.45	–	22.97	24.77	0.50	–	25.27
B030105E	soft chalk...............	m²	1.63	33.98	0.45	–	34.43	37.38	0.50	–	37.87
B030106	**Machine excavation to reduce level; load excavated material into:**										
B030106A	lorries.................	m³	1.00	20.85	7.39	–	28.24	22.94	8.13	–	31.06
B030107	**Hand excavation to reduce levels; remove excavated material by dumper 400 m and deposit:**										
B030107A	loose soil...............	m³	3.00	62.55	7.14	–	69.69	68.81	7.85	–	76.66
B030107B	firm soil; sand...........	m³	3.60	75.06	7.14	–	82.20	82.57	7.85	–	90.42
B030107C	light clay; compact soil; gravel..................	m³	3.75	78.19	7.14	–	85.33	86.01	7.85	–	93.86
B030107D	stiff heavy clay	m³	5.00	104.25	7.14	–	111.39	114.68	7.85	–	122.53
B030107E	soft chalk...............	m³	7.50	156.37	7.14	–	163.51	172.01	7.85	–	179.86
B030108	**Consolidate:**										
B030108A	formation...............	m²	0.10	2.09	–	–	2.09	2.30	–	–	2.30

Small Works 2009		Unit	Labour Hours	Labour Net	Plant Net	Materials Net	Unit Net	Labour Gross	Plant Gross	Materials Gross	Unit Price
								(Gross rates include 10% profit)			
				£	£	£	£	£	£	£	£
B03	**ROADS AND FOOTWAYS, KERBS ETC: WATER MAINS: CABLE LAYING: PILING**										
B0301	**ROADS**										
B030109	**Roll formation:**										
B030109B	8 Tonne roller	m²	0.10	2.08	0.42	–	2.50	2.29	0.46	–	2.75
B030110	**Break up 100 mm tarmacadam paving:**										
B030110A	by hand	m²	1.30	27.11	–	–	27.11	29.82	–	–	29.82
B030110B	by two tool compressor	m²	0.20	4.17	4.60	–	8.77	4.59	5.06	–	9.65
B030111	**Break up 100 mm tarmacadam paving and hardcore bed:**										
B030111A	by hand	m²	1.50	31.28	–	–	31.28	34.41	–	–	34.41
B030111B	by two tool compressor	m²	0.30	6.26	6.44	–	12.70	6.89	7.08	–	13.97
B030113	**Break up 150 mm surface concrete:**										
B030113A	by hand	m²	2.50	52.13	–	–	52.13	57.34	–	–	57.34
B030113B	by two tool compressor	m²	0.40	8.34	6.79	–	15.13	9.17	7.47	–	16.64
B030114	**Break up 150 mm surface concrete and 100 mm hardcore bed:**										
B030114A	by hand	m²	3.00	62.55	–	–	62.55	68.81	–	–	68.81
B030114B	by two tool compressor	m²	0.50	10.43	11.59	–	22.02	11.47	12.75	–	24.22
B030115	**Break up 225 mm surface concrete:**										
B030115A	by hand	m²	4.00	83.40	–	–	83.40	91.74	–	–	91.74
B030115B	by two tool compressor	m²	0.60	12.51	16.74	–	29.25	13.76	18.41	–	32.18
B030116	**Break up 300 mm surface concrete:**										
B030116A	by hand	m²	6.00	125.10	–	–	125.10	137.61	–	–	137.61
B030116B	by two tool compressor	m²	1.00	20.85	19.31	–	40.16	22.94	21.24	–	44.18
B030118	**Break up 150 mm reinforced surface concrete:**										
B030118A	by hand	m²	3.75	78.19	–	–	78.19	86.01	–	–	86.01
B030118B	by two tool compressor	m²	0.60	12.51	16.74	–	29.25	13.76	18.41	–	32.18
B030120	**Break up 225 mm reinforced surface concrete:**										
B030120A	by hand	m²	6.00	125.10	–	–	125.10	137.61	–	–	137.61
B030120B	by two tool compressor	m²	0.90	18.77	25.01	–	43.78	20.65	27.51	–	48.16
B030121	**Break up 300 mm reinforced surface concrete:**										
B030121A	by hand	m²	9.00	187.65	–	–	187.65	206.42	–	–	206.42
B030121B	by two tool compressor	m²	1.50	31.28	33.30	–	64.58	34.41	36.63	–	71.04
B030122	**Levelling off slightly uneven areas by bulldozer and remove arisings; distance**										
B030122A	20 m	m²	0.25	5.21	1.54	–	6.75	5.73	1.69	–	7.43
B030124	**Take up granite sets:**										
B030124A	set aside for reuse	m²	0.60	12.51	–	–	12.51	13.76	–	–	13.76
B030125	**Clean granite sets; relay on:**										
B030125A	25 mm cement and sand bed and grout joints	m²	2.70	56.29	–	4.58	60.87	61.92	–	5.04	66.96

Drainage, Sewerage and Public Works

Small Works 2009		Unit	Labour Hours	Labour Net	Plant Net	Materials Net	Unit Net	Labour Gross	Plant Gross	Materials Gross	Unit Price
								(Gross rates include 10% profit)			
				£	£	£	£	£	£	£	£
B03	**ROADS AND FOOTWAYS, KERBS ETC: WATER MAINS: CABLE LAYING: PILING**										
B0301	**ROADS**										
B030126	**Hand packed boulder stone pitching blinded with ashes or fine ballast and rolled with heavy roller:**										
B030126A	225 mm thick	m²	1.15	23.98	2.67	7.03	33.68	26.38	2.94	7.73	37.05
B030128	**Furnace clinker hardcore spread levelled and rolled; thickness:**										
B030128A	100 mm	m²	0.20	4.17	–	2.59	6.76	4.59	–	2.85	7.44
B030128B	150 mm	m²	0.25	5.21	–	3.90	9.11	5.73	–	4.29	10.02
B030129	**Brick hardcore bed spread levelled and rolled; thickness:**										
B030129A	100 mm	m²	0.36	7.51	–	2.59	10.10	8.26	–	2.85	11.11
B030129B	150 mm	m²	0.54	11.26	–	3.90	15.16	12.39	–	4.29	16.68
B030129C	225 mm	m²	0.81	16.89	–	5.83	22.72	18.58	–	6.41	24.99
B030130	**Blind hardcore with:**										
B030130A	ashes	m²	0.16	3.34	–	2.14	5.48	3.67	–	2.35	6.03
B030132	**Bitumen macadam 100 mm work to roads in two coats; 70 mm thick base course; 30 mm thick wearing course of 10 mm graded limestone aggregate; grit sprayed on:**										
B030132A	generally	m²	0.60	12.51	–	42.89	55.40	13.76	–	47.18	60.94
B030134	**Polythene building sheets; medium grade laying on:**										
B030134A	hardcore or ashes including laps.	m²	0.05	1.05	–	1.46	2.51	1.16	–	1.61	2.76
B030136	**Blinding layer:**										
B030136A	50 mm concrete 1:3:6	m²	0.35	7.29	–	5.70	12.99	8.02	–	6.27	14.29
B030138	**Surface concrete 1:2:4 spread and levelled to falls and cambers; tamped around reinforcement (measured separately); thickness:**										
B030138A	125 mm	m²	0.75	15.63	–	15.65	31.28	17.19	–	17.22	34.41
B030138B	150 mm	m²	0.85	17.72	–	17.90	35.62	19.49	–	19.69	39.18
B030138C	175 mm	m²	1.00	20.85	–	20.90	41.75	22.94	–	22.99	45.93
B030138D	225 mm	m²	1.15	23.98	–	26.79	50.77	26.38	–	29.47	55.85

Small Works 2009		Unit	Labour Hours	Labour Net	Plant Net	Materials Net	Unit Net	Labour Gross	Plant Gross	Materials Gross	Unit Price
								(Gross rates include 10% profit)			
				£	£	£	£	£	£	£	£
B03	**ROADS AND FOOTWAYS, KERBS ETC: WATER MAINS: CABLE LAYING: PILING**										
B0301	**ROADS**										
B030139	**Fabric reinforcement lapped in surface concrete; reference:**										
B030139A	C283 weighing 2.61 kg/m^2 .	m^2	0.12	2.93	–	3.31	6.24	3.22	–	3.64	6.86
B030139B	C385 weighing 3.41 kg/m^2 .	m^2	0.15	3.67	–	4.23	7.90	4.04	–	4.65	8.69
B030139C	C503 weighing 4.34 kg/m^2 .	m^2	0.20	4.88	–	5.28	10.16	5.37	–	5.81	11.18
B030139D	C636 weighing 5.55 kg/m^2 .	m^2	0.25	6.11	–	6.73	12.84	6.72	–	7.40	14.12
B030140	**Expansion joint:**										
B030140A	13 mm × 175 mm high including formwork	m	0.25	5.21	–	2.45	7.66	5.73	–	2.70	8.43
B030141	**Running top edge of expansion joint with:**										
B030141A	bitumen	m	0.18	3.76	–	0.19	3.95	4.14	–	0.21	4.35
B030142	**Extra over surface concrete for forming channel:**										
B030142A	300 mm wide including formwork.	m	0.25	5.22	–	0.50	5.72	5.74	–	0.55	6.29
B030144	**Treating surface of concrete with silicate of soda:**										
B030144A	two coats.	m^2	0.12	2.50	–	0.45	2.95	2.75	–	0.50	3.25
B030144B	three coats	m^2	0.20	4.17	–	0.67	4.84	4.59	–	0.74	5.32
B030146	**Formwork to edge of surface concrete; straight; height not exceeding:**										
B030146A	125 mm	m	0.19	5.28	–	0.43	5.71	5.81	–	0.47	6.28
B030146B	150 mm	m	0.23	6.39	–	0.51	6.90	7.03	–	0.56	7.59
B030146C	175 mm	m	0.27	7.51	–	0.59	8.10	8.26	–	0.65	8.91
B030146D	225 mm	m	0.34	9.45	–	0.68	10.13	10.40	–	0.75	11.14
B030147	**Formwork to edge of surface concrete; curved; height not exceeding:**										
B030147A	125 mm	m	0.38	10.56	–	0.88	11.44	11.62	–	0.97	12.58
B030147B	150 mm	m	0.46	12.79	–	1.02	13.81	14.07	–	1.12	15.19
B030147C	175 mm	m	0.54	15.01	–	1.06	16.07	16.51	–	1.17	17.68
B030147D	225 mm	m	0.68	18.91	–	1.63	20.54	20.80	–	1.79	22.59

Drainage, Sewerage and Public Works

Small Works 2009		Unit	Labour Hours	Labour Net	Plant Net	Materials Net	Unit Net	Labour Gross	Plant Gross	Materials Gross	Unit Price
				£	£	£	£	£	£	£	£
								(Gross rates include 10% profit)			
B03	ROADS AND FOOTWAYS, KERBS ETC: WATER MAINS: CABLE LAYING: PILING										
B0304	FOOTWAYS										
B030401	Take up precast concrete paving slabs; rebed in:										
B030401A	lime mortar 1:4, grout in cement mortar 1:3	m²	1.20	25.02	–	5.47	30.49	27.52	–	6.02	33.54
B030402	Precast concrete paving slabs 50 mm thick; bedding in:										
B030402A	lime mortar 1:4, grout in cement mortar 1:3	m²	0.65	13.55	–	15.33	28.88	14.91	–	16.86	31.77
B030403	Cutting on paving slabs:										
B030403A	raking..................	m	0.63	13.13	–	2.00	15.13	14.44	–	2.20	16.64
B030403B	curved	m	1.10	22.94	–	3.32	26.26	25.23	–	3.65	28.89
B030404	Gravel paving; two coats; rolled; thickness:										
B030404A	50 mm	m²	0.30	6.25	1.25	1.50	9.00	6.88	1.38	1.65	9.90
B030404B	63 mm	m²	0.35	7.30	1.57	1.95	10.82	8.03	1.73	2.15	11.90
B030405	Fine clinker ash bed; 75 mm thick:										
B030405A	spread, levelled and rolled..	m²	0.30	6.25	–	3.92	10.17	6.88	–	4.31	11.19
B030406	Sand bed; 25 mm thick:										
B030406A	spread, levelled and rolled..	m²	0.10	2.09	0.63	0.98	3.70	2.30	0.69	1.08	4.07
B030408	Bitumen macadam; 65 mm work to footway:										
B030408A	two coats; 45 mm base course; 20 mm wearing course of 6 mm medium graded limestone aggregate; 14 mm chippings sprinkled and rolled into wearing course	m²	0.85	17.72	2.67	32.17	52.56	19.49	2.94	35.39	57.82
B030410	Concrete 1:2:4 paving; thickness:										
B030410A	100 mm..................	m²	0.60	12.51	–	11.89	24.40	13.76	–	13.08	26.84
B030410B	150 mm..................	m²	0.85	17.72	–	17.90	35.62	19.49	–	19.69	39.18
B030411	Extra for marking out:										
B030411A	concrete paving in panels ..	m²	0.30	6.26	–	–	6.26	6.89	–	–	6.89
B030412	Precast concrete edging; bedded and pointed in cement mortar 1:3 on and including 150 mm × 75 mm concrete foundation and haunching:										
B030412A	38 mm × 125 mm	m	0.40	8.34	–	5.49	13.83	9.17	–	6.04	15.21
B030412B	50 mm × 150 mm	m	0.40	8.34	–	3.44	11.78	9.17	–	3.78	12.96
B030413	Creosoted softwood edging 150 mm × 38 mm staked at:										
B030413A	1050 mm centres	m	0.30	6.26	–	2.27	8.53	6.89	–	2.50	9.38

Small Works 2009		Unit	Labour Hours	Labour Net	Plant Net	Materials Net	Unit Net	Labour Gross	Plant Gross	Materials Gross	Unit Price
								(Gross rates include 10% profit)			
				£	£	£	£	£	£	£	£
B03	**ROADS AND FOOTWAYS, KERBS ETC: WATER MAINS: CABLE LAYING: PILING**										
B0305	**KERBS**										
B030501	**Hand excavation; 300 mm × 300 mm foundation trench:**										
B030501A	consolidate	m	0.20	4.17	–	–	4.17	4.59	–	–	4.59
B030502	**Concrete 1:3:6 bed and haunching to kerb:**										
B030502A	300 mm high overall	m	0.33	6.88	–	4.95	11.83	7.57	–	5.45	13.01
B030503	**Precast concrete kerb 152 mm × 305 mm; bedded, jointed and pointed in cement mortar 1:3, haunched both sides with concrete:**										
B030503A	straight	m	0.70	17.10	–	7.84	24.94	18.81	–	8.62	27.43
B030503B	curved	m	1.40	34.20	–	7.84	42.04	37.62	–	8.62	46.24
B030504	**Precast concrete channel 127 mm × 254 mm; bedded, jointed and pointed in cement mortar 1:3, haunched both sides with concrete:**										
B030504A	straight	m	0.50	12.22	–	3.67	15.89	13.44	–	4.04	17.48
B030504B	curved	m	1.00	24.43	–	3.67	28.10	26.87	–	4.04	30.91
B030505	**Precast concrete quadrant; bedded, jointed and pointed in cement mortar 1: haunched with concrete:**										
B030505A	300 mm radius × 250 mm deep	each	0.55	13.44	–	11.11	24.55	14.78	–	12.22	27.01
B030505B	450 mm radius × 250 mm deep	each	0.65	15.88	–	12.25	28.13	17.47	–	13.48	30.94

Drainage, Sewerage and Public Works

Small Works 2009		Unit	Labour Hours	Labour Net	Plant Net	Materials Net	Unit Net	Labour Gross	Plant Gross	Materials Gross	Unit Price
								(Gross rates include 10% profit)			
				£	£	£	£	£	£	£	£
B03	**ROADS AND FOOTWAYS, KERBS ETC: WATER MAINS: CABLE LAYING: PILING**										
B0306	**WATER MAINS**										
B030601	**Excavation of trenches to receive pipes 0.60 m wide × 1.00 m deep; grading bottom; earthwork support; backfilling; compacting; disposal of surplus excavated material; by hand:**										
B030601B	firm soil	m	2.63	54.84	–	–	54.84	60.32	–	–	60.32
B030602	**Excavation of trenches to receive pipes 0.60 m wide × 1.00 m deep; grading bottom; earthwork support; backfilling; compacting; disposal of surplus excavated material; by machine:**										
B030602B	firm soil	m	0.34	7.09	10.81	–	17.90	7.80	11.89	–	19.69
B030604	**Extra over excavating tarmacadam road surfacing:**										
B030604A	replacing with existing consolidated broken tarmacadam as temporary surfacing	m	0.70	14.60	–	–	14.60	16.06	–	–	16.06
B030604B	removing existing tarmacadam and reinstating with new tarmacadam	m	1.10	22.94	4.25	27.92	55.11	25.23	4.68	30.71	60.62
B030606	**Break up concrete paving by drill; replacing with existing broken concrete; consolidate as temporary surfacing:**										
B030606A	150 mm	m	1.00	20.85	–	–	20.85	22.94	–	–	22.94
B030610	**Hand excavation for hydrant pit beyond extent of pipe trench:**										
B030610A	part backfill and dispose of surplus excavated material .	each	1.50	31.28	–	–	31.28	34.41	–	–	34.41
B030611	**Class B engineering bricks; walls of hydrant pit; half brick thick:**										
B030611A	laid dry	each	2.00	48.86	–	48.66	97.52	53.75	–	53.53	107.27
B030611B	cement mortar 1:3	each	5.00	122.15	–	52.15	174.30	134.37	–	57.37	191.73
B030612	**Concrete surround to surface box:**										
B030612A	1:3:6	each	0.45	9.39	–	9.25	18.64	10.33	–	10.18	20.50
B030614	**Surface box; cast iron opening size 380 mm × 230 mm; 100 mm deep with drop-in lid and chain; bedded and flaunched in cement mortar 1:3:**										
B030614A	420 mm × 255 mm overall	each	1.00	24.43	–	51.18	75.61	26.87	–	56.30	83.17
B030614B	temporary reinstatement...	each	1.00	20.85	–	2.94	23.79	22.94	–	3.23	26.17
B030614C	cost per pit complete	each	8.95	208.09	–	115.42	323.51	228.90	–	126.96	355.86

Small Works 2009		Unit	Labour Hours	Labour Net	Plant Net	Materials Net	Unit Net	Labour Gross	Plant Gross	Materials Gross	Unit Price
								(Gross rates include 10% profit)			
				£	£	£	£	£	£	£	£
B03	**ROADS AND FOOTWAYS, KERBS ETC: WATER MAINS: CABLE LAYING: PILING**										
B0307	**CABLE LAYING FOR ELECTRICITY AUTHORITIES**										
B030701	**Excavation of trenches to receive cables; grading bottom; compacting; part backfill and dispose of surplus excavated material; by hand:**										
B030701A	300 mm wide × 525 mm deep..................	m	0.75	15.64	–	–	15.64	17.20	–	–	17.20
B030701B	373 mm wide × 675 mm deep..................	m	1.30	27.11	–	–	27.11	29.82	–	–	29.82
B030702	**Excavation of trenches to receive cables; grading bottom; compacting; part backfill and dispose of surplus excavated material; by machine:**										
B030702A	300 mm wide × 525 mm deep..................	m	0.40	8.34	1.11	–	9.45	9.17	1.22	–	10.40
B030702B	373 mm wide × 675 mm deep..................	m	0.70	14.60	1.71	–	16.31	16.06	1.88	–	17.94
B030703	**Break up 50 mm tarmacadam paving and 75 mm hardcore bed:**										
B030703A	450 mm wide	m	0.60	12.51	1.14	–	13.65	13.76	1.25	–	15.02
B030704	**Temporarily re-lay paving with existing broken tarmacadam and consolidate:**										
B030704A	450 mm wide	m	0.30	6.26	9.62	–	15.88	6.89	10.58	–	17.47
B030705	**Take up paving slabs and ash bed:**										
B030705A	450 mm wide	m	0.40	8.34	–	–	8.34	9.17	–	–	9.17
B030706	**Temporarily re-lay paving with:**										
B030706A	existing slabs on ash bed		0.45	9.38	–	12.15	21.53	10.32	–	13.37	23.68
B030708	**Take up granite sett paving:**										
B030708A	450 mm wide	m	0.55	11.47	–	–	11.47	12.62	–	–	12.62
B030709	**Temporarily re-lay paving with existing setts:**										
B030709A	450 mm wide	m	0.40	8.34	–	–	8.34	9.17	–	–	9.17

Drainage, Sewerage and Public Works

Small Works 2009		Unit	Labour Hours	Labour Net	Plant Net	Materials Net	Unit Net	Labour Gross	Plant Gross	Materials Gross	Unit Price
								(Gross rates include 10% profit)			
				£	£	£	£	£	£	£	£
B03	**ROADS AND FOOTWAYS, KERBS ETC: WATER MAINS: CABLE LAYING: PILING**										
B0307	**CABLE LAYING FOR ELECTRICITY AUTHORITIES**										
B030710	**Break up 75 mm tarmacadam road and 100 mm hardcore bed:**										
B030710A	450 mm wide	m	0.70	14.59	1.61	–	16.20	16.05	1.77	–	17.82
B030712	**Temporarily re-lay paving with existing broken tarmacadam and consolidate:**										
B030712A	450 mm wide	m	0.40	8.34	13.36	–	21.70	9.17	14.70	–	23.87
B030713	**Break up 150 mm concrete paving and 150 mm hardcore bed:**										
B030713A	450 mm wide	m	1.00	20.85	8.77	–	29.62	22.94	9.65	–	32.58
B030714	**Temporarily re-lay paving with existing broken concrete and consolidate:**										
B030714A	450 mm wide	m	0.60	12.51	9.62	–	22.13	13.76	10.58	–	24.34
B030716	**Labour unwinding and laying cable direct in trench:**										
B030716A	25 mm	m	0.10	2.09	–	–	2.09	2.30	–	–	2.30
B030716B	31 mm-50 mm	m	0.12	2.50	–	–	2.50	2.75	–	–	2.75
B030716C	50 mm-63 mm	m	0.14	2.92	–	–	2.92	3.21	–	–	3.21
B030716D	63 mm-75 mm	m	0.20	4.17	–	–	4.17	4.59	–	–	4.59
B030718	**Labour unwinding and drawing cable through ducts in trench:**										
B030718A	25 mm	m	0.22	4.59	–	–	4.59	5.05	–	–	5.05
B030718B	31 mm-50 mm	m	0.25	5.21	–	–	5.21	5.73	–	–	5.73
B030718C	50 mm-63 mm	m	0.30	6.26	–	–	6.26	6.89	–	–	6.89
B030718D	63 mm-75 mm	m	0.40	8.34	–	–	8.34	9.17	–	–	9.17
B030719	**Labour laying tile cable covers:**										
B030719A	300 mm × 100 mm	m	0.30	6.26	–	–	6.26	6.89	–	–	6.89
B030719B	225 mm × 150 mm	m	0.35	7.30	–	–	7.30	8.03	–	–	8.03
B030720	**Labour laying concrete cable covers:**										
B030720A	900 mm × 175 mm	m	0.40	8.34	–	–	8.34	9.17	–	–	9.17
B030720B	900 mm × 225 mm	m	0.50	10.43	–	–	10.43	11.47	–	–	11.47
B030721	**Labour laying stoneware ducts:**										
B030721A	100 mm	m	0.25	5.21	–	–	5.21	5.73	–	–	5.73

Small Works 2009		Unit			Specialist Net		Unit Net		Specialist Gross		Unit Price
									——— (Gross rates include 10% profit) ———		
				£	£	£	£	£	£	£	£
B03	**ROADS AND FOOTWAYS, KERBS ETC: WATER MAINS: CABLE LAYING: PILING**										
B0309	**PILING BY SPECIALISTS**										
B030901	**Driven mini-shell piles 340 mm diameter:**										
B030901A	maximum load 400 kN......	m	–	–	–	68.86	68.86	–	–	75.75	75.75
B030901B	Extra per metre over 250 m length..................	m	–	–	–	41.54	41.54	–	–	45.69	45.69
B030902	**Driven shell piles 400 mm diameter:**										
B030902A	maximum load 600 kN......	m	–	–	–	74.52	74.52	–	–	81.97	81.97
B030902B	Extra per metre over 250 m length..................	m	–	–	–	45.82	45.82	–	–	50.40	50.40
B030903	**Driven shell piles 440 mm diameter:**										
B030903A	maximum load 700 kN......	m	–	–	–	78.80	78.80	–	–	86.68	86.68
B030903B	Extra per metre over 250 m length..................	m	–	–	–	50.23	50.23	–	–	55.25	55.25
B030904	**Driven shell piles 530 mm diameter:**										
B030904A	maximum load 1000 kN	m	–	–	–	87.49	87.49	–	–	96.24	96.24
B030904B	Extra per metre over 250 m length..................	m	–	–	–	60.17	60.17	–	–	66.19	66.19
B030905	**Driven Hardrive piles 270 mm × 270 mm:**										
B030905A	maximum load 1200 kN	m	–	–	–	76.04	76.04	–	–	83.64	83.64
B030905B	Extra per metre over 250 mm length..................	m	–	–	–	45.82	45.82	–	–	50.40	50.40

**Construction Accounting
Solutions
for Small, Medium and Large Enterprises**

Operational and Estimating Systems for the Construction Industry
Summit the Award Wining Solution from RedSky IT

Integrated Solution

RedSky IT's Summit system is the only truly integrated, construction specific, enterprise solution on the UK market. Summit covers the complete process within a single product:

Estimating	Planning	Budgeting	Requisitions
Procurement	Plant	Valuations	CVR
Financials	Payroll	Housebuilding	Service Management

Scalability

Whether you are a small growing subcontractor or a top 100 construction business there is a Summit solution to suit you, and as you grow you can simply upgrade to the next level of software keeping all your existing data.

Choice

Summit gives you freedom of choice to choose the appropriate technology for your business:
Microsoft SQL or Oracle Database
Windows or Linux
Scalable thin client windows or web interface.

Pedigree

Over 1300 clients from your industry have chosen RedSky IT. These secure partnerships drive an unrivalled depth of functionality into our solutions, making RedSky IT the FD's choice of financial software provider for large implementations in the CBI/Real Finance survey 2006 and enabling us to win Product of the Year at the 2007 Construction Computing Awards.

Customer Driven Solutions

As authors of our solutions and not resellers of a 3rd party product, RedSky IT and our customers make the critical decisions regarding product direction and development.

Winner of Most Successful IT
return On Investment

For more information on the Summit Solution contact RedSky IT: 020 3002 8600
or visit www.redskyit.com

LANDSCAPING

Small Works 2009		Unit	Labour Hours	Labour Net	Plant Net	Materials Net	Unit Net	Labour Gross	Plant Gross	Materials Gross	Unit Price
								(Gross rates include 10% profit)			
				£	£	£	£	£	£	£	£
C01	**SEEDING, TURFING AND PLANTING**										
C0101	**PREPARATORY ITEMS**										
C010101	**Temporarily enclose site with chestnut fencing; up to twenty times used:**										
C010101A	1.35 m high	m	0.25	5.21	–	0.63	5.84	5.73	–	0.69	6.42
C010102	**Cut down hedge; grub up roots; burn or deposit in skip; height:**										
C010102A	600 mm	m	1.97	41.07	–	–	41.07	45.18	–	–	45.18
C010102B	900 mm	m	2.63	54.84	–	–	54.84	60.32	–	–	60.32
C010102C	1200 mm	m	3.12	65.05	–	–	65.05	71.56	–	–	71.56
C010102D	1500 mm	m	4.27	89.03	–	–	89.03	97.93	–	–	97.93
C010102E	1800 mm	m	5.74	119.68	–	–	119.68	131.65	–	–	131.65
C010103	**Cut down tree; lop off branches; grub u roots; burn or deposit in skip; fill hole with excavated material; girth and diameter:**										
C010103A	450 mm girth; 140 mm diameter	each	16.00	333.60	–	–	333.60	366.96	–	–	366.96
C010103B	900 mm girth; 290 mm diameter	each	28.00	583.80	–	–	583.80	642.18	–	–	642.18
C010103C	1350 mm girth; 430 mm diameter	each	42.00	875.70	–	–	875.70	963.27	–	–	963.27
C010103D	1800 mm girth; 570 mm diameter	each	56.00	1167.60	–	–	1167.60	1284.36	–	–	1284.36
C010103E	2250 mm girth; 720 mm diameter	each	69.00	1438.65	–	–	1438.65	1582.52	–	–	1582.52
C010103F	2700 mm girth; 860 mm diameter	each	81.00	1688.85	–	–	1688.85	1857.74	–	–	1857.74
C010103G	3150 mm girth; 1000 mm diameter	each	92.00	1918.20	–	–	1918.20	2110.02	–	–	2110.02
C010103H	3600 mm girth; 1150 mm diameter	each	102.00	2126.70	–	–	2126.70	2339.37	–	–	2339.37
C010104	**Clear site of bushes, scrub and undergrowth; cutting down small trees; grub up roots; burn or deposit in skip; average height:**										
C010104A	1.50 m	m²	0.30	6.26	0.99	–	7.25	6.89	1.09	–	7.98
C0102	**SEEDING**										
C010201	**Ground preparation:**										
C010201A	clear site of rubbish	m²	0.08	1.67	–	–	1.67	1.84	–	–	1.84
C010201B	strip site of surface vegetation	m²	0.07	1.46	–	–	1.46	1.61	–	–	1.61
C010201C	cultivate 150 mm deep; remove stones and vegetable matter	m²	0.12	2.50	–	–	2.50	2.75	–	–	2.75
C010201D	fill into barrows; wheel up to 20 m; deposit in skip	m²	0.17	3.54	–	–	3.54	3.89	–	–	3.89
C010201E	hire of 4.5 m³ skip; delivery to site; removing when full; disposal of contents; payment of tipping charges	m²	–	–	12.56	1.85	14.41	–	13.82	2.04	15.85
C010201F	grade	m²	0.08	1.67	–	–	1.67	1.84	–	–	1.84
C010201G	imported standard loam 150 mm deep; spread and levelled.	m²	0.41	8.55	–	6.37	14.92	9.41	–	7.01	16.41
C010201H	fork and rake	m²	0.06	1.25	–	–	1.25	1.38	–	–	1.38
C010201I	dress with bonemeal lightly raked in	m²	0.02	0.41	–	0.17	0.58	0.45	–	0.19	0.64

Landscaping

Small Works 2009		Unit	Labour Hours	Labour Net	Plant Net	Materials Net	Unit Net	Labour Gross	Plant Gross	Materials Gross	Unit Price
								(Gross rates include 10% profit)			
				£	£	£	£	£	£	£	£
C01	**SEEDING, TURFING AND PLANTING**										
C0102	**SEEDING**										
C010202	**Sowing and maintenance:**										
C010202A	seed with seed mixture	m²	0.10	2.08	–	0.20	2.28	2.29	–	0.22	2.51
C010202B	twice roll	m²	0.07	1.46	–	–	1.46	1.61	–	–	1.61
C010202C	scythe to top	m²	0.01	0.21	–	–	0.21	0.23	–	–	0.23
C010202D	scythe to reduce	m²	0.01	0.21	–	–	0.21	0.23	–	–	0.23
C010202E	keep grass mown to height of 50 mm during contract	m²	0.07	1.46	–	–	1.46	1.61	–	–	1.61
C010202F	keep area free of stones exceeding 12 mm	m²	0.07	1.46	–	–	1.46	1.61	–	–	1.61
C010202G	roll in two directions (maintenance)	m²	0.06	1.25	–	–	1.25	1.38	–	–	1.38
C010202H	scythe to top (maintenance)	m²	0.06	1.25	–	–	1.25	1.38	–	–	1.38
C010202I	scythe to reduce (maintenance)	m²	0.06	1.25	–	–	1.25	1.38	–	–	1.38
C010202J	twice box mow (maintenance)	m²	0.08	1.67	–	–	1.67	1.84	–	–	1.84
C010202K	dress with fish manure (maintenance)	m²	0.01	0.21	–	0.05	0.26	0.23	–	0.06	0.29
C010202L	water as necessary (maintenance)	m²	0.06	1.25	–	–	1.25	1.38	–	–	1.38

Small Works 2009		Unit	Labour Hours	Labour Net	Plant Net	Materials Net	Unit Net	Labour Gross	Plant Gross	Materials Gross	Unit Price
				£	£	£	£	£	£	£	£
								(Gross rates include 10% profit)			
C01	**SEEDING, TURFING AND PLANTING**										
C0103	**TURFING**										
C010301	**Ground preparation:**										
C010301A	clear site of rubbish	m²	0.08	1.67	–	–	1.67	1.84	–	–	1.84
C010301B	strip site of surface vegetation	m²	0.07	1.46	–	–	1.46	1.61	–	–	1.61
C010301C	cultivate 150 mm deep; remove stones and vegetable matter	m²	0.12	2.50	–	–	2.50	2.75	–	–	2.75
C010301D	fill into barrows; wheel up to 20 m deposit in skip	m²	0.17	3.54	–	–	3.54	3.89	–	–	3.89
C010301E	hire of 4.5 m³ skip; delivery to site; removing when full; disposal of contents; payment of tipping charges	m²	–	–	12.56	1.85	14.41	–	13.82	2.04	15.85
C010301F	grade	m²	0.08	1.67	–	–	1.67	1.84	–	–	1.84
C010301G	imported standard loam 100 mm deep; spread and levelled.................	m²	0.27	5.62	–	4.24	9.86	6.18	–	4.66	10.85
C010301H	fork and rake	m²	0.06	1.25	–	–	1.25	1.38	–	–	1.38
C010301I	dress with bonemeal lightly raked in	m²	0.02	0.42	–	0.12	0.54	0.46	–	0.13	0.59
C010302	**Laying and maintenance:**										
C010302A	25 mm turves and laying ...	m²	0.33	6.88	–	3.01	9.89	7.57	–	3.31	10.88
C010302B	twice roll	m²	0.07	1.46	–	–	1.46	1.61	–	–	1.61
C010302C	scythe to top	m²	0.01	0.21	–	–	0.21	0.23	–	–	0.23
C010302D	scythe to reduce	m²	0.01	0.21	–	–	0.21	0.23	–	–	0.23
C010302E	keep grass mown to height of 50 mm during contract	m²	0.07	1.46	–	–	1.46	1.61	–	–	1.61
C010302F	roll in two directions	m²	0.06	1.25	–	–	1.25	1.38	–	–	1.38
C010302G	scythe to top (maintenance)	m²	0.06	1.25	–	–	1.25	1.38	–	–	1.38
C010302H	scythe to reduce (maintenance)	m²	0.06	1.25	–	–	1.25	1.38	–	–	1.38
C010302I	twice box mow (maintenance)	m²	0.08	1.67	–	–	1.67	1.84	–	–	1.84
C010302J	top dress with fine sifted soil brushed into joints (maintenance)	m²	0.06	1.25	–	0.70	1.95	1.38	–	0.77	2.15
C010302K	dress with fish manure (maintenance)	m²	0.01	0.21	–	0.06	0.27	0.23	–	0.07	0.30
C010302L	water as necessary (maintenance)	m²	0.06	1.25	–	–	1.25	1.38	–	–	1.38

Landscaping

		Unit	Labour Hours	Labour Net	Plant Net	Materials Net	Unit Net	Labour Gross	Plant Gross	Materials Gross	Unit Price
								(Gross rates include 10% profit)			
				£	£	£	£	£	£	£	£
C01	**SEEDING, TURFING AND PLANTING**										
C0104	**SHRUB PLANTING**										
C010401	**Preparation:**										
C010401A	clear site of rubbish	m²	0.08	1.67	–	–	1.67	1.84	–	–	1.84
C010401B	excavation to reduce levels 300 mm deep	m²	1.08	22.52	–	–	22.52	24.77	–	–	24.77
C010401C	fill into barrows; wheel up to 20 m; deposit in skip	m²	0.33	6.88	–	–	6.88	7.57	–	–	7.57
C010401D	hire of 4.5 m³ skip; delivery to site; removing when full; disposal of contents; payment of tipping charges	m²	–	–	19.82	2.92	22.74	–	21.80	3.21	25.01
C010401E	cultivate 150 mm deep; remove stones and vegetable matter	m²	0.08	1.67	–	–	1.67	1.84	–	–	1.84
C010401F	manure 100 mm deep worked into subsoil	m²	0.17	3.55	–	3.65	7.20	3.91	–	4.02	7.92
C010401G	imported fibrous loam 375 mm deep	m²	1.00	20.85	–	14.51	35.36	22.94	–	15.96	38.90
C010401H	spread topsoil to even levels and camber where necessary	m²	0.05	1.04	–	–	1.04	1.14	–	–	1.14
C010402	**Preparation to existing areas:**										
C010402A	clear beds of rubbish; debris; vegetation	m²	0.08	1.67	–	–	1.67	1.84	–	–	1.84
C010402B	cultivate 150 mm deep; remove stones and vegetable matter	m²	0.08	1.67	–	–	1.67	1.84	–	–	1.84
C010402C	raking to even levels and camber where necessary. . .	m²	0.05	1.04	–	–	1.04	1.14	–	–	1.14
C010403	**Planting operations:**										
C010403A	clear weedgrowth and rubbish before planting	m²	0.08	1.67	–	–	1.67	1.84	–	–	1.84
C010403B	peat 50 mm deep forked into upper 200 mm of topsoil . . .	m²	0.25	5.21	–	2.81	8.02	5.73	–	3.09	8.82
C010403C	bulb planting in beds	each	0.04	0.84	–	0.24	1.08	0.92	–	0.26	1.19
C010403D	bulb planting in grassed areas with dibber; topped up with loose topsoil	each	0.09	1.88	–	0.24	2.12	2.07	–	0.26	2.33
C010403E	ground cover shrubs	each	0.22	4.59	–	10.52	15.11	5.05	–	11.57	16.62
C010403F	hedging plants	each	0.27	5.63	–	4.21	9.84	6.19	–	4.63	10.82
C010403G	plants; open ground grown .	each	0.28	5.84	–	10.52	16.36	6.42	–	11.57	18.00
C010403H	plants; container grown	each	0.30	6.25	–	14.72	20.97	6.88	–	16.19	23.07
C010403I	water at time of planting . . .	m²	0.15	3.13	–	–	3.13	3.44	–	–	3.44
C010403J	fertiliser; John Innes based .	m²	0.02	0.41	–	0.19	0.60	0.45	–	0.21	0.66
C010403K	cultivation, lightly, after planting	m²	0.08	1.67	–	–	1.67	1.84	–	–	1.84
C010404	**Maintenance:**										
C010404A	remove weedgrowth and rubbish; light cultivation; per visit.	m²	0.17	3.54	–	–	3.54	3.89	–	–	3.89
C010404B	water; per visit	m²	0.05	1.04	–	–	1.04	1.14	–	–	1.14
C010404C	mulching; spent mushroom compost; spread over area 80 mm deep; per visit.	m²	0.13	2.71	–	1.94	4.65	2.98	–	2.13	5.12
C010404D	prune shrubs; per visit.	each	0.07	1.46	–	–	1.46	1.61	–	–	1.61
C010404E	prune roses; per visit	each	0.12	2.50	–	–	2.50	2.75	–	–	2.75

Small Works 2009		Unit	Labour Hours	Labour Net	Plant Net	Materials Net	Unit Net	Labour Gross	Plant Gross	Materials Gross	Unit Price
				£	£	£	£	£	£	£	£
								(Gross rates include 10% profit)			
C01	**SEEDING, TURFING AND PLANTING**										
C0105	**CLIMBER PLANTING**										
C010501	**Preparation:**										
C010501A	clear rubbish, debris and vegetation from position . . .	each	0.08	1.67	–	–	1.67	1.84	–	–	1.84
C010501B	excavate position 900 × 230 × 450 mm deep	each	0.47	9.80	–	–	9.80	10.78	–	–	10.78
C010501C	fill into barrows; wheel up to 20 m; deposit in skip	each	0.19	3.96	–	–	3.96	4.36	–	–	4.36
C010501D	hire of 4.5 m³ skip; delivery to site; removing when full; disposal of contents; payment of tipping charges	each	–	–	7.92	1.17	9.09	–	8.71	1.29	10.00
C010501E	cultivate bottom of position to depth of 150 mm	each	0.03	0.63	–	–	0.63	0.69	–	–	0.69
C010501F	manure in bottom of position 100 mm deep	each	0.17	3.55	–	1.31	4.86	3.91	–	1.44	5.35
C010501G	imported fibrous loam 475 mm deep	each	0.71	14.80	–	4.26	19.06	16.28	–	4.69	20.97
C010501H	spread topsoil to even levels and camber	each	0.03	0.63	–	–	0.63	0.69	–	–	0.69
C010502	**Planting operations:**										
C010502A	clear weedgrowth and rubbish before planting	each	0.05	1.04	–	–	1.04	1.14	–	–	1.14
C010502B	peat 50 mm deep forked into upper 200 mm of topsoil . . .	each	0.22	4.59	–	0.94	5.53	5.05	–	1.03	6.08
C010502C	climber plant; open ground grown.	each	0.28	5.84	–	–	5.84	6.42	–	–	6.42
C010502D	climber plant; container grown.	each	0.30	6.26	–	–	6.26	6.89	–	–	6.89
C010502E	water at time of planting . . .	each	0.05	1.04	–	–	1.04	1.14	–	–	1.14
C010502F	fertiliser; John Innes based .	each	0.02	0.41	–	0.05	0.46	0.45	–	0.06	0.51
C010502G	cultivation; lightly; after planting	each	0.05	1.04	–	–	1.04	1.14	–	–	1.14
C010502H	climber guards; semi-circular section; secured to wall at 6 no points	each	1.75	36.49	–	16.57	53.06	40.14	–	18.23	58.37
C010503	**Maintenance:**										
C010503A	remove weedgrowth and rubbish; light cultivation; per visit.	each	0.10	2.09	–	–	2.09	2.30	–	–	2.30
C010503B	water; per visit	each	0.01	0.21	–	–	0.21	0.23	–	–	0.23
C010503C	mulching; spent mushroom compost; spread over area 80 mm deep; per visit.	each	0.07	1.46	–	1.77	3.23	1.61	–	1.95	3.55
C010503D	prune climber; per visit	each	0.10	2.09	–	–	2.09	2.30	–	–	2.30

Landscaping

	Unit	Labour Hours	Labour Net	Plant Net	Materials Net	Unit Net	Labour Gross	Plant Gross	Materials Gross	Unit Price
							— (Gross rates include 10% profit) —			
			£	£	£	£	£	£	£	£

C01 SEEDING, TURFING AND PLANTING

C0106 TREE PLANTING

	Unit	Labour Hours	Labour Net	Plant Net	Materials Net	Unit Net	Labour Gross	Plant Gross	Materials Gross	Unit Price
C010602 Preparation:										
C010602A clear rubbish, debris and vegetation from position; size: 300 × 300 × 300 mm; for transplants, whips and feathered trees	each	0.01	0.21	–	–	0.21	0.23	–	–	0.23
C010602B clear rubbish; debris and vegetation from position size: 900 × 900 × 600 mm for light standard and selected standard trees	each	0.07	1.46	–	–	1.46	1.61	–	–	1.61
C010602C clear rubbish; debris and vegetation from position size: 1200 × 1200 × 1000 mm for heavy and extra heavy standard trees	each	0.12	2.50	–	–	2.50	2.75	–	–	2.75
C010602D excavate to form tree pit size 300 × 300 × 300 mm ..	each	0.14	2.92	–	–	2.92	3.21	–	–	3.21
C010602E excavate to form tree pit size 900 × 900 × 600 mm ..	each	2.43	50.67	–	–	50.67	55.74	–	–	55.74
C010602F excavate to form tree pit size 1200 × 1200 × 1000 mm	each	7.20	150.12	–	–	150.12	165.13	–	–	165.13
C010602G fill into barrows; wheel up to 20 m; deposit in skip; tree pit size: 300 × 300 × 300 mm	each	0.03	0.63	–	–	0.63	0.69	–	–	0.69
C010602H fill into barrows; wheel up to 20 m; deposit in skip; tree pit size: 900 × 900 × 600 mm	each	0.54	11.26	–	–	11.26	12.39	–	–	12.39
C010602I fill into barrows; wheel up to 20 m; deposit in skip; tree pit size: 1200 × 1200 × 1000 mm	each	1.58	32.94	–	–	32.94	36.23	–	–	36.23
C010602J hire of 4.5 m³ skip; delivery to site; removing when full; disposal of contents; payment of tipping charges; 300 × 300 × 300 mm ..	each	–	–	2.32	0.34	2.66	–	2.55	0.37	2.93
C010602K hire of 4.5 m³ skip; delivery to site; removing when full; disposal of contents; payment of tipping charges; 900 × 900 × 600 mm ..	each	–	–	41.30	6.09	47.39	–	45.43	6.70	52.13
C010602L hire of 4.5 m³ skip; delivery to site; removing when full; disposal of contents; payment of tipping charges; 1200 × 1200 × 1000 mm	each	–	–	47.54	7.02	54.56	–	52.29	7.72	60.02

Small Works 2009		Unit	Labour Hours	Labour Net	Plant Net	Materials Net	Unit Net	Labour Gross	Plant Gross	Materials Gross	Unit Price
								(Gross rates include 10% profit)			
				£	£	£	£	£	£	£	£
C01	SEEDING, TURFING AND PLANTING										
C0106	TREE PLANTING										
C010602M	cultivate 150 mm deep to bottom of pit size: 300 × 300 mm	each	0.01	0.21	–	–	0.21	0.23	–	–	0.23
C010602N	cultivate 150 mm deep to bottom of pit size: 900 × 900 mm	each	0.07	1.46	–	–	1.46	1.61	–	–	1.61
C010602O	cultivate 150 mm deep to bottom of pit size: 1200 × 1200 mm	each	0.12	2.50	–	–	2.50	2.75	–	–	2.75
C010602P	manure 100 mm deep to bottom of pit size: 300 × 300 mm	each	0.02	0.42	–	0.50	0.92	0.46	–	0.55	1.01
C010602Q	manure 100 mm deep to bottom of pit size: 900 × 900 mm	each	0.13	2.71	–	4.46	7.17	2.98	–	4.91	7.89
C010602R	manure 100 mm deep to bottom of pit size: 1200 × 1200 mm	each	0.23	4.79	–	7.93	12.72	5.27	–	8.72	13.99
C010602S	imported fibrous loam to pit size: 300 × 300 × 300 mm	each	0.07	1.45	–	1.17	2.62	1.60	–	1.29	2.88
C010602T	imported fibrous loam to pit size: 900 × 900 × 600 mm	each	1.26	26.27	–	18.90	45.17	28.90	–	20.79	49.69
C010602U	imported fibrous loam to pit size: 1200 × 1200 × 1000 mm	each	3.73	77.77	–	55.56	133.33	85.55	–	61.12	146.66
C010602V	finish soil to even levels to pit size: 300 × 300 mm	each	0.01	0.21	–	–	0.21	0.23	–	–	0.23
C010602W	finish soil to even levels to pit size: 900 × 900 mm	each	0.03	0.63	–	–	0.63	0.69	–	–	0.69
C010602X	finish soil to even levels to pit size: 1200 × 1200 mm ...	each	0.04	0.83	–	–	0.83	0.91	–	–	0.91

Landscaping

Small Works 2009		Unit	Labour Hours	Labour Net	Plant Net	Materials Net	Unit Net	Labour Gross	Plant Gross	Materials Gross	Unit Price
								(Gross rates include 10% profit)			
				£	£	£	£	£	£	£	£
C01	**SEEDING, TURFING AND PLANTING**										
C0106	**TREE PLANTING**										
C010604	**Planting operations:**										
C010604A	clear weed growth and rubbish before planting to pit size: 300 mm × 300 m ...	each	0.01	0.21	–	–	0.21	0.23	–	–	0.23
C010604B	clear weedgrowth and rubbish before planting to pit size: 900 mm × 900 m ...	each	0.09	1.88	–	–	1.88	2.07	–	–	2.07
C010604C	clear weedgrowth and rubbish before planting to pit size: 1200 mm × 1200 mm	each	0.16	3.34	–	–	3.34	3.67	–	–	3.67
C010604D	peat 50 mm deep forked into upper 200 mm of topsoil to pit size: 300 mm × 300 mm	each	0.02	0.41	–	0.32	0.73	0.45	–	0.35	0.80
C010604E	peat 50 mm deep forked into upper 200 mm of topsoil to pit size: 900 mm × 900 mm	each	0.16	3.34	–	2.81	6.15	3.67	–	3.09	6.77
C010604F	peat 50 mm deep forked into upper 200 mm of topsoil to pit size: 1200 mm × 1200 mm	each	0.29	6.05	–	4.36	10.41	6.66	–	4.80	11.45
C010604G	tree planting; transplants ..	each	0.10	2.09	–	0.66	2.75	2.30	–	0.73	3.03
C010604H	tree planting; whips	each	0.12	2.50	–	0.89	3.39	2.75	–	0.98	3.73
C010604I	tree planting; feathered	each	0.15	3.13	–	8.83	11.96	3.44	–	9.71	13.16
C010604J	tree planting; light standard	each	0.19	3.96	–	19.87	23.83	4.36	–	21.86	26.21
C010604K	tree planting; standard.....	each	0.19	3.96	–	24.30	28.26	4.36	–	26.73	31.09
C010604L	tree planting; selected standard	each	0.22	4.59	–	41.96	46.55	5.05	–	46.16	51.21
C010604M	tree planting; heavy standard	each	0.24	5.00	–	53.02	58.02	5.50	–	58.32	63.82
C010604N	tree planting; extra heavy standard	each	0.27	5.63	–	61.84	67.47	6.19	–	68.02	74.22
C010604O	water at time of planting to pit size: 300 mm × 300 mm..	each	0.01	0.21	–	–	0.21	0.23	–	–	0.23
C010604P	water at time of planting to pit size: 900 mm × 900 mm..	each	0.05	1.04	–	–	1.04	1.14	–	–	1.14
C010604Q	water at time of planting to pit size: 1200 mm × 1200 mm	each	0.08	1.67	–	–	1.67	1.84	–	–	1.84
C010604R	fertiliser; John Innes based to pit size: 300 mm × 300 mm	each	0.01	0.21	–	0.09	0.30	0.23	–	0.10	0.33
C010604S	fertiliser; John Innes based to pit size: 900 mm × 900 mm	each	0.01	0.21	–	0.70	0.91	0.23	–	0.77	1.00
C010604T	fertiliser; John Innes based to pit size: 1200 mm × 1200 mm	each	0.02	0.42	–	1.17	1.59	0.46	–	1.29	1.75
C010604U	lightly cultivate after planting to pit size; 300 mm × 300 mm	each	0.01	0.21	–	–	0.21	0.23	–	–	0.23
C010604V	lightly cultivate after planting to pit size; 900 mm × 900 mm	each	0.03	0.63	–	–	0.63	0.69	–	–	0.69
C010604W	lightly cultivate after planting to pit size; 1200 mm × 1200 mm	each	0.04	0.83	–	–	0.83	0.91	–	–	0.91
C010604X	turf around tree position after planting to form opening 600 × 600mm to pit size: 900 mm × 900 mm......	each	0.25	5.21	–	1.43	6.64	5.73	–	1.57	7.30
C010604Y	turf around tree position after planting to form opening 600 mm × 600 mm to pit size: 1200 mm × 1200 m .	each	0.45	9.38	–	2.72	12.10	10.32	–	2.99	13.31

Small Works 2009		Unit	Labour Hours	Labour Net	Plant Net	Materials Net	Unit Net	Labour Gross	Plant Gross	Materials Gross	Unit Price
								(Gross rates include 10% profit)			
				£	£	£	£	£	£	£	£
C01	**SEEDING, TURFING AND PLANTING**										
C0106	**TREE PLANTING**										
C010605	**Maintenance:**										
C010605A	remove weedgrowth and rubbish; light cultivation; per visit; to pit size: 300 mm × 300 mm	each	0.01	0.21	–	–	0.21	0.23	–	–	0.23
C010605B	remove weedgrowth and rubbish; light cultivation; per visit; to pit size: 900 mm × 900 mm	each	0.06	1.25	–	–	1.25	1.38	–	–	1.38
C010605C	remove weedgrowth and rubbish; light cultivation; per visit; to pit size: 1200 mm × 1200 mm	each	0.11	2.29	–	–	2.29	2.52	–	–	2.52
C010605D	watering; per visit; to pit size: 300 mm × 300 mm	each	0.01	0.21	–	–	0.21	0.23	–	–	0.23
C010605E	watering; per visit; to pit size: 900 mm × 900 mm	each	0.04	0.83	–	–	0.83	0.91	–	–	0.91
C010605F	watering; per visit; to pit size: 1200 mm × 1200 mm	each	0.07	1.46	–	–	1.46	1.61	–	–	1.61
C010605G	mulching; spent mushroom compost; spread 80 mm deep; per visit; over pit size: 300 mm × 300 mm	each	0.01	0.21	–	0.56	0.77	0.23	–	0.62	0.85
C010605H	mulching; spent mushroom compost; spread 80 mm deep; per visit; over pit size: 900 mm × 900 mm	each	0.10	2.08	–	2.98	5.06	2.29	–	3.28	5.57
C010605I	mulching; spent mushroom compost; spread 80 mm deep; per visit; over pit size: 1200 mm × 1200 mm	each	0.17	3.54	–	5.29	8.83	3.89	–	5.82	9.71
C010605J	prune trees; per visit	each	0.17	3.54	–	–	3.54	3.89	–	–	3.89
C010606	**Sundry items:**										
C010606A	spiral tree guards for protection against rabbit damage	each	0.03	0.62	–	0.73	1.35	0.68	–	0.80	1.49
C010606B	tree spats	each	0.08	1.67	–	0.99	2.66	1.84	–	1.09	2.93
C010606E	tree stake	each	0.33	6.88	–	0.76	7.64	7.57	–	0.84	8.40
C010606F	tree stake ties (3 no.)	each	0.15	3.13	–	1.68	4.81	3.44	–	1.85	5.29
C010606G	tree guard	each	1.58	32.94	–	31.14	64.08	36.23	–	34.25	70.49

Landscaping

Small Works 2009		Unit	Labour Hours	Labour Net	Plant Net	Materials Net	Unit Net	Labour Gross	Plant Gross	Materials Gross	Unit Price
								(Gross rates include 10% profit)			
				£	£	£	£	£	£	£	£
C02	**PATHS AND WALLS**										
C0201	**PATHS**										
C020101	**Surface excavation:**										
C020101A	150 mm deep, remove soil up to 18 m; deposit; trim and consolidate new surface ...	m²	0.50	10.43	–	–	10.43	11.47	–	–	11.47
C020101B	fill into barrows; wheel up to 20 m deposit in skip	m²	0.15	3.13	–	–	3.13	3.44	–	–	3.44
C020101C	hire of 4.5 m³ skip; delivery to site; removing when full; disposal of contents; payment of tipping charges	m²	–	–	12.56	1.85	14.41	–	13.82	2.04	15.85
C020102	**Ash or fine clinker; spread, levelled and rolled:**										
C020102A	50 mm thick	m²	0.25	5.21	–	2.14	7.35	5.73	–	2.35	8.09
C020102B	75 mm thick	m²	0.30	6.26	–	3.25	9.51	6.89	–	3.58	10.46
C020103	**Brick hardcore 100 mm; spread, levelled watered, rammed, blinded with ashes and rolled; cambered surface:**										
C020103A	finished to receive surfacing material	m²	0.35	7.30	–	4.50	11.80	8.03	–	4.95	12.98
C020104	**Brick hardcore 75 mm; spread, levelled, watered, rammed and blinded with ashes; 100 mm concrete paving:**										
C020104A	to falls; in bays; formwork; expansion joints; spade finish to falls	m²	1.20	25.02	–	19.30	44.32	27.52	–	21.23	48.75
C020105	**Crazy paving; broken precast concrete slabs; mortar bed; pointing:**										
C020105A	50 mm	m²	0.85	21.80	–	13.33	35.13	23.98	–	14.66	38.64
C020106	**Precast concrete slabs 50 mm; natural finish; mortar bed; pointing:**										
C020106A	600 mm × 600 mm	m²	0.65	15.87	–	14.60	30.47	17.46	–	16.06	33.52
C020106B	600 mm × 750 mm	m²	0.55	13.44	–	15.09	28.53	14.78	–	16.60	31.38
C020106C	600 mm × 900 mm	m²	0.50	12.22	–	13.23	25.45	13.44	–	14.55	28.00
C020107	**Precast concrete slabs 50 mm; 25 mm sand bed:**										
C020107A	spread; levelled; consolidated 600 mm × 600 mm	m²	1.20	29.31	–	11.97	41.28	32.24	–	13.17	45.41
C020107B	75 mm fine clinker; spread; levelled consolidated 600 × 600 mm	m²	1.50	36.64	–	15.22	51.86	40.30	–	16.74	57.05
C020108	**Precast concrete edging to paths; bedding; pointing in cement mortar; haunched with concrete:**										
C020108A	50 mm × 150 mm; flat top	m	0.40	9.77	–	6.74	16.51	10.75	–	7.41	18.16
C020108B	50 mm × 150 mm; round top	m	0.40	9.77	–	6.74	16.51	10.75	–	7.41	18.16

Landscaping

Small Works 2009		Unit	Labour Hours	Labour Net	Plant Net	Materials Net	Unit Net	Labour Gross	Plant Gross	Materials Gross	Unit Price
								(Gross rates include 10% profit)			
				£	£	£	£	£	£	£	£
C02	PATHS AND WALLS										
C0201	PATHS										
C020109	Concrete (1:3:6) path; slightly cambered; formwork; trowelled smooth:										
C020109A	75 mm	m²	0.90	21.99	–	10.31	32.30	24.19	–	11.34	35.53
C020109B	100 mm	m²	1.10	26.87	–	13.71	40.58	29.56	–	15.08	44.64
C020109C	Extra for marking out concrete in square or crazy pattern	m²	0.30	7.33	–	–	7.33	8.06	–	–	8.06
C020110	Formwork to edge of path:										
C020110A	75 mm high	m	0.10	2.78	–	0.44	3.22	3.06	–	0.48	3.54
C020110B	100 mm high	m	0.11	3.06	–	0.56	3.62	3.37	–	0.62	3.98
C020110C	150 mm high	m	0.14	3.90	–	0.69	4.59	4.29	–	0.76	5.05
C020110D	75 mm high, left in	m	0.10	2.78	–	2.03	4.81	3.06	–	2.23	5.29
C020110E	100 mm high, left in	m	0.11	3.06	–	2.47	5.53	3.37	–	2.72	6.08
C020110F	150 mm high, left in	m	0.14	3.89	–	2.47	6.36	4.28	–	2.72	7.00
C020111	Paving; paviors laid to flats, falls, cross falls, slopes not exceeding 15 degrees from horizontal:										
C020111A	brick paviors; (PC 945.00 per 1000) 75 mm thick; bedding and jointing in cement mortar (1:3); laid stretcher bond	m²	2.76	67.43	–	54.24	121.67	74.17	–	59.66	133.84
C020111B	brick paviors; (PC 945.00 per 1000); 75 mm thick; bedding and jointing in cement mortar (1:3); laid in herringbone bond	m²	2.98	72.81	–	54.24	127.05	80.09	–	59.66	139.76
C020111C	Keyblok concrete block paviors; 200 mm × 100 mm; 65 mm thick; red colour; laid on 50 mm screeded bed; compacting and vibrating with hand operated vibrating plate; laid flat in herringbone bond	m²	1.50	36.64	7.38	25.33	69.35	40.30	8.12	27.86	76.29
C020111D	Keyblok concrete block paviors; 200 mm × 100 mm; 80 mm thick; red colour; laid on 50 mm screeded bed; compacting and vibrating with hand operated vibrating plate; laid flat in herringbone bond	m²	1.70	41.53	7.38	14.78	63.69	45.68	8.12	16.26	70.06
C020112	Kerb; brick on flat; brick paviors; (PC 945:00 per 1000); bedding and jointing; flush pointing; straight:										
C020112A	102.5 mm wide × 75 mm high	m	0.28	6.84	–	6.47	13.31	7.52	–	7.12	14.64
C020112B	215 mm wide × 75 mm high	m	0.50	12.22	–	13.05	25.27	13.44	–	14.36	27.80
C020113	Creosoted sawn timber edging, nailed to and including 50 mm × 50 mm creosoted and pointed stakes driven in at 1.50 m centres (one side only measured):										
C020113A	150 mm × 25 mm or 100 mm × 31 mm	m	0.30	7.33	–	2.26	9.59	8.06	–	2.49	10.55

Landscaping

Small Works 2009		Unit	Labour Hours	Labour Net	Plant Net	Materials Net	Unit Net	Labour Gross	Plant Gross	Materials Gross	Unit Price
				£	£	£	£	£	£	£	£
								<td colspan="4">—— (Gross rates include 10% profit) ——</td>
C02	**PATHS AND WALLS**										
C0202	**WALLS**										
C020201	**Excavate trench; garden wall foundations; part backfill; part wheel and disposal by skip:**										
C020201A	375 mm × 300 mm deep .	m	0.56	11.68	5.30	–	16.98	12.85	5.83	–	18.68
C020201B	375 mm × 450 mm deep .	m	0.80	16.68	7.92	–	24.60	18.35	8.71	–	27.06
C020202	**Concrete (1:3:6) in trench:**										
C020202A	375 mm wide × 150 mm thick	m	0.60	12.51	–	7.07	19.58	13.76	–	7.78	21.54
C020203	**Brick wall in common bricks:**										
C020203A	half brick thick; pointed both sides; brick-on-edge coping	m²	2.60	63.52	–	20.93	84.45	69.87	–	23.02	92.90
C020203B	one brick thick; pointed both sides; brick-on-edge coping	m²	4.50	109.93	–	43.81	153.74	120.92	–	48.19	169.11
C020203C	half brick thick; joints raked out; rendered in cement mortar both sides	m²	3.90	95.28	–	25.20	120.48	104.81	–	27.72	132.53
C020203D	one brick thick; joints raked out; rendered in cement mortar both sides	m²	5.60	136.80	–	48.09	184.89	150.48	–	52.90	203.38
C020204	**Brick wall in second hand stocks; (PC 650:00 per 1000); brick-on-edge coping:**										
C020204A	one brick thick; pointed both sides.	m²	4.50	109.93	–	108.10	218.03	120.92	–	118.91	239.83
C020204B	one brick thick; rendered in cement mortar both sides . .	m²	5.60	136.81	–	113.16	249.97	150.49	–	124.48	274.97
C020205	**Brick wall in facing bricks; (PC 325:00 per 1000); brick-on-edge coping:**										
C020205A	half brick thick; pointed both sides.	m²	2.60	63.51	–	27.98	91.49	69.86	–	30.78	100.64
C020205B	one brick thick; pointed both sides.	m²	4.50	109.93	–	57.80	167.73	120.92	–	63.58	184.50
C020206	**Double course tile creasing:**										
C020206A	brick-on-flat coping; cement mortar fillets	m	1.15	28.10	–	13.98	42.08	30.91	–	15.38	46.29
C020207	**Coping flat; twice throated; precast concrete:**										
C020207A	600 mm × 300 mm × 50 mm	m	1.20	29.31	–	9.61	38.92	32.24	–	10.57	42.81
C020208	**Metal coping:**										
C020208A	angle iron at ends	each	0.08	1.95	–	3.69	5.64	2.15	–	4.06	6.20
C020209	**Excavate pit; part backfill; part wheel and disposal by skip:**										
C020209A	525 mm × 525 mm × 300 mm deep for 225 mm × 225 mm brick pier	each	0.68	14.18	3.94	–	18.12	15.60	4.33	–	19.93
C020209B	650 mm × 650 mm × 300 mm deep for 338 mm × 338 mm brick pier	each	0.93	19.39	6.27	–	25.66	21.33	6.90	–	28.23
C020210	**Concrete (1:3:6) in pits:**										
C020210A	525 mm × 525 mm × 150 mm	each	0.30	6.26	–	5.14	11.40	6.89	–	5.65	12.54
C020210B	650 mm × 650 mm × 150 mm	each	0.40	8.34	–	7.93	16.27	9.17	–	8.72	17.90

Small Works 2009		Unit	Labour Hours	Labour Net	Plant Net	Materials Net	Unit Net	Labour Gross	Plant Gross	Materials Gross	Unit Price
								(Gross rates include 10% profit)			
				£	£	£	£	£	£	£	£
C02	**PATHS AND WALLS**										
C0202	**WALLS**										
C020211	**Brick piers; 225 mm × 225 mm; pointed o all faces:**										
C020211A	common bricks..........	m	1.80	43.98	–	10.07	54.05	48.38	–	11.08	59.46
C020211B	facing bricks; (PC 325:00 per 1000)..................	m	2.10	51.30	–	13.28	64.58	56.43	–	14.61	71.04
C020212	**Pier cap; weathered four ways; precast concrete:**										
C020212A	305 mm × 305 mm......	each	1.00	24.43	–	5.09	29.52	26.87	–	5.60	32.47
C020214	**Brick piers; 338 mm × 338 mm; pointed on all faces:**										
C020214A	common bricks..........	m	3.00	73.29	–	20.92	94.21	80.62	–	23.01	103.63
C020214B	facing bricks; (PC 325:00 per 1000)..................	m	3.50	85.50	–	29.72	115.22	94.05	–	32.69	126.74
C020215	**Pier cap; weathered four ways; precast concrete:**										
C020215A	420 mm × 420 mm......	each	1.30	31.76	–	6.79	38.55	34.94	–	7.47	42.41
C020216	**Flint stone (PC 180:00 m³) walling built in cement lime mortar and pointed both sides:**										
C020216A	225 mm thick	m²	6.25	152.69	–	85.66	238.35	167.96	–	94.23	262.19
C020217	**Flint stone (PC 180:00 m³) cavity walling comprising 100 mm flint facework to backing of:**										
C020217A	half brick inner skin in cement lime mortar and pointed one side	m²	4.91	119.95	–	67.55	187.50	131.95	–	74.31	206.25
C020218	**Marshalls Superscreen walling; 90 mm precast concrete blocks; type Porto, Virgo or Fargo; bedded in gauged mortar (1:1:6); jointing with flush joints both sides:**										
C020218A	290 mm × 290 mm open .	m²	2.20	53.74	–	26.15	79.89	59.11	–	28.77	87.88
C020218B	290 mm × 290 mm solid .	m²	2.20	53.75	–	31.59	85.34	59.13	–	34.75	93.87
C020218C	pilaster; 190 mm × 194 mm × 194 mm; pointed all round..........	m	2.20	53.75	–	17.96	71.71	59.13	–	19.76	78.88
C020218D	add for reinforcing pilasters over three courses high; 4 No.-12 mm diameter mild steel reinforcing rods set in concrete foundations (measured separately); placing pilaster blocks over rods; filling centre void with cement mortar packed around rods.............	m	1.10	26.87	–	7.14	34.01	29.56	–	7.85	37.41
C020218E	pilaster cap 194 mm × 194 mm × 51 mm.......	each	0.56	13.68	–	1.73	15.41	15.05	–	1.90	16.95
C020220	**Marshalite reconstructed Yorkstone walling; pitched faced stones and jumpers; 100 mm bedded and pointed in cement mortar (1:3):**										
C020220A	natural	m²	2.40	58.63	–	42.91	101.54	64.49	–	47.20	111.69
C020220B	red or buff	m²	2.40	58.64	–	46.47	105.11	64.50	–	51.12	115.62

Landscaping

		Unit	Labour Hours	Labour Net	Plant Net	Materials Net	Unit Net	Labour Gross	Plant Gross	Materials Gross	Unit Price
								(Gross rates include 10% profit)			
				£	£	£	£	£	£	£	£
C02	**PATHS AND WALLS**										
C0202	**WALLS**										
C020222	**Marshalite reconstructed Yorkstone walling; rustic faced stones and jumpers; 100 mm bedded and pointed in cement mortar (1:3):**										
C020222A	natural	m²	2.88	70.36	–	42.91	113.27	77.40	–	47.20	124.60
C020222B	red or buff	m²	2.40	58.64	–	46.47	105.11	64.50	–	51.12	115.62
C020224	**Marshalite reconstructed Yorkstone coping; Saxon textured split faced stone; 600 mm × 136 mm × 50 mm bedded and pointed in cement mortar (1:3):**										
C020224A	natural	m	3.99	97.48	–	6.76	104.24	107.23	–	7.44	114.66
C020224B	red or buff	m	3.99	97.48	–	7.20	104.68	107.23	–	7.92	115.15
C020226	**Marshalite reconstructed Yorkstone attached pier; pitched faced stone and jumpers; 300 mm × 300 mm; bedded and pointed in cement mortar (1:3):**										
C020226A	natural	m	3.00	73.29	–	32.04	105.33	80.62	–	35.24	115.86
C020226B	red or buff	m	3.00	73.29	–	34.89	108.18	80.62	–	38.38	119.00
C020228	**Marshalite reconstructed Yorkstone attached pier; pitched faced stone and jumpers; 400 mm × 400 mm; bedded and pointed in cement mortar (1:3):**										
C020228A	natural	m	4.00	97.72	–	48.00	145.72	107.49	–	52.80	160.29
C020228B	red or buff	m	4.00	97.72	–	52.28	150.00	107.49	–	57.51	165.00
C020230	**Marshalite reconstructed Yorkstone pillar cap; pitched faced stone; 350 mm × 350 mm × 50 mm; bedded and pointed in cement mortar (1:3):**										
C020230A	natural	each	1.00	24.43	–	9.18	33.61	26.87	–	10.10	36.97
C020230B	red or buff	each	1.00	24.43	–	10.23	34.66	26.87	–	11.25	38.13
C020232	**Marshalite reconstructed Yorkstone pillar cap; pitched faced stone; 450 mm × 450 mm × 50 mm; bedded and pointed in cement mortar (1:3):**										
C020232A	natural	each	1.50	36.65	–	10.13	46.78	40.32	–	11.14	51.46
C020232B	red or buff	each	1.50	36.65	–	10.84	47.49	40.32	–	11.92	52.24

Small Works 2009		Unit	Labour Hours	Labour Net	Plant Net	Materials Net	Unit Net	Labour Gross	Plant Gross	Materials Gross	Unit Price
								(Gross rates include 10% profit)			
				£	£	£	£	£	£	£	£
C03	**FENCING AND GATES**										
C0301	**PANEL FENCING**										
C030101	Lapped panels; 1800 mm wide; natural waney edged timber; overlapped; weathered capping strip; waney edged timber sandwiched between five pairs planed battens; timber posts; treated; including excavating holes, setting posts, backfilling with concrete; height:										
C030101A	900 mm	m	1.13	27.61	–	44.83	72.44	30.37	–	49.31	79.68
C030101B	1200 mm	m	1.27	31.03	–	46.17	77.20	34.13	–	50.79	84.92
C030101C	1500 mm	m	1.41	34.45	–	48.14	82.59	37.90	–	52.95	90.85
C030101D	1800 mm	m	1.55	37.87	–	56.37	94.24	41.66	–	62.01	103.66
C030102	Lapped panels; 1800 mm wide; natural waney edged timber; overlapped; weathered capping strip; waney edged timber sandwiched between five pairs planed battens treated; concrete gravel board; H section posts; including excavating holes, setting posts, backfilling; height:										
C030102A	1350 mm	m	1.00	24.43	–	60.54	84.97	26.87	–	66.59	93.47
C030102B	1650 mm	m	1.06	25.90	–	61.71	87.61	28.49	–	67.88	96.37
C030102C	1950 mm	m	1.13	27.60	–	62.90	90.50	30.36	–	69.19	99.55
C030105	Featherboard panels; 1800 mm wide; three horizontal rails; weathered; clad with 100 mm featherboard pales; timber posts; treated; chamfered post cap; timber gravel board including excavating, setting post and backfilling with concrete; height:										
C030105B	1200 mm	m	1.36	33.22	–	67.06	100.28	36.54	–	73.77	110.31
C030105C	1500 mm	m	1.51	36.89	–	73.92	110.81	40.58	–	81.31	121.89
C030105D	1800 mm	m	1.65	40.31	–	79.02	119.33	44.34	–	86.92	131.26
C030106	Featherboard panels; 1800 mm wide; three horizontal rails; weathered; clad with 100 mm featherboard pales; treated concrete gravel board; concrete H section posts; including excavating, setting posts and backfilling with concrete; height:										
C030106B	1200 mm	m	1.03	25.16	–	74.79	99.95	27.68	–	82.27	109.95
C030106C	1500 mm	m	1.11	27.11	–	80.86	107.97	29.82	–	88.95	118.77
C030106D	1800 mm	m	1.19	29.07	–	85.16	114.23	31.98	–	93.68	125.65

Landscaping

Small Works 2009		Unit	Labour Hours	Labour Net	Plant Net	Materials Net	Unit Net	Labour Gross	Plant Gross	Materials Gross	Unit Price
								(Gross rates include 10% profit)			
				£	£	£	£	£	£	£	£
C03	**FENCING AND GATES**										
C0301	**PANEL FENCING**										
C030107	**Trellis panels; square top 1800 mm wide 38mm × 19 mm softwood framing; weathered capping; 19 mm × 19 mm softwood horizontal and vertical infill at 150 m centres; timber posts; chamfered post cap; timber gravel board; treated; height:**										
C030107A	1350 mm..............	m	0.82	20.03	–	52.11	72.14	22.03	–	57.32	79.35
C030107B	1650 mm..............	m	1.10	26.87	–	58.98	85.85	29.56	–	64.88	94.44
C030109	**Trellis panels; square top; 1800 mm wide; 38 mm × 19 mm softwood framing; weathered capping; 19 mm × 19 mm softwood horizontal and vertical infill at 150 mm centres; treated; concrete gravel board; concrete H section posts; height:**										
C030109A	1350 mm..............	m	0.99	24.19	–	59.04	83.23	26.61	–	64.94	91.55
C030109B	1650 mm..............	m	1.27	31.03	–	64.23	95.26	34.13	–	70.65	104.79
C0303	**GATES**										
C030301	**Lapped panel gate; 900 mm wide; galvanised ring latch; heavy hinges; hanging:**										
C030301A	fence height 900 mm; gate height 850 mm..........	each	0.25	6.11	–	115.48	121.59	6.72	–	127.03	133.75
C030301B	fence height 1200 mm; gate height 1150 mm..........	each	0.50	12.21	–	118.16	130.37	13.43	–	129.98	143.41
C030301C	fence height 1500 mm; gate height 1450 mm..........	each	0.75	18.32	–	120.84	139.16	20.15	–	132.92	153.08
C030301D	fence height 1800 mm; gate height 1750 mm..........	each	0.95	23.21	–	123.51	146.72	25.53	–	135.86	161.39
C030303	**Featherboard panel gate; 1000 mm wide; galvanised ring latch; heavy hinges; hanging:**										
C030303A	fence height 1200 mm; gate height 1150 mm..........	each	0.75	18.32	–	118.16	136.48	20.15	–	129.98	150.13
C030303B	fence height 1500 mm; gate height 1450 mm..........	each	1.00	24.43	–	120.84	145.27	26.87	–	132.92	159.80
C030303C	fence height 1800 mm; gate height 1750 mm..........	each	1.20	29.32	–	123.51	152.83	32.25	–	135.86	168.11
C030305	**Trellis panel gate; square top; 900 mm wide; galvanised fittings; hanging:**										
C030305A	1750 mm high...........	each	0.95	23.21	–	122.62	145.83	25.53	–	134.88	160.41

Small Works 2009		Unit	Labour Hours	Labour Net	Plant Net	Materials Net	Unit Net	Labour Gross	Plant Gross	Materials Gross	Unit Price
								(Gross rates include 10% profit)			
				£	£	£	£	£	£	£	£
C03	**FENCING AND GATES**										
C0305	**WOOD PRESERVATIVES**										
C030501	**One coat timber preservative on wrought timber:**										
C030501A	general surfaces not exceeding 150 mm girth ...	m	0.04	1.11	–	0.02	1.13	1.22	–	0.02	1.24
C030501B	150-300 mm girth	m	0.09	2.50	–	0.05	2.55	2.75	–	0.06	2.81
C030501C	over 300 mm girth	m²	0.19	5.28	–	0.14	5.42	5.81	–	0.15	5.96
C030502	**One coat timber preservative on sawn timber:**										
C030502A	general surfaces not exceeding 150 mm girth ...	m	0.05	1.39	–	0.05	1.44	1.53	–	0.06	1.58
C030502B	150-300 mm girth	m	0.10	2.78	–	0.11	2.89	3.06	–	0.12	3.18
C030502C	over 300 mm girth	m²	0.20	5.56	–	0.36	5.92	6.12	–	0.40	6.51
C030503	**One coat Solignum preservative on wrought timber:**										
C030503A	general surfaces not exceeding 150 mm girth ...	m	0.04	1.11	–	0.07	1.18	1.22	–	0.08	1.30
C030503B	150-300 mm girth	m	0.07	1.95	–	0.14	2.09	2.15	–	0.15	2.30
C030503C	over 300 mm girth	m²	0.18	5.01	–	0.38	5.39	5.51	–	0.42	5.93
C030504	**One coat Solignum preservative on sawn timber:**										
C030504A	general surfaces not exceeding 150 mm girth ...	m	0.05	1.39	–	0.10	1.49	1.53	–	0.11	1.64
C030504B	150-300 mm girth	m	0.08	2.23	–	0.17	2.40	2.45	–	0.19	2.64
C030504C	over 300 mm girth	m²	0.19	5.28	–	0.59	5.87	5.81	–	0.65	6.46
C030505	**One coat Cuprinol preservative on wrought timber:**										
C030505A	general surfaces not exceeding 150 mm girth ...	m	0.04	1.11	–	0.19	1.30	1.22	–	0.21	1.43
C030505B	150-300 mm girth	m	0.08	2.22	–	0.32	2.54	2.44	–	0.35	2.79
C030505C	over 300 mm girth	m²	0.19	5.28	–	1.08	6.36	5.81	–	1.19	7.00
C030506	**One coat Cuprinol preservative on sawn timber:**										
C030506A	general surfaces not exceeding 150 mm girth ...	m	0.05	1.39	–	0.32	1.71	1.53	–	0.35	1.88
C030506B	150-300 mm girth	m	0.09	2.51	–	0.63	3.14	2.76	–	0.69	3.45
C030506C	over 300 mm girth	m²	0.20	5.56	–	1.78	7.34	6.12	–	1.96	8.07

Landscaping

Small Works 2009		Unit	Labour Hours	Labour Net	Plant Net	Materials Net	Unit Net	Labour Gross	Plant Gross	Materials Gross	Unit Price
								(Gross rates include 10% profit)			
				£	£	£	£	£	£	£	£
C04	**FENCING**										
C0401	**POST AND WIRE FENCING**										
C040101	**Fencing of five 4 mm line wires and 125 mm × 125 mm to 75 mm × 75 mm × 1670 mm reinforced concrete tapered posts at 3000 mm centres set 600 mm deep into ground in concrete:**										
C040101A	height; 1000 mm	m	0.56	13.68	–	4.73	18.41	15.05	–	5.20	20.25
C040101B	Extra for 125 mm × 125 mm end straining posts with 100 mm × 75 mm strut set in concrete	each	0.88	21.49	–	37.34	58.83	23.64	–	41.07	64.71
C040101C	Extra for corner straining posts with two struts set in concrete.................	each	1.32	32.25	–	42.70	74.95	35.48	–	46.97	82.45
C040102	**Fencing of seven 4 mm line wires and 125 mm × 125 mm to 75 mm × 2070 mm reinforced concrete tapered posts at centres set 600 mm deep into ground:**										
C040102A	height; 1400 mm	m	0.61	14.85	–	9.08	23.93	16.34	–	9.99	26.32
C040102B	Extra for 125 mm × 125 mm end straining posts with 100 mm × 75 mm strut set in concrete	each	0.44	10.74	–	37.34	48.08	11.81	–	41.07	52.89
C040102C	Extra for corner straining posts with two struts set in concrete.................	each	0.88	21.50	–	42.70	64.20	23.65	–	46.97	70.62

Small Works 2009		Unit	Labour Hours	Labour Net	Plant Net	Materials Net	Unit Net	Labour Gross	Plant Gross	Materials Gross	Unit Price
				£	£	£	£	£ (Gross rates include 10% profit) £	£	£	£
C04	**FENCING**										
C0402	**GALVANISED CHAIN-LINK FENCING**										
C040201	**Fencing of 50 mm mesh × 3 mm chain link two 3 mm line wires and 40 mm × 40 mm × 1500 mm steel angle posts at 3000 mm centres set 600 mm deep into ground in concrete:**										
C040201A	height; 900 mm	m	0.64	15.63	–	7.66	23.29	17.19	–	8.43	25.62
C040201B	Extra for 50 mm × 50 mm angle end straining posts with 40 mm × 40 mm steel angle strut, each bent over at bottom and set in concrete .	each	0.98	23.94	–	21.86	45.80	26.33	–	24.05	50.38
C040201C	Extra for corner straining posts with two struts set in concrete.	each	1.47	35.91	–	25.42	61.33	39.50	–	27.96	67.46
C040202	**Fencing of 50 mm mesh × 3 mm chain link three 3.55 mm line wires and 45 mm × 45 mm × 2000 mm steel angle posts at 3000 mm centres set 600 mm deep into ground in concrete:**										
C040202A	height; 1400 mm	m	0.75	18.33	–	10.43	28.76	20.16	–	11.47	31.64
C040202B	Extra for 50 mm × 50 mm angle end straining posts with 45 mm × 45 mm steel angle strut, each bent over at bottom and set in concrete .	each	1.15	28.09	–	18.94	47.03	30.90	–	20.83	51.73
C040202C	Extra for corner straining posts with two struts set in concrete.	each	1.72	42.02	–	26.76	68.78	46.22	–	29.44	75.66
C040203	**Fencing of 50 mm mesh × 3 mm chain link, three 3.55 mm line wires and 45 mm × 45 mm × 2600 mm steel angle posts at 3000 mm centres set 760 mm deep into ground in concrete:**										
C040203A	height; 1800 mm	m	0.96	23.45	–	12.48	35.93	25.80	–	13.73	39.52
C040203B	Extra for 60 mm × 60 mm angle end straining posts with 45 mm × 45 mm steel angle strut, each bent over at bottom and set in concrete .	each	1.48	36.15	–	25.52	61.67	39.77	–	28.07	67.84
C040203C	Extra for corner straining posts with two struts set in concrete.	each	2.21	53.99	–	26.61	80.60	59.39	–	29.27	88.66

Landscaping

Small Works 2009		Unit	Labour Hours	Labour Net	Plant Net	Materials Net	Unit Net	Labour Gross	Plant Gross	Materials Gross	Unit Price
								(Gross rates include 10% profit)			
				£	£	£	£	£	£	£	£
C04	**FENCING**										
C0402	**GALVANISED CHAIN-LINK FENCING**										
C040204	**Fencing of 50 mm mesh × 3 mm chain link, two 3 mm line wires and 120 mm × 120 mm to 75 mm × 75 mm × 1600 mm reinforced concrete tapered posts at 3000 mm centres set 600 mm deep into ground in concrete:**										
C040204A	height; 900 mm	m	0.60	14.66	–	20.21	34.87	16.13	–	22.23	38.36
C040204B	Extra for 125 mm × 125 mm end straining posts with 100 mm × 75 mm strut set in concrete	each	1.20	29.32	–	48.41	77.73	32.25	–	53.25	85.50
C040204C	Extra for corner, straining posts with two struts set in concrete	each	1.80	43.97	–	70.00	113.97	48.37	–	77.00	125.37
C040205	**Fencing of 50 mm mesh × 3 mm chain link, three 3.55 mm line wires and 125 mm × 125 mm to 75 × 75 mm × 2070 mm reinforced concrete tapered posts at 3000 mm centres set 600 mm deep into ground in concrete:**										
C040205A	height; 1400 mm	m	0.75	18.33	–	22.56	40.89	20.16	–	24.82	44.98
C040205B	Extra for 125 mm × 125 mm end straining posts with 100 mm × 75 mm strut set in concrete	each	1.41	34.45	–	54.52	88.97	37.90	–	59.97	97.87
C040205C	Extra for corner, straining posts with two struts set in concrete	each	2.13	62.44	–	78.91	141.35	68.68	–	86.80	155.49
C040206	**Fencing of 50 mm mesh × 3 mm chain link, three 3.55 mm line wires and 125 mm × 125 mm to 75 mm × 75 mm × 2630 mm reinforced concrete tapered posts at 3000 mm centres set 760 mm deep into ground in concrete:**										
C040206A	height; 1800 mm	m	0.94	22.96	–	16.06	39.02	25.26	–	17.67	42.92
C040206B	Extra for 125 mm × 125 mm end straining posts with 100 mm × 75 mm strut set in concrete	each	1.76	42.99	–	55.03	98.02	47.29	–	60.53	107.82
C040206C	Extra for corner straining posts with two struts set in concrete	each	2.64	64.49	–	69.98	134.47	70.94	–	76.98	147.92

Small Works 2009		Unit	Labour Hours	Labour Net	Plant Net	Materials Net	Unit Net	Labour Gross	Plant Gross	Materials Gross	Unit Price
								—— (Gross rates include 10% profit) ——			
				£	£	£	£	£	£	£	£
C04	FENCING										
C0402	GALVANISED CHAIN-LINK FENCING										
C040207	Security fencing of 50 mm mesh × 3 mm chain link, three 3.55 mm line wires, three rows of barbed wire and 125 mm × 125 mm to 75 mm × 75 mm × 3000 mm reinforced concrete tapered posts, with cranked top, at 3000 mm centres set 760 mm deep into ground in concrete:										
C040207A	height; 1820 mm	m	0.96	23.45	–	16.81	40.26	25.80	–	18.49	44.29
C040207B	Extra for 125 mm × 125 mm end straining posts with 100 mm × 75 mm strut set in concrete	each	1.76	42.99	–	55.03	98.02	47.29	–	60.53	107.82
C040207C	Extra for corner straining posts with two struts set in concrete.................	each	2.64	64.50	–	62.59	127.09	70.95	–	68.85	139.80
C0404	CLEFT-PALE FENCING										
C040401	Fencing of chestnut pales 75 mm apart, two lines of binding wire and 63 mm approximate diameter × 1670 mm chestnut posts at 2280 mm centres driven 600 mm into ground:										
C040401A	height; 1060 mm	m	0.64	15.63	–	5.90	21.53	17.19	–	6.49	23.68
C040401B	Extra for 75 mm to 85 mm approximate diameter straining posts with strut spiked to post	each	1.00	24.43	–	3.61	28.04	26.87	–	3.97	30.84
C040401C	Extra for corner straining posts with two struts spiked to post	each	1.50	36.65	–	5.36	42.01	40.32	–	5.90	46.21

Landscaping

Small Works 2009		Unit	Labour Hours	Labour Net	Plant Net	Materials Net	Unit Net	Labour Gross	Plant Gross	Materials Gross	Unit Price
								(Gross rates include 10% profit)			
				£	£	£	£	£	£	£	£
C04	FENCING										
C0406	GALVANISED STEEL PALISADE FENCING										
C040601	Fencing of triple pointed corrugated pales (1.9 Kg/m) fixed with 6 mm Avelok rivets to two 50 mm × 40 mm × 6 mm horizontal angle rails, bottom rail fitted with two support feet per bay set into ground in concrete and with 102 mm × 44 mm RSJ posts at 2750 mm centres set 760 mm deep into ground in concrete:										
C040601A	height; 1800 mm	m	1.33	32.49	–	45.25	77.74	35.74	–	49.78	85.51
C040601B	height; 2400 mm	m	1.50	36.64	–	58.54	95.18	40.30	–	64.39	104.70
C040602	Fencing of triple pointed corrugated pales (2.42 Kg/m) fixed with 8 mm Avelok rivets to two 50 mm × 40 mm × 6 mm horizontal angle rails, bottom rail fitted with two support feet per bay set into ground in concrete and with 102 mm × 44 mm RSJ posts at 2750 mm centres set 760 mm deep into ground in concrete:										
C040602A	height; 1800 mm	m	1.50	36.65	–	54.55	91.20	40.32	–	60.01	100.32
C040602B	height; 2400 mm	m	1.75	42.75	–	65.38	108.13	47.03	–	71.92	118.94
C0408	TREATED SOFTWOOD CLOSE-BOARDED FENCING										
C040801	Fencing of 14 mm to 7 mm × 100 mm feather edged boarding, two 75 mm × 75 mm arris rails, 100 mm × 100 mm × 1600 mm sawn posts at 3000 mm centres set 600 mm deep into ground in concrete, 32 mm × 200 mm gravel board with 50 mm × 50 mm centre stumps driven 600 mm into ground, 25 mm × 65 mm counter rail and 38 mm × 65 mm weather capping:										
C040801A	height; 1000 mm	m	1.45	35.42	–	18.73	54.15	38.96	–	20.60	59.57

Small Works 2009		Unit	Labour Hours	Labour Net	Plant Net	Materials Net	Unit Net	Labour Gross	Plant Gross	Materials Gross	Unit Price
								(Gross rates include 10% profit)			
				£	£	£	£	£	£	£	£
C04	**FENCING**										
C0406	**GALVANISED STEEL PALISADE FENCING**										
C040802	Fencing of 14 mm to 7 mm × 100 mm feather edged boarding, three 75 mm × 75 mm arris rails, 100 mm × 125 mm × 2350 mm sawn posts at 3000 mm centres set 760 mm deep into ground in concrete, 32 mm × 200 mm gravel board with 50 mm × 50 mm centre stumps driven 600 mm into ground, 25 mm × 65 mm counter rail and 38 mm × 65 mm weather capping:										
C040802A	height; 1600 mm	m	2.05	50.08	–	24.94	75.02	55.09	–	27.43	82.52
C040803	Fencing of 1830 mm × 910 mm interwoven panels, of 6 mm × 75 mm woven slats, 19 mm × 38 mm framing and weathered capping, nailed between 75 mm × 75 mm × 1520 mm capped posts at 1900 mm centres set 600 mm deep into ground in concrete:										
C040803A	height; 910 mm	m	0.90	21.98	–	15.79	37.77	24.18	–	17.37	41.55
C040804	Fencing of 1830 mm × 1830 mm interwoven panels, of 6 mm × 75 mm woven slats, 19 mm × 38 mm framing and weathered capping, nailed between 75 mm × 75 mm × 2590 mm capped posts at 1900 mm centres set 760 mm deep into ground in concrete:										
C040804A	height; 1830 mm	m	1.20	29.32	–	18.27	47.59	32.25	–	20.10	52.35
C040805	Fencing of 1830 mm × 910 mm waney edged panels, of 5 mm × 100 mm to 125 mm waney edged slats, 16 mm × 38 mm framing and weathered capping, nailed between 75 mm × 75 mm × 1520 mm capped posts at 1900 mm centres set 600 mm into ground set in concrete:										
C040805A	height; 910 mm	m	0.90	21.98	–	15.08	37.06	24.18	–	16.59	40.77
C040806	Fencing of 1830 mm × 1830 mm waney edge panels, of 5 mm × 100 mm to 125 mm waney edged slats, 16 mm × 38 mm framing and weathered capping, nailed between 75 mm × 75 mm × 2590 mm capped posts at 1900 mm centres set 760 mm into ground set in concrete:										
C040806A	height; 1830 mm	m	1.20	29.31	–	18.14	47.45	32.24	–	19.95	52.20

Landscaping

Small Works 2009		Unit	Labour Hours	Labour Net	Plant Net	Materials Net	Unit Net	Labour Gross	Plant Gross	Materials Gross	Unit Price
								(Gross rates include 10% profit)			
				£	£	£	£	£	£	£	£
C04	FENCING										
C0409	GATES										
C040901	42 mm (outside diameter) primed tubular steel single leaf gates filled in with chain link and with two 150 mm × 150 mm reinforced concrete gate posts each with strut and set of fittings including setting posts and struts in concrete and hanging gates:										
C040901A	1000 mm × 900 mm.....	each	4.75	116.04	–	218.56	334.60	127.64	–	240.42	368.06
C040901B	1000 mm × 1400 mm....	each	5.00	122.15	–	254.47	376.62	134.37	–	279.92	414.28
C040901C	1000 mm × 1800 mm....	each	5.25	128.26	–	294.12	422.38	141.09	–	323.53	464.62
C040902	48 mm (outside diameter) primed tubular steel single leaf gates filled in with chain link and with two 150 mm × 150 mm reinforced concrete gate posts each with strut and set of fittings including setting posts and struts in concrete and hanging gates:										
C040902A	3000 mm × 900 mm.....	pair	7.50	183.22	–	484.36	667.58	201.54	–	532.80	734.34
C040902B	3000 mm × 1400 mm....	pair	8.00	195.44	–	596.85	792.29	214.98	–	656.54	871.52
C040903	Galvanised steel single leaf gates, to match corrugated pale (1.9 Kg/m) fencing, with two 127 mm × 76 mm RSJ gate posts including setting posts in concrete and hanging gates:										
C040903A	1000 mm × 1800 mm....	each	7.50	183.23	–	416.19	599.42	201.55	–	457.81	659.36
C040903B	1000 mm × 2400 mm....	each	8.25	201.54	–	504.19	705.73	221.69	–	554.61	776.30
C040904	Galvanised steel double leaf gates, to match corrugated pale (1.9 Kg/m) fencing, with two 125 mm × 125 mm SHS gate posts including setting posts in concrete and hanging gates:										
C040904A	3000 mm × 1800 mm....	pair	18.00	439.74	–	1068.88	1508.62	483.71	–	1175.77	1659.48
C040905	Treated sawn softwood close-boarded gates, to match close-boarded fencing, complete with all necessary hanging and closing fittings including hanging gates:										
C040905A	3000 mm × 1800 mm....	each	5.50	134.37	–	328.20	462.57	147.81	–	361.02	508.83

HUTCHINS
SMALL WORKS INDEX

Small Works Index

Small Works Index

Small Works Index

HUTCHINS'
MAJOR WORKS
SECTION

EXISTING SITE, BUILDINGS, SERVICES

Major Works 2009		Unit	Labour Hours	Labour Net	Plant Net	Materials Net	Unit Net	Labour Gross	Plant Gross	Materials Gross	Unit Price
								(Gross rates include 10% profit)			
				£	£	£	£	£	£	£	£
C11	**C11: GROUND INVESTIGATION**										
C1101	**Machine excavation of trial holes**										
C110102	**Excavate trial holes; backfill with excavated material, compacted in 250 mm layers; maximum depth not exceeding:**										
C110102A	0.25 m	m³	0.30	3.81	9.72	–	13.53	4.19	10.69	–	14.88
C110102B	1.00 m	m³	0.30	3.81	8.92	–	12.73	4.19	9.81	–	14.00
C110102C	2.00 m	m³	0.30	3.81	9.56	–	13.37	4.19	10.52	–	14.71
C110102D	4.00 m	m³	0.35	4.44	10.58	–	15.02	4.88	11.64	–	16.52
C110102E	6.00 m	m³	0.35	4.44	12.04	–	16.48	4.88	13.24	–	18.13
C1105	**Hand excavation of trial holes**										
C110511	**Excavate trial holes; backfill with excavated material, compacted in 250 mm layers; maximum depth not exceeding:**										
C110511A	0.25 m	m³	3.15	40.01	0.86	–	40.87	44.01	0.95	–	44.96
C110511B	1.00 m	m³	3.30	41.92	0.86	–	42.78	46.11	0.95	–	47.06
C110511C	2.00 m	m³	3.75	47.63	0.86	–	48.49	52.39	0.95	–	53.34
C110511D	4.00 m	m³	4.80	60.96	1.00	–	61.96	67.06	1.10	–	68.16
C110511E	6.00 m	m³	5.95	75.56	1.00	–	76.56	83.12	1.10	–	84.22
C1111	**Extra over trial hole excavation and filling for removal of excavated material from site, filling with imported materials; by machine**										
C111104	**Filling with:**										
C111104A	sand	m³	–	–	20.80	22.21	43.01	–	22.88	24.43	47.31
C111104B	hardcore	m³	–	–	20.80	27.78	48.59	–	22.88	30.56	53.45
C111104C	hoggin	m³	–	–	20.80	24.45	45.25	–	22.88	26.90	49.78
C1112	**Extra over trial hole excavation and filling for removal of excavated material from site and filling with imported materials; by hand**										
C111213	**Filling with:**										
C111213A	sand	m³	1.25	15.88	25.50	22.21	63.59	17.47	28.05	24.43	69.95
C111213B	hardcore	m³	1.25	15.88	25.50	27.78	69.16	17.47	28.05	30.56	76.08
C111213C	hoggin	m³	1.25	15.88	25.50	24.45	65.83	17.47	28.05	26.90	72.41

Existing Site, Buildings, Services

Major Works 2009		Unit	Labour Hours	Labour Net	Plant Net	Materials Net	Unit Net	Labour Gross	Plant Gross	Materials Gross	Unit Price
								(Gross rates include 10% profit)			
				£	£	£	£	£	£	£	£
C20	**C20: DEMOLITION**										
C2003	**Demolition of concrete structural elements**										
C200343	**Reinforced concrete walls and attached columns:**										
C200343A	not exceeding 150 mm thick	m³	12.00	152.40	155.88	–	308.28	167.64	171.47	–	339.11
C200343B	150-300 mm thick	m³	14.00	177.80	181.86	–	359.66	195.58	200.05	–	395.63
C200343C	over 300 mm thick	m³	18.00	228.60	233.82	–	462.42	251.46	257.20	–	508.66
C200344	**Reinforced concrete ground slabs:**										
C200344A	not exceeding 150 mm thick	m³	6.00	76.20	77.94	–	154.14	83.82	85.73	–	169.55
C200344B	150-300 mm thick	m³	8.00	101.60	103.92	–	205.52	111.76	114.31	–	226.07
C200344C	over 300 mm thick	m³	10.00	127.00	129.90	–	256.90	139.70	142.89	–	282.59
C200345	**Reinforced concrete suspended slab and attached beams:**										
C200345A	not exceeding 150 mm thick	m³	10.00	127.00	129.90	–	256.90	139.70	142.89	–	282.59
C200345B	150-300 mm thick	m³	16.00	203.20	207.84	–	411.04	223.52	228.62	–	452.14
C200345C	over 300 mm thick	m³	19.00	241.30	246.81	–	488.11	265.43	271.49	–	536.92
C200346	**Reinforced concrete isolated beams:**										
C200346A	not exceeding 0.1 m² sectional area	m³	12.00	152.40	155.88	–	308.28	167.64	171.47	–	339.11
C200346B	0.1-0.25 m² sectional area .	m³	14.00	177.80	181.86	–	359.66	195.58	200.05	–	395.63
C200346C	over 0.25 m² sectional area.	m³	19.00	241.30	246.81	–	488.11	265.43	271.49	–	536.92
C200347	**Reinforced concrete isolated columns:**										
C200347A	not exceeding 0.1 m² sectional area	m³	10.00	127.00	129.90	–	256.90	139.70	142.89	–	282.59
C200347B	0.1-0.25 m² sectional area .	m³	13.00	165.11	130.59	–	295.70	181.62	143.65	–	325.27
C200347C	over 0.25 m² sectional area.	m³	18.00	228.60	180.81	–	409.41	251.46	198.89	–	450.35

Major Works 2009		Unit	Labour Hours	Labour Net	Plant Net	Materials Net	Unit Net	Labour Gross	Plant Gross	Materials Gross	Unit Price
								(Gross rates include 10% profit)			
				£	£	£	£	£	£	£	£
C20	**C20: DEMOLITION**										
C2005	**Demolition of masonry structural elements**										
C200548	**Brick walls:**										
C200548A	half brick thick	m²	0.80	10.16	1.33	–	11.49	11.18	1.46	–	12.64
C200548B	one brick thick	m²	1.40	17.78	2.32	–	20.10	19.56	2.55	–	22.11
C200548C	one and a half brick thick...	m²	2.10	26.67	3.49	–	30.16	29.34	3.84	–	33.18
C200548D	two brick thick	m²	2.70	34.29	4.48	–	38.77	37.72	4.93	–	42.65
C200549	**Block walls:**										
C200549A	50 mm thick	m²	0.50	6.35	–	–	6.35	6.99	–	–	6.99
C200549B	75 mm thick	m²	0.55	6.99	–	–	6.99	7.69	–	–	7.69
C200549C	100 mm thick	m²	0.60	7.62	1.00	–	8.62	8.38	1.10	–	9.48
C200549D	125 mm thick	m²	0.65	8.25	1.10	–	9.35	9.08	1.21	–	10.29
C200549E	150 mm thick	m²	0.70	8.89	1.16	–	10.05	9.78	1.28	–	11.06
C200549F	200 mm thick	m²	0.80	10.16	1.33	–	11.49	11.18	1.46	–	12.64
C200549G	225 mm thick	m²	1.10	13.97	1.83	–	15.80	15.37	2.01	–	17.38
C200553	**Attached chimney breasts:**										
C200553A	half brick common brickwork	m²	0.90	11.43	1.49	–	12.92	12.57	1.64	–	14.21
C200553B	one brick common brickwork	m²	1.60	20.32	2.66	–	22.98	22.35	2.93	–	25.28
C200553C	one and a half brick common brickwork	m²	2.30	29.21	3.82	–	33.03	32.13	4.20	–	36.33
C200553D	two brick common brickwork	m²	2.80	35.56	4.65	–	40.21	39.12	5.12	–	44.23
C200553E	100 mm blockwork	m²	0.70	8.89	1.16	–	10.05	9.78	1.28	–	11.06
C200553F	200 mm blockwork	m²	0.90	11.43	1.49	–	12.92	12.57	1.64	–	14.21
C200553G	300 mm blockwork	m²	1.40	17.78	2.32	–	20.10	19.56	2.55	–	22.11
C200553H	400 mm blockwork	m²	1.60	20.32	2.66	–	22.98	22.35	2.93	–	25.28
C200554	**Isolated chimney stacks:**										
C200554A	common brickwork; within building	m³	9.60	121.92	7.97	–	129.89	134.11	8.77	–	142.88
C200554B	common brickwork; above roof slope	m³	8.40	106.68	6.97	–	113.65	117.35	7.67	–	125.02
C200554C	facing brickwork; above roof slope	m³	8.70	110.49	7.30	–	117.79	121.54	8.03	–	129.57
C200554D	rendered blockwork; within building	m³	7.50	95.25	12.62	–	107.87	104.78	13.88	–	118.66
C200554E	rendered blockwork; above roof slope	m³	6.30	80.01	10.62	–	90.63	88.01	11.68	–	99.69

Existing Site, Buildings, Services

Major Works 2009		Unit	Labour Hours	Labour Net	Plant Net	Materials Net	Unit Net	Labour Gross	Plant Gross	Materials Gross	Unit Price
								(Gross rates include 10% profit)			
				£	£	£	£	£	£	£	£
C20	**C20: DEMOLITION**										
C2007	**Removal of roofs, ceilings and timber suspended floors**										
C200750	**Pitched roofs; placing debris in rubbish skips:**										
C200750A	tiles or slates on battens and underfelt; 50 × 150 mm softwood rafters at 400 mm centres; 50 × 200 mm softwood purlin at midspan; 50 × 100 mm softwood wall plate, binders, hangers and collars..............	m²	0.37	4.70	–	–	4.70	5.17	–	–	5.17
C200750B	50 × 100 mm ceiling joists; fibreglass insulation laid between joists; plasterboard ceiling	m²	0.15	1.91	–	–	1.91	2.10	–	–	2.10
C200751	**Flat roofs; placing debris in rubbish skips:**										
C200751A	three layer built up felt roofing on ply or chipboard decking; 50 × 200 mm ceiling joists at 400 mm centres with fibreglass laid between; 50 × 100 mm wall plate; plasterboard ceiling..	m²	0.45	5.72	–	–	5.72	6.29	–	–	6.29
C200752	**Timber suspended floors; placing debris in rubbish skips:**										
C200752A	softwood boarding on 50 × 200 mm softwood floor joists at 400 mm centres; plasterboard ceiling	m²	0.30	3.81	–	–	3.81	4.19	–	–	4.19
C200752B	chipboard flooring on 50 × 150 mm softwood floor joists at 400 mm centres; plasterboard ceiling	m²	0.25	3.18	–	–	3.18	3.50	–	–	3.50
C2010	**Removal of internal partitions**										
C201001	**Take down stud partitions, faced both sides; place debris in rubbish skip:**										
C201001A	lath and plaster finish......	m²	0.65	8.26	2.55	–	10.81	9.09	2.81	–	11.89
C201001B	plasterboard finish........	m²	0.60	7.62	2.55	–	10.17	8.38	2.81	–	11.19
C201001C	softwood board finish	m²	0.55	6.99	1.91	–	8.90	7.69	2.10	–	9.79

Major Works 2009		Unit	Labour Hours	Labour Net	Plant Net	Materials Net	Unit Net	Labour Gross	Plant Gross	Materials Gross	Unit Price
								—— (Gross rates include 10% profit) ——			
				£	£	£	£	£	£	£	£
C20	**C20: DEMOLITION**										
C2035	**Taking down, cleaning and setting aside materials for re-use**										
C203571	**Facing brickwork; placing debris in rubbish skips:**										
C203571A	half brick wall	m²	1.20	15.24	–	–	15.24	16.76	–	–	16.76
C203571B	one brick wall	m²	2.10	26.67	–	–	26.67	29.34	–	–	29.34
C203571C	one and a half brick wall . . .	m²	3.15	40.01	–	–	40.01	44.01	–	–	44.01
C203581	**Roof coverings; placing debris in rubbish skips:**										
C203581A	roof slating	m²	0.25	3.18	–	–	3.18	3.50	–	–	3.50
C203581B	roof tiling	m²	0.20	2.54	–	–	2.54	2.79	–	–	2.79
C2095	**Temporary roofs**										
C209599	**Temporary roofs; corrugated sheeting laid to slope on and including 50 × 150 mm softwood framing:**										
C209599A	fibre cement sheets	m²	0.48	8.15	–	34.74	42.89	8.97	–	38.21	47.18
C209599B	galvanised sheets	m²	0.48	8.15	–	30.83	38.98	8.97	–	33.91	42.88
C209599C	translucent PVC sheets	m²	0.48	8.15	–	28.26	36.41	8.97	–	31.09	40.05
C209599D	extra for 50 × 150 mm softwood posts	m²	0.35	5.95	–	0.48	6.43	6.55	–	0.53	7.07
C2097	**Temporary screens**										
C209792	**Temporary dustproof screens; 1200 gauge polythene sheeting on 50 × 100 mm sawn softwood framing; joints sealed with self adhesive PVC tape:**										
C209792A	vertical screens	m²	0.35	5.95	–	6.82	12.77	6.55	–	7.50	14.05
C209792B	extra for sealing perimeters with self adhesive PVC tape	m²	0.05	0.85	–	4.70	5.55	0.94	–	5.17	6.11
C209792C	extra for access door	m²	1.50	25.47	–	51.93	77.40	28.02	–	57.12	85.14

Major Works 2009		Unit	Labour Hours	Labour Net	Plant Net	Materials Net	Unit Net	Labour Gross	Plant Gross	Materials Gross	Unit Price
				£	£	£	£	(Gross rates include 10% profit)			
								£	£	£	£
C41	**C41: REPAIRING, RENOVATING, CONSERVING MASONRY**										
C4131	**Cutting out decayed and defective work and replacing with new**										
C413111	**Cut out damaged or decayed common brickwork; cut, tooth and bond new commons to existing in gauged mortar (1:1:6); half brick thick:**										
C413111A	stretcher bond; single brick	Nr	0.25	7.44	–	0.35	7.79	8.18	–	0.39	8.57
C413111B	stretcher bond; in areas not exceeding 0.50 m²	Nr	1.25	37.22	–	9.51	46.73	40.94	–	10.46	51.40
C413111C	stretcher bond; in areas 0.50-1.00 m²	Nr	2.40	71.47	–	19.02	90.49	78.62	–	20.92	99.54
C413111D	stretcher bond; crack repair average 225 mm wide	m	1.15	34.25	–	3.85	38.10	37.68	–	4.24	41.91
C413111E	stretcher bond; crack repair average 450 mm wide	m	1.65	49.14	–	7.70	56.84	54.05	–	8.47	62.52
C413111F	English or Flemish bond (snapped headers); single brick	Nr	0.23	6.85	–	0.35	7.20	7.54	–	0.39	7.92
C413111G	English or Flemish bond (snapped headers); in areas not exceeding 0.50 m²	Nr	1.45	43.18	–	11.60	54.78	47.50	–	12.76	60.26
C413111H	English or Flemish bond (snapped headers); in areas 0.50-1.00 m²	Nr	2.65	78.92	–	23.89	102.81	86.81	–	26.28	113.09
C413111I	English or Flemish bond (snapped headers); crack repair average 225 m wide .	m	1.35	40.21	–	6.05	46.26	44.23	–	6.66	50.89
C413111J	English or Flemish bond (snapped headers); crack repair average 450 m wide .	m	1.85	55.10	–	10.45	65.55	60.61	–	11.50	72.11

Major Works 2009		Unit	Labour Hours	Labour Net	Plant Net	Materials Net	Unit Net	Labour Gross	Plant Gross	Materials Gross	Unit Price
								——— (Gross rates include 10% profit) ———			
				£	£	£	£	£	£	£	£
C41	**C41: REPAIRING, RENOVATING, CONSERVING MASONRY**										
C4131	**Cutting out decayed and defective work and replacing with new**										
C413113	**Cut out damaged or decayed facing brickwork; cut, tooth and bond new facings to existing in gauged mortar (1:1:6); half brick thick:**										
C413113A	stretcher bond; single brick	Nr	0.30	8.94	–	0.41	9.35	9.83	–	0.45	10.29
C413113B	stretcher bond; in areas not exceeding 0.50 m²	Nr	1.65	49.14	–	11.65	60.79	54.05	–	12.82	66.87
C413113C	stretcher bond; in areas 0.50-1.00 m²	Nr	2.90	86.36	–	23.30	109.66	95.00	–	25.63	120.63
C413113D	stretcher bond; crack repair average 225 mm wide	m	1.55	46.16	–	5.12	51.28	50.78	–	5.63	56.41
C413113E	stretcher bond; crack repair average 450 mm wide	m	2.00	59.56	–	10.25	69.81	65.52	–	11.28	76.79
C413113F	English or Flemish bond (snapped headers); single brick...................	Nr	0.26	7.75	–	0.41	8.16	8.53	–	0.45	8.98
C413113G	English or Flemish bond (snapped headers); in areas not exceeding 0.50 m².....	Nr	1.85	55.09	–	14.23	69.32	60.60	–	15.65	76.25
C413113H	English or Flemish bond (snapped headers); in areas 0.50-1.00 m²............	Nr	3.15	93.81	–	29.28	123.09	103.19	–	32.21	135.40
C413113I	English or Flemish bond (snapped headers); crack repair average 225 m wide .	m	1.85	55.09	–	7.81	62.90	60.60	–	8.59	69.19
C413113J	English or Flemish bond (snapped headers); crack repair average 450 m wide .	m	2.20	65.51	–	15.62	81.13	72.06	–	17.18	89.24

Existing Site, Buildings, Services

Major Works 2009		Unit	Labour Hours	Labour Net	Plant Net	Materials Net	Unit Net	Labour Gross	Plant Gross	Materials Gross	Unit Price
								(Gross rates include 10% profit)			
				£	£	£	£	£	£	£	£
C41	**C41: REPAIRING, RENOVATING, CONSERVING MASONRY**										
C4141	**Repointing brickwork**										
C414111	**Rake out joints of brick walls and repoint in gauged mortar (1:1:6):**										
C414111A	flush pointing; stretcher bond....................	m²	0.50	14.89	–	0.44	15.33	16.38	–	0.48	16.86
C414111B	flush pointing; Flemish bond	m²	0.75	22.33	–	0.66	22.99	24.56	–	0.73	25.29
C414111C	flush pointing; English bond	m²	0.95	28.29	–	0.88	29.17	31.12	–	0.97	32.09
C414111D	tooled pointing; stretcher bond....................	m²	0.55	16.38	–	0.44	16.82	18.02	–	0.48	18.50
C414111E	tooled pointing; Flemish bond....................	m²	0.80	23.82	–	0.66	24.48	26.20	–	0.73	26.93
C414111F	tooled pointing; English bond	m²	1.00	29.78	–	0.88	30.66	32.76	–	0.97	33.73
C45	**C45: DAMP PROOF COURSE RENEWAL AND INSERTION**										
C4501	**Chemical damp proof course injection**										
C450190	**Silicone injection damp proof coursing:**										
C450190A	half brick walls	m	0.70	11.89	–	9.34	21.23	13.08	–	10.27	23.35
C450190B	one brick walls	m	0.75	12.74	–	18.68	31.42	14.01	–	20.55	34.56
C450190C	one and a half brick walls ..	m	0.75	12.74	–	28.02	40.76	14.01	–	30.82	44.84
C450190D	two brick walls	m	0.80	13.58	–	37.36	50.94	14.94	–	41.10	56.03

Major Works 2009		Unit	Labour Hours	Labour Net	Plant Net	Materials Net	Unit Net	Labour Gross	Plant Gross	Materials Gross	Unit Price
								(Gross rates include 10% profit)			
				£	£	£	£	£	£	£	£
C41	**C41: REPAIRING, RENOVATING, CONSERVING MASONRY**										
C4131	**Cutting out decayed and defective work and replacing with new**										
C452201	**Timber mouldings; setting aside for reuse:**										
C452201A	architraves	m	0.08	0.95	–	–	0.95	1.05	–	–	1.05
C452201B	dado rails.	m	0.10	1.27	–	–	1.27	1.40	–	–	1.40
C452201C	skirtings.	m	0.13	1.59	–	–	1.59	1.75	–	–	1.75
C452211	**Wall finishes; placing debris in rubbish skips:**										
C452211A	plaster	m²	0.60	7.63	0.77	–	8.40	8.39	0.85	–	9.24
C452211B	render	m²	0.85	10.80	0.77	–	11.57	11.88	0.85	–	12.73
C452211C	plasterboard and battens. . .	m²	0.45	5.71	1.15	–	6.86	6.28	1.27	–	7.55
C452211D	plaster, lath and battens . . .	m²	0.50	6.35	1.40	–	7.75	6.99	1.54	–	8.53
C452211E	asphalt.	m²	0.65	8.25	0.64	–	8.89	9.08	0.70	–	9.78
C452211F	ceramic tiles	m²	0.45	5.71	0.64	–	6.35	6.28	0.70	–	6.99
C452211G	softwood matching and battens.	m²	0.55	6.99	0.89	–	7.88	7.69	0.98	–	8.67

Major Works 2009		Unit	Labour Hours	Labour Net	Plant Net	Materials Net	Unit Net	Labour Gross	Plant Gross	Materials Gross	Unit Price
								(Gross rates include 10% profit)			
				£	£	£	£	£	£	£	£
C45	**C45: DAMP PROOF COURSE RENEWAL AND INSERTION**										
C4531	**Reinstatement of plaster finishes and refixing of salvaged joinery**										
C453101	**Refixing salvaged timber mouldings:**										
C453101A	architraves	m	0.25	4.25	–	–	4.25	4.68	–	–	4.68
C453101B	dado rails..............	m	0.45	7.64	–	–	7.64	8.40	–	–	8.40
C453101C	skirtings................	m	0.55	9.34	–	–	9.34	10.27	–	–	10.27
C453178	**Making good after damp course works in Carlite lightweight plaster; 2 mm finish on undercoat; jointing and finishing flush to existing; average 1.0 m high:**										
C453178A	13 mm two coat work to masonry walls browning undercoat	m	1.50	44.67	–	2.28	46.95	49.14	–	2.51	51.65
C453179	**Dubbing out with Carlite undercoat; average 1.0 m high:**										
C453179A	6 mm browning to walls ...	m	0.35	10.42	–	1.11	11.53	11.46	–	1.22	12.68
C453179B	12 mm browning to walls ..	m	0.50	14.89	–	2.00	16.89	16.38	–	2.20	18.58
C453179C	15 mm browning to walls ..	m	0.60	17.87	–	2.66	20.53	19.66	–	2.93	22.58
C453179D	20 mm browning to walls ..	m	0.75	22.34	–	3.33	25.67	24.57	–	3.66	28.24
C453179E	6 mm bonding to walls	m	0.35	10.43	–	1.29	11.72	11.47	–	1.42	12.89
C453179F	12 mm bonding to walls ...	m	0.50	14.89	–	2.59	17.48	16.38	–	2.85	19.23
C453179G	15 mm bonding to walls ...	m	0.60	17.87	–	3.23	21.10	19.66	–	3.55	23.21
C453179H	20 mm bonding to walls ...	m	0.75	22.34	–	4.31	26.65	24.57	–	4.74	29.32
C4539	**Cutting in physical damp course**										
C453989	**Cut out 1 metre alternate lengths of existing brick wall one course high; lay Hyload pitch polymer damp proof course and make good wall with bricks t match existing in cement mortar (1:3):**										
C453989A	half brick wall in commons .	m	1.15	34.24	–	3.04	37.28	37.66	–	3.34	41.01
C453989B	one brick wall in commons .	m	2.25	67.00	–	6.20	73.20	73.70	–	6.82	80.52
C453989C	half brick wall in facings ...	m	1.35	40.20	–	3.38	43.58	44.22	–	3.72	47.94
C453989D	one brick wall in facings ...	m	2.65	78.92	–	6.89	85.81	86.81	–	7.58	94.39

Major Works 2009		Unit	Labour Hours	Labour Net	Plant Net	Materials Net	Unit Net	Labour Gross	Plant Gross	Materials Gross	Unit Price
								(Gross rates include 10% profit)			
				£	£	£	£	£	£	£	£
C90	**C90: ALTERATIONS-SPOT ITEMS**										
C9011	**Removal of building fabric fittings and fixtures**										
C901101	**Timber mouldings:**										
C901101A	architraves	m	0.08	0.95	–	–	0.95	1.05	–	–	1.05
C901101B	picture and dado rails	m	0.10	1.27	–	–	1.27	1.40	–	–	1.40
C901101C	skirtings................	m	0.13	1.59	–	–	1.59	1.75	–	–	1.75
C901114	**Straight flight timber staircase; placing debris in rubbish skips:**										
C901114A	600 mm wide × 2600 mm rise.....................	Nr	2.00	25.40	10.20	–	35.60	27.94	11.22	–	39.16
C901114B	900 mm wide × 2600 mm rise.....................	Nr	2.20	27.94	12.75	–	40.69	30.73	14.03	–	44.76
C901114C	1200 mm wide × 2600 mm rise.....................	Nr	2.60	33.02	17.85	–	50.87	36.32	19.64	–	55.96
C901115	**Two flight timber staircase with landing; placing debris in rubbish skips:**										
C901115A	600 mm wide × 2600 mm rise.....................	Nr	3.00	38.10	10.20	–	48.30	41.91	11.22	–	53.13
C901115B	900 mm wide × 2600 mm rise.....................	Nr	3.20	40.64	12.75	–	53.39	44.70	14.03	–	58.73
C901115C	1200 mm wide × 2600 mm rise.....................	Nr	3.50	44.45	17.85	–	62.30	48.90	19.64	–	68.53
C901116	**Timber balustrading; placing debris in rubbish skips:**										
C901116A	horizontal	m	0.25	3.18	2.30	–	5.48	3.50	2.53	–	6.03
C901116B	raking.................	m	0.35	4.45	2.30	–	6.75	4.90	2.53	–	7.43

Existing Site, Buildings, Services

Major Works 2009		Unit	Labour Hours	Labour Net	Plant Net	Materials Net	Unit Net	Labour Gross	Plant Gross	Materials Gross	Unit Price
								(Gross rates include 10% profit)			
				£	£	£	£	£	£	£	£
C90	**C90: ALTERATIONS-SPOT ITEMS**										
C9012	**Removal of general fittings and fixtures and placing in rubbish skips**										
C901203	**Fire surround and hearth not exceeding 2 m² area:**										
C901203A	masonry	Nr	1.25	15.88	5.10	–	20.98	17.47	5.61	–	23.08
C901203B	cast iron................	Nr	0.50	6.35	2.55	–	8.90	6.99	2.81	–	9.79
C901203C	tiled concrete	Nr	0.75	9.53	5.10	–	14.63	10.48	5.61	–	16.09
C901203D	plaster	Nr	0.50	6.35	2.55	–	8.90	6.99	2.81	–	9.79
C901203E	timber	Nr	0.25	3.18	2.55	–	5.73	3.50	2.81	–	6.30
C901204	**Wall units:**										
C901204A	600 × 300 × 300 mm ..	Nr	0.25	3.18	1.28	–	4.46	3.50	1.41	–	4.91
C901204B	300 × 300 × 600 mm ..	Nr	0.25	3.18	1.28	–	4.46	3.50	1.41	–	4.91
C901204C	600 × 300 × 600 mm ..	Nr	0.25	3.18	2.55	–	5.73	3.50	2.81	–	6.30
C901204D	1000 × 300 × 600 mm .	Nr	0.30	3.82	3.83	–	7.65	4.20	4.21	–	8.42
C901204E	1200 × 300 × 600 mm .	Nr	0.30	3.82	3.83	–	7.65	4.20	4.21	–	8.42
C901204F	300 × 300 × 900 mm ..	Nr	0.25	3.18	1.28	–	4.46	3.50	1.41	–	4.91
C901204G	600 × 300 × 900 mm ..	Nr	0.25	3.18	2.04	–	5.22	3.50	2.24	–	5.74
C901204H	1000 × 300 × 900 mm .	Nr	0.30	3.82	3.32	–	7.14	4.20	3.65	–	7.85
C901204I	1200 × 300 × 900 mm .	Nr	0.30	3.82	4.34	–	8.16	4.20	4.77	–	8.98
C901205	**Base units:**										
C901205A	300 × 600 × 900 mm ..	Nr	0.18	2.29	2.04	–	4.33	2.52	2.24	–	4.76
C901205B	600 × 600 × 900 mm ..	Nr	0.18	2.29	4.08	–	6.37	2.52	4.49	–	7.01
C901205C	1000 × 600 × 900 mm .	Nr	0.25	3.18	6.89	–	10.07	3.50	7.58	–	11.08
C901205D	1200 × 600 × 900 mm .	Nr	0.25	3.18	8.16	–	11.34	3.50	8.98	–	12.47

Major Works 2009		Unit	Labour Hours	Labour Net	Plant Net	Materials Net	Unit Net	Labour Gross	Plant Gross	Materials Gross	Unit Price
								—— (Gross rates include 10% profit) ——			
				£	£	£	£	£	£	£	£
C90	**C90: ALTERATIONS-SPOT ITEMS**										
C9012	**Removal of general fittings and fixtures and placing in rubbish skips**										
C901206	**Sink base units:**										
C901206A	1000 × 600 × 900 mm .	Nr	0.25	3.18	6.89	–	10.07	3.50	7.58	–	11.08
C901206B	1200 × 600 × 900 mm .	Nr	0.25	3.18	8.16	–	11.34	3.50	8.98	–	12.47
C901206C	1500 × 600 × 900 mm .	Nr	0.30	3.81	10.20	–	14.01	4.19	11.22	–	15.41
C901207	**Corner base units:**										
C901207A	800 × 600 × 900 mm ..	Nr	0.18	2.29	10.20	–	12.49	2.52	11.22	–	13.74
C901207B	900 × 600 × 900 mm ..	Nr	0.18	2.29	10.20	–	12.49	2.52	11.22	–	13.74
C901207C	1000 × 600 × 900 mm ..	Nr	0.25	3.18	6.89	–	10.07	3.50	7.58	–	11.08
C901207D	1200 × 600 × 900 mm ..	Nr	0.25	3.18	8.16	–	11.34	3.50	8.98	–	12.47
C901208	**Appliance housing units:**										
C901208A	1200 × 600 × 900 mm ..	Nr	0.25	3.18	8.16	–	11.34	3.50	8.98	–	12.47
C901208B	600 × 600 × 1950 mm .	Nr	0.30	3.82	8.93	–	12.75	4.20	9.82	–	14.03
C901208C	600 × 600 × 900 mm ..	Nr	0.25	3.18	8.16	–	11.34	3.50	8.98	–	12.47
C901209	**Store units:**										
C901209A	600 × 600 × 300 mm ..	Nr	0.25	3.18	2.81	–	5.99	3.50	3.09	–	6.59
C901209B	600 × 600 × 1950 mm .	Nr	0.30	3.82	8.93	–	12.75	4.20	9.82	–	14.03
C901210	**Worktops:**										
C901210A	500 mm wide	m	0.25	3.18	1.28	–	4.46	3.50	1.41	–	4.91
C901210B	600 mm wide	m	0.25	3.18	1.53	–	4.71	3.50	1.68	–	5.18
C901211	**Draining boards:**										
C901211A	500 × 400 mm..........	Nr	0.15	1.91	0.26	–	2.17	2.10	0.29	–	2.39
C901211B	800 × 600 mm..........	Nr	0.18	2.29	0.51	–	2.80	2.52	0.56	–	3.08
C901212	**Shelving units:**										
C901212A	1500 × 300 × 1000 mm	Nr	0.25	3.18	7.65	–	10.83	3.50	8.42	–	11.91
C901212B	2000 × 300 × 1500 mm	Nr	0.30	3.81	7.65	–	11.46	4.19	8.42	–	12.61
C901213	**Shelving:**										
C901213A	not exceeding 300 mm wide	m	0.13	1.66	0.26	–	1.92	1.83	0.29	–	2.11
C901213B	300-600 mm wide	m	0.20	2.55	0.26	–	2.81	2.81	0.29	–	3.09

Existing Site, Buildings, Services

Major Works 2009		Unit	Labour Hours	Labour Net	Plant Net	Materials Net	Unit Net	Labour Gross	Plant Gross	Materials Gross	Unit Price
								(Gross rates include 10% profit)			
				£	£	£	£	£	£	£	£
C90	**C90: ALTERATIONS-SPOT ITEMS**										
C9015	**Removal of windows, doors and frames**										
C901572	**Timber doors, frames and linings; removing ironmongery and piecing out; placing debris in rubbish skips:**										
C901572A	timber doors	Nr	1.00	16.98	–	1.14	18.12	18.68	–	1.25	19.93
C901572B	timber door frames, linings and architraves	Nr	0.50	8.49	–	0.57	9.06	9.34	–	0.63	9.97

Major Works 2009		Unit	Labour Hours	Labour Net	Plant Net	Materials Net	Unit Net	Labour Gross	Plant Gross	Materials Gross	Unit Price
								(Gross rates include 10% profit)			
				£	£	£	£	£	£	£	£
C90	**C90: ALTERATIONS-SPOT ITEMS**										
C901575	**Timber window frames and linings; removing ironmongery and piecing out; placing debris in rubbish skips:**										
C901575A	timber window frames and linings; not exceeding 0.50 m²	Nr	0.75	12.73	–	0.69	13.42	14.00	–	0.76	14.76
C901575B	timber window frames and linings; 0.50-1.00 m²	Nr	1.00	16.98	–	0.81	17.79	18.68	–	0.89	19.57
C901575C	timber window frames and linings; 1.00-2.00 m²	Nr	1.25	21.23	–	0.91	22.14	23.35	–	1.00	24.35
C901575D	timber window frames and linings; 2.00-3.00 m²	Nr	1.50	25.47	–	1.03	26.50	28.02	–	1.13	29.15
C9023	**Removal of plumbing and engineering installations; fixtures and fittings**										
C902320	**Plumbing and heating installations; fixtures and fittings; placing debris in rubbish skips:**										
C902320A	back boiler	Nr	0.50	8.20	3.06	–	11.26	9.02	3.37	–	12.39
C902320B	boiler and flue pipe	Nr	0.80	13.12	5.10	–	18.22	14.43	5.61	–	20.04
C902320C	feed and expansion tank	Nr	0.50	8.20	2.55	–	10.75	9.02	2.81	–	11.83
C902320D	cold water storage tank	Nr	0.80	13.12	9.18	–	22.30	14.43	10.10	–	24.53
C902320E	hot water cylinder	Nr	1.00	16.40	4.59	–	20.99	18.04	5.05	–	23.09
C902320F	oil tank and supply pipe	Nr	2.00	32.80	17.85	–	50.65	36.08	19.64	–	55.72
C902320G	radiators	Nr	0.50	8.21	1.28	–	9.49	9.03	1.41	–	10.44
C902320H	circulating pump	Nr	0.50	8.20	–	–	8.20	9.02	–	–	9.02
C902320I	pipework to fittings not exceeding 5 m run	Nr	0.50	8.20	0.03	–	8.23	9.02	0.03	–	9.05
C902320J	pipework to fittings 5-10 m run	Nr	0.80	13.12	0.08	–	13.20	14.43	0.09	–	14.52
C902320K	drain down domestic hot and cold water system	Nr	1.00	16.40	–	–	16.40	18.04	–	–	18.04
C902320L	drain down central heating system no exceeding 10 radiators	Nr	1.00	16.40	–	–	16.40	18.04	–	–	18.04
C902320M	disconnect and make safe mains water supply	Nr	0.50	8.20	–	2.29	10.49	9.02	–	2.52	11.54

Existing Site, Buildings, Services

Major Works 2009		Unit	Labour Hours	Labour Net	Plant Net	Materials Net	Unit Net	Labour Gross	Plant Gross	Materials Gross	Unit Price
								(Gross rates include 10% profit)			
				£	£	£	£	£	£	£	£
C90	**C90: ALTERATIONS-SPOT ITEMS**										
C902321	**Sanitary fittings, complete with taps and traps; placing debris in rubbish skips:**										
C902321A	wc suite	Nr	0.50	8.20	2.55	–	10.75	9.02	2.81	–	11.83
C902321B	bidet....................	Nr	0.50	8.20	2.55	–	10.75	9.02	2.81	–	11.83
C902321C	bath	Nr	0.75	12.30	12.75	–	25.05	13.53	14.03	–	27.56
C902321D	shower tray	Nr	0.30	4.93	6.38	–	11.31	5.42	7.02	–	12.44
C902321E	hand basin..............	Nr	0.50	8.20	2.55	–	10.75	9.02	2.81	–	11.83
C902321F	sink....................	Nr	0.50	8.21	3.83	–	12.04	9.03	4.21	–	13.24
C902321G	w.c. or shower cubicle partition.................	Nr	0.30	3.82	1.28	–	5.10	4.20	1.41	–	5.61
C902321H	service and waste pipes to fittings not exceeding 5 m run	Nr	0.50	8.20	0.03	–	8.23	9.02	0.03	–	9.05
C902321I	service and waste pipes to fittings 5-10 m run	Nr	0.80	13.12	0.08	–	13.20	14.43	0.09	–	14.52
C9024	**Removal of electrical installations; fixtures and fittings**										
C902430	**Electrical fixtures and fittings; placing debris in rubbish skips:**										
C902430A	distribution and switch boards	Nr	0.50	8.33	0.77	–	9.10	9.16	0.85	–	10.01
C902430B	meters	Nr	0.30	5.00	0.26	–	5.26	5.50	0.29	–	5.79
C902430C	light fittings.............	Nr	0.15	2.50	–	–	2.50	2.75	–	–	2.75
C902430D	flush power sockets.......	Nr	0.20	3.33	–	–	3.33	3.66	–	–	3.66
C902430E	surface mounted power sockets	Nr	0.15	2.50	–	–	2.50	2.75	–	–	2.75
C902430F	flush switch boxes	Nr	0.20	3.33	–	–	3.33	3.66	–	–	3.66
C902430G	surface mounted switch boxes	Nr	0.15	2.50	–	–	2.50	2.75	–	–	2.75
C902430H	flush cooker outlets	Nr	0.22	3.66	–	–	3.66	4.03	–	–	4.03
C902430I	surface mounted cooker outlets	Nr	0.17	2.83	–	–	2.83	3.11	–	–	3.11
C902430J	immersion heaters	Nr	0.25	4.16	–	–	4.16	4.58	–	–	4.58
C902430K	night storage heaters......	Nr	0.45	7.49	5.10	–	12.59	8.24	5.61	–	13.85
C902430L	wall mounted extractor fans	Nr	0.30	5.00	–	–	5.00	5.50	–	–	5.50
C902430M	ceiling mounted extractor fans	Nr	0.40	6.66	–	–	6.66	7.33	–	–	7.33
C902430N	window mounted extractor fans	Nr	0.40	6.66	–	–	6.66	7.33	–	–	7.33
C902430O	surface mounted cabling or trunking not exceeding 5 m length...................	Nr	0.15	2.50	–	–	2.50	2.75	–	–	2.75
C902430P	surface mounted cabling or trunking 5-10 m length	Nr	0.30	5.00	–	–	5.00	5.50	–	–	5.50
C902430Q	cap off and make safe buried cables not exceeding 30 Amp	Nr	1.00	20.80	–	5.72	26.52	22.88	–	6.29	29.17
C902430R	disconnect and make safe mains supply.............	Nr	0.75	15.60	–	2.29	17.89	17.16	–	2.52	19.68

Major Works 2009		Unit	Labour Hours	Labour Net	Plant Net	Materials Net	Unit Net	Labour Gross	Plant Gross	Materials Gross	Unit Price
								(Gross rates include 10% profit)			
				£	£	£	£	£	£	£	£
C90	**C90: ALTERATIONS-SPOT ITEMS**										
C9031	**Removal of floor, wall and ceiling finishes**										
C903101	**Floor finishes; placing debris in rubbish skips:**										
C903101A	sand and cement screed ...	m²	0.80	10.16	1.91	–	12.07	11.18	2.10	–	13.28
C903101B	quarry tiles	m²	0.80	10.17	1.28	–	11.45	11.19	1.41	–	12.60
C903101C	ceramic tiles	m²	0.55	6.98	0.64	–	7.62	7.68	0.70	–	8.38
C903101D	plastic floor tiles	m²	0.65	8.25	0.64	–	8.89	9.08	0.70	–	9.78
C903101E	carpeting	m²	0.10	1.27	2.55	–	3.82	1.40	2.81	–	4.20
C903101F	asphalt.................	m²	0.75	9.53	1.28	–	10.81	10.48	1.41	–	11.89
C903101G	linoleum................	m²	0.08	1.02	0.51	–	1.53	1.12	0.56	–	1.68
C903111	**Wall finishes; placing debris in rubbish skips:**										
C903111A	plaster	m²	0.60	7.63	0.77	–	8.40	8.39	0.85	–	9.24
C903111B	render	m²	0.85	10.80	0.77	–	11.57	11.88	0.85	–	12.73
C903111C	plasterboard	m²	0.35	4.45	1.02	–	5.47	4.90	1.12	–	6.02
C903111D	lath and plaster	m²	0.45	5.72	1.28	–	7.00	6.29	1.41	–	7.70
C903111E	asphalt.................	m²	0.65	8.25	0.64	–	8.89	9.08	0.70	–	9.78
C903111F	ceramic tiles	m²	0.45	5.71	0.64	–	6.35	6.28	0.70	–	6.99
C903111G	matching	m²	0.50	6.36	0.77	–	7.13	7.00	0.85	–	7.84
C903121	**Ceiling finishes; placing debris in rubbish skips:**										
C903121A	lath and plaster	m²	0.45	5.72	1.28	–	7.00	6.29	1.41	–	7.70
C903121B	plasterboard	m²	0.40	5.08	1.02	–	6.10	5.59	1.12	–	6.71
C903121C	softwood matching	m²	0.50	6.36	0.77	–	7.13	7.00	0.85	–	7.84
C903121D	rigid sheeting	m²	0.25	3.17	0.64	–	3.81	3.49	0.70	–	4.19
C9041	**Removal of roof coverings**										
C904181	**Slates and tiles; taking off, cleaning and setting aside for re-use; placing debris in rubbish skips:**										
C904181A	roof slating	m²	0.25	3.18	–	–	3.18	3.50	–	–	3.50
C904181B	roof tiling...............	m²	0.20	2.54	–	–	2.54	2.79	–	–	2.79

Major Works 2009		Unit	Labour Hours	Labour Net	Plant Net	Materials Net	Unit Net	Labour Gross	Plant Gross	Materials Gross	Unit Price
								(Gross rates include 10% profit)			
				£	£	£	£	£	£	£	£
C90	**C90: ALTERATIONS-SPOT ITEMS**										
C9051	**Cutting openings in existing structures**										
C905161	**Cutting openings in load bearing walls; placing debris in rubbish skips:**										
C905161A	half brick common brickwork	m²	2.00	25.40	6.83	–	32.23	27.94	7.51	–	35.45
C905161B	one brick common brickwork	m²	2.30	29.21	7.33	–	36.54	32.13	8.06	–	40.19
C905161C	one and a half brick common brickwork	m²	3.00	38.10	9.19	–	47.29	41.91	10.11	–	52.02
C905161D	two brick common brickwork	m²	3.80	48.26	10.99	–	59.25	53.09	12.09	–	65.18
C905161E	half brick engineering brickwork	m²	2.20	27.94	7.16	–	35.10	30.73	7.88	–	38.61
C905161F	one brick engineering brickwork	m²	2.50	31.75	7.66	–	39.41	34.93	8.43	–	43.35
C905161G	one and a half brick engineering brickwork	m²	3.20	40.64	9.52	–	50.16	44.70	10.47	–	55.18
C905161H	two brick engineering brickwork	m²	4.00	50.80	11.32	–	62.12	55.88	12.45	–	68.33
C905161I	half brick facing brickwork	m²	1.90	24.13	6.66	–	30.79	26.54	7.33	–	33.87
C905161J	one brick facing brickwork	m²	2.20	27.94	7.16	–	35.10	30.73	7.88	–	38.61
C905161K	100 or 125 mm blockwork	m²	1.70	21.59	6.33	–	27.92	23.75	6.96	–	30.71
C905161L	150 mm blockwork	m²	1.80	22.86	6.50	–	29.36	25.15	7.15	–	32.30
C905161M	200 mm blockwork	m²	2.20	27.94	7.86	–	35.80	30.73	8.65	–	39.38
C905161N	225 mm blockwork	m²	2.40	30.48	8.66	–	39.14	33.53	9.53	–	43.05
C905161O	250 or 275 mm cavity wall (half facing brick outer, 100 or 125 mm block inner skin)	m²	2.50	31.75	8.36	–	40.11	34.93	9.20	–	44.12
C905161P	300 mm cavity wall (half brick outer 150 mm block inner skin)	m²	2.80	35.56	9.33	–	44.89	39.12	10.26	–	49.38
C905161Q	300 mm cavity wall (half brick outer 100 mm block inner skin)	m²	2.50	31.75	8.36	–	40.11	34.93	9.20	–	44.12
C905161R	100 mm reinforced concrete wall	m²	1.50	19.05	2.49	–	21.54	20.96	2.74	–	23.69
C905161S	150 mm reinforced concrete wall	m²	2.10	26.67	3.49	–	30.16	29.34	3.84	–	33.18
C905161T	200 mm reinforced concrete wall	m²	2.90	36.83	4.81	–	41.64	40.51	5.29	–	45.80
C905161U	250 mm reinforced concrete wall	m²	3.50	44.45	5.81	–	50.26	48.90	6.39	–	55.29
C905161V	300 mm reinforced concrete wall	m²	4.00	50.80	6.64	–	57.44	55.88	7.30	–	63.18
C905162	**Cutting openings in non-load bearing walls; placing debris in rubbish skips:**										
C905162A	half brick common brickwork	m²	0.75	9.53	–	–	9.53	10.48	–	–	10.48
C905162B	half brick facing brickwork	m²	0.60	7.62	–	–	7.62	8.38	–	–	8.38
C905162C	50 mm blockwork	m²	0.25	3.18	–	–	3.18	3.50	–	–	3.50
C905162D	75 mm blockwork	m²	0.30	3.81	–	–	3.81	4.19	–	–	4.19
C905162E	100 mm blockwork	m²	0.40	5.08	–	–	5.08	5.59	–	–	5.59

Major Works 2009		Unit	Labour Hours	Labour Net	Plant Net	Materials Net	Unit Net	Labour Gross	Plant Gross	Materials Gross	Unit Price
								(Gross rates include 10% profit)			
				£	£	£	£	£	£	£	£
C90	**C90: ALTERATIONS-SPOT ITEMS**										
C9051	**Cutting openings in existing structures**										
C905163	**Making good to reveals of openings with materials to match existing:**										
C905163A	half brick common brickwork	m	0.25	7.44	–	2.11	9.55	8.18	–	2.32	10.51
C905163B	one brick common brickwork	m	0.40	11.91	–	4.36	16.27	13.10	–	4.80	17.90
C905163C	one and a half brick common brickwork	m	0.65	19.36	–	6.46	25.82	21.30	–	7.11	28.40
C905163D	two brick common brickwork	m	0.85	25.31	–	8.48	33.79	27.84	–	9.33	37.17
C905163E	half brick engineering brickwork	m	0.30	8.93	–	3.30	12.23	9.82	–	3.63	13.45
C905163F	one brick engineering brickwork	m	0.45	13.40	–	6.96	20.36	14.74	–	7.66	22.40
C905163G	one and a half brick engineering brickwork.....	m	0.70	20.84	–	10.26	31.10	22.92	–	11.29	34.21
C905163H	two brick engineering brickwork	m	0.90	26.80	–	13.47	40.27	29.48	–	14.82	44.30
C905163I	half brick facing brickwork .	m	0.50	14.89	–	2.36	17.25	16.38	–	2.60	18.98
C905163J	one brick facing brickwork .	m	0.90	26.80	–	5.02	31.82	29.48	–	5.52	35.00
C905163K	250 or 275 mm cavity wall (100 or 125 mm inner and outer skins)..............	m	0.60	17.87	–	2.93	20.80	19.66	–	3.22	22.88
C905163M	250 or 275 mm cavity wall (half brick facings outer, 100 mm block inner skins) .	m	0.90	26.80	–	3.65	30.45	29.48	–	4.02	33.50
C905163N	300 mm cavity wall (half brick facing outer, 150 mm block inner skins).........	m	1.00	29.78	–	4.35	34.13	32.76	–	4.79	37.54
C905163O	300 mm cavity wall (half brick facing outer, 100 mm block inner skins).........	m	0.85	25.31	–	3.65	28.96	27.84	–	4.02	31.86
C905163P	50 mm blockwork.........	m	0.15	4.47	–	0.88	5.35	4.92	–	0.97	5.89
C905163Q	75 mm blockwork.........	m	0.18	5.36	–	1.00	6.36	5.90	–	1.10	7.00
C905163R	100 mm blockwork	m	0.20	5.96	–	1.29	7.25	6.56	–	1.42	7.98
C905163S	125 mm blockwork	m	0.25	7.45	–	1.63	9.08	8.20	–	1.79	9.99
C905163T	150 mm blockwork	m	0.35	10.43	–	1.99	12.42	11.47	–	2.19	13.66
C905163U	200 mm blockwork	m	0.45	13.40	–	2.59	15.99	14.74	–	2.85	17.59
C905163V	215 mm blockwork	m	0.55	16.38	–	2.84	19.22	18.02	–	3.12	21.14
C905163W	100 mm reinforced concrete wall....................	m	0.25	7.45	–	0.27	7.72	8.20	–	0.30	8.49
C905163X	150 mm reinforced concrete wall....................	m	0.30	8.94	–	0.36	9.30	9.83	–	0.40	10.23
C905163Y	300 mm reinforced concrete wall....................	m	0.40	11.91	–	0.73	12.64	13.10	–	0.80	13.90

Major Works 2009		Unit	Labour Hours	Labour Net	Plant Net	Materials Net	Unit Net	Labour Gross	Plant Gross	Materials Gross	Unit Price
								(Gross rates include 10% profit)			
				£	£	£	£	£	£	£	£
C90	**C90: ALTERATIONS-SPOT ITEMS**										
C9076	**Filling in openings in existing structures**										
C907601	**Infilling with brickwork in gauged mortar (1:1:6):**										
C907601A	half brick wall in commons .	m²	0.75	22.34	–	17.26	39.60	24.57	–	18.99	43.56
C907601B	one brick wall in commons .	m²	1.50	44.67	–	35.84	80.51	49.14	–	39.42	88.56
C907601C	one and a half brick wall in commons	m²	2.25	67.01	–	53.34	120.35	73.71	–	58.67	132.39
C907601D	two brick wall in commons .	m²	2.90	86.36	–	71.92	158.28	95.00	–	79.11	174.11
C907601E	half brick wall in engineering brick.	m²	0.90	26.80	–	29.60	56.40	29.48	–	32.56	62.04
C907601F	one brick wall in engineering bricks.	m²	1.65	49.14	–	60.52	109.66	54.05	–	66.57	120.63
C907601G	one and a half brick wall in engineering bricks	m²	2.40	71.47	–	90.57	162.04	78.62	–	99.63	178.24
C907601H	two brick wall in engineering bricks.	m²	3.10	92.32	–	121.48	213.80	101.55	–	133.63	235.18
C907601I	half brick wall in facing bricks	m²	1.00	29.78	–	21.22	51.00	32.76	–	23.34	56.10
C907601J	one brick wall in facing bricks	m²	1.80	53.61	–	43.53	97.14	58.97	–	47.88	106.85
C907603	**Infilling with blockwork in gauged mortar (1:1:6):**										
C907603A	50 mm blockwork.	m²	0.65	19.36	–	7.06	26.42	21.30	–	7.77	29.06
C907603B	75 mm blockwork.	m²	0.70	20.84	–	8.21	29.05	22.92	–	9.03	31.96
C907603C	100 mm blockwork	m²	0.75	22.34	–	10.91	33.25	24.57	–	12.00	36.58
C907603D	125 mm blockwork	m²	0.80	23.83	–	13.99	37.82	26.21	–	15.39	41.60
C907603E	150 mm blockwork	m²	0.85	25.31	–	16.41	41.72	27.84	–	18.05	45.89
C907603F	200 mm blockwork	m²	0.95	28.29	–	21.81	50.10	31.12	–	23.99	55.11
C907603G	215 mm blockwork	m²	1.10	32.76	–	24.37	57.13	36.04	–	26.81	62.84
C907605	**Infilling with composite walling in gauged mortar (1:1:6):**										
C907605A	250 or 275 mm cavity wall (100 or 125 mm block outer and inner skins)	m²	1.65	49.14	–	34.66	83.80	54.05	–	38.13	92.18
C907605B	250 or 275 mm cavity wall (half brick outer and 100 or 125 mm inner skins)	m²	1.90	56.58	–	35.21	91.79	62.24	–	38.73	100.97
C907605C	300 mm cavity wall (half brick facing outer, 150 mm inner skins)	m²	1.95	58.07	–	37.63	95.70	63.88	–	41.39	105.27
C907605D	300 mm cavity wall (half brick facing outer, 100 mm inner skins)	m²	1.85	55.09	–	32.13	87.22	60.60	–	35.34	95.94

Major Works 2009		Unit	Labour Hours	Labour Net	Plant Net	Materials Net	Unit Net	Labour Gross	Plant Gross	Materials Gross	Unit Price
								(Gross rates include 10% profit)			
				£	£	£	£	£	£	£	£
C90	**C90: ALTERATIONS-SPOT ITEMS**										
C9079	**Cutting, toothing and bonding ends of new walls into existing**										
C907901	**Common brickwork; in alternate courses:**										
C907901A	half brick wall	m	0.42	12.50	–	2.11	14.61	13.75	–	2.32	16.07
C907901B	one brick wall	m	0.62	18.46	–	4.36	22.82	20.31	–	4.80	25.10
C907901C	one and a half brick wall . . .	m	0.82	24.42	–	6.46	30.88	26.86	–	7.11	33.97
C907901D	two brick wall	m	1.22	36.33	–	8.48	44.81	39.96	–	9.33	49.29
C907903	**Engineering brickwork; in alternate courses:**										
C907903A	half brick wall	m	0.45	13.40	–	3.30	16.70	14.74	–	3.63	18.37
C907903B	one brick wall	m	0.65	19.35	–	6.96	26.31	21.29	–	7.66	28.94
C907903C	one and a half brick wall . . .	m	0.85	25.31	–	10.26	35.57	27.84	–	11.29	39.13
C907903D	two brick wall	m	1.25	37.22	–	13.47	50.69	40.94	–	14.82	55.76
C907905	**Facing brickwork; in alternate courses:**										
C907905A	half brick wall	m	0.60	17.87	–	2.32	20.19	19.66	–	2.55	22.21
C907905B	one brick wall	m	0.85	25.31	–	4.94	30.25	27.84	–	5.43	33.28
C907908	**Blockwork; in alternate courses:**										
C907908A	50 mm thick	m	0.25	7.45	–	1.50	8.95	8.20	–	1.65	9.85
C907908B	75 mm thick	m	0.28	8.34	–	1.72	10.06	9.17	–	1.89	11.07
C907908C	100 mm thick	m	0.32	9.53	–	2.26	11.79	10.48	–	2.49	12.97
C907908D	125 mm thick	m	0.35	10.43	–	2.88	13.31	11.47	–	3.17	14.64
C907908E	150 mm thick	m	0.40	11.91	–	3.44	15.35	13.10	–	3.78	16.89
C907908F	200 mm thick	m	0.50	14.89	–	4.52	19.41	16.38	–	4.97	21.35
C907908G	215 mm thick	m	0.55	16.38	–	4.99	21.37	18.02	–	5.49	23.51
C9082	**Making good to floors after alterations in materials to match existing**										
C908201	**Concrete floor slabs; jointing to existing; 100 mm thick:**										
C908201A	not exceeding 150 mm wide	m	0.30	3.81	–	2.00	5.81	4.19	–	2.20	6.39
C908201B	150-300 mm wide	m	0.40	5.08	–	3.89	8.97	5.59	–	4.28	9.87
C908201C	isolated areas; not exceeding 1.00 m	Nr	0.50	6.35	–	12.96	19.31	6.99	–	14.26	21.24
C908201D	isolated areas; 1.00-2.00 m^2	Nr	0.75	9.53	–	25.91	35.44	10.48	–	28.50	38.98
C908203	**Concrete floor slabs; jointing to existing; 150 mm thick:**										
C908203A	not exceeding 150 mm wide	m	0.33	4.20	–	2.94	7.14	4.62	–	3.23	7.85
C908203B	150-300 mm wide	m	0.43	5.46	–	5.89	11.35	6.01	–	6.48	12.49
C908203C	isolated areas; not exceeding 1.00 m	Nr	0.55	6.99	–	19.43	26.42	7.69	–	21.37	29.06
C908203D	isolated areas; 1.00-2.00 m^2	Nr	0.80	10.16	–	38.87	49.03	11.18	–	42.76	53.93

Major Works 2009		Unit	Labour Hours	Labour Net	Plant Net	Materials Net	Unit Net	Labour Gross	Plant Gross	Materials Gross	Unit Price
								(Gross rates include 10% profit)			
				£	£	£	£	£	£	£	£
C90	**C90: ALTERATIONS-SPOT ITEMS**										
C9082	**Making good to floors after alterations in materials to match existing**										
C908208	**Cement and sand (1:3) trowelled screed; jointing to existing:**										
C908208A	25 mm thick	m²	0.25	7.45	–	2.54	9.99	8.20	–	2.79	10.99
C908208B	38 mm thick	m²	0.28	8.34	–	3.81	12.15	9.17	–	4.19	13.37
C908208C	50 mm thick	m²	0.32	9.52	–	5.00	14.52	10.47	–	5.50	15.97
C908208D	65 mm thick	m²	0.40	11.91	–	6.54	18.45	13.10	–	7.19	20.30
C908211	**Timber floors; 25 mm thick tongued and grooved softwood boarding on 50 × 150 mm joists at 400 mm centres:**										
C908211A	not exceeding 150 mm wide	m	0.50	8.49	–	6.25	14.74	9.34	–	6.88	16.21
C908211B	150-300 mm wide	m	0.75	12.73	–	9.02	21.75	14.00	–	9.92	23.93
C908211C	over 300 mm wide	m²	1.00	16.98	–	27.78	44.76	18.68	–	30.56	49.24
C908211D	isolated areas; not exceeding 1.00 m	Nr	1.50	25.47	–	28.23	53.70	28.02	–	31.05	59.07
C908211E	isolated areas; 1.00-2.00 m²	Nr	2.00	33.96	–	36.60	70.56	37.36	–	40.26	77.62
C908213	**Timber floors; 25 mm thick tongued and grooved softwood boarding on 50 × 200 mm joists at 400 mm centres:**										
C908213A	not exceeding 150 mm wide	m	0.50	8.49	–	6.95	15.44	9.34	–	7.65	16.98
C908213B	150-300 mm wide	m	0.75	12.74	–	9.69	22.43	14.01	–	10.66	24.67
C908213C	over 300 mm wide	m²	1.00	16.98	–	29.38	46.36	18.68	–	32.32	51.00
C908213D	isolated areas; not exceeding 1.00 m	Nr	1.50	25.47	–	29.83	55.30	28.02	–	32.81	60.83
C908213E	isolated areas; 1.00-2.00 m²	Nr	2.00	33.96	–	39.81	73.77	37.36	–	43.79	81.15
C908215	**Timber floors; 22 mm thick tongued and grooved V313 moisture resistant chipboard, BS 5669, on 50 × 150 mm joists at 400 mm centres:**										
C908215A	not exceeding 150 mm wide	m	0.35	5.95	–	3.91	9.86	6.55	–	4.30	10.85
C908215B	150-300 mm wide	m	0.50	8.49	–	4.87	13.36	9.34	–	5.36	14.70
C908215C	over 300 mm wide	m²	0.65	11.04	–	12.96	24.00	12.14	–	14.26	26.40
C908215D	isolated areas; not exceeding 1.00 m	Nr	0.95	16.13	–	13.22	29.35	17.74	–	14.54	32.29
C908215E	isolated areas; 1.00-2.00 m²	Nr	1.75	29.72	–	25.92	55.64	32.69	–	28.51	61.20
C908217	**Timber floors; 25 mm thick tongued and grooved V313 moisture resistant chipboard, BS 5669, on 50 × 200 mm joists at 400 mm centres:**										
C908217A	not exceeding 150 mm wide	m	0.35	5.95	–	4.74	10.69	6.55	–	5.21	11.76
C908217B	150-300 mm wide	m	0.50	8.49	–	5.55	14.04	9.34	–	6.11	15.44
C908217C	over 300 mm wide	m²	0.65	11.04	–	14.56	25.60	12.14	–	16.02	28.16
C908217D	isolated areas; not exceeding 1.00 m	Nr	0.95	16.13	–	14.82	30.95	17.74	–	16.30	34.05
C908217E	isolated areas; 1.00-2.00 m²	Nr	1.75	29.71	–	29.13	58.84	32.68	–	32.04	64.72

Major Works 2009		Unit	Labour Hours	Labour Net	Plant Net	Materials Net	Unit Net	Labour Gross	Plant Gross	Materials Gross	Unit Price
								(Gross rates include 10% profit)			
				£	£	£	£	£	£	£	£
C90	**C90: ALTERATIONS-SPOT ITEMS**										
C9083	**Making good to faces of walls after alterations in materials to match existing**										
C908301	**Common brickwork; in cement mortar (1:3):**										
C908301A	half brick wide............	m	0.25	7.44	–	1.40	8.84	8.18	–	1.54	9.72
C908301B	one brick wide...........	m	0.40	11.91	–	2.47	14.38	13.10	–	2.72	15.82
C908301C	one and a half brick wide ...	m	0.60	17.87	–	3.87	21.74	19.66	–	4.26	23.91
C908301D	two brick wide...........	m	0.80	23.82	–	5.27	29.09	26.20	–	5.80	32.00
C908301E	isolated areas; not exceeding 0.01 m.................	Nr	0.10	2.97	–	0.33	3.30	3.27	–	0.36	3.63
C908301F	isolated areas; 0.01-0.05 m^2	Nr	0.25	7.45	–	0.98	8.43	8.20	–	1.08	9.27
C908301G	isolated areas; 0.05-0.10 m^2	Nr	0.40	11.91	–	2.29	14.20	13.10	–	2.52	15.62
C908303	**Engineering brickwork; in cement mortar (1:3):**										
C908303A	half brick wide...........	m	0.30	8.94	–	1.96	10.90	9.83	–	2.16	11.99
C908303B	one brick wide...........	m	0.45	13.40	–	3.39	16.79	14.74	–	3.73	18.47
C908303C	one and a half brick wide ...	m	0.65	19.35	–	5.36	24.71	21.29	–	5.90	27.18
C908303D	two brick wide...........	m	0.85	25.31	–	7.32	32.63	27.84	–	8.05	35.89
C908303E	isolated areas; not exceeding 0.01 m.................	Nr	0.13	3.87	–	0.54	4.41	4.26	–	0.59	4.85
C908303F	isolated areas; 0.01-0.05 m^2	Nr	0.28	8.34	–	1.52	9.86	9.17	–	1.67	10.85
C908303G	isolated areas; 0.05-0.10 m^2	Nr	0.43	12.81	–	3.48	16.29	14.09	–	3.83	17.92
C908305	**Facing brickwork; in cement mortar (1:3):**										
C908305A	half brick wide...........	m	0.40	11.91	–	1.40	13.31	13.10	–	1.54	14.64
C908305B	one brick wide...........	m	0.55	16.38	–	2.71	19.09	18.02	–	2.98	21.00
C908305C	one and a half brick wide ...	m	0.75	22.34	–	4.42	26.76	24.57	–	4.86	29.44
C908305D	two brick wide...........	m	0.95	28.29	–	5.82	34.11	31.12	–	6.40	37.52
C908305E	isolated areas; not exceeding 0.01 m.................	Nr	0.15	4.46	–	0.40	4.86	4.91	–	0.44	5.35
C908305F	isolated areas; 0.01-0.05 m^2	Nr	0.30	8.93	–	1.10	10.03	9.82	–	1.21	11.03
C908305G	isolated areas; 0.05-0.10 m^2	Nr	0.45	13.40	–	2.50	15.90	14.74	–	2.75	17.49
C908307	**Blockwork; in cement mortar (1:3):**										
C908307A	50 mm wide.............	m	0.20	5.96	–	0.86	6.82	6.56	–	0.95	7.50
C908307B	75 mm wide.............	m	0.23	6.85	–	0.98	7.83	7.54	–	1.08	8.61
C908307C	100 mm wide	m	0.27	8.04	–	1.28	9.32	8.84	–	1.41	10.25
C908307D	125 mm wide	m	0.30	8.94	–	1.61	10.55	9.83	–	1.77	11.61
C908307E	150 mm wide	m	0.35	10.42	–	1.96	12.38	11.46	–	2.16	13.62
C908307F	200 mm wide	m	0.45	13.40	–	2.55	15.95	14.74	–	2.81	17.55
C908307G	215 mm wide	m	0.50	14.89	–	2.80	17.69	16.38	–	3.08	19.46
C908309	**Concrete work; in cement mortar (1:3):**										
C908309A	not exceeding 250 mm wide	m	0.30	8.93	–	0.64	9.57	9.82	–	0.70	10.53
C908309B	250-500 mm wide	m	0.55	16.38	–	1.27	17.65	18.02	–	1.40	19.42
C908309C	500-1000 mm wide	m	0.90	26.80	–	2.54	29.34	29.48	–	2.79	32.27
C908309D	exceeding 1000 mm wide ..	m^2	0.75	22.34	–	2.54	24.88	24.57	–	2.79	27.37

Existing Site, Buildings, Services

Major Works 2009		Unit	Labour Hours	Labour Net	Plant Net	Materials Net	Unit Net	Labour Gross	Plant Gross	Materials Gross	Unit Price
								(Gross rates include 10% profit)			
				£	£	£	£	£	£	£	£
C90	**C90: ALTERATIONS-SPOT ITEMS**										
C9084	**Making good to roof coverings after alterations in materials to match existing**										
C908401	**600 × 300 mm natural slates on and including 25 × 38 mm treated softwood battens, underfelting and 50 × 150 mm treated sawn softwood infill rafters at 400 mm centres:**										
C908401A	areas not exceeding 1.00 m²	Nr	2.00	49.32	–	81.41	130.73	54.25	–	89.55	143.80
C908401B	areas 1.00-2.00 m²	Nr	2.80	71.87	–	155.61	227.48	79.06	–	171.17	250.23
C908401C	areas 2.00-3.00 m²	Nr	4.00	103.76	–	224.82	328.58	114.14	–	247.30	361.44
C908403	**268 × 165 mm plain concrete tiles on and including 25 × 38 mm treated softwood battens, underfelting and 50 × 150 mm treated sawn softwood infill rafters at 400 mm centres:**										
C908403A	areas not exceeding 1.00 m²	Nr	2.80	73.15	–	42.97	116.12	80.47	–	47.27	127.73
C908403B	areas 1.00-2.00 m²	Nr	4.40	119.51	–	82.53	202.04	131.46	–	90.78	222.24
C908403C	areas 2.00-3.00 m²	Nr	6.20	169.27	–	121.28	290.55	186.20	–	133.41	319.61
C908405	**381 × 227 mm interlocking concrete tiles on and including 25 × 38 mm treated softwood battens, underfelting and 50 × 150 mm treated sawn softwood infill rafters at 400 mm centres:**										
C908405A	areas not exceeding 1.00 m²	Nr	1.90	46.35	–	22.39	68.74	50.99	–	24.63	75.61
C908405B	areas 1.00-2.00 m²	Nr	2.70	68.89	–	41.90	110.79	75.78	–	46.09	121.87
C908405C	areas 2.00-3.00 m²	Nr	3.90	100.78	–	60.90	161.68	110.86	–	66.99	177.85
C908407	**381 × 227 mm secondhand clay pantiles (PC 900:00 per 1000) on and including 25 × 38 mm treated softwood battens, underfelting and 50 × 150 mm treated sawn softwood infill rafters at 400 mm centres:**										
C908407A	areas not exceeding 1.00 m²	Nr	2.10	52.30	–	28.36	80.66	57.53	–	31.20	88.73
C908407B	areas 1.00-2.00 m²	Nr	2.90	74.85	–	54.73	129.58	82.34	–	60.20	142.54
C908407C	areas 2.00-3.00 m²	Nr	4.10	106.73	–	79.26	185.99	117.40	–	87.19	204.59

Major Works 2009		Unit	Labour Hours	Labour Net	Plant Net	Materials Net	Unit Net	Labour Gross	Plant Gross	Materials Gross	Unit Price
								(Gross rates include 10% profit)			
				£	£	£	£	£	£	£	£
C90	**C90: ALTERATIONS-SPOT ITEMS**										
C9084	**Making good to roof coverings after alterations in materials to match existing**										
C908411	**Slating or tiling as reclaimed and previously removed and stacked; 75 mm lap with aluminium alloy nails on new 25 × 38 mm treated sawn softwood battens and underfelt; slate and tile costs included:**										
C908411A	600 × 300 mm slates	m²	1.20	35.73	–	71.12	106.85	39.30	–	78.23	117.54
C908411B	268 × 165 mm plain tiles .	m²	2.00	59.56	–	36.64	96.20	65.52	–	40.30	105.82
C908411C	381 × 227 mm interlocking tiles.....................	m²	1.10	32.76	–	16.17	48.93	36.04	–	17.79	53.82
C908411D	secondhand pantiles	m²	1.30	38.71	–	20.21	58.92	42.58	–	22.23	64.81
C908413	**Relaying roof coverings previously removed and stacked; 75 mm lap with aluminium alloy nails on new 25 × 38 mm treated sawn softwood battens and underfelt; allowing 20 per cent new samples:**										
C908413A	600 × 300 mm slates	m²	1.20	35.74	–	19.85	55.59	39.31	–	21.84	61.15
C908413B	268 × 165 mm plain tiles .	m²	2.00	59.56	–	12.96	72.52	65.52	–	14.26	79.77
C908413C	381 × 227 mm interlocking tiles.....................	m²	1.10	32.76	–	6.00	38.76	36.04	–	6.60	42.64
C908413D	secondhand pantiles (PC 850:00 per 1000)	m²	1.30	38.72	–	6.04	44.76	42.59	–	6.64	49.24

Existing Site, Buildings, Services

Major Works 2009		Unit	Labour Hours	Labour Net	Plant Net	Materials Net	Unit Net	Labour Gross	Plant Gross	Materials Gross	Unit Price
								(Gross rates include 10% profit)			
				£	£	£	£	£	£	£	£
C90	**C90: ALTERATIONS-SPOT ITEMS**										
C9086	**Making good to wall and ceiling finishes after alterations in materials to match existing**										
C908678	**Carlite lightweight plaster; 2 mm finish on undercoat; jointing and finishing flush to existing; to masonry walls:**										
C908678A	13 mm two coat work to masonry walls browning undercoat	m²	1.50	44.67	–	2.28	46.95	49.14	–	2.51	51.65
C908678F	10 mm two coat work to concrete walls; bonding undercoat	m²	1.45	43.18	–	2.23	45.41	47.50	–	2.45	49.95
C908679	**Dubbing out with Carlite undercoat to walls:**										
C908679A	6 mm browning to walls ...	m²	0.35	10.42	–	1.11	11.53	11.46	–	1.22	12.68
C908679B	12 mm browning to walls ..	m²	0.50	14.89	–	2.00	16.89	16.38	–	2.20	18.58
C908679C	15 mm browning to walls ..	m²	0.60	17.87	–	2.66	20.53	19.66	–	2.93	22.58
C908679D	20 mm browning to walls ..	m²	0.75	22.34	–	3.33	25.67	24.57	–	3.66	28.24
C908679E	6 mm bonding to walls	m²	0.35	10.43	–	1.29	11.72	11.47	–	1.42	12.89
C908679F	12 mm bonding to walls ...	m²	0.50	14.89	–	2.59	17.48	16.38	–	2.85	19.23
C908679G	15 mm bonding to walls ...	m²	0.60	17.87	–	3.23	21.10	19.66	–	3.55	23.21
C908679H	20 mm bonding to walls ...	m²	0.75	22.34	–	4.31	26.65	24.57	–	4.74	29.32

Major Works 2009		Unit	Labour Hours	Labour Net	Plant Net	Materials Net	Unit Net	Labour Gross	Plant Gross	Materials Gross	Unit Price
								(Gross rates include 10% profit)			
				£	£	£	£	£	£	£	£
C90	**C90: ALTERATIONS-SPOT ITEMS**										
C9086	**Making good to wall and ceiling finishes after alterations in materials to match existing**										
C908681	**12.5 mm Gypsum plasterboard and 5 mm Thistle board finish; jointing to existing; to walls:**										
C908681A	to woodwork backgrounds .	m²	0.75	22.33	–	4.98	27.31	24.56	–	5.48	30.04
C908681D	to masonry backgrounds ..	m²	0.55	16.38	–	4.96	21.34	18.02	–	5.46	23.47
C908681F	to concrete backgrounds...	m²	0.55	16.38	–	4.96	21.34	18.02	–	5.46	23.47
C908688	**Carlite lightweight plaster; 2 mm finish on undercoat; jointing and finishing flush to existing; to concrete ceilings:**										
C908688A	10 mm two coat work to concrete ceilings; bonding undercoat	m²	1.65	49.14	–	2.23	51.37	54.05	–	2.45	56.51
C908689	**Dubbing out with Carlite undercoat to ceilings:**										
C908689E	6 mm bonding to ceilings ..	m²	0.45	13.40	–	1.29	14.69	14.74	–	1.42	16.16
C908689F	12 mm bonding to ceilings .	m²	0.60	17.87	–	2.59	20.46	19.66	–	2.85	22.51
C908689G	15 mm bonding to ceilings .	m²	0.70	20.85	–	3.23	24.08	22.94	–	3.55	26.49
C908689H	20 mm bonding to ceilings .	m²	0.85	25.32	–	4.31	29.63	27.85	–	4.74	32.59
C908691	**12.5 mm Gypsum plasterboard and 5 mm Thistle board finish; jointing to existing; to ceilings:**										
C908691A	to woodwork backgrounds .	m²	0.95	28.29	–	4.98	33.27	31.12	–	5.48	36.60
C908691F	to concrete backgrounds...	m²	0.75	22.33	–	4.96	27.29	24.56	–	5.46	30.02

Existing Site, Buildings, Services

Major Works 2009		Unit	Labour Hours	Labour Net	Plant Net	Materials Net	Unit Net	Labour Gross	Plant Gross	Materials Gross	Unit Price
								(Gross rates include 10% profit)			
				£	£	£	£	£	£	£	£
C90	**C90: ALTERATIONS-SPOT ITEMS**										
C9089	**Making good to timber mouldings after alterations in materials to match existing**										
C908901	**Moulded softwood sections in lengths not exceeding 1000 mm; jointing to existing:**										
C908901A	19 × 50 mm............	Nr	0.30	5.10	–	0.76	5.86	5.61	–	0.84	6.45
C908901B	19 × 75 mm............	Nr	0.32	5.43	–	1.12	6.55	5.97	–	1.23	7.21
C908901C	19 × 100 mm...........	Nr	0.35	5.94	–	1.46	7.40	6.53	–	1.61	8.14
C908901D	25 × 125 mm...........	Nr	0.36	6.11	–	3.56	9.67	6.72	–	3.92	10.64
C908901E	25 × 150 mm...........	Nr	0.38	6.46	–	3.74	10.20	7.11	–	4.11	11.22
C908901F	25 × 175 mm...........	Nr	0.40	6.79	–	4.44	11.23	7.47	–	4.88	12.35
C9095	**Temporary roofs**										
C909599	**Temporary roofs; corrugated sheeting laid to slope on and including 50 × 150 mm softwood framing:**										
C909599A	fibre cement sheets.......	m²	0.35	5.94	–	24.41	30.35	6.53	–	26.85	33.39
C909599B	galvanised sheets........	m²	0.35	5.95	–	21.84	27.79	6.55	–	24.02	30.57
C909599C	translucent PVC sheets....	m²	0.35	5.95	–	20.22	26.17	6.55	–	22.24	28.79
C909599D	extra for 50 × 150 mm softwood posts...........	m	0.30	5.09	–	3.42	8.51	5.60	–	3.76	9.36
C9097	**Temporary screens**										
C909792	**Temporary dustproof screens; 1200 gauge polythene sheeting on 50 × 100 mm sawn softwood framing; joints sealed with self adhesive PVC tape:**										
C909792A	vertical screens..........	m²	0.35	5.94	–	4.87	10.81	6.53	–	5.36	11.89
C909792B	extra for sealing perimeters with self adhesive PVC tape	m	0.05	0.85	–	0.81	1.66	0.94	–	0.89	1.83
C909792C	extra for access door......	Nr	1.50	25.47	–	14.81	40.28	28.02	–	16.29	44.31

GROUNDWORK

Major Works 2009		Unit	Labour Hours	Labour Net	Plant Net	Materials Net	Unit Net	Labour Gross	Plant Gross	Materials Gross	Unit Price
								(Gross rates include 10% profit)			
				£	£	£	£	£	£	£	£
D20	D20: EXCAVATING AND FILLING										
D2011	Site preparation										
D201101	Removing trees; girth:										
D201101A	600 mm-1.50 m	Nr	4.00	50.80	77.43	–	128.23	55.88	85.17	–	141.05
D201101B	1.50-3.00 m	Nr	16.00	203.20	310.65	–	513.85	223.52	341.72	–	565.24
D201101C	3.00-4.50 m	Nr	36.00	457.20	697.80	–	1155.00	502.92	767.58	–	1270.50
D201101D	4.50-6.00 m	Nr	64.00	812.80	1242.60	–	2055.40	894.08	1366.86	–	2260.94
D201102	Removing trees; filling voids with topsoil; girth:										
D201102A	600 mm-1.50 m	Nr	4.00	50.80	77.62	8.48	136.90	55.88	85.38	9.33	150.59
D201102B	1.50-3.00 m	Nr	16.00	203.20	310.65	33.99	547.84	223.52	341.72	37.39	602.62
D201102C	3.00-4.50 m	Nr	36.00	457.20	697.80	76.12	1231.12	502.92	767.58	83.73	1354.23
D201102D	4.50-6.00 m	Nr	64.00	812.80	1242.60	135.86	2191.26	894.08	1366.86	149.45	2410.39
D201103	Removing trees; filling voids with DTp aggregate; girth:										
D201103A	600 mm-1.50 m	Nr	4.00	50.80	77.43	20.81	149.04	55.88	85.17	22.89	163.94
D201103B	1.50-3.00 m	Nr	16.00	203.20	310.65	83.44	597.29	223.52	341.72	91.78	657.02
D201103C	3.00-4.50 m	Nr	36.00	457.20	697.80	186.89	1341.89	502.92	767.58	205.58	1476.08
D201103D	4.50-6.00 m	Nr	64.00	812.80	1242.60	333.57	2388.97	894.08	1366.86	366.93	2627.87
D201110	Cut down hedges; grub up roots and remove from site; height:										
D201110A	not exceeding 2.00 m......	m	1.33	16.89	48.92	–	65.81	18.58	53.81	–	72.39
D201110B	2.00-3.00 m	m	5.33	67.69	190.47	–	258.16	74.46	209.52	–	283.98
D201110C	3.00-4.00 m	m	12.00	152.40	440.65	–	593.05	167.64	484.72	–	652.36
D201110D	4.00-5.00 m	m	21.70	275.59	801.13	–	1076.72	303.15	881.24	–	1184.39
D201111	Removing tree stumps; filling voids with topsoil; girth:										
D201111A	600 mm-1.50 m	m	1.33	16.89	48.92	8.48	74.29	18.58	53.81	9.33	81.72
D201111B	1.50-3.00 m	m	5.33	67.69	190.47	33.99	292.15	74.46	209.52	37.39	321.37
D201111C	3.00-4.50 m	m	12.00	152.40	440.65	76.12	669.17	167.64	484.72	83.73	736.09
D201111D	4.50-6.00 m	m	21.70	275.59	801.13	135.86	1212.58	303.15	881.24	149.45	1333.84
D201112	Removing tree stumps; filling voids with DTp type 2 aggregate; girth:										
D201112A	600 mm-1.50 m	m	1.33	16.89	48.92	20.81	86.62	18.58	53.81	22.89	95.28
D201112B	1.50-3.00 m	m	5.33	67.69	190.47	83.44	341.60	74.46	209.52	91.78	375.76
D201112C	3.00-4.50 m	m	12.00	152.40	440.65	186.89	779.94	167.64	484.72	205.58	857.93
D201112D	4.50-6.00 m	m	21.70	275.59	801.13	333.57	1410.29	303.15	881.24	366.93	1551.32
D201120	Clear site of vegetation, undergrowth, bushes, hedges, trees or the like and remove from site:										
D201120A	generally	m²	0.02	0.19	1.37	–	1.56	0.21	1.51	–	1.72
D201130	Lifting turf for preservation:										
D201130A	stacking on site..........	m²	0.06	0.76	0.24	–	1.00	0.84	0.26	–	1.10
D201140	Lifting turf for preservation:										
D201140A	stacking on site..........	m²	0.25	3.18	–	–	3.18	3.50	–	–	3.50

Groundwork

Major Works 2009		Unit	Labour Hours	Labour Net	Plant Net	Materials Net	Unit Net	Labour Gross	Plant Gross	Materials Gross	Unit Price
								(Gross rates include 10% profit)			
				£	£	£	£	£	£	£	£
D20	**D20: EXCAVATING AND FILLING**										
D2021	**Machine excavation**										
D202102	**Oversite excavation to remove topsoil, average depth:**										
D202102A	150 mm	m²	–	–	0.44	–	0.44	–	0.48	–	0.48
D202102B	300 mm	m²	–	–	0.55	–	0.55	–	0.61	–	0.61
D202103	**Excavation to reduce levels, depth not exceeding:**										
D202103A	0.25 m	m³	–	–	1.76	–	1.76	–	1.94	–	1.94
D202103B	1.00 m	m³	–	–	1.32	–	1.32	–	1.45	–	1.45
D202103C	2.00 m	m³	–	–	1.98	–	1.98	–	2.18	–	2.18
D202103D	4.00 m	m³	–	–	2.63	–	2.63	–	2.89	–	2.89
D202103E	6.00 m	m³	–	–	3.07	–	3.07	–	3.38	–	3.38
D202104	**Excavation in cuttings, depth not exceeding:**										
D202104A	0.25 m	m³	0.10	1.27	2.81	–	4.08	1.40	3.09	–	4.49
D202104B	1.00 m	m³	0.08	1.01	2.25	–	3.26	1.11	2.48	–	3.59
D202104C	2.00 m	m³	0.10	1.27	2.81	–	4.08	1.40	3.09	–	4.49
D202104D	4.00 m	m³	0.12	1.52	3.37	–	4.89	1.67	3.71	–	5.38
D202104E	6.00 m	m³	0.14	1.78	3.93	–	5.71	1.96	4.32	–	6.28
D202105	**Basement excavation, depth not exceeding:**										
D202105A	0.25 m	m³	0.12	1.52	3.37	–	4.89	1.67	3.71	–	5.38
D202105B	1.00 m	m³	0.10	1.27	2.81	–	4.08	1.40	3.09	–	4.49
D202105C	2.00 m	m³	0.12	1.52	3.37	–	4.89	1.67	3.71	–	5.38
D202105D	4.00 m	m³	0.14	1.78	3.93	–	5.71	1.96	4.32	–	6.28
D202105E	6.00 m	m³	0.16	2.03	4.49	–	6.52	2.23	4.94	–	7.17
D202106	**Trench excavation to receive foundations, pile caps and ground beams, depth not exceeding:**										
D202106A	0.25 m	m³	0.30	3.82	6.59	–	10.41	4.20	7.25	–	11.45
D202106B	1.00 m	m³	0.26	3.30	5.71	–	9.01	3.63	6.28	–	9.91
D202106C	2.00 m	m³	0.30	3.82	6.59	–	10.41	4.20	7.25	–	11.45
D202106D	4.00 m	m³	0.33	4.19	7.24	–	11.43	4.61	7.96	–	12.57
D202106E	6.00 m	m³	0.40	5.08	8.78	–	13.86	5.59	9.66	–	15.25

Major Works 2009		Unit	Labour Hours	Labour Net	Plant Net	Materials Net	Unit Net	Labour Gross	Plant Gross	Materials Gross	Unit Price
								(Gross rates include 10% profit)			
				£	£	£	£	£	£	£	£
D20	**D20: EXCAVATING AND FILLING**										
D2021	**Machine excavation**										
D202107	**Pit excavation to receive foundation bases (in Nr. 1-5), depth not exceeding:**										
D202107A	0.25 m	m³	0.35	4.45	7.68	–	12.13	4.90	8.45	–	13.34
D202107B	1.00 m	m³	0.31	3.94	6.80	–	10.74	4.33	7.48	–	11.81
D202107C	2.00 m	m³	0.35	4.45	7.68	–	12.13	4.90	8.45	–	13.34
D202107D	4.00 m	m³	0.40	5.08	8.78	–	13.86	5.59	9.66	–	15.25
D202107E	6.00 m	m³	0.44	5.59	9.66	–	15.25	6.15	10.63	–	16.78
D202108	**Pit excavation to receive foundation bases (in Nr. 6-10), depth not exceeding:**										
D202108A	0.25 m	m³	0.39	4.95	8.56	–	13.51	5.45	9.42	–	14.86
D202108B	1.00 m	m³	0.34	4.32	7.46	–	11.78	4.75	8.21	–	12.96
D202108C	2.00 m	m³	0.39	4.95	8.56	–	13.51	5.45	9.42	–	14.86
D202108D	4.00 m	m³	0.44	5.59	9.66	–	15.25	6.15	10.63	–	16.78
D202108E	6.00 m	m³	0.48	6.09	10.54	–	16.63	6.70	11.59	–	18.29
D202109	**Pit excavation to receive foundation bases (in Nr. 11-20), depth not exceeding:**										
D202109A	0.25 m	m³	0.44	5.59	9.66	–	15.25	6.15	10.63	–	16.78
D202109B	1.00 m	m³	0.39	4.95	8.56	–	13.51	5.45	9.42	–	14.86
D202109C	2.00 m	m³	0.44	5.59	9.66	–	15.25	6.15	10.63	–	16.78
D202109D	4.00 m	m³	0.50	6.36	10.98	–	17.34	7.00	12.08	–	19.07
D202109E	6.00 m	m³	0.55	6.99	12.07	–	19.06	7.69	13.28	–	20.97

Groundwork

Major Works 2009		Unit	Labour Hours	Labour Net	Plant Net	Materials Net	Unit Net	Labour Gross	Plant Gross	Materials Gross	Unit Price
								(Gross rates include 10% profit)			
				£	£	£	£	£	£	£	£
D20	**D20: EXCAVATING AND FILLING**										
D2021	**Machine excavation**										
D202110	**Pit excavation to receive foundation bases (in Nr. 21 or more), depth not exceeding:**										
D202110A	0.25 m	m³	0.53	6.73	11.63	–	18.36	7.40	12.79	–	20.20
D202110B	1.00 m	m³	0.45	5.71	9.88	–	15.59	6.28	10.87	–	17.15
D202110C	2.00 m	m³	0.53	6.73	11.63	–	18.36	7.40	12.79	–	20.20
D202110D	4.00 m	m³	0.60	7.62	13.17	–	20.79	8.38	14.49	–	22.87
D202110E	6.00 m	m³	0.66	8.38	14.49	–	22.87	9.22	15.94	–	25.16
D2026	**Hand excavation**										
D202631	**Oversite excavation to remove topsoil, average depth:**										
D202631A	150 mm	m²	0.18	2.29	–	–	2.29	2.52	–	–	2.52
D202631B	300 mm	m²	0.32	4.06	–	–	4.06	4.47	–	–	4.47
D202632	**Excavation to reduce levels, depth not exceeding:**										
D202632A	0.25 m	m³	1.50	19.05	–	–	19.05	20.96	–	–	20.96
D202632B	1.00 m	m³	2.00	25.40	–	–	25.40	27.94	–	–	27.94
D202632C	2.00 m	m³	2.30	29.21	–	–	29.21	32.13	–	–	32.13
D202632D	4.00 m	m³	2.60	33.02	–	–	33.02	36.32	–	–	36.32
D202632E	6.00 m	m³	3.20	40.64	–	–	40.64	44.70	–	–	44.70
D202633	**Excavation in cuttings, depth not exceeding:**										
D202633A	0.25 m	m³	1.80	22.86	–	–	22.86	25.15	–	–	25.15
D202633B	1.00 m	m³	2.20	27.94	–	–	27.94	30.73	–	–	30.73
D202633C	2.00 m	m³	2.45	31.12	–	–	31.12	34.23	–	–	34.23
D202633D	4.00 m	m³	3.50	44.45	–	–	44.45	48.90	–	–	48.90
D202633E	6.00 m	m³	4.30	54.61	–	–	54.61	60.07	–	–	60.07
D202634	**Basement excavations, depth not exceeding:**										
D202634A	0.25 m	m³	2.00	25.40	–	–	25.40	27.94	–	–	27.94
D202634B	1.00 m	m³	2.40	30.48	–	–	30.48	33.53	–	–	33.53
D202634C	2.00 m	m³	2.65	33.66	–	–	33.66	37.03	–	–	37.03
D202634D	4.00 m	m³	3.70	46.99	–	–	46.99	51.69	–	–	51.69
D202634E	6.00 m	m³	4.50	57.15	–	–	57.15	62.87	–	–	62.87
D202635	**Trench excavation to receive foundations, pile caps and ground beams, depth not exceeding:**										
D202635A	0.25 m	m³	2.30	29.21	–	–	29.21	32.13	–	–	32.13
D202635B	1.00 m	m³	2.85	36.20	–	–	36.20	39.82	–	–	39.82
D202635C	2.00 m	m³	3.30	41.91	–	–	41.91	46.10	–	–	46.10
D202635D	4.00 m	m³	3.80	48.26	–	–	48.26	53.09	–	–	53.09
D202635E	6.00 m	m³	5.00	63.50	–	–	63.50	69.85	–	–	69.85
D202636	**Pit excavation to receive foundation bases (in Nr. 1-5), depth not exceeding:**										
D202636A	0.25 m	m³	2.80	35.56	–	–	35.56	39.12	–	–	39.12
D202636B	1.00 m	m³	3.45	43.82	–	–	43.82	48.20	–	–	48.20
D202636C	2.00 m	m³	3.80	48.26	–	–	48.26	53.09	–	–	53.09
D202636D	4.00 m	m³	4.45	56.52	–	–	56.52	62.17	–	–	62.17
D202636E	6.00 m	m³	5.50	69.85	–	–	69.85	76.84	–	–	76.84

Major Works 2009		Unit	Labour Hours	Labour Net	Plant Net	Materials Net	Unit Net	Labour Gross	Plant Gross	Materials Gross	Unit Price
								(Gross rates include 10% profit)			
				£	£	£	£	£	£	£	£
D20	**D20: EXCAVATING AND FILLING**										
D2026	**Hand excavation**										
D202637	**Pit excavation to receive foundation bases (in Nr. 6-10), depth not exceeding:**										
D202637A	0.25 m	m³	3.10	39.37	–	–	39.37	43.31	–	–	43.31
D202637B	1.00 m	m³	3.80	48.26	–	–	48.26	53.09	–	–	53.09
D202637C	2.00 m	m³	4.20	53.34	–	–	53.34	58.67	–	–	58.67
D202637D	4.00 m	m³	4.90	62.23	–	–	62.23	68.45	–	–	68.45
D202637E	6.00 m	m³	6.10	77.47	–	–	77.47	85.22	–	–	85.22
D202638	**Pit excavation to receive foundation bases (in Nr. 10-20), depth not exceeding:**										
D202638A	0.25 m	m³	3.50	44.45	–	–	44.45	48.90	–	–	48.90
D202638B	1.00 m	m³	4.30	54.61	–	–	54.61	60.07	–	–	60.07
D202638C	2.00 m	m³	4.75	60.33	–	–	60.33	66.36	–	–	66.36
D202638D	4.00 m	m³	5.60	71.12	–	–	71.12	78.23	–	–	78.23
D202638E	6.00 m	m³	6.80	86.36	–	–	86.36	95.00	–	–	95.00
D202639	**Pit excavation to receive foundation bases (in Nr. 21 or more), depth not exceeding:**										
D202639A	0.25 m	m³	4.20	53.34	–	–	53.34	58.67	–	–	58.67
D202639B	1.00 m	m³	5.10	64.77	–	–	64.77	71.25	–	–	71.25
D202639C	2.00 m	m³	5.70	72.39	–	–	72.39	79.63	–	–	79.63
D202639D	4.00 m	m³	6.65	84.46	–	–	84.46	92.91	–	–	92.91
D202639E	6.00 m	m³	8.25	104.78	–	–	104.78	115.26	–	–	115.26
D2041	**Breaking up obstructions with machine driven hammer**										
D204142	**Extra over excavation for breaking out:**										
D204142A	soft rock or brickwork	m³	–	–	8.28	–	8.28	–	9.11	–	9.11
D204142B	hard rock	m³	–	–	13.01	–	13.01	–	14.31	–	14.31
D204142C	plain concrete	m³	–	–	10.64	–	10.64	–	11.70	–	11.70
D204142D	reinforced concrete	m³	–	–	15.37	–	15.37	–	16.91	–	16.91

Groundwork

Major Works 2009		Unit	Labour Hours	Labour Net	Plant Net	Materials Net	Unit Net	Labour Gross	Plant Gross	Materials Gross	Unit Price
									(Gross rates include 10% profit)		
				£	£	£	£	£	£	£	£
D20	**D20: EXCAVATING AND FILLING**										
D2043	**Breaking up obstructions with hand held mechanical tools**										
D204344	**Extra over excavation for breaking out:**										
D204344A	soft rock or brickwork	m³	3.60	45.72	46.76	–	92.48	50.29	51.44	–	101.73
D204344B	hard rock	m³	6.40	81.28	83.14	–	164.42	89.41	91.45	–	180.86
D204344C	plain concrete	m³	5.00	63.50	64.95	–	128.45	69.85	71.45	–	141.30
D204344D	reinforced concrete	m³	7.20	91.44	93.53	–	184.97	100.58	102.88	–	203.47
D2051	**Breaking out pavings with machine driven hammer**										
D205133	**Excavation in tarmac paving:**										
D205133A	not exceeding 150 mm thick	m²	–	–	0.71	–	0.71	–	0.78	–	0.78
D205133B	150-300 mm thick	m²	–	–	1.18	–	1.18	–	1.30	–	1.30
D205133C	300-450 mm thick	m²	–	–	1.89	–	1.89	–	2.08	–	2.08
D205134	**Excavation in plain concrete paving:**										
D205134A	not exceeding 150 mm thick	m²	–	–	1.42	–	1.42	–	1.56	–	1.56
D205134B	150-300 mm thick	m²	–	–	2.37	–	2.38	–	2.61	–	2.62
D205134C	300-450 mm thick	m²	–	–	3.78	–	3.78	–	4.16	–	4.16
D205135	**Excavation in reinforced concrete paving:**										
D205135A	not exceeding 150 mm thick	m²	0.08	1.02	2.59	–	3.61	1.12	2.85	–	3.97
D205135B	150-300 mm thick	m²	0.08	1.01	3.77	–	4.78	1.11	4.15	–	5.26
D205135C	300-450 mm thick	m²	0.08	1.02	4.95	–	5.97	1.12	5.45	–	6.57

Major Works 2009		Unit	Labour Hours	Labour Net	Plant Net	Materials Net	Unit Net	Labour Gross	Plant Gross	Materials Gross	Unit Price
								(Gross rates include 10% profit)			
				£	£	£	£	£	£	£	£
D20	**D20: EXCAVATING AND FILLING**										
D2052	**Breaking out pavings with hand held compressor tools**										
D205237	**Excavation in tarmac paving:**										
D205237A	not exceeding 150 mm thick	m²	0.40	5.08	2.60	–	7.68	5.59	2.86	–	8.45
D205237B	150-300 mm thick	m²	0.70	8.89	5.20	–	14.09	9.78	5.72	–	15.50
D205237C	300-450 mm thick	m²	1.00	12.70	7.79	–	20.49	13.97	8.57	–	22.54
D205238	**Excavation in plain concrete paving:**										
D205238A	not exceeding 150 mm thick	m²	0.60	7.62	5.20	–	12.82	8.38	5.72	–	14.10
D205238B	150-300 mm thick	m²	0.90	11.43	7.79	–	19.22	12.57	8.57	–	21.14
D205238C	300-450 mm thick	m²	0.12	1.53	10.39	–	11.92	1.68	11.43	–	13.11
D205239	**Excavation in reinforced concrete paving:**										
D205239A	not exceeding 150 mm thick	m²	0.80	10.16	8.21	–	18.37	11.18	9.03	–	20.21
D205239B	150-300 mm thick	m²	1.30	16.51	13.40	–	29.91	18.16	14.74	–	32.90
D205239C	300-450 mm thick	m²	2.00	25.40	21.20	–	46.60	27.94	23.32	–	51.26
D2061	**Working space allowance to excavations; by hand**										
D206101	**Excavating for working space, by hand, additional earthwork support, compacting in layers; backfilling with excavated material:**										
D206101A	basements..............	m²	1.59	20.20	0.86	–	21.06	22.22	0.95	–	23.17
D206101B	pits....................	m²	2.28	28.96	0.86	–	29.82	31.86	0.95	–	32.80
D206101C	trenches................	m²	1.98	25.15	0.86	–	26.01	27.67	0.95	–	28.61
D206101D	pile caps and ground beams	m²	1.98	25.15	0.86	–	26.01	27.67	0.95	–	28.61
D206111	**Excavating for working space, by hand, disposal, additional earthwork support, compacting in layers; backfilling with hardcore:**										
D206111A	basements..............	m²	2.95	37.47	11.67	14.67	63.81	41.22	12.84	16.14	70.19
D206111B	pits....................	m²	3.64	46.23	11.67	14.67	72.57	50.85	12.84	16.14	79.83
D206111C	trenches................	m²	3.34	42.42	11.67	14.67	68.76	46.66	12.84	16.14	75.64
D206111D	pile caps and ground beams	m²	3.34	42.42	11.67	14.67	68.76	46.66	12.84	16.14	75.64
D206121	**Excavating for working space, by hand, disposal, additional earthwork support, backfilling with concrete, mix C15P:**										
D206121A	basements..............	m²	2.95	37.46	11.16	59.68	108.30	41.21	12.28	65.65	119.13
D206121B	pits....................	m²	3.64	46.23	11.16	59.68	117.07	50.85	12.28	65.65	128.78
D206121C	trenches................	m²	3.34	42.42	11.16	59.68	113.26	46.66	12.28	65.65	124.59
D206121D	pile caps and ground beams	m²	3.34	42.42	11.16	59.68	113.26	46.66	12.28	65.65	124.59

Groundwork

Major Works 2009		Unit	Labour Hours	Labour Net	Plant Net	Materials Net	Unit Net	Labour Gross	Plant Gross	Materials Gross	Unit Price
								(Gross rates include 10% profit)			
				£	£	£	£	£	£	£	£
D20	**D20: EXCAVATING AND FILLING**										
D2062	**Working space allowance to excavations; by machine**										
D206201	**Excavating for working space, by machine, additional earthwork support, compacting in layers; backfilling with excavated material:**										
D206201A	basements..............	m²	0.25	3.20	5.83	–	9.03	3.52	6.41	–	9.93
D206201B	pits....................	m²	0.39	4.96	8.42	–	13.38	5.46	9.26	–	14.72
D206201C	trenches................	m²	0.36	4.57	7.76	–	12.33	5.03	8.54	–	13.56
D206201D	pile caps and ground beams	m²	0.36	4.57	7.76	–	12.33	5.03	8.54	–	13.56
D206211	**Excavating for working space, by machine, disposal, additional earthwork support, compacting in layers; backfilling with hardcore:**										
D206211A	basements..............	m²	0.25	3.20	18.57	14.67	36.44	3.52	20.43	16.14	40.08
D206211B	pits....................	m²	0.39	4.95	21.16	14.67	40.78	5.45	23.28	16.14	44.86
D206211C	trenches................	m²	0.36	4.57	20.50	14.67	39.74	5.03	22.55	16.14	43.71
D206211D	pile caps and ground beams	m²	0.36	4.57	20.50	14.67	39.74	5.03	22.55	16.14	43.71
D206221	**Excavating for working space, by machine, disposal, additional earthwork support, backfilling with concrete, mix C15P:**										
D206221A	basements..............	m²	0.61	7.77	14.10	59.68	81.55	8.55	15.51	65.65	89.71
D206221B	pits....................	m²	0.75	9.52	16.69	59.68	85.89	10.47	18.36	65.65	94.48
D206221C	trenches................	m²	0.72	9.14	16.03	59.68	84.85	10.05	17.63	65.65	93.34
D206221D	pile caps and ground beams	m²	0.72	9.14	16.03	59.68	84.85	10.05	17.63	65.65	93.34
D2070	**Timber earthwork support to firm ground open boarded (risk item)**										
D207003	**To sides of excavation not exceeding 2.00 m apart, depth not exceeding:**										
D207003A	1.00 m	m²	0.30	3.81	–	0.73	4.54	4.19	–	0.80	4.99
D207003B	2.00 m	m²	0.36	4.57	–	0.97	5.54	5.03	–	1.07	6.09
D207003C	4.00 m	m²	0.48	6.09	–	1.45	7.54	6.70	–	1.60	8.29
D207003D	6.00 m	m²	0.72	9.15	–	1.93	11.08	10.07	–	2.12	12.19
D207004	**To sides of excavation 2.00-4.00 m apart, depth not exceeding:**										
D207004A	1.00 m	m²	0.42	5.34	–	1.20	6.54	5.87	–	1.32	7.19
D207004B	2.00 m	m²	0.48	6.09	–	1.45	7.54	6.70	–	1.60	8.29
D207004C	4.00 m	m²	0.60	7.62	–	1.93	9.55	8.38	–	2.12	10.51
D207004D	6.00 m	m²	0.84	10.67	–	2.42	13.09	11.74	–	2.66	14.40
D207005	**To sides of excavation over 4.00 m apart, depth not exceeding:**										
D207005A	1.00 m	m²	0.36	4.57	–	0.73	5.30	5.03	–	0.80	5.83
D207005B	2.00 m	m²	0.60	7.62	–	1.45	9.07	8.38	–	1.60	9.98
D207005C	4.00 m	m²	0.72	9.15	–	2.41	11.56	10.07	–	2.65	12.72
D207005D	6.00 m	m²	0.96	12.19	–	3.38	15.57	13.41	–	3.72	17.13

Major Works 2009		Unit	Labour Hours	Labour Net	Plant Net	Materials Net	Unit Net	Labour Gross	Plant Gross	Materials Gross	Unit Price
								(Gross rates include 10% profit)			
				£	£	£	£	£	£	£	£
D20	**D20: EXCAVATING AND FILLING**										
D2071	**Timber earthwork support to firm ground**										
D207103	**To sides of excavation not exceeding 2.00 m apart, depth not exceeding:**										
D207103A	1.00 m	m²	1.00	12.70	–	1.45	14.15	13.97	–	1.60	15.57
D207103B	2.00 m	m²	1.20	15.24	–	1.93	17.17	16.76	–	2.12	18.89
D207103C	4.00 m	m²	1.60	20.32	–	2.90	23.22	22.35	–	3.19	25.54
D207103D	6.00 m	m²	2.40	30.48	–	3.86	34.34	33.53	–	4.25	37.77
D207104	**To sides of excavation 2.00-4.00 m apart, depth not exceeding:**										
D207104A	1.00 m	m²	1.40	17.78	–	2.41	20.19	19.56	–	2.65	22.21
D207104B	2.00 m	m²	1.60	20.32	–	2.90	23.22	22.35	–	3.19	25.54
D207104C	4.00 m	m²	2.00	25.40	–	3.86	29.26	27.94	–	4.25	32.19
D207104D	6.00 m	m²	2.80	35.56	–	4.84	40.40	39.12	–	5.32	44.44
D207105	**To sides of excavation over 4.00 m apart, depth not exceeding:**										
D207105A	1.00 m	m²	1.20	15.24	–	1.45	16.69	16.76	–	1.60	18.36
D207105B	2.00 m	m²	2.00	25.40	–	2.90	28.30	27.94	–	3.19	31.13
D207105C	4.00 m	m²	2.40	30.48	–	4.83	35.31	33.53	–	5.31	38.84
D207105D	6.00 m	m²	3.20	40.64	–	6.76	47.40	44.70	–	7.44	52.14
D2072	**Timber earthwork support to loose ground**										
D207207	**To sides of excavation not exceeding 2.00 m apart, depth not exceeding:**										
D207207A	1.00 m	m²	1.32	16.77	–	6.83	23.60	18.45	–	7.51	25.96
D207207B	2.00 m	m²	1.56	19.81	–	7.31	27.12	21.79	–	8.04	29.83
D207207C	4.00 m	m²	1.92	24.38	–	8.28	32.66	26.82	–	9.11	35.93
D207207D	6.00 m	m²	2.76	35.05	–	9.24	44.29	38.56	–	10.16	48.72
D207208	**To sides of excavation 2.00-4.00 m apart, depth not exceeding:**										
D207208A	1.00 m	m²	2.04	25.91	–	7.79	33.70	28.50	–	8.57	37.07
D207208B	2.00 m	m²	1.84	23.37	–	8.28	31.65	25.71	–	9.11	34.82
D207208C	4.00 m	m²	2.32	29.47	–	9.24	38.71	32.42	–	10.16	42.58
D207208D	6.00 m	m²	3.04	38.61	–	10.22	48.83	42.47	–	11.24	53.71
D207209	**To sides of excavation over 4.00 m apart, depth not exceeding:**										
D207209A	1.00 m	m²	1.52	19.31	–	6.83	26.14	21.24	–	7.51	28.75
D207209B	2.00 m	m²	2.28	28.95	–	8.28	37.23	31.85	–	9.11	40.95
D207209C	4.00 m	m²	2.76	35.05	–	10.21	45.26	38.56	–	11.23	49.79
D207209D	6.00 m	m²	3.44	43.69	–	12.14	55.83	48.06	–	13.35	61.41

Groundwork

Major Works 2009		Unit	Labour Hours	Labour Net	Plant Net	Materials Net	Unit Net	Labour Gross	Plant Gross	Materials Gross	Unit Price
								(Gross rates include 10% profit)			
				£	£	£	£	£	£	£	£
D20	**D20: EXCAVATING AND FILLING**										
D2075	**Steel trench sheeting to firm ground**										
D207511	**To sides of excavation not exceeding 2.00 m apart, depth not exceeding:**										
D207511A	1.00 m	m²	0.60	7.62	5.33	0.96	13.91	8.38	5.86	1.06	15.30
D207511B	2.00 m	m²	0.60	7.62	5.91	0.96	14.49	8.38	6.50	1.06	15.94
D207511C	4.00 m	m²	0.60	7.62	6.48	0.96	15.06	8.38	7.13	1.06	16.57
D207511D	6.00 m	m²	1.00	12.70	5.91	0.96	19.57	13.97	6.50	1.06	21.53
D207512	**To sides of excavation 2.00-4.00 m apart, depth not exceeding:**										
D207512A	1.00 m	m²	1.00	12.70	5.33	1.91	19.94	13.97	5.86	2.10	21.93
D207512B	2.00 m	m²	1.00	12.70	5.91	1.91	20.52	13.97	6.50	2.10	22.57
D207512C	4.00 m	m²	1.20	15.24	6.48	1.91	23.63	16.76	7.13	2.10	25.99
D207512D	6.00 m	m²	1.40	17.78	5.91	1.91	25.60	19.56	6.50	2.10	28.16
D207513	**To sides of excavation over 4.00 m apart, depth not exceeding:**										
D207513A	1.00 m	m²	0.60	7.62	5.33	0.96	13.91	8.38	5.86	1.06	15.30
D207513B	2.00 m	m²	0.80	10.16	5.91	1.13	17.20	11.18	6.50	1.24	18.92
D207513C	4.00 m	m²	1.00	12.70	6.48	1.39	20.57	13.97	7.13	1.53	22.63
D207513D	6.00 m	m²	1.20	15.24	5.91	1.57	22.72	16.76	6.50	1.73	24.99

Major Works 2009		Unit	Labour Hours	Labour Net	Plant Net	Materials Net	Unit Net	Labour Gross	Plant Gross	Materials Gross	Unit Price
								(Gross rates include 10% profit)			
				£	£	£	£	£	£	£	£
D20	**D20: EXCAVATING AND FILLING**										
D2076	**Steel trench sheeting to loose ground**										
D207615	**To sides of excavation not exceeding 2.00 m apart, depth not exceeding:**										
D207615A	1.00 m	m²	0.60	7.62	14.42	0.96	23.00	8.38	15.86	1.06	25.30
D207615B	2.00 m	m²	0.60	7.62	20.60	0.96	29.18	8.38	22.66	1.06	32.10
D207615C	4.00 m	m²	0.60	7.62	34.29	0.96	42.87	8.38	37.72	1.06	47.16
D207615D	6.00 m	m²	1.00	12.70	41.60	0.96	55.26	13.97	45.76	1.06	60.79
D207616	**To sides of excavation 2.00-4.00 m apart, depth not exceeding:**										
D207616A	1.00 m	m²	1.00	12.70	14.42	1.91	29.03	13.97	15.86	2.10	31.93
D207616B	2.00 m	m²	1.00	12.70	20.60	1.91	35.21	13.97	22.66	2.10	38.73
D207616C	4.00 m	m²	1.20	15.24	34.29	1.91	51.44	16.76	37.72	2.10	56.58
D207616D	6.00 m	m²	1.40	17.78	41.60	1.91	61.29	19.56	45.76	2.10	67.42
D207617	**To sides of excavation over 4.00 m apart, depth not exceeding:**										
D207617A	1.00 m	m²	0.60	7.62	14.42	0.96	23.00	8.38	15.86	1.06	25.30
D207617B	2.00 m	m²	0.80	10.16	20.60	1.13	31.89	11.18	22.66	1.24	35.08
D207617C	4.00 m	m²	1.00	12.70	34.29	1.39	48.38	13.97	37.72	1.53	53.22
D207617D	6.00 m	m²	1.20	15.24	41.60	1.57	58.41	16.76	45.76	1.73	64.25
D2082	**Off site disposal of material arising from earthworks**										
D208209	**Removed, including providing a suitable tip:**										
D208209A	hand loading	m³	1.37	17.40	18.60	3.29	39.29	19.14	20.46	3.62	43.22
D208209B	machine loading	m³	–	–	20.14	3.29	23.43	–	22.15	3.62	25.77

Groundwork

Major Works 2009		Unit	Labour Hours	Labour Net	Plant Net	Materials Net	Unit Net	Labour Gross	Plant Gross	Materials Gross	Unit Price
								(Gross rates include 10% profit)			
				£	£	£	£	£	£	£	£
D20	**D20: EXCAVATING AND FILLING**										
D2084	**On site disposal of material arising from earthworks**										
D208402	**Backfilled into excavation; compacting in 250 mm layers:**										
D208402A	by hand	m³	1.30	16.52	0.86	–	17.38	18.17	0.95	–	19.12
D208402B	by machine	m³	0.30	3.81	6.34	–	10.15	4.19	6.97	–	11.17
D208403	**Backfilled in making up levels; by hand; compacting in 250 mm layers; wheeling average:**										
D208403A	25 m	m³	1.66	21.08	0.63	–	21.71	23.19	0.69	–	23.88
D208403B	50 m	m³	2.00	25.40	0.63	–	26.03	27.94	0.69	–	28.63
D208403C	75 m	m³	2.33	29.59	0.63	–	30.22	32.55	0.69	–	33.24
D208403D	100 m	m³	2.66	33.78	0.63	–	34.41	37.16	0.69	–	37.85
D208404	**Backfilled in making up levels; by machine; compacting in 250 mm layers; transporting average:**										
D208404A	25 m	m³	0.27	3.43	3.35	–	6.78	3.77	3.69	–	7.46
D208404B	50 m	m³	0.33	4.20	3.76	–	7.96	4.62	4.14	–	8.76
D208404C	75 m	m³	0.40	5.08	4.25	–	9.33	5.59	4.68	–	10.26
D208404D	100 m	m³	0.47	5.97	4.73	–	10.70	6.57	5.20	–	11.77
D208405	**Backfilled oversite to make up levels; by hand; compacting in 250 mm layers; wheeling average:**										
D208405A	25 m	m³	1.86	23.63	0.82	–	24.45	25.99	0.90	–	26.90
D208405B	50 m	m³	2.20	27.94	0.82	–	28.76	30.73	0.90	–	31.64
D208405C	75 m	m³	2.53	32.14	0.82	–	32.96	35.35	0.90	–	36.26
D208405D	100 m	m³	2.86	36.33	0.82	–	37.15	39.96	0.90	–	40.87
D208406	**Backfilled oversite to make up levels; by machine; compacting in 250 mm layers; transporting average:**										
D208406A	25 m	m³	0.35	4.44	4.92	–	9.36	4.88	5.41	–	10.30
D208406B	50 m	m³	0.41	5.21	5.33	–	10.54	5.73	5.86	–	11.59
D208406C	75 m	m³	0.49	6.23	5.88	–	12.11	6.85	6.47	–	13.32
D208406D	100 m	m³	0.55	6.98	6.30	–	13.28	7.68	6.93	–	14.61
D208407	**Grading backfilled oversite to contours, embankments or the like; by hand:**										
D208407A	to falls	m³	0.08	1.02	–	–	1.02	1.12	–	–	1.12
D208407B	to falls and cross-falls	m³	0.14	1.78	–	–	1.78	1.96	–	–	1.96
D208407C	to slopes	m³	0.07	0.89	–	–	0.89	0.98	–	–	0.98
D208408	**Grading backfilled oversite to contours, embankments or the like; by machine:**										
D208408A	to falls	m³	0.03	0.38	0.66	–	1.04	0.42	0.73	–	1.14
D208408B	to falls and cross-falls	m³	0.05	0.63	1.10	–	1.73	0.69	1.21	–	1.90
D208408C	to slopes	m³	0.02	0.25	0.44	–	0.69	0.28	0.48	–	0.76

Major Works 2009		Unit	Labour Hours	Labour Net	Plant Net	Materials Net	Unit Net	Labour Gross	Plant Gross	Materials Gross	Unit Price
								(Gross rates include 10% profit)			
				£	£	£	£	£	£	£	£
D20	**D20: EXCAVATING AND FILLING**										
D2091	**Filling to excavations with materials arising from earthworks**										
D209102	**Backfilled into excavation; compacting in 250 mm layers:**										
D209102A	by hand	m³	1.30	16.52	0.86	–	17.38	18.17	0.95	–	19.12
D209102B	by machine	m³	0.30	3.81	6.34	–	10.15	4.19	6.97	–	11.17
D209103	**Backfilled in making up levels; by hand; compacting in 250 mm layers; wheeling average:**										
D209103A	25 m....................	m³	1.66	21.08	0.63	–	21.71	23.19	0.69	–	23.88
D209103B	50 m....................	m³	2.00	25.40	0.63	–	26.03	27.94	0.69	–	28.63
D209103C	75 m....................	m³	2.33	29.59	0.63	–	30.22	32.55	0.69	–	33.24
D209103D	100 m...................	m³	2.66	33.78	0.63	–	34.41	37.16	0.69	–	37.85
D209104	**Backfilled in making up levels; by machine; compacting in 250 mm layers; transporting average:**										
D209104A	25 m....................	m³	0.27	3.43	3.35	–	6.78	3.77	3.69	–	7.46
D209104B	50 m....................	m³	0.33	4.20	3.76	–	7.96	4.62	4.14	–	8.76
D209104C	75 m....................	m³	0.40	5.08	4.25	–	9.33	5.59	4.68	–	10.26
D209104D	100 m...................	m³	0.47	5.97	4.73	–	10.70	6.57	5.20	–	11.77
D209105	**Backfilled oversite to make up levels; by hand; compacting in 250 mm layers; wheeling average:**										
D209105A	25 m....................	m³	1.86	23.63	0.82	–	24.45	25.99	0.90	–	26.90
D209105B	50 m....................	m³	2.20	27.94	0.82	–	28.76	30.73	0.90	–	31.64
D209105C	75 m....................	m³	2.53	32.14	0.82	–	32.96	35.35	0.90	–	36.26
D209105D	100 m...................	m³	2.86	36.33	0.82	–	37.15	39.96	0.90	–	40.87
D209106	**Backfilled oversite to make up levels; by machine; compacting in 250 mm layers; transporting average:**										
D209106A	25 m....................	m³	0.35	4.44	4.92	–	9.36	4.88	5.41	–	10.30
D209106B	50 m....................	m³	0.41	5.21	5.33	–	10.54	5.73	5.86	–	11.59
D209106C	75 mm...................	m³	0.49	6.23	5.88	–	12.11	6.85	6.47	–	13.32
D209106D	100 m...................	m³	0.55	6.98	6.30	–	13.28	7.68	6.93	–	14.61
D209107	**Grading backfilled oversite to contours, embankments or the like; by hand:**										
D209107A	to falls	m³	0.08	1.02	–	–	1.02	1.12	–	–	1.12
D209107B	to falls and cross-falls	m³	0.14	1.78	–	–	1.78	1.96	–	–	1.96
D209107C	to slopes	m³	0.07	0.89	–	–	0.89	0.98	–	–	0.98
D209108	**Grading backfilled oversite to contours, embankments or the like; by machine:**										
D209108A	to falls	m³	0.03	0.38	0.66	–	1.04	0.42	0.73	–	1.14
D209108B	to falls and cross-falls	m³	0.05	0.63	1.10	–	1.73	0.69	1.21	–	1.90
D209108C	to slopes	m³	0.02	0.25	0.44	–	0.69	0.28	0.48	–	0.76

Groundwork

Major Works 2009		Unit	Labour Hours	Labour Net	Plant Net	Materials Net	Unit Net	Labour Gross	Plant Gross	Materials Gross	Unit Price
								(Gross rates include 10% profit)			
				£	£	£	£	£	£	£	£
D20	**D20: EXCAVATING AND FILLING**										
D2093	**Filling to excavations with imported materials**										
D209301	**Filled into excavation; by hand compacting in layers:**										
D209301A	sand	m³	0.80	10.16	0.86	22.21	33.23	11.18	0.95	24.43	36.55
D209301B	hardcore	m³	1.65	20.95	1.00	27.78	49.73	23.05	1.10	30.56	54.70
D209301C	hoggin	m³	0.90	11.43	0.86	24.45	36.74	12.57	0.95	26.90	40.41
D209301D	DTp type 1	m³	1.63	20.70	0.94	29.43	51.07	22.77	1.03	32.37	56.18
D209301E	DTp type 2	m³	1.63	20.71	0.94	27.01	48.66	22.78	1.03	29.71	53.53
D209301F	stone rejects	m³	1.65	20.95	1.00	28.00	49.95	23.05	1.10	30.80	54.95
D209301G	granite scalpings	m³	1.65	20.96	0.94	25.14	47.04	23.06	1.03	27.65	51.74
D209302	**Filled into excavation; by machine; compacting in layers:**										
D209302A	sand	m³	0.30	3.81	5.25	22.21	31.27	4.19	5.78	24.43	34.40
D209302B	hardcore	m³	0.35	4.45	8.68	27.78	40.91	4.90	9.55	30.56	45.00
D209302C	hoggin	m³	0.30	3.81	7.44	24.45	35.70	4.19	8.18	26.90	39.27
D209302D	DTp type 1	m³	0.33	4.19	8.62	29.43	42.24	4.61	9.48	32.37	46.46
D209302E	DTp type 2	m³	0.33	4.19	8.62	27.01	39.82	4.61	9.48	29.71	43.80
D209302F	stone rejects	m³	0.35	4.44	8.68	28.00	41.12	4.88	9.55	30.80	45.23
D209302G	granite scalpings	m³	0.33	4.19	8.62	25.14	37.95	4.61	9.48	27.65	41.75
D209303	**Filled in making up levels; by hand; compacting in layers:**										
D209303A	sand	m³	0.83	10.55	1.07	22.21	33.83	11.61	1.18	24.43	37.21
D209303B	hardcore	m³	1.46	18.54	1.07	27.78	47.39	20.39	1.18	30.56	52.13
D209303C	hoggin	m³	0.93	11.81	1.07	24.45	37.33	12.99	1.18	26.90	41.06
D209303D	DTp type 1	m³	1.40	17.78	1.07	29.43	48.28	19.56	1.18	32.37	53.11
D209303E	DTp type 2	m³	1.40	17.78	1.07	27.01	45.86	19.56	1.18	29.71	50.45
D209303F	stone rejects	m³	1.46	18.54	1.07	28.00	47.61	20.39	1.18	30.80	52.37
D209303G	granite scalpings	m³	1.46	18.54	1.07	25.14	44.75	20.39	1.18	27.65	49.23
D209304	**Filled in making up levels; by machine; compacting in layers:**										
D209304A	sand	m³	0.13	1.65	2.17	22.21	26.03	1.82	2.39	24.43	28.63
D209304B	hardcore	m³	0.13	1.65	3.27	27.78	32.70	1.82	3.60	30.56	35.97
D209304C	hoggin	m³	0.13	1.65	2.83	24.45	28.93	1.82	3.11	26.90	31.82
D209304D	DTp type 1	m³	0.13	1.65	2.83	29.43	33.91	1.82	3.11	32.37	37.30
D209304E	DTp type 2	m³	0.13	1.65	2.83	27.01	31.49	1.82	3.11	29.71	34.64
D209304F	stone rejects	m³	0.13	1.65	3.27	28.00	32.92	1.82	3.60	30.80	36.21
D209304G	granite scalpings	m³	0.13	1.65	3.27	25.14	30.06	1.82	3.60	27.65	33.07
D209305	**Filled into oversite to make up levels; by hand; compacting in layers; average 150 mm thick:**										
D209305A	sand	m³	1.03	13.09	1.40	22.21	36.70	14.40	1.54	24.43	40.37
D209305B	hardcore	m³	1.66	21.08	1.40	27.78	50.26	23.19	1.54	30.56	55.29
D209305C	hoggin	m³	1.13	14.35	1.40	24.45	40.20	15.79	1.54	26.90	44.22
D209305D	DTp type 1	m³	1.60	20.32	1.40	29.43	51.15	22.35	1.54	32.37	56.27
D209305E	DTp type 2	m³	1.60	20.32	1.40	27.01	48.73	22.35	1.54	29.71	53.60
D209305F	stone rejects	m³	1.66	21.08	1.40	28.00	50.48	23.19	1.54	30.80	55.53
D209305G	granite scalpings	m³	1.66	21.08	1.40	25.14	47.62	23.19	1.54	27.65	52.38

Major Works 2009		Unit	Labour Hours	Labour Net	Plant Net	Materials Net	Unit Net	Labour Gross	Plant Gross	Materials Gross	Unit Price
								——— (Gross rates include 10% profit) ———			
				£	£	£	£	£	£	£	£
D20	**D20: EXCAVATING AND FILLING**										
D2093	**Filling to excavations with imported materials**										
D209306	**Filled into oversite to make up levels; by machine; compacting in layers; average 150 mm thick:**										
D209306A	sand	m³	0.17	2.16	3.60	22.21	27.97	2.38	3.96	24.43	30.77
D209306B	hardcore	m³	0.17	2.16	4.70	27.78	34.64	2.38	5.17	30.56	38.10
D209306C	hoggin	m³	0.17	2.16	4.26	24.45	30.87	2.38	4.69	26.90	33.96
D209306D	DTp type 1	m³	0.17	2.16	4.26	29.43	35.85	2.38	4.69	32.37	39.44
D209306E	DTp type 2	m³	0.17	2.16	4.26	27.01	33.43	2.38	4.69	29.71	36.77
D209306F	stone rejects	m³	0.17	2.16	4.70	28.00	34.86	2.38	5.17	30.80	38.35
D209306G	granite scalpings	m³	0.17	2.16	4.70	25.14	32.00	2.38	5.17	27.65	35.20
D209307	**Grading filled oversite to contours, embankments or the like; by hand:**										
D209307A	to falls	m²	0.10	1.27	–	–	1.27	1.40	–	–	1.40
D209307B	to falls and cross-falls	m²	0.17	2.16	–	–	2.16	2.38	–	–	2.38
D209307C	to slopes	m²	0.09	1.14	–	–	1.14	1.25	–	–	1.25
D209308	**Grading filled oversite to contours, embankments or the like; by machine:**										
D209308A	to falls	m²	0.03	0.38	0.66	–	1.04	0.42	0.73	–	1.14
D209308B	to falls and cross-falls	m²	0.05	0.63	1.10	–	1.73	0.69	1.21	–	1.90
D209308C	to slopes	m²	0.02	0.25	0.44	–	0.69	0.28	0.48	–	0.76
D209309	**Blinding to hardcore:**										
D209309A	25 mm sand	m²	0.04	0.51	–	0.50	1.01	0.56	–	0.55	1.11
D209309B	50 mm sand	m²	0.06	0.70	–	0.98	1.68	0.77	–	1.08	1.85
D2095	**Surface treatment**										
D209520	**Level and compact:**										
D209520A	ground	m²	0.05	0.64	0.14	–	0.78	0.70	0.15	–	0.86
D209520B	filling	m²	0.05	0.64	0.14	–	0.78	0.70	0.15	–	0.86
D209520C	bottoms of excavations	m²	0.06	0.70	0.16	–	0.86	0.77	0.18	–	0.95

Groundwork

Major Works 2009		Unit				Specialist Net	Unit Net			Specialist Gross	Unit Price
									(Gross rates include 10% profit)		
			£	£	£	£	£	£	£	£	£
D30	**D30: CAST IN PLACE CONCRETE PILING**										
D3020	**Driven shell piles; rotary bored**										
D302010	**Provision of all plant including bringing to site and removal on completion; setting up and subsequent dismantling; general maintenance:**										
D302010A	average 100 nr piles	Item	–	–	–	11371.90	11371.90	–	–	12509.09	12509.09
D302020	**Piles 400 mm diameter:**										
D302020A	total number of piles	Nr	–	–	–	67.43	67.43	–	–	74.17	74.17
D302020B	total concreted length	m	–	–	–	63.56	63.56	–	–	69.92	69.92
D302020F	10 m max bored depth	m	–	–	–	49.17	49.17	–	–	54.09	54.09
D302020G	15 m max bored depth	m	–	–	–	54.43	54.43	–	–	59.87	59.87
D302020H	20 m max bored depth	m	–	–	–	59.63	59.63	–	–	65.59	65.59
D302020M	Extra over for enlarging bases 900 m extreme diameter	Nr	–	–	–	161.55	161.55	–	–	177.71	177.71
D302030	**Cutting off tops of piles; 400 mm dia:**										
D302030C	total length 2.0 m	m	–	–	–	33.01	33.01	–	–	36.31	36.31
D302050	**Pile tests; 400 mm dia:**										
D302050A	working piles; maintained loading 500 Kn	Nr	–	–	–	252.85	252.85	–	–	278.14	278.14
D31	**D31: PREFORMED CONCRETE PILES**										
D3120	**Reinforced concrete piles**										
D312010	**Provision of all plant including bringing to site and removal on completion; setting up and subsequent dismantling; general maintenance:**										
D312010A	average 100 nr piles	Item	–	–	–	8428.58	8428.58	–	–	9271.44	9271.44
D312020	**Sectional size; 600 mm dia:**										
D312020A	10 m max total driven depth	m	–	–	–	217.73	217.73	–	–	239.50	239.50
D312020B	15 m total driven depth	m	–	–	–	309.05	309.05	–	–	339.96	339.96
D312020C	20 m total driven depth	m	–	–	–	386.30	386.30	–	–	424.93	424.93
D312030	**Cutting off tops of piles; 600 mm dia:**										
D312030A	total length 2.0 m	Nr	–	–	–	68.12	68.12	–	–	74.93	74.93
D312050	**Pile tests; 600 mm dia:**										
D312050A	working pile; maintained loading 500 Kn	Nr	–	–	–	280.95	280.95	–	–	309.05	309.05

Major Works 2009		Unit	Labour Hours	Labour Net	Plant Net	Materials Net	Unit Net	Labour Gross	Plant Gross	Materials Gross	Unit Price
				£	£	£	£	£	£	£	£
								——— (Gross rates include 10% profit) ———			
D50	**D50: UNDERPINNING**										
D5021	**Machine excavation**										
D502102	**Excavation in preliminary trenches down to the base of the existing foundations, depth not exceeding:**										
D502102A	0.25 m	m³	0.30	3.82	6.59	–	10.41	4.20	7.25	–	11.45
D502102B	1.00 m	m³	0.25	3.17	5.49	–	8.66	3.49	6.04	–	9.53
D502102C	2.00 m	m³	0.35	4.45	7.68	–	12.13	4.90	8.45	–	13.34
D502102D	4.00 m	m³	0.45	5.71	9.88	–	15.59	6.28	10.87	–	17.15
D502102E	6.00 m	m³	0.50	6.36	10.98	–	17.34	7.00	12.08	–	19.07
D502103	**Excavation below the base of the existing foundations, depth not exceeding:**										
D502103A	1.00 m	m³	0.40	5.08	8.78	–	13.86	5.59	9.66	–	15.25
D502103B	2.00 m	m³	0.70	8.90	15.37	–	24.27	9.79	16.91	–	26.70
D502103C	4.00 m	m³	0.90	11.44	19.76	–	31.20	12.58	21.74	–	34.32
D502103D	6.00 m	m³	1.10	13.98	24.15	–	38.13	15.38	26.57	–	41.94
D5025	**Hand excavation**										
D502501	**Excavation in preliminary trenches down to the base of the existing foundations, depth not exceeding:**										
D502501A	0.25 m	m³	4.50	57.15	–	–	57.15	62.87	–	–	62.87
D502501B	1.00 m	m³	4.20	53.34	–	–	53.34	58.67	–	–	58.67
D502501C	2.00 m	m³	4.80	60.96	–	–	60.96	67.06	–	–	67.06
D502501D	4.00 m	m³	5.60	71.12	–	–	71.12	78.23	–	–	78.23
D502501E	6.00 m	m³	6.50	82.55	–	–	82.55	90.81	–	–	90.81
D502502	**Excavation below the base of the existing foundations, depth not exceeding:**										
D502502B	1.00 m	m³	5.70	72.39	–	–	72.39	79.63	–	–	79.63
D502502C	2.00 m	m³	6.60	83.82	–	–	83.82	92.20	–	–	92.20
D502502D	4.00 m	m³	7.50	95.25	–	–	95.25	104.78	–	–	104.78
D502502E	6.00 m	m³	9.20	116.84	–	–	116.84	128.52	–	–	128.52
D5031	**Breaking up obstructions with hand held mechanical tools**										
D503144	**Extra over excavation for breaking out:**										
D503144A	soft rock or brickwork	m³	3.60	45.72	46.76	–	92.48	50.29	51.44	–	101.73
D503144B	hard rock	m³	6.40	81.28	83.14	–	164.42	89.41	91.45	–	180.86
D503144C	plain concrete	m³	5.00	63.50	64.95	–	128.45	69.85	71.45	–	141.30
D503144D	reinforced concrete	m³	7.20	91.44	93.53	–	184.97	100.58	102.88	–	203.47
D5033	**Breaking out pavings with hand held compressor tools**										
D503337	**Excavation in tarmac paving:**										
D503337A	not exceeding 150 mm thick	m²	0.40	5.08	2.60	–	7.68	5.59	2.86	–	8.45
D503337B	150-300 mm thick	m²	0.70	8.89	5.20	–	14.09	9.78	5.72	–	15.50
D503337C	300-450 mm thick	m²	1.00	12.70	7.79	–	20.49	13.97	8.57	–	22.54
D503338	**Excavation in plain concrete paving:**										
D503338A	not exceeding 150 mm thick	m²	0.60	7.62	5.20	–	12.82	8.38	5.72	–	14.10
D503338B	150-300 mm thick	m²	0.90	11.43	7.79	–	19.22	12.57	8.57	–	21.14
D503338C	300-450 mm thick	m²	0.12	1.53	10.39	–	11.92	1.68	11.43	–	13.11

Groundwork

Major Works 2009		Unit	Labour Hours	Labour Net	Plant Net	Materials Net	Unit Net	Labour Gross	Plant Gross	Materials Gross	Unit Price
				£	£	£	£	£	£	£	£
									(Gross rates include 10% profit)		
D50	**D50: UNDERPINNING**										
D5033	**Breaking out pavings with hand held compressor tools**										
D503339	**Excavation in reinforced concrete paving:**										
D503339A	not exceeding 150 mm thick	m²	0.80	10.16	8.21	–	18.37	11.18	9.03	–	20.21
D503339B	150-300 mm thick	m²	1.30	16.51	13.40	–	29.91	18.16	14.74	–	32.90
D503339C	300-450 mm thick	m²	2.00	25.40	21.20	–	46.60	27.94	23.32	–	51.26
D5041	**Timber earthwork support to firm ground**										
D504103	**To sides of excavation not exceeding 2.0 m apart, depth not exceeding:**										
D504103A	1.00 m	m²	1.00	12.70	–	1.45	14.15	13.97	–	1.60	15.57
D504103B	2.00 m	m²	1.20	15.24	–	1.93	17.17	16.76	–	2.12	18.89
D504103C	4.00 m	m²	1.60	20.32	–	2.90	23.22	22.35	–	3.19	25.54
D504103D	6.00 m	m²	2.40	30.48	–	3.86	34.34	33.53	–	4.25	37.77
D504104	**To sides of excavation 2.00-4.00 m apart, depth not exceeding:**										
D504104A	1.00 m	m²	1.40	17.78	–	2.41	20.19	19.56	–	2.65	22.21
D504104B	2.00 m	m²	1.60	20.32	–	2.90	23.22	22.35	–	3.19	25.54
D504104C	4.00 m	m²	2.00	25.40	–	3.86	29.26	27.94	–	4.25	32.19
D504104D	6.00 m	m²	2.80	35.56	–	4.84	40.40	39.12	–	5.32	44.44
D504105	**To sides of excavation over 4.00 m apart, depth not exceeding:**										
D504105A	1.00 m	m²	1.20	15.24	–	1.45	16.69	16.76	–	1.60	18.36
D504105B	2.00 m	m²	2.00	25.40	–	2.90	28.30	27.94	–	3.19	31.13
D504105C	4.00 m	m²	2.40	30.48	–	4.83	35.31	33.53	–	5.31	38.84
D504105D	6.00 m	m²	3.20	40.64	–	6.76	47.40	44.70	–	7.44	52.14
D5042	**Timber earthwork support to loose ground**										
D504207	**To sides of excavation not exceeding 2.00 m apart, depth not exceeding:**										
D504207A	1.00 m	m²	1.32	16.77	–	6.83	23.60	18.45	–	7.51	25.96
D504207B	2.00 m	m²	1.56	19.81	–	7.31	27.12	21.79	–	8.04	29.83
D504207C	4.00 m	m²	1.92	24.38	–	8.28	32.66	26.82	–	9.11	35.93
D504207D	6.00 m	m²	2.76	35.05	–	9.24	44.29	38.56	–	10.16	48.72
D504208	**To sides of excavation 2.00-4.00 m apart, depth not exceeding:**										
D504208A	1.00 m	m²	2.04	25.91	–	7.79	33.70	28.50	–	8.57	37.07
D504208B	2.00 m	m²	1.84	23.37	–	8.28	31.65	25.71	–	9.11	34.82
D504208C	4.00 m	m²	2.32	29.47	–	9.24	38.71	32.42	–	10.16	42.58
D504208D	6.00 m	m²	3.04	38.61	–	10.22	48.83	42.47	–	11.24	53.71
D504209	**To sides of excavation over 4.00 m apart, depth not exceeding:**										
D504209A	1.00 m	m²	1.52	19.31	–	6.83	26.14	21.24	–	7.51	28.75
D504209B	2.00 m	m²	2.28	28.95	–	8.28	37.23	31.85	–	9.11	40.95
D504209C	4.00 m	m²	2.76	35.05	–	10.21	45.26	38.56	–	11.23	49.79
D504209D	6.00 m	m²	3.44	43.69	–	12.14	55.83	48.06	–	13.35	61.41

Major Works 2009		Unit	Labour Hours	Labour Net	Plant Net	Materials Net	Unit Net	Labour Gross	Plant Gross	Materials Gross	Unit Price
				£	£	£	£	£	£	£	£
D50	**D50: UNDERPINNING**										
D5045	**Steel trench sheeting to firm ground**										
D504511	**To sides of excavation not exceeding 2.00 m apart, depth not exceeding:**										
D504511A	1.00 m	m²	0.60	7.62	5.33	0.96	13.91	8.38	5.86	1.06	15.30
D504511B	2.00 m	m²	0.60	7.62	5.91	0.96	14.49	8.38	6.50	1.06	15.94
D504511C	4.00 m	m²	0.60	7.62	6.48	0.96	15.06	8.38	7.13	1.06	16.57
D504511D	6.00 m	m²	1.00	12.70	5.91	0.96	19.57	13.97	6.50	1.06	21.53
D504512	**To sides of excavation 2.00-4.00 m apart, depth not exceeding:**										
D504512A	1.00 m	m²	1.00	12.70	5.33	1.91	19.94	13.97	5.86	2.10	21.93
D504512B	2.00 m	m²	1.00	12.70	5.91	1.91	20.52	13.97	6.50	2.10	22.57
D504512C	4.00 m	m²	1.20	15.24	6.48	1.91	23.63	16.76	7.13	2.10	25.99
D504512D	6.00 m	m²	1.40	17.78	5.91	1.91	25.60	19.56	6.50	2.10	28.16
D504513	**To sides of excavation over 4.00 m apart, depth not exceeding:**										
D504513A	1.00 m	m²	0.60	7.62	5.33	0.96	13.91	8.38	5.86	1.06	15.30
D504513B	2.00 m	m²	0.80	10.16	5.91	1.13	17.20	11.18	6.50	1.24	18.92
D504513C	4.00 m	m²	1.00	12.70	6.48	1.39	20.57	13.97	7.13	1.53	22.63
D504513D	6.00 m	m²	1.20	15.24	5.91	1.57	22.72	16.76	6.50	1.73	24.99
D5046	**Steel trench sheeting to loose ground**										
D504615	**To sides of excavation not exceeding 2.00 m apart; depth not exceeding:**										
D504615A	1.00 m	m²	0.60	7.62	14.42	0.96	23.00	8.38	15.86	1.06	25.30
D504615B	2.00 m	m²	0.60	7.62	20.60	0.96	29.18	8.38	22.66	1.06	32.10
D504615C	4.00 m	m²	0.60	7.62	34.29	0.96	42.87	8.38	37.72	1.06	47.16
D504615D	6.00 m	m²	1.00	12.70	41.60	0.96	55.26	13.97	45.76	1.06	60.79
D504616	**To sides of excavation 2.00-4.00 m apart; depth not exceeding:**										
D504616A	1.00 m	m²	1.00	12.70	14.42	1.91	29.03	13.97	15.86	2.10	31.93
D504616B	2.00 m	m²	1.00	12.70	20.60	1.91	35.21	13.97	22.66	2.10	38.73
D504616C	4.00 m	m²	1.20	15.24	34.29	1.91	51.44	16.76	37.72	2.10	56.58
D504616D	6.00 m	m²	1.40	17.78	41.60	1.91	61.29	19.56	45.76	2.10	67.42
D504617	**To sides of excavation over 4.00 m apart; depth not exceeding:**										
D504617A	1.00 m	m²	0.60	7.62	14.42	0.96	23.00	8.38	15.86	1.06	25.30
D504617B	2.00 m	m²	0.80	10.16	20.60	1.13	31.89	11.18	22.66	1.24	35.08
D504617C	4.00 m	m²	1.00	12.70	34.29	1.39	48.38	13.97	37.72	1.53	53.22
D504617D	6.00 m	m²	1.20	15.24	41.60	1.57	58.41	16.76	45.76	1.73	64.25

(Gross rates include 10% profit)

Groundwork

Major Works 2009		Unit	Labour Hours	Labour Net	Plant Net	Materials Net	Unit Net	Labour Gross	Plant Gross	Materials Gross	Unit Price
								(Gross rates include 10% profit)			
				£	£	£	£	£	£	£	£
D50	**D50: UNDERPINNING**										
D5051	**Cutting away projecting foundations**										
D505121	**Brick:**										
D505121A	half brick thick, one course .	m	0.25	3.18	–	–	3.18	3.50	–	–	3.50
D505121B	half brick thick, two course .	m	0.40	5.08	–	–	5.08	5.59	–	–	5.59
D505121C	half brick thick, three course	m	0.20	2.54	0.33	–	2.87	2.79	0.36	–	3.16
D505121D	half brick thick, four course	m	0.30	3.81	0.50	–	4.31	4.19	0.55	–	4.74
D505121E	half brick thick, five course .	m	0.50	6.35	0.83	–	7.18	6.99	0.91	–	7.90
D505121F	one brick thick, one course .	m	0.25	3.18	0.43	–	3.61	3.50	0.47	–	3.97
D505121G	one brick thick, two course .	m	0.35	4.45	0.56	–	5.01	4.90	0.62	–	5.51
D505121H	one brick thick, three course	m	0.45	5.72	0.83	–	6.55	6.29	0.91	–	7.21
D505121I	one brick thick, four course	m	0.60	7.62	1.16	–	8.78	8.38	1.28	–	9.66
D505121J	one brick thick, five course .	m	0.75	9.52	1.33	–	10.85	10.47	1.46	–	11.94
D505121K	one and a half brick thick, one course	m	0.30	3.81	0.50	–	4.31	4.19	0.55	–	4.74
D505121L	one and a half brick thick, two course	m	0.45	5.72	0.76	–	6.48	6.29	0.84	–	7.13
D505121M	one and a half brick thick, three course	m	0.55	6.98	1.00	–	7.98	7.68	1.10	–	8.78
D505121N	one and a half brick thick, four course	m	0.35	4.45	0.88	–	5.33	4.90	0.97	–	5.86
D505121O	one and a half brick thick, five course	m	0.40	5.08	1.06	–	6.14	5.59	1.17	–	6.75
D505121P	two brick thick, one course .	m	0.40	5.08	0.66	–	5.74	5.59	0.73	–	6.31
D505121Q	two brick thick, two course .	m	0.50	6.35	0.83	–	7.18	6.99	0.91	–	7.90
D505121R	two brick thick, three course	m	0.40	5.08	0.88	–	5.96	5.59	0.97	–	6.56
D505121S	two brick thick, four course	m	0.50	6.35	1.18	–	7.53	6.99	1.30	–	8.28
D505121T	two brick thick, five course .	m	0.60	7.62	1.47	–	9.09	8.38	1.62	–	10.00
D505122	**Concrete:**										
D505122A	not exceeding 150 mm thick, not exceeding 150 mm wide	m	0.45	5.72	0.66	–	6.38	6.29	0.73	–	7.02
D505122B	not exceeding 150 mm thick, 150-300 mm wide	m	0.55	6.99	0.66	–	7.65	7.69	0.73	–	8.42
D505122C	not exceeding 150 mm thick, 300-450 mm wide	m	0.65	8.26	0.66	–	8.92	9.09	0.73	–	9.81
D505122D	150-300 mm thick, not exceeding 150 mm wide . . .	m	0.45	5.71	1.18	–	6.89	6.28	1.30	–	7.58
D505122E	150-300 mm thick, 150-300 mm wide	m	0.55	6.98	1.18	–	8.16	7.68	1.30	–	8.98
D505122F	150-300 mm thick, 300-450 mm wide	m	0.65	8.25	1.18	–	9.43	9.08	1.30	–	10.37
D505122G	300-450 mm thick, not exceeding 150 mm wide . . .	m	0.85	10.80	2.06	–	12.86	11.88	2.27	–	14.15
D505122H	300-450 mm thick, 150-300 mm wide	m	0.95	12.07	2.06	–	14.13	13.28	2.27	–	15.54
D505122I	300-450 mm thick, 300-450 mm wide	m	1.10	13.97	2.06	–	16.03	15.37	2.27	–	17.63

Major Works 2009		Unit	Labour Hours	Labour Net	Plant Net	Materials Net	Unit Net	Labour Gross	Plant Gross	Materials Gross	Unit Price
				£	£	£	£	£	£	£	£
								(Gross rates include 10% profit)			
D50	D50: UNDERPINNING										
D5061	Wedging and grouting up between new and existing work										
D506131	Slates in cement mortar (1:3):										
D506131A	half brick wide	m	0.75	22.33	–	1.43	23.76	24.56	–	1.57	26.14
D506131B	one brick wide	m	1.25	37.22	–	2.86	40.08	40.94	–	3.15	44.09
D506131C	one and a half brick wide	m	1.50	44.67	–	4.19	48.86	49.14	–	4.61	53.75
D506131D	two brick wide	m	1.75	52.12	–	5.62	57.74	57.33	–	6.18	63.51
D506132	Neat cement slurry:										
D506132A	not exceeding 150 mm wide	m	0.70	15.73	–	1.35	17.08	17.30	–	1.49	18.79
D506132B	150-300 mm wide	m	0.75	17.22	–	2.01	19.23	18.94	–	2.21	21.15
D506132C	300-450 mm wide	m	0.90	21.69	–	2.67	24.36	23.86	–	2.94	26.80
D506133	Epoxy cement non shrinking grout:										
D506133A	not exceeding 150 mm wide	m	0.70	15.73	–	1.82	17.55	17.30	–	2.00	19.31
D506133B	150-300 mm wide	m	0.75	17.21	–	2.93	20.14	18.93	–	3.22	22.15
D506133C	300-450 mm wide	m	0.90	21.68	–	4.06	25.74	23.85	–	4.47	28.31

Groundwork

Major Works 2009		Unit	Labour Hours	Labour Net	Plant Net	Materials Net	Unit Net	Labour Gross	Plant Gross	Materials Gross	Unit Price
								(Gross rates include 10% profit)			
				£	£	£	£	£	£	£	£
D50	**D50: UNDERPINNING**										
D5065	**Off site disposal of material arising from earthworks**										
D506509	**Removed, including providing a suitable tip:**										
D506509A	hand loading	m³	1.37	17.40	18.60	–	36.00	19.14	20.46	–	39.60
D506509B	machine loading	m³	–	–	20.14	–	20.14	–	22.15	–	22.15
D5066	**Filling to excavations with materials arising from earthworks**										
D506602	**Backfilled into excavation; compacting in layers:**										
D506602A	by hand	m³	1.30	16.52	0.86	–	17.38	18.17	0.95	–	19.12
D506603	**Backfilled in making up levels; by hand; compacting in layers; wheeling average:**										
D506603A	25 m	m³	1.66	21.08	0.63	–	21.71	23.19	0.69	–	23.88
D506603B	50 m	m³	2.00	25.40	0.63	–	26.03	27.94	0.69	–	28.63
D506603C	75 m	m³	2.33	29.59	0.63	–	30.22	32.55	0.69	–	33.24
D506603D	100 m	m³	2.66	33.78	0.63	–	34.41	37.16	0.69	–	37.85
D5069	**Filling to excavations with imported materials**										
D506901	**Filled into excavation; by hand; compacting in layers:**										
D506901A	sand	m³	0.80	10.16	0.86	22.21	33.23	11.18	0.95	24.43	36.55
D506901B	hardcore	m³	1.65	20.95	1.00	27.78	49.73	23.05	1.10	30.56	54.70
D506901C	hoggin	m³	0.90	11.43	0.86	24.45	36.74	12.57	0.95	26.90	40.41
D506901D	DTp type 1	m³	1.63	20.70	0.94	29.43	51.07	22.77	1.03	32.37	56.18
D506901E	DTp type 2	m³	1.63	20.71	0.94	27.01	48.66	22.78	1.03	29.71	53.53
D506901F	stone rejects	m³	1.65	20.95	1.00	28.00	49.95	23.05	1.10	30.80	54.95
D506901G	granite scalpings	m³	1.65	20.96	0.94	25.14	47.04	23.06	1.03	27.65	51.74
D506903	**Filled in making up levels; by hand; compacting in layers:**										
D506903A	sand	m³	0.83	10.55	1.07	22.21	33.83	11.61	1.18	24.43	37.21
D506903B	hardcore	m³	1.46	18.54	1.07	27.78	47.39	20.39	1.18	30.56	52.13
D506903C	hoggin	m³	0.93	11.81	1.07	24.45	37.33	12.99	1.18	26.90	41.06
D506903D	DTp type 1	m³	1.40	17.78	1.07	29.43	48.28	19.56	1.18	32.37	53.11
D506903E	DTp type 2	m³	1.40	17.78	1.07	27.01	45.86	19.56	1.18	29.71	50.45
D506903F	stone rejects	m³	1.46	18.54	1.07	28.00	47.61	20.39	1.18	30.80	52.37
D506903G	granite chippings	m³	1.46	18.54	1.07	25.14	44.75	20.39	1.18	27.65	49.23
D5071	**Plain in situ concrete; mix C15P**										
D507101	**Foundations; poured on or against earth or unblinded hardcore:**										
D507101B	generally	m³	0.90	11.43	–	99.46	110.89	12.57	–	109.41	121.98
D507103	**Isolated foundations; poured on or against earth or unblinded hardcore:**										
D507103B	generally	m³	1.90	24.13	–	97.20	121.33	26.54	–	106.92	133.46

Major Works 2009		Unit	Labour Hours	Labour Net	Plant Net	Materials Net	Unit Net	Labour Gross	Plant Gross	Materials Gross	Unit Price
								(Gross rates include 10% profit)			
				£	£	£	£	£	£	£	£
D50	**D50: UNDERPINNING**										
D5072	**Plain in situ concrete; mix C20P**										
D507201	**Foundations; poured on or against earth or unblinded hardcore:**										
D507201B	generally	m³	0.90	11.43	–	101.60	113.03	12.57	–	111.76	124.33
D507203	**Isolated foundations; poured on or against earth or unblinded hardcore:**										
D507203B	generally	m³	1.90	24.13	–	99.29	123.42	26.54	–	109.22	135.76
D5073	**Reinforced in situ concrete; mix C25P**										
D507301	**Foundations:**										
D507301B	generally	m³	1.10	13.97	9.50	101.38	124.85	15.37	10.45	111.52	137.34
D507303	**Isolated foundations:**										
D507303B	generally	m³	2.15	27.30	18.41	100.25	145.96	30.03	20.25	110.28	160.56
D507318	**Walls:**										
D507318A	not exceeding 150 mm thick	m³	2.31	29.33	19.60	99.03	147.96	32.26	21.56	108.93	162.76
D507318B	150-450 mm thick	m³	2.05	26.04	17.23	99.03	142.30	28.64	18.95	108.93	156.53
D507318C	over 450 mm thick	m³	1.40	17.78	11.88	99.03	128.69	19.56	13.07	108.93	141.56
D507326	**Upstands:**										
D507326B	generally	m³	2.75	34.92	23.17	101.38	159.47	38.41	25.49	111.52	175.42

Groundwork

Major Works 2009		Unit	Labour Hours	Labour Net	Plant Net	Materials Net	Unit Net	Labour Gross	Plant Gross	Materials Gross	Unit Price
								(Gross rates include 10% profit)			
				£	£	£	£	£	£	£	£
D50	**D50: UNDERPINNING**										
D5075	**Formwork to general finish**										
D507501	**Sides of foundations:**										
D507501A	not exceeding 250 mm high	m	0.76	12.91	–	50.57	63.48	14.20	–	55.63	69.83
D507501B	250-500 mm high.........	m	1.15	19.45	–	100.38	119.83	21.40	–	110.42	131.81
D507501C	500-1000 mm high	m	2.04	34.56	–	200.02	234.58	38.02	–	220.02	258.04
D507501D	over 1000 mm high	m²	1.86	31.49	–	183.23	214.72	34.64	–	201.55	236.19
D507504	**Sides of upstands:**										
D507504A	not exceeding 250 mm wide	m	0.71	11.97	–	5.82	17.79	13.17	–	6.40	19.57
D507504B	250-500 mm wide	m	0.90	15.29	–	8.96	24.25	16.82	–	9.86	26.68
D507504C	500-1000 mm wide	m	1.60	27.15	0.63	15.10	42.88	29.87	0.69	16.61	47.17
D507504D	over 1000 mm wide	m²	1.46	24.76	1.25	15.96	41.97	27.24	1.38	17.56	46.17
D507526	**Walls:**										
D507526A	vertical surfaces	m²	1.78	30.14	1.53	13.40	45.07	33.15	1.68	14.74	49.58
D507526B	curved surfaces	m²	2.00	33.91	1.53	14.59	50.03	37.30	1.68	16.05	55.03
D507526C	conical surfaces	m²	2.66	45.22	1.72	18.67	65.61	49.74	1.89	20.54	72.17
D507526D	spherical surfaces	m²	4.44	75.35	1.91	28.88	106.14	82.89	2.10	31.77	116.75
D507526E	battering surfaces	m²	2.13	36.10	1.53	15.36	52.99	39.71	1.68	16.90	58.29
D507563	**Wall ends and steps in walls:**										
D507563A	not exceeding 250 mm wide	m	0.50	8.54	–	5.72	14.26	9.39	–	6.29	15.69
D507563B	250-500 mm wide	m	0.69	11.68	–	15.42	27.10	12.85	–	16.96	29.81
D507563C	500-1000 mm wide	m	0.83	14.01	1.15	15.79	30.95	15.41	1.27	17.37	34.05
D507563D	over 1000 mm wide	m²	0.75	12.77	1.53	15.28	29.58	14.05	1.68	16.81	32.54
D507564	**Openings in walls:**										
D507564A	not exceeding 250 mm wide	m	0.50	8.54	–	5.72	14.26	9.39	–	6.29	15.69
D507564B	250-500 mm wide	m	0.69	11.68	–	15.42	27.10	12.85	–	16.96	29.81
D507564C	500-1000 mm wide	m	0.83	14.01	1.15	15.79	30.95	15.41	1.27	17.37	34.05
D507564D	over 1000 mm wide	m²	0.75	12.77	1.53	15.28	29.58	14.05	1.68	16.81	32.54

Major Works 2009		Unit	Labour Hours	Labour Net	Plant Net	Materials Net	Unit Net	Labour Gross	Plant Gross	Materials Gross	Unit Price
								(Gross rates include 10% profit)			
				£	£	£	£	£	£	£	£
D50	**D50: UNDERPINNING**										
D5081	**Bar reinforcement; high yield steel bars, BS 4449, delivered to site cut, bent and labelled**										
D508105	**Bars, fixing with tying wire:**										
D508105A	6 mm	Tonne	72.00	1065.60	–	1098.27	2163.87	1172.16	–	1208.10	2380.26
D508105B	8 mm	Tonne	54.00	799.20	–	1073.24	1872.44	879.12	–	1180.56	2059.68
D508105C	10 mm	Tonne	44.00	651.20	–	1004.79	1655.99	716.32	–	1105.27	1821.59
D508105D	12 mm	Tonne	38.00	562.40	–	958.98	1521.38	618.64	–	1054.88	1673.52
D508105E	16 mm	Tonne	30.00	444.00	–	894.29	1338.29	488.40	–	983.72	1472.12
D508105F	20 mm	Tonne	26.00	384.80	–	878.96	1263.76	423.28	–	966.86	1390.14
D508105G	25 mm	Tonne	23.00	340.40	–	853.94	1194.34	374.44	–	939.33	1313.77
D508105H	32 mm	Tonne	20.00	296.00	–	840.96	1136.96	325.60	–	925.06	1250.66
D508105I	40 mm	Tonne	17.00	251.60	–	827.06	1078.66	276.76	–	909.77	1186.53
D5086	**Walls**										
D508602	**Common bricks, BS 3921, in cement mortar (1:3):**										
D508602B	one brick thick	m²	1.83	45.97	–	34.71	80.68	50.57	–	38.18	88.75
D508602C	one and a half brick thick. . .	m²	2.74	68.83	–	51.76	120.59	75.71	–	56.94	132.65
D508602D	two brick thick	m²	3.66	91.94	–	69.66	161.60	101.13	–	76.63	177.76
D508603	**Class A engineering bricks, BS 3921, in cement mortar (1:3):**										
D508603B	one brick thick	m²	1.98	49.74	–	68.87	118.61	54.71	–	75.76	130.47
D508603C	one and a half brick thick. . .	m²	2.97	74.61	–	103.28	177.89	82.07	–	113.61	195.68
D508603D	two brick thick	m²	3.96	99.47	–	138.26	237.73	109.42	–	152.09	261.50
D508604	**Class B engineering bricks, BS 3921, in cement mortar (1:3):**										
D508604B	one brick thick	m²	1.90	47.72	–	59.62	107.34	52.49	–	65.58	118.07
D508604C	one and a half brick thick. . .	m²	2.86	71.84	–	89.33	161.17	79.02	–	98.26	177.29
D508604D	two brick thick	m²	3.81	95.71	–	119.68	215.39	105.28	–	131.65	236.93
D508605	**Facing bricks, PC 300:00 per 1000, in gauged mortar (1:1:6); flush pointing both sides:**										
D508605B	one brick thick; double stretcher bond	m²	2.03	51.00	–	43.53	94.53	56.10	–	47.88	103.98
D508605C	one brick thick; English bond	m²	2.13	53.58	–	43.86	97.44	58.94	–	48.25	107.18
D508605F	one brick thick; Flemish bond	m²	2.20	55.27	–	43.75	99.02	60.80	–	48.13	108.92

Groundwork

Major Works 2009		Unit	Labour Hours	Labour Net	Plant Net	Materials Net	Unit Net	Labour Gross	Plant Gross	Materials Gross	Unit Price
								(Gross rates include 10% profit)			
				£	£	£	£	£	£	£	£
D50	**D50: UNDERPINNING**										
D5088	**Extra over general brickwork for fair faced work**										
D508882	**Fair facing and flush pointing:**										
D508882A	stretcher bond	m²	0.06	1.41	–	0.18	1.59	1.55	–	0.20	1.75
D508882B	English bond	m²	0.06	1.49	–	0.36	1.85	1.64	–	0.40	2.04
D508882E	Flemish bond	m²	0.06	1.53	–	0.27	1.80	1.68	–	0.30	1.98
D508883	**Fair facing and struck or weather struck pointing:**										
D508883A	stretcher bond	m²	0.06	1.46	–	0.18	1.64	1.61	–	0.20	1.80
D508883B	English bond	m²	0.06	1.56	–	0.36	1.92	1.72	–	0.40	2.11
D508883E	Flemish bond	m²	0.06	1.61	–	0.27	1.88	1.77	–	0.30	2.07
D508884	**Fair facing and tooled or keyed pointing:**										
D508884A	stretcher bond	m²	0.06	1.56	–	0.18	1.74	1.72	–	0.20	1.91
D508884B	English bond	m²	0.07	1.64	–	0.36	2.00	1.80	–	0.40	2.20
D508884E	Flemish bond	m²	0.07	1.69	–	0.27	1.96	1.86	–	0.30	2.16
D5091	**Cutting, toothing and bonding ends of new walls into existing**										
D509101	**Common brickwork; in alternate courses:**										
D509101B	one brick wall	m	0.84	25.01	–	4.36	29.37	27.51	–	4.80	32.31
D509101C	one and a half brick wall ...	m	1.11	33.06	–	6.46	39.52	36.37	–	7.11	43.47
D509101D	two brick wall	m	1.65	49.14	–	8.48	57.62	54.05	–	9.33	63.38
D509103	**Engineering brickwork; in alternate courses:**										
D509103B	one brick wall	m	0.88	26.14	–	6.96	33.10	28.75	–	7.66	36.41
D509103C	one and a half brick wall ...	m	1.15	34.24	–	10.26	44.50	37.66	–	11.29	48.95
D509103D	two brick wall	m	1.69	50.33	–	13.47	63.80	55.36	–	14.82	70.18
D509105	**Facing brickwork; in alternate courses:**										
D509105B	one brick wall	m	1.15	34.25	–	4.94	39.19	37.68	–	5.43	43.11

IN-SITU CONCRETE AND
LARGE PC CONCRETE

Major Works 2009		Unit	Labour Hours	Labour Net	Plant Net	Materials Net	Unit Net	Labour Gross	Plant Gross	Materials Gross	Unit Price
								(Gross rates include 10% profit)			
				£	£	£	£	£	£	£	£
E10	**E10: MIXING, CASTING, CURING IN SITU CONCRETE**										
E1001	**Plain in situ concrete; mix C10P**										
E100101	**Foundations; poured on or against earth or unblinded hardcore:**										
E100101B	generally	m³	0.90	11.43	–	96.62	108.05	12.57	–	106.28	118.86
E100102	**Ground beams; poured on or against earth or unblinded hardcore:**										
E100102B	generally	m³	1.90	24.13	–	94.43	118.56	26.54	–	103.87	130.42
E100103	**Isolated foundations; poured on or against earth or unblinded hardcore:**										
E100103B	generally	m³	1.90	24.13	–	94.43	118.56	26.54	–	103.87	130.42
E100104	**Beds; poured on or against earth or unblinded hardcore:**										
E100104A	not exceeding 150 mm thick	m³	1.05	13.34	–	92.23	105.57	14.67	–	101.45	116.13
E100104B	150-450 mm thick	m³	0.70	8.89	–	92.23	101.12	9.78	–	101.45	111.23
E100104C	over 450 mm thick	m³	0.50	6.35	–	92.23	98.58	6.99	–	101.45	108.44
E100106	**Filling hollow walls:**										
E100106A	not exceeding 150 mm thick	m³	2.70	34.29	–	92.23	126.52	37.72	–	101.45	139.17
E1002	**Plain in situ concrete; mix C15P**										
E100201	**Foundations; poured on or against unblinded hardcore:**										
E100201B	generally	m³	0.90	11.43	–	99.46	110.89	12.57	–	109.41	121.98
E100202	**Ground beams; poured on or against earth or unblinded hardcore:**										
E100202B	generally	m³	1.90	24.13	–	97.20	121.33	26.54	–	106.92	133.46
E100203	**Isolated foundations; poured on or against earth or unblinded hardcore:**										
E100203B	generally	m³	1.90	24.13	–	97.20	121.33	26.54	–	106.92	133.46
E100204	**Beds; poured on or against earth or unblinded hardcore:**										
E100204A	not exceeding 150 mm thick	m³	1.05	13.34	–	94.94	108.28	14.67	–	104.43	119.11
E100204B	150-450 mm thick	m³	0.70	8.89	–	94.94	103.83	9.78	–	104.43	114.21
E100204C	over 450 mm thick	m³	0.50	6.35	–	94.94	101.29	6.99	–	104.43	111.42
E100205	**Walls:**										
E100205A	not exceeding 150 mm thick	m³	1.90	24.13	–	94.94	119.07	26.54	–	104.43	130.98
E100205B	150-450 mm thick	m³	1.60	20.32	–	94.94	115.26	22.35	–	104.43	126.79
E100205C	over 450 mm thick	m³	1.15	14.61	–	94.94	109.55	16.07	–	104.43	120.51
E100206	**Filling hollow walls:**										
E100206A	not exceeding 150 mm thick	m³	2.70	34.29	–	94.94	129.23	37.72	–	104.43	142.15

In Situ Concrete and Large PC Concrete

Major Works 2009		Unit	Labour Hours	Labour Net	Plant Net	Materials Net	Unit Net	Labour Gross	Plant Gross	Materials Gross	Unit Price
								(Gross rates include 10% profit)			
				£	£	£	£	£	£	£	£
E10	**E10: MIXING, CASTING, CURING IN SITU CONCRETE**										
E1005	**Plain in situ concrete; mix C20P**										
E100501	**Foundations; poured on or against earth or unblinded hardcore:**										
E100501B	generally	m³	0.90	11.43	–	101.60	113.03	12.57	–	111.76	124.33
E100502	**Ground beams; poured on or against earth or unblinded hardcore:**										
E100502B	generally	m³	1.90	24.13	–	99.29	123.42	26.54	–	109.22	135.76
E100503	**Isolated foundations; poured on or against earth or unblinded hardcore:**										
E100503B	generally	m³	1.90	24.13	–	99.29	123.42	26.54	–	109.22	135.76
E100504	**Beds; poured on or against earth or unblinded hardcore:**										
E100504A	not exceeding 150 mm thick	m³	1.05	13.33	–	96.98	110.31	14.66	–	106.68	121.34
E100504B	150-450 mm thick	m³	0.70	8.89	–	96.98	105.87	9.78	–	106.68	116.46
E100504C	over 450 mm thick	m³	0.50	6.35	–	96.98	103.33	6.99	–	106.68	113.66
E100505	**Walls:**										
E100505A	not exceeding 150 mm thick	m³	1.90	24.13	–	96.98	121.11	26.54	–	106.68	133.22
E100505B	150-450 mm thick	m³	1.60	20.32	–	96.98	117.30	22.35	–	106.68	129.03
E100505C	over 450 mm thick	m³	1.15	14.60	–	96.98	111.58	16.06	–	106.68	122.74
E100506	**Filling hollow walls:**										
E100506A	not exceeding 150 mm thick	m³	2.70	34.29	–	96.98	131.27	37.72	–	106.68	144.40
E100511	**Columns:**										
E100511B	generally	m³	2.15	27.30	–	99.29	126.59	30.03	–	109.22	139.25
E100512	**Column casings:**										
E100512B	generally	m³	2.47	31.37	–	99.29	130.66	34.51	–	109.22	143.73
E100601	**Foundations; poured on or against earth or unblinded hardcore:**										
E100601B	generally	m³	0.90	11.43	–	101.60	113.03	12.57	–	111.76	124.33
E100602	**Ground beams; poured on or against earth or unblinded hardcore:**										
E100602B	generally	m³	1.90	24.13	–	99.29	123.42	26.54	–	109.22	135.76
E100603	**Isolated foundations; poured on or against earth or unblinded hardcore:**										
E100603B	generally	m³	1.90	24.13	–	99.29	123.42	26.54	–	109.22	135.76

Major Works 2009		Unit	Labour Hours	Labour Net	Plant Net	Materials Net	Unit Net	Labour Gross	Plant Gross	Materials Gross	Unit Price
								(Gross rates include 10% profit)			
				£	£	£	£	£	£	£	£
E10	**E10: MIXING, CASTING, CURING IN SITU CONCRETE**										
E1006	**Plain in situ concrete; mix C25P**										
E100604	**Beds; poured on or against earth or unblinded hardcore:**										
E100604A	not exceeding 150 mm thick	m³	1.05	13.33	–	96.98	110.31	14.66	–	106.68	121.34
E100604B	150-450 mm thick	m³	0.70	8.89	–	96.98	105.87	9.78	–	106.68	116.46
E100604C	over 450 mm thick	m³	0.50	6.35	–	96.98	103.33	6.99	–	106.68	113.66
E100605	**Walls:**										
E100605A	not exceeding 150 mm thick	m³	1.90	24.13	–	96.98	121.11	26.54	–	106.68	133.22
E100605B	150-450 mm thick	m³	1.60	20.32	–	96.98	117.30	22.35	–	106.68	129.03
E100605C	over 450 mm thick	m³	1.15	14.60	–	96.98	111.58	16.06	–	106.68	122.74
E100606	**Filling hollow walls:**										
E100606A	not exceeding 150 mm thick	m³	2.70	34.29	–	96.98	131.27	37.72	–	106.68	144.40
E100611	**Columns:**										
E100611B	generally	m³	2.15	27.30	–	99.29	126.59	30.03	–	109.22	139.25
E100612	**Column casings:**										
E100612B	generally	m³	2.47	31.37	–	99.29	130.66	34.51	–	109.22	143.73
E1011	**Reinforced in situ concrete; mix C20P**										
E101101	**Foundations:**										
E101101B	generally	m³	1.10	13.97	9.50	99.29	122.76	15.37	10.45	109.22	135.04
E101102	**Ground beams:**										
E101102B	generally	m³	2.15	27.31	18.41	98.18	143.90	30.04	20.25	108.00	158.29
E101103	**Isolated foundations:**										
E101103B	generally	m³	2.15	27.31	18.41	98.18	143.90	30.04	20.25	108.00	158.29
E101116	**Beds:**										
E101116A	not exceeding 150 mm thick	m³	1.40	17.78	5.56	96.98	120.32	19.56	6.12	106.68	132.35
E101116B	150-450 mm thick	m³	1.00	12.70	3.89	96.98	113.57	13.97	4.28	106.68	124.93
E101116C	over 450 mm thick	m³	0.70	8.89	2.78	96.98	108.65	9.78	3.06	106.68	119.52
E101117	**Slabs:**										
E101117A	not exceeding 150 mm thick	m³	2.10	26.67	8.34	96.98	131.99	29.34	9.17	106.68	145.19
E101117B	150-450 mm thick	m³	1.55	19.69	6.12	96.98	122.79	21.66	6.73	106.68	135.07
E101117C	over 450 mm thick	m³	1.05	13.33	4.17	96.98	114.48	14.66	4.59	106.68	125.93
E101118	**Walls:**										
E101118A	not exceeding 150 mm thick	m³	2.31	29.34	19.60	96.98	145.92	32.27	21.56	106.68	160.51
E101118B	150-450 mm thick	m³	2.05	26.04	17.23	96.98	140.25	28.64	18.95	106.68	154.28
E101118C	over 450 mm thick	m³	1.40	17.78	11.88	96.98	126.64	19.56	13.07	106.68	139.30
E101119	**Diaphragm walls:**										
E101119A	not exceeding 150 mm thick	m³	3.00	38.10	25.54	96.98	160.62	41.91	28.09	106.68	176.68
E101119B	150-450 mm thick	m³	2.30	29.21	19.60	96.98	145.79	32.13	21.56	106.68	160.37
E101119C	over 450 mm thick	m³	2.05	26.04	17.23	96.98	140.25	28.64	18.95	106.68	154.28

In Situ Concrete and Large PC Concrete

Major Works 2009		Unit	Labour Hours	Labour Net	Plant Net	Materials Net	Unit Net	Labour Gross	Plant Gross	Materials Gross	Unit Price
								(Gross rates include 10% profit)			
				£	£	£	£	£	£	£	£
E10	**E10: MIXING, CASTING, CURING IN SITU CONCRETE**										
E1011	**Reinforced in situ concrete; mix C20P**										
E101120	**Beams:**										
E101120B	generally	m³	2.80	35.56	23.76	98.18	157.50	39.12	26.14	108.00	173.25
E101121	**Beam casings:**										
E101121B	generally	m³	3.22	40.90	27.32	98.18	166.40	44.99	30.05	108.00	183.04
E101123	**Columns:**										
E101123B	generally	m³	4.00	50.80	34.16	98.18	183.14	55.88	37.58	108.00	201.45
E101124	**Column casings:**										
E101124B	generally	m³	4.60	58.42	39.26	98.18	195.86	64.26	43.19	108.00	215.45
E101125	**Staircases:**										
E101125A	generally	m³	2.80	35.56	23.76	98.18	157.50	39.12	26.14	108.00	173.25
E101126	**Upstands:**										
E101126B	generally	m³	2.75	34.93	23.17	99.29	157.39	38.42	25.49	109.22	173.13

Major Works 2009		Unit	Labour Hours	Labour Net	Plant Net	Materials Net	Unit Net	Labour Gross	Plant Gross	Materials Gross	Unit Price
				£	£	£	£	(Gross rates include 10% profit)			
								£	£	£	£
E10	E10: MIXING, CASTING, CURING IN SITU CONCRETE										
E1012	Reinforced in situ concrete; mix C25P										
E101201	Foundations:										
E101201B	generally	m³	1.10	13.97	9.50	101.38	124.85	15.37	10.45	111.52	137.34
E101202	Ground beams:										
E101202B	generally	m³	2.15	27.30	18.41	100.25	145.96	30.03	20.25	110.28	160.56
E101203	Isolated foundations:										
E101203B	generally	m³	2.15	27.30	18.41	100.25	145.96	30.03	20.25	110.28	160.56
E101216	Beds:										
E101216A	not exceeding 150 mm thick	m³	1.40	17.78	5.56	99.03	122.37	19.56	6.12	108.93	134.61
E101216B	150-450 mm thick	m³	1.00	12.70	3.89	99.03	115.62	13.97	4.28	108.93	127.18
E101216C	over 450 mm thick	m³	0.70	8.89	2.78	99.03	110.70	9.78	3.06	108.93	121.77
E101217	Slabs:										
E101217A	not exceeding 150 mm thick	m³	2.10	26.67	8.34	99.03	134.04	29.34	9.17	108.93	147.44
E101217B	150-450 mm thick	m³	1.55	19.69	6.12	99.03	124.84	21.66	6.73	108.93	137.32
E101217C	over 450 mm thick	m³	1.05	13.33	4.17	99.03	116.53	14.66	4.59	108.93	128.18
E101218	Walls:										
E101218A	not exceeding 150 mm thick	m³	2.31	29.33	19.60	99.03	147.96	32.26	21.56	108.93	162.76
E101218B	150-450 mm thick	m³	2.05	26.04	17.23	99.03	142.30	28.64	18.95	108.93	156.53
E101218C	over 450 mm thick	m³	1.40	17.78	11.88	99.03	128.69	19.56	13.07	108.93	141.56
E101219	Diaphragm walls:										
E101219A	not exceeding 150 mm thick	m³	3.00	38.10	25.54	99.03	162.67	41.91	28.09	108.93	178.94
E101219B	150-450 mm thick	m³	2.30	29.21	19.60	99.03	147.84	32.13	21.56	108.93	162.62
E101219C	over 450 mm thick	m³	2.05	26.04	17.23	99.03	142.30	28.64	18.95	108.93	156.53
E101220	Beams:										
E101220B	generally	m³	2.80	35.56	23.76	100.25	159.57	39.12	26.14	110.28	175.53
E101221	Beam casings:										
E101221B	generally	m³	3.22	40.89	27.32	100.25	168.46	44.98	30.05	110.28	185.31
E101223	Columns:										
E101223B	generally	m³	4.00	50.80	34.16	100.25	185.21	55.88	37.58	110.28	203.73
E101224	Column casings:										
E101224B	generally	m³	4.60	58.42	39.26	100.25	197.93	64.26	43.19	110.28	217.72
E101225	Staircases:										
E101225A	generally	m³	2.80	35.56	23.76	100.25	159.57	39.12	26.14	110.28	175.53
E101226	Upstands:										
E101226B	generally	m³	2.75	34.92	23.17	101.38	159.47	38.41	25.49	111.52	175.42

In Situ Concrete and Large PC Concrete

Major Works 2009		Unit	Labour Hours	Labour Net	Plant Net	Materials Net	Unit Net	Labour Gross	Plant Gross	Materials Gross	Unit Price
								(Gross rates include 10% profit)			
				£	£	£	£	£	£	£	£
E10	**E10: MIXING, CASTING, CURING IN SITU CONCRETE**										
E1013	**Reinforced in situ concrete; mix C30P**										
E101301	**Foundations:**										
E101301B	generally	m³	1.10	13.97	9.50	104.17	127.64	15.37	10.45	114.59	140.40
E101302	**Ground beams:**										
E101302B	generally	m³	2.15	27.30	18.41	103.00	148.71	30.03	20.25	113.30	163.58
E101303	**Isolated foundations:**										
E101303B	generally	m³	2.15	27.30	18.41	103.00	148.71	30.03	20.25	113.30	163.58
E101316	**Beds:**										
E101316A	not exceeding 150 mm thick	m³	1.40	17.79	5.56	101.75	125.10	19.57	6.12	111.93	137.61
E101316B	150-450 mm thick	m³	1.00	12.70	3.89	101.75	118.34	13.97	4.28	111.93	130.17
E101316C	over 450 mm thick	m³	0.70	8.90	2.78	101.75	113.43	9.79	3.06	111.93	124.77
E101317	**Slabs:**										
E101317A	not exceeding 150 mm thick	m³	2.10	26.68	8.34	101.75	136.77	29.35	9.17	111.93	150.45
E101317B	150-450 mm thick	m³	1.55	19.69	6.12	101.75	127.56	21.66	6.73	111.93	140.32
E101317C	over 450 mm thick	m³	1.05	13.34	4.17	101.75	119.26	14.67	4.59	111.93	131.19
E101318	**Walls:**										
E101318A	not exceeding 150 mm thick	m³	2.31	29.33	19.60	101.75	150.68	32.26	21.56	111.93	165.75
E101318B	150-450 mm thick	m³	2.05	26.04	17.23	101.75	145.02	28.64	18.95	111.93	159.52
E101318C	over 450 mm thick	m³	1.40	17.79	11.88	101.75	131.42	19.57	13.07	111.93	144.56
E101319	**Diaphragm walls:**										
E101319A	not exceeding 150 mm thick	m³	3.00	38.10	25.54	101.75	165.39	41.91	28.09	111.93	181.93
E101319B	150-450 mm thick	m³	2.30	29.21	19.60	101.75	150.56	32.13	21.56	111.93	165.62
E101319C	over 450 mm thick	m³	2.05	26.04	17.23	101.75	145.02	28.64	18.95	111.93	159.52
E101320	**Beams:**										
E101320B	generally	m³	2.80	35.56	23.76	103.00	162.32	39.12	26.14	113.30	178.55
E101321	**Beam casings:**										
E101321B	generally	m³	3.22	40.89	27.32	103.00	171.21	44.98	30.05	113.30	188.33
E101323	**Columns:**										
E101323B	generally	m³	4.00	50.80	34.16	103.00	187.96	55.88	37.58	113.30	206.76
E101324	**Column casings:**										
E101324B	generally	m³	4.60	58.42	39.26	103.00	200.68	64.26	43.19	113.30	220.75
E101325	**Staircases:**										
E101325A	generally	m³	2.80	35.56	23.76	103.00	162.32	39.12	26.14	113.30	178.55
E101326	**Upstands:**										
E101326B	generally	m³	2.75	34.93	23.17	104.17	162.27	38.42	25.49	114.59	178.50

Major Works 2009		Unit	Labour Hours	Labour Net	Plant Net	Materials Net	Unit Net	Labour Gross	Plant Gross	Materials Gross	Unit Price
								(Gross rates include 10% profit)			
				£	£	£	£	£	£	£	£
E10	**E10: MIXING, CASTING, CURING IN SITU CONCRETE**										
E1014	**Reinforced in situ concrete; mix C35P**										
E101401	**Foundations:**										
E101401B	generally	m³	1.10	13.97	9.50	106.24	129.71	15.37	10.45	116.86	142.68
E101402	**Ground beams:**										
E101402B	generally	m³	2.15	27.31	18.41	105.06	150.78	30.04	20.25	115.57	165.86
E101403	**Isolated foundations:**										
E101403B	generally	m³	2.15	27.31	18.41	105.06	150.78	30.04	20.25	115.57	165.86
E101416	**Beds:**										
E101416A	not exceeding 150 mm thick	m³	1.40	17.78	5.56	103.77	127.11	19.56	6.12	114.15	139.82
E101416B	150-450 mm thick	m³	1.00	12.70	3.89	103.77	120.36	13.97	4.28	114.15	132.40
E101416C	over 450 mm thick	m³	0.70	8.89	2.78	103.77	115.44	9.78	3.06	114.15	126.98
E101417	**Slabs:**										
E101417A	not exceeding 150 mm thick	m³	2.10	26.67	8.34	103.77	138.78	29.34	9.17	114.15	152.66
E101417B	150-450 mm thick	m³	1.55	19.68	6.12	103.77	129.57	21.65	6.73	114.15	142.53
E101417C	over 450 mm thick	m³	1.05	13.34	4.17	103.77	121.28	14.67	4.59	114.15	133.41
E101418	**Walls:**										
E101418A	not exceeding 150 mm thick	m³	2.31	29.34	19.60	103.77	152.71	32.27	21.56	114.15	167.98
E101418B	150-450 mm thick	m³	2.05	26.03	17.23	103.77	147.03	28.63	18.95	114.15	161.73
E101418C	over 450 mm thick	m³	1.40	17.78	11.88	103.77	133.43	19.56	13.07	114.15	146.77
E101419	**Diaphragm walls:**										
E101419A	not exceeding 150 mm thick	m³	3.00	38.10	25.54	103.77	167.41	41.91	28.09	114.15	184.15
E101419B	150-450 mm thick	m³	2.30	29.21	19.60	103.77	152.58	32.13	21.56	114.15	167.84
E101419C	over 450 mm thick	m³	2.05	26.03	17.23	103.77	147.03	28.63	18.95	114.15	161.73
E101420	**Beams:**										
E101420B	generally	m³	2.80	35.56	23.76	105.06	164.38	39.12	26.14	115.57	180.82
E101421	**Beam casings:**										
E101421B	generally	m³	3.22	40.89	27.32	105.06	173.27	44.98	30.05	115.57	190.60
E101423	**Columns:**										
E101423B	generally	m³	4.00	50.80	34.16	105.06	190.02	55.88	37.58	115.57	209.02
E101424	**Column casings:**										
E101424B	generally	m³	4.60	58.42	39.26	105.06	202.74	64.26	43.19	115.57	223.01
E101425	**Staircases:**										
E101425A	generally	m³	2.80	35.56	23.76	105.06	164.38	39.12	26.14	115.57	180.82
E101426	**Upstands:**										
E101426B	generally	m³	2.75	34.92	23.17	106.24	164.33	38.41	25.49	116.86	180.76

In Situ Concrete and Large PC Concrete

		Unit	Labour Hours	Labour Net	Plant Net	Materials Net	Unit Net	Labour Gross	Plant Gross	Materials Gross	Unit Price
								(Gross rates include 10% profit)			
				£	£	£	£	£	£	£	£
E10	**E10: MIXING, CASTING, CURING IN SITU CONCRETE**										
E1015	**Reinforced in situ concrete; mix C40P**										
E101501	**Foundations:**										
E101501B	generally	m³	1.10	13.97	9.50	108.32	131.79	15.37	10.45	119.15	144.97
E101502	**Ground beams:**										
E101502B	generally	m³	2.15	27.31	18.41	107.11	152.83	30.04	20.25	117.82	168.11
E101503	**Isolated foundations:**										
E101503B	generally	m³	2.15	27.31	18.41	107.11	152.83	30.04	20.25	117.82	168.11
E101516	**Beds:**										
E101516A	not exceeding 150 mm thick	m³	1.40	17.78	5.56	105.80	129.14	19.56	6.12	116.38	142.05
E101516B	150-450 mm thick	m³	1.00	12.70	3.89	105.80	122.39	13.97	4.28	116.38	134.63
E101516C	over 450 mm thick	m³	0.70	8.89	2.78	105.80	117.47	9.78	3.06	116.38	129.22
E101517	**Slabs:**										
E101517A	not exceeding 150 mm thick	m³	2.10	26.67	8.34	105.80	140.81	29.34	9.17	116.38	154.89
E101517B	150-450 mm thick	m³	1.55	19.69	6.12	105.80	131.61	21.66	6.73	116.38	144.77
E101517C	over 450 mm thick	m³	1.05	13.33	4.17	105.80	123.30	14.66	4.59	116.38	135.63
E101518	**Walls:**										
E101518A	not exceeding 150 mm thick	m³	2.31	29.34	19.60	105.80	154.74	32.27	21.56	116.38	170.21
E101518B	150-450 mm thick	m³	2.05	26.04	17.23	105.80	149.07	28.64	18.95	116.38	163.98
E101518C	over 450 mm thick	m³	1.40	17.78	11.88	105.80	135.46	19.56	13.07	116.38	149.01
E101519	**Diaphragm walls:**										
E101519A	not exceeding 150 mm thick	m³	3.00	38.10	25.54	105.80	169.44	41.91	28.09	116.38	186.38
E101519B	150-450 mm thick	m³	2.30	29.21	19.60	105.80	154.61	32.13	21.56	116.38	170.07
E101519C	over 450 mm thick	m³	2.05	26.04	17.23	105.80	149.07	28.64	18.95	116.38	163.98
E101520	**Beams:**										
E101520B	generally	m³	2.80	35.56	23.76	107.11	166.43	39.12	26.14	117.82	183.07
E101521	**Beam casings:**										
E101521B	generally	m³	3.22	40.90	27.32	107.11	175.33	44.99	30.05	117.82	192.86
E101523	**Columns:**										
E101523B	generally	m³	4.00	50.80	34.16	107.11	192.07	55.88	37.58	117.82	211.28
E101524	**Column casings:**										
E101524B	generally	m³	4.60	58.42	39.26	107.11	204.79	64.26	43.19	117.82	225.27
E101525	**Staircases:**										
E101525A	generally	m³	2.80	35.56	23.76	107.11	166.43	39.12	26.14	117.82	183.07
E101526	**Upstands:**										
E101526B	generally	m³	2.75	34.93	23.17	108.32	166.42	38.42	25.49	119.15	183.06

In Situ Concrete and Large PC Concrete

Major Works 2009		Unit	Labour Hours	Labour Net	Plant Net	Materials Net	Unit Net	Labour Gross	Plant Gross	Materials Gross	Unit Price
				£	£	£	£	£	£	£	£
								—— (Gross rates include 10% profit) ——			
E10	**E10: MIXING, CASTING, CURING IN SITU CONCRETE**										
E1021	**Wedging and grouting bases or the like**										
E102101	**Wedging up with steel shims and grouting under bases with cement mortar (1:3); 25 mm thick:**										
E102101A	not exceeding 0.10 m²	Nr	0.20	2.54	–	0.27	2.81	2.79	–	0.30	3.09
E102101B	0.10-0.25 m²	Nr	0.35	4.45	–	0.54	4.99	4.90	–	0.59	5.49
E102101C	0.25-0.50 m²	Nr	0.50	6.35	–	1.18	7.53	6.99	–	1.30	8.28
E102102	**Wedging up with steel shims and grouting under bases with cement mortar (1:3); 50 mm thick:**										
E102102D	not exceeding 0.10 m²	Nr	0.40	5.08	–	0.54	5.62	5.59	–	0.59	6.18
E102102E	0.10-0.25 m²	Nr	0.70	8.89	–	1.18	10.07	9.78	–	1.30	11.08
E102102F	0.25-0.50 m²	Nr	1.00	12.70	–	2.27	14.97	13.97	–	2.50	16.47

In Situ Concrete and Large PC Concrete

Major Works 2009		Unit	Labour Hours	Labour Net	Plant Net	Materials Net	Unit Net	Labour Gross	Plant Gross	Materials Gross	Unit Price
				£	£	£	£	£	£	£	£
								(Gross rates include 10% profit)			
E20	E20: FORMWORK FOR IN SITU CONCRETE										
E2001	Formwork to general finish										
E200101	Sides of foundations:										
E200101A	not exceeding 250 mm high	m	0.76	12.91	–	6.71	19.62	14.20	–	7.38	21.58
E200101B	250-500 mm high........	m	1.15	19.44	–	12.66	32.10	21.38	–	13.93	35.31
E200101C	500-1000 mm high	m	2.04	34.56	–	24.58	59.14	38.02	–	27.04	65.05
E200101D	over 1000 mm high	m²	1.86	31.49	–	23.31	54.80	34.64	–	25.64	60.28
E200102	Sides of ground beams and edges of beds:										
E200102A	not exceeding 250 mm high	m	0.76	12.91	–	6.71	19.62	14.20	–	7.38	21.58
E200102B	250-500 mm high.........	m	1.15	19.44	–	12.66	32.10	21.38	–	13.93	35.31
E200102C	500-1000 mm high	m	2.04	34.56	–	24.51	59.07	38.02	–	26.96	64.98
E200102D	over 1000 mm high	m²	1.86	31.49	–	23.31	54.80	34.64	–	25.64	60.28
E200103	Edges of suspended slabs:										
E200103A	not exceeding 250 mm wide	m	0.71	11.97	–	5.82	17.79	13.17	–	6.40	19.57
E200103B	250-500 mm wide	m	0.90	15.29	–	8.96	24.25	16.82	–	9.86	26.68
E200103C	500-1000 mm wide	m	1.60	27.15	0.63	15.10	42.88	29.87	0.69	16.61	47.17
E200103D	over 1000 mm wide	m²	1.46	24.76	1.25	15.96	41.97	27.24	1.38	17.56	46.17
E200104	Sides of upstands:										
E200104A	not exceeding 250 mm wide	m	0.71	11.97	–	5.82	17.79	13.17	–	6.40	19.57
E200104B	250-500 mm wide	m	0.90	15.29	–	8.96	24.25	16.82	–	9.86	26.68
E200104C	500-1000 mm wide	m	1.60	27.15	0.63	15.10	42.88	29.87	0.69	16.61	47.17
E200104D	over 1000 mm wide	m²	1.46	24.76	1.25	15.96	41.97	27.24	1.38	17.56	46.17
E200105	Steps in top surfaces:										
E200105A	not exceeding 250 mm wide	m	0.71	11.97	–	5.82	17.79	13.17	–	6.40	19.57
E200105B	250-500 mm wide	m	0.90	15.29	–	8.96	24.25	16.82	–	9.86	26.68
E200105C	500-1000 mm wide	m	1.60	27.15	0.63	15.10	42.88	29.87	0.69	16.61	47.17
E200105D	over 1000 mm wide	m²	1.46	24.76	1.25	15.96	41.97	27.24	1.38	17.56	46.17
E200106	Steps in soffits:										
E200106A	not exceeding 250 mm wide	m	1.24	21.01	0.92	8.12	30.05	23.11	1.01	8.93	33.06
E200106B	250-500 mm wide	m	1.44	24.42	0.92	20.74	46.08	26.86	1.01	22.81	50.69
E200106C	500-1000 mm wide	m	1.77	30.12	1.83	22.91	54.86	33.13	2.01	25.20	60.35
E200106D	over 1000 mm wide	m²	2.34	39.70	1.53	21.70	62.93	43.67	1.68	23.87	69.22
E200107	Machine bases and plinths:										
E200107A	not exceeding 250 mm high	m	0.76	12.91	–	50.57	63.48	14.20	–	55.63	69.83
E200107B	250-500 mm high.........	m	1.15	19.45	–	100.38	119.83	21.40	–	110.42	131.81
E200107C	500-1000 mm high	m	2.04	34.56	–	200.02	234.58	38.02	–	220.02	258.04
E200107D	over 1000 mm high	m²	1.86	31.49	–	183.23	214.72	34.64	–	201.55	236.19

Major Works 2009		Unit	Labour Hours	Labour Net	Plant Net	Materials Net	Unit Net	Labour Gross	Plant Gross	Materials Gross	Unit Price
								(Gross rates include 10% profit)			
				£	£	£	£	£	£	£	£
E20	**E20: FORMWORK FOR IN SITU CONCRETE**										
E2001	**Formwork to general finish**										
E200111	**Soffits; not exceeding 1.5 mm above floor level:**										
E200111A	not exceeding 200 mm thick	m²	1.46	24.70	0.52	21.16	46.38	27.17	0.57	23.28	51.02
E200111B	200-300 mm thick	m²	2.04	34.55	0.52	21.16	56.23	38.01	0.57	23.28	61.85
E200112	**Soffits; 1.5-3.0 m above floor level:**										
E200112E	not exceeding 200 mm thick	m²	1.79	30.36	0.52	21.16	52.04	33.40	0.57	23.28	57.24
E200112F	200-300 mm thick	m²	2.50	42.45	0.52	21.16	64.13	46.70	0.57	23.28	70.54
E200113	**Sloping soffits; not exceeding 1.5 m above floor level:**										
E200113A	not exceeding 200 mm thick	m²	1.46	24.70	0.52	21.16	46.38	27.17	0.57	23.28	51.02
E200113B	200-300 mm thick	m²	2.04	34.60	0.52	21.16	56.28	38.06	0.57	23.28	61.91
E200114	**Sloping soffits; 1.5-3.0 m above floor level:**										
E200114E	not exceeding 200 mm thick	m²	1.79	30.36	0.52	21.16	52.04	33.40	0.57	23.28	57.24
E200114F	200-300 mm thick	m²	2.50	42.45	0.52	21.16	64.13	46.70	0.57	23.28	70.54
E200125	**Top formwork; over 15 degrees from horizontal:**										
E200125A	generally	m²	1.86	31.64	–	21.98	53.62	34.80	–	24.18	58.98
E200126	**Walls:**										
E200126A	vertical surfaces	m²	1.78	30.14	1.53	13.40	45.07	33.15	1.68	14.74	49.58
E200126B	curved surfaces	m²	2.00	33.91	1.53	14.59	50.03	37.30	1.68	16.05	55.03
E200126C	conical surfaces	m²	2.66	45.22	1.72	18.67	65.61	49.74	1.89	20.54	72.17
E200126D	spherical surfaces	m²	4.44	75.35	1.91	28.88	106.14	82.89	2.10	31.77	116.75
E200126E	battering surfaces	m²	2.13	36.10	1.53	15.36	52.99	39.71	1.68	16.90	58.29
E200129	**Sides and soffits of attached beams; height to soffit:**										
E200129A	not exceeding 1.50 m......	m²	2.08	35.32	1.53	22.13	58.98	38.85	1.68	24.34	64.88
E200129B	1.51-3.00 m	m²	2.03	34.47	1.53	21.57	57.57	37.92	1.68	23.73	63.33
E200129C	3.01-4.50 m	m²	2.08	35.32	1.53	21.57	58.42	38.85	1.68	23.73	64.26
E200129D	4.51-6.00 m	m²	2.25	38.21	1.53	21.56	61.30	42.03	1.68	23.72	67.43
E200130	**Sides and soffits of isolated beams; height to soffit:**										
E200130A	not exceeding 1.50 m......	m²	2.25	38.21	2.15	21.57	61.93	42.03	2.37	23.73	68.12
E200130B	1.51-3.00 m	m²	2.20	37.36	2.15	21.57	61.08	41.10	2.37	23.73	67.19
E200130C	3.01-4.50 m	m²	2.32	39.34	2.15	21.58	63.07	43.27	2.37	23.74	69.38
E200130D	4.51-6.00 m	m²	2.43	41.26	2.15	21.16	64.57	45.39	2.37	23.28	71.03

In Situ Concrete and Large PC Concrete

Major Works 2009		Unit	Labour Hours	Labour Net	Plant Net	Materials Net	Unit Net	Labour Gross	Plant Gross	Materials Gross	Unit Price
								(Gross rates include 10% profit)			
				£	£	£	£	£	£	£	£
E20	**E20: FORMWORK FOR IN SITU CONCRETE**										
E2001	**Formwork to general finish**										
E200131	**Sides and soffits of sloping attached beams; height to soffit:**										
E200131A	not exceeding 1.50 m......	m²	2.39	40.58	1.53	21.57	63.68	44.64	1.68	23.73	70.05
E200131B	1.51-3.00 m	m²	2.34	39.73	1.53	23.37	64.63	43.70	1.68	25.71	71.09
E200131C	3.01-4.50 m	m²	2.46	41.77	1.52	21.60	64.89	45.95	1.67	23.76	71.38
E200131D	4.51-6.00 m	m²	2.58	43.81	1.53	21.70	67.04	48.19	1.68	23.87	73.74
E200132	**Sides and soffits of sloping isolated beams; height to soffit:**										
E200132A	not exceeding 1.50 m......	m²	2.70	45.85	2.15	21.57	69.57	50.44	2.37	23.73	76.53
E200132B	1.51-3.00 m	m²	2.63	44.66	2.15	21.57	68.38	49.13	2.37	23.73	75.22
E200132C	3.01-4.50 m	m²	2.76	46.86	2.15	21.60	70.61	51.55	2.37	23.76	77.67
E200132D	4.51-6.00 m	m²	2.90	49.24	2.15	21.70	73.09	54.16	2.37	23.87	80.40
E200135	**Sides and soffits of attached beam casings; height to soffit:**										
E200135A	not exceeding 1.50 m......	m²	2.08	35.32	0.92	21.57	57.81	38.85	1.01	23.73	63.59
E200135B	1.51-3.00 m	m²	2.03	34.47	0.92	21.57	56.96	37.92	1.01	23.73	62.66
E200135C	3.01-4.50 m	m²	2.13	36.16	0.92	21.51	58.59	39.78	1.01	23.66	64.45
E200135D	4.51-6.00 m	m²	2.24	38.07	0.92	21.16	60.15	41.88	1.01	23.28	66.17
E200136	**Sides and soffits of isolated beam casings; height to soffit:**										
E200136A	not exceeding 1.50 m......	m²	2.26	38.38	2.15	21.57	62.10	42.22	2.37	23.73	68.31
E200136B	1.51-3.00 m	m²	2.20	37.36	2.15	21.57	61.08	41.10	2.37	23.73	67.19
E200136C	3.01-4.50 m	m²	2.31	39.22	2.15	21.86	63.23	43.14	2.37	24.05	69.55
E200136D	4.50-6.00 m	m²	2.43	41.26	2.15	21.16	64.57	45.39	2.37	23.28	71.03

In Situ Concrete and Large PC Concrete

Major Works 2009		Unit	Labour Hours	Labour Net	Plant Net	Materials Net	Unit Net	Labour Gross	Plant Gross	Materials Gross	Unit Price
				£	£	£	£	£	£	£	£
								(Gross rates include 10% profit)			
E20	E20: FORMWORK FOR IN SITU CONCRETE										
E2001	Formwork to general finish										
E200137	Sides of isolated rectangular columns:										
E200137A	not exceeding 250 mm wide	m²	2.26	38.38	0.92	21.57	60.87	42.22	1.01	23.73	66.96
E200137B	250-500 mm wide	m²	2.20	37.35	0.92	21.57	59.84	41.09	1.01	23.73	65.82
E200137C	500-1000 mm wide	m²	2.31	39.22	0.92	21.51	61.65	43.14	1.01	23.66	67.82
E200137D	over 1000 mm wide	m²	2.43	41.26	0.92	21.50	63.68	45.39	1.01	23.65	70.05
E200139	Sides of isolated circular columns:										
E200139A	not exceeding 300 mm diameter	m²	1.71	29.04	1.06	14.76	44.86	31.94	1.17	16.24	49.35
E200139B	300-600 mm diameter	m²	1.40	23.77	0.53	12.94	37.24	26.15	0.58	14.23	40.96
E200139C	600-900 mm diameter	m²	1.25	21.23	0.35	11.08	32.66	23.35	0.39	12.19	35.93
E200139D	over 900 mm diameter	m²	1.18	20.04	0.27	9.24	29.55	22.04	0.30	10.16	32.51
E200145	Grooves, throats, rebates, chamfers or the like; sectional area:										
E200145A	2500-5000 mm²	m	0.26	4.46	–	3.92	8.38	4.91	–	4.31	9.22
E200145B	5000-10000 mm²	m	0.69	11.68	–	7.73	19.41	12.85	–	8.50	21.35
E200145C	10000-20000 mm²	m	0.83	14.01	–	13.65	27.66	15.41	–	15.02	30.43
E200163	Wall ends, soffits and steps in walls:										
E200163A	not exceeding 250 mm wide	m	0.50	8.54	–	5.72	14.26	9.39	–	6.29	15.69
E200163B	250-500 mm wide	m	0.69	11.68	–	15.42	27.10	12.85	–	16.96	29.81
E200163C	500-1000 mm wide	m	0.83	14.01	1.15	15.79	30.95	15.41	1.27	17.37	34.05
E200163D	over 1000 mm wide	m²	0.75	12.77	1.53	15.28	29.58	14.05	1.68	16.81	32.54
E200164	Openings in walls:										
E200164A	not exceeding 250 mm wide	m	0.50	8.54	–	5.72	14.26	9.39	–	6.29	15.69
E200164B	250-500 mm wide	m	0.69	11.68	–	15.42	27.10	12.85	–	16.96	29.81
E200164C	500-1000 mm wide	m	0.83	14.01	1.15	15.79	30.95	15.41	1.27	17.37	34.05
E200164D	over 1000 mm wide	m²	0.75	12.77	1.53	15.28	29.58	14.05	1.68	16.81	32.54
E200175	Staircases:										
E200175A	not exceeding 250 mm wide	m	0.41	6.94	–	5.82	12.76	7.63	–	6.40	14.04
E200175B	250-500 mm wide	m	0.85	14.36	–	15.32	29.68	15.80	–	16.85	32.65
E200175C	500-1000 mm wide	m	1.02	17.24	–	15.11	32.35	18.96	–	16.62	35.59
E200175D	over 1000 mm wide	m²	0.93	15.71	–	15.02	30.73	17.28	–	16.52	33.80

In Situ Concrete and Large PC Concrete

Major Works 2009		Unit	Labour Hours	Labour Net	Plant Net	Materials Net	Unit Net	Labour Gross	Plant Gross	Materials Gross	Unit Price
								(Gross rates include 10% profit)			
				£	£	£	£	£	£	£	£
E20	E20: FORMWORK FOR IN SITU CONCRETE										
E2016	Holodeck galvanised steel permanent formwork weighing 14.3 Kg/m² ; laid horizontally										
E201642	Not exceeding 3.5 m above floor level; strutting and supports at:										
E201642A	2500-3000 mm centres....	m²	0.30	5.16	0.25	18.63	24.04	5.68	0.28	20.49	26.44
E201642B	3000-3500 mm centres....	m²	0.28	4.81	0.21	18.60	23.62	5.29	0.23	20.46	25.98
E201642C	3500-4000 mm centres....	m²	0.27	4.60	0.18	18.59	23.37	5.06	0.20	20.45	25.71
E201643	3.5-5.0 m above floor level; strutting and supports at:										
E201643A	2500-3000 mm centres....	m²	0.33	5.54	0.25	18.63	24.42	6.09	0.28	20.49	26.86
E201643B	3000-3500 mm centres....	m²	0.30	5.11	0.21	18.60	23.92	5.62	0.23	20.46	26.31
E201643C	3500-4000 mm centres....	m²	0.39	6.55	0.18	18.59	25.32	7.21	0.20	20.45	27.85
E2017	Super Holorib galvanised steel permanent formwork weighing 13.27 Kg/m² (0.9 mm gauge); laid horizontally										
E201745	Not exceeding 3.5 m above floor level; strutting and supports at:										
E201745A	2500-3000 mm centres....	m²	0.29	4.92	0.25	20.90	26.07	5.41	0.28	22.99	28.68
E201745B	3000-3500 mm centres....	m²	0.27	4.57	0.21	20.87	25.65	5.03	0.23	22.96	28.22
E201745C	3500-4000 mm centres....	m²	0.26	4.37	0.18	20.86	25.41	4.81	0.20	22.95	27.95
E201746	3.5-5.0 m above floor level; strutting and supports at:										
E201746A	2500-3000 mm centres....	m²	0.31	5.30	0.25	20.90	26.45	5.83	0.28	22.99	29.10
E201746B	3000-3500 mm centres....	m²	0.29	4.87	0.21	20.87	25.95	5.36	0.23	22.96	28.55
E201746C	3500-4000 mm centres....	m²	0.27	4.62	0.18	20.86	25.66	5.08	0.20	22.95	28.23
E2018	Super Holorib galvanised steel permanent formwork weighing 17.69 Kg/m² (1.2 mm gauge); laid horizontally										
E201848	Not exceeding 3.5 m above floor level; strutting and supports at:										
E201848A	2500-3000 mm centres....	m²	0.35	5.96	0.25	26.03	32.24	6.56	0.28	28.63	35.46
E201848B	3000-3500 mm centres....	m²	0.33	5.61	0.21	26.00	31.82	6.17	0.23	28.60	35.00
E201848C	3500-4000 mm centres....	m²	0.32	5.40	0.18	25.99	31.57	5.94	0.20	28.59	34.73
E201849	3.5-5.0 m above floor level; strutting and supports at:										
E201849A	2500-3000 mm centres....	m²	0.37	6.34	0.25	26.03	32.62	6.97	0.28	28.63	35.88
E201849B	3000-3500 mm centres....	m²	0.35	5.91	0.21	26.00	32.12	6.50	0.23	28.60	35.33
E201849C	3500-4000 mm centres....	m²	0.33	5.65	0.18	25.99	31.82	6.22	0.20	28.59	35.00

Major Works 2009		Unit	Labour Hours	Labour Net	Plant Net	Materials Net	Unit Net	Labour Gross	Plant Gross	Materials Gross	Unit Price
								(Gross rates include 10% profit)			
				£	£	£	£	£	£	£	£
E20	**E20: FORMWORK FOR IN SITU CONCRETE**										
E2020	**Formwork to provide special finishes**										
E202031	**Extra over formwork to general finish for fair face formed with:**										
E202031A	wrought face timber lining .	m²	0.17	2.88	–	7.42	10.30	3.17	–	8.16	11.33
E202031B	oil tempered hardboard lining	m²	–	–	–	0.61	0.61	–	–	0.67	0.67
E202031C	plastic faced plywood lining	m²	–	–	–	1.05	1.05	–	–	1.16	1.16
E202031D	application of silver sand and cement mortar to surface imperfections and rubbing down with a carborundum stone	m²	0.11	1.87	–	0.12	1.99	2.06	–	0.13	2.19
E202032	**Extra over formwork to general finish for forming ribbed or fluted finish; planted timber fillets:**										
E202032A	38 × 50 mm at 100 mm centres	m²	0.63	10.69	–	229.37	240.06	11.76	–	252.31	264.07
E202032B	50 × 50 mm at 150 mm centres	m²	0.43	7.30	–	153.76	161.06	8.03	–	169.14	177.17
E202032C	75 × 75 mm at 200 mm centres	m²	0.35	5.94	–	118.85	124.79	6.53	–	130.74	137.27
E202032D	50 × 100 mm at 300 mm centres	m²	0.27	4.58	–	78.27	82.85	5.04	–	86.10	91.14
E202033	**Extra over formwork to general finish for exposed aggregate finish:**										
E202033A	applying retarding agent to shutter face; brushing off concrete laitance after striking	m²	0.47	7.98	–	0.19	8.17	8.78	–	0.21	8.99

In Situ Concrete and Large PC Concrete

Major Works 2009		Unit	Labour Hours	Labour Net	Plant Net	Materials Net	Unit Net	Labour Gross	Plant Gross	Materials Gross	Unit Price
								(Gross rates include 10% profit)			
				£	£	£	£	£	£	£	£
E30	**E30: REINFORCEMENT FOR IN SITU CONCRETE**										
E3010	**Bar reinforcement; mild steel bars, BS 4449, delivered to site cut, bent and labelled**										
E301003	**Bars, fixing with tying wire:**										
E301003A	6 mm	Tonne	72.00	1065.60	–	1010.45	2076.05	1172.16	–	1111.50	2283.66
E301003B	8 mm	Tonne	54.00	799.20	–	983.46	1782.66	879.12	–	1081.81	1960.93
E301003C	10 mm	Tonne	44.00	651.20	–	920.30	1571.50	716.32	–	1012.33	1728.65
E301003D	12 mm	Tonne	38.00	562.40	–	878.02	1440.42	618.64	–	965.82	1584.46
E301003E	16 mm	Tonne	30.00	444.00	–	818.60	1262.60	488.40	–	900.46	1388.86
E301003F	20 mm	Tonne	26.00	384.80	–	804.14	1188.94	423.28	–	884.55	1307.83
E301003G	25 mm	Tonne	23.00	340.40	–	780.91	1121.31	374.44	–	859.00	1233.44
E301003H	32 mm	Tonne	20.00	296.00	–	768.81	1064.81	325.60	–	845.69	1171.29
E301003I	40 mm	Tonne	17.00	251.60	–	755.77	1007.37	276.76	–	831.35	1108.11
E3011	**Bar reinforcement; high yield steel bars, BS 4449, delivered to site cut, bent and labelled**										
E301105	**Bars, fixing with tying wire:**										
E301105A	6 mm	Tonne	72.00	1065.60	–	1098.27	2163.87	1172.16	–	1208.10	2380.26
E301105B	8 mm	Tonne	54.00	799.20	–	1073.24	1872.44	879.12	–	1180.56	2059.68
E301105C	10 mm	Tonne	44.00	651.20	–	1004.79	1655.99	716.32	–	1105.27	1821.59
E301105D	12 mm	Tonne	38.00	562.40	–	958.98	1521.38	618.64	–	1054.88	1673.52
E301105E	16 mm	Tonne	30.00	444.00	–	894.29	1338.29	488.40	–	983.72	1472.12
E301105F	20 mm	Tonne	26.00	384.80	–	878.96	1263.76	423.28	–	966.86	1390.14
E301105G	25 mm	Tonne	23.00	340.40	–	853.94	1194.34	374.44	–	939.33	1313.77
E301105H	32 mm	Tonne	20.00	296.00	–	840.96	1136.96	325.60	–	925.06	1250.66
E301105I	40 mm	Tonne	17.00	251.60	–	827.06	1078.66	276.76	–	909.77	1186.53
E3012	**Bar reinforcement; stainless steel bars type 316 S66, delivered to site cut, bent and labelled**										
E301207	**Plain bars, fixing with stainless steel tying wire:**										
E301207A	10 mm	Tonne	44.00	651.20	–	3785.23	4436.43	716.32	–	4163.75	4880.07
E301207B	12 mm	Tonne	38.00	562.40	–	3771.49	4333.89	618.64	–	4148.64	4767.28
E301207C	16 mm	Tonne	30.00	444.00	–	3697.86	4141.86	488.40	–	4067.65	4556.05
E301207D	20 mm	Tonne	26.00	384.80	–	3688.40	4073.20	423.28	–	4057.24	4480.52
E301207E	25 mm	Tonne	23.00	340.40	–	3846.46	4186.86	374.44	–	4231.11	4605.55
E301207F	32 mm	Tonne	20.00	296.00	–	3843.64	4139.64	325.60	–	4228.00	4553.60
E301208	**Ribbed bars, fixing with stainless steel tying wire:**										
E301208A	10 mm	Tonne	44.00	651.20	–	3785.23	4436.43	716.32	–	4163.75	4880.07
E301208B	12 mm	Tonne	38.00	562.40	–	3771.49	4333.89	618.64	–	4148.64	4767.28
E301208C	16 mm	Tonne	30.00	444.00	–	3697.86	4141.86	488.40	–	4067.65	4556.05
E301208D	20 mm	Tonne	26.00	384.80	–	3688.40	4073.20	423.28	–	4057.24	4480.52
E301208E	25 mm	Tonne	23.00	340.40	–	3846.46	4186.86	374.44	–	4231.11	4605.55
E301208F	32 mm	Tonne	20.00	296.00	–	3843.64	4139.64	325.60	–	4228.00	4553.60

Major Works 2009		Unit	Labour Hours	Labour Net	Plant Net	Materials Net	Unit Net	Labour Gross	Plant Gross	Materials Gross	Unit Price
									(Gross rates include 10% profit)		
				£	£	£	£	£	£	£	£
E30	**E30: REINFORCEMENT FOR IN SITU CONCRETE**										
E3040	**Steel fabric reinforcement, BS 4483, delivered to site in standard sheets**										
E304022	**Fabric reinforcement, laid horizontally; ref:**										
E304022A	A98; 1.54 kg/m^2	m^2	0.02	0.30	–	1.95	2.25	0.33	–	2.15	2.48
E304022B	A142; 2.22 kg/m^2	m^2	0.03	0.46	–	2.49	2.95	0.51	–	2.74	3.25
E304022C	A193; 3.02 kg/m^2	m^2	0.03	0.44	–	3.32	3.76	0.48	–	3.65	4.14
E304022D	A252; 3.95 kg/m^2	m^2	0.03	0.45	–	4.30	4.75	0.50	–	4.73	5.23
E304022E	A393; 6.16 kg/m^2	m^2	0.05	0.74	–	6.76	7.50	0.81	–	7.44	8.25
E304022F	B196; 3.05 kg/m^2	m^2	0.03	0.45	–	3.52	3.97	0.50	–	3.87	4.37
E304022G	B283; 3.73 kg/m^2	m^2	0.03	0.45	–	4.13	4.58	0.50	–	4.54	5.04
E304022H	B385; 4.53 kg/m^2	m^2	0.04	0.62	–	4.94	5.56	0.68	–	5.43	6.12
E304022I	B503; 5.93kg/m^2	m^2	0.05	0.75	–	6.31	7.06	0.83	–	6.94	7.77
E304022J	B785; 8.14 kg/m^2	m^2	0.05	0.74	–	8.05	8.79	0.81	–	8.86	9.67
E304022K	B1131; 10.90 kg/m^2	m^2	0.07	1.04	–	10.72	11.76	1.14	–	11.79	12.94
E304022L	C283; 2.61 kg/m^2	m^2	0.03	0.45	–	3.11	3.56	0.50	–	3.42	3.92
E304022M	C385; 3.41 kg/m^2	m^2	0.03	0.45	–	3.94	4.39	0.50	–	4.33	4.83
E304022N	C503; 4.34 kg/m^2	m^2	0.04	0.62	–	4.88	5.50	0.68	–	5.37	6.05
E304022O	C636; 5.55 kg/m^2	m^2	0.04	0.60	–	6.18	6.78	0.66	–	6.80	7.46
E304022P	C785; 6.72 kg/m^2	m^2	0.05	0.74	–	6.82	7.56	0.81	–	7.50	8.32
E304023	**Fabric reinforcement fixed vertically; ref:**										
E304023A	A98; 1.54 kg/m^2	m^2	0.08	1.18	–	1.89	3.07	1.30	–	2.08	3.38
E304023B	A142; 2.22 kg/m^2	m^2	0.09	1.33	–	2.43	3.76	1.46	–	2.67	4.14
E304023C	A193; 3.02 kg/m^2	m^2	0.09	1.33	–	3.26	4.59	1.46	–	3.59	5.05
E304023D	A252; 3.95 kg/m^2	m^2	0.09	1.33	–	4.24	5.57	1.46	–	4.66	6.13
E304023E	A393; 6.16 kg/m^2	m^2	0.02	0.23	–	6.70	6.93	0.25	–	7.37	7.62
E304023F	B196; 3.05 kg/m^2	m^2	0.09	1.33	–	3.46	4.79	1.46	–	3.81	5.27
E304023G	B283; 3.73 kg/m^2	m^2	0.10	1.48	–	4.07	5.55	1.63	–	4.48	6.11
E304023H	B385; 4.53 kg/m^2	m^2	0.12	1.78	–	4.87	6.65	1.96	–	5.36	7.32
E304023I	B503; 5.93 kg/m^2	m^2	0.16	2.37	–	6.24	8.61	2.61	–	6.86	9.47
E304023J	B785; 8.14 kg/m^2	m^2	0.20	2.96	–	7.99	10.95	3.26	–	8.79	12.05
E304023K	B1131; 10.90 kg/m^2	m^2	0.22	3.25	–	10.66	13.91	3.58	–	11.73	15.30
E304023L	C283; 2.61 kg/m^2	m^2	0.08	1.19	–	3.05	4.24	1.31	–	3.36	4.66
E304023M	C385; 3.41 kg/m^2	m^2	0.09	1.33	–	3.88	5.21	1.46	–	4.27	5.73
E304023N	C503; 4.34 kg/m^2	m^2	0.12	1.78	–	4.81	6.59	1.96	–	5.29	7.25
E304023O	C636; 5.55 kg/m^2	m^2	0.15	2.22	–	6.12	8.34	2.44	–	6.73	9.17
E304023P	C785; 6.72 kg/m^2	m^2	0.16	2.36	–	6.76	9.12	2.60	–	7.44	10.03
E304024	**Fabric wrapping to column and beam casings; ref:**										
E304024A	D49	m^2	0.32	4.74	–	0.74	5.48	5.21	–	0.81	6.03
E304024B	D98	m^2	0.32	4.74	–	1.70	6.44	5.21	–	1.87	7.08

In Situ Concrete and Large PC Concrete

Major Works 2009		Unit	Labour Hours	Labour Net	Plant Net	Materials Net	Unit Net	Labour Gross	Plant Gross	Materials Gross	Unit Price
								(Gross rates include 10% profit)			
				£	£	£	£	£	£	£	£
E30	**E30: REINFORCEMENT FOR IN SITU CONCRETE**										
E3041	**Expament Hy-rib self centering reinforcement and permanent formwork with one rib side laps and 150 mm end laps; laid horizontally; ref 2411 weighing 5.71 Kg/m^2**										
E304132	**Not exceeding 3.5 m above floor level; strutting and supports at:**										
E304132A	450 mm centres	m^2	0.65	11.04	1.39	16.80	29.23	12.14	1.53	18.48	32.15
E304132B	600 mm centres	m^2	0.60	10.19	1.04	16.61	27.84	11.21	1.14	18.27	30.62
E304132C	900 mm centres	m^2	0.45	7.64	0.69	16.42	24.75	8.40	0.76	18.06	27.23
E304132D	1200 mm centres	m^2	0.38	6.45	0.52	16.32	23.29	7.10	0.57	17.95	25.62
E304133	**3.5-5.0 m above floor level; strutting and supports at:**										
E304133A	450 mm centres	m^2	0.78	13.24	1.39	16.80	31.43	14.56	1.53	18.48	34.57
E304133B	600 mm centres	m^2	0.71	12.06	1.04	16.61	29.71	13.27	1.14	18.27	32.68
E304133C	900 mm centres	m^2	0.54	9.17	0.69	16.42	26.28	10.09	0.76	18.06	28.91
E304133D	1200 mm centres	m^2	0.45	7.64	0.52	16.32	24.48	8.40	0.57	17.95	26.93
E3042	**Expamet Hy-rib self centering reinforcement and permanent formwork with one rib side laps and 150 mm end laps; laid horizontally; ref 2611 weighing 4.02 Kg/m^2**										
E304235	**Not exceeding 3.5 m above floor level; strutting and supports at:**										
E304235A	450 mm centres	m^2	0.67	11.38	1.39	15.01	27.78	12.52	1.53	16.51	30.56
E304235B	600 mm centres	m^2	0.62	10.52	1.04	14.81	26.37	11.57	1.14	16.29	29.01
E304235C	900 mm centres	m^2	0.47	7.98	0.69	14.62	23.29	8.78	0.76	16.08	25.62
E304235D	1200 mm centres	m^2	0.40	6.79	0.52	14.53	21.84	7.47	0.57	15.98	24.02
E304236	**3.5-5.0 m above floor level; strutting and supports at:**										
E304236A	450 mm centres	m^2	0.80	13.59	1.39	15.01	29.99	14.95	1.53	16.51	32.99
E304236B	600 mm centres	m^2	0.64	10.86	1.04	14.81	26.71	11.95	1.14	16.29	29.38
E304236C	900 mm centres	m^2	0.49	8.32	0.69	14.62	23.63	9.15	0.76	16.08	25.99
E304236D	1200 mm centres	m^2	0.42	7.13	0.52	14.53	22.18	7.84	0.57	15.98	24.40

Major Works 2009		Unit	Labour Hours	Labour Net	Plant Net	Materials Net	Unit Net	Labour Gross	Plant Gross	Materials Gross	Unit Price
								(Gross rates include 10% profit)			
				£	£	£	£	£	£	£	£
E40	**E40: DESIGNED JOINTS IN IN SITU CONCRETE**										
E4002	**Plain joints**										
E400223	**Horizontal joints; including 4 uses of formwork materials and zero waste in use:**										
E400223B	not exceeding 150 mm high	m	0.72	12.22	–	7.44	19.66	13.44	–	8.18	21.63
E400223E	150-300 mm high........	m	0.82	13.93	–	29.80	43.73	15.32	–	32.78	48.10
E400224	**Vertical joints; including 4 uses of formwork materials and zero waste in use:**										
E400224B	not exceeding 150 mm wide	m	0.45	7.64	–	4.28	11.92	8.40	–	4.71	13.11
E400224E	150-300 mm wide	m	0.52	8.83	0.19	7.79	16.81	9.71	0.21	8.57	18.49
E4003	**Keyed joints**										
E400326	**Horizontal joints; including 4 uses of formwork materials and zero waste in use:**										
E400326B	not exceeding 150 mm high	m	0.77	13.08	–	7.64	20.72	14.39	–	8.40	22.79
E400326E	150-300 mm high........	m	0.82	13.93	–	30.21	44.14	15.32	–	33.23	48.55
E400327	**Vertical joints; including 4 uses of formwork materials and zero waste in use:**										
E400327B	not exceeding 150 mm wide	m	0.50	8.49	–	5.83	14.32	9.34	–	6.41	15.75
E400327E	150-300 mm wide	m	0.57	9.67	0.19	9.52	19.38	10.64	0.21	10.47	21.32
E4004	**Movement joints**										
E400429	**Horizontal joints; including formwork; 25 mm mild steel dowel bars 600 mm long debonded for half length, dowel caps with compressible filler; notching formwork for dowels at 300 mm centres:**										
E400429B	not exceeding 150 mm high	m	1.09	18.51	–	18.33	36.84	20.36	–	20.16	40.52
E400429E	150-300 mm high........	m	1.19	20.21	–	40.73	60.94	22.23	–	44.80	67.03
E400430	**Vertical joints; including formwork; 25 mm mild steel dowel bars 600 mm long debonded for half length, dowel caps with compressible filler; notching formwork for dowels at 300 mm centres:**										
E400430B	not exceeding 150 mm wide	m	0.82	13.92	–	15.13	29.05	15.31	–	16.64	31.96
E400430E	150-300 mm wide	m	0.89	15.11	0.19	18.65	33.95	16.62	0.21	20.52	37.35

In Situ Concrete and Large PC Concrete

Major Works 2009		Unit	Labour Hours	Labour Net	Plant Net	Materials Net	Unit Net	Labour Gross	Plant Gross	Materials Gross	Unit Price
								(Gross rates include 10% profit)			
				£	£	£	£	£	£	£	£
E40	**E40: DESIGNED JOINTS IN IN SITU CONCRETE**										
E4010	**Schlegal crack inducer**										
E401032	**Horizontal joints; placing in position:**										
E401032A	generally	m	0.25	4.24	–	1.59	5.83	4.66	–	1.75	6.41
E4011	**Serviseal PVC waterstops**										
E401142	**Flat dumbell:**										
E401142A	100 mm wide	m	0.12	2.04	–	4.07	6.11	2.24	–	4.48	6.72
E401142B	170 mm wide	m	0.13	2.21	–	5.71	7.92	2.43	–	6.28	8.71
E401142C	210 mm wide	m	0.16	2.72	–	7.33	10.05	2.99	–	8.06	11.06
E401142D	250 mm wide	m	0.18	3.05	–	8.55	11.60	3.36	–	9.41	12.76
E401143	**Centre bulb:**										
E401143A	160 mm wide	m	0.12	2.04	–	5.71	7.75	2.24	–	6.28	8.53
E401143B	210 mm wide	m	0.13	2.21	–	7.33	9.54	2.43	–	8.06	10.49
E401143C	260 mm wide	m	0.18	3.05	–	8.55	11.60	3.36	–	9.41	12.76
E401143D	325 mm wide	m	0.21	3.56	–	16.31	19.87	3.92	–	17.94	21.86
E401144	**Servi-tite flat dumbell CJ:**										
E401144A	150 mm wide	m	0.12	2.04	–	11.20	13.24	2.24	–	12.32	14.56
E401144B	230 mm wide	m	0.15	2.54	–	15.28	17.82	2.79	–	16.81	19.60
E401144C	305 mm wide	m	0.18	3.05	–	28.51	31.56	3.36	–	31.36	34.72
E401145	**Servi-tite centre bulb XJ:**										
E401145A	150 mm wide	m	0.12	2.04	–	12.22	14.26	2.24	–	13.44	15.69
E401145B	230 mm wide	m	0.15	2.55	–	16.80	19.35	2.81	–	18.48	21.29
E401145C	305 mm wide	m	0.18	3.05	–	28.51	31.56	3.36	–	31.36	34.72
E4021	**Sinkings, channels or the like**										
E402153	**Form sinkings, channels or the like in face of concrete; including 4 uses of formwork materials with zero waste in use; horizontally:**										
E402153A	not exceeding 150 mm girth	m	0.42	7.19	–	5.23	12.42	7.91	–	5.75	13.66
E402153B	150-300 mm girth	m	0.85	14.36	–	8.26	22.62	15.80	–	9.09	24.88
E402153C	over 300 mm girth	m²	1.46	24.76	–	15.83	40.59	27.24	–	17.41	44.65
E402154	**Form sinkings, channels or the like in face of concrete; including 4 uses of formwork materials with zero waste in use; vertically:**										
E402154A	not exceeding 150 mm girth	m	0.34	5.77	–	2.95	8.72	6.35	–	3.25	9.59
E402154B	150-300 mm girth	m	0.60	10.19	–	5.76	15.95	11.21	–	6.34	17.55
E402154C	over 300 mm girth	m²	0.75	12.73	–	15.28	28.01	14.00	–	16.81	30.81

In Situ Concrete and Large PC Concrete

Major Works 2009		Unit	Labour Hours	Labour Net	Plant Net	Materials Net	Unit Net	Labour Gross	Plant Gross	Materials Gross	Unit Price
								(Gross rates include 10% profit)			
				£	£	£	£	£	£	£	£
E40	**E40: DESIGNED JOINTS IN IN SITU CONCRETE**										
E4041	**Expansion materials**										
E404111	**Flexcell fibreboard compressible joint filler; 10 mm thick:**										
E404111A	not exceeding 150 mm wide	m	0.10	1.70	–	1.76	3.46	1.87	–	1.94	3.81
E404111B	150-300 mm wide	m	0.18	2.97	–	3.51	6.48	3.27	–	3.86	7.13
E404111C	300-450 mm wide	m	0.22	3.74	–	5.26	9.00	4.11	–	5.79	9.90
E404112	**Flexcell fibreboard compressible joint filler; 13 mm thick:**										
E404112A	not exceeding 150 mm wide	m	0.11	1.79	–	1.57	3.36	1.97	–	1.73	3.70
E404112B	150-300 mm wide	m	0.18	3.06	–	3.13	6.19	3.37	–	3.44	6.81
E404112C	300-450 mm wide	m	0.23	3.82	–	4.71	8.53	4.20	–	5.18	9.38
E404113	**Flexcell fibreboard compressible joint filler; 19 mm thick:**										
E404113A	not exceeding 150 mm wide	m	0.12	1.96	–	2.88	4.84	2.16	–	3.17	5.32
E404113B	150-300 mm wide	m	0.20	3.31	–	5.75	9.06	3.64	–	6.33	9.97
E404113C	300-450 mm wide	m	0.23	3.91	–	8.63	12.54	4.30	–	9.49	13.79
E404114	**Flexcell fibreboard compressible joint filler; 25 mm thick:**										
E404114A	not exceeding 150 mm wide	m	0.13	2.13	–	2.83	4.96	2.34	–	3.11	5.46
E404114B	150-300 mm wide	m	0.20	3.31	–	5.65	8.96	3.64	–	6.22	9.86
E404114C	300-450 mm wide	m	0.24	4.08	–	8.48	12.56	4.49	–	9.33	13.82

In Situ Concrete and Large PC Concrete

Major Works 2009		Unit	Labour Hours	Labour Net	Plant Net	Materials Net	Unit Net	Labour Gross	Plant Gross	Materials Gross	Unit Price
								—— (Gross rates include 10% profit) ——			
				£	£	£	£	£	£	£	£
E40	E40: DESIGNED JOINTS IN IN SITU CONCRETE										
E4042	Joint sealants										
E404234	Hot poured bituminous rubber compound:										
E404234A	10 × 25mm...........	m	0.03	0.42	0.21	1.77	2.40	0.46	0.23	1.95	2.64
E404234B	13 × 25mm...........	m	0.03	0.51	0.24	2.10	2.85	0.56	0.26	2.31	3.14
E404234C	19 × 25mm...........	m	0.04	0.68	0.26	3.32	4.26	0.75	0.29	3.65	4.69
E404234D	25 × 25mm...........	m	0.06	1.01	0.30	4.58	5.89	1.11	0.33	5.04	6.48
E404235	Cold poured polysulphide rubber compound:										
E404235A	10 × 25mm...........	m	0.03	0.52	–	3.89	4.41	0.57	–	4.28	4.85
E404235B	13 × 25mm...........	m	0.03	0.51	–	5.07	5.58	0.56	–	5.58	6.14
E404235C	19 × 25mm...........	m	0.04	0.70	–	7.41	8.11	0.77	–	8.15	8.92
E404235D	25 × 25mm...........	m	0.06	1.02	–	9.71	10.73	1.12	–	10.68	11.80
E404236	Cold poured polysulphide epoxy based compound:										
E404236A	10 × 25mm...........	m	0.03	0.52	–	0.64	1.16	0.57	–	0.70	1.28
E404236B	13 × 25mm...........	m	0.03	0.51	–	0.84	1.35	0.56	–	0.92	1.49
E404236C	19 × 25mm...........	m	0.04	0.70	–	1.21	1.91	0.77	–	1.33	2.10
E404236D	25 × 25mm...........	m	0.06	1.02	–	1.98	3.00	1.12	–	2.18	3.30
E404237	Gun grade polysulphide rubber compound:										
E404237A	10 × 10mm...........	m	0.04	0.68	–	0.49	1.17	0.75	–	0.54	1.29
E404237B	13 × 13mm...........	m	0.06	1.02	–	0.83	1.85	1.12	–	0.91	2.04
E404237C	19 × 19mm...........	m	0.13	2.21	–	1.75	3.96	2.43	–	1.93	4.36
E404237D	25 × 25mm...........	m	0.23	3.90	–	3.00	6.90	4.29	–	3.30	7.59

In Situ Concrete and Large PC Concrete

Major Works 2009		Unit	Labour Hours	Labour Net	Plant Net	Materials Net	Unit Net	Labour Gross	Plant Gross	Materials Gross	Unit Price
				£	£	£	£	£	£	£	£
								(Gross rates include 10% profit)			
E41	**E41: WORKED FINISHES AND CUTTING TO IN SITU CONCRETE**										
E4101	**Surface finishes**										
E410102	**Trowelling surfaces of concrete:**										
E410102A	to levels	m²	0.16	2.03	–	–	2.03	2.23	–	–	2.23
E410102B	to falls and crossfalls	m²	0.25	3.18	–	–	3.18	3.50	–	–	3.50
E410103	**Power floating and trowelling concrete surfaces:**										
E410103A	to levels	m²	0.15	1.91	0.59	–	2.50	2.10	0.65	–	2.75
E410103B	to falls and crossfalls	m²	0.18	2.29	0.70	–	2.99	2.52	0.77	–	3.29
E410104	**Lithurin surface hardener applied in accordance with manufacturer's instructions to surfaces of concrete; brush applied:**										
E410104A	two coats to general surfaces of floors	m²	0.16	2.03	–	2.27	4.30	2.23	–	2.50	4.73
E410105	**Bush hammer treatment to surfaces of concrete:**										
E410105A	vertical surfaces	m²	0.50	6.35	3.84	–	10.19	6.99	4.22	–	11.21
E410105B	horizontal upper faces	m²	0.40	5.08	3.07	–	8.15	5.59	3.38	–	8.97
E410105C	horizontal soffits	m²	0.65	8.26	4.99	–	13.25	9.09	5.49	–	14.58
E42	**E42: ACCESSORIES CAST INTO IN SITU CONCRETE**										
E4210	**Anchor bolts**										
E421010	**Steel anchor bolts; indented; with nut; BS 916: 1953; size:**										
E421010A	M10 100 mm	Nr	0.07	1.04	–	0.91	1.95	1.14	–	1.00	2.15
E421010B	M10 120 mm	Nr	0.08	1.18	–	0.92	2.10	1.30	–	1.01	2.31
E421010C	M10 140 mm	Nr	0.08	1.18	–	0.93	2.11	1.30	–	1.02	2.32
E421010D	M10 160 mm	Nr	0.09	1.33	–	0.95	2.28	1.46	–	1.05	2.51
E421010H	M12 100 mm	Nr	0.09	1.33	–	1.00	2.33	1.46	–	1.10	2.56
E421010I	M12 120 mm	Nr	0.09	1.33	–	1.05	2.38	1.46	–	1.16	2.62
E421010J	M12 140 mm	Nr	0.10	1.48	–	1.10	2.58	1.63	–	1.21	2.84
E421010K	M12 160 mm	Nr	0.11	1.63	–	1.16	2.79	1.79	–	1.28	3.07
E421010L	M12 180 mm	Nr	0.13	1.92	–	1.21	3.13	2.11	–	1.33	3.44
E421010M	M12 200 mm	Nr	0.13	1.92	–	1.26	3.18	2.11	–	1.39	3.50
E421010N	M12 220 mm	Nr	0.14	2.07	–	1.31	3.38	2.28	–	1.44	3.72
E421010O	M12 240 mm	Nr	0.14	2.07	–	1.38	3.45	2.28	–	1.52	3.80
E421010P	M12 260 mm	Nr	0.16	2.37	–	1.50	3.87	2.61	–	1.65	4.26
E421010V	M16 120 mm	Nr	0.17	2.52	–	1.52	4.04	2.77	–	1.67	4.44
E421010W	M16 140 mm	Nr	0.19	2.81	–	1.62	4.43	3.09	–	1.78	4.87

In Situ Concrete and Large PC Concrete

Major Works 2009		Unit	Labour Hours	Labour Net	Plant Net	Materials Net	Unit Net	Labour Gross	Plant Gross	Materials Gross	Unit Price
								(Gross rates include 10% profit)			
				£	£	£	£	£	£	£	£
E60	E60: PRECAST AND COMPOSITE CONCRETE DECKING										
E6010	Trent precast concrete block and plank composite flooring system; comprising precast planks at 650 mm centres with precast concrete block infill; cement slurry grouting to joints with (1:3) mix mortar										
E601003	Floors and roofs; suspended with soffit not exceeding 3.50 m above floor level;										
E601003A	standard JJ1	m²	0.43	10.81	–	26.42	37.23	11.89	–	29.06	40.95
E601003B	standard RJ1	m²	0.43	10.80	–	29.53	40.33	11.88	–	32.48	44.36
E601003C	Jetplus JP1	m²	0.29	7.29	–	33.71	41.00	8.02	–	37.08	45.10
E601003D	Jetplus RP1	m²	0.29	7.28	–	37.97	45.25	8.01	–	41.77	49.78

MASONRY

Major Works 2009		Unit	Labour Hours	Labour Net	Plant Net	Materials Net	Unit Net	Labour Gross	Plant Gross	Materials Gross	Unit Price
								(Gross rates include 10% profit)			
				£	£	£	£	£	£	£	£
F10	**F10: BRICK AND BLOCK WALLING**										
F1001	**Walls**										
F100102	**Common bricks, BS 3921, in cement mortar (1:3):**										
F100102A	half brick thick	m²	0.68	17.01	–	16.81	33.82	18.71	–	18.49	37.20
F100102B	one brick thick	m²	1.36	34.04	–	34.71	68.75	37.44	–	38.18	75.63
F100102C	one and a half brick thick...	m²	2.03	51.05	–	51.76	102.81	56.16	–	56.94	113.09
F100102D	two brick thick	m²	2.71	68.05	–	69.66	137.71	74.86	–	76.63	151.48
F100103	**Class A engineering bricks BS 3921, in cement mortar (1:3):**										
F100103A	half brick thick	m²	0.73	18.44	–	33.89	52.33	20.28	–	37.28	57.56
F100103B	one brick thick	m²	1.47	36.85	–	68.87	105.72	40.54	–	75.76	116.29
F100103C	one and a half brick thick...	m²	2.20	55.29	–	103.28	158.57	60.82	–	113.61	174.43
F100103D	two brick thick	m²	2.94	73.73	–	138.26	211.99	81.10	–	152.09	233.19
F100104	**Class B engineering bricks, BS 3921, in cement mortar (1:3):**										
F100104A	half brick thick	m²	0.71	17.71	–	29.26	46.97	19.48	–	32.19	51.67
F100104B	one brick thick	m²	1.41	35.44	–	59.62	95.06	38.98	–	65.58	104.57
F100104C	one and a half brick thick...	m²	2.12	53.15	–	89.33	142.48	58.47	–	98.26	156.73
F100104D	two brick thick	m²	2.82	70.89	–	119.68	190.57	77.98	–	131.65	209.63
F100105	**Facing bricks, PC 300:00 per 1000 in gauged mortar (1:1:6); flush pointing both sides:**										
F100105A	half brick thick; stretcher bond....................	m²	0.79	19.84	–	21.22	41.06	21.82	–	23.34	45.17
F100105B	one brick thick; double stretcher bond	m²	1.50	37.71	–	43.53	81.24	41.48	–	47.88	89.36
F100105C	one brick thick; English bond	m²	1.58	39.69	–	43.86	83.55	43.66	–	48.25	91.91
F100105D	one brick thick; English garden wall bond	m²	1.53	38.51	–	43.86	82.37	42.36	–	48.25	90.61
F100105E	one brick thick; English cross bond....................	m²	1.66	41.67	–	44.78	86.45	45.84	–	49.26	95.10
F100105F	one brick thick; Flemish bond	m²	1.63	40.87	–	43.75	84.62	44.96	–	48.13	93.08
F100105G	one brick thick; Flemish garden wall bond	m²	1.55	38.89	–	43.75	82.64	42.78	–	48.13	90.90
F100105H	one brick thick; Dutch bond	m²	1.74	43.66	–	44.36	88.02	48.03	–	48.80	96.82
F100105I	one brick thick; monk bond.	m²	1.61	40.50	–	43.53	84.03	44.55	–	47.88	92.43
F100106	**Precast concrete blocks, BS 6073, strength 3.5 N/mm²; in cement mortar (1:3):**										
F100106A	100 mm solid blocks	m²	0.54	13.61	–	12.03	25.64	14.97	–	13.23	28.20
F100106B	140 mm solid blocks	m²	0.60	15.03	–	16.76	31.79	16.53	–	18.44	34.97
F100106C	150 mm solid blocks	m²	0.60	15.02	–	18.01	33.03	16.52	–	19.81	36.33
F100106D	200 mm solid blocks	m²	0.67	16.94	–	23.92	40.86	18.63	–	26.31	44.95
F100106E	215 mm solid blocks	m²	0.68	17.18	–	25.74	42.92	18.90	–	28.31	47.21
F100106F	100 mm hollow blocks.....	m²	0.50	12.51	–	11.23	23.74	13.76	–	12.35	26.11
F100106G	140 mm hollow blocks.....	m²	0.56	13.97	–	15.47	29.44	15.37	–	17.02	32.38
F100106H	150 mm hollow blocks.....	m²	0.58	14.49	–	16.75	31.24	15.94	–	18.43	34.36
F100106I	200 mm hollow blocks.....	m²	0.62	15.62	–	22.19	37.81	17.18	–	24.41	41.59
F100106J	215 mm hollow blocks.....	m²	0.64	16.06	–	23.93	39.99	17.67	–	26.32	43.99

Masonry

		Unit	Labour Hours	Labour Net	Plant Net	Materials Net	Unit Net	Labour Gross	Plant Gross	Materials Gross	Unit Price
								(Gross rates include 10% profit)			
				£	£	£	£	£	£	£	£
F10	**F10: BRICK AND BLOCK WALLING**										
F1001	**Walls**										
F100107	**Precast concrete blocks, BS 6073, strength 7 N/mm^2, in cement mortar (1:3):**										
F100107A	60 mm solid blocks	m^2	0.53	13.21	–	7.51	20.72	14.53	–	8.26	22.79
F100107B	75 mm solid blocks	m^2	0.55	13.79	–	9.44	23.23	15.17	–	10.38	25.55
F100107C	90 mm solid blocks	m^2	0.57	14.34	–	11.23	25.57	15.77	–	12.35	28.13
F100107D	100 mm solid blocks	m^2	0.57	14.35	–	12.21	26.56	15.79	–	13.43	29.22
F100107E	125 mm solid blocks	m^2	0.59	14.92	–	15.28	30.20	16.41	–	16.81	33.22
F100107F	140 mm solid blocks	m^2	0.62	15.57	–	17.11	32.68	17.13	–	18.82	35.95
F100107G	150 mm solid blocks	m^2	0.63	15.80	–	18.39	34.19	17.38	–	20.23	37.61
F100107H	190 mm solid blocks	m^2	0.71	17.81	–	23.28	41.09	19.59	–	25.61	45.20
F100107I	200 mm solid blocks	m^2	0.71	17.81	–	25.44	43.25	19.59	–	27.98	47.58
F100107J	215 mm solid blocks	m^2	0.72	18.09	–	28.12	46.21	19.90	–	30.93	50.83
F100107K	100 mm hollow blocks.....	m^2	0.52	13.16	–	11.38	24.54	14.48	–	12.52	26.99
F100107L	140 mm hollow blocks.....	m^2	0.58	14.47	–	15.88	30.35	15.92	–	17.47	33.39
F100107M	215 mm hollow blocks.....	m^2	0.66	16.58	–	26.12	42.70	18.24	–	28.73	46.97
F100108	**Thermalite blocks in gauged mortar (1:1:6):**										
F100108A	50 mm Shield blocks	m^2	0.44	11.00	–	7.06	18.06	12.10	–	7.77	19.87
F100108B	60 mm Shield blocks	m^2	0.44	11.01	–	7.37	18.38	12.11	–	8.11	20.22
F100108C	75 mm Shield blocks	m^2	0.46	11.48	–	8.21	19.69	12.63	–	9.03	21.66
F100108D	90 mm Shield blocks	m^2	0.48	11.96	–	9.86	21.82	13.16	–	10.85	24.00
F100108E	100 mm Shield blocks	m^2	0.48	11.96	–	10.91	22.87	13.16	–	12.00	25.16
F100108F	140 mm Shield blocks	m^2	0.52	13.16	–	15.28	28.44	14.48	–	16.81	31.28
F100108G	150 mm Shield blocks	m^2	0.52	13.16	–	16.41	29.57	14.48	–	18.05	32.53
F100108H	190 mm Shield blocks	m^2	0.59	14.82	–	20.77	35.59	16.30	–	22.85	39.15
F100108I	200 mm Shield blocks	m^2	0.59	14.82	–	21.81	36.63	16.30	–	23.99	40.29
F100108J	215 mm Shield blocks	m^2	0.60	15.07	–	24.15	39.22	16.58	–	26.57	43.14
F100108K	255 mm Trench blocks	m^2	0.64	16.16	–	28.08	44.24	17.78	–	30.89	48.66
F100108L	305 mm Trench blocks	m^2	0.67	16.76	–	33.64	50.40	18.44	–	37.00	55.44
F100108M	100 mm Turbo blocks	m^2	0.48	11.96	–	11.26	23.22	13.16	–	12.39	25.54
F100108N	125 mm Turbo blocks	m^2	0.50	12.44	–	13.99	26.43	13.68	–	15.39	29.07
F100108O	150 mm Turbo blocks	m^2	0.52	13.16	–	16.77	29.93	14.48	–	18.45	32.92
F100109	**Lignacite blocks in gauged mortar (1:1:6):**										
F100109A	70 mm solid blocks	m^2	0.61	15.27	–	7.56	22.83	16.80	–	8.32	25.11
F100109B	100 mm solid blocks	m^2	0.63	15.90	–	10.49	26.39	17.49	–	11.54	29.03
F100109C	140 mm solid blocks	m^2	0.66	16.58	–	15.27	31.85	18.24	–	16.80	35.04
F100109D	150 mm solid blocks	m^2	0.70	17.54	–	15.76	33.30	19.29	–	17.34	36.63
F100109E	190 mm solid blocks	m^2	0.79	19.75	–	23.68	43.43	21.73	–	26.05	47.77
F100109F	100 mm cellular blocks	m^2	0.48	11.96	–	11.24	23.20	13.16	–	12.36	25.52
F100110	**Durox Supablocs in gauged mortar (1:1:6):**										
F100110A	100 mm 3.5 N/mm^2 blocks .	m^2	0.48	11.96	–	10.64	22.60	13.16	–	11.70	24.86
F100110B	125 mm 3.5 N/mm^2 blocks .	m^2	0.50	12.44	–	13.16	25.60	13.68	–	14.48	28.16
F100110C	150 mm 3.5 N/mm^2 blocks .	m^2	0.52	13.16	–	15.87	29.03	14.48	–	17.46	31.93
F100110D	200 mm 3.5 N/mm^2 blocks .	m^2	0.59	14.82	–	21.10	35.92	16.30	–	23.21	39.51
F100110E	100 mm 7 N/mm^2 blocks...	m^2	0.48	12.06	–	12.18	24.24	13.27	–	13.40	26.66
F100110F	125 mm 7 N/mm^2 blocks...	m^2	0.50	12.56	–	14.71	27.27	13.82	–	16.18	30.00
F100110G	150 mm 7 N/mm^2 blocks...	m^2	0.53	13.32	–	17.41	30.73	14.65	–	19.15	33.80
F100110H	200 mm 7 N/mm^2 blocks...	m^2	0.60	15.07	–	22.64	37.71	16.58	–	24.90	41.48

Major Works 2009		Unit	Labour Hours	Labour Net	Plant Net	Materials Net	Unit Net	Labour Gross	Plant Gross	Materials Gross	Unit Price
				£	£	£	£	£	£	£	£
								(Gross rates include 10% profit)			
F10	**F10: BRICK AND BLOCK WALLING**										
F1002	**Sloping walls**										
F100212	**Common bricks, BS 3921, in cement mortar (1:3):**										
F100212A	half brick thick	m²	0.75	18.72	–	16.81	35.53	20.59	–	18.49	39.08
F100212B	one brick thick	m²	1.49	37.46	–	34.71	72.17	41.21	–	38.18	79.39
F100212C	one and a half brick thick . . .	m²	2.24	56.15	–	51.76	107.91	61.77	–	56.94	118.70
F100212D	two brick thick	m²	2.98	74.86	–	69.66	144.52	82.35	–	76.63	158.97
F100213	**Class A engineering bricks, BS 3921, in cement mortar (1:3):**										
F100213A	half brick thick	m²	0.81	20.27	–	33.89	54.16	22.30	–	37.28	59.58
F100213B	one brick thick	m²	1.61	40.54	–	68.87	109.41	44.59	–	75.76	120.35
F100213C	one and a half brick thick . . .	m²	2.42	60.81	–	103.28	164.09	66.89	–	113.61	180.50
F100213D	two brick thick	m²	3.23	81.11	–	138.26	219.37	89.22	–	152.09	241.31
F100214	**Class B engineering bricks, BS 3921, in cement mortar (1:3):**										
F100214A	half brick thick	m²	0.78	19.50	–	29.26	48.76	21.45	–	32.19	53.64
F100214B	one brick thick	m²	1.55	38.98	–	59.62	98.60	42.88	–	65.58	108.46
F100214C	one and a half brick thick . . .	m²	2.33	58.47	–	89.33	147.80	64.32	–	98.26	162.58
F100214D	two brick thick	m²	3.10	77.97	–	119.68	197.65	85.77	–	131.65	217.42
F100215	**Facing bricks, PC 300:00 per 1000, in gauged mortar (1:1:6); flush pointing both sides:**										
F100215A	half brick thick, stretcher bond.	m²	0.87	21.83	–	21.22	43.05	24.01	–	23.34	47.36
F100215B	one brick thick, double stretcher bond	m²	1.65	41.48	–	43.53	85.01	45.63	–	47.88	93.51
F100215C	one brick thick, English bond	m²	1.74	43.66	–	43.86	87.52	48.03	–	48.25	96.27
F100215D	one brick thick, English garden wall bond	m²	1.69	42.36	–	43.86	86.22	46.60	–	48.25	94.84
F100215E	one brick thick, English cross bond.	m²	1.83	45.84	–	44.78	90.62	50.42	–	49.26	99.68
F100215F	one brick thick, Flemish bond	m²	1.79	44.97	–	43.75	88.72	49.47	–	48.13	97.59
F100215G	one brick thick, Flemish garden wall bond	m²	1.70	42.78	–	43.75	86.53	47.06	–	48.13	95.18
F100215H	one brick thick, Dutch bond	m²	1.91	48.03	–	44.36	92.39	52.83	–	48.80	101.63
F100215I	one brick thick, monk bond.	m²	1.77	44.54	–	43.53	88.07	48.99	–	47.88	96.88

Masonry

Major Works 2009		Unit	Labour Hours	Labour Net	Plant Net	Materials Net	Unit Net	Labour Gross	Plant Gross	Materials Gross	Unit Price
								(Gross rates include 10% profit)			
				£	£	£	£	£	£	£	£
F10	**F10: BRICK AND BLOCK WALLING**										
F1003	**Battering walls**										
F100317	**Common bricks, BS 3921, in cement mortar (1:3):**										
F100317A	half brick thick	m²	0.81	20.40	–	16.81	37.21	22.44	–	18.49	40.93
F100317B	one brick thick	m²	1.63	40.85	–	34.71	75.56	44.94	–	38.18	83.12
F100317C	one and a half brick thick...	m²	2.44	61.25	–	51.76	113.01	67.38	–	56.94	124.31
F100317D	two brick thick	m²	3.25	81.67	–	69.66	151.33	89.84	–	76.63	166.46
F100318	**Class A engineering bricks, BS 3921, in cement mortar (1:3):**										
F100318A	half brick thick	m²	0.88	22.13	–	33.89	56.02	24.34	–	37.28	61.62
F100318B	one brick thick	m²	1.76	44.21	–	68.87	113.08	48.63	–	75.76	124.39
F100318C	one and a half brick thick...	m²	2.64	66.34	–	103.28	169.62	72.97	–	113.61	186.58
F100318D	two brick thick	m²	3.52	88.47	–	138.26	226.73	97.32	–	152.09	249.40
F100319	**Class B engineering bricks, BS 3921, in cement mortar (1:3):**										
F100319A	half brick thick	m²	0.85	21.25	–	29.26	50.51	23.38	–	32.19	55.56
F100319B	one brick thick	m²	1.69	42.52	–	59.62	102.14	46.77	–	65.58	112.35
F100319C	one and a half brick thick...	m²	2.54	63.77	–	89.33	153.10	70.15	–	98.26	168.41
F100319D	two brick thick	m²	3.39	85.05	–	119.68	204.73	93.56	–	131.65	225.20
F100320	**Facing bricks, PC 300:00 per 1000, in gauged mortar (1:1:6); flush pointing both sides:**										
F100320A	half brick thick, stretcher bond.....................	m²	0.95	23.81	–	21.22	45.03	26.19	–	23.34	49.53
F100320B	one brick thick, double stretcher bond	m²	1.80	45.25	–	43.53	88.78	49.78	–	47.88	97.66
F100320C	one brick thick, English bond	m²	1.90	47.63	–	43.86	91.49	52.39	–	48.25	100.64
F100320D	one brick thick, English garden wall bond	m²	1.84	46.22	–	43.86	90.08	50.84	–	48.25	99.09
F100320E	one brick thick, English cross bond...................	m²	1.99	50.01	–	44.78	94.79	55.01	–	49.26	104.27
F100320F	one brick thick, Flemish bond	m²	1.95	49.04	–	43.75	92.79	53.94	–	48.13	102.07
F100320G	one brick thick, Flemish garden wall bond	m²	1.86	46.68	–	43.75	90.43	51.35	–	48.13	99.47
F100320H	one brick thick, Dutch bond	m²	2.09	52.40	–	44.36	96.76	57.64	–	48.80	106.44
F100320I	one brick thick, monk bond.	m²	1.93	48.59	–	43.53	92.12	53.45	–	47.88	101.33

Major Works 2009		Unit	Labour Hours	Labour Net	Plant Net	Materials Net	Unit Net	Labour Gross	Plant Gross	Materials Gross	Unit Price
								(Gross rates include 10% profit)			
				£	£	£	£	£	£	£	£
F10	**F10: BRICK AND BLOCK WALLING**										
F1004	**Curved walls**										
F100422	**Common bricks, BS 3921, in cement mortar (1:3):**										
F100422A	half brick thick	m²	1.02	25.52	–	16.81	42.33	28.07	–	18.49	46.56
F100422B	one brick thick	m²	2.03	51.07	–	34.71	85.78	56.18	–	38.18	94.36
F100422C	one and a half brick thick...	m²	3.05	76.57	–	51.76	128.33	84.23	–	56.94	141.16
F100422D	two brick thick	m²	4.06	102.09	–	69.66	171.75	112.30	–	76.63	188.93
F100423	**Class A engineering bricks, BS 3921, in cement mortar (1:3):**										
F100423A	half brick thick	m²	1.10	27.66	–	33.89	61.55	30.43	–	37.28	67.71
F100423B	one brick thick	m²	2.20	55.29	–	68.87	124.16	60.82	–	75.76	136.58
F100423C	one and a half brick thick...	m²	3.30	82.95	–	103.28	186.23	91.25	–	113.61	204.85
F100423D	two brick thick	m²	4.40	110.60	–	138.26	248.86	121.66	–	152.09	273.75
F100424	**Class B engineering bricks, BS 3921, in cement mortar (1:3):**										
F100424A	half brick thick	m²	1.06	26.58	–	29.26	55.84	29.24	–	32.19	61.42
F100424B	one brick thick	m²	2.12	53.18	–	59.62	112.80	58.50	–	65.58	124.08
F100424C	one and a half brick thick...	m²	3.17	79.73	–	89.33	169.06	87.70	–	98.26	185.97
F100424D	two brick thick	m²	4.23	106.33	–	119.68	226.01	116.96	–	131.65	248.61
F100425	**Facing bricks, PC 300:00 per 1000, in gauged mortar; flush pointing both sides:**										
F100425A	half brick thick, stretcher bond....................	m²	1.19	29.77	–	21.22	50.99	32.75	–	23.34	56.09
F100425B	one brick thick, double stretcher bond	m²	2.25	56.57	–	43.53	100.10	62.23	–	47.88	110.11
F100425C	one brick thick, English bond	m²	2.37	59.54	–	43.86	103.40	65.49	–	48.25	113.74
F100425D	one brick thick, English garden wall bond	m²	2.30	57.78	–	43.86	101.64	63.56	–	48.25	111.80
F100425E	one brick thick, English cross bond....................	m²	2.49	62.52	–	44.78	107.30	68.77	–	49.26	118.03
F100425F	one brick thick, Flemish bond	m²	2.44	61.32	–	43.75	105.07	67.45	–	48.13	115.58
F100425G	one brick thick, Flemish garden wall bond	m²	2.32	58.33	–	43.75	102.08	64.16	–	48.13	112.29
F100425H	one brick thick, Dutch bond	m²	2.61	65.49	–	44.67	110.16	72.04	–	49.14	121.18
F100425I	one brick thick, monk bond.	m²	2.42	60.74	–	42.56	103.30	66.81	–	46.82	113.63
F100426	**Precast concrete blocks, BS 6073, strength 3.5 N/mm²; in cement mortar (1:3):**										
F100426A	100 mm solid blocks	m²	0.81	20.42	–	12.03	32.45	22.46	–	13.23	35.70
F100426B	140 mm solid blocks	m²	0.90	22.54	–	16.76	39.30	24.79	–	18.44	43.23
F100426C	150 mm solid blocks	m²	0.91	22.86	–	18.01	40.87	25.15	–	19.81	44.96
F100426D	200 mm solid blocks	m²	1.01	25.40	–	23.92	49.32	27.94	–	26.31	54.25
F100426E	215 mm solid blocks	m²	1.03	25.77	–	25.74	51.51	28.35	–	28.31	56.66
F100427	**Precast concrete blocks, BS 6073, strength 7 N/mm²; in cement mortar (1:3):**										
F100427A	100 mm solid blocks	m²	0.86	21.52	–	12.21	33.73	23.67	–	13.43	37.10
F100427B	140 mm solid blocks	m²	0.93	23.36	–	17.11	40.47	25.70	–	18.82	44.52
F100427C	150 mm solid blocks	m²	0.94	23.70	–	18.39	42.09	26.07	–	20.23	46.30
F100427D	200 mm solid blocks	m²	1.06	26.71	–	25.44	52.15	29.38	–	27.98	57.37
F100427E	215 mm solid blocks	m²	1.08	27.13	–	28.12	55.25	29.84	–	30.93	60.78

Masonry

Major Works 2009		Unit	Labour Hours	Labour Net	Plant Net	Materials Net	Unit Net	Labour Gross	Plant Gross	Materials Gross	Unit Price
				£	£	£	£	£	£	£	£
								(Gross rates include 10% profit)			
F10	**F10: BRICK AND BLOCK WALLING**										
F1005	**Walls built against other construction**										
F100531	**Common bricks, BS 3921, in cement mortar (1:3):**										
F100531A	half brick thick	m²	0.75	18.71	–	17.36	36.07	20.58	–	19.10	39.68
F100531B	one brick thick	m²	1.49	37.45	–	36.08	73.53	41.20	–	39.69	80.88
F100531C	one and a half brick thick	m²	2.24	56.14	–	53.67	109.81	61.75	–	59.04	120.79
F100531D	two brick thick	m²	2.98	74.86	–	72.39	147.25	82.35	–	79.63	161.98
F100532	**Class A engineering bricks, BS 3921, in cement mortar (1:3):**										
F100532A	half brick thick	m²	0.81	20.28	–	34.34	54.62	22.31	–	37.77	60.08
F100532B	one brick thick	m²	1.61	40.54	–	69.96	110.50	44.59	–	76.96	121.55
F100532C	one and a half brick thick	m²	2.42	60.82	–	104.82	165.64	66.90	–	115.30	182.20
F100532D	two brick thick	m²	3.23	81.11	–	140.44	221.55	89.22	–	154.48	243.71
F100533	**Class B engineering bricks, BS 3921, in cement mortar (1:3):**										
F100533A	half brick thick	m²	0.78	19.49	–	29.72	49.21	21.44	–	32.69	54.13
F100533B	one brick thick	m²	1.55	38.98	–	60.71	99.69	42.88	–	66.78	109.66
F100533C	one and a half brick thick	m²	2.33	58.48	–	90.87	149.35	64.33	–	99.96	164.29
F100533D	two brick thick	m²	3.10	77.97	–	121.86	199.83	85.77	–	134.05	219.81
F100534	**Facing bricks, PC 300:00 per 1000, in gauged mortar (1:1:6); flush pointing one side:**										
F100534A	half brick thick; stretcher bond	m²	0.87	21.83	–	21.66	43.49	24.01	–	23.83	47.84
F100534B	half brick thick; English bond (snapped headers)	m²	0.97	24.44	–	24.21	48.65	26.88	–	26.63	53.52
F100534C	half brick thick; Flemish bond (snapped headers)	m²	1.00	25.09	–	24.21	49.30	27.60	–	26.63	54.23

Masonry

Major Works 2009		Unit	Labour Hours	Labour Net	Plant Net	Materials Net	Unit Net	Labour Gross	Plant Gross	Materials Gross	Unit Price
								(Gross rates include 10% profit)			
				£	£	£	£	£	£	£	£
F10	**F10: BRICK AND BLOCK WALLING**										
F1005	**Walls built against other construction**										
F100535	**Precast concrete blocks, BS 6073, strength 3.5 N/mm^2; in cement mortar (1:3):**										
F100535A	100 mm solid blocks	m^2	0.60	14.97	–	12.12	27.09	16.47	–	13.33	29.80
F100535B	140 mm solid blocks	m^2	0.66	16.52	–	16.95	33.47	18.17	–	18.65	36.82
F100535C	150 mm solid blocks	m^2	0.66	16.53	–	18.19	34.72	18.18	–	20.01	38.19
F100535D	200 mm solid blocks	m^2	0.74	18.61	–	24.20	42.81	20.47	–	26.62	47.09
F100535E	215 mm solid blocks	m^2	0.75	18.89	–	26.01	44.90	20.78	–	28.61	49.39
F100535F	100 mm hollow blocks.	m^2	0.55	13.76	–	11.42	25.18	15.14	–	12.56	27.70
F100536	**Precast concrete blocks, BS 6073, strength 7 N/mm^2; in cement mortar (1:3):**										
F100536A	60 mm solid blocks	m^2	0.58	14.54	–	7.60	22.14	15.99	–	8.36	24.35
F100536B	75 mm solid blocks	m^2	0.60	15.17	–	9.53	24.70	16.69	–	10.48	27.17
F100536C	90 mm solid blocks	m^2	0.63	15.77	–	11.32	27.09	17.35	–	12.45	29.80
F100536D	100 mm solid blocks	m^2	0.63	15.78	–	12.30	28.08	17.36	–	13.53	30.89
F100536E	125 mm solid blocks	m^2	0.65	16.40	–	15.46	31.86	18.04	–	17.01	35.05
F100536F	140 mm solid blocks	m^2	0.69	17.38	–	17.29	34.67	19.12	–	19.02	38.14
F100536G	150 mm solid blocks	m^2	0.69	17.38	–	18.57	35.95	19.12	–	20.43	39.55
F100536H	190 mm solid blocks	m^2	0.78	19.59	–	23.56	43.15	21.55	–	25.92	47.47
F100536I	200 mm solid blocks	m^2	0.78	19.59	–	25.71	45.30	21.55	–	28.28	49.83
F100536J	215 mm solid blocks	m^2	0.79	19.90	–	28.39	48.29	21.89	–	31.23	53.12
F100536K	100 mm hollow blocks.	m^2	0.58	14.47	–	11.56	26.03	15.92	–	12.72	28.63
F100536L	140 mm hollow blocks.	m^2	0.63	15.93	–	16.06	31.99	17.52	–	17.67	35.19
F100536M	215 mm hollow blocks.	m^2	0.73	18.24	–	26.39	44.63	20.06	–	29.03	49.09

Masonry

Major Works 2009		Unit	Labour Hours	Labour Net	Plant Net	Materials Net	Unit Net	Labour Gross	Plant Gross	Materials Gross	Unit Price
								— (Gross rates include 10% profit) —			
				£	£	£	£	£	£	£	£
F10	**F10: BRICK AND BLOCK WALLING**										
F1005	**Walls built against other construction**										
F100537	**Thermalite blocks in gauged mortar (1:1:6):**										
F100537A	50 mm Shield blocks	m²	0.48	12.11	–	7.17	19.28	13.32	–	7.89	21.21
F100537B	60 mm Shield blocks	m²	0.48	12.11	–	7.48	19.59	13.32	–	8.23	21.55
F100537C	75 mm Shield blocks	m²	0.50	12.63	–	8.32	20.95	13.89	–	9.15	23.05
F100537D	90 mm Shield blocks	m²	0.52	13.16	–	9.97	23.13	14.48	–	10.97	25.44
F100537E	100 mm Shield blocks	m²	0.52	13.16	–	11.02	24.18	14.48	–	12.12	26.60
F100537F	140 mm Shield blocks	m²	0.58	14.47	–	15.50	29.97	15.92	–	17.05	32.97
F100537G	150 mm Shield blocks	m²	0.58	14.46	–	16.63	31.09	15.91	–	18.29	34.20
F100537H	190 mm Shield blocks	m²	0.65	16.30	–	21.10	37.40	17.93	–	23.21	41.14
F100537I	200 mm Shield blocks	m²	0.65	16.30	–	22.14	38.44	17.93	–	24.35	42.28
F100537J	215 mm Shield blocks	m²	0.66	16.58	–	24.48	41.06	18.24	–	26.93	45.17
F100537K	255 mm Trench blocks	m²	0.71	17.76	–	28.41	46.17	19.54	–	31.25	50.79
F100537L	305 mm Trench blocks	m²	0.73	18.44	–	34.08	52.52	20.28	–	37.49	57.77
F100537M	100 mm Turbo blocks	m²	0.52	13.16	–	11.37	24.53	14.48	–	12.51	26.98
F100537N	125 mm Turbo blocks	m²	0.55	13.69	–	14.21	27.90	15.06	–	15.63	30.69
F100537O	150 mm Turbo blocks	m²	0.58	14.47	–	17.10	31.57	15.92	–	18.81	34.73
F100538	**Lignacite blocks in gauged mortar (1:1:6):**										
F100538A	70 mm solid blocks	m²	0.67	16.80	–	7.67	24.47	18.48	–	8.44	26.92
F100538B	100 mm solid blocks	m²	0.70	17.51	–	10.60	28.11	19.26	–	11.66	30.92
F100538C	140 mm solid blocks	m²	0.73	18.21	–	15.49	33.70	20.03	–	17.04	37.07
F100538D	150 mm solid blocks	m²	0.77	19.24	–	15.98	35.22	21.16	–	17.58	38.74
F100538E	190 mm solid blocks	m²	0.86	21.68	–	24.01	45.69	23.85	–	26.41	50.26
F100538F	100 mm cellular blocks	m²	0.52	13.16	–	11.46	24.62	14.48	–	12.61	27.08
F100539	**Durox Supablocs in gauged mortar (1:1:6):**										
F100539A	100 mm 3.5 N/mm² blocks .	m²	0.52	13.16	–	10.75	23.91	14.48	–	11.83	26.30
F100539B	125 mm 3.5 N/mm² blocks .	m²	0.54	13.67	–	13.38	27.05	15.04	–	14.72	29.76
F100539C	150 mm 3.5 N/mm² blocks .	m²	0.58	14.47	–	16.09	30.56	15.92	–	17.70	33.62
F100539D	200 mm 3.5 N/mm² blocks .	m²	0.65	16.30	–	21.43	37.73	17.93	–	23.57	41.50
F100539E	100 mm 7 N/mm² blocks...	m²	0.53	13.27	–	12.29	25.56	14.60	–	13.52	28.12
F100539F	125 mm 7 N/mm² blocks...	m²	0.55	13.81	–	14.93	28.74	15.19	–	16.42	31.61
F100539G	150 mm 7 N/mm² blocks...	m²	0.58	14.65	–	17.63	32.28	16.12	–	19.39	35.51
F100539H	200 mm 7 N/mm² blocks...	m²	0.66	16.58	–	21.94	38.52	18.24	–	24.13	42.37

Major Works 2009		Unit	Labour Hours	Labour Net	Plant Net	Materials Net	Unit Net	Labour Gross	Plant Gross	Materials Gross	Unit Price
								(Gross rates include 10% profit)			
				£	£	£	£	£	£	£	£
F10	**F10: BRICK AND BLOCK WALLING**										
F1006	**Cavity walls**										
F100641	**Common bricks, BS 3921, in cement mortar (1:3):**										
F100641A	half brick skins	m²	0.68	17.01	–	16.81	33.82	18.71	–	18.49	37.20
F100641B	one brick skins	m²	1.36	34.04	–	34.71	68.75	37.44	–	38.18	75.63
F100641C	one and a half brick skins ..	m²	2.03	51.05	–	51.76	102.81	56.16	–	56.94	113.09
F100641D	two brick skins	m²	2.71	68.05	–	69.66	137.71	74.86	–	76.63	151.48
F100642	**Class A engineering bricks, BS 3921, in cement mortar (1:3):**										
F100642A	half brick skins	m²	0.73	18.44	–	33.89	52.33	20.28	–	37.28	57.56
F100642B	one brick skins	m²	1.47	36.85	–	68.87	105.72	40.54	–	75.76	116.29
F100642C	one and a half brick skins ..	m²	2.20	55.29	–	103.28	158.57	60.82	–	113.61	174.43
F100642D	two brick skins	m²	2.94	73.73	–	138.26	211.99	81.10	–	152.09	233.19
F100643	**Class B engineering bricks, BS 3921, in cement mortar (1:3):**										
F100643A	half brick skins	m²	0.71	17.71	–	29.26	46.97	19.48	–	32.19	51.67
F100643B	one brick skins	m²	1.41	35.44	–	59.62	95.06	38.98	–	65.58	104.57
F100643C	one and a half brick skins ..	m²	2.12	53.15	–	89.33	142.48	58.47	–	98.26	156.73
F100643D	two brick skins	m²	2.82	70.89	–	119.68	190.57	77.98	–	131.65	209.63
F100644	**Facing bricks, PC 300:00 per 1000, in gauged mortar (1:1:6); flush pointing one side:**										
F100644A	half brick skins; stretcher bond....................	m²	0.77	19.44	–	21.11	40.55	21.38	–	23.22	44.61
F100644B	half brick skins; English bond (snapped headers)	m²	0.87	21.78	–	23.66	45.44	23.96	–	26.03	49.98
F100644C	half brick skins; Flemish bond (snapped headers) ...	m²	0.89	22.36	–	23.66	46.02	24.60	–	26.03	50.62
F100645	**Precast concrete blocks, BS 6073, strength 3.5 N/mm² in cement mortar (1:3):**										
F100645A	100 mm solid block skins ..	m²	0.54	13.61	–	12.12	25.73	14.97	–	13.33	28.30
F100645B	140 mm solid block skins ..	m²	0.60	15.02	–	16.95	31.97	16.52	–	18.65	35.17
F100645C	150 mm solid block skins ..	m²	0.60	15.02	–	18.19	33.21	16.52	–	20.01	36.53
F100645D	200 mm solid block skins ..	m²	0.67	16.93	–	24.20	41.13	18.62	–	26.62	45.24
F100645E	215 mm solid block skins ..	m²	0.68	17.18	–	26.01	43.19	18.90	–	28.61	47.51
F100645F	100 mm hollow block skins.	m²	0.50	12.51	–	11.42	23.93	13.76	–	12.56	26.32
F100646	**Precast concrete blocks, BS 6073, strength 7 N/mm², in cement mortar (1:3):**										
F100646A	60 mm solid block skins ...	m²	0.53	13.21	–	7.60	20.81	14.53	–	8.36	22.89
F100646B	75 mm solid block skins ...	m²	0.55	13.79	–	9.53	23.32	15.17	–	10.48	25.65
F100646C	90 mm solid block skins ...	m²	0.57	14.34	–	11.32	25.66	15.77	–	12.45	28.23
F100646D	100 mm solid block skins ..	m²	0.57	14.35	–	12.30	26.65	15.79	–	13.53	29.32
F100646E	125 mm solid block skins ..	m²	0.59	14.92	–	15.46	30.38	16.41	–	17.01	33.42
F100646F	140 mm solid block skins ..	m²	0.63	15.80	–	17.29	33.09	17.38	–	19.02	36.40
F100646G	150 mm solid block skins ..	m²	0.63	15.80	–	18.57	34.37	17.38	–	20.43	37.81
F100646H	190 mm solid block skins ..	m²	0.71	17.81	–	23.56	41.37	19.59	–	25.92	45.51
F100646I	200 mm solid block skins ..	m²	0.71	17.81	–	25.71	43.52	19.59	–	28.28	47.87
F100646J	215 mm solid block skins ..	m²	0.72	18.09	–	28.39	46.48	19.90	–	31.23	51.13
F100646K	100 mm hollow block skins.	m²	0.52	13.17	–	11.56	24.73	14.49	–	12.72	27.20
F100646L	140 mm hollow block skins.	m²	0.58	14.47	–	16.06	30.53	15.92	–	17.67	33.58
F100646M	215 mm hollow block skins.	m²	0.66	16.58	–	26.39	42.97	18.24	–	29.03	47.27

Masonry

Major Works 2009		Unit	Labour Hours	Labour Net	Plant Net	Materials Net	Unit Net	Labour Gross	Plant Gross	Materials Gross	Unit Price
								(Gross rates include 10% profit)			
				£	£	£	£	£	£	£	£
F10	**F10: BRICK AND BLOCK WALLING**										
F1006	**Cavity walls**										
F100647	**Thermalite blocks in gauged mortar (1:1:6):**										
F100647A	50 mm Shield block skins ..	m²	0.44	11.00	–	7.17	18.17	12.10	–	7.89	19.99
F100647B	60 mm Shield block skins ..	m²	0.44	11.01	–	7.48	18.49	12.11	–	8.23	20.34
F100647C	75 mm Shield block skins ..	m²	0.46	11.48	–	8.32	19.80	12.63	–	9.15	21.78
F100647D	90 mm Shield block skins ..	m²	0.48	11.96	–	9.97	21.93	13.16	–	10.97	24.12
F100647E	100 mm Shield block skins .	m²	0.48	11.96	–	11.02	22.98	13.16	–	12.12	25.28
F100647F	140 mm Shield block skins .	m²	0.52	13.16	–	15.50	28.66	14.48	–	17.05	31.53
F100647G	150 mm Shield block skins .	m²	0.52	13.16	–	16.63	29.79	14.48	–	18.29	32.77
F100647H	190 mm Shield block skins .	m²	0.59	14.82	–	21.10	35.92	16.30	–	23.21	39.51
F100647I	200 mm Shield block skins .	m²	0.59	14.82	–	22.14	36.96	16.30	–	24.35	40.66
F100647J	215 mm Shield block skins .	m²	0.60	15.07	–	24.48	39.55	16.58	–	26.93	43.51
F100647K	255 mm Trench block skins	m²	0.64	16.16	–	28.41	44.57	17.78	–	31.25	49.03
F100647L	305 mm Trench block skins	m²	0.67	16.76	–	34.08	50.84	18.44	–	37.49	55.92
F100647M	100 mm Turbo block skins .	m²	0.48	11.95	–	11.37	23.32	13.15	–	12.51	25.65
F100647N	125 mm Turbo block skins .	m²	0.50	12.44	–	14.21	26.65	13.68	–	15.63	29.32
F100647O	150 mm Turbo block skins .	m²	0.52	13.16	–	17.10	30.26	14.48	–	18.81	33.29
F100648	**Lignacite blocks in gauged mortar (1:1:6):**										
F100648A	70 mm solid block skins ...	m²	0.61	15.27	–	7.67	22.94	16.80	–	8.44	25.23
F100648B	100 mm solid block skins ..	m²	0.63	15.90	–	10.60	26.50	17.49	–	11.66	29.15
F100648C	140 mm solid block skins ..	m²	0.66	16.53	–	15.49	32.02	18.18	–	17.04	35.22
F100648D	150 mm solid block skins ..	m²	0.70	17.51	–	15.98	33.49	19.26	–	17.58	36.84
F100648E	190 mm solid block skins ..	m²	0.79	19.72	–	24.01	43.73	21.69	–	26.41	48.10
F100648F	100 mm cellular block skins	m²	0.63	15.90	–	11.46	27.36	17.49	–	12.61	30.10
F100649	**Durox Supablocs in gauged mortar (1:1:6):**										
F100649A	100 mm skins 3.5 N/mm² blocks	m²	0.48	11.96	–	10.75	22.71	13.16	–	11.83	24.98
F100649B	125 mm skins 3.5 N/mm² blocks	m²	0.50	12.44	–	13.38	25.82	13.68	–	14.72	28.40
F100649C	150 mm skins 3.5 N/mm² blocks	m²	0.52	13.16	–	16.09	29.25	14.48	–	17.70	32.18
F100649D	200 mm skins 3.5 N/mm² blocks	m²	0.59	14.82	–	21.43	36.25	16.30	–	23.57	39.88
F100649E	100 mm skins 7 N/mm² blocks	m²	0.48	12.06	–	12.18	24.24	13.27	–	13.40	26.66
F100649F	125 mm skins 7 N/mm² blocks	m²	0.50	12.56	–	14.71	27.27	13.82	–	16.18	30.00
F100649G	150 mm skins 7 N/mm² blocks	m²	0.53	13.32	–	17.41	30.73	14.65	–	19.15	33.80
F100649H	200 mm skins 7 N/mm² blocks	m²	0.60	15.07	–	22.64	37.71	16.58	–	24.90	41.48

Major Works 2009		Unit	Labour Hours	Labour Net	Plant Net	Materials Net	Unit Net	Labour Gross	Plant Gross	Materials Gross	Unit Price
								— (Gross rates include 10% profit) —			
				£	£	£	£	£	£	£	£
F10	**F10: BRICK AND BLOCK WALLING**										
F1007	**Isolated piers**										
F100761	**Common bricks, BS 3921, in cement mortar (1:3):**										
F100761A	half brick thick	m²	0.81	20.40	–	17.99	38.39	22.44	–	19.79	42.23
F100761B	one brick thick	m²	1.63	40.84	–	36.84	77.68	44.92	–	40.52	85.45
F100761C	one and a half brick thick...	m²	2.44	61.24	–	55.07	116.31	67.36	–	60.58	127.94
F100761D	two brick thick	m²	3.25	81.66	–	74.15	155.81	89.83	–	81.57	171.39
F100762	**Class A engineering bricks, BS 3921, in cement mortar (1:3):**										
F100762A	half brick thick	m²	0.88	22.13	–	36.49	58.62	24.34	–	40.14	64.48
F100762B	one brick thick	m²	1.76	44.21	–	73.55	117.76	48.63	–	80.91	129.54
F100762C	one and a half brick thick...	m²	2.64	66.34	–	110.56	176.90	72.97	–	121.62	194.59
F100762D	two brick thick	m²	3.52	88.48	–	148.14	236.62	97.33	–	162.95	260.28
F100763	**Class B engineering bricks, BS 3921, in cement mortar (1:3):**										
F100763A	half brick thick	m²	0.85	21.25	–	31.49	52.74	23.38	–	34.64	58.01
F100763B	one brick thick	m²	1.69	42.52	–	63.63	106.15	46.77	–	69.99	116.77
F100763C	one and a half brick thick...	m²	2.54	63.78	–	95.56	159.34	70.16	–	105.12	175.27
F100763D	two brick thick	m²	3.39	85.06	–	128.14	213.20	93.57	–	140.95	234.52
F100764	**Facing bricks, PC 300:00 per 1000, in gauged mortar (1:1:6); flush pointing all round:**										
F100764A	half brick thick; stretcher bond	m²	0.95	23.82	–	22.74	46.56	26.20	–	25.01	51.22
F100764B	one brick thick; English bond	m²	1.90	47.63	–	46.61	94.24	52.39	–	51.27	103.66
F100764C	one brick thick; English garden wall bond	m²	1.84	46.22	–	46.61	92.83	50.84	–	51.27	102.11
F100764D	one brick thick; English cross bond	m²	1.99	50.02	–	47.52	97.54	55.02	–	52.27	107.29
F100764E	one brick thick; Flemish bond	m²	1.95	49.03	–	46.50	95.53	53.93	–	51.15	105.08
F100764F	one brick thick; Flemish garden wall bond	m²	1.86	46.67	–	46.50	93.17	51.34	–	51.15	102.49
F100764G	one brick thick; Dutch bond	m²	2.09	52.40	–	47.11	99.51	57.64	–	51.82	109.46
F100764H	one brick thick; monk bond.	m²	1.93	48.58	–	46.28	94.86	53.44	–	50.91	104.35
F100765	**Precast concrete blocks, BS 6073, strength 3.5 N/mm²; in cement mortar (1:3):**										
F100765A	100 mm solid blocks	m²	0.65	16.33	–	12.85	29.18	17.96	–	14.14	32.10
F100765B	140 mm solid blocks	m²	0.72	18.03	–	17.92	35.95	19.83	–	19.71	39.55
F100765C	150 mm solid blocks	m²	0.72	18.04	–	19.24	37.28	19.84	–	21.16	41.01
F100765D	200 mm solid blocks	m²	0.81	20.32	–	25.57	45.89	22.35	–	28.13	50.48
F100765E	215 mm solid blocks	m²	0.82	20.63	–	27.50	48.13	22.69	–	30.25	52.94
F100765F	100 mm hollow blocks.....	m²	0.60	15.02	–	12.00	27.02	16.52	–	13.20	29.72
F100765G	140 mm hollow blocks.....	m²	0.66	16.48	–	16.53	33.01	18.13	–	18.18	36.31
F100765H	150 mm hollow blocks.....	m²	0.68	17.06	–	17.88	34.94	18.77	–	19.67	38.43
F100765I	200 mm hollow blocks.....	m²	0.73	18.39	–	23.70	42.09	20.23	–	26.07	46.30
F100765J	215 mm hollow blocks.....	m²	0.75	18.89	–	25.56	44.45	20.78	–	28.12	48.90

Masonry

Major Works 2009		Unit	Labour Hours	Labour Net	Plant Net	Materials Net	Unit Net	Labour Gross	Plant Gross	Materials Gross	Unit Price
								(Gross rates include 10% profit)			
				£	£	£	£	£	£	£	£
F10	**F10: BRICK AND BLOCK WALLING**										
F1007	**Isolated piers**										
F100766	**Precast concrete blocks, BS 6073, strength 7 N/mm^2; in cement mortar (1:3):**										
F100766A	60 mm solid blocks	m^2	0.63	15.85	–	8.02	23.87	17.44	–	8.82	26.26
F100766B	75 mm solid blocks	m^2	0.66	16.56	–	10.08	26.64	18.22	–	11.09	29.30
F100766C	90 mm solid blocks	m^2	0.69	17.20	–	12.00	29.20	18.92	–	13.20	32.12
F100766D	100 mm solid blocks	m^2	0.69	17.21	–	13.05	30.26	18.93	–	14.36	33.29
F100766E	125 mm solid blocks	m^2	0.71	17.91	–	16.33	34.24	19.70	–	17.96	37.66
F100766F	140 mm solid blocks	m^2	0.76	18.96	–	18.29	37.25	20.86	–	20.12	40.98
F100766G	150 mm solid blocks	m^2	0.76	18.96	–	19.65	38.61	20.86	–	21.62	42.47
F100766H	190 mm solid blocks	m^2	0.85	21.38	–	24.88	46.26	23.52	–	27.37	50.89
F100766I	200 mm solid blocks	m^2	0.85	21.38	–	27.19	48.57	23.52	–	29.91	53.43
F100766J	215 mm solid blocks	m^2	0.86	21.60	–	30.06	51.66	23.76	–	33.07	56.83
F100766K	100 mm hollow blocks.....	m^2	0.63	15.81	–	12.15	27.96	17.39	–	13.37	30.76
F100766L	140 mm hollow blocks.....	m^2	0.69	17.36	–	16.96	34.32	19.10	–	18.66	37.75
F100766M	215 mm hollow blocks.....	m^2	0.79	19.89	–	27.90	47.79	21.88	–	30.69	52.57
F100767	**Thermalite blocks in gauged mortar (1:1:6):**										
F100767A	50 mm Shield blocks	m^2	0.53	13.21	–	7.54	20.75	14.53	–	8.29	22.83
F100767B	60 mm Shield blocks	m^2	0.53	13.21	–	7.88	21.09	14.53	–	8.67	23.20
F100767C	75 mm Shield blocks	m^2	0.55	13.77	–	8.76	22.53	15.15	–	9.64	24.78
F100767D	90 mm Shield blocks	m^2	0.57	14.34	–	10.53	24.87	15.77	–	11.58	27.36
F100767E	100 mm Shield blocks	m^2	0.57	14.35	–	11.65	26.00	15.79	–	12.82	28.60
F100767F	140 mm Shield blocks	m^2	0.63	15.81	–	16.31	32.12	17.39	–	17.94	35.33
F100767G	150 mm Shield blocks	m^2	0.63	15.80	–	17.52	33.32	17.38	–	19.27	36.65
F100767H	190 mm Shield blocks	m^2	0.71	17.78	–	22.18	39.96	19.56	–	24.40	43.96
F100767I	200 mm Shield blocks	m^2	0.71	17.79	–	23.10	40.89	19.57	–	25.41	44.98
F100767J	215 mm Shield blocks	m^2	0.72	18.08	–	25.79	43.87	19.89	–	28.37	48.26
F100767K	255 mm Trench blocks	m^2	0.77	19.39	–	29.99	49.38	21.33	–	32.99	54.32
F100767L	305 mm Trench blocks	m^2	0.80	20.10	–	35.92	56.02	22.11	–	39.51	61.62
F100767M	100 mm Turbo blocks	m^2	0.57	14.35	–	12.02	26.37	15.79	–	13.22	29.01
F100767N	125 mm Turbo blocks	m^2	0.59	14.92	–	14.95	29.87	16.41	–	16.45	32.86
F100767O	150 mm Turbo blocks	m^2	0.63	15.80	–	17.91	33.71	17.38	–	19.70	37.08

Major Works 2009		Unit	Labour Hours	Labour Net	Plant Net	Materials Net	Unit Net	Labour Gross	Plant Gross	Materials Gross	Unit Price
								(Gross rates include 10% profit)			
				£	£	£	£	£	£	£	£
F10	**F10: BRICK AND BLOCK WALLING**										
F1007	**Isolated piers**										
F100768	**Lignacite blocks in gauged mortar (1:1:6):**										
F100768A	70 mm solid blocks	m²	0.73	18.31	–	8.07	26.38	20.14	–	8.88	29.02
F100768B	100 mm solid blocks	m²	0.76	19.07	–	11.20	30.27	20.98	–	12.32	33.30
F100768C	140 mm solid blocks	m²	0.79	19.94	–	16.32	36.26	21.93	–	17.95	39.89
F100768D	150 mm solid blocks	m²	0.84	21.03	–	16.83	37.86	23.13	–	18.51	41.65
F100768E	190 mm solid blocks	m²	0.94	23.67	–	25.29	48.96	26.04	–	27.82	53.86
F100768F	100 mm cellular blocks	m²	0.76	19.06	–	12.00	31.06	20.97	–	13.20	34.17
F100769	**Durox Supablocs in gauged mortar (1:1:6):**										
F100769A	100 mm 3.5 N/mm² blocks .	m²	0.57	14.34	–	11.36	25.70	15.77	–	12.50	28.27
F100769B	125 mm 3.5 N/mm² blocks .	m²	0.59	14.92	–	14.06	28.98	16.41	–	15.47	31.88
F100769C	150 mm 3.5 N/mm² blocks .	m²	0.63	15.80	–	16.94	32.74	17.38	–	18.63	36.01
F100769D	200 mm 3.5 N/mm² blocks .	m²	0.71	17.78	–	22.53	40.31	19.56	–	24.78	44.34
F100769E	100 mm 7 N/mm² blocks...	m²	0.57	14.35	–	13.01	27.36	15.79	–	14.31	30.10
F100769F	125 mm 7 N/mm² blocks...	m²	0.59	14.92	–	15.71	30.63	16.41	–	17.28	33.69
F100769G	150 mm 7 N/mm² blocks...	m²	0.63	15.80	–	18.60	34.40	17.38	–	20.46	37.84
F100769H	200 mm 7 N/mm² blocks...	m²	0.69	17.36	–	24.29	41.65	19.10	–	26.72	45.82

Masonry

Major Works 2009		Unit	Labour Hours	Labour Net	Plant Net	Materials Net	Unit Net	Labour Gross	Plant Gross	Materials Gross	Unit Price
								(Gross rates include 10% profit)			
				£	£	£	£	£	£	£	£
F10	**F10: BRICK AND BLOCK WALLING**										
F1008	**Extra over general brickwork for fair faced work**										
F100882	**Fair facing and flush pointing:**										
F100882A	stretcher bond	m²	0.06	1.41	–	0.18	1.59	1.55	–	0.20	1.75
F100882B	English bond	m²	0.06	1.49	–	0.36	1.85	1.64	–	0.40	2.04
F100882C	English garden wall bond . .	m²	0.06	1.43	–	0.27	1.70	1.57	–	0.30	1.87
F100882D	English cross bond.	m²	0.06	1.56	–	0.36	1.92	1.72	–	0.40	2.11
F100882E	Flemish bond	m²	0.06	1.53	–	0.27	1.80	1.68	–	0.30	1.98
F100882F	Flemish garden wall bond . .	m²	0.06	1.46	–	0.36	1.82	1.61	–	0.40	2.00
F100882G	Dutch bond	m²	0.07	1.64	–	0.45	2.09	1.80	–	0.50	2.30
F100882H	monk bond	m²	0.06	1.51	–	0.27	1.78	1.66	–	0.30	1.96
F100883	**Fair facing and struck or weather struck pointing:**										
F100883A	stretcher bond	m²	0.06	1.46	–	0.18	1.64	1.61	–	0.20	1.80
F100883B	English bond.	m²	0.06	1.56	–	0.36	1.92	1.72	–	0.40	2.11
F100883C	English garden wall bond . .	m²	0.06	1.51	–	0.27	1.78	1.66	–	0.30	1.96
F100883D	English cross bond.	m²	0.07	1.64	–	0.36	2.00	1.80	–	0.40	2.20
F100883E	Flemish bond	m²	0.06	1.61	–	0.27	1.88	1.77	–	0.30	2.07
F100883F	Flemish Garden wall bond. .	m²	0.06	1.54	–	0.36	1.90	1.69	–	0.40	2.09
F100883G	Dutch bond	m²	0.07	1.71	–	0.45	2.16	1.88	–	0.50	2.38
F100883H	monk bond	m²	0.06	1.59	–	0.27	1.86	1.75	–	0.30	2.05
F100884	**Fair facing and tooled or keyed pointing:**										
F100884A	stretcher bond	m²	0.06	1.56	–	0.18	1.74	1.72	–	0.20	1.91
F100884B	English bond.	m²	0.07	1.64	–	0.36	2.00	1.80	–	0.40	2.20
F100884C	English garden wall bond . .	m²	0.06	1.59	–	0.27	1.86	1.75	–	0.30	2.05
F100884D	English cross bond.	m²	0.07	1.71	–	0.36	2.07	1.88	–	0.40	2.28
F100884E	Flemish bond	m²	0.07	1.69	–	0.27	1.96	1.86	–	0.30	2.16
F100884F	Flemish garden wall bond . .	m²	0.06	1.61	–	0.36	1.97	1.77	–	0.40	2.17
F100884G	Dutch bond	m²	0.07	1.81	–	0.45	2.26	1.99	–	0.50	2.49
F100884H	monk bond	m²	0.07	1.66	–	0.27	1.93	1.83	–	0.30	2.12
F100887	**Extra over common brickwork in cement mortar (1:3) for facing brickwork, PC £300.00 per 1000, in gauged mortar (1:1:6); flush pointing one side:**										
F100887A	stretcher bond	m²	0.11	2.84	–	4.50	7.34	3.12	–	4.95	8.07
F100887B	English bond.	m²	0.17	4.24	–	6.87	11.11	4.66	–	7.56	12.22
F100887C	English garden wall bond . .	m²	0.14	3.54	–	5.72	9.26	3.89	–	6.29	10.19
F100887D	English cross bond.	m²	0.18	4.42	–	7.14	11.56	4.86	–	7.85	12.72
F100887E	Flemish bond	m²	0.15	3.77	–	6.06	9.83	4.15	–	6.67	10.81
F100887F	Flemish garden wall bond . .	m²	0.13	3.24	–	5.35	8.59	3.56	–	5.89	9.45
F100887G	Dutch bond	m²	0.19	4.67	–	7.67	12.34	5.14	–	8.44	13.57
F100887H	monk bond	m²	0.17	4.24	–	6.76	11.00	4.66	–	7.44	12.10

Masonry

Major Works 2009		Unit	Labour Hours	Labour Net £	Plant Net £	Materials Net £	Unit Net £	Labour Gross £	Plant Gross £	Materials Gross £	Unit Price £
								(Gross rates include 10% profit)			
F10	**F10: BRICK AND BLOCK WALLING**										
F1009	**Extra over general blockwork for fair faced work**										
F100986	**Fair facing and flush pointing:**										
F100986A	precast concrete blocks, BS 6073	m²	0.02	0.60	–	0.11	0.71	0.66	–	0.12	0.78
F100986B	Thermalite blocks	m²	0.02	0.60	–	0.11	0.71	0.66	–	0.12	0.78
F100986C	Lignacite blocks	m²	0.02	0.60	–	0.11	0.71	0.66	–	0.12	0.78
F100986D	Durox Supablocs	m²	0.02	0.60	–	0.11	0.71	0.66	–	0.12	0.78
F100987	**Extra over blockwork in cement mortar (1:3) for facing brickwork, PC 300:00 per 1000, in gauged mortar (1:1:6); flush pointing one side:**										
F100987A	stretcher bond	m²	0.11	2.84	–	7.38	10.22	3.12	–	8.12	11.24
F100987B	English bond	m²	0.17	4.25	–	11.15	15.40	4.68	–	12.27	16.94
F100987C	English garden wall bond	m²	0.14	3.54	–	9.40	12.94	3.89	–	10.34	14.23
F100987D	English cross bond	m²	0.18	4.43	–	12.37	16.80	4.87	–	13.61	18.48
F100987E	Flemish bond	m²	0.15	3.77	–	9.18	12.95	4.15	–	10.10	14.25
F100987F	Flemish garden wall bond	m²	0.13	3.24	–	7.37	10.61	3.56	–	8.11	11.67
F100987G	Dutch bond	m²	0.19	4.67	–	9.60	14.27	5.14	–	10.56	15.70
F100987H	monk bond	m²	0.17	4.25	–	12.23	16.48	4.68	–	13.45	18.13

Masonry

Major Works 2009		Unit	Labour Hours	Labour Net	Plant Net	Materials Net	Unit Net	Labour Gross	Plant Gross	Materials Gross	Unit Price
								(Gross rates include 10% profit)			
				£	£	£	£	£	£	£	£
F10	**F10: BRICK AND BLOCK WALLING**										
F1065	**Sills, bands and features**										
F106511	**Sills and copings; facing bricks, PC £300.00 per 1000, in gauged mortar (1:1:6); flush pointing all exposed edges:**										
F106511A	brick on edge sills; flush; flat top half brick wide (snapped headers)	m	0.24	6.03	–	3.07	9.10	6.63	–	3.38	10.01
F106511B	brick on edge sills; flush; flat top one brick wide	m	0.37	9.29	–	4.93	14.22	10.22	–	5.42	15.64
F106511C	brick on edge sills; 50 mm projection weathered; half brick wide (snapped headers)	m	0.47	11.81	–	4.60	16.41	12.99	–	5.06	18.05
F106511D	brick on edge sills; 50 mm projection weathered; one brick wide	m	0.53	13.31	–	5.54	18.85	14.64	–	6.09	20.74
F106511E	brick on edge copings; one brick wide	m	0.37	9.29	–	4.93	14.22	10.22	–	5.42	15.64
F106511F	brick on end copings; half brick wide	m	0.56	14.07	–	4.93	19.00	15.48	–	5.42	20.90
F106521	**Quoins and reveals; facing bricks, PC 300.00 per 1000, in gauged mortar (1:1:6); flush pointing all exposed edges:**										
F106521M	oversailing reveals; 25 mm projection toothed in three course bands; 161.2 mm average width	m	0.59	14.82	–	4.32	19.14	16.30	–	4.75	21.05
F106521N	oversailing quoins; 25 mm projection toothed in three course bands; 322.5 average girth	m	0.71	17.83	–	5.76	23.59	19.61	–	6.34	25.95
F106521U	receding reveals; 25 mm inset; toothed in three course bands; 161.25 mm average width	m	0.59	14.82	–	4.01	18.83	16.30	–	4.41	20.71
F106521V	receding quoins; 25 mm inset; toothed in three course bands; 322.5 mm average girth	m	0.71	17.83	–	5.15	22.98	19.61	–	5.67	25.28

Masonry

Major Works 2009		Unit	Labour Hours	Labour Net	Plant Net	Materials Net	Unit Net	Labour Gross	Plant Gross	Materials Gross	Unit Price
								(Gross rates include 10% profit)			
				£	£	£	£	£	£	£	£
F10	**F10: BRICK AND BLOCK WALLING**										
F1065	**Sills, bands and features**										
F106531	**Bands and plain courses; facing bricks, PC £300:00 per 1000, in gauged mortar (1:1:6); flush pointing all exposed edges:**										
F106531G	oversailing plain courses; 25 mm projection; one course	m	0.24	6.03	–	1.85	7.88	6.63	–	2.04	8.67
F106531H	oversailing plain courses; 25 mm projection; two course	m	0.37	9.30	–	4.01	13.31	10.23	–	4.41	14.64
F106531I	oversailing plain courses; 25 mm projection; three course	m	0.47	11.81	–	5.76	17.57	12.99	–	6.34	19.33
F106531J	oversailing brick on end bands; half brick thick	m	0.36	9.04	–	5.54	14.58	9.94	–	6.09	16.04
F106531K	oversailing brick on edge bands; half brick thick (snapped headers)	m	0.36	9.04	–	4.60	13.64	9.94	–	5.06	15.00
F106531L	oversailing brick on edge bands; one brick thick	m	0.56	14.07	–	5.54	19.61	15.48	–	6.09	21.57
F106531O	receding plain courses; 25 mm inset; one course	m	0.24	6.03	–	1.85	7.88	6.63	–	2.04	8.67
F106531P	receding plain course; 25 mm inset; two course	m	0.37	9.30	–	3.40	12.70	10.23	–	3.74	13.97
F106531Q	receding plain courses; 25 mm inset; three course	m	0.47	11.80	–	5.15	16.95	12.98	–	5.67	18.65
F106531R	receding brick on end bands; half brick thick	m	0.36	9.04	–	4.93	13.97	9.94	–	5.42	15.37
F106531S	receding brick on edge bands; half brick thick (snapped headers)	m	0.19	4.77	–	4.60	9.37	5.25	–	5.06	10.31
F106531T	receding brick on edge bands; one brick thick	m	0.56	14.07	–	4.93	19.00	15.48	–	5.42	20.90

Masonry

Major Works 2009	Unit	Labour Hours	Labour Net £	Plant Net £	Materials Net £	Unit Net £	Labour Gross £	Plant Gross £	Materials Gross £	Unit Price £
							(Gross rates include 10% profit)			
F10 **F10: BRICK AND BLOCK WALLING**										
F1066 **Arches**										
F106621 **Facing bricks, PC £300:00 per 1000, in gauged mortar (1:1:6); flush pointing all exposed edges:**										
F106621A brick on edge flat arches; half brick wide (snapped headers)	m	0.32	8.04	–	3.07	11.11	8.84	–	3.38	12.22
F106621B brick on edge flat arches; one brick wide	m	0.46	11.55	–	4.93	16.48	12.71	–	5.42	18.13
F106621C brick on end flat arches; half brick wide	m	0.66	16.58	–	4.93	21.51	18.24	–	5.42	23.66
F106621D brick on edge segmental arches; half brick wide (snapped headers)	m	0.39	9.80	–	3.07	12.87	10.78	–	3.38	14.16
F106621E brick on edge segmental arches; one brick wide; one course	m	0.57	14.32	–	4.93	19.25	15.75	–	5.42	21.18
F106621F brick on edge segmental arches; one brick wide; two course	m	0.83	20.85	–	9.86	30.71	22.94	–	10.85	33.78
F106621G brick on end segmental arches; half brick wide	m	0.83	20.85	–	4.93	25.78	22.94	–	5.42	28.36
F106621H brick on edge semi-circular arches; half brick wide (snapped headers)	m	0.78	19.60	–	3.07	22.67	21.56	–	3.38	24.94
F106621I brick on edge semi-circular arches; one brick wide; one course	m	1.04	26.12	–	4.93	31.05	28.73	–	5.42	34.16
F106621J brick on edge semi-circular arches; one brick wide; two course	m	1.66	41.70	–	9.86	51.56	45.87	–	10.85	56.72
F106621K brick on end semi-circular arches; half brick wide	m	1.66	41.70	–	4.93	46.63	45.87	–	5.42	51.29

Masonry

Major Works 2009		Unit	Labour Hours	Labour Net	Plant Net	Materials Net	Unit Net	Labour Gross	Plant Gross	Materials Gross	Unit Price
								(Gross rates include 10% profit)			
				£	£	£	£	£	£	£	£
F30	**F30: ACCESSORIES AND SUNDRY ITEMS**										
F3001	**Forming cavities**										
F300150	**Form cavity to hollow wall:**										
F300150A	25 mm wide.............	m²	0.02	0.60	–	–	0.60	0.66	–	–	0.66
F300150B	50 mm wide.............	m²	0.02	0.53	–	–	0.53	0.58	–	–	0.58
F300150C	75 mm wide.............	m²	0.02	0.48	–	–	0.48	0.53	–	–	0.53
F300150D	100 mm wide	m²	0.02	0.38	–	–	0.38	0.42	–	–	0.42
F300151	**Build in wall ties; 3 per m²:**										
F300151A	3 mm galvanised wire butterfly ties, 200 mm long .	m²	0.09	2.26	–	0.44	2.70	2.49	–	0.48	2.97
F300151B	3 mm stainless steel wire butterfly ties, 200 mm long .	m²	0.09	2.26	–	0.61	2.87	2.49	–	0.67	3.16
F300151C	3 × 19 mm galvanised steel twisted ties, 200 mm long ..	m²	0.09	2.26	–	1.14	3.40	2.49	–	1.25	3.74
F300151D	3 × 19 mm stainless steel twisted ties 200 mm long ..	m²	0.09	2.26	–	1.52	3.78	2.49	–	1.67	4.16
F300152	**Build in wall ties; 5 per m²:**										
F300152A	3 mm galvanised wire butterfly ties, 200 mm long .	m²	0.15	3.77	–	0.73	4.50	4.15	–	0.80	4.95
F300152B	3 mm stainless steel wire butterfly ties, 200 mm long .	m²	0.15	3.77	–	1.02	4.79	4.15	–	1.12	5.27
F300152C	3 × 19 mm galvanised steel twisted ties 200 mm long ..	m²	0.15	3.77	–	1.90	5.67	4.15	–	2.09	6.24
F300152D	3 × 19 mm stainless steel twisted ties 200 mm long ..	m²	0.15	3.77	–	2.53	6.30	4.15	–	2.78	6.93

Masonry

Major Works 2009		Unit	Labour Hours	Labour Net	Plant Net	Materials Net	Unit Net	Labour Gross	Plant Gross	Materials Gross	Unit Price
								(Gross rates include 10% profit)			
				£	£	£	£	£	£	£	£
F30	**F30: ACCESSORIES AND SUNDRY ITEMS**										
F3003	**Closing cavities**										
F300310	**Thermabate insulated cavity closer; hollow PVC-u extrusion with core of polyisocyanate foam; fixed in accordance with manufacturer's instructions; to suit cavity width:**										
F300310A	50-60 mm; Thermabate 50 .	m	0.11	2.76	–	5.45	8.21	3.04	–	6.00	9.03
F300310B	65-75 mm; Thermabate 65 .	m	0.13	3.26	–	6.01	9.27	3.59	–	6.61	10.20
F300310C	75-85 mm; Thermabate 75 .	m	0.14	3.52	–	6.57	10.09	3.87	–	7.23	11.10
F300310D	85-95 mm; Thermabate 85 .	m	0.14	3.52	–	7.17	10.69	3.87	–	7.89	11.76
F300310E	90-100 mm; Thermabate 90	m	0.15	3.76	–	7.70	11.46	4.14	–	8.47	12.61
F300310F	100-110 mm; Thermabate 100.	m	0.15	3.77	–	8.27	12.04	4.15	–	9.10	13.24
F3005	**Cavity wall insulation**										
F300508	**Jablite expanded polystyrene cavity wall insulation; fitting between wall ties:**										
F300508A	25 mm thick	m²	0.15	3.77	–	2.36	6.13	4.15	–	2.60	6.74
F300508B	50 mm thick	m²	0.16	4.02	–	3.34	7.36	4.42	–	3.67	8.10
F300508C	75 mm thick	m²	0.18	4.52	–	5.16	9.68	4.97	–	5.68	10.65
F300509	**Dritherm fibre glass cavity wall insulation slabs; fitting between wall ties:**										
F300509A	50 mm thick	m²	0.16	4.02	–	2.40	6.42	4.42	–	2.64	7.06
F300509B	75 mm thick	m²	0.18	4.52	–	2.89	7.41	4.97	–	3.18	8.15

Masonry

Major Works 2009		Unit	Labour Hours	Labour Net	Plant Net	Materials Net	Unit Net	Labour Gross	Plant Gross	Materials Gross	Unit Price
								——— (Gross rates include 10% profit) ———			
				£	£	£	£	£	£	£	£
F30	**F30: ACCESSORIES AND SUNDRY ITEMS**										
F3011	**Damp proof courses and cavity trays**										
F301113	**Hyload pitch polymer d.p.c.; horizontal:**										
F301113A	not exceeding 225 mm wide	m²	0.22	5.52	–	13.41	18.93	6.07	–	14.75	20.82
F301113C	over 225 mm wide	m²	0.17	4.27	–	13.41	17.68	4.70	–	14.75	19.45
F301115	**Hyload pitch polymer d.p.c.; vertical:**										
F301115A	not exceeding 225 mm wide	m²	0.30	7.53	–	13.41	20.94	8.28	–	14.75	23.03
F301115G	over 225 mm wide	m²	0.25	6.28	–	13.41	19.69	6.91	–	14.75	21.66
F301121	**Hyload pitch polymer d.p.c.; forming cavity trays:**										
F301121D	over 300 mm wide	m²	0.33	8.29	–	13.41	21.70	9.12	–	14.75	23.87
F3030	**Expanded metal reinforcement**										
F303001	**24 gauge galvanised mild steel expanded metal brick reinforcement:**										
F303001A	half brick wide............	m	0.15	3.77	–	0.59	4.36	4.15	–	0.65	4.80
F303001B	one brick wide............	m	0.17	4.27	–	1.02	5.29	4.70	–	1.12	5.82
F303001C	one and a half brick wide ...	m	0.19	4.77	–	1.58	6.35	5.25	–	1.74	6.99
F303001D	two brick wide............	m	0.21	5.28	–	2.06	7.34	5.81	–	2.27	8.07
F303002	**24 gauge stainless steel expanded metal brick reinforcement:**										
F303002A	half brick wide............	m	0.15	3.77	–	1.01	4.78	4.15	–	1.11	5.26
F303002B	one brick wide............	m	0.17	4.27	–	1.57	5.84	4.70	–	1.73	6.42
F303002C	one and a half brick wide ...	m	0.19	4.77	–	2.40	7.17	5.25	–	2.64	7.89
F303002D	two brick wide............	m	0.21	5.28	–	3.12	8.40	5.81	–	3.43	9.24
F3048	**Expansion joints or the like**										
F304811	**19 mm Flexcell compressible joint filler; fixing in place in brickwork or blockwork:**										
F304811A	half brick wide............	m	0.13	3.26	–	2.12	5.38	3.59	–	2.33	5.92
F304811B	one brick wide............	m	0.15	3.76	–	4.22	7.98	4.14	–	4.64	8.78
F304811C	one and a half brick wide ...	m	0.17	4.27	–	6.33	10.60	4.70	–	6.96	11.66
F304811D	two brick wide............	m	0.19	4.77	–	8.43	13.20	5.25	–	9.27	14.52
F304811E	50 mm	m	0.11	2.76	–	0.97	3.73	3.04	–	1.07	4.10
F304811F	60 mm	m	0.11	2.76	–	1.15	3.91	3.04	–	1.27	4.30
F304811G	70 mm	m	0.12	3.01	–	1.35	4.36	3.31	–	1.49	4.80
F304811H	75 mm	m	0.12	3.02	–	1.44	4.46	3.32	–	1.58	4.91
F304811I	90 mm	m	0.13	3.27	–	1.73	5.00	3.60	–	1.90	5.50
F304811J	100 mm	m	0.13	3.26	–	1.92	5.18	3.59	–	2.11	5.70
F304811K	125 mm	m	0.13	3.27	–	2.39	5.66	3.60	–	2.63	6.23
F304811L	140 mm	m	0.14	3.52	–	2.68	6.20	3.87	–	2.95	6.82
F304811M	150 mm	m	0.14	3.52	–	2.88	6.40	3.87	–	3.17	7.04
F304811N	190 mm	m	0.15	3.77	–	3.65	7.42	4.15	–	4.02	8.16
F304811O	200 mm	m	0.15	3.77	–	3.83	7.60	4.15	–	4.21	8.36
F304811P	215 mm	m	0.15	3.77	–	4.12	7.89	4.15	–	4.53	8.68
F304812	**Gun grade polysulphide rubber compound:**										
F304812A	19 × 19 mm............	m	0.14	2.45	–	1.75	4.20	2.70	–	1.93	4.62

Masonry

Major Works 2009		Unit	Labour Hours	Labour Net	Plant Net	Materials Net	Unit Net	Labour Gross	Plant Gross	Materials Gross	Unit Price
								(Gross rates include 10% profit)			
				£	£	£	£	£	£	£	£
F30	**F30: ACCESSORIES AND SUNDRY ITEMS**										
F3055	**Tile sills and creasings**										
F305502	**Sills; 265 × 165 mm plain concrete tiles in gauged mortar (1:1:6); double course breaking joint 50 mm projection; weathered; flush pointing all exposed edges:**										
F305502A	152 mm wide	m	0.25	6.28	–	6.38	12.66	6.91	–	7.02	13.93
F305502B	265 mm wide	m	0.25	6.28	–	6.60	12.88	6.91	–	7.26	14.17
F305512	**Creasings; 265 × 165 mm plain concrete tiles in gauged mortar (1:1:6); single course; 50 mm projection one side; flush pointing all exposed edges:**										
F305512C	152 mm wide	m	0.22	5.53	–	3.06	8.59	6.08	–	3.37	9.45
F305512D	265 mm wide	m	0.22	5.53	–	3.28	8.81	6.08	–	3.61	9.69
F305515	**Creasings; 265 × 165 mm plain concrete tiles in gauged mortar (1:1:6); single course; 50 mm projection both sides; flush pointing all exposed edges:**										
F305515E	202 mm wide	m	0.22	5.53	–	3.06	8.59	6.08	–	3.37	9.45
F305515F	315 mm wide	m	0.28	7.03	–	6.60	13.63	7.73	–	7.26	14.99
F305517	**Creasings; 265 × 165 mm plain concrete tiles in gauged mortar (1:1:6); double course; 50 mm projection one side; flush pointing all exposed edges:**										
F305517G	152 mm wide	m	0.38	9.55	–	3.17	12.72	10.51	–	3.49	13.99
F305517H	265 mm wide	m	0.38	9.54	–	6.82	16.36	10.49	–	7.50	18.00
F305519	**Creasings; 265 × 165 mm plain concrete tiles in gauged mortar (1:1:6); double course; 50 mm projection both sides; flush pointing all exposed edges:**										
F305519I	202 mm wide	m	0.47	11.80	–	6.60	18.40	12.98	–	7.26	20.24
F305519J	315 mm wide	m	0.61	15.32	–	12.61	27.93	16.85	–	13.87	30.72

Major Works 2009		Unit	Labour Hours	Labour Net	Plant Net	Materials Net	Unit Net	Labour Gross	Plant Gross	Materials Gross	Unit Price
				£	£	£	£	£	£	£	£
F30	**F30: ACCESSORIES AND SUNDRY ITEMS**										
F3061	**Flue linings, bends, chimney pots and terminals**										
F306101	**Clay circular section rebated and socketed flue liners; BS 1181; bedded and pointed in cement mortar (1:3); internal diameter:**										
F306101A	125 mm	m	0.20	5.03	–	20.09	25.12	5.53	–	22.10	27.63
F306101B	150 mm	m	0.22	5.53	–	19.70	25.23	6.08	–	21.67	27.75
F306101C	185 mm	m	0.24	6.02	–	25.50	31.52	6.62	–	28.05	34.67
F306101D	200 mm	m	0.24	6.02	–	35.37	41.39	6.62	–	38.91	45.53
F306101E	225 mm	m	0.25	6.28	–	42.16	48.44	6.91	–	46.38	53.28
F306101F	300 mm	m	0.28	7.03	–	101.07	108.10	7.73	–	111.18	118.91
F306106	**Clay square section rebated and socketed flue liners; BS 1181; bedded and pointed in cement mortar (1:3); internal size:**										
F306106A	185 × 185 mm	m	0.24	6.03	–	29.32	35.35	6.63	–	32.25	38.89
F306106B	200 × 200 mm	m	0.24	6.03	–	40.85	46.88	6.63	–	44.94	51.57
F306106C	225 × 225 mm	m	0.25	6.28	–	48.77	55.05	6.91	–	53.65	60.56
F306111	**Clay circular section rebated and socketed flue bends; BS 1181; bedded and pointed in cement mortar (1:3); internal diameter:**										
F306111A	125 mm	Nr	0.23	5.78	–	19.04	24.82	6.36	–	20.94	27.30
F306111B	150 mm	Nr	0.25	6.28	–	19.04	25.32	6.91	–	20.94	27.85
F306111C	185 mm	Nr	0.28	7.04	–	22.22	29.26	7.74	–	24.44	32.19
F306111D	200 mm	Nr	0.30	7.54	–	37.95	45.49	8.29	–	41.75	50.04
F306111E	225 mm	Nr	0.30	7.54	–	38.89	46.43	8.29	–	42.78	51.07
F306111F	300 mm	Nr	0.50	12.56	–	87.65	100.21	13.82	–	96.42	110.23
F306116	**Clay square section rebated and socketed flue bends; BS 1181; bedded and pointed in cement mortar (1:3); internal size:**										
F306116A	185 × 185 mm	Nr	0.25	6.28	–	22.80	29.08	6.91	–	25.08	31.99
F306116B	200 × 200 mm	Nr	0.28	7.04	–	37.07	44.11	7.74	–	40.78	48.52
F306116C	225 × 225 mm	Nr	0.30	7.53	–	41.33	48.86	8.28	–	45.46	53.75
F306121	**Clay chimney pots; set and flaunched in cement mortar (1:3); Cannon head pattern; height:**										
F306121A	300 mm	Nr	0.35	8.79	–	26.64	35.43	9.67	–	29.30	38.97
F306121B	450 mm	Nr	0.35	8.79	–	32.85	41.64	9.67	–	36.14	45.80
F306121C	600 mm	Nr	0.37	9.29	–	46.70	55.99	10.22	–	51.37	61.59
F306121D	750 mm	Nr	0.55	13.82	–	61.78	75.60	15.20	–	67.96	83.16
F306131	**Clay flue terminal; dry fitted to flue liner; internal diameter:**										
F306131A	185 mm	Nr	0.30	7.53	–	32.26	39.79	8.28	–	35.49	43.77
F306131B	225 mm	Nr	0.35	8.79	–	53.94	62.73	9.67	–	59.33	69.00

(Gross rates include 10% profit)

Masonry

Major Works 2009		Unit	Labour Hours	Labour Net	Plant Net	Materials Net	Unit Net	Labour Gross	Plant Gross	Materials Gross	Unit Price
								(Gross rates include 10% profit)			
				£	£	£	£	£	£	£	£
F30	**F30: ACCESSORIES AND SUNDRY ITEMS**										
F3082	**Air bricks or the like**										
F308221	**Form opening in wall; build in terracotta air brick; bed and point in cement mortar (1:3):**										
F308221A	225 × 75 mm	Nr	0.12	3.01	–	2.87	5.88	3.31	–	3.16	6.47
F308221B	225 × 150 mm	Nr	0.15	3.77	–	4.37	8.14	4.15	–	4.81	8.95
F308221C	225 × 225 mm	Nr	0.18	4.52	–	10.54	15.06	4.97	–	11.59	16.57
F308222	**Line opening with slates in cement mortar (1:3):**										
F308222A	225 × 75 mm; one brick wall	Nr	0.12	3.02	–	3.88	6.90	3.32	–	4.27	7.59
F308222B	225 × 75 mm; one and a half brick wall	Nr	0.15	3.76	–	5.83	9.59	4.14	–	6.41	10.55
F308222C	225 × 75 mm; two brick wall	Nr	0.18	4.52	–	5.83	10.35	4.97	–	6.41	11.39
F308222D	225 × 75 mm; 250 mm cavity wall	Nr	0.19	4.78	–	3.88	8.66	5.26	–	4.27	9.53
F308222E	225 × 75 mm; 275 mm cavity wall	Nr	0.20	5.02	–	5.83	10.85	5.52	–	6.41	11.94
F308222F	225 × 75 mm; 300 mm cavity wall	Nr	0.22	5.52	–	5.83	11.35	6.07	–	6.41	12.49
F308222G	225 × 150 mm; one brick wall	Nr	0.14	3.52	–	3.88	7.40	3.87	–	4.27	8.14
F308222H	225 × 150 mm; one and a half brick wall	Nr	0.17	4.27	–	7.77	12.04	4.70	–	8.55	13.24
F308222I	225 × 150 mm; two brick wall	Nr	0.20	5.02	–	7.77	12.79	5.52	–	8.55	14.07
F308222J	225 × 150 mm; 250 mm cavity wall	Nr	0.21	5.27	–	7.77	13.04	5.80	–	8.55	14.34
F308222K	225 × 150 mm; 275 mm cavity wall	Nr	0.22	5.53	–	7.77	13.30	6.08	–	8.55	14.63
F308222L	225 × 150 mm; 300 mm cavity wall	Nr	0.23	5.78	–	7.77	13.55	6.36	–	8.55	14.91
F308222M	225 × 225 mm; one brick wall	Nr	0.20	5.02	–	5.83	10.85	5.52	–	6.41	11.94
F308222N	225 × 225 mm; one and a half brick wall	Nr	0.22	5.53	–	9.71	15.24	6.08	–	10.68	16.76
F308222O	225 × 225 mm; two brick wall	Nr	0.24	6.03	–	9.71	15.74	6.63	–	10.68	17.31
F308222P	225 × 225 mm; 250 mm cavity wall	Nr	0.25	6.28	–	9.71	15.99	6.91	–	10.68	17.59
F308222Q	225 × 225 mm; 275 mm cavity wall	Nr	0.26	6.53	–	9.71	16.24	7.18	–	10.68	17.86
F308222R	225 × 225 mm; 300 mm cavity wall	Nr	0.27	6.78	–	9.71	16.49	7.46	–	10.68	18.14

Major Works 2009		Unit	Labour Hours	Labour Net	Plant Net	Materials Net	Unit Net	Labour Gross	Plant Gross	Materials Gross	Unit Price
								(Gross rates include 10% profit)			
				£	£	£	£	£	£	£	£
F30	F30: ACCESSORIES AND SUNDRY ITEMS										
F3082	Air bricks or the like										
F308223	Line opening with terracotta cavity wall liner in cement mortar (1:3):										
F308223A	225 × 75 mm; 250 mm cavity wall	Nr	0.12	3.01	–	3.90	6.91	3.31	–	4.29	7.60
F308223B	225 × 75 mm; 275 mm cavity wall	Nr	0.14	3.52	–	4.27	7.79	3.87	–	4.70	8.57
F308223C	225 × 75 mm; 300 mm cavity wall	Nr	0.16	4.02	–	4.67	8.69	4.42	–	5.14	9.56
F308223D	225 × 150 mm; 250 mm cavity wall	Nr	0.15	3.77	–	4.48	8.25	4.15	–	4.93	9.08
F308223E	225 × 150 mm; 275 mm cavity wall	Nr	0.17	4.27	–	4.86	9.13	4.70	–	5.35	10.04
F308223F	225 × 150 mm; 300 mm cavity wall	Nr	0.19	4.77	–	5.25	10.02	5.25	–	5.78	11.02
F308223G	225 × 225 mm; 250 mm cavity wall	Nr	0.18	4.52	–	12.28	16.80	4.97	–	13.51	18.48
F308223H	225 × 225 mm; 275 mm cavity wall	Nr	0.20	5.02	–	12.64	17.66	5.52	–	13.90	19.43
F308223I	225 × 225 mm; 300 mm cavity wall	Nr	0.22	5.53	–	13.03	18.56	6.08	–	14.33	20.42
F308224	Plug and screw plastic inner screen with hit and miss vent; to brickwork or blockwork:										
F308224A	225 × 75 mm..........	Nr	0.30	5.09	–	2.48	7.57	5.60	–	2.73	8.33
F308224B	225 × 150 mm..........	Nr	0.30	5.09	–	3.33	8.42	5.60	–	3.66	9.26
F308224C	225 × 225 mm..........	Nr	0.30	5.09	–	4.66	9.75	5.60	–	5.13	10.73

Masonry

Major Works 2009		Unit	Labour Hours	Labour Net	Plant Net	Materials Net	Unit Net	Labour Gross	Plant Gross	Materials Gross	Unit Price
								(Gross rates include 10% profit)			
				£	£	£	£	£	£	£	£
F30	**F30: ACCESSORIES AND SUNDRY ITEMS**										
F3085	**Proprietary steel lintels; Catnic galvanised polyester powder coated; insulated; built into brick or block walling**										
F308501	**Open back range; Cougar 50/ 100; length:**										
F308501A	750 mm	Nr	0.05	1.26	–	30.61	31.87	1.39	–	33.67	35.06
F308501B	900 mm	Nr	0.07	1.76	–	37.07	38.83	1.94	–	40.78	42.71
F308501C	1050 mm	Nr	0.10	2.51	–	42.55	45.06	2.76	–	46.81	49.57
F308501D	1200 mm	Nr	0.12	3.01	–	48.03	51.04	3.31	–	52.83	56.14
F308501E	1350 mm	Nr	0.13	3.27	–	55.05	58.32	3.60	–	60.56	64.15
F308501F	1500 mm	Nr	0.15	3.77	–	62.08	65.85	4.15	–	68.29	72.44
F308501G	1650 mm	Nr	0.17	4.27	–	69.61	73.88	4.70	–	76.57	81.27
F308501H	1800 mm	Nr	0.18	4.52	–	77.18	81.70	4.97	–	84.90	89.87
F308501I	1950 mm	Nr	0.20	5.02	–	84.19	89.21	5.52	–	92.61	98.13
F308501J	2100 mm	Nr	0.21	5.28	–	88.61	93.89	5.81	–	97.47	103.28
F308501K	2250 mm	Nr	0.22	5.53	–	103.22	108.75	6.08	–	113.54	119.63
F308501L	2400 mm	Nr	0.24	6.03	–	108.63	114.66	6.63	–	119.49	126.13
F308501M	2550 mm	Nr	0.26	6.53	–	115.99	122.52	7.18	–	127.59	134.77
F308501N	2700 mm	Nr	0.27	6.78	–	123.29	130.07	7.46	–	135.62	143.08
F308501O	2850 mm	Nr	0.28	7.03	–	154.58	161.61	7.73	–	170.04	177.77
F308501P	3000 mm	Nr	0.30	7.54	–	170.32	177.86	8.29	–	187.35	195.65
F308501Q	3300 mm	Nr	0.32	8.04	–	190.54	198.58	8.84	–	209.59	218.44
F308501R	3600 mm	Nr	0.34	8.54	–	209.11	217.65	9.39	–	230.02	239.42
F308501S	3900 mm	Nr	0.36	9.04	–	272.07	281.11	9.94	–	299.28	309.22
F308505	**Open back range; Cougar 50/ 125; length:**										
F308505A	750 mm	Nr	0.05	1.26	–	30.10	31.36	1.39	–	33.11	34.50
F308505B	900 mm	Nr	0.07	1.76	–	35.96	37.72	1.94	–	39.56	41.49
F308505C	1050 mm	Nr	0.10	2.51	–	42.55	45.06	2.76	–	46.81	49.57
F308505D	1200 mm	Nr	0.12	3.01	–	47.95	50.96	3.31	–	52.75	56.06
F308505E	1350 mm	Nr	0.13	3.27	–	54.81	58.08	3.60	–	60.29	63.89
F308505F	1500 mm	Nr	0.15	3.77	–	61.65	65.42	4.15	–	67.82	71.96
F308505G	1650 mm	Nr	0.17	4.27	–	68.68	72.95	4.70	–	75.55	80.25
F308505H	1800 mm	Nr	0.18	4.52	–	76.56	81.08	4.97	–	84.22	89.19
F308505I	1950 mm	Nr	0.20	5.02	–	84.36	89.38	5.52	–	92.80	98.32
F308505J	2100 mm	Nr	0.21	5.28	–	88.40	93.68	5.81	–	97.24	103.05
F308505K	2250 mm	Nr	0.22	5.53	–	101.17	106.70	6.08	–	111.29	117.37
F308505L	2400 mm	Nr	0.24	6.03	–	107.77	113.80	6.63	–	118.55	125.18
F308505M	2550 mm	Nr	0.26	6.53	–	115.53	122.06	7.18	–	127.08	134.27
F308505N	2700 mm	Nr	0.27	6.78	–	123.29	130.07	7.46	–	135.62	143.08
F308505O	2850 mm	Nr	0.29	7.28	–	154.32	161.60	8.01	–	169.75	177.76
F308505P	3000 mm	Nr	0.31	7.79	–	170.32	178.11	8.57	–	187.35	195.92

Major Works 2009		Unit	Labour Hours	Labour Net	Plant Net	Materials Net	Unit Net	Labour Gross	Plant Gross	Materials Gross	Unit Price
								(Gross rates include 10% profit)			
				£	£	£	£	£	£	£	£
F30	**F30: ACCESSORIES AND SUNDRY ITEMS**										
F3085	**Proprietary steel lintels; Catnic galvanised polyester powder coated; insulated; built into brick or block walling**										
F308509	**Open back range; Cougar 70/ 100; length:**										
F308509A	750 mm	Nr	0.06	1.51	–	30.10	31.61	1.66	–	33.11	34.77
F308509B	900 mm	Nr	0.08	2.01	–	35.96	37.97	2.21	–	39.56	41.77
F308509C	1050 mm	Nr	0.11	2.76	–	41.96	44.72	3.04	–	46.16	49.19
F308509D	1200 mm	Nr	0.13	3.27	–	47.95	51.22	3.60	–	52.75	56.34
F308509E	1350 mm	Nr	0.15	3.77	–	53.95	57.72	4.15	–	59.35	63.49
F308509F	1500 mm	Nr	0.17	4.27	–	59.93	64.20	4.70	–	65.92	70.62
F308509G	1650 mm	Nr	0.18	4.52	–	67.47	71.99	4.97	–	74.22	79.19
F308509H	1800 mm	Nr	0.19	4.77	–	75.01	79.78	5.25	–	82.51	87.76
F308509I	1950 mm	Nr	0.21	5.28	–	81.47	86.75	5.81	–	89.62	95.43
F308509J	2100 mm	Nr	0.22	5.53	–	85.80	91.33	6.08	–	94.38	100.46
F308509K	2250 mm	Nr	0.23	5.78	–	96.64	102.42	6.36	–	106.30	112.66
F308509L	2400 mm	Nr	0.25	6.28	–	101.72	108.00	6.91	–	111.89	118.80
F308509M	2550 mm	Nr	0.27	6.78	–	111.42	118.20	7.46	–	122.56	130.02
F308509N	2700 mm	Nr	0.28	7.03	–	117.39	124.42	7.73	–	129.13	136.86
F308509O	2850 mm	Nr	0.30	7.54	–	155.06	162.60	8.29	–	170.57	178.86
F308509P	3000 mm	Nr	0.32	8.04	–	167.04	175.08	8.84	–	183.74	192.59
F308509Q	3300 mm	Nr	0.34	8.54	–	185.39	193.93	9.39	–	203.93	213.32
F308509R	3600 mm	Nr	0.36	9.04	–	202.19	211.23	9.94	–	222.41	232.35
F308509S	3900 mm	Nr	0.37	9.29	–	249.46	258.75	10.22	–	274.41	284.63

Masonry

Major Works 2009		Unit	Labour Hours	Labour Net	Plant Net	Materials Net	Unit Net	Labour Gross	Plant Gross	Materials Gross	Unit Price
								(Gross rates include 10% profit)			
				£	£	£	£	£	£	£	£
F30	**F30: ACCESSORIES AND SUNDRY ITEMS**										
F3085	**Proprietary steel lintels; Catnic galvanised polyester powder coated; insulated; built into brick or block walling**										
F308512	**Open back range; Cougar 70/ 125; length:**										
F308512A	750 mm	Nr	0.06	1.51	–	38.33	39.84	1.66	–	42.16	43.82
F308512B	900 mm	Nr	0.08	2.01	–	45.78	47.79	2.21	–	50.36	52.57
F308512C	1050 mm	Nr	0.11	2.76	–	55.26	58.02	3.04	–	60.79	63.82
F308512D	1200 mm	Nr	0.13	3.27	–	60.17	63.44	3.60	–	66.19	69.78
F308512E	1350 mm	Nr	0.15	3.77	–	70.43	74.20	4.15	–	77.47	81.62
F308512F	1500 mm	Nr	0.17	4.27	–	75.71	79.98	4.70	–	83.28	87.98
F308512G	1650 mm	Nr	0.19	4.77	–	94.31	99.08	5.25	–	103.74	108.99
F308512H	1800 mm	Nr	0.21	5.28	–	103.91	109.19	5.81	–	114.30	120.11
F308512I	1950 mm	Nr	0.23	5.78	–	116.09	121.87	6.36	–	127.70	134.06
F308512J	2100 mm	Nr	0.24	6.03	–	122.36	128.39	6.63	–	134.60	141.23
F308512K	2250 mm	Nr	0.26	6.53	–	153.10	159.63	7.18	–	168.41	175.59
F308512L	2400 mm	Nr	0.28	7.03	–	168.93	175.96	7.73	–	185.82	193.56
F308512M	2550 mm	Nr	0.29	7.28	–	188.34	195.62	8.01	–	207.17	215.18
F308512N	2700 mm	Nr	0.31	7.79	–	198.36	206.15	8.57	–	218.20	226.77
F308512O	2850 mm	Nr	0.33	8.29	–	249.73	258.02	9.12	–	274.70	283.82
F308512P	3000 mm	Nr	0.34	8.54	–	276.17	284.71	9.39	–	303.79	313.18
F308515	**Open back range; Cougar 90/ 100; length:**										
F308515A	750 mm	Nr	0.07	1.76	–	31.91	33.67	1.94	–	35.10	37.04
F308515B	900 mm	Nr	0.09	2.26	–	37.39	39.65	2.49	–	41.13	43.62
F308515C	1050 mm	Nr	0.12	3.01	–	42.75	45.76	3.31	–	47.03	50.34
F308515D	1200 mm	Nr	0.14	3.52	–	49.84	53.36	3.87	–	54.82	58.70
F308515E	1350 mm	Nr	0.16	4.02	–	56.11	60.13	4.42	–	61.72	66.14
F308515F	1500 mm	Nr	0.18	4.52	–	62.32	66.84	4.97	–	68.55	73.52
F308515G	1650 mm	Nr	0.20	5.02	–	68.68	73.70	5.52	–	75.55	81.07
F308515H	1800 mm	Nr	0.22	5.53	–	75.01	80.54	6.08	–	82.51	88.59
F308515I	1950 mm	Nr	0.24	6.03	–	84.39	90.42	6.63	–	92.83	99.46
F308515J	2100 mm	Nr	0.26	6.53	–	89.22	95.75	7.18	–	98.14	105.33
F308515K	2250 mm	Nr	0.28	7.03	–	101.35	108.38	7.73	–	111.49	119.22
F308515L	2400 mm	Nr	0.30	7.54	–	107.60	115.14	8.29	–	118.36	126.65
F308515M	2550 mm	Nr	0.32	8.04	–	118.20	126.24	8.84	–	130.02	138.86
F308515N	2700 mm	Nr	0.34	8.54	–	128.84	137.38	9.39	–	141.72	151.11
F308515O	2850 mm	Nr	0.35	8.79	–	154.45	163.24	9.67	–	169.90	179.56
F308515P	3000 mm	Nr	0.35	8.79	–	167.62	176.41	9.67	–	184.38	194.05
F308515Q	3300 mm	Nr	0.37	9.29	–	189.98	199.27	10.22	–	208.98	219.20
F308515R	3600 mm	Nr	0.39	9.80	–	208.49	218.29	10.78	–	229.34	240.12
F308515S	3900 mm	Nr	0.39	9.80	–	269.43	279.23	10.78	–	296.37	307.15

Major Works 2009		Unit	Labour Hours	Labour Net	Plant Net	Materials Net	Unit Net	Labour Gross	Plant Gross	Materials Gross	Unit Price
								(Gross rates include 10% profit)			
				£	£	£	£	£	£	£	£
F30	**F30: ACCESSORIES AND SUNDRY ITEMS**										
F3085	**Proprietary steel lintels; Catnic galvanised polyester powder coated; insulated; built into brick or block walling**										
F308519	**Open back range; Cougar 90/ 125; length:**										
F308519A	750 mm	Nr	0.08	2.01	–	47.86	49.87	2.21	–	52.65	54.86
F308519B	900 mm	Nr	0.10	2.51	–	57.16	59.67	2.76	–	62.88	65.64
F308519C	1050 mm	Nr	0.12	3.01	–	63.49	66.50	3.31	–	69.84	73.15
F308519D	1200 mm	Nr	0.14	3.52	–	66.75	70.27	3.87	–	73.43	77.30
F308519E	1350 mm	Nr	0.16	4.02	–	79.32	83.34	4.42	–	87.25	91.67
F308519F	1500 mm	Nr	0.18	4.52	–	85.80	90.32	4.97	–	94.38	99.35
F308519G	1650 mm	Nr	0.20	5.02	–	117.36	122.38	5.52	–	129.10	134.62
F308519H	1800 mm	Nr	0.22	5.53	–	133.60	139.13	6.08	–	146.96	153.04
F308519I	1950 mm	Nr	0.24	6.03	–	158.62	164.65	6.63	–	174.48	181.12
F308519J	2100 mm	Nr	0.26	6.53	–	171.52	178.05	7.18	–	188.67	195.86
F308519K	2250 mm	Nr	0.28	7.03	–	202.42	209.45	7.73	–	222.66	230.40
F308519L	2400 mm	Nr	0.30	7.54	–	218.35	225.89	8.29	–	240.19	248.48
F308519M	2550 mm	Nr	0.32	8.04	–	222.67	230.71	8.84	–	244.94	253.78
F308519N	2700 mm	Nr	0.34	8.54	–	247.38	255.92	9.39	–	272.12	281.51
F308519O	2850 mm	Nr	0.36	9.04	–	330.49	339.53	9.94	–	363.54	373.48
F308519P	3000 mm	Nr	0.38	9.55	–	373.30	382.85	10.51	–	410.63	421.14
F308525	**Combined box lintel range; CN7A; length**										
F308525A	750 mm	Nr	0.05	1.26	–	35.94	37.20	1.39	–	39.53	40.92
F308525B	900 mm	Nr	0.07	1.76	–	43.51	45.27	1.94	–	47.86	49.80
F308525C	1050 mm	Nr	0.10	2.51	–	50.12	52.63	2.76	–	55.13	57.89
F308525D	1200 mm	Nr	0.12	3.01	–	56.39	59.40	3.31	–	62.03	65.34
F308525E	1350 mm	Nr	0.13	3.27	–	64.47	67.74	3.60	–	70.92	74.51
F308525F	1500 mm	Nr	0.15	3.77	–	68.11	71.88	4.15	–	74.92	79.07
F308525G	1650 mm	Nr	0.17	4.27	–	81.75	86.02	4.70	–	89.93	94.62
F308525H	1800 mm	Nr	0.18	4.52	–	88.82	93.34	4.97	–	97.70	102.67
F308525I	1950 mm	Nr	0.20	5.02	–	99.45	104.47	5.52	–	109.40	114.92
F308525J	2100 mm	Nr	0.20	5.02	–	104.94	109.96	5.52	–	115.43	120.96
F308525K	2250 mm	Nr	0.22	5.53	–	122.47	128.00	6.08	–	134.72	140.80
F308525L	2400 mm	Nr	0.24	6.03	–	132.33	138.36	6.63	–	145.56	152.20
F308525M	2550 mm	Nr	0.26	6.53	–	142.34	148.87	7.18	–	156.57	163.76
F308525N	2700 mm	Nr	0.27	6.78	–	150.20	156.98	7.46	–	165.22	172.68
F308527	**Combined box lintel range; CN8C; length**										
F308527A	2250 mm	Nr	0.22	5.53	–	187.45	192.98	6.08	–	206.20	212.28
F308527B	2400 mm	Nr	0.24	6.03	–	196.61	202.64	6.63	–	216.27	222.90
F308527C	2550 mm	Nr	0.26	6.53	–	202.88	209.41	7.18	–	223.17	230.35
F308527D	2700 mm	Nr	0.27	6.78	–	208.61	215.39	7.46	–	229.47	236.93
F308527E	2850 mm	Nr	0.29	7.28	–	221.01	228.29	8.01	–	243.11	251.12
F308527F	3000 mm	Nr	0.30	7.54	–	223.70	231.24	8.29	–	246.07	254.36
F308527G	3300 mm	Nr	0.33	8.29	–	259.14	267.43	9.12	–	285.05	294.17
F308527H	3600 mm	Nr	0.36	9.04	–	278.83	287.87	9.94	–	306.71	316.66
F308527I	3900 mm	Nr	0.39	9.80	–	298.34	308.14	10.78	–	328.17	338.95
F308527J	4200 mm	Nr	0.42	10.55	–	298.50	309.05	11.61	–	328.35	339.96
F308527K	4500 mm	Nr	0.46	11.56	–	344.91	356.47	12.72	–	379.40	392.12
F308527L	4800 mm	Nr	0.50	12.56	–	362.16	374.72	13.82	–	398.38	412.19

Masonry

Major Works 2009		Unit	Labour Hours	Labour Net	Plant Net	Materials Net	Unit Net	Labour Gross	Plant Gross	Materials Gross	Unit Price
								——— (Gross rates include 10% profit) ———			
				£	£	£	£	£	£	£	£
F30	**F30: ACCESSORIES AND SUNDRY ITEMS**										
F3085	**Proprietary steel lintels; Catnic galvanised polyester powder coated; insulated; built into brick or block walling**										
F308532	**Combined box lintel range; CN3A; length**										
F308532A	750 mm	Nr	0.05	1.26	–	35.33	36.59	1.39	–	38.86	40.25
F308532B	900 mm	Nr	0.07	1.76	–	42.21	43.97	1.94	–	46.43	48.37
F308532C	1050 mm	Nr	0.10	2.51	–	49.58	52.09	2.76	–	54.54	57.30
F308532D	1200 mm	Nr	0.12	3.01	–	56.26	59.27	3.31	–	61.89	65.20
F308532E	1350 mm	Nr	0.14	3.52	–	63.95	67.47	3.87	–	70.35	74.22
F308532F	1500 mm	Nr	0.15	3.77	–	68.72	72.49	4.15	–	75.59	79.74
F308532G	1650 mm	Nr	0.17	4.27	–	80.96	85.23	4.70	–	89.06	93.75
F308532H	1800 mm	Nr	0.18	4.52	–	88.05	92.57	4.97	–	96.86	101.83
F308532I	1950 mm	Nr	0.19	4.77	–	95.15	99.92	5.25	–	104.67	109.91
F308532J	2100 mm	Nr	0.20	5.02	–	100.72	105.74	5.52	–	110.79	116.31
F308532K	2250 mm	Nr	0.22	5.53	–	113.37	118.90	6.08	–	124.71	130.79
F308532L	2400 mm	Nr	0.25	6.28	–	119.43	125.71	6.91	–	131.37	138.28
F308532M	2550 mm	Nr	0.26	6.53	–	127.52	134.05	7.18	–	140.27	147.46
F308532N	2700 mm	Nr	0.27	6.78	–	135.63	142.41	7.46	–	149.19	156.65
F308533	**Combined box lintel range; CN3C; length**										
F308533A	750 mm	Nr	0.05	1.26	–	60.91	62.17	1.39	–	67.00	68.39
F308533B	900 mm	Nr	0.07	1.76	–	69.82	71.58	1.94	–	76.80	78.74
F308533C	1050 mm	Nr	0.10	2.51	–	85.19	87.70	2.76	–	93.71	96.47
F308533D	1200 mm	Nr	0.12	3.01	–	93.12	96.13	3.31	–	102.43	105.74
F308533E	1350 mm	Nr	0.14	3.52	–	108.49	112.01	3.87	–	119.34	123.21
F308533F	1500 mm	Nr	0.15	3.77	–	116.40	120.17	4.15	–	128.04	132.19
F308533G	1650 mm	Nr	0.17	4.27	–	121.53	125.80	4.70	–	133.68	138.38
F308533H	1800 mm	Nr	0.18	4.52	–	124.16	128.68	4.97	–	136.58	141.55
F308533I	1950 mm	Nr	0.19	4.77	–	144.51	149.28	5.25	–	158.96	164.21
F308534	**Combined box lintel range; CN4B; length**										
F308534A	2100 mm	Nr	0.22	5.53	–	130.94	136.47	6.08	–	144.03	150.12
F308534B	2250 mm	Nr	0.23	5.78	–	143.71	149.49	6.36	–	158.08	164.44
F308534C	2400 mm	Nr	0.24	6.03	–	169.51	175.54	6.63	–	186.46	193.09
F308534D	2550 mm	Nr	0.26	6.53	–	180.07	186.60	7.18	–	198.08	205.26
F308534E	2700 mm	Nr	0.27	6.78	–	183.02	189.80	7.46	–	201.32	208.78
F308534F	3000 mm	Nr	0.29	7.28	–	196.07	203.35	8.01	–	215.68	223.69
F308534G	3300 mm	Nr	0.31	7.79	–	215.67	223.46	8.57	–	237.24	245.81
F308534H	3600 mm	Nr	0.33	8.29	–	235.36	243.65	9.12	–	258.90	268.02
F308535	**Combined box lintel range; CN4C; length**										
F308535A	2100 mm	Nr	0.24	6.03	–	180.40	186.43	6.63	–	198.44	205.07
F308535B	2250 mm	Nr	0.25	6.28	–	183.25	189.53	6.91	–	201.58	208.48
F308535C	2400 mm	Nr	0.27	6.78	–	185.63	192.41	7.46	–	204.19	211.65
F308535D	2550 mm	Nr	0.28	7.03	–	187.94	194.97	7.73	–	206.73	214.47
F308535E	2700 mm	Nr	0.30	7.54	–	196.37	203.91	8.29	–	216.01	224.30
F308535F	3000 mm	Nr	0.32	8.04	–	216.67	224.71	8.84	–	238.34	247.18
F308535G	3300 mm	Nr	0.33	8.29	–	259.00	267.29	9.12	–	284.90	294.02
F308535H	3600 mm	Nr	0.35	8.79	–	278.83	287.62	9.67	–	306.71	316.38
F308535I	3900 mm	Nr	0.36	9.04	–	292.93	301.97	9.94	–	322.22	332.17
F308535J	4200 mm	Nr	0.38	9.55	–	298.50	308.05	10.51	–	328.35	338.86
F308535K	4575 mm	Nr	0.40	10.05	–	319.05	329.10	11.06	–	350.96	362.01
F308535L	4800 mm	Nr	0.41	10.30	–	335.01	345.31	11.33	–	368.51	379.84

Major Works 2009		Unit	Labour Hours	Labour Net	Plant Net	Materials Net	Unit Net	Labour Gross	Plant Gross	Materials Gross	Unit Price
				£	£	£	£	£	£	£	£
								(Gross rates include 10% profit)			

F30 **F30: ACCESSORIES AND SUNDRY ITEMS**

F3085 **Proprietary steel lintels; Catnic galvanised polyester powder coated; insulated; built into brick or block walling**

Major Works 2009		Unit	Labour Hours	Labour Net	Plant Net	Materials Net	Unit Net	Labour Gross	Plant Gross	Materials Gross	Unit Price
F308537	**Combined box lintel range; CN43A; length:**										
F308537A	750 mm	Nr	0.05	1.26	–	35.33	36.59	1.39	–	38.86	40.25
F308537B	900 mm	Nr	0.07	1.76	–	42.21	43.97	1.94	–	46.43	48.37
F308537C	1050 mm	Nr	0.10	2.51	–	49.58	52.09	2.76	–	54.54	57.30
F308537D	1200 mm	Nr	0.12	3.01	–	56.28	59.29	3.31	–	61.91	65.22
F308537E	1350 mm	Nr	0.14	3.52	–	63.95	67.47	3.87	–	70.35	74.22
F308537F	1500 mm	Nr	0.15	3.77	–	73.06	76.83	4.15	–	80.37	84.51
F308537G	1650 mm	Nr	0.17	4.27	–	82.49	86.76	4.70	–	90.74	95.44
F308537H	1800 mm	Nr	0.18	4.52	–	89.87	94.39	4.97	–	98.86	103.83
F308537I	1950 mm	Nr	0.19	4.77	–	98.18	102.95	5.25	–	108.00	113.25
F308537J	2100 mm	Nr	0.20	5.02	–	103.77	108.79	5.52	–	114.15	119.67
F308537K	2250 mm	Nr	0.22	5.53	–	118.94	124.47	6.08	–	130.83	136.92
F308537L	2400 mm	Nr	0.25	6.28	–	126.53	132.81	6.91	–	139.18	146.09
F308537M	2550 mm	Nr	0.26	6.53	–	136.65	143.18	7.18	–	150.32	157.50
F308537N	2700 mm	Nr	0.27	6.78	–	144.73	151.51	7.46	–	159.20	166.66
F308538	**Combined box lintel range; CN44C; length:**										
F308538A	750 mm	Nr	0.06	1.51	–	64.41	65.92	1.66	–	70.85	72.51
F308538B	900 mm	Nr	0.08	2.01	–	69.82	71.83	2.21	–	76.80	79.01
F308538C	1050 mm	Nr	0.10	2.51	–	85.19	87.70	2.76	–	93.71	96.47
F308538D	1200 mm	Nr	0.12	3.01	–	93.12	96.13	3.31	–	102.43	105.74
F308538E	1350 mm	Nr	0.14	3.52	–	106.41	109.93	3.87	–	117.05	120.92
F308538F	1500 mm	Nr	0.16	4.02	–	113.25	117.27	4.42	–	124.58	129.00
F308538G	1650 mm	Nr	0.18	4.52	–	123.22	127.74	4.97	–	135.54	140.51
F308538H	1800 mm	Nr	0.20	5.02	–	128.36	133.38	5.52	–	141.20	146.72
F308538I	1950 mm	Nr	0.21	5.28	–	143.33	148.61	5.81	–	157.66	163.47
F308538J	2100 mm	Nr	0.23	5.78	–	146.35	152.13	6.36	–	160.99	167.34
F308538K	2250 mm	Nr	0.25	6.28	–	169.27	175.55	6.91	–	186.20	193.11
F308538L	2400 mm	Nr	0.27	6.78	–	179.67	186.45	7.46	–	197.64	205.10
F308538M	2550 mm	Nr	0.29	7.28	–	189.73	197.01	8.01	–	208.70	216.71
F308538N	2700 mm	Nr	0.31	7.79	–	199.92	207.71	8.57	–	219.91	228.48
F308538O	2850 mm	Nr	0.33	8.29	–	208.65	216.94	9.12	–	229.52	238.63
F308538P	3000 mm	Nr	0.35	8.79	–	229.43	238.22	9.67	–	252.37	262.04
F308538Q	3300 mm	Nr	0.36	9.04	–	250.29	259.33	9.94	–	275.32	285.26
F308538R	3600 mm	Nr	0.38	9.55	–	269.33	278.88	10.51	–	296.26	306.77
F308538S	3900 mm	Nr	0.40	10.05	–	283.63	293.68	11.06	–	311.99	323.05
F308538T	4200 mm	Nr	0.42	10.55	–	298.34	308.89	11.61	–	328.17	339.78
F308538U	4575 mm	Nr	0.44	11.05	–	336.28	347.33	12.16	–	369.91	382.06
F308538V	4800 mm	Nr	0.45	11.30	–	422.03	433.33	12.43	–	464.23	476.66
F308539	**Combined box lintel range; CN11A; length:**										
F308539A	750 mm	Nr	0.05	1.26	–	35.33	36.59	1.39	–	38.86	40.25
F308539B	900 mm	Nr	0.07	1.76	–	42.21	43.97	1.94	–	46.43	48.37
F308539C	1050 mm	Nr	0.10	2.51	–	49.58	52.09	2.76	–	54.54	57.30
F308539D	1200 mm	Nr	0.12	3.01	–	56.26	59.27	3.31	–	61.89	65.20
F308539E	1350 mm	Nr	0.14	3.52	–	66.75	70.27	3.87	–	73.43	77.30
F308539F	1500 mm	Nr	0.15	3.77	–	75.85	79.62	4.15	–	83.44	87.58
F308539G	1650 mm	Nr	0.17	4.27	–	88.59	92.86	4.70	–	97.45	102.15
F308539H	1800 mm	Nr	0.18	4.52	–	94.05	98.57	4.97	–	103.46	108.43
F308539I	1950 mm	Nr	0.19	4.77	–	102.37	107.14	5.25	–	112.61	117.85
F308539J	2100 mm	Nr	0.21	5.28	–	110.53	115.81	5.81	–	121.58	127.39
F308539K	2250 mm	Nr	0.23	5.78	–	124.91	130.69	6.36	–	137.40	143.76
F308539L	2400 mm	Nr	0.24	6.03	–	127.93	133.96	6.63	–	140.72	147.36
F308539M	2550 mm	Nr	0.26	6.53	–	147.86	154.39	7.18	–	162.65	169.83
F308539N	2700 mm	Nr	0.27	6.78	–	150.35	157.13	7.46	–	165.39	172.84

Masonry

Major Works 2009		Unit	Labour Hours	Labour Net	Plant Net	Materials Net	Unit Net	Labour Gross	Plant Gross	Materials Gross	Unit Price
								(Gross rates include 10% profit)			
				£	£	£	£	£	£	£	£
F30	**F30: ACCESSORIES AND SUNDRY ITEMS**										
F3085	**Proprietary steel lintels; Catnic galvanised polyester powder coated; insulated; built into brick or block walling**										
F308558	**External solid wall range; CN71A; length:**										
F308558A	750 mm	Nr	0.05	1.26	–	39.29	40.55	1.39	–	43.22	44.61
F308558B	900 mm	Nr	0.07	1.76	–	47.18	48.94	1.94	–	51.90	53.83
F308558C	1050 mm	Nr	0.10	2.51	–	54.93	57.44	2.76	–	60.42	63.18
F308558D	1200 mm	Nr	0.11	2.76	–	60.90	63.66	3.04	–	66.99	70.03
F308558E	1350 mm	Nr	0.13	3.27	–	70.47	73.74	3.60	–	77.52	81.11
F308558F	1500 mm	Nr	0.15	3.77	–	79.77	83.54	4.15	–	87.75	91.89
F308558G	1650 mm	Nr	0.17	4.27	–	88.03	92.30	4.70	–	96.83	101.53
F308558H	1800 mm	Nr	0.18	4.52	–	96.29	100.81	4.97	–	105.92	110.89
F308558I	1950 mm	Nr	0.20	5.02	–	99.21	104.23	5.52	–	109.13	114.65
F308558J	2100 mm	Nr	0.20	5.02	–	112.22	117.24	5.52	–	123.44	128.96
F308558K	2250 mm	Nr	0.22	5.53	–	131.40	136.93	6.08	–	144.54	150.62
F308558L	2400 mm	Nr	0.24	6.03	–	139.75	145.78	6.63	–	153.73	160.36
F308558M	2550 mm	Nr	0.26	6.53	–	144.46	150.99	7.18	–	158.91	166.09
F308558N	2700 mm	Nr	0.27	6.78	–	152.91	159.69	7.46	–	168.20	175.66
F308560	**External solid wall range; CN81C; length:**										
F308560A	2100 mm	Nr	0.20	5.02	–	188.03	193.05	5.52	–	206.83	212.36
F308560B	2250 mm	Nr	0.22	5.53	–	250.41	255.94	6.08	–	275.45	281.53
F308560C	2400 mm	Nr	0.24	6.03	–	256.52	262.55	6.63	–	282.17	288.81
F308560D	2550 mm	Nr	0.26	6.53	–	265.36	271.89	7.18	–	291.90	299.08
F308560E	2700 mm	Nr	0.27	6.78	–	272.41	279.19	7.46	–	299.65	307.11
F308560F	2850 mm	Nr	0.29	7.28	–	294.46	301.74	8.01	–	323.91	331.91
F308560G	3000 mm	Nr	0.31	7.79	–	309.58	317.37	8.57	–	340.54	349.11
F308560H	3300 mm	Nr	0.33	8.29	–	320.38	328.67	9.12	–	352.42	361.54
F308560I	3600 mm	Nr	0.35	8.79	–	347.86	356.65	9.67	–	382.65	392.32
F308560J	3900 mm	Nr	0.37	9.29	–	375.49	384.78	10.22	–	413.04	423.26
F308560K	4200 mm	Nr	0.39	9.80	–	398.44	408.24	10.78	–	438.28	449.06
F308560L	4575 mm	Nr	0.41	10.30	–	417.65	427.95	11.33	–	459.42	470.75
F308560M	4800 mm	Nr	0.43	10.80	–	445.16	455.96	11.88	–	489.68	501.56
F308565	**Internal solid wall range; CN92; length**										
F308565A	900 mm	Nr	0.11	2.76	–	5.69	8.45	3.04	–	6.26	9.30
F308565B	1050 mm	Nr	0.11	2.76	–	6.49	9.25	3.04	–	7.14	10.18
F308565C	1200 mm	Nr	0.12	3.01	–	7.34	10.35	3.31	–	8.07	11.39
F308566	**Internal solid wall range; CN102; length:**										
F308566A	900 mm	Nr	0.11	2.76	–	7.00	9.76	3.04	–	7.70	10.74
F308566B	1050 mm	Nr	0.11	2.76	–	8.20	10.96	3.04	–	9.02	12.06
F308566C	1200 mm	Nr	0.12	3.01	–	9.04	12.05	3.31	–	9.94	13.26
F308567	**Internal solid wall range; CN100; length:**										
F308567A	1050 mm	Nr	0.11	2.76	–	20.01	22.77	3.04	–	22.01	25.05
F308567B	1200 mm	Nr	0.11	2.76	–	24.87	27.63	3.04	–	27.36	30.39
F308567C	1350 mm	Nr	0.12	3.01	–	29.06	32.07	3.31	–	31.97	35.28
F308567D	1500 mm	Nr	0.13	3.27	–	30.74	34.01	3.60	–	33.81	37.41
F308567E	1800 mm	Nr	0.14	3.52	–	31.14	34.66	3.87	–	34.25	38.13
F308567F	2100 mm	Nr	0.15	3.77	–	36.21	39.98	4.15	–	39.83	43.98

Masonry

Major Works 2009		Unit	Labour Hours	Labour Net	Plant Net	Materials Net	Unit Net	Labour Gross	Plant Gross	Materials Gross	Unit Price
								(Gross rates include 10% profit)			
				£	£	£	£	£	£	£	£
F30	**F30: ACCESSORIES AND SUNDRY ITEMS**										
F3085	**Proprietary steel lintels; Catnic galvanised polyester powder coated; insulated; built into brick or block walling**										
F308568	**Internal solid wall range; CN5XA; length:**										
F308568A	900 mm	Nr	0.07	1.76	–	34.28	36.04	1.94	–	37.71	39.64
F308568B	1050 mm	Nr	0.10	2.51	–	37.80	40.31	2.76	–	41.58	44.34
F308568C	1200 mm	Nr	0.12	3.01	–	38.78	41.79	3.31	–	42.66	45.97
F308568D	1350 mm	Nr	0.14	3.52	–	41.15	44.67	3.87	–	45.27	49.14
F308568E	1500 mm	Nr	0.15	3.77	–	43.56	47.33	4.15	–	47.92	52.06
F308568F	1650 mm	Nr	0.17	4.27	–	55.17	59.44	4.70	–	60.69	65.38
F308568G	1800 mm	Nr	0.18	4.52	–	60.35	64.87	4.97	–	66.39	71.36
F308568H	1950 mm	Nr	0.19	4.77	–	65.68	70.45	5.25	–	72.25	77.50
F308568I	2100 mm	Nr	0.20	5.02	–	68.98	74.00	5.52	–	75.88	81.40
F308568J	2250 mm	Nr	0.22	5.53	–	77.57	83.10	6.08	–	85.33	91.41
F308568K	2400 mm	Nr	0.25	6.28	–	82.78	89.06	6.91	–	91.06	97.97
F308568L	2550 mm	Nr	0.26	6.53	–	89.67	96.20	7.18	–	98.64	105.82
F308568M	2700 mm	Nr	0.27	6.78	–	94.83	101.61	7.46	–	104.31	111.77
F308570	**Internal solid wall range; CN6XC; length:**										
F308570A	2250 mm	Nr	0.22	5.53	–	178.42	183.95	6.08	–	196.26	202.35
F308570B	2400 mm	Nr	0.25	6.28	–	192.77	199.05	6.91	–	212.05	218.96
F308570C	2550 mm	Nr	0.26	6.53	–	193.47	200.00	7.18	–	212.82	220.00
F308570D	2700 mm	Nr	0.27	6.78	–	195.94	202.72	7.46	–	215.53	222.99
F308570E	2850 mm	Nr	0.29	7.28	–	197.46	204.74	8.01	–	217.21	225.21
F308570F	3000 mm	Nr	0.30	7.54	–	204.61	212.15	8.29	–	225.07	233.37
F308570G	3300 mm	Nr	0.33	8.29	–	207.41	215.70	9.12	–	228.15	237.27
F308570H	3600 mm	Nr	0.36	9.04	–	223.94	232.98	9.94	–	246.33	256.28
F308570I	3900 mm	Nr	0.39	9.80	–	235.42	245.22	10.78	–	258.96	269.74
F308570J	4200 mm	Nr	0.42	10.55	–	253.10	263.65	11.61	–	278.41	290.02
F308570K	4575 mm	Nr	0.46	11.56	–	312.75	324.31	12.72	–	344.03	356.74
F308570L	4800 mm	Nr	0.50	12.56	–	321.96	334.52	13.82	–	354.16	367.97
F308572	**Internal solid wall range; CN56XA; length:**										
F308572A	900 mm	Nr	0.07	1.76	–	32.35	34.11	1.94	–	35.59	37.52
F308572B	1050 mm	Nr	0.10	2.51	–	34.46	36.97	2.76	–	37.91	40.67
F308572C	1200 mm	Nr	0.12	3.01	–	40.80	43.81	3.31	–	44.88	48.19
F308572D	1350 mm	Nr	0.14	3.52	–	47.49	51.01	3.87	–	52.24	56.11
F308572E	1500 mm	Nr	0.15	3.77	–	50.96	54.73	4.15	–	56.06	60.20
F308572F	1650 mm	Nr	0.17	4.27	–	61.65	65.92	4.70	–	67.82	72.51
F308572G	1800 mm	Nr	0.18	4.52	–	68.38	72.90	4.97	–	75.22	80.19
F308572H	1950 mm	Nr	0.19	4.77	–	73.91	78.68	5.25	–	81.30	86.55
F308572I	2100 mm	Nr	0.20	5.02	–	80.09	85.11	5.52	–	88.10	93.62
F308572J	2250 mm	Nr	0.22	5.53	–	85.98	91.51	6.08	–	94.58	100.66
F308572K	2400 mm	Nr	0.24	6.03	–	91.77	97.80	6.63	–	100.95	107.58
F308572L	2550 mm	Nr	0.26	6.53	–	97.53	104.06	7.18	–	107.28	114.47
F308572M	2700 mm	Nr	0.27	6.78	–	103.38	110.16	7.46	–	113.72	121.18

Masonry

Major Works 2009		Unit	Labour Hours	Labour Net	Plant Net	Materials Net	Unit Net	Labour Gross	Plant Gross	Materials Gross	Unit Price
				£	£	£	£	£	£	£	£
								(Gross rates include 10% profit)			
F30	**F30: ACCESSORIES AND SUNDRY ITEMS**										
F3087	**Proprietary steel lintels; IG galvanise polyester powder coated; insulated; built into brick or block walling**										
F308702	**L1/S 50; standard duty; length:**										
F308702A	600 mm	Nr	0.06	1.51	–	29.17	30.68	1.66	–	32.09	33.75
F308702B	750 mm	Nr	0.08	2.01	–	29.17	31.18	2.21	–	32.09	34.30
F308702C	900 mm	Nr	0.10	2.51	–	34.99	37.50	2.76	–	38.49	41.25
F308702D	1050 mm	Nr	0.12	3.01	–	40.68	43.69	3.31	–	44.75	48.06
F308702E	1200 mm	Nr	0.13	3.27	–	46.26	49.53	3.60	–	50.89	54.48
F308702F	1350 mm	Nr	0.15	3.77	–	54.26	58.03	4.15	–	59.69	63.83
F308702G	1500 mm	Nr	0.17	4.27	–	60.39	64.66	4.70	–	66.43	71.13
F308702H	1650 mm	Nr	0.18	4.52	–	68.30	72.82	4.97	–	75.13	80.10
F308702I	1800 mm	Nr	0.19	4.77	–	74.46	79.23	5.25	–	81.91	87.15
F308702J	1950 mm	Nr	0.21	5.28	–	81.37	86.65	5.81	–	89.51	95.32
F308702K	2100 mm	Nr	0.22	5.53	–	87.03	92.56	6.08	–	95.73	101.82
F308702L	2250 mm	Nr	0.23	5.78	–	97.57	103.35	6.36	–	107.33	113.69
F308702M	2400 mm	Nr	0.24	6.03	–	104.16	110.19	6.63	–	114.58	121.21
F308702N	2550 mm	Nr	0.25	6.28	–	120.42	126.70	6.91	–	132.46	139.37
F308702O	2700 mm	Nr	0.26	6.53	–	126.63	133.16	7.18	–	139.29	146.48
F308702P	2850 mm	Nr	0.27	6.78	–	157.19	163.97	7.46	–	172.91	180.37
F308702Q	3000 mm	Nr	0.29	7.28	–	170.62	177.90	8.01	–	187.68	195.69
F308702R	3150 mm	Nr	0.30	7.54	–	202.26	209.80	8.29	–	222.49	230.78
F308702S	3300 mm	Nr	0.31	7.79	–	202.26	210.05	8.57	–	222.49	231.06
F308702T	3450 mm	Nr	0.33	8.29	–	225.06	233.35	9.12	–	247.57	256.69
F308702U	3600 mm	Nr	0.34	8.54	–	225.06	233.60	9.39	–	247.57	256.96
F308702V	3750 mm	Nr	0.35	8.79	–	264.50	273.29	9.67	–	290.95	300.62
F308702W	3900 mm	Nr	0.37	9.29	–	264.50	273.79	10.22	–	290.95	301.17
F308702X	4050 mm	Nr	0.38	9.55	–	308.08	317.63	10.51	–	338.89	349.39
F308702Y	4200 mm	Nr	0.39	9.80	–	308.08	317.88	10.78	–	338.89	349.67
F308705	**L1/S 75; standard duty; length:**										
F308705A	600 mm	Nr	0.06	1.51	–	29.17	30.68	1.66	–	32.09	33.75
F308705B	750 mm	Nr	0.08	2.01	–	29.17	31.18	2.21	–	32.09	34.30
F308705C	900 mm	Nr	0.10	2.51	–	34.99	37.50	2.76	–	38.49	41.25
F308705D	1050 mm	Nr	0.12	3.01	–	40.68	43.69	3.31	–	44.75	48.06
F308705E	1200 mm	Nr	0.14	3.52	–	40.68	44.20	3.87	–	44.75	48.62
F308705F	1350 mm	Nr	0.16	4.02	–	54.26	58.28	4.42	–	59.69	64.11
F308705G	1500 mm	Nr	0.18	4.52	–	60.39	64.91	4.97	–	66.43	71.40
F308705H	1650 mm	Nr	0.19	4.77	–	68.30	73.07	5.25	–	75.13	80.38
F308705I	1800 mm	Nr	0.21	5.28	–	74.46	79.74	5.81	–	81.91	87.71
F308705J	1950 mm	Nr	0.23	5.78	–	81.37	87.15	6.36	–	89.51	95.87
F308705K	2100 mm	Nr	0.24	6.03	–	87.03	93.06	6.63	–	95.73	102.37
F308705L	2250 mm	Nr	0.26	6.53	–	97.57	104.10	7.18	–	107.33	114.51
F308705M	2400 mm	Nr	0.27	6.78	–	104.16	110.94	7.46	–	114.58	122.03
F308705N	2550 mm	Nr	0.28	7.03	–	120.42	127.45	7.73	–	132.46	140.20
F308705O	2700 mm	Nr	0.30	7.54	–	126.63	134.17	8.29	–	139.29	147.59
F308705P	2850 mm	Nr	0.31	7.79	–	157.19	164.98	8.57	–	172.91	181.48
F308705Q	3000 mm	Nr	0.33	8.29	–	170.62	178.91	9.12	–	187.68	196.80
F308705R	3150 mm	Nr	0.34	8.54	–	202.26	210.80	9.39	–	222.49	231.88
F308705S	3300 mm	Nr	0.36	9.04	–	202.26	211.30	9.94	–	222.49	232.43
F308705T	3450 mm	Nr	0.37	9.29	–	225.06	234.35	10.22	–	247.57	257.79
F308705U	3600 mm	Nr	0.39	9.80	–	225.06	234.86	10.78	–	247.57	258.35
F308705V	3750 mm	Nr	0.40	10.05	–	264.50	274.55	11.06	–	290.95	302.01
F308705W	3900 mm	Nr	0.41	10.30	–	264.50	274.80	11.33	–	290.95	302.28
F308705X	4050 mm	Nr	0.42	10.55	–	308.08	318.63	11.61	–	338.89	350.49
F308705Y	4200 mm	Nr	0.43	10.80	–	308.08	318.88	11.88	–	338.89	350.77

Major Works 2009		Unit	Labour Hours	Labour Net	Plant Net	Materials Net	Unit Net	Labour Gross	Plant Gross	Materials Gross	Unit Price
								— (Gross rates include 10% profit) —			
				£	£	£	£	£	£	£	£
F30	**F30: ACCESSORIES AND SUNDRY ITEMS**										
F3087	**Proprietary steel lintels; IG galvanise polyester powder coated; insulated; built into brick or block walling**										
F308708	**L1/S 100; standard duty; length:**										
F308708A	600 mm	Nr	0.06	1.51	–	31.42	32.93	1.66	–	34.56	36.22
F308708B	750 mm	Nr	0.08	2.01	–	31.42	33.43	2.21	–	34.56	36.77
F308708C	900 mm	Nr	0.11	2.76	–	37.12	39.88	3.04	–	40.83	43.87
F308708D	1050 mm	Nr	0.13	3.27	–	43.88	47.15	3.60	–	48.27	51.87
F308708E	1200 mm	Nr	0.15	3.77	–	48.67	52.44	4.15	–	53.54	57.68
F308708F	1350 mm	Nr	0.17	4.27	–	56.62	60.89	4.70	–	62.28	66.98
F308708G	1500 mm	Nr	0.19	4.77	–	60.67	65.44	5.25	–	66.74	71.98
F308708H	1650 mm	Nr	0.21	5.28	–	68.62	73.90	5.81	–	75.48	81.29
F308708I	1800 mm	Nr	0.22	5.53	–	74.84	80.37	6.08	–	82.32	88.41
F308708J	1950 mm	Nr	0.24	6.03	–	85.72	91.75	6.63	–	94.29	100.93
F308708K	2100 mm	Nr	0.26	6.53	–	90.22	96.75	7.18	–	99.24	106.43
F308708L	2250 mm	Nr	0.28	7.03	–	107.33	114.36	7.73	–	118.06	125.80
F308708M	2400 mm	Nr	0.29	7.28	–	114.21	121.49	8.01	–	125.63	133.64
F308708N	2550 mm	Nr	0.31	7.79	–	114.21	122.00	8.57	–	125.63	134.20
F308708O	2700 mm	Nr	0.33	8.29	–	135.02	143.31	9.12	–	148.52	157.64
F308708P	2850 mm	Nr	0.34	8.54	–	156.37	164.91	9.39	–	172.01	181.40
F308708Q	3000 mm	Nr	0.36	9.04	–	169.12	178.16	9.94	–	186.03	195.98
F308708R	3150 mm	Nr	0.37	9.29	–	196.52	205.81	10.22	–	216.17	226.39
F308708S	3300 mm	Nr	0.39	9.80	–	196.52	206.32	10.78	–	216.17	226.95
F308708T	3450 mm	Nr	0.41	10.30	–	219.87	230.17	11.33	–	241.86	253.19
F308708U	3600 mm	Nr	0.42	10.55	–	219.87	230.42	11.61	–	241.86	253.46
F308708V	3750 mm	Nr	0.44	11.05	–	272.17	283.22	12.16	–	299.39	311.54
F308708W	3900 mm	Nr	0.45	11.30	–	272.17	283.47	12.43	–	299.39	311.82
F308708X	4050 mm	Nr	0.47	11.81	–	289.11	300.92	12.99	–	318.02	331.01
F308708Y	4200 mm	Nr	0.48	12.06	–	289.11	301.17	13.27	–	318.02	331.29

Masonry

Major Works 2009		Unit	Labour Hours	Labour Net	Plant Net	Materials Net	Unit Net	Labour Gross	Plant Gross	Materials Gross	Unit Price
				£	£	£	£	£	£	£	£
								(Gross rates include 10% profit)			
F31	**F31: PRECAST CONCRETE SILLS, LINTELS, COPINGS AND FEATURES**										
F3101	**Lintels; 20 N/mm² concrete; bedding and pointing in cement mortar (1:3)**										
F310112	**100 × 150 mm plain rectangular section:**										
F310112A	900 mm long	Nr	0.23	5.65	–	8.02	13.67	6.22	–	8.82	15.04
F310112B	1200 mm long	Nr	0.24	5.91	–	10.66	16.57	6.50	–	11.73	18.23
F310112C	1500 mm long	Nr	0.24	6.02	–	13.31	19.33	6.62	–	14.64	21.26
F310112D	1800 mm long	Nr	0.25	6.15	–	15.95	22.10	6.77	–	17.55	24.31
F310113	**100 × 225 mm plain rectangular section:**										
F310113A	900 mm long	Nr	0.24	6.03	–	11.98	18.01	6.63	–	13.18	19.81
F310113B	1200 mm long	Nr	0.25	6.16	–	15.94	22.10	6.78	–	17.53	24.31
F310113C	1500 mm long	Nr	0.25	6.28	–	19.91	26.19	6.91	–	21.90	28.81
F310113D	1800 mm long	Nr	0.26	6.40	–	23.87	30.27	7.04	–	26.26	33.30
F310113E	2100 mm long	Nr	0.27	6.78	–	27.83	34.61	7.46	–	30.61	38.07
F3103	**Prestressed lintels; bedding and pointing in cement mortar (1:3); temporary support**										
F310315	**65 × 100 mm rectangular section:**										
F310315A	450 mm long	Nr	0.14	3.52	–	2.80	6.32	3.87	–	3.08	6.95
F310315B	600 mm long	Nr	0.15	3.77	–	3.48	7.25	4.15	–	3.83	7.98
F310315C	900 mm long	Nr	0.16	4.02	–	5.20	9.22	4.42	–	5.72	10.14
F310315D	1050 mm long	Nr	0.17	4.27	–	6.02	10.29	4.70	–	6.62	11.32
F310315E	1200 mm long	Nr	0.18	4.52	–	6.87	11.39	4.97	–	7.56	12.53
F310315F	1500 mm long	Nr	0.20	5.02	–	8.58	13.60	5.52	–	9.44	14.96
F310315G	1800 mm long	Nr	0.22	5.53	–	10.29	15.82	6.08	–	11.32	17.40
F310315H	2100 mm long	Nr	0.25	6.28	–	11.97	18.25	6.91	–	13.17	20.08
F310315I	2400 mm long	Nr	0.28	7.03	–	13.69	20.72	7.73	–	15.06	22.79
F310316	**65 × 140 mm rectangular section:**										
F310316A	900 mm long	Nr	0.18	4.52	–	6.84	11.36	4.97	–	7.52	12.50
F310316B	1200 mm long	Nr	0.21	5.28	–	9.12	14.40	5.81	–	10.03	15.84
F310316C	1500 mm long	Nr	0.24	6.03	–	11.35	17.38	6.63	–	12.49	19.12
F310316D	1800 mm long	Nr	0.26	6.53	–	13.59	20.12	7.18	–	14.95	22.13
F310316E	2100 mm long	Nr	0.28	7.03	–	15.87	22.90	7.73	–	17.46	25.19
F310316F	2400 mm long	Nr	0.31	7.79	–	18.09	25.88	8.57	–	19.90	28.47
F310317	**65 × 220 mm rectangular section:**										
F310317A	900 mm long	Nr	0.20	5.02	–	11.21	16.23	5.52	–	12.33	17.85
F310317B	1200 mm long	Nr	0.23	5.78	–	15.02	20.80	6.36	–	16.52	22.88
F310317C	1500 mm long	Nr	0.26	6.53	–	18.66	25.19	7.18	–	20.53	27.71
F310317D	1800 mm long	Nr	0.30	7.54	–	22.39	29.93	8.29	–	24.63	32.92
F310317E	2100 mm long	Nr	0.33	8.29	–	26.10	34.39	9.12	–	28.71	37.83
F310317F	2400 mm long	Nr	0.36	9.04	–	29.77	38.81	9.94	–	32.75	42.69
F310317G	2700 mm long	Nr	0.38	9.55	–	34.70	44.25	10.51	–	38.17	48.68
F310318	**100 × 140 mm rectangular section:**										
F310318A	1200 mm long	Nr	0.25	6.28	–	16.30	22.58	6.91	–	17.93	24.84
F310318B	1500 mm long	Nr	0.28	7.03	–	20.35	27.38	7.73	–	22.39	30.12
F310318C	1800 mm long	Nr	0.31	7.79	–	24.38	32.17	8.57	–	26.82	35.39
F310318D	2100 mm long	Nr	0.35	8.79	–	28.44	37.23	9.67	–	31.28	40.95

Masonry

Major Works 2009		Unit	Labour Hours	Labour Net	Plant Net	Materials Net	Unit Net	Labour Gross	Plant Gross	Materials Gross	Unit Price
									(Gross rates include 10% profit)		
				£	£	£	£	£	£	£	£
F31	**F31: PRECAST CONCRETE SILLS, LINTELS, COPINGS AND FEATURES**										
F3105	**Padstones; 21 N/mm² concrete; bedding jointing and pointing in cement mortar (1:3)**										
F310522	**Plain rectangular section:**										
F310522A	225 × 100 × 225 mm ..	Nr	0.20	5.02	–	50.47	55.49	5.52	–	55.52	61.04
F310522B	225 × 150 × 225 mm ..	Nr	0.22	5.53	–	7.74	13.27	6.08	–	8.51	14.60
F310522C	225 × 225 × 225 mm ..	Nr	0.24	6.03	–	7.15	13.18	6.63	–	7.87	14.50
F310522D	450 × 100 × 450 mm ..	Nr	0.22	5.53	–	18.77	24.30	6.08	–	20.65	26.73
F310522E	450 × 150 × 450 mm ..	Nr	0.24	6.03	–	27.89	33.92	6.63	–	30.68	37.31
F310522F	450 × 225 × 450 mm ..	Nr	0.26	6.53	–	41.06	47.59	7.18	–	45.17	52.35
F3106	**Coping units; BS3798; bedding, jointing and pointing in cement mortar (1:3)**										
F310624	**Splayed copings:**										
F310624A	75 × 200 mm	m	0.45	11.30	–	10.63	21.93	12.43	–	11.69	24.12
F310624B	100 × 300 mm	m	0.65	16.33	–	20.01	36.34	17.96	–	22.01	39.97
F310625	**Saddleback copings:**										
F310625A	75 × 200 mm	m	0.50	12.56	–	11.29	23.85	13.82	–	12.42	26.24
F310625B	100 × 300 mm	m	0.75	18.84	–	22.32	41.16	20.72	–	24.55	45.28
F310626	**Pier caps, weathered four ways:**										
F310626A	425 × 425 × 125 mm ..	Nr	0.30	7.54	–	31.17	38.71	8.29	–	34.29	42.58

STRUCTURAL AND CARCASSING

Major Works 2009		Unit	Labour Hours	Labour Net	Plant Net	Materials Net	Unit Net	Labour Gross	Plant Gross	Materials Gross	Unit Price
								——— (Gross rates include 10% profit) ———			
				£	£	£	£	£	£	£	£
G10	**G10: STRUCTURAL STEEL FRAMING**										
G1011	**Columns**										
G101111	**Universal columns; BS 4360; shot blasted and primed at works:**										
G101111A	356 × 406 mm × 634 Kg/m	Tonne	10.00	208.50	87.50	951.70	1247.70	229.35	96.25	1046.87	1372.47
G101111B	356 × 406 mm × 235 Kg/m	Tonne	13.00	271.05	113.75	951.70	1336.50	298.16	125.13	1046.87	1470.15
G101111C	356 × 368 mm × 202 Kg/m	Tonne	14.00	291.90	122.50	951.70	1366.10	321.09	134.75	1046.87	1502.71
G101111D	305 × 305 mm × 283 Kg/m	Tonne	12.00	250.20	105.00	951.70	1306.90	275.22	115.50	1046.87	1437.59
G101111E	305 × 305 mm × 96 Kg/m	Tonne	15.00	312.75	131.25	919.99	1363.99	344.03	144.38	1011.99	1500.39
G101111F	254 × 254 mm × 167 Kg/m	Tonne	15.00	312.75	131.25	919.99	1363.99	344.03	144.38	1011.99	1500.39
G101111G	203 × 203 mm × 52 Kg/m	Tonne	18.00	375.30	11.25	888.26	1274.81	412.83	12.38	977.09	1402.29
G101111H	152 × 152 mm × 37 Kg/m	Tonne	20.00	417.00	12.50	972.86	1402.36	458.70	13.75	1070.15	1542.60
G101112	**Rectangular hollow sections; BS 4360; shot blasted and primed at works:**										
G101112A	450 × 250 × 16.0 mm × 167.0 Kg/m	Tonne	15.00	312.75	131.25	1077.07	1521.07	344.03	144.38	1184.78	1673.18
G101112B	400 × 200 × 16.0 mm × 142.0 Kg/m	Tonne	16.00	333.60	140.00	1077.07	1550.67	366.96	154.00	1184.78	1705.74
G101112C	300 × 200 × 12.5 mm × 92.6 Kg/m	Tonne	17.00	354.45	10.63	1042.34	1407.42	389.90	11.69	1146.57	1548.16
G101112D	250 × 150 × 12.5 mm × 73.0 Kg/m	Tonne	18.00	375.30	11.25	1042.34	1428.89	412.83	12.38	1146.57	.1571.78
G101112E	200 × 100 × 10.0 mm × 43.6 Kg/m	Tonne	19.00	396.15	11.88	1007.61	1415.64	435.77	13.07	1108.37	1557.20
G101112F	150 × 100 × 10.0 mm × 35.7 Kg/m	Tonne	20.00	417.00	12.50	1007.61	1437.11	458.70	13.75	1108.37	1580.82
G101112G	120 × 60 × 6.3 mm × 16.4 Kg/m	Tonne	21.00	437.85	13.13	938.12	1389.10	481.64	14.44	1031.93	1528.01
G101112H	100 × 50 × 5.0 mm × 10.9 Kg/m	Tonne	22.00	458.70	13.75	903.37	1375.82	504.57	15.13	993.71	1513.40
G101112I	60 × 40 × 4.0 mm × 5.72 Kg/m	Tonne	23.00	479.55	14.38	886.00	1379.93	527.51	15.82	974.60	1517.92
G101112J	50 × 30 × 2.6 mm × 3.03 Kg/m	Tonne	24.00	500.40	15.00	886.00	1401.40	550.44	16.50	974.60	1541.54
G101113	**Square hollow sections; BS 4360; shot blasted and primed at works:**										
G101113A	400 × 400 × 12.5 mm × 152.0 Kg/m	Tonne	15.00	312.75	131.25	1077.07	1521.07	344.03	144.38	1184.78	1673.18
G101113B	300 × 300 × 12.5 mm × 112.0 Kg/m	Tonne	16.00	333.60	140.00	1042.34	1515.94	366.96	154.00	1146.57	1667.53
G101113C	200 × 200 × 10.0 mm × 59.3 Kg/m	Tonne	18.00	375.30	11.25	1007.61	1394.16	412.83	12.38	1108.37	1533.58
G101113D	150 × 150 × 10.0 mm × 43.6 Kg/m	Tonne	19.00	396.15	11.88	1007.61	1415.64	435.77	13.07	1108.37	1557.20
G101113E	100 × 100 × 8.0 mm × 22.9 Kg/m	Tonne	20.00	417.00	12.50	972.86	1402.36	458.70	13.75	1070.15	1542.60
G101113F	70 × 70 × 5.0 mm × 10.1 Kg/m	Tonne	22.00	458.70	13.75	903.37	1375.82	504.57	15.13	993.71	1513.40
G101113G	50 × 50 × 5.0 mm × 6.97 Kg/m	Tonne	23.00	479.55	14.38	886.00	1379.93	527.51	15.82	974.60	1517.92

Structural and Carcassing

Major Works 2009		Unit	Labour Hours	Labour Net	Plant Net	Materials Net	Unit Net	Labour Gross	Plant Gross	Materials Gross	Unit Price
								(Gross rates include 10% profit)			
				£	£	£	£	£	£	£	£
G10	**G10: STRUCTURAL STEEL FRAMING**										
G1011	**Columns**										
G101114	**Circular hollow sections; BS 4360; shot blasted and primed at works:**										
G101114A	457.0 mm dia × 40.0 mm × 411.0 Kg/m	Tonne	13.00	271.05	113.75	1077.07	1461.87	298.16	125.13	1184.78	1608.06
G101114B	355.6 mm dia × 25.0 mm × 204.0 Kg/m	Tonne	14.00	291.90	122.50	1077.07	1491.47	321.09	134.75	1184.78	1640.62
G101114C	273.0 mm dia × 20.0 mm × 125.0 Kg/m	Tonne	15.00	312.75	131.25	1059.72	1503.72	344.03	144.38	1165.69	1654.09
G101114D	193.7 mm dia × 16.0 mm × 70.1 Kg/m	Tonne	18.00	375.30	11.25	1042.34	1428.89	412.83	12.38	1146.57	1571.78
G101114E	139.7 mm dia × 10.0 mm × 32.0 Kg/m	Tonne	20.00	417.00	12.50	1007.61	1437.11	458.70	13.75	1108.37	1580.82
G101114F	88.9 mm dia × 5.0 mm × 10.3 Kg/m	Tonne	22.00	458.70	13.75	1048.26	1520.71	504.57	15.13	1153.09	1672.78
G101114G	60.3 mm dia × 5.0 mm × 6.82 Kg/m	Tonne	23.00	479.55	14.38	1028.10	1522.03	527.51	15.82	1130.91	1674.23
G101114H	33.7 mm dia × 4.0 mm × 2.93 Kg/m	Tonne	24.00	500.40	15.00	1028.10	1543.50	550.44	16.50	1130.91	1697.85
G1012	**Beams**										
G101206	**Universal beams; BS 4360; shot blasted and primed at works:**										
G101206A	914 × 305 mm × 289 Kg/m	Tonne	10.00	208.50	87.50	951.70	1247.70	229.35	96.25	1046.87	1372.47
G101206B	838 × 292 mm × 226 Kg/m	Tonne	13.00	271.05	113.75	951.70	1336.50	298.16	125.13	1046.87	1470.15
G101206C	610 × 305 mm × 238 Kg/m	Tonne	13.00	271.05	113.75	951.70	1336.50	298.16	125.13	1046.87	1470.15
G101206D	533 × 210 mm × 122 Kg/m	Tonne	14.00	291.90	8.75	919.99	1220.64	321.09	9.63	1011.99	1342.70
G101206E	457 × 191 mm × 98 Kg/m	Tonne	15.00	312.75	9.38	919.99	1242.12	344.03	10.32	1011.99	1366.33
G101206F	406 × 178 mm × 74 Kg/m	Tonne	16.00	333.60	10.00	888.26	1231.86	366.96	11.00	977.09	1355.05
G101206G	356 × 171 mm × 67 Kg/m	Tonne	17.00	354.45	10.63	888.26	1253.34	389.90	11.69	977.09	1378.67
G101206H	305 × 165 mm × 54 Kg/m	Tonne	18.00	375.30	11.25	888.26	1274.81	412.83	12.38	977.09	1402.29
G101206I	254 × 146 mm × 43 Kg/m	Tonne	19.00	396.15	11.88	888.26	1296.29	435.77	13.07	977.09	1425.92
G101206J	203 × 133 mm × 30 Kg/m	Tonne	20.00	417.01	12.50	856.55	1286.06	458.71	13.75	942.21	1414.67
G101207	**Rolled steel joists; BS 4360; shot blasted and primed at works:**										
G101207A	254 × 203 mm × 81.85 Kg/m	Tonne	12.00	250.20	7.50	888.26	1145.96	275.22	8.25	977.09	1260.56
G101207B	254 × 114 mm × 37.20 Kg/m	Tonne	15.00	312.75	9.38	888.26	1210.39	344.03	10.32	977.09	1331.43
G101207C	203 × 152 mm × 52.09 Kg/m	Tonne	18.00	375.30	11.25	888.26	1274.81	412.83	12.38	977.09	1402.29
G101207D	203 × 102 mm × 25.33 Kg/m	Tonne	24.00	500.41	15.00	856.55	1371.96	550.45	16.50	942.21	1509.16
G101207E	152 × 89 mm × 17.09 Kg/m	Tonne	24.00	500.41	15.00	856.55	1371.96	550.45	16.50	942.21	1509.16
G101207F	127 × 76 mm × 16.37 Kg/m	Tonne	24.00	500.41	15.00	856.55	1371.96	550.45	16.50	942.21	1509.16
G101207G	102 × 102 mm × 23.06 Kg/m	Tonne	24.00	500.41	15.00	856.55	1371.96	550.45	16.50	942.21	1509.16
G101207H	89 × 89 mm × 19.35 Kg/m	Tonne	24.00	500.41	15.00	856.55	1371.96	550.45	16.50	942.21	1509.16
G101207I	76 × 76 mm × 12.65 Kg/m	Tonne	24.00	500.40	15.00	824.83	1340.23	550.44	16.50	907.31	1474.25

Major Works 2009		Unit	Labour Hours	Labour Net	Plant Net	Materials Net	Unit Net	Labour Gross	Plant Gross	Materials Gross	Unit Price
								(Gross rates include 10% profit)			
				£	£	£	£	£	£	£	£
G10	**G10: STRUCTURAL STEEL FRAMING**										
G1012	**Beams**										
G101208	**Rolled steel channels; BS 4360; shot blasted and primed at works:**										
G101208A	432 × 102 mm × 65.54 Kg/m	Tonne	15.00	312.75	9.38	967.56	1289.69	344.03	10.32	1064.32	1418.66
G101208B	305 × 89 mm × 41.69 Kg/m	Tonne	18.00	375.30	11.25	967.56	1354.11	412.83	12.38	1064.32	1489.52
G101208C	254 × 76 mm × 28.89 Kg/m	Tonne	22.00	458.70	13.75	951.70	1424.15	504.57	15.13	1046.87	1566.57
G101208D	203 × 89 mm × 29.78 Kg/m	Tonne	22.00	458.70	13.75	951.70	1424.15	504.57	15.13	1046.87	1566.57
G101208E	178 × 76 mm × 20.84 Kg/m	Tonne	24.00	500.40	15.00	951.70	1467.10	550.44	16.50	1046.87	1613.81
G101208F	152 × 76 mm × 17.88 Kg/m	Tonne	24.00	500.40	15.00	951.70	1467.10	550.44	16.50	1046.87	1613.81
G101208G	127 × 64 mm × 14.90 Kg/m	Tonne	24.00	500.40	15.00	951.70	1467.10	550.44	16.50	1046.87	1613.81
G101208H	76 × 51 mm × 9.34 Kg/m	Tonne	24.00	500.40	15.00	919.99	1435.39	550.44	16.50	1011.99	1578.93
G101208I	51 × 38 mm × 5.81 Kg/m	Tonne	24.00	500.40	15.00	919.99	1435.39	550.44	16.50	1011.99	1578.93
G1013	**Support steelwork and bracings**										
G101326	**Equal angles; BS 4360; shot blasted and primed at works:**										
G101326A	250 × 250 × 25 mm × 93.60 Kg/m	Tonne	14.00	291.90	8.75	1088.56	1389.21	321.09	9.63	1197.42	1528.13
G101326B	200 × 200 × 16 mm × 48.50 Kg/m	Tonne	15.00	312.75	9.38	1088.56	1410.69	344.03	10.32	1197.42	1551.76
G101326C	150 × 150 × 10 mm × 23.00 Kg/m	Tonne	17.00	354.45	10.63	1068.42	1433.50	389.90	11.69	1175.26	1576.85
G101326D	100 × 100 × 15 mm × 21.90 Kg/m	Tonne	18.00	375.30	11.25	1068.42	1454.97	412.83	12.38	1175.26	1600.47
G101326E	80 × 80 × 10 mm × 11.90 Kg/m	Tonne	24.00	500.40	15.00	1048.26	1563.66	550.44	16.50	1153.09	1720.03
G101326F	50 × 50 × 8 mm × 5.82 Kg/m	Tonne	26.00	542.10	16.25	1048.26	1606.61	596.31	17.88	1153.09	1767.27
G101326G	40 × 40 × 6 mm × 3.52 Kg/m	Tonne	28.00	583.80	17.50	1048.26	1649.56	642.18	19.25	1153.09	1814.52
G101326H	25 × 25 × 5 mm × 1.77 Kg/m	Tonne	30.00	625.50	18.75	1048.26	1692.51	688.05	20.63	1153.09	1861.76

Structural and Carcassing

Major Works 2009		Unit	Labour Hours	Labour Net	Plant Net	Materials Net	Unit Net	Labour Gross	Plant Gross	Materials Gross	Unit Price
								(Gross rates include 10% profit)			
				£	£	£	£	£	£	£	£
G10	**G10: STRUCTURAL STEEL FRAMING**										
G1013	**Support steelwork and bracings**										
G101327	**Unequal angles; BS 4360; shot blasted and primed at works:**										
G101327A	200 × 150 × 18 mm × 47.10 Kg/m	Tonne	15.00	312.75	9.38	1088.56	1410.69	344.03	10.32	1197.42	1551.76
G101327B	200 × 100 × 15 mm × 33.70 Kg/m	Tonne	16.00	333.60	10.00	1088.56	1432.16	366.96	11.00	1197.42	1575.38
G101327C	150 × 75 × 15 mm × 24.80 Kg/m	Tonne	17.00	354.45	10.63	1088.56	1453.64	389.90	11.69	1197.42	1599.00
G101327D	100 × 75 × 12 mm × 15.40 Kg/m	Tonne	22.00	458.70	13.75	1088.56	1561.01	504.57	15.13	1197.42	1717.11
G101327E	75 × 50 × 8 mm × 7.39 Kg/m	Tonne	26.00	542.10	16.25	1048.26	1606.61	596.31	17.88	1153.09	1767.27
G101327F	65 × 50 × 8 mm × 6.75 Kg/m	Tonne	26.00	542.10	16.25	1048.26	1606.61	596.31	17.88	1153.09	1767.27
G101327G	60 × 30 × 6 mm × 3.99 Kg/m	Tonne	28.00	583.80	17.50	1048.26	1649.56	642.18	19.25	1153.09	1814.52
G101327H	40 × 25 × 4 mm × 1.93 Kg/m	Tonne	30.00	625.50	18.75	1048.26	1692.51	688.05	20.63	1153.09	1861.76
G1018	**Framing; erection**										
G101810	**Trial erection:**										
G101810A	at shop.................	Tonne	–	–	–	351.22	351.22	–	–	386.34	386.34
G101820	**Permanent erection:**										
G101820A	on site	Tonne	–	–	–	279.79	279.79	–	–	307.77	307.77

Major Works 2009		Unit	Labour Hours	Labour Net	Plant Net	Materials Net	Unit Net	Labour Gross	Plant Gross	Materials Gross	Unit Price
								(Gross rates include 10% profit)			
				£	£	£	£	£	£	£	£
G10	**G10: STRUCTURAL STEEL FRAMING**										
G1021	**Fixings**										
G102151	**Bolts; BS 4190 high strength friction grip (HSFG) black metric hexagon head with nut and washer:**										
G102151A	M6 × 25 mm	Nr	0.05	1.04	–	0.10	1.14	1.14	–	0.11	1.25
G102151B	M6 × 50 mm	Nr	0.06	1.26	–	0.22	1.48	1.39	–	0.24	1.63
G102151C	M6 × 75 mm	Nr	0.07	1.46	–	0.29	1.75	1.61	–	0.32	1.93
G102151D	M6 × 100 mm	Nr	0.08	1.67	–	0.43	2.10	1.84	–	0.47	2.31
G102151E	M8 × 25 mm	Nr	0.07	1.46	–	0.29	1.75	1.61	–	0.32	1.93
G102151F	M8 × 50 mm	Nr	0.08	1.66	–	0.33	1.99	1.83	–	0.36	2.19
G102151G	M8 × 75 mm	Nr	0.09	1.87	–	0.36	2.23	2.06	–	0.40	2.45
G102151H	M8 × 100 mm	Nr	0.10	2.09	–	0.51	2.60	2.30	–	0.56	2.86
G102151I	M10 × 50 mm	Nr	0.11	2.29	–	0.51	2.80	2.52	–	0.56	3.08
G102151J	M10 × 75 mm	Nr	0.12	2.50	–	0.58	3.08	2.75	–	0.64	3.39
G102151K	M10 × 100 mm	Nr	0.13	2.71	–	0.85	3.56	2.98	–	0.94	3.92
G102151L	M10 × 150 mm	Nr	0.14	2.91	–	1.29	4.20	3.20	–	1.42	4.62
G102151M	M12 × 50 mm	Nr	0.13	2.71	–	0.71	3.42	2.98	–	0.78	3.76
G102151N	M12 × 75 mm	Nr	0.14	2.92	–	0.85	3.77	3.21	–	0.94	4.15
G102151O	M12 × 100 mm	Nr	0.15	3.13	–	0.99	4.12	3.44	–	1.09	4.53
G102151P	M12 × 150 mm	Nr	0.16	3.33	–	1.86	5.19	3.66	–	2.05	5.71
G102151Q	M12 × 200 mm	Nr	0.17	3.55	–	3.14	6.69	3.91	–	3.45	7.36
G102151R	M12 × 300 mm	Nr	0.20	4.17	–	3.67	7.84	4.59	–	4.04	8.62
G102151S	M16 × 100 mm	Nr	0.18	3.76	–	1.71	5.47	4.14	–	1.88	6.02
G102151T	M16 × 150 mm	Nr	0.19	3.96	–	2.85	6.81	4.36	–	3.14	7.49
G102151U	M16 × 200 mm	Nr	0.20	4.17	–	4.27	8.44	4.59	–	4.70	9.28
G102151V	M16 × 300 mm	Nr	0.23	4.79	–	4.97	9.76	5.27	–	5.47	10.74
G102151W	M20 × 100 mm	Nr	0.20	4.17	–	3.43	7.60	4.59	–	3.77	8.36
G102151X	M20 × 150 mm	Nr	0.21	4.38	–	4.63	9.01	4.82	–	5.09	9.91
G102151Y	M20 × 200 mm	Nr	0.22	4.59	–	6.33	10.92	5.05	–	6.96	12.01
G102151Z	M20 × 300 mm	Nr	0.25	5.22	–	7.84	13.06	5.74	–	8.62	14.37
G102152	**Drill steelwork for bolts:**										
G102152A	6 mm steel for M6 bolt.....	Nr	0.20	4.17	–	–	4.17	4.59	–	–	4.59
G102152B	6 mm steel for M8 bolt.....	Nr	0.22	4.59	–	–	4.59	5.05	–	–	5.05
G102152C	6 mm steel for M10 bolt....	Nr	0.24	5.00	–	–	5.00	5.50	–	–	5.50
G102152D	6 mm steel for M12 bolt....	Nr	0.28	5.84	–	–	5.84	6.42	–	–	6.42
G102152E	6 mm steel for M16 bolt....	Nr	0.32	6.67	–	–	6.67	7.34	–	–	7.34
G102152F	6 mm steel for M20 bolt....	Nr	0.40	8.34	–	–	8.34	9.17	–	–	9.17
G102152G	10 mm steel for M6 bolt....	Nr	0.22	4.59	–	–	4.59	5.05	–	–	5.05
G102152H	10 mm steel for M8 bolt....	Nr	0.25	5.21	–	–	5.21	5.73	–	–	5.73
G102152I	10 mm steel for M10 bolt ..	Nr	0.27	5.63	–	–	5.63	6.19	–	–	6.19
G102152J	10 mm steel for M12 bolt ..	Nr	0.32	6.67	–	–	6.67	7.34	–	–	7.34
G102152K	10 mm steel for M16 bolt ..	Nr	0.36	7.51	–	–	7.51	8.26	–	–	8.26
G102152L	10 mm steel for M20 bolt ..	Nr	0.45	9.38	–	–	9.38	10.32	–	–	10.32
G102152M	13 mm steel for M6 bolt....	Nr	0.25	5.21	–	–	5.21	5.73	–	–	5.73
G102152N	13 mm steel for M8 bolt....	Nr	0.28	5.84	–	–	5.84	6.42	–	–	6.42
G102152O	13 mm steel for M10 bolt ..	Nr	0.30	6.26	–	–	6.26	6.89	–	–	6.89
G102152P	13 mm steel for M12 bolt ..	Nr	0.36	7.51	–	–	7.51	8.26	–	–	8.26
G102152Q	13 mm steel for M16 bolt ..	Nr	0.40	8.34	–	–	8.34	9.17	–	–	9.17
G102152R	13 mm steel for M20 bolt ..	Nr	0.50	10.43	–	–	10.43	11.47	–	–	11.47

Structural and Carcassing

Major Works 2009		Unit				Specialist Net	Unit Net			Specialist Gross	Unit Price
								(Gross rates include 10% profit)			
				£	£	£	£	£	£	£	£
G10	**G10: STRUCTURAL STEEL FRAMING**										
G1070	**Surface preparation**										
G107010	**Blast cleaning:**										
G107010A	at works................	m²	–	–	–	2.38	2.38	–	–	2.62	2.62
G107030	**Wire brushing:**										
G107030A	at works................	m²	–	–	–	2.68	2.68	–	–	2.95	2.95
G1080	**Surface treatment**										
G108010	**Galvanising:**										
G108010A	at works................	m²	–	–	–	13.99	13.99	–	–	15.39	15.39
G108030	**Protective painting; at works:**										
G108030A	zinc chromate primer; one coat	m²	–	–	–	1.96	1.96	–	–	2.16	2.16

Major Works 2009		Unit	Labour Hours	Labour Net	Plant Net	Materials Net	Unit Net	Labour Gross	Plant Gross	Materials Gross	Unit Price
								(Gross rates include 10% profit)			
				£	£	£	£	£	£	£	£
G20	**G20: CARPENTRY, TIMBER FRAMING AND FIRST FIXING**										
G2001	**Trussed rafters; preservative treated and stress graded softwood**										
G200101	**Standard trusses; 450 mm overhang at eaves; 22.5 degree pitch; span:**										
G200101A	5.00 m	Nr	0.80	13.58	–	33.79	47.37	14.94	–	37.17	52.11
G200101B	6.00 m	Nr	0.83	14.09	–	37.32	51.41	15.50	–	41.05	56.55
G200101C	7.00 m	Nr	0.85	14.43	–	42.25	56.68	15.87	–	46.48	62.35
G200101D	8.00 m	Nr	0.90	15.28	–	49.30	64.58	16.81	–	54.23	71.04
G200101E	9.00 m	Nr	0.95	16.13	–	58.44	74.57	17.74	–	64.28	82.03
G200101F	10.00 m	Nr	1.00	16.98	–	69.72	86.70	18.68	–	76.69	95.37
G200102	**Standard trusses; 450 mm overhang at eaves; 35 degree pitch; span:**										
G200102G	5.00 m	Nr	0.85	14.43	–	36.31	50.74	15.87	–	39.94	55.81
G200102H	6.00 m	Nr	0.88	14.94	–	39.61	54.55	16.43	–	43.57	60.01
G200102I	7.00 m	Nr	0.90	15.28	–	44.23	59.51	16.81	–	48.65	65.46
G200102J	8.00 m	Nr	0.95	16.13	–	50.83	66.96	17.74	–	55.91	73.66
G200102K	9.00 m	Nr	1.00	16.98	–	59.42	76.40	18.68	–	65.36	84.04
G200102L	10.00 m	Nr	1.05	17.83	–	69.99	87.82	19.61	–	76.99	96.60
G200106	**Standard trusses; 450 mm overhang at eaves; 45 degree pitch; span:**										
G200106M	5.00 m	Nr	0.90	15.28	–	58.94	74.22	16.81	–	64.83	81.64
G200106N	6.00 m	Nr	0.93	15.79	–	63.69	79.48	17.37	–	70.06	87.43
G200106O	7.00 m	Nr	0.95	16.13	–	70.35	86.48	17.74	–	77.39	95.13
G200106P	8.00 m	Nr	1.00	16.98	–	79.85	96.83	18.68	–	87.84	106.51
G200106Q	9.00 m	Nr	1.05	17.83	–	92.21	110.04	19.61	–	101.43	121.04
G200106R	10.00 m	Nr	1.10	18.68	–	107.42	126.10	20.55	–	118.16	138.71
G200113	**Monopitch trusses; 450 mm overhang at eaves; 22.5 degree pitch; span:**										
G200113A	2.00 m	Nr	0.55	9.34	–	38.73	48.07	10.27	–	42.60	52.88
G200113B	3.00 m	Nr	0.58	9.85	–	40.14	49.99	10.84	–	44.15	54.99
G200113C	4.00 m	Nr	0.60	10.19	–	42.25	52.44	11.21	–	46.48	57.68
G200113D	5.00 m	Nr	0.65	11.04	–	43.67	54.71	12.14	–	48.04	60.18
G200113E	6.00 m	Nr	0.70	11.89	–	47.17	59.06	13.08	–	51.89	64.97
G200114	**Monopitch trusses; 450 mm overhang at eaves; 35 degree pitch; span:**										
G200114F	2.00 m	Nr	0.60	10.19	–	38.96	49.15	11.21	–	42.86	54.07
G200114G	3.00 m	Nr	0.63	10.70	–	40.59	51.29	11.77	–	44.65	56.42
G200114H	4.00 m	Nr	0.65	11.04	–	42.25	53.29	12.14	–	46.48	58.62
G200114I	5.00 m	Nr	0.70	11.89	–	43.57	55.46	13.08	–	47.93	61.01
G200114J	6.00 m	Nr	0.75	12.74	–	46.87	59.61	14.01	–	51.56	65.57
G200115	**Monopitch trusses; 450 mm overhang at eaves; 45 degree pitch; span:**										
G200115K	2.00 m	Nr	0.65	11.04	–	59.90	70.94	12.14	–	65.89	78.03
G200115L	3.00 m	Nr	0.68	11.55	–	62.25	73.80	12.71	–	68.48	81.18
G200115M	4.00 m	Nr	0.70	11.89	–	64.63	76.52	13.08	–	71.09	84.17
G200115N	5.00 m	Nr	0.75	12.74	–	66.55	79.29	14.01	–	73.21	87.22
G200115O	6.00 m	Nr	0.80	13.58	–	71.30	84.88	14.94	–	78.43	93.37

Structural and Carcassing

Major Works 2009		Unit	Labour Hours	Labour Net	Plant Net	Materials Net	Unit Net	Labour Gross	Plant Gross	Materials Gross	Unit Price
								(Gross rates include 10% profit)			
				£	£	£	£	£	£	£	£
G20	**G20: CARPENTRY, TIMBER FRAMING AND FIRST FIXING**										
G2001	**Trussed rafters; preservative treated and stress graded softwood**										
G200121	**Girder trusses; 22.5 degree pitch; span:**										
G200121A	5.00 m	Nr	0.75	12.74	–	121.12	133.86	14.01	–	133.23	147.25
G200121B	6.00 m	Nr	0.78	13.24	–	138.01	151.25	14.56	–	151.81	166.38
G200121C	7.00 m	Nr	0.80	13.58	–	149.28	162.86	14.94	–	164.21	179.15
G200121D	8.00 m	Nr	0.85	14.43	–	169.00	183.43	15.87	–	185.90	201.77
G200121E	9.00 m	Nr	0.90	15.28	–	197.17	212.45	16.81	–	216.89	233.70
G200121F	10.00 m	Nr	0.95	16.13	–	225.32	241.45	17.74	–	247.85	265.60
G200122	**Girder trusses; 35 degree pitch; span:**										
G200122G	5.00 m	Nr	0.80	13.58	–	118.83	132.41	14.94	–	130.71	145.65
G200122H	6.00 m	Nr	0.83	14.09	–	136.00	150.09	15.50	–	149.60	165.10
G200122I	7.00 m	Nr	0.85	14.43	–	146.57	161.00	15.87	–	161.23	177.10
G200122J	8.00 m	Nr	0.90	15.28	–	166.35	181.63	16.81	–	182.99	199.79
G200122K	9.00 m	Nr	0.95	16.13	–	194.08	210.21	17.74	–	213.49	231.23
G200122L	10.00 m	Nr	1.00	16.98	–	221.80	238.78	18.68	–	243.98	262.66
G200123	**Girder trusses; 45 degree pitch; span:**										
G200123M	5.00 m	Nr	0.85	14.43	–	186.30	200.73	15.87	–	204.93	220.80
G200123N	6.00 m	Nr	0.88	14.94	–	218.65	233.59	16.43	–	240.52	256.95
G200123O	7.00 m	Nr	0.90	15.28	–	231.94	247.22	16.81	–	255.13	271.94
G200123P	8.00 m	Nr	0.95	16.13	–	262.38	278.51	17.74	–	288.62	306.36
G200123Q	9.00 m	Nr	1.00	16.98	–	308.01	324.99	18.68	–	338.81	357.49
G200123R	10.00 m	Nr	1.05	17.83	–	351.74	369.57	19.61	–	386.91	406.53
G200131	**Hip reducing set; 22.5 degree pitch; span:**										
G200131A	5.00 m	Nr	2.00	33.96	–	67.60	101.56	37.36	–	74.36	111.72
G200131B	6.00 m	Nr	2.91	49.41	–	90.13	139.54	54.35	–	99.14	153.49
G200131C	7.00 m	Nr	3.83	65.03	–	98.58	163.61	71.53	–	108.44	179.97
G200131D	8.00 m	Nr	4.05	68.77	–	101.39	170.16	75.65	–	111.53	187.18
G200131E	9.00 m	Nr	5.70	96.79	–	104.21	201.00	106.47	–	114.63	221.10
G200131F	10.00 m	Nr	7.00	118.86	–	107.04	225.90	130.75	–	117.74	248.49
G200132	**Hip reducing set; 35 degree pitch; span:**										
G200132G	5.00 m	Nr	2.13	36.17	–	68.67	104.84	39.79	–	75.54	115.32
G200132H	6.00 m	Nr	3.08	52.30	–	89.78	142.08	57.53	–	98.76	156.29
G200132I	7.00 m	Nr	4.05	68.77	–	97.70	166.47	75.65	–	107.47	183.12
G200132J	8.00 m	Nr	5.23	88.81	–	100.35	189.16	97.69	–	110.39	208.08
G200132K	9.00 m	Nr	6.00	101.88	–	105.61	207.49	112.07	–	116.17	228.24
G200132L	10.00 m	Nr	7.35	124.80	–	110.92	235.72	137.28	–	122.01	259.29
G200133	**Hip reducing set; 45 degree pitch; span:**										
G200133M	5.00 m	Nr	2.25	38.21	–	114.09	152.30	42.03	–	125.50	167.53
G200133N	6.00 m	Nr	3.26	55.35	–	144.49	199.84	60.89	–	158.94	219.82
G200133O	7.00 m	Nr	4.28	72.67	–	155.90	228.57	79.94	–	171.49	251.43
G200133P	8.00 m	Nr	5.50	93.39	–	159.71	253.10	102.73	–	175.68	278.41
G200133Q	9.00 m	Nr	6.30	106.97	–	167.29	274.26	117.67	–	184.02	301.69
G200133R	10.00 m	Nr	7.70	130.75	–	174.92	305.67	143.83	–	192.41	336.24

Major Works 2009		Unit	Labour Hours	Labour Net	Plant Net	Materials Net	Unit Net	Labour Gross	Plant Gross	Materials Gross	Unit Price
				£	£	£	£	£	£	£	£
G20	**G20: CARPENTRY, TIMBER FRAMING AND FIRST FIXING**										
G2001	**Trussed rafters; preservative treated and stress graded softwood**										
G200141	**Gable ladders; length:**										
G200141A	2.5-3.0 m	Nr	0.75	12.74	–	32.52	45.26	14.01	–	35.77	49.79
G200141B	3.0-3.5 m	Nr	0.80	13.59	–	35.15	48.74	14.95	–	38.67	53.61
G200141C	3.5-4.0 m	Nr	0.85	14.43	–	38.08	52.51	15.87	–	41.89	57.76
G200141D	4.0-4.5 m	Nr	0.90	15.28	–	43.35	58.63	16.81	–	47.69	64.49
G200141E	4.5-5.0 m	Nr	0.95	16.13	–	48.91	65.04	17.74	–	53.80	71.54
G200141F	5.0-5.5 m	Nr	1.00	16.98	–	54.18	71.16	18.68	–	59.60	78.28
G200141G	5.5-6.0 m	Nr	1.10	18.67	–	59.77	78.44	20.54	–	65.75	86.28
G200141H	6.0-6.5 m	Nr	1.20	20.37	–	65.03	85.40	22.41	–	71.53	93.94
G2005	**Glued laminated timber beams**										
G200521	**Beams, BS 4169, treated wrought softwood:**										
G200521A	65 × 150 mm	m	0.17	2.89	–	17.70	20.59	3.18	–	19.47	22.65
G200521B	65 × 200 mm	m	0.17	2.89	–	23.04	25.93	3.18	–	25.34	28.52
G200521C	65 × 300 mm	m	0.18	3.06	–	34.47	37.53	3.37	–	37.92	41.28
G200521D	90 × 150 mm	m	0.18	3.06	–	22.65	25.71	3.37	–	24.92	28.28
G200521E	90 × 200 mm	m	0.18	3.06	–	30.06	33.12	3.37	–	33.07	36.43
G200521F	90 × 300 mm	m	0.20	3.40	–	44.88	48.28	3.74	–	49.37	53.11
G200521G	90 × 400 mm	m	0.22	3.74	–	61.33	65.07	4.11	–	67.46	71.58
G200521H	90 × 450 mm	m	0.23	3.91	–	68.75	72.66	4.30	–	75.63	79.93
G200521I	115 × 250 mm	m	0.25	4.25	–	46.82	51.07	4.68	–	51.50	56.18
G200521J	115 × 300 mm	m	0.25	4.25	–	56.82	61.07	4.68	–	62.50	67.18
G200521K	115 × 400 mm	m	0.27	4.58	–	77.68	82.26	5.04	–	85.45	90.49
G200521L	115 × 500 mm	m	0.27	4.58	–	92.09	96.67	5.04	–	101.30	106.34
G200521M	140 × 350 mm	m	0.28	4.75	–	79.44	84.19	5.23	–	87.38	92.61
G200521N	140 × 400 mm	m	0.28	4.75	–	90.04	94.79	5.23	–	99.04	104.27
G200521O	140 × 475 mm	m	0.30	5.09	–	114.03	119.12	5.60	–	125.43	131.03
G200521P	165 × 425 mm	m	0.32	5.43	–	117.73	123.16	5.97	–	129.50	135.48
G200521Q	165 × 450 mm	m	0.32	5.43	–	124.30	129.73	5.97	–	136.73	142.70
G200521R	165 × 475 mm	m	0.34	5.77	–	132.15	137.92	6.35	–	145.37	151.71
G200521S	190 × 475 mm	m	0.37	6.28	–	153.84	160.12	6.91	–	169.22	176.13
G2021	**Floors**										
G202102	**Treated sawn softwood; grade SC3; basic sizes:**										
G202102A	38 × 100 mm	m	0.12	2.03	–	1.16	3.19	2.23	–	1.28	3.51
G202102B	38 × 150 mm	m	0.13	2.21	–	1.72	3.93	2.43	–	1.89	4.32
G202102C	50 × 100 mm	m	0.13	2.21	–	1.51	3.72	2.43	–	1.66	4.09
G202102D	50 × 150 mm	m	0.14	2.38	–	2.28	4.66	2.62	–	2.51	5.13
G202102E	50 × 200 mm	m	0.15	2.54	–	3.04	5.58	2.79	–	3.34	6.14
G202102F	50 × 225 mm	m	0.15	2.55	–	3.41	5.96	2.81	–	3.75	6.56
G202102H	75 × 150 mm	m	0.15	2.55	–	3.41	5.96	2.81	–	3.75	6.56
G202102I	75 × 200 mm	m	0.19	3.23	–	4.55	7.78	3.55	–	5.01	8.56
G202102J	75 × 225 mm	m	0.22	3.74	–	5.12	8.86	4.11	–	5.63	9.75
G202102M	100 × 200 mm	m	0.26	4.42	–	6.06	10.48	4.86	–	6.67	11.53
G202102N	100 × 225 mm	m	0.29	4.93	–	6.83	11.76	5.42	–	7.51	12.94
G202102O	100 × 300 mm	m	0.39	6.62	–	9.10	15.72	7.28	–	10.01	17.29

Structural and Carcassing

Major Works 2009		Unit	Labour Hours	Labour Net	Plant Net	Materials Net	Unit Net	Labour Gross	Plant Gross	Materials Gross	Unit Price
								(Gross rates include 10% profit)			
				£	£	£	£	£	£	£	£
G20	**G20: CARPENTRY, TIMBER FRAMING AND FIRST FIXING**										
G2023	**Walls**										
G202321	**Treated sawn softwood; grade GS; basic sizes:**										
G202321A	38 × 75 mm	m	0.10	1.70	–	0.80	2.50	1.87	–	0.88	2.75
G202321B	38 × 100 mm	m	0.12	2.04	–	1.04	3.08	2.24	–	1.14	3.39
G202321C	50 × 50 mm	m	0.10	1.70	–	0.71	2.41	1.87	–	0.78	2.65
G202321D	50 × 75 mm	m	0.12	2.04	–	1.03	3.07	2.24	–	1.13	3.38
G202321E	50 × 100 mm	m	0.15	2.55	–	1.38	3.93	2.81	–	1.52	4.32
G202321G	75 × 100 mm	m	0.17	2.88	–	2.12	5.00	3.17	–	2.33	5.50
G202321H	100 × 100 mm	m	0.20	3.40	–	2.77	6.17	3.74	–	3.05	6.79
G2025	**Plates or the like**										
G202531	**Treated sawn softwood; grade GS; basic sizes:**										
G202531A	19 × 38 mm	m	0.08	1.36	–	0.24	1.60	1.50	–	0.26	1.76
G202531B	19 × 50 mm	m	0.08	1.36	–	0.30	1.66	1.50	–	0.33	1.83
G202531C	25 × 50 mm	m	0.09	1.53	–	0.38	1.91	1.68	–	0.42	2.10
G202531D	25 × 75 mm	m	0.09	1.53	–	0.54	2.07	1.68	–	0.59	2.28
G202531E	25 × 100 mm	m	0.10	1.70	–	0.71	2.41	1.87	–	0.78	2.65
G202531F	38 × 38 mm	m	0.08	1.36	–	0.43	1.79	1.50	–	0.47	1.97
G202531G	38 × 50 mm	m	0.09	1.53	–	0.55	2.08	1.68	–	0.61	2.29
G202531H	38 × 100 mm	m	0.10	1.70	–	1.04	2.74	1.87	–	1.14	3.01
G202531I	50 × 50 mm	m	0.09	1.53	–	0.71	2.24	1.68	–	0.78	2.46
G202531J	50 × 75 mm	m	0.09	1.53	–	1.03	2.56	1.68	–	1.13	2.82
G202531K	50 × 100 mm	m	0.10	1.70	–	1.38	3.08	1.87	–	1.52	3.39
G202531L	50 × 150 mm	m	0.12	2.03	–	2.12	4.15	2.23	–	2.33	4.57
G202531M	75 × 100 mm	m	0.14	2.37	–	2.12	4.49	2.61	–	2.33	4.94
G202531N	75 × 150 mm	m	0.16	2.72	–	3.10	5.82	2.99	–	3.41	6.40
G202531O	75 × 200 mm	m	0.22	3.74	–	4.15	7.89	4.11	–	4.57	8.68
G202531P	100 × 100 mm	m	0.15	2.55	–	2.77	5.32	2.81	–	3.05	5.85
G2027	**Flat roofs**										
G202702	**Treated sawn softwood; grade SC3; basic sizes:**										
G202702A	38 × 100 mm	m	0.12	2.03	–	1.16	3.19	2.23	–	1.28	3.51
G202702B	38 × 150 mm	m	0.13	2.21	–	1.72	3.93	2.43	–	1.89	4.32
G202702C	50 × 100 mm	m	0.13	2.21	–	1.51	3.72	2.43	–	1.66	4.09
G202702D	50 × 150 mm	m	0.14	2.38	–	2.28	4.66	2.62	–	2.51	5.13
G202702E	50 × 200 mm	m	0.15	2.54	–	3.04	5.58	2.79	–	3.34	6.14
G202702F	50 × 225 mm	m	0.15	2.55	–	3.41	5.96	2.81	–	3.75	6.56
G202702H	75 × 150 mm	m	0.15	2.55	–	3.41	5.96	2.81	–	3.75	6.56
G202702I	75 × 200 mm	m	0.19	3.23	–	4.55	7.78	3.55	–	5.01	8.56
G202702J	75 × 225 mm	m	0.22	3.74	–	5.12	8.86	4.11	–	5.63	9.75
G202702M	100 × 200 mm	m	0.26	4.42	–	6.06	10.48	4.86	–	6.67	11.53
G202702N	100 × 225 mm	m	0.29	4.93	–	6.83	11.76	5.42	–	7.51	12.94
G202702O	100 × 300 mm	m	0.39	6.62	–	9.10	15.72	7.28	–	10.01	17.29

Major Works 2009		Unit	Labour Hours	Labour Net	Plant Net	Materials Net	Unit Net	Labour Gross	Plant Gross	Materials Gross	Unit Price
								(Gross rates include 10% profit)			
				£	£	£	£	£	£	£	£
G20	**G20: CARPENTRY, TIMBER FRAMING AND FIRST FIXING**										
G2029	**Pitched roofs**										
G202911	**Treated sawn softwood; grade SC3; basic sizes:**										
G202911A	25 × 100 mm..........	m	0.12	2.04	–	0.75	2.79	2.24	–	0.83	3.07
G202911B	25 × 150 mm..........	m	0.14	2.38	–	1.12	3.50	2.62	–	1.23	3.85
G202911C	25 × 175 mm..........	m	0.16	2.71	–	1.31	4.02	2.98	–	1.44	4.42
G202911D	25 × 200 mm..........	m	0.17	2.89	–	1.49	4.38	3.18	–	1.64	4.82
G202911E	38 × 100 mm..........	m	0.14	2.38	–	1.14	3.52	2.62	–	1.25	3.87
G202911F	38 × 150 mm..........	m	0.19	3.23	–	1.70	4.93	3.55	–	1.87	5.42
G202911G	38 × 200 mm..........	m	0.22	3.73	–	2.28	6.01	4.10	–	2.51	6.61
G202911H	50 × 50 mm..........	m	0.12	2.04	–	0.75	2.79	2.24	–	0.83	3.07
G202911I	50 × 100 mm..........	m	0.14	2.38	–	1.51	3.89	2.62	–	1.66	4.28
G202911J	50 × 150 mm..........	m	0.16	2.72	–	2.28	5.00	2.99	–	2.51	5.50
G202911K	50 × 200 mm..........	m	0.17	2.88	–	3.04	5.92	3.17	–	3.34	6.51
G202911L	50 × 225 mm..........	m	0.19	3.23	–	3.41	6.64	3.55	–	3.75	7.30
G202911M	75 × 100 mm..........	m	0.23	3.91	–	2.28	6.19	4.30	–	2.51	6.81
G202911N	75 × 150 mm..........	m	0.25	4.25	–	3.41	7.66	4.68	–	3.75	8.43
G202911O	75 × 200 mm..........	m	0.28	4.75	–	4.55	9.30	5.23	–	5.01	10.23
G202911P	75 × 250 mm..........	m	0.32	5.43	–	5.69	11.12	5.97	–	6.26	12.23
G202911Q	75 × 300 mm..........	m	0.38	6.46	–	6.83	13.29	7.11	–	7.51	14.62
G202911R	100 × 100 mm..........	m	0.25	4.24	–	3.04	7.28	4.66	–	3.34	8.01
G202911S	100 × 150 mm..........	m	0.28	4.75	–	4.55	9.30	5.23	–	5.01	10.23
G202911T	100 × 200 mm..........	m	0.30	5.10	–	6.06	11.16	5.61	–	6.67	12.28
G2031	**Strutting and bridging; treated sawn softwood; grade GS; basic sizes:**										
G203152	**Solid strutting:**										
G203152A	50 × 100 mm..........	m	0.28	4.75	–	1.80	6.55	5.23	–	1.98	7.21
G203152B	50 × 150 mm..........	m	0.30	5.09	–	2.46	7.55	5.60	–	2.71	8.31
G203152C	50 × 200 mm..........	m	0.35	5.95	–	3.11	9.06	6.55	–	3.42	9.97
G203152D	50 × 225 mm..........	m	0.37	6.29	–	3.44	9.73	6.92	–	3.78	10.70
G203152E	50 × 250 mm..........	m	0.39	6.62	–	3.78	10.40	7.28	–	4.16	11.44
G203153	**Herringbone strutting:**										
G203153A	38 × 38 × 100 mm deep	m	0.35	5.95	–	0.80	6.75	6.55	–	0.88	7.43
G203153B	38 × 38 × 150 mm deep	m	0.38	6.45	–	0.83	7.28	7.10	–	0.91	8.01
G203153C	38 × 38 × 200 mm deep	m	0.40	6.80	–	0.86	7.66	7.48	–	0.95	8.43
G203153D	38 × 38 × 225 mm deep	m	0.42	7.13	–	0.88	8.01	7.84	–	0.97	8.81
G203153E	38 × 38 × 250 mm deep	m	0.45	7.65	–	0.90	8.55	8.42	–	0.99	9.41
G203153F	50 × 50 × 100 mm deep	m	0.35	5.95	–	1.31	7.26	6.55	–	1.44	7.99
G203153G	50 × 50 × 125 mm deep	m	0.38	6.45	–	1.33	7.78	7.10	–	1.46	8.56
G203153H	50 × 50 × 150 mm deep	m	0.38	6.45	–	1.36	7.81	7.10	–	1.50	8.59
G203153I	50 × 50 × 200 mm deep	m	0.40	6.79	–	1.42	8.21	7.47	–	1.56	9.03
G203153J	50 × 50 × 225 mm deep	m	0.42	7.13	–	1.45	8.58	7.84	–	1.60	9.44

Structural and Carcassing

Major Works 2009	Unit	Labour Hours	Labour Net	Plant Net	Materials Net	Unit Net	Labour Gross	Plant Gross	Materials Gross	Unit Price
			£	£	£	£	£	£	£	£
							\multicolumn{4}{c}{(Gross rates include 10% profit)}			

G20   **G20: CARPENTRY, TIMBER FRAMING AND FIRST FIXING**

G2032   **Catnic galvanised mild steel herringbone joist struts; fixing between joists:**

G203241   **To suit joist size:**

Code	Description	Unit	Labour Hours	Labour Net	Plant Net	Materials Net	Unit Net	Labour Gross	Plant Gross	Materials Gross	Unit Price
G203241A	38 × 150/175 mm; 400 mm centres	m	0.35	5.95	–	3.28	9.23	6.55	–	3.61	10.15
G203241B	38 × 150/175 mm; 450 mm centres	m	0.30	5.09	–	2.93	8.02	5.60	–	3.22	8.82
G203241C	38 × 150/175 mm; 600 mm centres	m	0.25	4.24	–	2.20	6.44	4.66	–	2.42	7.08
G203241D	50 × 150/175 mm; 400 mm centres	m	0.35	5.95	–	3.28	9.23	6.55	–	3.61	10.15
G203241E	50 × 150/175 mm; 450 mm centres	m	0.30	5.09	–	2.93	8.02	5.60	–	3.22	8.82
G203241F	50 × 150/175 mm; 600 mm centres	m	0.25	4.24	–	2.20	6.44	4.66	–	2.42	7.08
G203241G	63 × 150/175 mm; 400 mm centres	m	0.35	5.95	–	3.28	9.23	6.55	–	3.61	10.15
G203241H	63 × 150/175 mm; 450 mm centres	m	0.30	5.09	–	2.93	8.02	5.60	–	3.22	8.82
G203241I	63 × 150/175 mm; 600 mm centres	m	0.25	4.24	–	2.20	6.44	4.66	–	2.42	7.08
G203241J	38 × 200/225 mm; 400 mm centres	m	0.35	5.95	–	3.28	9.23	6.55	–	3.61	10.15
G203241K	38 × 200/225 mm; 450 mm centres	m	0.30	5.09	–	2.93	8.02	5.60	–	3.22	8.82
G203241L	38 × 200/225 mm; 600 mm centres	m	0.25	4.24	–	2.20	6.44	4.66	–	2.42	7.08
G203241M	50 × 200/225 mm; 400 mm centres	m	0.35	5.95	–	3.28	9.23	6.55	–	3.61	10.15
G203241N	50 × 200/225 mm; 450 mm centres	m	0.30	5.09	–	2.93	8.02	5.60	–	3.22	8.82
G203241O	50 × 200/225 mm; 600 mm centres	m	0.25	4.24	–	2.20	6.44	4.66	–	2.42	7.08
G203241P	63 × 200/225 mm; 400 mm centres	m	0.35	5.95	–	3.28	9.23	6.55	–	3.61	10.15
G203241Q	63 × 200/225 mm; 450 mm centres	m	0.30	5.09	–	2.93	8.02	5.60	–	3.22	8.82
G203241R	63 × 200/225 mm; 600 mm centres	m	0.25	4.24	–	2.20	6.44	4.66	–	2.42	7.08

Major Works 2009		Unit	Labour Hours	Labour Net	Plant Net	Materials Net	Unit Net	Labour Gross	Plant Gross	Materials Gross	Unit Price
								(Gross rates include 10% profit)			
				£	£	£	£	£	£	£	£
G20	**G20: CARPENTRY, TIMBER FRAMING AND FIRST FIXING**										
G2033	**Supports, kerbs, bearers or the like**										
G203331	**Treated sawn softwood; grade GS; basic sizes:**										
G203331A	19 × 38 mm	m	0.08	1.36	–	0.24	1.60	1.50	–	0.26	1.76
G203331B	19 × 50 mm	m	0.08	1.36	–	0.30	1.66	1.50	–	0.33	1.83
G203331C	25 × 50 mm	m	0.09	1.53	–	0.38	1.91	1.68	–	0.42	2.10
G203331D	25 × 75 mm	m	0.09	1.53	–	0.54	2.07	1.68	–	0.59	2.28
G203331E	25 × 100 mm	m	0.10	1.70	–	0.71	2.41	1.87	–	0.78	2.65
G203331F	38 × 38 mm	m	0.08	1.36	–	0.43	1.79	1.50	–	0.47	1.97
G203331G	38 × 50 mm	m	0.09	1.53	–	0.55	2.08	1.68	–	0.61	2.29
G203331H	38 × 100 mm	m	0.10	1.70	–	1.04	2.74	1.87	–	1.14	3.01
G203331I	50 × 50 mm	m	0.09	1.53	–	0.71	2.24	1.68	–	0.78	2.46
G203331J	50 × 75 mm	m	0.09	1.53	–	1.03	2.56	1.68	–	1.13	2.82
G203331K	50 × 100 mm	m	0.10	1.70	–	1.38	3.08	1.87	–	1.52	3.39
G203331L	50 × 150 mm	m	0.12	2.03	–	2.12	4.15	2.23	–	2.33	4.57
G203331M	75 × 100 mm	m	0.14	2.37	–	2.12	4.49	2.61	–	2.33	4.94
G203331N	75 × 150 mm	m	0.16	2.72	–	3.10	5.82	2.99	–	3.41	6.40
G203331O	75 × 200 mm	m	0.22	3.74	–	4.15	7.89	4.11	–	4.57	8.68
G203331P	100 × 100 mm	m	0.15	2.55	–	2.77	5.32	2.81	–	3.05	5.85
G2039	**Fillets and rolls; treated sawn softwood grade GS; basic sizes**										
G203992	**Angle fillets:**										
G203992A	ex-25 × 50 mm	m	0.12	2.04	–	0.38	2.42	2.24	–	0.42	2.66
G203992B	ex-38 × 38 mm	m	0.13	2.21	–	0.47	2.68	2.43	–	0.52	2.95
G203992C	ex-38 × 75 mm	m	0.14	2.38	–	0.73	3.11	2.62	–	0.80	3.42
G203992D	ex-50 × 50 mm	m	0.15	2.55	–	0.57	3.12	2.81	–	0.63	3.43
G203992E	ex-75 × 75 mm	m	0.17	2.89	–	1.12	4.01	3.18	–	1.23	4.41
G203993	**Rolls:**										
G203993A	ex-50 × 50 mm	m	0.25	4.25	–	1.35	5.60	4.68	–	1.49	6.16
G203993B	ex-50 × 75 mm	m	0.27	4.59	–	1.75	6.34	5.05	–	1.93	6.97

Major Works 2009	Unit	Labour Hours	Labour Net	Plant Net	Materials Net	Unit Net	Labour Gross	Plant Gross	Materials Gross	Unit Price
							(Gross rates include 10% profit)			
			£	£	£	£	£	£	£	£
G20	**G20: CARPENTRY, TIMBER FRAMING AND FIRST FIXING**									
G2041	**Grounds and battens; treated sawn softwood, grade GS; basic sizes**									
G204102	**Open spaced grounds and battens:**									
G204102A	13 × 38 mm; 300 mm centres one way	m²	0.38	6.45	–	0.52	6.97	7.10	–	0.57	7.67
G204102B	13 × 38 mm; 450 centres one way	m²	0.29	4.92	–	0.38	5.30	5.41	–	0.42	5.83
G204102C	13 × 38 mm; 600 centres one way	m²	0.24	4.07	–	0.26	4.33	4.48	–	0.29	4.76
G204102D	13 × 38 mm; 900 centres one way	m²	0.19	3.23	–	0.19	3.42	3.55	–	0.21	3.76
G204102E	13 × 38 mm; 300 mm centres both ways	m²	0.71	12.06	–	1.08	13.14	13.27	–	1.19	14.45
G204102F	13 × 38 mm; 450 mm centres both ways	m²	0.52	8.83	–	0.71	9.54	9.71	–	0.78	10.49
G204102G	13 × 38 mm; 600 mm centres both ways	m²	0.43	7.30	–	0.52	7.82	8.03	–	0.57	8.60
G204102H	13 × 38 mm; 900 mm centres both ways	m²	0.34	5.77	–	0.38	6.15	6.35	–	0.42	6.77
G204102I	25 × 38 mm; 300 mm centres one way	m²	0.45	7.64	–	0.90	8.54	8.40	–	0.99	9.39
G204102J	25 × 38 mm; 450 mm centres one way	m²	0.33	5.61	–	0.63	6.24	6.17	–	0.69	6.86
G204102K	25 × 38 mm; 600 mm centres one way	m²	0.28	4.76	–	0.45	5.21	5.24	–	0.50	5.73
G204102L	25 × 38 mm; 900 mm centres one way	m²	0.22	3.73	–	0.32	4.05	4.10	–	0.35	4.46
G204102M	25 × 38 mm; 300 mm centres both ways	m²	0.85	14.44	–	1.85	16.29	15.88	–	2.04	17.92
G204102N	25 × 38 mm; 450 mm centres both ways	m²	0.62	10.53	–	1.22	11.75	11.58	–	1.34	12.93
G204102O	25 × 38 mm; 600 mm centres both ways	m²	0.50	8.49	–	0.90	9.39	9.34	–	0.99	10.33
G204102P	25 × 38 mm; 900 mm centres both ways	m²	0.38	6.45	–	0.64	7.09	7.10	–	0.70	7.80
G204102Q	38 × 50 mm; 300 mm centres one way	m²	0.49	8.32	–	1.74	10.06	9.15	–	1.91	11.07
G204102R	38 × 50 mm; 450 mm centres one way	m²	0.36	6.12	–	1.19	7.31	6.73	–	1.31	8.04
G204102S	38 × 50 mm; 600 mm centres one way	m²	0.29	4.93	–	0.87	5.80	5.42	–	0.96	6.38
G204102T	38 × 50 mm; 900 mm centres one way	m²	0.23	3.90	–	0.60	4.50	4.29	–	0.66	4.95
G204102U	38 × 50 mm; 300 mm centres both ways	m²	0.92	15.63	–	3.53	19.16	17.19	–	3.88	21.08
G204102V	38 × 50 mm; 450 mm centres both ways	m²	0.66	11.20	–	2.34	13.54	12.32	–	2.57	14.89
G204102W	38 × 50 mm; 600 mm centres both ways	m²	0.54	9.17	–	1.74	10.91	10.09	–	1.91	12.00
G204102X	38 × 50 mm; 900 mm centres both ways	m²	0.41	6.96	–	1.20	8.16	7.66	–	1.32	8.98

Major Works 2009		Unit	Labour Hours	Labour Net	Plant Net	Materials Net	Unit Net	Labour Gross	Plant Gross	Materials Gross	Unit Price
				£	£	£	£	£	£	£	£
								\multicolumn{4}{c}{(Gross rates include 10% profit)}
G20	**G20: CARPENTRY, TIMBER FRAMING AND FIRST FIXING**										
G2041	**Grounds and battens; treated sawn softwood, grade GS; basic sizes**										
G204110	**Individual grounds and battens:**										
G204110A	13 × 25 mm	m	0.08	1.36	–	0.13	1.49	1.50	–	0.14	1.64
G204110B	13 × 38 mm	m	0.08	1.36	–	0.17	1.53	1.50	–	0.19	1.68
G204110C	13 × 50 mm	m	0.08	1.36	–	0.22	1.58	1.50	–	0.24	1.74
G204110D	19 × 38 mm	m	0.09	1.53	–	0.24	1.77	1.68	–	0.26	1.95
G204110E	19 × 50 mm	m	0.09	1.53	–	0.29	1.82	1.68	–	0.32	2.00
G204110G	25 × 25 mm	m	0.10	1.69	–	0.21	1.90	1.86	–	0.23	2.09
G204110H	25 × 38 mm	m	0.10	1.70	–	0.29	1.99	1.87	–	0.32	2.19
G204110I	25 × 50 mm	m	0.10	1.70	–	0.37	2.07	1.87	–	0.41	2.28
G204110J	38 × 50 mm	m	0.11	1.87	–	0.54	2.41	2.06	–	0.59	2.65
G204110K	50 × 50 mm	m	0.13	2.21	–	0.70	2.91	2.43	–	0.77	3.20
G2043	**Framework; treated sawn softwood, grade GS; basic sizes**										
G204302	**Framework to receive boarded finish:**										
G204302A	19 × 38 mm; 300 mm centres both ways	m²	0.75	12.74	–	1.50	14.24	14.01	–	1.65	15.66
G204302B	25 × 50 mm; 300 mm centres both ways	m²	0.83	14.10	–	2.41	16.51	15.51	–	2.65	18.16
G204302C	50 × 50 mm; 300 mm centres both ways	m²	1.08	18.34	–	4.58	22.92	20.17	–	5.04	25.21
G204302D	50 × 75 mm; 450 mm centres both ways	m²	0.72	12.23	–	4.44	16.67	13.45	–	4.88	18.34
G204303	**Framework around structural metalwork:**										
G204303A	50 × 50 mm horizontally at 450 mm centres and 38 × 38 mm vertically at 600 mm centres	m²	1.30	22.08	–	2.22	24.30	24.29	–	2.44	26.73
G204303B	50 × 75 mm horizontally at 450 mm centres and 50 × 50 mm vertically at 600 mm centres	m²	1.36	23.09	–	3.38	26.47	25.40	–	3.72	29.12
G204310	**Framework to receive pipe casings and the like; 25 × 38 mm vertically; 25 × 25 mm horizontally at 450 mm centres:**										
G204310A	one sided; not exceeding 150 mm wide	m	0.40	6.80	–	0.68	7.48	7.48	–	0.75	8.23
G204310B	one sided; 150-300 mm wide	m	0.43	7.30	–	0.74	8.04	8.03	–	0.81	8.84
G204310C	two sided; 150-300 mm girth	m	0.54	9.17	–	1.03	10.20	10.09	–	1.13	11.22
G204310D	two sided; 300-450 mm girth	m	0.57	9.68	–	1.13	10.81	10.65	–	1.24	11.89
G204310E	two sided; 450-600 mm girth	m	0.61	10.36	–	1.18	11.54	11.40	–	1.30	12.69
G204310F	three sided; 300-450 mm girth	m	0.68	11.55	–	1.42	12.97	12.71	–	1.56	14.27
G204310G	three sided; 450-600 mm girth	m	0.71	12.06	–	1.47	13.53	13.27	–	1.62	14.88
G204310H	three sided; 600-900 mm girth	m	0.78	13.24	–	1.63	14.87	14.56	–	1.79	16.36

Major Works 2009		Unit	Labour Hours	Labour Net	Plant Net	Materials Net	Unit Net	Labour Gross	Plant Gross	Materials Gross	Unit Price
								(Gross rates include 10% profit)			
				£	£	£	£	£	£	£	£
G20	**G20: CARPENTRY, TIMBER FRAMING AND FIRST FIXING**										
G2051	**Eaves, verges, soffits, fascias, barge boards or the like**										
G205181	**Wrought softwood cross-tongued boarding; basic sizes:**										
G205181A	16 mm thick; not exceeding 150 mm wide	m	0.11	1.87	–	2.37	4.24	2.06	–	2.61	4.66
G205181B	16 mm thick; 150-300 mm wide	m	0.15	2.55	–	4.60	7.15	2.81	–	5.06	7.87
G205181C	16 mm thick; 300-450 mm wide	m	0.19	3.22	–	6.97	10.19	3.54	–	7.67	11.21
G205181D	16 mm thick; 450-600 mm wide	m	0.22	3.74	–	9.01	12.75	4.11	–	9.91	14.03
G205181E	19 mm thick; not exceeding 150 mm wide	m	0.12	2.04	–	2.56	4.60	2.24	–	2.82	5.06
G205181F	19 mm thick; 150-300 mm wide	m	0.16	2.72	–	4.97	7.69	2.99	–	5.47	8.46
G205181G	19 mm thick; 300-450 mm wide	m	0.20	3.39	–	7.54	10.93	3.73	–	8.29	12.02
G205181H	19 mm thick; 450-600 mm wide	m	0.23	3.90	–	9.76	13.66	4.29	–	10.74	15.03
G205181I	25 mm thick; not exceeding 150 mm wide	m	0.13	2.21	–	3.02	5.23	2.43	–	3.32	5.75
G205181J	25 mm thick; 150-300 mm wide	m	0.17	2.89	–	5.87	8.76	3.18	–	6.46	9.64
G205181K	25 mm thick; 300-450 mm wide	m	0.21	3.57	–	8.89	12.46	3.93	–	9.78	13.71
G205181L	25 mm thick; 450-600 mm wide	m	0.24	4.07	–	11.52	15.59	4.48	–	12.67	17.15
G205182	**Wrought softwood tongued and grooved and V-jointed one side matchboarding; basic sizes:**										
G205182A	13 mm thick; not exceeding 150 mm wide	m	0.15	2.55	–	2.61	5.16	2.81	–	2.87	5.68
G205182B	13 mm thick; 150-300 mm wide	m	0.30	5.09	–	5.07	10.16	5.60	–	5.58	11.18
G205182C	13 mm thick; 300-450 mm wide	m	0.40	6.79	–	7.68	14.47	7.47	–	8.45	15.92
G205182D	13 mm thick; 450-600 mm thick	m	0.55	9.34	–	9.94	19.28	10.27	–	10.93	21.21
G205182E	19 mm thick; not exceeding 150 mm wide	m	0.15	2.55	–	3.26	5.81	2.81	–	3.59	6.39
G205182F	19 mm thick; 150-300 mm wide	m	0.30	5.10	–	6.33	11.43	5.61	–	6.96	12.57
G205182G	19 mm thick; 300-450 mm wide	m	0.40	6.79	–	9.59	16.38	7.47	–	10.55	18.02
G205182H	19 mm thick; 450-600 mm wide	m	0.55	9.34	–	12.43	21.77	10.27	–	13.67	23.95

Major Works 2009		Unit	Labour Hours	Labour Net	Plant Net	Materials Net	Unit Net	Labour Gross	Plant Gross	Materials Gross	Unit Price
								(Gross rates include 10% profit)			
				£	£	£	£	£	£	£	£
G20	**G20: CARPENTRY, TIMBER FRAMING AND FIRST FIXING**										
G2051	**Eaves, verges, soffits, fascias, barge boards or the like**										
G205183	**Marine plywood; BS 1088:**										
G205183A	12 mm thick; not exceeding 150 mm wide	m	0.11	1.86	–	2.21	4.07	2.05	–	2.43	4.48
G205183B	12 mm thick; 150-300 mm wide	m	0.15	2.55	–	4.28	6.83	2.81	–	4.71	7.51
G205183C	12 mm thick; 300-450 mm wide	m	0.19	3.23	–	6.49	9.72	3.55	–	7.14	10.69
G205183D	12 mm thick; 450-600 mm wide	m	0.22	3.73	–	8.40	12.13	4.10	–	9.24	13.34
G205183I	18 mm thick; not exceeding 150 mm wide	m	0.12	2.04	–	3.22	5.26	2.24	–	3.54	5.79
G205183J	18 mm thick; 150-300 mm wide	m	0.16	2.72	–	6.26	8.98	2.99	–	6.89	9.88
G205183K	18 mm thick; 300-450 mm wide	m	0.20	3.39	–	9.48	12.87	3.73	–	10.43	14.16
G205183L	18 mm thick; 450-600 mm wide	m	0.23	3.90	–	12.28	16.18	4.29	–	13.51	17.80
G205183M	25 mm thick; not exceeding 150 mm wide	m	0.13	2.20	–	4.81	7.01	2.42	–	5.29	7.71
G205183N	25 mm thick; 150-300 mm wide	m	0.17	2.89	–	9.33	12.22	3.18	–	10.26	13.44
G205183O	25 mm thick; 300-450 mm wide	m	0.21	3.56	–	14.14	17.70	3.92	–	15.55	19.47
G205183P	25 mm thick; 450-600 mm wide	m	0.24	4.07	–	18.34	22.41	4.48	–	20.17	24.65
G205186	**Non-asbestos flameproof class 1 boarding; BS 476:**										
G205186A	6 mm thick; not exceeding 150 mm wide	m	0.25	4.25	–	1.95	6.20	4.68	–	2.15	6.82
G205186B	6 mm thick; 150-300 mm wide	m	0.28	4.75	–	3.68	8.43	5.23	–	4.05	9.27
G205186C	6 mm thick; 300-450 mm wide	m	0.35	5.94	–	5.56	11.50	6.53	–	6.12	12.65
G205186D	6 mm thick; 450-600 mm wide	m	0.38	6.45	–	7.17	13.62	7.10	–	7.89	14.98
G205186E	9 mm thick; not exceeding 150 mm wide	m	0.25	4.25	–	2.90	7.15	4.68	–	3.19	7.87
G205186F	9 mm thick; 150-300 mm wide	m	0.28	4.76	–	5.52	10.28	5.24	–	6.07	11.31
G205186G	9 mm thick; 300-450 mm wide	m	0.35	5.94	–	8.35	14.29	6.53	–	9.19	15.72
G205186H	9 mm thick; 450-600 mm wide	m	0.38	6.46	–	10.80	17.26	7.11	–	11.88	18.99
G205186I	12 mm thick; not exceeding 150 mm wide	m	0.25	4.24	–	3.81	8.05	4.66	–	4.19	8.86
G205186J	12 mm thick; 150-300 mm wide	m	0.28	4.76	–	7.27	12.03	5.24	–	8.00	13.23
G205186K	12 mm thick; 300-450 mm wide	m	0.35	5.94	–	11.01	16.95	6.53	–	12.11	18.65
G205186L	12 mm thick; 450-600 mm wide	m	0.38	6.45	–	14.26	20.71	7.10	–	15.69	22.78

Structural and Carcassing

Major Works 2009		Unit	Labour Hours	Labour Net	Plant Net	Materials Net	Unit Net	Labour Gross	Plant Gross	Materials Gross	Unit Price
								(Gross rates include 10% profit)			
				£	£	£	£	£	£	£	£
G20	**G20: CARPENTRY, TIMBER FRAMING AND FIRST FIXING**										
G2067	**Cleats, sprockets or the like**										
G206741	**Treated sawn softwood; grade GS; basic sizes:**										
G206741A	ex-38 × 100 × 200 mm long	Nr	0.12	2.04	–	0.15	2.19	2.24	–	0.17	2.41
G206741B	ex-38 × 150 × 300 mm long	Nr	0.16	2.72	–	0.27	2.99	2.99	–	0.30	3.29
G206741C	ex-50 × 100 × 300 mm long	Nr	0.16	2.71	–	0.25	2.96	2.98	–	0.28	3.26
G206741D	ex-50 × 150 × 400 mm long	Nr	0.20	3.39	–	0.44	3.83	3.73	–	0.48	4.21
G206741E	ex-75 × 150 × 300 mm long	Nr	0.20	3.40	–	0.49	3.89	3.74	–	0.54	4.28
G206741F	ex-75 × 150 × 450 mm long	Nr	0.22	3.74	–	0.71	4.45	4.11	–	0.78	4.90
G206741G	ex-100 × 200 × 400 mm long	Nr	0.23	3.91	–	1.08	4.99	4.30	–	1.19	5.49
G206741H	ex-100 × 200 × 600 mm long	Nr	0.25	4.25	–	1.62	5.87	4.68	–	1.78	6.46
G2071	**Finished surfaces on sawn items**										
G207102	**Hand labours:**										
G207102A	wrought face; not exceeding 150 mm wide	m	0.08	1.36	–	–	1.36	1.50	–	–	1.50
G207102B	wrought face; 150-300 mm wide	m	0.12	2.04	–	–	2.04	2.24	–	–	2.24
G207102C	wrought face; over 300 mm wide	m	0.33	5.60	–	–	5.60	6.16	–	–	6.16
G207102D	rounds	m	0.15	2.55	–	–	2.55	2.81	–	–	2.81
G207102E	rebates	m	0.18	3.06	–	–	3.06	3.37	–	–	3.37
G207102F	tongues	m	0.25	4.25	–	–	4.25	4.68	–	–	4.68
G207102G	grooves	m	0.18	3.06	–	–	3.06	3.37	–	–	3.37
G207102H	chamfers	m	0.13	2.21	–	–	2.21	2.43	–	–	2.43
G207102I	throats	m	0.18	3.06	–	–	3.06	3.37	–	–	3.37
G207102J	mouldings; not exceeding 50 mm girth	m	0.20	3.40	–	–	3.40	3.74	–	–	3.74
G207102K	mouldings; 50-100 mm girth	m	0.32	5.43	–	–	5.43	5.97	–	–	5.97
G207102L	mouldings; 100-150 mm girth	m	0.45	7.64	–	–	7.64	8.40	–	–	8.40

Major Works 2009		Unit	Labour Hours	Labour Net	Plant Net	Materials Net	Unit Net	Labour Gross	Plant Gross	Materials Gross	Unit Price
								(Gross rates include 10% profit)			
				£	£	£	£	£	£	£	£
G20	**G20: CARPENTRY, TIMBER FRAMING AND FIRST FIXING**										
G2081	**Straps and frame cramps**										
G208107	**Galvanised mild steel fish-tail frame cramps; fixing to woodwork and masonry:**										
G208107A	200 × 25 × 2 mm......	Nr	0.11	1.87	–	0.65	2.52	2.06	–	0.72	2.77
G208107B	250 × 25 × 2 mm......	Nr	0.11	1.87	–	0.68	2.55	2.06	–	0.75	2.81
G208108	**30 × 2.5 mm BAT galvanised mild steel restraint straps; fixing to woodwork:**										
G208108A	600 mm long; straight.....	Nr	0.08	1.36	–	1.03	2.39	1.50	–	1.13	2.63
G208108B	800 mm long; straight.....	Nr	0.08	1.36	–	1.45	2.81	1.50	–	1.60	3.09
G208108C	1000 mm long; straight....	Nr	0.10	1.70	–	91.79	93.49	1.87	–	100.97	102.84
G208108D	1200 mm long; straight....	Nr	0.10	1.70	–	2.26	3.96	1.87	–	2.49	4.36
G208108E	1600 mm long; straight....	Nr	0.12	2.04	–	3.06	5.10	2.24	–	3.37	5.61
G208108F	600 mm long; straight; once twisted.................	Nr	0.08	1.36	–	1.11	2.47	1.50	–	1.22	2.72
G208108G	800 mm long; straight; once twisted.................	Nr	0.08	1.36	–	1.59	2.95	1.50	–	1.75	3.25
G208108H	1000 mm long; straight; once twisted	Nr	0.10	1.70	–	1.98	3.68	1.87	–	2.18	4.05
G208108I	1200 mm long; straight; once twisted	Nr	0.10	1.70	–	2.37	4.07	1.87	–	2.61	4.48
G208108J	1600 mm long; straight; once twisted	Nr	0.12	2.04	–	3.19	5.23	2.24	–	3.51	5.75
G208108K	600 mm long; once bent ...	Nr	0.08	1.36	–	1.21	2.57	1.50	–	1.33	2.83
G208108L	800 mm long; once bent ...	Nr	0.08	1.36	–	1.66	3.02	1.50	–	1.83	3.32
G208108M	1000 mm long; once bent ..	Nr	0.10	1.70	–	2.06	3.76	1.87	–	2.27	4.14
G208108N	1200 mm long; once bent ..	Nr	0.10	1.70	–	2.42	4.12	1.87	–	2.66	4.53
G208108O	1600 mm long; once bent ..	Nr	0.12	2.03	–	3.29	5.32	2.23	–	3.62	5.85
G208108P	600 mm long; once bent; once twisted	Nr	0.08	1.36	–	1.30	2.66	1.50	–	1.43	2.93
G208108Q	800 mm long; once bent; once twisted	Nr	0.08	1.35	–	1.76	3.11	1.49	–	1.94	3.42
G208108R	1000 mm long; once bent; once twisted	Nr	0.10	1.70	–	88.77	90.47	1.87	–	97.65	99.52
G208108S	1200 mm long; once bent; once twisted	Nr	0.10	1.70	–	2.50	4.20	1.87	–	2.75	4.62
G208108T	1600 mm long; once bent; once twisted	Nr	0.12	2.04	–	3.39	5.43	2.24	–	3.73	5.97
G208109	**30 × 5 mm BAT galvanised mild steel restraint straps; fixing to woodwork and masonry:**										
G208109A	700 mm long; once bent ...	Nr	0.20	3.40	–	2.76	6.16	3.74	–	3.04	6.78
G208109B	800 mm long; once bent ...	Nr	0.25	4.25	–	3.19	7.44	4.68	–	3.51	8.18
G208109C	1000 mm long; once bent ..	Nr	0.30	5.09	–	71.80	76.89	5.60	–	78.98	84.58
G208109D	1200 mm long; once bent ..	Nr	0.30	5.10	–	4.61	9.71	5.61	–	5.07	10.68
G208109E	1300 mm long; once bent ..	Nr	0.36	6.11	–	4.66	10.77	6.72	–	5.13	11.85
G208109F	1500 mm long; once bent ..	Nr	0.36	6.12	–	5.28	11.40	6.73	–	5.81	12.54
G208109G	1700 mm long; once bent ..	Nr	0.42	7.13	–	6.12	13.25	7.84	–	6.73	14.58

Structural and Carcassing

Major Works 2009		Unit	Labour Hours	Labour Net	Plant Net	Materials Net	Unit Net	Labour Gross	Plant Gross	Materials Gross	Unit Price
				£	£	£	£	(Gross rates include 10% profit) £		£	£
G20	**G20: CARPENTRY, TIMBER FRAMING AND FIRST FIXING**										
G2083	**BAT SPW galvanised joist hangers; building into masonry**										
G208312	**Type S; joist size:**										
G208312A	38 × 100 mm	Nr	0.05	1.26	–	1.62	2.88	1.39	–	1.78	3.17
G208312B	38 × 125 mm	Nr	0.05	1.26	–	1.66	2.92	1.39	–	1.83	3.21
G208312C	38 × 150 mm	Nr	0.05	1.26	–	1.66	2.92	1.39	–	1.83	3.21
G208312D	38 × 175 mm	Nr	0.05	1.26	–	1.78	3.04	1.39	–	1.96	3.34
G208312E	38 × 200 mm	Nr	0.05	1.25	–	1.91	3.16	1.38	–	2.10	3.48
G208312F	38 × 225 mm	Nr	0.05	1.25	–	2.27	3.52	1.38	–	2.50	3.87
G208312G	38 × 250 mm	Nr	0.05	1.25	–	2.39	3.64	1.38	–	2.63	4.00
G208312H	50 × 100 mm	Nr	0.05	1.26	–	1.42	2.68	1.39	–	1.56	2.95
G208312I	50 × 125 mm	Nr	0.05	1.26	–	1.42	2.68	1.39	–	1.56	2.95
G208312J	50 × 150 mm	Nr	0.05	1.25	–	1.56	2.81	1.38	–	1.72	3.09
G208312K	50 × 175 mm	Nr	0.05	1.25	–	1.56	2.81	1.38	–	1.72	3.09
G208312L	50 × 200 mm	Nr	0.05	1.26	–	1.66	2.92	1.39	–	1.83	3.21
G208312M	50 × 225 mm	Nr	0.05	1.25	–	1.91	3.16	1.38	–	2.10	3.48
G208312N	50 × 250 mm	Nr	0.05	1.26	–	2.14	3.40	1.39	–	2.35	3.74
G208312O	63 × 100 mm	Nr	0.05	1.26	–	1.66	2.92	1.39	–	1.83	3.21
G208312P	63 × 125 mm	Nr	0.05	1.26	–	1.73	2.99	1.39	–	1.90	3.29
G208312Q	63 × 150 mm	Nr	0.05	1.25	–	1.91	3.16	1.38	–	2.10	3.48
G208312R	63 × 175 mm	Nr	0.05	1.26	–	2.04	3.30	1.39	–	2.24	3.63
G208312S	63 × 200 mm	Nr	0.05	1.26	–	2.04	3.30	1.39	–	2.24	3.63
G208312T	63 × 225 mm	Nr	0.05	1.26	–	2.14	3.40	1.39	–	2.35	3.74
G208312U	63 × 250 mm	Nr	0.05	1.25	–	2.27	3.52	1.38	–	2.50	3.87
G208312V	75 × 100 mm	Nr	0.05	1.26	–	1.72	2.98	1.39	–	1.89	3.28
G208312W	75 × 125 mm	Nr	0.05	1.26	–	2.04	3.30	1.39	–	2.24	3.63
G208312X	75 × 150 mm	Nr	0.05	1.26	–	2.22	3.48	1.39	–	2.44	3.83
G208312Y	75 × 175 mm	Nr	0.05	1.26	–	2.22	3.48	1.39	–	2.44	3.83
G208312Z	75 × 200 mm	Nr	0.05	1.25	–	2.27	3.52	1.38	–	2.50	3.87
G208313	**Type S; joist size:**										
G208313A	75 × 225 mm	Nr	0.05	1.25	–	2.32	3.57	1.38	–	2.55	3.93
G208313B	75 × 250 mm	Nr	0.05	1.26	–	2.43	3.69	1.39	–	2.67	4.06
G208313C	100 × 100 mm	Nr	0.08	2.00	–	2.27	4.27	2.20	–	2.50	4.70
G208313D	100 × 125 mm	Nr	0.08	2.01	–	2.32	4.33	2.21	–	2.55	4.76
G208313E	100 × 150 mm	Nr	0.08	2.01	–	2.39	4.40	2.21	–	2.63	4.84
G208313F	100 × 175 mm	Nr	0.08	2.01	–	2.51	4.52	2.21	–	2.76	4.97
G208313G	100 × 200 mm	Nr	0.08	2.01	–	2.57	4.58	2.21	–	2.83	5.04
G208313H	100 × 225 mm	Nr	0.08	2.01	–	2.69	4.70	2.21	–	2.96	5.17
G208313I	100 × 250 mm	Nr	0.08	2.01	–	2.81	4.82	2.21	–	3.09	5.30
G208314	**Type ST; joist size:**										
G208314A	38 × 100 mm	Nr	0.05	1.26	–	3.28	4.54	1.39	–	3.61	4.99
G208314B	38 × 125 mm	Nr	0.05	1.26	–	3.34	4.60	1.39	–	3.67	5.06
G208314C	38 × 150 mm	Nr	0.05	1.26	–	3.34	4.60	1.39	–	3.67	5.06
G208314D	38 × 175 mm	Nr	0.05	1.25	–	3.52	4.77	1.38	–	3.87	5.25
G208314E	38 × 200 mm	Nr	0.05	1.26	–	3.81	5.07	1.39	–	4.19	5.58
G208314F	38 × 225 mm	Nr	0.05	1.25	–	4.05	5.30	1.38	–	4.46	5.83
G208314G	50 × 100 mm	Nr	0.05	1.26	–	3.28	4.54	1.39	–	3.61	4.99
G208314H	50 × 125 mm	Nr	0.05	1.26	–	3.34	4.60	1.39	–	3.67	5.06
G208314I	50 × 150 mm	Nr	0.05	1.26	–	3.34	4.60	1.39	–	3.67	5.06
G208314J	50 × 175 mm	Nr	0.05	1.25	–	3.52	4.77	1.38	–	3.87	5.25
G208314K	50 × 200 mm	Nr	0.05	1.26	–	3.81	5.07	1.39	–	4.19	5.58
G208314L	50 × 225 mm	Nr	0.05	1.25	–	4.05	5.30	1.38	–	4.46	5.83
G208314M	50 × 250 mm	Nr	0.05	1.26	–	5.07	6.33	1.39	–	5.58	6.96
G208314N	63 × 100 mm	Nr	0.05	1.25	–	3.64	4.89	1.38	–	4.00	5.38
G208314O	63 × 125 mm	Nr	0.05	1.26	–	3.70	4.96	1.39	–	4.07	5.46
G208314P	63 × 150 mm	Nr	0.05	1.26	–	3.70	4.96	1.39	–	4.07	5.46

Major Works 2009		Unit	Labour Hours	Labour Net	Plant Net	Materials Net	Unit Net	Labour Gross	Plant Gross	Materials Gross	Unit Price
								(Gross rates include 10% profit)			
				£	£	£	£	£	£	£	£
G20	**G20: CARPENTRY, TIMBER FRAMING AND FIRST FIXING**										
G2083	**BAT SPW galvanised joist hangers; building into masonry**										
G208314	**Type ST; joist size:**										
G208314Q	63 × 175 mm	Nr	0.05	1.26	–	3.88	5.14	1.39	–	4.27	5.65
G208314R	63 × 200 mm	Nr	0.05	1.26	–	4.18	5.44	1.39	–	4.60	5.98
G208314S	63 × 225 mm	Nr	0.05	1.25	–	4.42	5.67	1.38	–	4.86	6.24
G208314T	63 × 250 mm	Nr	0.05	1.26	–	5.43	6.69	1.39	–	5.97	7.36
G208314U	75 × 100 mm	Nr	0.05	1.26	–	4.23	5.49	1.39	–	4.65	6.04
G208314V	75 × 125 mm	Nr	0.05	1.26	–	4.29	5.55	1.39	–	4.72	6.11
G208314W	75 × 150 mm	Nr	0.05	1.26	–	4.29	5.55	1.39	–	4.72	6.11
G208314X	75 × 175 mm	Nr	0.05	1.26	–	4.47	5.73	1.39	–	4.92	6.30
G208314Y	75 × 200 mm	Nr	0.05	1.25	–	4.78	6.03	1.38	–	5.26	6.63
G208315	**Type ST; joist size:**										
G208315A	75 × 225 mm	Nr	0.05	1.26	–	5.00	6.26	1.39	–	5.50	6.89
G208315B	75 × 250 mm	Nr	0.05	1.26	–	5.90	7.16	1.39	–	6.49	7.88
G208315C	100 × 100 mm	Nr	0.08	2.01	–	4.83	6.84	2.21	–	5.31	7.52
G208315D	100 × 125 mm	Nr	0.08	2.01	–	4.91	6.92	2.21	–	5.40	7.61
G208315E	100 × 150 mm	Nr	0.08	2.01	–	4.91	6.92	2.21	–	5.40	7.61
G208315F	100 × 175 mm	Nr	0.08	2.01	–	5.07	7.08	2.21	–	5.58	7.79
G208315G	100 × 200 mm	Nr	0.08	2.01	–	5.38	7.39	2.21	–	5.92	8.13
G208315H	100 × 225 mm	Nr	0.08	2.01	–	5.61	7.62	2.21	–	6.17	8.38
G208315I	100 × 250 mm	Nr	0.08	2.01	–	6.50	8.51	2.21	–	7.15	9.36
G208316	**Type R; joist size:**										
G208316A	38 × 100 mm	Nr	0.05	1.26	–	2.43	3.69	1.39	–	2.67	4.06
G208316B	38 × 125 mm	Nr	0.05	1.26	–	2.51	3.77	1.39	–	2.76	4.15
G208316C	38 × 150 mm	Nr	0.05	1.25	–	2.69	3.94	1.38	–	2.96	4.33
G208316D	38 × 175 mm	Nr	0.05	1.25	–	2.69	3.94	1.38	–	2.96	4.33
G208316E	38 × 200 mm	Nr	0.05	1.26	–	2.99	4.25	1.39	–	3.29	4.68
G208316F	38 × 225 mm	Nr	0.05	1.26	–	3.28	4.54	1.39	–	3.61	4.99
G208316G	38 × 250 mm	Nr	0.05	1.26	–	3.46	4.72	1.39	–	3.81	5.19
G208316H	50 × 100 mm	Nr	0.05	1.26	–	2.57	3.83	1.39	–	2.83	4.21
G208316I	50 × 125 mm	Nr	0.05	1.26	–	2.62	3.88	1.39	–	2.88	4.27
G208316J	50 × 150 mm	Nr	0.05	1.25	–	2.88	4.13	1.38	–	3.17	4.54
G208316K	50 × 175 mm	Nr	0.05	1.25	–	2.81	4.06	1.38	–	3.09	4.47
G208316L	50 × 200 mm	Nr	0.05	1.25	–	3.09	4.34	1.38	–	3.40	4.77
G208316M	50 × 225 mm	Nr	0.05	1.26	–	3.39	4.65	1.39	–	3.73	5.12
G208316N	50 × 250 mm	Nr	0.05	1.25	–	3.59	4.84	1.38	–	3.95	5.32
G208316O	63 × 100 mm	Nr	0.05	1.26	–	2.93	4.19	1.39	–	3.22	4.61
G208316P	63 × 125 mm	Nr	0.05	1.26	–	2.99	4.25	1.39	–	3.29	4.68
G208316Q	63 × 150 mm	Nr	0.05	1.25	–	3.17	4.42	1.38	–	3.49	4.86
G208316R	63 × 175 mm	Nr	0.05	1.25	–	3.17	4.42	1.38	–	3.49	4.86
G208316S	63 × 200 mm	Nr	0.05	1.26	–	3.46	4.72	1.39	–	3.81	5.19
G208316T	63 × 225 mm	Nr	0.05	1.26	–	3.75	5.01	1.39	–	4.13	5.51
G208316U	63 × 250 mm	Nr	0.05	1.25	–	3.95	5.20	1.38	–	4.35	5.72
G208316V	75 × 100 mm	Nr	0.05	1.26	–	3.39	4.65	1.39	–	3.73	5.12
G208316W	75 × 125 mm	Nr	0.05	1.26	–	3.46	4.72	1.39	–	3.81	5.19
G208316X	75 × 150 mm	Nr	0.05	1.25	–	3.64	4.89	1.38	–	4.00	5.38
G208316Y	75 × 175 mm	Nr	0.05	1.25	–	3.64	4.89	1.38	–	4.00	5.38
G208316Z	75 × 200 mm	Nr	0.05	1.25	–	3.95	5.20	1.38	–	4.35	5.72

Structural and Carcassing

Major Works 2009		Unit	Labour Hours	Labour Net	Plant Net	Materials Net	Unit Net	Labour Gross	Plant Gross	Materials Gross	Unit Price
				£	£	£	£	£	£	£	£
G20	**G20: CARPENTRY, TIMBER FRAMING AND FIRST FIXING**										
G2083	**BAT SPW galvanised joist hangers; building into masonry**										
G208317	**Type R; joist size:**										
G208317A	75 × 225 mm..........	Nr	0.05	1.26	–	4.23	5.49	1.39	–	4.65	6.04
G208317B	75 × 250 mm..........	Nr	0.05	1.25	–	4.42	5.67	1.38	–	4.86	6.24
G208317C	100 × 100 mm..........	Nr	0.08	2.01	–	3.81	5.82	2.21	–	4.19	6.40
G208317D	100 × 125 mm..........	Nr	0.08	2.01	–	3.88	5.89	2.21	–	4.27	6.48
G208317E	100 × 150 mm..........	Nr	0.08	2.01	–	4.05	6.06	2.21	–	4.46	6.67
G208317F	100 × 175 mm..........	Nr	0.08	2.01	–	4.47	6.48	2.21	–	4.92	7.13
G208317G	100 × 200 mm..........	Nr	0.08	2.01	–	4.78	6.79	2.21	–	5.26	7.47
G208317H	100 × 225 mm..........	Nr	0.08	2.01	–	4.91	6.92	2.21	–	5.40	7.61
G208317I	100 × 250 mm..........	Nr	0.08	2.01	–	5.07	7.08	2.21	–	5.58	7.79
G2084	**BAT SPW joist hangers; fixing to masonry or concrete**										
G208419	**Type FF; joist width:**										
G208419A	38 mm.................	Nr	0.35	5.94	–	1.11	7.05	6.53	–	1.22	7.76
G208419B	50 mm.................	Nr	0.35	5.94	–	1.11	7.05	6.53	–	1.22	7.76
G208419C	63 mm.................	Nr	0.35	5.94	–	1.21	7.15	6.53	–	1.33	7.87
G208419D	75 mm.................	Nr	0.35	5.94	–	1.21	7.15	6.53	–	1.33	7.87
G208419E	100 mm.................	Nr	0.35	5.95	–	1.26	7.21	6.55	–	1.39	7.93
G2085	**BAT truss clips; fixing to woodwork**										
G208531	**To suit truss width:**										
G208531A	38 mm.................	Nr	0.15	2.54	–	0.74	3.28	2.79	–	0.81	3.61
G208531B	50 mm.................	Nr	0.15	2.54	–	0.79	3.33	2.79	–	0.87	3.66

Major Works 2009		Unit	Labour Hours	Labour Net	Plant Net	Materials Net	Unit Net	Labour Gross	Plant Gross	Materials Gross	Unit Price
								(Gross rates include 10% profit)			
				£	£	£	£	£	£	£	£
G20	**G20: CARPENTRY, TIMBER FRAMING AND FIRST FIXING**										
G2091	**Dowels, bolts, water bars**										
G209102	**Galvanised mild steel dowels:**										
G209102A	8 mm diameter	m	0.30	5.10	–	3.17	8.27	5.61	–	3.49	9.10
G209102B	10 mm diameter	m	0.30	5.09	–	3.61	8.70	5.60	–	3.97	9.57
G209102C	12 mm diameter	m	0.30	5.09	–	4.03	9.12	5.60	–	4.43	10.03
G209102D	16 mm diameter	m	0.30	5.10	–	5.31	10.41	5.61	–	5.84	11.45
G209103	**Black hexagon head bolts BS 4190 with nut and washer:**										
G209103A	M10 × 50 mm	Nr	0.08	1.36	–	0.26	1.62	1.50	–	0.29	1.78
G209103B	M10 × 75 mm	Nr	0.08	1.36	–	0.30	1.66	1.50	–	0.33	1.83
G209103C	M10 × 100 mm	Nr	0.09	1.53	–	0.45	1.98	1.68	–	0.50	2.18
G209103D	M10 × 150 mm	Nr	0.09	1.53	–	0.95	2.48	1.68	–	1.05	2.73
G209103E	M12 × 100 mm	Nr	0.10	1.69	–	0.58	2.27	1.86	–	0.64	2.50
G209103F	M12 × 150 mm	Nr	0.10	1.70	–	1.03	2.73	1.87	–	1.13	3.00
G209103G	M12 × 200 mm	Nr	0.11	1.86	–	1.61	3.47	2.05	–	1.77	3.82
G209103H	M12 × 250 mm	Nr	0.11	1.87	–	1.84	3.71	2.06	–	2.02	4.08
G209103I	M12 × 300 mm	Nr	0.11	1.87	–	2.00	3.87	2.06	–	2.20	4.26
G209103J	M16 × 100 mm	Nr	0.11	1.87	–	0.94	2.81	2.06	–	1.03	3.09
G209103K	M16 × 150 mm	Nr	0.12	2.04	–	1.49	3.53	2.24	–	1.64	3.88
G209103L	M16 × 200 mm	Nr	0.13	2.20	–	2.25	4.45	2.42	–	2.48	4.90
G209103M	M16 × 250 mm	Nr	0.13	2.20	–	3.30	5.50	2.42	–	3.63	6.05
G209103N	M16 × 300 mm	Nr	0.13	2.21	–	3.61	5.82	2.43	–	3.97	6.40
G2091030	M20 × 100 mm	Nr	0.13	2.21	–	1.68	3.89	2.43	–	1.85	4.28
G209103P	M20 × 150 mm	Nr	0.14	2.38	–	2.36	4.74	2.62	–	2.60	5.21
G209103Q	M20 × 200 mm	Nr	0.15	2.54	–	3.35	5.89	2.79	–	3.69	6.48
G209103R	M20 × 250 mm	Nr	0.15	2.55	–	3.82	6.37	2.81	–	4.20	7.01
G209103S	M20 × 300 mm	Nr	0.15	2.55	–	4.08	6.63	2.81	–	4.49	7.29
G209104	**Rawlbolt projecting expansion bolt with nut and washer; to masonry:**										
G209104A	M10 15	Nr	0.17	2.88	–	2.24	5.12	3.17	–	2.46	5.63
G209104B	M10 30	Nr	0.17	2.88	–	2.34	5.22	3.17	–	2.57	5.74
G209104C	M10 60	Nr	0.17	2.89	–	2.43	5.32	3.18	–	2.67	5.85
G209104D	M12 15	Nr	0.20	3.39	–	3.39	6.78	3.73	–	3.73	7.46
G209104E	M12 30	Nr	0.20	3.39	–	3.64	7.03	3.73	–	4.00	7.73
G209104F	M12 75	Nr	0.20	3.40	–	4.54	7.94	3.74	–	4.99	8.73
G209104G	M16 15	Nr	0.23	3.91	–	7.25	11.16	4.30	–	7.98	12.28
G209104H	M16 35	Nr	0.23	3.91	–	8.68	12.59	4.30	–	9.55	13.85
G209104I	M16 75	Nr	0.23	3.90	–	9.21	13.11	4.29	–	10.13	14.42
G209104J	M20 15	Nr	0.27	4.58	–	12.25	16.83	5.04	–	13.48	18.51
G209104K	M20 30	Nr	0.27	4.59	–	13.21	17.80	5.05	–	14.53	19.58
G209104L	M20 100	Nr	0.27	4.58	–	15.06	19.64	5.04	–	16.57	21.60

Structural and Carcassing

Major Works 2009		Unit	Labour Hours	Labour Net	Plant Net	Materials Net	Unit Net	Labour Gross	Plant Gross	Materials Gross	Unit Price
								(Gross rates include 10% profit)			
				£	£	£	£	£	£	£	£
G20	**G20: CARPENTRY, TIMBER FRAMING AND FIRST FIXING**										
G2091	**Dowels, bolts, water bars**										
G209105	**Rawlbolt loose expansion bolt; to concrete:**										
G209105A	M6 10...................	Nr	0.16	2.72	–	1.52	4.24	2.99	–	1.67	4.66
G209105B	M6 25...................	Nr	0.16	2.72	–	1.53	4.25	2.99	–	1.68	4.68
G209105C	M6 40...................	Nr	0.16	2.72	–	1.64	4.36	2.99	–	1.80	4.80
G209105D	M8 10...................	Nr	0.20	3.40	–	1.71	5.11	3.74	–	1.88	5.62
G209105E	M8 25...................	Nr	0.20	3.40	–	1.76	5.16	3.74	–	1.94	5.68
G209105F	M8 40...................	Nr	0.20	3.39	–	1.88	5.27	3.73	–	2.07	5.80
G209105G	M10 10	Nr	0.25	4.25	–	2.22	6.47	4.68	–	2.44	7.12
G209105H	M10 25	Nr	0.25	4.25	–	2.30	6.55	4.68	–	2.53	7.21
G209105I	M10 50	Nr	0.25	4.24	–	2.39	6.63	4.66	–	2.63	7.29
G209105J	M10 75	Nr	0.25	4.24	–	2.49	6.73	4.66	–	2.74	7.40
G209105K	M12 10	Nr	0.30	5.10	–	3.28	8.38	5.61	–	3.61	9.22
G209105L	M12 25	Nr	0.30	5.10	–	3.66	8.76	5.61	–	4.03	9.64
G209105M	M12 40	Nr	0.30	5.10	–	3.80	8.90	5.61	–	4.18	9.79
G209105N	M12 60	Nr	0.30	5.09	–	4.03	9.12	5.60	–	4.43	10.03
G209105O	M16 15	Nr	0.35	5.95	–	7.34	13.29	6.55	–	8.07	14.62
G209105P	M16 30	Nr	0.35	5.94	–	8.60	14.54	6.53	–	9.46	15.99
G209105Q	M16 60	Nr	0.35	5.94	–	9.11	15.05	6.53	–	10.02	16.56
G209105R	M20 60	Nr	0.40	6.80	–	13.41	20.21	7.48	–	14.75	22.23
G209105S	M20 100	Nr	0.40	6.79	–	13.79	20.58	7.47	–	15.17	22.64
G209106	**Galvanised mild steel round toothed-plate connectors; BS 1579 Table 4:**										
G209106A	38 mm diameter; single sided	Nr	0.02	0.34	–	0.47	0.81	0.37	–	0.52	0.89
G209106B	51 mm diameter; single sided	Nr	0.02	0.34	–	0.47	0.81	0.37	–	0.52	0.89
G209106C	64 mm diameter; single sided	Nr	0.02	0.34	–	0.71	1.05	0.37	–	0.78	1.16
G209106D	76 mm diameter; single sided	Nr	0.02	0.34	–	0.71	1.05	0.37	–	0.78	1.16
G209106E	38 mm diameter; double sided	Nr	0.02	0.34	–	0.47	0.81	0.37	–	0.52	0.89
G209106F	51 mm diameter; double sided	Nr	0.02	0.34	–	0.48	0.82	0.37	–	0.53	0.90
G209106G	64 mm diameter; double sided	Nr	0.02	0.34	–	0.71	1.05	0.37	–	0.78	1.16
G209106H	76 mm diameter; double sided	Nr	0.02	0.34	–	0.93	1.27	0.37	–	1.02	1.40
G209107	**Galvanised mild steel fish tailed frame cramps:**										
G209107A	200 × 25 × 2 mm......	Nr	0.11	1.87	–	0.65	2.52	2.06	–	0.72	2.77
G209107B	250 × 25 × 2 mm......	Nr	0.11	1.87	–	0.68	2.55	2.06	–	0.75	2.81

Structural and Carcassing

Major Works 2009		Unit	Labour Hours	Labour Net	Plant Net	Materials Net	Unit Net	Labour Gross	Plant Gross	Materials Gross	Unit Price
								(Gross rates include 10% profit)			
				£	£	£	£	£	£	£	£
G20	**G20: CARPENTRY, TIMBER FRAMING AND FIRST FIXING**										
G2091	**Dowels, bolts, water bars**										
G209108	**30 × 2.5 mm BAT galvanised mild steel restraint straps; fixing to wood work:**										
G209108A	600 mm long; straight	Nr	0.08	1.36	–	1.03	2.39	1.50	–	1.13	2.63
G209108B	800 mm long; straight	Nr	0.08	1.36	–	1.45	2.81	1.50	–	1.60	3.09
G209108C	1000 mm long; straight	Nr	0.10	1.70	–	91.79	93.49	1.87	–	100.97	102.84
G209108D	1200 mm long; straight	Nr	0.10	1.70	–	2.26	3.96	1.87	–	2.49	4.36
G209108E	1600 mm long; straight	Nr	0.12	2.04	–	3.06	5.10	2.24	–	3.37	5.61
G209108F	600 mm long; straight; once twisted	Nr	0.08	1.36	–	1.11	2.47	1.50	–	1.22	2.72
G209108G	800 mm long; straight; once twisted	Nr	0.08	1.36	–	1.59	2.95	1.50	–	1.75	3.25
G209108H	1000 mm long; straight; once twisted	Nr	0.10	1.70	–	1.98	3.68	1.87	–	2.18	4.05
G209108I	1200 mm long; straight; once twisted	Nr	0.10	1.70	–	2.37	4.07	1.87	–	2.61	4.48
G209108J	1600 mm long; straight; once twisted	Nr	0.12	2.04	–	3.19	5.23	2.24	–	3.51	5.75
G209108K	600 mm long; once bent . . .	Nr	0.08	1.36	–	1.21	2.57	1.50	–	1.33	2.83
G209108L	800 mm long; once bent . . .	Nr	0.08	1.36	–	1.66	3.02	1.50	–	1.83	3.32
G209108M	1000 mm long; once bent . .	Nr	0.10	1.70	–	2.06	3.76	1.87	–	2.27	4.14
G209108N	1200 mm long; once bent . .	Nr	0.10	1.70	–	2.42	4.12	1.87	–	2.66	4.53
G209108O	1600 mm long; once bent . .	Nr	0.12	2.03	–	3.29	5.32	2.23	–	3.62	5.85
G209108P	600 mm long; once bent; once twisted	Nr	0.08	1.36	–	1.30	2.66	1.50	–	1.43	2.93
G209108Q	800 mm long; once bent; once twisted	Nr	0.08	1.35	–	1.76	3.11	1.49	–	1.94	3.42
G209108R	1000 mm long; once bent; once twisted	Nr	0.10	1.70	–	88.77	90.47	1.87	–	97.65	99.52
G209108S	1200 mm long; once bent; once twisted	Nr	0.10	1.70	–	2.50	4.20	1.87	–	2.75	4.62
G209108T	1600 mm long; once bent; once twisted	Nr	0.12	2.04	–	3.39	5.43	2.24	–	3.73	5.97
G209109	**30 × 5 mm BAT galvanised mild steel restraint straps; fixing to woodwork and masonry:**										
G209109A	700 mm long; once bent . . .	Nr	0.20	3.40	–	2.76	6.16	3.74	–	3.04	6.78
G209109B	800 mm long; once bent . . .	Nr	0.25	4.25	–	3.19	7.44	4.68	–	3.51	8.18
G209109C	1000 mm long; once bent . .	Nr	0.30	5.09	–	71.80	76.89	5.60	–	78.98	84.58
G209109D	1200 mm long; once bent . .	Nr	0.30	5.10	–	4.61	9.71	5.61	–	5.07	10.68
G209109E	1300 mm long; once bent . .	Nr	0.36	6.11	–	4.66	10.77	6.72	–	5.13	11.85
G209109F	1500 mm long; once bent . .	Nr	0.36	6.12	–	5.28	11.40	6.73	–	5.81	12.54
G209109G	1700 mm long; once bent . .	Nr	0.42	7.13	–	6.12	13.25	7.84	–	6.73	14.58

Structural and Carcassing

Major Works 2009		Unit	Labour Hours	Labour Net	Plant Net	Materials Net	Unit Net	Labour Gross	Plant Gross	Materials Gross	Unit Price
								(Gross rates include 10% profit)			
				£	£	£	£	£	£	£	£
G20	**G20: CARPENTRY, TIMBER FRAMING AND FIRST FIXING**										
G2091	**Dowels, bolts, water bars**										
G209110	**Galvanised mild steel water bars:**										
G209110A	25 × 3 mm............	m	0.20	3.40	–	5.94	9.34	3.74	–	6.53	10.27
G209110B	40 × 3 mm............	m	0.20	3.39	–	6.23	9.62	3.73	–	6.85	10.58
G209110C	40 × 6 mm............	m	0.20	3.40	–	9.43	12.83	3.74	–	10.37	14.11
G209110D	50 × 6 mm............	m	0.20	3.40	–	13.08	16.48	3.74	–	14.39	18.13
G2097	**Additional fixings for woodwork**										
G209711	**Drilling and plugging concrete; plastic plugs:**										
G209711A	No.8; isolated...........	Nr	0.08	1.36	–	0.01	1.37	1.50	–	0.01	1.51
G209711B	No.8; 300 mm centres.....	m	0.28	4.76	–	0.03	4.79	5.24	–	0.03	5.27
G209711C	No.8; 450 mm centres.....	m	0.19	3.23	–	0.02	3.25	3.55	–	0.02	3.58
G209711D	No.8; 600 mm centres.....	m	0.14	2.38	–	0.02	2.40	2.62	–	0.02	2.64
G209711E	No.8; 750 mm centres.....	m	0.11	1.87	–	0.01	1.88	2.06	–	0.01	2.07
G209711F	No.8; 1200 mm centres....	m	0.07	1.19	–	0.01	1.20	1.31	–	0.01	1.32
G209711G	No.10; isolated..........	Nr	0.10	1.70	–	0.01	1.71	1.87	–	0.01	1.88
G209711H	No.10; 300 mm centres....	m	0.33	5.60	–	0.04	5.64	6.16	–	0.04	6.20
G209711I	No.10; 450 mm centres....	m	0.22	3.73	–	0.03	3.76	4.10	–	0.03	4.14
G209711J	No.10; 600 mm centres....	m	0.17	2.88	–	0.03	2.91	3.17	–	0.03	3.20
G209711K	No.10; 750 mm centres....	m	0.13	2.21	–	0.01	2.22	2.43	–	0.01	2.44
G209711L	No.10; 1200 mm centres...	m	0.08	1.36	–	0.01	1.37	1.50	–	0.01	1.51
G209711M	No.12; isolated..........	Nr	0.11	1.87	–	0.02	1.89	2.06	–	0.02	2.08
G209711N	No.12; 300 mm centres....	m	0.38	6.45	–	0.06	6.51	7.10	–	0.07	7.16
G2097110	No.12; 450 mm centres....	m	0.26	4.41	–	0.04	4.45	4.85	–	0.04	4.90
G209711P	No.12; 600 mm centres....	m	0.19	3.22	–	0.04	3.26	3.54	–	0.04	3.59
G209711Q	No.12; 750 mm centres....	m	0.16	2.72	–	0.02	2.74	2.99	–	0.02	3.01
G209711R	No.12; 1200 mm centres...	m	0.10	1.70	–	0.02	1.72	1.87	–	0.02	1.89
G209712	**Drilling and plugging masonry; plastic plugs:**										
G209712A	No.8; isolated...........	Nr	0.03	0.51	–	0.01	0.52	0.56	–	0.01	0.57
G209712B	No.8; 300 mm centres.....	m	0.10	1.70	–	0.03	1.73	1.87	–	0.03	1.90
G209712C	No.8; 450 mm centres.....	m	0.07	1.19	–	0.02	1.21	1.31	–	0.02	1.33
G209712D	No.8; 600 mm centres.....	m	0.06	1.02	–	0.02	1.04	1.12	–	0.02	1.14
G209712E	No.8; 750 mm centres.....	m	0.04	0.68	–	0.01	0.69	0.75	–	0.01	0.76
G209712F	No.8; 1200 mm centres....	m	0.03	0.51	–	0.01	0.52	0.56	–	0.01	0.57
G209712G	No.10; isolated..........	Nr	0.05	0.85	–	0.01	0.86	0.94	–	0.01	0.95
G209712H	No.10; 300 mm centres....	m	0.17	2.88	–	0.04	2.92	3.17	–	0.04	3.21
G209712I	No.10; 450 mm centres....	m	0.11	1.86	–	0.03	1.89	2.05	–	0.03	2.08
G209712J	No.10; 600 mm centres....	m	0.08	1.35	–	0.03	1.38	1.49	–	0.03	1.52
G209712K	No.10; 750 mm centres....	m	0.07	1.19	–	0.01	1.20	1.31	–	0.01	1.32
G209712L	No.10; 1200 mm centres...	m	0.04	0.68	–	0.01	0.69	0.75	–	0.01	0.76
G209712M	No.12; isolated..........	Nr	0.06	1.02	–	0.02	1.04	1.12	–	0.02	1.14
G209712N	No.12; 300 mm centres....	m	0.19	3.22	–	0.06	3.28	3.54	–	0.07	3.61
G2097120	No.12; 450 mm centres....	m	0.13	2.20	–	0.04	2.24	2.42	–	0.04	2.46
G209712P	No.12; 600 mm centres....	m	0.10	1.69	–	0.04	1.73	1.86	–	0.04	1.90
G209712Q	No.12; 750 mm centres....	m	0.08	1.36	–	0.02	1.38	1.50	–	0.02	1.52
G209712R	No.12; 1200 mm centres...	m	0.05	0.85	–	0.02	0.87	0.94	–	0.02	0.96

Major Works 2009		Unit	Labour Hours	Labour Net	Plant Net	Materials Net	Unit Net	Labour Gross	Plant Gross	Materials Gross	Unit Price
								(Gross rates include 10% profit)			
				£	£	£	£	£	£	£	£
G20	**G20: CARPENTRY, TIMBER FRAMING AND FIRST FIXING**										
G2097	**Additional fixings for woodwork**										
G209713	**Fixing with steel countersunk wood screws:**										
G209713A	38 mm No.8; isolated......	Nr	0.03	0.51	–	0.02	0.53	0.56	–	0.02	0.58
G209713B	38 mm No.8; 300 mm centres..................	m	0.11	1.87	–	0.07	1.94	2.06	–	0.08	2.13
G209713C	38 mm No.8; 450 mm centres..................	m	0.07	1.19	–	0.05	1.24	1.31	–	0.06	1.36
G209713D	38 mm No.8; 600 mm centres..................	m	0.06	1.02	–	0.05	1.07	1.12	–	0.06	1.18
G209713E	38 mm No.8; 750 mm centres..................	m	0.04	0.68	–	0.02	0.70	0.75	–	0.02	0.77
G209713F	38 mm No.8; 1200 mm centres..................	m	0.03	0.51	–	0.02	0.53	0.56	–	0.02	0.58
G209713G	50 mm No.8; isolated......	Nr	0.03	0.51	–	0.04	0.55	0.56	–	0.04	0.61
G209713H	50 mm No.8; 300 mm centres..................	m	0.11	1.87	–	0.11	1.98	2.06	–	0.12	2.18
G209713I	50 mm No.8; 450 mm centres..................	m	0.07	1.19	–	0.07	1.26	1.31	–	0.08	1.39
G209713J	50 mm No.8; 600 mm centres..................	m	0.06	1.02	–	0.07	1.09	1.12	–	0.08	1.20
G209713K	50 mm No.8; 750 mm centres..................	m	0.04	0.68	–	0.04	0.72	0.75	–	0.04	0.79
G209713L	50 mm No.8; 1200 mm centres..................	m	0.03	0.51	–	0.04	0.55	0.56	–	0.04	0.61
G209713M	75 mm No.10; isolated.....	Nr	0.04	0.68	–	0.05	0.73	0.75	–	0.06	0.80
G209713N	75 mm No.10; 300 mm centres..................	m	0.13	2.21	–	0.16	2.37	2.43	–	0.18	2.61
G209713O	75 mm No.10; 450 mm centres..................	m	0.09	1.52	–	0.11	1.63	1.67	–	0.12	1.79
G209713P	75 mm No.10; 600 mm centres..................	m	0.07	1.18	–	0.11	1.29	1.30	–	0.12	1.42
G209713Q	75 mm No.10; 750 mm centres..................	m	0.05	0.85	–	0.05	0.90	0.94	–	0.06	0.99
G209713R	75 mm No.10; 1200 mm centres..................	m	0.03	0.51	–	0.05	0.56	0.56	–	0.06	0.62
G209713S	100 mm No.12; isolated ...	Nr	0.05	0.85	–	0.08	0.93	0.94	–	0.09	1.02
G209713T	100 mm No.12; 300 mm centres..................	m	0.17	2.88	–	0.25	3.13	3.17	–	0.28	3.44
G209713U	100 mm No.12; 450 mm centres..................	m	0.11	1.87	–	0.16	2.03	2.06	–	0.18	2.23
G209713V	100 mm No.12; 600 mm centres..................	m	0.08	1.36	–	0.16	1.52	1.50	–	0.18	1.67
G209713W	100 mm No.12; 750 mm centres..................	m	0.07	1.19	–	0.08	1.27	1.31	–	0.09	1.40
G209713X	100 mm No.12; 1200 mm centres..................	m	0.04	0.68	–	0.08	0.76	0.75	–	0.09	0.84

CLADDING AND COVERING

Major Works 2009		Unit				Specialist Net	Unit Net			Specialist Gross	Unit Price
									(Gross rates include 10% profit)		
			£	£	£	£	£	£	£	£	£
H10	**H10: PATENT GLAZING**										
H1010	**Patent glazing; aluminium alloy glazing bars 2400 mm long at 600 mm centres**										
H101010	**In roofing areas; single tier:**										
H101010A	7 mm Georgian wired cast glass	m²	–	–	–	157.77	157.77	–	–	173.55	173.55
H101010B	6 mm Georgian polished plate glass	m²	–	–	–	227.19	227.19	–	–	249.91	249.91
H101020	**In roofing areas; multi-tier:**										
H101020A	7 mm Georgian wired cast glass	m²	–	–	–	173.54	173.54	–	–	190.89	190.89
H101020B	6 mm Georgian polished plate glass	m²	–	–	–	246.12	246.12	–	–	270.73	270.73
H101030	**In vertical areas; single tier:**										
H101030A	7 mm Georgian wired cast glass	m²	–	–	–	173.54	173.54	–	–	190.89	190.89
H101030B	6 mm Georgian polished plate glass	m²	–	–	–	246.12	246.12	–	–	270.73	270.73
H101040	**In vertical areas; multi-tier:**										
H101040A	7 mm Georgian wired cast glass	m²	–	–	–	187.43	187.44	–	–	206.17	206.18
H101040B	6 mm Georgian polished plate glass	m²	–	–	–	265.05	265.05	–	–	291.56	291.56

Cladding and Covering

Major Works 2009		Unit				Specialist Net	Unit Net			Specialist Gross	Unit Price
			£	£	£	£	£	£	£	£	£
								(Gross rates include 10% profit)			
H11	**H11: CURTAIN WALLING**										
H1110	**Curtain walling system; extruded powder coated aluminium; insulated spandrel panels; double glazed vision panels and opening casement lights; fixed to supporting structure**										
H111010	**Flat vertical curtain walling in sections:**										
H111010A	185 mm thick	m²	–	–	–	410.19	410.19	–	–	451.21	451.21
H111010B	250 mm thick	m²	–	–	–	580.59	580.59	–	–	638.65	638.65
H111012	**Flat sloping curtain walling in sections:**										
H111012A	185 mm thick	m²	–	–	–	471.84	471.84	–	–	519.02	519.02
H111012B	250 mm thick	m²	–	–	–	667.59	667.59	–	–	734.35	734.35
H111013	**Curved vertical curtain walling in sections:**										
H111013A	185 mm thick	m²	–	–	–	512.75	512.75	–	–	564.03	564.03
H111013B	250 mm thick	m²	–	–	–	725.73	725.73	–	–	798.30	798.30
H111014	**Curved sloping curtain walling in sections:**										
H111014A	185 mm thick	m²	–	–	–	589.88	589.88	–	–	648.87	648.87
H111014B	250 mm thick	m²	–	–	–	834.71	834.71	–	–	918.18	918.18
H111015	**Extra over curtain walling for:**										
H111015A	insulated spandrel panels; 185 mm thick	m	–	–	–	23.67	23.67	–	–	26.04	26.04
H111015B	insulated spandrel panels; 250 mm thick	m	–	–	–	23.67	23.67	–	–	26.04	26.04
H111015E	insulated extruded aluminium channel 75 × 250 mm high.............	m	–	–	–	90.25	90.25	–	–	99.28	99.28
H111015F	insulated parapet flashing; vertical 600 mm girth......	m	–	–	–	88.98	88.98	–	–	97.88	97.88
H111015G	bottom flashing; horizontal; 195 mm.................	m	–	–	–	60.52	60.52	–	–	66.57	66.57
H111015H	abutment to corner profile panel; vertical	m	–	–	–	21.46	21.46	–	–	23.61	23.61
H111015K	abutment to metal composite panel cladding; vertical.................	m	–	–	–	21.46	21.46	–	–	23.61	23.61
H111015N	opening light; 1500 × 900 mm; 90 mm thick	Nr	–	–	–	423.44	423.44	–	–	465.78	465.78

Major Works 2009		Unit	Labour Hours	Labour Net	Plant Net	Materials Net	Unit Net	Labour Gross	Plant Gross	Materials Gross	Unit Price
				£	£	£	£	(Gross rates include 10% profit)			
								£	£	£	£
H20	**H20: RIGID SHEET CLADDING**										
H2021	**Marine plywood square edged boarding; BS1088**										
H202158	**Flat; firring pieces and bearers included:**										
H202158A	18 mm thick	m²	0.85	14.43	–	23.49	37.92	15.87	–	25.84	41.71
H202158B	25 mm thick	m²	0.85	14.43	–	33.55	47.98	15.87	–	36.91	52.78
H202159	**Sloping; bearers included:**										
H202159A	18 mm thick	m²	0.66	11.21	–	21.92	33.13	12.33	–	24.11	36.44
H202159B	25 mm thick	m²	0.66	11.20	–	31.99	43.19	12.32	–	35.19	47.51
H202160	**Vertical; bearers included:**										
H202160A	18 mm thick	m²	0.81	13.76	–	21.56	35.32	15.14	–	23.72	38.85
H202160B	25 mm thick	m²	0.81	13.75	–	31.63	45.38	15.13	–	34.79	49.92
H2031	**Marine plywood tongued and grooved boarding; BS1088**										
H203162	**Flat; firring pieces and bearers included:**										
H203162A	18 mm thick	m²	0.95	16.14	–	25.49	41.63	17.75	–	28.04	45.79
H203162B	25 mm thick	m²	0.95	16.13	–	36.58	52.71	17.74	–	40.24	57.98
H203163	**Sloping; bearers included:**										
H203163A	18 mm thick	m²	0.76	12.91	–	23.93	36.84	14.20	–	26.32	40.52
H203163B	25 mm thick	m²	0.76	12.91	–	35.01	47.92	14.20	–	38.51	52.71
H203164	**Vertical; bearers included:**										
H203164A	18 mm thick	m²	0.91	15.46	–	23.57	39.03	17.01	–	25.93	42.93
H203164B	25 mm thick	m²	0.91	15.46	–	34.65	50.11	17.01	–	38.12	55.12

Cladding and Covering

Major Works 2009		Unit	Labour Hours	Labour Net	Plant Net	Materials Net	Unit Net	Labour Gross	Plant Gross	Materials Gross	Unit Price
								(Gross rates include 10% profit)			
				£	£	£	£	£	£	£	£
H20	**H20: RIGID SHEET CLADDING**										
H2041	**Roofing grade chipboard square edged boarding; BS 5669**										
H204166	**Flat; firring pieces and bearers included:**										
H204166A	18 mm thick	m²	0.80	13.59	–	6.85	20.44	14.95	–	7.54	22.48
H204166B	22 mm thick	m²	0.80	13.58	–	7.89	21.47	14.94	–	8.68	23.62
H204167	**Sloping; bearers included:**										
H204167A	18 mm thick	m²	0.61	10.36	–	5.29	15.65	11.40	–	5.82	17.22
H204167B	22 mm thick	m²	0.61	10.35	–	6.33	16.68	11.39	–	6.96	18.35
H204168	**Vertical; bearers included:**										
H204168A	18 mm thick	m²	0.76	12.91	–	4.93	17.84	14.20	–	5.42	19.62
H204168B	22 mm thick	m²	0.76	12.90	–	5.97	18.87	14.19	–	6.57	20.76
H2051	**Roofing grade chipboard tongued and grooved boarding; BS 5669**										
H205170	**Flat; firring pieces and bearers included:**										
H205170A	18 mm thick	m²	0.90	15.28	–	7.04	22.32	16.81	–	7.74	24.55
H205170B	22 mm thick	m²	0.90	15.28	–	8.10	23.38	16.81	–	8.91	25.72
H205171	**Sloping; bearers included:**										
H205171A	18 mm thick	m²	0.71	12.06	–	5.47	17.53	13.27	–	6.02	19.28
H205171B	22 mm thick	m²	0.71	12.06	–	6.53	18.59	13.27	–	7.18	20.45
H205172	**Vertical; bearers included:**										
H205172A	18 mm thick	m²	0.86	14.60	–	5.12	19.72	16.06	–	5.63	21.69
H205172B	22 mm thick	m²	0.86	14.61	–	6.17	20.78	16.07	–	6.79	22.86

Major Works 2009		Unit	Labour Hours	Labour Net	Plant Net	Materials Net	Unit Net	Labour Gross	Plant Gross	Materials Gross	Unit Price
				£	£	£	£	£	£	£	£
								(Gross rates include 10% profit)			
H21	**H21: TIMBER WEATHERBOARDING**										
H2110	**Shiplap boarding; wrought softwood; nominal 125 mm board face; fixing to timber backgrounds**										
H211010	**To walls:**										
H211010A	19 mm thick; over 300 mm wide	m²	0.65	11.04	–	22.36	33.40	12.14	–	24.60	36.74
H211010B	19 mm thick; not exceeding 300 mm wide	m	0.24	4.08	–	6.71	10.79	4.49	–	7.38	11.87
H211010C	19 mm thick; in areas not exceeding 1.00 m²	Nr	0.80	13.58	–	22.41	35.99	14.94	–	24.65	39.59
H211010D	25 mm thick; over 300 mm wide	m²	0.70	11.89	–	27.88	39.77	13.08	–	30.67	43.75
H211010E	25 mm thick; not exceeding 300 mm wide	m	0.27	4.50	–	8.37	12.87	4.95	–	9.21	14.16
H211010F	25 mm thick; in areas not exceeding 1.00 m²	Nr	0.88	14.94	–	27.93	42.87	16.43	–	30.72	47.16
H2120	**Feather-edge boarding; sawn softwood; nominal 150 mm board face; fixing to timber backgrounds**										
H212010	**To walls:**										
H212010A	14-7 mm thick; over 300 mm wide	m²	0.65	11.04	–	11.56	22.60	12.14	–	12.72	24.86
H212010B	14-7 mm thick; not exceeding 300 mm wide ...	m	0.24	4.08	–	3.47	7.55	4.49	–	3.82	8.31
H212010C	14-7 mm thick; in areas not exceeding 1.00 m²	Nr	0.80	13.58	–	11.61	25.19	14.94	–	12.77	27.71
H212010D	19-9 mm thick; over 300 mm wide	m²	0.70	11.89	–	19.03	30.92	13.08	–	20.93	34.01
H212010E	19-9 mm thick; not exceeding 300 mm wide ...	m	0.27	4.59	–	5.71	10.30	5.05	–	6.28	11.33
H212010F	19-9 mm thick; in areas not exceeding 1.00 m²	Nr	0.88	14.95	–	19.07	34.02	16.45	–	20.98	37.42

Cladding and Covering

Major Works 2009		Unit	Labour Hours	Labour Net	Plant Net	Materials Net	Unit Net	Labour Gross	Plant Gross	Materials Gross	Unit Price
								(Gross rates include 10% profit)			
				£	£	£	£	£	£	£	£
H30	**H30: FIBRE CEMENT PROFILED SHEET CLADDING, COVERING AND SIDING**										
H3005	**Roof coverings**										
H300510	**Eternit 2000 asbestos free corrugated sheeting; sloping not exceeding 50 degrees; fixing to timber members with drive screws:**										
H300510A	Profile 3 natural finish	m²	0.25	4.25	–	16.50	20.75	4.68	–	18.15	22.83
H300510F	Profile 6R natural finish	m²	0.28	4.76	–	19.02	23.78	5.24	–	20.92	26.16
H300510G	Profile 6R painted finish . . .	m²	0.28	4.75	–	22.54	27.29	5.23	–	24.79	30.02
H300510K	Extra for 60 mm glassfibre infill insulation and lining panel	m²	0.50	8.49	–	36.11	44.60	9.34	–	39.72	49.06
H300520	**Eternit 2000 asbestos free corrugated sheeting; sloping not exceeding 50 degrees; fixing to steel members with hook bolts:**										
H300520A	Profile 3 natural finish	m²	0.30	5.09	–	15.72	20.81	5.60	–	17.29	22.89
H300520F	Profile 6R natural finish	m²	0.35	5.94	–	18.24	24.18	6.53	–	20.06	26.60
H300520G	Profile 6R painted finish . . .	m²	0.35	5.95	–	21.75	27.70	6.55	–	23.93	30.47
H300520K	Extra for 60 mm glass fibre infill insulation and lining panel	m²	0.55	9.34	–	3.25	12.59	10.27	–	3.58	13.85
H300525	**Eternit 2000 accessories:**										
H300525A	Profile 3 two piece close fitting ridge; natural finish . .	m	0.20	3.39	–	26.13	29.52	3.73	–	28.74	32.47
H300525B	Profile 3 eaves filler piece; natural finish	m	0.13	2.21	–	18.26	20.47	2.43	–	20.09	22.52
H300525C	Profile 3 eaves corrugation closure piece; natural finish	m	0.19	3.23	–	18.26	21.49	3.55	–	20.09	23.64
H300525D	Profile 3 roll top barge board; natural finish	m	0.19	3.22	–	14.57	17.79	3.54	–	16.03	19.57
H300525J	Profile 6R two piece close fitting ridge; natural finish . .	m	0.22	3.73	–	22.20	25.93	4.10	–	24.42	28.52
H300525K	Profile 6R eaves filler piece; natural finish	m	0.17	2.89	–	12.41	15.30	3.18	–	13.65	16.83
H300525L	Profile 6R eaves corrugation closure piece; natural finish	m	0.25	4.25	–	12.41	16.66	4.68	–	13.65	18.33
H300525M	Profile 6R roll top barge board; natural finish	m	0.25	4.24	–	14.64	18.88	4.66	–	16.10	20.77
H300525Q	Profile 6R two piece close fitting ridge; painted finish .	m	0.22	3.73	–	27.59	31.32	4.10	–	30.35	34.45
H300525R	Profile 6R eaves filler piece; painted finish	m	0.17	2.88	–	15.31	18.19	3.17	–	16.84	20.01
H300525S	Profile 6R eaves corrugation closure piece; painted finish	m	0.25	4.24	–	15.35	19.59	4.66	–	16.89	21.55
H300525T	Profile 6R roll top barge board; painted finish	m	0.25	4.25	–	18.12	22.37	4.68	–	19.93	24.61

Major Works 2009		Unit			Specialist Net	Unit Net		Specialist Gross	Unit Price
							(Gross rates include 10% profit)		
			£	£	£	£	£	£	£
H31	H31: METAL PROFILED AND FLAT SHEET CLADDING, COVERING AND SIDING								
H3110	Aluminium mill finished standing seam roofing; 0.9 mm nominal thickness; 65 m standing seam; mechanically sealed end laps								
H311010	Mechanically fixed to structural frame; 15 degree pitch:								
H311010A	over 300 mm wide	m^2	–	–	–	86.14	86.14	–	–	94.75	94.75

Cladding and Covering

Major Works 2009		Unit	Labour Hours	Labour Net	Plant Net	Materials Net	Unit Net	Labour Gross	Plant Gross	Materials Gross	Unit Price
								(Gross rates include 10% profit)			
				£	£	£	£	£	£	£	£
H60	**H60: PLAIN ROOF TILING H65: SINGLE LAP ROOF TILING**										
H6011	**Sloping coverings**										
H601133	**Clay tile roofing; Redland; alloy nailed every fifth course; 38 × 25 mm tanalised softwood battens; Type 1F underfelt; 65 mm lap:**										
H601133A	265 × 165 mm Rosemary Plain, red	m²	1.64	27.85	–	43.84	71.69	30.64	–	48.22	78.86
H601133B	265 × 165 mm Rosemary Plain, red sanded	m²	1.64	27.85	–	43.84	71.69	30.64	–	48.22	78.86
H601133C	265 × 165 mm Rosemary Plain, brindle	m²	1.64	27.84	–	53.47	81.31	30.62	–	58.82	89.44
H601133D	265 × 165 mm Rosemary Plain, russet mix	m²	1.64	27.85	–	43.84	71.69	30.64	–	48.22	78.86
H601133E	265 × 165 mm Rosemary Plain, Cheslyn	m²	1.64	27.84	–	66.50	94.34	30.62	–	73.15	103.77
H601133F	380 × 260 mm Clay Pantile, red	m²	0.56	9.51	–	21.71	31.22	10.46	–	23.88	34.34
H601133G	380 × 260 mm Clay Pantile, brindled	m²	0.56	9.51	–	23.33	32.84	10.46	–	25.66	36.12
H601134	**Clay tile roofing; Sandtoft Goxhill; alloy nailed alternate courses; 38 × 25 mm tanalised softwood battens; Type 1F underfelt:**										
H601134A	384 × 267 mm County Pantiles; 58 mm lap; red . . .	m²	0.54	9.17	–	16.60	25.77	10.09	–	18.26	28.35
H601134B	384 × 267 mm County Pantiles; 58 mm lap; mixed russet	m²	0.54	9.17	–	17.52	26.69	10.09	–	19.27	29.36
H601134C	384 × 267 mm County Pantiles; 58 mm lap; brown/ antique	m²	0.54	9.17	–	18.31	27.48	10.09	–	20.14	30.23
H601134D	342 × 252 mm Old English Pantiles; 72 mm lap; red . . .	m²	0.56	9.51	–	23.18	32.69	10.46	–	25.50	35.96
H601134E	342 × 252 mm Old English Pantiles; 72 mm lap; mixed russet	m²	0.56	9.51	–	21.87	31.38	10.46	–	24.06	34.52
H601134F	342 × 252 mm Old English Pantiles; 72 mm lap; brown/ antique	m²	0.56	9.51	–	22.82	32.33	10.46	–	25.10	35.56
H601134G	342 × 255 mm Gaelic tiles; 75 mm lap red	m²	0.56	9.51	–	22.35	31.86	10.46	–	24.59	35.05
H601134H	342 × 255 mm Gaelic tiles; 75 mm lap mixed russet . . .	m²	0.56	9.51	–	23.46	32.97	10.46	–	25.81	36.27
H601134I	342 × 255 mm Gaelic tiles; 75 mm lap brown/antique . .	m²	0.56	9.51	–	24.41	33.92	10.46	–	26.85	37.31
H601134J	342 × 253 Greenwood Pantiles; 75 mm lap; red . . .	m²	0.56	9.51	–	22.14	31.65	10.46	–	24.35	34.82
H601134K	342 × 276 mm Provincial Pantiles; 75 mm lap; red . . .	m²	0.56	9.51	–	25.78	35.29	10.46	–	28.36	38.82
H601134L	342 × 267 mm Barrow Bold Roman tiles 75 mm lap; red	m²	0.56	9.51	–	32.40	41.91	10.46	–	35.64	46.10

Major Works 2009		Unit	Labour Hours	Labour Net	Plant Net	Materials Net	Unit Net	Labour Gross	Plant Gross	Materials Gross	Unit Price
				£	£	£	£	£	£	£	£
								(Gross rates include 10% profit)			
H60	**H60: PLAIN ROOF TILING H65: SINGLE LAP ROOF TILING**										
H6011	**Sloping coverings**										
H601135	**Concrete tile roofing; Redland, laid unfixed; 38 × 25 mm tanalised softwood battens; Type 1F underfelt:**										
H601135A	412 × 332 mm Richmond; 112 mm lap	m²	0.44	7.47	–	21.21	28.68	8.22	–	23.33	31.55
H601135B	412 × 332 mm Saxon; 112 mm lap	m²	0.44	7.47	–	24.93	32.40	8.22	–	27.42	35.64
H601135C	430 × 380 mm Stonewold II; 75 mm lap	m²	0.38	6.46	–	18.17	24.63	7.11	–	19.99	27.09
H601135D	418 × 334 mm Mini Stonewold; 75 mm lap	m²	0.40	6.79	–	15.18	21.97	7.47	–	16.70	24.17
H601135E	418 × 334 mm Mini Stonewold; 100 mm lap	m²	0.42	7.13	–	16.47	23.60	7.84	–	18.12	25.96
H601135F	430 × 380 mm Delta; 75 mm lap	m²	0.38	6.46	–	24.53	30.99	7.11	–	26.98	34.09
H601135G	430 × 380 mm Delta and Stonewold combination in equal numbers; 75 mm lap	m²	0.38	6.45	–	23.41	29.86	7.10	–	25.75	32.85
H601135H	418 × 332 mm Regent; 75 mm lap	m²	0.40	6.79	–	14.01	20.80	7.47	–	15.41	22.88
H601135I	418 × 332 mm Regent; 100 mm lap	m²	0.42	7.13	–	15.18	22.31	7.84	–	16.70	24.54
H601135J	418 × 332 mm Grovebury; 75 mm lap	m²	0.40	6.79	–	14.01	20.80	7.47	–	15.41	22.88
H601135K	418 × 332 mm Grovebury; 100 mm lap	m²	0.42	7.13	–	15.18	22.31	7.84	–	16.70	24.54
H601135L	418 × 330 mm Redland 50; 75 mm lap	m²	0.40	6.79	–	13.80	20.59	7.47	–	15.18	22.65
H601135M	418 × 330 mm Redland 50; 100 mm lap	m²	0.42	7.13	–	14.95	22.08	7.84	–	16.45	24.29
H601135N	418 × 330 mm Bridgewater; 75 mm lap	m²	0.40	6.80	–	16.96	23.76	7.48	–	18.66	26.14
H601135O	418 × 330 mm Renown; 75 mm lap	m²	0.40	6.79	–	15.23	22.02	7.47	–	16.75	24.22
H601135P	418 × 330 mm Renown; 100 mm lap	m²	0.42	7.13	–	16.52	23.65	7.84	–	18.17	26.02
H601135Q	381 × 227 mm Norfolk Pantile; 75 mm lap	m²	0.52	8.83	–	18.30	27.13	9.71	–	20.13	29.84
H601135R	381 × 227 mm Norfolk Pantile; 100 mm lap	m²	0.56	9.51	–	20.22	29.73	10.46	–	22.24	32.70
H601135S	381 × 227 mm Redland 49; 75 mm lap	m²	0.52	8.83	–	15.35	24.18	9.71	–	16.89	26.60
H601135T	381 × 227 mm Redland 49; 100 mm lap	m²	0.56	9.50	–	16.93	26.43	10.45	–	18.62	29.07
H601135U	268 × 165 mm Downland Plain tile; 65 mm lap	m²	1.64	27.85	–	39.72	67.57	30.64	–	43.69	74.33
H601135V	268 × 165 mm Redland Plain tile; 65 mm lap	m²	1.64	27.85	–	35.31	63.16	30.64	–	38.84	69.48

Cladding and Covering

Major Works 2009		Unit	Labour Hours	Labour Net	Plant Net	Materials Net	Unit Net	Labour Gross	Plant Gross	Materials Gross	Unit Price
								(Gross rates include 10% profit)			
				£	£	£	£	£	£	£	£
H60	**H60: PLAIN ROOF TILING H65: SINGLE LAP ROOF TILING**										
H6011	**Sloping coverings**										
H601136	**Underslating felt; fixing with battens (measured separately), 150 mm laps all round:**										
H601136A	BS 747; Type 1B	m²	0.04	0.68	–	1.06	1.74	0.75	–	1.17	1.91
H601136B	BS 747; Type 1F	m²	0.04	0.68	–	1.84	2.52	0.75	–	2.02	2.77
H601136C	BS 747; Type 1F aluminium foil faced	m²	0.04	0.68	–	3.35	4.03	0.75	–	3.69	4.43
H60	**H60: PLAIN ROOF TILING H65: SINGLE LAP ROOF TILING**										
H6021	**Vertical coverings**										
H602158	**Clay plain tile and ornamental tile cladding; Redland Rosemary; two alloy nails per tile; 38 × 25 mm tanalised softwood battens; 35 mm lap:**										
H602158A	265 × 165 mm; plain tiles; Red	m²	1.98	33.63	–	38.21	71.84	36.99	–	42.03	79.02
H602158B	265 × 165 mm; ornamental tiles, Bullnose	m²	1.98	33.62	–	56.51	90.13	36.98	–	62.16	99.14
H602158C	265 × 165 mm; alternate courses plain and ornamental, Red and Bullnose	m²	1.98	33.62	–	48.13	81.75	36.98	–	52.94	89.93
H602159	**Concrete plain tile cladding; Redland Plain tile two alloy nails per tile; 38 × 25 mm tanalised softwood battens; 35 mm lap:**										
H602159A	265 × 165 mm; plain tiles	m²	1.98	33.63	–	31.13	64.76	36.99	–	34.24	71.24
H602159B	265 × 165 mm; ornamental tiles, Club	m²	1.98	33.62	–	44.13	77.75	36.98	–	48.54	85.53
H602159C	265 × 165 mm; alternate courses plain and ornamental, Club	m²	1.98	33.62	–	38.23	71.85	36.98	–	42.05	79.04

Major Works 2009		Unit	Labour Hours	Labour Net	Plant Net	Materials Net	Unit Net	Labour Gross	Plant Gross	Materials Gross	Unit Price
				£	£	£	£	£	£	£	£
								(Gross rates include 10% profit)			
H60	**H60: PLAIN ROOF TILING H65: SINGLE LAP ROOF TILING**										
H6031	**Eaves, verges, ridges, hips or the like**										
H603183	**Clay tile roofing; Sandtoft Goxhill; 38 × 25 mm tanalised softwood battens; extra for:**										
H603183A	eaves with plastic filler, County pantiles..........	m	0.20	3.39	–	2.15	5.54	3.73	–	2.37	6.09
H603183B	eaves with undercloak; bed and point in cement mortar (1:3); Old English, Greenwood, Provincial or Barrow.................	m	0.40	6.79	–	4.22	11.01	7.47	–	4.64	12.11
H603183C	right hand verge with undercloak; be and point in cement mortar (1:3); County, Old English, Gaelic, Greenwood, Provincial or Barrow.................	m	0.80	13.59	–	3.65	17.24	14.95	–	4.02	18.96
H603183D	left hand verge with undercloak; bed and point in cement mortar (1:3); County or Old English; red or mixed russet.................	m	0.80	13.58	–	20.40	33.98	14.94	–	22.44	37.38
H603183E	left hand verge with undercloak; bed and point in cement mortar (1:3); Old English or County; brown or antique.................	m	0.80	13.58	–	21.31	34.89	14.94	–	23.44	38.38
H603183F	left hand verge tiles with undercloak bed and point in cement mortar (1:3) Gaelic.	m	0.80	13.59	–	3.65	17.24	14.95	–	4.02	18.96
H603183G	left hand verge with undercloak bed and point in cement mortar (1:3); Greenwood; red	m	0.80	13.59	–	21.71	35.30	14.95	–	23.88	38.83
H603183H	left hand verge with undercloak bed and point in cement mortar (1:3); Provincial; red............	m	0.80	13.58	–	31.38	44.96	14.94	–	34.52	49.46
H603183I	left hand verge with undercloak; bed and point in cement mortar (1:3); Barrow; red	m	0.80	13.58	–	36.37	49.95	14.94	–	40.01	54.95
H603183J	Goxhill concrete valley trough; battens both sides; red or antique	m	0.40	6.79	–	15.87	22.66	7.47	–	17.46	24.93
H603183K	cutting against valley gutters with undercloak; bed and point in cement mortar (1:3); County red.............	m	0.30	5.10	0.28	5.64	11.02	5.61	0.31	6.20	12.12
H603183L	cutting against valley gutters with undercloak; bed and point in cement mortar (1:3); Old English red	m	0.30	5.09	0.28	6.04	11.41	5.60	0.31	6.64	12.55
H603183M	cutting against valley gutters with undercloak; bed and point in cement mortar (1:3); Gaelic red	m	0.30	5.10	0.28	5.95	11.33	5.61	0.31	6.55	12.46

Cladding and Covering

Major Works 2009		Unit	Labour Hours	Labour Net	Plant Net	Materials Net	Unit Net	Labour Gross	Plant Gross	Materials Gross	Unit Price
									(Gross rates include 10% profit)		
				£	£	£	£	£	£	£	£
H60	**H60: PLAIN ROOF TILING H65: SINGLE LAP ROOF TILING**										
H6031	**Eaves, verges, ridges, hips or the like**										
H603183	**Clay tile roofing; Sandtoft Goxhill; 38 × 25 mm tanalised softwood battens; extra for:**										
H603183N	cutting against valley gutters with undercloak; bed and point in cement mortar (1:3); Greenwood red	m	0.30	5.09	0.28	5.92	11.29	5.60	0.31	6.51	12.42
H603183O	cutting against valley gutters with undercloak; bed and point in cement mortar (1:3); Provincial red	m	0.30	5.10	0.28	6.48	11.86	5.61	0.31	7.13	13.05
H603183P	cutting against valley gutters with undercloak; bed and point in cement mortar (1:3); Barrow red.	m	0.30	5.09	0.28	7.06	12.43	5.60	0.31	7.77	13.67
H603183Q	half or third round ridge and hip tiles; bedding and pointing in cement mortar (1:3); double dentil slips both sides; County, Old English, half or third round ridge and hip tiles;	m	0.80	13.59	–	21.57	35.16	14.95	–	23.73	38.68
H603183R	half or third round ridge and hip tiles; bedding and pointing in cement mortar (1:3); double dentil slips both sides; County or Old English half or third round ridge and hip tiles;	m	0.80	13.59	–	21.81	35.40	14.95	–	23.99	38.94
H603183S	half or third round ridge and hip tiles; bedding and pointing in cement mortar (1:3); Gaelic red or russet . .	m	0.80	13.58	–	15.69	29.27	14.94	–	17.26	32.20
H603183T	half or third round ridge and hip tiles; bedding and pointing in cement mortar (1:3); Gaelic brown or antique.	m	0.80	13.58	–	15.93	29.51	14.94	–	17.52	32.46
H603183U	half round monopitch ridge; bedding and pointing in cement mortar (1:3); double dentil slips one side; County Old English, Greenwood, Provincial o Barrow; red, russet, brown or antique . . .	m	0.80	13.59	–	38.27	51.86	14.95	–	42.10	57.05
H603183V	half round monopitch ridge; bedding and pointing in cement mortar (1:3); Gaelic; red, russet, brown or antique	m	0.80	13.59	–	35.33	48.92	14.95	–	38.86	53.81

Major Works 2009		Unit	Labour Hours	Labour Net	Plant Net	Materials Net	Unit Net	Labour Gross	Plant Gross	Materials Gross	Unit Price
								(Gross rates include 10% profit)			
				£	£	£	£	£	£	£	£
H60	**H60: PLAIN ROOF TILING H65: SINGLE LAP ROOF TILING**										
H6031	**Eaves, verges, ridges, hips or the like**										
H603184	**Clay plain tile roofing; Redland Rosemary 265 × 165 mm; 38 × 25 mm tanalised softwood battens; extra for:**										
H603184A	double course at eaves	m	0.40	6.79	–	4.47	11.26	7.47	–	4.92	12.39
H603184B	verge with undercloak; bed and point cement mortar (1:3)..................	m	0.80	13.59	–	7.73	21.32	14.95	–	8.50	23.45
H603184C	universal angular valley....	m	0.50	8.49	–	88.41	96.90	9.34	–	97.25	106.59
H603184D	universal curved valley	m	0.50	8.49	–	88.41	96.90	9.34	–	97.25	106.59
H603184E	cutting against valley gutters; bed and point in cement mortar (1:3).......	m	0.64	10.87	0.28	11.35	22.50	11.96	0.31	12.49	24.75
H603184F	half round ridge; bed and point in cement mortar (1:3)	m	0.80	13.59	–	30.62	44.21	14.95	–	33.68	48.63
H603184G	plain angle ridge; bed and point in cement mortar (1:3)	m	0.80	13.58	–	23.28	36.86	14.94	–	25.61	40.55
H603184H	hogsback ridge; bed and point in cement mortar (1:3)	m	0.80	13.59	–	30.62	44.21	14.95	–	33.68	48.63
H603184I	baby ridge; bed and point in cement mortar (1:3).......	m	0.80	13.59	–	30.62	44.21	14.95	–	33.68	48.63
H603184J	third round hip; bed and point in cement mortar (1:3).....	m	1.00	16.98	–	43.90	60.88	18.68	–	48.29	66.97
H603184K	universal bonnet hip.......	m	0.50	8.49	–	88.58	97.07	9.34	–	97.44	106.78
H603184L	universal arris hip........	m	0.50	8.49	–	88.58	97.07	9.34	–	97.44	106.78
H603184M	half round monoridge; bed and point in cement mortar (1:3)..................	m	0.80	13.58	–	8.39	21.97	14.94	–	9.23	24.17

Cladding and Covering

Major Works 2009		Unit	Labour Hours	Labour Net	Plant Net	Materials Net	Unit Net	Labour Gross	Plant Gross	Materials Gross	Unit Price
								(Gross rates include 10% profit)			
				£	£	£	£	£	£	£	£
H60	H60: PLAIN ROOF TILING H65: SINGLE LAP ROOF TILING										
H6031	Eaves, verges, ridges, hips or the like										
H603185	Concrete tile roofing; Redland; 38 × 25 mm tanalised softwood battens; extra for:										
H603185A	eaves; Richmond	m	0.10	1.70	–	11.80	13.50	1.87	–	12.98	14.85
H603185B	eaves; Saxon	m	0.10	1.70	–	11.80	13.50	1.87	–	12.98	14.85
H603185C	eaves; Stonewold II, Mini Stonewold, 50, Bridgewater, Renown, 49	m	0.10	1.69	–	0.43	2.12	1.86	–	0.47	2.33
H603185D	eaves; Delta, Regent, Grovebury, Norfolk.	m	0.10	1.70	–	1.18	2.88	1.87	–	1.30	3.17
H603185E	eaves; Downland/Plain	m	0.40	6.79	–	3.57	10.36	7.47	–	3.93	11.40
H603185F	Ambi-dry verges; Richmond	m	0.30	5.09	–	17.93	23.02	5.60	–	19.72	25.32
H603185G	Ambi-dry verges; Saxon . . .	m	0.30	5.09	–	18.75	23.84	5.60	–	20.63	26.22
H603185H	right hand verge with undercloak; be and point in cement mortar (1:3); Stonewold II	m	0.40	6.79	–	9.06	15.85	7.47	–	9.97	17.44
H603185I	left hand verge with undercloak; bed and point in cement mortar (1:3); Stonewold II	m	0.50	8.49	–	15.77	24.26	9.34	–	17.35	26.69
H603185J	verge with undercloak; bed and point in cement mortar (1:3); Mini, Stonewold, Renown, Norfolk, 49	m	0.40	6.79	–	4.99	11.78	7.47	–	5.49	12.96
H603185K	right hand verge with undercloak; be and point in cement mortar (1:3); Delta, Regent, Grovebury, 50, Bridgewater.	m	0.40	6.79	–	4.86	11.65	7.47	–	5.35	12.82
H603185L	left hand verge with undercloak; bed and point in cement mortar (1:3); Delta .	m	0.40	6.79	–	26.19	32.98	7.47	–	28.81	36.28
H603185M	left hand verge with undercloak; bed and point in cement mortar (1:3); Regent	m	0.40	6.79	–	16.61	23.40	7.47	–	18.27	25.74
H603185N	left hand verge with undercloak; bed and point in cement mortar (1:3); Grovebury	m	0.40	6.79	–	16.61	23.40	7.47	–	18.27	25.74
H603185O	left hand verge with undercloak bed and point in cement mortar (1:3); Redland 50	m	0.40	6.79	–	15.69	22.48	7.47	–	17.26	24.73
H603185P	left hand verge with undercloak; bed and point in cement mortar (1:3); Bridgewater.	m	0.40	6.79	–	17.74	24.53	7.47	–	19.51	26.98
H603185Q	verge with undercloak; bed and point in cement mortar; plain, Downland	m	0.80	13.59	–	6.21	19.80	14.95	–	6.83	21.78
H603185R	cloaked verge: Regent	m	0.20	3.40	–	13.74	17.14	3.74	–	15.11	18.85
H603185S	cloaked verge; Grovebury . .	m	0.20	3.40	–	13.74	17.14	3.74	–	15.11	18.85
H603185T	cloaked verge; Redland 50 .	m	0.20	3.40	–	13.68	17.08	3.74	–	15.05	18.79
H603185U	cloaked verge; Renown	m	0.20	3.40	–	14.11	17.51	3.74	–	15.52	19.26
H603185V	Redland Universal valley troughs; battens both sides	m	0.40	6.79	–	25.33	32.12	7.47	–	27.86	35.33

Major Works 2009		Unit	Labour Hours	Labour Net	Plant Net	Materials Net	Unit Net	Labour Gross	Plant Gross	Materials Gross	Unit Price
								(Gross rates include 10% profit)			
				£	£	£	£	£	£	£	£
H60	**H60: PLAIN ROOF TILING H65: SINGLE LAP ROOF TILING**										
H6031	**Eaves, verges, ridges, hips or the like**										
H603185	**Concrete tile roofing; Redland; 38 × 25 mm tanalised softwood battens; extra for:**										
H603185W	Cutting against valley gutters; bed and point in cement mortar (1:3); Richmond	m	0.24	4.08	0.28	3.39	7.75	4.49	0.31	3.73	8.53
H603185X	Cutting against valley gutters; bed and point in cement mortar (1:3); Saxon	m	0.24	4.08	0.28	4.01	8.37	4.49	0.31	4.41	9.21
H603185Y	Cutting against valley gutters; bed and point in cement mortar (1:3); Stonewold II	m	0.30	5.09	0.28	2.05	7.42	5.60	0.31	2.26	8.16
H603185Z	Cutting against valley gutters; bed and point in cement mortar (1:3); Mini Stonewold	m	0.30	5.10	0.28	2.81	8.19	5.61	0.31	3.09	9.01

Cladding and Covering

Major Works 2009		Unit	Labour Hours	Labour Net	Plant Net	Materials Net	Unit Net	Labour Gross	Plant Gross	Materials Gross	Unit Price
								(Gross rates include 10% profit)			
				£	£	£	£	£	£	£	£
H60	**H60: PLAIN ROOF TILING H65: SINGLE LAP ROOF TILING**										
H6031	**Eaves, verges, ridges, hips or the like**										
H603186	**Concrete tile roofing; Redland; 38 × 25 mm tanalised softwood battens; extra for:**										
H603186A	Cutting against valley gutters; bed and point in cement mortar (1:3); Delta .	m	0.32	5.43	0.28	5.17	10.88	5.97	0.31	5.69	11.97
H603186B	Cutting against valley gutters; bed and point in cement mortar (1:3); Regent	m	0.32	5.43	0.28	2.57	8.28	5.97	0.31	2.83	9.11
H603186C	Cutting against valley gutters; bed and point in cement mortar (1:3); Grovebury	m	0.32	5.43	0.28	2.57	8.28	5.97	0.31	2.83	9.11
H603186D	Cutting against valley gutters; bed and point in cement mortar (1:3); 50 ...	m	0.32	5.43	0.47	2.53	8.43	5.97	0.52	2.78	9.27
H603186E	Cutting against valley gutters; bed and point in cement mortar (1:3); Bridgewater.............	m	0.32	5.44	0.47	3.17	9.08	5.98	0.52	3.49	9.99
H603186F	Cutting against valley gutters; bed and point in cement mortar (1:3); Renown	m	0.30	5.09	0.47	2.82	8.38	5.60	0.52	3.10	9.22
H603186G	Cutting against valley gutters; bed and point in cement mortar (1:3); Norfolk	m	0.30	5.10	0.47	2.16	7.73	5.61	0.52	2.38	8.50
H603186H	Cutting against valley gutters; bed and point in cement mortar (1:3); 49 ...	m	0.30	5.09	0.47	1.81	7.37	5.60	0.52	1.99	8.11
H603186I	Cutting against valley gutters; bed and point in cement mortar (1:3); Downland	m	0.64	10.87	0.47	9.62	20.96	11.96	0.52	10.58	23.06

Major Works 2009		Unit	Labour Hours	Labour Net	Plant Net	Materials Net	Unit Net	Labour Gross	Plant Gross	Materials Gross	Unit Price
								(Gross rates include 10% profit)			
				£	£	£	£	£	£	£	£
H60	**H60: PLAIN ROOF TILING H65: SINGLE LAP ROOF TILING**										
H6031	**Eaves, verges, ridges, hips or the like**										
H603186J	Cutting against valley gutters; bed and point in cement mortar (1:3); Plain tiles....................	m	0.64	10.87	0.47	9.06	20.40	11.96	0.52	9.97	22.44
H603186K	Universal angle dry ridge; Richmond or Saxon.......	m	0.50	8.49	–	35.50	43.99	9.34	–	39.05	48.39
H603186L	Universal angle dry hip; Richmond or Saxon.......	m	0.50	8.49	–	22.63	31.12	9.34	–	24.89	34.23
H603186M	Universal angle Dry Mono ridge; Richmond or Saxon .	m	0.50	8.49	–	16.99	25.48	9.34	–	18.69	28.03
H603186N	Angular hip and ridge tiles; bedding and pointing in cement mortar (1:3); Stonewold II or Mini-Stonewold..............	m	0.80	13.59	–	11.21	24.80	14.95	–	12.33	27.28
H6031860	Universal angle monoridge; bedding and pointing in cement mortar (1:3); Stonewold II or Mini Stonewold..............	m	0.80	13.59	–	19.05	32.64	14.95	–	20.96	35.90
H603186P	Delta ridge and hip tiles; bedding and pointing in cement mortar (1:3); Delta .	m	0.80	13.58	–	17.60	31.18	14.94	–	19.36	34.30
H603186Q	Delta Mono ridge tiles; bedding and pointing in cement mortar (1:3); Delta .	m	0.80	13.59	–	26.15	39.74	14.95	–	28.77	43.71
H603186R	half round ridge and hip tiles; bedding and pointing in cement mortar (1:3); Redland 49 or Renown	m	0.80	13.59	–	9.39	22.98	14.95	–	10.33	25.28

Cladding and Covering

Major Works 2009		Unit	Labour Hours	Labour Net	Plant Net	Materials Net	Unit Net	Labour Gross	Plant Gross	Materials Gross	Unit Price
								(Gross rates include 10% profit)			
				£	£	£	£	£	£	£	£
H60	**H60: PLAIN ROOF TILING H65: SINGLE LAP ROOF TILING**										
H6031	**Eaves, verges, ridges, hips or the like**										
H603186S	half round mono ridge tiles; bedding and pointing in cement mortar (1:3); Redland 49 or Renown	m	0.80	13.58	–	18.22	31.80	14.94	–	20.04	34.98
H603186T	half round ridge and hip tiles; bedding and pointing in cement mortar (1:3); dentil slips; Regent, Grovebury, Redland 50, Bridgewater o Norfolk.................	m	0.80	13.59	–	12.56	26.15	14.95	–	13.82	28.77
H603186U	half round mono ridge tiles; bedding and pointing in cement mortar (1:3); dentil slips; Regent, Grovebury, Redland 50, Bridgewater or Norfolk.................	m	0.80	13.58	–	19.80	33.38	14.94	–	21.78	36.72
H603186V	half round ridge and hip tiles; bedding and pointing in cement mortar (1:3); Plain tiles or Downland	m	0.80	13.59	–	20.59	34.18	14.95	–	22.65	37.60
H603186W	half round monoridge; bedding and pointing in cement mortar (1:3); Plain or Downland	m	0.80	13.58	–	23.08	36.66	14.94	–	25.39	40.33
H603186X	bonnet hip tiles; Plain or Downland	m	0.50	8.49	–	52.08	60.57	9.34	–	57.29	66.63
H603186Y	arris hip tiles; Plain or Downland	m	0.50	8.49	–	52.08	60.57	9.34	–	57.29	66.63
H603186Z	valley tiles; Plain or Downland	m	0.50	8.49	–	51.91	60.40	9.34	–	57.10	66.44

Major Works 2009		Unit	Labour Hours	Labour Net	Plant Net	Materials Net	Unit Net	Labour Gross	Plant Gross	Materials Gross	Unit Price
								(Gross rates include 10% profit)			
				£	£	£	£	£	£	£	£
H60	**H60: PLAIN ROOF TILING H65: SINGLE LAP ROOF TILING**										
H603187	**Clay plain tiles and ornamental tile cladding; Redland Rosemary; 38 × 25 mm tanalised softwood battens; extra for:**										
H603187A	double course at eaves	m	0.40	6.79	–	4.47	11.26	7.47	–	4.92	12.39
H603187B	external angle tiles	m	0.50	8.49	–	88.58	97.07	9.34	–	97.44	106.78
H603187C	top edge tiling	m	0.40	6.79	–	4.47	11.26	7.47	–	4.92	12.39
H603188	**Concrete plain tile and ornamental tile cladding; Redland; 38 × 25 mm tanalised softwood battens; extra for:**										
H603188A	double course at eaves	m	0.40	6.79	–	3.57	10.36	7.47	–	3.93	11.40
H603188B	external angle tiles	m	0.50	8.49	–	52.08	60.57	9.34	–	57.29	66.63
H603188C	top edge tiling	m	0.40	6.79	–	3.57	10.36	7.47	–	3.93	11.40
H603189	**Redland ventilation systems; extra over tiling for:**										
H603189A	Redvent eaves vent	m	0.20	3.40	–	10.37	13.77	3.74	–	11.41	15.15
H603189B	ridge vents; half round or Universal angle concrete ...	Nr	–	–	–	97.91	97.91	–	–	107.70	107.70
H603189C	ridge vents; Delta	Nr	–	–	–	119.40	119.40	–	–	131.34	131.34
H603189D	ridge vents; Rosemary half round	Nr	–	–	–	109.73	109.73	–	–	120.70	120.70
H603189E	gas flue ridge vent and accessories; half round or universal angle concrete ...	Nr	–	–	–	129.36	129.36	–	–	142.30	142.30
H603189F	gas flue ridge vent; Delta ...	Nr	–	–	–	150.86	150.86	–	–	165.95	165.95
H603189G	Thruvent; Rosemary	Nr	–	–	–	78.99	78.99	–	–	86.89	86.89
H603189H	Thruvent; Cambrian	Nr	–	–	–	65.37	65.37	–	–	71.91	71.91
H603189I	Thruvent; concrete tiles....	Nr	–	–	–	58.35	58.35	–	–	64.19	64.19

Cladding and Covering

Major Works 2009		Unit	Labour Hours	Labour Net	Plant Net	Materials Net	Unit Net	Labour Gross	Plant Gross	Materials Gross	Unit Price
								— (Gross rates include 10% profit) —			
				£	£	£	£	£	£	£	£
H62	**H62: NATURAL SLATING**										
H6211	**Sloping coverings**										
H621130	**Natural blue/grey roofing; 75 mm lap; two aluminium alloy nails per slate; 38 × 25 mm tanalised softwood battens; Type 1F underfelt:**										
H621130A	600 × 300 mm	m²	0.62	10.53	–	65.12	75.65	11.58	–	71.63	83.22
H621130B	500 × 250 mm	m²	0.86	14.60	–	57.08	71.68	16.06	–	62.79	78.85
H621130C	450 × 225 mm	m²	1.00	16.98	–	51.33	68.31	18.68	–	56.46	75.14
H621136	**Underslating felt; fixing with battens (measured separately), 150 mm laps all round:**										
H621136A	BS 747; Type 1B	m²	0.04	0.68	–	1.06	1.74	0.75	–	1.17	1.91
H621136B	BS 747; Type 1F	m²	0.04	0.68	–	1.84	2.52	0.75	–	2.02	2.77
H621136C	BS 747; Type 1F aluminium foil faced	m²	0.04	0.68	–	3.35	4.03	0.75	–	3.69	4.43
H6231	**Eaves, verges, ridges, hips or the like**										
H623180	**Natural blue/grey slate roofing; 75 mm lap; two aluminium alloy nails per slate; 38 × 25 mm tanalised softwood battens; extra for:**										
H623180A	double course at eaves; 600 × 300 mm	m	0.28	4.75	–	21.01	25.76	5.23	–	23.11	28.34
H623180B	double course at eaves; 500 × 250 mm	m	0.30	5.10	–	11.64	16.74	5.61	–	12.80	18.41
H623180C	double course at eaves; 450 × 225 mm	m	0.32	5.43	–	10.25	15.68	5.97	–	11.28	17.25
H623180D	verge with undercloak; bed and point cement mortar (1:3): 600 × 300 mm	m	0.32	5.43	–	10.80	16.23	5.97	–	11.88	17.85
H623180E	verge with undercloak; bed and point cement mortar (1:3): 500 × 250 mm	m	0.34	5.77	–	10.80	16.57	6.35	–	11.88	18.23
H623180F	verge with undercloak; bed and point cement mortar (1:3): 450 × 225 mm	m	0.34	5.77	–	10.80	16.57	6.35	–	11.88	18.23
H623180G	laced valleys; 600 × 300 mm	m	0.50	8.49	–	51.78	60.27	9.34	–	56.96	66.30
H623180H	laced valleys; 500 × 250 mm	m	0.50	8.49	–	35.86	44.35	9.34	–	39.45	48.79
H623180I	laced valleys; 450 × 225 mm	m	0.50	8.49	–	29.90	38.39	9.34	–	32.89	42.23
H623180J	cutting against valley gutters; 600 300 mm	m	0.24	4.08	–	10.25	14.33	4.49	–	11.28	15.76
H623180K	cutting against valley gutters; 500 250 mm	m	0.28	4.75	–	5.56	10.31	5.23	–	6.12	11.34
H623180L	cutting against valley gutters; 450 225 mm	m	0.28	4.75	–	5.83	10.58	5.23	–	6.41	11.64
H623180M	mitred hips; 600 × 300 mm	m	0.50	8.49	–	83.05	91.54	9.34	–	91.36	100.69
H623180N	mitred hips; 500 × 250 mm	m	0.60	10.19	–	53.43	63.62	11.21	–	58.77	69.98
H623180O	mitred hips; 450 × 225 mm	m	0.80	13.58	–	43.18	56.76	14.94	–	47.50	62.44
H623180P	clay angular ridge or hip tiles; bed and point in cement mortar (1:3)	m	0.52	8.83	–	9.11	17.94	9.71	–	10.02	19.73

Major Works 2009		Unit	Labour Hours	Labour Net	Plant Net	Materials Net	Unit Net	Labour Gross	Plant Gross	Materials Gross	Unit Price
				£	£	£	£	£	£	£	£
								—— (Gross rates include 10% profit) ——			
H63	**H63: RECONSTRUCTED STONE SLATING AND TILING**										
H6311	**Sloping coverings**										
H631131	**Asbestos free cement slate roofing; Eternit 2000; two copper nails and one copper disc rivet per slate; 38 × 25 mm tanalised softwood battens; Type 1F underfelt:**										
H631131A	600 × 300 mm; 100 mm lap	m²	0.66	11.20	–	20.50	31.70	12.32	–	22.55	34.87
H631131B	600 × 300 mm; 110 mm lap	m²	0.68	11.55	–	20.52	32.07	12.71	–	22.57	35.28
H631131C	500 × 250 mm; 80 mm lap	m²	0.84	14.26	–	23.61	37.87	15.69	–	25.97	41.66
H631131D	500 × 250 mm; 100 mm lap	m²	0.88	14.95	–	24.68	39.63	16.45	–	27.15	43.59
H631132	**Reconstituted slate interlocking roofing; Redland Cambrian; two stainless steel ring shank nails and one stainless steel clip per slate; 38 × 25 mm tanalised softwood battens; Type 1F underfelt:**										
H631132A	330 × 336 mm; 50 mm lap	m²	0.60	10.18	–	43.02	53.20	11.20	–	47.32	58.52
H631132B	330 × 336 mm; 90 mm lap	m²	0.68	11.55	–	51.79	63.34	12.71	–	56.97	69.67
H631136	**Underslating felt; fixing with battens (measured separately), 150 mm laps all round:**										
H631136A	BS 747; Type 1B	m²	0.04	0.68	–	1.06	1.74	0.75	–	1.17	1.91
H631136B	BS 747; Type 1F	m²	0.04	0.68	–	1.84	2.52	0.75	–	2.02	2.77
H631136C	BS 747; Type 1F aluminium foil faced	m²	0.04	0.68	–	3.35	4.03	0.75	–	3.69	4.43
H631136D .	Klober Span-Flex Type 1F . .	m²	0.05	0.85	–	1.09	1.94	0.94	–	1.20	2.13
H631136E	Klober Permo Forte breather membrane	m²	0.05	0.85	–	1.96	2.81	0.94	–	2.16	3.09

Cladding and Covering

Major Works 2009		Unit	Labour Hours	Labour Net	Plant Net	Materials Net	Unit Net	Labour Gross	Plant Gross	Materials Gross	Unit Price
								(Gross rates include 10% profit)			
				£	£	£	£	£	£	£	£
H63	**H63: RECONSTRUCTED STONE SLATING AND TILING**										
H6331	**Eaves, verges, ridges, hips or the like**										
H633181	**Asbestos-free cement slate roofing; Eternit 2000; 38 × 25 mm tanalised softwood battens; extra for:**										
H633181A	double course at eaves; 600 × 300 mm..............	m	0.26	4.41	–	5.29	9.70	4.85	–	5.82	10.67
H633181B	double course at eaves; 500 × 250 mm..............	m	0.26	4.42	–	4.38	8.80	4.86	–	4.82	9.68
H633181D	verge with undercloak; bed and point cement mortar (1:3); 600 × 300 mm, 90 mm lap..............	m	0.26	4.41	–	2.86	7.27	4.85	–	3.15	8.00
H633181E	verge with undercloak; bed and point cement mortar (1:3); 600 × 300 mm 11 mm lap..............	m	0.26	4.41	–	2.86	7.27	4.85	–	3.15	8.00
H633181F	verge with undercloak; bed and point cement mortar (1:3); 500 × 250 mm, 90 mm lap..............	m	0.28	4.75	–	2.86	7.61	5.23	–	3.15	8.37
H633181G	verge with undercloak; bed and point cement mortar (1:3); 500 × 250 mm 11 mm lap..............	m	0.28	4.75	–	2.86	7.61	5.23	–	3.15	8.37
H633181J	cutting against valley gutters; 600 300 mm......	m	0.24	4.08	–	2.31	6.39	4.49	–	2.54	7.03
H633181K	cutting against valley gutters; 500 250 mm......	m	0.28	4.75	–	1.86	6.61	5.23	–	2.05	7.27
H633181M	mitred hips; 600 × 300 mm, 90 mm lap..............	m	0.50	8.49	–	23.24	31.73	9.34	–	25.56	34.90
H633181N	mitred hips; 600 × 300 mm, 110 mm la..............	m	0.50	8.49	–	23.24	31.73	9.34	–	25.56	34.90
H633181O	mitred hips; 500 × 250 mm, 90 mm lap..............	m	0.70	11.89	–	23.40	35.29	13.08	–	25.74	38.82
H633181P	mitred hips; 500 × 250 mm, 110 mm la..............	m	0.70	11.89	–	23.40	35.29	13.08	–	25.74	38.82
H633181S	half round ridge or hip coverings...............	m	0.50	8.49	–	29.29	37.78	9.34	–	32.22	41.56
H633181T	roll top angular ridge coverings...............	m	0.40	6.79	–	35.89	42.68	7.47	–	39.48	46.95
H633181U	internally socketed ridge coverings...............	m	0.40	6.80	–	33.32	40.12	7.48	–	36.65	44.13
H633181V	externally socketed monopitch ridge coverings.	m	0.40	6.79	–	40.81	47.60	7.47	–	44.89	52.36

Major Works 2009		Unit	Labour Hours	Labour Net	Plant Net	Materials Net	Unit Net	Labour Gross	Plant Gross	Materials Gross	Unit Price
								(Gross rates include 10% profit)			
				£	£	£	£	£	£	£	£
H63	**H63: RECONSTRUCTED STONE SLATING AND TILING**										
H6331	**Eaves, verges, ridges, hips or the like**										
H633182	**Reconstituted slate interlocking roofing; Redland Cambrian; 38 × 25 mm tanalised softwood battens; extra for Drytech detailing:**										
H633182A	stainless steel clips at eaves	m	0.10	1.70	–	1.09	2.79	1.87	–	1.20	3.07
H633182B	right hand Ambi-dry verges	m	0.30	5.10	–	34.69	39.79	5.61	–	38.16	43.77
H633182C	left hand Ambi-dry verges; special slates.	m	0.30	5.09	–	44.54	49.63	5.60	–	48.99	54.59
H633182D	mitred hip	m	0.50	8.49	–	17.56	26.05	9.34	–	19.32	28.66
H633182E	universal angle Dry Hip	m	0.50	8.49	–	35.50	43.99	9.34	–	39.05	48.39
H633182F	universal angle Dry Ridge . .	m	0.50	8.49	–	22.63	31.12	9.34	–	24.89	34.23
H633182G	universal angle Dry Mono ridge.	m	0.50	8.49	–	17.82	26.31	9.34	–	19.60	28.94
H633182H	Redland GRP valley; battens both sides	m	0.40	6.79	–	10.33	17.12	7.47	–	11.36	18.83
H633182I	cutting against valley gutters	m	0.24	4.07	0.28	50.52	54.87	4.48	0.31	55.57	60.36

Cladding and Covering

Major Works 2009		Unit	Labour Hours	Labour Net	Plant Net	Materials Net	Unit Net	Labour Gross	Plant Gross	Materials Gross	Unit Price
									(Gross rates include 10% profit)		
				£	£	£	£	£	£	£	£
H71	**H71: LEAD SHEET COVERINGS AND FLASHINGS**										
H7101	**Flat coverings**										
H710103	**Sheet lead roofing; BS 1178; waterproof building paper underlay; wood cored roll joints in direction of falls; welted joints across falls:**										
H710103B	Code 4	m²	3.50	59.43	–	61.60	121.03	65.37	–	67.76	133.13
H710103C	Code 5	m²	3.80	64.52	–	72.19	136.71	70.97	–	79.41	150.38
H710103D	Code 6	m²	4.10	69.62	–	77.67	147.29	76.58	–	85.44	162.02
H710103E	Code 7	m²	4.40	74.72	–	97.38	172.10	82.19	–	107.12	189.31
H7111	**Sloping coverings**										
H711122	**Sheet lead roofing; BS 1178; waterproof building paper underlay; wood cored roll joints in direction of falls; welted joints across falls:**										
H711122B	Code 4	m²	3.80	64.53	–	61.60	126.13	70.98	–	67.76	138.74
H711122C	Code 5	m²	4.10	69.62	–	72.19	141.81	76.58	–	79.41	155.99
H711122D	Code 6	m²	4.40	74.71	–	79.86	154.57	82.18	–	87.85	170.03
H711122E	Code 7	m²	4.70	79.81	–	97.38	177.19	87.79	–	107.12	194.91
H7121	**Vertical coverings**										
H712152	**Sheet lead roofing; BS 1178; waterproof building paper underlay; wood cored roll joints vertically; welted joints horizontally:**										
H712152B	Code 4	m²	4.00	67.92	–	59.67	127.59	74.71	–	65.64	140.35
H712152C	Code 5	m²	4.30	73.01	–	71.70	144.71	80.31	–	78.87	159.18
H712152D	Code 6	m²	4.60	78.11	–	76.43	154.54	85.92	–	84.07	169.99

Major Works 2009		Unit	Labour Hours	Labour Net	Plant Net	Materials Net	Unit Net	Labour Gross	Plant Gross	Materials Gross	Unit Price
								(Gross rates include 10% profit)			
				£	£	£	£	£	£	£	£
H71	**H71: LEAD SHEET COVERINGS AND FLASHINGS**										
H7141	**Eaves, ridges, skirtings, fascias, flashings, aprons or the like**										
H714172	**Sheet lead; BS 1178; working over fillets, slating or tiling:**										
H714172A	Code 3 flashings, aprons, soakers or the like; wedging into grooves with lead wedges; not exceeding 150 mm girth	m	0.35	5.94	–	4.58	10.52	6.53	–	5.04	11.57
H714172B	Code 3 lead flashings, aprons, soakers or the like; wedging into grooves with lead wedges; 150-300 mm girth	m	0.60	10.19	–	8.89	19.08	11.21	–	9.78	20.99
H714172C	Code 4 lead flashings, aprons, soakers or the like; wedging into grooves with lead wedges; not exceeding 150 mm girth	m	0.40	6.79	–	6.59	13.38	7.47	–	7.25	14.72
H714172D	Code 4 lead flashings, aprons, soakers or the like; wedging into grooves with lead wedges; 150-300 mm girth	m	0.69	11.72	–	12.79	24.51	12.89	–	14.07	26.96
H714172E	Code 4 stepped flashings; wedging into grooves with lead wedges; 150-300 mm girth	m	0.92	15.63	–	12.79	28.42	17.19	–	14.07	31.26

Cladding and Covering

Major Works 2009		Unit	Labour Hours	Labour Net	Plant Net	Materials Net	Unit Net	Labour Gross	Plant Gross	Materials Gross	Unit Price
									(Gross rates include 10% profit)		
				£	£	£	£	£	£	£	£
H71	**H71: LEAD SHEET COVERINGS AND FLASHINGS**										
H7141	**Eaves, ridges, skirtings, fascias, flashings, aprons or the like**										
H714172	**Sheet lead; BS 1178; working over fillets, slating or tiling:**										
H714172F	Code 4 stepped flashings; wedging into grooves with lead wedges; 300-450 mm girth	m	1.25	21.23	–	19.39	40.62	23.35	–	21.33	44.68
H714172G	Code 4 cappings to ridges and hips, valley gutters or the like; 300-450 mm girth	m	1.03	17.49	–	19.39	36.88	19.24	–	21.33	40.57
H714172H	Code 4 cappings to ridges and hips, valley gutters or the like; working over fillets, slating or tiling; 450-600 mm girth	m	1.38	23.43	–	25.59	49.02	25.77	–	28.15	53.92
H714172I	Code 5 flashings, aprons or the like wedging into grooves with lead wedges; not exceeding 150 mm girth	m	0.43	7.30	–	8.20	15.50	8.03	–	9.02	17.05
H714172J	Code 5 flashings, aprons or the like wedging into grooves with lead wedges; 150-300 mm girth	m	0.74	12.57	–	15.92	28.49	13.83	–	17.51	31.34
H714172K	Code 5 stepped flashings; wedging into grooves with lead wedges; 150-300 mm girth	m	1.00	16.98	–	15.92	32.90	18.68	–	17.51	36.19
H714172L	Code 5 stepped flashings; wedging into grooves with lead wedges; 300-450 mm girth	m	1.34	22.76	–	24.13	46.89	25.04	–	26.54	51.58
H714172M	Code 5 cappings to ridges and hips, valley gutters or the like; 300-450 mm girth	m	1.10	18.68	–	24.13	42.81	20.55	–	26.54	47.09
H714172N	Code 5 cappings to ridges and hips, valley gutters or the like; 450-600 mm girth	m	1.48	25.14	–	31.85	56.99	27.65	–	35.04	62.69
H714172O	Code 6 flashings, aprons or the like wedging into grooves with lead wedges; not exceeding 150 mm girth	m	0.48	8.15	–	9.16	17.31	8.97	–	10.08	19.04
H714172P	Code 6 flashings, aprons or the like wedging into grooves with lead wedges; 150-300 mm girth	m	0.80	13.58	–	17.78	31.36	14.94	–	19.56	34.50
H714172Q	Code 6 stepped flashings; wedging into grooves with lead wedges; 150-300 mm girth	m	1.10	18.68	–	17.78	36.46	20.55	–	19.56	40.11
H714172R	Code 6 stepped flashings; wedging into grooves with lead wedges; 300-450 mm girth	m	1.45	24.63	–	26.94	51.57	27.09	–	29.63	56.73
H714172S	Code 6 cappings to ridges and hips, valley gutters or the like; 300-450 mm girth	m	1.18	20.04	–	26.94	46.98	22.04	–	29.63	51.68
H714172T	Code 6 cappings to ridges and hips, valley gutters or the like; 450-600 mm girth	m	1.59	27.00	–	35.55	62.55	29.70	–	39.11	68.81

Major Works 2009		Unit	Labour Hours	Labour Net	Plant Net	Materials Net	Unit Net	Labour Gross	Plant Gross	Materials Gross	Unit Price
								(Gross rates include 10% profit)			
				£	£	£	£	£	£	£	£
H71	**H71: LEAD SHEET COVERINGS AND FLASHINGS**										
H7191	**Soaker collars**										
H719197	**Sheet lead soaker collars; fixing around pipes, standards or the like; dressing over roof coverings; mastic joint at top; 300 mm high:**										
H719197A	Code 3; not exceeding 150 mm girth	Nr	0.18	3.06	–	1.60	4.66	3.37	–	1.76	5.13
H719197B	Code 3; 150-300 mm girth	Nr	0.30	5.09	–	3.21	8.30	5.60	–	3.53	9.13
H719197C	Code 3; 300-450 mm girth	Nr	0.50	8.49	–	4.81	13.30	9.34	–	5.29	14.63
H719197D	Code 3; 450-600 mm girth	Nr	0.65	11.03	–	6.42	17.45	12.13	–	7.06	19.20
H719197E	Code 4; not exceeding 150 mm girth	Nr	0.28	4.75	–	2.20	6.95	5.23	–	2.42	7.65
H719197F	Code 4; 150-300 mm girth	Nr	0.50	8.49	–	4.39	12.88	9.34	–	4.83	14.17
H719197G	Code 4; 300-450 mm girth	Nr	0.75	12.73	–	6.59	19.32	14.00	–	7.25	21.25
H719197H	Code 4; 450-600 mm girth	Nr	0.90	15.29	–	8.78	24.07	16.82	–	9.66	26.48
H73	**H73: COPPER STRIP AND SHEET COVERINGS AND FLASHINGS**										
H7301	**Flat coverings**										
H730105	**Sheet copper roofing; BS 2870; waterproof inodorous felt No.1 underlay wood cored roll joints in direction of falls; double lock cross welts across falls:**										
H730105A	0.45 mm thick	m²	4.00	67.92	–	57.81	125.73	74.71	–	63.59	138.30
H730105B	0.60 mm thick	m²	4.30	73.02	–	67.44	140.46	80.32	–	74.18	154.51
H730105C	0.70 mm thick	m²	4.50	76.41	–	78.47	154.88	84.05	–	86.32	170.37
H7311	**Sloping coverings**										
H731124	**Sheet copper roofing; BS 2870; inodorous felt No.1 underlay; wood cored roll joints in direction of falls; double lock cross welts across falls:**										
H731124A	0.45 mm thick	m²	4.50	76.41	–	57.81	134.22	84.05	–	63.59	147.64
H731124B	0.60 mm thick	m²	4.80	81.51	–	67.44	148.95	89.66	–	74.18	163.85
H731124C	0.70 mm thick	m²	5.00	84.90	–	78.47	163.37	93.39	–	86.32	179.71
H7321	**Vertical coverings**										
H732154	**Sheet copper roofing; BS 2870; inodorous felt No.1 underlay; wood cored roll joints in direction of falls; double lock cross welts across falls:**										
H732154A	0.45 mm thick	m²	5.00	84.90	–	57.81	142.71	93.39	–	63.59	156.98
H732154B	0.60 mm thick	m²	5.30	90.00	–	67.44	157.44	99.00	–	74.18	173.18
H732154C	0.70 mm thick	m²	5.50	93.39	–	78.47	171.86	102.73	–	86.32	189.05

Cladding and Covering

Major Works 2009		Unit	Labour Hours	Labour Net	Plant Net	Materials Net	Unit Net	Labour Gross	Plant Gross	Materials Gross	Unit Price
								(Gross rates include 10% profit)			
				£	£	£	£	£	£	£	£
H73	H73: COPPER STRIP AND SHEET COVERINGS AND FLASHINGS										
H7341	Eaves, ridges, skirtings, fascias, flashings, aprons or the like										
H734174	Sheet copper; BS 2870; working over fillets and into grooves as necessary:										
H734174A	0.45 mm flashings, aprons, soakers o the like; not exceeding 150 mm girth ...	m	0.48	8.15	–	5.31	13.46	8.97	–	5.84	14.81
H734174B	0.45 mm flashings, aprons, soakers o the like; 150-300 mm girth	m	0.91	15.45	–	10.32	25.77	17.00	–	11.35	28.35
H734174C	0.45 mm stepped flashings; 150-300 mm girth	m	1.20	20.37	–	10.32	30.69	22.41	–	11.35	33.76
H734174D	0.45 mm stepped flashings; 300-450 mm girth	m	1.60	27.17	–	15.63	42.80	29.89	–	17.19	47.08
H734174E	0.45 mm cappings to ridges and hips, valley gutters or the like; 300-450 mm girth	m	1.35	22.92	–	15.63	38.55	25.21	–	17.19	42.41
H734174F	0.45 mm cappings to ridges and hips, valley gutters or the like; 450-600 mm girth	m	1.80	30.56	–	24.31	54.87	33.62	–	26.74	60.36
H734174G	0.60 mm flashings, aprons, soakers o the like; not exceeding 150 mm girth ...	m	0.50	8.49	–	6.26	14.75	9.34	–	6.89	16.23
H734174H	0.60 mm flashings, aprons, soakers o the like; 150-300 mm girth	m	0.95	16.13	–	12.15	28.28	17.74	–	13.37	31.11
H734174I	0.60 mm stepped flashings; 150-300 mm girth	m	1.25	21.23	–	12.15	33.38	23.35	–	13.37	36.72
H734174J	0.60 mm stepped flashings; 300-450 mm girth	m	1.70	28.87	–	18.42	47.29	31.76	–	20.26	52.02
H734174K	0.60 mm cappings to ridges and hips, valley gutters or the like; 300-450 mm girth	m	1.45	24.63	–	18.42	43.05	27.09	–	20.26	47.36
H734174L	0.60 mm cappings to ridges and hips, valley gutters or the like; 450-600 mm girth	m	1.90	32.26	–	24.31	56.57	35.49	–	26.74	62.23
H734174M	0.70 mm flashings, aprons, soakers o the like; not exceeding 150 mm girth ...	m	0.53	9.00	–	8.03	17.03	9.90	–	8.83	18.73
H734174N	0.70 mm flashings, aprons, soakers o the like; 150-300 mm girth	m	1.05	17.82	–	15.60	33.42	19.60	–	17.16	36.76
H734174O	0.70 mm stepped flashing; 150-300 mm girth	m	1.30	22.07	–	15.60	37.67	24.28	–	17.16	41.44
H734174P	0.70 mm stepped flashing; 300-450 mm girth	m	1.75	29.72	–	23.63	53.35	32.69	–	25.99	58.69
H734174Q	0.70 mm cappings to ridges and hips valley gutters or the like; 300-450 mm girth	m	1.55	26.32	–	23.63	49.95	28.95	–	25.99	54.95
H734174R	0.70 mm cappings to ridges and hips valley gutters or the like; 450-600 mm girth	m	2.00	33.96	–	31.19	65.15	37.36	–	34.31	71.67

Major Works 2009		Unit	Labour Hours	Labour Net	Plant Net	Materials Net	Unit Net	Labour Gross	Plant Gross	Materials Gross	Unit Price
				£	£	£	£	£	£	£	£
								(Gross rates include 10% profit)			
H74	**H74: ZINC STRIP AND SHEET COVERINGS AND FLASHINGS**										
H7401	**Flat coverings**										
H740104	**Sheet zinc roofing; BS 849; waterproof building paper underlay; wood cored roll joints in direction of falls; beaded drip joints across falls:**										
H740104A	0.80 mm thick...........	m²	4.00	67.92	–	47.64	115.56	74.71	–	52.40	127.12
H740104B	1.00 mm thick...........	m²	4.40	74.71	–	53.99	128.70	82.18	–	59.39	141.57
H7411	**Sloping coverings**										
H741123	**Sheet zinc roofing; BS 849; waterproof building paper underlay; wood cored roll joints in direction of falls; welted joints across falls:**										
H741123A	0.80 mm thick...........	m²	4.50	76.41	–	47.06	123.47	84.05	–	51.77	135.82
H741123B	1.00 mm thick...........	m²	4.90	83.21	–	53.32	136.53	91.53	–	58.65	150.18
H7421	**Vertical coverings**										
H742153	**Sheet zinc roofing; BS 849; waterproof building paper underlay; welted joints vertically and horizontally:**										
H742153A	0.80 mm thick...........	m²	4.80	81.51	–	41.69	123.20	89.66	–	45.86	135.52
H742153B	1.00 mm thick...........	m²	5.20	88.29	–	47.28	135.57	97.12	–	52.01	149.13

Cladding and Covering

Major Works 2009		Unit	Labour Hours	Labour Net	Plant Net	Materials Net	Unit Net	Labour Gross	Plant Gross	Materials Gross	Unit Price
								(Gross rates include 10% profit)			
				£	£	£	£	£	£	£	£
H74	**H74: ZINC STRIP AND SHEET COVERINGS AND FLASHINGS**										
H7441	**Eaves, ridges, skirtings, fascias, flashings, aprons or the like**										
H744173	**Sheet zinc; BS 849; working over fillets and into grooves as necessary:**										
H744173A	0.80 mm flashings, aprons, soakers o the like; not exceeding 150 mm girth . . .	m	0.45	7.64	–	5.16	12.80	8.40	–	5.68	14.08
H744173B	0.80 mm flashings, aprons, soakers o the like; 150-300 mm girth	m	0.87	14.77	–	10.02	24.79	16.25	–	11.02	27.27
H744173C	0.80 mm stepped flashings; 150-300 mm girth	m	1.15	19.53	–	10.02	29.55	21.48	–	11.02	32.51
H744173D	0.80 mm stepped flashings; 300-450 mm girth	m	1.55	26.32	–	15.19	41.51	28.95	–	16.71	45.66
H744173E	0.80 mm cappings to ridges and hips, valley gutters or the like; 300-450 mm girth	m	1.30	22.08	–	15.19	37.27	24.29	–	16.71	41.00
H744173F	0.80 mm cappings to ridges and hips, valley gutters or the like; 450-600 mm girth	m	1.75	29.72	–	20.04	49.76	32.69	–	22.04	54.74
H744173G	1.00 mm flashings, aprons, soakers o the like; not exceeding 150 mm girth . . .	m	0.50	8.49	–	5.88	14.37	9.34	–	6.47	15.81
H744173H	1.00 mm flashings, aprons, soakers o the like; 150-300 mm girth	m	1.00	16.98	–	11.42	28.40	18.68	–	12.56	31.24
H744173I	1.00 mm stepped flashings; 150-300 mm girth	m	1.25	21.22	–	11.42	32.64	23.34	–	12.56	35.90
H744173J	1.00 mm stepped flashings; 300-450 mm girth	m	1.65	28.02	–	17.30	45.32	30.82	–	19.03	49.85
H744173K	1.00 mm cappings to ridges and hips, valley gutters or the like; 300-450 mm girth	m	1.45	24.62	–	17.30	41.92	27.08	–	19.03	46.11
H744173L	1.00 mm cappings to ridges and hips, valley gutters or the like; 450-600 mm girth	m	1.90	32.26	–	22.84	55.10	35.49	–	25.12	60.61

Major Works 2009		Unit				Specialist Net	Unit Net			Specialist Gross	Unit Price
									(Gross rates include 10% profit)		
				£	£	£	£	£	£	£	£
H92	**H92: RAINSCREEN CLADDING**										
H9210	**Rainscreen cladding to walls**										
H921010	**7.5 mm Eternit Glasal cladding rivet fixed with Eternit Astro rivet system on and including Eternit Ventisol aluminium support framework on 80 mm stand-off brackets to form 100 mm void; fixing to substrate with mechanical fixings:**										
H921010A	over 300 mm wide	m²	–	–	–	155.52	155.52	–	–	171.07	171.07
H9220	**Rainscreen cladding to soffits**										
H922010	**7.5 mm Eternit Glasal cladding; rivet fixed with Eternit Astro rivet system on and including Eternit Omega and Zed 40 mm aluminium support framework; fixing to substrate with screws:**										
H922010A	over 300 mm wide	m²	–	–	–	153.79	153.79	–	–	169.17	169.17
H922020	**4 mm Eternit Alucomat aluminium composite cladding; rivet fixed with Alucomat matched rivets on and including Eternit Omega and Zed 40 mm aluminium support framework; fixing to substrate with screws:**										
H922020A	over 300 mm wide	m²	–	–	–	216.90	216.90	–	–	238.59	238.59
H9230	**Rainscreen cladding to fascias**										
H923010	**7.5 mm Eternit Glasal cladding; secret fixed with Eternit Sikatack structural adhesive system on and including Eternit Omega and Zed 40 mm aluminium support framework; fixing to substrate with screws:**										
H923010A	not exceeding 300 mm wide	m	–	–	–	77.70	77.70	–	–	85.47	85.47
H9250	**Rainscreen accessories**										
H925010	**Cladding profiles:**										
H925010A	horizontal joint profile	m	–	–	–	8.89	8.89	–	–	9.78	9.78
H925010B	universal corner profile	m	–	–	–	15.28	15.28	–	–	16.81	16.81
H925010C	50 mm perforated vent profile.	m	–	–	–	7.03	7.03	–	–	7.73	7.73
H925010D	100 mm perforated vent profile.	m	–	–	–	12.93	12.93	–	–	14.22	14.22

LANSDOWNE ROAD STADIUM, DUBLIN

OPTIMUM SOLUTIONS

At Franklin Sports Business we provide timely, accurate and professional cost consultancy advice to the sport and leisure industry – but what makes us different is that we do this in the context of the overall business equation. We guide our clients to invest in an efficient manner so that the end product represents a sustainable optimum solution.

We have worked on some of the world's highest-profile projects including England's new Wembley Stadium, the Lansdowne Road Stadium in Ireland and the new National Indoor Sports Arena and Velodrome in Scotland. We have worked with local, national and international sporting organisations including Fulham FC (UK), FC Internazionale (Italy), Galatasaray FC (Turkey) and the City of Warsaw for a new Polish national stadium.

For more information please contact Barry Winterton:
T +44 (0)20 7803 4501
E sport&leisure@franklinandrews.com

Franklin Sports Business is a member of the Mott MacDonald Group

www.franklinandrews.com

FRANKLIN SPORTS BUSINESS

WATERPROOFING

Major Works 2009		Unit	Labour Hours	Labour Net	Plant Net	Materials Net	Unit Net	Labour Gross	Plant Gross	Materials Gross	Unit Price
								(Gross rates include 10% profit)			
				£	£	£	£	£	£	£	£
J20	**J20: MASTIC ASPHALT TANKING AND DAMP PROOFING**										
J2011	**Flat coverings**										
J201108	**Mastic asphalt tanking; BS 1097; limestone aggregate:**										
J201108A	20 mm two coat work	m²	0.50	11.71	–	10.24	21.95	12.88	–	11.26	24.15
J201108B	30 mm three coat work	m²	0.70	16.40	–	15.36	31.76	18.04	–	16.90	34.94
J2013	**Sloping coverings**										
J201327	**Mastic asphalt tanking; BS 1097; limestone aggregate:**										
J201327A	20 mm two coat work	m²	0.65	15.23	–	10.24	25.47	16.75	–	11.26	28.02
J201327B	30 mm three coat work	m²	0.91	21.32	–	15.36	36.68	23.45	–	16.90	40.35
J2015	**Vertical coverings**										
J201557	**Mastic asphalt tanking; BS 1097; limestone aggregate:**										
J201557A	20 mm two coat work	m²	0.82	19.21	–	10.24	29.45	21.13	–	11.26	32.40
J201557B	30 mm three coat work	m²	1.14	26.71	–	15.36	42.07	29.38	–	16.90	46.28
J2061	**Skirtings, upstands or the like**										
J206177	**Mastic asphalt tanking; BS 1097; limestone aggregate; skirtings, upstand or the like; rounded arrises and internal angle fillet; turning nib into groove:**										
J206177A	20 mm two coat work; not exceeding 150 mm high ...	m	0.25	5.85	–	2.05	7.90	6.44	–	2.26	8.69
J206177B	20 mm two coat work; 150-300 mm high.............	m	0.40	9.37	–	3.59	12.96	10.31	–	3.95	14.26
J206177E	30 mm three coat work; not exceeding 150 mm high ...	m	0.35	8.20	–	3.07	11.27	9.02	–	3.38	12.40
J206177F	30 mm three coat work; 150-300 mm high.............	m	0.55	12.88	–	5.38	18.26	14.17	–	5.92	20.09

Waterproofing

Major Works 2009		Unit	Labour Hours	Labour Net	Plant Net	Materials Net	Unit Net	Labour Gross	Plant Gross	Materials Gross	Unit Price
								(Gross rates include 10% profit)			
				£	£	£	£	£	£	£	£
J21	**J21: MASTIC ASPHALT ROOFING, INSULATION AND FINISHES**										
J2131	**Flat coverings**										
J213106	**Mastic asphalt roofing; BS 988; limestone aggregate; sheathing felt underlay; BS 747; rubbing surface with fine sand:**										
J213106A	20 mm two coat work	m²	0.50	11.72	–	12.15	23.87	12.89	–	13.37	26.26
J213107	**Mastic asphalt roofing; BS 1162; natural rock aggregate; sheathing felt underlay; BS 747; rubbing surface with fine sand:**										
J213107A	20 mm two coat work	m²	0.50	11.71	–	14.00	25.71	12.88	–	15.40	28.28
J2133	**Sloping coverings**										
J213325	**Mastic asphalt roofing; BS 988; limestone aggregate; sheathing felt underlay; BS 747; rubbing surface with fine sand:**										
J213325A	20 mm two coat work	m²	0.65	15.23	–	12.15	27.38	16.75	–	13.37	30.12
J213326	**Mastic asphalt roofing; BS 1162; natural rock aggregate; sheathing felt underlay; BS 747; rubbing surface with fine sand:**										
J213326A	20 mm two coat work	m²	0.65	15.23	–	14.00	29.23	16.75	–	15.40	32.15
J2135	**Vertical coverings**										
J213555	**Mastic asphalt roofing; BS 988; limestone aggregate; sheathing felt underlay; BS 747; rubbing with fine sand:**										
J213555A	20 mm two coat work	m²	0.82	19.22	–	12.15	31.37	21.14	–	13.37	34.51
J213556	**Mastic asphalt roofing; BS 1162; natural rock aggregate; sheathing felt underlay; BS 747; rubbing surface with fine sand:**										
J213556A	20 mm two coat work	m²	0.82	19.21	–	14.00	33.21	21.13	–	15.40	36.53

Major Works 2009		Unit	Labour Hours	Labour Net	Plant Net	Materials Net	Unit Net	Labour Gross	Plant Gross	Materials Gross	Unit Price
								——— (Gross rates include 10% profit) ———			
				£	£	£	£	£	£	£	£
J21	**J21: MASTIC ASPHALT ROOFING, INSULATION AND FINISHES**										
J2161	**Skirtings, upstands or the like**										
J216175	**Mastic asphalt; BS 988; limestone aggregate; sheathing felt underlay; BS 747; rubbing surface with fine sand; 20 mm two coat skirtings, upstands or the like; rounded arrises and internal angle fillet; turning nib into groove:**										
J216175A	not exceeding 150 mm high	m	0.25	5.85	–	2.39	8.24	6.44	–	2.63	9.06
J216175B	150-300 mm high.........	m	0.40	9.37	–	4.21	13.58	10.31	–	4.63	14.94
J216176	**Mastic asphalt; BS 1162; natural rock aggregate; sheathing felt underlay BS 747; rubbing surface with fine sand; 20 mm two coat skirtings, upstands or the like; rounded arrises and internal angle fillet; turning nib into groove:**										
J216176A	not exceeding 150 mm high	m	0.25	5.85	–	2.76	8.61	6.44	–	3.04	9.47
J216176B	150-300 mm high.........	m	0.40	9.37	–	4.86	14.23	10.31	–	5.35	15.65

Waterproofing

Major Works 2009		Unit	Labour Hours	Labour Net	Plant Net	Materials Net	Unit Net	Labour Gross	Plant Gross	Materials Gross	Unit Price
								(Gross rates include 10% profit)			
				£	£	£	£	£	£	£	£
J30	**J30: LIQUID APPLIED TANKING AND DAMP PROOFING**										
J3011	**Membranes and compounds**										
J301103	**RIW liquid asphaltic composition; two coats on concrete surfaces:**										
J301103A	horizontal; not exceeding 150 mm wide	m	0.02	0.20	–	1.48	1.68	0.22	–	1.63	1.85
J301103B	horizontal; 150-300 mm wide	m	0.03	0.32	–	2.95	3.27	0.35	–	3.25	3.60
J301103C	horizontal; over 300 mm wide	m²	0.08	0.95	–	9.91	10.86	1.05	–	10.90	11.95
J301103D	vertical; not exceeding 150 mm high.	m	0.02	0.26	–	1.48	1.74	0.29	–	1.63	1.91
J301103E	vertical; 150-300 mm high .	m	0.03	0.38	–	2.95	3.33	0.42	–	3.25	3.66
J301103F	vertical; over 300 mm high .	m²	0.09	1.08	–	9.91	10.99	1.19	–	10.90	12.09
J301104	**RIW liquid asphaltic composition; three coats on masonry surfaces:**										
J301104A	vertical; not exceeding 150 mm high.	m	0.03	0.31	–	1.42	1.73	0.34	–	1.56	1.90
J301104B	vertical; 150-300 mm high .	m	0.04	0.45	–	2.83	3.28	0.50	–	3.11	3.61
J301104C	vertical; over 300 mm high .	m²	0.10	1.27	–	9.38	10.65	1.40	–	10.32	11.72
J301105	**Synthaprufe waterproofing compound; two coats on concrete surfaces; final coat dusted with sharp sand:**										
J301105A	horizontal; not exceeding 150 mm wide	m	0.02	0.23	–	0.91	1.14	0.25	–	1.00	1.25
J301105B	horizontal; 150-300 mm wide	m	0.03	0.36	–	1.82	2.18	0.40	–	2.00	2.40
J301105C	horizontal; over 300 mm wide	m²	0.09	1.12	–	6.10	7.22	1.23	–	6.71	7.94
J301105D	vertical; not exceeding 150 mm high	m	0.02	0.29	–	0.91	1.20	0.32	–	1.00	1.32
J301105E	vertical; 150-300 mm high .	m	0.03	0.42	–	1.82	2.24	0.46	–	2.00	2.46
J301105F	vertical; over 300 mm high .	m²	0.10	1.25	–	6.10	7.35	1.38	–	6.71	8.09
J301106	**Synthaprufe waterproofing compound; three coats on concrete surfaces; final coat dusted with sharp sand:**										
J301106A	horizontal; not exceeding 150 mm wide	m	0.03	0.33	–	1.37	1.70	0.36	–	1.51	1.87
J301106B	horizontal; 150-300 mm wide	m	0.04	0.46	–	2.75	3.21	0.51	–	3.03	3.53
J301106C	horizontal; over 300 mm wide	m²	0.11	1.40	–	9.10	10.50	1.54	–	10.01	11.55
J301106D	vertical; not exceeding 150 mm high.	m	0.03	0.36	–	1.37	1.73	0.40	–	1.51	1.90
J301106E	vertical; 150-300 mm high .	m	0.04	0.48	–	2.75	3.23	0.53	–	3.03	3.55
J301106F	vertical; over 300 mm high .	m²	0.11	1.44	–	9.10	10.54	1.58	–	10.01	11.59
J301107	**Synthaprufe waterproofing compound; three coats on masonry surfaces; final coat dusted with sharp sand:**										
J301107A	vertical; not exceeding 150 mm high.	m	0.03	0.35	–	0.86	1.21	0.39	–	0.95	1.33
J301107B	vertical; 150-300 mm high .	m	0.04	0.49	–	1.71	2.20	0.54	–	1.88	2.42
J301107C	vertical; over 300 mm high .	m²	0.11	1.43	–	5.68	7.11	1.57	–	6.25	7.82

Major Works 2009		Unit	Labour Hours	Labour Net	Plant Net	Materials Net	Unit Net	Labour Gross	Plant Gross	Materials Gross	Unit Price
								—— (Gross rates include 10% profit) ——			
				£	£	£	£	£	£	£	£
J40	**J40: FLEXIBLE SHEET TANKING AND DAMP PROOFING**										
J4011	**Membranes**										
J401101	**1200 gauge polythene sheeting; 150 mm side and end laps:**										
J401101A	horizontal; over 300 mm wide	m²	0.04	0.51	–	1.10	1.61	0.56	–	1.21	1.77
J401101B	vertical; not exceeding 150 mm high.............	m	0.01	0.06	–	0.17	0.23	0.07	–	0.19	0.25
J401101C	vertical; 150-300 mm high .	m	0.01	0.13	–	0.33	0.46	0.14	–	0.36	0.51
J401101D	vertical; over 300 mm high .	m²	0.05	0.64	–	1.10	1.74	0.70	–	1.21	1.91
J401102	**500 gauge polythene sheeting; 150 mm side and end laps:**										
J401102A	horizontal; over 300 mm wide	m²	0.04	0.51	–	1.10	1.61	0.56	–	1.21	1.77
J401102B	vertical; not exceeding 150 mm high.............	m	0.01	0.06	–	0.17	0.23	0.07	–	0.19	0.25
J401102C	vertical; 150-300 mm high .	m	0.01	0.13	–	0.33	0.46	0.14	–	0.36	0.51
J401102D	vertical; over 300 mm high .	m²	0.05	0.64	–	1.10	1.74	0.70	–	1.21	1.91
J401108	**Bituthene bitumen coated 1000 gauge polythene sheeting; sticking to concrete surfaces primed with bituthene primer:**										
J401108A	horizontal; not exceeding 150 mm wide	m	0.02	0.19	–	1.70	1.89	0.21	–	1.87	2.08
J401108B	horizontal; 150-300 mm wide	m	0.03	0.39	–	3.48	3.87	0.43	–	3.83	4.26
J401108C	horizontal; over 300 mm wide	m²	0.10	1.27	–	11.56	12.83	1.40	–	12.72	14.11
J401108D	vertical; not exceeding 150 mm high.............	m	0.02	0.24	–	1.77	2.01	0.26	–	1.95	2.21
J401108E	vertical; 150-300 mm high .	m	0.04	0.48	–	3.67	4.15	0.53	–	4.04	4.57
J401108F	vertical; over 300 mm high .	m²	0.13	1.59	–	12.11	13.70	1.75	–	13.32	15.07
J401109	**Bituthene bitumen coated 1000 gauge polythene sheeting; sticking to masonry surfaces primed with bituthene primer:**										
J401109A	horizontal; not exceeding 150 mm wide	m	0.02	0.19	–	1.77	1.96	0.21	–	1.95	2.16
J401109B	horizontal; 150-300 mm wide	m	0.03	0.38	–	3.67	4.05	0.42	–	4.04	4.46
J401109C	horizontal; over 300 mm wide	m²	0.10	1.27	–	12.11	13.38	1.40	–	13.32	14.72
J401109D	vertical; not exceeding 150 mm high.............	m	0.02	0.24	–	1.70	1.94	0.26	–	1.87	2.13
J401109E	vertical; 150-300 mm high .	m	0.04	0.49	–	3.48	3.97	0.54	–	3.83	4.37
J401109F	vertical; over 300 mm high .	m²	0.13	1.59	–	11.56	13.15	1.75	–	12.72	14.47

Waterproofing

Major Works 2009		Unit	Labour Hours	Labour Net	Plant Net	Materials Net	Unit Net	Labour Gross	Plant Gross	Materials Gross	Unit Price
								(Gross rates include 10% profit)			
				£	£	£	£	£	£	£	£
J40	**J40: FLEXIBLE SHEET TANKING AND DAMP PROOFING**										
J4011	**Membranes**										
J401110	**Bituthene bitumen coated 500 gauge polythene sheeting; sticking to concrete surfaces primed with bituthene primer:**										
J401110A	horizontal; not exceeding 150 mm wide	m	0.02	0.26	–	1.46	1.72	0.29	–	1.61	1.89
J401110B	horizontal; 150-300 mm wide	m	0.03	0.35	–	3.00	3.35	0.39	–	3.30	3.69
J401110C	horizontal; over 300 mm wide	m²	0.09	1.14	–	9.98	11.12	1.25	–	10.98	12.23
J401110D	vertical; not exceeding 150 mm high............	m	0.02	0.23	–	1.54	1.77	0.25	–	1.69	1.95
J401110E	vertical; 150-300 mm high .	m	0.04	0.44	–	3.19	3.63	0.48	–	3.51	3.99
J401110F	vertical; over 300 mm high .	m²	0.12	1.46	–	10.52	11.98	1.61	–	11.57	13.18
J401111	**Bituthene bitumen coated 500 gauge polythene sheeting; sticking to masonry surfaces primed with bituthene primer:**										
J401111A	horizontal; not exceeding 150 mm wide	m	0.02	0.25	–	1.54	1.79	0.28	–	1.69	1.97
J401111B	horizontal; 150-300 mm wide	m	0.03	0.34	–	3.19	3.53	0.37	–	3.51	3.88
J401111C	horizontal; over 300 mm wide	m²	0.09	1.15	–	10.52	11.67	1.27	–	11.57	12.84
J401111D	vertical; not exceeding 150 mm high............	m	0.02	0.23	–	1.46	1.69	0.25	–	1.61	1.86
J401111E	vertical; 150-300 mm high .	m	0.04	0.45	–	3.00	3.45	0.50	–	3.30	3.80
J401111F	vertical; over 300 mm high .	m²	0.12	1.46	–	9.98	11.44	1.61	–	10.98	12.58
J401112	**Waterproof building paper; BS 1521:**										
J401112A	horizontal; over 300 mm wide	m²	0.03	0.42	–	1.36	1.78	0.46	–	1.50	1.96
J401112B	vertical; over 300 mm high; fixing with staples........	m²	0.04	0.64	–	1.36	2.00	0.70	–	1.50	2.20

Waterproofing

Major Works 2009		Unit	Labour Hours	Labour Net	Plant Net	Materials Net	Unit Net	Labour Gross	Plant Gross	Materials Gross	Unit Price
				£	£	£	£	£	£	£	£
								(Gross rates include 10% profit)			
J40	J40: FLEXIBLE SHEET TANKING AND DAMP PROOFING										
J4011	Membranes										
J401113	Hyload pitch polymer d.p.c.; horizontal:										
J401113A	not exceeding 150 mm wide	m	0.03	0.83	–	2.04	2.87	0.91	–	2.24	3.16
J401113B	150-300 mm wide	m	0.05	1.25	–	4.09	5.34	1.38	–	4.50	5.87
J401113C	over 300 mm wide	m²	0.15	3.77	–	13.41	17.18	4.15	–	14.75	18.90
J401114	Hyload pitch polymer d.p.c.; forming cavity trays:										
J401114D	over 300 mm girth	m²	0.33	8.29	–	13.41	21.70	9.12	–	14.75	23.87
J401115	Hyload pitch polymer d.p.c.; vertical:										
J401115E	not exceeding 150 mm high	m	0.05	1.26	–	2.04	3.30	1.39	–	2.24	3.63
J401115F	150-300 mm high	m	0.09	2.26	–	4.09	6.35	2.49	–	4.50	6.99
J401115G	over 300 mm high	m²	0.25	6.28	–	13.41	19.69	6.91	–	14.75	21.66
J4016	Newtonite lathing to concrete or masonry backgrounds										
J401651	To walls, returns, reveals of openings or recesses, attached and unattached columns:										
J401651A	lathing	m²	0.12	2.81	–	11.57	14.38	3.09	–	12.73	15.82

Waterproofing

Major Works 2009		Unit	Labour Hours	Labour Net	Plant Net	Materials Net	Unit Net	Labour Gross	Plant Gross	Materials Gross	Unit Price
								(Gross rates include 10% profit)			
				£	£	£	£	£	£	£	£
J41	**J41: BUILT UP FELT ROOF COVERINGS**										
J4121	**Flat coverings**										
J412102	**Built up bituminous felt roofing; BS 747; bedding in hot bitumen; laying on timber or screeded backings:**										
J412102A	Type 1B; one layer	m²	0.15	3.51	0.35	3.68	7.54	3.86	0.39	4.05	8.29
J412102B	Type 1B; two layers	m²	0.28	6.56	0.35	6.11	13.02	7.22	0.39	6.72	14.32
J412102C	Type 1B; three layers	m²	0.40	9.37	0.70	9.79	19.86	10.31	0.77	10.77	21.85
J412102D	Type 2B; one layer	m²	0.16	3.75	0.35	6.05	10.15	4.13	0.39	6.66	11.17
J412102E	Type 2B; two layers	m²	0.29	6.80	0.35	10.86	18.01	7.48	0.39	11.95	19.81
J412102F	Type 2B; three layers	m²	0.41	9.61	0.70	16.91	27.22	10.57	0.77	18.60	29.94
J412102G	Type 3B; one layer	m²	0.17	3.99	0.35	7.32	11.66	4.39	0.39	8.05	12.83
J412102H	Type 3B; two layers	m²	0.30	7.03	0.35	13.41	20.79	7.73	0.39	14.75	22.87
J412102I	Type 3B; three layers	m²	0.42	9.84	0.70	20.73	31.27	10.82	0.77	22.80	34.40
J412102J	Type 1E; one layer	m²	0.20	4.69	0.35	4.47	9.51	5.16	0.39	4.92	10.46
J412102K	Type 2E; one layer	m²	0.21	4.92	0.35	6.83	12.10	5.41	0.39	7.51	13.31
J412102L	Type 3E; one layer	m²	0.22	5.16	0.35	8.44	13.95	5.68	0.39	9.28	15.35
J412102M	Limestone chippings in cold gritting compound; 6 mm thick	m²	0.17	3.99	–	2.76	6.75	4.39	–	3.04	7.43
J412102N	Limestone chippings in cold gritting compound; 13 mm thick	m²	0.22	5.16	–	4.13	9.29	5.68	–	4.54	10.22
J4131	**Sloping coverings**										
J413121	**Built up bituminous felt roofing; BS 747; bedding in hot bitumen; laying on timber or screeded backings:**										
J413121A	Type 1B; one layer	m²	0.20	4.68	0.35	3.68	8.71	5.15	0.39	4.05	9.58
J413121B	Type 1B; two layers	m²	0.37	8.67	0.35	6.11	15.13	9.54	0.39	6.72	16.64
J413121C	Type 1B; three layers	m²	0.53	12.42	0.70	9.79	22.91	13.66	0.77	10.77	25.20
J413121D	Type 2B; one layer	m²	0.21	4.92	0.35	6.05	11.32	5.41	0.39	6.66	12.45
J413121E	Type 2B; two layers	m²	0.39	9.14	0.35	10.86	20.35	10.05	0.39	11.95	22.39
J413121F	Type 2B; three layers	m²	0.55	12.90	0.70	16.91	30.51	14.19	0.77	18.60	33.56
J413121G	Type 3B; one layer	m²	0.23	5.39	0.35	7.32	13.06	5.93	0.39	8.05	14.37
J413121H	Type 3B; two layers	m²	0.40	9.37	0.35	13.41	23.13	10.31	0.39	14.75	25.44
J413121I	Type 3B; three layers	m²	0.56	13.13	0.70	20.73	34.56	14.44	0.77	22.80	38.02
J413121J	Type 1E; one layer	m²	0.27	6.33	0.35	4.47	11.15	6.96	0.39	4.92	12.27
J413121K	Type 2E; one layer	m²	0.28	6.56	0.35	6.87	13.78	7.22	0.39	7.56	15.16
J413121L	Type 3E; one layer	m²	0.29	6.80	0.70	8.47	15.97	7.48	0.77	9.32	17.57
J4141	**Vertical coverings**										
J414151	**Built up bituminous felt roofing; BS 747; bedding in hot bitumen; laying on timber or screeded backings:**										
J414151A	Type 1B; one layer	m²	0.25	5.86	0.35	3.68	9.89	6.45	0.39	4.05	10.88
J414151B	Type 1B; two layers	m²	0.46	10.78	0.35	6.11	17.24	11.86	0.39	6.72	18.96
J414151C	Type 1B; three layers	m²	0.66	15.47	0.70	9.79	25.96	17.02	0.77	10.77	28.56
J414151D	Type 2B; one layer	m²	0.26	6.10	0.35	6.05	12.50	6.71	0.39	6.66	13.75
J414151E	Type 2B; two layers	m²	0.49	11.49	0.35	10.86	22.70	12.64	0.39	11.95	24.97
J414151F	Type 2B; three layers	m²	0.69	16.18	0.70	16.91	33.79	17.80	0.77	18.60	37.17
J414151G	Type 3B; one layer	m²	0.29	6.80	0.35	7.32	14.47	7.48	0.39	8.05	15.92
J414151H	Type 3B; two layers	m²	0.50	11.72	0.35	13.41	25.48	12.89	0.39	14.75	28.03
J414151I	Type 3B; three layers	m²	0.70	16.41	0.70	20.73	37.84	18.05	0.77	22.80	41.62
J414151J	Type 1E; one layer	m²	0.34	7.97	0.35	4.47	12.79	8.77	0.39	4.92	14.07
J414151K	Type 2E; one layer	m²	0.35	8.21	0.35	6.83	15.39	9.03	0.39	7.51	16.93
J414151L	Type 3E; one layer	m²	0.36	8.44	0.70	8.44	17.58	9.28	0.77	9.28	19.34

Waterproofing

Major Works 2009		Unit	Labour Hours	Labour Net	Plant Net	Materials Net	Unit Net	Labour Gross	Plant Gross	Materials Gross	Unit Price
								(Gross rates include 10% profit)			
				£	£	£	£	£	£	£	£
J41	**J41: BUILT UP FELT ROOF COVERINGS**										
J4161	**Skirtings, upstands, downstands or the like**										
J416171	**Mineral surfaced bituminous felt skirtings, upstands or downstands; BS 747; bedding in hot bitumen on timber, screeded or masonry backings:**										
J416171A	Type 1E plain skirting; not exceeding 150 mm high ...	m	0.10	2.35	0.14	0.67	3.16	2.59	0.15	0.74	3.48
J416171B	Type 1E plain skirting; 150-300 mm high.............	m	0.15	3.51	0.21	1.35	5.07	3.86	0.23	1.49	5.58
J416171C	Type 1E upstand; working over fillet and into groove; not exceeding 150 m girth	m	0.17	3.99	0.14	0.89	5.02	4.39	0.15	0.98	5.52
J416171D	Type 1E upstand; working over fillet and into groove; 150-300 mm girth	m	0.22	5.15	0.21	1.57	6.93	5.67	0.23	1.73	7.62
J416171E	Type 1E downstand; working over fillets and with welted drip; not exceeding 150 mm girth	m	0.25	5.86	0.21	1.18	7.25	6.45	0.23	1.30	7.98
J416171F	Type 1E downstand; working over fillets and with welted drip; 150-300 mm girth	m	0.35	8.20	0.28	1.86	10.34	9.02	0.31	2.05	11.37
J416171G	Type 2E plain skirting; not exceeding 150 mm high ...	m	0.10	2.34	0.14	1.03	3.51	2.57	0.15	1.13	3.86
J416171H	Type 2E plain skirting; 150-300 mm high.............	m	0.15	3.52	0.21	2.05	5.78	3.87	0.23	2.26	6.36
J416171I	Type 2E upstand; working over fillet and into groove; not exceeding 150 m girth	m	0.18	4.22	0.14	1.37	5.73	4.64	0.15	1.51	6.30
J416171J	Type 2E upstand; working over fillet and into groove; 150-300 mm girth	m	0.23	5.39	0.21	2.39	7.99	5.93	0.23	2.63	8.79
J416171K	Type 2E downstand; working over fillets and with welted drip; not exceeding 150 mm girth	m	0.26	6.09	0.21	1.78	8.08	6.70	0.23	1.96	8.89
J416171L	Type 2E downstand; working over fillets and with welted drip; 150-300 mm girth	m	0.36	8.44	0.28	2.80	11.52	9.28	0.31	3.08	12.67
J416171M	Type 3E plain skirting; not exceeding 150 mm girth ...	m	0.11	2.58	0.14	1.27	3.99	2.84	0.15	1.40	4.39
J416171N	Type 3E plain skirting; 150-300 mm girth	m	0.16	3.75	0.21	2.54	6.50	4.13	0.23	2.79	7.15
J416171O	Type 3E upstand; working over fillet and into groove; not exceeding 150 m girth	m	0.19	4.45	0.14	1.69	6.28	4.90	0.15	1.86	6.91
J416171P	Type 3E upstand; working over fillet and into groove; 150-300 mm girth	m	0.24	5.62	0.21	2.96	8.79	6.18	0.23	3.26	9.67
J416171Q	Type 3E downstand; working over fillets and with welted drip; not exceeding 150 mm girth	m	0.27	6.33	0.21	2.18	8.72	6.96	0.23	2.40	9.59
J416171R	Type 3E downstand; working over fillets and with welted drip; 150-300 mm girth	m	0.37	8.67	0.28	3.45	12.40	9.54	0.31	3.80	13.64

Waterproofing

Major Works 2009		Unit			Specialist Net	Unit Net		Specialist Gross	Unit Price
			£	£	£	£	(Gross rates include 10% profit)	
							£ £ £	£
J42	**J42: SINGLE LAYER POLYMERIC ROOF COVERINGS**							
J4210	**Flat coverings**							
J421010	**Sarnafil membrane G410-EL; adhesive fixed to insulation board substrate (measured separately); on vapour barrier; to concrete base:**							
J421010A	horizontal; over 300 mm wide	m²	–	–	–	27.75	27.75	– – 30.53	30.53
J421010B	horizontal; not exceeding 300 mm wide	m²	–	–	–	34.67	34.67	– – 38.14	38.14

LININGS, SHEATHING
AND DRY PARTITIONING

Major Works 2009		Unit	Labour Hours	Labour Net	Plant Net	Materials Net	Unit Net	Labour Gross	Plant Gross	Materials Gross	Unit Price
								(Gross rates include 10% profit)			
				£	£	£	£	£	£	£	£
K10	**K10: PLASTERBOARD DRY LINING, PARTITIONS AND CEILINGS**										
K1001	**Proprietary partition; Gyproc metal stud partitions and walls**										
K100110	**GypWall Robust system; Gypframe 70 mm Gyproc C studs at 600 mm centres; 13 mm DuraLine each side; joints filled and taped to receive direct decoration:**										
K100110A	not exceeding 1200 mm high	m	1.66	38.91	–	20.54	59.45	42.80	–	22.59	65.40
K100110B	1200-1500 mm high	m	1.77	41.49	–	24.08	65.57	45.64	–	26.49	72.13
K100110C	1500-1800 mm high	m	1.89	44.30	–	28.23	72.53	48.73	–	31.05	79.78
K100110D	1800-2100 mm high	m	2.18	51.10	–	32.47	83.57	56.21	–	35.72	91.93
K100110E	2100-2400 mm high	m	2.49	58.36	–	36.49	94.85	64.20	–	40.14	104.34
K100110F	2400-2700 mm high	m	2.86	67.04	–	40.52	107.56	73.74	–	44.57	118.32
K100110G	2700-3000 mm high	m	3.20	75.01	–	44.67	119.68	82.51	–	49.14	131.65
K100115	**Glasroc FireWall system; Gypframe 92 mm Gyproc I studs at 600 mm centres; 15 mm FireLine board outer layer over 25 mm Glasroc board inner layer; 40 mm and 50 mm Rock mineral wool batts to void; joints filled and taped to receive direct decoration:**										
K100115A	not exceeding 1200 mm high	m	3.13	73.37	–	88.93	162.30	80.71	–	97.82	178.53
K100115B	1200-1500 mm high	m	3.90	91.41	–	109.29	200.70	100.55	–	120.22	220.77
K100115C	1500-1800 mm high	m	4.67	109.47	–	129.79	239.26	120.42	–	142.77	263.19
K100115D	1800-2100 mm high	m	5.47	128.22	–	150.59	278.81	141.04	–	165.65	306.69
K100115E	2100-2400 mm high	m	6.24	146.27	–	171.02	317.29	160.90	–	188.12	349.02
K100115F	2400-2700 mm high	m	7.03	164.79	–	191.35	356.14	181.27	–	210.49	391.75
K100115G	2700-3000 mm high	m	7.80	182.83	–	211.64	394.47	201.11	–	232.80	433.92

Major Works 2009		Unit	Labour Hours	Labour Net	Plant Net	Materials Net	Unit Net	Labour Gross	Plant Gross	Materials Gross	Unit Price
								(Gross rates include 10% profit)			
				£	£	£	£	£	£	£	£
K10	**K10: PLASTERBOARD DRY LINING, PARTITIONS AND CEILINGS**										
K1011	**Gyproc linings; 9.5 mm wallboard to woodwork backgrounds**										
K101101	**Linings to walls:**										
K101101A	not exceeding 1200 mm high	m	0.16	3.75	–	3.38	7.13	4.13	–	3.72	7.84
K101101B	1200-1500 mm high	m	0.19	4.45	–	4.23	8.68	4.90	–	4.65	9.55
K101101C	1500-1800 mm high	m	0.22	5.06	–	5.06	10.12	5.57	–	5.57	11.13
K101101D	1800-2100 mm high	m	0.25	5.91	–	5.90	11.81	6.50	–	6.49	12.99
K101101E	2100-2400 mm high	m	0.29	6.75	–	6.75	13.50	7.43	–	7.43	14.85
K101101F	2400-2700 mm high	m	0.32	7.60	–	7.59	15.19	8.36	–	8.35	16.71
K101101G	2700-3000 mm high	m	0.36	8.44	–	8.44	16.88	9.28	–	9.28	18.57
K101111	**Linings to beams; 3 nr faces:**										
K101111A	not exceeding 600 mm girth	m	0.13	3.05	–	1.69	4.74	3.36	–	1.86	5.21
K101111B	600-1200 mm girth	m	0.25	5.86	–	3.38	9.24	6.45	–	3.72	10.16
K101111C	1200-1800 mm girth	m	0.38	8.91	–	5.07	13.98	9.80	–	5.58	15.38
K101121	**Linings to columns; 4 nr faces:**										
K101121A	not exceeding 600 mm girth	m	0.12	2.81	–	1.69	4.50	3.09	–	1.86	4.95
K101121B	600-1200 mm girth	m	0.23	5.39	–	3.38	8.77	5.93	–	3.72	9.65
K101121C	1200-1800 mm girth	m	0.39	9.15	–	5.07	14.22	10.07	–	5.58	15.64
K101131	**Linings to reveals and soffits:**										
K101131A	not exceeding 300 mm wide	m	0.10	2.34	–	0.85	3.19	2.57	–	0.94	3.51
K101131B	300-600 mm wide	m	0.12	2.81	–	1.69	4.50	3.09	–	1.86	4.95
K101141	**Linings to ceilings:**										
K101141A	over 300 mm wide	m²	0.15	3.52	–	2.81	6.33	3.87	–	3.09	6.96
K101141B	over 300 mm wide; in staircase areas	m²	0.17	3.87	–	2.81	6.68	4.26	–	3.09	7.35
K1012	**Gyproc linings; 9.5 mm Duplex wallboard to woodwork backgrounds**										
K101201	**Linings to walls:**										
K101201A	not exceeding 1200 mm high	m	0.16	3.76	–	4.60	8.36	4.14	–	5.06	9.20
K101201B	1200-1500 mm high	m	0.19	4.45	–	5.76	10.21	4.90	–	6.34	11.23
K101201C	1500-1800 mm high	m	0.22	5.06	–	6.89	11.95	5.57	–	7.58	13.15
K101201D	1800-2100 mm high	m	0.25	5.91	–	8.04	13.95	6.50	–	8.84	15.35
K101201E	2100-2400 mm high	m	0.29	6.75	–	9.19	15.94	7.43	–	10.11	17.53
K101201F	2400-2700 mm high	m	0.32	7.60	–	10.34	17.94	8.36	–	11.37	19.73
K101201G	2700-3000 mm high	m	0.36	8.44	–	11.49	19.93	9.28	–	12.64	21.92
K101211	**Linings to beams; 3 nr faces:**										
K101211A	not exceeding 600 mm girth	m	0.13	3.05	–	2.30	5.35	3.36	–	2.53	5.89
K101211B	600-1200 mm girth	m	0.25	5.86	–	4.60	10.46	6.45	–	5.06	11.51
K101211C	1200-1800 mm girth	m	0.38	8.90	–	6.91	15.81	9.79	–	7.60	17.39
K101221	**Linings to columns; 4 nr faces:**										
K101221A	not exceeding 600 mm girth	m	0.12	2.82	–	2.30	5.12	3.10	–	2.53	5.63
K101221B	600-1200 mm girth	m	0.23	5.40	–	4.60	10.00	5.94	–	5.06	11.00
K101221C	1200-1800 mm girth	m	0.39	9.14	–	6.91	16.05	10.05	–	7.60	17.66
K101231	**Linings to reveals and soffits:**										
K101231A	not exceeding 300 mm wide	m	0.10	2.35	–	1.15	3.50	2.59	–	1.27	3.85
K101231B	300-600 mm wide	m	0.12	2.82	–	2.30	5.12	3.10	–	2.53	5.63
K101241	**Linings to ceilings:**										
K101241A	over 300 mm wide	m²	0.15	3.52	–	3.83	7.35	3.87	–	4.21	8.09
K101241B	over 300 mm wide; in staircase areas	m²	0.17	3.87	–	3.83	7.70	4.26	–	4.21	8.47

Major Works 2009		Unit	Labour Hours	Labour Net	Plant Net	Materials Net	Unit Net	Labour Gross	Plant Gross	Materials Gross	Unit Price
								(Gross rates include 10% profit)			
				£	£	£	£	£	£	£	£
K10	**K10: PLASTERBOARD DRY LINING, PARTITIONS AND CEILINGS**										
K1013	**Gyproc linings; 9.5 mm plaster lath to woodwork backgrounds**										
K101301	**Linings to walls:**										
K101301A	not exceeding 1200 mm high	m	0.16	3.75	–	3.53	7.28	4.13	–	3.88	8.01
K101301B	1200-1500 mm high	m	0.19	4.45	–	4.42	8.87	4.90	–	4.86	9.76
K101301C	1500-1800 mm high	m	0.22	5.07	–	5.28	10.35	5.58	–	5.81	11.39
K101301D	1800-2100 mm high	m	0.25	5.90	–	6.17	12.07	6.49	–	6.79	13.28
K101301E	2100-2400 mm high	m	0.29	6.75	–	7.05	13.80	7.43	–	7.76	15.18
K101301F	2400-2700 mm high	m	0.32	7.60	–	7.93	15.53	8.36	–	8.72	17.08
K101301G	2700-3000 mm high	m	0.36	8.44	–	8.82	17.26	9.28	–	9.70	18.99
K101311	**Linings to beams; 3 nr faces:**										
K101311A	not exceeding 600 mm girth	m	0.13	3.04	–	1.77	4.81	3.34	–	1.95	5.29
K101311B	600-1200 mm girth	m	0.25	5.86	–	3.53	9.39	6.45	–	3.88	10.33
K101311C	1200-1800 mm girth	m	0.38	8.91	–	5.30	14.21	9.80	–	5.83	15.63
K101321	**Linings to columns; 4 nr faces:**										
K101321A	not exceeding 600 mm girth	m	0.12	2.81	–	1.77	4.58	3.09	–	1.95	5.04
K101321B	600-1200 mm girth	m	0.23	5.40	–	3.53	8.93	5.94	–	3.88	9.82
K101321C	1200-1800 mm girth	m	0.39	9.14	–	5.30	14.44	10.05	–	5.83	15.88
K101331	**Linings to reveals and soffits:**										
K101331A	not exceeding 300 mm wide	m	0.10	2.35	–	0.88	3.23	2.59	–	0.97	3.55
K101331B	300-600 mm wide	m	0.12	2.81	–	1.77	4.58	3.09	–	1.95	5.04
K101341	**Linings to ceilings:**										
K101341A	over 300 mm wide	m²	0.15	3.52	–	2.94	6.46	3.87	–	3.23	7.11
K101341B	over 300 mm wide; in staircase areas	m²	0.17	3.87	–	2.94	6.81	4.26	–	3.23	7.49

Linings, Sheathing and Dry Partitioning

Major Works 2009		Unit	Labour Hours	Labour Net	Plant Net	Materials Net	Unit Net	Labour Gross	Plant Gross	Materials Gross	Unit Price
								(Gross rates include 10% profit)			
				£	£	£	£	£	£	£	£
K10	**K10: PLASTERBOARD DRY LINING, PARTITIONS AND CEILINGS**										
K1014	**Gyproc linings; 12.5 mm wallboard to woodwork backgrounds**										
K101401	**Linings to walls:**										
K101401A	not exceeding 1200 mm high	m	0.19	4.38	–	4.03	8.41	4.82	–	4.43	9.25
K101401B	1200-1500 mm high	m	0.22	5.21	–	5.03	10.24	5.73	–	5.53	11.26
K101401C	1500-1800 mm high	m	0.25	5.91	–	6.02	11.93	6.50	–	6.62	13.12
K101401D	1800-2100 mm high	m	0.29	6.89	–	7.03	13.92	7.58	–	7.73	15.31
K101401E	2100-2400 mm high	m	0.34	7.88	–	8.03	15.91	8.67	–	8.83	17.50
K101401F	2400-2700 mm high	m	0.38	8.86	–	9.04	17.90	9.75	–	9.94	19.69
K101401G	2700-3000 mm high	m	0.42	9.84	–	10.05	19.89	10.82	–	11.06	21.88
K101411	**Linings to beams; 3 nr faces:**										
K101411A	not exceeding 600 mm girth	m	0.15	3.57	–	2.01	5.58	3.93	–	2.21	6.14
K101411B	600-1200 mm girth	m	0.29	6.84	–	4.03	10.87	7.52	–	4.43	11.96
K101411C	1200-1800 mm girth	m	0.44	10.38	–	6.04	16.42	11.42	–	6.64	18.06
K101421	**Linings to columns; 4 nr faces:**										
K101421A	not exceeding 600 mm girth	m	0.14	3.28	–	2.01	5.29	3.61	–	2.21	5.82
K101421B	600-1200 mm girth	m	0.27	6.28	–	4.03	10.31	6.91	–	4.43	11.34
K101421C	1200-1800 mm girth	m	0.46	10.66	–	6.04	16.70	11.73	–	6.64	18.37
K101431	**Linings to reveals and soffits:**										
K101431A	not exceeding 300 mm wide	m	0.12	2.74	–	1.01	3.75	3.01	–	1.11	4.13
K101431B	300-600 mm wide	m	0.14	3.28	–	2.01	5.29	3.61	–	2.21	5.82
K101441	**Linings to ceilings:**										
K101441A	over 300 mm wide	m²	0.17	3.98	–	3.35	7.33	4.38	–	3.69	8.06
K101441B	over 300 mm wide; in staircase areas	m²	0.19	4.38	–	3.35	7.73	4.82	–	3.69	8.50

Major Works 2009		Unit	Labour Hours	Labour Net	Plant Net	Materials Net	Unit Net	Labour Gross	Plant Gross	Materials Gross	Unit Price
								—	(Gross rates include 10% profit)	—	
				£	£	£	£	£	£	£	£
K10	**K10: PLASTERBOARD DRY LINING, PARTITIONS AND CEILINGS**										
K1015	**Gyproc linings; 12.5 mm Duplex wallboard to woodwork backgrounds**										
K101501	**Linings to walls:**										
K101501A	not exceeding 1200 mm high	m	0.19	4.38	–	5.26	9.64	4.82	–	5.79	10.60
K101501B	1200-1500 mm high	m	0.22	5.21	–	6.58	11.79	5.73	–	7.24	12.97
K101501C	1500-1800 mm high	m	0.25	5.91	–	7.87	13.78	6.50	–	8.66	15.16
K101501D	1800-2100 mm high	m	0.29	6.89	–	9.19	16.08	7.58	–	10.11	17.69
K101501E	2100-2400 mm high	m	0.34	7.88	–	10.50	18.38	8.67	–	11.55	20.22
K101501F	2400-2700 mm high	m	0.38	8.86	–	11.82	20.68	9.75	–	13.00	22.75
K101501G	2700-3000 mm high	m	0.42	9.85	–	13.13	22.98	10.84	–	14.44	25.28
K101511	**Linings to beams; 3 nr faces:**										
K101511A	not exceeding 600 mm girth	m	0.15	3.56	–	2.63	6.19	3.92	–	2.89	6.81
K101511B	600-1200 mm girth	m	0.29	6.84	–	5.26	12.10	7.52	–	5.79	13.31
K101511C	1200-1800 mm girth	m	0.44	10.38	–	7.89	18.27	11.42	–	8.68	20.10
K101521	**Linings to columns; 4 nr faces:**										
K101521A	not exceeding 600 mm girth	m	0.14	3.28	–	2.63	5.91	3.61	–	2.89	6.50
K101521B	600-1200 mm girth	m	0.27	6.28	–	5.26	11.54	6.91	–	5.79	12.69
K101521C	1200-1800 mm girth	m	0.46	10.67	–	7.89	18.56	11.74	–	8.68	20.42
K101531	**Linings to reveals and soffits:**										
K101531A	not exceeding 300 mm wide	m	0.12	2.75	–	1.32	4.07	3.03	–	1.45	4.48
K101531B	300-600 mm wide	m	0.14	3.28	–	2.63	5.91	3.61	–	2.89	6.50
K101541	**Linings to ceilings:**										
K101541A	over 300 mm wide	m²	0.17	3.98	–	4.38	8.36	4.38	–	4.82	9.20
K101541B	over 300 mm wide; in staircase areas	m²	0.19	4.38	–	4.38	8.76	4.82	–	4.82	9.64

Linings, Sheathing and Dry Partitioning

Major Works 2009		Unit	Labour Hours	Labour Net	Plant Net	Materials Net	Unit Net	Labour Gross	Plant Gross	Materials Gross	Unit Price
								(Gross rates include 10% profit)			
				£	£	£	£	£	£	£	£
K10	**K10: PLASTERBOARD DRY LINING, PARTITIONS AND CEILINGS**										
K1016	**Gyproc linings; 12.5 mm plaster lath to woodwork backgrounds**										
K101601	**Linings to walls:**										
K101601A	not exceeding 1200 mm high	m	0.19	4.38	–	4.28	8.66	4.82	–	4.71	9.53
K101601B	1200-1500 mm high	m	0.22	5.20	–	5.35	10.55	5.72	–	5.89	11.61
K101601C	1500-1800 mm high	m	0.25	5.91	–	6.40	12.31	6.50	–	7.04	13.54
K101601D	1800-2100 mm high	m	0.29	6.89	–	7.47	14.36	7.58	–	8.22	15.80
K101601E	2100-2400 mm high	m	0.34	7.87	–	8.54	16.41	8.66	–	9.39	18.05
K101601F	2400-2700 mm high	m	0.38	8.86	–	9.61	18.47	9.75	–	10.57	20.32
K101601G	2700-3000 mm high	m	0.42	9.84	–	10.68	20.52	10.82	–	11.75	22.57
K101611	**Linings to beams; 3 nr faces:**										
K101611A	not exceeding 600 mm girth	m	0.15	3.56	–	2.14	5.70	3.92	–	2.35	6.27
K101611B	600-1200 mm girth	m	0.29	6.84	–	4.28	11.12	7.52	–	4.71	12.23
K101611C	1200-1800 mm girth	m	0.44	10.38	–	6.42	16.80	11.42	–	7.06	18.48
K101621	**Linings to columns; 4 nr faces:**										
K101621A	not exceeding 600 mm girth	m	0.14	3.28	–	2.14	5.42	3.61	–	2.35	5.96
K101621B	600-1200 mm girth	m	0.27	6.28	–	4.28	10.56	6.91	–	4.71	11.62
K101621C	1200-1800 mm girth	m	0.46	10.66	–	6.42	17.08	11.73	–	7.06	18.79
K101631	**Linings to reveals and soffits:**										
K101631A	not exceeding 300 mm wide	m	0.12	2.74	–	1.07	3.81	3.01	–	1.18	4.19
K101631B	300-600 mm wide	m	0.14	3.28	–	2.14	5.42	3.61	–	2.35	5.96
K101641	**Linings to ceilings:**										
K101641A	over 300 mm wide	m²	0.17	3.98	–	3.56	7.54	4.38	–	3.92	8.29
K101641B	over 300 mm wide; in staircase areas	m²	0.19	4.38	–	3.56	7.94	4.82	–	3.92	8.73

Major Works 2009		Unit	Labour Hours	Labour Net	Plant Net	Materials Net	Unit Net	Labour Gross	Plant Gross	Materials Gross	Unit Price
									(Gross rates include 10% profit)		
				£	£	£	£	£	£	£	£
K10	**K10: PLASTERBOARD DRY LINING, PARTITIONS AND CEILINGS**										
K1017	**Gyproc linings; 12.5 mm Fireline board to woodwork backgrounds**										
K101701	**Linings to walls:**										
K101701A	not exceeding 1200 mm high	m	0.19	4.38	–	5.93	10.31	4.82	–	6.52	11.34
K101701B	1200-1500 mm high	m	0.22	5.20	–	7.41	12.61	5.72	–	8.15	13.87
K101701C	1500-1800 mm high	m	0.25	5.91	–	8.87	14.78	6.50	–	9.76	16.26
K101701D	1800-2100 mm high	m	0.29	6.89	–	10.36	17.25	7.58	–	11.40	18.98
K101701E	2100-2400 mm high	m	0.34	7.87	–	11.84	19.71	8.66	–	13.02	21.68
K101701F	2400-2700 mm high	m	0.38	8.86	–	13.32	22.18	9.75	–	14.65	24.40
K101701G	2700-3000 mm high	m	0.42	9.85	–	14.80	24.65	10.84	–	16.28	27.12
K101711	**Linings to beams; 3 nr faces:**										
K101711A	not exceeding 600 mm girth	m	0.15	3.57	–	2.96	6.53	3.93	–	3.26	7.18
K101711B	600-1200 mm girth	m	0.29	6.84	–	5.93	12.77	7.52	–	6.52	14.05
K101711C	1200-1800 mm girth	m	0.44	10.39	–	8.89	19.28	11.43	–	9.78	21.21
K101721	**Linings to columns; 4 nr faces:**										
K101721A	not exceeding 600 mm girth	m	0.14	3.29	–	2.96	6.25	3.62	–	3.26	6.88
K101721B	600-1200 mm girth	m	0.27	6.28	–	5.93	12.21	6.91	–	6.52	13.43
K101721C	1200-1800 mm girth	m	0.46	10.67	–	8.89	19.56	11.74	–	9.78	21.52
K101731	**Linings to reveals and soffits:**										
K101731A	not exceeding 300 mm wide	m	0.12	2.74	–	1.48	4.22	3.01	–	1.63	4.64
K101731B	300-600 mm wide	m	0.14	3.29	–	2.96	6.25	3.62	–	3.26	6.88
K101741	**Linings to ceilings:**										
K101741A	over 300 mm wide	m²	0.17	3.99	–	4.93	8.92	4.39	–	5.42	9.81
K101741B	over 300 mm wide; in staircase areas	m²	0.19	4.39	–	4.93	9.32	4.83	–	5.42	10.25

Linings, Sheathing and Dry Partitioning

Major Works 2009		Unit	Labour Hours	Labour Net	Plant Net	Materials Net	Unit Net	Labour Gross	Plant Gross	Materials Gross	Unit Price
								(Gross rates include 10% profit)			
				£	£	£	£	£	£	£	£
K10	**K10: PLASTERBOARD DRY LINING, PARTITIONS AND CEILINGS**										
K1021	**Gyproc linings; 9.5 mm tapered edge wallboard to woodwork backgrounds**										
K102101	**Linings to walls:**										
K102101A	not exceeding 1200 mm high	m	0.16	3.75	–	3.72	7.47	4.13	–	4.09	8.22
K102101B	1200-1500 mm high	m	0.19	4.45	–	4.66	9.11	4.90	–	5.13	10.02
K102101C	1500-1800 mm high	m	0.22	5.06	–	5.58	10.64	5.57	–	6.14	11.70
K102101D	1800-2100 mm high	m	0.25	5.91	–	6.44	12.35	6.50	–	7.08	13.59
K102101E	2100-2400 mm high	m	0.29	6.75	–	7.43	14.18	7.43	–	8.17	15.60
K102101F	2400-2700 mm high	m	0.32	7.60	–	8.37	15.97	8.36	–	9.21	17.57
K102101G	2700-3000 mm high	m	0.36	8.44	–	9.30	17.74	9.28	–	10.23	19.51
K102111	**Linings to beams; 3 nr faces:**										
K102111A	not exceeding 600 mm girth	m	0.13	3.04	–	1.87	4.91	3.34	–	2.06	5.40
K102111B	600-1200 mm girth	m	0.25	5.86	–	3.72	9.58	6.45	–	4.09	10.54
K102111C	1200-1800 mm girth	m	0.38	8.91	–	5.58	14.49	9.80	–	6.14	15.94
K102121	**Linings to columns; 4 nr faces:**										
K102121A	not exceeding 600 mm girth	m	0.12	2.81	–	1.87	4.68	3.09	–	2.06	5.15
K102121B	600-1200 mm girth	m	0.23	5.39	–	3.72	9.11	5.93	–	4.09	10.02
K102121C	1200-1800 mm girth	m	0.39	9.14	–	5.58	14.72	10.05	–	6.14	16.19
K102131	**Linings to reveals and soffits:**										
K102131A	not exceeding 300 mm wide	m	0.10	2.35	–	0.92	3.27	2.59	–	1.01	3.60
K102131B	300-600 mm wide	m	0.12	2.81	–	1.87	4.68	3.09	–	2.06	5.15
K102141	**Linings to ceilings:**										
K102141A	over 300 mm wide	m²	0.15	3.52	–	3.08	6.60	3.87	–	3.39	7.26
K102141B	over 300 mm wide; in staircase areas	m²	0.17	3.87	–	3.08	6.95	4.26	–	3.39	7.65

Major Works 2009		Unit	Labour Hours	Labour Net	Plant Net	Materials Net	Unit Net	Labour Gross	Plant Gross	Materials Gross	Unit Price
								— (Gross rates include 10% profit) —			
				£	£	£	£	£	£	£	£
K10	**K10: PLASTERBOARD DRY LINING, PARTITIONS AND CEILINGS**										
K1022	**Gyproc linings; 9.5 mm tapered edge Duplex wallboard to woodwork backgrounds**										
K102201	**Linings to walls:**										
K102201A	not exceeding 1200 mm high	m	0.16	3.75	–	4.94	8.69	4.13	–	5.43	9.56
K102201B	1200-1500 mm high	m	0.19	4.46	–	6.18	10.64	4.91	–	6.80	11.70
K102201C	1500-1800 mm high	m	0.22	5.07	–	7.41	12.48	5.58	–	8.15	13.73
K102201D	1800-2100 mm high	m	0.25	5.91	–	8.58	14.49	6.50	–	9.44	15.94
K102201E	2100-2400 mm high	m	0.29	6.75	–	9.88	16.63	7.43	–	10.87	18.29
K102201F	2400-2700 mm high	m	0.32	7.60	–	11.12	18.72	8.36	–	12.23	20.59
K102201G	2700-3000 mm high	m	0.36	8.44	–	12.35	20.79	9.28	–	13.59	22.87
K102211	**Linings to beams; 3 nr faces:**										
K102211A	not exceeding 600 mm girth	m	0.13	3.04	–	2.48	5.52	3.34	–	2.73	6.07
K102211B	600-1200 mm girth	m	0.25	5.86	–	4.94	10.80	6.45	–	5.43	11.88
K102211C	1200-1800 mm girth	m	0.38	8.91	–	7.41	16.32	9.80	–	8.15	17.95
K102221	**Linings to columns; 4 nr faces:**										
K102221A	not exceeding 600 mm girth	m	0.12	2.81	–	2.48	5.29	3.09	–	2.73	5.82
K102221B	600-1200 mm girth	m	0.23	5.39	–	4.94	10.33	5.93	–	5.43	11.36
K102221C	1200-1800 mm girth	m	0.39	9.15	–	7.41	16.56	10.07	–	8.15	18.22
K102231	**Linings to reveals and soffits:**										
K102231A	not exceeding 300 mm wide	m	0.10	2.34	–	1.23	3.57	2.57	–	1.35	3.93
K102231B	300-600 mm wide	m	0.12	2.81	–	2.48	5.29	3.09	–	2.73	5.82
K102241	**Linings to ceilings:**										
K102241A	over 300 mm wide	m²	0.15	3.52	–	4.10	7.62	3.87	–	4.51	8.38
K102241B	over 300 mm wide; in staircase areas	m²	0.17	3.87	–	4.10	7.97	4.26	–	4.51	8.77

Linings, Sheathing and Dry Partitioning

Major Works 2009		Unit	Labour Hours	Labour Net	Plant Net	Materials Net	Unit Net	Labour Gross	Plant Gross	Materials Gross	Unit Price
								(Gross rates include 10% profit)			
				£	£	£	£	£	£	£	£
K10	**K10: PLASTERBOARD DRY LINING, PARTITIONS AND CEILINGS**										
K1023	**Gyproc linings; 12.5 mm tapered edge wallboard to woodwork backgrounds**										
K102301	**Linings to walls:**										
K102301A	not exceeding 1200 mm high	m	0.19	4.38	–	4.36	8.74	4.82	–	4.80	9.61
K102301B	1200-1500 mm high	m	0.22	5.20	–	5.46	10.66	5.72	–	6.01	11.73
K102301C	1500-1800 mm high	m	0.25	5.90	–	6.55	12.45	6.49	–	7.21	13.70
K102301D	1800-2100 mm high	m	0.29	6.89	–	7.63	14.52	7.58	–	8.39	15.97
K102301E	2100-2400 mm high	m	0.34	7.87	–	8.72	16.59	8.66	–	9.59	18.25
K102301F	2400-2700 mm high	m	0.38	8.86	–	9.82	18.68	9.75	–	10.80	20.55
K102301G	2700-3000 mm high	m	0.42	9.85	–	10.90	20.75	10.84	–	11.99	22.83
K102311	**Linings to beams; 3 nr faces:**										
K102311A	not exceeding 600 mm girth	m	0.15	3.56	–	2.19	5.75	3.92	–	2.41	6.33
K102311B	600-1200 mm girth	m	0.29	6.84	–	4.36	11.20	7.52	–	4.80	12.32
K102311C	1200-1800 mm girth	m	0.44	10.38	–	6.55	16.93	11.42	–	7.21	18.62
K102321	**Linings to columns; 4 nr faces:**										
K102321A	not exceeding 600 mm girth	m	0.14	3.28	–	2.19	5.47	3.61	–	2.41	6.02
K102321B	600-1200 mm girth	m	0.27	6.28	–	4.36	10.64	6.91	–	4.80	11.70
K102321C	1200-1800 mm girth	m	0.46	10.66	–	6.55	17.21	11.73	–	7.21	18.93
K102331	**Linings to reveals and soffits:**										
K102331A	not exceeding 300 mm wide	m	0.12	2.74	–	1.09	3.83	3.01	–	1.20	4.21
K102331B	300-600 mm wide	m	0.14	3.28	–	2.19	5.47	3.61	–	2.41	6.02
K102341	**Linings to ceilings:**										
K102341A	over 300 mm wide	m²	0.17	3.98	–	3.62	7.60	4.38	–	3.98	8.36
K102341B	over 300 mm wide; in staircase areas	m²	0.19	4.38	–	3.62	8.00	4.82	–	3.98	8.80

Major Works 2009		Unit	Labour Hours	Labour Net	Plant Net	Materials Net	Unit Net	Labour Gross	Plant Gross	Materials Gross	Unit Price
								(Gross rates include 10% profit)			
				£	£	£	£	£	£	£	£
K10	**K10: PLASTERBOARD DRY LINING, PARTITIONS AND CEILINGS**										
K1024	**Gyproc linings; 12.5 mm tapered edge Duplex wallboard to woodwork backgrounds**										
K102401	**Linings to walls:**										
K102401A	not exceeding 1200 mm high	m	0.19	4.39	–	5.59	9.98	4.83	–	6.15	10.98
K102401B	1200-1500 mm high	m	0.22	5.21	–	7.00	12.21	5.73	–	7.70	13.43
K102401C	1500-1800 mm high	m	0.25	5.90	–	8.40	14.30	6.49	–	9.24	15.73
K102401D	1800-2100 mm high	m	0.29	6.89	–	9.79	16.68	7.58	–	10.77	18.35
K102401E	2100-2400 mm high	m	0.34	7.87	–	11.19	19.06	8.66	–	12.31	20.97
K102401F	2400-2700 mm high	m	0.38	8.86	–	12.60	21.46	9.75	–	13.86	23.61
K102401G	2700-3000 mm high	m	0.42	9.85	–	13.99	23.84	10.84	–	15.39	26.22
K102411	**Linings to beams; 3 nr faces:**										
K102411A	not exceeding 600 mm girth	m	0.15	3.57	–	2.80	6.37	3.93	–	3.08	7.01
K102411B	600-1200 mm girth	m	0.29	6.85	–	5.59	12.44	7.54	–	6.15	13.68
K102411C	1200-1800 mm girth	m	0.44	10.38	–	8.40	18.78	11.42	–	9.24	20.66
K102421	**Linings to columns; 4 nr faces:**										
K102421A	not exceeding 600 mm girth	m	0.14	3.29	–	2.80	6.09	3.62	–	3.08	6.70
K102421B	600-1200 mm girth	m	0.27	6.28	–	5.59	11.87	6.91	–	6.15	13.06
K102421C	1200-1800 mm girth	m	0.46	10.66	–	8.40	19.06	11.73	–	9.24	20.97
K102431	**Linings to reveals and soffits:**										
K102431A	not exceeding 300 mm wide	m	0.12	2.75	–	1.39	4.14	3.03	–	1.53	4.55
K102431B	300-600 mm wide	m	0.14	3.29	–	2.80	6.09	3.62	–	3.08	6.70
K102441	**Linings to ceilings:**										
K102441A	over 300 mm wide	m²	0.17	3.98	–	4.65	8.63	4.38	–	5.12	9.49
K102441B	over 300 mm wide; in staircase areas	m²	0.19	4.38	–	4.65	9.03	4.82	–	5.12	9.93

Major Works 2009		Unit	Labour Hours	Labour Net	Plant Net	Materials Net	Unit Net	Labour Gross	Plant Gross	Materials Gross	Unit Price
								(Gross rates include 10% profit)			
				£	£	£	£	£	£	£	£
K10	**K10: PLASTERBOARD DRY LINING, PARTITIONS AND CEILINGS**										
K1025	**Gyproc linings; 12.5 mm tapered edge Fireline wallboard to woodwork backgrounds**										
K102501	**Linings to walls:**										
K102501A	not exceeding 1200 mm high	m	0.19	4.38	–	6.35	10.73	4.82	–	6.99	11.80
K102501B	1200-1500 mm high	m	0.22	5.20	–	7.95	13.15	5.72	–	8.75	14.47
K102501C	1500-1800 mm high	m	0.25	5.91	–	9.53	15.44	6.50	–	10.48	16.98
K102501D	1800-2100 mm high	m	0.29	6.90	–	11.11	18.01	7.59	–	12.22	19.81
K102501E	2100-2400 mm high	m	0.34	7.87	–	12.70	20.57	8.66	–	13.97	22.63
K102501F	2400-2700 mm high	m	0.38	8.86	–	14.30	23.16	9.75	–	15.73	25.48
K102501G	2700-3000 mm high	m	0.42	9.85	–	15.88	25.73	10.84	–	17.47	28.30
K102511	**Linings to beams; 3 nr faces:**										
K102511A	not exceeding 600 mm girth	m	0.15	3.57	–	3.18	6.75	3.93	–	3.50	7.43
K102511B	600-1200 mm girth	m	0.29	6.84	–	6.35	13.19	7.52	–	6.99	14.51
K102511C	1200-1800 mm girth	m	0.44	10.39	–	9.53	19.92	11.43	–	10.48	21.91
K102521	**Linings to columns; 4 nr faces:**										
K102521A	not exceeding 600 mm girth	m	0.14	3.28	–	3.18	6.46	3.61	–	3.50	7.11
K102521B	600-1200 mm girth	m	0.27	6.28	–	6.35	12.63	6.91	–	6.99	13.89
K102521C	1200-1800 mm girth	m	0.46	10.67	–	9.53	20.20	11.74	–	10.48	22.22
K102531	**Linings to reveals and soffits:**										
K102531A	not exceeding 300 mm wide	m	0.12	2.75	–	1.58	4.33	3.03	–	1.74	4.76
K102531B	300-600 mm wide	m	0.14	3.28	–	3.18	6.46	3.61	–	3.50	7.11
K102541	**Linings to ceilings:**										
K102541A	over 300 mm wide	m²	0.17	3.98	–	5.28	9.26	4.38	–	5.81	10.19
K102541B	over 300 mm wide; in staircase areas	m²	0.19	4.38	–	5.28	9.66	4.82	–	5.81	10.63

Major Works 2009		Unit	Labour Hours	Labour Net	Plant Net	Materials Net	Unit Net	Labour Gross	Plant Gross	Materials Gross	Unit Price
								(Gross rates include 10% profit)			
				£	£	£	£	£	£	£	£
K10	**K10: PLASTERBOARD DRY LINING, PARTITIONS AND CEILINGS**										
K1026	**Gyproc linings; 15.0 mm tapered edge wallboard to woodwork backgrounds**										
K102601	**Linings to walls:**										
K102601A	not exceeding 1200 mm high	m	0.24	5.62	–	5.95	11.57	6.18	–	6.55	12.73
K102601B	1200-1500 mm high	m	0.29	6.68	–	7.44	14.12	7.35	–	8.18	15.53
K102601C	1500-1800 mm high	m	0.32	7.59	–	8.93	16.52	8.35	–	9.82	18.17
K102601D	1800-2100 mm high	m	0.38	8.86	–	10.41	19.27	9.75	–	11.45	21.20
K102601E	2100-2400 mm high	m	0.43	10.13	–	11.89	22.02	11.14	–	13.08	24.22
K102601F	2400-2700 mm high	m	0.49	11.39	–	13.39	24.78	12.53	–	14.73	27.26
K102601G	2700-3000 mm high	m	0.54	12.66	–	14.87	27.53	13.93	–	16.36	30.28
K102611	**Linings to beams; 3 nr faces:**										
K102611A	not exceeding 600 mm girth	m	0.20	4.57	–	2.98	7.55	5.03	–	3.28	8.31
K102611B	600-1200 mm girth	m	0.38	8.81	–	5.95	14.76	9.69	–	6.55	16.24
K102611C	1200-1800 mm girth	m	0.57	13.36	–	8.93	22.29	14.70	–	9.82	24.52
K102621	**Linings to columns; 4 nr faces:**										
K102621A	not exceeding 600 mm girth	m	0.18	4.22	–	2.98	7.20	4.64	–	3.28	7.92
K102621B	600-1200 mm girth	m	0.35	8.08	–	5.95	14.03	8.89	–	6.55	15.43
K102621C	1200-1800 mm girth	m	0.59	13.71	–	8.93	22.64	15.08	–	9.82	24.90
K102631	**Linings to reveals and soffits:**										
K102631A	not exceeding 300 mm wide	m	0.15	3.52	–	1.48	5.00	3.87	–	1.63	5.50
K102631B	300-600 mm wide	m	0.18	4.22	–	2.98	7.20	4.64	–	3.28	7.92
K102641	**Linings to ceilings:**										
K102641A	over 300 mm wide	m²	0.21	4.92	–	4.94	9.86	5.41	–	5.43	10.85
K102641B	over 300 mm wide; in staircase areas	m²	0.23	5.39	–	4.94	10.33	5.93	–	5.43	11.36

Linings, Sheathing and Dry Partitioning

Major Works 2009		Unit	Labour Hours	Labour Net	Plant Net	Materials Net	Unit Net	Labour Gross	Plant Gross	Materials Gross	Unit Price
				£	£	£	£	£	£	£	£
								—— (Gross rates include 10% profit) ——			
K10	**K10: PLASTERBOARD DRY LINING, PARTITIONS AND CEILINGS**										
K1027	**Gyproc linings; 15.0 mm tapered edge Duplex wallboard to woodwork backgrounds**										
K102701	**Linings to walls:**										
K102701A	not exceeding 1200 mm high	m	0.24	5.62	–	7.16	12.78	6.18	–	7.88	14.06
K102701B	1200-1500 mm high	m	0.29	6.68	–	8.96	15.64	7.35	–	9.86	17.20
K102701C	1500-1800 mm high	m	0.32	7.60	–	10.74	18.34	8.36	–	11.81	20.17
K102701D	1800-2100 mm high	m	0.38	8.86	–	12.53	21.39	9.75	–	13.78	23.53
K102701E	2100-2400 mm high	m	0.43	10.13	–	14.31	24.44	11.14	–	15.74	26.88
K102701F	2400-2700 mm high	m	0.49	11.39	–	16.11	27.50	12.53	–	17.72	30.25
K102701G	2700-3000 mm high	m	0.54	12.65	–	17.90	30.55	13.92	–	19.69	33.61
K102711	**Linings to beams; 3 nr faces:**										
K102711A	not exceeding 600 mm girth	m	0.20	4.57	–	3.59	8.16	5.03	–	3.95	8.98
K102711B	600-1200 mm girth	m	0.38	8.81	–	7.16	15.97	9.69	–	7.88	17.57
K102711C	1200-1800 mm girth	m	0.57	13.36	–	10.74	24.10	14.70	–	11.81	26.51
K102721	**Linings to columns; 4 nr faces:**										
K102721A	not exceeding 600 mm girth	m	0.18	4.21	–	3.59	7.80	4.63	–	3.95	8.58
K102721B	600-1200 mm girth	m	0.35	8.08	–	7.16	15.24	8.89	–	7.88	16.76
K102721C	1200-1800 mm girth	m	0.59	13.71	–	10.74	24.45	15.08	–	11.81	26.90
K102731	**Linings to reveals and soffits:**										
K102731A	not exceeding 300 mm wide	m	0.15	3.52	–	1.78	5.30	3.87	–	1.96	5.83
K102731B	300-600 mm wide	m	0.18	4.21	–	3.59	7.80	4.63	–	3.95	8.58
K102741	**Linings to ceilings:**										
K102741A	over 300 mm wide	m²	0.21	4.92	–	5.95	10.87	5.41	–	6.55	11.96
K102741B	over 300 mm wide; in staircase areas	m²	0.23	5.39	–	5.95	11.34	5.93	–	6.55	12.47

Major Works 2009		Unit	Labour Hours	Labour Net	Plant Net	Materials Net	Unit Net	Labour Gross	Plant Gross	Materials Gross	Unit Price
								—— (Gross rates include 10% profit) ——			
				£	£	£	£	£	£	£	£
K10	**K10: PLASTERBOARD DRY LINING, PARTITIONS AND CEILINGS**										
K1028	**Gyproc linings; 15.0 mm tapered edge Fireline wallboard to woodwork backgrounds**										
K102801	**Linings to walls:**										
K102801A	not exceeding 1200 mm high	m	0.24	5.62	–	7.21	12.83	6.18	–	7.93	14.11
K102801B	1200-1500 mm high	m	0.29	6.68	–	9.02	15.70	7.35	–	9.92	17.27
K102801C	1500-1800 mm high	m	0.32	7.59	–	10.82	18.41	8.35	–	11.90	20.25
K102801D	1800-2100 mm high	m	0.38	8.86	–	12.61	21.47	9.75	–	13.87	23.62
K102801E	2100-2400 mm high	m	0.43	10.13	–	14.41	24.54	11.14	–	15.85	26.99
K102801F	2400-2700 mm high	m	0.49	11.40	–	16.22	27.62	12.54	–	17.84	30.38
K102801G	2700-3000 mm high	m	0.54	12.66	–	18.02	30.68	13.93	–	19.82	33.75
K102811	**Linings to beams; 3 nr faces:**										
K102811A	not exceeding 600 mm girth	m	0.20	4.57	–	3.61	8.18	5.03	–	3.97	9.00
K102811B	600-1200 mm girth	m	0.38	8.81	–	7.21	16.02	9.69	–	7.93	17.62
K102811C	1200-1800 mm girth	m	0.57	13.36	–	10.82	24.18	14.70	–	11.90	26.60
K102821	**Linings to columns; 4 nr faces:**										
K102821A	not exceeding 600 mm girth	m	0.18	4.22	–	3.61	7.83	4.64	–	3.97	8.61
K102821B	600-1200 mm girth	m	0.35	8.08	–	7.21	15.29	8.89	–	7.93	16.82
K102821C	1200-1800 mm girth	m	0.59	13.71	–	10.82	24.53	15.08	–	11.90	26.98
K102831	**Linings to reveals and soffits:**										
K102831A	not exceeding 300 mm wide	m	0.15	3.51	–	1.80	5.31	3.86	–	1.98	5.84
K102831B	300-600 mm wide	m	0.18	4.22	–	3.61	7.83	4.64	–	3.97	8.61
K102841	**Linings to ceilings:**										
K102841A	over 300 mm wide	m²	0.21	4.92	–	5.99	10.91	5.41	–	6.59	12.00
K102841B	over 300 mm wide; in staircase areas	m²	0.23	5.39	–	5.99	11.38	5.93	–	6.59	12.52

Linings, Sheathing and Dry Partitioning

Major Works 2009		Unit	Labour Hours	Labour Net	Plant Net	Materials Net	Unit Net	Labour Gross	Plant Gross	Materials Gross	Unit Price
								(Gross rates include 10% profit)			
				£	£	£	£	£	£	£	£
K10	**K10: PLASTERBOARD DRY LINING, PARTITIONS AND CEILINGS**										
K1029	**Gyproc linings; 19.0 mm tapered edge plank to woodwork backgrounds**										
K102901	**Linings to walls:**										
K102901A	not exceeding 1200 mm high	m	0.28	6.56	–	7.37	13.93	7.22	–	8.11	15.32
K102901B	1200-1500 mm high	m	0.33	7.81	–	9.22	17.03	8.59	–	10.14	18.73
K102901C	1500-1800 mm high	m	0.38	8.86	–	11.06	19.92	9.75	–	12.17	21.91
K102901D	1800-2100 mm high	m	0.44	10.34	–	12.90	23.24	11.37	–	14.19	25.56
K102901E	2100-2400 mm high	m	0.50	11.81	–	14.74	26.55	12.99	–	16.21	29.21
K102901F	2400-2700 mm high	m	0.57	13.29	–	16.59	29.88	14.62	–	18.25	32.87
K102901G	2700-3000 mm high	m	0.63	14.77	–	18.43	33.20	16.25	–	20.27	36.52
K102911	**Linings to beams; 3 nr faces:**										
K102911A	not exceeding 600 mm girth	m	0.23	5.35	–	3.69	9.04	5.89	–	4.06	9.94
K102911B	600-1200 mm girth	m	0.44	10.29	–	7.37	17.66	11.32	–	8.11	19.43
K102911C	1200-1800 mm girth	m	0.67	15.59	–	11.06	26.65	17.15	–	12.17	29.32
K102921	**Linings to columns; 4 nr faces:**										
K102921A	not exceeding 600 mm girth	m	0.21	4.93	–	3.69	8.62	5.42	–	4.06	9.48
K102921B	600-1200 mm girth	m	0.40	9.45	–	7.37	16.82	10.40	–	8.11	18.50
K102921C	1200-1800 mm girth	m	0.68	16.01	–	11.06	27.07	17.61	–	12.17	29.78
K102931	**Linings to reveals and soffits:**										
K102931A	not exceeding 300 mm wide	m	0.18	4.10	–	1.84	5.94	4.51	–	2.02	6.53
K102931B	300-600 mm wide	m	0.21	4.93	–	3.69	8.62	5.42	–	4.06	9.48
K102941	**Linings to ceilings:**										
K102941A	over 300 mm wide	m²	0.24	5.62	–	6.13	11.75	6.18	–	6.74	12.93
K102941B	over 300 mm wide; in staircase areas	m²	0.26	6.19	–	6.13	12.32	6.81	–	6.74	13.55

Linings, Sheathing and Dry Partitioning

Major Works 2009		Unit	Labour Hours	Labour Net	Plant Net	Materials Net	Unit Net	Labour Gross	Plant Gross	Materials Gross	Unit Price
								(Gross rates include 10% profit)			
				£	£	£	£	£	£	£	£
K10	**K10: PLASTERBOARD DRY LINING, PARTITIONS AND CEILINGS**										
K1065	**Gyproc linings; 12.5 mm tapered edge wallboard to woodwork backgrounds; fixing with screws; joints flush filled, taped and finished for direct decoration**										
K106501	**Linings to walls; height:**										
K106501A	not exceeding 1200 mm high	m	0.26	6.07	–	5.62	11.69	6.68	–	6.18	12.86
K106501B	1200-1500 mm high	m	0.31	7.31	–	6.33	13.64	8.04	–	6.96	15.00
K106501C	1500-1800 mm high	m	0.36	8.44	–	7.59	16.03	9.28	–	8.35	17.63
K106501D	1800-2100 mm high	m	0.42	9.85	–	8.85	18.70	10.84	–	9.74	20.57
K106501E	2100-2400 mm high	m	0.48	11.25	–	10.11	21.36	12.38	–	11.12	23.50
K106501F	2400-2700 mm high	m	0.54	12.65	–	11.39	24.04	13.92	–	12.53	26.44
K106501G	2700-3000 mm high	m	0.60	14.06	–	12.65	26.71	15.47	–	13.92	29.38
K106511	**Linings to beams; 3 nr faces; girth:**										
K106511A	not exceeding 600 mm girth	m	0.20	4.61	–	3.40	8.01	5.07	–	3.74	8.81
K106511B	600-1200 mm girth	m	0.36	8.53	–	5.86	14.39	9.38	–	6.45	15.83
K106511C	1200-1800 mm girth	m	0.55	12.91	–	8.33	21.24	14.20	–	9.16	23.36
K106521	**Linings to columns; 4 nr faces; girth:**										
K106521A	not exceeding 600 mm girth	m	0.18	4.12	–	3.85	7.97	4.53	–	4.24	8.77
K106521B	600-1200 mm girth	m	0.34	7.97	–	6.31	14.28	8.77	–	6.94	15.71
K106521C	1200-1800 mm girth	m	0.56	13.20	–	8.79	21.99	14.52	–	9.67	24.19
K106531	**Linings to reveals and soffits; width:**										
K106531A	not exceeding 300 mm wide	m	0.14	3.28	–	1.73	5.01	3.61	–	1.90	5.51
K106531B	300-600 mm wide	m	0.18	4.12	–	2.95	7.07	4.53	–	3.25	7.78
K106541	**Linings to ceilings:**										
K106541A	over 300 mm wide	m²	0.23	5.39	–	4.06	9.45	5.93	–	4.47	10.40
K106541B	over 300 mm wide; in staircase areas	m²	0.25	5.86	–	4.06	9.92	6.45	–	4.47	10.91

Linings, Sheathing and Dry Partitioning

Major Works 2009		Unit	Labour Hours	Labour Net	Plant Net	Materials Net	Unit Net	Labour Gross	Plant Gross	Materials Gross	Unit Price
								(Gross rates include 10% profit)			
				£	£	£	£	£	£	£	£
K10	**K10: PLASTERBOARD DRY LINING, PARTITIONS AND CEILINGS**										
K1066	**Gyproc linings; 9.5 mm wallboard to masonry or concrete walls; fixing by Thistlebond system; joints flush filled, taped and finished for direct decoration**										
K106601	**Linings to walls; height:**										
K106601A	not exceeding 1200 mm ...	m	0.28	6.47	–	4.60	11.07	7.12	–	5.06	12.18
K106601B	1200-1500 mm.	m	0.35	8.08	–	5.76	13.84	8.89	–	6.34	15.22
K106601C	1500-1800 mm.	m	0.41	9.70	–	6.90	16.60	10.67	–	7.59	18.26
K106601D	1800-2100 mm.	m	0.48	11.32	–	8.06	19.38	12.45	–	8.87	21.32
K106601E	2100-2400 mm.	m	0.55	12.94	–	9.19	22.13	14.23	–	10.11	24.34
K106601F	2400-2700 mm.	m	0.62	14.56	–	10.35	24.91	16.02	–	11.39	27.40
K106601G	2700-3000 mm.	m	0.69	16.18	–	11.49	27.67	17.80	–	12.64	30.44
K106611	**Linings to beams; 3 nr faces; girth:**										
K106611A	not exceeding 600 mm	m	0.15	3.51	–	3.15	6.66	3.86	–	3.47	7.33
K106611B	600-1200 mm.	m	0.30	7.03	–	5.37	12.40	7.73	–	5.91	13.64
K106611C	1200-1800 mm.	m	0.45	10.55	–	7.59	18.14	11.61	–	8.35	19.95
K106621	**Linings to columns; 4 nr faces; girth:**										
K106621A	not exceeding 600 mm	m	0.15	3.51	–	3.60	7.11	3.86	–	3.96	7.82
K106621B	600-1200 mm.	m	0.30	7.04	–	5.82	12.86	7.74	–	6.40	14.15
K106621C	1200-1800 mm.	m	0.45	10.54	–	8.05	18.59	11.59	–	8.86	20.45
K106631	**Linings to reveals and soffits; width:**										
K106631A	not exceeding 300 mm	m	0.11	2.58	–	1.58	4.16	2.84	–	1.74	4.58
K106631B	300-600 mm.	m	0.15	3.52	–	2.68	6.20	3.87	–	2.95	6.82

Major Works 2009		Unit	Labour Hours	Labour Net	Plant Net	Materials Net	Unit Net	Labour Gross	Plant Gross	Materials Gross	Unit Price
								(Gross rates include 10% profit)			
				£	£	£	£	£	£	£	£
K10	**K10: PLASTERBOARD DRY LINING, PARTITIONS AND CEILINGS**										
K1067	**Gyproc linings; 12.5 mm wallboard to masonry or concrete walls; fixing by Thistlebond system; joints flush filled, taped and finished for direct decoration**										
K106701	**Linings to walls; height:**										
K106701A	not exceeding 1200 mm ...	m	0.30	7.03	–	5.24	12.27	7.73	–	5.76	13.50
K106701B	1200-1500 mm..........	m	0.38	8.79	–	6.56	15.35	9.67	–	7.22	16.89
K106701C	1500-1800 mm..........	m	0.45	10.55	–	7.86	18.41	11.61	–	8.65	20.25
K106701D	1800-2100 mm..........	m	0.53	12.30	–	8.62	20.92	13.53	–	9.48	23.01
K106701E	2100-2400 mm..........	m	0.60	14.06	–	10.48	24.54	15.47	–	11.53	26.99
K106701F	2400-2700 mm..........	m	0.68	15.82	–	11.80	27.62	17.40	–	12.98	30.38
K106701G	2700-3000 mm..........	m	0.75	17.58	–	13.10	30.68	19.34	–	14.41	33.75
K106711	**Linings to beams; 3 nr faces; girth:**										
K106711A	not exceeding 600 mm	m	0.15	3.51	–	3.47	6.98	3.86	–	3.82	7.68
K106711B	600-1200 mm..........	m	0.30	7.03	–	6.02	13.05	7.73	–	6.62	14.36
K106711C	1200-1800 mm..........	m	0.45	10.55	–	8.56	19.11	11.61	–	9.42	21.02
K106721	**Linings to columns; 4 nr faces; girth:**										
K106721A	not exceeding 600 mm	m	0.15	3.51	–	3.92	7.43	3.86	–	4.31	8.17
K106721B	600-1200 mm..........	m	0.30	7.03	–	6.47	13.50	7.73	–	7.12	14.85
K106721C	1200-1800 mm..........	m	0.45	10.55	–	9.01	19.56	11.61	–	9.91	21.52
K106731	**Linings to reveals and soffits; width:**										
K106731A	not exceeding 300 mm	m	0.11	2.57	–	1.74	4.31	2.83	–	1.91	4.74
K106731B	300-600 mm.............	m	0.15	3.52	–	3.00	6.52	3.87	–	3.30	7.17

Linings, Sheathing and Dry Partitioning

Major Works 2009		Unit	Labour Hours	Labour Net	Plant Net	Materials Net	Unit Net	Labour Gross	Plant Gross	Materials Gross	Unit Price
								—— (Gross rates include 10% profit) ——			
				£	£	£	£	£	£	£	£
K10	**K10: PLASTERBOARD DRY LINING, PARTITIONS AND CEILINGS**										
K1068	**Gyproc linings; 12.5 mm Fireline board to masonry or concrete walls; fixing by Thistlebond system; joints flush filled, taped and finished for direct decoration**										
K106801	**Linings to walls; height:**										
K106801A	not exceeding 1200 mm ...	m	0.30	7.03	–	7.23	14.26	7.73	–	7.95	15.69
K106801B	1200-1500 mm..........	m	0.38	8.79	–	9.05	17.84	9.67	–	9.96	19.62
K106801C	1500-1800 mm..........	m	0.45	10.54	–	10.85	21.39	11.59	–	11.94	23.53
K106801D	1800-2100 mm..........	m	0.53	12.31	–	11.81	24.12	13.54	–	12.99	26.53
K106801E	2100-2400 mm..........	m	0.60	14.07	–	14.46	28.53	15.48	–	15.91	31.38
K106801F	2400-2700 mm..........	m	0.68	15.82	–	16.28	32.10	17.40	–	17.91	35.31
K106801G	2700-3000 mm..........	m	0.75	17.58	–	18.08	35.66	19.34	–	19.89	39.23
K106811	**Linings to beams; 3 nr faces; girth:**										
K106811A	not exceeding 600 mm	m	0.15	3.52	–	4.46	7.98	3.87	–	4.91	8.78
K106811B	600-1200 mm............	m	0.30	7.03	–	8.01	15.04	7.73	–	8.81	16.54
K106811C	1200-1800 mm..........	m	0.45	10.55	–	11.54	22.09	11.61	–	12.69	24.30
K106821	**Linings to columns; 4 nr faces; girth:**										
K106821A	not exceeding 600 mm	m	0.15	3.52	–	4.91	8.43	3.87	–	5.40	9.27
K106821B	600-1200 mm............	m	0.30	7.03	–	8.46	15.49	7.73	–	9.31	17.04
K106821C	1200-1800 mm..........	m	0.45	10.54	–	12.00	22.54	11.59	–	13.20	24.79
K106831	**Linings to reveals and soffits; width:**										
K106831A	not exceeding 300 mm	m	0.11	2.58	–	2.23	4.81	2.84	–	2.45	5.29
K106831B	300-600 mm............	m	0.15	3.51	–	4.00	7.51	3.86	–	4.40	8.26

Linings, Sheathing and Dry Partitioning

Major Works 2009		Unit	Labour Hours	Labour Net	Plant Net	Materials Net	Unit Net	Labour Gross	Plant Gross	Materials Gross	Unit Price
								(Gross rates include 10% profit)			
				£	£	£	£	£	£	£	£
K10	**K10: PLASTERBOARD DRY LINING, PARTITIONS AND CEILINGS**										
K1069	**Gyproc linings; 25 mm thermal board to masonry or concrete walls; fixing by Thistlebond TL system; joints flush filled, taped and finished for direct decoration**										
K106901	**Linings to walls; height:**										
K106901A	not exceeding 1200 mm ...	m	0.34	7.88	–	11.91	19.79	8.67	–	13.10	21.77
K106901B	1200-1500 mm..........	m	0.42	9.84	–	14.90	24.74	10.82	–	16.39	27.21
K106901C	1500-1800 mm..........	m	0.50	11.81	–	17.87	29.68	12.99	–	19.66	32.65
K106901D	1800-2100 mm..........	m	0.59	13.78	–	20.86	34.64	15.16	–	22.95	38.10
K106901E	2100-2400 mm..........	m	0.67	15.76	–	23.82	39.58	17.34	–	26.20	43.54
K106901F	2400-2700 mm..........	m	0.76	17.72	–	26.81	44.53	19.49	–	29.49	48.98
K106901G	2700-3000 mm..........	m	0.84	19.69	–	29.78	49.47	21.66	–	32.76	54.42
K106911	**Linings to beams; 3 nr faces; girth:**										
K106911A	not exceeding 600 mm	m	0.15	3.52	–	6.79	10.31	3.87	–	7.47	11.34
K106911B	600-1200 mm..........	m	0.30	7.03	–	12.67	19.70	7.73	–	13.94	21.67
K106911C	1200-1800 mm..........	m	0.45	10.54	–	18.54	29.08	11.59	–	20.39	31.99
K106921	**Linings to columns; 4 nr faces; girth:**										
K106921A	not exceeding 600 mm	m	0.15	3.52	–	7.24	10.76	3.87	–	7.96	11.84
K106921B	600-1200 mm..........	m	0.30	7.03	–	13.12	20.15	7.73	–	14.43	22.17
K106921C	1200-1800 mm..........	m	0.45	10.55	–	18.99	29.54	11.61	–	20.89	32.49
K106931	**Linings to reveals and soffits; width:**										
K106931A	not exceeding 300 mm	m	0.11	2.58	–	3.40	5.98	2.84	–	3.74	6.58
K106931B	300-600 mm.............	m	0.15	3.52	–	6.37	9.89	3.87	–	7.01	10.88

Linings, Sheathing and Dry Partitioning

Major Works 2009		Unit	Labour Hours	Labour Net	Plant Net	Materials Net	Unit Net	Labour Gross	Plant Gross	Materials Gross	Unit Price
								(Gross rates include 10% profit)			
				£	£	£	£	£	£	£	£
K10	**K10: PLASTERBOARD DRY LINING, PARTITIONS AND CEILINGS**										
K1070	**Gyproc linings; 32 mm thermal board to masonry or concrete walls; fixing by Thistlebond TL system; joints flush filled, taped and finished for direct decoration**										
K107001	**Linings to walls; height:**										
K107001A	not exceeding 1200 mm ...	m	0.36	8.43	–	13.10	21.53	9.27	–	14.41	23.68
K107001B	1200-1500 mm..........	m	0.45	10.55	–	16.38	26.93	11.61	–	18.02	29.62
K107001C	1500-1800 mm..........	m	0.54	12.66	–	19.64	32.30	13.93	–	21.60	35.53
K107001D	1800-2100 mm..........	m	0.63	14.77	–	22.93	37.70	16.25	–	25.22	41.47
K107001E	2100-2400 mm..........	m	0.72	16.86	–	26.19	43.05	18.55	–	28.81	47.36
K107001F	2400-2700 mm..........	m	0.81	18.96	–	29.48	48.44	20.86	–	32.43	53.28
K107001G	2700-3000 mm..........	m	0.90	21.07	–	32.74	53.81	23.18	–	36.01	59.19
K107011	**Linings to beams; 3 nr faces; girth:**										
K107011A	not exceeding 600 mm	m	0.16	3.75	–	7.39	11.14	4.13	–	8.13	12.25
K107011B	600-1200 mm..........	m	0.32	7.50	–	13.85	21.35	8.25	–	15.24	23.49
K107011C	1200-1800 mm..........	m	0.47	11.02	–	20.31	31.33	12.12	–	22.34	34.46
K107021	**Linings to columns; 4 nr faces; girth:**										
K107021A	not exceeding 600 mm	m	0.16	3.75	–	7.84	11.59	4.13	–	8.62	12.75
K107021B	600-1200 mm..........	m	0.32	7.51	–	14.30	21.81	8.26	–	15.73	23.99
K107021C	1200-1800 mm..........	m	0.47	11.01	–	20.77	31.78	12.11	–	22.85	34.96
K107031	**Linings to reveals and soffits; width:**										
K107031A	not exceeding 300 mm	m	0.12	2.81	–	3.70	6.51	3.09	–	4.07	7.16
K107031B	300-600 mm.............	m	0.16	3.75	–	6.96	10.71	4.13	–	7.66	11.78

Linings, Sheathing and Dry Partitioning

Major Works 2009		Unit	Labour Hours	Labour Net	Plant Net	Materials Net	Unit Net	Labour Gross	Plant Gross	Materials Gross	Unit Price
								(Gross rates include 10% profit)			
				£	£	£	£	£	£	£	£
K10	**K10: PLASTERBOARD DRY LINING, PARTITIONS AND CEILINGS**										
K1071	**Gyproc linings; 40 mm thermal board to masonry or concrete walls; fixing by Thistlebond TL system; joints flush filled, taped and finished for direct decoration**										
K107101	**Linings to walls; height:**										
K107101A	not exceeding 1200 mm ...	m	0.38	9.00	–	15.53	24.53	9.90	–	17.08	26.98
K107101B	1200-1500 mm..........	m	0.48	11.25	–	19.42	30.67	12.38	–	21.36	33.74
K107101C	1500-1800 mm..........	m	0.58	13.50	–	23.29	36.79	14.85	–	25.62	40.47
K107101D	1800-2100 mm..........	m	0.67	15.76	–	27.18	42.94	17.34	–	29.90	47.23
K107101E	2100-2400 mm..........	m	0.77	17.97	–	31.06	49.03	19.77	–	34.17	53.93
K107101F	2400-2700 mm..........	m	0.86	20.23	–	34.95	55.18	22.25	–	38.45	60.70
K107101G	2700-3000 mm..........	m	0.96	22.48	–	38.82	61.30	24.73	–	42.70	67.43
K107111	**Linings to beams; 3 nr faces; girth:**										
K107111A	not exceeding 600 mm	m	0.17	3.99	–	8.60	12.59	4.39	–	9.46	13.85
K107111B	600-1200 mm..........	m	0.34	7.97	–	16.28	24.25	8.77	–	17.91	26.68
K107111C	1200-1800 mm..........	m	0.49	11.49	–	23.96	35.45	12.64	–	26.36	39.00
K107121	**Linings to columns; 4 nr faces; girth:**										
K107121A	not exceeding 600 mm	m	0.17	3.99	–	9.05	13.04	4.39	–	9.96	14.34
K107121B	600-1200 mm..........	m	0.34	7.97	–	16.74	24.71	8.77	–	18.41	27.18
K107121C	1200-1800 mm..........	m	0.49	11.49	–	24.41	35.90	12.64	–	26.85	39.49
K107131	**Linings to reveals and soffits; width:**										
K107131A	not exceeding 300 mm	m	0.13	3.04	–	4.31	7.35	3.34	–	4.74	8.09
K107131B	300-600 mm.............	m	0.17	3.98	–	8.18	12.16	4.38	–	9.00	13.38

Linings, Sheathing and Dry Partitioning

Major Works 2009		Unit	Labour Hours	Labour Net	Plant Net	Materials Net	Unit Net	Labour Gross	Plant Gross	Materials Gross	Unit Price
								(Gross rates include 10% profit)			
				£	£	£	£	£	£	£	£
K10	**K10: PLASTERBOARD DRY LINING, PARTITIONS AND CEILINGS**										
K1072	**Gyproc linings; 50 mm thermal board to masonry or concrete walls; fixing by Thistlebond TL system; joints flush filled, taped and finished for direct decoration**										
K107201	**Linings to walls; height:**										
K107201A	not exceeding 1200 mm ...	m	0.41	9.57	–	16.73	26.30	10.53	–	18.40	28.93
K107201B	1200-1500 mm..........	m	0.51	11.95	–	20.92	32.87	13.15	–	23.01	36.16
K107201C	1500-1800 mm..........	m	0.61	14.34	–	25.09	39.43	15.77	–	27.60	43.37
K107201D	1800-2100 mm..........	m	0.71	16.74	–	29.28	46.02	18.41	–	32.21	50.62
K107201E	2100-2400 mm..........	m	0.82	19.10	–	33.45	52.55	21.01	–	36.80	57.81
K107201F	2400-2700 mm..........	m	0.92	21.50	–	37.64	59.14	23.65	–	41.40	65.05
K107201G	2700-3000 mm..........	m	1.02	23.89	–	41.81	65.70	26.28	–	45.99	72.27
K107211	**Linings to beams; 3 nr faces; girth:**										
K107211A	not exceeding 600 mm	m	0.18	4.22	–	9.20	13.42	4.64	–	10.12	14.76
K107211B	600-1200 mm...........	m	0.36	8.44	–	17.48	25.92	9.28	–	19.23	28.51
K107211C	1200-1800 mm..........	m	0.51	11.95	–	25.76	37.71	13.15	–	28.34	41.48
K107221	**Linings to columns; 4 nr faces; girth:**										
K107221A	not exceeding 600 mm	m	0.18	4.22	–	9.65	13.87	4.64	–	10.62	15.26
K107221B	600-1200 mm...........	m	0.36	8.44	–	17.93	26.37	9.28	–	19.72	29.01
K107221C	1200-1800 mm..........	m	0.51	11.95	–	26.21	38.16	13.15	–	28.83	41.98
K107231	**Linings to reveals and soffits; width:**										
K107231A	not exceeding 300 mm	m	0.14	3.28	–	4.61	7.89	3.61	–	5.07	8.68
K107231B	300-600 mm............	m	0.18	4.22	–	8.78	13.00	4.64	–	9.66	14.30

Major Works 2009		Unit	Labour Hours	Labour Net	Plant Net	Materials Net	Unit Net	Labour Gross	Plant Gross	Materials Gross	Unit Price
								(Gross rates include 10% profit)			
				£	£	£	£	£	£	£	£
K10	**K10: PLASTERBOARD DRY LINING, PARTITIONS AND CEILINGS**										
K1073	**Gyproc linings; 25 mm vapour check thermal board to masonry or concrete walls; fixing by Thistlebond TL system; joints flush filled, taped and finished for direct decoration**										
K107301	**Linings to walls; height:**										
K107301A	not exceeding 1200 mm ...	m	0.34	7.88	–	12.88	20.76	8.67	–	14.17	22.84
K107301B	1200-1500 mm..........	m	0.42	9.85	–	16.11	25.96	10.84	–	17.72	28.56
K107301C	1500-1800 mm..........	m	0.50	11.82	–	19.32	31.14	13.00	–	21.25	34.25
K107301D	1800-2100 mm..........	m	0.59	13.79	–	22.55	36.34	15.17	–	24.81	39.97
K107301E	2100-2400 mm..........	m	0.67	15.76	–	25.76	41.52	17.34	–	28.34	45.67
K107301F	2400-2700 mm..........	m	0.76	17.73	–	28.99	46.72	19.50	–	31.89	51.39
K107301G	2700-3000 mm..........	m	0.84	19.69	–	32.21	51.90	21.66	–	35.43	57.09
K107311	**Linings to beams; 3 nr faces; girth:**										
K107311A	not exceeding 600 mm	m	0.15	3.51	–	7.28	10.79	3.86	–	8.01	11.87
K107311B	600-1200 mm..........	m	0.30	7.03	–	13.64	20.67	7.73	–	15.00	22.74
K107311C	1200-1800 mm..........	m	0.45	10.55	–	19.99	30.54	11.61	–	21.99	33.59
K107321	**Linings to columns; 4 nr faces; girth:**										
K107321A	not exceeding 600 mm	m	0.15	3.52	–	7.73	11.25	3.87	–	8.50	12.38
K107321B	600-1200 mm..........	m	0.30	7.03	–	14.09	21.12	7.73	–	15.50	23.23
K107321C	1200-1800 mm..........	m	0.45	10.55	–	20.44	30.99	11.61	–	22.48	34.09
K107331	**Linings to reveals and soffits; width:**										
K107331A	not exceeding 300 mm	m	0.11	2.57	–	3.65	6.22	2.83	–	4.02	6.84
K107331B	300-600 mm.............	m	0.15	3.51	–	6.86	10.37	3.86	–	7.55	11.41

Linings, Sheathing and Dry Partitioning

Major Works 2009		Unit	Labour Hours	Labour Net	Plant Net	Materials Net	Unit Net	Labour Gross	Plant Gross	Materials Gross	Unit Price
								(Gross rates include 10% profit)			
				£	£	£	£	£	£	£	£
K10	**K10: PLASTERBOARD DRY LINING, PARTITIONS AND CEILINGS**										
K1074	**Gyproc linings; 32 mm vapour check thermal board to masonry or concrete walls; fixing by Thistlebond TL system; joints flush filled, taped and finished for direct decoration**										
K107401	**Linings to walls; height:**										
K107401A	not exceeding 1200 mm ...	m	0.36	8.44	–	14.09	22.53	9.28	–	15.50	24.78
K107401B	1200-1500 mm...........	m	0.45	10.55	–	17.62	28.17	11.61	–	19.38	30.99
K107401C	1500-1800 mm...........	m	0.54	12.66	–	21.14	33.80	13.93	–	23.25	37.18
K107401D	1800-2100 mm...........	m	0.63	14.77	–	24.67	39.44	16.25	–	27.14	43.38
K107401E	2100-2400 mm...........	m	0.72	16.86	–	28.18	45.04	18.55	–	31.00	49.54
K107401F	2400-2700 mm...........	m	0.81	18.96	–	31.72	50.68	20.86	–	34.89	55.75
K107401G	2700-3000 mm...........	m	0.90	21.07	–	35.23	56.30	23.18	–	38.75	61.93
K107411	**Linings to beams; 3 nr faces; girth:**										
K107411A	not exceeding 600 mm	m	0.16	3.75	–	7.88	11.63	4.13	–	8.67	12.79
K107411B	600-1200 mm...........	m	0.32	7.50	–	14.85	22.35	8.25	–	16.34	24.59
K107411C	1200-1800 mm...........	m	0.47	11.01	–	21.81	32.82	12.11	–	23.99	36.10
K107421	**Linings to columns; 4 nr faces; girth:**										
K107421A	not exceeding 600 mm	m	0.16	3.76	–	8.33	12.09	4.14	–	9.16	13.30
K107421B	600-1200 mm...........	m	0.32	7.50	–	15.30	22.80	8.25	–	16.83	25.08
K107421C	1200-1800 mm...........	m	0.47	11.02	–	22.26	33.28	12.12	–	24.49	36.61
K107431	**Linings to reveals and soffits; width:**										
K107431A	not exceeding 300 mm	m	0.12	2.81	–	3.95	6.76	3.09	–	4.35	7.44
K107431B	300-600 mm............	m	0.16	3.75	–	7.46	11.21	4.13	–	8.21	12.33

Major Works 2009		Unit	Labour Hours	Labour Net	Plant Net	Materials Net	Unit Net	Labour Gross	Plant Gross	Materials Gross	Unit Price
								(Gross rates include 10% profit)			
				£	£	£	£	£	£	£	£
K10	**K10: PLASTERBOARD DRY LINING, PARTITIONS AND CEILINGS**										
K1075	**Gyproc linings; 40 mm vapour check thermal board to masonry or concrete walls; fixing by Thistlebond TL system; joints flush filled, taped and finished for direct decoration**										
K107501	**Linings to walls; height:**										
K107501A	not exceeding 1200 mm ...	m	0.38	9.00	–	16.46	25.46	9.90	–	18.11	28.01
K107501B	1200-1500 mm...........	m	0.48	11.25	–	20.59	31.84	12.38	–	22.65	35.02
K107501C	1500-1800 mm...........	m	0.58	13.50	–	24.69	38.19	14.85	–	27.16	42.01
K107501D	1800-2100 mm...........	m	0.67	15.75	–	28.82	44.57	17.33	–	31.70	49.03
K107501E	2100-2400 mm...........	m	0.77	17.98	–	32.92	50.90	19.78	–	36.21	55.99
K107501F	2400-2700 mm...........	m	0.86	20.22	–	37.05	57.27	22.24	–	40.76	63.00
K107501G	2700-3000 mm...........	m	0.96	22.48	–	41.15	63.63	24.73	–	45.27	69.99
K107511	**Linings to beams; 3 nr faces; girth:**										
K107511A	not exceeding 600 mm	m	0.17	3.98	–	9.07	13.05	4.38	–	9.98	14.36
K107511B	600-1200 mm...........	m	0.34	7.97	–	17.22	25.19	8.77	–	18.94	27.71
K107511C	1200-1800 mm...........	m	0.49	11.49	–	25.36	36.85	12.64	–	27.90	40.54
K107521	**Linings to columns; 4 nr faces; girth:**										
K107521A	not exceeding 600 mm	m	0.17	3.98	–	9.52	13.50	4.38	–	10.47	14.85
K107521B	600-1200 mm...........	m	0.34	7.97	–	17.67	25.64	8.77	–	19.44	28.20
K107521C	1200-1800 mm...........	m	0.49	11.49	–	25.81	37.30	12.64	–	28.39	41.03
K107531	**Linings to reveals and soffits; width:**										
K107531A	not exceeding 300 mm	m	0.13	3.05	–	4.54	7.59	3.36	–	4.99	8.35
K107531B	300-600 mm.............	m	0.17	3.99	–	8.64	12.63	4.39	–	9.50	13.89

Linings, Sheathing and Dry Partitioning

Major Works 2009		Unit	Labour Hours	Labour Net	Plant Net	Materials Net	Unit Net	Labour Gross	Plant Gross	Materials Gross	Unit Price
								(Gross rates include 10% profit)			
				£	£	£	£	£	£	£	£
K10	**K10: PLASTERBOARD DRY LINING, PARTITIONS AND CEILINGS**										
K1076	**Gyproc linings; 50 mm vapour check thermal board to masonry or concrete walls; fixing by Thistlebond TL system; joints flush filled, taped and finished for direct decoration**										
K107601	**Linings to walls; height:**										
K107601A	not exceeding 1200 mm ...	m	0.41	9.56	–	17.67	27.23	10.52	–	19.44	29.95
K107601B	1200-1500 mm..........	m	0.51	11.95	–	22.10	34.05	13.15	–	24.31	37.46
K107601C	1500-1800 mm..........	m	0.61	14.35	–	26.51	40.86	15.79	–	29.16	44.95
K107601D	1800-2100 mm..........	m	0.71	16.74	–	30.93	47.67	18.41	–	34.02	52.44
K107601E	2100-2400 mm..........	m	0.82	19.10	–	35.34	54.44	21.01	–	38.87	59.88
K107601F	2400-2700 mm..........	m	0.92	21.49	–	39.77	61.26	23.64	–	43.75	67.39
K107601G	2700-3000 mm..........	m	1.02	23.89	–	44.18	68.07	26.28	–	48.60	74.88
K107611	**Linings to beams; 3 nr faces; girth:**										
K107611A	not exceeding 600 mm	m	0.18	4.22	–	9.67	13.89	4.64	–	10.64	15.28
K107611B	600-1200 mm..........	m	0.36	8.43	–	18.43	26.86	9.27	–	20.27	29.55
K107611C	1200-1800 mm..........	m	0.51	11.96	–	27.17	39.13	13.16	–	29.89	43.04
K107621	**Linings to columns; 4 nr faces; girth:**										
K107621A	not exceeding 600 mm	m	0.18	4.22	–	10.12	14.34	4.64	–	11.13	15.77
K107621B	600-1200 mm..........	m	0.36	8.44	–	18.88	27.32	9.28	–	20.77	30.05
K107621C	1200-1800 mm..........	m	0.51	11.95	–	27.63	39.58	13.15	–	30.39	43.54
K107631	**Linings to reveals and soffits; width:**										
K107631A	not exceeding 300 mm	m	0.14	3.28	–	4.84	8.12	3.61	–	5.32	8.93
K107631B	300-600 mm............	m	0.18	4.22	–	9.25	13.47	4.64	–	10.18	14.82

Linings, Sheathing and Dry Partitioning

Major Works 2009		Unit	Labour Hours	Labour Net	Plant Net	Materials Net	Unit Net	Labour Gross	Plant Gross	Materials Gross	Unit Price
								(Gross rates include 10% profit)			
				£	£	£	£	£	£	£	£
K10	**K10: PLASTERBOARD DRY LINING, PARTITIONS AND CEILINGS**										
K1077	**Gyproc linings; 25 mm urethane laminate board to masonry or concrete walls; fixing by Thistlebond TL system; joints flush filled, taped and finished for direct decoration**										
K107701	**Linings to walls; height:**										
K107701A	not exceeding 1200 mm ...	m	0.34	7.88	–	20.20	28.08	8.67	–	22.22	30.89
K107701B	1200-1500 mm..........	m	0.42	9.85	–	25.26	35.11	10.84	–	27.79	38.62
K107701C	1500-1800 mm..........	m	0.50	11.82	–	30.30	42.12	13.00	–	33.33	46.33
K107701D	1800-2100 mm..........	m	0.59	13.79	–	35.36	49.15	15.17	–	38.90	54.07
K107701E	2100-2400 mm..........	m	0.67	15.75	–	40.41	56.16	17.33	–	44.45	61.78
K107701F	2400-2700 mm..........	m	0.76	17.72	–	45.47	63.19	19.49	–	50.02	69.51
K107701G	2700-3000 mm..........	m	0.84	19.69	–	50.51	70.20	21.66	–	55.56	77.22
K107711	**Linings to beams; 3 nr faces; girth:**										
K107711A	not exceeding 600 mm	m	0.15	3.51	–	10.94	14.45	3.86	–	12.03	15.90
K107711B	600-1200 mm..........	m	0.30	7.03	–	20.96	27.99	7.73	–	23.06	30.79
K107711C	1200-1800 mm..........	m	0.45	10.55	–	30.97	41.52	11.61	–	34.07	45.67
K107721	**Linings to columns; 4 nr faces; girth:**										
K107721A	not exceeding 600 mm	m	0.15	3.52	–	11.39	14.91	3.87	–	12.53	16.40
K107721B	600-1200 mm..........	m	0.30	7.03	–	21.41	28.44	7.73	–	23.55	31.28
K107721C	1200-1800 mm..........	m	0.45	10.55	–	31.42	41.97	11.61	–	34.56	46.17
K107731	**Linings to reveals and soffits; width:**										
K107731A	not exceeding 300 mm	m	0.11	2.57	–	5.48	8.05	2.83	–	6.03	8.86
K107731B	300-600 mm.............	m	0.15	3.51	–	10.52	14.03	3.86	–	11.57	15.43

Linings, Sheathing and Dry Partitioning

Major Works 2009		Unit	Labour Hours	Labour Net	Plant Net	Materials Net	Unit Net	Labour Gross	Plant Gross	Materials Gross	Unit Price
								(Gross rates include 10% profit)			
				£	£	£	£	£	£	£	£
K10	**K10: PLASTERBOARD DRY LINING, PARTITIONS AND CEILINGS**										
K1078	**Gyproc linings; 32 mm urethane laminate board to masonry or concrete walls; fixing by Thistlebond TL system; joints flush filled, taped and finished for direct decoration**										
K107801	**Linings to walls; height:**										
K107801A	not exceeding 1200 mm ...	m	0.36	8.44	–	22.13	30.57	9.28	–	24.34	33.63
K107801B	1200-1500 mm..........	m	0.45	10.55	–	27.67	38.22	11.61	–	30.44	42.04
K107801C	1500-1800 mm..........	m	0.54	12.65	–	33.20	45.85	13.92	–	36.52	50.44
K107801D	1800-2100 mm..........	m	0.63	14.77	–	38.74	53.51	16.25	–	42.61	58.86
K107801E	2100-2400 mm..........	m	0.72	16.85	–	44.26	61.11	18.54	–	48.69	67.22
K107801F	2400-2700 mm..........	m	0.81	18.97	–	49.80	68.77	20.87	–	54.78	75.65
K107801G	2700-3000 mm..........	m	0.90	21.07	–	55.33	76.40	23.18	–	60.86	84.04
K107811	**Linings to beams; 3 nr faces; girth:**										
K107811A	not exceeding 600 mm	m	0.16	3.75	–	11.90	15.65	4.13	–	13.09	17.22
K107811B	600-1200 mm..........	m	0.32	7.50	–	22.89	30.39	8.25	–	25.18	33.43
K107811C	1200-1800 mm..........	m	0.47	11.02	–	33.86	44.88	12.12	–	37.25	49.37
K107821	**Linings to columns; 4 nr faces; girth:**										
K107821A	not exceeding 600 mm	m	0.16	3.75	–	12.35	16.10	4.13	–	13.59	17.71
K107821B	600-1200 mm..........	m	0.32	7.50	–	23.34	30.84	8.25	–	25.67	33.92
K107821C	1200-1800 mm..........	m	0.47	11.01	–	34.32	45.33	12.11	–	37.75	49.86
K107831	**Linings to reveals and soffits; width:**										
K107831A	not exceeding 300 mm	m	0.12	2.81	–	5.96	8.77	3.09	–	6.56	9.65
K107831B	300-600 mm.............	m	0.16	3.75	–	11.48	15.23	4.13	–	12.63	16.75

Major Works 2009		Unit	Labour Hours	Labour Net	Plant Net	Materials Net	Unit Net	Labour Gross	Plant Gross	Materials Gross	Unit Price
								(Gross rates include 10% profit)			
				£	£	£	£	£	£	£	£
K10	**K10: PLASTERBOARD DRY LINING, PARTITIONS AND CEILINGS**										
K1079	**Gyproc linings; 40 mm urethane laminate board to masonry or concrete walls; fixing by Thistlebond TL system; joints flush filled, taped and finished for direct decoration**										
K107901	**Linings to walls; height:**										
K107901A	not exceeding 1200 mm ...	m	0.38	9.00	–	24.54	33.54	9.90	–	26.99	36.89
K107901B	1200-1500 mm.	m	0.48	11.25	–	30.68	41.93	12.38	–	33.75	46.12
K107901C	1500-1800 mm.	m	0.58	13.50	–	36.81	50.31	14.85	–	40.49	55.34
K107901D	1800-2100 mm.	m	0.67	15.75	–	42.95	58.70	17.33	–	47.25	64.57
K107901E	2100-2400 mm.	m	0.77	17.98	–	49.07	67.05	19.78	–	53.98	73.76
K107901F	2400-2700 mm.	m	0.86	20.23	–	55.22	75.45	22.25	–	60.74	83.00
K107901G	2700-3000 mm.	m	0.96	22.48	–	61.34	83.82	24.73	–	67.47	92.20
K107911	**Linings to beams; 3 nr faces; girth:**										
K107911A	not exceeding 600 mm	m	0.17	3.98	–	13.11	17.09	4.38	–	14.42	18.80
K107911B	600-1200 mm.	m	0.34	7.97	–	25.29	33.26	8.77	–	27.82	36.59
K107911C	1200-1800 mm.	m	0.49	11.49	–	37.47	48.96	12.64	–	41.22	53.86
K107921	**Linings to columns; 4 nr faces; girth:**										
K107921A	not exceeding 600 mm	m	0.17	3.98	–	13.56	17.54	4.38	–	14.92	19.29
K107921B	600-1200 mm.	m	0.34	7.96	–	25.75	33.71	8.76	–	28.33	37.08
K107921C	1200-1800 mm.	m	0.49	11.48	–	37.93	49.41	12.63	–	41.72	54.35
K107931	**Linings to reveals and soffits; width:**										
K107931A	not exceeding 300 mm	m	0.13	3.05	–	6.56	9.61	3.36	–	7.22	10.57
K107931B	300-600 mm.	m	0.17	3.99	–	12.68	16.67	4.39	–	13.95	18.34

Linings, Sheathing and Dry Partitioning

Major Works 2009		Unit	Labour Hours	Labour Net	Plant Net	Materials Net	Unit Net	Labour Gross	Plant Gross	Materials Gross	Unit Price
								(Gross rates include 10% profit)			
				£	£	£	£	£	£	£	£
K10	**K10: PLASTERBOARD DRY LINING, PARTITIONS AND CEILINGS**										
K1085	**Gyproc linings; 32 mm tapered edge Tri-line laminate board to masonry or concrete walls; fixing by Gyplyner system; joints flush filled, taped and finished for direct decoration**										
K108501	**Linings to walls; height:**										
K108501A	not exceeding 1200 mm ...	m	0.30	6.91	–	22.82	29.73	7.60	–	25.10	32.70
K108501B	1200-1500 mm..........	m	0.45	10.55	–	28.52	39.07	11.61	–	31.37	42.98
K108501C	1500-1800 mm..........	m	0.54	12.62	–	34.22	46.84	13.88	–	37.64	51.52
K108501D	1800-2100 mm..........	m	0.63	14.77	–	39.93	54.70	16.25	–	43.92	60.17
K108501E	2100-2400 mm..........	m	0.72	16.88	–	45.63	62.51	18.57	–	50.19	68.76
K108501F	2400-2700 mm..........	m	0.81	18.94	–	51.34	70.28	20.83	–	56.47	77.31
K108501G	2700-3000 mm..........	m	0.90	21.10	–	57.04	78.14	23.21	–	62.74	85.95
K108511	**Linings to beams; 3 nr faces; girth:**										
K108511A	not exceeding 600 mm	m	0.15	3.52	–	12.99	16.51	3.87	–	14.29	18.16
K108511B	600-1200 mm............	m	0.30	7.03	–	24.17	31.20	7.73	–	26.59	34.32
K108511C	1200-1800 mm..........	m	0.45	10.55	–	35.29	45.84	11.61	–	38.82	50.42
K108521	**Linings to columns; 4 nr faces; girth:**										
K108521A	not exceeding 600 mm	m	0.15	3.51	–	13.75	17.26	3.86	–	15.13	18.99
K108521B	600-1200 mm............	m	0.30	7.03	–	24.92	31.95	7.73	–	27.41	35.15
K108521C	1200-1800 mm..........	m	0.45	10.54	–	36.05	46.59	11.59	–	39.66	51.25
K108531	**Linings to reveals and soffits; width:**										
K108531A	not exceeding 300 mm	m	0.11	2.58	–	6.34	8.92	2.84	–	6.97	9.81
K108531B	300-600 mm.............	m	0.15	3.51	–	11.93	15.44	3.86	–	13.12	16.98

Major Works 2009		Unit	Labour Hours	Labour Net	Plant Net	Materials Net	Unit Net	Labour Gross	Plant Gross	Materials Gross	Unit Price
								(Gross rates include 10% profit)			
				£	£	£	£	£	£	£	£
K10	**K10: PLASTERBOARD DRY LINING, PARTITIONS AND CEILINGS**										
K1086	**Gyproc linings; 40 mm tapered edge Tri-line laminate board to masonry or concrete walls; fixing by Gyplyner system; joints flush filled, taped and finished for direct decoration**										
K108601	**Linings to walls; height:**										
K108601A	not exceeding 1200 mm ...	m	0.32	7.50	–	26.72	34.22	8.25	–	29.39	37.64
K108601B	1200-1500 mm	m	0.49	11.41	–	33.40	44.81	12.55	–	36.74	49.29
K108601C	1500-1800 mm	m	0.58	13.66	–	40.08	53.74	15.03	–	44.09	59.11
K108601D	1800-2100 mm	m	0.68	15.98	–	46.76	62.74	17.58	–	51.44	69.01
K108601E	2100-2400 mm	m	0.78	18.28	–	53.44	71.72	20.11	–	58.78	78.89
K108601F	2400-2700 mm	m	0.88	20.51	–	60.12	80.63	22.56	–	66.13	88.69
K108601G	2700-3000 mm	m	0.98	22.85	–	66.80	89.65	25.14	–	73.48	98.62
K108611	**Linings to beams; 3 nr faces; girth:**										
K108611A	not exceeding 600 mm	m	0.16	3.80	–	15.09	18.89	4.18	–	16.60	20.78
K108611B	600-1200 mm	m	0.33	7.62	–	28.18	35.80	8.38	–	31.00	39.38
K108611C	1200-1800 mm	m	0.49	11.41	–	41.22	52.63	12.55	–	45.34	57.89
K108621	**Linings to columns; 4 nr faces; girth:**										
K108621A	not exceeding 600 mm	m	0.16	3.80	–	15.90	19.70	4.18	–	17.49	21.67
K108621B	600-1200 mm	m	0.30	7.03	–	28.99	36.02	7.73	–	31.89	39.62
K108621C	1200-1800 mm	m	0.49	11.42	–	42.03	53.45	12.56	–	46.23	58.80
K108631	**Linings to reveals and soffits; width:**										
K108631A	not exceeding 300 mm	m	0.12	2.81	–	7.36	10.17	3.09	–	8.10	11.19
K108631B	300-600 mm	m	0.16	3.80	–	13.90	17.70	4.18	–	15.29	19.47

Linings, Sheathing and Dry Partitioning

Major Works 2009		Unit	Labour Hours	Labour Net	Plant Net	Materials Net	Unit Net	Labour Gross	Plant Gross	Materials Gross	Unit Price
								(Gross rates include 10% profit)			
				£	£	£	£	£	£	£	£
K10	**K10: PLASTERBOARD DRY LINING, PARTITIONS AND CEILINGS**										
K1087	**Gyproc linings; 50 mm tapered edge Tri-line laminate board to masonry or concrete walls; fixing by Gyplyner system; joints flush filled, taped and finished for direct decoration**										
K108701	**Linings to walls; height:**										
K108701A	not exceeding 1200 mm ...	m	0.34	8.07	–	31.53	39.60	8.88	–	34.68	43.56
K108701B	1200-1500 mm..........	m	0.52	12.12	–	39.41	51.53	13.33	–	43.35	56.68
K108701C	1500-1800 mm..........	m	0.62	14.51	–	47.30	61.81	15.96	–	52.03	67.99
K108701D	1800-2100 mm..........	m	0.72	16.97	–	55.18	72.15	18.67	–	60.70	79.37
K108701E	2100-2400 mm..........	m	0.83	19.41	–	63.06	82.47	21.35	–	69.37	90.72
K108701F	2400-2700 mm..........	m	0.93	21.77	–	70.95	92.72	23.95	–	78.05	101.99
K108701G	2700-3000 mm..........	m	1.04	24.26	–	78.83	103.09	26.69	–	86.71	113.40
K108711	**Linings to beams; 3 nr faces; girth:**										
K108711A	not exceeding 600 mm	m	0.17	4.08	–	17.49	21.57	4.49	–	19.24	23.73
K108711B	600-1200 mm............	m	0.35	8.18	–	32.99	41.17	9.00	–	36.29	45.29
K108711C	1200-1800 mm..........	m	0.52	12.26	–	48.44	60.70	13.49	–	53.28	66.77
K108721	**Linings to columns; 4 nr faces; girth:**										
K108721A	not exceeding 600 mm	m	0.17	4.08	–	18.31	22.39	4.49	–	20.14	24.63
K108721B	600-1200 mm............	m	0.32	7.60	–	33.80	41.40	8.36	–	37.18	45.54
K108721C	1200-1800 mm..........	m	0.52	12.26	–	49.25	61.51	13.49	–	54.18	67.66
K108731	**Linings to reveals and soffits; width:**										
K108731A	not exceeding 300 mm	m	0.13	2.96	–	8.56	11.52	3.26	–	9.42	12.67
K108731B	300-600 mm.............	m	0.17	4.08	–	16.31	20.39	4.49	–	17.94	22.43

Major Works 2009		Unit	Labour Hours	Labour Net	Plant Net	Materials Net	Unit Net	Labour Gross	Plant Gross	Materials Gross	Unit Price
								(Gross rates include 10% profit)			
				£	£	£	£	£	£	£	£
K10	**K10: PLASTERBOARD DRY LINING, PARTITIONS AND CEILINGS**										
K1088	**Gyproc linings; 32 mm tapered edge vapour check Tri-line laminate board to masonry or concrete walls; fixing by Gyplyner system; joints flush filled, taped and finished for direct decoration**										
K108801	**Linings to walls; height:**										
K108801A	not exceeding 1200 mm ...	m	0.30	6.92	–	24.00	30.92	7.61	–	26.40	34.01
K108801B	1200-1500 mm...........	m	0.45	10.55	–	30.00	40.55	11.61	–	33.00	44.61
K108801C	1500-1800 mm...........	m	0.54	12.61	–	36.00	48.61	13.87	–	39.60	53.47
K108801D	1800-2100 mm...........	m	0.63	14.77	–	42.00	56.77	16.25	–	46.20	62.45
K108801E	2100-2400 mm...........	m	0.72	16.88	–	48.00	64.88	18.57	–	52.80	71.37
K108801F	2400-2700 mm...........	m	0.81	18.94	–	54.00	72.94	20.83	–	59.40	80.23
K108801G	2700-3000 mm...........	m	0.90	21.10	–	60.00	81.10	23.21	–	66.00	89.21
K108811	**Linings to beams; 3 nr faces; girth:**										
K108811A	not exceeding 600 mm	m	0.15	3.51	–	13.59	17.10	3.86	–	14.95	18.81
K108811B	600-1200 mm...........	m	0.30	7.03	–	25.35	32.38	7.73	–	27.89	35.62
K108811C	1200-1800 mm...........	m	0.45	10.55	–	37.07	47.62	11.61	–	40.78	52.38
K108821	**Linings to columns; 4 nr faces; girth:**										
K108821A	not exceeding 600 mm	m	0.15	3.51	–	14.34	17.85	3.86	–	15.77	19.64
K108821B	600-1200 mm...........	m	0.30	7.04	–	26.10	33.14	7.74	–	28.71	36.45
K108821C	1200-1800 mm...........	m	0.45	10.55	–	37.82	48.37	11.61	–	41.60	53.21
K108831	**Linings to reveals and soffits; width:**										
K108831A	not exceeding 300 mm	m	0.11	2.58	–	6.64	9.22	2.84	–	7.30	10.14
K108831B	300-600 mm.............	m	0.15	3.52	–	12.52	16.04	3.87	–	13.77	17.64

Linings, Sheathing and Dry Partitioning

Major Works 2009		Unit	Labour Hours	Labour Net	Plant Net	Materials Net	Unit Net	Labour Gross	Plant Gross	Materials Gross	Unit Price
								(Gross rates include 10% profit)			
				£	£	£	£	£	£	£	£
K10	**K10: PLASTERBOARD DRY LINING, PARTITIONS AND CEILINGS**										
K1089	**Gyproc linings; 40 mm tapered edge vapour check Tri-line laminate board to masonry or concrete walls; fixing by Gyplyner system; joints flush filled, taped and finished for direct decoration**										
K108901	**Linings to walls; height:**										
K108901A	not exceeding 1200 mm ...	m	0.32	7.50	–	27.69	35.19	8.25	–	30.46	38.71
K108901B	1200-1500 mm..........	m	0.49	11.42	–	34.61	46.03	12.56	–	38.07	50.63
K108901C	1500-1800 mm..........	m	0.58	13.67	–	41.53	55.20	15.04	–	45.68	60.72
K108901D	1800-2100 mm..........	m	0.68	15.98	–	48.46	64.44	17.58	–	53.31	70.88
K108901E	2100-2400 mm..........	m	0.78	18.28	–	55.38	73.66	20.11	–	60.92	81.03
K108901F	2400-2700 mm..........	m	0.88	20.51	–	62.30	82.81	22.56	–	68.53	91.09
K108901G	2700-3000 mm..........	m	0.98	22.86	–	69.22	92.08	25.15	–	76.14	101.29
K108911	**Linings to beams; 3 nr faces; girth:**										
K108911A	not exceeding 600 mm	m	0.16	3.80	–	15.57	19.37	4.18	–	17.13	21.31
K108911B	600-1200 mm..........	m	0.33	7.62	–	29.15	36.77	8.38	–	32.07	40.45
K108911C	1200-1800 mm..........	m	0.49	11.42	–	42.67	54.09	12.56	–	46.94	59.50
K108921	**Linings to columns; 4 nr faces; girth:**										
K108921A	not exceeding 600 mm	m	0.16	3.79	–	16.39	20.18	4.17	–	18.03	22.20
K108921B	600-1200 mm..........	m	0.30	7.03	–	29.96	36.99	7.73	–	32.96	40.69
K108921C	1200-1800 mm..........	m	0.49	11.41	–	43.49	54.90	12.55	–	47.84	60.39
K108931	**Linings to reveals and soffits; width:**										
K108931A	not exceeding 300 mm	m	0.12	2.82	–	7.60	10.42	3.10	–	8.36	11.46
K108931B	300-600 mm.............	m	0.16	3.79	–	14.39	18.18	4.17	–	15.83	20.00

Major Works 2009		Unit	Labour Hours	Labour Net	Plant Net	Materials Net	Unit Net	Labour Gross	Plant Gross	Materials Gross	Unit Price
								(Gross rates include 10% profit)			
				£	£	£	£	£	£	£	£
K10	**K10: PLASTERBOARD DRY LINING, PARTITIONS AND CEILINGS**										
K1090	**Gyproc linings; 50 mm tapered edge vapour check Tri-line laminate board to masonry or concrete walls; fixing by Gyplyner system; joints flush filled, taped and finished for direct decoration**										
K109001	**Linings to walls; height:**										
K109001A	not exceeding 1200 mm ...	m	0.34	8.06	–	30.10	38.16	8.87	–	33.11	41.98
K109001B	1200-1500 mm...........	m	0.52	12.12	–	37.62	49.74	13.33	–	41.38	54.71
K109001C	1500-1800 mm...........	m	0.62	14.51	–	45.14	59.65	15.96	–	49.65	65.62
K109001D	1800-2100 mm...........	m	0.72	16.97	–	52.67	69.64	18.67	–	57.94	76.60
K109001E	2100-2400 mm...........	m	0.83	19.41	–	60.19	79.60	21.35	–	66.21	87.56
K109001F	2400-2700 mm...........	m	0.93	21.78	–	67.71	89.49	23.96	–	74.48	98.44
K109001G	2700-3000 mm...........	m	1.04	24.26	–	75.24	99.50	26.69	–	82.76	109.45
K109011	**Linings to beams; 3 nr faces; girth:**										
K109011A	not exceeding 600 mm	m	0.17	4.08	–	16.78	20.86	4.49	–	18.46	22.95
K109011B	600-1200 mm............	m	0.35	8.18	–	31.56	39.74	9.00	–	34.72	43.71
K109011C	1200-1800 mm...........	m	0.52	12.26	–	46.28	58.54	13.49	–	50.91	64.39
K109021	**Linings to columns; 4 nr faces; girth:**										
K109021A	not exceeding 600 mm	m	0.17	4.08	–	17.59	21.67	4.49	–	19.35	23.84
K109021B	600-1200 mm............	m	0.32	7.59	–	32.37	39.96	8.35	–	35.61	43.96
K109021C	1200-1800 mm...........	m	0.52	12.26	–	47.10	59.36	13.49	–	51.81	65.30
K109031	**Linings to reveals and soffits; width:**										
K109031A	not exceeding 300 mm	m	0.13	2.95	–	8.21	11.16	3.25	–	9.03	12.28
K109031B	300-600 mm.............	m	0.17	4.08	–	15.59	19.67	4.49	–	17.15	21.64

Linings, Sheathing and Dry Partitioning

Major Works 2009		Unit	Labour Hours	Labour Net	Plant Net	Materials Net	Unit Net	Labour Gross	Plant Gross	Materials Gross	Unit Price
								(Gross rates include 10% profit)			
				£	£	£	£	£	£	£	£
K10	**K10: PLASTERBOARD DRY LINING, PARTITIONS AND CEILINGS**										
K1094	**Gyproc Drywall topcoat**										
K109401	**One coat Gyproc Drywall topcoat to surfaces of tapered edge boarding including filling, taping and finishing joints flush; ready for direct decoration:**										
K109401A	walls, returns, reveals of openings or recesses, attached and unattached columns................	m²	0.17	3.98	–	1.04	5.02	4.38	–	1.14	5.52
K109401B	ceilings, attached and unattached beams and soffits of staircases	m²	0.21	4.92	–	0.90	5.82	5.41	–	0.99	6.40
K109401C	skirtings, bands, strings, coverings kerbs, mouldings, channels or the like; not exceeding 300 mm wide ...	m	0.10	2.34	–	0.29	2.63	2.57	–	0.32	2.89
K109440	**One coat Gyproc Drywall topcoat to surfaces of boarding excluding filling, taping and finishing joints; ready for direct decoration:**										
K109440A	walls, returns, reveals of openings or recesses, attached and unattached columns................	m²	0.12	2.82	–	0.45	3.27	3.10	–	0.50	3.60
K109440B	ceilings, attached and unattached beams and soffits of staircases	m²	0.15	3.52	–	0.45	3.97	3.87	–	0.50	4.37
K109440C	skirtings, bands, strings, coverings kerbs, mouldings, channels or the like; not exceeding 300 mm wide ...	m	0.07	1.64	–	0.15	1.79	1.80	–	0.17	1.97

Major Works 2009		Unit	Labour Hours	Labour Net	Plant Net	Materials Net	Unit Net	Labour Gross	Plant Gross	Materials Gross	Unit Price
								(Gross rates include 10% profit)			
				£	£	£	£	£	£	£	£
K10	**K10: PLASTERBOARD DRY LINING, PARTITIONS AND CEILINGS**										
K1095	**Dry-lining beads, stops, edgings and arches**										
K109504	**Expamet galvanised mild steel plaster beads and stops; fixing in accordance with manufacturer's instructions:**										
K109504P	10 mm architrave bead ref 513	m	0.04	0.68	–	1.05	1.73	0.75	–	1.16	1.90
K109504Q	10 mm architrave bead ref 514	m	0.04	0.68	–	1.22	1.90	0.75	–	1.34	2.09
K109504X	dry wall corner bead ref 548	m	0.04	0.68	–	0.98	1.66	0.75	–	1.08	1.83
K109504Y	10 mm edge bead ref 567 . .	m	0.04	0.68	–	1.58	2.26	0.75	–	1.74	2.49
K109504Z	12 mm edge bead ref 568 . .	m	. 0.04	0.68	–	1.58	2.26	0.75	–	1.74	2.49
K109511	**Expamet galvanised mild steel dry-lining arch formers; fixing in accordance with manufacturer's instructions:**										
K109511A	380 mm radius semi-circle ref DSC 30	Nr	0.35	8.20	–	18.27	26.47	9.02	–	20.10	29.12
K109511B	405 mm radius semi-circle ref DSC 32	Nr	0.35	8.20	–	18.81	27.01	9.02	–	20.69	29.71
K109511C	420 mm radius semi-circle ref DSC 33	Nr	0.35	8.20	–	18.81	27.01	9.02	–	20.69	29.71
K109511D	455 mm radius semi-circle ref DSC 36	Nr	0.35	8.20	–	19.94	28.14	9.02	–	21.93	30.95
K109511E	610 mm radius semi-circle ref DSC 48	Nr	0.35	8.20	–	23.48	31.68	9.02	–	25.83	34.85
K109511F	760 mm radius semi-circle ref DSC 60	Nr	0.35	8.20	–	26.47	34.67	9.02	–	29.12	38.14
K109511G	1520 mm wide elliptical ref DEL 60	Nr	0.35	8.20	–	25.90	34.10	9.02	–	28.49	37.51
K109511H	1830 mm wide elliptical ref DEL 72	Nr	0.50	11.72	–	28.70	40.42	12.89	–	31.57	44.46
K109511I	2130 mm wide elliptical ref DEL 84	Nr	0.50	11.72	–	29.99	41.71	12.89	–	32.99	45.88
K109511J	2440 mm wide elliptical ref DEL 96	Nr	0.50	11.72	–	34.66	46.38	12.89	–	38.13	51.02
K109511L	soffit strip 80 mm wide	m	0.12	2.81	–	2.23	5.04	3.09	–	2.45	5.54
K109511M	dry-lining bead ref 553	m	0.04	0.94	–	0.92	1.86	1.03	–	1.01	2.05

Linings, Sheathing and Dry Partitioning

Major Works 2009		Unit	Labour Hours	Labour Net	Plant Net	Materials Net	Unit Net	Labour Gross	Plant Gross	Materials Gross	Unit Price
								(Gross rates include 10% profit)			
				£	£	£	£	£	£	£	£
K11	**K11: RIGID SHEET FLOORING, SHEATHING, LININGS AND CASINGS**										
K1111	**Walls**										
K111101	**Hardboard; 3.2 mm standard:**										
K111101A	over 300 mm wide	m²	0.25	4.25	–	1.76	6.01	4.68	–	1.94	6.61
K111101B	n.e. 300 mm wide	m	0.10	1.70	–	0.56	2.26	1.87	–	0.62	2.49
K111102	**Hardboard; 6.0 mm standard:**										
K111102C	over 300 mm wide	m²	0.30	5.09	–	4.69	9.78	5.60	–	5.16	10.76
K111102D	n.e. 300 mm wide	m	0.12	2.04	–	1.48	3.52	2.24	–	1.63	3.87
K111103	**Hardboard; 3.2 mm perforated:**										
K111103E	over 300 mm wide	m²	0.28	4.75	–	1.83	6.58	5.23	–	2.01	7.24
K111103F	n.e. 300 mm wide	m	0.12	1.96	–	0.58	2.54	2.16	–	0.64	2.79
K111104	**Hardboard; 6.0 mm perforated:**										
K111104G	over 300 mm wide	m²	0.32	5.44	–	3.57	9.01	5.98	–	3.93	9.91
K111104H	n.e. 300 mm wide	m	0.13	2.21	–	1.13	3.34	2.43	–	1.24	3.67
K111105	**Hardboard; 6.0 mm flameproof Class 1:**										
K111105I	over 300 mm wide	m²	0.30	5.10	–	12.78	17.88	5.61	–	14.06	19.67
K111105J	n.e. 300 mm wide	m	0.12	2.04	–	4.02	6.06	2.24	–	4.42	6.67
K111106	**Hardboard; 3.2 mm stove enamelled one side:**										
K111106K	over 300 mm wide	m²	0.28	4.76	–	2.57	7.33	5.24	–	2.83	8.06
K111106L	n.e. 300 mm wide	m	0.12	1.95	–	0.82	2.77	2.15	–	0.90	3.05
K111111	**Insulation board; 6.4 mm Sundeala A:**										
K111111A	over 300 mm wide	m²	0.35	5.94	–	9.05	14.99	6.53	–	9.96	16.49
K111111B	n.e. 300 mm wide	m	0.14	2.43	–	2.85	5.28	2.67	–	3.14	5.81
K111112	**Insulation board; 9.5 mm Sundeala A:**										
K111112C	over 300 mm wide	m²	0.38	6.45	–	11.68	18.13	7.10	–	12.85	19.94
K111112D	n.e. 300 mm wide	m	0.15	2.55	–	3.67	6.22	2.81	–	4.04	6.84
K111113	**Insulation board; 12.5 mm Sundeala A:**										
K111113E	over 300 mm wide	m²	0.40	6.79	–	13.36	20.15	7.47	–	14.70	22.17
K111113F	n.e. 300 mm wide	m	0.16	2.72	–	4.19	6.91	2.99	–	4.61	7.60
K111114	**Insulation board; 6.4 mm Sundeala K:**										
K111114G	over 300 mm wide	m²	0.35	5.94	–	8.02	13.96	6.53	–	8.82	15.36
K111114H	n.e. 300 mm wide	m	0.14	2.38	–	2.52	4.90	2.62	–	2.77	5.39
K111115	**Insulation board; 9.5 mm Sundeala K:**										
K111115I	over 300 mm wide	m²	0.38	6.45	–	11.68	18.13	7.10	–	12.85	19.94
K111115J	n.e. 300 mm wide	m	0.15	2.55	–	3.67	6.22	2.81	–	4.04	6.84
K111116	**Insulation board; 12.5 mm Unitex ivory faced:**										
K111116K	over 300 mm wide	m²	0.45	7.64	–	3.67	11.31	8.40	–	4.04	12.44
K111116L	n.e. 300 mm wide	m	0.18	3.05	–	1.15	4.20	3.36	–	1.27	4.62

Major Works 2009		Unit	Labour Hours	Labour Net	Plant Net	Materials Net	Unit Net	Labour Gross	Plant Gross	Materials Gross	Unit Price
								(Gross rates include 10% profit)			
				£	£	£	£	£	£	£	£
K11	**K11: RIGID SHEET FLOORING, SHEATHING, LININGS AND CASINGS**										
K1111	**Walls**										
K111117	**Insulation board; 12.5 mm Unitex white faced:**										
K111117M	over 300 mm wide	m²	0.45	7.65	–	4.45	12.10	8.42	–	4.90	13.31
K111117N	n.e. 300 mm wide	m	0.18	3.05	–	1.40	4.45	3.36	–	1.54	4.90
K111121	**Chipboard; standard grade; 12 mm:**										
K111121A	over 300 mm wide	m²	0.30	5.09	–	2.46	7.55	5.60	–	2.71	8.31
K111121B	n.e. 300 mm wide	m	0.12	2.03	–	0.78	2.81	2.23	–	0.86	3.09
K111122	**Chipboard; standard grade; 15 mm:**										
K111122C	over 300 mm wide	m²	0.35	5.95	–	3.59	9.54	6.55	–	3.95	10.49
K111122D	n.e. 300 mm wide	m	0.14	2.38	–	1.14	3.52	2.62	–	1.25	3.87
K111123	**Chipboard; standard grade; 18 mm:**										
K111123E	over 300 mm wide	m²	0.40	6.79	–	4.32	11.11	7.47	–	4.75	12.22
K111123F	n.e. 300 mm wide	m	0.16	2.71	–	1.37	4.08	2.98	–	1.51	4.49
K111124	**Chipboard; standard grade; 25 mm:**										
K111124E	over 300 mm wide	m²	0.45	7.64	–	5.11	12.75	8.40	–	5.62	14.03
K111124F	n.e. 300 mm wide	m	0.18	3.06	–	1.61	4.67	3.37	–	1.77	5.14
K111126	**Chipboard; faced one side with 1.5 mm Class 1 laminated plastic covering and balancing veneer other side; 15 mm:**										
K111126A	over 300 mm wide	m²	0.50	8.49	–	4.72	13.21	9.34	–	5.19	14.53
K111126B	n.e. 300 mm wide	m	0.20	3.40	–	1.40	4.80	3.74	–	1.54	5.28
K111127	**Chipboard; faced one side with 1.5 mm Class 1 laminated plastic covering and balancing veneer other side; 18 mm:**										
K111127C	over 300 mm wide	m²	0.60	10.19	–	5.01	15.20	11.21	–	5.51	16.72
K111127D	n.e. 300 mm wide	m	0.24	4.07	–	1.60	5.67	4.48	–	1.76	6.24
K111131	**Finnish birch faced 5 ply blockboard; grade BB; 12 mm:**										
K111131A	over 300 mm wide	m²	0.68	11.46	–	11.31	22.77	12.61	–	12.44	25.05
K111131B	n.e. 300 mm wide	m	0.27	4.58	–	3.58	8.16	5.04	–	3.94	8.98
K111132	**Finnish birch faced 5 ply blockboard; grade BB; 18 mm:**										
K111132A	over 300 mm wide	m²	0.75	12.74	–	14.72	27.46	14.01	–	16.19	30.21
K111132B	n.e. 300 mm wide	m	0.30	5.10	–	4.65	9.75	5.61	–	5.12	10.73
K111133	**Finnish birch faced 5 ply blockboard; grade BB; 25 mm:**										
K111133C	over 300 mm wide	m²	0.80	13.58	–	20.86	34.44	14.94	–	22.95	37.88
K111133D	n.e. 300 mm wide	m	0.32	5.43	–	6.58	12.01	5.97	–	7.24	13.21
K111135	**Far Eastern hardwood faced MR boarding ply; grade B/BB; 4 mm:**										
K111135A	over 300 mm wide	m²	0.38	6.45	–	3.53	9.98	7.10	–	3.88	10.98
K111135B	n.e. 300 mm wide	m	0.15	2.55	–	1.11	3.66	2.81	–	1.22	4.03

Linings, Sheathing and Dry Partitioning

Major Works 2009		Unit	Labour Hours	Labour Net	Plant Net	Materials Net	Unit Net	Labour Gross	Plant Gross	Materials Gross	Unit Price
								— (Gross rates include 10% profit) —			
				£	£	£	£	£	£	£	£
K11	**K11: RIGID SHEET FLOORING, SHEATHING, LININGS AND CASINGS**										
K1111	**Walls**										
K111136	**Far Eastern hardwood faced MR boarding ply; grade B/BB; 6 mm:**										
K111136C	over 300 wide	m²	0.42	7.13	–	4.54	11.67	7.84	–	4.99	12.84
K111136D	n.e. 300 mm wide	m	0.17	2.89	–	1.43	4.32	3.18	–	1.57	4.75
K111137	**Far Eastern hardwood faced MR boarding ply; grade B/BB; 9 mm:**										
K111137E	over 300 mm wide	m²	0.46	7.81	–	6.38	14.19	8.59	–	7.02	15.61
K111137F	n.e. 300 mm wide	m	0.18	3.06	–	2.01	5.07	3.37	–	2.21	5.58
K111138	**Far Eastern hardwood faced MR boarding ply; grade B/BB; 12 mm:**										
K111138G	over 300 mm wide	m²	0.50	8.49	–	8.09	16.58	9.34	–	8.90	18.24
K111138H	n.e. 300 mm wide	m	0.20	3.40	–	8.06	11.46	3.74	–	8.87	12.61
K111139	**Far Eastern hardwood faced MR boarding ply; grade B/BB; 15 mm:**										
K111139I	over 300 mm wide	m²	0.56	9.51	–	10.29	19.80	10.46	–	11.32	21.78
K111139J	n.e. 300 mm wide	m	0.23	3.82	–	3.24	7.06	4.20	–	3.56	7.77
K111140	**Far Eastern hardwood faced MR boarding ply; grade B/BB; 18 mm:**										
K111140K	over 300 mm wide	m²	0.60	10.19	–	11.75	21.94	11.21	–	12.93	24.13
K111140L	n.e. 300 mm wide	m	0.24	4.07	–	3.70	7.77	4.48	–	4.07	8.55
K111141	**Far Eastern hardwood faced MR boarding ply; grade B/BB; 22 mm:**										
K111141M	over 300 mm wide	m²	0.64	10.86	–	14.05	24.91	11.95	–	15.46	27.40
K111141N	n.e. 300 mm wide	m	0.26	4.35	–	4.42	8.77	4.79	–	4.86	9.65
K111142	**Far Eastern hardwood faced MR boarding ply; grade B/BB; 25 mm:**										
K111142O	over 300 mm wide	m²	0.69	11.71	–	16.32	28.03	12.88	–	17.95	30.83
K111142P	n.e. 300 mm wide	m	0.28	4.67	–	5.13	9.80	5.14	–	5.64	10.78
K111145	**Finnish birch faced WBP boarding ply; grade BB; 4 mm:**										
K111145A	over 300 mm wide	m²	0.35	5.94	–	7.01	12.95	6.53	–	7.71	14.25
K111145B	n.e. 300 mm wide	m	0.14	2.37	–	2.21	4.58	2.61	–	2.43	5.04
K111146	**Finnish birch faced WBP boarding ply; grade BB; 6 mm:**										
K111146C	over 300 mm wide	m²	0.38	6.46	–	10.30	16.76	7.11	–	11.33	18.44
K111146D	n.e. 300 mm wide	m	0.15	2.55	–	3.24	5.79	2.81	–	3.56	6.37
K111147	**Finnish birch faced WBP boarding ply; grade BB; 9 mm:**										
K111147E	over 300 mm wide	m²	0.40	6.79	–	12.68	19.47	7.47	–	13.95	21.42
K111147F	n.e. 300 mm wide	m	0.16	2.72	–	3.99	6.71	2.99	–	4.39	7.38
K111148	**Finnish birch faced WBP boarding ply; grade BB; 12 mm:**										
K111148G	over 300 mm wide	m²	0.45	7.64	–	14.87	22.51	8.40	–	16.36	24.76
K111148H	n.e. 300 mm wide	m	0.18	3.05	–	4.68	7.73	3.36	–	5.15	8.50

Major Works 2009		Unit	Labour Hours	Labour Net	Plant Net	Materials Net	Unit Net	Labour Gross	Plant Gross	Materials Gross	Unit Price
								(Gross rates include 10% profit)			
				£	£	£	£	£	£	£	£
K11	**K11: RIGID SHEET FLOORING, SHEATHING, LININGS AND CASINGS**										
K1111	**Walls**										
K111149	**Finnish birch faced WBP boarding ply; grade BB; 15 mm:**										
K1111491	over 300 mm wide	m²	0.48	8.15	–	20.00	28.15	8.97	–	22.00	30.97
K111149J	n.e. 300 mm wide	m	0.19	3.22	–	6.29	9.51	3.54	–	6.92	10.46
K111150	**Finnish birch faced WBP boarding ply; grade BB; 18 mm:**										
K111150K	over 300 mm wide	m²	0.52	8.83	–	23.84	32.67	9.71	–	26.22	35.94
K111150L	n.e. 300 mm wide	m	0.21	3.56	–	7.50	11.06	3.92	–	8.25	12.17
K111151	**Finnish birch faced WBP boarding ply; grade BB; 22 mm:**										
K111151M	over 300 mm wide	m²	0.56	9.51	–	28.22	37.73	10.46	–	31.04	41.50
K111151N	n.e. 300 mm wide	m	0.23	3.82	–	8.87	12.69	4.20	–	9.76	13.96
K111152	**Finnish birch faced WBP boarding ply; grade BB; 25 mm:**										
K1111520	over 300 mm wide	m²	0.60	10.19	–	32.61	42.80	11.21	–	35.87	47.08
K111152P	n.e. 300 mm wide	m	0.24	4.08	–	10.25	14.33	4.49	–	11.28	15.76
K111155	**Non-asbestos, flameproof Class O boards; BS 476; 6 mm:**										
K111155A	over 300 mm wide	m²	0.28	4.76	–	9.07	13.83	5.24	–	9.98	15.21
K111155B	n.e. 300 mm wide	m	0.11	1.87	–	2.86	4.73	2.06	–	3.15	5.20
K111156	**Non-asbestos, flameproof Class O boards; BS 476; 9 mm:**										
K111156C	over 300 mm wide	m²	0.30	5.09	–	24.56	29.65	5.60	–	27.02	32.62
K111156D	n.e. 300 mm wide	m	0.12	2.04	–	7.73	9.77	2.24	–	8.50	10.75
K111157	**Non-asbestos, flameproof Class O boards; BS 476; 12 mm:**										
K111157E	over 300 mm wide	m²	0.35	5.94	–	37.00	42.94	6.53	–	40.70	47.23
K111157F	n.e. 300 mm wide	m	0.14	2.38	–	11.64	14.02	2.62	–	12.80	15.42
K111158	**Non-asbestos, flameproof Class O boards; BS 476; 15 mm:**										
K111158G	over 300 mm wide	m²	0.40	6.79	–	46.34	53.13	7.47	–	50.97	58.44
K111158H	n.e. 300 mm wide	m	0.16	2.72	–	14.58	17.30	2.99	–	16.04	19.03
K111161	**Medium density fibreboard; MDF; 9 mm:**										
K111161A	over 300 mm wide	m²	0.32	5.44	–	4.36	9.80	5.98	–	4.80	10.78
K111161B	n.e. 300 mm wide	m	0.19	3.23	–	1.35	4.58	3.55	–	1.49	5.04
K111162	**Medium density fibreboard; MDF; 12 mm:**										
K111162A	over 300 mm wide	m²	0.33	5.60	–	5.00	10.60	6.16	–	5.50	11.66
K111162B	n.e. 300 mm wide	m	0.20	3.40	–	1.55	4.95	3.74	–	1.71	5.45
K111163	**Medium density fibreboard; MDF; 15 mm:**										
K111163A	over 300 mm wide	m²	0.34	5.78	–	5.03	10.81	6.36	–	5.53	11.89
K111163B	n.e. 300 mm wide	m	0.21	3.56	–	1.56	5.12	3.92	–	1.72	5.63
K111164	**Medium density fibreboard; MDF; 18 mm:**										
K111164A	over 300 mm wide	m²	0.36	6.11	–	6.94	13.05	6.72	–	7.63	14.36
K111164B	n.e. 300 mm wide	m	0.22	3.74	–	2.15	5.89	4.11	–	2.37	6.48

Linings, Sheathing and Dry Partitioning

Major Works 2009		Unit	Labour Hours	Labour Net	Plant Net	Materials Net	Unit Net	Labour Gross	Plant Gross	Materials Gross	Unit Price
								(Gross rates include 10% profit)			
				£	£	£	£	£	£	£	£
K11	**K11: RIGID SHEET FLOORING, SHEATHING, LININGS AND CASINGS**										
K1111	**Walls**										
K111165	**Medium density fibreboard; MDF; 25 mm:**										
K111165A	over 300 mm wide	m²	0.38	6.45	–	9.97	16.42	7.10	–	10.97	18.06
K111165B	n.e. 300 mm wide	m	0.23	3.91	–	3.08	6.99	4.30	–	3.39	7.69
K1113	**Floors**										
K111304	**Marine plywood square edged boarding; BS1088:**										
K111304A	12 mm thick; over 300 mm wide	m²	0.35	5.95	–	13.65	19.60	6.55	–	15.02	21.56
K111304B	12 mm thick; n.e. 300 mm wide	m	0.14	2.38	–	4.34	6.72	2.62	–	4.77	7.39
K111304C	18 mm thick; over 300 mm wide	m²	0.35	5.95	–	19.98	25.93	6.55	–	21.98	28.52
K111304D	18 mm thick; n.e. 300 mm wide	m	0.14	2.38	–	6.35	8.73	2.62	–	6.99	9.60
K111304E	25 mm thick; over 300 mm wide	m²	0.35	5.94	–	29.86	35.80	6.53	–	32.85	39.38
K111304F	25 mm thick; n.e. 300 mm wide	m	0.14	2.38	–	9.48	11.86	2.62	–	10.43	13.05
K111305	**Marine plywood tongued and grooved boarding; BS1088:**										
K111305A	12 mm thick; over 300 mm wide	m²	0.45	7.64	–	15.00	22.64	8.40	–	16.50	24.90
K111305B	12 mm thick; n.e. 300 mm wide	m	0.18	3.06	–	4.77	7.83	3.37	–	5.25	8.61
K111305C	18 mm thick; over 300 mm wide	m²	0.45	7.64	–	21.95	29.59	8.40	–	24.15	32.55
K111305D	18 mm thick; n.e. 300 mm wide	m	0.18	3.06	–	6.97	10.03	3.37	–	7.67	11.03
K111305E	25 mm thick; over 300 mm wide	m²	0.45	7.64	–	32.83	40.47	8.40	–	36.11	44.52
K111305F	25 mm thick; n.e. 300 mm wide	m	0.18	3.06	–	10.42	13.48	3.37	–	11.46	14.83
K111306	**WBP bonding plywood square edged boarding; grade BB:**										
K111306A	12 mm thick; over 300 mm wide	m²	0.35	5.94	–	9.01	14.95	6.53	–	9.91	16.45
K111306B	12 mm thick; n.e. 300 mm wide	m	0.14	2.38	–	2.87	5.25	2.62	–	3.16	5.78
K111306C	18 mm thick; over 300 mm wide	m²	0.35	5.94	–	13.08	19.02	6.53	–	14.39	20.92
K111306D	18 mm thick; n.e. 300 mm wide	m	0.14	2.38	–	4.16	6.54	2.62	–	4.58	7.19
K111306E	25 mm thick; over 300 mm wide	m²	0.35	5.94	–	18.63	24.57	6.53	–	20.49	27.03
K111306F	25 mm thick; n.e. 300 mm wide	m	0.14	2.38	–	5.92	8.30	2.62	–	6.51	9.13

Major Works 2009		Unit	Labour Hours	Labour Net	Plant Net	Materials Net	Unit Net	Labour Gross	Plant Gross	Materials Gross	Unit Price
								(Gross rates include 10% profit)			
				£	£	£	£	£	£	£	£
K11	**K11: RIGID SHEET FLOORING, SHEATHING, LININGS AND CASINGS**										
K1111	**Walls**										
K111307	**V313 moisture resistant chipboard square edged boarding; BS5669:**										
K111307A	18 mm thick; over 300 mm wide	m²	0.30	5.10	–	4.65	9.75	5.61	–	5.12	10.73
K111307B	18 mm thick; n.e. 300 mm wide	m	0.12	2.04	–	1.49	3.53	2.24	–	1.64	3.88
K111307C	22 mm thick; over 300 mm wide	m²	0.30	5.09	–	5.75	10.84	5.60	–	6.33	11.92
K111307D	22 mm thick; n.e. 300 mm wide	m	0.12	2.03	–	1.84	3.87	2.23	–	2.02	4.26
K111308	**V313 moisture resistant tongued and grooved chipboard boarding; BS5669:**										
K111308A	18 mm thick; over 300 mm wide	m²	0.40	6.79	–	5.91	12.70	7.47	–	6.50	13.97
K111308B	18 mm thick; n.e. 300 mm wide	m	0.16	2.71	–	1.89	4.60	2.98	–	2.08	5.06
K111308C	22 mm thick; over 300 mm wide	m²	0.40	6.79	–	6.99	13.78	7.47	–	7.69	15.16
K111308D	22 mm thick; n.e. 300 mm wide	m	0.16	2.72	–	2.23	4.95	2.99	–	2.45	5.45

Linings, Sheathing and Dry Partitioning

Major Works 2009		Unit	Labour Hours	Labour Net	Plant Net	Materials Net	Unit Net	Labour Gross	Plant Gross	Materials Gross	Unit Price
				£	£	£	£	(Gross rates include 10% profit)			
								£	£	£	£
K11	**K11: RIGID SHEET FLOORING, SHEATHING, LININGS AND CASINGS**										
K1115	**Ceilings**										
K111501	**Hardboard; 3.2 mm standard:**										
K111501A	over 300 mm wide	m²	0.30	5.10	–	1.76	6.86	5.61	–	1.94	7.55
K111501B	n.e. 300 mm wide	m	0.12	2.04	–	0.56	2.60	2.24	–	0.62	2.86
K111502	**Hardboard; 6.0 mm standard:**										
K111502C	over 300 mm wide	m²	0.35	5.94	–	4.69	10.63	6.53	–	5.16	11.69
K111502D	n.e. 300 mm wide	m	0.14	2.38	–	1.48	3.86	2.62	–	1.63	4.25
K111503	**Hardboard; 6.0 mm flameproof Class 1:**										
K111503E	over 300 mm wide	m²	0.35	5.95	–	12.78	18.73	6.55	–	14.06	20.60
K111503F	n.e. 300 mm wide	m	0.14	2.38	–	4.02	6.40	2.62	–	4.42	7.04
K111511	**Insulation board; 6.4 mm Sundeala A:**										
K111511A	over 300 mm wide	m²	0.40	6.79	–	9.05	15.84	7.47	–	9.96	17.42
K111511B	n.e. 300 mm wide	m	0.16	2.71	–	2.86	5.57	2.98	–	3.15	6.13
K111512	**Insulation board; 9.5 mm Sundeala A:**										
K111512C	over 300 mm wide	m²	0.43	7.30	–	11.68	18.98	8.03	–	12.85	20.88
K111512D	n.e. 300 mm wide	m	0.17	2.89	–	3.68	6.57	3.18	–	4.05	7.23
K111513	**Insulation board; 12.5 mm Sundeala A:**										
K111513E	over 300 mm wide	m²	0.45	7.64	–	13.36	21.00	8.40	–	14.70	23.10
K111513F	n.e. 300 mm wide	m	0.18	3.06	–	4.22	7.28	3.37	–	4.64	8.01
K111514	**Insulation board; 6.4 mm Sundeala K:**										
K111514G	over 300 mm wide	m²	0.40	6.79	–	8.02	14.81	7.47	–	8.82	16.29
K111514H	n.e. 300 mm wide	m	0.16	2.72	–	2.53	5.25	2.99	–	2.78	5.78
K111515	**Insulation board; 9.5 mm Sundeala K:**										
K111515I	over 300 mm wide	m²	0.43	7.30	–	11.68	18.98	8.03	–	12.85	20.88
K111515J	n.e. 300 mm wide	m	0.17	2.89	–	3.68	6.57	3.18	–	4.05	7.23
K111516	**Insulation board; 12.5 mm ivory faced:**										
K111516K	over 300 mm wide	m²	0.50	8.49	–	3.67	12.16	9.34	–	4.04	13.38
K111516L	n.e. 300 mm wide	m	0.20	3.39	–	1.18	4.57	3.73	–	1.30	5.03

Major Works 2009		Unit	Labour Hours	Labour Net	Plant Net	Materials Net	Unit Net	Labour Gross	Plant Gross	Materials Gross	Unit Price
								(Gross rates include 10% profit)			
				£	£	£	£	£	£	£	£
K11	**K11: RIGID SHEET FLOORING, SHEATHING, LININGS AND CASINGS**										
K1115	**Ceilings**										
K111517	**Insulation board; 12.5 mm white faced:**										
K111517M	over 300 mm wide	m²	0.50	8.49	–	4.45	12.94	9.34	–	4.90	14.23
K111517N	n.e. 300 mm wide	m	0.20	3.40	–	1.42	4.82	3.74	–	1.56	5.30
K111521	**Non-asbestos flameproof Class O boards; BS 476; 6 mm:**										
K111521A	over 300 mm wide	m²	0.33	5.60	–	9.12	14.72	6.16	–	10.03	16.19
K111521B	300 mm wide	m	0.13	2.21	–	2.88	5.09	2.43	–	3.17	5.60
K111522	**Non-asbestos flameproof Class O boards; BS 476; 9 mm:**										
K111522C	over 300 mm wide	m²	0.35	5.94	–	24.61	30.55	6.53	–	27.07	33.61
K111522D	n.e. 300 mm wide	m	0.14	2.38	–	7.75	10.13	2.62	–	8.53	11.14
K111523	**Non-asbestos flameproof Class O boards; BS 476; 12 mm:**										
K111523E	over 300 mm wide	m²	0.40	6.79	–	37.05	43.84	7.47	–	40.76	48.22
K111523F	n.e. 300 mm wide	m	0.16	2.72	–	11.66	14.38	2.99	–	12.83	15.82
K111524	**Non-asbestos flameproof Class O boards; BS 476; 15 mm:**										
K111524G	over 300 mm wide	m²	0.45	7.64	–	46.39	54.03	8.40	–	51.03	59.43
K111524H	n.e. 300 mm wide	m	0.18	3.06	–	14.60	17.66	3.37	–	16.06	19.43

Linings, Sheathing and Dry Partitioning

Major Works 2009		Unit	Labour Hours	Labour Net	Plant Net	Materials Net	Unit Net	Labour Gross	Plant Gross	Materials Gross	Unit Price
								(Gross rates include 10% profit)			
				£	£	£	£	£	£	£	£
K11	**K11: RIGID SHEET FLOORING, SHEATHING, LININGS AND CASINGS**										
K1120	**Isolated beams**										
K112001	**Hardboard; 3.2 mm standard:**										
K112001A	not exceeding 600 mm girth	m²	0.45	7.64	–	1.84	9.48	8.40	–	2.02	10.43
K112001B	600-1200 mm girth	m²	0.36	6.12	–	1.80	7.92	6.73	–	1.98	8.71
K112001C	1200-1800 mm girth	m²	0.30	5.10	–	1.76	6.86	5.61	–	1.94	7.55
K112002	**Hardboard; 6.0 mm standard:**										
K112002A	not exceeding 600 mm girth	m²	0.53	8.91	–	4.91	13.82	9.80	–	5.40	15.20
K112002B	600-1200 mm girth	m²	0.42	7.13	–	4.80	11.93	7.84	–	5.28	13.12
K112002C	1200-1800 mm girth	m²	0.35	5.94	–	4.69	10.63	6.53	–	5.16	11.69
K112003	**Hardboard; 6.0 mm flameproof Class 1:**										
K112003A	not exceeding 600 mm girth	m²	0.53	8.91	–	13.39	22.30	9.80	–	14.73	24.53
K112003B	600-1200 mm girth	m²	0.42	7.13	–	13.09	20.22	7.84	–	14.40	22.24
K112003C	1200-1800 mm girth	m²	0.35	5.95	–	12.78	18.73	6.55	–	14.06	20.60
K112011	**Insulation board; 6.4 mm Sundeala A:**										
K112011A	not exceeding 600 mm girth	m²	0.60	10.19	–	9.47	19.66	11.21	–	10.42	21.63
K112011B	600-1200 mm girth	m²	0.48	8.15	–	9.26	17.41	8.97	–	10.19	19.15
K112011C	1200-1800 mm girth	m²	0.40	6.79	–	9.05	15.84	7.47	–	9.96	17.42
K112012	**Insulation board; 9.5 mm Sundeala A:**										
K112012A	not exceeding 600 mm girth	m²	0.65	10.96	–	12.22	23.18	12.06	–	13.44	25.50
K112012B	600-1200 mm girth	m²	0.52	8.83	–	11.95	20.78	9.71	–	13.15	22.86
K112012C	1200-1800 mm girth	m²	0.43	7.30	–	11.68	18.98	8.03	–	12.85	20.88
K112013	**Insulation board; 12.5 mm Sundeala A:**										
K112013A	not exceeding 600 mm girth	m²	0.68	11.46	–	13.98	25.44	12.61	–	15.38	27.98
K112013B	600-1200 mm girth	m²	0.54	9.17	–	13.67	22.84	10.09	–	15.04	25.12
K112013C	1200-1800 mm girth	m²	0.45	7.64	–	13.36	21.00	8.40	–	14.70	23.10
K112014	**Insulation board; 6.4 mm Sundeala K:**										
K112014A	not exceeding 600 mm girth	m²	0.60	10.18	–	8.40	18.58	11.20	–	9.24	20.44
K112014B	600-1200 mm girth	m²	0.48	8.15	–	8.21	16.36	8.97	–	9.03	18.00
K112014C	1200-1800 mm girth	m²	0.40	6.79	–	8.02	14.81	7.47	–	8.82	16.29
K112015	**Insulation board; 9.5 mm Sundeala K:**										
K112015A	not exceeding 600 mm girth	m²	0.65	10.96	–	12.22	23.18	12.06	–	13.44	25.50
K112015B	600-1200 mm girth	m²	0.52	8.83	–	11.95	20.78	9.71	–	13.15	22.86
K112015C	1200-1800 mm girth	m²	0.43	7.30	–	11.68	18.98	8.03	–	12.85	20.88
K112016	**Insulation board; 12.5 mm Pilkington ivory faced:**										
K112016A	not exceeding 600 mm girth	m²	0.75	12.73	–	3.83	16.56	14.00	–	4.21	18.22
K112016B	600-1200 mm girth	m²	0.60	10.19	–	3.75	13.94	11.21	–	4.13	15.33
K112016C	1200-1800 mm girth	m²	0.50	8.49	–	3.67	12.16	9.34	–	4.04	13.38

Major Works 2009		Unit	Labour Hours	Labour Net	Plant Net	Materials Net	Unit Net	Labour Gross	Plant Gross	Materials Gross	Unit Price
								—— (Gross rates include 10% profit) ——			
				£	£	£	£	£	£	£	£
K11	**K11: RIGID SHEET FLOORING, SHEATHING, LININGS AND CASINGS**										
K1120	**Isolated beams**										
K112017	**Insulation board; 12.5 mm Unitex white faced:**										
K112017A	not exceeding 600 mm girth	m²	0.75	12.74	–	4.65	17.39	14.01	–	5.12	19.13
K112017B	600-1200 mm girth	m²	0.60	10.19	–	4.55	14.74	11.21	–	5.01	16.21
K112017C	1200-1800 mm girth	m²	0.50	8.49	–	4.45	12.94	9.34	–	4.90	14.23
K112021	**Non-asbestos flameproof Class O boards; BS 476; 6 mm:**										
K112021A	not exceeding 600 mm girth	m²	0.50	8.40	–	9.55	17.95	9.24	–	10.51	19.75
K112021B	600-1200 mm girth	m²	0.40	6.79	–	9.33	16.12	7.47	–	10.26	17.73
K112021C	1200-1800 mm girth	m²	0.33	5.60	–	9.12	14.72	6.16	–	10.03	16.19
K112022	**Non-asbestos flameproof Class O boards; BS 476; 9 mm:**										
K112022A	not exceeding 600 mm girth	m²	0.53	8.91	–	25.77	34.68	9.80	–	28.35	38.15
K112022B	600-1200 mm girth	m²	0.42	7.13	–	25.19	32.32	7.84	–	27.71	35.55
K112022C	1200-1800 mm girth	m²	0.35	5.94	–	24.61	30.55	6.53	–	27.07	33.61
K112023	**Non-asbestos flameproof Class O boards; BS 476; 12 mm:**										
K112023A	not exceeding 600 mm girth	m²	0.60	10.19	–	38.80	48.99	11.21	–	42.68	53.89
K112023B	600-1200 mm girth	m²	0.48	8.15	–	37.92	46.07	8.97	–	41.71	50.68
K112023C	1200-1800 mm girth	m²	0.40	6.79	–	37.05	43.84	7.47	–	40.76	48.22
K112024	**Non-asbestos flameproof Class O boards; BS 476; 15 mm:**										
K112024A	not exceeding 600 mm girth	m²	0.68	11.46	–	48.59	60.05	12.61	–	53.45	66.06
K112024B	600-1200 mm girth	m²	0.54	9.17	–	47.49	56.66	10.09	–	52.24	62.33
K112024C	1200-1800 mm girth	m²	0.45	7.64	–	46.39	54.03	8.40	–	51.03	59.43

Linings, Sheathing and Dry Partitioning

		Unit	Labour Hours	Labour Net	Plant Net	Materials Net	Unit Net	Labour Gross	Plant Gross	Materials Gross	Unit Price
								(Gross rates include 10% profit)			
				£	£	£	£	£	£	£	£
K11	**K11: RIGID SHEET FLOORING, SHEATHING, LININGS AND CASINGS**										
K1121	**Isolated columns**										
K112101	**Hardboard; 3.2 mm standard:**										
K112101A	not exceeding 600 mm girth	m²	0.38	6.37	–	1.84	8.21	7.01	–	2.02	9.03
K112101B	600-1200 mm girth	m²	0.30	5.10	–	1.80	6.90	5.61	–	1.98	7.59
K112101C	1200-1800 mm girth	m²	0.25	4.25	–	1.76	6.01	4.68	–	1.94	6.61
K112102	**Hardboard; 6.0 mm standard:**										
K112102A	not exceeding 600 mm girth	m²	0.45	7.64	–	4.91	12.55	8.40	–	5.40	13.81
K112102B	600-1200 mm girth	m²	0.36	6.11	–	4.80	10.91	6.72	–	5.28	12.00
K112102C	1200-1800 mm girth	m²	0.30	5.09	–	4.69	9.78	5.60	–	5.16	10.76
K112103	**Hardboard; 3.2 mm perforated:**										
K112103A	not exceeding 600 mm girth	m²	0.42	7.13	–	1.91	9.04	7.84	–	2.10	9.94
K112103B	600-1200 mm girth	m²	0.34	5.70	–	1.87	7.57	6.27	–	2.06	8.33
K112103C	1200-1800 mm girth	m²	0.28	4.75	–	1.83	6.58	5.23	–	2.01	7.24
K112104	**Hardboard; 6.0 mm perforated:**										
K112104A	not exceeding 600 mm girth	m²	0.48	8.15	–	3.74	11.89	8.97	–	4.11	13.08
K112104B	600-1200 mm girth	m²	0.38	6.52	–	3.66	10.18	7.17	–	4.03	11.20
K112104C	1200-1800 mm girth	m²	0.32	5.44	–	3.57	9.01	5.98	–	3.93	9.91
K112105	**Hardboard; 6.0 mm flameproof Class 1:**										
K112105A	not exceeding 600 mm girth	m²	0.45	7.64	–	13.39	21.03	8.40	–	14.73	23.13
K112105B	600-1200 mm girth	m²	0.36	6.11	–	13.09	19.20	6.72	–	14.40	21.12
K112105C	1200-1800 mm girth	m²	0.30	5.10	–	12.78	17.88	5.61	–	14.06	19.67
K112106	**Hardboard; 3.2 mm stove enamelled one side:**										
K112106A	not exceeding 600 mm girth	m²	0.42	7.13	–	2.69	9.82	7.84	–	2.96	10.80
K112106B	600-1200 mm girth	m²	0.34	5.71	–	2.63	8.34	6.28	–	2.89	9.17
K112106C	1200-1800 mm girth	m²	0.28	4.76	–	2.57	7.33	5.24	–	2.83	8.06
K112111	**Insulation board; 6.4 mm Sundeala A:**										
K112111A	not exceeding 600 mm girth	m²	0.53	8.92	–	9.47	18.39	9.81	–	10.42	20.23
K112111B	600-1200 mm girth	m²	0.42	7.13	–	9.26	16.39	7.84	–	10.19	18.03
K112111C	1200-1800 mm girth	m²	0.35	5.94	–	9.05	14.99	6.53	–	9.96	16.49
K112112	**Insulation board; 9.5 mm Sundeala A:**										
K112112A	not exceeding 600 mm girth	m²	0.57	9.68	–	12.22	21.90	10.65	–	13.44	24.09
K112112B	600-1200 mm girth	m²	0.46	7.74	–	11.95	19.69	8.51	–	13.15	21.66
K112112C	1200-1800 mm girth	m²	0.38	6.45	–	11.68	18.13	7.10	–	12.85	19.94
K112113	**Insulation board; 12.5 mm Sundeala A:**										
K112113A	not exceeding 600 mm girth	m²	0.60	10.19	–	13.98	24.17	11.21	–	15.38	26.59
K112113B	600-1200 mm girth	m²	0.48	8.15	–	13.67	21.82	8.97	–	15.04	24.00
K112113C	1200-1800 mm girth	m²	0.40	6.79	–	13.36	20.15	7.47	–	14.70	22.17
K112114	**Insulation board; 6.4 mm Sundeala K:**										
K112114A	not exceeding 600 mm girth	m²	0.53	8.91	–	8.40	17.31	9.80	–	9.24	19.04
K112114B	600-1200 mm girth	m²	0.42	7.13	–	8.21	15.34	7.84	–	9.03	16.87
K112114C	1200-1800 mm girth	m²	0.35	5.94	–	8.02	13.96	6.53	–	8.82	15.36

Major Works 2009		Unit	Labour Hours	Labour Net	Plant Net	Materials Net	Unit Net	Labour Gross	Plant Gross	Materials Gross	Unit Price
								(Gross rates include 10% profit)			
				£	£	£	£	£	£	£	£
K11	**K11: RIGID SHEET FLOORING, SHEATHING, LININGS AND CASINGS**										
K1121	**Isolated columns**										
K112115	**Insulation board; 9.5 mm Sundeala K:**										
K112115A	not exceeding 600 mm girth	m²	0.57	9.68	–	12.22	21.90	10.65	–	13.44	24.09
K112115B	600-1200 mm girth	m²	0.46	7.74	–	11.95	19.69	8.51	–	13.15	21.66
K112115C	1200-1800 mm girth	m²	0.38	6.45	–	11.68	18.13	7.10	–	12.85	19.94
K112116	**Insulation board; 12.5 mm Pilkington ivory faced:**										
K112116A	not exceeding 600 mm girth	m²	0.68	11.46	–	3.83	15.29	12.61	–	4.21	16.82
K112116B	600-1200 mm girth	m²	0.54	9.17	–	3.75	12.92	10.09	–	4.13	14.21
K112116C	1200-1800 mm girth	m²	0.45	7.64	–	3.67	11.31	8.40	–	4.04	12.44
K112117	**Insulation board; 12.5 mm Unitex ivory faced:**										
K112117A	not exceeding 600 mm girth	m²	0.68	11.46	–	4.65	16.11	12.61	–	5.12	17.72
K112117B	600-1200 mm girth	m²	0.54	9.17	–	4.55	13.72	10.09	–	5.01	15.09
K112117C	1200-1800 mm girth	m²	0.45	7.65	–	4.45	12.10	8.42	–	4.90	13.31
K112121	**Chipboard; 12 mm:**										
K112121A	not exceeding 600 mm girth	m²	0.45	7.64	–	2.57	10.21	8.40	–	2.83	11.23
K112121B	600-1200 mm girth	m²	0.36	6.11	–	2.52	8.63	6.72	–	2.77	9.49
K112121C	1200-1800 mm girth	m²	0.30	5.09	–	2.46	7.55	5.60	–	2.71	8.31
K112122	**Chipboard; 15 mm:**										
K112122A	not exceeding 600 mm girth	m²	0.53	8.92	–	3.76	12.68	9.81	–	4.14	13.95
K112122B	600-1200 mm girth	m²	0.42	7.13	–	3.68	10.81	7.84	–	4.05	11.89
K112122C	1200-1800 mm girth	m²	0.35	5.95	–	3.59	9.54	6.55	–	3.95	10.49
K112123	**Chipboard; 18 mm:**										
K112123A	not exceeding 600 mm girth	m²	0.60	10.19	–	4.52	14.71	11.21	–	4.97	16.18
K112123B	600-1200 mm girth	m²	0.48	8.15	–	4.42	12.57	8.97	–	4.86	13.83
K112123C	1200-1800 mm girth	m²	0.40	6.79	–	4.32	11.11	7.47	–	4.75	12.22
K112127	**Chipboard faced one side with 1.5 mm Class 1 laminated plastic covering and balancing veneer other side; 15 mm:**										
K112127A	not exceeding 600 mm girth	m²	0.75	12.73	–	4.93	17.66	14.00	–	5.42	19.43
K112127B	600-1200 mm girth	m²	0.60	10.19	–	4.82	15.01	11.21	–	5.30	16.51
K112127C	1200-1800 mm girth	m²	0.50	8.49	–	4.72	13.21	9.34	–	5.19	14.53
K112128	**Chipboard faced one side with 1.5 mm Class 1 laminated plastic covering and balancing veneer other side; 18 mm:**										
K112128A	not exceeding 600 mm girth	m²	0.90	15.28	–	5.24	20.52	16.81	–	5.76	22.57
K112128B	600-1200 mm girth	m²	0.72	12.23	–	5.12	17.35	13.45	–	5.63	19.09
K112128C	1200-1800 mm girth	m²	0.60	10.19	–	5.01	15.20	11.21	–	5.51	16.72
K112131	**Finnish birch faced 5-ply blockboard; grade BB; 18 mm:**										
K112131A	not exceeding 600 mm girth	m²	1.13	19.10	–	15.41	34.51	21.01	–	16.95	37.96
K112131B	600-1200 mm girth	m²	0.90	15.28	–	15.07	30.35	16.81	–	16.58	33.39
K112131C	1200-1800 mm girth	m²	0.75	12.74	–	14.72	27.46	14.01	–	16.19	30.21

Linings, Sheathing and Dry Partitioning

									(Gross rates include 10% profit)		
				£	£	£	£	£	£	£	£
K11	**K11: RIGID SHEET FLOORING, SHEATHING, LININGS AND CASINGS**										
K1121	**Isolated columns**										
K112132	**Finnish birch faced 5-ply blockboard; grade BB; 25 mm:**										
K112132A	not exceeding 600 mm wide	m²	1.20	20.37	–	21.84	42.21	22.41	–	24.02	46.43
K112132B	600-1200 mm wide	m²	0.96	16.30	–	21.35	37.65	17.93	–	23.49	41.42
K112132C	1200-1800 mm wide	m²	0.80	13.58	–	20.86	34.44	14.94	–	22.95	37.88
K112136	**Far Eastern hardwood faced MR boarding ply; grade B/BB; 4 mm:**										
K112136A	not exceeding 600 mm girth	m²	0.57	9.68	–	3.70	13.38	10.65	–	4.07	14.72
K112136B	600-1200 mm girth	m²	0.46	7.75	–	3.61	11.36	8.53	–	3.97	12.50
K112136C	1200-1800 mm girth	m²	0.38	6.45	–	3.53	9.98	7.10	–	3.88	10.98
K112137	**Far Eastern hardwood faced MR boarding ply; grade B/BB; 6 mm:**										
K112137A	not exceeding 600 mm girth	m²	0.63	10.70	–	4.75	15.45	11.77	–	5.23	17.00
K112137B	600-1200 mm girth	m²	0.50	8.49	–	4.65	13.14	9.34	–	5.12	14.45
K112137C	1200-1800 mm girth	m²	0.42	7.13	–	4.54	11.67	7.84	–	4.99	12.84
K112138	**Far Eastern hardwood faced MR boarding ply; grade B/BB; 9 mm:**										
K112138A	not exceeding 600 mm girth	m²	0.69	11.71	–	6.68	18.39	12.88	–	7.35	20.23
K112138B	600-1200 mm girth	m²	0.55	9.34	–	6.53	15.87	10.27	–	7.18	17.46
K112138C	1200-1800 mm girth	m²	0.46	7.81	–	6.38	14.19	8.59	–	7.02	15.61
K112139	**Far Eastern hardwood faced MR boarding ply; grade B/BB; 12 mm:**										
K112139A	not exceeding 600 mm girth	m²	0.75	12.74	–	8.47	21.21	14.01	–	9.32	23.33
K112139B	600-1200 mm girth	m²	0.60	10.19	–	8.28	18.47	11.21	–	9.11	20.32
K112139C	1200-1800 mm girth	m²	0.50	8.49	–	8.09	16.58	9.34	–	8.90	18.24
K112140	**Far Eastern hardwood faced MR boarding ply; grade B/BB; 15 mm:**										
K112140A	not exceeding 600 mm girth	m²	0.84	14.26	–	10.78	25.04	15.69	–	11.86	27.54
K112140B	600-1200 mm girth	m²	0.67	11.37	–	10.54	21.91	12.51	–	11.59	24.10
K112140C	1200-1800 mm girth	m²	0.56	9.51	–	10.29	19.80	10.46	–	11.32	21.78
K112141	**Far Eastern hardwood faced MR boarding ply; grade B/BB; 18 mm:**										
K112141A	not exceeding 600 mm girth	m²	0.90	15.28	–	12.31	27.59	16.81	–	13.54	30.35
K112141B	600-1200 mm girth	m²	0.72	12.22	–	12.03	24.25	13.44	–	13.23	26.68
K112141C	1200-1800 mm girth	m²	0.60	10.19	–	11.75	21.94	11.21	–	12.93	24.13
K112142	**Far Eastern hardwood faced MR boarding ply; grade B/BB; 22 mm:**										
K112142A	not exceeding 600 mm girth	m²	0.96	16.31	–	14.71	31.02	17.94	–	16.18	34.12
K112142B	600-1200 mm girth	m²	0.77	13.08	–	14.38	27.46	14.39	–	15.82	30.21
K112142C	1200-1800 mm girth	m²	0.64	10.86	–	14.05	24.91	11.95	–	15.46	27.40
K112143	**Far Eastern hardwood faced MR boarding ply; grade B/BB; 25 mm:**										
K112143A	not exceeding 600 mm girth	m²	1.04	17.57	–	17.09	34.66	19.33	–	18.80	38.13
K112143B	600-1200 mm girth	m²	0.83	14.10	–	16.70	30.80	15.51	–	18.37	33.88
K112143C	1200-1800 mm girth	m²	0.69	11.71	–	16.32	28.03	12.88	–	17.95	30.83

Major Works 2009		Unit	Labour Hours	Labour Net	Plant Net	Materials Net	Unit Net	Labour Gross	Plant Gross	Materials Gross	Unit Price
								(Gross rates include 10% profit)			
				£	£	£	£	£	£	£	£
K11	**K11: RIGID SHEET FLOORING, SHEATHING, LININGS AND CASINGS**										
K1121	**Isolated columns**										
K112150	**Finnish birch faced WBP boarding ply; grade BB; 4 mm:**										
K112150A	not exceeding 600 mm girth	m²	0.53	8.91	–	7.34	16.25	9.80	–	8.07	17.88
K112150B	600-1200 mm girth	m²	0.42	7.13	–	7.17	14.30	7.84	–	7.89	15.73
K112150C	1200-1800 mm girth	m²	0.35	5.94	–	7.01	12.95	6.53	–	7.71	14.25
K112151	**Finnish birch faced WBP boarding ply; grade BB; 6 mm:**										
K112151A	not exceeding 600 mm girth	m²	0.57	9.68	–	10.79	20.47	10.65	–	11.87	22.52
K112151B	600-1200 mm girth	m²	0.46	7.74	–	10.55	18.29	8.51	–	11.61	20.12
K112151C	1200-1800 mm girth	m²	0.38	6.46	–	10.30	16.76	7.11	–	11.33	18.44
K112152	**Finnish birch faced WBP boarding ply; grade BB; 9 mm:**										
K112152A	not exceeding 600 mm girth	m²	0.60	10.19	–	13.28	23.47	11.21	–	14.61	25.82
K112152B	600-1200 mm girth	m²	0.48	8.15	–	12.98	21.13	8.97	–	14.28	23.24
K112152C	1200-1800 mm girth	m²	0.40	6.79	–	12.68	19.47	7.47	–	13.95	21.42
K112153	**Finnish birch faced WBP boarding ply; grade BB; 12 mm:**										
K112153A	not exceeding 600 mm girth	m²	0.68	11.46	–	15.58	27.04	12.61	–	17.14	29.74
K112153B	600-1200 mm girth	m²	0.54	9.17	–	15.22	24.39	10.09	–	16.74	26.83
K112153C	1200-1800 mm girth	m²	0.45	7.64	–	14.87	22.51	8.40	–	16.36	24.76
K112154	**Finnish birch faced WBP boarding ply; grade BB; 15 mm:**										
K112154A	not exceeding 600 mm girth	m²	0.72	12.22	–	20.95	33.17	13.44	–	23.05	36.49
K112154B	600-1200 mm girth	m²	0.58	9.85	–	20.47	30.32	10.84	–	22.52	33.35
K112154C	1200-1800 mm girth	m²	0.48	8.15	–	20.00	28.15	8.97	–	22.00	30.97
K112155	**Finnish birch faced WBP boarding ply; grade BB; 18 mm:**										
K112155A	not exceeding 600 mm girth	m²	0.78	13.24	–	24.98	38.22	14.56	–	27.48	42.04
K112155B	600-1200 mm girth	m²	0.63	10.61	–	24.41	35.02	11.67	–	26.85	38.52
K112155C	1200-1800 mm girth	m²	0.52	8.83	–	23.84	32.67	9.71	–	26.22	35.94
K112156	**Finnish birch faced WBP boarding ply; grade BB; 22 mm:**										
K112156A	not exceeding 600 mm girth	m²	0.84	14.27	–	29.56	43.83	15.70	–	32.52	48.21
K112156B	600-1200 mm girth	m²	0.67	11.38	–	28.89	40.27	12.52	–	31.78	44.30
K112156C	1200-1800 mm girth	m²	0.56	9.51	–	28.22	37.73	10.46	–	31.04	41.50
K112157	**Finnish birch faced WBP boarding ply; grade BB; 25 mm:**										
K112157A	not exceeding 600 mm girth	m²	0.90	15.28	–	34.16	49.44	16.81	–	37.58	54.38
K112157B	600-1200 mm girth	m²	0.72	12.22	–	33.39	45.61	13.44	–	36.73	50.17
K112157C	1200-1800 mm girth	m²	0.60	10.19	–	32.61	42.80	11.21	–	35.87	47.08
K112161	**Non-asbestos, flameproof Class O boards; BS 476; 6 mm:**										
K112161A	not exceeding 600 mm girth	m²	0.42	7.13	–	9.50	16.63	7.84	–	10.45	18.29
K112161B	600-1200 mm girth	m²	0.34	5.71	–	9.28	14.99	6.28	–	10.21	16.49
K112161C	1200-1800 mm girth	m²	0.28	4.76	–	9.07	13.83	5.24	–	9.98	15.21
K112162	**Non-asbestos, flameproof Class O boards; BS 476; 9 mm:**										
K112162A	not exceeding 600 mm girth	m²	0.45	7.64	–	25.72	33.36	8.40	–	28.29	36.70
K112162B	600-1200 mm girth	m²	0.36	6.11	–	25.14	31.25	6.72	–	27.65	34.38
K112162C	1200-1800 mm girth	m²	0.30	5.09	–	24.56	29.65	5.60	–	27.02	32.62

Linings, Sheathing and Dry Partitioning

Major Works 2009		Unit	Labour Hours	Labour Net	Plant Net	Materials Net	Unit Net	Labour Gross	Plant Gross	Materials Gross	Unit Price
								(Gross rates include 10% profit)			
				£	£	£	£	£	£	£	£
K11	**K11: RIGID SHEET FLOORING, SHEATHING, LININGS AND CASINGS**										
K1121	**Isolated columns**										
K112163	**Non-asbestos, flameproof Class O boards; BS 476; 12 mm:**										
K112163A	not exceeding 600 mm girth	m²	0.53	8.91	–	38.75	47.66	9.80	–	42.63	52.43
K112163B	600-1200 mm girth	m²	0.42	7.14	–	37.87	45.01	7.85	–	41.66	49.51
K112163C	1200-1800 mm girth	m²	0.35	5.94	–	37.00	42.94	6.53	–	40.70	47.23
K112164	**Non-asbestos, flameproof Class O boards; BS 476; 15 mm:**										
K112164A	not exceeding 600 mm girth	m²	0.60	10.19	–	48.54	58.73	11.21	–	53.39	64.60
K112164B	600-1200 mm girth	m²	0.48	8.15	–	47.44	55.59	8.97	–	52.18	61.15
K112164C	1200-1800 mm girth	m²	0.40	6.79	–	46.34	53.13	7.47	–	50.97	58.44

Major Works 2009		Unit	Labour Hours	Labour Net	Plant Net	Materials Net	Unit Net	Labour Gross	Plant Gross	Materials Gross	Unit Price
									(Gross rates include 10% profit)		
				£	£	£	£	£	£	£	£
K13	**K13: RIGID SHEET FINE LININGS AND PANELLING**										
K1311	**Walls**										
K131101	**Hardboard; 3.2 mm standard:**										
K131101A	over 300 mm wide	m²	0.25	4.25	–	1.84	6.09	4.68	–	2.02	6.70
K131101B	n.e. 300 mm wide.	m	0.10	1.72	–	0.55	2.27	1.89	–	0.61	2.50
K131101C	areas n.e. 1.0 m²	Nr	0.19	3.19	–	0.88	4.07	3.51	–	0.97	4.48
K131102	**Hardboard; 6.0 mm standard:**										
K131102A	over 300 mm wide	m²	0.30	5.09	–	4.91	10.00	5.60	–	5.40	11.00
K131102B	n.e. 300 mm wide.	m	0.12	2.07	–	1.47	3.54	2.28	–	1.62	3.89
K131102C	areas n.e. 1.0 m²	Nr	0.23	3.82	–	2.34	6.16	4.20	–	2.57	6.78
K131103	**Hardboard; 3.2 mm perforated:**										
K131103A	over 300 mm wide	m²	0.28	4.75	–	1.91	6.66	5.23	–	2.10	7.33
K131103B	n.e. 300 mm wide.	m	0.11	1.92	–	0.57	2.49	2.11	–	0.63	2.74
K131103C	areas n.e. 1.0 m²	Nr	0.21	3.57	–	0.91	4.48	3.93	–	1.00	4.93
K131104	**Hardboard; 6.0 mm perforated:**										
K131104A	over 300 mm wide	m²	0.32	5.44	–	3.74	9.18	5.98	–	4.11	10.10
K131104B	n.e. 300 mm wide.	m	0.13	2.21	–	1.12	3.33	2.43	–	1.23	3.66
K131104C	areas n.e. 1.0 m²	Nr	0.24	4.07	–	1.79	5.86	4.48	–	1.97	6.45
K131105	**Hardboard; 6.0 mm flameproof Class 1:**										
K131105A	over 300 mm wide	m²	0.30	5.09	–	13.39	18.48	5.60	–	14.73	20.33
K131105B	n.e. 300 mm wide.	m	0.12	2.07	–	4.02	6.09	2.28	–	4.42	6.70
K131105C	areas n.e. 1.0 m²	Nr	0.23	3.82	–	6.39	10.21	4.20	–	7.03	11.23
K131106	**Hardboard; 3.2 mm stove enamelled one side:**										
K131106A	over 300 mm wide	m²	0.28	4.75	–	2.69	7.44	5.23	–	2.96	8.18
K131106B	n.e. 300 mm wide.	m	0.11	1.92	–	0.81	2.73	2.11	–	0.89	3.00
K131106C	areas n.e. 1.0 m²	Nr	0.21	3.56	–	1.29	4.85	3.92	–	1.42	5.34
K131111	**Insulation board; 6.4 mm Sundeala A:**										
K131111A	over 300 mm wide	m²	0.35	5.95	–	9.47	15.42	6.55	–	10.42	16.96
K131111B	n.e. 300 mm wide.	m	0.14	2.41	–	2.84	5.25	2.65	–	3.12	5.78
K131111C	areas n.e. 1.0 m²	Nr	0.26	4.46	–	4.53	8.99	4.91	–	4.98	9.89
K131112	**Insulation board; 9.5 mm Sundeala A:**										
K131112A	over 300 mm wide	m²	0.38	6.46	–	12.22	18.68	7.11	–	13.44	20.55
K131112B	n.e. 300 mm wide.	m	0.15	2.61	–	3.67	6.28	2.87	–	4.04	6.91
K131112C	areas n.e. 1.0 m²	Nr	0.29	4.84	–	5.84	10.68	5.32	–	6.42	11.75
K131113	**Insulation board; 12.5 mm Sundeala A:**										
K131113A	over 300 mm wide	m²	0.40	6.79	–	13.98	20.77	7.47	–	15.38	22.85
K131113B	n.e. 300 mm wide.	m	0.16	2.76	–	4.19	6.95	3.04	–	4.61	7.65
K131113C	areas n.e. 1.0 m²	Nr	0.30	5.09	–	6.68	11.77	5.60	–	7.35	12.95
K131114	**Insulation board; 6.4 mm Sundeala K:**										
K131114A	over 300 mm wide	m²	0.35	5.94	–	8.40	14.34	6.53	–	9.24	15.77
K131114B	n.e. 300 mm wide.	m	0.14	2.41	–	2.52	4.93	2.65	–	2.77	5.42
K131114C	areas n.e. 1.0 m²	Nr	0.26	4.47	–	4.01	8.48	4.92	–	4.41	9.33

Linings, Sheathing and Dry Partitioning

		Unit	Labour Hours	Labour Net	Plant Net	Materials Net	Unit Net	Labour Gross	Plant Gross	Materials Gross	Unit Price
									(Gross rates include 10% profit)		
				£	£	£	£	£	£	£	£
K13	**K13: RIGID SHEET FINE LININGS AND PANELLING**										
K1311	**Walls**										
K131115	**Insulation board; 9.5 mm Sundeala K:**										
K131115A	over 300 mm wide	m²	0.38	6.46	–	12.22	18.68	7.11	–	13.44	20.55
K131115B	n.e. 300 mm wide	m	0.15	2.61	–	3.67	6.28	2.87	–	4.04	6.91
K131115C	areas n.e. 1.0 m²	Nr	0.29	4.84	–	5.84	10.68	5.32	–	6.42	11.75
K131116	**Insulation board; 12.5 mm Pilkington ivory faced:**										
K131116A	over 300 mm wide	m²	0.45	7.64	–	3.83	11.47	8.40	–	4.21	12.62
K131116B	n.e. 300 mm wide	m	0.18	3.09	–	1.15	4.24	3.40	–	1.27	4.66
K131116C	areas n.e. 1.0 m²	Nr	0.34	5.74	–	1.83	7.57	6.31	–	2.01	8.33
K131117	**Insulation board; 12.5 mm Unitex ivory faced:**										
K131117A	over 300 mm wide	m²	0.45	7.64	–	4.65	12.29	8.40	–	5.12	13.52
K131117B	n.e. 300 mm wide	m	0.18	3.09	–	1.40	4.49	3.40	–	1.54	4.94
K131117C	areas n.e. 1.0 m²	Nr	0.34	5.74	–	2.23	7.97	6.31	–	2.45	8.77
K131121	**Chipboard; 12 mm:**										
K131121A	over 300 mm wide	m²	0.30	5.10	–	2.57	7.67	5.61	–	2.83	8.44
K131121B	n.e. 300 mm wide	m	0.12	2.07	–	0.77	2.84	2.28	–	0.85	3.12
K131121C	areas n.e. 1.0 m²	Nr	0.23	3.82	–	1.23	5.05	4.20	–	1.35	5.56
K131122	**Chipboard; 15 mm:**										
K131122A	over 300 mm wide	m²	0.35	5.94	–	3.76	9.70	6.53	–	4.14	10.67
K131122B	n.e. 300 mm wide	m	0.14	2.41	–	1.13	3.54	2.65	–	1.24	3.89
K131122C	areas n.e. 1.0 m²	Nr	0.26	4.46	–	1.80	6.26	4.91	–	1.98	6.89
K131123	**Chipboard; 18 mm:**										
K131123A	over 300 mm wide	m²	0.40	6.79	–	4.52	11.31	7.47	–	4.97	12.44
K131123B	n.e. 300 mm wide	m	0.16	2.75	–	1.36	4.11	3.03	–	1.50	4.52
K131123C	areas n.e. 1.0 m²	Nr	0.30	5.09	–	2.16	7.25	5.60	–	2.38	7.98
K131127	**Chipboard faced one side with 1.5 mm Class 1 laminated plastic covering and balancing veneer other side; 15 mm:**										
K131127A	over 300 mm wide	m²	0.50	8.49	–	4.93	13.42	9.34	–	5.42	14.76
K131127B	n.e. 300 mm wide	m	0.20	3.45	–	1.48	4.93	3.80	–	1.63	5.42
K131127C	areas n.e. 1.0 m²	Nr	0.38	6.37	–	2.36	8.73	7.01	–	2.60	9.60
K131128	**Chipboard faced one side with 1.5 mm Class 1 laminated plastic covering and balancing veneer other side; 18 mm:**										
K131128A	over 300 mm wide	m²	0.60	10.18	–	5.24	15.42	11.20	–	5.76	16.96
K131128B	n.e. 300 mm wide	m	0.24	4.13	–	1.57	5.70	4.54	–	1.73	6.27
K131128C	areas n.e. 1.0 m²	Nr	0.45	7.64	–	2.51	10.15	8.40	–	2.76	11.17
K131131	**Finnish birch faced 5 ply blockboard; grade BB; 18 mm:**										
K131131A	over 300 mm wide	m²	0.75	12.74	–	15.41	28.15	14.01	–	16.95	30.97
K131131B	n.e. 300 mm wide	m	0.30	5.17	–	4.62	9.79	5.69	–	5.08	10.77
K131131C	areas n.e. 1.0 m²	Nr	0.56	9.56	–	7.36	16.92	10.52	–	8.10	18.61
K131132	**Finnish birch faced 5 ply blockboard; grade BB; 25 mm:**										
K131132A	over 300 mm wide	m²	0.80	13.58	–	21.84	35.42	14.94	–	24.02	38.96
K131132B	n.e. 300 mm wide	m	0.32	5.50	–	6.55	12.05	6.05	–	7.21	13.26
K131132C	areas n.e. 1.0 m²	Nr	0.60	10.19	–	10.43	20.62	11.21	–	11.47	22.68

Major Works 2009		Unit	Labour Hours	Labour Net	Plant Net	Materials Net	Unit Net	Labour Gross	Plant Gross	Materials Gross	Unit Price
								(Gross rates include 10% profit)			
				£	£	£	£	£	£	£	£
K13	**K13: RIGID SHEET FINE LININGS AND PANELLING**										
K1311	**Walls**										
K131136	**Far Eastern hardwood faced MR boarding ply; grade B/BB; 4 mm:**										
K131136A	over 300 mm wide	m²	0.38	6.45	–	3.70	10.15	7.10	–	4.07	11.17
K131136B	n.e. 300 mm wide	m	0.15	2.61	–	1.11	3.72	2.87	–	1.22	4.09
K131136C	areas n.e. 1.0 m²	Nr	0.29	4.84	–	1.77	6.61	5.32	–	1.95	7.27
K131137	**Far Eastern hardwood faced MR boarding ply; grade B/BB; 6 mm:**										
K131137A	over 300 mm wide	m²	0.42	7.14	–	4.75	11.89	7.85	–	5.23	13.08
K131137B	n.e. 300 mm wide	m	0.17	2.88	–	1.43	4.31	3.17	–	1.57	4.74
K131137C	areas n.e. 1.0 m²	Nr	0.32	5.35	–	2.27	7.62	5.89	–	2.50	8.38
K131138	**Far Eastern hardwood faced MR boarding ply; grade B/BB; 9 mm:**										
K131138A	over 300 mm wide	m²	0.46	7.81	–	6.68	14.49	8.59	–	7.35	15.94
K131138B	n.e. 300 mm wide	m	0.19	3.16	–	2.00	5.16	3.48	–	2.20	5.68
K131138C	areas n.e. 1.0 m²	Nr	0.35	5.86	–	3.19	9.05	6.45	–	3.51	9.96
K131139	**Far Eastern hardwood faced MR boarding ply; grade B/BB; 12 mm:**										
K131139A	over 300 mm wide	m²	0.50	8.49	–	8.47	16.96	9.34	–	9.32	18.66
K131139B	n.e. 300 mm wide	m	0.20	3.45	–	2.54	5.99	3.80	–	2.79	6.59
K131139C	areas n.e. 1.0 m²	Nr	0.38	6.37	–	4.04	10.41	7.01	–	4.44	11.45
K131140	**Far Eastern hardwood faced MR boarding ply; grade B/BB; 15 mm:**										
K131140A	over 300 mm wide	m²	0.56	9.51	–	10.78	20.29	10.46	–	11.86	22.32
K131140B	n.e. 300 mm wide	m	0.23	3.86	–	3.23	7.09	4.25	–	3.55	7.80
K131140C	areas n.e. 1.0 m²	Nr	0.42	7.13	–	5.15	12.28	7.84	–	5.67	13.51
K131141	**Far Eastern hardwood faced MR boarding ply; grade B/BB; 18 mm:**										
K131141A	over 300 mm wide	m²	0.60	10.18	–	12.31	22.49	11.20	–	13.54	24.74
K131141B	n.e. 300 mm wide	m	0.24	4.13	–	3.69	7.82	4.54	–	4.06	8.60
K131141C	areas n.e. 1.0 m²	Nr	0.45	7.65	–	5.87	13.52	8.42	–	6.46	14.87
K131142	**Far Eastern hardwood faced MR boarding ply; grade B/BB; 22 mm:**										
K131142A	over 300 mm wide	m²	0.64	10.87	–	14.71	25.58	11.96	–	16.18	28.14
K131142B	n.e. 300 mm wide	m	0.48	8.15	–	4.41	12.56	8.97	–	4.85	13.82
K131142C	areas n.e. 1.0 m²	Nr	0.48	8.15	–	7.02	15.17	8.97	–	7.72	16.69
K131143	**Far Eastern hardwood faced MR boarding ply; grade B/BB; 25 mm:**										
K131143A	over 300 mm wide	m²	0.69	11.72	–	17.09	28.81	12.89	–	18.80	31.69
K131143B	n.e. 300 mm wide	m	0.28	4.73	–	5.13	9.86	5.20	–	5.64	10.85
K131143C	areas n.e. 1.0 m²	Nr	0.52	8.83	–	8.16	16.99	9.71	–	8.98	18.69
K131150	**Finnish birch faced WBP boarding ply; grade BB; 4 mm:**										
K131150A	over 300 mm wide	m²	0.35	5.94	–	7.34	13.28	6.53	–	8.07	14.61
K131150B	n.e. 300 mm wide	m	0.14	2.41	–	2.20	4.61	2.65	–	2.42	5.07
K131150C	areas n.e. 1.0 m²	Nr	0.26	4.47	–	3.50	7.97	4.92	–	3.85	8.77

Linings, Sheathing and Dry Partitioning

Major Works 2009		Unit	Labour Hours	Labour Net	Plant Net	Materials Net	Unit Net	Labour Gross	Plant Gross	Materials Gross	Unit Price
								— (Gross rates include 10% profit) —			
				£	£	£	£	£	£	£	£
K13	**K13: RIGID SHEET FINE LININGS AND PANELLING**										
K1311	**Walls**										
K131151	**Finnish birch faced WBP boarding ply; grade BB; 6 mm:**										
K131151A	over 300 mm wide	m²	0.38	6.45	–	10.79	17.24	7.10	–	11.87	18.96
K131151B	n.e. 300 mm wide	m	0.15	2.61	–	3.24	5.85	2.87	–	3.56	6.44
K131151C	areas n.e. 1.0 m²	Nr	0.29	4.84	–	5.15	9.99	5.32	–	5.67	10.99
K131152	**Finnish birch faced WBP boarding ply; grade BB; 9 mm:**										
K131152A	over 300 mm wide	m²	0.40	6.79	–	13.28	20.07	7.47	–	14.61	22.08
K131152B	n.e. 300 mm wide	m	0.16	2.75	–	3.98	6.73	3.03	–	4.38	7.40
K131152C	areas n.e. 1.0 m²	Nr	0.30	5.09	–	6.34	11.43	5.60	–	6.97	12.57
K131153	**Finnish birch faced WBP boarding ply; grade BB; 12 mm:**										
K131153A	over 300 mm wide	m²	0.45	7.64	–	15.58	23.22	8.40	–	17.14	25.54
K131153B	n.e. 300 mm wide	m	0.18	3.09	–	4.67	7.76	3.40	–	5.14	8.54
K131153C	areas n.e. 1.0 m²	Nr	0.34	5.73	–	7.44	13.17	6.30	–	8.18	14.49
K131154	**Finnish birch faced WBP boarding ply; grade BB; 15 mm:**										
K131154A	over 300 mm wide	m²	0.48	8.15	–	20.95	29.10	8.97	–	23.05	32.01
K131154B	n.e. 300 mm wide	m	0.19	3.30	–	6.28	9.58	3.63	–	6.91	10.54
K131154C	areas n.e. 1.0 m²	Nr	0.36	6.11	–	10.00	16.11	6.72	–	11.00	17.72
K131155	**Finnish birch faced WBP boarding ply; grade BB; 18 mm:**										
K131155A	over 300 mm wide	m²	0.52	8.83	–	24.98	33.81	9.71	–	27.48	37.19
K131155B	n.e. 300 mm wide	m	0.21	3.59	–	7.49	11.08	3.95	–	8.24	12.19
K131155C	areas n.e. 1.0 m²	Nr	0.39	6.62	–	11.92	18.54	7.28	–	13.11	20.39
K131156	**Finnish birch faced WBP boarding ply; grade BB; 22 mm:**										
K131156A	over 300 mm wide	m²	0.56	9.51	–	29.56	39.07	10.46	–	32.52	42.98
K131156B	n.e. 300 mm wide	m	0.23	3.85	–	8.87	12.72	4.24	–	9.76	13.99
K131156C	areas n.e. 1.0 m²	Nr	0.42	7.13	–	14.11	21.24	7.84	–	15.52	23.36
K131157	**Finnish birch faced WBP boarding ply; grade BB; 25 mm:**										
K131157A	over 300 mm wide	m²	0.60	10.19	–	34.16	44.35	11.21	–	37.58	48.79
K131157B	n.e. 300 mm wide	m	0.24	4.12	–	10.25	14.37	4.53	–	11.28	15.81
K131157C	areas n.e. 1.0 m²	Nr	0.45	7.64	–	16.31	23.95	8.40	–	17.94	26.35
K131161	**Non-asbestos, flameproof Class O boards; BS 476; 6 mm:**										
K131161A	over 300 mm wide	m²	0.28	4.75	–	9.50	14.25	5.23	–	10.45	15.68
K131161B	n.e. 300 mm wide	m	0.11	1.92	–	2.85	4.77	2.11	–	3.14	5.25
K131161C	areas n.e. 1.0 m²	Nr	0.21	3.56	–	4.54	8.10	3.92	–	4.99	8.91
K131162	**Non-asbestos, flameproof Class O boards; BS 476; 9 mm:**										
K131162A	over 300 mm wide	m²	0.30	5.10	–	25.72	30.82	5.61	–	28.29	33.90
K131162B	n.e. 300 mm wide	m	0.12	2.07	–	7.72	9.79	2.28	–	8.49	10.77
K131162C	areas n.e. 1.0 m²	Nr	0.23	3.82	–	12.28	16.10	4.20	–	13.51	17.71
K131163	**Non-asbestos, flameproof Class O boards; BS 476; 12 mm:**										
K131163A	over 300 mm wide	m²	0.35	5.94	–	38.75	44.69	6.53	–	42.63	49.16
K131163B	n.e. 300 mm wide	m	0.14	2.41	–	11.63	14.04	2.65	–	12.79	15.44
K131163C	areas n.e. 1.0 m²	Nr	0.26	4.46	–	18.50	22.96	4.91	–	20.35	25.26

Major Works 2009		Unit	Labour Hours	Labour Net	Plant Net	Materials Net	Unit Net	Labour Gross	Plant Gross	Materials Gross	Unit Price
								(Gross rates include 10% profit)			
				£	£	£	£	£	£	£	£
K13	**K13: RIGID SHEET FINE LININGS AND PANELLING**										
K1311	**Walls**										
K131164	**Non-asbestos, flameproof Class O boards; BS 476; 15 mm:**										
K131164A	over 300 mm wide	m²	0.40	6.79	–	48.54	55.33	7.47	–	53.39	60.86
K131164B	n.e. 300 mm wide	m	0.16	2.75	–	14.56	17.31	3.03	–	16.02	19.04
K131164C	areas n.e. 1.0 m²	Nr	0.30	5.10	–	23.17	28.27	5.61	–	25.49	31.10
K131171	**MDF board; 12 mm:**										
K131171A	over 300 mm wide	m²	0.40	6.79	–	4.96	11.75	7.47	–	5.46	12.93
K131171B	n.e. 300 mm wide	m	0.16	2.75	–	1.49	4.24	3.03	–	1.64	4.66
K131171C	areas n.e. 1.0 m²	Nr	0.30	5.09	–	2.37	7.46	5.60	–	2.61	8.21
K131172	**MDF board; 15 mm:**										
K131172A	over 300 mm wide	m²	0.45	7.64	–	4.99	12.63	8.40	–	5.49	13.89
K131172B	n.e. 300 mm wide	m	0.18	3.11	–	1.50	4.61	3.42	–	1.65	5.07
K131172C	areas n.e. 1.0 m²	Nr	0.34	5.73	–	2.39	8.12	6.30	–	2.63	8.93
K131173	**MDF board; 18 mm:**										
K131173A	over 300 mm wide	m²	0.50	8.49	–	6.87	15.36	9.34	–	7.56	16.90
K131173B	n.e. 300 mm wide	m	0.20	3.45	–	2.06	5.51	3.80	–	2.27	6.06
K131173C	areas n.e. 1.0 m²	Nr	0.38	6.37	–	3.28	9.65	7.01	–	3.61	10.62

Linings, Sheathing and Dry Partitioning

Major Works 2009		Unit	Labour Hours	Labour Net	Plant Net	Materials Net	Unit Net	Labour Gross	Plant Gross	Materials Gross	Unit Price
								(Gross rates include 10% profit)			
				£	£	£	£	£	£	£	£
K13	**K13: RIGID SHEET FINE LININGS AND PANELLING**										
K1315	**Ceilings**										
K131501	**Hardboard; 3.2 mm standard:**										
K131501A	over 300 mm wide	m²	0.28	4.76	–	1.84	6.60	5.24	–	2.02	7.26
K131501B	n.e. 300 mm wide	m	0.11	1.94	–	0.55	2.49	2.13	–	0.61	2.74
K131501C	areas n.e. 1.0 m²	Nr	0.21	3.58	–	0.88	4.46	3.94	–	0.97	4.91
K131502	**Hardboard; 6.0 mm standard:**										
K131502A	over 300 mm wide	m²	0.34	5.74	–	4.91	10.65	6.31	–	5.40	11.72
K131502B	n.e. 300 mm wide	m	0.14	2.33	–	1.47	3.80	2.56	–	1.62	4.18
K131502C	areas n.e. 1.0 m²	Nr	0.25	4.32	–	2.34	6.66	4.75	–	2.57	7.33
K131503	**Hardboard; 3.2 mm perforated:**										
K131503A	over 300 mm wide	m²	0.32	5.35	–	1.91	7.26	5.89	–	2.10	7.99
K131503B	n.e. 300 mm wide	m	0.13	2.18	–	0.57	2.75	2.40	–	0.63	3.03
K131503C	areas n.e. 1.0 m²	Nr	0.24	4.01	–	0.91	4.92	4.41	–	1.00	5.41
K131504	**Hardboard; 6.0 mm perforated:**										
K131504A	over 300 mm wide	m²	0.36	6.11	–	3.74	9.85	6.72	–	4.11	10.84
K131504B	n.e. 300 mm wide	m	0.15	2.48	–	1.12	3.60	2.73	–	1.23	3.96
K131504C	areas n.e. 1.0 m²	Nr	0.27	4.58	–	1.79	6.37	5.04	–	1.97	7.01
K131505	**Hardboard; 6.0 mm flameproof Class 1:**										
K131505A	over 300 mm wide	m²	0.34	5.74	–	13.39	19.13	6.31	–	14.73	21.04
K131505B	n.e. 300 mm wide	m	0.14	2.32	–	4.02	6.34	2.55	–	4.42	6.97
K131505C	areas n.e. 1.0 m²	Nr	0.25	4.31	–	6.39	10.70	4.74	–	7.03	11.77
K131506	**Hardboard; 3.2 mm stove enamelled one side:**										
K131506A	over 300 mm wide	m²	0.32	5.35	–	2.69	8.04	5.89	–	2.96	8.84
K131506B	n.e. 300 mm wide	m	0.13	2.17	–	0.81	2.98	2.39	–	0.89	3.28
K131506C	areas n.e. 1.0 m²	Nr	0.24	4.00	–	1.29	5.29	4.40	–	1.42	5.82
K131511	**Insulation board; 6.4 mm Sundeala A:**										
K131511A	over 300 mm wide	m²	0.39	6.69	–	9.47	16.16	7.36	–	10.42	17.78
K131511B	n.e. 300 mm wide	m	0.16	2.70	–	2.84	5.54	2.97	–	3.12	6.09
K131511C	areas n.e. 1.0 m²	Nr	0.30	5.02	–	4.53	9.55	5.52	–	4.98	10.51
K131512	**Insulation board; 9.5 mm Sundeala A:**										
K131512A	over 300 mm wide	m²	0.43	7.27	–	12.22	19.49	8.00	–	13.44	21.44
K131512B	n.e. 300 mm wide	m	0.17	2.93	–	3.67	6.60	3.22	–	4.04	7.26
K131512C	areas n.e. 1.0 m²	Nr	0.32	5.45	–	5.84	11.29	6.00	–	6.42	12.42
K131513	**Insulation board; 12.5 mm Sundeala A:**										
K131513A	over 300 mm wide	m²	0.45	7.64	–	13.98	21.62	8.40	–	15.38	23.78
K131513B	n.e. 300 mm wide	m	0.18	3.09	–	4.19	7.28	3.40	–	4.61	8.01
K131513C	areas n.e. 1.0 m²	Nr	0.34	5.74	–	6.68	12.42	6.31	–	7.35	13.66
K131514	**Insulation board; 6.4 mm Sundeala K:**										
K131514A	over 300 mm wide	m²	0.39	6.69	–	8.40	15.09	7.36	–	9.24	16.60
K131514B	n.e. 300 mm wide	m	0.16	2.70	–	2.52	5.22	2.97	–	2.77	5.74
K131514C	areas n.e. 1.0 m²	Nr	0.30	5.03	–	4.01	9.04	5.53	–	4.41	9.94

Major Works 2009		Unit	Labour Hours	Labour Net	Plant Net	Materials Net	Unit Net	Labour Gross	Plant Gross	Materials Gross	Unit Price
								(Gross rates include 10% profit)			
				£	£	£	£	£	£	£	£
K13	**K13: RIGID SHEET FINE LININGS AND PANELLING**										
K1315	**Ceilings**										
K131515	**Insulation board; 9.5 mm Sundeala K:**										
K131515A	over 300 mm wide	m²	0.43	7.27	–	12.22	19.49	8.00	–	13.44	21.44
K131515B	n.e. 300 mm wide.........	m	0.17	2.93	–	3.67	6.60	3.22	–	4.04	7.26
K131515C	areas n.e. 1.0 m²	Nr	0.32	5.45	–	5.84	11.29	6.00	–	6.42	12.42
K131516	**Insulation board; 12.5 mm Pilkington ivory faced:**										
K131516A	over 300 mm wide	m²	0.51	8.59	–	3.83	12.42	9.45	–	4.21	13.66
K131516B	n.e. 300 mm wide.........	m	0.21	3.48	–	1.15	4.63	3.83	–	1.27	5.09
K131516C	areas n.e. 1.0 m²	Nr	0.38	6.46	–	1.83	8.29	7.11	–	2.01	9.12
K131517	**Insulation board; 12.5 mm Unitex ivory faced:**										
K131517A	over 300 mm wide	m²	0.51	8.60	–	4.65	13.25	9.46	–	5.12	14.58
K131517B	n.e. 300 mm wide.........	m	0.21	3.48	–	1.40	4.88	3.83	–	1.54	5.37
K131517C	areas n.e. 1.0 m²	Nr	0.38	6.45	–	2.23	8.68	7.10	–	2.45	9.55
K131521	**Chipboard; 12 mm:**										
K131521A	over 300 mm wide	m²	0.34	5.74	–	2.57	8.31	6.31	–	2.83	9.14
K131521B	n.e. 300 mm wide.........	m	0.14	2.33	–	0.77	3.10	2.56	–	0.85	3.41
K131521C	areas n.e. 1.0 m²	Nr	0.25	4.31	–	1.23	5.54	4.74	–	1.35	6.09
K131522	**Chipboard; 15 mm:**										
K131522A	over 300 mm wide	m²	0.39	6.69	–	3.76	10.45	7.36	–	4.14	11.50
K131522B	n.e. 300 mm wide.........	m	0.16	2.70	–	1.13	3.83	2.97	–	1.24	4.21
K131522C	areas n.e. 1.0 m²	Nr	0.30	5.02	–	1.80	6.82	5.52	–	1.98	7.50
K131523	**Chipboard; 18 mm:**										
K131523A	over 300 mm wide	m²	0.45	7.64	–	4.52	12.16	8.40	–	4.97	13.38
K131523B	n.e. 300 mm wide.........	m	0.18	3.09	–	1.36	4.45	3.40	–	1.50	4.90
K131523C	areas n.e. 1.0 m²	Nr	0.34	5.74	–	2.16	7.90	6.31	–	2.38	8.69
K131527	**Chipboard faced one side with 1.5 mm Class 1 laminated plastic covering and balancing veneer other side; 15 mm:**										
K131527A	over 300 mm wide	m²	0.56	9.56	–	4.93	14.49	10.52	–	5.42	15.94
K131527B	n.e. 300 mm wide.........	m	0.23	3.87	–	1.48	5.35	4.26	–	1.63	5.89
K131527C	areas n.e. 1.0 m²	Nr	0.42	7.16	–	2.36	9.52	7.88	–	2.60	10.47
K131528	**Chipboard faced one side with 1.5 mm Class 1 laminated plastic covering and balancing veneer other side; 18 mm:**										
K131528A	over 300 mm wide	m²	0.68	11.46	–	5.24	16.70	12.61	–	5.76	18.37
K131528B	n.e. 300 mm wide.........	m	0.27	4.64	–	1.57	6.21	5.10	–	1.73	6.83
K131528C	areas n.e. 1.0 m²	Nr	0.51	8.59	–	2.51	11.10	9.45	–	2.76	12.21
K131531	**Finnish birch faced 5 ply blockboard; grade BB; 18 mm:**										
K131531A	over 300 mm wide	m²	0.84	14.33	–	15.41	29.74	15.76	–	16.95	32.71
K131531B	n.e. 300 mm wide.........	m	0.34	5.81	–	4.62	10.43	6.39	–	5.08	11.47
K131531C	areas n.e. 1.0 m²	Nr	0.63	10.75	–	7.36	18.11	11.83	–	8.10	19.92
K131532	**Finnish birch faced 5 ply blockboard; grade BB; 25 mm:**										
K131532A	over 300 mm wide	m²	0.90	15.28	–	21.84	37.12	16.81	–	24.02	40.83
K131532B	n.e. 300 mm wide.........	m	0.37	6.20	–	6.55	12.75	6.82	–	7.21	14.03
K131532C	areas n.e. 1.0 m²	Nr	0.68	11.46	–	10.43	21.89	12.61	–	11.47	24.08

Linings, Sheathing and Dry Partitioning

Major Works 2009		Unit	Labour Hours	Labour Net	Plant Net	Materials Net	Unit Net	Labour Gross	Plant Gross	Materials Gross	Unit Price
								(Gross rates include 10% profit)			
				£	£	£	£	£	£	£	£
K13	**K13: RIGID SHEET FINE LININGS AND PANELLING**										
K1315	**Ceilings**										
K131536	**Far Eastern hardwood faced MR boarding ply; grade B/BB; 4 mm:**										
K131536A	over 300 mm wide	m²	0.43	7.26	–	3.70	10.96	7.99	–	4.07	12.06
K131536B	n.e. 300 mm wide	m	0.17	2.94	–	1.11	4.05	3.23	–	1.22	4.46
K131536C	areas n.e. 1.0 m²	Nr	0.32	5.45	–	1.77	7.22	6.00	–	1.95	7.94
K131537	**Far Eastern hardwood faced MR boarding ply; grade B/BB; 6 mm:**										
K131537A	over 300 mm wide	m²	0.47	8.04	–	4.75	12.79	8.84	–	5.23	14.07
K131537B	n.e. 300 mm wide	m	0.19	3.24	–	1.43	4.67	3.56	–	1.57	5.14
K131537C	areas n.e. 1.0 m²	Nr	0.36	6.03	–	2.27	8.30	6.63	–	2.50	9.13
K131538	**Far Eastern hardwood faced MR boarding ply; grade B/BB; 9 mm:**										
K131538A	over 300 mm wide	m²	0.52	8.79	–	6.68	15.47	9.67	–	7.35	17.02
K131538B	n.e. 300 mm wide	m	0.21	3.57	–	2.00	5.57	3.93	–	2.20	6.13
K131538C	areas n.e. 1.0 m²	Nr	0.39	6.60	–	3.19	9.79	7.26	–	3.51	10.77
K131539	**Far Eastern hardwood faced MR boarding ply; grade B/BB; 12 mm:**										
K131539A	over 300 mm wide	m²	0.56	9.56	–	8.47	18.03	10.52	–	9.32	19.83
K131539B	n.e. 300 mm wide	m	0.23	3.87	–	2.54	6.41	4.26	–	2.79	7.05
K131539C	areas n.e. 1.0 m²	Nr	0.42	7.17	–	4.04	11.21	7.89	–	4.44	12.33
K131540	**Far Eastern hardwood faced MR boarding ply; grade B/BB; 15 mm:**										
K131540A	over 300 mm wide	m²	0.63	10.70	–	10.78	21.48	11.77	–	11.86	23.63
K131540B	n.e. 300 mm wide	m	0.26	4.33	–	3.23	7.56	4.76	–	3.55	8.32
K131540C	areas n.e. 1.0 m²	Nr	0.47	8.03	–	5.15	13.18	8.83	–	5.67	14.50
K131541	**Far Eastern hardwood faced MR boarding ply; grade B/BB; 18 mm:**										
K131541A	over 300 mm wide	m²	0.68	11.46	–	12.31	23.77	12.61	–	13.54	26.15
K131541B	n.e. 300 mm wide	m	0.27	4.64	–	3.69	8.33	5.10	–	4.06	9.16
K131541C	areas n.e. 1.0 m²	Nr	0.51	8.60	–	5.87	14.47	9.46	–	6.46	15.92
K131542	**Far Eastern hardwood faced MR boarding ply; grade B/BB; 22 mm:**										
K131542A	over 300 mm wide	m²	0.72	12.23	–	14.71	26.94	13.45	–	16.18	29.63
K131542B	n.e. 300 mm wide	m	0.29	4.96	–	4.41	9.37	5.46	–	4.85	10.31
K131542C	areas n.e. 1.0 m²	Nr	0.54	9.17	–	7.02	16.19	10.09	–	7.72	17.81
K131543	**Far Eastern hardwood faced MR boarding ply; grade B/BB; 25 mm:**										
K131543A	over 300 mm wide	m²	0.78	13.18	–	17.09	30.27	14.50	–	18.80	33.30
K131543B	n.e. 300 mm wide	m	0.31	5.33	–	5.13	10.46	5.86	–	5.64	11.51
K131543C	areas n.e. 1.0 m²	Nr	0.58	9.88	–	8.16	18.04	10.87	–	8.98	19.84

Linings, Sheathing and Dry Partitioning

Major Works 2009		Unit	Labour Hours	Labour Net	Plant Net	Materials Net	Unit Net	Labour Gross	Plant Gross	Materials Gross	Unit Price
				£	£	£	£	£	£	£	£
								(Gross rates include 10% profit)			
K13	K13: RIGID SHEET FINE LININGS AND PANELLING										
K1315	Ceilings										
K131550	Finnish birch faced WBP boarding ply; grade BB; 4 mm:										
K131550A	over 300 mm wide	m²	0.39	6.69	–	7.34	14.03	7.36	–	8.07	15.43
K131550B	n.e. 300 mm wide	m	0.16	2.70	–	2.20	4.90	2.97	–	2.42	5.39
K131550C	areas n.e. 1.0 m²	Nr	0.30	5.03	–	3.50	8.53	5.53	–	3.85	9.38
K131551	Finnish birch faced WBP boarding ply; grade BB; 6 mm:										
K131551A	over 300 mm wide	m²	0.43	7.27	–	10.79	18.06	8.00	–	11.87	19.87
K131551B	n.e. 300 mm wide	m	0.17	2.94	–	3.24	6.18	3.23	–	3.56	6.80
K131551C	areas n.e. 1.0 m²	Nr	0.32	5.45	–	5.15	10.60	6.00	–	5.67	11.66
K131552	Finnish birch faced WBP boarding ply; grade BB; 9 mm:										
K131552A	over 300 mm wide	m²	0.45	7.64	–	13.28	20.92	8.40	–	14.61	23.01
K131552B	n.e. 300 mm wide	m	0.18	3.09	–	3.98	7.07	3.40	–	4.38	7.78
K131552C	areas n.e. 1.0 m²	Nr	0.34	5.74	–	6.34	12.08	6.31	–	6.97	13.29
K131553	Finnish birch faced WBP boarding ply; grade BB; 12 mm:										
K131553A	over 300 mm wide	m²	0.51	8.59	–	15.58	24.17	9.45	–	17.14	26.59
K131553B	n.e. 300 mm wide	m	0.21	3.48	–	4.67	8.15	3.83	–	5.14	8.97
K131553C	areas n.e. 1.0 m²	Nr	0.38	6.45	–	7.44	13.89	7.10	–	8.18	15.28
K131554	Finnish birch faced WBP boarding ply; grade BB; 15 mm:										
K131554A	over 300 mm wide	m²	0.54	9.16	–	20.95	30.11	10.08	–	23.05	33.12
K131554B	n.e. 300 mm wide	m	0.22	3.72	–	6.28	10.00	4.09	–	6.91	11.00
K131554C	areas n.e. 1.0 m²	Nr	0.41	6.87	–	10.00	16.87	7.56	–	11.00	18.56
K131555	Finnish birch faced WBP boarding ply; grade BB; 18 mm:										
K131555A	over 300 mm wide	m²	0.59	9.93	–	24.98	34.91	10.92	–	27.48	38.40
K131555B	n.e. 300 mm wide	m	0.24	4.03	–	7.49	11.52	4.43	–	8.24	12.67
K131555C	areas n.e. 1.0 m²	Nr	0.44	7.46	–	11.92	19.38	8.21	–	13.11	21.32
K131556	Finnish birch faced WBP boarding ply; grade BB; 22 mm:										
K131556A	over 300 mm wide	m²	0.63	10.70	–	29.56	40.26	11.77	–	32.52	44.29
K131556B	n.e. 300 mm wide	m	0.26	4.33	–	8.87	13.20	4.76	–	9.76	14.52
K131556C	areas n.e. 1.0 m²	Nr	0.47	8.03	–	14.11	22.14	8.83	–	15.52	24.35

Linings, Sheathing and Dry Partitioning

Major Works 2009		Unit	Labour Hours	Labour Net	Plant Net	Materials Net	Unit Net	Labour Gross	Plant Gross	Materials Gross	Unit Price
								(Gross rates include 10% profit)			
				£	£	£	£	£	£	£	£
K13	**K13: RIGID SHEET FINE LININGS AND PANELLING**										
K1315	**Ceilings**										
K131557	**Finnish birch faced WBP boarding ply; grade BB; 25 mm:**										
K131557A	over 300 mm wide	m²	0.68	11.46	–	34.16	45.62	12.61	–	37.58	50.18
K131557B	n.e. 300 mm wide	m	0.27	4.63	–	10.25	14.88	5.09	–	11.28	16.37
K131557C	areas n.e. 1.0 m²	Nr	0.51	8.59	–	16.31	24.90	9.45	–	17.94	27.39
K131561	**Non-asbestos, flameproof Class O boards; BS 476; 6 mm:**										
K131561A	over 300 mm wide	m²	0.32	5.35	–	9.50	14.85	5.89	–	10.45	16.34
K131561B	n.e. 300 mm wide	m	0.13	2.17	–	2.85	5.02	2.39	–	3.14	5.52
K131561C	areas n.e. 1.0 m²	Nr	0.24	4.00	–	4.54	8.54	4.40	–	4.99	9.39
K131562	**Non-asbestos, flameproof Class O boards; BS 476; 9 mm:**										
K131562A	over 300 mm wide	m²	0.34	5.74	–	25.72	31.46	6.31	–	28.29	34.61
K131562B	n.e. 300 mm wide	m	0.14	2.32	–	7.72	10.04	2.55	–	8.49	11.04
K131562C	areas n.e. 1.0 m²	Nr	0.25	4.31	–	12.28	16.59	4.74	–	13.51	18.25
K131563	**Non-asbestos, flameproof Class O boards; BS 476; 12 mm:**										
K131563A	over 300 mm wide	m²	0.39	6.69	–	38.75	45.44	7.36	–	42.63	49.98
K131563B	n.e. 300 mm wide	m	0.16	2.69	–	11.63	14.32	2.96	–	12.79	15.75
K131563C	areas n.e. 1.0 m²	Nr	0.30	5.02	–	18.50	23.52	5.52	–	20.35	25.87
K131564	**Non-asbestos, flameproof Class O boards; BS 476; 15 mm:**										
K131564A	over 300 mm wide	m²	0.45	7.64	–	48.54	56.18	8.40	–	53.39	61.80
K131564B	n.e. 300 mm wide	m	0.18	3.09	–	14.56	17.65	3.40	–	16.02	19.42
K131564C	areas n.e. 1.0 m²	Nr	0.34	5.74	–	23.17	28.91	6.31	–	25.49	31.80
K131571	**MDF board; 12 mm:**										
K131571A	over 300 mm wide	m²	0.45	7.64	–	4.96	12.60	8.40	–	5.46	13.86
K131571B	n.e. 300 mm wide	m	0.18	3.09	–	1.49	4.58	3.40	–	1.64	5.04
K131571C	areas n.e. 1.0 m²	Nr	0.34	5.74	–	2.37	8.11	6.31	–	2.61	8.92
K131572	**MDF board; 15 mm:**										
K131572A	over 300 mm wide	m²	0.51	8.59	–	4.99	13.58	9.45	–	5.49	14.94
K131572B	n.e. 300 mm wide	m	0.21	3.48	–	1.50	4.98	3.83	–	1.65	5.48
K131572C	areas n.e. 1.0 m²	Nr	0.38	6.45	–	2.39	8.84	7.10	–	2.63	9.72
K131573	**MDF board; 18 mm:**										
K131573A	over 300 mm wide	m²	0.56	9.56	–	6.87	16.43	10.52	–	7.56	18.07
K131573B	n.e. 300 mm wide	m	0.23	3.87	–	2.06	5.93	4.26	–	2.27	6.52
K131573C	areas n.e. 1.0 m²	Nr	0.42	7.17	–	3.28	10.45	7.89	–	3.61	11.50

Major Works 2009		Unit	Labour Hours	Labour Net	Plant Net	Materials Net	Unit Net	Labour Gross	Plant Gross	Materials Gross	Unit Price
								(Gross rates include 10% profit)			
				£	£	£	£	£	£	£	£
K13	**K13: RIGID SHEET FINE LININGS AND PANELLING**										
K1319	**Isolated beams**										
K131901	**Hardboard; 3.2 mm standard:**										
K131901A	not exceeding 600 mm girth	m²	0.42	7.13	–	1.84	8.97	7.84	–	2.02	9.87
K131901B	600-1200 mm girth	m²	0.34	5.74	–	1.80	7.54	6.31	–	1.98	8.29
K131901C	1200-1800 mm girth	m²	0.28	4.76	–	1.76	6.52	5.24	–	1.94	7.17
K131902	**Hardboard; 6.0 mm standard:**										
K131902A	not exceeding 600 mm girth	m²	0.51	8.59	–	4.91	13.50	9.45	–	5.40	14.85
K131902B	600-1200 mm girth	m²	0.41	6.87	–	4.80	11.67	7.56	–	5.28	12.84
K131902C	1200-1800 mm girth	m²	0.34	5.74	–	4.69	10.43	6.31	–	5.16	11.47
K131903	**Hardboard; 3.2 mm perforated:**										
K131903A	not exceeding 600 mm girth	m²	0.47	8.03	–	1.91	9.94	8.83	–	2.10	10.93
K131903B	600-1200 mm girth	m²	0.38	6.45	–	1.87	8.32	7.10	–	2.06	9.15
K131903C	1200-1800 mm girth	m²	0.32	5.35	–	1.83	7.18	5.89	–	2.01	7.90
K131904	**Hardboard; 6.0 mm perforated:**										
K131904A	not exceeding 600 mm girth	m²	0.54	9.17	–	3.74	12.91	10.09	–	4.11	14.20
K131904B	600-1200 mm girth	m²	0.43	7.33	–	3.66	10.99	8.06	–	4.03	12.09
K131904C	1200-1800 mm girth	m²	0.36	6.12	–	3.57	9.69	6.73	–	3.93	10.66
K131905	**Hardboard; 6.0 mm flameproof Class 1:**										
K131905A	not exceeding 600 mm girth	m²	0.51	8.59	–	13.39	21.98	9.45	–	14.73	24.18
K131905B	600-1200 mm girth	m²	0.41	6.87	–	13.09	19.96	7.56	–	14.40	21.96
K131905C	1200-1800 mm girth	m²	0.34	5.74	–	12.78	18.52	6.31	–	14.06	20.37
K131906	**Hardboard; 3.2 mm stove enamelled one side:**										
K131906A	not exceeding 600 mm girth	m²	0.47	8.03	–	2.69	10.72	8.83	–	2.96	11.79
K131906B	600-1200 mm girth	m²	0.38	6.45	–	2.63	9.08	7.10	–	2.89	9.99
K131906C	1200-1800 mm girth	m²	0.32	5.35	–	2.57	7.92	5.89	–	2.83	8.71
K131911	**Insulation board; 6.4 mm Sundeala A:**										
K131911A	not exceeding 600 mm girth	m²	0.59	10.02	–	9.47	19.49	11.02	–	10.42	21.44
K131911B	600-1200 mm girth	m²	0.47	8.03	–	9.26	17.29	8.83	–	10.19	19.02
K131911C	1200-1800 mm girth	m²	0.39	6.69	–	9.05	15.74	7.36	–	9.96	17.31
K131912	**Insulation board; 9.5 mm Sundeala A:**										
K131912A	not exceeding 600 mm girth	m²	0.64	10.87	–	12.22	23.09	11.96	–	13.44	25.40
K131912B	600-1200 mm girth	m²	0.51	8.71	–	11.95	20.66	9.58	–	13.15	22.73
K131912C	1200-1800 mm girth	m²	0.43	7.30	–	11.68	18.98	8.03	–	12.85	20.88
K131913	**Insulation board; 12.5 mm Sundeala A:**										
K131913A	not exceeding 600 mm girth	m²	0.68	11.46	–	13.98	25.44	12.61	–	15.38	27.98
K131913B	600-1200 mm girth	m²	0.54	9.17	–	13.67	22.84	10.09	–	15.04	25.12
K131913C	1200-1800 mm girth	m²	0.45	7.64	–	13.36	21.00	8.40	–	14.70	23.10
K131914	**Insulation board; 6.4 mm Sundeala K:**										
K131914A	not exceeding 600 mm girth	m²	0.59	10.01	–	8.40	18.41	11.01	–	9.24	20.25
K131914B	600-1200 mm girth	m²	0.47	8.03	–	8.21	16.24	8.83	–	9.03	17.86
K131914C	1200-1800 mm girth	m²	0.39	6.69	–	8.02	14.71	7.36	–	8.82	16.18

Linings, Sheathing and Dry Partitioning

Major Works 2009		Unit	Labour Hours	Labour Net	Plant Net	Materials Net	Unit Net	Labour Gross	Plant Gross	Materials Gross	Unit Price
								(Gross rates include 10% profit)			
				£	£	£	£	£	£	£	£
K13	**K13: RIGID SHEET FINE LININGS AND PANELLING**										
K1319	**Isolated beams**										
K131915	**Insulation board; 9.5 mm Sundeala K:**										
K131915A	not exceeding 600 mm girth	m²	0.64	10.87	–	12.22	23.09	11.96	–	13.44	25.40
K131915B	600-1200 mm girth	m²	0.51	8.71	–	11.95	20.66	9.58	–	13.15	22.73
K131915C	1200-1800 mm girth	m²	0.43	7.30	–	11.68	18.98	8.03	–	12.85	20.88
K131916	**Insulation board; 12.5 mm Pilkington ivory faced:**										
K131916A	not exceeding 600 mm girth	m²	0.76	12.90	–	3.83	16.73	14.19	–	4.21	18.40
K131916B	600-1200 mm girth	m²	0.61	10.32	–	3.75	14.07	11.35	–	4.13	15.48
K131916C	1200-1800 mm girth	m²	0.51	8.59	–	3.67	12.26	9.45	–	4.04	13.49
K131917	**Insulation board; 12.5 mm Unitex ivory faced:**										
K131917A	not exceeding 600 mm girth	m²	0.76	12.91	–	4.65	17.56	14.20	–	5.12	19.32
K131917B	600-1200 mm girth	m²	0.61	10.33	–	4.55	14.88	11.36	–	5.01	16.37
K131917C	1200-1800 mm girth	m²	0.51	8.60	–	4.45	13.05	9.46	–	4.90	14.36
K131921	**Chipboard; 12 mm:**										
K131921A	not exceeding 600 mm girth	m²	0.51	8.59	–	2.57	11.16	9.45	–	2.83	12.28
K131921B	600-1200 mm girth	m²	0.41	6.87	–	2.52	9.39	7.56	–	2.77	10.33
K131921C	1200-1800 mm girth	m²	0.34	5.74	–	2.46	8.20	6.31	–	2.71	9.02
K131922	**Chipboard; 15 mm:**										
K131922A	not exceeding 600 mm girth	m²	0.59	10.02	–	3.76	13.78	11.02	–	4.14	15.16
K131922B	600-1200 mm girth	m²	0.47	8.03	–	3.68	11.71	8.83	–	4.05	12.88
K131922C	1200-1800 mm girth	m²	0.39	6.69	–	3.59	10.28	7.36	–	3.95	11.31
K131923	**Chipboard; 18 mm:**										
K131923A	not exceeding 600 mm girth	m²	0.68	11.46	–	4.52	15.98	12.61	–	4.97	17.58
K131923B	600-1200 mm girth	m²	0.54	9.17	–	4.42	13.59	10.09	–	4.86	14.95
K131923C	1200-1800 mm girth	m²	0.45	7.64	–	4.32	11.96	8.40	–	4.75	13.16
K131927	**Chipboard faced one side with 1.5 mm Class 1 laminated plastic covering and balancing veneer other side; 15 mm:**										
K131927A	not exceeding 600 mm girth	m²	0.84	14.33	–	4.93	19.26	15.76	–	5.42	21.19
K131927B	600-1200 mm girth	m²	0.68	11.46	–	4.82	16.28	12.61	–	5.30	17.91
K131927C	1200-1800 mm girth	m²	0.56	9.56	–	4.72	14.28	10.52	–	5.19	15.71
K131928	**Chipboard faced one side with 1.5 mm Class 1 laminated plastic covering and balancing veneer other side; 18 mm:**										
K131928A	not exceeding 600 mm girth	m²	1.01	17.20	–	5.24	22.44	18.92	–	5.76	24.68
K131928B	600-1200 mm girth	m²	0.81	13.76	–	5.12	18.88	15.14	–	5.63	20.77
K131928C	1200-1800 mm girth	m²	0.68	11.46	–	5.01	16.47	12.61	–	5.51	18.12
K131931	**Finnish birch faced 5 ply blockboard; grade BB; 18 mm:**										
K131931A	not exceeding 600 mm girth	m²	1.27	21.50	–	15.41	36.91	23.65	–	16.95	40.60
K131931B	600-1200 mm girth	m²	1.01	17.20	–	15.07	32.27	18.92	–	16.58	35.50
K131931C	1200-1800 mm girth	m²	0.84	14.34	–	14.72	29.06	15.77	–	16.19	31.97
K131932	**Finnish birch faced 5 ply blockboard; grade BB; 25 mm:**										
K131932A	not exceeding 600 mm girth	m²	1.35	22.92	–	21.84	44.76	25.21	–	24.02	49.24
K131932B	600-1200 mm girth	m²	1.08	18.33	–	21.35	39.68	20.16	–	23.49	43.65
K131932C	1200-1800 mm girth	m²	0.90	15.28	–	20.86	36.14	16.81	–	22.95	39.75

Major Works 2009		Unit	Labour Hours	Labour Net	Plant Net	Materials Net	Unit Net	Labour Gross	Plant Gross	Materials Gross	Unit Price
								(Gross rates include 10% profit)			
				£	£	£	£	£	£	£	£
K13	**K13: RIGID SHEET FINE LININGS AND PANELLING**										
K1319	**Isolated beams**										
K131936	**Far Eastern hardwood faced MR boarding ply; grade B/BB; 4 mm:**										
K131936A	not exceeding 600 mm girth	m²	0.64	10.86	–	3.70	14.56	11.95	–	4.07	16.02
K131936B	600-1200 mm girth	m²	0.51	8.72	–	3.61	12.33	9.59	–	3.97	13.56
K131936C	1200-1800 mm girth	m²	0.43	7.27	–	3.53	10.80	8.00	–	3.88	11.88
K131937	**Far Eastern hardwood faced MR boarding ply; grade B/BB; 6 mm:**										
K131937A	not exceeding 600 mm girth	m²	0.71	12.04	–	4.75	16.79A	13.24	–	5.23	18.47
K131937B	600-1200 mm girth	m²	0.56	9.56	–	4.65	14.21	10.52	–	5.12	15.63
K131937C	1200-1800 mm girth	m²	0.47	8.03	–	4.54	12.57	8.83	–	4.99	13.83
K131938	**Far Eastern hardwood faced MR boarding ply; grade B/BB; 9 mm:**										
K131938A	not exceeding 600 mm girth	m²	0.78	13.17	–	6.68	19.85	14.49	–	7.35	21.84
K131938B	600-1200 mm girth	m²	0.62	10.51	–	6.53	17.04	11.56	–	7.18	18.74
K131938C	1200-1800 mm girth	m²	0.52	8.79	–	6.38	15.17	9.67	–	7.02	16.69
K131939	**Far Eastern hardwood faced MR boarding ply; grade B/BB; 12 mm:**										
K131939A	not exceeding 600 mm girth	m²	0.84	14.33	–	8.47	22.80	15.76	–	9.32	25.08
K131939B	600-1200 mm girth	m²	0.68	11.46	–	8.28	19.74	12.61	–	9.11	21.71
K131939C	1200-1800 mm girth	m²	0.56	9.56	–	8.09	17.65	10.52	–	8.90	19.42
K131940	**Far Eastern hardwood faced MR boarding ply; grade B/BB; 15 mm:**										
K131940A	not exceeding 600 mm girth	m²	0.95	16.05	–	10.78	26.83	17.66	–	11.86	29.51
K131940B	600-1200 mm girth	m²	0.75	12.80	–	10.54	23.34	14.08	–	11.59	25.67
K131940C	1200-1800 mm girth	m²	0.63	10.70	–	10.29	20.99	11.77	–	11.32	23.09
K131941	**Far Eastern hardwood faced MR boarding ply; grade B/BB; 18 mm:**										
K131941A	not exceeding 600 mm girth	m²	1.01	17.20	–	12.31	29.51	18.92	–	13.54	32.46
K131941B	600-1200 mm girth	m²	0.81	13.75	–	12.03	25.78	15.13	–	13.23	28.36
K131941C	1200-1800 mm girth	m²	0.68	11.46	–	11.75	23.21	12.61	–	12.93	25.53
K131942	**Far Eastern hardwood faced MR boarding ply; grade B/BB; 22 mm:**										
K131942A	not exceeding 600 mm girth	m²	1.08	18.34	–	14.71	33.05	20.17	–	16.18	36.36
K131942B	600-1200 mm girth	m²	0.87	14.71	–	14.38	29.09	16.18	–	15.82	32.00
K131942C	1200-1800 mm girth	m²	0.72	12.22	–	14.05	26.27	13.44	–	15.46	28.90
K131943	**Far Eastern hardwood faced MR boarding ply; grade B/BB; 25 mm:**										
K131943A	not exceeding 600 mm girth	m²	1.16	19.77	–	17.09	36.86	21.75	–	18.80	40.55
K131943B	600-1200 mm girth	m²	0.93	15.86	–	16.70	32.56	17.45	–	18.37	35.82
K131943C	1200-1800 mm girth	m²	0.78	13.17	–	16.32	29.49	14.49	–	17.95	32.44
K131950	**Finnish birch faced WBP boarding ply; grade BB; 4 mm:**										
K131950A	not exceeding 600 mm girth	m²	0.59	10.02	–	7.34	17.36	11.02	–	8.07	19.10
K131950B	600-1200 mm girth	m²	0.47	8.03	–	7.17	15.20	8.83	–	7.89	16.72
K131950C	1200-1800 mm girth	m²	0.39	6.69	–	7.01	13.70	7.36	–	7.71	15.07

Major Works 2009		Unit	Labour Hours	Labour Net	Plant Net	Materials Net	Unit Net	Labour Gross	Plant Gross	Materials Gross	Unit Price
								(Gross rates include 10% profit)			
				£	£	£	£	£	£	£	£
K13	**K13: RIGID SHEET FINE LININGS AND PANELLING**										
K1319	**Isolated beams**										
K131951	**Finnish birch faced WBP boarding ply; grade BB; 6 mm:**										
K131951A	not exceeding 600 mm girth	m²	0.64	10.87	–	10.79	21.66	11.96	–	11.87	23.83
K131951B	600-1200 mm girth	m²	0.51	8.71	–	10.55	19.26	9.58	–	11.61	21.19
K131951C	1200-1800 mm girth	m²	0.43	7.27	–	10.30	17.57	8.00	–	11.33	19.33
K131952	**Finnish birch faced WBP boarding ply; grade BB; 9 mm:**										
K131952A	not exceeding 600 mm girth	m²	0.68	11.46	–	13.28	24.74	12.61	–	14.61	27.21
K131952B	600-1200 mm girth	m²	0.54	9.17	–	12.98	22.15	10.09	–	14.28	24.37
K131952C	1200-1800 mm girth	m²	0.45	7.64	–	12.68	20.32	8.40	–	13.95	22.35
K131953	**Finnish birch faced WBP boarding ply; grade BB; 12 mm:**										
K131953A	not exceeding 600 mm girth	m²	0.76	12.90	–	15.58	28.48	14.19	–	17.14	31.33
K131953B	600-1200 mm girth	m²	0.61	10.33	–	15.22	25.55	11.36	–	16.74	28.11
K131953C	1200-1800 mm girth	m²	1.19	20.21	–	14.87	35.08	22.23	–	16.36	38.59
K131954	**Finnish birch faced WBP boarding ply; grade BB; 15 mm:**										
K131954A	not exceeding 600 mm girth	m²	0.81	13.75	–	20.95	34.70	15.13	–	23.05	38.17
K131954B	600-1200 mm girth	m²	0.65	11.09	–	20.47	31.56	12.20	–	22.52	34.72
K131954C	1200-1800 mm girth	m²	0.54	9.16	–	20.00	29.16	10.08	–	22.00	32.08
K131955	**Finnish birch faced WBP boarding ply; grade BB; 18 mm:**										
K131955A	not exceeding 600 mm girth	m²	0.88	14.91	–	24.98	39.89	16.40	–	27.48	43.88
K131955B	600-1200 mm girth	m²	0.70	11.94	–	24.41	36.35	13.13	–	26.85	39.99
K131955C	1200-1800 mm girth	m²	0.59	9.94	–	23.84	33.78	10.93	–	26.22	37.16
K131956	**Finnish birch faced WBP boarding ply; grade BB; 22 mm:**										
K131956A	not exceeding 600 mm girth	m²	0.95	16.05	–	29.56	45.61	17.66	–	32.52	50.17
K131956B	600-1200 mm girth	m²	0.75	12.81	–	28.89	41.70	14.09	–	31.78	45.87
K131956C	1200-1800 mm girth	m²	0.63	10.70	–	28.22	38.92	11.77	–	31.04	42.81
K131957	**Finnish birch faced WBP boarding ply; grade BB; 25 mm:**										
K131957A	not exceeding 600 mm girth	m²	1.01	17.20	–	34.16	51.36	18.92	–	37.58	56.50
K131957B	600-1200 mm girth	m²	0.81	13.75	–	33.39	47.14	15.13	–	36.73	51.85
K131957C	1200-1800 mm girth	m²	0.68	11.46	–	32.61	44.07	12.61	–	35.87	48.48
K131961	**Non-asbestos, flameproof Class O boards; BS 476; 6 mm:**										
K131961A	not exceeding 600 mm girth	m²	0.47	8.03	–	9.50	17.53	8.83	–	10.45	19.28
K131961B	600-1200 mm girth	m²	0.38	6.42	–	9.28	15.70	7.06	–	10.21	17.27
K131961C	1200-1800 mm girth	m²	0.32	5.35	–	9.07	14.42	5.89	–	9.98	15.86
K131962	**Non-asbestos, flameproof Class O boards; BS 476; 9 mm:**										
K131962A	not exceeding 600 mm girth	m²	0.51	8.59	–	25.72	34.31	9.45	–	28.29	37.74
K131962B	600-1200 mm girth	m²	0.41	6.88	–	25.14	32.02	7.57	–	27.65	35.22
K131962C	1200-1800 mm girth	m²	0.34	5.74	–	24.56	30.30	6.31	–	27.02	33.33
K131963	**Non-asbestos, flameproof Class O boards; BS 476; 12 mm:**										
K131963A	not exceeding 600 mm girth	m²	0.59	10.02	–	38.75	48.77	11.02	–	42.63	53.65
K131963B	600-1200 mm girth	m²	0.47	8.04	–	37.87	45.91	8.84	–	41.66	50.50
K131963C	1200-1800 mm girth	m²	0.39	6.69	–	37.00	43.69	7.36	–	40.70	48.06

Linings, Sheathing and Dry Partitioning

Major Works 2009		Unit	Labour Hours	Labour Net	Plant Net	Materials Net	Unit Net	Labour Gross	Plant Gross	Materials Gross	Unit Price
				£	£	£	£	£	£	£	£
								——— (Gross rates include 10% profit) ———			
K13	K13: RIGID SHEET FINE LININGS AND PANELLING										
K1319	Isolated beams										
K131964	Non-asbestos, flameproof Class O boards; BS 476; 15 mm:										
K131964A	not exceeding 600 mm girth	m²	0.68	11.46	–	48.54	60.00	12.61	–	53.39	66.00
K131964B	600-1200 mm girth	m²	0.54	9.17	–	47.44	56.61	10.09	–	52.18	62.27
K131964C	1200-1800 mm girth	m²	0.45	7.64	–	46.34	53.98	8.40	–	50.97	59.38
K131971	MDF board; 12 mm:										
K131971A	not exceeding 600 mm girth	m²	0.68	11.46	–	4.96	16.42	12.61	–	5.46	18.06
K131971B	600-1200 mm girth	m²	0.54	9.17	–	4.85	14.02	10.09	–	5.34	15.42
K131971C	1200-1800 mm girth	m²	0.45	7.64	–	4.74	12.38	8.40	–	5.21	13.62
K131972	MDF board; 15 mm:										
K131972A	not exceeding 600 mm girth	m²	0.76	12.91	–	4.99	17.90	14.20	–	5.49	19.69
K131972B	600-1200 mm girth	m²	0.61	10.33	–	4.88	15.21	11.36	–	5.37	16.73
K131972C	1200-1800 mm girth	m²	0.51	8.59	–	4.77	13.36	9.45	–	5.25	14.70
K131973	MDF board; 18 mm:										
K131973A	not exceeding 600 mm girth	m²	0.84	14.33	–	6.87	21.20	15.76	–	7.56	23.32
K131973B	600-1200 mm girth	m²	0.68	11.46	–	6.72	18.18	12.61	–	7.39	20.00
K131973C	1200-1800 mm girth	m²	0.56	9.56	–	6.57	16.13	10.52	–	7.23	17.74

Linings, Sheathing and Dry Partitioning

Major Works 2009		Unit	Labour Hours	Labour Net	Plant Net	Materials Net	Unit Net	Labour Gross	Plant Gross	Materials Gross	Unit Price
								(Gross rates include 10% profit)			
				£	£	£	£	£	£	£	£
K13	**K13: RIGID SHEET FINE LININGS AND PANELLING**										
K1321	**Isolated columns**										
K132101	**Hardboard; 3.2 mm standard:**										
K132101A	not exceeding 600 mm girth	m²	0.38	6.37	–	1.84	8.21	7.01	–	2.02	9.03
K132101B	600-1200 mm girth	m²	0.30	5.10	–	1.80	6.90	5.61	–	1.98	7.59
K132101C	1200-1800 mm girth	m²	0.25	4.25	–	1.76	6.01	4.68	–	1.94	6.61
K132102	**Hardboard; 6.0 mm standard:**										
K132102A	not exceeding 600 mm girth	m²	0.45	7.64	–	4.91	12.55	8.40	–	5.40	13.81
K132102B	600-1200 mm girth	m²	0.36	6.11	–	4.80	10.91	6.72	–	5.28	12.00
K132102C	1200-1800 mm girth	m²	0.30	5.09	–	4.69	9.78	5.60	–	5.16	10.76
K132103	**Hardboard; 3.2 mm perforated:**										
K132103A	not exceeding 600 mm girth	m²	0.42	7.13	–	1.91	9.04	7.84	–	2.10	9.94
K132103B	600-1200 mm girth	m²	0.34	5.70	–	1.87	7.57	6.27	–	2.06	8.33
K132103C	1200-1800 mm girth	m²	0.28	4.75	–	1.83	6.58	5.23	–	2.01	7.24
K132104	**Hardboard; 6.0 mm perforated:**										
K132104A	not exceeding 600 mm girth	m²	0.48	8.15	–	3.74	11.89	8.97	–	4.11	13.08
K132104B	600-1200 mm girth	m²	0.38	6.52	–	3.66	10.18	7.17	–	4.03	11.20
K132104C	1200-1800 mm girth	m²	0.32	5.44	–	3.57	9.01	5.98	–	3.93	9.91
K132105	**Hardboard; 6.0 mm flameproof Class 1:**										
K132105A	not exceeding 600 mm girth	m²	0.45	7.64	–	13.39	21.03	8.40	–	14.73	23.13
K132105B	600-1200 mm girth	m²	0.36	6.11	–	13.09	19.20	6.72	–	14.40	21.12
K132105C	1200-1800 mm girth	m²	0.30	5.10	–	12.78	17.88	5.61	–	14.06	19.67
K132106	**Hardboard; 3.2 mm stove enamelled one side:**										
K132106A	not exceeding 600 mm girth	m²	0.42	7.13	–	2.69	9.82	7.84	–	2.96	10.80
K132106B	600-1200 mm girth	m²	0.34	5.71	–	2.63	8.34	6.28	–	2.89	9.17
K132106C	1200-1800 mm girth	m²	0.28	4.76	–	2.57	7.33	5.24	–	2.83	8.06
K132111	**Insulation board; 6.4 mm Sundeala A:**										
K132111A	not exceeding 600 mm girth	m²	0.53	8.92	–	9.47	18.39	9.81	–	10.42	20.23
K132111B	600-1200 mm girth	m²	0.42	7.13	–	9.26	16.39	7.84	–	10.19	18.03
K132111C	1200-1800 mm girth	m²	0.35	5.94	–	9.05	14.99	6.53	–	9.96	16.49
K132112	**Insulation board; 9.5 mm Sundeala A:**										
K132112A	not exceeding 600 mm girth	m²	0.57	9.68	–	12.22	21.90	10.65	–	13.44	24.09
K132112B	600-1200 mm girth	m²	0.46	7.74	–	11.95	19.69	8.51	–	13.15	21.66
K132112C	1200-1800 mm girth	m²	0.38	6.45	–	11.68	18.13	7.10	–	12.85	19.94
K132113	**Insulation board; 12.5 mm Sundeala A:**										
K132113A	not exceeding 600 mm girth	m²	0.60	10.19	–	13.98	24.17	11.21	–	15.38	26.59
K132113B	600-1200 mm girth	m²	0.48	8.15	–	13.67	21.82	8.97	–	15.04	24.00
K132113C	1200-1800 mm girth	m²	0.40	6.79	–	13.36	20.15	7.47	–	14.70	22.17
K132114	**Insulation board; 6.4 mm Sundeala K:**										
K132114A	not exceeding 600 mm girth	m²	0.53	8.91	–	8.40	17.31	9.80	–	9.24	19.04
K132114B	600-1200 mm girth	m²	0.42	7.13	–	8.21	15.34	7.84	–	9.03	16.87
K132114C	1200-1800 mm girth	m²	0.35	5.94	–	8.02	13.96	6.53	–	8.82	15.36

Major Works 2009		Unit	Labour Hours	Labour Net	Plant Net	Materials Net	Unit Net	Labour Gross	Plant Gross	Materials Gross	Unit Price
								——— (Gross rates include 10% profit) ———			
				£	£	£	£	£	£	£	£
K13	**K13: RIGID SHEET FINE LININGS AND PANELLING**										
K1321	**Isolated columns**										
K132115	**Insulation board; 9.5 mm Sundeala K:**										
K132115A	not exceeding 600 mm girth	m²	0.57	9.68	–	12.22	21.90	10.65	–	13.44	24.09
K132115B	600-1200 mm girth	m²	0.46	7.74	–	11.95	19.69	8.51	–	13.15	21.66
K132115C	1200-1800 mm girth	m²	0.38	6.45	–	11.68	18.13	7.10	–	12.85	19.94
K132116	**Insulation board; 12.5 mm Pilkington ivory faced:**										
K132116A	not exceeding 600 mm girth	m²	0.68	11.46	–	3.83	15.29	12.61	–	4.21	16.82
K132116B	600-1200 mm girth	m²	0.54	9.17	–	3.75	12.92	10.09	–	4.13	14.21
K132116C	1200-1800 mm girth	m²	0.45	7.64	–	3.67	11.31	8.40	–	4.04	12.44
K132117	**Insulation board; 12.5 mm Unitex ivory faced:**										
K132117A	not exceeding 600 mm girth	m²	0.68	11.46	–	4.65	16.11	12.61	–	5.12	17.72
K132117B	600-1200 mm girth	m²	0.54	9.17	–	4.55	13.72	10.09	–	5.01	15.09
K132117C	1200-1800 mm girth	m²	0.45	7.65	–	4.45	12.10	8.42	–	4.90	13.31
K132121	**Chipboard; 12 mm:**										
K132121A	not exceeding 600 mm girth	m²	0.45	7.64	–	2.57	10.21	8.40	–	2.83	11.23
K132121B	600-1200 mm girth	m²	0.36	6.11	–	2.52	8.63	6.72	–	2.77	9.49
K132121C	1200-1800 mm girth	m²	0.30	5.09	–	2.46	7.55	5.60	–	2.71	8.31
K132122	**Chipboard; 15 mm:**										
K132122A	not exceeding 600 mm girth	m²	0.53	8.92	–	3.76	12.68	9.81	–	4.14	13.95
K132122B	600-1200 mm girth	m²	0.42	7.13	–	3.68	10.81	7.84	–	4.05	11.89
K132122C	1200-1800 mm girth	m²	0.35	5.95	–	3.59	9.54	6.55	–	3.95	10.49
K132123	**Chipboard; 18 mm:**										
K132123A	not exceeding 600 mm girth	m²	0.60	10.19	–	4.52	14.71	11.21	–	4.97	16.18
K132123B	600-1200 mm girth	m²	0.48	8.15	–	4.42	12.57	8.97	–	4.86	13.83
K132123C	1200-1800 mm girth	m²	0.40	6.79	–	4.32	11.11	7.47	–	4.75	12.22
K132127	**Chipboard faced one side with 1.5 mm Class 1 laminated plastic covering and balancing veneer other side; 15 mm:**										
K132127A	not exceeding 600 mm girth	m²	0.75	12.73	–	4.93	17.66	14.00	–	5.42	19.43
K132127B	600-1200 mm girth	m²	0.60	10.19	–	4.82	15.01	11.21	–	5.30	16.51
K132127C	1200-1800 mm girth	m²	0.50	8.49	–	4.72	13.21	9.34	–	5.19	14.53
K132128	**Chipboard faced one side with 1.5 mm Class 1 laminated plastic covering and balancing veneer other side; 18 mm:**										
K132128A	not exceeding 600 mm girth	m²	0.90	15.28	–	5.24	20.52	16.81	–	5.76	22.57
K132128B	600-1200 mm girth	m²	0.72	12.23	–	5.12	17.35	13.45	–	5.63	19.09
K132128C	1200-1800 mm girth	m²	0.60	10.19	–	5.01	15.20	11.21	–	5.51	16.72
K132131	**Finnish birch faced 5 ply blockboard; grade BB; 18 mm:**										
K132131A	not exceeding 600 mm girth	m²	1.13	19.10	–	15.41	34.51	21.01	–	16.95	37.96
K132131B	600-1200 mm girth	m²	0.90	15.28	–	15.07	30.35	16.81	–	16.58	33.39
K132131C	1200-1800 mm girth	m²	0.75	12.74	–	14.72	27.46	14.01	–	16.19	30.21
K132132	**Finnish birch faced 5 ply blockboard; grade BB; 25 mm:**										
K132132A	not exceeding 600 mm girth	m²	1.20	20.37	–	21.84	42.21	22.41	–	24.02	46.43
K132132B	600-1200 mm girth	m²	0.96	16.30	–	21.35	37.65	17.93	–	23.49	41.42
K132132C	1200-1800 mm girth	m²	0.80	13.58	–	20.86	34.44	14.94	–	22.95	37.88

Major Works 2009		Unit	Labour Hours	Labour Net	Plant Net	Materials Net	Unit Net	Labour Gross	Plant Gross	Materials Gross	Unit Price
									(Gross rates include 10% profit)		
				£	£	£	£	£	£	£	£
K13	**K13: RIGID SHEET FINE LININGS AND PANELLING**										
K1321	**Isolated columns**										
K132136	**Far Eastern hardwood faced MR boarding ply; grade B/BB; 4 mm:**										
K132136A	not exceeding 600 mm girth	m²	0.57	9.68	–	3.70	13.38	10.65	–	4.07	14.72
K132136B	600-1200 mm girth	m²	0.46	7.75	–	3.61	11.36	8.53	–	3.97	12.50
K132136C	1200-1800 mm girth	m²	0.38	6.45	–	3.53	9.98	7.10	–	3.88	10.98
K132137	**Far Eastern hardwood faced MR boarding ply; grade B/BB; 6 mm:**										
K132137A	not exceeding 600 mm girth	m²	0.63	10.70	–	4.75	15.45	11.77	–	5.23	17.00
K132137B	600-1200 mm girth	m²	0.50	8.49	–	4.65	13.14	9.34	–	5.12	14.45
K132137C	1200-1800 mm girth	m²	0.42	7.13	–	4.54	11.67	7.84	–	4.99	12.84
K132138	**Far Eastern hardwood faced MR boarding ply; grade B/BB; 9 mm:**										
K132138A	not exceeding 600 mm girth	m²	0.69	11.71	–	6.68	18.39	12.88	–	7.35	20.23
K132138B	600-1200 mm girth	m²	0.55	9.34	–	6.53	15.87	10.27	–	7.18	17.46
K132138C	1200-1800 mm girth	m²	0.46	7.81	–	6.38	14.19	8.59	–	7.02	15.61
K132139	**Far Eastern hardwood faced MR boarding ply; grade B/BB; 12 mm:**										
K132139A	not exceeding 600 mm girth	m²	0.75	12.74	–	8.47	21.21	14.01	–	9.32	23.33
K132139B	600-1200 mm girth	m²	0.60	10.19	–	8.28	18.47	11.21	–	9.11	20.32
K132139C	1200-1800 mm girth	m²	0.50	8.49	–	8.09	16.58	9.34	–	8.90	18.24
K132140	**Far Eastern hardwood faced MR boarding ply; grade B/BB; 15 mm:**										
K132140A	not exceeding 600 mm girth	m²	0.84	14.26	–	10.78	25.04	15.69	–	11.86	27.54
K132140B	600-1200 mm girth	m²	0.67	11.37	–	10.54	21.91	12.51	–	11.59	24.10
K132140C	1200-1800 mm girth	m²	0.56	9.51	–	10.29	19.80	10.46	–	11.32	21.78
K132141	**Far Eastern hardwood faced MR boarding ply; grade B/BB; 18 mm:**										
K132141A	not exceeding 600 mm girth	m²	0.90	15.28	–	12.31	27.59	16.81	–	13.54	30.35
K132141B	600-1200 mm girth	m²	0.72	12.22	–	12.03	24.25	13.44	–	13.23	26.68
K132141C	1200-1800 mm girth	m²	0.60	10.19	–	11.75	21.94	11.21	–	12.93	24.13
K132142	**Far Eastern hardwood faced MR boarding ply; grade B/BB; 22 mm:**										
K132142A	not exceeding 600 mm girth	m²	0.96	16.31	–	14.71	31.02	17.94	–	16.18	34.12
K132142B	600-1200 mm girth	m²	0.77	13.08	–	14.38	27.46	14.39	–	15.82	30.21
K132142C	1200-1800 mm girth	m²	0.64	10.86	–	14.05	24.91	11.95	–	15.46	27.40
K132143	**Far Eastern hardwood faced MR boarding ply; grade B/BB; 25 mm:**										
K132143A	not exceeding 600 mm girth	m²	1.04	17.57	–	17.09	34.66	19.33	–	18.80	38.13
K132143B	600-1200 mm girth	m²	0.83	14.10	–	16.70	30.80	15.51	–	18.37	33.88
K132143C	1200-1800 mm girth	m²	0.69	11.71	–	16.32	28.03	12.88	–	17.95	30.83
K132150	**Finnish birch faced WBP boarding ply; grade BB; 4 mm:**										
K132150A	not exceeding 600 mm girth	m²	0.53	8.91	–	7.34	16.25	9.80	–	8.07	17.88
K132150B	600-1200 mm girth	m²	0.42	7.13	–	7.17	14.30	7.84	–	7.89	15.73
K132150C	1200-1800 mm girth	m²	0.35	5.94	–	7.01	12.95	6.53	–	7.71	14.25

Major Works 2009		Unit	Labour Hours	Labour Net	Plant Net	Materials Net	Unit Net	Labour Gross	Plant Gross	Materials Gross	Unit Price
								(Gross rates include 10% profit)			
				£	£	£	£	£	£	£	£
K13	**K13: RIGID SHEET FINE LININGS AND PANELLING**										
K1321	**Isolated columns**										
K132151	**Finnish birch faced WBP boarding ply; grade BB; 6 mm:**										
K132151A	not exceeding 600 mm girth	m²	0.57	9.68	–	10.79	20.47	10.65	–	11.87	22.52
K132151B	600-1200 mm girth	m²	0.46	7.74	–	10.55	18.29	8.51	–	11.61	20.12
K132151C	1200-1800 mm girth	m²	0.38	6.46	–	10.30	16.76	7.11	–	11.33	18.44
K132152	**Finnish birch faced WBP boarding ply; grade BB; 9 mm:**										
K132152A	not exceeding 600 mm girth	m²	0.60	10.19	–	13.28	23.47	11.21	–	14.61	25.82
K132152B	600-1200 mm girth	m²	0.48	8.15	–	12.98	21.13	8.97	–	14.28	23.24
K132152C	1200-1800 mm girth	m²	0.40	6.79	–	12.68	19.47	7.47	–	13.95	21.42
K132153	**Finnish birch faced WBP boarding ply; grade BB; 12 mm:**										
K132153A	not exceeding 600 mm girth	m²	0.68	11.46	–	15.58	27.04	12.61	–	17.14	29.74
K132153B	600-1200 mm girth	m²	0.54	9.17	–	15.22	24.39	10.09	–	16.74	26.83
K132153C	1200-1800 mm girth	m²	0.45	7.64	–	14.87	22.51	8.40	–	16.36	24.76
K132154	**Finnish birch faced WBP boarding ply; grade BB; 15 mm:**										
K132154A	not exceeding 600 mm girth	m²	0.72	12.22	–	20.95	33.17	13.44	–	23.05	36.49
K132154B	600-1200 mm girth	m²	0.58	9.85	–	20.47	30.32	10.84	–	22.52	33.35
K132154C	1200-1800 mm girth	m²	0.48	8.15	–	20.00	28.15	8.97	–	22.00	30.97
K132155	**Finnish birch faced WBP boarding ply; grade BB; 18 mm:**										
K132155A	not exceeding 600 mm girth	m²	0.78	13.24	–	24.98	38.22	14.56	–	27.48	42.04
K132155B	600-1200 mm girth	m²	0.63	10.61	–	24.41	35.02	11.67	–	26.85	38.52
K132155C	1200-1800 mm girth	m²	0.52	8.83	–	23.84	32.67	9.71	–	26.22	35.94
K132156	**Finnish birch faced WBP boarding ply; grade BB; 22 mm:**										
K132156A	not exceeding 600 mm girth	m²	0.84	14.27	–	29.56	43.83	15.70	–	32.52	48.21
K132156B	600-1200 mm girth	m²	0.67	11.38	–	28.89	40.27	12.52	–	31.78	44.30
K132156C	1200-1800 mm girth	m²	0.56	9.51	–	28.22	37.73	10.46	–	31.04	41.50
K132157	**Finnish birch faced WBP boarding ply; grade BB; 25 mm:**										
K132157A	not exceeding 600 mm girth	m²	0.90	15.28	–	34.16	49.44	16.81	–	37.58	54.38
K132157B	600-1200 mm girth	m²	0.72	12.22	–	33.39	45.61	13.44	–	36.73	50.17
K132157C	1200-1800 mm girth	m²	0.60	10.19	–	32.61	42.80	11.21	–	35.87	47.08
K132161	**Non-asbestos, flameproof Class O boards; BS 476; 6 mm:**										
K132161A	not exceeding 600 mm girth	m²	0.42	7.13	–	9.50	16.63	7.84	–	10.45	18.29
K132161B	600-1200 mm girth	m²	0.34	5.71	–	9.28	14.99	6.28	–	10.21	16.49
K132161C	1200-1800 mm girth	m²	0.28	4.76	–	9.07	13.83	5.24	–	9.98	15.21
K132162	**Non-asbestos, flameproof Class O boards; BS 476; 9 mm:**										
K132162A	not exceeding 600 mm girth	m²	0.45	7.64	–	25.72	33.36	8.40	–	28.29	36.70
K132162B	600-1200 mm girth	m²	0.36	6.11	–	25.14	31.25	6.72	–	27.65	34.38
K132162C	1200-1800 mm girth	m²	0.30	5.09	–	24.56	29.65	5.60	–	27.02	32.62
K132163	**Non-asbestos, flameproof Class O boards; BS 476; 12 mm:**										
K132163A	not exceeding 600 mm girth	m²	0.53	8.91	–	38.75	47.66	9.80	–	42.63	52.43
K132163B	600-1200 mm girth	m²	0.42	7.14	–	37.87	45.01	7.85	–	41.66	49.51
K132163C	1200-1800 mm girth	m²	0.35	5.94	–	37.00	42.94	6.53	–	40.70	47.23

Linings, Sheathing and Dry Partitioning

Major Works 2009		Unit	Labour Hours	Labour Net	Plant Net	Materials Net	Unit Net	Labour Gross	Plant Gross	Materials Gross	Unit Price
								(Gross rates include 10% profit)			
				£	£	£	£	£	£	£	£
K13	**K13: RIGID SHEET FINE LININGS AND PANELLING**										
K1321	**Isolated columns**										
K132164	**Non-asbestos, flameproof Class 0 boards; BS 476; 15 mm:**										
K132164A	not exceeding 600 mm girth	m²	0.60	10.19	–	48.54	58.73	11.21	–	53.39	64.60
K132164B	600-1200 mm girth	m²	0.48	8.15	–	47.44	55.59	8.97	–	52.18	61.15
K132164C	1200-1800 mm girth	m²	0.40	6.79	–	46.34	53.13	7.47	–	50.97	58.44
K132171	**MDF board; 12 mm:**										
K132171A	not exceeding 600 mm girth	m²	0.52	8.86	–	4.96	13.82	9.75	–	5.46	15.20
K132171B	600-1200 mm girth	m²	0.42	7.13	–	4.85	11.98	7.84	–	5.34	13.18
K132171C	1200-1800 mm girth	m²	0.35	5.94	–	4.74	10.68	6.53	–	5.21	11.75
K132172	**MDF board; 15 mm:**										
K132172A	not exceeding 600 mm girth	m²	0.60	10.19	–	4.99	15.18	11.21	–	5.49	16.70
K132172B	600-1200 mm girth	m²	0.48	8.15	–	4.88	13.03	8.97	–	5.37	14.33
K132172C	1200-1800 mm girth	m²	0.40	6.79	–	4.77	11.56	7.47	–	5.25	12.72
K132173	**MDF board; 18 mm:**										
K132173A	not exceeding 600 mm girth	m²	0.67	11.38	–	6.87	18.25	12.52	–	7.56	20.08
K132173B	600-1200 mm girth	m²	0.54	9.17	–	6.72	15.89	10.09	–	7.39	17.48
K132173C	1200-1800 mm girth	m²	0.45	7.64	–	6.57	14.21	8.40	–	7.23	15.63

Major Works 2009		Unit	Labour Hours	Labour Net	Plant Net	Materials Net	Unit Net	Labour Gross	Plant Gross	Materials Gross	Unit Price
								(Gross rates include 10% profit)			
				£	£	£	£	£	£	£	£
K20	**K20: TIMBER BOARD FLOORING, SHEATHING, LININGS AND CASINGS**										
K2006	**Walls**										
K200601	**Wrought softwood shiplap boarding; basic sizes; 19 mm thick:**										
K200601A	over 300 mm wide	m²	0.75	12.74	–	22.75	35.49	14.01	–	25.03	39.04
K200601B	n.e. 300 mm wide	m	0.45	7.64	–	7.51	15.15	8.40	–	8.26	16.67
K200601C	area n.e. 1.0 m²	Nr	1.13	19.10	–	23.59	42.69	21.01	–	25.95	46.96
K200603	**Wrought softwood shiplap boarding; basic sizes; 25 mm thick:**										
K200603E	over 300 mm wide	m²	0.75	12.73	–	28.33	41.06	14.00	–	31.16	45.17
K200603F	n.e. 300 mm wide	m	0.45	7.65	–	9.35	17.00	8.42	–	10.29	18.70
K200603G	area n.e. 1.0 m²	Nr	1.13	19.11	–	29.37	48.48	21.02	–	32.31	53.33
K200611	**Wrought softwood tongued and grooved and V-jointed one side matchboarding; basic sizes; 13 mm thick:**										
K200611A	over 300 mm wide	m²	0.80	13.59	–	16.24	29.83	14.95	–	17.86	32.81
K200611B	n.e. 300 mm wide	m	0.48	8.16	–	5.36	13.52	8.98	–	5.90	14.87
K200611C	area n.e. 1.0 m²	Nr	1.20	20.38	–	16.83	37.21	22.42	–	18.51	40.93
K200613	**Wrought softwood tongued and grooved and V-jointed one side matchboarding; basic sizes; 19 mm thick:**										
K200613E	over 300 mm wide	m²	0.80	13.59	–	20.30	33.89	14.95	–	22.33	37.28
K200613F	n.e. 300 mm wide	m	0.48	8.15	–	6.71	14.86	8.97	–	7.38	16.35
K200613G	area n.e. 1.0 m²	Nr	1.20	20.37	–	21.05	41.42	22.41	–	23.16	45.56
K2011	**Floors**										
K201101	**Wrought softwood square edged boarding; basic sizes; 19 mm thick:**										
K201101A	over 300 mm wide	m²	0.55	9.34	–	17.93	27.27	10.27	–	19.72	30.00
K201101B	n.e. 300 mm wide	m	0.33	5.61	–	5.85	11.46	6.17	–	6.44	12.61
K201101C	area n.e. 1.0 m²	Nr	0.83	14.01	–	18.52	32.53	15.41	–	20.37	35.78
K201102	**Wrought softwood square edged boarding; basic sizes; 22 mm thick:**										
K201102D	over 300 mm wide	m²	0.55	9.34	–	19.38	28.72	10.27	–	21.32	31.59
K201102E	n.e. 300 mm wide	m	0.33	5.60	–	6.33	11.93	6.16	–	6.96	13.12
K201102F	area n.e. 1.0 m²	Nr	0.83	14.01	–	20.03	34.04	15.41	–	22.03	37.44
K201103	**Wrought softwood square edged boarding; basic sizes; 25 mm thick:**										
K201103G	over 300 mm wide	m²	0.55	9.34	–	20.80	30.14	10.27	–	22.88	33.15
K201103H	n.e. 300 mm wide	m	0.33	5.60	–	6.80	12.40	6.16	–	7.48	13.64
K201103I	area n.e. 1.0 m²	Nr	0.83	14.01	–	21.50	35.51	15.41	–	23.65	39.06
K201111	**Wrought softwood tongued and grooved boarding; basic sizes; 19 mm thick:**										
K201111A	over 300 mm wide	m²	0.65	11.04	–	19.89	30.93	12.14	–	21.88	34.02
K201111B	n.e. 300 mm wide	m	0.39	6.62	–	6.50	13.12	7.28	–	7.15	14.43
K201111C	area n.e. 1.0 m²	Nr	0.98	16.56	–	20.56	37.12	18.22	–	22.62	40.83

Linings, Sheathing and Dry Partitioning

Major Works 2009		Unit	Labour Hours	Labour Net	Plant Net	Materials Net	Unit Net	Labour Gross	Plant Gross	Materials Gross	Unit Price
								(Gross rates include 10% profit)			
				£	£	£	£	£	£	£	£
K20	**K20: TIMBER BOARD FLOORING, SHEATHING, LININGS AND CASINGS**										
K2011	**Floors**										
K201112	**Wrought softwood tongued and grooved boarding; basic sizes; 22 mm thick:**										
K201112D	over 300 mm wide	m²	0.65	11.04	–	20.63	31.67	12.14	–	22.69	34.84
K201112E	n.e. 300 mm wide	m	0.39	6.63	–	6.74	13.37	7.29	–	7.41	14.71
K201112F	area n.e. 1.0 m²	Nr	0.98	16.56	–	21.33	37.89	18.22	–	23.46	41.68
K201113	**Wrought softwood tongued and grooved boarding; basic sizes; 25 mm thick:**										
K201113G	over 300 mm wide	m²	0.65	11.04	–	21.37	32.41	12.14	–	23.51	35.65
K201113H	n.e. 300 mm wide	m	0.39	6.62	–	6.99	13.61	7.28	–	7.69	14.97
K201113I	area n.e. 1.0 m²	Nr	0.98	16.56	–	22.10	38.66	18.22	–	24.31	42.53
K2016	**Ceilings**										
K201601	**Wrought softwood tongued and grooved and V-jointed one side matchboarding; basic sizes; 13 mm thick:**										
K201601A	over 300 mm wide	m²	0.95	16.13	–	16.24	32.37	17.74	–	17.86	35.61
K201601B	n.e. 300 mm wide	m	0.57	9.68	–	5.36	15.04	10.65	–	5.90	16.54
K201601C	area n.e. 1.0 m²	Nr	1.43	24.20	–	16.83	41.03	26.62	–	18.51	45.13
K201631	**Wrought softwood tongued and grooved and V-jointed one side matchboarding; basic sizes; 19 mm thick:**										
K201631D	over 300 mm wide	m²	0.95	16.13	–	20.30	36.43	17.74	–	22.33	40.07
K201631E	n.e. 300 mm wide	m	0.57	9.67	–	6.71	16.38	10.64	–	7.38	18.02
K201631F	area n.e. 1.0 m²	Nr	1.43	24.19	–	21.05	45.24	26.61	–	23.16	49.76

Major Works 2009		Unit	Labour Hours	Labour Net	Plant Net	Materials Net	Unit Net	Labour Gross	Plant Gross	Materials Gross	Unit Price
								(Gross rates include 10% profit)			
				£	£	£	£	£	£	£	£
K20	**K20: TIMBER BOARD FLOORING, SHEATHING, LININGS AND CASINGS**										
K2021	**Roofs**										
K202101	**Wrought softwood square edged boarding; basic sizes; 19 mm thick:**										
K202101A	over 300 mm wide	m²	0.60	10.19	–	17.93	28.12	11.21	–	19.72	30.93
K202101B	n.e. 300 mm wide	m	0.35	5.95	–	5.85	11.80	6.55	–	6.44	12.98
K202101C	area n.e. 1.0 m²	Nr	0.90	15.28	–	18.52	33.80	16.81	–	20.37	37.18
K202102	**Wrought softwood square edged boarding; basic sizes; 22 mm thick:**										
K202102D	over 300 mm wide	m²	0.60	10.19	–	19.38	29.57	11.21	–	21.32	32.53
K202102E	n.e. 300 mm wide	m	0.35	5.94	–	6.33	12.27	6.53	–	6.96	13.50
K202102F	area n.e. 1.0 m²	Nr	0.90	15.28	–	20.03	35.31	16.81	–	22.03	38.84
K202103	**Wrought softwood square edged boarding; basic sizes; 25 mm thick:**										
K202103G	over 300 mm wide	m²	0.60	10.19	–	20.80	30.99	11.21	–	22.88	34.09
K202103H	n.e. 300 mm wide	m	0.35	5.94	–	6.80	12.74	6.53	–	7.48	14.01
K202103I	area n.e. 1.0 m²	Nr	0.90	15.28	–	21.50	36.78	16.81	–	23.65	40.46
K202111	**Wrought softwood tongued and grooved boarding; basic sizes; 19 mm thick:**										
K202111A	over 300 mm wide	m²	0.70	11.89	–	19.89	31.78	13.08	–	21.88	34.96
K202111B	n.e. 300 mm wide	m	0.40	6.79	–	6.50	13.29	7.47	–	7.15	14.62
K202111C	area n.e. 1.0 m²	Nr	1.05	17.83	–	20.56	38.39	19.61	–	22.62	42.23
K202112	**Wrought softwood tongued and grooved boarding; basic sizes; 22 mm thick:**										
K202112D	over 300 mm wide	m²	0.70	11.89	–	20.63	32.52	13.08	–	22.69	35.77
K202112E	n.e. 300 mm wide	m	0.40	6.80	–	6.74	13.54	7.48	–	7.41	14.89
K202112F	area n.e. 1.0 m²	Nr	1.05	17.83	–	21.33	39.16	19.61	–	23.46	43.08
K202113	**Wrought softwood tongued and grooved boarding; basic sizes; 25 mm thick:**										
K202113G	over 300 mm wide	m²	0.70	11.89	–	21.37	33.26	13.08	–	23.51	36.59
K202113H	n.e. 300 mm wide	m	0.40	6.79	–	6.99	13.78	7.47	–	7.69	15.16
K202113I	area n.e. 1.0 m²	Nr	1.05	17.83	–	22.10	39.93	19.61	–	24.31	43.92

Linings, Sheathing and Dry Partitioning

Major Works 2009		Unit	Labour Hours	Labour Net	Plant Net	Materials Net	Unit Net	Labour Gross	Plant Gross	Materials Gross	Unit Price
				£	£	£	£	£ (Gross rates include 10% profit)	£	£	£
K20	**K20: TIMBER BOARD FLOORING, SHEATHING, LININGS AND CASINGS**										
K2025	**Tops and cheeks of dormers**										
K202501	**Wrought softwood square edged boarding; basic sizes; firrings and bearers included as necessary; 19 mm thick:**										
K202501A	flat; over 300 mm wide	m²	1.05	17.83	–	19.28	37.11	19.61	–	21.21	40.82
K202501B	flat; n.e. 300 mm wide	m	0.58	9.85	–	5.91	15.76	10.84	–	6.50	17.34
K202501C	flat; area n.e. 1.0 m²	Nr	1.58	26.75	–	19.28	46.03	29.43	–	21.21	50.63
K202501D	sloping; over 300 mm wide.	m²	0.86	14.61	–	17.85	32.46	16.07	–	19.64	35.71
K202501E	sloping; n.e. 300 mm wide .	m	0.50	8.49	–	5.53	14.02	9.34	–	6.08	15.42
K202501F	sloping; area n.e. 1.0 m² ...	Nr	1.29	21.91	–	17.85	39.76	24.10	–	19.64	43.74
K202501G	vertical; over 300 mm wide.	m²	1.04	17.66	–	17.50	35.16	19.43	–	19.25	38.68
K202501H	vertical; n.e. 300 mm wide .	m	0.57	9.68	–	5.42	15.10	10.65	–	5.96	16.61
K202501I	vertical; area n.e. 1.0 m² ...	Nr	1.56	26.49	–	17.50	43.99	29.14	–	19.25	48.39
K202502	**Wrought softwood square edged boarding; basic sizes; firrings and bearers included as necessary; 22 mm thick:**										
K202502A	flat; over 300 mm wide	m²	1.05	17.83	–	20.73	38.56	19.61	–	22.80	42.42
K202502B	flat; n.e. 300 mm wide	m	0.58	9.85	–	6.36	16.21	10.84	–	7.00	17.83
K202502C	flat; area n.e. 1.0 m²	Nr	1.58	26.75	–	20.73	47.48	29.43	–	22.80	52.23
K202502D	sloping; over 300 mm wide.	m²	0.86	14.60	–	19.31	33.91	16.06	–	21.24	37.30
K202502E	sloping; n.e. 300 mm wide .	m	0.50	8.49	–	5.98	14.47	9.34	–	6.58	15.92
K202502F	sloping; area n.e. 1.0 m² ...	Nr	1.29	21.90	–	19.31	41.21	24.09	–	21.24	45.33
K202502G	vertical; over 300 mm wide.	m²	1.04	17.66	–	18.95	36.61	19.43	–	20.85	40.27
K202502H	vertical; n.e. 300 mm wide .	m	0.57	9.68	–	5.87	15.55	10.65	–	6.46	17.11
K202502I	vertical; area n.e. 1.0 m² ...	Nr	1.56	26.49	–	18.95	45.44	29.14	–	20.85	49.98
K202503	**Wrought softwood square edged boarding; basic sizes; firrings and bearers included as necessary; 25 mm thick:**										
K202503A	flat; over 300 mm wide	m²	1.05	17.83	–	22.15	39.98	19.61	–	24.37	43.98
K202503B	flat; n.e. 300 mm wide	m	0.58	9.85	–	6.85	16.70	10.84	–	7.54	18.37
K202503C	flat; area n.e. 1.0 m²	Nr	1.58	26.75	–	22.15	48.90	29.43	–	24.37	53.79
K202503D	sloping; over 300 mm wide.	m²	0.86	14.60	–	20.73	35.33	16.06	–	22.80	38.86
K202503E	sloping; n.e. 300 mm wide .	m	0.50	8.49	–	6.42	14.91	9.34	–	7.06	16.40
K202503F	sloping; area n.e. 1.0 m² ...	Nr	1.29	21.91	–	36.41	58.32	24.10	–	40.05	64.15
K202503G	vertical; over 300 mm wide.	m²	1.04	17.66	–	20.37	38.03	19.43	–	22.41	41.83
K202503H	vertical; n.e. 300 mm wide .	m	0.57	9.68	–	6.32	16.00	10.65	–	6.95	17.60
K202503I	vertical; area n.e. 1.0 m² ...	Nr	1.56	26.49	–	20.37	46.86	29.14	–	22.41	51.55
K202521	**Wrought softwood tongued and grooved boarding; basic sizes; firrings and bearers included as necessary; 19 mm thick:**										
K202521A	flat; over 300 mm wide	m²	1.15	19.52	–	21.76	41.28	21.47	–	23.94	45.41
K202521B	flat; n.e. 300 mm wide	m	0.64	10.87	–	6.69	17.56	11.96	–	7.36	19.32
K202521C	flat; area n.e. 1.0 m²	Nr	1.73	29.29	–	21.88	51.17	32.22	–	24.07	56.29
K202521D	sloping; over 300 mm wide.	m²	0.94	15.97	–	20.36	36.33	17.57	–	22.40	39.96
K202521E	sloping; n.e. 300 mm wide .	m	0.55	9.34	–	6.22	15.56	10.27	–	6.84	17.12
K202521F	sloping; area n.e. 1.0 m² ...	Nr	1.41	23.95	–	20.36	44.31	26.35	–	22.40	48.74
K202521G	vertical; over 300 mm wide.	m²	1.14	19.35	–	20.01	39.36	21.29	–	22.01	43.30
K202521H	vertical; n.e. 300 mm wide .	m	0.63	10.70	–	6.12	16.82	11.77	–	6.73	18.50
K202521I	vertical; area n.e. 1.0 m² ...	Nr	1.71	29.03	–	20.01	49.04	31.93	–	22.01	53.94

Major Works 2009		Unit	Labour Hours	Labour Net	Plant Net	Materials Net	Unit Net	Labour Gross	Plant Gross	Materials Gross	Unit Price
								——— (Gross rates include 10% profit) ———			
				£	£	£	£	£	£	£	£
K20	**K20: TIMBER BOARD FLOORING, SHEATHING, LININGS AND CASINGS**										
K2025	**Tops and cheeks of dormers**										
K202522	**Wrought softwood tongued and grooved boarding; basic sizes; firrings and bearers included as necessary; 22 mm thick:**										
K202522A	flat; over 300 mm wide	m²	1.15	19.53	–	22.51	42.04	21.48	–	24.76	46.24
K202522B	flat; n.e. 300 mm wide	m	0.64	10.87	–	6.92	17.79	11.96	–	7.61	19.57
K202522C	flat; area n.e. 1.0 m²	Nr	1.73	29.30	–	22.63	51.93	32.23	–	24.89	57.12
K202522D	sloping; over 300 mm wide .	m²	0.94	15.96	–	21.12	37.08	17.56	–	23.23	40.79
K202522E	sloping; n.e. 300 mm wide .	m	0.55	9.33	–	6.46	15.79	10.26	–	7.11	17.37
K202522F	sloping; area n.e. 1.0 m² ...	Nr	1.41	23.94	–	21.12	45.06	26.33	–	23.23	49.57
K202522G	vertical; over 300 mm wide .	m²	1.14	19.36	–	20.76	40.12	21.30	–	22.84	44.13
K202522H	vertical; n.e. 300 mm wide .	m	0.63	10.70	–	6.35	17.05	11.77	–	6.99	18.76
K202522I	vertical; area n.e. 1.0 m² ...	Nr	1.71	29.04	–	20.76	49.80	31.94	–	22.84	54.78
K202523	**Wrought softwood tongued and grooved boarding; basic sizes; firrings and bearers included as necessary; 25 mm thick:**										
K202523A	flat; over 300 mm wide	m²	1.15	19.53	–	23.27	42.80	21.48	–	25.60	47.08
K202523B	flat; n.e. 300 mm wide	m	0.64	10.86	–	7.16	18.02	11.95	–	7.88	19.82
K202523C	flat; area n.e. 1.0 m²	Nr	1.73	29.29	–	23.39	52.68	32.22	–	25.73	57.95
K202523D	sloping; over 300 mm wide .	m²	0.94	15.96	–	21.88	37.84	17.56	–	24.07	41.62
K202523E	sloping; n.e. 300 mm wide .	m	0.55	9.34	–	6.69	16.03	10.27	–	7.36	17.63
K202523F	sloping; area n.e. 1.0 m² ...	Nr	1.41	23.94	–	21.88	45.82	26.33	–	24.07	50.40
K202523G	vertical; over 300 mm wide .	m²	1.14	19.36	–	21.52	40.88	21.30	–	23.67	44.97
K202523H	vertical; n.e. 300 mm wide .	m	0.63	10.70	–	6.58	17.28	11.77	–	7.24	19.01
K202523I	vertical; area n.e. 1.0 m² ...	Nr	1.71	29.04	–	21.52	50.56	31.94	–	23.67	55.62
K2066	**Isolated beams**										
K206601	**Wrought softwood tongued and grooved and V-jointed one side matchboarding; basic sizes; 13 mm thick:**										
K206601A	not exceeding 600 mm girth	m²	1.43	24.20	–	17.13	41.33	26.62	–	18.84	45.46
K206601B	600-1200 mm girth	m²	1.14	19.36	–	16.54	35.90	21.30	–	18.19	39.49
K206601C	1200-1800 mm girth	m²	0.95	16.13	–	16.24	32.37	17.74	–	17.86	35.61
K206631	**Wrought softwood tongued and grooved and V-jointed one side matchboarding; basic sizes; 19 mm thick:**										
K206631A	not exceeding 600 mm girth	m²	1.43	24.20	–	21.42	45.62	26.62	–	23.56	50.18
K206631B	600-1200 mm girth	m²	1.14	19.36	–	20.67	40.03	21.30	–	22.74	44.03
K206631C	1200-1800 mm girth	m²	0.95	16.13	–	20.30	36.43	17.74	–	22.33	40.07

Linings, Sheathing and Dry Partitioning

		Unit	Labour Hours	Labour Net	Plant Net	Materials Net	Unit Net	Labour Gross	Plant Gross	Materials Gross	Unit Price
								(Gross rates include 10% profit)			
				£	£	£	£	£	£	£	£
K20	**K20: TIMBER BOARD FLOORING, SHEATHING, LININGS AND CASINGS**										
K2076	**Isolated columns**										
K207601	**Wrought softwood shiplap boarding; basic sizes; 19 mm thick:**										
K207601A	not exceeding 600 mm girth	m²	1.13	19.10	–	24.01	43.11	21.01	–	26.41	47.42
K207601B	600-1200 mm girth	m²	0.90	15.28	–	23.17	38.45	16.81	–	25.49	42.30
K207601C	1200-1800 mm girth	m²	0.75	12.74	–	22.75	35.49	14.01	–	25.03	39.04
K207603	**Wrought softwood shiplap boarding; basic sizes; 25 mm thick:**										
K207603A	not exceeding 600 mm girth	m²	1.13	19.10	–	29.90	49.00	21.01	–	32.89	53.90
K207603B	600-1200 mm girth	m²	0.90	15.28	–	28.85	44.13	16.81	–	31.74	48.54
K207603C	1200-1800 mm girth	m²	0.75	12.73	–	28.33	41.06	14.00	–	31.16	45.17
K207611	**Wrought softwood tongued and grooved and V-jointed one side matchboarding; basic sizes; 13 mm thick:**										
K207611A	not exceeding 600 mm girth	m²	1.20	20.38	–	17.13	37.51	22.42	–	18.84	41.26
K207611B	600-1200 mm girth	m²	0.96	16.30	–	16.54	32.84	17.93	–	18.19	36.12
K207611C	1200-1800 mm girth	m²	0.80	13.59	–	16.24	29.83	14.95	–	17.86	32.81
K207613	**Wrought softwood tongued and grooved and V-jointed one side matchboarding; basic sizes; 19 mm thick:**										
K207613A	not exceeding 600 mm girth	m²	1.20	20.38	–	21.42	41.80	22.42	–	23.56	45.98
K207613B	600-1200 mm girth	m²	0.96	16.31	–	20.67	36.98	17.94	–	22.74	40.68
K207613C	1200-1800 mm girth	m²	0.80	13.59	–	20.30	33.89	14.95	–	22.33	37.28

Linings, Sheathing and Dry Partitioning

Major Works 2009		Unit	Labour Hours	Labour Net	Plant Net	Materials Net	Unit Net	Labour Gross	Plant Gross	Materials Gross	Unit Price
								(Gross rates include 10% profit)			
				£	£	£	£	£	£	£	£
K21	**K21: TIMBER STRIP AND BOARD FINE FLOORING AND LININGS**										
K2110	**Prime maple strip flooring; 19 mm thick pre-finished; tongued and grooved joint clipped and laid on and including Sylvaform 4 mm thick and 1000 gauge polythene**										
K211010 K211010A	To floors: over 300 mm wide	m²	2.10	35.66	–	65.38	101.04	39.23	–	71.92	111.14
K2115	**Natural oak strip flooring; 19 mm thick pre-finished; tongued and grooved joint clipped and laid on and including Sylvaform 4 mm thick and 1000 gauge polythene**										
K211510 K211510A	To floors: over 300 mm wide	m²	2.00	33.96	–	49.21	83.17	37.36	–	54.13	91.49
K2120	**Ash strip flooring; 19 mm thick; pre-finished; tongued and grooved joint clipped and laid on and including Sylvaform 4 mm thick and 1000 gauge polythene**										
K212010 K212010A	To floors: over 300 mm wide	m²	2.00	33.96	–	56.15	90.11	37.36	–	61.77	99.12

Linings, Sheathing and Dry Partitioning

Major Works 2009		Unit	Labour Hours	Labour Net	Plant Net	Materials Net	Unit Net	Labour Gross	Plant Gross	Materials Gross	Unit Price
								(Gross rates include 10% profit)			
				£	£	£	£	£	£	£	£
K32	**K32: PANEL CUBICLES**										
K3210	**Cubicles; Twyford Bushboard System One**										
K321010	**DriCor cubicles against walls; 1800 mm deep × 2000 mm high; cubicle up to 900 mm wide; one panel and door in line; to form:**										
K321010A	set of one..............	Set	4.00	67.92	–	336.62	404.54	74.71	–	370.28	444.99
K321010B	set of two..............	Set	7.00	118.86	–	772.25	891.11	130.75	–	849.48	980.22
K321010D	set of four	Set	12.00	203.76	–	1372.90	1576.66	224.14	–	1510.19	1734.33
K321010F	set of six	Set	16.00	271.68	–	1994.67	2266.35	298.85	–	2194.14	2492.99
K321020	**DriCor cubicles against walls; disabled panel and door in line; outward opening door; up to 1800 mm deep × 2208 mm wide × 2000 mm high; to form:**										
K321020A	set of one...............	Set	5.00	84.90	–	489.75	574.65	93.39	–	538.73	632.12
K321030	**DriCor cubicles between walls; up to 1800 mm deep × 2000 mm high; one panel and door in line; to form:**										
K321030C	set of six	Set	16.00	271.68	–	1994.67	2266.35	298.85	–	2194.14	2492.99

Major Works 2009		Unit	Labour Hours	Labour Net	Plant Net	Materials Net	Unit Net	Labour Gross	Plant Gross	Materials Gross	Unit Price
									(Gross rates include 10% profit)		
				£	£	£	£	£	£	£	£
K40	**K40: DEMOUNTABLE SUSPENDED CEILINGS**										
K4011	**Gyproc M/F metal framed suspended ceilings; boards to receive direct decoration**										
K401102	**Suspended ceilings with 500 mm drop:**										
K401102A	12.5 mm wallboard	m²	0.22	6.54	–	13.63	20.17	7.19	–	14.99	22.19
K401102B	12.5 mm Fireline board	m²	0.22	6.54	–	15.29	21.83	7.19	–	16.82	24.01
K401102C	12.5 mm Duplex board	m²	0.22	6.54	–	14.66	21.20	7.19	–	16.13	23.32
K401103	**Suspended ceilings with 1000 mm drop:**										
K401103A	12.5 mm wallboard	m²	0.23	6.84	–	13.63	20.47	7.52	–	14.99	22.52
K401103B	12.5 mm Fireline board	m²	0.23	6.84	–	15.29	22.13	7.52	–	16.82	24.34
K401103C	12.5 mm Duplex board	m²	0.23	6.84	–	14.66	21.50	7.52	–	16.13	23.65
K401104	**Suspended ceilings with 1500 mm drop:**										
K401104A	12.5 mm wallboard	m²	0.23	6.84	–	13.63	20.47	7.52	–	14.99	22.52
K401104B	12.5 mm Fireline board	m²	0.23	6.84	–	15.29	22.13	7.52	–	16.82	24.34
K401104C	12.5 mm Duplex board	m²	0.23	6.84	–	14.66	21.50	7.52	–	16.13	23.65
K401105	**Sides and soffits of beams or upstands:**										
K401105A	12.5 mm wallboard	m²	0.25	7.44	–	14.77	22.21	8.18	–	16.25	24.43
K401105B	12.5 mm Fireline board	m²	0.25	7.44	–	16.43	23.87	8.18	–	18.07	26.26
K401105C	12.5 mm Duplex board	m²	0.25	7.44	–	15.80	23.24	8.18	–	17.38	25.56
K4013	**Armstrong concealed grid suspended ceilings; factory finished lay-in-grid tiles**										
K401311	**Suspended ceilings with 500 mm drop:**										
K401311A	Minaboard 600 × 600 mm	m²	0.35	10.41	–	12.34	22.75	11.45	–	13.57	25.03
K401311B	Minaboard 600 × 1200 mm	m²	0.35	10.41	–	11.32	21.73	11.45	–	12.45	23.90
K401311C	Minatone Tegular 600 × 600 mm..................	m²	0.35	10.41	–	14.97	25.38	11.45	–	16.47	27.92
K401311D	Minatone Tegular 600 × 1200 mm...............	m²	0.35	10.41	–	13.95	24.36	11.45	–	15.35	26.80
K401311E	ML Second Look 600 × 1200 mm...............	m²	0.35	10.41	–	28.36	38.77	11.45	–	31.20	42.65
K401312	**Suspended ceilings with 1000 mm drop:**										
K401312A	Minaboard 600 × 600 mm	m²	0.35	10.41	–	12.46	22.87	11.45	–	13.71	25.16
K401312B	Minaboard 600 × 1200 mm	m²	0.35	10.41	–	11.45	21.86	11.45	–	12.60	24.05
K401312C	Minatone Tegular 600 × 600 mm..................	m²	0.35	10.41	–	15.10	25.51	11.45	–	16.61	28.06
K401312D	Minatone Tegular 600 × 1200 mm...............	m²	0.35	10.41	–	14.08	24.49	11.45	–	15.49	26.94
K401312E	ML Second Look 600 × 1200 mm...............	m²	0.35	10.41	–	28.49	38.90	11.45	–	31.34	42.79

Linings, Sheathing and Dry Partitioning

Major Works 2009		Unit	Labour Hours	Labour Net	Plant Net	Materials Net	Unit Net	Labour Gross	Plant Gross	Materials Gross	Unit Price
								\u2014 (Gross rates include 10% profit) \u2014			
				£	£	£	£	£	£	£	£
K40	**K40: DEMOUNTABLE SUSPENDED CEILINGS**										
K4013	**Armstrong concealed grid suspended ceilings; factory finished lay-in-grid tiles**										
K401313	**Suspended ceilings with 1500 mm drop:**										
K401313A	Minaboard 600 × 600 mm	m²	0.35	10.41	–	12.78	23.19	11.45	–	14.06	25.51
K401313B	Minaboard 600 × 1200 mm	m²	0.35	10.41	–	11.76	22.17	11.45	–	12.94	24.39
K401313C	Minatone Tegular 600 × 600 mm	m²	0.35	10.41	–	15.41	25.82	11.45	–	16.95	28.40
K401313D	Minatone Tegular 600 × 1200 mm	m²	0.35	10.40	–	14.40	24.80	11.44	–	15.84	27.28
K401313E	ML Second Look 600 × 1200 mm	m²	0.35	10.41	–	28.80	39.21	11.45	–	31.68	43.13
K401314	**Sides and soffits of beams or upstands:**										
K401314A	Minaboard 600 × 600 mm	m²	0.40	11.90	–	13.59	25.49	13.09	–	14.95	28.04
K401314B	Minaboard 600 × 1200 mm	m²	0.40	11.89	–	12.52	24.41	13.08	–	13.77	26.85
K401314C	Minatone Tegular 600 × 600 mm	m²	0.40	11.89	–	16.35	28.24	13.08	–	17.99	31.06
K401314D	Minatone Tegular 600 × 1200 mm	m²	0.40	11.90	–	15.28	27.18	13.09	–	16.81	29.90
K401314E	ML Second Look 600 × 1200 mm	m²	0.40	11.90	–	30.37	42.27	13.09	–	33.41	46.50

Major Works 2009		Unit	Labour Hours	Labour Net	Plant Net	Materials Net	Unit Net	Labour Gross	Plant Gross	Materials Gross	Unit Price
								(Gross rates include 10% profit)			
				£	£	£	£	£	£	£	£
K40	**K40: DEMOUNTABLE SUSPENDED CEILINGS**										
K4015	**Treetex Spa Range suspended ceilings; factory finished 'lay-in-grid' tiles**										
K401516	**Suspended ceilings with 500 mm drop:**										
K401516A	Leamington Shadow 24....	m²	0.35	10.41	–	17.19	27.60	11.45	–	18.91	30.36
K401516B	Leamington Slimtree 15 ...	m²	0.35	10.41	–	17.41	27.82	11.45	–	19.15	30.60
K401516C	Leamington Slimline 15....	m²	0.35	10.41	–	17.63	28.04	11.45	–	19.39	30.84
K401516D	Leamington Square edge ..	m²	0.35	10.41	–	13.65	24.06	11.45	–	15.02	26.47
K401516E	Bath Shadow 24	m²	0.35	10.41	–	17.41	27.82	11.45	–	19.15	30.60
K401516F	Bath Slimtree 15	m²	0.35	10.41	–	17.73	28.14	11.45	–	19.50	30.95
K401516G	Bath Slimline 15	m²	0.35	10.41	–	18.55	28.96	11.45	–	20.41	31.86
K401516H	Bath Square edge	m²	0.35	10.41	–	16.16	26.57	11.45	–	17.78	29.23
K401517	**Suspended ceilings with 1000 mm drop:**										
K401517A	Leamington Shadow 24....	m²	0.35	10.41	–	17.31	27.72	11.45	–	19.04	30.49
K401517B	Leamington Slimtree 15 ...	m²	0.35	10.41	–	17.54	27.95	11.45	–	19.29	30.75
K401517C	Leamington Slimline 15....	m²	0.35	10.40	–	17.76	28.16	11.44	–	19.54	30.98
K401517D	Leamington Square edge ..	m²	0.35	10.41	–	13.78	24.19	11.45	–	15.16	26.61
K401517E	Bath Shadow 24	m²	0.35	10.41	–	17.54	27.95	11.45	–	19.29	30.75
K401517F	Bath Slimtree 15	m²	0.35	10.41	–	17.86	28.27	11.45	–	19.65	31.10
K401517G	Bath Slimline 15	m²	0.35	10.41	–	18.68	29.09	11.45	–	20.55	32.00
K401517H	Bath Square edge	m²	0.35	10.40	–	16.29	26.69	11.44	–	17.92	29.36
K401518	**Suspended ceilings with 1500 mm drop:**										
K401518A	Leamington Shadow 24....	m²	0.35	10.41	–	17.63	28.04	11.45	–	19.39	30.84
K401518B	Leamington Slimtree 15 ...	m²	0.35	10.41	–	17.85	28.26	11.45	–	19.64	31.09
K401518C	Leamington Slimline 15....	m²	0.35	10.41	–	18.07	28.48	11.45	–	19.88	31.33
K401518D	Leamington Square edge ..	m²	0.35	10.41	–	14.09	24.50	11.45	–	15.50	26.95
K401518E	Bath Shadow 24	m²	0.35	10.41	–	17.85	28.26	11.45	–	19.64	31.09
K401518F	Bath Slimtree 15	m²	0.35	10.40	–	18.18	28.58	11.44	–	20.00	31.44
K401518G	Bath Slimline 15	m²	0.35	10.41	–	18.99	29.40	11.45	–	20.89	32.34
K401518H	Bath Square edge	m²	0.35	10.41	–	16.60	27.01	11.45	–	18.26	29.71
K401519	**Sides and soffits of beams or upstands:**										
K401519A	Leamington Shadow 24....	m²	0.40	11.89	–	17.82	29.71	13.08	–	19.60	32.68
K401519B	Leamington Slimtree 15 ...	m²	0.40	11.90	–	18.04	29.94	13.09	–	19.84	32.93
K401519C	Leamington Slimline 15....	m²	0.40	11.90	–	18.26	30.16	13.09	–	20.09	33.18
K401519D	Leamington Square edge ..	m²	0.40	11.90	–	20.48	32.38	13.09	–	22.53	35.62
K401519E	Bath Shadow 24	m²	0.40	11.90	–	18.04	29.94	13.09	–	19.84	32.93
K401519F	Bath Slimtree 15	m²	0.40	11.90	–	18.36	30.26	13.09	–	20.20	33.29
K401519G	Bath Slimline 15	m²	0.40	11.90	–	19.18	31.08	13.09	–	21.10	34.19
K401519H	Bath Square edge	m²	0.40	11.90	–	16.79	28.69	13.09	–	18.47	31.56

Linings, Sheathing and Dry Partitioning

Major Works 2009		Unit	Labour Hours	Labour Net	Plant Net	Materials Net	Unit Net	Labour Gross	Plant Gross	Materials Gross	Unit Price
								(Gross rates include 10% profit)			
				£	£	£	£	£	£	£	£
K40	**K40: DEMOUNTABLE SUSPENDED CEILINGS**										
K4017	**Hunter Douglas Luxalon cell system suspended ceilings**										
K401721	**Suspended ceilings with 500 mm drop:**										
K401721A	Cell module 75; tone white .	m²	0.48	14.27	–	70.75	85.02	15.70	–	77.83	93.52
K401721B	Cell module 75; coloured...	m²	0.48	14.28	–	84.90	99.18	15.71	–	93.39	109.10
K401721C	Cell module 75; mirror or brushed finish............	m²	0.48	14.28	–	113.25	127.53	15.71	–	124.58	140.28
K401721D	Cell module 100; tone white	m²	0.45	13.39	–	52.13	65.52	14.73	–	57.34	72.07
K401721E	Cell module 100; coloured .	m²	0.45	13.39	–	61.40	74.79	14.73	–	67.54	82.27
K401721F	Cell module 100; mirror or brushed finish............	m²	0.45	13.38	–	78.45	91.83	14.72	–	86.30	101.01
K401721G	Cell module 150; tone white	m²	0.42	12.50	–	34.34	46.84	13.75	–	37.77	51.52
K401721H	Cell module 150; coloured .	m²	0.42	12.49	–	37.95	50.44	13.74	–	41.75	55.48
K401721I	Cell module 150; mirror or brushed finish............	m²	0.42	12.49	–	51.52	64.01	13.74	–	56.67	70.41
K401722	**Suspended ceilings with 1000 mm drop:**										
K401722A	Cell module 75; tone white .	m²	0.48	14.28	–	71.07	85.35	15.71	–	78.18	93.89
K401722B	Cell module 75; coloured...	m²	0.48	14.27	–	85.23	99.50	15.70	–	93.75	109.45
K401722C	Cell module 75; mirror or brushed finish............	m²	0.48	14.27	–	113.58	127.85	15.70	–	124.94	140.64
K401722D	Cell module 100; tone white	m²	0.45	13.38	–	52.46	65.84	14.72	–	57.71	72.42
K401722E	Cell module 100; coloured .	m²	0.45	13.38	–	61.73	75.11	14.72	–	67.90	82.62
K401722F	Cell module 100; mirror or brushed finish............	m²	0.45	13.38	–	78.77	92.15	14.72	–	86.65	101.37
K401722G	Cell module 150; tone white	m²	0.42	12.49	–	34.66	47.15	13.74	–	38.13	51.87
K401722H	Cell module 150; coloured .	m²	0.42	12.49	–	38.27	50.76	13.74	–	42.10	55.84
K401722I	Cell module 150; mirror or brushed finish............	m²	0.42	12.49	–	51.85	64.34	13.74	–	57.04	70.77
K401723	**Suspended ceilings with 1500 mm drop:**										
K401723A	Cell module 75; tone white .	m²	0.48	14.27	–	71.59	85.86	15.70	–	78.75	94.45
K401723B	Cell module 75; coloured...	m²	0.48	14.28	–	85.74	100.02	15.71	–	94.31	110.02
K401723C	Cell module 75; mirror or brushed finish............	m²	0.48	14.28	–	114.09	128.37	15.71	–	125.50	141.21
K401723D	Cell module 100; tone white	m²	0.45	13.39	–	52.97	66.36	14.73	–	58.27	73.00
K401723E	Cell module 100; coloured .	m²	0.45	13.39	–	62.24	75.63	14.73	–	68.46	83.19
K401723F	Cell module 100; mirror or brushed finish............	m²	0.45	13.38	–	79.29	92.67	14.72	–	87.22	101.94
K401723G	Cell module 150; tone white	m²	0.42	12.50	–	35.18	47.68	13.75	–	38.70	52.45
K401723H	Cell module 150; coloured .	m²	0.42	12.49	–	38.79	51.28	13.74	–	42.67	56.41
K401723I	Cell module 150; mirror or brushed finish............	m²	0.42	12.49	–	52.36	64.85	13.74	–	57.60	71.34
K401724	**Sides and soffits of beams or upstands:**										
K401724A	Cell module 75; tone white .	m²	0.50	14.87	–	72.33	87.20	16.36	–	79.56	95.92
K401724B	Cell module 75; coloured...	m²	0.50	14.87	–	86.49	101.36	16.36	–	95.14	111.50
K401724C	Cell module 75; mirror or brushed finish............	m²	0.50	14.87	–	114.84	129.71	16.36	–	126.32	142.68
K401724D	Cell module 100; tone white	m²	0.47	13.98	–	53.72	67.70	15.38	–	59.09	74.47
K401724E	Cell module 100; coloured .	m²	0.47	13.98	–	62.99	76.97	15.38	–	69.29	84.67
K401724F	Cell module 100; mirror or brushed finish............	m²	0.47	13.98	–	80.03	94.01	15.38	–	88.03	103.41
K401724G	Cell module 150; tone white	m²	0.44	13.09	–	35.92	49.01	14.40	–	39.51	53.91
K401724H	Cell module 150; coloured .	m²	0.44	13.09	–	39.53	52.62	14.40	–	43.48	57.88
K401724I	Cell module 150; mirror or brushed finish............	m²	0.44	13.08	–	53.11	66.19	14.39	–	58.42	72.81

Major Works 2009		Unit	Labour Hours	Labour Net	Plant Net	Materials Net	Unit Net	Labour Gross	Plant Gross	Materials Gross	Unit Price
									(Gross rates include 10% profit)		
				£	£	£	£	£	£	£	£
K40	**K40: DEMOUNTABLE SUSPENDED CEILINGS**										
K4080	**Metal framed suspended ceiling grids**										
K408002	**Suspended ceilings; drop:**										
K408002A	500 mm................	m²	0.22	6.54	–	9.13	15.67	7.19	–	10.04	17.24
K408002B	1000 mm...............	m²	0.22	6.54	–	9.55	16.09	7.19	–	10.51	17.70
K408002C	1500 mm...............	m²	0.23	6.84	–	9.55	16.39	7.52	–	10.51	18.03
K408005	**Sides and soffits:**										
K408005A	beams and upstands......	m²	0.25	7.43	–	10.70	18.13	8.17	–	11.77	19.94
K4081	**Suspended ceiling grid trims**										
K408110	**Gyproc M/F suspended ceiling edge trim:**										
K408110A	MF6A..................	m	0.20	5.95	–	2.82	8.77	6.55	–	3.10	9.65
K408111	**Armstrong suspended ceiling edge trim:**										
K408111A	998...................	m	0.20	5.94	–	2.37	8.31	6.53	–	2.61	9.14
K408112	**Treetex Spa Range suspended ceiling edge trim:**										
K408112A	Shadow 24.............	m	0.20	5.94	–	2.56	8.50	6.53	–	2.82	9.35
K408112B	Slimtree 15............	m	0.20	5.94	–	2.37	8.31	6.53	–	2.61	9.14
K408112C	Slimline 15............	m	0.20	5.94	–	2.37	8.31	6.53	–	2.61	9.14
K408112D	square edge...........	m	0.20	5.95	–	2.26	8.21	6.55	–	2.49	9.03
K408113	**Hunter Luxalon suspended ceiling edge trim:**										
K408113A	cover strip and edge cover profile.................	m	0.20	5.94	–	2.56	8.50	6.53	–	2.82	9.35

WINDOWS, DOORS
AND STAIRS

Major Works 2009		Unit	Labour Hours	Labour Net	Plant Net	Materials Net	Unit Net	Labour Gross	Plant Gross	Materials Gross	Unit Price
								(Gross rates include 10% profit)			
				£	£	£	£	£	£	£	£
L10	**L10: WINDOWS, ROOFLIGHTS, SCREENS AND LOUVRES**										
L1000	**Proprietary PVC-u windows**										
L100072	**Side hung casement window; fully welded fitted 24 mm Low E insulating double glazing units; including ironmongery; size:**										
L100072A	1000 × 600 mm high	Nr	1.00	16.98	–	90.78	107.76	18.68	–	99.86	118.54
L100072B	1000 × 900 mm high	Nr	1.15	19.52	–	104.57	124.09	21.47	–	115.03	136.50
L100072C	1000 × 1200 mm high ...	Nr	1.30	22.07	–	119.16	141.23	24.28	–	131.08	155.35
L100072D	1200 × 600 mm high	Nr	1.25	21.22	–	101.98	123.20	23.34	–	112.18	135.52
L100072E	1200 × 900 mm high	Nr	1.40	23.77	–	113.37	137.14	26.15	–	124.71	150.85
L100072F	1200 × 1200 mm high ...	Nr	1.55	26.32	–	128.76	155.08	28.95	–	141.64	170.59
L100072G	1500 × 600 mm high	Nr	1.50	25.47	–	113.18	138.65	28.02	–	124.50	152.52
L100072H	1500 × 900 mm high	Nr	1.65	28.01	–	128.57	156.58	30.81	–	141.43	172.24
L100072I	1500 × 1200 mm high ...	Nr	1.80	30.56	–	140.76	171.32	33.62	–	154.84	188.45
L100072J	1800 × 600 mm high	Nr	1.75	29.71	–	128.38	158.09	32.68	–	141.22	173.90
L100072K	1800 × 900 mm high	Nr	1.90	32.26	–	140.57	172.83	35.49	–	154.63	190.11
L100072L	1800 × 1200 mm high ...	Nr	2.05	34.81	–	157.56	192.37	38.29	–	173.32	211.61
L100072M	2100 × 600 mm high	Nr	2.00	33.96	–	140.38	174.34	37.36	–	154.42	191.77
L100072N	2100 × 900 mm high	Nr	2.15	36.50	–	157.37	193.87	40.15	–	173.11	213.26
L100072O	2100 × 1200 mm high ...	Nr	2.30	39.05	–	178.36	217.41	42.96	–	196.20	239.15
L100072P	2400 × 600 mm high	Nr	2.50	42.45	–	157.18	199.63	46.70	–	172.90	219.59
L100072Q	2400 × 900 mm high	Nr	2.65	44.99	–	178.17	223.16	49.49	–	195.99	245.48
L100072R	2400 × 1200 mm high ...	Nr	2.80	47.54	–	229.56	277.10	52.29	–	252.52	304.81
L100073	**Top hung and side casement window; full welded; fitted 24 mm Low E double insulating double glazing units; including ironmongery; size:**										
L100073A	1000 × 600 mm high	Nr	1.00	16.98	–	117.98	134.96	18.68	–	129.78	148.46
L100073B	1000 × 900 mm high	Nr	1.15	19.52	–	135.77	155.29	21.47	–	149.35	170.82
L100073C	1000 × 1200 mm high ...	Nr	1.30	22.07	–	149.56	171.63	24.28	–	164.52	188.79
L100073D	1200 × 600 mm high	Nr	1.25	21.22	–	126.78	148.00	23.34	–	139.46	162.80
L100073E	1200 × 900 mm high	Nr	1.40	23.77	–	145.37	169.14	26.15	–	159.91	186.05
L100073F	1200 × 1200 mm high ...	Nr	1.55	26.32	–	159.16	185.48	28.95	–	175.08	204.03
L100073G	1500 × 600 mm high	Nr	1.50	25.47	–	145.18	170.65	28.02	–	159.70	187.72
L100073H	1500 × 900 mm high	Nr	1.65	28.01	–	158.97	186.98	30.81	–	174.87	205.68
L100073I	1500 × 1200 mm high ...	Nr	1.80	30.56	–	175.96	206.52	33.62	–	193.56	227.17
L100073J	1800 × 600 mm high	Nr	1.75	29.71	–	158.78	188.49	32.68	–	174.66	207.34
L100073K	1800 × 900 mm high	Nr	1.90	32.26	–	175.77	208.03	35.49	–	193.35	228.83
L100073L	1800 × 1200 mm high ...	Nr	2.05	34.81	–	191.96	226.77	38.29	–	211.16	249.45

Windows, Doors and Stairs

Major Works 2009		Unit	Labour Hours	Labour Net	Plant Net	Materials Net	Unit Net	Labour Gross	Plant Gross	Materials Gross	Unit Price
								(Gross rates include 10% profit)			
				£	£	£	£	£	£	£	£
L10	**L10: WINDOWS, ROOFLIGHTS, SCREENS AND LOUVRES**										
L1011	**Standard softwood windows**										
L101101	**Boulton and Paul softwood windows; Sovereign; casement; plain; fitted with standard sill; complete with ironmongery; size:**										
L101101A	630 × 750 mm; W107C ..	Nr	0.20	5.03	–	88.55	93.58	5.53	–	97.41	102.94
L101101B	630 × 900 mm; W109C ..	Nr	0.20	5.03	–	93.85	98.88	5.53	–	103.24	108.77
L101101C	630 × 1050 mm; W110C .	Nr	0.20	5.03	–	94.24	99.27	5.53	–	103.66	109.20
L101101D	630 × 1200 mm; W112C .	Nr	0.20	5.03	–	97.67	102.70	5.53	–	107.44	112.97
L101101E	630 × 1350 mm; W113C .	Nr	0.20	5.03	–	109.28	114.31	5.53	–	120.21	125.74
L101101F	1200 × 750 mm; W207C .	Nr	0.25	6.28	–	115.05	121.33	6.91	–	126.56	133.46
L101101G	1200 × 900 mm; W209C .	Nr	0.25	6.28	–	117.66	123.94	6.91	–	129.43	136.33
L101101H	1200 × 1050 mm; W210C	Nr	0.25	6.28	–	119.97	126.25	6.91	–	131.97	138.88
L101101I	1200 × 1200 mm; W212C	Nr	0.25	6.28	–	122.27	128.55	6.91	–	134.50	141.41
L101101J	1200 × 1350 mm; W213C	Nr	0.25	6.28	–	136.82	143.10	6.91	–	150.50	157.41
L101101K	1200 × 750 mm; W207CC	Nr	0.25	6.28	–	156.37	162.65	6.91	–	172.01	178.92
L101101L	1200 × 900 mm; W209CC	Nr	0.25	6.28	–	163.82	170.10	6.91	–	180.20	187.11
L101101M	1200 × 1050 mm; W210CC	Nr	0.25	6.28	–	171.08	177.36	6.91	–	188.19	195.10
L101101N	1200 × 1200 mm; W212CC	Nr	0.25	6.28	–	177.80	184.08	6.91	–	195.58	202.49
L101101O	1200 × 1350 mm; W213CC	Nr	0.25	6.28	–	191.58	197.86	6.91	–	210.74	217.65
L101101P	1770 × 750 mm; W307CC	Nr	0.30	7.54	–	168.49	176.03	8.29	–	185.34	193.63
L101101Q	1770 × 900 mm; W309CC	Nr	0.30	7.54	–	172.48	180.02	8.29	–	189.73	198.02
L101101R	1770 × 1050 mm; W310CC	Nr	0.30	7.54	–	173.15	180.69	8.29	–	190.47	198.76
L101101S	1770 × 1200 mm; W312CC	Nr	0.30	7.54	–	179.36	186.90	8.29	–	197.30	205.59
L101101T	1770 × 1350 mm; W313CC	Nr	0.30	7.54	–	202.07	209.61	8.29	–	222.28	230.57
L101101W	2339 × 900 mm; W409CMC..............	Nr	0.35	8.80	–	215.13	223.93	9.68	–	236.64	246.32
L101101X	2339 × 1050 mm; W410CMC..............	Nr	0.35	8.80	–	224.18	232.98	9.68	–	246.60	256.28
L101101Y	2339 × 1200 mm; W412CMC..............	Nr	0.35	8.80	–	233.56	242.36	9.68	–	256.92	266.60
L101101Z	2339 × 1350 mm; W413CMC..............	Nr	0.35	8.80	–	248.33	257.13	9.68	–	273.16	282.84

Major Works 2009		Unit	Labour Hours	Labour Net	Plant Net	Materials Net	Unit Net	Labour Gross	Plant Gross	Materials Gross	Unit Price
								(Gross rates include 10% profit)			
				£	£	£	£	£	£	£	£
L10	**L10: WINDOWS, ROOFLIGHTS, SCREENS AND LOUVRES**										
L1011	**Standard softwood windows**										
L101102	**Boulton and Paul softwood windows; Sovereign; casement; landscape; fitted with standard sill; complete with ironmongery; size:**										
L101102A	1770 × 1050 mm; W310C	Nr	0.30	7.54	–	145.48	153.02	8.29	–	160.03	168.32
L101102B	1770 × 1200 mm; W312C	Nr	0.30	7.54	–	149.70	157.24	8.29	–	164.67	172.96
L101102C	1770 × 1350 mm; W313C	Nr	0.30	7.54	–	157.15	164.69	8.29	–	172.87	181.16
L101102D	1770 × 1050 mm; W310WW	Nr	0.30	7.54	–	199.41	206.95	8.29	–	219.35	227.65
L101102E	1770 × 1200 mm; W312WW	Nr	0.30	7.54	–	204.47	212.01	8.29	–	224.92	233.21
L101102F	1770 × 1350 mm; W313WW	Nr	0.30	7.54	–	209.13	216.67	8.29	–	230.04	238.34
L101102G	2339 × 1050 mm; W410CWC..............	Nr	0.35	8.80	–	224.18	232.98	9.68	–	246.60	256.28
L101102H	2339 × 1200 mm; W412CWC..............	Nr	0.35	8.80	–	233.56	242.36	9.68	–	256.92	266.60
L101102I	2339 × 1350 mm; W413CWC..............	Nr	0.35	8.80	–	248.33	257.13	9.68	–	273.16	282.84
L101102N	915 × 900 mm; W2N09W	Nr	0.23	5.78	–	105.89	111.67	6.36	–	116.48	122.84
L101102O	915 × 1050 mm; W2N10W	Nr	0.23	5.78	–	107.33	113.11	6.36	–	118.06	124.42
L101102P	915 × 1200 mm; W2N12W	Nr	0.23	5.78	–	115.66	121.44	6.36	–	127.23	133.58
L101102Q	915 × 1350 mm; W2N13W	Nr	0.23	5.78	–	117.95	123.73	6.36	–	129.75	136.10
L101102R	915 × 1500 mm; W2N15W	Nr	0.23	5.78	–	119.49	125.27	6.36	–	131.44	137.80
L101102S	1200 × 900 mm; W209W	Nr	0.25	6.28	–	125.62	131.90	6.91	–	138.18	145.09
L101102T	1200 × 1050 mm; W210W	Nr	0.25	6.28	–	127.76	134.04	6.91	–	140.54	147.44
L101102U	1200 × 1200 mm; W212W	Nr	0.25	6.28	–	130.16	136.44	6.91	–	143.18	150.08
L101102V	1200 × 1350 mm; W213W	Nr	0.25	6.28	–	132.77	139.05	6.91	–	146.05	152.96

Windows, Doors and Stairs

Major Works 2009		Unit	Labour Hours	Labour Net	Plant Net	Materials Net	Unit Net	Labour Gross	Plant Gross	Materials Gross	Unit Price
								(Gross rates include 10% profit)			
				£	£	£	£	£	£	£	£
L10	**L10: WINDOWS, ROOFLIGHTS, SCREENS AND LOUVRES**										
L1011	**Standard softwood windows**										
L101102	**Boulton and Paul softwood windows; Sovereign; casement; landscape; fitted with standard sill; complete with ironmongery; size:**										
L101102W	1200 × 1500 mm; W215W	Nr	0.25	6.28	–	135.84	142.12	6.91	–	149.42	156.33
L101102X	1770 × 1050 mm;										
	W310CW	Nr	0.30	7.54	–	186.19	193.73	8.29	–	204.81	213.10
L101102Y	1700 × 1200 mm;										
	W312CW	Nr	0.30	7.54	–	191.02	198.56	8.29	–	210.12	218.42
L101102Z	1700 × 1350 mm;										
	W313CW	Nr	0.30	7.54	–	198.47	206.01	8.29	–	218.32	226.61
L101103	**Boulton and Paul softwood windows; Sovereign; casement; with vents; fitted with standard sill; complete with ironmongery; size:**										
L101103A	630 × 750 mm; W107V	Nr	0.20	5.03	–	86.84	91.87	5.53	–	95.52	101.06
L101103B	630 × 900 mm; W109V	Nr	0.20	5.03	–	87.12	92.15	5.53	–	95.83	101.37
L101103C	630 × 1050 mm; W110V	Nr	0.20	5.03	–	89.13	94.16	5.53	–	98.04	103.58
L101103D	630 × 1200 mm; W112V	Nr	0.20	5.03	–	96.00	101.03	5.53	–	105.60	111.13
L101103E	630 × 1350 mm; W113V	Nr	0.20	5.03	–	98.67	103.70	5.53	–	108.54	114.07
L101103F	630 × 1500 mm; W115V	Nr	0.20	5.03	–	102.02	107.05	5.53	–	112.22	117.76
L101103G	1200 × 900 mm; W209T	Nr	0.25	6.28	–	148.37	154.65	6.91	–	163.21	170.12
L101103H	1200 × 1050 mm; W210T	Nr	0.25	6.28	–	155.38	161.66	6.91	–	170.92	177.83
L101103I	1200 × 1200 mm; W212T	Nr	0.25	6.28	–	160.37	166.65	6.91	–	176.41	183.32
L101103J	1200 × 1350 mm; W213T	Nr	0.25	6.28	–	164.87	171.15	6.91	–	181.36	188.27
L101103K	1200 × 1500 mm; W215T	Nr	0.25	6.28	–	176.42	182.70	6.91	–	194.06	200.97
L101103L	1200 × 750 mm; W207CV	Nr	0.25	6.28	–	143.39	149.67	6.91	–	157.73	164.64
L101103M	1200 × 900 mm; W209CV	Nr	0.25	6.28	–	144.76	151.04	6.91	–	159.24	166.14
L101103N	1200 × 1050 mm; W210CV	Nr	0.25	6.28	–	144.94	151.22	6.91	–	159.43	166.34
L101103O	1200 × 1200 mm; W212CV	Nr	0.25	6.28	–	149.48	155.76	6.91	–	164.43	171.34
L101103P	1200 × 1350 mm; W213CV	Nr	0.25	6.28	–	165.31	171.59	6.91	–	181.84	188.75
L101103Q	1770 × 900 mm; W309CVC	Nr	0.30	7.54	–	204.47	212.01	8.29	–	224.92	233.21
L101103R	1779 × 1050 mm;										
	W310CVC	Nr	0.30	7.54	–	211.07	218.61	8.29	–	232.18	240.47
L101103S	1770 × 1200 mm;										
	W312CVC	Nr	0.30	7.54	–	218.29	225.83	8.29	–	240.12	248.41
L101103T	1770 × 1350 mm;										
	W313CVC	Nr	0.30	7.54	–	230.93	238.47	8.29	–	254.02	262.32
L101103U	2339 × 1200 mm;										
	W412CVVC	Nr	0.35	8.80	–	270.71	279.51	9.68	–	297.78	307.46
L101103V	2339 × 1350 mm;										
	W413CVVC	Nr	0.35	8.80	–	285.14	293.94	9.68	–	313.65	323.33
L101103W	2339 × 1200 mm; W412TT	Nr	0.35	8.80	–	268.47	277.27	9.68	–	295.32	305.00
L101103X	2339 × 1350 mm; W413TT	Nr	0.35	8.80	–	275.54	284.34	9.68	–	303.09	312.77
L101103Y	1770 × 1050 mm; W310T	Nr	0.30	7.54	–	172.80	180.34	8.29	–	190.08	198.37
L101103Z	1770 × 1200 mm; W312T	Nr	0.30	7.54	–	177.52	185.06	8.29	–	195.27	203.57

Major Works 2009		Unit	Labour Hours	Labour Net	Plant Net	Materials Net	Unit Net	Labour Gross	Plant Gross	Materials Gross	Unit Price
								(Gross rates include 10% profit)			
				£	£	£	£	£	£	£	£
L10	**L10: WINDOWS, ROOFLIGHTS, SCREENS AND LOUVRES**										
L1011	**Standard softwood windows**										
L101105	**Boulton and Paul softwood windows; Sovereign; casement; transom; fitted with standard sill; complete with ironmongery; size:**										
L101105A	630 × 900 mm; W109T	Nr	0.20	5.03	–	123.99	129.02	5.53	–	136.39	141.92
L101105B	630 × 1050 mm; W110T	Nr	0.20	5.03	–	127.60	132.63	5.53	–	140.36	145.89
L101105C	630 × 1200 mm; W112T	Nr	0.20	5.03	–	131.17	136.20	5.53	–	144.29	149.82
L101105D	630 × 1350 mm; W113T	Nr	0.20	5.03	–	134.76	139.79	5.53	–	148.24	153.77
L101105E	630 × 1500 mm; W115T	Nr	0.20	5.03	–	145.27	150.30	5.53	–	159.80	165.33
L101105F	1200 × 1050 mm; W210TX	Nr	0.25	6.28	–	155.38	161.66	6.91	–	170.92	177.83
L101105G	1200 × 1200 mm; W212TX	Nr	0.25	6.28	–	160.37	166.65	6.91	–	176.41	183.32
L101105H	1200 × 1350 mm; W213TX	Nr	0.25	6.28	–	164.87	171.15	6.91	–	181.36	188.27
L101105I	1200 × 1500 mm; W215TX	Nr	0.25	6.28	–	176.42	182.70	6.91	–	194.06	200.97
L101105J	1770 × 1050 mm; W310TXT	Nr	0.30	7.54	–	241.78	249.32	8.29	–	265.96	274.25
L101105K	1770 × 1200 mm; W312TXT	Nr	0.30	7.54	–	249.31	256.85	8.29	–	274.24	282.54
L101105L	1770 × 1350 mm; W313TXT	Nr	0.30	7.54	–	254.83	262.37	8.29	–	280.31	288.61
L101105M	1770 × 1500 mm; W315TXT	Nr	0.30	7.54	–	276.50	284.04	8.29	–	304.15	312.44

Windows, Doors and Stairs

Major Works 2009		Unit	Labour Hours	Labour Net	Plant Net	Materials Net	Unit Net	Labour Gross	Plant Gross	Materials Gross	Unit Price
								(Gross rates include 10% profit)			
				£	£	£	£	£	£	£	£
L10	**L10: WINDOWS, ROOFLIGHTS, SCREENS AND LOUVRES**										
L1011	**Standard softwood windows**										
L101106	**Boulton and Paul softwood windows; Sovereign; casement; narrow module; fitted with standard sill; complete with ironmongery; size:**										
L101106A	488 × 750 mm; WN07C ..	Nr	0.18	4.52	–	77.90	82.42	4.97	–	85.69	90.66
L101106B	488 × 900 mm; WN09C ..	Nr	0.18	4.52	–	80.90	85.42	4.97	–	88.99	93.96
L101106C	488 × 1050 mm; WN10C .	Nr	0.18	4.52	–	84.40	88.92	4.97	–	92.84	97.81
L101106D	488 × 1200 mm; WN12C .	Nr	0.18	4.52	–	87.12	91.64	4.97	–	95.83	100.80
L101106E	488 × 1350 mm; WN13C .	Nr	0.18	4.52	–	92.29	96.81	4.97	–	101.52	106.49
L101106F	915 × 750 mm; W2N07C .	Nr	0.23	5.78	–	111.72	117.50	6.36	–	122.89	129.25
L101106G	915 × 900 mm; W2N09C .	Nr	0.23	5.78	–	113.88	119.66	6.36	–	125.27	131.63
L101106H	915 × 1050 mm; W2N10C	Nr	0.23	5.78	–	120.26	126.04	6.36	–	132.29	138.64
L101106I	915 × 1200 mm; W2N12C	Nr	0.23	5.78	–	124.17	129.95	6.36	–	136.59	142.95
L101106J	915 × 1350 mm; W2N13C	Nr	0.23	5.78	–	128.05	133.83	6.36	–	140.86	147.21
L101106K	915 × 750 mm; W2N07CC	Nr	0.23	5.78	–	151.54	157.32	6.36	–	166.69	173.05
L101106L	915 × 900 mm; W2N09CC	Nr	0.23	5.78	–	152.14	157.92	6.36	–	167.35	173.71
L101106M	915 × 1050 mm; W2N10CC	Nr	0.23	5.78	–	158.36	164.14	6.36	–	174.20	180.55
L101106N	915 × 1200 mm; W2N12CC	Nr	0.23	5.78	–	164.31	170.09	6.36	–	180.74	187.10
L1011060	915 × 1350 mm; W2N13CC	Nr	0.23	5.78	–	170.04	175.82	6.36	–	187.04	193.40
L101106P	1342 × 750 mm; W3N07CC	Nr	0.28	7.04	–	161.60	168.64	7.74	–	177.76	185.50
L101106Q	1342 × 900 mm; W3N09CC	Nr	0.28	7.04	–	168.11	175.15	7.74	–	184.92	192.67
L101106R	1342 × 1050 mm; W3N10CC	Nr	0.28	7.04	–	174.08	181.12	7.74	–	191.49	199.23
L101106S	1342 × 1200 mm; W3N12CC	Nr	0.28	7.04	–	180.08	187.12	7.74	–	198.09	205.83
L101106T	1342 × 1350 mm; W3N13CC	Nr	0.28	7.04	–	186.19	193.23	7.74	–	204.81	212.55
L101106U	1770 × 900 mm; W4N09CMC	Nr	0.33	8.29	–	207.62	215.91	9.12	–	228.38	237.50
L101106V	1770 × 1050 mm; W4N10CMC	Nr	0.33	8.29	–	216.06	224.35	9.12	–	237.67	246.79
L101106W	1770 × 1200 mm; W4N12CMC	Nr	0.33	8.29	–	224.33	232.62	9.12	–	246.76	255.88
L101106X	1770 × 1350 mm; W4N13CMC	Nr	0.33	8.29	–	236.23	244.52	9.12	–	259.85	268.97
L101107	**Boulton and Paul softwood windows; Sovereign; casement; narrow module; with vents; fitted with standard sill; complete with ironmongery; size:**										
L101107K	488 × 750 mm; WN07V ..	Nr	0.18	4.52	–	71.75	76.27	4.97	–	78.93	83.90
L101107L	488 × 900 mm; WN09V ..	Nr	0.18	4.52	–	74.09	78.61	4.97	–	81.50	86.47
L101107M	488 × 1050 mm; WN10V .	Nr	0.18	4.52	–	76.35	80.87	4.97	–	83.99	88.96
L101107N	488 × 1200 mm; WN12V .	Nr	0.18	4.52	–	79.01	83.53	4.97	–	86.91	91.88
L1011070	915 × 900 mm; W2N09CV	Nr	0.23	5.78	–	146.04	151.82	6.36	–	160.64	167.00
L101107P	915 × 1050 mm; W2N10CV	Nr	0.23	5.78	–	149.09	154.87	6.36	–	164.00	170.36
L101107Q	915 × 1200 mm; W2N12CV	Nr	0.23	5.78	–	154.61	160.39	6.36	–	170.07	176.43

Major Works 2009		Unit	Labour Hours	Labour Net	Plant Net	Materials Net	Unit Net	Labour Gross	Plant Gross	Materials Gross	Unit Price
								(Gross rates include 10% profit)			
				£	£	£	£	£	£	£	£
L10	**L10: WINDOWS, ROOFLIGHTS, SCREENS AND LOUVRES**										
L1011	**Standard softwood windows**										
L101108	**Boulton and Paul softwood windows; Sovereign; all bar; fitted 24 mm Low E insulating glass units; fitted with standard sill; complete with ironmongery; size:**										
L101108A	630 × 750 mm; LEWB107C	Nr	0.20	5.03	–	162.46	167.49	5.53	–	178.71	184.24
L101108B	630 × 900 mm; LEWB109C	Nr	0.20	5.03	–	183.47	188.50	5.53	–	201.82	207.35
L101108C	630 × 1050 mm; LEWB110C	Nr	0.20	5.03	–	193.14	198.17	5.53	–	212.45	217.99
L101108D	630 × 1200 mm; LEWB112C	Nr	0.20	5.03	–	212.16	217.19	5.53	–	233.38	238.91
L101108E	630 × 1350 mm; LEWB113C	Nr	0.20	5.03	–	238.37	243.40	5.53	–	262.21	267.74
L101108F	1200 × 750 mm; LEWB207C	Nr	0.25	6.28	–	294.06	300.34	6.91	–	323.47	330.37
L101108G	1200 × 900 mm; LEWB209C	Nr	0.25	6.28	–	329.74	336.02	6.91	–	362.71	369.62
L101108H	1200 × 1050 mm; LEWB210C	Nr	0.25	6.28	–	350.42	356.70	6.91	–	385.46	392.37
L101108I	1200 × 1200 mm; LEWB212C	Nr	0.25	6.28	–	369.65	375.93	6.91	–	406.62	413.52
L101108J	1200 × 1350 mm; LEWB213C	Nr	0.25	6.28	–	433.37	439.65	6.91	–	476.71	483.62
L101108K	1770 × 900 mm; LEWB309CC	Nr	0.30	7.54	–	472.32	479.86	8.29	–	519.55	527.85
L101108L	1770 × 1050 mm; LEWB310CC	Nr	0.30	7.54	–	502.84	510.38	8.29	–	553.12	561.42
L101108M	1770 × 1200 mm; LEWB312CC	Nr	0.30	7.54	–	557.69	565.23	8.29	–	613.46	621.75
L101108N	1770 × 1300 mm; LEWB313CC	Nr	0.30	7.54	–	625.63	633.17	8.29	–	688.19	696.49

Windows, Doors and Stairs

Major Works 2009		Unit	Labour Hours	Labour Net	Plant Net	Materials Net	Unit Net	Labour Gross	Plant Gross	Materials Gross	Unit Price
								(Gross rates include 10% profit)			
				£	£	£	£	£	£	£	£
L10	**L10: WINDOWS, ROOFLIGHTS, SCREENS AND LOUVRES**										
L1011	**Standard softwood windows**										
L101109	**Boulton and Paul softwood windows; Sovereign; all bar; with vents; fitted 24 mm Low E insulating glazing units; fitted with standard sill; complete with ironmongery; size:**										
L101109A	630 × 1050 mm; LEWB110T	Nr	0.20	5.03	–	261.67	266.70	5.53	–	287.84	293.37
L101109B	630 × 1200 mm; LEWB112T	Nr	0.20	5.03	–	293.40	298.43	5.53	–	322.74	328.27
L101109C	630 × 1350 mm; LEWB113T	Nr	0.20	5.03	–	306.43	311.46	5.53	–	337.07	342.61
L101109D	630 × 750 mm; LEWB107V	Nr	0.20	5.03	–	238.31	243.34	5.53	–	262.14	267.67
L101109E	630 × 900 mm; LEWB109V	Nr	0.20	5.03	–	247.03	252.06	5.53	–	271.73	277.27
L101109F	630 × 1050 mm; LEWB110V	Nr	0.20	5.03	–	255.47	260.50	5.53	–	281.02	286.55
L101109G	630 × 1200 mm; LEWB112V	Nr	0.20	5.03	–	280.20	285.23	5.53	–	308.22	313.75
L101109H	630 × 1350 mm; LEWB113V	Nr	0.20	5.03	–	294.29	299.32	5.53	–	323.72	329.25
L101109I	1200 × 750 mm; LEWB207CV	Nr	0.25	6.28	–	367.25	373.53	6.91	–	403.98	410.88
L101109J	1200 × 900 mm; LEWB209CV	Nr	0.25	6.28	–	392.59	398.87	6.91	–	431.85	438.76
L101109K	1200 × 1050 mm; LEWB210CV	Nr	0.25	6.28	–	408.37	414.65	6.91	–	449.21	456.12
L101109L	1200 × 1200 mm; LEWB212CV	Nr	0.25	6.28	–	446.05	452.33	6.91	–	490.66	497.56
L101109M	1200 × 1350 mm; LEWB213CV	Nr	0.25	6.28	–	487.99	494.27	6.91	–	536.79	543.70
L101109N	1770 × 900 mm; LEWB309CVC	Nr	0.30	7.54	–	540.31	547.85	8.29	–	594.34	602.64

Major Works 2009		Unit	Labour Hours	Labour Net	Plant Net	Materials Net	Unit Net	Labour Gross	Plant Gross	Materials Gross	Unit Price
								(Gross rates include 10% profit)			
				£	£	£	£	£	£	£	£
L10	**L10: WINDOWS, ROOFLIGHTS, SCREENS AND LOUVRES**										
L1011	**Standard softwood windows**										
L101109	**Boulton and Paul softwood windows; Sovereign; all bar; with vents; fitted 24 mm Low E insulating glazing units; fitted with standard sill; complete with ironmongery; size:**										
L101109O	1770 × 1050 mm; LEWB310CVC............	Nr	0.30	7.54	–	572.10	579.64	8.29	–	629.31	637.60
L101109P	1770 × 1200 mm; LEWB312CVC............	Nr	0.30	7.54	–	628.02	635.56	8.29	–	690.82	699.12
L101109Q	1770 × 1350 mm; LEWB313CVC............	Nr	0.30	7.54	–	680.63	688.17	8.29	–	748.69	756.99
L101110	**Boulton and Paul softwood windows; Sovereign; all bar; transom; fitted wit 24 mm Low E insulating glazing units; fitted with standard sill; complete with ironmongery; size:**										
L101110A	1200 × 1350 mm; LEWB213TX.............	Nr	0.25	6.28	–	545.90	552.18	6.91	–	600.49	607.40
L101110B	1200 × 1500 mm; LEWB215TX.............	Nr	0.25	6.28	–	630.66	636.94	6.91	–	693.73	700.63
L101110C	1770 × 1350 mm; LEWB313TXT............	Nr	0.30	7.54	–	792.85	800.39	8.29	–	872.14	880.43
L101110D	1770 × 1500 mm; LEWB315TXT............	Nr	0.30	7.54	–	920.83	928.37	8.29	–	1012.91	1021.21
L101110E	2339 × 1500 mm; LEWB415TXXT..........	Nr	0.35	8.80	–	1211.40	1220.20	9.68	–	1332.54	1342.22
L101110F	2339 × 1050 mm; LEWB410CVVC..........	Nr	0.35	8.80	–	789.95	798.75	9.68	–	868.95	878.63
L101110G	2339 × 1200 mm; LEWB412CVVC..........	Nr	0.35	8.80	–	862.71	871.51	9.68	–	948.98	958.66
L101110H	2339 × 1350 mm; LEWB413CVVC..........	Nr	0.35	8.80	–	928.33	937.13	9.68	–	1021.16	1030.84

Windows, Doors and Stairs

Major Works 2009		Unit	Labour Hours	Labour Net	Plant Net	Materials Net	Unit Net	Labour Gross	Plant Gross	Materials Gross	Unit Price
								(Gross rates include 10% profit)			
				£	£	£	£	£	£	£	£
L10	**L10: WINDOWS, ROOFLIGHTS, SCREENS AND LOUVRES**										
L1011	**Standard softwood windows**										
L101111	**Boulton and Paul softwood windows; Sovereign; all bar; narrow module; fitted with 24 mm Low E glazing units; fitted with standard sill; complete with ironmongery; size:**										
L101111A	488 × 750 mm; LEWBN07C	Nr	0.18	4.52	–	140.05	144.57	4.97	–	154.06	159.03
L101111B	488 × 900 mm; LEWBN09C	Nr	0.18	4.52	–	149.20	153.72	4.97	–	164.12	169.09
L101111C	488 × 1050 mm; LEWBN10C	Nr	0.18	4.52	–	159.77	164.29	4.97	–	175.75	180.72
L101111D	488 × 1200 mm; LEWBN12C	Nr	0.18	4.52	–	174.88	179.40	4.97	–	192.37	197.34
L101111E	488 × 900 mm; LEWBN09V	Nr	0.18	4.52	–	223.17	227.69	4.97	–	245.49	250.46
L101111F	488 × 1050 mm; LEWBN10V	Nr	0.18	4.52	–	225.46	229.98	4.97	–	248.01	252.98
L101111G	488 × 1200 mm; LEWBN12V	Nr	0.18	4.52	–	239.87	244.39	4.97	–	263.86	268.83
L101111H	915 × 1050 mm; LEWB2N10CV	Nr	0.23	5.78	–	377.17	382.95	6.36	–	414.89	421.25
L101111I	915 × 1200 mm; LEWB2N12CV	Nr	0.23	5.78	–	404.80	410.58	6.36	–	445.28	451.64
L101111J	915 × 1050 mm; LEWB2N10W	Nr	0.23	5.78	–	321.03	326.81	6.36	–	353.13	359.49
L101111K	915 × 1200 mm; LEWB2N12W	Nr	0.23	5.78	–	362.36	368.14	6.36	–	398.60	404.95

Major Works 2009		Unit	Labour Hours	Labour Net	Plant Net	Materials Net	Unit Net	Labour Gross	Plant Gross	Materials Gross	Unit Price
								(Gross rates include 10% profit)			
				£	£	£	£	£	£	£	£
L10	**L10: WINDOWS, ROOFLIGHTS, SCREENS AND LOUVRES**										
L1011	**Standard softwood windows**										
L101112	**Boulton and Paul softwood windows; Sovereign; Cottage; plain; fitted with standard sill; complete with ironmongery; size:**										
L101112A	630 × 900 mm; WC109C .	Nr	0.20	5.02	–	1.72	6.74	5.52	–	1.89	7.41
L101112B	630 × 1050 mm; WC110C	Nr	0.20	5.03	–	124.16	129.19	5.53	–	136.58	142.11
L101112C	630 × 1200 mm; WC112C	Nr	0.20	5.03	–	128.34	133.37	5.53	–	141.17	146.71
L101112D	630 × 1350 mm; WC113C	Nr	0.20	5.03	–	136.63	141.66	5.53	–	150.29	155.83
L101112E	1200 × 900 mm; WC209C	Nr	0.25	6.28	–	168.23	174.51	6.91	–	185.05	191.96
L101112F	1200 × 1050 mm; WC210C	Nr	0.25	6.28	–	174.33	180.61	6.91	–	191.76	198.67
L101112G	1200 × 1200 mm; WC212C	Nr	0.25	6.28	–	180.50	186.78	6.91	–	198.55	205.46
L101112H	1200 × 1350 mm; WC213C	Nr	0.25	6.28	–	190.30	196.58	6.91	–	209.33	216.24
L101112I	1200 × 900 mm; WC209CC	Nr	0.25	6.28	–	219.60	225.88	6.91	–	241.56	248.47
L101112J	1200 × 1050 mm; WC210CC	Nr	0.25	6.28	–	227.94	234.22	6.91	–	250.73	257.64
L101112K	1200 × 1200 mm; WC212CC	Nr	0.25	6.28	–	236.20	242.48	6.91	–	259.82	266.73
L101112L	1200 × 1350 mm; WC213CC	Nr	0.25	6.28	–	252.89	259.17	6.91	–	278.18	285.09
L101112M	1770 × 900 mm; WC309CC	Nr	0.30	7.54	–	254.35	261.89	8.29	–	279.79	288.08
L101112N	1770 × 1050 mm; WC310CC	Nr	0.30	7.54	–	263.25	270.79	8.29	–	289.58	297.87
L101112O	1770 × 1200 mm; WC312CC	Nr	0.30	7.54	–	272.32	279.86	8.29	–	299.55	307.85
L101112P	1770 × 1350 mm; WC313CC	Nr	0.30	7.54	–	288.36	295.90	8.29	–	317.20	325.49
L101112Q	2339 × 1050 mm; WC410CMC.............	Nr	0.35	8.80	–	333.07	341.87	9.68	–	366.38	376.06
L101112R	2339 × 1200 mm; WC412CMC.............	Nr	0.35	8.80	–	344.95	353.75	9.68	–	379.45	389.13
L101112S	2339 × 1350 mm; WC413CMC.............	Nr	0.35	8.80	–	364.36	373.16	9.68	–	400.80	410.48

Windows, Doors and Stairs

Major Works 2009		Unit	Labour Hours	Labour Net	Plant Net	Materials Net	Unit Net	Labour Gross	Plant Gross	Materials Gross	Unit Price
								(Gross rates include 10% profit)			
				£	£	£	£	£	£	£	£
L10	**L10: WINDOWS, ROOFLIGHTS, SCREENS AND LOUVRES**										
L1011	**Standard softwood windows**										
L101113	**Boulton and Paul softwood windows; Sovereign; Cottage; divided casement; fitted with standard sill; complete with ironmongery; size:**										
L101113A	630 × 900 mm; WC109D .	Nr	0.20	5.03	–	146.62	151.65	5.53	–	161.28	166.82
L101113B	630 × 1050 mm; WC110D	Nr	0.20	5.03	–	150.81	155.84	5.53	–	165.89	171.42
L101113C	630 × 1200 mm; WC112D	Nr	0.20	5.03	–	155.32	160.35	5.53	–	170.85	176.39
L101113D	630 × 1350 mm; WC113D	Nr	0.20	5.03	–	159.64	164.67	5.53	–	175.60	181.14
L101113E	915 × 1050 mm; WC2N10D	Nr	0.23	5.78	–	174.96	180.74	6.36	–	192.46	198.81
L101113F	915 × 1200 mm; WC2N12D	Nr	0.23	5.78	–	179.65	185.43	6.36	–	197.62	203.97
L101113G	915 × 1350 mm; WC2N13D	Nr	0.23	5.78	–	184.03	189.81	6.36	–	202.43	208.79
L101113H	1200 × 900 mm; WC209CD	Nr	0.25	6.28	–	250.10	256.38	6.91	–	275.11	282.02
L101113I	1200 × 1050 mm; WC210CD	Nr	0.25	6.28	–	257.96	264.24	6.91	–	283.76	290.66
L101113J	1200 × 1200 mm; WC212CD	Nr	0.25	6.28	–	267.42	273.70	6.91	–	294.16	301.07
L101113K	1200 × 1350 mm; WC213CD	Nr	0.25	6.28	–	277.36	283.64	6.91	–	305.10	312.00
L101113L	1770 × 900 mm; WC309CDC	Nr	0.30	7.54	–	343.19	350.73	8.29	–	377.51	385.80
L101113M	1770 × 1050 mm; WC310CDC	Nr	0.30	7.54	–	353.45	360.99	8.29	–	388.80	397.09
L101113N	1770 × 1200 mm; WC312CDC	Nr	0.30	7.54	–	367.34	374.88	8.29	–	404.07	412.37
L101113O	1770 × 1350 mm; WC313CDC	Nr	0.30	7.54	–	383.38	390.92	8.29	–	421.72	430.01
L101113P	2339 × 1050 mm; WC410CDDC	Nr	0.35	8.80	–	500.65	509.45	9.68	–	550.72	560.40
L101113Q	2339 × 1200 mm; WC412CDDC	Nr	0.35	8.80	–	519.12	527.92	9.68	–	571.03	580.71
L101113R	2339 × 1350 mm; WC413CDDC	Nr	0.35	8.80	–	538.12	546.92	9.68	–	591.93	601.61

Major Works 2009		Unit	Labour Hours	Labour Net	Plant Net	Materials Net	Unit Net	Labour Gross	Plant Gross	Materials Gross	Unit Price
								(Gross rates include 10% profit)			
				£	£	£	£	£	£	£	£
L10	**L10: WINDOWS, ROOFLIGHTS, SCREENS AND LOUVRES**										
L1011	**Standard softwood windows**										
L101114	**Boulton and Paul softwood windows; Sovereign; horizontal bar; plain; fitted with standard sill; complete with ironmongery; size:**										
L101114A	630 × 750 mm; WH107C .	Nr	0.20	5.03	–	108.86	113.89	5.53	–	119.75	125.28
L101114B	630 × 900 mm; WH109C .	Nr	0.20	5.03	–	112.80	117.83	5.53	–	124.08	129.61
L101114C	630 × 1050 mm; WH110C	Nr	0.20	5.03	–	116.71	121.74	5.53	–	128.38	133.91
L101114D	630 × 1200 mm; WH112C	Nr	0.20	5.03	–	120.89	125.92	5.53	–	132.98	138.51
L101114E	1200 × 1350 mm; WH113C	Nr	0.20	5.03	–	128.99	134.02	5.53	–	141.89	147.42
L101114F	1200 × 750 mm; WH207C	Nr	0.25	6.28	–	146.76	153.04	6.91	–	161.44	168.34
L101114G	1200 × 900 mm; WH209C	Nr	0.25	6.28	–	148.25	154.53	6.91	–	163.08	169.98
L101114H	1200 × 1050 mm; WH210C	Nr	0.25	6.28	–	149.09	155.37	6.91	–	164.00	170.91
L101114I	1200 × 1200 mm; WH212C	Nr	0.25	6.28	–	154.61	160.89	6.91	–	170.07	176.98
L101114J	1200 × 1350 mm; WH213C	Nr	0.25	6.28	–	173.22	179.50	6.91	–	190.54	197.45
L101114K	1770 × 900 mm; WH309CC	Nr	0.30	7.54	–	230.73	238.27	8.29	–	253.80	262.10
L101114L	1770 × 1050 mm; WH310CC	Nr	0.30	7.54	–	238.65	246.19	8.29	–	262.52	270.81
L101114M	1770 × 1200 mm; WH312CC	Nr	0.30	7.54	–	247.01	254.55	8.29	–	271.71	280.01
L101114N	1770 × 1350 mm; WH313CC	Nr	0.30	7.54	–	262.54	270.08	8.29	–	288.79	297.09
L101114O	2339 × 1050 mm; WH410CMC	Nr	0.35	8.80	–	300.41	309.21	9.68	–	330.45	340.13
L101114P	2339 × 1200 mm; WH412CMC	Nr	0.35	8.80	–	311.10	319.90	9.68	–	342.21	351.89
L101114Q	2339 × 1350 mm; WH413CMC	Nr	0.35	8.80	–	329.64	338.44	9.68	–	362.60	372.28

Windows, Doors and Stairs

Major Works 2009		Unit	Labour Hours	Labour Net	Plant Net	Materials Net	Unit Net	Labour Gross	Plant Gross	Materials Gross	Unit Price
								(Gross rates include 10% profit)			
				£	£	£	£	£	£	£	£
L10	**L10: WINDOWS, ROOFLIGHTS, SCREENS AND LOUVRES**										
L1011	**Standard softwood windows**										
L101115	**Boulton and Paul softwood windows; Sovereign; horizontal bar; narrow module; fitted with standard sill; complete with ironmongery; size:**										
L101115A	488 × 900 mm; WHN09C.	Nr	0.18	4.52	–	94.18	98.70	4.97	–	103.60	108.57
L101115B	488 × 1050 mm; WHN10C	Nr	0.18	4.52	–	98.41	102.93	4.97	–	108.25	113.22
L101115C	488 × 1200 mm; WHN12C	Nr	0.18	4.52	–	102.61	107.13	4.97	–	112.87	117.84
L101115D	488 × 1350 mm; WHN13C	Nr	0.18	4.52	–	111.27	115.79	4.97	–	122.40	127.37
L101115E	915 × 900 mm; WH2N09C	Nr	0.23	5.78	–	146.76	152.54	6.36	–	161.44	167.79
L101115F	915 × 1050 mm; WH2N10C	Nr	0.23	5.78	–	152.67	158.45	6.36	–	167.94	174.30
L101115G	915 × 1200 mm; WH2N12C	Nr	0.23	5.78	–	158.71	164.49	6.36	–	174.58	180.94
L101115H	915 × 1350 mm; WH2N13C	Nr	0.23	5.78	–	168.52	174.30	6.36	–	185.37	191.73
L101115I	915 × 900 mm; WH2N09CC..............	Nr	0.23	5.78	–	195.26	201.04	6.36	–	214.79	221.14
L101115J	915 × 1050 mm; WH2N10CC..............	Nr	0.23	5.78	–	203.20	208.98	6.36	–	223.52	229.88
L101115K	915 × 1200 mm; WH2N12CC..............	Nr	0.23	5.78	–	211.19	216.97	6.36	–	232.31	238.67
L101115L	915 × 1350 mm; WH2N13CC..............	Nr	0.23	5.78	–	225.29	231.07	6.36	–	247.82	254.18
L101115M	1342 × 900 mm; WH3N09CC..............	Nr	0.28	7.04	–	219.52	226.56	7.74	–	241.47	249.22
L101115N	1342 × 1050 mm; WH3N10CC..............	Nr	0.28	7.04	–	228.48	235.52	7.74	–	251.33	259.07
L101115O	1342 × 1200 mm; WH3N12CC..............	Nr	0.28	7.04	–	237.31	244.35	7.74	–	261.04	268.79
L101115P	1342 × 1350 mm; WH3N13CC..............	Nr	0.28	7.04	–	253.17	260.21	7.74	–	278.49	286.23
L101115Q	1770 × 1050 mm; W4N10CMC..............	Nr	0.33	8.29	–	290.06	298.35	9.12	–	319.07	328.19
L101115R	1770 × 1200 mm; W4N12CMC..............	Nr	0.33	8.29	–	300.83	309.12	9.12	–	330.91	340.03
L101115S	1770 × 1350 mm; W4N13CMC..............	Nr	0.33	8.29	–	320.03	328.32	9.12	–	352.03	361.15

Major Works 2009		Unit	Labour Hours	Labour Net	Plant Net	Materials Net	Unit Net	Labour Gross	Plant Gross	Materials Gross	Unit Price
				£	£	£	£	£	£	£	£
								(Gross rates include 10% profit)			
L10	**L10: WINDOWS, ROOFLIGHTS, SCREENS AND LOUVRES**										
L1011	**Standard softwood windows**										
L101116	**Boulton and Paul softwood windows; Sovereign; horizontal bar; divided casement; fitted with standard sill; complete with ironmongery; size:**										
L101116B	630 × 900 mm; WH109D.	Nr	0.20	5.03	–	139.57	144.60	5.53	–	153.53	159.06
L101116C	630 × 1050 mm; WH110D	Nr	0.20	5.03	–	143.84	148.87	5.53	–	158.22	163.76
L101116D	630 × 1200 mm; WH112D	Nr	0.20	5.03	–	148.00	153.03	5.53	–	162.80	168.33
L101116E	1200 × 1350 mm; WH113D	Nr	0.20	5.03	–	151.84	156.87	5.53	–	167.02	172.56
L101116G	1200 × 900 mm; WH209CD	Nr	0.25	6.28	–	235.62	241.90	6.91	–	259.18	266.09
L101116H	1200 × 1050 mm; WH210CD	Nr	0.25	6.28	–	243.00	249.28	6.91	–	267.30	274.21
L101116I	1200 × 1200 mm; WH212CD	Nr	0.25	6.28	–	252.08	258.36	6.91	–	277.29	284.20
L101116J	1200 × 1350 mm; WH213CD	Nr	0.25	6.28	–	261.42	267.70	6.91	–	287.56	294.47
L101116K	1770 × 900 mm; WH309CDC	Nr	0.30	7.54	–	326.37	333.91	8.29	–	359.01	367.30
L101116L	1770 × 1050 mm; WH310CDC.	Nr	0.30	7.54	–	336.14	343.68	8.29	–	369.75	378.05
L101116M	1770 × 1200 mm; WH312CDC	Nr	0.30	7.54	–	349.85	357.39	8.29	–	384.84	393.13
L101116N	1770 × 1350 mm; WH313CDC.	Nr	0.30	7.54	–	365.60	373.14	8.29	–	402.16	410.45
L101116O	2339 × 1050 mm; WH4N410CDDC	Nr	0.35	8.80	–	478.52	487.32	9.68	–	526.37	536.05
L101116P	2339 × 1200 mm; WH4N412CDDC	Nr	0.35	8.80	–	496.30	505.10	9.68	–	545.93	555.61
L101116Q	2339 × 1350 mm; WH4N413CDDC	Nr	0.35	8.80	–	514.99	523.79	9.68	–	566.49	576.17

Windows, Doors and Stairs

Major Works 2009		Unit	Labour Hours	Labour Net	Plant Net	Materials Net	Unit Net	Labour Gross	Plant Gross	Materials Gross	Unit Price
								(Gross rates include 10% profit)			
				£	£	£	£	£	£	£	£
L10	**L10: WINDOWS, ROOFLIGHTS, SCREENS AND LOUVRES**										
L101117	**Boulton and Paul softwood windows; Sovereign; top hung; fitted with standard sill; complete with ironmongery; size:**										
L101117A	630 × 450 mm; W104A ..	Nr	0.20	5.03	–	90.02	95.05	5.53	–	99.02	104.56
L101117B	630 × 600 mm; W106A ..	Nr	0.20	5.03	–	94.40	99.43	5.53	–	103.84	109.37
L101117C	630 × 750 mm; W107A ..	Nr	0.20	5.03	–	98.40	103.43	5.53	–	108.24	113.77
L101117D	630 × 900 mm; W109A ..	Nr	0.20	5.03	–	101.35	106.38	5.53	–	111.49	117.02
L101117E	630 × 1050 mm; W110A .	Nr	0.20	5.03	–	105.28	110.31	5.53	–	115.81	121.34
L101117F	630 × 1200 mm; W112A .	Nr	0.20	5.03	–	108.83	113.86	5.53	–	119.71	125.25
L101117G	915 × 450 mm; W2N04A.	Nr	0.23	5.78	–	108.83	114.61	6.36	–	119.71	126.07
L101117H	915 × 600 mm; W2N06A.	Nr	0.23	5.78	–	113.17	118.95	6.36	–	124.49	130.85
L101117I	915 × 750 mm; W2N07A.	Nr	0.23	5.78	–	116.99	122.77	6.36	–	128.69	135.05
L101117J	915 × 900 mm; W2N09A.	Nr	0.23	5.78	–	125.17	130.95	6.36	–	137.69	144.05
L101117K	915 × 1050 mm; W2N10A	Nr	0.23	5.78	–	129.55	135.33	6.36	–	142.51	148.86
L101117L	915 × 1200 mm; W2N12A	Nr	0.23	5.78	–	133.11	138.89	6.36	–	146.42	152.78
L101117M	915 × 1350 mm; W2N13AS	Nr	0.25	6.28	–	146.27	152.55	6.91	–	160.90	167.81
L101117N	1200 × 450 mm; W204A .	Nr	0.20	5.03	–	116.39	121.42	5.53	–	128.03	133.56
L101117O	1200 × 600 mm; W206A .	Nr	0.25	6.28	–	126.94	133.22	6.91	–	139.63	146.54
L101117P	1200 × 750 mm; W207A .	Nr	0.25	6.28	–	116.99	123.27	6.91	–	128.69	135.60
L101117Q	1200 × 900 mm; W209A .	Nr	0.25	6.28	–	138.55	144.83	6.91	–	152.41	159.31
L101117R	1200 × 1050 mm; W210A	Nr	0.25	6.28	–	142.88	149.16	6.91	–	157.17	164.08
L101117S	1200 × 1200 mm; W212A	Nr	0.25	6.28	–	147.05	153.33	6.91	–	161.76	168.66
L101117T	1200 × 1350 mm; W213AS	Nr	0.25	6.28	–	160.37	166.65	6.91	–	176.41	183.32
L101117U	1770 × 450 mm; W304AE	Nr	0.30	7.54	–	132.32	139.86	8.29	–	145.55	153.85
L101117V	1770 × 600 mm; W306AE	Nr	0.30	7.54	–	148.04	155.58	8.29	–	162.84	171.14
L101117W	1770 × 750 mm; W307AE	Nr	0.30	7.54	–	153.21	160.75	8.29	–	168.53	176.83
L101117X	1770 × 900 mm; W309AE	Nr	0.30	7.54	–	161.85	169.39	8.29	–	178.04	186.33
L101117Y	1770 × 1050 mm; W310AE	Nr	0.30	7.54	–	167.48	175.02	8.29	–	184.23	192.52
L101117Z	1770 × 1200 mm; W312AE	Nr	0.30	7.54	–	172.37	179.91	8.29	–	189.61	197.90

Major Works 2009		Unit	Labour Hours	Labour Net	Plant Net	Materials Net	Unit Net	Labour Gross	Plant Gross	Materials Gross	Unit Price
								(Gross rates include 10% profit)			
				£	£	£	£	£	£	£	£
L10	**L10: WINDOWS, ROOFLIGHTS, SCREENS AND LOUVRES**										
L1011	**Standard softwood windows**										
L101119	**Boulton and Paul softwood windows; Sovereign; direct glazed; fitted with standard sill; size:**										
L101119A	630 × 1050 mm; W110DG	Nr	0.20	5.03	–	59.75	64.78	5.53	–	65.73	71.26
L101119B	630 × 1200 mm; W112DG	Nr	0.20	5.03	–	61.53	66.56	5.53	–	67.68	73.22
L101119C	630 × 1350 mm; W113DG	Nr	0.20	5.03	–	66.18	71.21	5.53	–	72.80	78.33
L101119D	1200 × 450 mm; W204DG	Nr	0.25	6.28	–	74.12	80.40	6.91	–	81.53	88.44
L101119E	1200 × 600 mm; W206DG	Nr	0.25	6.28	–	75.01	81.29	6.91	–	82.51	89.42
L101119F	1200 × 750 mm; W207DG	Nr	0.25	6.28	–	76.97	83.25	6.91	–	84.67	91.58
L101119G	1200 × 900 mm; W209DG	Nr	0.25	6.28	–	82.62	88.90	6.91	–	90.88	97.79
L101119H	1200 × 1050 mm; W210DG	Nr	0.25	6.28	–	85.23	91.51	6.91	–	93.75	100.66
L101119I	1200 × 1200 mm; W212DG	Nr	0.25	6.28	–	87.35	93.63	6.91	–	96.09	102.99
L101119J	1200 × 1350 mm; W213DG	Nr	0.25	6.28	–	90.08	96.36	6.91	–	99.09	106.00
L101121	**Boulton and Paul softwood windows; Sovereign; Regency; non bar; fitted with standard sill; complete with ironmongery; size:**										
L101121A	488 × 750 mm; WSRN07.	Nr	0.15	3.77	–	147.06	150.83	4.15	–	161.77	165.91
L101121B	488 × 900 mm; WSRN09.	Nr	0.15	3.77	–	152.64	156.41	4.15	–	167.90	172.05
L101121C	488 × 1050 mm; WSRN10	Nr	0.15	3.77	–	158.25	162.02	4.15	–	174.08	178.22
L101121D	488 × 1200 mm; WSRN12	Nr	0.15	3.77	–	163.84	167.61	4.15	–	180.22	184.37
L101121E	488 × 1350 mm; WSRN13	Nr	0.15	3.77	–	169.35	173.12	4.15	–	186.29	190.43
L101121F	488 × 1500 mm; WSRN15	Nr	0.15	3.77	–	174.91	178.68	4.15	–	192.40	196.55
L101121G	630 × 750 mm; WSR107.	Nr	0.20	5.03	–	153.71	158.74	5.53	–	169.08	174.61
L101121H	630 × 900 mm; WSR109.	Nr	0.20	5.03	–	159.30	164.33	5.53	–	175.23	180.76
L101121I	630 × 1050 mm; WSR110	Nr	0.20	5.03	–	164.83	169.86	5.53	–	181.31	186.85
L101121J	630 × 1200 mm; WSR112	Nr	0.20	5.03	–	170.38	175.41	5.53	–	187.42	192.95
L101121K	630 × 1350 mm; WSR113	Nr	0.20	5.03	–	175.91	180.94	5.53	–	193.50	199.03
L101121L	630 × 1500 mm; WSR115	Nr	0.20	5.03	–	181.58	186.61	5.53	–	199.74	205.27
L101121M	630 × 1650 mm; WSR116	Nr	0.20	5.03	–	187.16	192.19	5.53	–	205.88	211.41
L101121N	915 × 750 mm; WSR2N07	Nr	0.25	6.28	–	164.83	171.11	6.91	–	181.31	188.22
L101121O	915 × 900 mm; WSR2N09	Nr	0.25	6.28	–	170.38	176.66	6.91	–	187.42	194.33
L101121P	915 × 1050 mm; WSR2N10	Nr	0.25	6.28	–	175.91	182.19	6.91	–	193.50	200.41
L101121Q	915 × 1200 mm; WSR2N12	Nr	0.25	6.28	–	181.58	187.86	6.91	–	199.74	206.65
L101121R	915 × 1350 mm; WSR2N13	Nr	0.25	6.28	–	187.09	193.37	6.91	–	205.80	212.71
L101121S	915 × 1500 mm; WSR2N15	Nr	0.25	6.28	–	192.10	198.38	6.91	–	211.31	218.22
L101121T	915 × 1650 mm; WSR2N16	Nr	0.25	6.28	–	198.24	204.52	6.91	–	218.06	224.97
L101121U	1200 × 900 mm; WSR209	Nr	0.25	6.28	–	180.43	186.71	6.91	–	198.47	205.38
L101121V	1200 × 1050 mm; WSR210	Nr	0.25	6.28	–	187.09	193.37	6.91	–	205.80	212.71
L101121W	1200 × 1200 mm; WSR212	Nr	0.25	6.28	–	192.50	198.78	6.91	–	211.75	218.66
L101121X	1200 × 1350 mm; WSR213	Nr	0.25	6.28	–	198.18	204.46	6.91	–	218.00	224.91
L101121Y	1200 × 1500 mm; WSR215	Nr	0.25	6.28	–	203.70	209.98	6.91	–	224.07	230.98
L101121Z	1200 × 1650 mm; WSR216	Nr	0.25	6.28	–	210.18	216.46	6.91	–	231.20	238.11

Windows, Doors and Stairs

Major Works 2009		Unit	Labour Hours	Labour Net	Plant Net	Materials Net	Unit Net	Labour Gross	Plant Gross	Materials Gross	Unit Price
								(Gross rates include 10% profit)			
				£	£	£	£	£	£	£	£
L10	**L10: WINDOWS, ROOFLIGHTS, SCREENS AND LOUVRES**										
L1011	**Standard softwood windows**										
L101122	**Boulton and Paul softwood windows; Sovereign; Regency; non bar; fitted with standard sill; complete with ironmongery; size:**										
L101122B	1200 × 1050 mm; WSR210D	Nr	0.25	6.28	–	323.62	329.90	6.91	–	355.98	362.89
L101122C	1200 × 1200 mm; WSR212D	Nr	0.25	6.28	–	334.82	341.10	6.91	–	368.30	375.21
L101122D	1200 × 1350 mm; WSR213D	Nr	0.25	6.28	–	345.83	352.11	6.91	–	380.41	387.32
L101122E	1200 × 1500 mm; WSR215D	Nr	0.25	6.28	–	356.91	363.19	6.91	–	392.60	399.51
L101122F	1200 × 1650 mm; WSR216D	Nr	0.25	6.28	–	369.62	375.90	6.91	–	406.58	413.49
L101122G	1770 × 1050 mm; WSR4N10	Nr	0.30	7.54	–	345.83	353.37	8.29	–	380.41	388.71
L101122H	1770 × 1200 mm; WSR4N12	Nr	0.30	7.54	–	356.91	364.45	8.29	–	392.60	400.90
L101122I	1770 × 1350 mm; WSR4N13	Nr	0.30	7.54	–	367.93	375.47	8.29	–	404.72	413.02
L101122J	1770 × 1500 mm; WSR4N15	Nr	0.30	7.54	–	379.01	386.55	8.29	–	416.91	425.21

Major Works 2009		Unit	Labour Hours	Labour Net	Plant Net	Materials Net	Unit Net	Labour Gross	Plant Gross	Materials Gross	Unit Price
								(Gross rates include 10% profit)			
				£	£	£	£	£	£	£	£
L10	**L10: WINDOWS, ROOFLIGHTS, SCREENS AND LOUVRES**										
L1011	**Standard softwood windows**										
L101123	**Boulton and Paul softwood windows; Sovereign; Regency; vertical bar; fitted with standard sill; complete with ironmongery; size:**										
L101123G	630 × 750 mm; WSRV107	Nr	0.20	5.03	–	187.33	192.36	5.53	–	206.06	211.60
L101123H	630 × 900 mm; WSRV109	Nr	0.20	5.03	–	193.95	198.98	5.53	–	213.35	218.88
L101123I	630 × 1050 mm; WSRV110	Nr	0.20	5.03	–	200.44	205.47	5.53	–	220.48	226.02
L101123J	630 × 1200 mm; WSRV112	Nr	0.20	5.03	–	207.03	212.06	5.53	–	227.73	233.27
L101123K	630 × 1350 mm; WSRV113	Nr	0.20	5.03	–	213.80	218.83	5.53	–	235.18	240.71
L101123L	630 × 1500 mm; WSRV115	Nr	0.20	5.03	–	220.31	225.34	5.53	–	242.34	247.87
L101123M	630 × 1650 mm; WSRV116	Nr	0.20	5.03	–	226.90	231.93	5.53	–	249.59	255.12
L101123N	915 × 750 mm; WSRV2N07	Nr	0.25	6.28	–	199.53	205.81	6.91	–	219.48	226.39
L101123O	915 × 900 mm; WSRV2N09	Nr	0.25	6.28	–	206.04	212.32	6.91	–	226.64	233.55
L101123P	915 × 1050 mm; WSRV2N10	Nr	0.25	6.28	–	212.60	218.88	6.91	–	233.86	240.77
L101123Q	915 × 1200 mm; WSRV2N12	Nr	0.25	6.28	–	219.18	225.46	6.91	–	241.10	248.01
L101123R	915 × 1350 mm; WSRV2N13	Nr	0.25	6.28	–	225.78	232.06	6.91	–	248.36	255.27
L101123S	915 × 1500 mm; WSRV2N15	Nr	0.25	6.28	–	232.26	238.54	6.91	–	255.49	262.39
L101123T	915 × 1650 mm; WSRV2N16	Nr	0.25	6.28	–	239.10	245.38	6.91	–	263.01	269.92
L101123U	1200 × 900 mm; WSRV209	Nr	0.25	6.28	–	219.18	225.46	6.91	–	241.10	248.01
L101123V	1200 × 1050 mm; WSRV210	Nr	0.25	6.28	–	224.59	230.87	6.91	–	247.05	253.96
L101123W	1200 × 1200 mm; WSRV212	Nr	0.25	6.28	–	231.28	237.56	6.91	–	254.41	261.32
L101123X	1200 × 1350 mm; WSRV213	Nr	0.25	6.28	–	237.78	244.06	6.91	–	261.56	268.47
L101123Y	1200 × 1500 mm; WSRV215	Nr	0.25	6.28	–	244.48	250.76	6.91	–	268.93	275.84
L101123Z	1200 × 1650 mm; WSRV216	Nr	0.25	6.28	–	254.26	260.54	6.91	–	279.69	286.59
L101124	**Boulton and Paul softwood windows; Sovereign; Regency; vertical bar; fitted with standard sill; complete with ironmongery; size:**										
L101124C	1770 × 1050 mm; WSRV4N10	Nr	0.30	7.54	–	430.77	438.31	8.29	–	473.85	482.14
L101124D	1770 × 1200 mm; WSRV4N12	Nr	0.30	7.54	–	445.12	452.66	8.29	–	489.63	497.93
L101124E	1770 × 1350 mm; WSRV4N13	Nr	0.30	7.54	–	459.22	466.76	8.29	–	505.14	513.44
L101124F	1770 × 1500 mm; WSRV4N15	Nr	0.30	7.54	–	472.98	480.52	8.29	–	520.28	528.57
L101124G	1770 × 1600 mm; WSRV4N16	Nr	0.30	7.54	–	496.89	504.43	8.29	–	546.58	554.87
L101124H	2339 × 1050 mm; WSRV410	Nr	0.35	8.80	–	437.47	446.27	9.68	–	481.22	490.90
L101124I	2339 × 1200 mm; WSRV412	Nr	0.35	8.80	–	451.56	460.36	9.68	–	496.72	506.40
L101124J	2339 × 1350 mm; WSRV413	Nr	0.35	8.80	–	465.65	474.45	9.68	–	512.22	521.90

Major Works 2009		Unit	Labour Hours	Labour Net	Plant Net	Materials Net	Unit Net	Labour Gross	Plant Gross	Materials Gross	Unit Price
								—— (Gross rates include 10% profit) ——			
				£	£	£	£	£	£	£	£
L10	**L10: WINDOWS, ROOFLIGHTS, SCREENS AND LOUVRES**										
L1011	**Standard softwood windows**										
L101125	**Boulton and Paul softwood windows; Sovereign; designer range; size:**										
L101125L	630 × 345 mm; semi-circular; W638C	Nr	0.25	6.28	–	193.88	200.16	6.91	–	213.27	220.18
L101125M	915 × 488 mm; semi-circular; W952D	Nr	0.30	7.54	–	222.23	229.77	8.29	–	244.45	252.75
L101125N	1200 × 630 mm; semi-circular; W1267E	Nr	0.35	8.80	–	227.24	236.04	9.68	–	249.96	259.64
L101125O	630 × 345 mm; semi-circular; W638CRB........	Nr	0.25	6.28	–	225.95	232.23	6.91	–	248.55	255.45
L101125P	915 × 488 mm; semi-circular; W952DRB	Nr	0.30	7.54	–	255.27	262.81	8.29	–	280.80	289.09
L101125Q	1200 × 630 mm; semi-circular; W1267ERB.......	Nr	0.35	8.80	–	261.04	269.84	9.68	–	287.14	296.82
L101125T	600 mm diameter; circular; W120BE................	Nr	0.30	7.54	–	145.47	153.01	8.29	–	160.02	168.31
L101125U	600 mm diameter; circular; W120BP	Nr	0.30	7.54	–	316.43	323.97	8.29	–	348.07	356.37
L101127	**Boulton and Paul softwood windows; sliding sash; non bar; fitted standard sill; complete with ironmongery; size:**										
L101127A	410 × 1050 mm; TVS0410	Nr	0.50	8.49	–	352.30	360.79	9.34	–	387.53	396.87
L101127B	410 × 1350 mm; TVS0413	Nr	0.50	8.49	–	376.51	385.00	9.34	–	414.16	423.50
L101127C	410 × 1650 mm; TVS0416	Nr	0.50	8.49	–	404.13	412.62	9.34	–	444.54	453.88
L101127D	635 × 1050 mm; TVS0610	Nr	0.60	10.19	–	400.88	411.07	11.21	–	440.97	452.18
L101127E	635 × 1350 mm; TVS0613	Nr	0.60	10.19	–	425.61	435.80	11.21	–	468.17	479.38
L101127F	635 × 1650 mm; TVS0616	Nr	0.60	10.19	–	450.05	460.24	11.21	–	495.06	506.26
L101127G	860 × 1050 mm; TVS0810	Nr	0.70	11.88	–	425.61	437.49	13.07	–	468.17	481.24
L101127H	860 × 1350 mm; TVS0813	Nr	0.70	11.88	–	450.05	461.93	13.07	–	495.06	508.12
L101127I	860 × 1650 mm; TVS0816	Nr	0.70	11.88	–	480.87	492.75	13.07	–	528.96	542.03
L101127J	1085 × 1050 mm; TVS1010	Nr	0.80	13.58	–	450.05	463.63	14.94	–	495.06	509.99
L101127K	1085 × 1350 mm; TVS1013	Nr	0.80	20.09	–	480.87	500.96	22.10	–	528.96	551.06
L101127L	1085 × 1650 mm; TVS1016	Nr	0.80	13.58	–	502.34	515.92	14.94	–	552.57	567.51
L101127M	1699 × 1050 mm; TVS1710	Nr	0.90	15.28	–	808.45	823.73	16.81	–	889.30	906.10
L101127N	1699 × 1350 mm; TVS1713	Nr	0.90	15.28	–	865.07	880.35	16.81	–	951.58	968.39
L101127O	1699 × 1650 mm; TVS1716	Nr	0.90	15.28	–	915.40	930.68	16.81	–	1006.94	1023.75
L101127P	1638 × 1050 mm; TVS1610	Nr	0.90	15.28	–	891.11	906.39	16.81	–	980.22	997.03
L101127Q	1638 × 1350 mm; TVS1613	Nr	0.90	15.28	–	964.58	979.86	16.81	–	1061.04	1077.85
L101127R	1638 × 1650 mm; TVS1616	Nr	0.90	15.28	–	1041.31	1056.59	16.81	–	1145.44	1162.25
L101127S	1863 × 1050 mm; TVS1810	Nr	0.90	15.28	–	921.69	936.97	16.81	–	1013.86	1030.67
L101127T	1863 × 1350 mm; TVS1813	Nr	0.90	15.28	–	995.32	1010.60	16.81	–	1094.85	1111.66
L101127U	1863 × 1650 mm; TVS1816	Nr	0.90	15.28	–	1069.16	1084.44	16.81	–	1176.08	1192.88

Major Works 2009		Unit	Labour Hours	Labour Net	Plant Net	Materials Net	Unit Net	Labour Gross	Plant Gross	Materials Gross	Unit Price
								(Gross rates include 10% profit)			
				£	£	£	£	£	£	£	£
L10	**L10: WINDOWS, ROOFLIGHTS, SCREENS AND LOUVRES**										
L1011	**Standard softwood windows**										
L101128	**Boulton and Paul softwood windows; semi-circular feature for site coupling with sliding sash windows; fitted with standard sill; complete with ironmongery; size:**										
L101128A	635 × 343 mm; VSSEM6 .	Nr	0.25	4.24	–	284.32	288.56	4.66	–	312.75	317.42
L101128B	860 × 458 mm; VSSEM8 .	Nr	0.30	5.09	–	305.81	310.90	5.60	–	336.39	341.99
L101128C	1085 × 568 mm; VSSEM10	Nr	0.35	5.94	–	334.43	340.37	6.53	–	367.87	374.41
L101128D	635 × 343 mm; VSSEM6B	Nr	0.25	4.24	–	351.27	355.51	4.66	–	386.40	391.06
L101128E	860 × 458 mm; VSSEM8B	Nr	0.30	5.09	–	375.76	380.85	5.60	–	413.34	418.94
L101128F	1085 × 568 mm; VSSEM10B	Nr	0.35	5.94	–	415.49	421.43	6.53	–	457.04	463.57
L101130	**Boulton and Paul softwood square bay assemblies; including softwood joining and make-up kit; extra over cost of frames; ref:**										
L101130A	Two return ends; SQ2	Nr	0.70	11.88	–	215.30	227.18	13.07	–	236.83	249.90
L101130B	Two return ends; SQ3	Nr	0.90	15.28	–	215.30	230.58	16.81	–	236.83	253.64
L101130C	Two return ends; SQ4	Nr	1.20	20.37	–	215.30	235.67	22.41	–	236.83	259.24
L101130D	Two return ends; SQ5	Nr	1.50	25.47	–	215.30	240.77	28.02	–	236.83	264.85
L101130E	One return end; SQR2	Nr	0.70	11.88	–	103.32	115.20	13.07	–	113.65	126.72
L101130F	One return end; SQR3	Nr	0.90	15.28	–	103.32	118.60	16.81	–	113.65	130.46
L101130G	One return end; SQR4	Nr	1.20	30.14	–	103.32	133.46	33.15	–	113.65	146.81
L101130H	One return end; SQR5	Nr	1.50	25.47	–	103.32	128.79	28.02	–	113.65	141.67
L101130I	Narrow module; two return ends; SQ2N	Nr	0.70	11.88	–	215.30	227.18	13.07	–	236.83	249.90
L101130J	Narrow module; two return ends; SQ3N	Nr	0.90	15.28	–	215.30	230.58	16.81	–	236.83	253.64
L101130K	Narrow module; two return ends; SQ4N	Nr	1.20	20.37	–	215.30	235.67	22.41	–	236.83	259.24
L101130L	Narrow module; one return end; SQR2N	Nr	0.70	11.88	–	103.32	115.20	13.07	–	113.65	126.72
L101130M	Narrow module; one return end; SQR3N	Nr	0.90	15.28	–	103.32	118.60	16.81	–	113.65	130.46
L101130N	Narrow module; one return end; SQR4N	Nr	1.20	20.37	–	103.32	123.69	22.41	–	113.65	136.06

Windows, Doors and Stairs

Major Works 2009		Unit	Labour Hours	Labour Net	Plant Net	Materials Net	Unit Net	Labour Gross	Plant Gross	Materials Gross	Unit Price
				£	£	£	£	£ (Gross rates include 10% profit) £	£	£	£
L10	**L10: WINDOWS, ROOFLIGHTS, SCREENS AND LOUVRES**										
L1011	**Standard softwood windows**										
L101131	**Boulton and Paul softwood splay bay assemblies; including softwood joining and make-up kit; extra over cost of frames; ref:**										
L101131B	Two return ends; SP2	Nr	0.90	15.28	–	215.30	230.58	16.81	–	236.83	253.64
L101131C	Two return ends; SP3	Nr	1.20	20.37	–	215.30	235.67	22.41	–	236.83	259.24
L101131D	Two return ends; SP4	Nr	1.50	25.47	–	215.30	240.77	28.02	–	236.83	264.85
L101131F	One return end; SPR2	Nr	0.90	15.28	–	103.32	118.60	16.81	–	113.65	130.46
L101131G	One return end; SPR3	Nr	1.20	20.37	–	103.32	123.69	22.41	–	113.65	136.06
L101131H	One return end; SPR4	Nr	1.50	25.47	–	103.32	128.79	28.02	–	113.65	141.67
L101131I	Narrow module; two return ends; SP2N	Nr	0.90	15.28	–	215.30	230.58	16.81	–	236.83	253.64
L101131J	Narrow module; two return ends; SP3N	Nr	1.20	20.37	–	215.30	235.67	22.41	–	236.83	259.24
L101131K	Narrow module; two return ends; SP4N	Nr	1.50	25.47	–	215.30	240.77	28.02	–	236.83	264.85
L101131L	Narrow module; one return end; SPR2N	Nr	0.90	15.28	–	103.32	118.60	16.81	–	113.65	130.46
L101131M	Narrow module; one return end; SPR3N	Nr	1.20	20.37	–	103.32	123.69	22.41	–	113.65	136.06
L101131N	Narrow module; one return end; SPR4N	Nr	1.50	25.47	–	103.32	128.79	28.02	–	113.65	141.67
L101143	**Boulton and Paul softwood windows; Hi-Profile Combi; bespoke manufacture; complete with all ironmongery:**										
L101143A	450 × 900 mm	Nr	0.15	3.77	–	211.78	215.55	4.15	–	232.96	237.11
L101143B	450 × 1050 mm	Nr	0.15	3.77	–	216.61	220.38	4.15	–	238.27	242.42
L101143C	450 × 1200 mm	Nr	0.15	3.77	–	222.04	225.81	4.15	–	244.24	248.39
L101143D	600 × 600 mm	Nr	0.20	5.03	–	199.17	204.20	5.53	–	219.09	224.62
L101143E	600 × 900 mm	Nr	0.20	5.03	–	208.04	213.07	5.53	–	228.84	234.38
L101143F	600 × 1050 mm	Nr	0.20	5.03	–	212.98	218.01	5.53	–	234.28	239.81
L101143G	600 × 1200 mm	Nr	0.20	5.03	–	218.19	223.22	5.53	–	240.01	245.54
L101143H	600 × 1350 mm	Nr	0.20	5.03	–	239.72	244.75	5.53	–	263.69	269.23
L101143I	600 × 1500 mm	Nr	0.20	5.03	–	246.80	251.83	5.53	–	271.48	277.01
L101143J	600 × 1600 mm	Nr	0.20	5.03	–	251.73	256.76	5.53	–	276.90	282.44
L101143K	900 × 600 mm	Nr	0.25	6.28	–	218.29	224.57	6.91	–	240.12	247.03
L101143L	900 × 900 mm	Nr	0.25	6.28	–	227.23	233.51	6.91	–	249.95	256.86
L101143M	900 × 1050 mm	Nr	0.25	6.28	–	231.67	237.95	6.91	–	254.84	261.75
L101143N	900 × 1200 mm	Nr	0.25	6.28	–	237.98	244.26	6.91	–	261.78	268.69
L101143O	900 × 1350 mm	Nr	0.25	6.28	–	261.55	267.83	6.91	–	287.71	294.61
L101143P	900 × 1500 mm	Nr	0.25	6.28	–	269.27	275.55	6.91	–	296.20	303.11
L101143Q	900 × 1600 mm	Nr	0.25	6.28	–	274.66	280.94	6.91	–	302.13	309.03
L101143R	1200 × 600 mm	Nr	0.25	6.28	–	237.98	244.26	6.91	–	261.78	268.69
L101143S	1200 × 900 mm	Nr	0.25	6.28	–	246.62	252.90	6.91	–	271.28	278.19
L101143T	1200 × 1050 mm	Nr	0.25	6.28	–	252.44	258.72	6.91	–	277.68	284.59
L101143U	1200 × 1200 mm	Nr	0.25	6.28	–	259.14	265.42	6.91	–	285.05	291.96
L101143V	1200 × 1350 mm	Nr	0.25	6.28	–	284.75	291.03	6.91	–	313.23	320.13
L101143W	1200 × 1500 mm	Nr	0.25	6.28	–	293.27	299.55	6.91	–	322.60	329.51
L101143X	1200 × 1600 mm	Nr	0.25	6.28	–	299.18	305.46	6.91	–	329.10	336.01
L101143Y	1350 × 600 mm	Nr	0.28	6.91	–	243.56	250.47	7.60	–	267.92	275.52
L101143Z	1350 × 900 mm	Nr	0.28	6.91	–	253.81	260.72	7.60	–	279.19	286.79

Major Works 2009		Unit	Labour Hours	Labour Net	Plant Net	Materials Net	Unit Net	Labour Gross	Plant Gross	Materials Gross	Unit Price
								— (Gross rates include 10% profit) —			
				£	£	£	£	£	£	£	£
L10	**L10: WINDOWS, ROOFLIGHTS, SCREENS AND LOUVRES**										
L1011	**Standard softwood windows**										
L101145	**Boulton and Paul softwood windows; Hi-Profile Combi; bespoke manufacture; complete with all ironmongery:**										
L101145A	1350 × 1050 mm	Nr	0.28	6.91	–	260.05	266.96	7.60	–	286.06	293.66
L101145B	1350 × 1200 mm	Nr	0.28	6.91	–	268.36	275.27	7.60	–	295.20	302.80
L101145C	1350 × 1350 mm	Nr	0.28	6.91	–	295.00	301.91	7.60	–	324.50	332.10
L101145D	1500 × 600 mm.........	Nr	0.29	7.16	–	256.59	263.75	7.88	–	282.25	290.13
L101145E	1500 × 900 mm.........	Nr	0.29	7.16	–	263.29	270.45	7.88	–	289.62	297.50
L101145F	1500 × 1050 mm	Nr	0.29	7.16	–	280.85	288.01	7.88	–	308.94	316.81
L101145G	1500 × 1200 mm	Nr	0.29	7.16	–	290.48	297.64	7.88	–	319.53	327.40
L101145H	1500 × 1350 mm	Nr	0.29	7.16	–	304.15	311.31	7.88	–	334.57	342.44
L101145I	1500 × 1500 mm	Nr	0.29	7.16	–	311.43	318.59	7.88	–	342.57	350.45
L101145J	1800 × 1050 mm	Nr	0.30	7.54	–	303.26	310.80	8.29	–	333.59	341.88
L101145K	1800 × 1200 mm	Nr	0.30	7.54	–	308.66	316.20	8.29	–	339.53	347.82
L101145L	1800 × 1500 mm	Nr	0.30	7.54	–	331.15	338.69	8.29	–	364.27	372.56
L101147	**Boulton and Paul softwood windows; Hi-Profile; single casement and direct glazed; complete with all ironmongery:**										
L101147D	R2109D; 2100 × 900 mm	Nr	0.32	8.04	–	295.98	304.02	8.84	–	325.58	334.42
L101147E	R2110D; 2100 × 1050 mm	Nr	0.32	8.04	–	312.03	320.07	8.84	–	343.23	352.08
L101147F	R2112D; 2100 × 1200 mm	Nr	0.32	8.04	–	321.42	329.46	8.84	–	353.56	362.41
L101147G	R2209D; 2250 × 900 mm	Nr	0.32	8.04	–	300.73	308.77	8.84	–	330.80	339.65
L101147H	R2210D; 2250 × 1050 mm	Nr	0.32	8.04	–	316.82	324.86	8.84	–	348.50	357.35
L101147I	R2212D; 2250 × 1200 mm	Nr	0.32	8.04	–	326.22	334.26	8.84	–	358.84	367.69
L101147J	R2409D; 2400 × 900 mm	Nr	0.35	8.80	–	307.10	315.90	9.68	–	337.81	347.49
L101147K	R2410D; 2400 × 1050 mm	Nr	0.35	8.80	–	323.78	332.58	9.68	–	356.16	365.84
L101147L	R2412D; 2400 × 1200 mm	Nr	0.35	8.80	–	333.50	342.30	9.68	–	366.85	376.53
L101147M	R2415D; 2400 × 1500 mm	Nr	0.35	8.80	–	367.13	375.93	9.68	–	403.84	413.52
L101147N	R3015D; 3000 × 1500 mm	Nr	0.37	9.17	–	396.26	405.43	10.09	–	435.89	445.97
L101147O	R3615D; 3600 × 1500 mm	Nr	0.38	9.42	–	425.34	434.76	10.36	–	467.87	478.24
L101149	**Boulton and Paul softwood windows; Hi-Profile; feature windows; complete with all ironmongery:**										
L101149A	R04F12; 450 × 2100 mm.	Nr	0.20	5.03	–	315.65	320.68	5.53	–	347.22	352.75
L101149B	R06F12; 600 × 2100 mm.	Nr	0.23	5.78	–	412.27	418.05	6.36	–	453.50	459.86
L101149C	R09F12; 900 × 2100 mm.	Nr	0.23	5.78	–	424.14	429.92	6.36	–	466.55	472.91
L101149D	R12F12; 1200 × 2100 mm	Nr	0.27	6.78	–	478.85	485.63	7.46	–	526.74	534.19
L101149E	R15F12; 1500 × 2100 mm	Nr	0.33	8.16	–	640.20	648.36	8.98	–	704.22	713.20
L101151	**Boulton and Paul softwood windows; Skyview reversible roof windows; complete with ironmongery:**										
L101151A	550 × 780 mm; RL508...	Nr	0.85	14.43	–	170.27	184.70	15.87	–	187.30	203.17
L101151B	550 × 980 mm; RL510...	Nr	0.90	15.28	–	188.51	203.79	16.81	–	207.36	224.17
L101151C	780 × 980 mm; RL810...	Nr	1.00	16.98	–	214.15	231.13	18.68	–	235.57	254.24
L101151D	780 × 1180 mm; RL812..	Nr	1.30	22.07	–	222.49	244.56	24.28	–	244.74	269.02
L101151E	780 × 1400 mm; RL814FE	Nr	1.50	25.47	–	377.69	403.16	28.02	–	415.46	443.48
L101151F	1140 × 1180 mm; RL1112	Nr	1.50	25.47	–	273.32	298.79	28.02	–	300.65	328.67
L101151G	450 × 550 mm; RL555...	Nr	0.85	14.43	–	126.51	140.94	15.87	–	139.16	155.03

Windows, Doors and Stairs

Major Works 2009		Unit	Labour Hours	Labour Net	Plant Net	Materials Net	Unit Net	Labour Gross	Plant Gross	Materials Gross	Unit Price
								(Gross rates include 10% profit)			
				£	£	£	£	£	£	£	£
L10	**L10: WINDOWS, ROOFLIGHTS, SCREENS AND LOUVRES**										
L1012	**Softwood window sundries and accessories**										
L101251	**Boulton and Paul Skyview roof window tile flashing units:**										
L101251A	RL508TF	Nr	0.90	15.28	–	50.29	65.57	16.81	–	55.32	72.13
L101251B	RL510TF	Nr	0.95	16.13	–	54.08	70.21	17.74	–	59.49	77.23
L101251C	RL810TF	Nr	1.00	16.98	–	58.05	75.03	18.68	–	63.86	82.53
L101251D	RL812TF	Nr	1.25	21.23	–	64.67	85.90	23.35	–	71.14	94.49
L101251E	RL814TF	Nr	1.25	21.23	–	69.61	90.84	23.35	–	76.57	99.92
L101251F	RL1112TF	Nr	1.55	26.32	–	72.57	98.89	28.95	–	79.83	108.78
L101252	**Boulton and Paul softwood window surround sets; to suit window size:**										
L101252A	488 × 450 mm	Set	0.20	3.40	–	52.44	55.84	3.74	–	57.68	61.42
L101252B	488 × 600 mm	Set	0.20	3.40	–	56.69	60.09	3.74	–	62.36	66.10
L101252C	488 × 750 mm	Set	0.20	3.40	–	61.63	65.03	3.74	–	67.79	71.53
L101252D	488 × 900 mm	Set	0.20	3.40	–	66.13	69.53	3.74	–	72.74	76.48
L101252E	488 × 1050 mm	Set	0.20	3.40	–	70.24	73.64	3.74	–	77.26	81.00
L101252F	488 × 1200 mm	Set	0.20	3.40	–	75.31	78.71	3.74	–	82.84	86.58
L101252G	488 × 1350 mm	Set	0.20	3.40	–	79.87	83.27	3.74	–	87.86	91.60
L101252H	488 × 1500 mm	Set	0.20	3.40	–	84.24	87.64	3.74	–	92.66	96.40
L101252I	630 × 450 mm	Set	0.23	3.82	–	54.67	58.49	4.20	–	60.14	64.34
L101252J	630 × 600 mm	Set	0.23	3.82	–	59.17	62.99	4.20	–	65.09	69.29
L101252K	630 × 750 mm	Set	0.23	3.82	–	63.61	67.43	4.20	–	69.97	74.17
L101252L	630 × 900 mm	Set	0.23	3.82	–	68.50	72.32	4.20	–	75.35	79.55
L101252M	630 × 1050 mm	Set	0.23	3.82	–	72.42	76.24	4.20	–	79.66	83.86
L101252N	630 × 1200 mm	Set	0.23	3.82	–	77.62	81.44	4.20	–	85.38	89.58
L101252O	630 × 1350 mm	Set	0.23	3.82	–	82.57	86.39	4.20	–	90.83	95.03
L101252P	630 × 1500 mm	Set	0.23	3.82	–	85.69	89.51	4.20	–	94.26	98.46
L101252Q	915 × 450 mm	Set	0.25	4.25	–	59.17	63.42	4.68	–	65.09	69.76
L101252R	915 × 600 mm	Set	0.25	4.25	–	61.61	65.86	4.68	–	67.77	72.45
L101252S	915 × 750 mm	Set	0.25	4.25	–	68.50	72.75	4.68	–	75.35	80.03
L101252T	915 × 900 mm	Set	0.25	4.25	–	72.42	76.67	4.68	–	79.66	84.34
L101252U	915 × 1050 mm	Set	0.25	4.25	–	77.62	81.87	4.68	–	85.38	90.06
L101252V	915 × 1200 mm	Set	0.25	4.25	–	82.57	86.82	4.68	–	90.83	95.50
L101252W	915 × 1350 mm	Set	0.25	4.25	–	85.69	89.94	4.68	–	94.26	98.93
L101252X	915 × 1500 mm	Set	0.25	4.25	–	95.08	99.33	4.68	–	104.59	109.26
L101252Y	1200 × 450 mm	Set	0.30	5.10	–	63.61	68.71	5.61	–	69.97	75.58
L101252Z	1200 × 600 mm	Set	0.30	5.10	–	68.50	73.60	5.61	–	75.35	80.96

Major Works 2009		Unit	Labour Hours	Labour Net	Plant Net	Materials Net	Unit Net	Labour Gross	Plant Gross	Materials Gross	Unit Price
								(Gross rates include 10% profit)			
				£	£	£	£	£	£	£	£

L10   **L10: WINDOWS, ROOFLIGHTS, SCREENS AND LOUVRES**

L1012   **Softwood window sundries and accessories**

L101253   **Boulton and Paul softwood window surround sets; to suit window size:**

Code	Size	Unit	Labour Hours	Labour Net	Plant Net	Materials Net	Unit Net	Labour Gross	Plant Gross	Materials Gross	Unit Price
L101253A	1200 × 750 mm	Set	0.30	5.10	–	72.42	77.52	5.61	–	79.66	85.27
L101253B	1200 × 900 mm	Set	0.30	5.10	–	77.62	82.72	5.61	–	85.38	90.99
L101253C	1200 × 1050 mm	Set	0.30	5.10	–	82.47	87.57	5.61	–	90.72	96.33
L101253D	1200 × 1200 mm	Set	0.30	5.10	–	85.69	90.79	5.61	–	94.26	99.87
L101253E	1200 × 1350 mm	Set	0.30	5.10	–	95.08	100.18	5.61	–	104.59	110.20
L101253F	1200 × 1500 mm	Set	0.30	5.10	–	99.82	104.92	5.61	–	109.80	115.41
L101253G	1342 × 450 mm	Set	0.30	5.10	–	66.60	71.70	5.61	–	73.26	78.87
L101253H	1342 × 600 mm	Set	0.30	5.10	–	71.39	76.49	5.61	–	78.53	84.14
L101253I	1342 × 750 mm	Set	0.30	5.10	–	75.77	80.87	5.61	–	83.35	88.96
L101253J	1342 × 900 mm	Set	0.30	5.10	–	78.33	83.43	5.61	–	86.16	91.77
L101253K	1342 × 1050 mm	Set	0.30	5.10	–	86.68	91.78	5.61	–	95.35	100.96
L101253L	1342 × 1200 mm	Set	0.30	5.10	–	90.47	95.57	5.61	–	99.52	105.13
L101253M	1342 × 1350 mm	Set	0.30	5.10	–	98.26	103.36	5.61	–	108.09	113.70
L101253N	1342 × 1500 mm	Set	0.30	5.10	–	102.70	107.80	5.61	–	112.97	118.58
L101253O	1770 × 450 mm	Set	0.35	5.95	–	72.09	78.04	6.55	–	79.30	85.84
L101253P	1770 × 600 mm	Set	0.35	5.95	–	77.62	83.57	6.55	–	85.38	91.93
L101253Q	1770 × 750 mm	Set	0.35	5.95	–	82.57	88.52	6.55	–	90.83	97.37
L101253R	1770 × 900 mm	Set	0.35	5.95	–	88.39	94.34	6.55	–	97.23	103.77
L101253S	1770 × 1050 mm	Set	0.35	5.95	–	95.08	101.03	6.55	–	104.59	111.13
L101253T	1770 × 1200 mm	Set	0.35	5.95	–	99.82	105.77	6.55	–	109.80	116.35
L101253U	1770 × 1350 mm	Set	0.35	5.95	–	104.35	110.30	6.55	–	114.79	121.33
L101253V	1770 × 1500 mm	Set	0.35	5.95	–	108.82	114.77	6.55	–	119.70	126.25
L101253W	2339 × 450 mm	Set	0.40	6.79	–	82.57	89.36	7.47	–	90.83	98.30
L101253X	2339 × 600 mm	Set	0.40	6.79	–	85.59	92.38	7.47	–	94.15	101.62
L101253Y	2339 × 750 mm	Set	0.40	6.79	–	95.08	101.87	7.47	–	104.59	112.06
L101253Z	2339 × 900 mm	Set	0.40	6.79	–	99.82	106.61	7.47	–	109.80	117.27

L101254   **Boulton and Paul softwood window surround sets; to suit window size:**

Code	Size	Unit	Labour Hours	Labour Net	Plant Net	Materials Net	Unit Net	Labour Gross	Plant Gross	Materials Gross	Unit Price
L101254A	2339 × 1050 mm	Set	0.50	8.49	–	104.38	112.87	9.34	–	114.82	124.16
L101254B	2339 × 1200 mm	Set	0.50	8.49	–	108.98	117.47	9.34	–	119.88	129.22
L101254C	2339 × 1350 mm	Set	0.50	8.49	–	113.14	121.63	9.34	–	124.45	133.79
L101254D	2339 × 1500 mm	Set	0.50	8.49	–	122.19	130.68	9.34	–	134.41	143.75

L101255   **Boulton and Paul softwood cambered heads:**

Code	Size	Unit	Labour Hours	Labour Net	Plant Net	Materials Net	Unit Net	Labour Gross	Plant Gross	Materials Gross	Unit Price
L101255A	483 mm wide; CAM483	Nr	0.15	2.55	–	9.05	11.60	2.81	–	9.96	12.76
L101255B	626 mm wide; CAM626	Nr	0.15	2.55	–	9.80	12.35	2.81	–	10.78	13.59
L101255C	913 mm wide; CAM913	Nr	0.20	3.40	–	11.87	15.27	3.74	–	13.06	16.80
L101255D	1200 mm wide; CAM1200	Nr	0.25	4.24	–	13.84	18.08	4.66	–	15.22	19.89
L101255E	1343 mm wide; CAM1343	Nr	0.30	5.09	–	15.09	20.18	5.60	–	16.60	22.20
L101255F	1774 mm wide; CAM1774	Nr	0.35	5.94	–	16.26	22.20	6.53	–	17.89	24.42
L101255G	2348 mm wide; CAM2348	Nr	0.40	6.79	–	22.67	29.46	7.47	–	24.94	32.41

L101258   **Boulton and Paul softwood window board; 32 × 225 mm; fixing with ties to masonry backgrounds:**

Code	Size	Unit	Labour Hours	Labour Net	Plant Net	Materials Net	Unit Net	Labour Gross	Plant Gross	Materials Gross	Unit Price
L101258A	488 mm long	Set	0.60	10.19	–	20.16	30.35	11.21	–	22.18	33.39
L101258B	630 mm long	Set	0.75	12.74	–	23.90	36.64	14.01	–	26.29	40.30
L101258C	915 mm long	Set	0.85	14.44	–	31.00	45.44	15.88	–	34.10	49.98
L101258D	1200 mm long	Set	0.95	16.14	–	38.11	54.25	17.75	–	41.92	59.68
L101258E	1342 mm long	Set	1.15	19.52	–	41.85	61.37	21.47	–	46.04	67.51
L101258F	1770 mm long	Set	1.20	20.37	–	51.80	72.17	22.41	–	56.98	79.39
L101258G	2339 mm long	Set	1.25	21.22	–	64.22	85.44	23.34	–	70.64	93.98

Windows, Doors and Stairs

Major Works 2009		Unit	Labour Hours	Labour Net	Plant Net	Materials Net	Unit Net	Labour Gross	Plant Gross	Materials Gross	Unit Price
								— (Gross rates include 10% profit) —			
				£	£	£	£	£	£	£	£
L10	**L10: WINDOWS, ROOFLIGHTS, SCREENS AND LOUVRES**										
L1013	**Purpose made window frames; treated softwood; casement style**										
L101382	**Casement style frames; rebated moulded sections; frame size not exceeding 1.0 m²:**										
L101382X	small pane, not exceeding 0.10 m²	m²	0.25	6.28	–	232.14	238.42	6.91	–	255.35	262.26
L101382Y	medium pane, 0.10-0.50 m²	m²	0.23	5.66	–	191.35	197.01	6.23	–	210.49	216.71
L101382Z	large pane, over 0.50 m² ...	m²	0.20	5.02	–	174.47	179.49	5.52	–	191.92	197.44
L101383	**Casement style frames; rebated moulded sections; frame size 1.0-2.0 m²:**										
L101383A	small pane, not exceeding 0.10 m²	m²	0.25	6.28	–	190.81	197.09	6.91	–	209.89	216.80
L101383B	medium pane, 0.10-0.50 m²	m²	0.23	5.65	–	162.90	168.55	6.22	–	179.19	185.41
L101383C	large pane, over 0.50 m² ...	m²	0.20	5.03	–	153.76	158.79	5.53	–	169.14	174.67
L101384	**Casement style frames; rebated moulded sections; frame size over 2.0 m²:**										
L101384A	small pane, not exceeding 0.10 m²	m²	0.25	6.28	–	177.28	183.56	6.91	–	195.01	201.92
L101384B	medium pane, 0.10-0.50 m²	m²	0.23	5.65	–	145.40	151.05	6.22	–	159.94	166.16
L101384C	large pane, over 0.50 m² ...	m²	0.20	5.02	–	136.73	141.75	5.52	–	150.40	155.93
L1014	**Purpose made window frames; treated softwood; sliding sash style**										
L101486	**Sliding sash style; rebated moulded sections; including spiral spring balances; frame size not exceeding 1.5 m²:**										
L101486A	small pane, not exceeding 0.10 m²	m²	0.75	14.77	–	358.42	373.19	16.25	–	394.26	410.51
L101486B	medium pane, 0.10-0.50 m²	m²	0.75	14.77	–	295.21	309.98	16.25	–	324.73	340.98
L101486C	large pane, over 0.50 m² ...	m²	0.75	14.77	–	269.02	283.79	16.25	–	295.92	312.17
L101487	**Sliding sash style; rebated moulded sections; including spiral spring balances; frame size over 1.5 m²:**										
L101487A	small pane, not exceeding 0.10 m²	m²	0.75	14.77	–	336.85	351.62	16.25	–	370.54	386.78
L101487B	medium pane, 0.10-0.50 m²	m²	0.75	14.77	–	277.47	292.24	16.25	–	305.22	321.46
L101487C	large pane, over 0.50 m² ...	m²	0.75	14.77	–	252.85	267.62	16.25	–	278.14	294.38

Major Works 2009		Unit	Labour Hours	Labour Net	Plant Net	Materials Net	Unit Net	Labour Gross	Plant Gross	Materials Gross	Unit Price
								(Gross rates include 10% profit)			
				£	£	£	£	£	£	£	£
L10	**L10: WINDOWS, ROOFLIGHTS, SCREENS AND LOUVRES**										
L1016	**Standard hardwood windows**										
L101630	**Boulton and Paul hardwood windows; Sovereign; casement; plain, transom and landscape; insulating glass units; standard sill; complete with ironmongery; size:**										
L101630A	630 × 750 mm; W107CH .	Nr	0.20	3.39	–	216.39	219.78	3.73	–	238.03	241.76
L101630B	630 × 900 mm; W109CH .	Nr	0.20	3.39	–	228.74	232.13	3.73	–	251.61	255.34
L101630C	630 × 1050 mm; W110CH	Nr	0.20	3.39	–	181.39	184.78	3.73	–	199.53	203.26
L101630D	630 × 1200 mm; W112CH	Nr	0.20	3.39	–	105.77	109.16	3.73	–	116.35	120.08
L101630E	630 × 1350 mm; W113CH	Nr	0.20	3.39	–	202.53	205.92	3.73	–	222.78	226.51
L101630F	1200 × 750 mm; W207CH	Nr	0.25	4.24	–	214.31	218.55	4.66	–	235.74	240.41
L101630G	1200 × 900 mm; W209CH	Nr	0.25	4.24	–	224.94	229.18	4.66	–	247.43	252.10
L101630H	1200 × 1050 mm; W210CH	Nr	0.25	4.24	–	233.06	237.30	4.66	–	256.37	261.03
L101630I	1200 × 1200 mm; W212CH	Nr	0.25	4.24	–	242.90	247.14	4.66	–	267.19	271.85
L101630J	1200 × 1350 mm; W213CH	Nr	0.25	4.24	–	259.40	263.64	4.66	–	285.34	290.00
L101630K	1200 × 900 mm; W209CCH	Nr	0.25	4.24	–	315.57	319.81	4.66	–	347.13	351.79
L101630L	1200 × 1050 mm; W210CCH	Nr	0.25	4.24	–	330.68	334.92	4.66	–	363.75	368.41
L101630M	1200 × 1200 mm; W212CCH	Nr	0.25	4.24	–	344.16	348.40	4.66	–	378.58	383.24
L101630N	1200 × 1350 mm; W213CCH	Nr	0.25	4.24	–	372.65	376.89	4.66	–	409.92	414.58
L101630O	1770 × 750 mm; W307CCH	Nr	0.30	5.09	–	324.88	329.97	5.60	–	357.37	362.97
L101630P	1770 × 900 mm; W309CCH	Nr	0.30	5.09	–	340.70	345.79	5.60	–	374.77	380.37
L101630Q	1770 × 1050 mm; W310CCH	Nr	0.30	5.09	–	354.28	359.37	5.60	–	389.71	395.31
L101630R	1770 × 1200 mm; W312CCH	Nr	0.30	5.09	–	368.21	373.30	5.60	–	405.03	410.63
L101630S	1770 × 1350 mm; W313CCH	Nr	0.30	5.09	–	394.52	399.61	5.60	–	433.97	439.57
L101630T	2339 × 900 mm; W409CMCH	Nr	0.35	5.94	–	429.77	435.71	6.53	–	472.75	479.28
L101630U	2339 × 1050 mm; W410CMCH	Nr	0.35	5.94	–	440.00	445.94	6.53	–	484.00	490.53
L101630V	2339 × 1200 mm; W412CMCH	Nr	0.35	5.94	–	459.51	465.45	6.53	–	505.46	512.00
L101630W	2339 × 1350 mm; W413CMCH	Nr	0.35	5.94	–	489.92	495.86	6.53	–	538.91	545.45
L101630X	630 × 1050 mm; W110TH	Nr	0.20	3.39	–	240.29	243.68	3.73	–	264.32	268.05
L101630Y	630 × 1200 mm; W112TH	Nr	0.20	3.39	–	247.73	251.12	3.73	–	272.50	276.23
L101630Z	915 × 900 mm; W2N09WH	Nr	0.25	4.24	–	206.98	211.22	4.66	–	227.68	232.34

Windows, Doors and Stairs

Major Works 2009		Unit	Labour Hours	Labour Net	Plant Net	Materials Net	Unit Net	Labour Gross	Plant Gross	Materials Gross	Unit Price
								— (Gross rates include 10% profit) —			
				£	£	£	£	£	£	£	£
L10	**L10: WINDOWS, ROOFLIGHTS, SCREENS AND LOUVRES**										
L1016	**Standard hardwood windows**										
L101631	**Boulton and Paul hardwood windows; Sovereign; casement; landscape; narrow module; casement vents; standard sill; complete with ironmongery; size:**										
L101631A	915 × 1050 mm; W2N10WH	Nr	0.25	4.24	–	210.33	214.57	4.66	–	231.36	236.03
L101631B	915 × 1200 mm; W2N12WH	Nr	0.25	4.24	–	215.55	219.79	4.66	–	237.11	241.77
L101631C	915 × 1350 mm; W2N13WH	Nr	0.25	4.24	–	220.45	224.69	4.66	–	242.50	247.16
L101631D	1200 × 900 mm; W209WH	Nr	0.28	4.67	–	236.24	240.91	5.14	–	259.86	265.00
L101631E	1200 × 1050 mm; W210WH	Nr	0.28	4.67	–	240.80	245.47	5.14	–	264.88	270.02
L101631F	1200 × 1200 mm; W212WH	Nr	0.28	4.67	–	245.63	250.30	5.14	–	270.19	275.33
L101631G	1770 × 1050 mm; W310CWH	Nr	0.30	5.09	–	361.73	366.82	5.60	–	397.90	403.50
L101631H	1770 × 1200 mm; W312CWH	Nr	0.30	5.09	–	371.51	376.60	5.60	–	408.66	414.26
L101631I	630 × 750 mm; W107VH	Nr	0.20	3.39	–	160.13	163.52	3.73	–	176.14	179.87
L101631J	630 × 900 mm; W109VH	Nr	0.20	3.39	–	165.74	169.13	3.73	–	182.31	186.04
L101631K	630 × 1050 mm; W110VH	Nr	0.20	3.39	–	169.97	173.36	3.73	–	186.97	190.70
L101631L	630 × 1200 mm; W112VH	Nr	0.20	3.39	–	174.74	178.13	3.73	–	192.21	195.94
L101631M	630 × 1350 mm; W113VH	Nr	0.20	3.39	–	180.48	183.87	3.73	–	198.53	202.26
L101631N	1200 × 900 mm; W209CVH	Nr	0.28	4.67	–	283.82	288.49	5.14	–	312.20	317.34
L101631O	1200 × 1050 mm; W210CVH	Nr	0.28	4.67	–	292.54	297.21	5.14	–	321.79	326.93
L101631P	1200 × 1200 mm; W212CVH	Nr	0.28	4.67	–	302.83	307.50	5.14	–	333.11	338.25
L101631Q	1200 × 1350 mm; W213CVH	Nr	0.28	4.67	–	318.45	323.12	5.14	–	350.30	355.43
L101631R	1770 × 900 mm; W309CVCH	Nr	0.30	5.09	–	399.29	404.38	5.60	–	439.22	444.82
L101631S	1770 × 1050 mm; W310CVCH	Nr	0.30	5.09	–	412.94	418.03	5.60	–	454.23	459.83
L101631T	1770 × 1200 mm; W312CVCH	Nr	0.30	5.09	–	427.95	433.04	5.60	–	470.75	476.34
L101631U	1770 × 1350 mm; W313CVCH	Nr	0.30	5.09	–	454.22	459.31	5.60	–	499.64	505.24
L101631V	2339 × 1200 mm; W412CVVH	Nr	0.35	5.94	–	536.54	542.48	6.53	–	590.19	596.73
L101631W	2339 × 1350 mm; W413CVVCH	Nr	0.35	5.94	–	566.66	572.60	6.53	–	623.33	629.86
L101631X	488 × 750 mm; WN07VH	Nr	0.15	2.54	–	133.91	136.45	2.79	–	147.30	150.10
L101631Y	488 × 900 mm; WN09VH	Nr	0.15	2.54	–	138.82	141.36	2.79	–	152.70	155.50
L101631Z	488 × 1050 mm; WN10VH	Nr	0.15	2.54	–	143.74	146.28	2.79	–	158.11	160.91

Major Works 2009		Unit	Labour Hours	Labour Net	Plant Net	Materials Net	Unit Net	Labour Gross	Plant Gross	Materials Gross	Unit Price
								(Gross rates include 10% profit)			
			£	£	£	£	£	£	£	£	£
L10	**L10: WINDOWS, ROOFLIGHTS, SCREENS AND LOUVRES**										
L1016	**Standard hardwood windows**										
L101632	**Boulton and Paul hardwood windows; Sovereign; casement, narrow module; standard sill; complete with ironmongery; size:**										
L101632A	488 × 750 mm; WN07CH.	Nr	0.15	2.54	–	146.84	149.38	2.79	–	161.52	164.32
L101632B	488 × 900 mm; WN09CH.	Nr	0.15	2.54	–	153.24	155.78	2.79	–	168.56	171.36
L101632C	488 × 1050 mm; WN10CH	Nr	0.15	2.54	–	160.47	163.01	2.79	–	176.52	179.31
L101632D	488 × 1200 mm; WN12CH	Nr	0.15	2.54	–	166.21	168.75	2.79	–	182.83	185.63
L101632E	915 × 750 mm; W2N07CH	Nr	0.25	4.24	–	207.82	212.06	4.66	–	228.60	233.27
L101632F	915 × 900 mm; W2N09CH	Nr	0.25	4.24	–	216.97	221.21	4.66	–	238.67	243.33
L101632G	915 × 1050 mm; W2N10CH	Nr	0.25	4.24	–	224.76	229.00	4.66	–	247.24	251.90
L101632H	915 × 1200 mm; W2N12CH	Nr	0.25	4.24	–	233.18	237.42	4.66	–	256.50	261.16
L101632I	915 × 900 mm; W2N09CCH.	Nr	0.25	4.24	–	291.27	295.51	4.66	–	320.40	325.06
L101632J	915 × 1050 mm; W2N10CCH.	Nr	0.25	4.24	–	303.90	308.14	4.66	–	334.29	338.95
L101632K	915 × 1200 mm; W2N12CCH.	Nr	0.25	4.24	–	316.06	320.30	4.66	–	347.67	352.33
L101632L	1342 × 1050 mm; W3N10CCH.	Nr	0.29	4.84	–	336.31	341.15	5.32	–	369.94	375.27
L101632M	1342 × 1200 mm; W3N12CCH.	Nr	0.29	4.84	–	348.86	353.70	5.32	–	383.75	389.07
L101632N	1770 × 1050 mm; W4N10CMCH.	Nr	0.30	5.09	–	423.23	428.32	5.60	–	465.55	471.15
L101632O	1700 × 1200 mm; W4N12CMCH.	Nr	0.30	5.09	–	440.08	445.17	5.60	–	484.09	489.69
L101633	**Boulton and Paul hardwood windows; Sovereign; top hung; standard sill; complete with ironmongery; size:**										
L101633A	630 × 450 mm; W104AH.	Nr	0.28	4.67	–	238.97	243.64	5.14	–	262.87	268.00
L101633B	630 × 600 mm; W106AH.	Nr	0.28	4.67	–	247.39	252.06	5.14	–	272.13	277.27
L101633C	630 × 750 mm; W107AH.	Nr	0.28	4.67	–	262.58	267.25	5.14	–	288.84	293.98
L101633D	630 × 900 mm; W109AH.	Nr	0.28	4.67	–	272.18	276.85	5.14	–	299.40	304.54
L101633E	915 × 450 mm; W2N04AH	Nr	0.28	4.67	–	280.59	285.26	5.14	–	308.65	313.79
L101633F	915 × 600 mm; W2N06AH	Nr	0.25	4.24	–	210.60	214.84	4.66	–	231.66	236.32
L101633G	915 × 750 mm; W2N07AH	Nr	0.25	4.24	–	218.23	222.47	4.66	–	240.05	244.72
L101633H	915 × 900 mm; W2N09AH	Nr	0.25	4.24	–	235.10	239.34	4.66	–	258.61	263.27
L101633I	915 × 1050 mm; W2N10AH	Nr	0.25	4.24	–	244.34	248.58	4.66	–	268.77	273.44
L101633J	915 × 1200 mm; W2N12AH	Nr	0.25	4.24	–	251.90	256.14	4.66	–	277.09	281.75
L101633K	1200 × 450 mm; W204AH	Nr	0.28	4.67	–	217.22	221.89	5.14	–	238.94	244.08
L101633L	1200 × 600 mm; W206AH	Nr	0.28	4.67	–	238.97	243.64	5.14	–	262.87	268.00
L101633M	1200 × 750 mm; W207AH	Nr	0.28	4.67	–	247.39	252.06	5.14	–	272.13	277.27
L101633N	1200 × 900 mm; W209AH	Nr	0.28	4.67	–	262.58	267.25	5.14	–	288.84	293.98
L101633O	1200 × 1050 mm; W210AH	Nr	0.28	4.67	–	272.18	276.85	5.14	–	299.40	304.54
L101633P	1200 × 1200 mm; W212AH	Nr	0.28	4.67	–	280.59	285.26	5.14	–	308.65	313.79

Windows, Doors and Stairs

Major Works 2009		Unit	Labour Hours	Labour Net	Plant Net	Materials Net	Unit Net	Labour Gross	Plant Gross	Materials Gross	Unit Price
								(Gross rates include 10% profit)			
				£	£	£	£	£	£	£	£
L10	**L10: WINDOWS, ROOFLIGHTS, SCREENS AND LOUVRES**										
L1016	**Standard hardwood windows**										
L101634	**Boulton and Paul hardwood square bay assemblies:**										
L101634A	two return ends; SQ2H	Nr	0.30	5.09	–	220.66	225.75	5.60	–	242.73	248.33
L101634B	two return ends; SQ3H	Nr	0.45	7.64	–	220.66	228.30	8.40	–	242.73	251.13
L101634C	two return ends; SQ4H	Nr	0.60	10.19	–	220.66	230.85	11.21	–	242.73	253.94
L101634D	one return end; SQR2H ...	Nr	0.30	5.09	–	105.89	110.98	5.60	–	116.48	122.08
L101634E	one return end; SQR3H	Nr	0.45	7.64	–	105.89	113.53	8.40	–	116.48	124.88
L101634F	one return end; SQR4H ..	Nr	0.60	10.19	–	105.89	116.08	11.21	–	116.48	127.69
L101634G	narrow module two return ends; SQ2NH	Nr	0.30	5.09	–	220.66	225.75	5.60	–	242.73	248.33
L101634H	narrow module two return ends; SQ3NH	Nr	0.45	7.64	–	220.66	228.30	8.40	–	242.73	251.13
L101634I	narrow module two return ends; SQ4NH	Nr	0.60	10.19	–	220.66	230.85	11.21	–	242.73	253.94
L101634J	narrow module; one return end; SQR2N	Nr	0.30	5.09	–	105.89	110.98	5.60	–	116.48	122.08
L101634K	narrow module; one return end; SQR3N	Nr	0.45	7.64	–	105.89	113.53	8.40	–	116.48	124.88
L101634L	narrow module; one return end; SQR4N	Nr	0.60	10.19	–	105.89	116.08	11.21	–	116.48	127.69
L101635	**Boulton and Paul hardwood splay bay assemblies:**										
L101635A	two return ends; SP145H ..	Nr	0.30	5.09	–	220.66	225.75	5.60	–	242.73	248.33
L101635B	two return ends; SP245H ..	Nr	0.45	7.64	–	220.66	228.30	8.40	–	242.73	251.13
L101635C	two return ends; SP345H ..	Nr	0.60	10.19	–	220.66	230.85	11.21	–	242.73	253.94
L101635D	two return ends; SP445H ..	Nr	0.75	12.73	–	220.66	233.39	14.00	–	242.73	256.73
L101635E	one return end; SPR145H ..	Nr	0.30	5.09	–	105.89	110.98	5.60	–	116.48	122.08
L101635F	one return end; SPR245H ..	Nr	0.45	7.64	–	105.89	113.53	8.40	–	116.48	124.88
L101635G	one return end; SPR345H ..	Nr	0.60	10.19	–	105.89	116.08	11.21	–	116.48	127.69
L101635H	one return end; SPR445H ..	Nr	0.75	12.73	–	105.89	118.62	14.00	–	116.48	130.48
L101635I	narrow module; two return ends; SP2N45H	Nr	0.45	7.64	–	220.66	228.30	8.40	–	242.73	251.13
L101635J	narrow module; two return ends; SP3N45H	Nr	0.60	10.19	–	220.66	230.85	11.21	–	242.73	253.94
L101635K	narrow module; two return ends; SP4N45H	Nr	0.75	12.73	–	220.66	233.39	14.00	–	242.73	256.73
L101635L	narrow module; one return end; SPR2N45H	Nr	0.45	7.64	–	105.89	113.53	8.40	–	116.48	124.88
L101635M	narrow module; one return end; SPR3N45H	Nr	0.60	10.19	–	105.89	116.08	11.21	–	116.48	127.69
L101635N	narrow module; one return end; SPR4N45H	Nr	0.75	12.73	–	105.89	118.62	14.00	–	116.48	130.48

Major Works 2009		Unit	Labour Hours	Labour Net	Plant Net	Materials Net	Unit Net	Labour Gross	Plant Gross	Materials Gross	Unit Price
								(Gross rates include 10% profit)			
				£	£	£	£	£	£	£	£
L10	**L10: WINDOWS, ROOFLIGHTS, SCREENS AND LOUVRES**										
L1016	**Standard hardwood windows**										
L101639	**Boulton and Paul hardwood casement windows; horizontal bar; narrow module; standard sill; complete with ironmongery; size:**										
L101639A	488 × 1050 mm; WHN10CH..............	Nr	0.30	5.09	–	160.47	165.56	5.60	–	176.52	182.12
L101639B	488 × 1200 mm; WHN12CH..............	Nr	0.30	5.09	–	166.21	171.30	5.60	–	182.83	188.43
L101639C	488 × 1350 mm; WHN13CH..............	Nr	0.30	5.09	–	197.87	202.96	5.60	–	217.66	223.26
L101639D	915 × 1050 mm; WH2N10CH.............	Nr	0.32	5.43	–	259.28	264.71	5.97	–	285.21	291.18
L101639E	915 × 1200 mm; WH2N12CH.............	Nr	0.32	5.43	–	269.51	274.94	5.97	–	296.46	302.43
L101639F	915 × 1350 mm; WH2N13CH.............	Nr	0.32	5.43	–	286.27	291.70	5.97	–	314.90	320.87
L101639G	915 × 1050 mm; WH2N10CCH...........	Nr	0.33	5.60	–	345.11	350.71	6.16	–	379.62	385.78
L101639H	915 × 1200 mm; WH2N12CCH...........	Nr	0.33	5.60	–	358.76	364.36	6.16	–	394.64	400.80
L101639I	915 × 1350 mm; WH2N13CCH...........	Nr	0.33	5.60	–	382.76	388.36	6.16	–	421.04	427.20
L101639J	1342 × 1050 mm; WH3N10CCH...........	Nr	0.35	5.94	–	388.50	394.44	6.53	–	427.35	433.88
L101639K	1342 × 1200 mm; WH3N12CCH...........	Nr	0.35	5.94	–	403.28	409.22	6.53	–	443.61	450.14
L101639L	1342 × 1350 mm; WH3N13CCH...........	Nr	0.35	5.94	–	430.64	436.58	6.53	–	473.70	480.24
L101639M	1770 × 1050 mm; W4N10CMCH...........	Nr	0.35	5.94	–	480.03	485.97	6.53	–	528.03	534.57
L101639N	1770 × 1200 mm; W4N12CMCH...........	Nr	0.36	6.11	–	511.70	517.81	6.72	–	562.87	569.59
L101639O	1770 × 1350 mm; W4N13CMCH...........	Nr	0.38	6.45	–	710.03	716.48	7.10	–	781.03	788.13

Major Works 2009		Unit	Labour Hours	Labour Net	Plant Net	Materials Net	Unit Net	Labour Gross	Plant Gross	Materials Gross	Unit Price
				£	£	£	£	£	£	£	£
								— (Gross rates include 10% profit) —			
L10	**L10: WINDOWS, ROOFLIGHTS, SCREENS AND LOUVRES**										
L1017	**Hardwood window sundries and accessories**										
L101759	**Boulton and Paul hardwood window surround sets; to suit window size:**										
L101759A	488 × 750 mm	Set	0.25	4.25	–	122.13	126.38	4.68	–	134.34	139.02
L101759B	488 × 900 mm	Set	0.25	4.25	–	131.48	135.73	4.68	–	144.63	149.30
L101759C	488 × 1050 mm	Set	0.25	4.25	–	139.73	143.98	4.68	–	153.70	158.38
L101759D	488 × 1200 mm	Set	0.25	4.25	–	149.48	153.73	4.68	–	164.43	169.10
L101759E	488 × 1350 mm	Set	0.25	4.25	–	158.48	162.73	4.68	–	174.33	179.00
L101759F	630 × 750 mm	Set	0.28	4.67	–	126.23	130.90	5.14	–	138.85	143.99
L101759G	630 × 900 mm	Set	0.28	4.67	–	135.98	140.65	5.14	–	149.58	154.72
L101759H	630 × 1050 mm	Set	0.28	4.67	–	143.48	148.15	5.14	–	157.83	162.97
L101759I	630 × 1200 mm	Set	0.28	4.67	–	154.73	159.40	5.14	–	170.20	175.34
L101759J	630 × 1350 mm	Set	0.28	4.67	–	164.48	169.15	5.14	–	180.93	186.07
L101759K	915 × 750 mm	Set	0.30	5.10	–	135.98	141.08	5.61	–	149.58	155.19
L101759L	915 × 900 mm	Set	0.30	5.10	–	143.48	148.58	5.61	–	157.83	163.44
L101759M	915 × 1050 mm	Set	0.30	5.10	–	154.73	159.83	5.61	–	170.20	175.81
L101759N	915 × 1200 mm	Set	0.30	5.10	–	164.48	169.58	5.61	–	180.93	186.54
L101759O	915 × 1350 mm	Set	0.30	5.10	–	170.48	175.58	5.61	–	187.53	193.14
L101759P	1200 × 750 mm	Set	0.33	5.61	–	143.48	149.09	6.17	–	157.83	164.00
L101759Q	1200 × 900 mm	Set	0.33	5.61	–	154.73	160.34	6.17	–	170.20	176.37
L101759R	1200 × 1050 mm	Set	0.33	5.61	–	162.98	168.59	6.17	–	179.28	185.45
L101759S	1200 × 1200 mm	Set	0.33	5.61	–	169.73	175.34	6.17	–	186.70	192.87
L101759T	1200 × 1350 mm	Set	0.33	5.61	–	188.48	194.09	6.17	–	207.33	213.50
L101759U	1342 × 750 mm	Set	0.33	5.61	–	149.48	155.09	6.17	–	164.43	170.60
L101759V	1342 × 900 mm	Set	0.33	5.61	–	155.48	161.09	6.17	–	171.03	177.20
L101759W	1342 × 1050 mm	Set	0.33	5.61	–	171.98	177.59	6.17	–	189.18	195.35
L101759X	1342 × 1200 mm	Set	0.33	5.61	–	179.48	185.09	6.17	–	197.43	203.60
L101759Y	1342 × 1350 mm	Set	0.33	5.61	–	195.98	201.59	6.17	–	215.58	221.75
L101759Z	1770 × 750 mm	Set	0.39	6.54	–	162.98	169.52	7.19	–	179.28	186.47
L101760	**Boulton and Paul hardwood window surround sets; to suit window size:**										
L101760A	1770 × 900 mm	Set	0.39	6.54	–	175.73	182.27	7.19	–	193.30	200.50
L101760B	1770 × 1050 mm	Set	0.39	6.54	–	188.48	195.02	7.19	–	207.33	214.52
L101760C	1770 × 1200 mm	Set	0.39	6.54	–	197.48	204.02	7.19	–	217.23	224.42
L101760D	1770 × 1350 mm	Set	0.39	6.54	–	206.48	213.02	7.19	–	227.13	234.32
L101760E	2339 × 750 mm	Set	0.45	7.64	–	188.48	196.12	8.40	–	207.33	215.73
L101760F	2339 × 900 mm	Set	0.45	7.64	–	197.48	205.12	8.40	–	217.23	225.63
L101760G	2339 × 1050 mm	Set	0.45	7.64	–	206.48	214.12	8.40	–	227.13	235.53
L101760H	2339 × 1200 mm	Set	0.45	7.64	–	216.98	224.62	8.40	–	238.68	247.08
L101760I	2339 × 1350 mm	Set	0.45	7.64	–	224.48	232.12	8.40	–	246.93	255.33
L101761	**Proprietary hardwood cambered heads:**										
L101761A	483 mm wide; CAM483H...	Nr	0.20	3.40	–	22.85	26.25	3.74	–	25.14	28.88
L101761B	626 mm wide; CAM626H...	Nr	0.20	3.40	–	25.33	28.73	3.74	–	27.86	31.60
L101761C	913 mm wide; CAM913H...	Nr	0.25	4.25	–	29.95	34.20	4.68	–	32.95	37.62
L101761D	1200 mm wide; CAM1200H	Nr	0.30	5.09	–	35.58	40.67	5.60	–	39.14	44.74
L101761E	1343 mm wide; CAM1343H	Nr	0.35	5.94	–	38.47	44.41	6.53	–	42.32	48.85
L101761F	1774 mm wide; CAM1774H	Nr	0.35	5.94	–	41.71	47.65	6.53	–	45.88	52.42
L101761G	2348 mm wide; CAM2348H	Nr	0.45	7.64	–	55.91	63.55	8.40	–	61.50	69.91

Major Works 2009		Unit	Labour Hours	Labour Net	Plant Net	Materials Net	Unit Net	Labour Gross	Plant Gross	Materials Gross	Unit Price
								(Gross rates include 10% profit)			
				£	£	£	£	£	£	£	£
L10	**L10: WINDOWS, ROOFLIGHTS, SCREENS AND LOUVRES**										
L1018	**Purpose made window frames; hardwood; casement style**										
L101892	**Casement style frames; rebated moulded sections; frame size not exceeding 1.0 m²:**										
L101892A	medium pane, not exceeding 0.50 m²	m²	0.25	6.28	–	247.84	254.12	6.91	–	272.62	279.53
L101892B	large pane, over 0.50 m² ...	m²	0.23	5.65	–	318.11	323.76	6.22	–	349.92	356.14
L101893	**Casement style frames; rebated moulded sections; frame size 1.0-2.0 m²:**										
L101893A	medium pane, not exceeding 0.50 m²	m²	0.25	6.28	–	216.46	222.74	6.91	–	238.11	245.01
L101893B	large pane, over 0.50 m² ...	m²	0.23	5.65	–	196.20	201.85	6.22	–	215.82	222.04
L101894	**Casement style frames; rebated moulded sections; frame size over 2.0 m²:**										
L101894A	medium pane, not exceeding 0.50 m²	m²	0.25	6.28	–	186.96	193.24	6.91	–	205.66	212.56
L101894B	large pane, over 0.50 m² ...	m²	0.23	5.65	–	170.25	175.90	6.22	–	187.28	193.49
L1019	**Purpose made window frames; hardwood; sliding sash style**										
L101996	**Sliding sash style frames; rebated moulded sections; including spiral spring balances; frame size not exceeding 1.5 m²:**										
L101996A	medium pane, not exceeding 0.50 m²	m²	0.90	17.32	–	380.36	397.68	19.05	–	418.40	437.45
L101996B	large pane, over 0.50 m² ...	m²	0.90	17.31	–	349.44	366.75	19.04	–	384.38	403.43
L101997	**Sliding sash style frames; rebated moulded sections; including spiral spring balances; frame size over 1.5 m²**										
L101997A	medium pane, not exceeding 0.50 m²	m²	0.90	17.31	–	360.93	378.24	19.04	–	397.02	416.06
L101997B	large pane, over 0.50 m² ...	m²	0.90	17.32	–	328.85	346.17	19.05	–	361.74	380.79

Windows, Doors and Stairs

Major Works 2009		Unit	Labour Hours	Labour Net	Plant Net	Materials Net	Unit Net	Labour Gross	Plant Gross	Materials Gross	Unit Price
								(Gross rates include 10% profit)			
				£	£	£	£	£	£	£	£
L10	**L10: WINDOWS, ROOFLIGHTS, SCREENS AND LOUVRES**										
L1040	**Rooflights; PVC single skin dome lights complete with outer flange, rubber seal and fixings**										
L104093	**Square rooflights; fixing to upstands:**										
L104093A	650 × 650 mm..........	Nr	0.50	8.49	–	99.46	107.95	9.34	–	109.41	118.75
L104093B	800 × 800 mm..........	Nr	0.50	8.49	–	118.05	126.54	9.34	–	129.86	139.19
L104093C	950 × 950 mm..........	Nr	0.50	8.49	–	164.67	173.16	9.34	–	181.14	190.48
L104093D	1100 × 1000 mm	Nr	0.50	8.49	–	195.73	204.22	9.34	–	215.30	224.64
L104093E	1250 × 1250 mm	Nr	0.50	8.49	–	332.43	340.92	9.34	–	365.67	375.01
L104093F	1400 × 1400 mm	Nr	0.50	8.49	–	354.17	362.66	9.34	–	389.59	398.93
L104094	**Circular rooflights; fixing to upstands:**										
L104094A	800 mm diameter........	Nr	0.50	8.49	–	136.71	145.20	9.34	–	150.38	159.72
L104094B	950 mm diameter........	Nr	0.50	8.49	–	177.10	185.59	9.34	–	194.81	204.15
L104094C	1100 mm diameter.......	Nr	0.50	8.49	–	214.37	222.86	9.34	–	235.81	245.15
L104094D	1250 mm diameter.......	Nr	0.50	8.49	–	332.43	340.92	9.34	–	365.67	375.01
L104094E	1400 mm diameter.......	Nr	0.50	8.49	–	354.17	362.66	9.34	–	389.59	398.93
L104094F	1550 mm diameter.......	Nr	0.50	8.49	–	434.95	443.44	9.34	–	478.45	487.78
L104094G	1700 mm diameter.......	Nr	0.50	8.49	–	515.73	524.22	9.34	–	567.30	576.64
L104095	**Rectangular rooflights; fixing to upstands:**										
L104095A	650 × 950 mm..........	Nr	0.50	8.49	–	139.79	148.28	9.34	–	153.77	163.11
L104095B	650 × 1250 mm.........	Nr	0.50	8.49	–	205.04	213.53	9.34	–	225.54	234.88
L104095C	800 × 950 mm..........	Nr	0.50	8.49	–	155.34	163.83	9.34	–	170.87	180.21
L104095D	800 × 1100 mm.........	Nr	0.50	8.49	–	161.57	170.06	9.34	–	177.73	187.07
L104095E	800 × 1400 mm.........	Nr	0.50	8.49	–	214.37	222.86	9.34	–	235.81	245.15
L104095F	950 × 1250 mm.........	Nr	0.50	8.49	–	254.77	263.26	9.34	–	280.25	289.59
L104095G	1100 × 1400 mm	Nr	0.50	8.49	–	273.37	281.86	9.34	–	300.71	310.05

Major Works 2009		Unit	Labour Hours	Labour Net	Plant Net	Materials Net	Unit Net	Labour Gross	Plant Gross	Materials Gross	Unit Price
								(Gross rates include 10% profit)			
			£	£	£	£	£	£	£	£	£
L10	**L10: WINDOWS, ROOFLIGHTS, SCREENS AND LOUVRES**										
L1041	**Velux roof windows and accessories**										
L104166	**Velux roof windows; type GGL 3073:**										
L104166A	C02: 550 × 780 mm	Nr	0.85	14.43	–	192.70	207.13	15.87	–	211.97	227.84
L104166B	C04: 550 × 980 mm	Nr	0.90	15.28	–	206.80	222.08	16.81	–	227.48	244.29
L104166C	F06: 660 × 1180 mm	Nr	1.00	16.98	–	249.10	266.08	18.68	–	274.01	292.69
L104166D	M04: 780 × 980 mm	Nr	1.00	16.98	–	235.00	251.98	18.68	–	258.50	277.18
L104166E	M08: 780 × 1400 mm	Nr	1.30	22.07	–	277.30	299.37	24.28	–	305.03	329.31
L104166F	P10: 940 × 1600 mm	Nr	1.35	22.92	–	347.80	370.72	25.21	–	382.58	407.79
L104166G	S06: 1140 × 1180 mm	Nr	1.25	21.23	–	324.30	345.53	23.35	–	356.73	380.08
L104166H	U04: 1340 × 980 mm	Nr	1.25	21.23	–	319.60	340.83	23.35	–	351.56	374.91
L104166I	U08: 1340 × 1400 mm ...	Nr	1.40	23.77	–	375.24	399.01	26.15	–	412.76	438.91
L104167	**Velux RNL roller blinds; type GGL:**										
L104167A	C02	Nr	0.30	5.09	–	28.40	33.49	5.60	–	31.24	36.84
L104167B	C04	Nr	0.35	5.94	–	28.90	34.84	6.53	–	31.79	38.32
L104167C	F06	Nr	0.42	7.13	–	37.38	44.51	7.84	–	41.12	48.96
L104167D	M04	Nr	0.40	6.79	–	34.89	41.68	7.47	–	38.38	45.85
L104167E	M08	Nr	0.45	7.64	–	42.34	49.98	8.40	–	46.57	54.98
L104167F	P10	Nr	0.50	8.49	–	51.80	60.29	9.34	–	56.98	66.32
L104167G	S06	Nr	0.45	7.64	–	50.33	57.97	8.40	–	55.36	63.77
L104167H	U04	Nr	0.40	6.79	–	51.32	58.11	7.47	–	56.45	63.92
L104167I	U08	Nr	0.50	8.49	–	61.28	69.77	9.34	–	67.41	76.75
L104168	**Velux EDZ flashings; type GGL:**										
L104168A	C02	Nr	0.85	14.43	–	28.20	42.63	15.87	–	31.02	46.89
L104168B	C04	Nr	0.90	15.28	–	32.90	48.18	16.81	–	36.19	53.00
L104168C	F06	Nr	1.00	16.98	–	37.60	54.58	18.68	–	41.36	60.04
L104168D	M04	Nr	0.95	16.13	–	32.90	49.03	17.74	–	36.19	53.93
L104168E	M08	Nr	1.20	20.38	–	37.60	57.98	22.42	–	41.36	63.78
L104168F	P10	Nr	1.30	22.07	–	42.30	64.37	24.28	–	46.53	70.81
L104168G	S06	Nr	1.20	20.38	–	42.30	62.68	22.42	–	46.53	68.95
L104168H	U04	Nr	1.25	21.23	–	42.30	63.53	23.35	–	46.53	69.88
L104168I	U08	Nr	1.35	22.92	–	42.30	65.22	25.21	–	46.53	71.74
L1051	**Screens, borrowed lights and frames**										
L105101	**Proprietary softwood exterior screens with hardwood sills:**										
L105101A	1530 × 2100 mm	Nr	0.35	8.80	–	288.11	296.91	9.68	–	316.92	326.60
L105101B	2100 × 2100 mm	Nr	0.40	10.05	–	348.41	358.46	11.06	–	383.25	394.31
L105101C	2100 × 2100 mm	Nr	0.40	10.05	–	362.10	372.15	11.06	–	398.31	409.37
L105101D	2100 × 2100 mm	Nr	0.40	10.05	–	362.10	372.15	11.06	–	398.31	409.37
L105101E	2100 × 2100 mm	Nr	0.40	10.05	–	362.10	372.15	11.06	–	398.31	409.37
L105150	**Steel framed glazed screens; 6 mm clear toughened glass; fixing with screws; size:**										
L105150A	250 × 1200 mm	Nr	3.00	44.52	–	114.13	158.65	48.97	–	125.54	174.52
L105150D	300 × 2100 mm	Nr	3.00	44.52	–	209.30	253.82	48.97	–	230.23	279.20
L105150G	700 × 2100 mm	Nr	5.00	74.20	–	356.60	430.80	81.62	–	392.26	473.88
L105150L	1200 × 2100 mm	Nr	7.00	103.88	–	540.73	644.61	114.27	–	594.80	709.07
L105150P	1400 × 1200 mm	Nr	5.50	81.62	–	379.31	460.93	89.78	–	417.24	507.02
L105151	**Steel framed glazed screens; bullet proof glass, ballistic rating to G2 requirements; fixing with screws; size:**										
L105151D	1200 × 900 mm	Nr	4.50	66.78	–	392.78	459.56	73.46	–	432.06	505.52

Windows, Doors and Stairs

Major Works 2009		Unit	Labour Hours	Labour Net	Plant Net	Materials Net	Unit Net	Labour Gross	Plant Gross	Materials Gross	Unit Price
									(Gross rates include 10% profit)		
				£	£	£	£	£	£	£	£
L10	**L10: WINDOWS, ROOFLIGHTS, SCREENS AND LOUVRES**										
L1051	**Screens, borrowed lights and frames**										
L105160	**Brise-soleil; extruded aluminium blades fixed horizontally on brackets; to frame (measure separately); size:**										
L105160A	2.5 × 1.0 m	Nr	–	–	–	715.50	715.50	–	–	787.05	787.05
L105160B	5.0 × 1.5 m	Nr	–	–	–	2056.93	2056.93	–	–	2262.62	2262.62
L105160C	7.5 × 2.0 m	Nr	–	–	–	3935.25	3935.25	–	–	4328.78	4328.78
L105160D	10.0 × 2.5 m	Nr	–	–	–	6259.30	6259.30	–	–	6885.23	6885.23
L1096	**Mastic pointing**										
L109699	**Pointing frames one side with mastic sealant:**										
L109699A	standard	m	0.05	0.63	–	0.31	0.94	0.69	–	0.34	1.03
L109699B	coloured	m	0.05	0.64	–	0.34	0.98	0.70	–	0.37	1.08
L20	**L20: DOORS, SHUTTERS AND HATCHES**										
L2011	**Standard softwood exterior doors**										
L201120	**John Carr softwood exterior casement an panel doors; 44 mm thick:**										
L201120A	762 × 1981 mm; 26E2XGG	Nr	1.15	19.53	–	53.12	72.65	21.48	–	58.43	79.92
L201120B	838 × 1981 mm; 29E2XGG	Nr	1.20	20.38	–	53.15	73.53	22.42	–	58.47	80.88
L201120C	762 × 1981 mm; 26ESA..	Nr	1.15	19.53	–	128.53	148.06	21.48	–	141.38	162.87
L201120D	838 × 1981 mm; 29ESA..	Nr	1.20	20.38	–	132.10	152.48	22.42	–	145.31	167.73
L201120E	762 × 1981 mm; 26ESC..	Nr	1.15	19.53	–	142.54	162.07	21.48	–	156.79	178.28
L201120F	838 × 1981 mm; 29ESC..	Nr	1.20	20.38	–	145.78	166.16	22.42	–	160.36	182.78
L201120G	762 × 1981 mm; 26E10..	Nr	1.15	19.53	–	77.63	97.16	21.48	–	85.39	106.88
L201120H	838 × 1981 mm; 29E10..	Nr	1.20	20.38	–	80.87	101.25	22.42	–	88.96	111.38
L201120I	762 × 1981 mm; 26EKXT.	Nr	1.15	19.53	–	151.06	170.59	21.48	–	166.17	187.65
L201120J	838 × 1981 mm; 29EKXT.	Nr	1.20	20.38	–	154.67	175.05	22.42	–	170.14	192.56
L201120K	762 × 1981 mm; 26ESCP	Nr	1.15	19.53	–	157.37	176.90	21.48	–	173.11	194.59
L201120L	838 × 1981 mm; 20ESCP	Nr	1.20	20.38	–	160.99	181.37	22.42	–	177.09	199.51
L201120M	762 × 1981 mm; 26E4XPP	Nr	1.15	19.53	–	139.45	158.98	21.48	–	153.40	174.88
L201120N	838 × 1981 mm; 29E4XPP	Nr	1.20	20.38	–	142.36	162.74	22.42	–	156.60	179.01
L201120O	762 × 1981 mm; 26E50..	Nr	1.15	19.53	–	92.38	111.91	21.48	–	101.62	123.10
L201120P	838 × 1981 mm; 29E50..	Nr	1.20	20.38	–	95.40	115.78	22.42	–	104.94	127.36
L201120Q	762 × 1981 mm; 26E4XG	Nr	1.15	19.53	–	126.33	145.86	21.48	–	138.96	160.45
L201120R	838 × 1981 mm; 29E4XG	Nr	1.20	20.38	–	129.26	149.64	22.42	–	142.19	164.60
L201120S	762 × 1981 mm; 26E2XG	Nr	1.15	19.53	–	94.70	114.23	21.48	–	104.17	125.65
L201120T	838 × 1981 mm; 29E2XG	Nr	1.20	20.38	–	98.47	118.85	22.42	–	108.32	130.74

Major Works 2009		Unit	Labour Hours	Labour Net	Plant Net	Materials Net	Unit Net	Labour Gross	Plant Gross	Materials Gross	Unit Price
								(Gross rates include 10% profit)			
				£	£	£	£	£	£	£	£
L20	**L20: DOORS, SHUTTERS AND HATCHES**										
L2011	**Standard softwood exterior doors**										
L201121	**Premdor feature softwood exterior panel doors; mortice and tenon construction; 44 mm thick:**										
L201121A	838 × 1981 mm; 3-panel; ref 33124	Nr	1.20	20.38	–	319.28	339.66	22.42	–	351.21	373.63
L201121B	813 × 2032 mm; 3-panel; ref 33129	Nr	1.20	20.38	–	319.28	339.66	22.42	–	351.21	373.63
L201121C	762 × 1981 mm; 3-panel; ref 33121	Nr	1.15	19.53	–	319.28	338.81	21.48	–	351.21	372.69
L201121D	807 × 2000 mm; 3-panel; ref 33128	Nr	1.20	20.38	–	319.28	339.66	22.42	–	351.21	373.63
L201121E	838 × 1981 mm; 4-panel; ref 26024	Nr	1.20	20.38	–	340.24	360.62	22.42	–	374.26	396.68
L201121F	813 × 2032 mm; 4-panel; ref 26029	Nr	1.20	20.38	–	340.24	360.62	22.42	–	374.26	396.68
L201121G	762 × 1981 mm; 4-panel; ref 26021	Nr	1.15	19.53	–	340.24	359.77	21.48	–	374.26	395.75
L201121H	807 × 2000 mm; 4-panel; ref 26028	Nr	1.20	20.38	–	340.24	360.62	22.42	–	374.26	396.68
L201121I	838 × 1981 mm; 6-panel; ref 91514	Nr	1.20	20.38	–	318.47	338.85	22.42	–	350.32	372.74
L201121J	813 × 2032 mm; 6-panel; ref 91539	Nr	1.20	20.38	–	318.47	338.85	22.42	–	350.32	372.74
L201121K	762 × 1981 mm; 6-panel; ref 91511	Nr	1.15	19.53	–	318.47	338.00	21.48	–	350.32	371.80
L201121L	807 × 2000 mm; 6-panel; ref 91548	Nr	1.15	19.53	–	318.47	338.00	21.48	–	350.32	371.80
L201121M	838 × 1981 mm; 6-panel toplight; ref 28324	Nr	1.20	20.38	–	298.31	318.69	22.42	–	328.14	350.56
L201121N	813 × 2032 mm; 6-panel toplight; ref 28329	Nr	1.20	20.38	–	298.31	318.69	22.42	–	328.14	350.56
L201121O	762 × 1981 mm; 6-panel toplight; ref 28321	Nr	1.15	19.53	–	298.31	317.84	21.48	–	328.14	349.62
L201121P	807 × 2000 mm; 6-panel toplight; ref 28328	Nr	1.20	20.38	–	298.31	318.69	22.42	–	328.14	350.56
L201121Q	838 × 1981 mm; 8-panel; ref 28924	Nr	1.20	20.38	–	366.04	386.42	22.42	–	402.64	425.06
L201121R	813 × 2032 mm; 8-panel toplight; ref 28929	Nr	1.20	20.38	–	366.04	386.42	22.42	–	402.64	425.06
L201121S	762 × 1981 mm; 8-panel toplight; ref 28921	Nr	1.15	19.53	–	366.04	385.57	21.48	–	402.64	424.13
L201121T	807 × 2000 mm; 8-panel toplight; ref 28928	Nr	1.20	20.38	–	366.04	386.42	22.42	–	402.64	425.06

Windows, Doors and Stairs

Major Works 2009		Unit	Labour Hours	Labour Net	Plant Net	Materials Net	Unit Net	Labour Gross	Plant Gross	Materials Gross	Unit Price
								(Gross rates include 10% profit)			
				£	£	£	£	£	£	£	£
L20	**L20: DOORS, SHUTTERS AND HATCHES**										
L2012	**Standard softwood utility doors and gates**										
L201223	**John Carr softwood preservative treated utility doors and gates; 44 mm thick:**										
L201223A	610 × 1981 mm; 20LB; ledged and braced	Nr	0.70	11.89	–	72.45	84.34	13.08	–	79.70	92.77
L201223B	686 × 1981 mm; 23LB; ledged and braced	Nr	0.75	12.74	–	72.45	85.19	14.01	–	79.70	93.71
L201223C	762 × 1981 mm; 26LB; ledged and braced	Nr	0.75	12.74	–	72.45	85.19	14.01	–	79.70	93.71
L201223D	838 × 1981 mm; 29LB; ledged and braced	Nr	0.80	13.58	–	77.96	91.54	14.94	–	85.76	100.69
L201223E	813 × 2032 mm; 28LB; ledged and braced	Nr	0.80	13.58	–	77.96	91.54	14.94	–	85.76	100.69
L201223F	686 × 1981 mm; 23FLB; framed, ledged and braced .	Nr	0.75	12.74	–	93.74	106.48	14.01	–	103.11	117.13
L201223G	762 × 1981 mm; 26FLB; framed, ledged and braced .	Nr	0.75	12.74	–	93.74	106.48	14.01	–	103.11	117.13
L201223H	838 × 1981 mm; 29FLB; framed, ledged and braced .	Nr	0.80	13.58	–	98.44	112.02	14.94	–	108.28	123.22
L201223I	813 × 2032 mm; 28FLB; framed, ledged and braced .	Nr	0.80	13.58	–	98.44	112.02	14.94	–	108.28	123.22
L201223J	726 × 2040 mm; 726FLB; framed, ledge and braced ..	Nr	0.75	12.74	–	93.71	106.45	14.01	–	103.08	117.10
L201223K	826 × 2040 mm; 826FLB; framed, ledge and braced ..	Nr	0.80	13.58	–	93.71	107.29	14.94	–	103.08	118.02
L201223L	807 × 2000 mm; 807FLB; framed, ledge and braced ..	Nr	0.80	13.58	–	98.44	112.02	14.94	–	108.28	123.22
L201223M	762 × 1981 mm; 26SD; stable door	Nr	1.40	23.77	–	179.55	203.32	26.15	–	197.51	223.65
L201223N	838 × 1981 mm; 29SD; stable door	Nr	1.50	25.47	–	179.55	205.02	28.02	–	197.51	225.52
L2012230	813 × 2032 mm; 28SD; stable door	Nr	1.50	25.47	–	179.55	205.02	28.02	–	197.51	225.52
L201223P	914 × 1981 mm; 3060GS arch top gate.............	Nr	0.85	14.43	–	123.20	137.63	15.87	–	135.52	151.39
L201223Q	914 × 1041 mm; 30GTE gate	Nr	0.60	10.19	–	65.36	75.55	11.21	–	71.90	83.11
L201223R	1067 × 1041 mm; 36GTE gate	Nr	0.75	12.74	–	74.03	86.77	14.01	–	81.43	95.45
L2013	**Standard timber patio door sets**										
L201326	**John Carr 'Ledbury' patio door sets complete with frames, clear double glazing and all fittings:**										
L201326A	1590 × 2073 mm; LED16LE	Nr	5.00	84.90	–	827.32	912.22	93.39	–	910.05	1003.44
L201326B	1790 × 2073 mm; LED18LE	Nr	6.00	101.88	–	875.63	977.51	112.07	–	963.19	1075.26
L201326C	2090 × 2073 mm; LED21LE	Nr	7.00	118.86	–	1049.03	1167.89	130.75	–	1153.93	1284.68
L201326D	2390 × 2073 mm; LED24LE	Nr	8.00	135.84	–	1131.47	1267.31	149.42	–	1244.62	1394.04

Major Works 2009		Unit	Labour Hours	Labour Net	Plant Net	Materials Net	Unit Net	Labour Gross	Plant Gross	Materials Gross	Unit Price
								(Gross rates include 10% profit)			
				£	£	£	£	£	£	£	£
L20	**L20: DOORS, SHUTTERS AND HATCHES**										
L2015	**Standard plywood faced external doors**										
L201524	**John Carr plywood faced lipped exterior flush doors; 44 mm thick:**										
L201524A	686 × 1981 mm; 23F1X ..	Nr	0.90	15.28	–	62.51	77.79	16.81	–	68.76	85.57
L201524B	762 × 1981 mm; 26F1X ..	Nr	0.85	14.43	–	62.00	76.43	15.87	–	68.20	84.07
L201524C	838 × 1981 mm; 29F1X ..	Nr	0.90	15.28	–	62.51	77.79	16.81	–	68.76	85.57
L201524D	762 × 1981 mm; 26F2X ..	Nr	0.85	14.43	–	69.44	83.87	15.87	–	76.38	92.26
L201524E	838 × 1981 mm; 29F2X ..	Nr	0.90	15.28	–	69.44	84.72	16.81	–	76.38	93.19
L201524F	762 × 1981 mm; 26F3X ..	Nr	0.85	14.43	–	62.00	76.43	15.87	–	68.20	84.07
L201524G	838 × 1981 mm; 29F3X ..	Nr	0.90	15.28	–	62.00	77.28	16.81	–	68.20	85.01
L201525	**John Carr half hour firecheck plywood faced lipped exterior flush doors; 44 m thick:**										
L201525A	762 × 1981 mm; 26F3XBF	Nr	1.10	18.68	–	105.17	123.85	20.55	–	115.69	136.24
L201525B	838 × 1981 mm; 29F3XBF	Nr	1.05	17.83	–	105.17	123.00	19.61	–	115.69	135.30
L201525C	813 × 2032 mm; 28F3XBF	Nr	1.15	19.53	–	105.17	124.70	21.48	–	115.69	137.17
L2018	**Standard hardwood exterior doors**										
L201830	**John Carr hardwood panel doors; 44 mm thick:**										
L201830A	762 × 1981 mm; 26H2XGG	Nr	1.25	21.23	–	129.95	151.18	23.35	–	142.95	166.30
L201830B	838 × 1981 mm; 29H2XGG	Nr	1.30	22.07	–	133.43	155.50	24.28	–	146.77	171.05
L201830C	813 × 2032 mm; 28H2XGG	Nr	1.25	21.23	–	133.43	154.66	23.35	–	146.77	170.13
L201830D	807 × 2000 mm; 807H2XGG	Nr	1.25	21.23	–	133.43	154.66	23.35	–	146.77	170.13
L201830E	762 × 1981 mm; 26H10..	Nr	1.25	21.23	–	127.48	148.71	23.35	–	140.23	163.58
L201830F	838 × 1981 mm; 29H10..	Nr	1.25	21.23	–	130.89	152.12	23.35	–	143.98	167.33
L201830G	813 × 2032 mm; 28H10..	Nr	1.25	21.23	–	130.89	152.12	23.35	–	143.98	167.33
L201830H	807 × 2000 mm; 807H10.	Nr	1.25	21.23	–	130.89	152.12	23.35	–	143.98	167.33
L201832	**John Carr hardwood feature doors; 44 mm thick:**										
L201832A	838 × 1981 mm; N29HART	Nr	1.30	22.07	–	304.76	326.83	24.28	–	335.24	359.51
L201832B	838 × 1981 mm; 29CARL	Nr	1.30	22.07	–	304.76	326.83	24.28	–	335.24	359.51
L201832C	838 × 1981 mm; 29CLAR	Nr	1.30	22.07	–	304.76	326.83	24.28	–	335.24	359.51

Windows, Doors and Stairs

Major Works 2009		Unit	Labour Hours	Labour Net	Plant Net	Materials Net	Unit Net	Labour Gross	Plant Gross	Materials Gross	Unit Price
				£	£	£	£	\u2014\u2014 (Gross rates include 10% profit) \u2014\u2014 £		£	£
L20	**L20: DOORS, SHUTTERS AND HATCHES**										
L2019	**Standard PVC-u patio door sets**										
L201936	**John Carr 'Ingleby' PVC-u French doors; white polyester paint finish; 24 mm Low E insulating glass units; toughened inner pane, laminated outer pane; complete with all fittings; size:**										
L201936A	1184 × 2090 mm; ING12E	Nr	4.50	76.41	–	797.92	874.33	84.05	–	877.71	961.76
L201936B	1484 × 2090 mm; ING15E	Nr	4.75	80.66	–	854.82	935.48	88.73	–	940.30	1029.03
L201936C	1784 × 2090 mm; ING18E	Nr	5.25	89.15	–	901.58	990.73	98.07	–	991.74	1089.80
L201937	**John Carr 'Ingleby' PVC-u French doors; white polyester paint finish; 24 mm Low E insulating glass units; toughened inner and outer panes; complete with al fittings; size:**										
L201937A	1184 × 2090 mm; ING12.	Nr	4.50	76.41	–	797.92	874.33	84.05	–	877.71	961.76
L201937B	1484 × 2090 mm; ING15.	Nr	4.75	80.66	–	901.58	982.24	88.73	–	991.74	1080.46
L201937C	1784 × 2090 mm; ING18.	Nr	5.25	89.15	–	854.82	943.97	98.07	–	940.30	1038.37
L201940	**John Carr 'Claydon' sliding patio doors white PVC-u finish; 24 mm Low E insulating glass units; toughened inner laminated outer pane; complete with all fittings; size:**										
L201940A	1790 × 2090 mm; CLAY18	Nr	5.25	89.15	–	1047.84	1136.99	98.07	–	1152.62	1250.69
L201940B	2090 × 2090 mm; CLAY21	Nr	6.00	101.88	–	1141.69	1243.57	112.07	–	1255.86	1367.93
L201940C	2390 × 2090 mm; CLAY24	Nr	7.00	118.86	–	1235.54	1354.40	130.75	–	1359.09	1489.84
L201941	**John Carr 'Claydon' sliding patio doors white PVC-u finish; 24 mm Low E insulating glass units; toughened inner and outer panes; complete with all fittings; size:**										
L201941A	1790 × 2090 mm; CLAY18	Nr	5.25	89.15	–	1205.06	1294.21	98.07	–	1325.57	1423.63
L201941B	2090 × 2090 mm; CLAY21	Nr	6.00	101.88	–	1320.36	1422.24	112.07	–	1452.40	1564.46
L201941C	2390 × 2090 mm; CLAY24	Nr	7.00	118.86	–	1437.87	1556.73	130.75	–	1581.66	1712.40
L201950	**Premdor PVC-u patio door sets; 24 mm Low E sealed toughened insulating double glazing units; complete with locking system and all fittings; size:**										
L201950A	1490 × 2090 mm; 60131.	Nr	4.75	80.66	–	748.20	828.86	88.73	–	823.02	911.75
L201950B	1790 × 2090 mm; 60132.	Nr	5.25	89.15	–	807.06	896.21	98.07	–	887.77	985.83
L201950C	2090 × 2090 mm; 60133.	Nr	6.00	101.88	–	880.43	982.31	112.07	–	968.47	1080.54
L201950D	2390 × 2090 mm; 60134.	Nr	7.00	118.86	–	953.79	1072.65	130.75	–	1049.17	1179.92

Major Works 2009		Unit	Labour Hours	Labour Net	Plant Net	Materials Net	Unit Net	Labour Gross	Plant Gross	Materials Gross	Unit Price
								——— (Gross rates include 10% profit) ———			
				£	£	£	£	£	£	£	£
L20	**L20: DOORS, SHUTTERS AND HATCHES**										
L2023	**Interior doors**										
L202301	**John Carr Premium softwood interior panel doors; 35 mm thick:**										
L202301A	686 × 1981 mm; 23ISC ..	Nr	1.15	19.53	–	127.51	147.04	21.48	–	140.26	161.74
L202301B	762 × 1981 mm; 26ISC ..	Nr	1.20	20.38	–	128.59	148.97	22.42	–	141.45	163.87
L202301C	838 × 1981 mm; 29ISC ..	Nr	1.25	21.23	–	133.43	154.66	23.35	–	146.77	170.13
L202301D	686 × 1981 mm; 23ISA ..	Nr	1.10	18.68	–	119.97	138.65	20.55	–	131.97	152.52
L202301E	762 × 1981 mm; 26ISA ..	Nr	1.20	20.38	–	120.94	141.32	22.42	–	133.03	155.45
L202302	**John Carr 'Eskdale' veneered panel effect feature doors; 35 mm thick:**										
L202302A	762 × 1981 mm; 26ESK2P	Nr	1.20	20.38	–	126.66	147.04	22.42	–	139.33	161.74
L202302B	762 × 1981 mm; 26ESK4P	Nr	1.20	20.38	–	142.84	163.22	22.42	–	157.12	179.54
L202302C	610 × 1981 mm; 20ESK2P	Nr	1.10	18.68	–	125.30	143.98	20.55	–	137.83	158.38
L202302D	686 × 1981 mm; 23ESK2P	Nr	1.15	19.53	–	125.30	144.83	21.48	–	137.83	159.31
L202302E	686 × 1981 mm; 23ESK4P	Nr	1.20	20.38	–	141.45	161.83	22.42	–	155.60	178.01
L202303	**John Carr 'Newstead' oak veneered panel feature doors; 35 mm thick:**										
L202303A	686 × 1981 mm; 23NEWS	Nr	1.10	18.68	–	187.60	206.28	20.55	–	206.36	226.91
L202303B	762 × 1981 mm; 26NEWS	Nr	1.10	18.68	–	187.60	206.28	20.55	–	206.36	226.91
L202303C	838 × 1981 mm; 29NEWS	Nr	1.20	20.38	–	196.98	217.36	22.42	–	216.68	239.10
L202304	**John Carr 'Chateau' wood grain moulded panel doors; 35 mm thick:**										
L202304A	457 × 1981 mm; 16CLAS	Nr	1.05	17.83	–	58.65	76.48	19.61	–	64.52	84.13
L202304B	533 × 1981 mm; 19CLAS	Nr	1.05	17.83	–	58.65	76.48	19.61	–	64.52	84.13
L202304C	610 × 1981 mm; 20CLAS	Nr	1.05	17.83	–	58.65	76.48	19.61	–	64.52	84.13
L202304D	686 × 1981 mm; 23CLAS	Nr	1.10	18.68	–	58.65	77.33	20.55	–	64.52	85.06
L202304E	762 × 1981 mm; 26CLAS	Nr	1.10	18.68	–	58.91	77.59	20.55	–	64.80	85.35
L202305	**John Carr 'Cambridge' smooth-skin moulded panel doors; 35 mm thick:**										
L202305A	457 × 1981 mm; 16CAMB	Nr	1.05	17.83	–	48.95	66.78	19.61	–	53.85	73.46
L202305B	533 × 1981 mm; 19CAMB	Nr	1.05	17.83	–	48.95	66.78	19.61	–	53.85	73.46
L202305C	610 × 1981 mm; 20CAMB	Nr	1.05	17.83	–	48.95	66.78	19.61	–	53.85	73.46
L202305D	686 × 1981 mm; 23CAMB	Nr	1.10	18.68	–	48.95	67.63	20.55	–	53.85	74.39
L202305E	762 × 1981 mm; 26CAMB	Nr	1.10	18.68	–	48.95	67.63	20.55	–	53.85	74.39
L202306	**John Carr 'Carrwood' hardboard faced flush interior door; lipped two edges; 35 mm thick:**										
L202306A	457 × 1981 mm; 16HBL..	Nr	1.05	17.83	–	42.47	60.30	19.61	–	46.72	66.33
L202306B	533 × 1981 mm; 19HBL..	Nr	1.05	17.83	–	42.47	60.30	19.61	–	46.72	66.33
L202306C	610 × 1981 mm; 20HBL..	Nr	1.05	17.83	–	42.47	60.30	19.61	–	46.72	66.33
L202306D	686 × 1981 mm; 23HBL..	Nr	1.10	18.68	–	42.47	61.15	20.55	–	46.72	67.27
L202306E	762 × 1981 mm; 26HBL..	Nr	1.10	18.68	–	42.47	61.15	20.55	–	46.72	67.27
L202306F	838 × 1981 mm; 29HBL..	Nr	1.15	19.53	–	44.38	63.91	21.48	–	48.82	70.30
L202306G	813 × 2032 mm; 28HBL..	Nr	1.15	19.53	–	44.38	63.91	21.48	–	48.82	70.30

Windows, Doors and Stairs

Major Works 2009		Unit	Labour Hours	Labour Net	Plant Net	Materials Net	Unit Net	Labour Gross	Plant Gross	Materials Gross	Unit Price
								(Gross rates include 10% profit)			
				£	£	£	£	£	£	£	£
L20	**L20: DOORS, SHUTTERS AND HATCHES**										
L2023	**Interior doors**										
L202307	**John Carr 'Carrwood' hardboard faced interior flush doors; lipped two edges; 40 mm thick:**										
L202307A	626 × 2040 mm; 626HBL	Nr	1.05	17.83	–	44.38	62.21	19.61	–	48.82	68.43
L202307B	726 × 2040 mm; 726HBL	Nr	1.10	18.68	–	44.38	63.06	20.55	–	48.82	69.37
L202307C	826 × 2040 mm; 826HBL	Nr	1.15	19.53	–	44.38	63.91	21.48	–	48.82	70.30
L202308	**John Carr 'Silverwood' hardboard faced interior flush doors; unlipped; 35 mm thick:**										
L202308A	457 × 1981 mm; 16HB...	Nr	1.05	17.83	–	38.60	56.43	19.61	–	42.46	62.07
L202308B	533 × 1981 mm; 19HB...	Nr	1.05	17.83	–	38.60	56.43	19.61	–	42.46	62.07
L202308C	610 × 1981 mm; 20HB...	Nr	1.05	17.83	–	38.60	56.43	19.61	–	42.46	62.07
L202308D	686 × 1981 mm; 23HB...	Nr	1.10	18.68	–	38.60	57.28	20.55	–	42.46	63.01
L202308E	762 × 1981 mm; 26HB...	Nr	1.10	18.68	–	38.60	57.28	20.55	–	42.46	63.01
L202308F	838 × 1981 mm; 29HB...	Nr	1.15	19.53	–	40.34	59.87	21.48	–	44.37	65.86
L202308G	813 × 2032 mm; 28HB...	Nr	1.15	19.53	–	40.34	59.87	21.48	–	44.37	65.86
L202309	**John Carr 'Silverwood' hardboard faced interior flush doors; unlipped; 40 mm thick:**										
L202309A	626 × 2040 mm; 626HB..	Nr	1.15	19.53	–	40.34	59.87	21.48	–	44.37	65.86
L202309B	726 × 2040 mm; 726HB..	Nr	1.20	20.38	–	40.34	60.72	22.42	–	44.37	66.79
L202309C	826 × 2040 mm; 826HB..	Nr	1.25	21.23	–	42.00	63.23	23.35	–	46.20	69.55
L202310	**Proprietary serving hatch in plywood; assembled; rebated meeting tiles; hung on 2 pr nylon hinges; 133 mm rebated softwood linings; 170 mm sill:**										
L202310A	648 × 533 mm..........	Nr	0.75	12.74	–	95.51	108.25	14.01	–	105.06	119.08

Major Works 2009		Unit	Labour Hours	Labour Net	Plant Net	Materials Net	Unit Net	Labour Gross	Plant Gross	Materials Gross	Unit Price
				£	£	£	£	£	£	£	£
								——— (Gross rates include 10% profit) ———			
L20	**L20: DOORS, SHUTTERS AND HATCHES**										
L2023	**Interior doors**										
L202312	**John Carr factory finished wood veneered interior flush doors; clear lacquer finish; 35 mm thick:**										
L202312A	457 × 1981 mm; Sapele 16SDL	Nr	1.10	18.68	–	61.34	80.02	20.55	–	67.47	88.02
L202312B	533 × 1981 mm; Sapele 19SDL	Nr	1.10	18.68	–	61.34	80.02	20.55	–	67.47	88.02
L202312C	610 × 1981 mm; Sapele 20SDL	Nr	1.15	19.53	–	61.34	80.87	21.48	–	67.47	88.96
L202312D	686 × 1981 mm; Sapele 23SDL	Nr	1.15	19.53	–	61.34	80.87	21.48	–	67.47	88.96
L202312E	762 × 1981 mm; Sapele 26SDL	Nr	1.20	20.38	–	61.34	81.72	22.42	–	67.47	89.89
L202312F	838 × 1981 mm; Sapele 29SDL	Nr	1.25	21.23	–	66.32	87.55	23.35	–	72.95	96.31
L202312G	864 × 1981 mm; Sapele 210SDL	Nr	1.25	21.23	–	73.10	94.33	23.35	–	80.41	103.76
L202312H	457 × 1981 mm; Koto 16KOT	Nr	1.25	21.23	–	68.06	89.29	23.35	–	74.87	98.22
L202312I	533 × 1981 mm; Koto 19KOT	Nr	1.10	18.68	–	68.06	86.74	20.55	–	74.87	95.41
L202312J	610 × 1981 mm; Koto 20KOT	Nr	1.10	18.68	–	68.06	86.74	20.55	–	74.87	95.41
L202312K	686 × 1981 mm; Koto 23KOT	Nr	1.15	19.53	–	68.06	87.59	21.48	–	74.87	96.35
L202312L	762 × 1981 mm; Koto 26KOT	Nr	1.15	19.53	–	68.06	87.59	21.48	–	74.87	96.35
L202312M	838 × 1981 mm; Koto 29KOT	Nr	1.20	20.38	–	77.29	97.67	22.42	–	85.02	107.44
L202312N	457 × 1981 mm; Ash 16ASH	Nr	1.25	21.23	–	89.06	110.29	23.35	–	97.97	121.32
L202312O	533 × 1981 mm; Ash 19ASH	Nr	1.10	18.68	–	89.06	107.74	20.55	–	97.97	118.51
L202312P	610 × 1981 mm; Ash 20ASH	Nr	1.10	18.68	–	89.06	107.74	20.55	–	97.97	118.51
L202312Q	686 × 1981 mm; Ash 23ASH	Nr	1.15	19.53	–	89.06	108.59	21.48	–	97.97	119.45
L202312R	762 × 1981 mm; Ash 26ASH	Nr	1.15	19.53	–	89.06	108.59	21.48	–	97.97	119.45
L202312S	838 × 1981 mm; Ash 29ASH	Nr	1.20	20.38	–	94.03	114.41	22.42	–	103.43	125.85
L202312T	457 × 1981 mm; African Maple 16MPL	Nr	1.25	21.23	–	73.10	94.33	23.35	–	80.41	103.76
L202312U	533 × 1981 mm; African Maple 19MPL	Nr	1.10	18.68	–	73.10	91.78	20.55	–	80.41	100.96
L202312V	610 × 1981 mm; African Maple 20MPL	Nr	1.10	18.68	–	73.10	91.78	20.55	–	80.41	100.96
L202312W	686 × 1981 mm; African Maple 23MPL	Nr	1.15	19.53	–	73.10	92.63	21.48	–	80.41	101.89
L202312X	762 × 1981 mm; African Maple 26MPL	Nr	1.15	19.53	–	73.10	92.63	21.48	–	80.41	101.89
L202312Y	838 × 1981 mm; African Maple 29MPL	Nr	1.25	21.23	–	77.29	98.52	23.35	–	85.02	108.37

Windows, Doors and Stairs

Major Works 2009		Unit	Labour Hours	Labour Net	Plant Net	Materials Net	Unit Net	Labour Gross	Plant Gross	Materials Gross	Unit Price
								——— (Gross rates include 10% profit) ———			
				£	£	£	£	£	£	£	£
L20	**L20: DOORS, SHUTTERS AND HATCHES**										
L2023	**Interior doors**										
L202313	**John Carr Sapele factory finished wood veneered interior flush doors; clear lacquer finish; 40 mm thick:**										
L202313A	526 × 2040 mm; 526SDL	Nr	1.10	18.68	–	63.87	82.55	20.55	–	70.26	90.81
L202313B	626 × 2040 mm; 626SDL	Nr	1.15	19.53	–	63.87	83.40	21.48	–	70.26	91.74
L202313C	726 × 2040 mm; 726SDL	Nr	1.20	20.38	–	63.87	84.25	22.42	–	70.26	92.68
L202313D	826 × 2040 mm; 826SDL	Nr	1.25	21.23	–	68.06	89.29	23.35	–	74.87	98.22
L202314	**John Carr 'Silverwood' half hour fire check hardboard faced interior flush doors; unlipped; 44 mm thick:**										
L202314A	686 × 1981 mm; 23HBF..	Nr	1.15	19.53	–	65.21	84.74	21.48	–	71.73	93.21
L202314B	762 × 1981 mm; 26HBF..	Nr	1.20	20.38	–	65.21	85.59	22.42	–	71.73	94.15
L202314C	838 × 1981 mm; 29HBF..	Nr	1.25	21.23	–	67.82	89.05	23.35	–	74.60	97.96
L202314D	726 × 2040 mm; 726HBF.	Nr	1.20	20.38	–	67.82	88.20	22.42	–	74.60	97.02
L202314E	826 × 2040 mm; 826HBF.	Nr	1.25	21.23	–	68.69	89.92	23.35	–	75.56	98.91
L202316	**John Carr half hour firecheck factory finished wood veneered lipped interior flush doors; clear lacquer finish; 44 m thick:**										
L202316A	686 × 1981 mm; Sapele 23SDLF	Nr	1.30	22.07	–	86.60	108.67	24.28	–	95.26	119.54
L202316B	762 × 1981 mm; Sapele 26SDLF	Nr	1.35	22.92	–	86.60	109.52	25.21	–	95.26	120.47
L202316C	838 × 1981 mm; Sapele 29SDLF	Nr	1.40	23.77	–	93.40	117.17	26.15	–	102.74	128.89
L202316D	726 × 2040 mm; Sapele 726SDLF	Nr	1.35	22.92	–	89.13	112.05	25.21	–	98.04	123.26
L202316E	826 × 2040 mm; Sapele 826SDLF	Nr	1.40	23.77	–	95.92	119.69	26.15	–	105.51	131.66
L202316F	762 × 1981 mm; Ash 26ASHF	Nr	1.35	22.92	–	113.37	136.29	25.21	–	124.71	149.92
L202316G	838 × 1981 mm; Ash 29ASHF	Nr	1.40	23.77	–	120.08	143.85	26.15	–	132.09	158.24
L202316H	762 × 1981 mm; African Maple 26MPL	Nr	1.35	22.92	–	98.45	121.37	25.21	–	108.30	133.51
L202316I	838 × 1981 mm; African Maple 29MPL	Nr	1.40	23.77	–	110.37	134.14	26.15	–	121.41	147.55
L202316J	762 × 1981 mm; Koto 26KOTF	Nr	1.35	22.92	–	105.24	128.16	25.21	–	115.76	140.98
L202316K	838 × 1981 mm; Koto 29KOTF	Nr	1.40	23.77	–	101.06	124.83	26.15	–	111.17	137.31
L202317	**John Carr half hour firecheck interior doors with one piece moulded skin both sides; 44 mm thick:**										
L202317A	762 × 1981 mm; Chateau 26CLASF	Nr	1.35	22.92	–	147.93	170.85	25.21	–	162.72	187.94
L202317B	838 × 1981 mm; Chateau 29CLASF	Nr	1.40	23.77	–	155.04	178.81	26.15	–	170.54	196.69
L202317C	762 × 1981 mm; Cambridge 26CAMBF	Nr	1.35	22.92	–	105.56	128.48	25.21	–	116.12	141.33
L202317D	838 × 1981 mm; Cambridge 29CAMBF	Nr	1.40	23.77	–	108.16	131.93	26.15	–	118.98	145.12

Major Works 2009		Unit	Labour Hours	Labour Net	Plant Net	Materials Net	Unit Net	Labour Gross	Plant Gross	Materials Gross	Unit Price
				£	£	£	£	£	£	£	£
								(Gross rates include 10% profit)			
L20	**L20: DOORS, SHUTTERS AND HATCHES**										
L2071	**Standard softwood external door frames**										
L207102	**Boulton and Paul softwood exterior door frames; hardwood sills; heavy duty PVC waterbar; for 686 × 1981 mm doors:**										
L207102A	780 × 2079 mm; FN23M; opening inward weatherstripped	Nr	0.35	8.80	–	70.11	78.91	9.68	–	77.12	86.80
L207102B	780 × 2079 mm; FX23M; opening outward; weatherstripped	Nr	0.35	8.80	–	70.11	78.91	9.68	–	77.12	86.80
L207102C	780 × 2035 mm; F23; opening inward and outward; weatherstripped; no sill	Nr	0.35	8.80	–	75.01	83.81	9.68	–	82.51	92.19
L207102D	780 × 2035 mm; DF23; opening inward and outward; non-weatherstripped; no sill	Nr	0.35	8.80	–	60.57	69.37	9.68	–	66.63	76.31
L207103	**Boulton and Paul softwood exterior door frames; hardwood sills; heavy duty PVC waterbar; for 762 × 1981 mm doors:**										
L207103A	856 × 2079 mm; FN26M; opening inward weatherstripped	Nr	0.35	8.80	–	72.23	81.03	9.68	–	79.45	89.13
L207103B	856 × 2079 mm; FX26M; opening outward; weatherstripped	Nr	0.35	8.80	–	72.23	81.03	9.68	–	79.45	89.13
L207103C	856 × 2035; F26; opening inward and outward; weatherstripped; no sill	Nr	0.35	8.80	–	75.01	83.81	9.68	–	82.51	92.19
L207103D	856 × 2035 mm; DF26IN; opening inward; non-weatherstripped	Nr	0.35	8.80	–	84.38	93.18	9.68	–	92.82	102.50
L207103E	856 × 2079 mm; DF26OUT; opening outward; non-weatherstripped	Nr	0.35	8.80	–	84.38	93.18	9.68	–	92.82	102.50
L207103F	856 × 2035 mm; DF26; opening inward and outward; non-weatherstripped; no sill	Nr	0.35	8.80	–	61.47	70.27	9.68	–	67.62	77.30
L207104	**Boulton and Paul softwood exterior door frames; hardwood sills; heavy duty PVC waterbar; for 838 × 1981 mm doors:**										
L207104A	932 × 2079 mm; FN29M; opening inward weatherstripped	Nr	0.35	8.80	–	75.01	83.81	9.68	–	82.51	92.19
L207104B	932 × 2079 mm; FX29M; opening outward; weatherstripped	Nr	0.35	8.80	–	75.01	83.81	9.68	–	82.51	92.19
L207104C	932 × 2035; F29; opening inward and outward; weatherstripped; no sill	Nr	0.35	8.80	–	75.01	83.81	9.68	–	82.51	92.19
L207104D	932 × 2079 mm; DF29IN; opening inward; non-weatherstripped	Nr	0.35	8.80	–	87.23	96.03	9.68	–	95.95	105.63
L207104E	932 × 2079 mm; DF29OUT; opening outward; non-weatherstripped	Nr	0.35	8.80	–	87.23	96.03	9.68	–	95.95	105.63
L207104F	932 × 2035 mm; DF29; opening inward and outward; non-weatherstripped; no sill	Nr	0.35	8.80	–	64.14	72.94	9.68	–	70.55	80.23

Windows, Doors and Stairs

Major Works 2009		Unit	Labour Hours	Labour Net	Plant Net	Materials Net	Unit Net	Labour Gross	Plant Gross	Materials Gross	Unit Price
								(Gross rates include 10% profit)			
				£	£	£	£	£	£	£	£
L20	**L20: DOORS, SHUTTERS AND HATCHES**										
L2071	**Standard softwood external door frames**										
L207105	**Boulton and Paul softwood exterior door frames; hardwood sills; heavy duty PVC waterbar; for 914 × 1981 mm doors:**										
L207105A	1008 × 2130 mm; FN30M; opening inward; weatherstripped	Nr	0.35	8.80	–	104.94	113.74	9.68	–	115.43	125.11
L207105B	1008 × 2130 mm; FX30M; opening outward; weatherstripped	Nr	0.35	8.80	–	104.94	113.74	9.68	–	115.43	125.11
L207105C	1008 × 2086 mm; F30; opening inward and outward; weatherstripped; no sill	Nr	0.35	8.80	–	70.14	78.94	9.68	–	77.15	86.83
L207106	**Boulton and Paul softwood exterior door frames; hardwood sills; heavy duty PVC waterbar; for 813 × 2032 mm doors:**										
L207106A	907 × 2130 mm; FN28M; opening inward weatherstripped	Nr	0.35	8.80	–	75.01	83.81	9.68	–	82.51	92.19
L207106B	907 × 2130 mm; FX28M; opening outward; weatherstripped	Nr	0.35	8.80	–	75.01	83.81	9.68	–	82.51	92.19
L207106C	907 × 2086 mm; F28; opening inward and outward; weatherstripped; no sill	Nr	0.35	8.80	–	75.01	83.81	9.68	–	82.51	92.19
L207106D	907 × 2086 mm; DF28IN; opening inward; non-weatherstripped	Nr	0.35	8.80	–	87.23	96.03	9.68	–	95.95	105.63
L207106E	907 × 2086 mm; DF28OUT; opening outward; non-weatherstripped	Nr	0.35	8.80	–	87.23	96.03	9.68	–	95.95	105.63
L207106F	907 × 2086 mm; DF28; opening inward and outward; non-weatherstripped; no sill	Nr	0.35	8.80	–	64.14	72.94	9.68	–	70.55	80.23
L207110	**Boulton and Paul softwood garage door frames; supplied unassembled; overall frame size:**										
L207110A	2271 × 2052 mm; UF7066NS..............	Nr	0.50	12.56	–	69.73	82.29	13.82	–	76.70	90.52
L207110B	2271 × 2205 mm; UF7070NS..............	Nr	0.50	12.56	–	71.87	84.43	13.82	–	79.06	92.87
L207110C	2423 × 2052 mm; UF7666NS..............	Nr	0.50	12.56	–	71.00	83.56	13.82	–	78.10	91.92
L207110D	2423 × 2205 mm; UF7670NS..............	Nr	0.50	12.56	–	74.23	86.79	13.82	–	81.65	95.47
L207110E	2575 × 2052 mm; UF8066NS..............	Nr	0.50	12.56	–	79.54	92.10	13.82	–	87.49	101.31
L207110F	2575 × 2205 mm; UF8070NS..............	Nr	0.50	12.56	–	81.67	94.23	13.82	–	89.84	103.65
L207110G	4404 × 2052 mm; UF14066NS..............	Nr	0.70	17.59	–	120.74	138.33	19.35	–	132.81	152.16
L207110H	4404 × 2205 mm; UF14070NS..............	Nr	0.70	17.59	–	120.74	138.33	19.35	–	132.81	152.16

Major Works 2009		Unit	Labour Hours	Labour Net	Plant Net	Materials Net	Unit Net	Labour Gross	Plant Gross	Materials Gross	Unit Price
								(Gross rates include 10% profit)			
				£	£	£	£	£	£	£	£
L20	**L20: DOORS, SHUTTERS AND HATCHES**										
L2072	**Standard softwood external door frames and side lights**										
L207270	**Boulton and Paul softwood exterior door frames; hardwood sills; factory fitted sidelights; for 838 × 1981 mm doors:**										
L207270A	1307 × 2079 mm; FE13029; 332 mm wide sidelight; SL3366SHX	Nr	0.35	8.80	–	231.21	240.01	9.68	–	254.33	264.01
L207270B	1532 × 2079 mm; FE1529; 557 mm wide sidelight; SL5566SHX.	Nr	0.35	8.80	–	258.64	267.44	9.68	–	284.50	294.18
L207270C	1682 × 2079 mm; FED16829; 332 mm wide sidelight; SL3366SHX	Nr	0.35	8.80	–	269.41	278.21	9.68	–	296.35	306.03
L207270D	2132 × 2079 mm; FED21329; 557 mm wide sidelight; SL5566SHX	Nr	0.35	8.80	–	309.99	318.79	9.68	–	340.99	350.67
L207271	**Boulton and Paul softwood half hour firecheck exterior door frames; fitted with 15 × 4 mm intumescent strip; for 762 × 1981 mm doors:**										
L207271A	856 × 2035 mm; DF26FCA2; opening inward and outward; no sill	Nr	0.25	6.28	–	65.30	71.58	6.91	–	71.83	78.74
L207271B	856 × 2035 mm; DF26FCA1; opening inward; standard sill.	Nr	0.25	6.28	–	84.09	90.37	6.91	–	92.50	99.41
L207271C	856 × 2035 mm; DF26FCA3; opening inward and outward; flush sill	Nr	0.25	6.28	–	84.09	90.37	6.91	–	92.50	99.41
L207272	**Boulton and Paul softwood half hour fir check door frames; 15 × 4 mm intumescent strip; for 838 × 1981 mm doors:**										
L207272A	932 × 2035 mm; DF29FCA2; opening inward and outward; no sill	Nr	0.25	6.28	–	75.01	81.29	6.91	–	82.51	89.42
L207272B	932 × 2035 mm; DF29FCA1; opening inward; standard sill.	Nr	0.25	6.28	–	75.01	81.29	6.91	–	82.51	89.42
L207272C	932 × 2035 mm; DF29FCA3; opening inward and outward; flush sill	Nr	0.25	6.28	–	70.11	76.39	6.91	–	77.12	84.03
L207273	**Boulton and Paul softwood half hour fir check exterior door frames; hardwood sills; 15 × 4 mm intumescent strip; for 813 × 2032 mm doors:**										
L207273A	906 × 2086 mm; DF28FCA2; opening inward and outward; no sill	Nr	0.25	6.28	–	93.21	99.49	6.91	–	102.53	109.44

Windows, Doors and Stairs

Major Works 2009		Unit	Labour Hours	Labour Net	Plant Net	Materials Net	Unit Net	Labour Gross	Plant Gross	Materials Gross	Unit Price
								(Gross rates include 10% profit)			
				£	£	£	£	£	£	£	£
L20	**L20: DOORS, SHUTTERS AND HATCHES**										
L2072	**Standard softwood external door frames and side lights**										
L207275	**Boulton and Paul softwood exterior garage door frames:**										
L207275I	2427 × 2054 mm; UF7666NS.............	Nr	0.50	12.56	–	71.00	83.56	13.82	–	78.10	91.92
L207275J	2275 × 2054 mm; UF7066NS.............	Nr	0.50	12.56	–	69.73	82.29	13.82	–	76.70	90.52
L207275K	2275 × 2207 mm; UF7070NS.............	Nr	0.50	12.56	–	71.87	84.43	13.82	–	79.06	92.87
L207275L	4408 × 2254 mm; UF14066NS...........	Nr	0.70	17.59	–	120.74	138.33	19.35	–	132.81	152.16
L207275M	4408 × 2207 mm; UF14070NS...........	Nr	0.70	17.59	–	120.74	138.33	19.35	–	132.81	152.16
L207276	**Boulton and Paul softwood side lights; fitting to exterior frames (measured separately); to suit imperial doors:**										
L207276A	SL3366PX; 332 mm wide ..	Nr	0.50	8.49	–	95.56	104.05	9.34	–	105.12	114.46
L207276B	SL5566PX; 557 mm wide ..	Nr	0.55	9.34	–	131.19	140.53	10.27	–	144.31	154.58
L207276C	SL3366RX; 332 mm wide ..	Nr	0.50	8.49	–	102.57	111.06	9.34	–	112.83	122.17
L207276D	SL5566RX; 557 mm wide ..	Nr	0.55	9.34	–	152.87	162.21	10.27	–	168.16	178.43
L207276E	SL3366SBX; 332 mm wide .	Nr	0.50	8.49	–	100.11	108.60	9.34	–	110.12	119.46
L207276F	SL5566SBX; 557 mm wide .	Nr	0.55	9.34	–	113.93	123.27	10.27	–	125.32	135.60
L207276G	SL3366SHX; 332 mm wide .	Nr	0.50	8.49	–	93.93	102.42	9.34	–	103.32	112.66
L207276H	SL5566SHX; 557 mm wide .	Nr	0.55	9.34	–	114.26	123.60	10.27	–	125.69	135.96
L207276I	SL3366TBX; 332 mm wide .	Nr	0.50	8.49	–	328.62	337.11	9.34	–	361.48	370.82
L207276J	SL5566TBX; 557 mm wide .	Nr	0.55	9.34	–	328.62	337.96	10.27	–	361.48	371.76
L207276K	SL3366THX; 332 mm wide .	Nr	0.50	8.49	–	182.92	191.41	9.34	–	201.21	210.55
L207276L	SL5566THX; 557 mm wide .	Nr	0.55	9.34	–	197.88	207.22	10.27	–	217.67	227.94
L207290	**Boulton and Paul softwood interior door frames:**										
L207290A	225DF23 or 26	Nr	0.40	6.79	–	29.00	35.79	7.47	–	31.90	39.37
L207290B	25DF23 or 26	Nr	0.40	6.79	–	29.00	35.79	7.47	–	31.90	39.37
L207290C	4DF23 or 26	Nr	0.40	6.79	–	41.18	47.97	7.47	–	45.30	52.77
L207290D	45DF23 or 26	Nr	0.40	6.79	–	47.40	54.19	7.47	–	52.14	59.61
L207290E	225SF23 or 26	Nr	0.40	6.79	–	31.04	37.83	7.47	–	34.14	41.61
L207290F	25SF23 or 26	Nr	0.40	6.79	–	33.14	39.93	7.47	–	36.45	43.92
L207290G	4SF23 or 26.............	Nr	0.40	6.79	–	49.12	55.91	7.47	–	54.03	61.50
L207290H	45SF23 or 26	Nr	0.40	6.79	–	55.37	62.16	7.47	–	60.91	68.38
L207290I	225FF23 or 26...........	Nr	0.40	6.79	–	37.94	44.73	7.47	–	41.73	49.20
L207290J	25FF23 or 26...........	Nr	0.40	6.79	–	39.75	46.54	7.47	–	43.73	51.19
L207290K	4FF23 or 26.............	Nr	0.40	6.79	–	57.50	64.29	7.47	–	63.25	70.72
L207290L	45FF23 or 26	Nr	0.40	6.79	–	63.43	70.22	7.47	–	69.77	77.24
L207291	**Boulton and Paul softwood interior door lining sets:**										
L207291A	94DL8 or 9	Nr	0.40	6.79	–	35.76	42.55	7.47	–	39.34	46.81
L207291B	107DL8 or 9	Nr	0.40	6.79	–	42.07	48.86	7.47	–	46.28	53.75
L207291C	133DL8 or 9	Nr	0.40	6.79	–	47.03	53.82	7.47	–	51.73	59.20
L207291D	94FL8 or 9..............	Nr	0.40	6.79	–	51.10	57.89	7.47	–	56.21	63.68
L207291E	107FL8 or 9.............	Nr	0.40	6.79	–	57.59	64.38	7.47	–	63.35	70.82
L207291F	133FL8 or 9.............	Nr	0.40	6.79	–	62.03	68.82	7.47	–	68.23	75.70
L207291G	4DL23 or 26	Nr	0.40	6.79	–	30.85	37.64	7.47	–	33.94	41.40
L207291H	45DL23 or 26	Nr	0.40	6.79	–	32.41	39.20	7.47	–	35.65	43.12
L207291I	5DL23 or 26	Nr	0.40	6.79	–	34.99	41.78	7.47	–	38.49	45.96
L207291J	55DL23 or 26	Nr	0.40	6.79	–	37.66	44.45	7.47	–	41.43	48.90
L207291K	5FL23 or 26.............	Nr	0.40	6.79	–	49.26	56.05	7.47	–	54.19	61.66
L207291L	55FL23 or 26............	Nr	0.40	6.79	–	52.81	59.60	7.47	–	58.09	65.56
L207291M	45DLR23A or 26A	Nr	0.40	6.79	–	33.59	40.38	7.47	–	36.95	44.42
L207291N	55DLR23A or 26A	Nr	0.40	6.79	–	38.64	45.43	7.47	–	42.50	49.97

Major Works 2009		Unit	Labour Hours	Labour Net	Plant Net	Materials Net	Unit Net	Labour Gross	Plant Gross	Materials Gross	Unit Price
								(Gross rates include 10% profit)			
				£	£	£	£	£	£	£	£
L20	**L20: DOORS, SHUTTERS AND HATCHES**										
L2073	**Softwood jambs, heads, sills, mullions, transoms or the like**										
L207351	**Wrought softwood plain jambs or heads:**										
L207351A	25 × 75 mm	m	0.27	4.59	–	2.21	6.80	5.05	–	2.43	7.48
L207351B	25 × 100 mm	m	0.29	4.92	–	2.68	7.60	5.41	–	2.95	8.36
L207351C	25 × 125 mm	m	0.32	5.43	–	3.28	8.71	5.97	–	3.61	9.58
L207351D	25 × 150 mm	m	0.35	5.94	–	3.94	9.88	6.53	–	4.33	10.87
L207351E	32 × 75 mm	m	0.27	4.58	–	2.68	7.26	5.04	–	2.95	7.99
L207351F	32 × 100 mm	m	0.29	4.93	–	3.51	8.44	5.42	–	3.86	9.28
L207351G	32 × 125 mm	m	0.32	5.43	–	4.01	9.44	5.97	–	4.41	10.38
L207351H	32 × 150 mm	m	0.35	5.94	–	5.13	11.07	6.53	–	5.64	12.18
L207351I	50 × 75 mm	m	0.30	5.09	–	3.81	8.90	5.60	–	4.19	9.79
L207351J	50 × 100 mm	m	0.32	5.43	–	5.10	10.53	5.97	–	5.61	11.58
L207351K	50 × 125 mm	m	0.35	5.95	–	6.39	12.34	6.55	–	7.03	13.57
L207351L	50 × 150 mm	m	0.38	6.45	–	7.64	14.09	7.10	–	8.40	15.50
L207352	**Wrought softwood once rebated jambs or heads:**										
L207352A	38 × 100 mm	m	0.36	6.11	–	4.24	10.35	6.72	–	4.66	11.39
L207352B	38 × 125 mm	m	0.38	6.45	–	5.18	11.63	7.10	–	5.70	12.79
L207352C	38 × 150 mm	m	0.40	6.79	–	6.10	12.89	7.47	–	6.71	14.18
L207352D	50 × 75 mm	m	0.35	5.95	–	4.02	9.97	6.55	–	4.42	10.97
L207352E	50 × 100 mm	m	0.37	6.28	–	5.31	11.59	6.91	–	5.84	12.75
L207352F	50 × 150 mm	m	0.43	7.30	–	7.82	15.12	8.03	–	8.60	16.63
L207352G	63 × 75 mm	m	0.37	6.28	–	5.06	11.34	6.91	–	5.57	12.47
L207352H	63 × 100 mm	m	0.40	6.80	–	6.64	13.44	7.48	–	7.30	14.78
L207352I	63 × 125 mm	m	0.43	7.31	–	8.17	15.48	8.04	–	8.99	17.03
L207352J	63 × 150 mm	m	0.45	7.64	–	9.74	17.38	8.40	–	10.71	19.12
L207353	**Wrought softwood once rebated and once grooved jambs or heads:**										
L207353A	50 × 100 mm	m	0.37	6.28	–	5.53	11.81	6.91	–	6.08	12.99
L207353B	50 × 125 mm	m	0.40	6.79	–	6.83	13.62	7.47	–	7.51	14.98
L207353C	50 × 150 mm	m	0.43	7.30	–	8.07	15.37	8.03	–	8.88	16.91
L207353D	63 × 75 mm	m	0.37	6.28	–	5.29	11.57	6.91	–	5.82	12.73
L207353E	63 × 100 mm	m	0.40	6.79	–	6.88	13.67	7.47	–	7.57	15.04
L207353F	63 × 125 mm	m	0.43	7.31	–	8.40	15.71	8.04	–	9.24	17.28
L207353G	63 × 150 mm	m	0.45	7.64	–	9.96	17.60	8.40	–	10.96	19.36
L207354	**Wrought softwood once sunk weathered, once rebated and three times grooved sills:**										
L207354A	63 × 75 mm	m	0.35	5.95	–	5.98	11.93	6.55	–	6.58	13.12
L207354B	75 × 150 mm	m	0.48	8.15	–	12.33	20.48	8.97	–	13.56	22.53
L207355	**Wrought softwood mullions or transoms:**										
L207355A	32 × 63 mm	m	0.30	5.09	–	2.05	7.14	5.60	–	2.26	7.85
L207355B	32 × 100 mm	m	0.31	5.27	–	3.34	8.61	5.80	–	3.67	9.47
L207355C	32 × 150 mm	m	0.35	5.94	–	4.96	10.90	6.53	–	5.46	11.99
L207356	**Wrought softwood twice rebated mullions or transoms:**										
L207356A	38 × 115 mm	m	0.38	6.45	–	5.30	11.75	7.10	–	5.83	12.93
L207356B	38 × 150 mm	m	0.40	6.79	–	6.24	13.03	7.47	–	6.86	14.33
L207356C	50 × 100 mm	m	0.37	6.28	–	5.39	11.67	6.91	–	5.93	12.84
L207356D	63 × 115 mm	m	0.42	7.13	–	7.99	15.12	7.84	–	8.79	16.63
L207356E	63 × 150 mm	m	0.45	7.65	–	9.72	17.37	8.42	–	10.69	19.11

Windows, Doors and Stairs

Major Works 2009		Unit	Labour Hours	Labour Net	Plant Net	Materials Net	Unit Net	Labour Gross	Plant Gross	Materials Gross	Unit Price
								(Gross rates include 10% profit)			
				£	£	£	£	£	£	£	£
L20	**L20: DOORS, SHUTTERS AND HATCHES**										
L2076	**Standard hardwood external door frames**										
L207606	**Boulton and Paul hardwood exterior door frames; standard sills; heavy duty PVC waterbar; for 762 × 1981 mm doors:**										
L207606A	856 × 2079 mm; FN26MH; opening inward; weatherstripped	Nr	0.50	8.49	–	354.71	363.20	9.34	–	390.18	399.52
L207606B	856 × 2035 mm; F26H; opening inward and outward; weatherstripped	Nr	0.50	8.49	–	368.28	376.77	9.34	–	405.11	414.45
L207606C	FE127RH; 1275 × 2100 mm	Nr	0.50	8.49	–	387.63	396.12	9.34	–	426.39	435.73
L207606D	FE135RH; 1350 × 2100 mm	Nr	0.50	8.49	–	404.51	413.00	9.34	–	444.96	454.30
L207606E	FE127FH; 1275 × 2100 mm	Nr	0.50	8.49	–	421.76	430.25	9.34	–	463.94	473.28
L207606F	FE135FH; 1350 × 2100 mm	Nr	0.50	8.49	–	446.59	455.08	9.34	–	491.25	500.59
L207606G	FED165PPH; 1650 × 2100 mm	Nr	0.50	8.49	–	541.45	549.94	9.34	–	595.60	604.93
L207606H	FED180PPH; 1800 × 2100 mm	Nr	0.50	8.49	–	569.99	578.48	9.34	–	626.99	636.33
L207606I	FED165RRH; 1650 × 2100 mm	Nr	0.50	8.49	–	607.32	615.81	9.34	–	668.05	677.39
L207606J	FED180RRH; 1800 × 2100 mm	Nr	0.50	8.49	–	642.45	650.94	9.34	–	706.70	716.03
L207606K	FED165FFH; 1650 × 2100 mm	Nr	0.50	8.49	–	675.51	684.00	9.34	–	743.06	752.40
L207606L	FED180FFH; 1800 × 2100 mm	Nr	0.50	8.49	–	726.64	735.13	9.34	–	799.30	808.64
L207607	**Boulton and Paul hardwood exterior door frames; standard sill; heavy duty PVC waterbar; for 838 × 1981 mm doors:**										
L207607A	932 × 2079 mm; FN29MH; opening inward; weatherstripped	Nr	0.50	8.49	–	123.77	132.26	9.34	–	136.15	145.49
L207607B	932 × 2079 mm; FX29MH; opening outward; weatherstripped	Nr	0.50	8.49	–	123.77	132.26	9.34	–	136.15	145.49
L207607C	932 × 2079 mm; F29H; opening inward and outward; weatherstripped	Nr	0.50	8.49	–	105.74	114.23	9.34	–	116.31	125.65

Major Works 2009		Unit	Labour Hours	Labour Net	Plant Net	Materials Net	Unit Net	Labour Gross	Plant Gross	Materials Gross	Unit Price
								(Gross rates include 10% profit)			
				£	£	£	£	£	£	£	£
L20	**L20: DOORS, SHUTTERS AND HATCHES**										
L2076	**Standard hardwood external door frames**										
L207608	**Boulton and Paul hardwood exterior door frames; standard sills; heavy duty PVC waterbar; for 807 × 2000 mm doors:**										
L207608A	900 × 2100 mm; FNSH; opening inward; weatherstripped	Nr	0.50	8.49	–	118.82	127.31	9.34	–	130.70	140.04
L207608B	900 × 2100 mm; FXSH; opening outward weatherstripped	Nr	0.50	8.49	–	118.82	127.31	9.34	–	130.70	140.04
L207608C	900 × 2100 mm; FDH; opening inward and outward; weatherstripped	Nr	0.50	8.49	–	105.74	114.23	9.34	–	116.31	125.65
L2077	**Standard hardwood door frames**										
L207782	**Boulton and Paul hardwood side lights; fitting to exterior frames (measured separately):**										
L207782A	SL25PXH; 257 mm wide	Nr	0.40	6.79	–	158.60	165.39	7.47	–	174.46	181.93
L207782B	SL33PXH; 332 mm wide	Nr	0.45	7.64	–	169.15	176.79	8.40	–	186.07	194.47
L207782C	SL40PXH; 407 mm wide	Nr	0.40	6.79	–	156.41	163.20	7.47	–	172.05	179.52
L207782D	SL48PXH; 482 mm wide	Nr	0.45	7.64	–	198.58	206.22	8.40	–	218.44	226.84
L207782E	SL55PXH; 557 mm wide	Nr	0.40	6.79	–	172.84	179.63	7.47	–	190.12	197.59

Windows, Doors and Stairs

Major Works 2009		Unit	Labour Hours	Labour Net	Plant Net	Materials Net	Unit Net	Labour Gross	Plant Gross	Materials Gross	Unit Price
								——— (Gross rates include 10% profit) ———			
				£	£	£	£	£	£	£	£
L20	**L20: DOORS, SHUTTERS AND HATCHES**										
L2078	**Hardwood jambs, heads, sills, mullions, transoms or the like**										
L207860	**Wrought hardwood; Sapele; plain jambs or heads:**										
L207860A	20 × 68 mm	m	0.30	5.10	–	1.64	6.74	5.61	–	1.80	7.41
L207860B	20 × 93 mm	m	0.32	5.43	–	2.24	7.67	5.97	–	2.46	8.44
L207860C	20 × 118 mm	m	0.35	5.94	–	2.81	8.75	6.53	–	3.09	9.63
L207860D	20 × 143 mm	m	0.38	6.46	–	3.40	9.86	7.11	–	3.74	10.85
L207860E	26 × 56 mm	m	0.33	5.60	–	1.81	7.41	6.16	–	1.99	8.15
L207860F	26 × 93 mm	m	0.35	5.95	–	2.92	8.87	6.55	–	3.21	9.76
L207860G	26 × 118 mm	m	0.38	6.45	–	3.67	10.12	7.10	–	4.04	11.13
L207860H	26 × 143 mm	m	0.42	7.13	–	4.43	11.56	7.84	–	4.87	12.72
L207860I	44 × 56 mm	m	0.42	7.13	–	3.01	10.14	7.84	–	3.31	11.15
L207860J	44 × 68 mm	m	0.45	7.64	–	3.64	11.28	8.40	–	4.00	12.41
L207860K	44 × 93 mm	m	0.47	7.98	–	4.92	12.90	8.78	–	5.41	14.19
L207860L	44 × 118 mm	m	0.52	8.83	–	6.18	15.01	9.71	–	6.80	16.51
L207860M	44 × 143 mm	m	0.55	9.34	–	7.46	16.80	10.27	–	8.21	18.48
L207861	**Wrought hardwood; Sapele; once rebated jambs or heads:**										
L207861A	32 × 93 mm	m	0.35	5.94	–	3.73	9.67	6.53	–	4.10	10.64
L207861B	32 × 118 mm	m	0.38	6.45	–	4.67	11.12	7.10	–	5.14	12.23
L207861C	32 × 143 mm	m	0.42	7.13	–	5.60	12.73	7.84	–	6.16	14.00
L207861D	44 × 68 mm	m	0.45	7.64	–	3.82	11.46	8.40	–	4.20	12.61
L207861E	44 × 93 mm	m	0.47	7.98	–	5.09	13.07	8.78	–	5.60	14.38
L207861F	44 × 118 mm	m	0.52	8.83	–	6.36	15.19	9.71	–	7.00	16.71
L207861G	44 × 143 mm	m	0.55	9.34	–	7.64	16.98	10.27	–	8.40	18.68
L207861H	56 × 68 mm	m	0.50	8.49	–	4.85	13.34	9.34	–	5.34	14.67
L207861I	56 × 93 mm	m	0.52	8.83	–	6.48	15.31	9.71	–	7.13	16.84
L207861J	56 × 118 mm	m	0.57	9.68	–	8.11	17.79	10.65	–	8.92	19.57
L207861K	56 × 143 mm	m	0.60	10.19	–	9.72	19.91	11.21	–	10.69	21.90
L207862	**Wrought hardwood; Sapele; once rebated and once grooved jambs or heads:**										
L207862A	44 × 93 mm	m	0.47	7.98	–	5.27	13.25	8.78	–	5.80	14.58
L207862B	44 × 118 mm	m	0.52	8.83	–	6.54	15.37	9.71	–	7.19	16.91
L207862C	44 × 143 mm	m	0.55	9.34	–	7.81	17.15	10.27	–	8.59	18.87
L207862D	56 × 68 mm	m	0.50	8.49	–	5.03	13.52	9.34	–	5.53	14.87
L207862E	56 × 93 mm	m	0.52	8.83	–	6.58	15.41	9.71	–	7.24	16.95
L207862F	56 × 118 mm	m	0.57	9.68	–	8.27	17.95	10.65	–	9.10	19.75
L207862G	56 × 143 mm	m	0.60	10.19	–	9.92	20.11	11.21	–	10.91	22.12
L207863	**Wrought hardwood; Sapele; once sunk weathered, once rebated and three times grooved sills:**										
L207863A	56 × 168 mm	m	0.60	10.19	–	11.86	22.05	11.21	–	13.05	24.26
L207863B	68 × 143 mm	m	0.65	11.04	–	12.21	23.25	12.14	–	13.43	25.58
L207864	**Wrought hardwood; Sapele; plain mullion or transoms:**										
L207864A	26 × 56 mm	m	0.33	5.60	–	1.72	7.32	6.16	–	1.89	8.05
L207864B	26 × 93 mm	m	0.35	5.94	–	2.83	8.77	6.53	–	3.11	9.65
L207864C	26 × 143 mm	m	0.42	7.14	–	4.33	11.47	7.85	–	4.76	12.62
L207865	**Wrought hardwood; Sapele; twice rebated mullions or transoms:**										
L207865A	32 × 118 mm	m	0.38	6.45	–	4.75	11.20	7.10	–	5.23	12.32
L207865B	32 × 143 mm	m	0.42	7.13	–	5.68	12.81	7.84	–	6.25	14.09
L207865C	44 × 93 mm	m	0.47	7.98	–	5.13	13.11	8.78	–	5.64	14.42
L207865D	56 × 118 mm	m	0.57	9.68	–	8.04	17.72	10.65	–	8.84	19.49
L207865E	56 × 143 mm	m	0.60	10.19	–	9.69	19.88	11.21	–	10.66	21.87

Major Works 2009		Unit	Labour Hours	Labour Net	Plant Net	Materials Net	Unit Net	Labour Gross	Plant Gross	Materials Gross	Unit Price
								(Gross rates include 10% profit)			
				£	£	£	£	£	£	£	£
L20	**L20: DOORS, SHUTTERS AND HATCHES**										
L2085	**Standard metal garage doors**										
L208541	**Henderson galvanised steel up-and-over garage doors complete with all gear; to suit opening size:**										
L208541A	1981 × 1981 mm; Merlin 6666; canopy	Nr	3.00	50.94	–	268.80	319.74	56.03	–	295.68	351.71
L208541B	2134 × 1981 mm; Merlin 7066; canopy	Nr	3.25	55.19	–	252.80	307.99	60.71	–	278.08	338.79
L208541C	2286 × 1981 mm; Merlin 7666; canopy	Nr	3.50	59.43	–	300.80	360.23	65.37	–	330.88	396.25
L208541D	2438 × 1981 mm; Merlin 8066; canopy	Nr	3.75	63.68	–	348.00	411.68	70.05	–	382.80	452.85
L208541E	1981 × 2134 mm; Merlin 6670; canopy	Nr	3.25	55.19	–	278.40	333.59	60.71	–	306.24	366.95
L208541F	2134 × 2134 mm; Merlin 7070; canopy	Nr	3.75	63.68	–	289.60	353.28	70.05	–	318.56	388.61
L208541G	2286 × 2134 mm; Merlin 7670; canopy	Nr	3.75	63.68	–	344.80	408.48	70.05	–	379.28	449.33
L208541H	2438 × 2134 mm; Merlin 8070; canopy	Nr	4.00	67.92	–	356.00	423.92	74.71	–	391.60	466.31
L208541I	1981 × 1981 mm; Regent 6666; canopy	Nr	3.00	50.94	–	308.80	359.74	56.03	–	339.68	395.71
L208541J	2134 × 1981 mm; Regent 7066; canopy	Nr	3.25	55.19	–	308.00	363.19	60.71	–	338.80	399.51
L208541K	2286 × 1981 mm; Regent 7666; canopy	Nr	3.50	59.43	–	335.20	394.63	65.37	–	368.72	434.09
L208541L	2438 × 1981 mm; Regent 8066; canopy	Nr	3.75	63.68	–	397.60	461.28	70.05	–	437.36	507.41
L208541M	1981 × 2134 mm; Regent 6670; canopy	Nr	3.25	55.19	–	309.60	364.79	60.71	–	340.56	401.27
L208541N	2134 × 2134 mm; Regent 7070; canopy	Nr	3.75	63.68	–	320.00	383.68	70.05	–	352.00	422.05
L208541O	2286 × 2134 mm; Regent 7670; canopy	Nr	3.75	63.68	–	376.80	440.48	70.05	–	414.48	484.53
L208541P	2438 × 2134 mm; Regent 8070; canopy	Nr	4.00	67.92	–	455.20	523.12	74.71	–	500.72	575.43
L208541Q	2743 × 2134 mm; Regent 9070; canopy	Nr	4.50	76.41	–	608.80	685.21	84.05	–	669.68	753.73
L208541R	2134 × 1981 mm; Doric 7066; canopy	Nr	3.25	55.19	–	380.80	435.99	60.71	–	418.88	479.59
L208541S	2134 × 2134 mm; Doric 7070; canopy	Nr	3.75	63.68	–	401.60	465.28	70.05	–	441.76	511.81
L208541T	4267 × 1981 mm; Doric 1466; tracked	Nr	5.00	84.90	–	1115.20	1200.10	93.39	–	1226.72	1320.11
L208541U	4267 × 2134 mm; Doric 1470; tracked	Nr	5.50	93.39	–	1115.20	1208.59	102.73	–	1226.72	1329.45
L208541V	2134 × 1981 mm; Regent Chevron 7066; canopy.....	Nr	3.25	55.19	–	320.00	375.19	60.71	–	352.00	412.71
L208541W	2134 × 2134 mm; Regent Chevron 7070; canopy.....	Nr	3.75	63.68	–	337.60	401.28	70.05	–	371.36	441.41
L208541X	4267 × 1981 mm; Regent Chevron 1466; canopy.....	Nr	5.00	84.90	–	967.20	1052.10	93.39	–	1063.92	1157.31
L208541Y	4267 × 2134 mm; Regent Chevron 1470; canopy.....	Nr	5.50	93.39	–	967.20	1060.59	102.73	–	1063.92	1166.65

Windows, Doors and Stairs

Major Works 2009		Unit	Labour Hours	Labour Net	Plant Net	Materials Net	Unit Net	Labour Gross	Plant Gross	Materials Gross	Unit Price
								(Gross rates include 10% profit)			
				£	£	£	£	£	£	£	£
L20	**L20: DOORS, SHUTTERS AND HATCHES**										
L2090	**Standard GRP and plastic coated garage doors**										
L209042	**Henderson GRP up-and-over garage doors complete with all gear; to suit opening size:**										
L209042A	4267 × 1981 mm; Consort 1466; tracked	Nr	4.50	76.41	–	1488.00	1564.41	84.05	–	1636.80	1720.85
L209042B	4267 × 2134 mm; Consort 1470; tracked	Nr	5.00	84.90	–	1488.00	1572.90	93.39	–	1636.80	1730.19
L209042C	4267 × 1981 mm; Caversham 1466; tracked ..	Nr	4.50	76.41	–	1780.00	1856.41	84.05	–	1958.00	2042.05
L209042D	4267 × 2134 mm; Caversham 1470; tracked ..	Nr	5.00	84.90	–	1780.00	1864.90	93.39	–	1958.00	2051.39
L209042E	2134 × 1981 mm; Consort 7066; tracked	Nr	3.25	55.19	–	738.40	793.59	60.71	–	812.24	872.95
L209042F	2134 × 2134 mm; Consort 7070; tracked	Nr	3.75	63.68	–	738.40	802.08	70.05	–	812.24	882.29
L209042G	2134 × 1981 mm; Caversham 7066; tracked ..	Nr	3.25	55.19	–	960.00	1015.19	60.71	–	1056.00	1116.71
L209042H	2134 × 2134 mm; Caversham 7070; tracked ..	Nr	3.75	63.68	–	960.00	1023.68	70.05	–	1056.00	1126.05
L209043	**Henderson roller doors complete with al gear; HP 200 High Performance Plastisol finish; curtain width and height:**										
L209043A	2185 × 1829-2133 mm ..	Nr	3.00	50.94	–	424.80	475.74	56.03	–	467.28	523.31
L209043B	2490 × 1829-2133 mm ..	Nr	3.10	52.64	–	433.60	486.24	57.90	–	476.96	534.86
L209043C	2800 × 1829-2133 mm ..	Nr	3.25	55.19	–	479.20	534.39	60.71	–	527.12	587.83
L209043D	3400 × 1829-2133 mm ..	Nr	3.50	59.43	–	601.60	661.03	65.37	–	661.76	727.13
L209043E	4370 × 1829-2133 mm ..	Nr	3.75	63.68	–	855.20	918.88	70.05	–	940.72	1010.77
L209043F	5000 × 1829-2133 mm ..	Nr	4.00	67.92	–	1035.20	1103.12	74.71	–	1138.72	1213.43
L209043G	2185 × 2160-2440 mm ..	Nr	3.50	59.43	–	453.60	513.03	65.37	–	498.96	564.33
L209043H	2490 × 2160-2440 mm ..	Nr	3.60	61.13	–	471.20	532.33	67.24	–	518.32	585.56
L209043I	2800 × 2160-2440 mm ..	Nr	3.75	63.68	–	536.80	600.48	70.05	–	590.48	660.53
L209043J	3400 × 2160-2440 mm ..	Nr	4.00	67.92	–	676.00	743.92	74.71	–	743.60	818.31
L209043K	4370 × 2160-2440 mm ..	Nr	4.30	73.01	–	962.40	1035.41	80.31	–	1058.64	1138.95
L209043L	5000 × 2160-2440 mm ..	Nr	4.60	78.11	–	1109.60	1187.71	85.92	–	1220.56	1306.48
L209043M	2185 × 2465-2745 mm ..	Nr	4.00	67.92	–	522.40	590.32	74.71	–	574.64	649.35
L209043N	2490 × 2465-2745 mm ..	Nr	4.15	70.47	–	575.20	645.67	77.52	–	632.72	710.24
L209043O	2800 × 2465-2745 mm ..	Nr	4.25	72.17	–	600.00	672.17	79.39	–	660.00	739.39
L209043P	3400 × 2465-2745 mm ..	Nr	4.55	77.26	–	703.20	780.46	84.99	–	773.52	858.51
L209043Q	4375 × 2465-2745 mm ..	Nr	4.85	82.35	–	1040.00	1122.35	90.59	–	1144.00	1234.59
L209043R	5000 × 2465-2745 mm ..	Nr	5.20	88.30	–	1160.00	1248.30	97.13	–	1276.00	1373.13
L209043S	2185 × 2770-3000 mm ..	Nr	4.40	74.71	–	554.40	629.11	82.18	–	609.84	692.02
L209043T	2490 × 2770-3000 mm ..	Nr	4.55	77.26	–	591.20	668.46	84.99	–	650.32	735.31
L209043U	2800 × 2770-3000 mm ..	Nr	4.70	79.81	–	649.60	729.41	87.79	–	714.56	802.35
L209043V	3400 × 2770-3000 mm ..	Nr	5.00	84.90	–	792.80	877.70	93.39	–	872.08	965.47
L209043W	4370 × 2770-3000 mm ..	Nr	5.35	90.84	–	1103.20	1194.04	99.92	–	1213.52	1313.94
L209043X	5000 × 2770-3000 mm ..	Nr	5.75	97.64	–	1182.40	1280.04	107.40	–	1300.64	1408.04
L209044	**Henderson roller shutter garage doors; accessories:**										
L209044A	heavy duty remote control .	Nr	–	–	–	276.00	276.00	–	–	303.60	303.60
L209044B	dual remote control	Nr	–	–	–	336.00	336.00	–	–	369.60	369.60
L209044C	external manual release and electric key switch	Nr	–	–	–	44.00	44.00	–	–	48.40	48.40
L209044D	two function transmitter ...	Nr	–	–	–	33.60	33.60	–	–	36.96	36.96
L2096	**Mastic pointing**										
L209699	**Pointing frames one side with mastic sealant:**										
L209699A	standard	m	0.05	0.63	–	0.31	0.94	0.69	–	0.34	1.03
L209699B	coloured	m	0.05	0.64	–	0.34	0.98	0.70	–	0.37	1.08

Major Works 2009		Unit	Labour Hours	Labour Net	Plant Net	Materials Net	Unit Net	Labour Gross	Plant Gross	Materials Gross	Unit Price
								(Gross rates include 10% profit)			
				£	£	£	£	£	£	£	£
L30	**L30: STAIRS, WALKWAYS AND BALUSTRADES**										
L3011	**Staircases, handrails and balustrades**										
L301101	**Boulton and Paul standard stock flight staircases; closed riser straight flight unit; 13 riser; 855 mm overall width; total rise 2600 mm; model ref:**										
L301101A	STAIR M; Parana Pine strings and treads	Nr	8.00	135.84	–	447.59	583.43	149.42	–	492.35	641.77
L301101B	STAIR WM; whitewood/ composite string and treads	Nr	8.00	135.84	–	306.49	442.33	149.42	–	337.14	486.56
L301111	**Boulton and Paul standard staircase; winder design; o/a size 2940 × 1027 mm; newels and raking balustrade; 13 riser; total rise 2600 mm; model ref:**										
L301111A	W4DBTW; whitewood	Nr	18.00	305.64	–	1229.90	1535.54	336.20	–	1352.89	1689.09
L301111B	W4DBTP; parana pine	Nr	18.00	305.64	–	1309.06	1614.70	336.20	–	1439.97	1776.17
L301111C	W4DBTP; hardwood	Nr	27.00	458.46	–	1697.49	2155.95	504.31	–	1867.24	2371.55
L301152	**Handrails:**										
L301152A	50 mm dia; softwood mopstick	m	0.40	6.79	–	2.95	9.74	7.47	–	3.25	10.71
L301152B	50 mm dia; hardwood mopstick	m	0.40	6.79	–	4.09	10.88	7.47	–	4.50	11.97
L301152C	50 × 75 mm; softwood moulded	m	0.45	7.64	–	6.16	13.80	8.40	–	6.78	15.18
L301152D	50 × 75 mm; hardwood moulded	m	0.45	7.64	–	7.43	15.07	8.40	–	8.17	16.58
L301152E	75 × 100 mm; moulded . .	m	0.50	8.49	–	9.14	17.63	9.34	–	10.05	19.39
L301153	**Balustrades; stair and landing kits; hemlock spindles and newels; string capping and moulded handrail; newel caps; type:**										
L301153A	SMRKIT36 square stair kit .	Nr	2.80	47.54	–	36.42	83.96	52.29	–	40.06	92.36
L301153B	SMLKIT24 square landing kit	Nr	2.80	47.54	–	39.38	86.92	52.29	–	43.32	95.61
L301153C	SKGE Georgian stair kit	Nr	3.60	61.12	–	36.42	97.54	67.23	–	40.06	107.29
L301153D	LKGE Georgian landing kit. .	Nr	3.60	61.12	–	39.38	100.50	67.23	–	43.32	110.55
L301154	**Newels, caps and accessories:**										
L301154A	82 × 82 mm newel; turned softwood	Nr	0.50	8.49	–	75.42	83.91	9.34	–	82.96	92.30
L301154B	82 × 82 mm newel; turned hardwood	Nr	0.75	12.73	–	108.46	121.19	14.00	–	119.31	133.31
L301154C	82 × 82 mm newel; square softwood	Nr	0.50	8.49	–	45.32	53.81	9.34	–	49.85	59.19
L301154D	82 × 82 mm newel; square hardwood	Nr	0.75	12.73	–	70.14	82.87	14.00	–	77.15	91.16
L301154E	caps to suit newels; softwood	Nr	0.22	3.74	–	4.94	8.68	4.11	–	5.43	9.55
L301154F	caps to suit newels; hardwood	Nr	0.25	4.25	–	6.92	11.17	4.68	–	7.61	12.29

Windows, Doors and Stairs

Major Works 2009		Unit	Labour Hours	Labour Net	Plant Net	Materials Net	Unit Net	Labour Gross	Plant Gross	Materials Gross	Unit Price
								(Gross rates include 10% profit)			
				£	£	£	£	£	£	£	£
L40	**L40: GENERAL GLAZING**										
L4011	**Plain glazing**										
L401102	**Clear sheet or float glass to wood with putty:**										
L401102A	3 mm	m²	0.60	10.19	–	33.10	43.29	11.21	–	36.41	47.62
L401102B	4 mm	m²	0.60	10.19	–	37.49	47.68	11.21	–	41.24	52.45
L401102C	5 mm	m²	0.70	11.89	–	55.12	67.01	13.08	–	60.63	73.71
L401102D	6 mm	m²	0.70	11.89	–	62.01	73.90	13.08	–	68.21	81.29
L401102E	10 mm	m²	0.90	15.29	–	150.53	165.82	16.82	–	165.58	182.40
L401103	**Clear sheet or float glass to wood with beads (beads measured separately):**										
L401103A	3 mm	m²	0.70	11.89	–	32.62	44.51	13.08	–	35.88	48.96
L401103B	4 mm	m²	0.70	11.89	–	37.01	48.90	13.08	–	40.71	53.79
L401103C	5 mm	m²	0.80	13.59	–	54.64	68.23	14.95	–	60.10	75.05
L401103D	6 mm	m²	0.80	13.58	–	61.53	75.11	14.94	–	67.68	82.62
L401103E	10 mm	m²	1.00	16.99	–	150.05	167.04	18.69	–	165.06	183.74
L401104	**Georgian wired glass to wood with putty:**										
L401104A	6 mm polished plate.......	m²	0.70	11.89	–	99.50	111.39	13.08	–	109.45	122.53
L401104B	7 mm cast glass	m²	0.75	12.73	–	40.57	53.30	14.00	–	44.63	58.63
L401105	**Georgian wired glass to wood with beads (beads measured separately):**										
L401105A	6 mm polished plate.......	m²	0.80	13.59	–	99.02	112.61	14.95	–	108.92	123.87
L401105B	7 mm cast glass	m²	0.85	14.43	–	40.09	54.52	15.87	–	44.10	59.97
L401106	**Toughened safety glass to wood with putty:**										
L401106A	4 mm	m²	0.60	10.18	–	63.39	73.57	11.20	–	69.73	80.93
L401106B	5 mm	m²	0.60	10.19	–	71.70	81.89	11.21	–	78.87	90.08
L401106C	6 mm	m²	0.70	11.89	–	78.02	89.91	13.08	–	85.82	98.90
L401106D	10 mm	m²	0.90	15.28	–	154.35	169.63	16.81	–	169.79	186.59
L401107	**Toughened safety glass to wood with beads (beads measured separately):**										
L401107A	4 mm	m²	0.70	11.88	–	62.91	74.79	13.07	–	69.20	82.27
L401107B	5 mm	m²	0.70	11.89	–	71.22	83.11	13.08	–	78.34	91.42
L401107C	6 mm	m²	0.80	13.59	–	77.54	91.13	14.95	–	85.29	100.24
L401107D	10 mm	m²	1.00	16.98	–	153.87	170.85	18.68	–	169.26	187.94
L401108	**Clear laminated safety glass to wood with beads (beads measured separately):**										
L401108A	4.4 mm	m²	0.75	12.74	–	86.80	99.54	14.01	–	95.48	109.49
L401108B	5.4 mm	m²	0.80	13.58	–	88.78	102.36	14.94	–	97.66	112.60
L401108C	6.4 mm	m²	0.90	15.29	–	94.59	109.88	16.82	–	104.05	120.87
L401108D	6.8 mm	m²	0.95	16.14	–	116.64	132.78	17.75	–	128.30	146.06

Major Works 2009		Unit	Labour Hours	Labour Net	Plant Net	Materials Net	Unit Net	Labour Gross	Plant Gross	Materials Gross	Unit Price
								(Gross rates include 10% profit)			
				£	£	£	£	£	£	£	£
L40	**L40: GENERAL GLAZING**										
L4011	**Plain glazing**										
L401109	**Clear laminated anti-bandit glass to wood with beads (beads measured separately):**										
L401109A	7.5 mm	m²	0.90	15.29	–	178.99	194.28	16.82	–	196.89	213.71
L401109B	9.5 mm	m²	1.00	16.98	–	188.10	205.08	18.68	–	206.91	225.59
L401109C	11.5 mm	m²	1.10	18.68	–	220.48	239.16	20.55	–	242.53	263.08
L401110	**Antisun float glass to wood with putty:**										
L401110A	4 mm	m²	0.65	11.04	–	75.06	86.10	12.14	–	82.57	94.71
L401110B	6 mm	m²	0.75	12.73	–	113.24	125.97	14.00	–	124.56	138.57
L401110C	10 mm	m²	0.95	16.13	–	252.61	268.74	17.74	–	277.87	295.61
L401111	**Antisun float glass to wood with beads (beads measured separately):**										
L401111A	4 mm	m²	0.75	12.74	–	74.58	87.32	14.01	–	82.04	96.05
L401111B	6 mm	m²	0.85	14.43	–	112.76	127.19	15.87	–	124.04	139.91
L401111C	10 mm	m²	1.05	17.83	–	252.13	269.96	19.61	–	277.34	296.96
L401112	**Extra over clear sheet or float glass for:**										
L401112A	white patterned glass; 4 mm	m²	–	–	–	5.68	5.68	–	–	6.25	6.25
L401112B	white patterned glass; 6 mm	m²	–	–	–	13.02	13.02	–	–	14.32	14.32
L401112C	tinted patterned glass; 4 mm	m²	–	–	–	29.96	29.96	–	–	32.96	32.96
L401112D	tinted patterned glass; 6 mm	m²	–	–	–	21.48	21.48	–	–	23.63	23.63
L401113	**Extra over toughened safety glass for:**										
L401113A	tempered safety glass; 4 mm	m²	–	–	–	2.13	2.13	–	–	2.34	2.34
L401113B	tempered safety glass; 6 mm	m²	–	–	–	7.22	7.22	–	–	7.94	7.94
L401113C	white patterned safety glass; 4 mm	m²	–	–	–	2.13	2.13	–	–	2.34	2.34
L401113D	white patterned safety glass; 6 mm	m²	–	–	–	7.22	7.22	–	–	7.94	7.94
L401113E	tinted patterned safety glass; 4 mm	m²	–	–	–	54.52	54.52	–	–	59.97	59.97
L401113F	tinted patterned safety glass; 6 mm	m²	–	–	–	59.60	59.60	–	–	65.56	65.56

Windows, Doors and Stairs

Major Works 2009		Unit	Labour Hours	Labour Net	Plant Net	Materials Net	Unit Net	Labour Gross	Plant Gross	Materials Gross	Unit Price
								(Gross rates include 10% profit)			
				£	£	£	£	£	£	£	£
L40	**L40: GENERAL GLAZING**										
L4031	**Special glazing**										
L403121	**Boulton and Paul hermetically sealed annealed double glazing units to wood with beads (beads measured separately); to suit window ref:**										
L403121A	WN07C/WN07CH.........	Set	0.55	9.34	–	32.83	42.17	10.27	–	36.11	46.39
L403121B	WN09C/WN09CH.........	Set	0.66	11.21	–	32.84	44.05	12.33	–	36.12	48.46
L403121C	WN10C/WN10CH.........	Set	0.76	12.90	–	38.14	51.04	14.19	–	41.95	56.14
L403121D	WN12C/WN12CH.........	Set	0.88	14.94	–	120.66	135.60	16.43	–	132.73	149.16
L403121E	WN07V/WN07VH.........	Set	0.55	9.34	–	65.68	75.02	10.27	–	72.25	82.52
L403121F	WN09V/WN09VH.........	Set	0.66	11.21	–	65.68	76.89	12.33	–	72.25	84.58
L403121G	WN10V/WN10VH.........	Set	0.77	13.07	–	65.82	78.89	14.38	–	72.40	86.78
L403121H	WN12V	Set	0.88	14.94	–	73.84	88.78	16.43	–	81.22	97.66
L403121I	W107C/W107CH	Set	0.71	12.06	–	37.15	49.21	13.27	–	40.87	54.13
L403121J	W109C/W109CH	Set	0.85	14.43	–	41.47	55.90	15.87	–	45.62	61.49
L403121K	W110C/W110CH	Set	0.99	16.81	–	45.80	62.61	18.49	–	50.38	68.87
L403121L	W112C/W112CH	Set	1.13	19.19	–	50.10	69.29	21.11	–	55.11	76.22
L403121M	W113C/W113CH	Set	1.28	21.73	–	58.67	80.40	23.90	–	64.54	88.44
L403121N	W110T/W110TH..........	Set	0.99	16.81	–	69.99	86.80	18.49	–	76.99	95.48
L403121O	W112T/W112TH..........	Set	1.13	19.19	–	74.32	93.51	21.11	–	81.75	102.86
L403121P	W107V/W107VH	Set	0.71	12.06	–	65.68	77.74	13.27	–	72.25	85.51
L403121Q	W109V/W109VH	Set	0.86	14.60	–	70.68	85.28	16.06	–	77.75	93.81
L403121R	W110V/W110VH	Set	0.99	16.81	–	75.78	92.59	18.49	–	83.36	101.85
L403121S	W112V/W112VH	Set	1.13	19.19	–	80.91	100.10	21.11	–	89.00	110.11
L403121T	W113V/W113VH	Set	1.28	21.73	–	86.03	107.76	23.90	–	94.63	118.54
L403121U	W115V..................	Set	1.42	24.11	–	108.40	132.51	26.52	–	119.24	145.76
L403121V	W2N09W/W2N09WH	Set	1.23	20.89	–	83.66	104.55	22.98	–	92.03	115.01
L403121W	W2N10W/W2N10WH	Set	1.44	24.45	–	91.49	115.94	26.90	–	100.64	127.53
L403121X	W2N12W/W2N12WH	Set	1.65	28.02	–	106.01	134.03	30.82	–	116.61	147.43
L403121Y	W2N13W/W2N13WH	Set	1.85	31.41	–	107.15	138.56	34.55	–	117.87	152.42
L403121Z	W2N15W................	Set	2.06	34.98	–	134.86	169.84	38.48	–	148.35	186.82

Major Works 2009		Unit	Labour Hours	Labour Net	Plant Net	Materials Net	Unit Net	Labour Gross	Plant Gross	Materials Gross	Unit Price
								——— (Gross rates include 10% profit) ———			
				£	£	£	£	£	£	£	£
L40	**L40: GENERAL GLAZING**										
L4031	**Special glazing**										
L403122	**Boulton and Paul hermetically sealed annealed double glazing units to wood with beads (beads measured separately); to suit window ref:**										
L403122A	W207C/W207CH	Set	1.35	22.92	–	80.10	103.02	25.21	–	88.11	113.32
L403122B	W209C/W209CH	Set	1.62	27.51	–	89.54	117.05	30.26	–	98.49	128.76
L403122C	W210C/W210CH	Set	1.89	32.09	–	99.01	131.10	35.30	–	108.91	144.21
L403122D	W212C/W212CH	Set	2.16	36.68	–	106.12	142.80	40.35	–	116.73	157.08
L403122E	W213C/W213CH	Set	2.43	41.26	–	126.37	167.63	45.39	–	139.01	184.39
L403122F	W207CV	Set	1.35	22.92	–	74.30	97.22	25.21	–	81.73	106.94
L403122G	W209CV/W209CVH	Set	1.62	27.51	–	82.96	110.47	30.26	–	91.26	121.52
L403122H	W210CV/W210CVH	Set	1.89	32.09	–	91.62	123.71	35.30	–	100.78	136.08
L403122I	W212CV/W212CVH	Set	2.16	36.68	–	131.00	167.68	40.35	–	144.10	184.45
L403122J	W213CV/W213CVH	Set	2.43	41.26	–	144.72	185.98	45.39	–	159.19	204.58
L403122K	W204DG	Set	0.81	13.75	–	44.81	58.56	15.13	–	49.29	64.42
L403122L	W206DG	Set	1.08	18.34	–	59.59	77.93	20.17	–	65.55	85.72
L403122M	W207DG	Set	1.35	22.92	–	70.12	93.04	25.21	–	77.13	102.34
L403122N	W210T	Set	1.89	32.09	–	123.19	155.28	35.30	–	135.51	170.81
L403122O	W212T	Set	2.16	36.68	–	136.86	173.54	40.35	–	150.55	190.89
L403122P	W209W/W209WH	Set	1.62	27.51	–	92.43	119.94	30.26	–	101.67	131.93
L403122Q	W210W/W210WH	Set	1.89	32.09	–	102.96	135.05	35.30	–	113.26	148.56
L403122R	W212W/W212WH	Set	2.16	36.68	–	113.47	150.15	40.35	–	124.82	165.17
L403122S	W213W	Set	2.43	41.26	–	128.26	169.52	45.39	–	141.09	186.47
L403122T	W215W	Set	2.70	45.85	–	165.55	211.40	50.44	–	182.11	232.54
L403122U	W312C	Set	3.06	51.96	–	156.04	208.00	57.16	–	171.64	228.80
L403122V	W307CC/W307CCH	Set	1.91	32.43	–	117.26	149.69	35.67	–	128.99	164.66
L403122W	W309CC/W309CCH	Set	2.30	39.05	–	131.03	170.08	42.96	–	144.13	187.09
L403122X	W310CC/W310CCH	Set	2.68	45.51	–	144.82	190.33	50.06	–	159.30	209.36
L403122Y	W312CC/W312CCH	Set	3.06	51.96	–	162.77	214.73	57.16	–	179.05	236.20
L403122Z	W313CC/W313CCH	Set	3.44	58.41	–	185.06	243.47	64.25	–	203.57	267.82

Windows, Doors and Stairs

Major Works 2009		Unit	Labour Hours	Labour Net	Plant Net	Materials Net	Unit Net	Labour Gross	Plant Gross	Materials Gross	Unit Price
								(Gross rates include 10% profit)			
				£	£	£	£	£	£	£	£
L40	**L40: GENERAL GLAZING**										
L4031	**Special glazing**										
L403123	**Boulton and Paul hermetically sealed annealed double glazing units to wood with beads (beads measured separately); to suit window ref:**										
L403123A	W309CVC/W309CVCH	Set	2.30	39.05	–	153.64	192.69	42.96	–	169.00	211.96
L403123B	W310CVC/W310CVCH	Set	2.68	45.51	–	167.41	212.92	50.06	–	184.15	234.21
L403123C	W312CVC/W312CVCH	Set	3.06	51.96	–	181.13	233.09	57.16	–	199.24	256.40
L403123D	W313CVC/W313CVCH	Set	3.44	58.41	–	203.41	261.82	64.25	–	223.75	288.00
L403123E	W310CW/W310CWH......	Set	2.68	45.51	–	148.77	194.28	50.06	–	163.65	213.71
L403123F	W312CW/W312CWH......	Set	3.06	51.96	–	163.57	215.53	57.16	–	179.93	237.08
L403123G	W313CW.................	Set	3.44	58.41	–	186.95	245.36	64.25	–	205.65	269.90
L403123H	W310WW	Set	2.68	45.51	–	167.18	212.69	50.06	–	183.90	233.96
L403123I	W312WW	Set	3.06	51.96	–	187.38	239.34	57.16	–	206.12	263.27
L403123J	W310T.................	Set	2.68	45.51	–	165.42	210.93	50.06	–	181.96	232.02
L403123K	W312T.................	Set	3.06	51.96	–	188.50	240.46	57.16	–	207.35	264.51
L403123L	W313T.................	Set	3.44	58.41	–	199.40	257.81	64.25	–	219.34	283.59
L403123M	W315T.................	Set	3.83	65.03	–	262.74	327.77	71.53	–	289.01	360.55
L403123N	W410CMC/W410CMCH ...	Set	3.68	62.49	–	165.84	228.33	68.74	–	182.42	251.16
L403123O	W412CMC/W412CMCH ...	Set	4.21	71.49	–	185.97	257.46	78.64	–	204.57	283.21
L403123P	W413CMC/W413CMCH ...	Set	4.74	80.49	–	192.79	273.28	88.54	–	212.07	300.61
L403123Q	W410CWC...............	Set	3.68	62.49	–	194.58	257.07	68.74	–	214.04	282.78
L403123R	W412CWC...............	Set	4.21	71.49	–	213.70	285.19	78.64	–	235.07	313.71
L403123S	W413CWC...............	Set	4.74	80.49	–	245.63	326.12	88.54	–	270.19	358.73
L403123T	W410TT................	Set	3.68	62.49	–	235.42	297.91	68.74	–	258.96	327.70
L403123U	W412TT................	Set	4.21	71.49	–	254.60	326.09	78.64	–	280.06	358.70
L403123V	W413TT................	Set	4.74	80.49	–	278.03	358.52	88.54	–	305.83	394.37
L403123W	W415TT................	Set	5.26	89.31	–	355.83	445.14	98.24	–	391.41	489.65
L403123X	W104A/W104AH	Set	0.43	7.30	–	33.28	40.58	8.03	–	36.61	44.64
L403123Y	W106A/W106AH	Set	0.57	9.68	–	32.83	42.51	10.65	–	36.11	46.76
L403123Z	W107A/W107AH	Set	0.71	12.06	–	37.15	49.21	13.27	–	40.87	54.13

Major Works 2009		Unit	Labour Hours	Labour Net	Plant Net	Materials Net	Unit Net	Labour Gross	Plant Gross	Materials Gross	Unit Price
								(Gross rates include 10% profit)			
				£	£	£	£	£	£	£	£
L40	**L40: GENERAL GLAZING**										
L4031	**Special glazing**										
L403124	**Boulton and Paul hermetically sealed annealed double glazing units to wood with beads (beads measured separately); to suit window ref:**										
L403124A	W109A/W109AH	Set	0.86	14.60	–	41.48	56.08	16.06	–	45.63	61.69
L403124B	W110A.................	Set	0.99	16.81	–	45.81	62.62	18.49	–	50.39	68.88
L403124C	W112A.................	Set	1.13	19.19	–	50.10	69.29	21.11	–	55.11	76.22
L403124D	W2N04A/W2N04AH.......	Set	0.62	10.53	–	37.10	47.63	11.58	–	40.81	52.39
L403124E	W2N06A/W2N06AH.......	Set	0.83	14.09	–	37.10	51.19	15.50	–	40.81	56.31
L403124F	W2N07A/W2N07AH.......	Set	1.03	17.49	–	40.08	57.57	19.24	–	44.09	63.33
L403124G	W2N09A/W2N09AH.......	Set	1.23	20.89	–	58.39	79.28	22.98	–	64.23	87.21
L403124H	W2N10A/W2N10AH.......	Set	1.44	24.45	–	65.41	89.86	26.90	–	71.95	98.85
L403124I	W2N12A/W2N12AH.......	Set	1.65	28.02	–	72.41	100.43	30.82	–	79.65	110.47
L403124J	W2N13AS	Set	1.85	31.41	–	98.96	130.37	34.55	–	108.86	143.41
L403124L	W204A/W204AH	Set	0.81	13.75	–	37.75	51.50	15.13	–	41.53	56.65
L403124M	W206A/W206AH	Set	1.13	19.19	–	47.30	66.49	21.11	–	52.03	73.14
L403124N	W207A/W207AH	Set	1.35	22.92	–	61.29	84.21	25.21	–	67.42	92.63
L403124O	W209A/W209AH	Set	1.62	27.51	–	71.02	98.53	30.26	–	78.12	108.38
L403124P	W210A/W210AH	Set	1.89	32.09	–	80.74	112.83	35.30	–	88.81	124.11
L403124Q	W212A/W212AH	Set	2.16	36.68	–	94.72	131.40	40.35	–	104.19	144.54
L403124R	W213AS	Set	2.43	41.26	–	120.98	162.24	45.39	–	133.08	178.46
L403124S	W215AS	Set	2.70	45.85	–	141.62	187.47	50.44	–	155.78	206.22
L403124X	W310AE................	Set	2.68	45.51	–	139.73	185.24	50.06	–	153.70	203.76
L403124Y	W312AE................	Set	3.06	51.96	–	154.55	206.51	57.16	–	170.01	227.16
L403125	**Boulton and Paul hermetically sealed annealed double glazing units to wood with beads (beads measured separately); to suit window ref:**										
L403125D	WHN09C/WHN09CH	Set	0.65	11.04	–	65.69	76.73	12.14	–	72.26	84.40
L403125E	WHN10C/WHN10CH	Set	0.77	13.07	–	65.69	78.76	14.38	–	72.26	86.64
L403125F	WH109C/WH109CH.......	Set	0.86	14.60	–	65.69	80.29	16.06	–	72.26	88.32
L403125G	WH110C/WH110CH.......	Set	0.99	16.81	–	65.69	82.50	18.49	–	72.26	90.75
L403125H	WH112C/WH112CH.......	Set	1.13	19.19	–	65.69	84.88	21.11	–	72.26	93.37
L403125I	WH113C/WH113CH.......	Set	1.28	21.73	–	75.08	96.81	23.90	–	82.59	106.49
L403125J	WH209C/WH209CH.......	Set	1.62	27.51	–	131.38	158.89	30.26	–	144.52	174.78
L403125K	WH210C/WH210CH.......	Set	1.89	32.09	–	131.37	163.46	35.30	–	144.51	179.81
L403125L	WH212C/WH212CH.......	Set	2.16	36.68	–	144.56	181.24	40.35	–	159.02	199.36
L403125M	WH213C/WH213CH.......	Set	2.43	41.26	–	159.09	200.35	45.39	–	175.00	220.39
L403125N	WH309CC/WH309CCH	Set	2.30	39.05	–	197.03	236.08	42.96	–	216.73	259.69
L403125O	WH310CC/WH310CCH	Set	2.68	45.51	–	197.03	242.54	50.06	–	216.73	266.79
L403125P	WH312CC/WH312CCH	Set	3.06	51.96	–	210.24	262.20	57.16	–	231.26	288.42
L403125Q	WH313CC/WH313CCH	Set	3.44	58.41	–	234.22	292.63	64.25	–	257.64	321.89

Windows, Doors and Stairs

Major Works 2009		Unit	Labour Hours	Labour Net	Plant Net	Materials Net	Unit Net	Labour Gross	Plant Gross	Materials Gross	Unit Price
								(Gross rates include 10% profit)			
				£	£	£	£	£	£	£	£
L40	**L40: GENERAL GLAZING**										
L4031	**Special glazing**										
L403126	**Boulton and Paul hermetically sealed toughened double glazing units to wood with beads (beads measured separately); to suit window ref:**										
L403126A	WN07C/WN07CH	Set	0.55	9.34	–	26.74	36.08	10.27	–	29.41	39.69
L403126B	WN09C/WN09CH	Set	0.66	11.21	–	31.45	42.66	12.33	–	34.60	46.93
L403126C	WN10C/WN10CH	Set	0.76	12.90	–	37.99	50.89	14.19	–	41.79	55.98
L403126D	WN12C/WN12CH	Set	0.88	14.94	–	44.54	59.48	16.43	–	48.99	65.43
L403126E	WN07V/WN07VH	Set	0.55	9.34	–	53.49	62.83	10.27	–	58.84	69.11
L403126F	WN09V/WN09VH	Set	0.66	11.21	–	53.49	64.70	12.33	–	58.84	71.17
L403126G	WN10V/WN10VH	Set	0.77	13.07	–	60.24	73.31	14.38	–	66.26	80.64
L403126H	WN12V	Set	0.88	14.94	–	68.02	82.96	16.43	–	74.82	91.26
L403126I	W107C/W107CH	Set	0.71	12.06	–	35.69	47.75	13.27	–	39.26	52.53
L403126J	W109C/W109CH	Set	0.85	14.43	–	45.06	59.49	15.87	–	49.57	65.44
L403126K	W110C/W110CH	Set	0.99	16.81	–	43.17	59.98	18.49	–	47.49	65.98
L403126L	W112C/W112CH	Set	1.13	19.19	–	50.63	69.82	21.11	–	55.69	76.80
L403126M	W113C/W113CH	Set	1.28	21.73	–	49.20	70.93	23.90	–	54.12	78.02
L403126N	W110T/W110TH	Set	0.99	16.81	–	62.42	79.23	18.49	–	68.66	87.15
L403126O	W112T/W112TH	Set	1.13	19.19	–	71.82	91.01	21.11	–	79.00	100.11
L403126P	W107V/W107VH	Set	0.71	12.06	–	53.49	65.55	13.27	–	58.84	72.11
L403126Q	W109V/W109VH	Set	0.86	14.60	–	61.77	76.37	16.06	–	67.95	84.01
L403126R	W110V/W110VH	Set	0.99	16.81	–	72.46	89.27	18.49	–	79.71	98.20
L403126S	W112V/W112VH	Set	1.13	19.19	–	71.44	90.63	21.11	–	78.58	99.69
L403126T	W113V/W113VH	Set	1.28	21.73	–	71.82	93.55	23.90	–	79.00	102.91
L403126U	W115V	Set	1.42	24.11	–	78.85	102.96	26.52	–	86.74	113.26
L403126V	W2N09W/W2N09WH	Set	1.23	20.89	–	69.34	90.23	22.98	–	76.27	99.25
L403126W	W2N10W/W2N10WH	Set	1.44	24.45	–	73.77	98.22	26.90	–	81.15	108.04
L403126X	W2N12W/W2N12WH	Set	1.65	28.02	–	84.82	112.84	30.82	–	93.30	124.12
L403126Y	W2N13W/W2N13WH	Set	1.85	31.41	–	95.08	126.49	34.55	–	104.59	139.14
L403126Z	W2N15W	Set	2.06	34.98	–	105.97	140.95	38.48	–	116.57	155.05

Major Works 2009		Unit	Labour Hours	Labour Net	Plant Net	Materials Net	Unit Net	Labour Gross	Plant Gross	Materials Gross	Unit Price
								(Gross rates include 10% profit)			
				£	£	£	£	£	£	£	£
L40	**L40: GENERAL GLAZING**										
L4031	**Special glazing**										
L403127	**Boulton and Paul hermetically sealed toughened double glazing units to wood with beads (beads measured separately); to suit window ref:**										
L403127A	W207C/W207CH	Set	1.35	22.92	–	81.39	104.31	25.21	–	89.53	114.74
L403127B	W209C/W209CH	Set	1.62	27.51	–	89.76	117.27	30.26	–	98.74	129.00
L403127C	W210C/W210CH	Set	1.89	32.09	–	88.22	120.31	35.30	–	97.04	132.34
L403127D	W212C/W212CH	Set	2.16	36.68	–	102.75	139.43	40.35	–	113.03	153.37
L403127E	W213C/W213CH	Set	2.43	41.26	–	108.58	149.84	45.39	–	119.44	164.82
L403127F	W207CV	Set	1.35	22.92	–	89.18	112.10	25.21	–	98.10	123.31
L403127G	W209CV/W209CVH	Set	1.62	27.51	–	106.82	134.33	30.26	–	117.50	147.76
L403127H	W210CV/W210CVH	Set	1.89	32.09	–	115.64	147.73	35.30	–	127.20	162.50
L403127I	W212CV/W212CVH	Set	2.16	36.68	–	122.10	158.78	40.35	–	134.31	174.66
L403127J	W213CV/W213CVH	Set	2.43	41.26	–	120.99	162.25	45.39	–	133.09	178.48
L403127K	W204DG	Set	0.81	13.75	–	39.85	53.60	15.13	–	43.84	58.96
L403127L	W206DG	Set	1.08	18.34	–	48.47	66.81	20.17	–	53.32	73.49
L403127M	W207DG	Set	1.35	22.92	–	63.38	86.30	25.21	–	69.72	94.93
L403127N	W210T	Set	1.89	32.09	–	107.50	139.59	35.30	–	118.25	153.55
L403127O	W212T	Set	2.16	36.68	–	123.90	160.58	40.35	–	136.29	176.64
L403127P	W209W/W209WH	Set	1.62	27.51	–	76.38	103.89	30.26	–	84.02	114.28
L403127Q	W210W/W210WH	Set	1.89	32.09	–	91.29	123.38	35.30	–	100.42	135.72
L403127R	W212W/W212WH	Set	2.16	36.68	–	105.38	142.06	40.35	–	115.92	156.27
L403127S	W213W	Set	2.43	41.26	–	112.06	153.32	45.39	–	123.27	168.65
L403127T	W215W	Set	2.70	45.85	–	125.50	171.35	50.44	–	138.05	188.49
L403127U	W310C	Set	2.68	45.51	–	127.34	172.85	50.06	–	140.07	190.14
L403127V	W312C	Set	3.06	51.96	–	148.26	200.22	57.16	–	163.09	220.24
L403127W	W307CC/W307CCH	Set	1.91	32.43	–	117.08	149.51	35.67	–	128.79	164.46
L403127X	W309CC/W309CCH	Set	2.30	39.05	–	134.82	173.87	42.96	–	148.30	191.26
L403127Y	W310CC/W310CCH	Set	2.68	45.51	–	131.39	176.90	50.06	–	144.53	194.59
L403127Z	W312CC/W312CCH	Set	3.06	51.96	–	153.42	205.38	57.16	–	168.76	225.92

Major Works 2009		Unit	Labour Hours	Labour Net	Plant Net	Materials Net	Unit Net	Labour Gross	Plant Gross	Materials Gross	Unit Price
				£	£	£	£	£	£	£	£
									(Gross rates include 10% profit)		
L40	**L40: GENERAL GLAZING**										
L4031	**Special glazing**										
L403128	**Boulton and Paul hermetically sealed toughened double glazing units to wood with beads (beads measured separately); to suit window ref:**										
L403128A	W313CC/W313CCH	Set	3.44	58.41	–	157.77	216.18	64.25	–	173.55	237.80
L403128B	W309CVC/W309CVCH	Set	2.30	39.05	–	151.89	190.94	42.96	–	167.08	210.03
L403128C	W310CVC/W310CVCH	Set	2.68	45.51	–	158.78	204.29	50.06	–	174.66	224.72
L403128D	W312CVC/W312CVCH	Set	3.06	51.96	–	172.73	224.69	57.16	–	190.00	247.16
L403128E	W313CVC/W313CVCH	Set	3.44	58.41	–	170.20	228.61	64.25	–	187.22	251.47
L403128F	W310CW/W310CWH	Set	2.68	45.51	–	134.46	179.97	50.06	–	147.91	197.97
L403128G	W312CW/W312CWH	Set	3.06	51.96	–	156.02	207.98	57.16	–	171.62	228.78
L403128H	W313CW	Set	3.44	58.41	–	161.26	219.67	64.25	–	177.39	241.64
L403128I	W310WW	Set	2.68	45.51	–	140.42	185.93	50.06	–	154.46	204.52
L403128J	W312WW	Set	3.06	51.96	–	160.53	212.49	57.16	–	176.58	233.74
L403128K	W310T	Set	2.68	45.51	–	146.57	192.08	50.06	–	161.23	211.29
L403128L	W312T	Set	3.06	51.96	–	169.41	221.37	57.16	–	186.35	243.51
L403128M	W313T	Set	3.44	58.41	–	180.87	239.28	64.25	–	198.96	263.21
L403128N	W315T	Set	3.83	65.03	–	201.80	266.83	71.53	–	221.98	293.51
L403128O	W410CMC/W410CMCH . . .	Set	3.68	62.49	–	176.47	238.96	68.74	–	194.12	262.86
L403128P	W412CMC/W412CMCH . . .	Set	4.21	71.49	–	205.54	277.03	78.64	–	226.09	304.73
L403128Q	W413CMC/W413CMCH . . .	Set	4.74	80.49	–	217.18	297.67	88.54	–	238.90	327.44
L403128R	W410CWC.	Set	3.68	62.49	–	177.63	240.12	68.74	–	195.39	264.13
L403128S	W412CWC.	Set	4.21	71.49	–	206.71	278.20	78.64	–	227.38	306.02
L403128T	W413CWC.	Set	4.74	80.49	–	210.49	290.98	88.54	–	231.54	320.08
L403128U	W410TT.	Set	3.68	62.49	–	209.03	271.52	68.74	–	229.93	298.67
L403128V	W412TT.	Set	4.21	71.49	–	241.21	312.70	78.64	–	265.33	343.97
L403128W	W413TT.	Set	4.74	80.49	–	250.80	331.29	88.54	–	275.88	364.42
L403128X	W415TT.	Set	5.26	89.31	–	279.22	368.53	98.24	–	307.14	405.38
L403128Y	W104A/W104AH	Set	0.43	7.30	–	26.74	34.04	8.03	–	29.41	37.44
L403128Z	W106A/W106AH	Set	0.57	9.68	–	26.74	36.42	10.65	–	29.41	40.06
L403129	**Boulton and Paul hermetically sealed toughened double glazing units to wood with beads (beads measured separately); to suit window ref:**										
L403129A	W107A/W107AH	Set	0.71	12.06	–	35.10	47.16	13.27	–	38.61	51.88
L403129B	W109A/W109AH	Set	0.86	14.60	–	44.54	59.14	16.06	–	48.99	65.05
L403129C	W110A.	Set	0.99	16.81	–	42.80	59.61	18.49	–	47.08	65.57
L403129D	W112A.	Set	1.13	19.19	–	50.21	69.40	21.11	–	55.23	76.34
L403129E	W2N04A/W2N04AH.	Set	0.62	10.53	–	26.74	37.27	11.58	–	29.41	41.00
L403129F	W2N06A/W2N06AH.	Set	0.83	14.09	–	40.18	54.27	15.50	–	44.20	59.70
L403129G	W2N07A/W2N07AH.	Set	1.03	17.49	–	43.61	61.10	19.24	–	47.97	67.21
L403129H	W2N09A/W2N09AH.	Set	1.23	20.89	–	46.87	67.76	22.98	–	51.56	74.54
L403129I	W2N10A/W2N10AH.	Set	1.44	24.45	–	56.70	81.15	26.90	–	62.37	89.27
L403129J	W2N12A/W2N12AH.	Set	1.65	28.02	–	66.64	94.66	30.82	–	73.30	104.13
L403129K	W2N13AS	Set	1.85	31.41	–	85.51	116.92	34.55	–	94.06	128.61
L403129M	W204A/W204AH	Set	0.81	13.75	–	35.30	49.05	15.13	–	38.83	53.96
L403129N	W206A/W206AH	Set	1.13	19.19	–	44.33	63.52	21.11	–	48.76	69.87
L403129O	W207A/W207AH	Set	1.35	22.92	–	51.21	74.13	25.21	–	56.33	81.54
L403129P	W209A/W209AH	Set	1.62	27.51	–	64.95	92.46	30.26	–	71.45	101.71
L403129Q	W210A/W210AH	Set	1.89	32.09	–	77.90	109.99	35.30	–	85.69	120.99
L403129R	W212A/W212AH	Set	2.16	36.68	–	83.58	120.26	40.35	–	91.94	132.29
L403129S	W213AS	Set	2.43	41.26	–	116.70	157.96	45.39	–	128.37	173.76
L403129T	W215AS	Set	2.70	45.85	–	122.40	168.25	50.44	–	134.64	185.08
L403129Y	W310AE.	Set	2.68	45.51	–	125.01	170.52	50.06	–	137.51	187.57
L403129Z	W312AE.	Set	3.06	51.96	–	145.86	197.82	57.16	–	160.45	217.60

Major Works 2009		Unit	Labour Hours	Labour Net	Plant Net	Materials Net	Unit Net	Labour Gross	Plant Gross	Materials Gross	Unit Price
				£	£	£	£	£	£	£	£
								(Gross rates include 10% profit)			
L40	**L40: GENERAL GLAZING**										
L4031	**Special glazing**										
L403130	**Boulton and Paul hermetically sealed toughened double glazing units to wood with beads (beads measured separately); to suit window ref:**										
L403130A	W310AV	Set	2.68	45.51	–	150.36	195.87	50.06	–	165.40	215.46
L403130E	WHN09C/WHN09CH	Set	0.65	11.04	–	53.49	64.53	12.14	–	58.84	70.98
L403130F	WHN10C/WHN10CH	Set	0.77	13.07	–	53.49	66.56	14.38	–	58.84	73.22
L403130G	WH109C/WH109CH......	Set	0.86	14.60	–	53.49	68.09	16.06	–	58.84	74.90
L403130H	WH110C/WH110CH.......	Set	0.99	16.81	–	53.49	70.30	18.49	–	58.84	77.33
L403130I	WH112C/WH112CH.......	Set	1.13	19.19	–	62.63	81.82	21.11	–	68.89	90.00
L403130J	WH113C/WH113CH.......	Set	1.28	21.73	–	72.10	93.83	23.90	–	79.31	103.21
L403130K	WH209C/WH209CH.......	Set	1.62	27.51	–	108.87	136.38	30.26	–	119.76	150.02
L403130L	WH210C/WH210CH.......	Set	1.89	32.09	–	119.61	151.70	35.30	–	131.57	166.87
L403130M	WH212C/WH212CH.......	Set	2.16	36.68	–	139.39	176.07	40.35	–	153.33	193.68
L403130N	WH213C/WH213CH.......	Set	2.43	41.26	–	159.45	200.71	45.39	–	175.40	220.78
L403130O	WH309CC/WH309CCH	Set	2.30	39.05	–	162.35	201.40	42.96	–	178.59	221.54
L403130P	WH310CC/WH310CCH	Set	2.68	45.51	–	173.12	218.63	50.06	–	190.43	240.49
L403130Q	WH312CC/WH312CCH	Set	3.06	51.96	–	202.05	254.01	57.16	–	222.26	279.41
L403130R	WH313CC/WH313CCH	Set	3.44	58.41	–	231.55	289.96	64.25	–	254.71	318.96
L403131	**John Carr sealed toughened double glazing units; to suit door ref:**										
L403131A	231SC	Set	1.71	29.04	–	149.47	178.51	31.94	–	164.42	196.36
L403131B	261SC	Set	1.71	29.04	–	152.38	181.42	31.94	–	167.62	199.56
L403131C	291SC	Set	1.85	31.41	–	164.39	195.80	34.55	–	180.83	215.38
L403131D	231SA	Set	1.65	28.02	–	145.81	173.83	30.82	–	160.39	191.21
L403131E	261SA	Set	1.75	29.72	–	153.82	183.54	32.69	–	169.20	201.89
L403131F	26E2XGG	Set	1.38	23.43	–	112.16	135.59	25.77	–	123.38	149.15
L403131G	29E2XGG	Set	1.40	23.77	–	122.89	146.66	26.15	–	135.18	161.33
L403131H	26ESA	Set	2.00	33.96	–	175.98	209.94	37.36	–	193.58	230.93
L403131I	29ESA	Set	2.10	35.66	–	187.35	223.01	39.23	–	206.09	245.31
L403131J	26ESC	Set	2.55	43.30	–	224.56	267.86	47.63	–	247.02	294.65
L403131K	29ESC	Set	2.55	43.30	–	224.56	267.86	47.63	–	247.02	294.65
L403131L	26E10.................	Set	1.32	22.41	–	116.02	138.43	24.65	–	127.62	152.27
L403131M	29E10.................	Set	1.45	24.62	–	127.71	152.33	27.08	–	140.48	167.56
L403131N	26EKXT	Set	1.51	25.64	–	131.93	157.57	28.20	–	145.12	173.33
L403131O	29EKXT	Set	1.51	25.64	–	131.93	157.57	28.20	–	145.12	173.33
L403131P	26ESCP	Set	1.82	30.90	–	159.60	190.50	33.99	–	175.56	209.55
L403131Q	29ESCP	Set	1.82	30.90	–	159.62	190.52	33.99	–	175.58	209.57
L403131R	26E50.................	Set	1.62	27.51	–	144.06	171.57	30.26	–	158.47	188.73
L403131S	29E50.................	Set	1.72	29.21	–	151.14	180.35	32.13	–	166.25	198.39
L403131T	26E4XG	Set	0.92	15.62	–	80.34	95.96	17.18	–	88.37	105.56
L403131U	29E4XG	Set	1.00	16.98	–	88.52	105.50	18.68	–	97.37	116.05
L403131V	26E2XG	Set	0.85	14.43	–	72.55	86.98	15.87	–	79.81	95.68
L403131W	29E2XG	Set	0.83	14.09	–	72.56	86.65	15.50	–	79.82	95.32
L403131X	26F2X..................	Set	0.68	11.46	–	58.64	70.10	12.61	–	64.50	77.11
L403131Y	29F2X..................	Set	0.70	11.89	–	58.64	70.53	13.08	–	64.50	77.58

Major Works 2009		Unit	Labour Hours	Labour Net	Plant Net	Materials Net	Unit Net	Labour Gross	Plant Gross	Materials Gross	Unit Price
									(Gross rates include 10% profit)		
				£	£	£	£	£	£	£	£
L40	**L40: GENERAL GLAZING**										
L4031	**Special glazing**										
L403132	**John Carr hermetically sealed toughened double glazing units to wood with beads (beads measured separately); to suit door ref:**										
L403132A	26F3X...................	Set	1.15	19.53	–	58.64	78.17	21.48	–	64.50	85.99
L403132B	29F3X...................	Set	1.20	20.38	–	58.64	79.02	22.42	–	64.50	86.92
L403132C	26F3XBF	Set	1.15	19.53	–	62.82	82.35	21.48	–	69.10	90.59
L403132D	29F3XBF	Set	1.20	20.38	–	62.82	83.20	22.42	–	69.10	91.52
L403132E	28F3XBF	Set	1.18	20.04	–	62.82	82.86	22.04	–	69.10	91.15
L403132F	26H2XGG	Set	1.75	29.72	–	115.95	145.67	32.69	–	127.55	160.24
L403132G	29H2XGG	Set	1.75	29.72	–	115.96	145.68	32.69	–	127.56	160.25
L403132H	807H2XGG	Set	1.75	29.72	–	115.96	145.68	32.69	–	127.56	160.25
L403132I	26H10	Set	1.60	27.17	–	107.79	134.96	29.89	–	118.57	148.46
L403132J	29H10	Set	1.65	28.02	–	118.46	146.48	30.82	–	130.31	161.13
L403132K	807H10	Set	1.65	28.02	–	118.46	146.48	30.82	–	130.31	161.13
L403132L	29CARL	Set	1.85	31.41	–	167.38	198.79	34.55	–	184.12	218.67
L403132M	29CLAR	Set	2.17	36.85	–	115.58	152.43	40.54	–	127.14	167.67
L403133	**Boulton and Paul factory glazing; 20 mm Low E clear insulating units; to suit sidelights (measured separately); ref:**										
L403133A	SL3366PX	Set	0.80	13.58	–	72.02	85.60	14.94	–	79.22	94.16
L403133B	SL5566PX	Set	1.20	20.38	–	98.91	119.29	22.42	–	108.80	131.22
L403133C	SL3366RX	Set	0.80	13.58	–	77.31	90.89	14.94	–	85.04	99.98
L403133D	SL5566RX	Set	1.20	20.38	–	115.28	135.66	22.42	–	126.81	149.23
L403133E	SL3366SBX.............	Set	0.80	13.58	–	108.80	122.38	14.94	–	119.68	134.62
L403133F	SL5566SBX.............	Set	1.20	20.38	–	172.50	192.88	22.42	–	189.75	212.17
L403133G	SL3366SHX.............	Set	0.80	13.58	–	105.11	118.69	14.94	–	115.62	130.56
L403133H	SL5566SHX.............	Set	1.20	20.38	–	132.01	152.39	22.42	–	145.21	167.63
L403133I	SL3366TBX.............	Set	0.80	13.58	–	135.65	149.23	14.94	–	149.22	164.15
L403133J	SL5566TBX.............	Set	1.20	20.38	–	247.90	268.28	22.42	–	272.69	295.11
L403133K	SL3366THX.............	Set	0.80	13.58	–	137.94	151.52	14.94	–	151.73	166.67
L403133L	SL5566THX.............	Set	1.20	20.38	–	149.24	169.62	22.42	–	164.16	186.58

SURFACE FINISHES

Major Works 2009		Unit	Labour Hours	Labour Net	Plant Net	Materials Net	Unit Net	Labour Gross	Plant Gross	Materials Gross	Unit Price
								(Gross rates include 10% profit)			
				£	£	£	£	£	£	£	£
M10	**M10: CEMENT : SAND, CONCRETE SCREEDS AND TOPPINGS**										
M1011	**Cement and sand (1:3); trowelled finish**										
M101103	To floors and landings:										
M101103A	25 mm thick	m²	0.25	5.86	–	2.54	8.40	6.45	–	2.79	9.24
M101103B	32 mm thick	m²	0.27	6.33	–	3.18	9.51	6.96	–	3.50	10.46
M101103C	38 mm thick	m²	0.29	6.80	–	3.81	10.61	7.48	–	4.19	11.67
M101103D	50 mm thick	m²	0.32	7.50	–	5.00	12.50	8.25	–	5.50	13.75
M101103E	65 mm thick	m²	0.36	8.44	–	6.54	14.98	9.28	–	7.19	16.48
M1012	**Cement and sand (1:3); screeded finish**										
M101206	To floors and landings:										
M101206A	25 mm thick	m²	0.19	4.46	–	2.54	7.00	4.91	–	2.79	7.70
M101206B	32 mm thick	m²	0.20	4.69	–	3.18	7.87	5.16	–	3.50	8.66
M101206C	38 mm thick	m²	0.22	5.16	–	3.81	8.97	5.68	–	4.19	9.87
M101206D	50 mm thick	m²	0.24	5.62	–	5.00	10.62	6.18	–	5.50	11.68
M101206E	65 mm thick	m²	0.27	6.33	–	6.54	12.87	6.96	–	7.19	14.16
M1013	**Cement and sand (1:3); floated finish**										
M101309	To floors and landings:										
M101309A	25 mm thick	m²	0.23	5.39	–	2.54	7.93	5.93	–	2.79	8.72
M101309B	32 mm thick	m²	0.24	5.62	–	3.18	8.80	6.18	–	3.50	9.68
M101309C	38 mm thick	m²	0.26	6.10	–	3.81	9.91	6.71	–	4.19	10.90
M101309D	50 mm thick	m²	0.29	6.79	–	5.00	11.79	7.47	–	5.50	12.97
M101309E	65 mm thick	m²	0.32	7.50	–	6.54	14.04	8.25	–	7.19	15.44
M1016	**Granolithic paving (two parts cement to five parts dustless granite chippings); trowelled finish**										
M101602	To floors and landings:										
M101602A	25 mm thick	m²	0.30	7.04	–	5.08	12.12	7.74	–	5.59	13.33
M101602B	32 mm thick	m²	0.32	7.50	–	6.35	13.85	8.25	–	6.99	15.24
M101602C	38 mm thick	m²	0.34	7.97	–	7.62	15.59	8.77	–	8.38	17.15
M101602D	50 mm thick	m²	0.37	8.68	–	9.98	18.66	9.55	–	10.98	20.53
M101603	To staircases, treads, risers and edges of landings:										
M101603A	25 mm thick	m²	0.88	20.63	–	5.08	25.71	22.69	–	5.59	28.28
M101603B	32 mm thick	m²	0.94	22.04	–	6.35	28.39	24.24	–	6.99	31.23
M101603C	38 mm thick	m²	1.00	23.44	–	7.62	31.06	25.78	–	8.38	34.17
M101603D	50 mm thick	m²	1.09	25.55	–	9.98	35.53	28.11	–	10.98	39.08
M101604	To skirtings, bands, strings, coverings to kerbs, mouldings, channels or the like; not exceeding 300 mm wide:										
M101604A	25 mm thick	m	0.22	5.16	–	1.45	6.61	5.68	–	1.60	7.27
M101604B	32 mm thick	m	0.24	5.62	–	2.00	7.62	6.18	–	2.20	8.38
M101604C	38 mm thick	m	0.25	5.86	–	2.36	8.22	6.45	–	2.60	9.04
M101604D	50 mm thick	m	0.27	6.32	–	3.09	9.41	6.95	–	3.40	10.35
M101605	To risers and edges of landings; not exceeding 150 mm wide:										
M101605A	25 mm thick	m	0.15	3.49	–	0.73	4.22	3.84	–	0.80	4.64
M101605B	32 mm thick	m	0.16	3.80	–	1.09	4.89	4.18	–	1.20	5.38
M101605C	38 mm thick	m	0.17	3.99	–	1.27	5.26	4.39	–	1.40	5.79
M101605D	50 mm thick	m	0.17	3.97	–	1.63	5.60	4.37	–	1.79	6.16
M101606	To risers and edges of landings; 150-300 mm wide:										
M101606A	25 mm thick	m	0.26	6.19	–	1.45	7.64	6.81	–	1.60	8.40
M101606B	32 mm thick	m	0.29	6.75	–	2.00	8.75	7.43	–	2.20	9.63
M101606C	38 mm thick	m	0.30	7.03	–	2.36	9.39	7.73	–	2.60	10.33
M101606D	50 mm thick	m	0.32	7.50	–	3.09	10.59	8.25	–	3.40	11.65

Surface Finishes

Major Works 2009		Unit	Labour Hours	Labour Net	Plant Net	Materials Net	Unit Net	Labour Gross	Plant Gross	Materials Gross	Unit Price
								(Gross rates include 10% profit)			
				£	£	£	£	£	£	£	£
M11	**M11: MASTIC ASPHALT FLOORING AND FLOOR UNDERLAYS**										
M1121	**Flat coverings**										
M112109	**Mastic asphalt paving; BS 1076; limestone aggregate; rubbing surface with fine sand:**										
M112109A	20 mm two coat work	m²	0.50	11.72	–	11.79	23.51	12.89	–	12.97	25.86
M112110	**Mastic asphalt coloured flooring; BS1451; limestone aggregate; rubbing surface with fine sand**										
M112110A	20 mm two coat work	m²	0.50	11.71	–	13.13	24.84	12.88	–	14.44	27.32
M112110B	15 mm one coat work	m²	0.30	7.03	–	10.23	17.26	7.73	–	11.25	18.99
M1123	**Sloping coverings**										
M112328	**Mastic asphalt paving; BS 1076; limestone aggregate; rubbing surface with fine sand:**										
M112328A	20 mm two coat work	m²	0.65	15.23	–	11.79	27.02	16.75	–	12.97	29.72
M112329	**Mastic asphalt coloured flooring; BS 1451; limestone aggregate; rubbing surface with fine sand:**										
M112329A	20 mm two coat work	m²	0.65	15.23	–	13.13	28.36	16.75	–	14.44	31.20
M112329B	15 mm one coat work	m²	0.40	9.37	–	10.23	19.60	10.31	–	11.25	21.56
M1161	**Skirtings, upstands or the like**										
M116179	**Mastic asphalt coloured flooring; BS 1451; limestone aggregate; rubbing surface with fine sand; skirtings, upstands or the like; rounded arrises and internal angle fillet; turning nib into groove; 20 mm two coat work:**										
M116179A	not exceeding 150 mm high	m	0.25	5.86	–	2.41	8.27	6.45	–	2.65	9.10
M116179B	150-300 mm high.........	m	0.40	9.38	–	4.21	13.59	10.32	–	4.63	14.95
M116189	**Mastic asphalt coloured flooring; BS 1451; limestone aggregate; rubbing surface with fine sand; skirtings, upstands or the like; rounded arrises and internal angle fillet; turning nib into groove; 15 mm one coat work:**										
M116189E	not exceeding 150 mm high	m	0.15	3.51	–	1.82	5.33	3.86	–	2.00	5.86
M116189F	150-300 mm high.........	m	0.25	5.86	–	3.16	9.02	6.45	–	3.48	9.92
M12	**M12: TROWELLED BITUMEN, RESIN AND RUBBER-LATEX FLOORING**										
M1211	**Evostik floor levelling compound, laid in accordance with the manufacturer's instructions**										
M121118	**To floors and landings:**										
M121118A	2 mm nominal thickness ...	m²	0.13	3.04	–	3.83	6.87	3.34	–	4.21	7.56
M121118B	5 mm nominal thickness ...	m²	0.15	3.52	–	9.56	13.08	3.87	–	10.52	14.39

Major Works 2009		Unit	Labour Hours	Labour Net	Plant Net	Materials Net	Unit Net	Labour Gross	Plant Gross	Materials Gross	Unit Price
				£	£	£	£	£	£	£	£
								(Gross rates include 10% profit)			
M20	**M20: PLASTERED, RENDERED AND ROUGHCAST COATINGS**										
M2011	**Cement and sand (1:3); trowelled finish**										
M201104	**To walls; 12 mm thick; one coat work:**										
M201104A	over 300 mm wide	m²	0.20	4.69	–	1.18	5.87	5.16	–	1.30	6.46
M201104B	not exceeding 300 mm wide	m	0.08	1.90	–	0.36	2.26	2.09	–	0.40	2.49
M201105	**To walls; 18 mm thick; two coat work:**										
M201105A	over 300 mm wide	m²	0.30	7.03	–	1.82	8.85	7.73	–	2.00	9.74
M201105B	not exceeding 300 mm wide	m	0.12	2.86	–	0.54	3.40	3.15	–	0.59	3.74
M201114	**To isolated columns; 12 mm thick; one coat work:**										
M201114A	over 300 mm wide	m²	0.20	4.69	–	1.18	5.87	5.16	–	1.30	6.46
M201114B	not exceeding 300 mm wide	m	0.08	1.90	–	0.36	2.26	2.09	–	0.40	2.49
M201115	**To isolated columns; 18 mm thick; two coat work:**										
M201115A	over 300 mm wide	m²	0.30	7.03	–	1.82	8.85	7.73	–	2.00	9.74
M201115B	not exceeding 300 mm wide	m	0.12	2.86	–	0.54	3.40	3.15	–	0.59	3.74
M2012	**Cement and sand (1:3); screeded finish**										
M201201	**To walls; 6 mm thick; one coat work:**										
M201201A	over 300 mm wide	m²	0.14	3.28	–	0.64	3.92	3.61	–	0.70	4.31
M201201B	not exceeding 300 mm wide	m	0.06	1.34	–	0.18	1.52	1.47	–	0.20	1.67
M201202	**To walls; 12 mm thick; one coat work:**										
M201202A	over 300 mm wide	m²	0.18	4.22	–	1.18	5.40	4.64	–	1.30	5.94
M201202B	not exceeding 300 mm wide	m	0.07	1.71	–	0.36	2.07	1.88	–	0.40	2.28
M201203	**To walls; 18 mm thick; two coat work:**										
M201203A	over 300 mm wide	m²	0.27	6.33	–	1.82	8.15	6.96	–	2.00	8.97
M201203C	not exceeding 300 mm wide	m	0.11	2.56	–	0.54	3.10	2.82	–	0.59	3.41
M201207	**To isolated columns; 6 mm thick; one coat work:**										
M201207A	over 300 mm wide	m²	0.14	3.28	–	0.64	3.92	3.61	–	0.70	4.31
M201207B	not exceeding 300 mm wide	m	0.06	1.34	–	0.36	1.70	1.47	–	0.40	1.87
M201208	**To isolated columns; 12 mm thick; one coat work:**										
M201208A	over 300 mm wide	m²	0.18	4.22	–	1.18	5.40	4.64	–	1.30	5.94
M201208B	not exceeding 300 mm wide	m	0.07	1.71	–	0.36	2.07	1.88	–	0.40	2.28
M201209	**To isolated columns; 18 mm thick; two coat work:**										
M201209A	over 300 mm wide	m²	0.27	6.33	–	1.82	8.15	6.96	–	2.00	8.97
M201209C	not exceeding 300 mm wide	m	0.11	2.56	–	0.54	3.10	2.82	–	0.59	3.41

Surface Finishes

Major Works 2009		Unit	Labour Hours	Labour Net	Plant Net	Materials Net	Unit Net	Labour Gross	Plant Gross	Materials Gross	Unit Price
								——— (Gross rates include 10% profit) ———			
				£	£	£	£	£	£	£	£
M20	**M20: PLASTERED, RENDERED AND ROUGHCAST COATINGS**										
M2013	**Cement and sand (1:3); floated finish**										
M201301	**To walls; 12 mm thick; one coat work:**										
M201301A	over 300 mm wide	m²	0.19	4.45	–	1.18	5.63	4.90	–	1.30	6.19
M201301B	not exceeding 300 mm wide	m	0.08	1.81	–	0.36	2.17	1.99	–	0.40	2.39
M201302	**To walls; 18 mm thick; two coat work:**										
M201302A	over 300 mm wide	m²	0.29	6.79	–	1.82	8.61	7.47	–	2.00	9.47
M201302B	not exceeding 300 mm wide	m	0.12	2.75	–	0.54	3.29	3.03	–	0.59	3.62
M201310	**To isolated columns; 12 mm thick; one coat work:**										
M201310A	over 300 mm wide	m²	0.19	4.45	–	1.18	5.63	4.90	–	1.30	6.19
M201310B	not exceeding 300 mm wide	m	0.08	1.81	–	0.36	2.17	1.99	–	0.40	2.39
M201311	**To isolated columns; 18 mm thick; two coat work:**										
M201311A	over 300 mm wide	m²	0.29	6.79	–	1.82	8.61	7.47	–	2.00	9.47
M201311B	not exceeding 300 mm wide	m	0.12	2.75	–	0.54	3.29	3.03	–	0.59	3.62
M2014	**Cement and sand (1:4); screeded finish**										
M201412	**To walls; 12 mm thick; one coat work:**										
M201412A	over 300 mm wide	m²	0.18	4.22	–	1.03	5.25	4.64	–	1.13	5.78
M201412B	not exceeding 300 mm wide	m	0.07	1.71	–	0.32	2.03	1.88	–	0.35	2.23
M201414	**To walls; 18 mm thick; two coat work:**										
M201414A	over 300 mm wide	m²	0.27	6.33	–	1.58	7.91	6.96	–	1.74	8.70
M201414B	not exceeding 300 mm wide	m	0.11	2.55	–	0.48	3.03	2.81	–	0.53	3.33
M201422	**To isolated columns; 12 mm thick; one coat work:**										
M201422A	over 300 mm wide	m²	0.18	4.22	–	1.03	5.25	4.64	–	1.13	5.78
M201422B	not exceeding 300 mm wide	m	0.07	1.71	–	0.32	2.03	1.88	–	0.35	2.23
M201424	**To isolated columns; 18 mm thick; two coat work:**										
M201424A	over 300 mm wide	m²	0.27	6.33	–	1.58	7.91	6.96	–	1.74	8.70
M201424B	not exceeding 300 mm wide	m	0.11	2.55	–	0.48	3.03	2.81	–	0.53	3.33

Surface Finishes

Major Works 2009		Unit	Labour Hours	Labour Net	Plant Net	Materials Net	Unit Net	Labour Gross	Plant Gross	Materials Gross	Unit Price
								(Gross rates include 10% profit)			
				£	£	£	£	£	£	£	£
M20	**M20: PLASTERED, RENDERED AND ROUGHCAST COATINGS**										
M2015	**Cement, lime and sand (1:1:6); screeded finish**										
M201501	**To walls; 12 mm thick; one coat work:**										
M201501A	over 300 mm wide	m²	0.18	4.22	–	1.42	5.64	4.64	–	1.56	6.20
M201501B	not exceeding 300 mm wide	m	0.07	1.71	–	0.44	2.15	1.88	–	0.48	2.37
M201502	**To walls; 18 mm thick; two coat work:**										
M201502A	over 300 mm wide	m²	0.27	6.33	–	2.19	8.52	6.96	–	2.41	9.37
M201502B	not exceeding 300 mm wide	m	0.11	2.55	–	0.66	3.21	2.81	–	0.73	3.53
M201511	**To isolated columns; 12 mm thick; one coat work:**										
M201511A	over 300 mm wide	m²	0.18	4.22	–	1.42	5.64	4.64	–	1.56	6.20
M201511B	not exceeding 300 mm wide	m	0.07	1.71	–	0.44	2.15	1.88	–	0.48	2.37
M201512	**To isolated columns; 18 mm thick; two coat work:**										
M201512A	over 300 mm wide	m²	0.27	6.33	–	2.19	8.52	6.96	–	2.41	9.37
M201512B	not exceeding 300 mm wide	m	0.11	2.55	–	0.66	3.21	2.81	–	0.73	3.53
M2016	**Cement, lime and sand (1:1:6); trowelled finish**										
M201601	**To walls; 12 mm thick; one coat work:**										
M201601A	over 300 mm wide	m²	0.20	4.69	–	1.42	6.11	5.16	–	1.56	6.72
M201601B	not exceeding 300 mm wide	m	0.08	1.90	–	0.44	2.34	2.09	–	0.48	2.57
M201602	**To walls; 18 mm thick; two coat work:**										
M201602A	over 300 mm wide	m²	0.30	7.03	–	2.19	9.22	7.73	–	2.41	10.14
M201602B	not exceeding 300 mm wide	m	0.12	2.86	–	0.66	3.52	3.15	–	0.73	3.87
M201611	**To isolated columns; 12 mm thick; one coat work:**										
M201611A	over 300 mm wide	m²	0.20	4.69	–	1.42	6.11	5.16	–	1.56	6.72
M201611B	not exceeding 300 mm wide	m	0.08	1.90	–	0.44	2.34	2.09	–	0.48	2.57
M201612	**To isolated columns; 18 mm thick; two coat work:**										
M201612A	over 300 mm wide	m²	0.30	7.03	–	2.19	9.22	7.73	–	2.41	10.14
M201612B	not exceeding 300 mm wide	m	0.12	2.86	–	0.66	3.52	3.15	–	0.73	3.87

Surface Finishes

Major Works 2009		Unit	Labour Hours	Labour Net	Plant Net	Materials Net	Unit Net	Labour Gross	Plant Gross	Materials Gross	Unit Price
								(Gross rates include 10% profit)			
				£	£	£	£	£	£	£	£
M20	**M20: PLASTERED, RENDERED AND ROUGHCAST COATINGS**										
M2021	**Carlite lightweight plastering with 2 mm Carlite finish plaster**										
M202101	**To walls; 10 mm thick; two coat work; to concrete backgrounds with bonding backings:**										
M202101A	over 300 mm wide	m²	0.30	7.03	–	1.85	8.88	7.73	–	2.04	9.77
M202101B	not exceeding 300 mm wide	m	0.12	2.86	–	0.60	3.46	3.15	–	0.66	3.81
M202102	**To walls; 10 mm thick; two coat work; to plasterboard backgrounds with bonding backings; including scrimming joints:**										
M202102A	over 300 mm wide	m²	0.30	7.03	–	2.07	9.10	7.73	–	2.28	10.01
M202102B	not exceeding 300 mm wide	m	0.12	2.86	–	0.67	3.53	3.15	–	0.74	3.88
M202103	**To walls; 13 mm thick; two coat work; to masonry backgrounds with browning backings:**										
M202103A	over 300 mm wide	m²	0.30	7.04	–	2.11	9.15	7.74	–	2.32	10.07
M202103C	not exceeding 300 mm wide	m	0.12	2.86	–	0.61	3.47	3.15	–	0.67	3.82
M202104	**To walls; 13 mm thick; two coat work; to masonry backgrounds with special browning backings:**										
M202104A	over 300 mm wide	m²	0.30	7.03	–	2.20	9.23	7.73	–	2.42	10.15
M202104D	not exceeding 300 mm wide	m	0.12	2.86	–	0.63	3.49	3.15	–	0.69	3.84
M202105	**To walls; 13 mm thick; two coat work; to masonry backgrounds with browning HSB backings:**										
M202105A	over 300 mm wide	m²	0.30	7.03	–	2.23	9.26	7.73	–	2.45	10.19
M202105E	not exceeding 300 mm wide	m	0.12	2.86	–	0.64	3.50	3.15	–	0.70	3.85
M202106	**To walls; 13 mm thick; three coat work; metal lathing backgrounds with metal lathing backings:**										
M202106A	over 300 mm wide	m²	0.40	9.38	–	3.72	13.10	10.32	–	4.09	14.41
M202106B	not exceeding 300 mm wide	m	0.16	3.79	–	1.23	5.02	4.17	–	1.35	5.52
M202111	**To ceilings; 10 mm thick; two coat work; to concrete backgrounds with bonding backings:**										
M202111A	over 300 mm wide	m²	0.34	7.97	–	1.85	9.82	8.77	–	2.04	10.80
M202111B	not exceeding 300 mm wide	m	0.14	3.24	–	0.60	3.84	3.56	–	0.66	4.22
M202112	**To ceilings; 10 mm thick; two coat work; to plasterboard backgrounds with bonding backings; including scrimming joints:**										
M202112A	over 300 mm wide	m²	0.34	7.97	–	2.07	10.04	8.77	–	2.28	11.04
M202112B	not exceeding 300 mm wide	m	0.14	3.23	–	0.67	3.90	3.55	–	0.74	4.29

Major Works 2009		Unit	Labour Hours	Labour Net	Plant Net	Materials Net	Unit Net	Labour Gross	Plant Gross	Materials Gross	Unit Price
								(Gross rates include 10% profit)			
				£	£	£	£	£	£	£	£
M20	**M20: PLASTERED, RENDERED AND ROUGHCAST COATINGS**										
M2021	**Carlite lightweight plastering with 2 mm Carlite finish plaster**										
M202116	**To ceilings; 13 mm thick; three coat work; to metal lathing backgrounds with metal lathing backings:**										
M202116A	over 300 mm wide	m²	0.45	10.55	–	3.72	14.27	11.61	–	4.09	15.70
M202116B	not exceeding 300 mm wide	m	0.18	4.29	–	1.23	5.52	4.72	–	1.35	6.07
M202121	**To isolated beams; 10 mm thick; two coat work; to concrete backgrounds with bonding backings:**										
M202121A	over 300 mm wide	m²	0.34	7.97	–	1.85	9.82	8.77	–	2.04	10.80
M202121B	not exceeding 300 mm wide	m	0.14	3.24	–	0.60	3.84	3.56	–	0.66	4.22
M202122	**To isolated beams; 10 mm thick; two coat work; to plasterboard backgrounds with bonding backings; including scrimming joints:**										
M202122A	over 300 mm wide	m²	0.34	7.97	–	2.07	10.04	8.77	–	2.28	11.04
M202122B	not exceeding 300 mm wide	m	0.14	3.23	–	0.67	3.90	3.55	–	0.74	4.29
M202126	**To isolated beams; 13 mm thick; three coat work; to metal lathing backgrounds with metal lathing backings:**										
M202126A	over 300 mm wide	m²	0.45	10.55	–	3.72	14.27	11.61	–	4.09	15.70
M202126B	not exceeding 300 mm wide	m	0.18	4.29	–	1.23	5.52	4.72	–	1.35	6.07
M202141	**To isolated columns; 10 mm thick; two coat work; to concrete backgrounds with bonding backings:**										
M202141A	over 300 mm wide	m²	0.30	7.03	–	1.85	8.88	7.73	–	2.04	9.77
M202141B	not exceeding 300 mm wide	m	0.12	2.86	–	0.60	3.46	3.15	–	0.66	3.81
M202142	**To isolated columns; 10 mm thick; two coat work; to plasterboard backgrounds with bonding backings; including scrimming joints:**										
M202142A	over 300 mm wide	m²	0.30	7.03	–	2.07	9.10	7.73	–	2.28	10.01
M202142B	not exceeding 300 mm wide	m	0.12	2.86	–	0.67	3.53	3.15	–	0.74	3.88
M202143	**To isolated columns; 13 mm thick; two coat work; to masonry backgrounds with browning backings:**										
M202143A	over 300 mm wide	m²	0.30	7.04	–	2.11	9.15	7.74	–	2.32	10.07
M202143B	not exceeding 300 mm wide	m	0.12	2.86	–	0.61	3.47	3.15	–	0.67	3.82
M202144	**To isolated columns; 13 mm thick; two coat work; to masonry backgrounds with special browning backings:**										
M202144A	over 300 mm wide	m²	0.30	7.03	–	2.20	9.23	7.73	–	2.42	10.15
M202144B	not exceeding 300 mm wide	m	0.12	2.86	–	0.63	3.49	3.15	–	0.69	3.84

Surface Finishes

Major Works 2009		Unit	Labour Hours	Labour Net	Plant Net	Materials Net	Unit Net	Labour Gross	Plant Gross	Materials Gross	Unit Price
								(Gross rates include 10% profit)			
				£	£	£	£	£	£	£	£
M20	**M20: PLASTERED, RENDERED AND ROUGHCAST COATINGS**										
M2021	**Carlite lightweight plastering with 2 mm Carlite finish plaster**										
M202145	**To isolated columns; 13 mm thick; two coat work; to masonry backgrounds with browning HSB backings:**										
M202145A	over 300 mm wide	m²	0.30	7.03	–	2.23	9.26	7.73	–	2.45	10.19
M202145E	not exceeding 300 mm wide	m	0.12	2.86	–	0.64	3.50	3.15	–	0.70	3.85
M202146	**To isolated columns; 13 mm thick; three coat work; metal lathing backgrounds with metal lathing backings:**										
M202146A	over 300 mm wide	m²	0.40	9.38	–	3.72	13.10	10.32	–	4.09	14.41
M202146B	not exceeding 300 mm wide	m	0.16	3.79	–	1.23	5.02	4.17	–	1.35	5.52
M202161	**To skirtings, bands, strings, coverings to kerbs, mouldings, channels or the like; 10 mm thick; two coat work; to concrete backgrounds with bonding backings:**										
M202161A	not exceeding 300 mm wide	m	0.18	4.22	–	0.60	4.82	4.64	–	0.66	5.30
M202162	**To skirtings, bands, strings, coverings to kerbs, mouldings, channels or the like; 10 mm thick; two coat work; to plasterboard backgrounds with bonding backings; including scrimming joints:**										
M202162B	not exceeding 300 mm wide	m	0.18	4.22	–	0.67	4.89	4.64	–	0.74	5.38
M202163	**To skirtings, bands, strings, coverings to kerbs, mouldings, channels or the like; 13 mm thick; two coat work; to masonry backgrounds with browning backings:**										
M202163C	not exceeding 300 mm wide	m	0.18	4.21	–	0.84	5.05	4.63	–	0.92	5.56
M202164	**To skirtings, bands, strings, coverings to kerbs, mouldings, channels or the like; 13 mm thick; two coat work; to masonry backgrounds with special browning backings:**										
M202164D	not exceeding 300 mm wide	m	0.18	4.22	–	0.87	5.09	4.64	–	0.96	5.60

Major Works 2009		Unit	Labour Hours	Labour Net	Plant Net	Materials Net	Unit Net	Labour Gross	Plant Gross	Materials Gross	Unit Price
								— (Gross rates include 10% profit) —			
				£	£	£	£	£	£	£	£
M20	**M20: PLASTERED, RENDERED AND ROUGHCAST COATINGS**										
M2021	**Carlite lightweight plastering with 2 mm Carlite finish plaster**										
M202165	**To skirtings, bands, strings, coverings to kerbs, mouldings, channels or the like; 13 mm thick; two coat work; to masonry backgrounds with browning HSB backings:**										
M202165E	not exceeding 300 mm wide	m	0.18	4.22	–	0.88	5.10	4.64	–	0.97	5.61
M202166	**To skirtings, bands, strings, coverings to kerbs, mouldings, channels or the like; 13 mm thick; three coat work; to metal lathing backgrounds with metal lathing backings:**										
M202166F	not exceeding 300 mm wide	m	0.24	5.62	–	1.23	6.85	6.18	–	1.35	7.54
M2022	**Thistle 2 mm finish on Thistle renovating plaster**										
M202201	**To walls; 13 mm thick; two coat work:**										
M202201A	over 300 mm wide	m²	0.30	7.04	–	2.84	9.88	7.74	–	3.12	10.87
M202201B	not exceeding 300 mm wide	m	0.12	2.86	–	0.95	3.81	3.15	–	1.05	4.19
M202211	**To isolated columns; 13 mm thick; two coat work:**										
M202211A	over 300 mm wide	m²	0.30	7.04	–	2.84	9.88	7.74	–	3.12	10.87
M202211B	not exceeding 300 mm wide	m	0.12	2.86	–	0.95	3.81	3.15	–	1.05	4.19
M202226	**To skirtings, bands, strings, coverings to kerbs, mouldings, channels or the like; 13 mm thick; two coat work:**										
M202226A	not exceeding 300 mm wide	m	0.18	4.22	–	0.95	5.17	4.64	–	1.05	5.69

Surface Finishes

Major Works 2009		Unit	Labour Hours	Labour Net	Plant Net	Materials Net	Unit Net	Labour Gross	Plant Gross	Materials Gross	Unit Price
								(Gross rates include 10% profit)			
				£	£	£	£	£	£	£	£
M20	M20: PLASTERED, RENDERED AND ROUGHCAST COATINGS										
M2023	Thistle finishing plaster										
M202301	To walls; 2 mm thick; one coat work; to plasterboard backgrounds including scrimming joints and filling nail holes; board finish:										
M202301A	2 mm one coat work to plasterboard backgrounds including scrimming join and filling nail holes; board finish	m²	0.14	3.28	–	0.79	4.07	3.61	–	0.87	4.48
M202301B	not exceeding 300 mm wide	m	0.06	1.33	–	0.26	1.59	1.46	–	0.29	1.75
M202302	To walls; 5 mm thick; two coat work; to plasterboard backgrounds including scrimming joints and filling nail holes; board finish:										
M202302A	over 300 mm wide	m²	0.20	4.69	–	1.36	6.05	5.16	–	1.50	6.66
M202302B	not exceeding 300 mm wide	m	0.08	1.89	–	0.45	2.34	2.08	–	0.50	2.57
M202303	To walls; 2 mm thick; one coat work; to sanded backgrounds:										
M202303A	over 300 mm wide	m²	0.08	1.87	–	0.38	2.25	2.06	–	0.42	2.48
M202303B	not exceeding 300 mm wide	m	0.03	0.75	–	0.19	0.94	0.83	–	0.21	1.03
M202313	To ceilings; 2 mm thick; one coat work; to plasterboard backgrounds including scrimming joints and filling nail holes; board finish:										
M202313A	over 300 mm wide	m²	0.16	3.75	–	0.79	4.54	4.13	–	0.87	4.99
M202313B	not exceeding 300 mm wide	m	0.07	1.52	–	0.26	1.78	1.67	–	0.29	1.96
M202314	To ceilings; 5 mm thick; two coat work; to plasterboard backgrounds including scrimming joints and filling nail holes; board finish:										
M202314A	over 300 mm wide	m²	0.23	5.39	–	1.36	6.75	5.93	–	1.50	7.43
M202314B	not exceeding 300 mm wide	m	0.09	2.18	–	0.45	2.63	2.40	–	0.50	2.89
M202315	To ceilings; 2 mm thick; one coat work; to sanded backgrounds:										
M202315A	over 300 mm wide	m²	0.10	2.34	–	0.38	2.72	2.57	–	0.42	2.99
M202315B	not exceeding 300 mm wide	m	0.04	0.96	–	0.19	1.15	1.06	–	0.21	1.27
M202323	To isolated beams; 2 mm thick; one coat work; to plasterboard backgrounds including scrimming joints and filling nail holes; board finish:										
M202323A	over 300 mm wide	m²	0.16	3.75	–	0.79	4.54	4.13	–	0.87	4.99
M202323B	not exceeding 300 mm wide	m	0.07	1.52	–	0.26	1.78	1.67	–	0.29	1.96

Major Works 2009		Unit	Labour Hours	Labour Net	Plant Net	Materials Net	Unit Net	Labour Gross	Plant Gross	Materials Gross	Unit Price
								(Gross rates include 10% profit)			
				£	£	£	£	£	£	£	£
M20	**M20: PLASTERED, RENDERED AND ROUGHCAST COATINGS**										
M2023	**Thistle finishing plaster**										
M202324	**To isolated beams; 5 mm thick; two coat work; to plasterboard backgrounds including scrimming joints and filling nail holes; board finish:**										
M202324A	over 300 mm wide	m²	0.23	5.39	–	1.36	6.75	5.93	–	1.50	7.43
M202324B	not exceeding 300 mm wide	m	0.09	2.18	–	0.45	2.63	2.40	–	0.50	2.89
M202325	**To isolated beams; 2 mm thick; one coat work; to sanded backgrounds:**										
M202325A	over 300 mm wide	m²	0.10	2.34	–	0.38	2.72	2.57	–	0.42	2.99
M202325B	not exceeding 300 mm wide	m	0.04	0.96	–	0.19	1.15	1.06	–	0.21	1.27
M202341	**To isolated columns; 2 mm thick; one coat work; to plasterboard backgrounds including scrimming joints and filling nail holes; board finish:**										
M202341A	over 300 mm wide	m²	0.14	3.28	–	0.79	4.07	3.61	–	0.87	4.48
M202341B	not exceeding 300 mm wide	m	0.06	1.33	–	0.26	1.59	1.46	–	0.29	1.75
M202342	**To isolated columns; 5 mm thick; two coat work; to plasterboard backgrounds including scrimming joints and filling nail holes; board finish:**										
M202342A	over 300 mm wide	m²	0.20	4.69	–	1.36	6.05	5.16	–	1.50	6.66
M202342B	not exceeding 300 mm wide	m	0.08	1.89	–	0.45	2.34	2.08	–	0.50	2.57
M202343	**To isolated columns; 2 mm thick; one coat work; to sanded backgrounds:**										
M202343A	over 300 mm wide	m²	0.08	1.87	–	0.38	2.25	2.06	–	0.42	2.48
M202343B	not exceeding 300 mm wide	m	0.03	0.75	–	0.19	0.94	0.83	–	0.21	1.03

Surface Finishes

Major Works 2009		Unit	Labour Hours	Labour Net	Plant Net	Materials Net	Unit Net	Labour Gross	Plant Gross	Materials Gross	Unit Price
								(Gross rates include 10% profit)			
				£	£	£	£	£	£	£	£
M20	**M20: PLASTERED, RENDERED AND ROUGHCAST COATINGS**										
M2023	**Thistle finishing plaster**										
M202361	**To skirtings, bands, strings, coverings to kerbs, mouldings, channels or the like; 2 mm thick; one coat work; to plasterboard backgrounds including scrimming joints and filling nail holes; board finish:**										
M202361A	not exceeding 300 mm wide	m	0.08	1.87	–	0.26	2.13	2.06	–	0.29	2.34
M202362	**To skirtings, bands, strings, coverings to kerbs, mouldings, channels or the like; 5 mm thick; two coat work; to plasterboard backgrounds including scrimming joints and filling nail holes; board finish:**										
M202362B	not exceeding 300 mm wide	m	0.12	2.81	–	0.45	3.26	3.09	–	0.50	3.59
M202363	**To skirtings, bands, strings, coverings to kerbs, mouldings, channels or the like; 2 mm thick; one coat work; to sanded backgrounds:**										
M202363C	not exceeding 300 mm wide	m	0.05	1.17	–	0.19	1.36	1.29	–	0.21	1.50

Major Works 2009		Unit	Labour Hours	Labour Net	Plant Net	Materials Net	Unit Net	Labour Gross	Plant Gross	Materials Gross	Unit Price
								(Gross rates include 10% profit)			
				£	£	£	£	£	£	£	£
M20	**M20: PLASTERED, RENDERED AND ROUGHCAST COATINGS**										
M2024	**Thistle Universal one coat plaster**										
M202401	**To walls; 10 mm thick; to concrete backgrounds:**										
M202401A	over 300 mm wide	m²	0.20	4.69	–	2.09	6.78	5.16	–	2.30	7.46
M202401B	not exceeding 300 mm wide	m	0.08	1.89	–	0.70	2.59	2.08	–	0.77	2.85
M202402	**To walls; 5 mm thick; to plasterboard backgrounds including scrimming joints and filling nail holes:**										
M202402A	over 300 mm wide	m²	0.16	3.75	–	1.16	4.91	4.13	–	1.28	5.40
M202402B	not exceeding 300 mm wide	m	0.07	1.53	–	0.46	1.99	1.68	–	0.51	2.19
M202403	**To walls; 13 mm thick; to masonry backgrounds:**										
M202403A	over 300 mm wide	m²	0.20	4.69	–	2.78	7.47	5.16	–	3.06	8.22
M202403B	not exceeding 300 mm wide	m	0.08	1.90	–	0.93	2.83	2.09	–	1.02	3.11
M202411	**To ceilings; 10 mm thick; to concrete backgrounds:**										
M202411A	over 300 mm wide	m²	0.23	5.39	–	2.09	7.48	5.93	–	2.30	8.23
M202411B	not exceeding 300 mm wide	m	0.09	2.18	–	0.70	2.88	2.40	–	0.77	3.17
M202412	**To ceilings; 5 mm thick; to plasterboard backgrounds including scrimming joints and filling nail holes:**										
M202412A	over 300 mm wide	m²	0.18	4.22	–	1.16	5.38	4.64	–	1.28	5.92
M202412B	not exceeding 300 mm wide	m	0.07	1.72	–	0.46	2.18	1.89	–	0.51	2.40
M202421	**To isolated beams; 10 mm thick; to concrete backgrounds:**										
M202421A	over 300 mm wide	m²	0.23	5.39	–	2.09	7.48	5.93	–	2.30	8.23
M202421B	not exceeding 300 mm wide	m	0.09	2.18	–	0.70	2.88	2.40	–	0.77	3.17
M202422	**To isolated beams; 5 mm thick; to plasterboard backgrounds including scrimming joints and filling nail holes:**										
M202422A	over 300 mm wide	m²	0.18	4.22	–	1.16	5.38	4.64	–	1.28	5.92
M202422B	not exceeding 300 mm wide	m	0.07	1.72	–	0.46	2.18	1.89	–	0.51	2.40
M202441	**To isolated columns; 10 mm thick; to concrete backgrounds:**										
M202441A	over 300 mm wide	m²	0.20	4.69	–	2.09	6.78	5.16	–	2.30	7.46
M202441B	not exceeding 300 mm wide	m	0.08	1.89	–	0.70	2.59	2.08	–	0.77	2.85
M202442	**To isolated columns; 5 mm thick; to plasterboard backgrounds including scrimming joints and filling nail holes:**										
M202442A	over 300 mm wide	m²	0.16	3.75	–	1.16	4.91	4.13	–	1.28	5.40
M202442B	not exceeding 300 mm wide	m	0.07	1.53	–	0.46	1.99	1.68	–	0.51	2.19

Surface Finishes

Major Works 2009		Unit	Labour Hours	Labour Net	Plant Net	Materials Net	Unit Net	Labour Gross	Plant Gross	Materials Gross	Unit Price
								— (Gross rates include 10% profit) —			
				£	£	£	£	£	£	£	£
M20	**M20: PLASTERED, RENDERED AND ROUGHCAST COATINGS**										
M2024	**Thistle Universal one coat plaster**										
M202443	**To isolated columns; 13 mm thick; to masonry backgrounds:**										
M202443A	over 300 mm wide	m²	0.20	4.69	–	2.78	7.47	5.16	–	3.06	8.22
M202443B	not exceeding 300 mm wide	m	0.08	1.90	–	0.93	2.83	2.09	–	1.02	3.11
M202461	**To skirtings, bands, strings, coverings to kerbs, mouldings, channels or the like; 10 mm thick; to concrete backgrounds:**										
M202461A	not exceeding 300 mm wide	m	0.12	2.81	–	0.70	3.51	3.09	–	0.77	3.86
M202462	**To skirtings, bands, strings, coverings to kerbs, mouldings, channels or the like; 5 mm thick; to plasterboard backgrounds including scrimming joints and filling nail holes:**										
M202462B	not exceeding 300 mm wide	m	0.10	2.35	–	0.46	2.81	2.59	–	0.51	3.09
M202463	**To skirtings, bands, strings, coverings to kerbs, mouldings, channels or the like; 13 mm thick; to masonry backgrounds:**										
M202463C	not exceeding 300 mm wide	m	0.12	2.81	–	0.93	3.74	3.09	–	1.02	4.11
M2025	**Sirapite B finish plaster**										
M202501	**To walls; 3 mm thick; to sanded backgrounds:**										
M202501A	over 300 mm wide	m²	0.08	1.88	–	0.86	2.74	2.07	–	0.95	3.01
M202501B	not exceeding 300 mm wide	m	0.03	0.75	–	0.22	0.97	0.83	–	0.24	1.07
M202511	**To ceilings; 3 mm thick; to sanded backgrounds:**										
M202511A	over 300 mm wide	m²	0.10	2.35	–	0.86	3.21	2.59	–	0.95	3.53
M202511B	not exceeding 300 mm wide	m	0.04	0.96	–	0.22	1.18	1.06	–	0.24	1.30
M202521	**To isolated beams; 3 mm thick; to sanded backgrounds:**										
M202521A	over 300 mm wide	m²	0.10	2.35	–	0.86	3.21	2.59	–	0.95	3.53
M202521B	not exceeding 300 mm wide	m	0.04	0.96	–	0.22	1.18	1.06	–	0.24	1.30
M202541	**To isolated columns; 3 mm thick; to sanded backgrounds:**										
M202541A	over 300 mm wide	m²	0.08	1.88	–	0.86	2.74	2.07	–	0.95	3.01
M202541B	not exceeding 300 mm wide	m	0.03	0.75	–	0.22	0.97	0.83	–	0.24	1.07
M202561	**To skirtings, bands, strings, coverings to kerbs, mouldings, channels or the like; 3 mm thick; to sanded backgrounds:**										
M202561A	not exceeding 300 mm wide	m	0.05	1.17	–	0.22	1.39	1.29	–	0.24	1.53

Major Works 2009		Unit	Labour Hours	Labour Net	Plant Net	Materials Net	Unit Net	Labour Gross	Plant Gross	Materials Gross	Unit Price
				£	£	£	£	£ (Gross rates include 10% profit)	£	£	£
M20	**M20: PLASTERED, RENDERED AND ROUGHCAST COATINGS**										
M2026	**Gyproc Drywall topcoat**										
M202601	**To walls; one coat Gyproc Drywall top coat to surfaces of tapered edge boarding including filling, taping and finishing joints flush; ready for direct decoration:**										
M202601A	over 300 mm wide	m²	0.17	3.98	–	1.04	5.02	4.38	–	1.14	5.52
M202601B	not exceeding 300 mm wide	m	0.07	1.62	–	0.31	1.93	1.78	–	0.34	2.12
M202611	**To ceilings; one coat Gyproc Drywall top coat to surfaces of tapered edge boarding including filling, taping and finishing joints flush; ready for direct decoration:**										
M202611A	over 300 mm wide	m²	0.21	4.92	–	0.90	5.82	5.41	–	0.99	6.40
M202611B	not exceeding 300 mm wide	m	0.09	1.99	–	0.27	2.26	2.19	–	0.30	2.49
M202621	**To isolated beams; one coat Gyproc Drywall top coat to surfaces of tapered edge boarding including filling, taping and finishing joints flush; ready for direct decoration:**										
M202621A	over 300 mm wide	m²	0.21	4.92	–	0.90	5.82	5.41	–	0.99	6.40
M202621B	not exceeding 300 mm wide	m	0.09	1.99	–	0.27	2.26	2.19	–	0.30	2.49
M202641	**To isolated columns; one coat Gyproc Drywall top coat to surfaces of tapered edge boarding including filling, taping and finishing joints flush; ready for direct decoration:**										
M202641A	over 300 mm wide	m²	0.17	3.98	–	1.04	5.02	4.38	–	1.14	5.52
M202641B	not exceeding 300 mm wide	m	0.07	1.62	–	0.31	1.93	1.78	–	0.34	2.12
M202661	**To skirtings, bands, strings, coverings to kerbs or the like; one coat Gyproc Drywall top coat to surfaces of tapered edge boarding including filling, taping and finishing joints flush; ready for direct decoration:**										
M202661C	not exceeding 300 mm wide	m	0.10	2.34	–	0.29	2.63	2.57	–	0.32	2.89

Surface Finishes

Major Works 2009		Unit	Labour Hours	Labour Net	Plant Net	Materials Net	Unit Net	Labour Gross	Plant Gross	Materials Gross	Unit Price
									(Gross rates include 10% profit)		
				£	£	£	£	£	£	£	£
M20	**M20: PLASTERED, RENDERED AND ROUGHCAST COATINGS**										
M2031	**Tyrolean 7 mm three coat rendering to sanded backgrounds**										
M203101	**To walls; honeycomb finish:**										
M203101A	over 300 mm wide	m²	0.40	9.38	0.19	2.40	11.97	10.32	0.21	2.64	13.17
M203101B	not exceeding 300 mm wide	m	0.16	3.80	0.08	0.60	4.48	4.18	0.09	0.66	4.93
M203102	**To walls; rubbed finish:**										
M203102A	over 300 mm wide	m²	0.55	12.90	0.26	2.40	15.56	14.19	0.29	2.64	17.12
M203102B	not exceeding 300 mm wide	m	0.23	5.34	0.11	0.60	6.05	5.87	0.12	0.66	6.66
M203111	**To isolated columns; honeycomb finish:**										
M203111A	over 300 mm wide	m²	0.40	9.38	0.19	2.40	11.97	10.32	0.21	2.64	13.17
M203111B	not exceeding 300 mm wide	m	0.16	3.80	0.08	0.60	4.48	4.18	0.09	0.66	4.93
M203112	**To isolated columns; rubbed finish:**										
M203112A	over 300 mm wide	m²	0.55	12.90	0.26	2.40	15.56	14.19	0.29	2.64	17.12
M203112B	not exceeding 300 mm wide	m	0.23	5.34	0.11	0.60	6.05	5.87	0.12	0.66	6.66
M203161	**To skirtings, bands, strings, coverings to kerbs, mouldings, channels or the like; honeycomb finish:**										
M203161A	not exceeding 300 mm wide	m	0.20	4.68	0.10	0.60	5.38	5.15	0.11	0.66	5.92
M203162	**To skirtings, bands, strings, coverings to kerbs, mouldings, channels or the like; rubbed finish:**										
M203162B	not exceeding 300 mm wide	m	0.30	7.04	0.14	0.60	7.78	7.74	0.15	0.66	8.56

Major Works 2009		Unit	Labour Hours	Labour Net	Plant Net	Materials Net	Unit Net	Labour Gross	Plant Gross	Materials Gross	Unit Price
								(Gross rates include 10% profit)			
				£	£	£	£	£	£	£	£
M20	**M20: PLASTERED, RENDERED AND ROUGHCAST COATINGS**										
M2033	**Roughcast rendering to sanded backgrounds**										
M203301	**To walls:**										
M203301A	over 300 mm wide	m²	0.22	5.16	0.11	0.99	6.26	5.68	0.12	1.09	6.89
M203301B	not exceeding 300 mm wide	m	0.09	2.09	0.04	0.28	2.41	2.30	0.04	0.31	2.65
M203341	**To isolated columns:**										
M203341A	over 300 mm wide	m²	0.22	5.16	0.11	0.99	6.26	5.68	0.12	1.09	6.89
M203341B	not exceeding 300 mm wide	m	0.09	2.09	0.04	0.28	2.41	2.30	0.04	0.31	2.65
M203361	**To skirtings, bands, strings, coverings to kerbs, mouldings, channels or the like:**										
M203361A	not exceeding 300 mm wide	m	0.13	3.04	0.06	0.99	4.09	3.34	0.07	1.09	4.50
M2035	**Pebbledash finish to sanded backgrounds**										
M203501	**To walls:**										
M203501A	over 300 mm wide	m²	0.30	7.03	0.14	0.52	7.69	7.73	0.15	0.57	8.46
M203501B	not exceeding 300 mm wide	m	0.12	2.86	0.06	0.14	3.06	3.15	0.07	0.15	3.37
M203541	**To isolated columns:**										
M203541A	over 300 mm wide	m²	0.30	7.03	0.14	0.52	7.69	7.73	0.15	0.57	8.46
M203541B	not exceeding 300 mm wide	m	0.12	2.86	0.06	0.14	3.06	3.15	0.07	0.15	3.37
M203561	**To skirtings, bands, strings, coverings to kerbs, mouldings, channels or the like:**										
M203561A	not exceeding 300 mm wide	m	0.18	4.22	0.09	0.52	4.83	4.64	0.10	0.57	5.31

Surface Finishes

Major Works 2009		Unit	Labour Hours	Labour Net	Plant Net	Materials Net	Unit Net	Labour Gross	Plant Gross	Materials Gross	Unit Price
								(Gross rates include 10% profit)			
				£	£	£	£	£	£	£	£
M20	**M20: PLASTERED, RENDERED AND ROUGHCAST COATINGS**										
M2074	**Beads, stops, edging strips and arches**										
M207401	**Division strips; embedding in pavings:**										
M207401A	5 × 25 mm brass........	m	0.06	1.41	–	9.89	11.30	1.55	–	10.88	12.43
M207401B	5 × 25 mm aluminium ...	m	0.06	1.40	–	4.12	5.52	1.54	–	4.53	6.07
M207402	**Ferodo nosings; plugging and screwing to concrete backgrounds:**										
M207402A	type SD1	m	0.30	5.10	–	20.32	25.42	5.61	–	22.35	27.96
M207402B	type SD2	m	0.30	5.09	–	23.63	28.72	5.60	–	25.99	31.59
M207402C	type HD1	m	0.30	5.10	–	21.98	27.08	5.61	–	24.18	29.79
M207402D	type HD2	m	0.30	5.10	–	25.52	30.62	5.61	–	28.07	33.68
M207403	**Division strips; plugging and screwing to concrete backgrounds:**										
M207403A	aluminium; carpet to carpet	m	0.25	4.25	–	9.84	14.09	4.68	–	10.82	15.50
M207403B	aluminium; carpet to stop edge....................	m	0.25	4.24	–	9.09	13.33	4.66	–	10.00	14.66
M207403C	aluminium; carpet to vinyl flooring	m	0.25	4.25	–	9.84	14.09	4.68	–	10.82	15.50
M207403D	aluminium; carpet to vinyl flooring stop edge	m	0.25	4.24	–	9.09	13.33	4.66	–	10.00	14.66
M207403E	brass anodised aluminium; carpet to carpet...........	m	0.25	4.24	–	12.56	16.80	4.66	–	13.82	18.48
M207403F	brass anodised aluminium; carpet to carpet stop edge..	m	0.25	4.24	–	12.01	16.25	4.66	–	13.21	17.88
M207403G	brass anodised aluminium; carpet to vinyl flooring.....	m	0.25	4.24	–	12.56	16.80	4.66	–	13.82	18.48
M207403H	brass anodised aluminium; vinyl flooring to stop edge..	m	0.25	4.24	–	12.01	16.25	4.66	–	13.21	17.88

Major Works 2009		Unit	Labour Hours	Labour Net	Plant Net	Materials Net	Unit Net	Labour Gross	Plant Gross	Materials Gross	Unit Price
								(Gross rates include 10% profit)			
				£	£	£	£	£	£	£	£
M20	**M20: PLASTERED, RENDERED AND ROUGHCAST COATINGS**										
M2024	**Thistle Universal one coat plaster**										
M207404	**Expamet galvanised mild steel plaster beads and stops; fixing in accordance with manufacturer's instructions:**										
M207404A	angle bead ref 550	m	0.04	0.68	–	0.92	1.60	0.75	–	1.01	1.76
M207404B	maxicon bead ref 558	m	0.04	0.68	–	0.88	1.56	0.75	–	0.97	1.72
M207404C	10 mm plaster stop ref 562 .	m	0.04	0.68	–	1.10	1.78	0.75	–	1.21	1.96
M207404D	13 mm plaster stop ref 563 .	m	0.04	0.68	–	1.10	1.78	0.75	–	1.21	1.96
M207404E	16 mm plaster stop ref 565 .	m	0.04	0.68	–	1.39	2.07	0.75	–	1.53	2.28
M207404F	19 mm plaster stop ref 566 .	m	0.04	0.68	–	1.39	2.07	0.75	–	1.53	2.28
M207404G	depth gauge bead ref 569 ..	m	0.04	0.68	–	0.89	1.57	0.75	–	0.98	1.73
M207404H	12 mm movement bead ref 588....................	m	0.04	0.68	–	4.79	5.47	0.75	–	5.27	6.02
M207404I	18 mm movement bead ref 589....................	m	0.04	0.68	–	4.83	5.51	0.75	–	5.31	6.06
M207404J	21 mm movement bead ref 590....................	m	0.04	0.68	–	5.43	6.11	0.75	–	5.97	6.72
M207404K	corner movement bead ref 587....................	m	0.04	0.68	–	4.79	5.47	0.75	–	5.27	6.02
M207404L	13 mm architrave bead ref 580....................	m	0.04	0.68	–	1.41	2.09	0.75	–	1.55	2.30
M207404M	10 mm architrave bead ref 586....................	m	0.04	0.68	–	1.28	1.96	0.75	–	1.41	2.16
M207404N	13 mm architrave bead ref 579....................	m	0.04	0.68	–	1.42	2.10	0.75	–	1.56	2.31
M207404O	10 mm architrave bead ref 585....................	m	0.04	0.68	–	1.29	1.97	0.75	–	1.42	2.17
M207404P	10 mm architrave bead ref 513....................	m	0.04	0.68	–	1.05	1.73	0.75	–	1.16	1.90
M207404Q	10 mm architrave bead ref 514....................	m	0.04	0.68	–	1.22	1.90	0.75	–	1.34	2.09
M207404R	square nose angle bead ref 559....................	m	0.04	0.68	–	1.03	1.71	0.75	–	1.13	1.88
M207404S	3 mm angle bead ref 553...	m	0.04	0.68	–	0.92	1.60	0.75	–	1.01	1.76
M207404T	6 mm angle bead ref 554...	m	0.04	0.68	–	1.21	1.89	0.75	–	1.33	2.08
M207404U	3 mm stop bead ref 560....	m	0.04	0.68	–	1.20	1.88	0.75	–	1.32	2.07
M207404V	6 mm stop bead ref 561....	m	0.04	0.68	–	1.20	1.88	0.75	–	1.32	2.07
M207404W	thin coat angle bead ref 595	m	0.04	0.68	–	3.18	3.86	0.75	–	3.50	4.25
M207404X	dry wall corner bead ref 548	m	0.04	0.68	–	0.98	1.66	0.75	–	1.08	1.83
M207404Y	10 mm edge bead ref 567 ..	m	0.04	0.68	–	1.58	2.26	0.75	–	1.74	2.49
M207404Z	12 mm edge bead ref 568 ..	m	0.04	0.68	–	1.58	2.26	0.75	–	1.74	2.49

Surface Finishes

		Unit	Labour Hours	Labour Net	Plant Net	Materials Net	Unit Net	Labour Gross	Plant Gross	Materials Gross	Unit Price
				£	£	£	£	(Gross rates include 10% profit)			
								£	£	£	£
M20	**M20: PLASTERED, RENDERED AND ROUGHCAST COATINGS**										
M2024	**Thistle Universal one coat plaster**										
M207405	**Expamet galvanised mild steel render beads and stops; fixing in accordance with manufacturer's instructions:**										
M207405A	bellmouth stop ref 570	m	0.04	0.68	–	1.11	1.79	0.75	–	1.22	1.97
M207405B	stop bead ref 1222	m	0.04	0.68	–	3.18	3.86	0.75	–	3.50	4.25
M207405C	bellmouth stop ref 1229 ...	m	0.04	0.68	–	3.18	3.86	0.75	–	3.50	4.25
M207405D	angle bead ref 1019	m	0.04	0.68	–	2.81	3.49	0.75	–	3.09	3.84
M207405E	stripmesh ref 584	m	0.04	0.68	–	1.20	1.88	0.75	–	1.32	2.07
M207405F	corner mesh ref 583	m	0.04	0.68	–	1.20	1.88	0.75	–	1.32	2.07
M207406	**Expamet austenitic stainless steel render beads and stops; fixing in accordance with manufacturer's instructions:**										
M207406A	angle bead ref 545	m	0.04	0.68	–	3.20	3.88	0.75	–	3.52	4.27
M207406B	19 mm stop bead ref 546...	m	0.04	0.68	–	2.86	3.54	0.75	–	3.15	3.89
M207406C	16 mm stop bead ref 526...	m	0.04	0.68	–	2.86	3.54	0.75	–	3.15	3.89
M207406D	13 mm stop bead ref 533...	m	0.04	0.68	–	2.86	3.54	0.75	–	3.15	3.89
M207406E	10 mm stop bead ref 534...	m	0.04	0.68	–	2.86	3.54	0.75	–	3.15	3.89
M207406F	bellmouth stop ref 547	m	0.04	0.68	–	2.86	3.54	0.75	–	3.15	3.89
M207406G	movement joint ref 544	m	0.04	0.68	–	7.90	8.58	0.75	–	8.69	9.44
M207406H	movement joint ref 538	m	0.04	0.68	–	3.03	3.71	0.75	–	3.33	4.08
M207406I	stripmesh ref 522	m	0.04	0.68	–	2.99	3.67	0.75	–	3.29	4.04
M207406J	corner mesh ref 521	m	0.04	0.68	–	3.07	3.75	0.75	–	3.38	4.13

Major Works 2009		Unit	Labour Hours	Labour Net	Plant Net	Materials Net	Unit Net	Labour Gross	Plant Gross	Materials Gross	Unit Price
				£	£	£	£	£	£	£	£
								Gross rates include 10% profit			
M20	**M20: PLASTERED, RENDERED AND ROUGHCAST COATINGS**										
M2074	**Beads, stops, edging strips and arches**										
M207407	**Expamet galvanised mild steel arch formers; fixing in accordance with manufacturer's instructions:**										
M207407A	380 mm radius half semi-circle; ref EAC15	Nr	0.20	4.69	–	17.68	22.37	5.16	–	19.45	24.61
M207407B	460 mm radius half semi-circle; ref EAC18	Nr	0.20	4.69	–	21.42	26.11	5.16	–	23.56	28.72
M207407C	610 mm radius half semi-circle; ref EAC24	Nr	0.20	4.69	–	26.61	31.30	5.16	–	29.27	34.43
M207407D	760 mm radius half semi-circle; ref EAC30	Nr	0.20	4.69	–	37.62	42.31	5.16	–	41.38	46.54
M207407E	380 mm radius full semi-circle; ref ESC30	Nr	0.35	8.20	–	34.80	43.00	9.02	–	38.28	47.30
M207407F	410 mm radius full semi-circle; ref ESC32	Nr	0.35	8.20	–	35.37	43.57	9.02	–	38.91	47.93
M207407G	420 mm radius full semi-circle; ref ESC33	Nr	0.35	8.20	–	36.51	44.71	9.02	–	40.16	49.18
M207407H	460 mm radius full semi-circle; ref ESC36	Nr	0.35	8.20	–	42.83	51.03	9.02	–	47.11	56.13
M207407I	610 mm radius full semi-circle; ref ESC48	Nr	0.35	8.20	–	52.70	60.90	9.02	–	57.97	66.99
M207407J	760 mm radius full semi-circle; ref ESC60	Nr	0.35	8.20	–	74.12	82.32	9.02	–	81.53	90.55
M207407K	230 mm radius full circle; ref BE18	Nr	0.40	9.37	–	44.14	53.51	10.31	–	48.55	58.86
M207407L	1220 mm wide elliptical arch; ref EEL48	Nr	0.50	11.72	–	66.76	78.48	12.89	–	73.44	86.33
M207407M	1370 mm wide elliptical arch; ref EEL54	Nr	0.50	11.72	–	69.92	81.64	12.89	–	76.91	89.80
M207407N	1520 mm wide elliptical arch; ref EEL60	Nr	0.50	11.72	–	74.20	85.92	12.89	–	81.62	94.51
M207407O	1830 mm wide elliptical arch; ref EEL72	Nr	0.67	15.70	–	79.80	95.50	17.27	–	87.78	105.05
M207407P	2130 mm wide elliptical arch; ref EEL84	Nr	0.67	15.70	–	87.44	103.14	17.27	–	96.18	113.45
M207407Q	2440 mm wide elliptical arch; ref EEL96	Nr	0.67	15.70	–	91.73	107.43	17.27	–	100.90	118.17
M207407R	3050 mm wide elliptical arch; ref EEL120	Nr	0.67	15.70	–	93.59	109.29	17.27	–	102.95	120.22
M207407S	760 mm wide spandrel arch; ref ESP30	Nr	0.40	9.37	–	44.22	53.59	10.31	–	48.64	58.95
M207407T	910 mm wide spandrel arch; ref ESP36	Nr	0.40	9.37	–	46.27	55.64	10.31	–	50.90	61.20
M207407U	1220 mm wide spandrel arch; ref ESP4	Nr	0.40	9.37	–	59.12	68.49	10.31	–	65.03	75.34
M207407V	1520 mm wide spandrel arch; ref ESP6	Nr	0.40	9.37	–	65.65	75.02	10.31	–	72.22	82.52
M207407W	1830 mm wide spandrel arch; ref ESP7	Nr	0.40	9.37	–	72.14	81.51	10.31	–	79.35	89.66
M207407X	2130 mm wide spandrel arch; ref ESP8	Nr	0.40	9.37	–	78.50	87.87	10.31	–	86.35	96.66
M207407Y	2440 mm wide spandrel arch; ref ESP9	Nr	0.67	15.70	–	83.15	98.85	17.27	–	91.47	108.74
M207407Z	3050 mm wide spandrel arch; ref ESP120	Nr	0.67	15.70	–	87.44	103.14	17.27	–	96.18	113.45

Surface Finishes

Major Works 2009		Unit	Labour Hours	Labour Net	Plant Net	Materials Net	Unit Net	Labour Gross	Plant Gross	Materials Gross	Unit Price
				£	£	£	£	£	£	£	£
								(Gross rates include 10% profit)			
M20	**M20: PLASTERED, RENDERED AND ROUGHCAST COATINGS**										
M2074	**Beads, stops, edging strips and arches**										
M207408	**Expamet galvanised mild steel arch formers; fixing in accordance with manufacturer's instructions:**										
M207408A	155 mm wide lath soffit strip; ref LSS6	m	0.12	2.82	–	2.57	5.39	3.10	–	2.83	5.93
M207408B	600 mm long extender piece; ref MP24	Nr	0.10	2.34	–	5.21	7.55	2.57	–	5.73	8.31
M207408C	610 mm diameter internal liner for circular windows; ref WBE24	Nr	0.15	3.52	–	37.44	40.96	3.87	–	41.18	45.06
M30	**M30: METAL MESH LATHING AND ANCHORED REINFORCEMENT FOR PLASTERED COATING**										
M3021	**Expamet expanded metal lathing to woodwork backgrounds**										
M302101	**To walls; over 300 mm wide:**										
M302101A	ref BB263	m²	0.10	2.34	–	6.26	8.60	2.57	–	6.89	9.46
M302101B	ref BB264	m²	0.10	2.34	–	7.19	9.53	2.57	–	7.91	10.48
M302101C	ref 94G	m²	0.10	2.35	–	10.79	13.14	2.59	–	11.87	14.45
M302101D	rib lath ref 269	m²	0.10	2.34	–	7.75	10.09	2.57	–	8.53	11.10
M302101E	rib lath ref 271	m²	0.10	2.34	–	8.82	11.16	2.57	–	9.70	12.28
M302101F	spray lath ref 273	m²	0.10	2.35	–	10.64	12.99	2.59	–	11.70	14.29
M302101G	red-rib lath ref 274	m²	0.10	2.34	–	9.65	11.99	2.57	–	10.62	13.19
M302101H	stainless steel rib lath ref 267	m²	0.10	2.35	–	20.19	22.54	2.59	–	22.21	24.79
M302101I	stainless steel lath ref 95S	m²	0.10	2.34	–	18.19	20.53	2.57	–	20.01	22.58
M302102	**To walls; not exceeding 300 mm wide:**										
M302102A	ref BB263	m	0.04	0.96	–	1.88	2.84	1.06	–	2.07	3.12
M302102B	ref BB264	m	0.04	0.96	–	2.16	3.12	1.06	–	2.38	3.43
M302102C	ref 94G	m	0.04	0.96	–	3.24	4.20	1.06	–	3.56	4.62
M302102D	rib lath ref 269	m	0.04	0.97	–	2.32	3.29	1.07	–	2.55	3.62
M302102E	rib lath ref 271	m	0.04	0.96	–	2.65	3.61	1.06	–	2.92	3.97
M302102F	spray lath ref 273	m	0.04	0.99	–	3.19	4.18	1.09	–	3.51	4.60
M302102G	red-rib lath ref 274	m	0.04	0.97	–	2.89	3.86	1.07	–	3.18	4.25
M302102H	stainless steel rib lath ref 267	m	0.04	0.96	–	6.06	7.02	1.06	–	6.67	7.72
M302102I	stainless steel lath ref 95S	m	0.04	0.96	–	5.46	6.42	1.06	–	6.01	7.06
M302111	**To ceilings; over 300 mm wide:**										
M302111A	ref BB263	m²	0.15	3.51	–	7.27	10.78	3.86	–	8.00	11.86
M302111B	ref BB264	m²	0.15	3.52	–	8.20	11.72	3.87	–	9.02	12.89
M302111C	ref 94G	m²	0.15	3.52	–	11.80	15.32	3.87	–	12.98	16.85
M302111D	rib lath ref 269	m²	0.15	3.51	–	8.76	12.27	3.86	–	9.64	13.50
M302111E	rib lath ref 271	m²	0.15	3.51	–	9.83	13.34	3.86	–	10.81	14.67
M302111F	spray lath ref 273	m²	0.15	3.52	–	11.66	15.18	3.87	–	12.83	16.70
M302111G	red-rib lath ref 274	m²	0.15	3.51	–	10.66	14.17	3.86	–	11.73	15.59
M302111H	stainless steel rib lath ref 267	m²	0.15	3.51	–	21.68	25.19	3.86	–	23.85	27.71
M302111I	stainless steel lath ref 95S	m²	0.15	3.52	–	19.67	23.19	3.87	–	21.64	25.51

Major Works 2009		Unit	Labour Hours	Labour Net	Plant Net	Materials Net	Unit Net	Labour Gross	Plant Gross	Materials Gross	Unit Price
								— (Gross rates include 10% profit) —			
				£	£	£	£	£	£	£	£
M30	**M30: METAL MESH LATHING AND ANCHORED REINFORCEMENT FOR PLASTERED COATING**										
M3021	**Expamet expanded metal lathing to woodwork backgrounds**										
M302112	**To ceilings; not exceeding 300 mm wide:**										
M302112A	ref BB263..............	m	0.06	1.43	–	2.18	3.61	1.57	–	2.40	3.97
M302112B	ref BB264..............	m	0.06	1.43	–	2.46	3.89	1.57	–	2.71	4.28
M302112C	ref 94G...............	m	0.06	1.43	–	3.54	4.97	1.57	–	3.89	5.47
M302112D	rib lath ref 269...........	m	0.06	1.43	–	2.63	4.06	1.57	–	2.89	4.47
M302112E	rib lath ref 271...........	m	0.06	1.43	–	2.95	4.38	1.57	–	3.25	4.82
M302112F	spray lath ref 273	m	0.06	1.43	–	3.50	4.93	1.57	–	3.85	5.42
M302112G	red-rib lath ref 274	m	0.06	1.43	–	3.20	4.63	1.57	–	3.52	5.09
M302112H	stainless steel rib lath ref 267	m	0.06	1.43	–	6.50	7.93	1.57	–	7.15	8.72
M302112I	stainless steel lath ref 95S..	m	0.06	1.43	–	5.90	7.33	1.57	–	6.49	8.06
M302121	**To isolated beams; over 300 mm wide:**										
M302121A	ref BB263..............	m²	0.15	3.51	–	7.27	10.78	3.86	–	8.00	11.86
M302121B	ref BB264..............	m²	0.15	3.52	–	8.20	11.72	3.87	–	9.02	12.89
M302121C	ref 94G...............	m²	0.15	3.52	–	11.80	15.32	3.87	–	12.98	16.85
M302121D	rib lath ref 269...........	m²	0.15	3.51	–	8.76	12.27	3.86	–	9.64	13.50
M302121E	rib lath ref 271...........	m²	0.15	3.51	–	9.83	13.34	3.86	–	10.81	14.67
M302121F	spray lath ref 273	m²	0.15	3.52	–	11.66	15.18	3.87	–	12.83	16.70
M302121G	red-rib lath ref 274	m²	0.15	3.51	–	10.66	14.17	3.86	–	11.73	15.59
M302121H	stainless steel rib lath ref 267	m²	0.15	3.51	–	21.68	25.19	3.86	–	23.85	27.71
M302121I	stainless steel lath ref 95S..	m²	0.15	3.52	–	19.67	23.19	3.87	–	21.64	25.51
M302122	**To isolated beams; not exceeding 300 mm wide:**										
M302122A	ref BB263..............	m	0.06	1.43	–	2.18	3.61	1.57	–	2.40	3.97
M302122B	ref BB264..............	m	0.06	1.43	–	2.46	3.89	1.57	–	2.71	4.28
M302122C	ref 94G...............	m	0.06	1.43	–	3.54	4.97	1.57	–	3.89	5.47
M302122D	rib lath ref 269...........	m	0.06	1.43	–	2.63	4.06	1.57	–	2.89	4.47
M302122E	rib lath ref 271...........	m	0.06	1.43	–	2.95	4.38	1.57	–	3.25	4.82
M302122F	spray lath ref 273	m	0.06	1.43	–	3.50	4.93	1.57	–	3.85	5.42
M302122G	red-rib lath ref 274	m	0.06	1.43	–	3.20	4.63	1.57	–	3.52	5.09
M302122H	stainless steel rib lath ref 267	m	0.06	1.43	–	6.50	7.93	1.57	–	7.15	8.72
M302122I	stainless steel lath ref 95S..	m	0.06	1.43	–	5.90	7.33	1.57	–	6.49	8.06
M302141	**To isolated columns; over 300 mm wide:**										
M302141A	ref BB263..............	m²	0.10	2.34	–	6.26	8.60	2.57	–	6.89	9.46
M302141B	ref BB264..............	m²	0.10	2.34	–	7.19	9.53	2.57	–	7.91	10.48
M302141C	ref 94G...............	m²	0.10	2.35	–	10.79	13.14	2.59	–	11.87	14.45
M302141D	rib lath ref 269...........	m²	0.10	2.34	–	7.75	10.09	2.57	–	8.53	11.10
M302141E	rib lath ref 271...........	m²	0.10	2.34	–	8.82	11.16	2.57	–	9.70	12.28
M302141F	spray lath ref 273	m²	0.10	2.35	–	10.64	12.99	2.59	–	11.70	14.29
M302141G	red-rib lath ref 274	m²	0.10	2.34	–	9.65	11.99	2.57	–	10.62	13.19
M302141H	stainless steel rib lath ref 267	m²	0.10	2.35	–	20.19	22.54	2.59	–	22.21	24.79
M302141I	stainless steel lath ref 95S..	m²	0.10	2.34	–	18.19	20.53	2.57	–	20.01	22.58
M302142	**To isolated columns; not exceeding 300 mm wide:**										
M302142A	ref BB263..............	m	0.04	0.96	–	1.88	2.84	1.06	–	2.07	3.12
M302142B	ref BB264..............	m	0.04	0.96	–	2.16	3.12	1.06	–	2.38	3.43
M302142C	ref 94G...............	m	0.04	0.96	–	3.24	4.20	1.06	–	3.56	4.62
M302142D	rib lath ref 269...........	m	0.04	0.97	–	2.32	3.29	1.07	–	2.55	3.62
M302142E	rib lath ref 271...........	m	0.04	0.96	–	2.65	3.61	1.06	–	2.92	3.97
M302142F	spray lath ref 273	m	0.04	0.99	–	3.19	4.18	1.09	–	3.51	4.60
M302142G	red-rib lath ref 274	m	0.04	0.97	–	2.89	3.86	1.07	–	3.18	4.25
M302142H	stainless steel rib lath ref 267	m	0.04	0.96	–	6.06	7.02	1.06	–	6.67	7.72
M302142I	stainless steel lath ref 95S..	m	0.04	0.96	–	5.46	6.42	1.06	–	6.01	7.06

Surface Finishes

Major Works 2009		Unit	Labour Hours	Labour Net	Plant Net	Materials Net	Unit Net	Labour Gross	Plant Gross	Materials Gross	Unit Price
								(Gross rates include 10% profit)			
				£	£	£	£	£	£	£	£
M30	**M30: METAL MESH LATHING AND ANCHORED REINFORCEMENT FOR PLASTERED COATING**										
M3022	**Expamet expanded metal lathing to metalwork backgrounds with tying wire**										
M302201	**To walls; over 300 mm wide:**										
M302201A	ref BB263.	m²	0.15	3.52	–	5.71	9.23	3.87	–	6.28	10.15
M302201B	ref BB264.	m²	0.15	3.51	–	6.65	10.16	3.86	–	7.32	11.18
M302201C	ref 94G.	m²	0.15	3.51	–	10.25	13.76	3.86	–	11.28	15.14
M302201D	rib lath ref 269.	m²	0.15	3.52	–	7.20	10.72	3.87	–	7.92	11.79
M302201E	rib lath ref 271.	m²	0.15	3.52	–	8.27	11.79	3.87	–	9.10	12.97
M302201F	spray lath ref 273	m²	0.15	3.52	–	10.10	13.62	3.87	–	11.11	14.98
M302201G	red-rib lath ref 274	m²	0.15	3.52	–	9.10	12.62	3.87	–	10.01	13.88
M302201H	stainless steel rib lath ref 267	m²	0.15	3.52	–	19.39	22.91	3.87	–	21.33	25.20
M302201I	stainless steel lath ref 95S. .	m²	0.15	3.51	–	17.39	20.90	3.86	–	19.13	22.99
M302202	**To walls; not exceeding 300 mm wide:**										
M302202A	ref BB263.	m	0.06	1.43	–	1.71	3.14	1.57	–	1.88	3.45
M302202B	ref BB264.	m	0.06	1.43	–	1.99	3.42	1.57	–	2.19	3.76
M302202C	ref 94G.	m	0.06	1.43	–	3.07	4.50	1.57	–	3.38	4.95
M302202D	rib lath ref 269.	m	0.06	1.43	–	2.16	3.59	1.57	–	2.38	3.95
M302202E	rib lath ref 271.	m	0.06	1.43	–	2.48	3.91	1.57	–	2.73	4.30
M302202F	spray lath ref 273	m	0.06	1.43	–	3.03	4.46	1.57	–	3.33	4.91
M302202G	red-rib lath ref 274	m	0.06	1.43	–	2.73	4.16	1.57	–	3.00	4.58
M302202H	stainless steel rib lath ref 267	m	0.06	1.43	–	5.82	7.25	1.57	–	6.40	7.98
M302202I	stainless steel lath ref 95S. .	m	0.06	1.43	–	5.22	6.65	1.57	–	5.74	7.32
M302211	**To ceilings; over 300 mm wide:**										
M302211A	ref BB263.	m²	0.23	5.39	–	5.71	11.10	5.93	–	6.28	12.21
M302211B	ref BB264.	m²	0.23	5.39	–	6.65	12.04	5.93	–	7.32	13.24
M302211C	ref 94G.	m²	0.23	5.39	–	10.25	15.64	5.93	–	11.28	17.20
M302211D	rib lath ref 269.	m²	0.23	5.39	–	7.20	12.59	5.93	–	7.92	13.85
M302211E	rib lath ref 271.	m²	0.23	5.40	–	8.27	13.67	5.94	–	9.10	15.04
M302211F	spray lath ref 273	m²	0.23	5.39	–	10.10	15.49	5.93	–	11.11	17.04
M302211G	red-rib lath ref 274	m²	0.23	5.39	–	9.10	14.49	5.93	–	10.01	15.94
M302211H	stainless steel rib lath ref 267	m²	0.23	5.39	–	19.39	24.78	5.93	–	21.33	27.26
M302211I	stainless steel lath ref 95S. .	m²	0.23	5.39	–	17.39	22.78	5.93	–	19.13	25.06
M302212	**To ceilings; not exceeding 300 mm wide:**										
M302212A	ref BB263.	m	0.09	2.18	–	1.71	3.89	2.40	–	1.88	4.28
M302212B	ref BB264.	m	0.09	2.18	–	1.99	4.17	2.40	–	2.19	4.59
M302212C	ref 94G.	m	0.09	2.18	–	3.07	5.25	2.40	–	3.38	5.78
M302212D	rib lath ref 269.	m	0.09	2.18	–	2.16	4.34	2.40	–	2.38	4.77
M302212E	rib lath ref 271.	m	0.09	2.18	–	2.48	4.66	2.40	–	2.73	5.13
M302212F	spray lath ref 273	m	0.09	2.18	–	3.03	5.21	2.40	–	3.33	5.73
M302212G	red-rib lath ref 274	m	0.09	2.18	–	2.73	4.91	2.40	–	3.00	5.40
M302212H	stainless steel rib lath ref 267	m	0.09	2.18	–	5.82	8.00	2.40	–	6.40	8.80
M302212I	stainless steel lath ref 95S. .	m	0.09	2.18	–	5.22	7.40	2.40	–	5.74	8.14

Major Works 2009		Unit	Labour Hours	Labour Net	Plant Net	Materials Net	Unit Net	Labour Gross	Plant Gross	Materials Gross	Unit Price
								(Gross rates include 10% profit)			
				£	£	£	£	£	£	£	£
M30	**M30: METAL MESH LATHING AND ANCHORED REINFORCEMENT FOR PLASTERED COATING**										
M3022	**Expamet expanded metal lathing to metalwork backgrounds with tying wire**										
M302221	**To isolated beams; over 300 mm wide:**										
M302221A	ref BB263	m²	0.23	5.39	–	5.71	11.10	5.93	–	6.28	12.21
M302221B	ref BB264	m²	0.23	5.39	–	6.65	12.04	5.93	–	7.32	13.24
M302221C	ref 94G	m²	0.23	5.39	–	10.25	15.64	5.93	–	11.28	17.20
M302221D	rib lath ref 269	m²	0.23	5.39	–	7.20	12.59	5.93	–	7.92	13.85
M302221E	rib lath ref 271	m²	0.23	5.40	–	8.27	13.67	5.94	–	9.10	15.04
M302221F	spray lath ref 273	m²	0.23	5.39	–	10.10	15.49	5.93	–	11.11	17.04
M302221G	red-rib lath ref 274	m²	0.23	5.39	–	9.10	14.49	5.93	–	10.01	15.94
M302221H	stainless steel rib lath ref 267	m²	0.23	5.39	–	19.39	24.78	5.93	–	21.33	27.26
M302221I	stainless steel lath ref 95S	m²	0.23	5.39	–	17.39	22.78	5.93	–	19.13	25.06
M302222	**To isolated beams; not exceeding 300 mm wide:**										
M302222A	ref BB263	m	0.09	2.18	–	1.71	3.89	2.40	–	1.88	4.28
M302222B	ref BB264	m	0.09	2.18	–	1.99	4.17	2.40	–	2.19	4.59
M302222C	ref 94G	m	0.09	2.18	–	3.07	5.25	2.40	–	3.38	5.78
M302222D	rib lath ref 269	m	0.09	2.18	–	2.16	4.34	2.40	–	2.38	4.77
M302222E	rib lath ref 271	m	0.09	2.18	–	2.48	4.66	2.40	–	2.73	5.13
M302222F	spray lath ref 273	m	0.09	2.18	–	3.03	5.21	2.40	–	3.33	5.73
M302222G	red-rib lath ref 274	m	0.09	2.18	–	2.73	4.91	2.40	–	3.00	5.40
M302222H	stainless steel rib lath ref 267	m	0.09	2.18	–	5.82	8.00	2.40	–	6.40	8.80
M302222I	stainless steel lath ref 95S	m	0.09	2.18	–	5.22	7.40	2.40	–	5.74	8.14
M302241	**To isolated columns; over 300 mm wide:**										
M302241A	ref BB263	m²	0.15	3.52	–	5.71	9.23	3.87	–	6.28	10.15
M302241B	ref BB264	m²	0.15	3.51	–	6.65	10.16	3.86	–	7.32	11.18
M302241C	ref 94G	m²	0.15	3.51	–	10.25	13.76	3.86	–	11.28	15.14
M302241D	rib lath ref 269	m²	0.15	3.52	–	7.20	10.72	3.87	–	7.92	11.79
M302241E	rib lath ref 271	m²	0.15	3.52	–	8.27	11.79	3.87	–	9.10	12.97
M302241F	spray lath ref 273	m²	0.15	3.52	–	10.10	13.62	3.87	–	11.11	14.98
M302241G	red-rib lath ref 274	m²	0.15	3.52	–	9.10	12.62	3.87	–	10.01	13.88
M302241H	stainless steel rib lath ref 267	m²	0.15	3.52	–	19.39	22.91	3.87	–	21.33	25.20
M302241I	stainless steel lath ref 95S	m²	0.15	3.51	–	17.39	20.90	3.86	–	19.13	22.99
M302242	**To isolated columns; not exceeding 300 mm wide:**										
M302242A	ref BB263	m	0.06	1.43	–	1.71	3.14	1.57	–	1.88	3.45
M302242B	ref BB264	m	0.06	1.43	–	1.99	3.42	1.57	–	2.19	3.76
M302242C	ref 94G	m	0.06	1.43	–	3.07	4.50	1.57	–	3.38	4.95
M302242D	rib lath ref 269	m	0.06	1.43	–	2.16	3.59	1.57	–	2.38	3.95
M302242E	rib lath ref 271	m	0.06	1.43	–	2.48	3.91	1.57	–	2.73	4.30
M302242F	spray lath ref 273	m	0.06	1.43	–	3.03	4.46	1.57	–	3.33	4.91
M302242G	red-rib lath ref 274	m	0.06	1.43	–	2.73	4.16	1.57	–	3.00	4.58
M302242H	stainless steel rib lath ref 267	m	0.06	1.43	–	5.82	7.25	1.57	–	6.40	7.98
M302242I	stainless steel lath ref 95S	m	0.06	1.43	–	5.22	6.65	1.57	–	5.74	7.32

Surface Finishes

Major Works 2009		Unit	Labour Hours	Labour Net	Plant Net	Materials Net	Unit Net	Labour Gross	Plant Gross	Materials Gross	Unit Price
				£	£	£	£	£	£	£	£
								(Gross rates include 10% profit)			
M30	**M30: METAL MESH LATHING AND ANCHORED REINFORCEMENT FOR PLASTERED COATING**										
M3023	**Expamet expanded metal lathing to concrete, masonry or metalwork backgrounds with cartridge fired nails**										
M302301	**To walls; over 300 mm wide:**										
M302301A	ref BB263...............	m²	0.10	2.35	0.28	9.71	12.34	2.59	0.31	10.68	13.57
M302301B	ref BB264...............	m²	0.10	2.34	0.28	10.65	13.27	2.57	0.31	11.72	14.60
M302301C	ref 94G.................	m²	0.10	2.34	0.28	14.25	16.87	2.57	0.31	15.68	18.56
M302301D	rib lath ref 269...........	m²	0.10	2.35	0.28	11.20	13.83	2.59	0.31	12.32	15.21
M302301E	rib lath ref 271...........	m²	0.10	2.35	0.28	12.27	14.90	2.59	0.31	13.50	16.39
M302301F	spray lath ref 273	m²	0.10	2.35	0.28	14.10	16.73	2.59	0.31	15.51	18.40
M302301G	red-rib lath ref 274	m²	0.10	2.35	0.28	13.10	15.73	2.59	0.31	14.41	17.30
M302301H	stainless steel rib lath ref 267	m²	0.10	2.35	0.28	23.39	26.02	2.59	0.31	25.73	28.62
M3023011	stainless steel lath ref 95S..	m²	0.10	2.34	0.28	21.39	24.01	2.57	0.31	23.53	26.41
M302302	**To walls; not exceeding 300 mm wide:**										
M302302A	ref BB263...............	m	0.04	0.96	0.11	2.91	3.98	1.06	0.12	3.20	4.38
M302302B	ref BB264...............	m	0.04	0.96	0.11	3.19	4.26	1.06	0.12	3.51	4.69
M302302C	ref 94G.................	m	0.04	0.96	0.11	4.27	5.34	1.06	0.12	4.70	5.87
M302302D	rib lath ref 269...........	m	0.04	0.97	0.11	3.36	4.44	1.07	0.12	3.70	4.88
M302302E	rib lath ref 271...........	m	0.04	0.93	0.11	3.68	4.72	1.02	0.12	4.05	5.19
M302302F	spray lath ref 273	m	0.04	0.96	0.11	4.23	5.30	1.06	0.12	4.65	5.83
M302302G	red-rib lath ref 274	m	0.04	0.97	0.11	3.93	5.01	1.07	0.12	4.32	5.51
M302302H	stainless steel rib lath ref 267	m	0.04	0.96	0.11	7.02	8.09	1.06	0.12	7.72	8.90
M3023021	stainless steel lath ref 95S..	m	0.04	0.96	0.11	6.42	7.49	1.06	0.12	7.06	8.24
M302311	**To ceilings; over 300 mm wide:**										
M302311A	ref BB263...............	m²	0.15	3.52	0.84	17.71	22.07	3.87	0.92	19.48	24.28
M302311B	ref BB264...............	m²	0.15	3.51	0.84	18.65	23.00	3.86	0.92	20.52	25.30
M302311C	ref 94G.................	m²	0.15	3.51	0.84	22.25	26.60	3.86	0.92	24.48	29.26
M302311D	rib lath ref 269...........	m²	0.15	3.52	0.84	19.20	23.56	3.87	0.92	21.12	25.92
M302311E	rib lath ref 271...........	m²	0.15	3.52	0.84	20.27	24.63	3.87	0.92	22.30	27.09
M302311F	spray lath ref 273	m²	0.15	3.52	0.84	22.10	26.46	3.87	0.92	24.31	29.11
M302311G	red rib lath ref 274	m²	0.15	3.52	0.84	21.10	25.46	3.87	0.92	23.21	28.01
M302311H	stainless steel rib lath ref 267	m²	0.15	3.52	0.84	31.39	35.75	3.87	0.92	34.53	39.33
M3023111	stainless steel lath ref 95S..	m²	0.15	3.51	0.84	29.39	33.74	3.86	0.92	32.33	37.11
M302312	**To ceilings; not exceeding 300 mm wide:**										
M302312A	ref BB263...............	m	0.06	1.43	0.25	5.31	6.99	1.57	0.28	5.84	7.69
M302312B	ref BB264...............	m	0.06	1.43	0.25	5.59	7.27	1.57	0.28	6.15	8.00
M302312C	ref 94G.................	m	0.06	1.43	0.25	6.67	8.35	1.57	0.28	7.34	9.19
M302312D	rib lath ref 269...........	m	0.06	1.43	0.25	5.76	7.44	1.57	0.28	6.34	8.18
M302312E	rib lath ref 271...........	m	0.06	1.43	0.25	6.08	7.76	1.57	0.28	6.69	8.54
M302312F	spray lath ref 273	m	0.06	1.43	0.25	6.63	8.31	1.57	0.28	7.29	9.14
M302312G	red rib lath ref 274	m	0.06	1.43	0.25	6.33	8.01	1.57	0.28	6.96	8.81
M302312H	stainless steel rib lath ref 267	m	0.06	1.43	0.25	9.42	11.10	1.57	0.28	10.36	12.21
M3023121	stainless steel lath ref 95S..	m	0.06	1.43	0.25	8.82	10.50	1.57	0.28	9.70	11.55

Surface Finishes

Major Works 2009		Unit	Labour Hours	Labour Net	Plant Net	Materials Net	Unit Net	Labour Gross	Plant Gross	Materials Gross	Unit Price
								(Gross rates include 10% profit)			
				£	£	£	£	£	£	£	£
M30	**M30: METAL MESH LATHING AND ANCHORED REINFORCEMENT FOR PLASTERED COATING**										
M3022	**Expamet expanded metal lathing to metalwork backgrounds with tying wire**										
M302321	**To isolated beams; over 300 mm wide:**										
M302321A	ref BB263...............	m²	0.15	3.52	0.84	17.71	22.07	3.87	0.92	19.48	24.28
M302321B	ref BB264...............	m²	0.15	3.51	0.84	18.65	23.00	3.86	0.92	20.52	25.30
M302321C	ref 94G.................	m²	0.15	3.51	0.84	22.25	26.60	3.86	0.92	24.48	29.26
M302321D	rib lath ref 269...........	m²	0.15	3.52	0.84	19.20	23.56	3.87	0.92	21.12	25.92
M302321E	rib lath ref 271...........	m²	0.15	3.52	0.84	20.27	24.63	3.87	0.92	22.30	27.09
M302321F	spray lath ref 273	m²	0.15	3.52	0.84	22.10	26.46	3.87	0.92	24.31	29.11
M302321G	red rib lath ref 274	m²	0.15	3.52	0.84	21.10	25.46	3.87	0.92	23.21	28.01
M302321H	stainless steel rib lath ref 267	m²	0.15	3.52	0.84	31.39	35.75	3.87	0.92	34.53	39.33
M302321I	stainless steel lath ref 95S..	m²	0.15	3.51	0.84	29.39	33.74	3.86	0.92	32.33	37.11
M302322	**To isolated beams; not exceeding 300 mm wide:**										
M302322A	ref BB263...............	m	0.06	1.43	0.25	5.31	6.99	1.57	0.28	5.84	7.69
M302322B	ref BB264...............	m	0.06	1.43	0.25	5.59	7.27	1.57	0.28	6.15	8.00
M302322C	ref 94G.................	m	0.06	1.43	0.25	6.67	8.35	1.57	0.28	7.34	9.19
M302322D	rib lath ref 269...........	m	0.06	1.43	0.25	5.76	7.44	1.57	0.28	6.34	8.18
M302322E	rib lath ref 271...........	m	0.06	1.43	0.25	6.08	7.76	1.57	0.28	6.69	8.54
M302322F	spray lath ref 273	m	0.06	1.43	0.25	6.63	8.31	1.57	0.28	7.29	9.14
M302322G	red rib lath ref 274	m	0.06	1.43	0.25	6.33	8.01	1.57	0.28	6.96	8.81
M302322H	stainless steel rib lath ref 267	m	0.06	1.43	0.25	9.42	11.10	1.57	0.28	10.36	12.21
M302322I	stainless steel lath ref 95S..	m	0.06	1.43	0.25	8.82	10.50	1.57	0.28	9.70	11.55
M302341	**To isolated columns; over 300 mm wide:**										
M302341A	ref BB263...............	m²	0.10	2.35	0.28	9.71	12.34	2.59	0.31	10.68	13.57
M302341B	ref BB264...............	m²	0.10	2.34	0.28	10.65	13.27	2.57	0.31	11.72	14.60
M302341C	ref 94G.................	m²	0.10	2.34	0.28	14.25	16.87	2.57	0.31	15.68	18.56
M302341D	rib lath ref 269...........	m²	0.10	2.35	0.28	11.20	13.83	2.59	0.31	12.32	15.21
M302341E	rib lath ref 271...........	m²	0.10	2.35	0.28	12.27	14.90	2.59	0.31	13.50	16.39
M302341F	spray lath ref 273	m²	0.10	2.35	0.28	14.10	16.73	2.59	0.31	15.51	18.40
M302341G	red-rib lath ref 274	m²	0.10	2.35	0.28	13.10	15.73	2.59	0.31	14.41	17.30
M302341H	stainless steel rib lath ref 267	m²	0.10	2.35	0.28	23.39	26.02	2.59	0.31	25.73	28.62
M302341I	stainless steel lath ref 95S..	m²	0.10	2.34	0.28	21.39	24.01	2.57	0.31	23.53	26.41
M302342	**To isolated columns; not exceeding 300 mm wide:**										
M302342A	ref BB263...............	m	0.04	0.96	0.11	2.91	3.98	1.06	0.12	3.20	4.38
M302342B	ref BB264...............	m	0.04	0.96	0.11	3.19	4.26	1.06	0.12	3.51	4.69
M302342C	ref 94G.................	m	0.04	0.96	0.11	4.27	5.34	1.06	0.12	4.70	5.87
M302342D	rib lath ref 269...........	m	0.04	0.97	0.11	3.36	4.44	1.07	0.12	3.70	4.88
M302342E	rib lath ref 271...........	m	0.04	0.93	0.11	3.68	4.72	1.02	0.12	4.05	5.19
M302342F	spray lath ref 273	m	0.04	0.96	0.11	4.23	5.30	1.06	0.12	4.65	5.83
M302342G	red-rib lath ref 274	m	0.04	0.97	0.11	3.93	5.01	1.07	0.12	4.32	5.51
M302342H	stainless steel rib lath ref 267	m	0.04	0.96	0.11	7.02	8.09	1.06	0.12	7.72	8.90
M302342I	stainless steel lath ref 95S..	m	0.04	0.96	0.11	6.42	7.49	1.06	0.12	7.06	8.24
M31	**M31: FIBROUS PLASTER**										
M3111	**Gyproc coving**										
M311161	**Gyproc coving; fixing with adhesive:**										
M311161A	100 mm girth	m	0.12	2.81	–	2.35	5.16	3.09	–	2.59	5.68
M311161B	127 mm girth	m	0.13	3.05	–	2.12	5.17	3.36	–	2.33	5.69

Surface Finishes

Major Works 2009		Unit	Labour Hours	Labour Net	Plant Net	Materials Net	Unit Net	Labour Gross	Plant Gross	Materials Gross	Unit Price
				£	£	£	£	£ (Gross rates include 10% profit)	£	£	£
M40	**M40: STONE, CONCRETE, QUARRY AND CERAMIC TILING AND MOSAIC**										
M4011	**Glazed ceramic tiling; BS6431; fixing with tile adhesive, grouting with neat white cement; to floated backings**										
M401101	**To walls; 108 × 108 × 4 mm plain tiles:**										
M401101A	over 300 mm wide	m²	1.63	27.68	–	22.99	50.67	30.45	–	25.29	55.74
M401101B	not exceeding 300 mm wide	m	0.66	11.21	–	6.90	18.11	12.33	–	7.59	19.92
M401102	**To walls; 108 × 108 × 4 mm patterned tiles:**										
M401102A	over 300 mm wide	m²	1.63	27.68	–	27.30	54.98	30.45	–	30.03	60.48
M401102B	not exceeding 300 mm wide	m	0.66	11.21	–	8.19	19.40	12.33	–	9.01	21.34
M401103	**To walls; 152 × 152 × 5.5 mm plain tiles:**										
M401103A	over 300 mm wide	m²	1.22	20.72	–	23.62	44.34	22.79	–	25.98	48.77
M401103B	not exceeding 300 mm wide	m	0.50	8.40	–	7.09	15.49	9.24	–	7.80	17.04
M401104	**To walls; 152 × 152 × 5.5 mm patterned tiles:**										
M401104A	over 300 mm wide	m²	1.22	20.71	–	27.91	48.62	22.78	–	30.70	53.48
M401104B	not exceeding 300 mm wide	m	0.50	8.41	–	8.37	16.78	9.25	–	9.21	18.46
M401141	**To isolated columns; 108 × 108 × 4 mm plain tiles:**										
M401141A	over 300 mm wide	m²	1.63	27.68	–	22.99	50.67	30.45	–	25.29	55.74
M401141B	not exceeding 300 mm wide	m	0.66	11.21	–	6.90	18.11	12.33	–	7.59	19.92
M401142	**To isolated columns; 108 × 108 × 4 mm patterned tiles:**										
M401142A	over 300 mm wide	m²	1.63	27.68	–	27.30	54.98	30.45	–	30.03	60.48
M401142B	not exceeding 300 mm wide	m	0.66	11.21	–	8.19	19.40	12.33	–	9.01	21.34
M401143	**To isolated columns; 152 × 152 × 5.5 mm plain tiles:**										
M401143A	over 300 mm wide	m²	1.22	20.72	–	23.62	44.34	22.79	–	25.98	48.77
M401143B	not exceeding 300 mm wide	m	0.50	8.40	–	7.09	15.49	9.24	–	7.80	17.04
M401144	**To isolated columns; 152 × 152 × 5.5 mm patterned tiles:**										
M401144A	over 300 mm wide	m²	1.22	20.71	–	27.91	48.62	22.78	–	30.70	53.48
M401144B	not exceeding 300 mm wide	m	0.50	8.41	–	8.37	16.78	9.25	–	9.21	18.46
M401161	**To skirtings, bands, strings, coverings to kerbs, mouldings, channels or the like; 108 × 108 × 4 mm plain tiles:**										
M401161A	not exceeding 300 mm wide	m	0.52	8.83	–	7.34	16.17	9.71	–	8.07	17.79

Major Works 2009		Unit	Labour Hours	Labour Net	Plant Net	Materials Net	Unit Net	Labour Gross	Plant Gross	Materials Gross	Unit Price
								(Gross rates include 10% profit)			
				£	£	£	£	£	£	£	£
M40	**M40: STONE, CONCRETE, QUARRY AND CERAMIC TILING AND MOSAIC**										
M4011	**Glazed ceramic tiling; BS6431; fixing with tile adhesive, grouting with neat white cement; to floated backings**										
M401162	**To skirtings, bands, strings, coverings to kerbs, mouldings, channels or the like; 108 × 108 × 4 mm patterned tiles:**										
M401162B	not exceeding 300 mm wide	m	0.52	8.83	–	8.69	17.52	9.71	–	9.56	19.27
M401163	**To skirtings, bands, strings, coverings to kerbs, mouldings, channels or the like; 152 × 152 × 5.5 mm plain tiles:**										
M401163C	not exceeding 300 mm wide	m	0.40	6.79	–	7.50	14.29	7.47	–	8.25	15.72
M401164	**To skirtings, bands, strings, coverings to kerbs, mouldings, channels or the like; 152 × 152 × 5.5 mm patterned tiles:**										
M401164D	not exceeding 300 mm wide	m	0.40	6.79	–	8.85	15.64	7.47	–	9.74	17.20

Surface Finishes

Major Works 2009		Unit	Labour Hours	Labour Net	Plant Net	Materials Net	Unit Net	Labour Gross	Plant Gross	Materials Gross	Unit Price
				£	£	£	£	£	£	£	£
								(Gross rates include 10% profit)			
M40	**M40: STONE, CONCRETE, QUARRY AND CERAMIC TILING AND MOSAIC**										
M4051	**Quarry tiles; BS 6431; bedded, jointed and pointed in cement mortar (1:3)**										
M405101	**To floors; 150 × 150 × 12.5 mm:**										
M405101A	over 300 mm wide	m²	1.00	16.98	–	21.55	38.53	18.68	–	23.71	42.38
M405101B	not exceeding 300 mm wide	m	0.41	6.88	–	6.50	13.38	7.57	–	7.15	14.72
M405102	**To floors; 150 × 150 × 20 mm:**										
M405102A	over 300 mm wide	m²	1.03	17.49	–	23.93	41.42	19.24	–	26.32	45.56
M405102B	not exceeding 300 mm wide	m	0.42	7.09	–	7.21	14.30	7.80	–	7.93	15.73
M405103	**To floors; 225 × 225 × 25 mm:**										
M405103A	over 300 mm wide	m²	1.05	17.83	–	40.80	58.63	19.61	–	44.88	64.49
M405103B	not exceeding 300 mm wide	m	0.43	7.21	–	12.25	19.46	7.93	–	13.48	21.41
M405111	**To treads; 150 × 150 × 12.5 mm:**										
M405111B	150-300 mm wide	m	0.38	6.53	–	6.79	13.32	7.18	–	7.47	14.65
M405111C	300-450 mm wide	m	0.58	9.78	–	10.10	19.88	10.76	–	11.11	21.87
M405112	**To treads; 150 × 150 × 20 mm:**										
M405112B	150-300 mm wide	m	0.41	6.88	–	7.54	14.42	7.57	–	8.29	15.86
M405112C	300-450 mm wide	m	0.61	10.32	–	11.22	21.54	11.35	–	12.34	23.69
M405113	**To treads; 225 × 225 × 25 mm:**										
M405113B	150-300 mm wide	m	0.42	7.19	–	12.81	20.00	7.91	–	14.09	22.00
M405113C	300-450 mm wide	m	0.64	10.78	–	19.22	30.00	11.86	–	21.14	33.00
M405121	**To risers; 150 × 150 × 12.5 mm:**										
M405121A	not exceeding 150 mm high	m	0.20	3.31	–	3.40	6.71	3.64	–	3.74	7.38
M405121B	150-300 mm high.........	m	0.38	6.53	–	6.79	13.32	7.18	–	7.47	14.65
M405122	**To risers; 150 × 150 × 20 mm:**										
M405122A	not exceeding 150 mm high	m	0.20	3.45	–	3.77	7.22	3.80	–	4.15	7.94
M405122B	150-300 mm high.........	m	0.41	6.88	–	7.54	14.42	7.57	–	8.29	15.86
M405123	**To risers; 225 × 225 × 25 mm:**										
M405123A	not exceeding 150 mm high	m	0.21	3.60	–	6.41	10.01	3.96	–	7.05	11.01
M405123C	150-300 mm high.........	m	0.42	7.19	–	12.81	20.00	7.91	–	14.09	22.00

Major Works 2009		Unit	Labour Hours	Labour Net	Plant Net	Materials Net	Unit Net	Labour Gross	Plant Gross	Materials Gross	Unit Price
								(Gross rates include 10% profit)			
				£	£	£	£	£	£	£	£
M40	**M40: STONE, CONCRETE, QUARRY AND CERAMIC TILING AND MOSAIC**										
M4051	**Quarry tiles; BS 6431; bedded, jointed and pointed in cement mortar (1:3)**										
M405161	**To skirtings, bands, strings, coverings to kerbs, mouldings, channels or the like; not exceeding 300 mm wide:**										
M405161A	150 × 150 × 12.5 mm..	m	0.44	7.47	–	21.80	29.27	8.22	–	23.98	32.20
M405161B	150 × 150 × 20 mm....	m	0.48	8.15	–	24.29	32.44	8.97	–	26.72	35.68
M405161C	225 × 225 × 25 mm....	m	0.35	5.94	–	41.87	47.81	6.53	–	46.06	52.59
M405171	**To skirtings; rounded top; not exceeding 150 mm wide:**										
M405171D	150 × 150 × 12.5 mm..	m	0.44	7.47	–	4.74	12.21	8.22	–	5.21	13.43
M405171E	150 × 150 × 20 mm....	m	0.48	8.15	–	5.43	13.58	8.97	–	5.97	14.94
M405172	**To skirtings; square top; not exceeding 150 mm wide:**										
M405172F	150 × 150 × 12.5 mm..	m	0.44	7.47	–	3.97	11.44	8.22	–	4.37	12.58
M405172G	150 × 150 × 20 mm....	m	0.48	8.15	–	4.80	12.95	8.97	–	5.28	14.25
M405173	**To skirtings; rounded top cove base; not exceeding 150 mm wide:**										
M405173H	150 × 150 × 12.5 mm..	m	0.44	7.47	–	5.39	12.86	8.22	–	5.93	14.15
M405173I	150 × 150 × 20 mm....	m	0.48	8.15	–	7.80	15.95	8.97	–	8.58	17.55
M405174	**To skirtings; square top cove base; not exceeding 150 mm wide:**										
M405174J	150 × 150 × 12.5 mm..	m	0.44	7.47	–	4.74	12.21	8.22	–	5.21	13.43
M405174K	150 × 150 × 20 mm....	m	0.48	8.15	–	7.15	15.30	8.97	–	7.87	16.83
M405175	**To edgings; twice rounded; not exceeding 150 mm wide:**										
M405175L	150 × 150 × 12.5 mm..	m	0.23	3.91	–	26.15	30.06	4.30	–	28.77	33.07
M405175M	150 × 150 × 20 mm....	m	0.23	3.91	–	37.63	41.54	4.30	–	41.39	45.69

Surface Finishes

Major Works 2009		Unit	Labour Hours	Labour Net	Plant Net	Materials Net	Unit Net	Labour Gross	Plant Gross	Materials Gross	Unit Price
								(Gross rates include 10% profit)			
				£	£	£	£	£	£	£	£
M40	**M40: STONE, CONCRETE, QUARRY AND CERAMIC TILING AND MOSAIC**										
M4054	**Vitrified ceramic floor tiles; BS 6431; bedded, jointed and pointed in cement mortar (1:3)**										
M405401	**To floors; 150 × 150 × 9 mm:**										
M405401A	over 300 mm wide	m²	0.93	15.79	–	31.09	46.88	17.37	–	34.20	51.57
M405401B	not exceeding 300 mm wide	m	0.38	6.40	–	9.36	15.76	7.04	–	10.30	17.34
M405402	**To floors; 150 × 150 × 12 mm:**										
M405402A	over 300 mm wide	m²	0.98	16.64	–	37.09	53.73	18.30	–	40.80	59.10
M405402B	not exceeding 300 mm wide	m	0.40	6.75	–	11.16	17.91	7.43	–	12.28	19.70
M405403	**To floors; 150 × 75 × 12 mm:**										
M405403A	over 300 mm wide	m²	1.59	27.00	–	44.29	71.29	29.70	–	48.72	78.42
M405403B	not exceeding 300 mm wide	m	0.64	10.94	–	13.32	24.26	12.03	–	14.65	26.69
M405421	**To treads; 150 × 150 × 9 mm:**										
M405421A	150-300 mm wide	m	0.42	7.13	–	9.79	16.92	7.84	–	10.77	18.61
M405421B	300-450 mm wide	m	0.63	10.69	–	14.60	25.29	11.76	–	16.06	27.82
M405422	**To treads; 150 × 150 × 12 mm:**										
M405422A	150-300 mm wide	m	0.44	7.49	–	11.68	19.17	8.24	–	12.85	21.09
M405422B	300-450 mm wide	m	0.66	11.24	–	17.43	28.67	12.36	–	19.17	31.54
M405423	**To treads; 150 × 75 × 12 mm:**										
M405423A	150-300 mm wide	m	0.72	12.23	–	13.94	26.17	13.45	–	15.33	28.79
M405423B	300-450 mm wide	m	1.08	18.34	–	20.82	39.16	20.17	–	22.90	43.08
M405431	**To risers; 150 × 150 × 9 mm:**										
M405431A	not exceeding 150 mm high	m	0.21	3.56	–	4.90	8.46	3.92	–	5.39	9.31
M405431B	150-300 mm high.	m	0.42	7.13	–	9.79	16.92	7.84	–	10.77	18.61
M405432	**To risers; 150 × 150 × 12 mm:**										
M405432A	not exceeding 150 mm high	m	0.22	3.75	–	5.84	9.59	4.13	–	6.42	10.55
M405432B	150-300 mm high.	m	0.44	7.49	–	11.68	19.17	8.24	–	12.85	21.09
M405433	**To risers; 150 × 75 × 12 mm:**										
M405433A	not exceeding 150 mm wide	m	0.36	6.11	–	6.97	13.08	6.72	–	7.67	14.39
M405433B	150-300 mm wide	m	0.72	12.23	–	13.94	26.17	13.45	–	15.33	28.79

Major Works 2009		Unit	Labour Hours	Labour Net	Plant Net	Materials Net	Unit Net	Labour Gross	Plant Gross	Materials Gross	Unit Price
				£	£	£	£	£	£	£	£
								(Gross rates include 10% profit)			
M40	**M40: STONE, CONCRETE, QUARRY AND CERAMIC TILING AND MOSAIC**										
M4054	**Vitrified ceramic floor tiles; BS 6431; bedded, jointed and pointed in cement mortar (1:3)**										
M405461	**To skirtings, bands, strings, coverings to kerbs, mouldings, channels or the like; not exceeding 300 mm wide:**										
M405461A	150 × 150 × 9mm.....	m	0.42	7.13	–	9.79	16.92	7.84	–	10.77	18.61
M405461B	150 × 150 × 12mm....	m	0.44	7.47	–	11.68	19.15	8.22	–	12.85	21.07
M405461C	150 × 75 × 12mm.....	m	0.72	12.22	–	13.76	25.98	13.44	–	15.14	28.58
M405462	**To skirtings; rounded top; not exceeding 150 mm wide:**										
M405462D	150 × 150 × 9mm.....	m	0.41	6.96	–	3.57	10.53	7.66	–	3.93	11.58
M405462E	150 × 150 × 12mm....	m	0.44	7.47	–	6.02	13.49	8.22	–	6.62	14.84
M405462F	150 × 75 × 12mm.....	m	0.71	12.06	–	5.56	17.62	13.27	–	6.12	19.38
M405463	**To skirtings; square top; not exceeding 150 mm wide:**										
M405463G	150 × 150 × 9mm.....	m	0.41	6.97	–	3.69	10.66	7.67	–	4.06	11.73
M405463H	150 × 150 × 12mm....	m	0.44	7.47	–	6.27	13.74	8.22	–	6.90	15.11
M405463I	150 × 75 × 12mm.....	m	0.71	12.06	–	5.78	17.84	13.27	–	6.36	19.62
M405464	**To skirtings; rounded top cove base; not exceeding 150 mm wide:**										
M405464J	150 × 150 × 9mm.....	m	0.41	6.96	–	6.94	13.90	7.66	–	7.63	15.29
M405464K	150 × 150 × 12mm....	m	0.44	7.47	–	9.62	17.09	8.22	–	10.58	18.80
M405464L	150 × 75 × 12mm.....	m	0.71	12.06	–	9.15	21.21	13.27	–	10.07	23.33
M405465	**To skirtings; square top cove base; not exceeding 150 mm wide:**										
M405465M	150 × 150 × 9mm.....	m	0.41	6.96	–	6.69	13.65	7.66	–	7.36	15.02
M405465N	150 × 150 × 12mm....	m	0.44	7.47	–	9.39	16.86	8.22	–	10.33	18.55
M405465O	150 × 75 × 12mm.....	m	0.71	12.05	–	8.90	20.95	13.26	–	9.79	23.05
M405469	**To edgings; twice rounded; not exceeding 150 mm wide:**										
M405469P	150 × 150 × 9mm.....	m	0.21	3.56	–	5.93	9.49	3.92	–	6.52	10.44
M405469Q	150 × 150 × 12mm....	m	0.18	3.06	–	46.59	49.65	3.37	–	51.25	54.62
M405469R	150 × 75 × 12mm.....	m	0.36	6.11	–	43.37	49.48	6.72	–	47.71	54.43
M4083	**Division strips and nosings**										
M408301	**Division strips; embedding in pavings:**										
M408301A	5 × 25 mm brass........	m	0.06	1.41	–	9.89	11.30	1.55	–	10.88	12.43
M408301B	5 × 25 mm aluminium ...	m	0.06	1.40	–	4.12	5.52	1.54	–	4.53	6.07
M408302	**Ferodo nosings; plugging and screwing to concrete backgrounds; ref:**										
M408302A	type SD1	m	0.30	5.10	–	20.32	25.42	5.61	–	22.35	27.96
M408302B	type SD2	m	0.30	5.09	–	23.63	28.72	5.60	–	25.99	31.59
M408302C	type HD1	m	0.30	5.10	–	21.98	27.08	5.61	–	24.18	29.79
M408302D	type HD2	m	0.30	5.10	–	25.52	30.62	5.61	–	28.07	33.68

Surface Finishes

Major Works 2009		Unit	Labour Hours	Labour Net	Plant Net	Materials Net	Unit Net	Labour Gross	Plant Gross	Materials Gross	Unit Price
								(Gross rates include 10% profit)			
				£	£	£	£	£	£	£	£
M50	**M50: RUBBER, PLASTIC, CORK, LINO AND CARPET TILING AND SHEETING**										
M5051	**Vinyl sheet flooring**										
M505101	**Standard grade; 2.5 mm thick:**										
M505101A	PC 10·00 m^2	m^2	0.50	8.49	–	11.10	19.59	9.34	–	12.21	21.55
M505101B	PC 12·50 m^2	m^2	0.50	8.50	–	13.88	22.38	9.35	–	15.27	24.62
M505101C	PC 15·00 m^2	m^2	0.50	8.49	–	16.65	25.14	9.34	–	18.32	27.65
M505102	**Heavy duty grade; 2.5 mm thick:**										
M505102A	PC 10·00 m^2	m^2	0.50	8.49	–	11.10	19.59	9.34	–	12.21	21.55
M505102B	PC 12·50 m^2	m^2	0.50	8.50	–	13.88	22.38	9.35	–	15.27	24.62
M505102C	PC 15·00 m^2	m^2	0.50	8.49	–	16.65	25.14	9.34	–	18.32	27.65
M5053	**Vinyl floor tiling**										
M505301	**Standard grade**										
M505301A	PC 10·00 m^2	m^2	0.50	8.49	–	11.10	19.59	9.34	–	12.21	21.55
M505301B	PC 12·50 m^2	m^2	0.50	8.50	–	13.88	22.38	9.35	–	15.27	24.62
M505301C	PC 15·00 m^2	m^2	0.50	8.49	–	16.65	25.14	9.34	–	18.32	27.65
M505302	**Heavy duty grade**										
M505302A	PC 10·00 m^2	m^2	0.50	8.49	–	11.10	19.59	9.34	–	12.21	21.55
M505302B	PC 12·50 m^2	m^2	0.50	8.50	–	13.88	22.38	9.35	–	15.27	24.62
M505302C	PC 15·00 m^2	m^2	0.50	8.49	–	16.65	25.14	9.34	–	18.32	27.65
M5055	**Carpet tiling**										
M505502	**Carpet tiles**										
M505502A	PC 10·00 m^2	m^2	0.50	8.49	–	11.10	19.59	9.34	–	12.21	21.55
M505502B	PC 12·50 m^2	m^2	0.50	8.50	–	13.88	22.38	9.35	–	15.27	24.62
M505502C	PC 15·00 m^2	m^2	0.50	8.49	–	16.65	25.14	9.34	–	18.32	27.65

Major Works 2009		Unit	Labour Hours	Labour Net	Plant Net	Materials Net	Unit Net	Labour Gross	Plant Gross	Materials Gross	Unit Price
								(Gross rates include 10% profit)			
				£	£	£	£	£	£	£	£
M50	**M50: RUBBER, PLASTIC, CORK, LINO AND CARPET TILING AND SHEETING**										
M5083	**Division strips and nosings**										
M508301	**Division strips; embedding in pavings:**										
M508301A	5 × 25 mm brass........	m	0.06	1.41	–	9.89	11.30	1.55	–	10.88	12.43
M508301B	5 × 25 mm aluminium ...	m	0.06	1.40	–	4.12	5.52	1.54	–	4.53	6.07
M508302	**Ferodo nosings; plugging and screwing to concrete backgrounds:**										
M508302A	type SD1	m	0.30	5.10	–	20.32	25.42	5.61	–	22.35	27.96
M508302B	type SD2	m	0.30	5.09	–	23.75	28.84	5.60	–	26.13	31.72
M508302C	type HD1	m	0.30	5.10	–	21.98	27.08	5.61	–	24.18	29.79
M508302D	type HD2	m	0.30	5.10	–	25.52	30.62	5.61	–	28.07	33.68
M508303	**Division strips; plugging and screwing to concrete backgrounds:**										
M508303A	aluminium; carpet to carpet	m	0.25	4.25	–	9.84	14.09	4.68	–	10.82	15.50
M508303B	aluminium; carpet to stop edge....................	m	0.25	4.24	–	9.09	13.33	4.66	–	10.00	14.66
M508303C	aluminium; carpet to vinyl flooring	m	0.25	4.25	–	9.84	14.09	4.68	–	10.82	15.50
M508303D	aluminium; carpet to vinyl flooring stop edge	m	0.25	4.24	–	9.09	13.33	4.66	–	10.00	14.66
M508303E	brass anodised aluminium; carpet to carpet..........	m	0.25	4.24	–	12.56	16.80	4.66	–	13.82	18.48
M508303F	brass anodised aluminium; carpet to carpet stop edge..	m	0.25	4.24	–	12.01	16.25	4.66	–	13.21	17.88
M508303G	brass anodised aluminium; carpet to vinyl flooring.....	m	0.25	4.24	–	12.56	16.80	4.66	–	13.82	18.48
M508303H	brass anodised aluminium; vinyl flooring to stop edge..	m	0.25	4.24	–	12.01	16.25	4.66	–	13.21	17.88
M51	**M51: EDGE FIXED CARPETING**										
M5155	**Carpeting**										
M515501	**Carpet:**										
M515501A	PC 10.00 m²	m²	0.50	8.49	–	11.10	19.59	9.34	–	12.21	21.55
M515501B	PC 12.50 m²	m²	0.50	8.50	–	13.88	22.38	9.35	–	15.27	24.62
M515501C	PC 15.00 m²	m²	0.50	8.49	–	16.65	25.14	9.34	–	18.32	27.65

Surface Finishes

Major Works 2009		Unit	Labour Hours	Labour Net	Plant Net	Materials Net	Unit Net	Labour Gross	Plant Gross	Materials Gross	Unit Price
								—— (Gross rates include 10% profit) ——			
				£	£	£	£	£	£	£	£
M52	**M52: DECORATIVE PAPERS AND FABRICS**										
M5212	**Plain or woodchip lining paper; (PC £1.50 per roll)**										
M521201	**Walls and columns; stop, rub down, size and hang to plastered backgrounds:**										
M521201A	areas over 0.5 m²	m²	0.26	4.41	–	0.48	4.89	4.85	–	0.53	5.38
M521201B	areas not exceeding 0.5 m².	Nr	0.20	3.31	–	0.25	3.56	3.64	–	0.28	3.92
M521202	**Walls and columns; stop, rub down, size and hang to plasterboard backgrounds:**										
M521202A	areas over 0.5 m²	m²	0.25	4.24	–	0.48	4.72	4.66	–	0.53	5.19
M521202B	areas not exceeding 0.5 m².	Nr	0.19	3.20	–	0.25	3.45	3.52	–	0.28	3.80
M521211	**Ceilings and beams; stop, rub down, size and hang to plastered backgrounds:**										
M521211A	areas over 0.5 m²	m²	0.31	5.26	–	0.48	5.74	5.79	–	0.53	6.31
M521211B	areas not exceeding 0.5 m².	Nr	0.23	3.96	–	0.25	4.21	4.36	–	0.28	4.63
M521212	**Ceilings and beams; stop, rub down, size and hang to plasterboard backgrounds:**										
M521212A	areas over 0.5 m²	m²	0.30	5.09	–	0.48	5.57	5.60	–	0.53	6.13
M521212B	areas not exceeding 0.5 m².	Nr	0.23	3.82	–	0.25	4.07	4.20	–	0.28	4.48
M5214	**Decorative wallpaper; (PC £6:50 per roll)**										
M521401	**Walls and columns; stop, rub down, size and hang to plastered backgrounds:**										
M521401A	areas over 0.5 m²	m²	0.30	5.09	–	2.29	7.38	5.60	–	2.52	8.12
M521401B	areas not exceeding 0.5 m².	Nr	0.23	3.82	–	1.16	4.98	4.20	–	1.28	5.48
M521402	**Walls and columns; stop, rub down, size and hang to plasterboard backgrounds:**										
M521402A	areas over 0.5 m²	m²	0.31	5.26	–	2.29	7.55	5.79	–	2.52	8.31
M521402B	areas not exceeding 0.5 m².	Nr	0.23	3.96	–	1.16	5.12	4.36	–	1.28	5.63
M521411	**Ceilings and beams; stop, rub down, size and hang to plastered backgrounds:**										
M521411A	areas over 0.5 m²	m²	0.35	5.94	–	2.29	8.23	6.53	–	2.52	9.05
M521411B	areas not exceeding 0.5 m².	Nr	0.26	4.46	–	1.16	5.62	4.91	–	1.28	6.18
M521412	**Ceilings and beams; stop, rub down, size and hang to plasterboard backgrounds:**										
M521412A	areas over 0.5 m²	m²	0.36	6.11	–	2.29	8.40	6.72	–	2.52	9.24
M521412B	areas not exceeding 0.5 m².	Nr	0.27	4.58	–	1.16	5.74	5.04	–	1.28	6.31

Major Works 2009		Unit	Labour Hours	Labour Net	Plant Net	Materials Net	Unit Net	Labour Gross	Plant Gross	Materials Gross	Unit Price
								\multicolumn{4}{}{—— (Gross rates include 10% profit) ——}			
				£	£	£	£	£	£	£	£
M52	**M52: DECORATIVE PAPERS AND FABRICS**										
M5216	**Decorative wallpaper; (PC £9:00 per roll)**										
M521601	**Walls and columns; stop, rub down, size and hang to plastered backgrounds:**										
M521601A	areas over 0.5 m²	m²	0.30	5.10	–	2.17	7.27	5.61	–	2.39	8.00
M521601B	areas not exceeding 0.5 m².	Nr	0.23	3.82	–	1.10	4.92	4.20	–	1.21	5.41
M521602	**Walls and columns; stop, rub down, size and hang to plasterboard backgrounds:**										
M521602A	areas over 0.5 m²	m²	0.31	5.27	–	2.17	7.44	5.80	–	2.39	8.18
M521602B	areas not exceeding 0.5 m².	Nr	0.23	3.96	–	1.10	5.06	4.36	–	1.21	5.57
M521611	**Ceilings and beams; stop, rub down, size and hang to plastered backgrounds:**										
M521611A	areas over 0.5 m²	m²	0.35	5.94	–	2.17	8.11	6.53	–	2.39	8.92
M521611B	areas not exceeding 0.5 m².	Nr	0.26	4.47	–	1.10	5.57	4.92	–	1.21	6.13
M521612	**Ceilings and beams; stop, rub down, size and hang to plasterboard backgrounds:**										
M521612A	areas over 0.5 m²	m²	0.36	6.11	–	2.17	8.28	6.72	–	2.39	9.11
M521612B	areas not exceeding 0.5 m².	Nr	0.27	4.58	–	1.10	5.68	5.04	–	1.21	6.25

Surface Finishes

Major Works 2009		Unit	Labour Hours	Labour Net	Plant Net	Materials Net	Unit Net	Labour Gross	Plant Gross	Materials Gross	Unit Price
								(Gross rates include 10% profit)			
				£	£	£	£	£	£	£	£
M60	**M60: PAINTING AND CLEAR FINISHING**										
M6010	**Emulsion paint**										
M601001	**Prepare, apply one mist coat and two full coats; plaster backgrounds:**										
M601001A	walls....................	m²	0.18	3.06	–	2.06	5.12	3.37	–	2.27	5.63
M601001B	walls; 3.5-5.0 m high	m²	0.21	3.48	–	2.06	5.54	3.83	–	2.27	6.09
M601001D	walls; n.e. 300 mm girth ...	m	0.07	1.24	–	0.62	1.86	1.36	–	0.68	2.05
M601001E	walls; areas n.e. 0.5 m²	Nr	0.14	2.29	–	1.03	3.32	2.52	–	1.13	3.65
M601001F	ceilings	m²	0.20	3.36	–	2.06	5.42	3.70	–	2.27	5.96
M601001G	ceilings; 3.5-5.0 m high....	m²	0.22	3.68	–	2.06	5.74	4.05	–	2.27	6.31
M601001I	ceilings; n.e. 300 mm girth .	m	0.08	1.36	–	0.62	1.98	1.50	–	0.68	2.18
M601001J	ceilings; areas n.e. 0.5 m²..	Nr	0.15	2.51	–	1.03	3.54	2.76	–	1.13	3.89
M601002	**Prepare, apply one mist coat and two full coats; plasterboard backgrounds:**										
M601002A	walls....................	m²	0.18	3.06	–	2.06	5.12	3.37	–	2.27	5.63
M601002B	walls; 3.5-5.0 m high	m²	0.21	3.48	–	2.06	5.54	3.83	–	2.27	6.09
M601002D	walls; n.e. 300 mm girth ...	m	0.07	1.24	–	0.62	1.86	1.36	–	0.68	2.05
M601002E	walls; areas n.e. 0.5 m²	Nr	0.14	2.29	–	1.03	3.32	2.52	–	1.13	3.65
M601002F	ceilings	m²	0.20	3.36	–	2.06	5.42	3.70	–	2.27	5.96
M601002G	ceilings; 3.5-5.0 m high....	m²	0.22	3.68	–	2.06	5.74	4.05	–	2.27	6.31
M601002I	ceilings; n.e. 300 mm girth .	m	0.08	1.36	–	0.62	1.98	1.50	–	0.68	2.18
M601002J	ceilings; areas n.e. 0.5 m²..	Nr	0.15	2.51	–	1.03	3.54	2.76	–	1.13	3.89
M601003	**Prepare, apply one mist coat and two full coats; lining paper backgrounds:**										
M601003A	walls....................	m²	0.19	3.14	–	2.23	5.37	3.45	–	2.45	5.91
M601003B	walls; 3.5-5.0 m high	m²	0.21	3.57	–	2.23	5.80	3.93	–	2.45	6.38
M601003D	walls; n.e. 300 mm girth ...	m	0.08	1.27	–	0.69	1.96	1.40	–	0.76	2.16
M601003E	walls; areas n.e. 0.5 m²	Nr	0.14	2.36	–	1.13	3.49	2.60	–	1.24	3.84
M601003F	ceilings	m²	0.20	3.46	–	2.23	5.69	3.81	–	2.45	6.26
M601003G	ceilings; 3.5-5.0 m high....	m²	0.23	3.92	–	2.23	6.15	4.31	–	2.45	6.77
M601003I	ceilings; n.e. 300 mm girth .	m	0.08	1.41	–	0.69	2.10	1.55	–	0.76	2.31
M601003J	ceilings; areas n.e. 0.5 m²..	Nr	0.15	2.60	–	1.13	3.73	2.86	–	1.24	4.10
M601004	**Prepare, apply one mist coat and two full coats; concrete backgrounds:**										
M601004A	walls....................	m²	0.20	3.31	–	2.40	5.71	3.64	–	2.64	6.28
M601004B	walls; 3.5-5.0 m high	m²	0.22	3.74	–	2.40	6.14	4.11	–	2.64	6.75
M601004D	walls; n.e. 300 mm girth ...	m	0.09	1.51	–	0.72	2.23	1.66	–	0.79	2.45
M601004E	walls; areas n.e. 0.5 m²	Nr	0.17	2.80	–	1.20	4.00	3.08	–	1.32	4.40
M601004F	ceilings	m²	0.22	3.65	–	2.40	6.05	4.02	–	2.64	6.66
M601004G	ceilings; 3.5-5.0 m high....	m²	0.27	4.52	–	2.40	6.92	4.97	–	2.64	7.61
M601004I	ceilings; n.e. 300 mm girth .	m	0.10	1.66	–	0.72	2.38	1.83	–	0.79	2.62
M601004J	ceilings; areas n.e. 0.5 m²..	Nr	0.18	3.09	–	1.20	4.29	3.40	–	1.32	4.72

Major Works 2009		Unit	Labour Hours	Labour Net	Plant Net	Materials Net	Unit Net	Labour Gross	Plant Gross	Materials Gross	Unit Price
								(Gross rates include 10% profit)			
				£	£	£	£	£	£	£	£
M60	**M60: PAINTING AND CLEAR FINISHING**										
M6010	**Emulsion paint**										
M601005	**Prepare, apply one mist coat and two full coats; brickwork backgrounds:**										
M601005A	walls...................	m²	0.25	4.24	–	3.09	7.33	4.66	–	3.40	8.06
M601005B	walls; 3.5-5.0 m high......	m²	0.27	4.58	–	3.09	7.67	5.04	–	3.40	8.44
M601005D	walls; n.e. 300 mm girth ...	m	0.10	1.69	–	0.93	2.62	1.86	–	1.02	2.88
M601005E	walls; areas n.e. 0.5 m²....	Nr	0.19	3.23	–	1.54	4.77	3.55	–	1.69	5.25
M601006	**Prepare, apply one mist coat and two full coats; blockwork backgrounds:**										
M601006A	walls...................	m²	0.27	4.58	–	3.09	7.67	5.04	–	3.40	8.44
M601006B	walls; 3.5-5.0 m high......	m²	0.29	4.92	–	3.09	8.01	5.41	–	3.40	8.81
M601006D	walls; n.e. 300 mm girth ...	m	0.11	1.86	–	0.93	2.79	2.05	–	1.02	3.07
M601006E	walls; areas n.e. 0.5 m²....	Nr	0.20	3.40	–	1.54	4.94	3.74	–	1.69	5.43
M601007	**Prepare, apply one mist coat and two full coats; rendered backgrounds:**										
M601007A	walls...................	m²	0.27	4.58	–	3.09	7.67	5.04	–	3.40	8.44
M601007B	walls; 3.5-5.0 m high......	m²	0.29	4.92	–	3.09	8.01	5.41	–	3.40	8.81
M601007D	walls; n.e. 300 mm girth ...	m	0.11	1.86	–	0.93	2.79	2.05	–	1.02	3.07
M601007E	walls; areas n.e. 0.5 m²....	Nr	0.20	3.40	–	1.54	4.94	3.74	–	1.69	5.43
M601008	**Prepare, apply one mist coat and two full coats; textured plastic coating backgrounds:**										
M601008A	walls...................	m²	0.25	4.25	–	2.57	6.82	4.68	–	2.83	7.50
M601008B	walls; 3.5-5.0 m high......	m²	0.27	4.59	–	2.57	7.16	5.05	–	2.83	7.88
M601008D	walls; n.e. 300 mm girth ...	m	0.10	1.70	–	0.79	2.49	1.87	–	0.87	2.74
M601008E	walls; areas n.e. 0.5 m²....	Nr	0.19	3.20	–	1.30	4.50	3.52	–	1.43	4.95
M601008F	ceilings	m²	0.28	4.67	–	2.57	7.24	5.14	–	2.83	7.96
M601008G	ceilings; 3.5-5.0 m high....	m²	0.30	5.13	–	2.57	7.70	5.64	–	2.83	8.47
M601008I	ceilings; n.e. 300 mm girth .	m	0.11	1.87	–	0.79	2.66	2.06	–	0.87	2.93
M601008J	ceilings; areas n.e. 0.5 m²..	Nr	0.21	3.50	–	1.30	4.80	3.85	–	1.43	5.28

Surface Finishes

Major Works 2009		Unit	Labour Hours	Labour Net	Plant Net	Materials Net	Unit Net	Labour Gross	Plant Gross	Materials Gross	Unit Price
								——— (Gross rates include 10% profit) ———			
				£	£	£	£	£	£	£	£
M60	**M60: PAINTING AND CLEAR FINISHING**										
M6011	**Eggshell paint**										
M601101	**Prepare, apply one undercoat and two full coats; plaster backgrounds:**										
M601101A	walls....................	m²	0.36	6.11	–	1.95	8.06	6.72	–	2.15	8.87
M601101B	walls; 3.5-5.0 m high	m²	0.39	6.54	–	1.95	8.49	7.19	–	2.15	9.34
M601101D	walls; n.e. 300 mm girth ...	m	0.15	2.48	–	0.65	3.13	2.73	–	0.72	3.44
M601101E	walls; areas n.e. 0.5 m²	Nr	0.27	4.59	–	0.89	5.48	5.05	–	0.98	6.03
M601101F	ceilings	m²	0.38	6.42	–	1.95	8.37	7.06	–	2.15	9.21
M601101G	ceilings; 3.5-5.0 m high	m²	0.40	6.84	–	1.95	8.79	7.52	–	2.15	9.67
M601101I	ceilings; n.e. 300 mm girth .	m	0.15	2.60	–	0.65	3.25	2.86	–	0.72	3.58
M601101J	ceilings; areas n.e. 0.5 m² ..	Nr	0.28	4.82	–	0.95	5.77	5.30	–	1.05	6.35
M601102	**Prepare, apply one undercoat and two full coats; plasterboard backgrounds:**										
M601102A	walls....................	m²	0.36	6.11	–	1.95	8.06	6.72	–	2.15	8.87
M601102B	walls; 3.5-5.0 m high	m²	0.39	6.54	–	1.95	8.49	7.19	–	2.15	9.34
M601102D	walls; n.e. 300 mm girth ...	m	0.15	2.48	–	0.65	3.13	2.73	–	0.72	3.44
M601102E	walls; areas n.e. 0.5 m²	Nr	0.27	4.59	–	0.89	5.48	5.05	–	0.98	6.03
M601102F	ceilings	m²	0.38	6.42	–	1.95	8.37	7.06	–	2.15	9.21
M601102G	ceilings; 3.5-5.0 m high	m²	0.40	6.84	–	1.95	8.79	7.52	–	2.15	9.67
M601102I	ceilings; n.e. 300 mm girth .	m	0.15	2.60	–	0.65	3.25	2.86	–	0.72	3.58
M601102J	ceilings; areas n.e. 0.5 m² ..	Nr	0.28	4.82	–	0.95	5.77	5.30	–	1.05	6.35
M601103	**Prepare, apply one undercoat and two full coats; lining paper backgrounds:**										
M601103A	walls....................	m²	0.37	6.28	–	1.95	8.23	6.91	–	2.15	9.05
M601103B	walls; 3.5-5.0 m high	m²	0.40	6.71	–	1.95	8.66	7.38	–	2.15	9.53
M601103D	walls; n.e. 300 mm girth ...	m	0.15	2.55	–	0.65	3.20	2.81	–	0.72	3.52
M601103E	walls; areas n.e. 0.5 m²	Nr	0.28	4.72	–	0.89	5.61	5.19	–	0.98	6.17
M601103F	ceilings	m²	0.39	6.60	–	1.95	8.55	7.26	–	2.15	9.41
M601103G	ceilings; 3.5-5.0 m high	m²	0.41	7.03	–	1.95	8.98	7.73	–	2.15	9.88
M601103I	ceilings; n.e. 300 mm girth .	m	0.16	2.66	–	0.65	3.31	2.93	–	0.72	3.64
M601103J	ceilings; areas n.e. 0.5 m² ..	Nr	0.29	4.94	–	0.95	5.89	5.43	–	1.05	6.48
M601104	**Prepare, apply one undercoat and two full coats; concrete backgrounds:**										
M601104A	walls....................	m²	0.38	6.45	–	1.95	8.40	7.10	–	2.15	9.24
M601104B	walls; 3.5-5.0 m high	m²	0.04	0.69	–	1.95	2.64	0.76	–	2.15	2.90
M601104D	walls; n.e. 300 mm girth ...	m	0.15	2.61	–	0.65	3.26	2.87	–	0.72	3.59
M601104E	walls; areas n.e. 0.5 m²	Nr	0.29	4.84	–	0.89	5.73	5.32	–	0.98	6.30
M601104F	ceilings	m²	0.40	6.77	–	1.95	8.72	7.45	–	2.15	9.59
M601104G	ceilings; 3.5-5.0 m high....	m²	0.43	7.21	–	1.95	9.16	7.93	–	2.15	10.08
M601104I	ceilings; n.e. 300 mm girth .	m	0.16	2.75	–	0.65	3.40	3.03	–	0.72	3.74
M601104J	ceilings; areas n.e. 0.5 m² ..	Nr	0.30	5.07	–	0.95	6.02	5.58	–	1.05	6.62

Surface Finishes

Major Works 2009		Unit	Labour Hours	Labour Net	Plant Net	Materials Net	Unit Net	Labour Gross	Plant Gross	Materials Gross	Unit Price
								(Gross rates include 10% profit)			
				£	£	£	£	£	£	£	£
M60	**M60: PAINTING AND CLEAR FINISHING**										
M6011	**Eggshell paint**										
M601105	**Prepare, apply one undercoat and two full coats; brickwork backgrounds:**										
M601105A	walls....................	m²	0.50	8.49	–	2.70	11.19	9.34	–	2.97	12.31
M601105B	walls; 3.5-5.0 m high	m²	0.53	8.92	–	2.70	11.62	9.81	–	2.97	12.78
M601105D	walls; n.e. 300 mm girth ...	m	0.20	3.44	–	0.84	4.28	3.78	–	0.92	4.71
M601105E	walls; areas n.e. 0.5 m²	Nr	0.38	6.37	–	1.30	7.67	7.01	–	1.43	8.44
M601106	**Prepare, apply one undercoat and two full coats; blockwork backgrounds:**										
M601106A	walls....................	m²	0.60	10.18	–	3.24	13.42	11.20	–	3.56	14.76
M601106B	walls; 3.5-5.0 m high	m²	0.63	10.61	–	3.24	13.85	11.67	–	3.56	15.24
M601106D	walls; n.e. 300 mm girth ...	m	0.24	4.13	–	0.97	5.10	4.54	–	1.07	5.61
M601106E	walls; areas n.e. 0.5 m²	Nr	0.45	7.64	–	1.67	9.31	8.40	–	1.84	10.24
M601107	**Prepare, apply one undercoat and two full coats; rendered backgrounds:**										
M601107A	walls....................	m²	0.47	7.98	–	2.59	10.57	8.78	–	2.85	11.63
M601107B	walls; 3.5-5.0 m high	m²	0.50	8.41	–	2.59	11.00	9.25	–	2.85	12.10
M601107D	walls; n.e. 300 mm girth ...	m	0.19	3.23	–	0.81	4.04	3.55	–	0.89	4.44
M601107E	walls; areas n.e. 0.5 m²	Nr	0.35	5.99	–	1.30	7.29	6.59	–	1.43	8.02
M601107F	ceilings	m²	0.49	8.39	–	2.59	10.98	9.23	–	2.85	12.08
M601107G	ceilings; 3.5-5.0 m high....	m²	0.52	8.82	–	2.59	11.41	9.70	–	2.85	12.55
M601107I	ceilings; n.e. 300 mm girth .	m	0.20	3.38	–	0.81	4.19	3.72	–	0.89	4.61
M601107J	ceilings; areas n.e. 0.5 m² .	Nr	0.37	6.26	–	1.30	7.56	6.89	–	1.43	8.32
M601108	**Prepare, apply one undercoat and two full coats; textured plastic coating backgrounds:**										
M601108A	walls....................	m²	0.50	8.49	–	2.59	11.08	9.34	–	2.85	12.19
M601108B	walls; 3.5-5.0 m high	m²	0.53	8.92	–	2.59	11.51	9.81	–	2.85	12.66
M601108D	walls; n.e. 300 mm girth ...	m	0.20	3.45	–	0.81	4.26	3.80	–	0.89	4.69
M601108E	walls; areas n.e. 0.5 m²	Nr	0.38	6.36	–	1.30	7.66	7.00	–	1.43	8.43
M601108F	ceilings	m²	0.53	8.92	–	2.59	11.51	9.81	–	2.85	12.66
M601108G	ceilings; 3.5-5.0 m high....	m²	0.55	9.34	–	2.59	11.93	10.27	–	2.85	13.12
M601108I	ceilings; n.e. 300 mm girth .	m	0.21	3.62	–	0.81	4.43	3.98	–	0.89	4.87
M601108J	ceilings; areas n.e. 0.5 m² ..	Nr	0.39	6.69	–	1.30	7.99	7.36	–	1.43	8.79

Surface Finishes

Major Works 2009		Unit	Labour Hours	Labour Net	Plant Net	Materials Net	Unit Net	Labour Gross	Plant Gross	Materials Gross	Unit Price
								(Gross rates include 10% profit)			
				£	£	£	£	£	£	£	£
M60	**M60: PAINTING AND CLEAR FINISHING**										
M6015	**Flame retardant coatings**										
M601501	**Prepare and apply two coats Timonox vinyl matt emulsion; to plastered, woodwork or intumescent paint backgrounds; general surfaces:**										
M601501A	over 300 mm girth	m²	0.16	2.72	–	3.22	5.94	2.99	–	3.54	6.53
M601501B	n.e. 300 mm girth	m	0.07	1.10	–	1.02	2.12	1.21	–	1.12	2.33
M601501C	areas n.e. 0.5 m²	Nr	0.12	2.04	–	1.64	3.68	2.24	–	1.80	4.05
M601502	**Prepare and apply two coats Timonox vinyl silk emulsion; to plastered, woodwork or intumescent paint backgrounds; general surfaces:**										
M601502A	over 300 mm girth	m²	0.16	2.72	–	3.73	6.45	2.99	–	4.10	7.10
M601502B	n.e. 300 mm girth	m	0.07	1.10	–	1.13	2.23	1.21	–	1.24	2.45
M601502C	areas n.e. 0.5 m²	Nr	0.12	2.03	–	1.87	3.90	2.23	–	2.06	4.29
M601503	**Prepare and apply one coat Timonox alkali resisting primer, one coat Timonox undercoat and one coat Timonox gloss; to plastered backgrounds; general surfaces:**										
M601503A	over 300 mm girth	m²	0.36	6.11	–	3.06	9.17	6.72	–	3.37	10.09
M601503B	n.e. 300 mm girth	m	0.15	2.46	–	1.04	3.50	2.71	–	1.14	3.85
M601503C	areas n.e. 0.5 m²	Nr	0.27	4.59	–	1.57	6.16	5.05	–	1.73	6.78
M601504	**Prepare and apply one coat Timonox alkali resisting primer, two coats Timonox eggshell; to plastered backgrounds; general surfaces:**										
M601504A	over 300 mm girth	m²	0.36	6.11	–	3.00	9.11	6.72	–	3.30	10.02
M601504B	n.e. 300 mm girth	m	0.15	2.48	–	0.92	3.40	2.73	–	1.01	3.74
M601504C	areas n.e. 0.5 m²	Nr	0.27	4.59	–	1.51	6.10	5.05	–	1.66	6.71
M601511	**Prepare and apply one coat Timonox undercoat and one coat Timonox gloss to intumescent painted backgrounds; general surfaces:**										
M601511A	over 300 mm girth	m²	0.27	4.58	–	1.81	6.39	5.04	–	1.99	7.03
M601511B	n.e. 300 mm girth	m	0.11	1.85	–	0.60	2.45	2.04	–	0.66	2.70
M601511C	areas n.e. 0.5 m²	Nr	0.20	3.44	–	0.97	4.41	3.78	–	1.07	4.85
M601512	**Prepare and apply one coat Timonox undercoat and one coat Timonox gloss to intumescent painted backgrounds; glazed windows and screens; in panes n.e. 0.10 m²:**										
M601512A	over 300 mm girth	m²	0.75	12.70	–	1.81	14.51	13.97	–	1.99	15.96
M601512B	n.e. 300 mm girth	m	0.30	5.15	–	0.60	5.75	5.67	–	0.66	6.33
M601512C	areas n.e. 0.5 m²	Nr	0.56	9.52	–	0.97	10.49	10.47	–	1.07	11.54

Major Works 2009		Unit	Labour Hours	Labour Net	Plant Net	Materials Net	Unit Net	Labour Gross	Plant Gross	Materials Gross	Unit Price
				£	£	£	£	£	£	£	£
								─── (Gross rates include 10% profit) ───			
M60	**M60: PAINTING AND CLEAR FINISHING**										
M6015	**Flame retardant coatings**										
M601513	**Prepare and apply one coat Timonox undercoat and one coat Timonox gloss to intumescent painted backgrounds; glazed windows and screens; in panes 0.10-0.50 m²:**										
M601513A	over 300 mm girth	m²	0.55	9.34	–	1.81	11.15	10.27	–	1.99	12.27
M601513B	n.e. 300 mm girth	m	0.22	3.79	–	0.60	4.39	4.17	–	0.66	4.83
M601513C	areas n.e. 0.5 m²	Nr	0.41	7.01	–	0.97	7.98	7.71	–	1.07	8.78
M601514	**Prepare and apply one coat Timonox undercoat and one coat Timonox gloss to intumescent painted backgrounds; glazed windows and screens; in panes 0.50-1.00 m²:**										
M601514A	over 300 mm girth	m²	0.48	8.10	–	1.81	9.91	8.91	–	1.99	10.90
M601514B	n.e. 300 mm girth	m	0.19	3.28	–	0.60	3.88	3.61	–	0.66	4.27
M601515	**Prepare and apply one coat Timonox undercoat and one coat Timonox gloss to intumescent painted backgrounds; glazed windows and screens; in panes over 1.00 m²:**										
M601515A	over 300 mm girth	m²	0.43	7.35	–	1.81	9.16	8.09	–	1.99	10.08
M601515B	n.e. 300 mm girth	m	0.18	2.97	–	0.60	3.57	3.27	–	0.66	3.93
M601516	**Prepare and apply one coat Timonox undercoat and one coat Timonox gloss to intumescent painted backgrounds; glazed sash windows; in panes n.e. 0.10 m²:**										
M601516A	over 300 mm girth	m²	0.82	13.97	–	1.81	15.78	15.37	–	1.99	17.36
M601516B	n.e. 300 mm girth	m	0.33	5.66	–	0.60	6.26	6.23	–	0.66	6.89
M601516C	areas n.e. 0.5 m²	Nr	0.62	10.47	–	0.97	11.44	11.52	–	1.07	12.58
M601517	**Prepare and apply one coat Timonox undercoat and one coat Timonox gloss to intumescent painted backgrounds; glazed sash windows; in panes 0.10-0.50 m²:**										
M601517A	over 300 mm girth	m²	0.61	10.27	–	1.81	12.08	11.30	–	1.99	13.29
M601517B	n.e. 300 mm girth	m	0.25	4.16	–	0.60	4.76	4.58	–	0.66	5.24
M601517C	areas n.e. 0.5 m²	Nr	0.45	7.70	–	0.97	8.67	8.47	–	1.07	9.54
M601518	**Prepare and apply one coat Timonox undercoat and one coat Timonox gloss to intumescent painted backgrounds; glazed sash windows; in panes 0.50-1.00 m²:**										
M601518A	over 300 mm girth	m²	0.53	8.91	–	1.81	10.72	9.80	–	1.99	11.79
M601518B	n.e. 300 mm girth	m	0.21	3.60	–	0.60	4.20	3.96	–	0.66	4.62

Surface Finishes

Major Works 2009		Unit	Labour Hours	Labour Net	Plant Net	Materials Net	Unit Net	Labour Gross	Plant Gross	Materials Gross	Unit Price
								<td colspan="4" align="center">—— (Gross rates include 10% profit) ——</td>
				£	£	£	£	£	£	£	£
M60	**M60: PAINTING AND CLEAR FINISHING**										
M6015	**Flame retardant coatings**										
M601519	**Prepare and apply one coat Timonox undercoat and one coat Timonox gloss to intumescent painted backgrounds; glazed sash windows; in panes over 1.00 m²:**										
M601519A	over 300 mm girth	m²	0.48	8.08	–	1.81	9.89	8.89	–	1.99	10.88
M601519B	n.e. 300 mm girth	m	0.19	3.28	–	0.60	3.88	3.61	–	0.66	4.27
M601520	**Prepare and apply one coat Timonox undercoat and one coat Timonox gloss to intumescent painted backgrounds; glazed doors; in panes n.e. 0.10 m²:**										
M601520A	over 300 mm girth	m²	0.75	12.70	–	1.81	14.51	13.97	–	1.99	15.96
M601520B	n.e. 300 mm girth	m	0.30	5.15	–	0.60	5.75	5.67	–	0.66	6.33
M601520C	areas n.e. 0.5 m²	Nr	0.56	9.52	–	0.97	10.49	10.47	–	1.07	11.54
M601521	**Prepare and apply one coat Timonox undercoat and one coat Timonox gloss to intumescent painted backgrounds; glazed doors; in panes 0.10-0.50 m²:**										
M601521A	over 300 mm girth	m²	0.55	9.34	–	1.81	11.15	10.27	–	1.99	12.27
M601521B	n.e. 300 mm girth	m	0.22	3.79	–	0.60	4.39	4.17	–	0.66	4.83
M601521C	areas n.e. 0.5 m²	Nr	0.41	7.01	–	0.97	7.98	7.71	–	1.07	8.78
M601522	**Prepare and apply one coat Timonox undercoat and one coat Timonox gloss to intumescent painted backgrounds; glazed doors; in panes 0.50-1.00 m²:**										
M601522A	over 300 mm girth	m²	0.48	8.10	–	1.81	9.91	8.91	–	1.99	10.90
M601522B	n.e. 300 mm girth	m	0.19	3.28	–	0.60	3.88	3.61	–	0.66	4.27
M601523	**Prepare and apply one coat Timonox undercoat and one coat Timonox gloss to intumescent painted backgrounds; glazed doors; in panes over 1.00 m²:**										
M601523A	over 300 mm girth	m²	0.43	7.35	–	1.81	9.16	8.09	–	1.99	10.08
M601523B	n.e. 300 mm girth	m	0.18	2.97	–	0.60	3.57	3.27	–	0.66	3.93
M601531	**Prepare and apply two coats Timonox eggshell to intumescent painted backgrounds; general surfaces:**										
M601531A	over 300 mm girth	m²	0.27	4.58	–	1.81	6.39	5.04	–	1.99	7.03
M601531B	n.e. 300 mm girth	m	0.11	1.85	–	0.54	2.39	2.04	–	0.59	2.63
M601531C	areas n.e. 0.5 m²	Nr	0.20	3.44	–	0.91	4.35	3.78	–	1.00	4.79

Major Works 2009		Unit	Labour Hours	Labour Net	Plant Net	Materials Net	Unit Net	Labour Gross	Plant Gross	Materials Gross	Unit Price
								(Gross rates include 10% profit)			
				£	£	£	£	£	£	£	£
M60	**M60: PAINTING AND CLEAR FINISHING**										
M6015	**Flame retardant coatings**										
M601532	**Prepare and apply two coats Timonox eggshell to intumescent painted backgrounds; glazed windows and screens; in panes n.e. 0.10 m²:**										
M601532A	over 300 mm girth	m²	0.75	12.70	–	1.81	14.51	13.97	–	1.99	15.96
M601532B	n.e. 300 mm girth	m	0.12	2.09	–	0.54	2.63	2.30	–	0.59	2.89
M601532C	areas n.e. 0.5 m²	Nr	0.42	7.14	–	0.91	8.05	7.85	–	1.00	8.86
M601533	**Prepare and apply two coats Timonox eggshell to intumescent painted backgrounds; glazed windows and screens; in panes 0.10-0.50 m²:**										
M601533A	over 300 mm girth	m²	0.55	9.34	–	1.81	11.15	10.27	–	1.99	12.27
M601533B	n.e. 300 mm girth	m	0.22	3.79	–	0.54	4.33	4.17	–	0.59	4.76
M601533C	areas n.e. 0.5 m²	Nr	0.41	7.01	–	0.91	7.92	7.71	–	1.00	8.71
M601534	**Prepare and apply two coats Timonox eggshell to intumescent painted backgrounds; glazed windows and screens; in panes 0.50-1.00 m²:**										
M601534A	over 300 mm girth	m²	0.48	8.10	–	1.81	9.91	8.91	–	1.99	10.90
M601534B	n.e. 300 mm girth	m	0.19	3.28	–	0.54	3.82	3.61	–	0.59	4.20
M601535	**Prepare and apply two coats Timonox eggshell to intumescent painted backgrounds; glazed windows and screens; in panes over 1.00 m²:**										
M601535A	over 300 mm girth	m²	0.43	7.35	–	1.81	9.16	8.09	–	1.99	10.08
M601535B	n.e. 300 mm girth	m	0.18	2.97	–	0.54	3.51	3.27	–	0.59	3.86
M601536	**Prepare and apply two coats Timonox eggshell to intumescent painted backgrounds; glazed sash windows; in panes n.e. 0.10 m²:**										
M601536A	over 300 mm girth	m²	0.82	13.97	–	1.81	15.78	15.37	–	1.99	17.36
M601536B	n.e. 300 mm girth	m	0.14	2.30	–	0.54	2.84	2.53	–	0.59	3.12
M601536C	areas n.e. 0.5 m²	Nr	0.46	7.86	–	0.91	8.77	8.65	–	1.00	9.65
M601537	**Prepare and apply two coats Timonox eggshell to intumescent painted backgrounds; glazed sash windows; in panes 0.10-0.50 m²:**										
M601537A	over 300 mm girth	m²	0.61	10.27	–	1.81	12.08	11.30	–	1.99	13.29
M601537B	n.e. 300 mm girth	m	0.25	4.16	–	0.54	4.70	4.58	–	0.59	5.17
M601537C	areas n.e. 0.5 m²	Nr	0.45	7.70	–	0.91	8.61	8.47	–	1.00	9.47
M601538	**Prepare and apply two coats Timonox eggshell to intumescent painted backgrounds; glazed sash windows; in panes 0.50-1.00 m²:**										
M601538A	over 300 mm girth	m²	0.53	8.91	–	1.81	10.72	9.80	–	1.99	11.79
M601538B	n.e. 300 mm girth	m	0.21	3.60	–	0.54	4.14	3.96	–	0.59	4.55

Surface Finishes

Major Works 2009		Unit	Labour Hours	Labour Net	Plant Net	Materials Net	Unit Net	Labour Gross	Plant Gross	Materials Gross	Unit Price
								(Gross rates include 10% profit)			
				£	£	£	£	£	£	£	£
M60	**M60: PAINTING AND CLEAR FINISHING**										
M6015	**Flame retardant coatings**										
M601539	**Prepare and apply two coats Timonox eggshell to intumescent painted backgrounds; glazed sash windows; in panes over 1.00 m²:**										
M601539A	over 300 mm girth	m²	0.48	8.08	–	1.81	9.89	8.89	–	1.99	10.88
M601539B	n.e. 300 mm girth	m	0.19	3.28	–	0.54	3.82	3.61	–	0.59	4.20
M601540	**Prepare and apply two coats Timonox eggshell to intumescent painted backgrounds; glazed doors; in panes n.e. 0.10 m²:**										
M601540A	over 300 mm girth	m²	0.75	12.70	–	1.81	14.51	13.97	–	1.99	15.96
M601540B	n.e. 300 mm girth	m	0.12	2.09	–	0.54	2.63	2.30	–	0.59	2.89
M601540C	areas n.e. 0.5 m²	Nr	0.42	7.14	–	0.91	8.05	7.85	–	1.00	8.86
M601541	**Prepare and apply two coats Timonox eggshell to intumescent painted backgrounds; glazed doors; in panes 0.10-0.50 m²:**										
M601541A	over 300 mm girth	m²	0.55	9.34	–	1.81	11.15	10.27	–	1.99	12.27
M601541B	n.e. 300 mm girth	m	0.22	3.79	–	0.54	4.33	4.17	–	0.59	4.76
M601541C	areas n.e. 0.5 m²	Nr	0.41	7.01	–	0.91	7.92	7.71	–	1.00	8.71
M601542	**Prepare and apply two coats Timonox eggshell to intumescent painted backgrounds; glazed doors; in panes 0.50-1.00 m²:**										
M601542A	over 300 mm girth	m²	0.48	8.10	–	1.81	9.91	8.91	–	1.99	10.90
M601542B	n.e. 300 mm girth	m	0.19	3.28	–	0.54	3.82	3.61	–	0.59	4.20
M601543	**Prepare and apply two coats Timonox eggshell to intumescent painted backgrounds; glazed doors; in panes over 1.00 m²:**										
M601543A	over 300 mm girth	m²	0.43	7.35	–	1.81	9.16	8.09	–	1.99	10.08
M601543B	n.e. 300 mm girth	m	0.18	2.97	–	0.54	3.51	3.27	–	0.59	3.86
M601581	**Prepare and apply two coats Timonox intumescent paint to woodwork backgrounds; general surfaces:**										
M601581A	over 300 mm girth	m²	0.75	12.74	–	5.42	18.16	14.01	–	5.96	19.98
M601581B	n.e. 300 mm girth	m	0.30	5.17	–	1.61	6.78	5.69	–	1.77	7.46
M601581C	areas n.e. 0.5 m²	Nr	0.56	9.56	–	2.71	12.27	10.52	–	2.98	13.50

Major Works 2009		Unit	Labour Hours	Labour Net	Plant Net	Materials Net	Unit Net	Labour Gross	Plant Gross	Materials Gross	Unit Price
				£	£	£	£	£	£	£	£
								(Gross rates include 10% profit)			
M60	**M60: PAINTING AND CLEAR FINISHING**										
M6015	**Flame retardant coatings**										
M601582	**Prepare and apply two coats Timonox intumescent paint to woodwork backgrounds; glazed windows and screens; in panes n.e. 0.10 m²:**										
M601582A	over 300 mm girth	m²	2.29	38.80	–	5.42	44.22	42.68	–	5.96	48.64
M601582B	n.e. 300 mm girth	m	0.93	15.71	–	1.61	17.32	17.28	–	1.77	19.05
M601582C	areas n.e. 0.5 m²	Nr	1.71	29.11	–	2.71	31.82	32.02	–	2.98	35.00
M601583	**Prepare and apply two coats Timonox intumescent paint to woodwork backgrounds; glazed windows and screens; in panes 0.10-0.50 m²:**										
M601583A	over 300 mm girth	m²	1.68	28.53	–	5.42	33.95	31.38	–	5.96	37.35
M601583B	n.e. 300 mm girth	m	0.68	11.55	–	1.61	13.16	12.71	–	1.77	14.48
M601583C	areas n.e. 0.5 m²	Nr	1.26	21.40	–	2.71	24.11	23.54	–	2.98	26.52
M601584	**Prepare and apply two coats Timonox intumescent paint to woodwork backgrounds; glazed windows and screens; in panes 0.50-1.00 m²:**										
M601584A	over 300 mm girth	m²	1.46	24.74	–	5.42	30.16	27.21	–	5.96	33.18
M601584B	n.e. 300 mm girth	m	0.59	10.02	–	1.61	11.63	11.02	–	1.77	12.79
M601585	**Prepare and apply two coats Timonox intumescent paint to woodwork backgrounds; glazed windows and screens; in panes over 1.00 m²:**										
M601585A	over 300 mm girth	m²	1.32	22.47	–	5.42	27.89	24.72	–	5.96	30.68
M601585B	n.e. 300 mm girth	m	0.54	9.11	–	1.61	10.72	10.02	–	1.77	11.79

Surface Finishes

Major Works 2009		Unit	Labour Hours	Labour Net	Plant Net	Materials Net	Unit Net	Labour Gross	Plant Gross	Materials Gross	Unit Price
								(Gross rates include 10% profit)			
				£	£	£	£	£	£	£	£
M60	**M60: PAINTING AND CLEAR FINISHING**										
M6015	**Flame retardant coatings**										
M601586	**Prepare and apply two coats Timonox intumescent paint to woodwork backgrounds; glazed sash windows; in panes n.e. 0.10 m²:**										
M601586A	over 300 mm girth	m²	2.51	42.69	–	5.42	48.11	46.96	–	5.96	52.92
M601586B	n.e. 300 mm girth	m	1.11	18.82	–	1.61	20.43	20.70	–	1.77	22.47
M601586C	areas n.e. 0.5 m²	Nr	1.89	32.01	–	2.71	34.72	35.21	–	2.98	38.19
M601587	**Prepare and apply two coats Timonox intumescent paint to woodwork backgrounds; glazed sash windows; in panes 0.10-0.50 m²:**										
M601587A	over 300 mm girth	m²	1.85	31.38	–	5.42	36.80	34.52	–	5.96	40.48
M601587B	n.e. 300 mm girth	m	0.75	12.71	–	1.61	14.32	13.98	–	1.77	15.75
M601587C	areas n.e. 0.5 m²	Nr	1.39	23.54	–	2.71	26.25	25.89	–	2.98	28.88
M601588	**Prepare and apply two coats Timonox intumescent paint to woodwork backgrounds; glazed sash windows; in panes 0.50-1.00 m²:**										
M601588A	over 300 mm girth	m²	1.60	27.22	–	5.42	32.64	29.94	–	5.96	35.90
M601588B	n.e. 300 mm girth	m	0.65	11.02	–	1.61	12.63	12.12	–	1.77	13.89
M601589	**Prepare and apply two coats Timonox intumescent paint to woodwork backgrounds; glazed sash windows; in panes over 1.00 m²:**										
M601589A	over 300 mm girth	m²	1.46	24.71	–	5.42	30.13	27.18	–	5.96	33.14
M601589B	n.e. 300 mm girth	m	0.59	10.02	–	1.61	11.63	11.02	–	1.77	12.79

Major Works 2009		Unit	Labour Hours	Labour Net	Plant Net	Materials Net	Unit Net	Labour Gross	Plant Gross	Materials Gross	Unit Price
								(Gross rates include 10% profit)			
				£	£	£	£	£	£	£	£
M60	**M60: PAINTING AND CLEAR FINISHING**										
M6015	**Flame retardant coatings**										
M601590	**Prepare and apply two coats Timonox intumescent paint to woodwork backgrounds; glazed doors; in panes n.e. 0.10 m²:**										
M601590A	over 300 mm girth	m²	2.29	38.80	–	5.42	44.22	42.68	–	5.96	48.64
M601590B	n.e. 300 mm girth	m	0.93	15.71	–	1.61	17.32	17.28	–	1.77	19.05
M601590C	areas n.e. 0.5 m²	Nr	1.71	29.11	–	2.71	31.82	32.02	–	2.98	35.00
M601591	**Prepare and apply two coats Timonox intumescent paint to woodwork backgrounds; glazed doors; in panes 0.10- 0.50 m²:**										
M601591A	over 300 mm girth	m²	1.68	28.53	–	5.42	33.95	31.38	–	5.96	37.35
M601591B	n.e. 300 mm girth	m	0.68	11.55	–	1.61	13.16	12.71	–	1.77	14.48
M601591C	areas n.e. 0.5 m²	Nr	1.26	21.40	–	2.71	24.11	23.54	–	2.98	26.52
M601592	**Prepare and apply two coats Timonox intumescent paint to woodwork backgrounds; glazed doors; in panes 0.50- 1.00 m²:**										
M601592A	over 300 mm girth	m²	1.46	24.74	–	5.42	30.16	27.21	–	5.96	33.18
M601592B	n.e. 300 mm girth	m	0.59	10.02	–	1.61	11.63	11.02	–	1.77	12.79
M601593	**Prepare and apply two coats Timonox intumescent paint to woodwork backgrounds; glazed doors; in panes over 1.00 m²:**										
M601593A	over 300 mm girth	m²	1.32	22.47	–	5.42	27.89	24.72	–	5.96	30.68
M601593B	n.e. 300 mm girth	m	0.54	9.11	–	1.61	10.72	10.02	–	1.77	11.79
M6017	**Textured plastic finish**										
M601722	**Prepare, apply one coat Artex sealer and one coat Artex compound textured finish:**										
M601722A	ceilings	m²	0.30	5.10	–	1.13	6.23	5.61	–	1.24	6.85
M601722B	ceilings; 3.5-5.0 m high	m²	0.33	5.51	–	1.25	6.76	6.06	–	1.38	7.44
M601722C	ceilings; n.e. 300 mm girth .	m	0.12	2.07	–	0.38	2.45	2.28	–	0.42	2.70
M601722D	ceilings; areas n.e. 0.5 m² . .	Nr	0.23	3.82	–	0.64	4.46	4.20	–	0.70	4.91

Surface Finishes

Major Works 2009		Unit	Labour Hours	Labour Net	Plant Net	Materials Net	Unit Net	Labour Gross	Plant Gross	Materials Gross	Unit Price
								(Gross rates include 10% profit)			
				£	£	£	£	£	£	£	£
M60	**M60: PAINTING AND CLEAR FINISHING**										
M6018	**Masonry paint**										
M601801	**Prepare, apply masonry base coat sealer and two coats of masonry paint finish; rendered backgrounds:**										
M601801A	walls....................	m²	0.27	4.59	–	3.64	8.23	5.05	–	4.00	9.05
M601801B	walls; 3.5-5.0 m high	m²	0.30	5.01	–	3.64	8.65	5.51	–	4.00	9.52
M601801C	walls; n.e. 300 mm girth ...	m	0.11	1.87	–	3.94	5.81	2.06	–	4.33	6.39
M601801D	walls; areas n.e. 0.5 m²	Nr	0.20	3.45	–	1.79	5.24	3.80	–	1.97	5.76
M601801F	ceilings	m²	0.28	4.82	–	3.64	8.46	5.30	–	4.00	9.31
M601801G	ceilings; 3.5-5.0 m high....	m²	0.31	5.25	–	3.64	8.89	5.78	–	4.00	9.78
M601801H	ceilings; n.e. 300 mm girth .	m	0.12	1.97	–	3.94	5.91	2.17	–	4.33	6.50
M601801I	ceilings; areas n.e. 0.5 m²..	Nr	0.21	3.61	–	1.79	5.40	3.97	–	1.97	5.94
M601802	**Prepare, apply masonry base coat sealer and two coats of masonry paint finish; concrete backgrounds:**										
M601802A	walls....................	m²	0.25	4.16	–	3.32	7.48	4.58	–	3.65	8.23
M601802B	walls; 3.5-5.0 m high	m²	0.27	4.58	–	3.32	7.90	5.04	–	3.65	8.69
M601802C	walls; n.e. 300 mm girth ...	m	0.10	1.68	–	1.02	2.70	1.85	–	1.12	2.97
M601802D	walls; areas n.e. 0.5 m²	Nr	0.18	3.12	–	1.68	4.80	3.43	–	1.85	5.28
M601802F	ceilings	m²	0.26	4.36	–	3.32	7.68	4.80	–	3.65	8.45
M601802G	ceilings; 3.5-5.0 m high....	m²	0.28	4.79	–	3.32	8.11	5.27	–	3.65	8.92
M601802H	ceilings; n.e. 300 mm girth .	m	0.08	1.31	–	1.02	2.33	1.44	–	1.12	2.56
M601802I	ceilings; areas n.e. 0.5 m²..	Nr	0.19	3.28	–	1.68	4.96	3.61	–	1.85	5.46
M601803	**Prepare, apply masonry base coat sealer and two coats of masonry paint finish; brickwork backgrounds:**										
M601803A	walls....................	m²	0.30	5.09	–	3.87	8.96	5.60	–	4.26	9.86
M601803B	walls; 3.5-5.0 m high	m²	0.33	5.52	–	3.87	9.39	6.07	–	4.26	10.33
M601803C	walls; n.e. 300 mm girth ...	m	0.12	2.07	–	1.17	3.24	2.28	–	1.29	3.56
M601803D	walls; areas n.e. 0.5 m²	Nr	0.23	3.82	–	1.86	5.68	4.20	–	2.05	6.25
M601804	**Prepare, apply masonry base coat sealer and two coats of masonry paint finish; blockwork backgrounds:**										
M601804A	walls....................	m²	0.34	5.78	–	4.53	10.31	6.36	–	4.98	11.34
M601804B	walls; 3.5-5.0 m high	m²	0.37	6.20	–	4.53	10.73	6.82	–	4.98	11.80
M601804C	walls; n.e. 300 mm girth ...	m	0.14	2.35	–	1.35	3.70	2.59	–	1.49	4.07
M601804D	walls; areas n.e. 0.5 m²	Nr	0.26	4.33	–	2.30	6.63	4.76	–	2.53	7.29

Major Works 2009		Unit	Labour Hours	Labour Net	Plant Net	Materials Net	Unit Net	Labour Gross	Plant Gross	Materials Gross	Unit Price
								(Gross rates include 10% profit)			
				£	£	£	£	£	£	£	£
M60	**M60: PAINTING AND CLEAR FINISHING**										
M6019	**Cement paint**										
M601901	**Prepare, apply one coat stabiliser and two coats Sandtex textured finish; rendered backgrounds:**										
M601901A	walls....................	m²	0.19	3.22	–	1.56	4.78	3.54	–	1.72	5.26
M601901B	walls; 3.5-5.0 m high	m²	0.22	3.65	–	1.56	5.21	4.02	–	1.72	5.73
M601901C	walls; n.e. 300 mm girth ...	m	0.08	1.31	–	0.44	1.75	1.44	–	0.48	1.93
M601901D	walls; areas n.e. 0.5 m²	Nr	0.14	2.30	–	0.76	3.06	2.53	–	0.84	3.37
M601901F	ceilings	m²	0.20	3.39	–	1.56	4.95	3.73	–	1.72	5.45
M601901G	ceilings; 3.5-5.0 m high....	m²	0.23	3.82	–	1.56	5.38	4.20	–	1.72	5.92
M601901H	ceilings; n.e. 300 mm girth .	m	0.08	1.38	–	0.44	1.82	1.52	–	0.48	2.00
M601901I	ceilings; areas n.e. 0.5 m²..	Nr	0.15	2.55	–	0.76	3.31	2.81	–	0.84	3.64
M601902	**Prepare, apply one coat stabiliser and two coats Sandtex textured finish; concrete backgrounds:**										
M601902A	walls....................	m²	0.20	3.39	–	1.21	4.60	3.73	–	1.33	5.06
M601902B	walls; 3.5-5.0 m high	m²	0.23	3.82	–	1.21	5.03	4.20	–	1.33	5.53
M601902C	walls; n.e. 300 mm girth ...	m	0.08	1.38	–	0.35	1.73	1.52	–	0.39	1.90
M601902D	walls; areas n.e. 0.5 m²	Nr	0.15	2.54	–	0.15	2.69	2.79	–	0.17	2.96
M601902F	ceilings	m²	0.21	3.56	–	1.21	4.77	3.92	–	1.33	5.25
M601902G	ceilings; 3.5-5.0 m high....	m²	0.24	3.99	–	1.21	5.20	4.39	–	1.33	5.72
M601902H	ceilings; n.e. 300 mm girth .	m	0.09	1.45	–	0.35	1.80	1.60	–	0.39	1.98
M601902I	ceilings; areas n.e. 0.5 m²..	Nr	0.16	2.68	–	0.15	2.83	2.95	–	0.17	3.11
M601903	**Prepare, apply one coat stabiliser and two coats Sandtex textured finish; brickwork backgrounds:**										
M601903A	walls....................	m²	0.24	4.07	–	1.71	5.78	4.48	–	1.88	6.36
M601903B	walls; 3.5-5.0 m high	m²	0.27	4.49	–	1.71	6.20	4.94	–	1.88	6.82
M601903C	walls; n.e. 300 mm girth ...	m	0.10	1.65	–	0.50	2.15	1.82	–	0.55	2.37
M601903D	walls; areas n.e. 0.5 m²	Nr	0.18	3.06	–	0.88	3.94	3.37	–	0.97	4.33
M601904	**Prepare, apply one coat stabiliser and two coats Sandtex textured finish; blockwork backgrounds:**										
M601904A	walls....................	m²	0.27	4.58	–	1.71	6.29	5.04	–	1.88	6.92
M601904B	walls; 3.5-5.0 m high	m²	0.30	5.00	–	1.71	6.71	5.50	–	1.88	7.38
M601904C	walls; n.e. 300 mm girth ...	m	0.11	1.87	–	0.50	2.37	2.06	–	0.55	2.61
M601904D	walls; areas n.e. 0.5 m²	Nr	0.20	3.45	–	0.88	4.33	3.80	–	0.97	4.76

Surface Finishes

Major Works 2009		Unit	Labour Hours	Labour Net	Plant Net	Materials Net	Unit Net	Labour Gross	Plant Gross	Materials Gross	Unit Price
								(Gross rates include 10% profit)			
				£	£	£	£	£	£	£	£
M60	**M60: PAINTING AND CLEAR FINISHING**										
M6021	**Oil paint; woodwork backgrounds; one undercoat, one top coat**										
M602101	**Prepare, knot, prime and stop, apply one undercoat and one top coat gloss paint; general surfaces:**										
M602101A	over 300 mm girth	m²	0.33	5.60	–	2.65	8.25	6.16	–	2.92	9.08
M602101B	n.e. 300 mm girth	m	0.14	2.29	–	0.77	3.06	2.52	–	0.85	3.37
M602101C	areas n.e. 0.5 m²	Nr	0.25	4.21	–	1.37	5.58	4.63	–	1.51	6.14
M602102	**Prepare, knot, prime and stop, apply one undercoat and one top coat gloss paint; glazed windows and screens; in panes n.e. 0.10 m²:**										
M602102A	over 300 mm girth	m²	1.02	17.32	–	4.06	21.38	19.05	–	4.47	23.52
M602102B	n.e. 300 mm girth	m	0.41	7.01	–	1.22	8.23	7.71	–	1.34	9.05
M602102C	areas n.e. 0.5 m²	Nr	0.77	12.99	–	1.88	14.87	14.29	–	2.07	16.36
M602103	**Prepare, knot, prime and stop, apply one undercoat and one top coat gloss paint; glazed windows and screens; in panes 0.10-0.50 m²:**										
M602103A	over 300 mm girth	m²	0.75	12.73	–	2.93	15.66	14.00	–	3.22	17.23
M602103B	n.e. 300 mm girth	m	0.31	5.18	–	0.90	6.08	5.70	–	0.99	6.69
M602103C	areas n.e. 0.5 m²	Nr	0.56	9.56	–	1.52	11.08	10.52	–	1.67	12.19
M602104	**Prepare, knot, prime and stop, apply one undercoat and one top coat gloss paint; glazed windows and screens; in panes 0.50-1.00 m²:**										
M602104A	over 300 mm girth	m²	0.65	11.03	–	2.61	13.64	12.13	–	2.87	15.00
M602104B	n.e. 300 mm girth	m	0.26	4.46	–	0.88	5.34	4.91	–	0.97	5.87
M602105	**Prepare, knot, prime and stop, apply one undercoat and one top coat gloss paint; glazed windows and screens; in panes over 1.00 m²:**										
M602105A	over 300 mm girth	m²	0.59	10.02	–	2.64	12.66	11.02	–	2.90	13.93
M602105B	n.e. 300 mm girth	m	0.24	4.06	–	0.75	4.81	4.47	–	0.83	5.29
M602106	**Prepare, knot, prime and stop, apply one undercoat and one top coat gloss paint; glazed sash windows; in panes n.e. 0.10 m²:**										
M602106A	over 300 mm girth	m²	1.12	19.05	–	4.06	23.11	20.96	–	4.47	25.42
M602106B	n.e. 300 mm girth	m	0.45	7.71	–	1.22	8.93	8.48	–	1.34	9.82
M602106C	areas n.e. 0.5 m²	Nr	0.84	14.30	–	1.88	16.18	15.73	–	2.07	17.80

Major Works 2009		Unit	Labour Hours	Labour Net	Plant Net	Materials Net	Unit Net	Labour Gross	Plant Gross	Materials Gross	Unit Price
								(Gross rates include 10% profit)			
				£	£	£	£	£	£	£	£
M60	**M60: PAINTING AND CLEAR FINISHING**										
M6021	**Oil paint; woodwork backgrounds; one undercoat, one top coat**										
M602107	**Prepare, knot, prime and stop, apply one undercoat and one top coat gloss paint; glazed sash windows; in panes 0.10-0.50 m²:**										
M602107A	over 300 mm girth	m²	0.83	14.01	–	2.93	16.94	15.41	–	3.22	18.63
M602107B	n.e. 300 mm girth	m	0.33	5.67	–	0.90	6.57	6.24	–	0.99	7.23
M602107C	areas n.e. 0.5 m²	Nr	0.62	10.51	–	1.52	12.03	11.56	–	1.67	13.23
M602108	**Prepare, knot, prime and stop, apply one undercoat and one top coat gloss paint; glazed sash windows; in panes 0.50-1.00 m²:**										
M602108A	over 300 mm girth	m²	0.72	12.14	–	2.61	14.75	13.35	–	2.87	16.23
M602108B	n.e. 300 mm girth	m	0.29	4.92	–	0.88	5.80	5.41	–	0.97	6.38
M602109	**Prepare, knot, prime and stop, apply one undercoat and one top coat gloss paint; glazed sash windows; in panes over 1.00 m²:**										
M602109A	over 300 mm girth	m²	0.65	11.02	–	2.64	13.66	12.12	–	2.90	15.03
M602109B	n.e. 300 mm girth	m	0.26	4.47	–	0.75	5.22	4.92	–	0.83	5.74
M602110	**Prepare, knot, prime and stop, apply one undercoat and one top coat gloss paint; glazed doors; in panes n.e. 1.00 m²:**										
M602110A	over 300 mm girth	m²	1.02	17.32	–	2.93	20.25	19.05	–	3.22	22.28
M602110B	n.e. 300 mm girth	m	0.41	7.01	–	0.90	7.91	7.71	–	0.99	8.70
M602110C	areas n.e. 0.5 m²	Nr	0.77	12.99	–	1.52	14.51	14.29	–	1.67	15.96
M602111	**Prepare, knot, prime and stop, apply one undercoat and one top coat gloss paint; glazed doors; in panes 0.10-0.50 m²:**										
M602111A	over 300 mm girth	m²	0.75	12.73	–	2.93	15.66	14.00	–	3.22	17.23
M602111B	n.e. 300 mm girth	m	0.31	5.18	–	0.90	6.08	5.70	–	0.99	6.69
M602111C	areas n.e. 0.5 m²	Nr	0.56	9.56	–	1.52	11.08	10.52	–	1.67	12.19
M602112	**Prepare, knot, prime and stop, apply one undercoat and one top coat gloss paint; glazed doors; in panes 0.50-1.00 m²:**										
M602112A	over 300 mm girth	m²	0.65	11.03	–	2.93	13.96	12.13	–	3.22	15.36
M602112B	n.e. 300 mm girth	m	0.26	4.47	–	0.90	5.37	4.92	–	0.99	5.91
M602113	**Prepare, knot, prime and stop, apply one undercoat and one top coat gloss paint; glazed doors; in panes over 1.00 m²:**										
M602113A	over 300 mm girth	m²	0.59	10.02	–	2.93	12.95	11.02	–	3.22	14.25
M602113B	n.e. 300 mm girth	m	0.24	4.06	–	0.90	4.96	4.47	–	0.99	5.46

Surface Finishes

Major Works 2009		Unit	Labour Hours	Labour Net	Plant Net	Materials Net	Unit Net	Labour Gross	Plant Gross	Materials Gross	Unit Price
								(Gross rates include 10% profit)			
				£	£	£	£	£	£	£	£
M60	**M60: PAINTING AND CLEAR FINISHING**										
M6023	**Oil paint; woodwork backgrounds; two undercoats, one top coat**										
M602301	**Prepare, knot, prime and stop, apply two undercoats and one top coat gloss paint; general surfaces:**										
M602301A	over 300 mm girth	m²	0.44	7.39	–	3.39	10.78	8.13	–	3.73	11.86
M602301B	n.e. 300 mm girth	m	0.18	2.99	–	1.02	4.01	3.29	–	1.12	4.41
M602301C	areas n.e. 0.5 m²	Nr	0.33	5.53	–	1.74	7.27	6.08	–	1.91	8.00
M602302	**Prepare, knot, prime and stop, apply two undercoats and one top coat gloss paint; glazed windows and screens; in panes n.e. 0.10 m²:**										
M602302A	over 300 mm girth	m²	1.35	22.84	–	5.13	27.97	25.12	–	5.64	30.77
M602302B	n.e. 300 mm girth	m	0.55	9.26	–	1.59	10.85	10.19	–	1.75	11.94
M602302C	areas n.e. 0.5 m²	Nr	1.01	17.13	–	2.58	19.71	18.84	–	2.84	21.68
M602303	**Prepare, knot, prime and stop, apply two undercoats and one top coat gloss paint; glazed windows and screens; in panes 0.10-0.50 m²:**										
M602303A	over 300 mm girth	m²	0.96	16.27	–	3.75	20.02	17.90	–	4.13	22.02
M602303B	n.e. 300 mm girth	m	0.39	6.59	–	1.15	7.74	7.25	–	1.27	8.51
M602303C	areas n.e. 0.5 m²	Nr	0.72	12.21	–	1.93	14.14	13.43	–	2.12	15.55
M602304	**Prepare, knot, prime and stop, apply two undercoats and one top coat gloss paint; glazed windows and screens; in panes 0.50-1.00 m²:**										
M602304A	over 300 mm girth	m²	0.85	14.35	–	3.26	17.61	15.79	–	3.59	19.37
M602304B	n.e. 300 mm girth	m	0.34	5.81	–	1.04	6.85	6.39	–	1.14	7.54
M602305	**Prepare, knot, prime and stop, apply two undercoats and one top coat gloss paint; glazed windows and screens; in panes over 1.00 m²:**										
M602305A	over 300 mm girth	m²	0.77	13.01	–	3.75	16.76	14.31	–	4.13	18.44
M602305B	n.e. 300 mm girth	m	0.31	5.26	–	1.15	6.41	5.79	–	1.27	7.05
M602306	**Prepare, knot, prime and stop, apply two undercoats and one top coat gloss paint; glazed sash windows; in panes n.e. 0.10 m²:**										
M602306A	over 300 mm girth	m²	1.48	25.13	–	5.13	30.26	27.64	–	5.64	33.29
M602306B	n.e. 300 mm girth	m	0.60	10.19	–	1.59	11.78	11.21	–	1.75	12.96
M602306C	areas n.e. 0.5 m²	Nr	1.11	18.85	–	2.50	21.35	20.74	–	2.75	23.49

Major Works 2009		Unit	Labour Hours	Labour Net	Plant Net	Materials Net	Unit Net	Labour Gross	Plant Gross	Materials Gross	Unit Price
									(Gross rates include 10% profit)		
				£	£	£	£	£	£	£	£
M60	**M60: PAINTING AND CLEAR FINISHING**										
M6021	**Oil paint; woodwork backgrounds; one undercoat, one top coat**										
M602307	Prepare, knot, prime and stop, apply two undercoats and one top coat gloss paint; glazed sash windows; in panes 0.10-0.50 m²:										
M602307A	over 300 mm girth	m²	1.05	17.90	–	3.75	21.65	19.69	–	4.13	23.82
M602307B	n.e. 300 mm girth	m	0.43	7.25	–	1.15	8.40	7.98	–	1.27	9.24
M602307C	areas n.e. 0.5 m²	Nr	0.79	13.42	–	1.93	15.35	14.76	–	2.12	16.89
M602308	Prepare, knot, prime and stop, apply two undercoats and one top coat gloss paint; glazed sash windows; in panes 0.50-1.00 m²:										
M602308A	over 300 mm girth	m²	0.93	15.80	–	3.26	19.06	17.38	–	3.59	20.97
M602308B	n.e. 300 mm girth	m	0.38	6.41	–	1.04	7.45	7.05	–	1.14	8.20
M602309	Prepare, knot, prime and stop, apply two undercoats and one top coat gloss paint; glazed sash windows; in panes over 1.00 m²:										
M602309A	over 300 mm girth	m²	0.84	14.30	–	3.75	18.05	15.73	–	4.13	19.86
M602309B	n.e. 300 mm girth	m	0.63	10.73	–	1.15	11.88	11.80	–	1.27	13.07
M602310	Prepare, knot, prime and stop, apply two undercoats and one top coat gloss paint; glazed doors; in panes n.e. 1.00 m²:										
M602310A	over 300 mm girth	m²	1.33	22.50	–	3.75	26.25	24.75	–	4.13	28.88
M602310B	n.e. 300 mm girth	m	0.54	9.08	–	1.15	10.23	9.99	–	1.27	11.25
M602310C	areas n.e. 0.5 m²	Nr	0.99	16.81	–	1.93	18.74	18.49	–	2.12	20.61
M602311	Prepare, knot, prime and stop, apply two undercoats and one top coat gloss paint; glazed doors; in panes 0.10-0.50 m²:										
M602311A	over 300 mm girth	m²	0.96	16.30	–	3.75	20.05	17.93	–	4.13	22.06
M602311B	n.e. 300 mm girth	m	0.39	6.59	–	1.15	7.74	7.25	–	1.27	8.51
M602311C	areas n.e. 0.5 m²	Nr	0.72	12.23	–	1.93	14.16	13.45	–	2.12	15.58
M602312	Prepare, knot, prime and stop, apply two undercoats and one top coat gloss paint; glazed doors; in panes 0.50-1.00 m²:										
M602312A	over 300 mm girth	m²	0.85	14.35	–	3.75	18.10	15.79	–	4.13	19.91
M602312B	n.e. 300 mm girth	m	0.34	5.81	–	1.15	6.96	6.39	–	1.27	7.66
M602313	Prepare, knot, prime and stop, apply two undercoats and one top coat gloss paint; glazed doors; in panes over 1.00 m²:										
M602313A	over 300 mm girth	m²	0.77	13.01	–	3.75	16.76	14.31	–	4.13	18.44
M602313B	n.e. 300 mm girth	m	0.31	5.26	–	1.15	6.41	5.79	–	1.27	7.05

Surface Finishes

Major Works 2009		Unit	Labour Hours	Labour Net	Plant Net	Materials Net	Unit Net	Labour Gross	Plant Gross	Materials Gross	Unit Price
								(Gross rates include 10% profit)			
				£	£	£	£	£	£	£	£
M60	**M60: PAINTING AND CLEAR FINISHING**										
M6024	**Oil paint; metalwork backgrounds; two undercoats, one top coat**										
M602401	**Prepare, apply etching primer, two undercoats and one top coat gloss paint; general surfaces:**										
M602401A	over 300 mm girth	m²	0.36	6.11	–	3.99	10.10	6.72	–	4.39	11.11
M602401B	n.e. 300 mm girth	m	0.15	2.46	–	1.23	3.69	2.71	–	1.35	4.06
M602401C	areas n.e. 0.5 m²	Nr	0.27	4.59	–	1.99	6.58	5.05	–	2.19	7.24
M602402	**Prepare, apply etching primer, two undercoats and top coat gloss paint; glazed windows and screens; in panes n.e. 0.10 m²:**										
M602402A	over 300 mm girth	m²	1.14	19.39	–	3.99	23.38	21.33	–	4.39	25.72
M602402B	n.e. 300 mm girth	m	0.46	7.86	–	1.23	9.09	8.65	–	1.35	10.00
M602402C	areas n.e. 0.5 m²	Nr	0.86	14.55	–	1.99	16.54	16.01	–	2.19	18.19
M602403	**Prepare, apply etching primer, two undercoats and top coat gloss paint; glazed windows and screens; in panes 0.10-0.50 m²:**										
M602403A	over 300 mm girth	m²	0.84	14.26	–	2.99	17.25	15.69	–	3.29	18.98
M602403B	n.e. 300 mm girth	m	0.34	5.78	–	0.91	6.69	6.36	–	1.00	7.36
M602403C	areas n.e. 0.5 m²	Nr	0.63	10.70	–	1.49	12.19	11.77	–	1.64	13.41
M602404	**Prepare, apply etching primer, two undercoats and top coat gloss paint; glazed windows and screens; in panes 0.50-1.00 m²:**										
M602404A	over 300 mm girth	m²	0.73	12.36	–	2.54	14.90	13.60	–	2.79	16.39
M602404B	n.e. 300 mm girth	m	0.30	5.01	–	0.82	5.83	5.51	–	0.90	6.41
M602405	**Prepare, apply etching primer, two undercoats and top coat gloss paint; glazed windows and screens; in panes over 1.0 m²:**										
M602405A	over 300 mm girth	m²	0.66	11.22	–	2.36	13.58	12.34	–	2.60	14.94
M602405B	n.e. 300 mm girth	m	0.27	4.55	–	0.63	5.18	5.01	–	0.69	5.70
M602410	**Prepare, apply etching primer, two undercoats and top coat gloss paint; glazed doors; in panes n.e. 0.10 m²:**										
M602410A	over 300 mm girth	m²	1.14	19.39	–	3.99	23.38	21.33	–	4.39	25.72
M602410B	n.e. 300 mm girth	m	0.46	7.86	–	1.23	9.09	8.65	–	1.35	10.00
M602410C	areas n.e. 0.5 m²	Nr	0.86	14.55	–	1.99	16.54	16.01	–	2.19	18.19
M602411	**Prepare, apply etching primer, two undercoats and top coat gloss paint; glazed doors; in panes 0.10-0.50 m²:**										
M602411A	over 300 mm girth	m²	0.84	14.26	–	2.99	17.25	15.69	–	3.29	18.98
M602411B	n.e. 300 mm girth	m	0.34	5.78	–	0.91	6.69	6.36	–	1.00	7.36
M602411C	areas n.e. 0.5 m²	Nr	0.63	10.70	–	1.49	12.19	11.77	–	1.64	13.41

Major Works 2009		Unit	Labour Hours	Labour Net	Plant Net	Materials Net	Unit Net	Labour Gross	Plant Gross	Materials Gross	Unit Price
								(Gross rates include 10% profit)			
				£	£	£	£	£	£	£	£
M60	**M60: PAINTING AND CLEAR FINISHING**										
M6024	**Oil paint; metalwork backgrounds; two undercoats, one top coat**										
M602412	**Prepare, apply etching primer, two undercoats and top coat gloss paint; glazed doors; in panes 0.50-1.00 m²:**										
M602412A	over 300 mm girth	m²	0.73	12.36	–	2.54	14.90	13.60	–	2.79	16.39
M602412B	n.e. 300 mm girth	m	0.30	5.01	–	0.82	5.83	5.51	–	0.90	6.41
M602413	**Prepare, apply etching primer, two undercoats and top coat gloss paint; glazed doors; in panes over 1.0 m²:**										
M602413A	over 300 mm girth	m²	0.66	11.22	–	2.36	13.58	12.34	–	2.60	14.94
M602413B	n.e. 300 mm girth	m	0.27	4.55	–	0.63	5.18	5.01	–	0.69	5.70
M602415	**Prepare, apply etching primer, two undercoats and top coat gloss paint; structural metalwork:**										
M602415A	over 300 mm girth	m²	0.60	10.18	–	3.99	14.17	11.20	–	4.39	15.59
M602415B	n.e. 300 mm girth	m	0.24	4.12	–	1.23	5.35	4.53	–	1.35	5.89
M602415C	areas n.e. 0.5 m²	Nr	0.45	7.64	–	1.99	9.63	8.40	–	2.19	10.59
M602417	**Prepare, apply etching primer, two undercoats and top coat gloss paint; radiators:**										
M602417A	over 300 mm girth	m²	0.36	6.11	–	3.99	10.10	6.72	–	4.39	11.11
M602417B	n.e. 300 mm girth	m	0.15	2.48	–	1.23	3.71	2.73	–	1.35	4.08
M602417C	areas n.e. 0.5 m²	Nr	0.27	4.59	–	1.99	6.58	5.05	–	2.19	7.24
M602418	**Prepare, apply etching primer, two undercoats and top coat of gloss paint; railings, fences and gates:**										
M602418A	over 300 mm girth	m²	0.60	10.18	–	3.99	14.17	11.20	–	4.39	15.59
M602418B	n.e. 300 mm girth	m	0.24	4.12	–	1.23	5.35	4.53	–	1.35	5.89
M602418C	areas n.e. 0.5 m²	Nr	0.45	7.64	–	1.99	9.63	8.40	–	2.19	10.59
M602419	**Prepare, apply etching primer, two undercoats and top coat gloss paint; staircases and balustrades:**										
M602419A	over 300 mm girth	m²	0.51	8.66	–	3.58	12.24	9.53	–	3.94	13.46
M602419B	n.e. 300 mm girth	m	0.21	3.51	–	1.23	4.74	3.86	–	1.35	5.21
M602419C	areas n.e. 0.5 m²	Nr	0.38	6.51	–	1.99	8.50	7.16	–	2.19	9.35
M602420	**Prepare, apply etching primer, two undercoats and top coat gloss paint; gutters:**										
M602420A	over 300 mm girth	m²	0.55	9.33	–	3.58	12.91	10.26	–	3.94	14.20
M602420B	n.e. 300 mm girth	m	0.22	3.78	–	1.23	5.01	4.16	–	1.35	5.51
M602420C	areas n.e. 0.5 m²	Nr	0.41	7.02	–	1.99	9.01	7.72	–	2.19	9.91
M602421	**Prepare, apply etching primer, two undercoats and top coat gloss paint; services:**										
M602421A	over 300 mm girth	m²	0.55	9.33	–	3.58	12.91	10.26	–	3.94	14.20
M602421B	n.e. 300 mm girth	m	0.22	3.78	–	1.23	5.01	4.16	–	1.35	5.51
M602421C	areas n.e. 0.5 m²	Nr	0.41	7.02	–	1.99	9.01	7.72	–	2.19	9.91

Surface Finishes

Major Works 2009		Unit	Labour Hours	Labour Net	Plant Net	Materials Net	Unit Net	Labour Gross	Plant Gross	Materials Gross	Unit Price
								(Gross rates include 10% profit)			
				£	£	£	£	£	£	£	£
M60	**M60: PAINTING AND CLEAR FINISHING**										
M6025	**Preservative stain**										
M602501	**Prepare, apply one coat Sadolins base and two coats Sadolins Classic finish; general surfaces:**										
M602501A	over 300 mm girth	m²	0.51	8.66	–	2.26	10.92	9.53	–	2.49	12.01
M602501B	n.e. 300 mm girth	m	0.21	3.51	–	0.71	4.22	3.86	–	0.78	4.64
M602501C	areas n.e. 0.5 m²	Nr	0.38	6.45	–	2.26	8.71	7.10	–	2.49	9.58
M602502	**Prepare, apply one coat Sadolins base and two coats Sadolins Classic finish; glazed windows and screens; in panes n.e. 0.10 m²:**										
M602502A	over 300 mm girth	m²	1.55	26.32	–	2.99	29.31	28.95	–	3.29	32.24
M602502B	n.e. 300 mm girth	m	0.63	10.66	–	0.90	11.56	11.73	–	0.99	12.72
M602502C	areas n.e. 0.5 m²	Nr	1.16	19.75	–	1.23	20.98	21.73	–	1.35	23.08
M602503	**Prepare, apply one coat Sadolins base and two coats Sadolins Classic finish; glazed windows and screens; in panes 0.10-0.50 m²:**										
M602503A	over 300 mm girth	m²	1.14	19.35	–	2.26	21.61	21.29	–	2.49	23.77
M602503B	n.e. 300 mm girth	m	0.46	7.84	–	0.71	8.55	8.62	–	0.78	9.41
M602503C	areas n.e. 0.5 m²	Nr	0.86	14.52	–	1.17	15.69	15.97	–	1.29	17.26
M602504	**Prepare, apply one coat Sadolins base and two coats Sadolins Classic finish; glazed windows and screens; in panes 0.50-1.00 m²:**										
M602504A	over 300 mm girth	m²	0.99	16.81	–	1.95	18.76	18.49	–	2.15	20.64
M602504B	n.e. 300 mm girth	m	0.40	6.79	–	0.60	7.39	7.47	–	0.66	8.13
M602505	**Prepare, apply one coat Sadolins base and two coats Sadolins Classic finish; glazed windows and screens; in panes over 1.00 m²:**										
M602505A	over 300 mm girth	m²	0.90	15.28	–	1.77	17.05	16.81	–	1.95	18.76
M602505B	n.e. 300 mm girth	m	0.37	6.19	–	0.60	6.79	6.81	–	0.66	7.47
M602506	**Prepare, apply one coat Sadolins base and two coats Sadolins Classic finish; glazed sash windows; in panes n.e. 0.10 m²:**										
M602506A	over 300 mm girth	m²	1.71	28.95	–	2.99	31.94	31.85	–	3.29	35.13
M602506B	n.e. 300 mm girth	m	0.69	11.73	–	0.90	12.63	12.90	–	0.99	13.89
M602506C	areas n.e. 0.5 m²	Nr	1.28	21.71	–	1.23	22.94	23.88	–	1.35	25.23

Surface Finishes

Major Works 2009		Unit	Labour Hours	Labour Net	Plant Net	Materials Net	Unit Net	Labour Gross	Plant Gross	Materials Gross	Unit Price
									(Gross rates include 10% profit)		
				£	£	£	£	£	£	£	£
M60	**M60: PAINTING AND CLEAR FINISHING**										
M6025	**Preservative stain**										
M602507	**Prepare, apply one coat Sadolins base and two coats Sadolins Classic finish; glazed sash windows; in panes 0.10-0.50 m²:**										
M602507A	over 300 mm girth	m²	1.25	21.29	–	2.26	23.55	23.42	–	2.49	25.91
M602507B	n.e. 300 mm girth	m	0.51	8.62	–	0.71	9.33	9.48	–	0.78	10.26
M602507C	areas n.e. 0.5 m²	Nr	0.94	15.98	–	1.17	17.15	17.58	–	1.29	18.87
M602508	**Prepare, apply one coat Sadolins base and two coats Sadolins Classic finish; glazed sash windows; in panes 0.50-1.00 m²:**										
M602508A	over 300 mm girth	m²	1.09	18.50	–	1.95	20.45	20.35	–	2.15	22.50
M602508B	n.e. 300 mm girth	m	0.44	7.47	–	0.60	8.07	8.22	–	0.66	8.88
M602509	**Prepare, apply one coat Sadolins base and two coats Sadolins Classic finish; glazed sash windows; in panes over 1.00 m²:**										
M602509A	over 300 mm girth	m²	0.99	16.81	–	1.77	18.58	18.49	–	1.95	20.44
M602509B	n.e. 300 mm girth	m	0.40	6.82	–	0.60	7.42	7.50	–	0.66	8.16
M602510	**Prepare, apply one coat Sadolins base and two coats Sadolins Classic finish; glazed doors; in panes n.e. 0.10 m²:**										
M602510A	over 300 mm girth	m²	1.55	26.32	–	2.99	29.31	28.95	–	3.29	32.24
M602510B	n.e. 300 mm girth	m	0.63	10.66	–	0.90	11.56	11.73	–	0.99	12.72
M602510C	areas n.e. 0.5 m²	Nr	1.16	19.75	–	1.23	20.98	21.73	–	1.35	23.08
M602511	**Prepare, apply one coat Sadolins base and two coats Sadolins Classic finish; glazed doors; in panes 0.10-0.50 m²:**										
M602511A	over 300 mm girth	m²	1.14	19.35	–	2.26	21.61	21.29	–	2.49	23.77
M602511B	n.e. 300 mm girth	m	0.46	7.84	–	0.71	8.55	8.62	–	0.78	9.41
M602511C	areas n.e. 0.5 m²	Nr	0.86	14.52	–	1.17	15.69	15.97	–	1.29	17.26
M602512	**Prepare, apply one coat Sadolins base and two coats Sadolins Classic finish; glazed doors; in panes 0.50-1.00 m²:**										
M602512A	over 300 mm girth	m²	0.99	16.81	–	1.95	18.76	18.49	–	2.15	20.64
M602512B	n.e. 300 mm girth	m	0.40	6.79	–	0.60	7.39	7.47	–	0.66	8.13
M602513	**Prepare, apply one coat Sadolins base and two coats Sadolins Classic finish; glazed doors; in panes over 1.00 m²:**										
M602513A	over 300 mm girth	m²	0.90	15.28	–	1.77	17.05	16.81	–	1.95	18.76
M602513B	n.e. 300 mm girth	m	0.37	6.19	–	0.60	6.79	6.81	–	0.66	7.47

Surface Finishes

		Unit	Labour Hours	Labour Net	Plant Net	Materials Net	Unit Net	Labour Gross	Plant Gross	Materials Gross	Unit Price
								——— (Gross rates include 10% profit) ———			
				£	£	£	£	£	£	£	£
M60	**M60: PAINTING AND CLEAR FINISHING**										
M6028	**Microporous paint**										
M602801	**Prepare, apply one coat Hicksons base and two coats Hicksons Decor finish; general surfaces:**										
M602801A	over 300 mm girth	m²	0.51	8.66	–	3.64	12.30	9.53	–	4.00	13.53
M602801B	n.e. 300 mm girth	m	0.21	3.52	–	1.17	4.69	3.87	–	1.29	5.16
M602801C	areas n.e. 0.5 m²	Nr	0.38	6.45	–	1.90	8.35	7.10	–	2.09	9.19
M602802	**Prepare, apply one coat Hicksons base and two coats Hicksons Decor finish; glazed windows and screens; in panes n.e. 0.10 m²:**										
M602802A	over 300 mm girth	m²	1.55	26.32	–	4.81	31.13	28.95	–	5.29	34.24
M602802B	n.e. 300 mm girth	m	0.63	10.66	–	0.90	11.56	11.73	–	0.99	12.72
M602802C	areas n.e. 0.5 m²	Nr	1.16	19.75	–	1.17	20.92	21.73	–	1.29	23.01
M602803	**Prepare, apply one coat Hicksons base and two coats Hicksons Decor finish; glazed windows and screens; in panes 0.10-0.50 m²:**										
M602803A	over 300 mm girth	m²	1.14	19.36	–	3.64	23.00	21.30	–	4.00	25.30
M602803B	n.e. 300 mm girth	m	0.46	7.84	–	4.60	12.44	8.62	–	5.06	13.68
M602803C	areas n.e. 0.5 m²	Nr	0.86	14.52	–	1.17	15.69	15.97	–	1.29	17.26
M602804	**Prepare, apply one coat Hicksons base and two coats Hicksons Decor finish; glazed windows and screens; in panes 0.50-1.00 m²:**										
M602804A	over 300 mm girth	m²	0.99	16.81	–	3.13	19.94	18.49	–	3.44	21.93
M602804B	n.e. 300 mm girth	m	0.40	6.80	–	0.94	7.74	7.48	–	1.03	8.51
M602805	**Prepare, apply one coat Hicksons base and two coats Hicksons Decor finish; glazed windows and screens; in panes over 1.00 m²:**										
M602805A	over 300 mm girth	m²	0.90	15.28	–	2.84	18.12	16.81	–	3.12	19.93
M602805B	n.e. 300 mm girth	m	0.37	6.20	–	0.94	7.14	6.82	–	1.03	7.85
M602806	**Prepare, apply one coat Hicksons base and two coats Hicksons Decor finish; glazed sash windows; in panes n.e. 0.10 m²:**										
M602806A	over 300 mm girth	m²	1.71	28.95	–	4.81	33.76	31.85	–	5.29	37.14
M602806B	n.e. 300 mm girth	m	0.69	11.73	–	0.90	12.63	12.90	–	0.99	13.89
M602806C	areas n.e. 0.5 m²	Nr	1.28	21.72	–	1.17	22.89	23.89	–	1.29	25.18

Surface Finishes

Major Works 2009		Unit	Labour Hours	Labour Net	Plant Net	Materials Net	Unit Net	Labour Gross	Plant Gross	Materials Gross	Unit Price
								(Gross rates include 10% profit)			
				£	£	£	£	£	£	£	£
M60	**M60: PAINTING AND CLEAR FINISHING**										
M6028	**Microporous paint**										
M602807	**Prepare, apply one coat Hicksons base and two coats Hicksons Decor finish; glazed sash windows; in panes 0.10-0.50 m²:**										
M602807A	over 300 mm girth	m²	1.25	21.30	–	3.64	24.94	23.43	–	4.00	27.43
M602807B	n.e. 300 mm girth	m	0.51	8.62	–	4.60	13.22	9.48	–	5.06	14.54
M602807C	areas n.e. 0.5 m²	Nr	0.94	15.98	–	1.17	17.15	17.58	–	1.29	18.87
M602808	**Prepare, apply one coat Hicksons base and two coats Hicksons Decor finish; glazed sash windows; in panes 0.50-1.00 m²:**										
M602808A	over 300 mm girth	m²	1.09	18.51	–	3.13	21.64	20.36	–	3.44	23.80
M602808B	n.e. 300 mm girth	m	0.44	7.48	–	0.94	8.42	8.23	–	1.03	9.26
M602809	**Prepare, apply one coat Hicksons base and two coats Hicksons Decor finish; glazed sash windows; in panes over 1.00 m²:**										
M602809A	over 300 mm girth	m²	0.99	16.81	–	2.84	19.65	18.49	–	3.12	21.62
M602809B	n.e. 300 mm girth	m	0.40	6.83	–	0.94	7.77	7.51	–	1.03	8.55
M602810	**Prepare, apply one coat Hicksons base and two coats Hicksons Decor finish; glazed doors; in panes n.e. 0.10 m²:**										
M602810A	over 300 mm girth	m²	1.55	26.32	–	4.81	31.13	28.95	–	5.29	34.24
M602810B	n.e. 300 mm girth	m	0.63	10.66	–	0.90	11.56	11.73	–	0.99	12.72
M602810C	areas n.e. 0.5 m²	Nr	1.16	19.75	–	1.17	20.92	21.73	–	1.29	23.01
M602811	**Prepare, apply one coat Hicksons base and two coats Hicksons Decor finish; glazed doors; in panes 0.10-0.50 m²:**										
M602811A	over 300 mm girth	m²	1.14	19.36	–	3.64	23.00	21.30	–	4.00	25.30
M602811B	n.e. 300 mm girth	m	0.46	7.84	–	4.60	12.44	8.62	–	5.06	13.68
M602811C	areas n.e. 0.5 m²	Nr	0.86	14.52	–	1.17	15.69	15.97	–	1.29	17.26
M602812	**Prepare, apply one coat Hicksons base and two coats Hicksons Decor finish; glazed doors; in panes 0.50-1.00 m²:**										
M602812A	over 300 mm girth	m²	0.99	16.81	–	3.13	19.94	18.49	–	3.44	21.93
M602812B	n.e. 300 mm girth	m	0.40	6.80	–	0.94	7.74	7.48	–	1.03	8.51
M602813	**Prepare, apply one coat Hicksons base and two coats Hicksons Decor finish; glazed doors; in panes over 1.00 m²:**										
M602813A	over 300 mm girth	m²	0.90	15.28	–	2.84	18.12	16.81	–	3.12	19.93
M602813B	n.e. 300 mm girth	m	0.37	6.20	–	0.94	7.14	6.82	–	1.03	7.85

Surface Finishes

Major Works 2009		Unit	Labour Hours	Labour Net	Plant Net	Materials Net	Unit Net	Labour Gross	Plant Gross	Materials Gross	Unit Price
								——— (Gross rates include 10% profit) ———			
				£	£	£	£	£	£	£	£
M60	**M60: PAINTING AND CLEAR FINISHING**										
M6030	**Polyurethane lacquer**										
M603001	**Prepare, apply one thinned coat and two full coats varnish; general surfaces:**										
M603001A	over 300 mm girth	m²	0.51	8.66	–	3.42	12.08	9.53	–	3.76	13.29
M603001B	n.e. 300 mm girth	m	0.21	3.51	–	1.06	4.57	3.86	–	1.17	5.03
M603001C	areas n.e. 0.5 m²	Nr	0.38	6.50	–	1.78	8.28	7.15	–	1.96	9.11
M603002	**Prepare, apply one thinned coat and two full coats varnish; glazed windows and screens; in panes n.e. 0.1 m²:**										
M603002A	over 300 mm girth	m²	1.28	21.65	–	3.42	25.07	23.82	–	3.76	27.58
M603002B	n.e. 300 mm girth	m	0.52	8.76	–	1.06	9.82	9.64	–	1.17	10.80
M603002C	areas n.e. 0.5 m²	Nr	0.96	16.23	–	1.78	18.01	17.85	–	1.96	19.81
M603003	**Prepare, apply one thinned coat and two full coats varnish; glazed windows and screens; in panes 0.1-0.5 m²:**										
M603003A	over 300 mm girth	m²	0.94	15.96	–	3.42	19.38	17.56	–	3.76	21.32
M603003B	n.e. 300 mm girth	m	0.38	6.47	–	1.06	7.53	7.12	–	1.17	8.28
M603003C	areas n.e. 0.5 m²	Nr	0.71	11.97	–	1.78	13.75	13.17	–	1.96	15.13
M603004	**Prepare, apply one thinned coat and two full coats varnish; glazed windows and screens; in panes 0.5-1.0 m²:**										
M603004A	over 300 mm girth	m²	0.82	13.84	–	3.42	17.26	15.22	–	3.76	18.99
M603004B	n.e. 300 mm girth	m	0.33	5.60	–	1.06	6.66	6.16	–	1.17	7.33
M603005	**Prepare, apply one thinned coat and two full coats varnish; glazed windows and screens; in panes over 1.0 m²:**										
M603005A	over 300 mm girth	m²	0.74	12.48	–	3.42	15.90	13.73	–	3.76	17.49
M603005B	n.e. 300 mm girth	m	0.30	5.09	–	1.06	6.15	5.60	–	1.17	6.77
M603006	**Prepare, apply one thinned coat and two full coats varnish; glazed doors; in panes n.e. 0.1 m²:**										
M603006A	over 300 mm girth	m²	1.28	21.65	–	3.42	25.07	23.82	–	3.76	27.58
M603006B	n.e. 300 mm girth	m	0.52	8.76	–	1.06	9.82	9.64	–	1.17	10.80
M603006C	areas n.e. 0.5 m²	Nr	0.96	16.23	–	1.78	18.01	17.85	–	1.96	19.81

Major Works 2009		Unit	Labour Hours	Labour Net	Plant Net	Materials Net	Unit Net	Labour Gross	Plant Gross	Materials Gross	Unit Price
								—— (Gross rates include 10% profit) ——			
				£	£	£	£	£	£	£	£
M60	**M60: PAINTING AND CLEAR FINISHING**										
M6028	**Microporous paint**										
M603007	**Prepare, apply one thinned coat and two full coats varnish; glazed doors: in panes 0.1-0.5 m²:**										
M603007A	over 300 mm girth	m²	0.94	15.96	–	3.42	19.38	17.56	–	3.76	21.32
M603007B	n.e. 300 mm girth	m	0.38	6.47	–	1.06	7.53	7.12	–	1.17	8.28
M603007C	areas n.e. 0.5 m²	Nr	0.71	11.97	–	1.78	13.75	13.17	–	1.96	15.13
M603008	**Prepare, apply one thinned coat and two full coats varnish; glazed doors; in panes 0.5-1.0 m²:**										
M603008A	over 300 mm girth	m²	0.82	13.84	–	3.42	17.26	15.22	–	3.76	18.99
M603008B	n.e. 300 mm girth	m	0.33	5.60	–	1.06	6.66	6.16	–	1.17	7.33
M603009	**Prepare, apply one thinned coat and two full coats varnish; glazed doors; in panes over 1.0 m²:**										
M603009A	over 300 mm girth	m²	0.74	12.48	–	3.42	15.90	13.73	–	3.76	17.49
M603009B	n.e. 300 mm girth	m	0.30	5.09	–	1.06	6.15	5.60	–	1.17	6.77
M6041	**Wood preservative treatment**										
M604101	**Prepare for and apply one coat; general surfaces:**										
M604101A	over 300 mm girth	m²	0.10	1.70	–	0.25	1.95	1.87	–	0.28	2.15
M604101B	n.e. 300 mm girth	m	0.04	0.69	–	0.08	0.77	0.76	–	0.09	0.85
M604101C	areas n.e. 0.5 m²	Nr	0.08	1.27	–	0.13	1.40	1.40	–	0.14	1.54
M604102	**Prepare for and apply one coat; railings, fences and gates:**										
M604102A	over 300 mm girth	m²	0.14	2.38	–	0.25	2.63	2.62	–	0.28	2.89
M604102B	n.e. 300 mm girth	m	0.06	0.96	–	0.08	1.04	1.06	–	0.09	1.14
M604102C	areas n.e. 0.5 m²	Nr	0.11	1.78	–	0.13	1.91	1.96	–	0.14	2.10
M604111	**Prepare for and apply two coats; general surfaces:**										
M604111A	over 300 mm girth	m²	0.18	3.06	–	0.46	3.52	3.37	–	0.51	3.87
M604111B	n.e. 300 mm girth	m	0.07	1.24	–	0.14	1.38	1.36	–	0.15	1.52
M604111C	areas n.e. 0.5 m²	Nr	0.14	2.29	–	0.12	2.41	2.52	–	0.13	2.65
M604112	**Prepare for and apply two coats; railings, fences and gates:**										
M604112A	over 300 mm girth	m²	0.25	4.24	–	0.46	4.70	4.66	–	0.51	5.17
M604112B	n.e. 300 mm girth	m	0.10	1.75	–	0.14	1.89	1.93	–	0.15	2.08
M604112C	areas n.e. 0.5 m²	Nr	0.19	3.23	–	0.24	3.47	3.55	–	0.26	3.82

Surface Finishes

Major Works 2009		Unit	Labour Hours	Labour Net	Plant Net	Materials Net	Unit Net	Labour Gross	Plant Gross	Materials Gross	Unit Price
								(Gross rates include 10% profit)			
				£	£	£	£	£	£	£	£
M60	**M60: PAINTING AND CLEAR FINISHING**										
M6051	**Intumescent fire protection; woodwork backgrounds**										
M605101	**Prepare and apply three coats Intuclear decorative translucent intumescent varnish to a total loading of 1 litre per 3 m² for Class 1/0 fire protection; general surfaces:**										
M605101A	over 300 mm girth	m²	0.51	8.66	–	4.01	12.67	9.53	–	4.41	13.94
M605101B	n.e. 300 mm girth	m	0.21	3.51	–	1.21	4.72	3.86	–	1.33	5.19
M605101C	areas n.e. 0.5 m²	Nr	0.38	6.51	–	2.03	8.54	7.16	–	2.23	9.39
M605102	**Prepare and apply three coats Intuclear decorative translucent intumescent varnish to a total loading of 1 litre per 3 m² for Class 1/0 fire protection; glazed windows and screens; in panes n.e. 0.1 m²:**										
M605102A	over 300 mm girth	m²	1.55	26.26	–	4.01	30.27	28.89	–	4.41	33.30
M605102B	n.e. 300 mm girth	m	0.63	10.63	–	0.12	10.75	11.69	–	0.13	11.83
M605102C	areas n.e. 0.5 m²	Nr	1.16	19.70	–	2.03	21.73	21.67	–	2.23	23.90
M605103	**Prepare and apply three coats Intuclear decorative translucent intumescent varnish to a total loading of 1 litre per 3 m² for Class 1/0 fire protection; glazed windows and screens; in panes 0.1-0.5 m²:**										
M605103A	over 300 mm girth	m²	1.14	19.36	–	4.01	23.37	21.30	–	4.41	25.71
M605103B	n.e. 300 mm girth	m	0.46	7.84	–	1.21	9.05	8.62	–	1.33	9.96
M605103C	areas n.e. 0.5 m²	Nr	0.86	14.52	–	2.03	16.55	15.97	–	2.23	18.21
M605104	**Prepare and apply three coats Intuclear decorative translucent intumescent varnish to a total loading of 1 litre per 3 m² for Class 1/0 fire protection; glazed windows and screens; in panes 0.5-1.0 m²:**										
M605104A	over 300 mm girth	m²	0.99	16.73	–	4.01	20.74	18.40	–	4.41	22.81
M605104B	n.e. 300 mm girth	m	0.40	6.79	–	1.21	8.00	7.47	–	1.33	8.80
M605105	**Prepare and apply three coats Intuclear decorative translucent intumescent varnish to a total loading of 1 litre per 3 m² for Class 1/0 fire protection; glazed windows and screens; in panes over 1.0 m²:**										
M605105A	over 300 mm girth	m²	0.89	15.12	–	4.01	19.13	16.63	–	4.41	21.04
M605105B	n.e. 300 mm girth	m	0.36	6.11	–	1.21	7.32	6.72	–	1.33	8.05

Major Works 2009		Unit	Labour Hours	Labour Net	Plant Net	Materials Net	Unit Net	Labour Gross	Plant Gross	Materials Gross	Unit Price
								(Gross rates include 10% profit)			
				£	£	£	£	£	£	£	£
M60	**M60: PAINTING AND CLEAR FINISHING**										
M6051	**Intumescent fire protection; woodwork backgrounds**										
M605106	**Prepare and apply three coats Intuclear decorative translucent intumescent varnish to a total loading of 1 litre per 3 m² for Class 1/0 fire protection; glazed doors; in panes n.e. 0.1 m²:**										
M605106A	over 300 mm girth	m²	1.55	26.26	–	4.01	30.27	28.89	–	4.41	33.30
M605106B	n.e. 300 mm girth	m	0.63	10.63	–	0.12	10.75	11.69	–	0.13	11.83
M605106C	areas n.e. 0.5 m²	Nr	1.16	19.70	–	2.03	21.73	21.67	–	2.23	23.90
M605107	**Prepare and apply three coats Intuclear decorative translucent intumescent varnish to a total loading of 1 litre per 3 m² for Class 1/0 fire protection; glazed doors; in panes 0.1-0.5 m²:**										
M605107A	over 300 mm girth	m²	1.14	19.36	–	4.01	23.37	21.30	–	4.41	25.71
M605107B	n.e. 300 mm girth	m	0.46	7.84	–	1.21	9.05	8.62	–	1.33	9.96
M605107C	areas n.e. 0.5 m²	Nr	0.86	14.52	–	2.03	16.55	15.97	–	2.23	18.21
M605108	**Prepare and apply three coats Intuclear decorative translucent intumescent varnish to a total loading of 1 litre per 3 m² for Class 1/0 fire protection; glazed doors; in panes 0.5-1.0 m²:**										
M605108A	over 300 mm girth	m²	0.99	16.73	–	4.01	20.74	18.40	–	4.41	22.81
M605108B	n.e. 300 mm girth	m	0.40	6.79	–	1.21	8.00	7.47	–	1.33	8.80
M605109	**Prepare and apply three coats Intuclear decorative translucent intumescent varnish to a total loading of 1 litre per 3 m² for Class 1/0 fire protection; glazed doors; in panes over 1.0 m²:**										
M605109A	over 300 mm girth	m²	0.89	15.12	–	4.01	19.13	16.63	–	4.41	21.04
M605109B	n.e. 300 mm girth	m	0.36	6.11	–	1.21	7.32	6.72	–	1.33	8.05
M605151	**Prepare and apply one coat Intuclear decorative gloss overcoat; to intumescent varnish backgrounds; general surfaces:**										
M605151A	over 300 mm girth	m²	0.15	2.54	–	1.13	3.67	2.79	–	1.24	4.04
M605151B	n.e. 300 mm girth	m	0.06	1.03	–	0.34	1.37	1.13	–	0.37	1.51
M605151C	areas n.e. 0.5 m²	Nr	0.11	1.92	–	0.56	2.48	2.11	–	0.62	2.73
M605152	**Prepare and apply one coat Intuclear decorative gloss overcoat; to intumescent varnish backgrounds; glazed windows and screens; in panes n.e. 0.1 m²:**										
M605152A	over 300 mm girth	m²	0.48	8.06	–	1.13	9.19	8.87	–	1.24	10.11
M605152B	n.e. 300 mm girth	m	0.19	3.26	–	0.34	3.60	3.59	–	0.37	3.96
M605152C	areas n.e. 0.5 m²	Nr	0.36	6.05	–	0.56	6.61	6.66	–	0.62	7.27

Surface Finishes

Major Works 2009		Unit	Labour Hours	Labour Net	Plant Net	Materials Net	Unit Net	Labour Gross	Plant Gross	Materials Gross	Unit Price
								—— (Gross rates include 10% profit) ——			
				£	£	£	£	£	£	£	£
M60	**M60: PAINTING AND CLEAR FINISHING**										
M6051	**Intumescent fire protection; woodwork backgrounds**										
M605153	**Prepare and apply one coat Intuclear decorative gloss overcoat; to intumescent varnish backgrounds; glazed windows and screens; in panes 0.1-0.5 m²:**										
M605153A	over 300 mm girth	m²	0.35	5.94	–	1.13	7.07	6.53	–	1.24	7.78
M605153B	n.e. 300 mm girth	m	0.14	2.41	–	0.34	2.75	2.65	–	0.37	3.03
M605153C	areas n.e. 0.5 m²	Nr	0.26	4.47	–	0.56	5.03	4.92	–	0.62	5.53
M605154	**Prepare and apply one coat Intuclear decorative gloss overcoat; to intumescent varnish backgrounds; glazed windows and screens; in panes 0.5-1.0 m²:**										
M605154A	over 300 mm girth	m²	0.30	5.09	–	1.13	6.22	5.60	–	1.24	6.84
M605154B	n.e. 300 mm girth	m	0.12	2.07	–	0.34	2.41	2.28	–	0.37	2.65
M605155	**Prepare and apply one coat Intuclear decorative gloss overcoat; to intumescent varnish backgrounds; glazed windows and screens; in panes over 1.0 m²:**										
M605155A	over 300 mm girth	m²	0.27	4.58	–	1.13	5.71	5.04	–	1.24	6.28
M605155B	n.e. 300 mm girth	m	0.11	1.85	–	0.34	2.19	2.04	–	0.37	2.41
M605156	**Prepare and apply one coat Intuclear decorative gloss overcoat; to intumescent varnish backgrounds; glazed doors; in panes n.e. 0.1 m²:**										
M605156A	over 300 mm girth	m²	0.48	8.06	–	1.13	9.19	8.87	–	1.24	10.11
M605156B	n.e. 300 mm girth	m	0.19	3.26	–	0.34	3.60	3.59	–	0.37	3.96
M605156C	areas n.e. 0.5 m²	Nr	0.36	6.05	–	0.56	6.61	6.66	–	0.62	7.27
M605157	**Prepare and apply one coat Intuclear decorative gloss overcoat; to intumescent varnish backgrounds; glazed doors; in panes 0.1-0.5 m²:**										
M605157A	over 300 mm girth	m²	0.35	5.94	–	1.13	7.07	6.53	–	1.24	7.78
M605157B	n.e. 300 mm girth	m	0.14	2.41	–	0.34	2.75	2.65	–	0.37	3.03
M605157C	areas n.e. 0.5 m²	Nr	0.26	4.47	–	0.56	5.03	4.92	–	0.62	5.53
M605158	**Prepare and apply one coat Intuclear decorative gloss overcoat; to intumescent varnish backgrounds; glazed doors; in panes 0.5-1.0 m²:**										
M605158A	over 300 mm girth	m²	0.30	5.09	–	1.13	6.22	5.60	–	1.24	6.84
M605158B	n.e. 300 mm girth	m	0.12	2.07	–	0.34	2.41	2.28	–	0.37	2.65
M605159	**Prepare and apply one coat Intuclear decorative gloss overcoat; to intumescent varnish backgrounds; glazed doors; in panes over 1.0 m²:**										
M605159A	over 300 mm girth	m²	0.27	4.58	–	1.13	5.71	5.04	–	1.24	6.28
M605159B	n.e. 300 mm girth	m	0.11	1.85	–	0.34	2.19	2.04	–	0.37	2.41

Major Works 2009	Unit	Labour Hours	Labour Net	Plant Net	Materials Net	Unit Net	Labour Gross	Plant Gross	Materials Gross	Unit Price
			£	£	£	£	(Gross rates include 10% profit) £	£	£	£
M61 **M61: INTUMESCENT COATINGS FOR FIRE PROTECTION OF STEELWORK**										
M6161 **Intumescent fire protection; structural steelwork**										
M616101 **Prepare, epoxy zinc phosphate primer, intumescent Interbond FP build coating to required thickness, Intersheen 54 colour coating overseal; steel sections exposed on three sides; half hour fire protection; FP dry film thickness:**										
M616101A 525 microns; over 300 mm girth	m²	1.60	27.16	–	15.94	43.10	29.88	–	17.53	47.41
M616101B 525 microns; n.e. 300 mm girth	m	0.65	11.01	–	4.79	15.80	12.11	–	5.27	17.38
M616101C 525 microns; areas n.e. 0.5 m²	Nr	1.20	20.38	–	7.98	28.36	22.42	–	8.78	31.20
M616102 **Prepare, epoxy zinc phosphate primer, intumescent Interbond FP build coating to required thickness, Intersheen 54 colour coating overseal; steel sections exposed on three sides; one hour fire protection; FP dry film thickness:**										
M616102A 625 microns; over 300 mm girth	m²	1.60	27.17	–	17.92	45.09	29.89	–	19.71	49.60
M616102B 625 microns; n.e. 300 mm girth	m	0.65	11.03	–	5.39	16.42	12.13	–	5.93	18.06
M616102C 625 microns; areas n.e. 0.5 m²	Nr	1.20	20.38	–	8.97	29.35	22.42	–	9.87	32.29
M616102D 825 microns; over 300 mm girth	m²	2.00	33.96	–	22.05	56.01	37.36	–	24.26	61.61
M616102E 825 microns; n.e. 300 mm girth	m	0.81	13.76	–	6.61	20.37	15.14	–	7.27	22.41
M616102F 825 microns; areas n.e. 0.5 m²	Nr	1.50	25.47	–	11.03	36.50	28.02	–	12.13	40.15
M616102G 1025 microns; over 300 mm girth	m²	2.40	40.75	–	26.03	66.78	44.83	–	28.63	73.46
M616102H 1025 microns; n.e. 300 mm girth	m	0.97	16.47	–	7.82	24.29	18.12	–	8.60	26.72
M616102I 1025 microns; areas n.e. 0.5 m²	Nr	1.80	30.56	–	13.02	43.58	33.62	–	14.32	47.94
M616102J 1125 microns; over 300 mm girth	m²	2.40	40.75	–	28.16	68.91	44.83	–	30.98	75.80
M616102K 1125 microns; n.e. 300 mm girth	m	0.97	16.47	–	8.45	24.92	18.12	–	9.30	27.41
M616102L 1125 microns; areas n.e. 0.5 m²	Nr	1.80	30.56	–	14.09	44.65	33.62	–	15.50	49.12
M616102M 1225 microns; over 300 mm girth	m²	2.40	40.75	–	30.15	70.90	44.83	–	33.17	77.99
M616102N 1225 microns; n.e. 300 mm girth	m	0.97	16.50	–	9.06	25.56	18.15	–	9.97	28.12
M616102O 1225 microns; areas n.e. 0.5 m²	Nr	1.80	30.56	–	15.09	45.65	33.62	–	16.60	50.22
M616102P 1325 microns; over 300 mm girth	m²	2.80	47.54	–	32.14	79.68	52.29	–	35.35	87.65
M616102Q 1325 microns; n.e. 300 mm girth	m	1.13	19.26	–	9.65	28.91	21.19	–	10.62	31.80
M616102R 1325 microns; areas n.e. 0.5 m²	Nr	2.10	35.66	–	16.08	51.74	39.23	–	17.69	56.91
M616102S 1625 microns; over 300 mm girth	m²	3.20	54.33	–	38.25	92.58	59.76	–	42.08	101.84
M616102T 1625 microns; n.e. 300 mm girth	m	1.30	22.01	–	11.48	33.49	24.21	–	12.63	36.84
M616102U 1625 microns; areas n.e. 0.5 m²	Nr	2.40	40.75	–	19.13	59.88	44.83	–	21.04	65.87

Surface Finishes

Major Works 2009		Unit	Labour Hours	Labour Net	Plant Net	Materials Net	Unit Net	Labour Gross	Plant Gross	Materials Gross	Unit Price
								(Gross rates include 10% profit)			
				£	£	£	£	£	£	£	£
M61	**M61: INTUMESCENT COATINGS FOR FIRE PROTECTION OF STEELWORK**										
M6161	**Intumescent fire protection; structural steelwork**										
M616103	**Prepare, epoxy zinc phosphate primer, intumescent Interbond FP build coating to required thickness, Intersheen 54 colour coating overseal; steel sections exposed three sides; one and half hour fire protection; FP dry film thickness:**										
M616103A	2335 microns; over 300 mm girth	m²	4.00	67.92	–	47.95	115.87	74.71	–	52.75	127.46
M616103B	2335 microns; n.e. 300 mm girth	m	1.62	27.50	–	15.83	43.33	30.25	–	17.41	47.66
M616103C	2335 microns; areas n.e. 0.5 m²	Nr	3.00	50.94	–	26.38	77.32	56.03	–	29.02	85.05
M616104	**Prepare, epoxy zinc phosphate primer, intumescent Interbond FP build coating to required thickness, Intersheen 54 colour coating overseal; steel sections exposed four sides; half hour fire protection; FP dry film thickness:**										
M616104A	525 microns; over 300 mm girth	m²	1.60	27.16	–	15.94	43.10	29.88	–	17.53	47.41
M616104B	525 microns; n.e. 300 mm girth	m	0.65	11.01	–	4.79	15.80	12.11	–	5.27	17.38
M616104C	525 microns; areas n.e. 0.5 m²	Nr	1.20	20.38	–	7.98	28.36	22.42	–	8.78	31.20

Major Works 2009		Unit	Labour Hours	Labour Net	Plant Net	Materials Net	Unit Net	Labour Gross	Plant Gross	Materials Gross	Unit Price
								(Gross rates include 10% profit)			
				£	£	£	£	£	£	£	£
M61	**M61: INTUMESCENT COATINGS FOR FIRE PROTECTION OF STEELWORK**										
M6161	**Intumescent fire protection; structural steelwork**										
M616105	**Prepare, epoxy zinc phosphate primer, intumescent Interbond FP build coating to required thickness, Intersheen 54 colour coating overseal; steel sections exposed four sides; one hour fire protection; FP dry film thickness:**										
M616105A	825 microns; over 300 mm girth	m²	2.00	33.96	–	22.05	56.01	37.36	–	24.26	61.61
M616105B	825 microns; n.e. 300 mm girth	m	0.81	13.76	–	6.61	20.37	15.14	–	7.27	22.41
M616105C	825 microns; areas n.e. 0.5 m²	Nr	1.50	25.47	–	11.03	36.50	28.02	–	12.13	40.15
M616105D	1325 microns; over 300 mm girth	m²	2.80	47.54	–	32.14	79.68	52.29	–	35.35	87.65
M616105E	1325 microns; n.e. 300 mm girth	m	1.13	19.19	–	9.65	28.84	21.11	–	10.62	31.72
M616105F	1325 microns; areas n.e. 0.5 m²	Nr	2.10	35.66	–	16.08	51.74	39.23	–	17.69	56.91
M616105G	1625 microns; over 300 mm girth	m²	3.20	54.33	–	38.25	92.58	59.76	–	42.08	101.84
M616105H	1625 microns; n.e. 300 mm girth	m	1.30	22.08	–	11.48	33.56	24.29	–	12.63	36.92
M616105I	1625 microns; areas n.e. 0.5 m²	Nr	2.40	40.75	–	19.13	59.88	44.83	–	21.04	65.87
M616105J	1825 microns; over 300 mm girth	m²	3.20	54.34	–	42.37	96.71	59.77	–	46.61	106.38
M616105K	1825 microns; n.e. 300 mm girth	m	1.30	22.08	–	12.71	34.79	24.29	–	13.98	38.27
M616105L	1825 microns; areas n.e. 0.5 m²	Nr	2.40	40.75	–	21.20	61.95	44.83	–	23.32	68.15
M616105M	2325 microns; over 300 mm girth	m²	4.00	67.92	–	52.46	120.38	74.71	–	57.71	132.42
M616105N	2325 microns; n.e. 300 mm girth	m	1.60	27.17	–	15.75	42.92	29.89	–	17.33	47.21
M616105O	2325 microns; areas n.e. 0.5 m²	Nr	3.00	50.94	–	26.27	77.21	56.03	–	28.90	84.93

FURNITURE AND EQUIPMENT

Major Works 2009		Unit	Labour Hours	Labour Net	Plant Net	Materials Net	Unit Net	Labour Gross	Plant Gross	Materials Gross	Unit Price
								(Gross rates include 10% profit)			
				£	£	£	£	£	£	£	£
N10	**N10: GENERAL FIXTURES, FURNISHINGS AND EQUIPMENT**										
N1004	**Mirrors**										
N100410	**Mirrors; 6 mm thick safety glass; polished bevelled edges; fixing with brass screws including polyethylene washers and screw caps; size:**										
N100410A	450 × 600 mm	Nr	0.75	12.74	–	33.78	46.52	14.01	–	37.16	51.17
N100410C	450 × 900 mm	Nr	0.80	13.59	–	48.51	62.10	14.95	–	53.36	68.31
N100410E	450 × 1200 mm	Nr	0.95	16.13	–	60.26	76.39	17.74	–	66.29	84.03
N100410G	600 × 900 mm	Nr	1.10	18.68	–	63.24	81.92	20.55	–	69.56	90.11
N100410I	600 × 1200 mm	Nr	1.25	21.23	–	84.07	105.30	23.35	–	92.48	115.83
N100410K	600 × 1500 mm	Nr	1.50	25.47	–	101.85	127.32	28.02	–	112.04	140.05
N100410M	750 × 1200 mm	Nr	1.50	25.47	–	104.39	129.86	28.02	–	114.83	142.85
N100410O	750 × 1500 mm	Nr	1.75	29.72	–	126.24	155.96	32.69	–	138.86	171.56
N100410Q	750 × 1800 mm	Nr	2.00	33.96	–	150.11	184.07	37.36	–	165.12	202.48
N1028	**Door mats**										
N102810	**Entrance mats; William Armes Fitzwell; 17 mm thick; laying loose or in matwell frames:**										
N102810A	600 × 450 mm	Nr	0.10	1.70	–	8.71	10.41	1.87	–	9.58	11.45
N102810B	750 × 450 mm	Nr	0.10	1.70	–	10.86	12.56	1.87	–	11.95	13.82
N102810C	750 × 600 mm	Nr	0.11	1.86	–	14.51	16.37	2.05	–	15.96	18.01
N102810D	900 × 600 mm	Nr	0.11	1.87	–	17.39	19.26	2.06	–	19.13	21.19
N102810E	1200 × 750 mm	Nr	0.12	2.04	–	28.98	31.02	2.24	–	31.88	34.12
N1029	**Matwell frames; fabricated, welded or brazed construction with lugs**										
N102922	**Galvanised mild steel angle section; 32 × 32 × 6 mm:**										
N102922A	600 × 450 mm	Nr	0.80	13.58	–	71.17	84.75	14.94	–	78.29	93.23
N102922B	750 × 450 mm	Nr	0.90	15.28	–	77.46	92.74	16.81	–	85.21	102.01
N102922C	750 × 600 mm	Nr	1.00	16.98	–	83.74	100.72	18.68	–	92.11	110.79
N102922D	900 × 600 mm	Nr	1.10	18.68	–	90.03	108.71	20.55	–	99.03	119.58
N102922E	1200 × 750 mm	Nr	1.20	20.38	–	102.58	122.96	22.42	–	112.84	135.26
N102923	**Polished brass angle section; 32 × 32 × 6 mm:**										
N102923A	600 × 450 mm	Nr	1.20	20.38	–	154.16	174.54	22.42	–	169.58	191.99
N102923B	750 × 450 mm	Nr	1.30	22.07	–	172.50	194.57	24.28	–	189.75	214.03
N102923C	750 × 600 mm	Nr	1.40	23.77	–	190.86	214.63	26.15	–	209.95	236.09
N102923D	900 × 600 mm	Nr	1.50	25.47	–	209.22	234.69	28.02	–	230.14	258.16
N102923E	1200 × 750 mm	Nr	1.60	27.17	–	268.42	295.59	29.89	–	295.26	325.15
N102924	**Aluminium angle section; 32 × 32 × 6 mm:**										
N102924A	600 × 450 mm	Nr	1.10	18.68	–	76.33	95.01	20.55	–	83.96	104.51
N102924B	750 × 450 mm	Nr	1.20	20.38	–	85.42	105.80	22.42	–	93.96	116.38
N102924C	750 × 600 mm	Nr	1.30	22.07	–	94.51	116.58	24.28	–	103.96	128.24
N102924D	900 × 600 mm	Nr	1.40	23.77	–	103.60	127.37	26.15	–	113.96	140.11
N102924E	1200 × 750 mm	Nr	1.50	25.47	–	118.14	143.61	28.02	–	129.95	157.97
N1060	**Fire extinguishers**										
N106010	**Halon Small Automatics; fixing support bracket to masonry backgrounds:**										
N106010A	GTP1000	Nr	0.50	8.49	–	42.84	51.33	9.34	–	47.12	56.46
N106010C	GTP2000	Nr	0.60	10.19	–	58.98	69.17	11.21	–	64.88	76.09

Furniture and Equipment

Major Works 2009		Unit	Labour Hours	Labour Net	Plant Net	Materials Net	Unit Net	Labour Gross	Plant Gross	Materials Gross	Unit Price
								(Gross rates include 10% profit)			
				£	£	£	£	£	£	£	£
N11	**N11: DOMESTIC KITCHEN FITTINGS**										
N1110	**Kitchen units; proprietary standard ready assembled; Jewson range**										
N111001	**Base units:**										
N111001A	Flair 1203; 300 × 600 mm drawerline	Nr	0.70	11.89	–	182.77	194.66	13.08	–	201.05	214.13
N111001B	Flair 1204; 400 × 600 mm drawerline	Nr	0.80	13.58	–	199.53	213.11	14.94	–	219.48	234.42
N111001C	Flair 1245; 450 × 600 mm drawerline	Nr	0.85	14.43	–	201.83	216.26	15.87	–	222.01	237.89
N111001D	Flair 1205; 500 × 600 mm drawerline	Nr	0.90	15.28	–	204.30	219.58	16.81	–	224.73	241.54
N111001E	Flair 1206; 600 × 600 mm drawerline	Nr	1.00	16.98	–	221.43	238.41	18.68	–	243.57	262.25
N111001F	Flair 1208; 800 × 600 mm drawerline	Nr	1.20	20.38	–	327.52	347.90	22.42	–	360.27	382.69
N111001G	Flair 1210; 1000 × 600 mm drawerline	Nr	1.40	23.77	–	342.29	366.06	26.15	–	376.52	402.67
N111001H	Flair 1103; 300 × 600 mm highline	Nr	0.70	11.89	–	105.95	117.84	13.08	–	116.55	129.62
N111001I	Flair 1104; 400 × 600 mm highline	Nr	0.80	13.58	–	110.67	124.25	14.94	–	121.74	136.68
N111001J	Flair 1145; 450 × 600 mm highline	Nr	0.85	14.43	–	113.05	127.48	15.87	–	124.36	140.23
N111001K	Flair 1106; 600 × 600 mm highline	Nr	0.90	15.28	–	115.42	130.70	16.81	–	126.96	143.77
N111001L	Flair 1106; 600 × 600 mm highline	Nr	1.00	16.98	–	122.54	139.52	18.68	–	134.79	153.47
N111001M	Flair 1108; 800 × 600 mm highline	Nr	1.20	20.38	–	155.40	175.78	22.42	–	170.94	193.36
N111001N	Flair 1110; 1000 × 600 mm highline	Nr	1.40	23.77	–	167.25	191.02	26.15	–	183.98	210.12
N111011	**Corner base units:**										
N111011A	Flair 2508; 800 × 600 mm; 300 mm door; drawerline	Nr	1.20	20.38	–	221.20	241.58	22.42	–	243.32	265.74
N111011B	Flair 3208; 800 × 600 mm; 400 mm door; drawerline	Nr	1.20	20.38	–	221.36	241.74	22.42	–	243.50	265.91
N111011C	Flair 2608; 800 × 600 mm; 500 mm door; drawerline	Nr	1.20	20.38	–	221.20	241.58	22.42	–	243.32	265.74
N111011D	Flair 2710; 1000 × 600 mm; 400 mm door; drawerline	Nr	1.40	23.77	–	233.20	256.97	26.15	–	256.52	282.67
N111011E	Flair 3210; 1000 × 600 mm; 500 mm door; drawerline	Nr	1.40	23.77	–	233.28	257.05	26.15	–	256.61	282.76
N111011F	Flair 2810; 1000 × 600 mm; 600 mm door; drawerline	Nr	1.40	23.77	–	233.77	257.54	26.15	–	257.15	283.29
N111011G	Flair 2908; 800 × 600 mm; 300 mm door; highline	Nr	1.20	20.38	–	136.44	156.82	22.42	–	150.08	172.50
N111011H	Flair 3410; 800 × 600 mm; 400 mm door; highline	Nr	1.20	20.38	–	148.29	168.67	22.42	–	163.12	185.54
N111011I	Flair 3108; 800 × 600 mm; 400 mm door; highline	Nr	1.20	20.38	–	136.42	156.80	22.42	–	150.06	172.48
N111011J	Flair 3110; 1000 × 600 mm; 500 mm door; highline	Nr	1.40	23.77	–	148.29	172.06	26.15	–	163.12	189.27
N111011K	Flair 3008; 800 × 600 mm; 500 mm door; highline	Nr	1.20	20.38	–	136.44	156.82	22.42	–	150.08	172.50
N111011L	Flair 3101; 925 × 600 mm; L-shaped; highline	Nr	1.60	27.17	–	243.13	270.30	29.89	–	267.44	297.33
N111011M	Flair 3310; 1000 × 600 mm; 600 door; highline	Nr	1.40	23.77	–	148.29	172.06	26.15	–	163.12	189.27

Major Works 2009	Unit	Labour Hours	Labour Net	Plant Net	Materials Net	Unit Net	Labour Gross	Plant Gross	Materials Gross	Unit Price
							(Gross rates include 10% profit)			
			£	£	£	£	£	£	£	£
N11 **N11: DOMESTIC KITCHEN FITTINGS**										
N1110 Kitchen units; proprietary standard ready assembled; Jewson range										
N111021 Sink base units:										
N111021A Flair 2105; 500 × 600 mm sink unit; drawerline.......	Nr	0.90	15.28	–	167.58	182.86	16.81	–	184.34	201.15
N111021B Flair 2106; 600 × 600 mm sink unit................	Nr	1.00	16.98	–	184.16	201.14	18.68	–	202.58	221.25
N111021C Flair 2108; 800 × 600 mm sink unit; drawerline.......	Nr	1.20	20.38	–	293.82	314.20	22.42	–	323.20	345.62
N111021D Flair 2110; 1000 × 600 mm sink unit; drawerline.......	Nr	1.40	23.77	–	277.48	301.25	26.15	–	305.23	331.38
N111031 Store units:										
N111031A Flair 5003; 300 × 600 × 2193 mm high medium larder unit	Nr	1.75	29.72	–	253.10	282.82	32.69	–	278.41	311.10
N111031B Flair 5005; 500 × 600 × 2193 mm high medium larder unit	Nr	1.85	31.41	–	253.10	284.51	34.55	–	278.41	312.96
N111031C Flair 5006; 600 × 600 × 2193 mm high medium larder unit	Nr	1.95	33.11	–	347.91	381.02	36.42	–	382.70	419.12
N111031D Flair 5205; 500 × 600 × 2193 mm high medium broom cupboard..........	Nr	1.85	31.41	–	253.10	284.51	34.55	–	278.41	312.96
N111031E Flair 5203; 300 × 600 × 1485 mm high studio larder unit...................	Nr	1.35	22.92	–	246.30	269.22	25.21	–	270.93	296.14
N111031F Flair 4805; 500 × 600 × 1485 mm high studio larder unit...................	Nr	1.45	24.62	–	246.30	270.92	27.08	–	270.93	298.01
N111031G Flair 7506; 600 × 600 × 1485 mm high studio larder unit...................	Nr	1.55	26.32	–	341.13	367.45	28.95	–	375.24	404.20
N111031H Flair 4705; 500 × 600 × 1485 mm high studio broom cupboard...............	Nr	1.45	24.62	–	246.30	270.92	27.08	–	270.93	298.01
N111041 Appliance housings:										
N111041A Flair 4606; 600 × 600 × 1485 mm high studio appliance housing Type A1 .	Nr	1.55	26.32	–	343.51	369.83	28.95	–	377.86	406.81
N111041B Flair 4706; 600 × 600 × 1485 mm high studio appliance housing Type A2 .	Nr	1.55	26.32	–	414.31	440.63	28.95	–	455.74	484.69
N111041C Flair 5967; 600 × 600 × 1485 mm high studio appliance housing Type B ..	Nr	1.55	26.32	–	414.31	440.63	28.95	–	455.74	484.69
N111041D Flair 5946; 600 × 600 × 1485 mm high studio appliance housing Type C1 .	Nr	1.55	26.32	–	343.51	369.83	28.95	–	377.86	406.81
N111041E Flair 7206; 600 × 600 × 1485 mm high studio appliance housing Type E ..	Nr	1.55	26.32	–	415.13	441.45	28.95	–	456.64	485.60
N111041F Flair 6016; 600 × 600 × 2193 mm high medium appliance housing Type C1 .	Nr	1.95	33.11	–	350.30	383.41	36.42	–	385.33	421.75
N111041G Flair 6026; 600 × 600 × 2193 mm high medium appliance housing Type C2 .	Nr	1.95	33.11	–	350.30	383.41	36.42	–	385.33	421.75
N111041H Flair 6606; 600 × 600 × 2193 mm high medium appliance housing Type F ..	Nr	1.95	33.11	–	366.89	400.00	36.42	–	403.58	440.00

Furniture and Equipment

Major Works 2009		Unit	Labour Hours	Labour Net	Plant Net	Materials Net	Unit Net	Labour Gross	Plant Gross	Materials Gross	Unit Price
								(Gross rates include 10% profit)			
				£	£	£	£	£	£	£	£
N11	**N11: DOMESTIC KITCHEN FITTINGS**										
N1110	**Kitchen units; proprietary standard ready assembled; Jewson range**										
N111051	**Wall units:**										
N111051A	Flair 7703; 300 × 284 × 588 mm high; wall unit	Nr	0.90	15.28	–	86.97	102.25	16.81	–	95.67	112.48
N111051B	Flair 7704; 400 × 284 × 588 mm high; wall unit	Nr	0.95	16.13	–	96.46	112.59	17.74	–	106.11	123.85
N111051C	Flair 7745; 450 × 284 × 588 mm high; wall unit	Nr	1.10	18.68	–	98.82	117.50	20.55	–	108.70	129.25
N111051D	Flair 7705; 500 × 284 × 588 mm high; wall unit	Nr	1.15	19.53	–	101.20	120.73	21.48	–	111.32	132.80
N111051E	Flair 7706; 600 × 284 × 588 mm high; wall unit	Nr	1.35	22.92	–	113.05	135.97	25.21	–	124.36	149.57
N111051F	Flair 7708; 800 × 284 × 588 mm high; wall unit	Nr	1.55	26.32	–	150.66	176.98	28.95	–	165.73	194.68
N111051G	Flair 7710; 1000 × 284 × 588 mm high wall unit	Nr	1.80	30.56	–	157.78	188.34	33.62	–	173.56	207.17
N111051H	Flair 8103; 300 × 284 × 735 mm high; wall unit	Nr	1.00	16.98	–	86.97	103.95	18.68	–	95.67	114.35
N111051I	Flair 8104; 400 × 284 × 735 mm high; wall unit	Nr	1.15	19.53	–	96.46	115.99	21.48	–	106.11	127.59
N111051J	Flair 8145; 450 × 284 × 735 mm high; wall unit	Nr	1.20	20.38	–	98.82	119.20	22.42	–	108.70	131.12
N111051K	Flair 8105; 500 × 284 × 735 mm high; wall unit	Nr	1.25	21.23	–	101.20	122.43	23.35	–	111.32	134.67
N111051L	Flair 8106; 600 × 284 × 735 mm high; wall unit	Nr	1.50	25.47	–	113.05	138.52	28.02	–	124.36	152.37
N111051M	Flair 8108; 800 × 284 × 735 mm high; wall unit	Nr	1.70	28.87	–	150.67	179.54	31.76	–	165.74	197.49
N111051N	Flair 8110; 1000 × 284 × 735 mm high wall unit	Nr	2.00	33.96	–	157.78	191.74	37.36	–	173.56	210.91
N111051O	Flair 8103; 300 × 284 × 735 mm high; wall unit	Nr	0.90	15.28	–	86.97	102.25	16.81	–	95.67	112.48
N111061	**Corner wall units:**										
N111061A	Flair 8306; 625 × 284 × 735 mm high; L-shaped corner wall unit..........	Nr	1.80	30.56	–	207.55	238.11	33.62	–	228.31	261.92
N111061B	Flair 8506; 600 × 284 × 735 mm high; closed corner wall unit................	Nr	1.70	28.87	–	117.80	146.67	31.76	–	129.58	161.34
N111081	**Worktops:**										
N111081A	600 × 30 mm thick; lipped long edges..............	m	1.50	25.47	–	23.66	49.13	28.02	–	26.03	54.04
N111081B	600 × 30 mm thick; double roll edge................	m	1.50	25.47	–	37.22	62.69	28.02	–	40.94	68.96
N111081C	600 × 40 mm thick; single roll edge................	m	1.70	28.87	–	37.22	66.09	31.76	–	40.94	72.70
N111086	**Worktop sundries:**										
N111086A	30 mm jointing strip; rolled edge....................	m	0.60	10.19	–	6.45	16.64	11.21	–	7.10	18.30
N111086B	40 mm jointing strip; rolled edge....................	m	0.70	11.89	–	6.45	18.34	13.08	–	7.10	20.17
N111086C	30 mm jointing strip; square edge....................	m	0.55	9.34	–	6.24	15.58	10.27	–	6.86	17.14
N111086D	30 mm end capping; rolled edge....................	m	0.65	11.04	–	6.24	17.28	12.14	–	6.86	19.01

Major Works 2009		Unit	Labour Hours	Labour Net	Plant Net	Materials Net	Unit Net	Labour Gross	Plant Gross	Materials Gross	Unit Price
				£	£	£	£	£	£	£	£
								(Gross rates include 10% profit)			
N13	**N13: SANITARY APPLIANCES AND FITTINGS**										
N1301	**Sanitary fittings**										
N130101	**Baths; complete with taps and associated fittings; fixing in position:**										
N130101A	pressed steel; PC £200:00..	Nr	3.25	126.72	–	210.00	336.72	139.39	–	231.00	370.39
N130101B	cast iron; PC £350:00	Nr	3.75	146.21	–	367.50	513.71	160.83	–	404.25	565.08
N130101C	acrylic; PC £150:00	Nr	3.00	116.97	–	157.50	274.47	128.67	–	173.25	301.92
N130102	**Basins; complete with taps and associated fittings; fixing in position:**										
N130102A	enamelled steel; PC £50:00.	Nr	2.00	77.98	–	52.50	130.48	85.78	–	57.75	143.53
N130102B	vitreous china; PC £75:00 ..	Nr	2.25	87.73	–	78.75	166.48	96.50	–	86.63	183.13
N130102C	acrylic; PC £60:00	Nr	1.50	58.49	–	63.00	121.49	64.34	–	69.30	133.64
N130112	**Sinks; complete with taps and associated fittings; fixing in position:**										
N130112A	glazed fireclay; PC 140:00..	Nr	1.75	68.23	–	147.00	215.23	75.05	–	161.70	236.75
N130112B	stainless steel; PC 100:00 ..	Nr	1.50	58.49	–	105.00	163.49	64.34	–	115.50	179.84
N130112C	resin; PC 120:00	Nr	1.50	58.49	–	126.00	184.49	64.34	–	138.60	202.94
N130121	**WC suites; complete with cistern, seat and flap and associated fittings; fixing in position:**										
N130121A	high level washdown; PC £175:00................	Nr	2.50	97.48	–	183.75	281.23	107.23	–	202.13	309.35
N130121B	low level washdown; PC £150:00................	Nr	2.00	77.98	–	157.50	235.48	85.78	–	173.25	259.03
N130121C	low level syphonic; PC £300:00................	Nr	2.25	87.73	–	315.00	402.73	96.50	–	346.50	443.00
N130126	**Bidets; complete with taps and associated fittings; fixing in position:**										
N130126A	vitreous china; PC £150:00.	Nr	2.00	77.98	–	157.50	235.48	85.78	–	173.25	259.03
N130131	**Shower trays; complete with fittings; fixing in position:**										
N130131A	fireclay; PC £60:00........	Nr	1.25	48.74	–	63.00	111.74	53.61	–	69.30	122.91
N130131B	acrylic; PC £100:00	Nr	0.75	29.24	–	105.00	134.24	32.16	–	115.50	147.66
N130141	**Shower enclosures; complete with fittings; fixing in position:**										
N130141A	acrylic, three sided; front or side entry; PC £150:00	Nr	1.75	68.23	–	157.50	225.73	75.05	–	173.25	248.30
N130141B	acrylic, two sided; corner entry; PC £250:00.........	Nr	1.50	58.49	–	262.50	320.99	64.34	–	288.75	353.09
N130141C	plastic curtain and rail, one sided; PC £25:00	Nr	0.50	19.50	–	26.25	45.75	21.45	–	28.88	50.33
N130143	**Showers; complete with taps and associated fittings; fixing in position:**										
N130143A	recessed mechanical valve and spray head; PC £150:00	Nr	2.00	77.98	–	157.50	235.48	85.78	–	173.25	259.03
N130143B	recessed thermostatic valve and spray head; PC £300:00	Nr	2.00	77.98	–	315.00	392.98	85.78	–	346.50	432.28
N130143C	surface mounted mechanical valve and spray head; PC £100:00................	Nr	1.00	38.99	–	105.00	143.99	42.89	–	115.50	158.39
N130143D	surface mounted thermostatic valve and spray head; PC £200:00.........	Nr	1.00	38.99	–	210.00	248.99	42.89	–	231.00	273.89

Furniture and Equipment

Major Works 2009		Unit	Labour Hours	Labour Net	Plant Net	Materials Net	Unit Net	Labour Gross	Plant Gross	Materials Gross	Unit Price
								(Gross rates include 10% profit)			
				£	£	£	£	£	£	£	£
N15	**N15: SIGNS AND NOTICES**										
N1510	**Internal signage**										
N151010	**Aluminium plate signage; lettered with lacquer finish; drilled and countersunk four times; fixing to timber substrate with screws; size:**										
N151010B	150 × 75 mm..........	Nr	0.40	6.79	–	3.68	10.47	7.47	–	4.05	11.52
N151010D	200 × 100 mm..........	Nr	0.60	10.19	–	8.28	18.47	11.21	–	9.11	20.32
N151010G	600 × 300 mm..........	Nr	0.80	13.59	–	19.14	32.73	14.95	–	21.05	36.00

BUILDING FABRIC SUNDRIES

Major Works 2009		Unit	Labour Hours	Labour Net	Plant Net	Materials Net	Unit Net	Labour Gross	Plant Gross	Materials Gross	Unit Price
								(Gross rates include 10% profit)			
				£	£	£	£	£	£	£	£
P10	**P10: SUNDRY INSULATION, PROOFING WORK AND FIRE STOPS**										
P1020	**Insulation quilts**										
P102010	**Crown glass fibre insulation quilt; generally; thickness:**										
P102010A	horizontal; 60 mm thick....	m²	0.07	1.19	–	1.54	2.73	1.31	–	1.69	3.00
P102010B	horizontal; 80 mm thick....	m²	0.08	1.36	–	1.83	3.19	1.50	–	2.01	3.51
P102010C	horizontal; 100 mm thick...	m²	0.09	1.52	–	2.27	3.79	1.67	–	2.50	4.17
P102010D	horizontal; 150 mm thick...	m²	0.14	2.37	–	4.42	6.79	2.61	–	4.86	7.47
P102010E	vertical; 60 mm thick	m²	0.12	2.04	–	1.54	3.58	2.24	–	1.69	3.94
P102010F	vertical; 80 mm thick	m²	0.14	2.38	–	1.83	4.21	2.62	–	2.01	4.63
P102010G	vertical; 100 mm thick	m²	0.18	3.05	–	2.27	5.32	3.36	–	2.50	5.85
P102010H	vertical; 150 mm thick	m²	0.25	4.24	–	4.42	8.66	4.66	–	4.86	9.53
P102020	**Crown glass fibre insulation roll; laid horizontally between joists at 400 mm centres; thickness:**										
P102020A	60 mm thick	m²	0.10	1.70	–	1.54	3.24	1.87	–	1.69	3.56
P102020B	80 mm thick	m²	0.12	2.04	–	1.83	3.87	2.24	–	2.01	4.26
P102020C	100 mm thick	m²	0.14	2.37	–	2.27	4.64	2.61	–	2.50	5.10
P102020D	150 mm thick	m²	0.20	3.39	–	4.42	7.81	3.73	–	4.86	8.59
P102020E	170 mm thick	m²	0.21	3.57	–	5.07	8.64	3.93	–	5.58	9.50
P102020F	200 mm thick	m²	0.22	3.73	–	6.06	9.79	4.10	–	6.67	10.77
P102022	**Crown glass fibre insulation roll; laid horizontally between joists at 600 mm centres; thickness:**										
P102022A	60 mm thick	m²	0.08	1.36	–	1.54	2.90	1.50	–	1.69	3.19
P102022B	80 mm thick	m²	0.10	1.70	–	1.83	3.53	1.87	–	2.01	3.88
P102022C	100 mm thick	m²	0.12	2.03	–	2.27	4.30	2.23	–	2.50	4.73
P102022D	150 mm thick	m²	0.18	3.05	–	4.42	7.47	3.36	–	4.86	8.22
P102022E	170 mm thick	m²	0.19	3.23	–	5.07	8.30	3.55	–	5.58	9.13
P102022F	200 mm thick	m²	0.20	3.39	–	6.06	9.45	3.73	–	6.67	10.40
P102025	**Crown glass fibre insulation roll; laid horizontally over joists; thickness:**										
P102025C	100 mm thick	m²	0.10	1.69	–	2.27	3.96	1.86	–	2.50	4.36
P102025D	150 mm thick	m²	0.16	2.71	–	4.42	7.13	2.98	–	4.86	7.84
P102025E	170 mm thick	m²	0.17	2.89	–	5.07	7.96	3.18	–	5.58	8.76
P102025F	200 mm thick	m²	0.18	3.05	–	6.06	9.11	3.36	–	6.67	10.02
P102030	**DriTherm Cavity Slab glass fibre wall insulation; medium density; fitting between wall ties; securing with retaining clips; thickness:**										
P102030A	50 mm thick	m²	0.16	4.02	–	2.40	6.42	4.42	–	2.64	7.06
P102030B	65 mm thick	m²	0.17	4.27	–	3.78	8.05	4.70	–	4.16	8.86
P102030C	75 mm thick	m²	0.18	4.53	–	4.08	8.61	4.98	–	4.49	9.47
P102030D	85 mm thick	m²	0.19	4.77	–	4.48	9.25	5.25	–	4.93	10.18
P102030E	100 mm thick	m²	0.21	5.27	–	5.18	10.45	5.80	–	5.70	11.50

Building Fabric Sundries

Major Works 2009		Unit	Labour Hours	Labour Net	Plant Net	Materials Net	Unit Net	Labour Gross	Plant Gross	Materials Gross	Unit Price
								(Gross rates include 10% profit)			
				£	£	£	£	£	£	£	£
P10	**P10: SUNDRY INSULATION, PROOFING WORK AND FIRE STOPS**										
P1020	**Insulation quilts**										
P102032	**DriTherm Cavity Slab 32 glassfibre wall insulation; high density; fitting between wall ties; securing with retaining clips; thickness:**										
P102032A	50 mm thick	m²	0.15	3.77	–	6.09	9.86	4.15	–	6.70	10.85
P102032B	65 mm thick	m²	0.17	4.28	–	7.98	12.26	4.71	–	8.78	13.49
P102032C	75 mm thick	m²	0.18	4.53	–	9.21	13.74	4.98	–	10.13	15.11
P102032D	85 mm thick	m²	0.19	4.78	–	10.39	15.17	5.26	–	11.43	16.69
P102032E	100 mm thick	m²	0.21	5.28	–	12.02	17.30	5.81	–	13.22	19.03
P102034	**DriTherm Cavity Slab 34 glass fibre wall insulation; medium to high density; fitting between wall ties; securing with retaining clips; thickness:**										
P102034A	50 mm thick	m²	0.16	4.02	–	4.88	8.90	4.42	–	5.37	9.79
P102034B	65 mm thick	m²	0.17	4.27	–	6.04	10.31	4.70	–	6.64	11.34
P102034C	75 mm thick	m²	0.18	4.52	–	6.98	11.50	4.97	–	7.68	12.65
P102034D	85 mm thick	m²	0.19	4.77	–	7.85	12.62	5.25	–	8.64	13.88
P102034E	100 mm thick	m²	0.21	5.28	–	9.09	14.37	5.81	–	10.00	15.81
P102040	**Actis Tri-Iso pitched roof insulation; fixed to roof timbers by stapling at 50 mm centres; taping with Isodhesif Alu tape at overlapping joints; over or under rafters:**										
P102040A	Tri-Iso Super 9	m²	0.33	5.61	–	14.16	19.77	6.17	–	15.58	21.75
P102040B	Triso-Super 10	m²	0.33	5.60	–	15.96	21.56	6.16	–	17.56	23.72

Major Works 2009		Unit	Labour Hours	Labour Net	Plant Net	Materials Net	Unit Net	Labour Gross	Plant Gross	Materials Gross	Unit Price
								(Gross rates include 10% profit)			
				£	£	£	£	£	£	£	£
P10	**P10: SUNDRY INSULATION, PROOFING WORK AND FIRE STOPS**										
P1030	**Insulation boards**										
P103010	**Dow Floormate expanded polystyrene boards; fixed horizontally with wedges to floors; thickness:**										
P103010A	25 mm thick	m²	0.12	2.04	–	5.43	7.47	2.24	–	5.97	8.22
P103010B	50 mm thick	m²	0.13	2.21	–	10.46	12.67	2.43	–	11.51	13.94
P103010C	70 mm thick	m²	0.14	2.38	–	14.78	17.16	2.62	–	16.26	18.88
P103010D	100 mm thick	m²	0.16	2.72	–	19.09	21.81	2.99	–	21.00	23.99
P103015	**VR Jablite Jabfloor 70 polystyrene thermal insulation sheets to concrete slab ground floor construction; laid to floors; thickness:**										
P103015A	25 mm	m²	0.12	2.03	–	3.90	5.93	2.23	–	4.29	6.52
P103015B	40 mm	m²	0.13	2.20	–	6.24	8.44	2.42	–	6.86	9.28
P103015C	50 mm	m²	0.13	2.21	–	7.81	10.02	2.43	–	8.59	11.02
P103015D	60 mm	m²	0.14	2.37	–	9.37	11.74	2.61	–	10.31	12.91
P103015E	75 mm	m²	0.14	2.37	–	11.70	14.07	2.61	–	12.87	15.48
P103015F	100 mm	m²	0.15	2.55	–	15.61	18.16	2.81	–	17.17	19.98
P103015G	125 mm	m²	0.16	2.72	–	22.66	25.38	2.99	–	24.93	27.92
P103015H	30 × 150 mm high edge trim..................	m	0.05	0.85	–	0.76	1.61	0.94	–	0.84	1.77
P103020	**Glass fibre medium density insulation boards; laid horizontally or fixed vertically; thickness:**										
P103020A	horizontal; 25 mm thick....	m²	0.12	2.04	–	5.57	7.61	2.24	–	6.13	8.37
P103020B	horizontal; 50 mm thick....	m²	0.14	2.38	–	6.98	9.36	2.62	–	7.68	10.30
P103020C	horizontal; 75 mm thick....	m²	0.17	2.88	–	10.87	13.75	3.17	–	11.96	15.13
P103020D	vertical; 25 mm thick	m²	0.18	3.06	–	5.57	8.63	3.37	–	6.13	9.49
P103020E	vertical; 50 mm thick	m²	0.21	3.57	–	6.98	10.55	3.93	–	7.68	11.61
P103020F	vertical; 75 mm thick	m²	0.25	4.24	–	10.87	15.11	4.66	–	11.96	16.62
P103030	**Glass fibre medium density insulation board underlay to roofing; bedding in hot bitumen; thickness:**										
P103030A	25 mm thick	m²	0.15	3.52	0.35	6.84	10.71	3.87	0.39	7.52	11.78
P103030B	50 mm thick	m²	0.15	3.51	0.35	8.26	12.12	3.86	0.39	9.09	13.33
P103030C	75 mm thick	m²	0.15	3.52	0.35	12.14	16.01	3.87	0.39	13.35	17.61
P103040	**Insulation board underlay to roofing; BS 1142 part 3; bedding in hot bitumen; thickness:**										
P103040A	12 mm thick	m²	0.15	3.51	0.35	4.03	7.89	3.86	0.39	4.43	8.68
P103050	**Jablite expanded polystyrene cavity wall insulation; fitting between wall ties; securing with retaining clips; thickness:**										
P103050A	25 mm thick	m²	0.15	3.77	–	2.36	6.13	4.15	–	2.60	6.74
P103050B	50 mm thick	m²	0.16	4.02	–	3.34	7.36	4.42	–	3.67	8.10
P103050C	75 mm thick	m²	0.18	4.52	–	5.16	9.68	4.97	–	5.68	10.65
P103050D	100 mm thick	m²	0.21	5.27	–	19.09	24.36	5.80	–	21.00	26.80

Building Fabric Sundries

Major Works 2009		Unit	Labour Hours	Labour Net	Plant Net	Materials Net	Unit Net	Labour Gross	Plant Gross	Materials Gross	Unit Price
				£	£	£	£	£	£	£	£
								(Gross rates include 10% profit)			
P10	**P10: SUNDRY INSULATION, PROOFING WORK AND FIRE STOPS**										
P1030	**Insulation boards**										
P103060	**Celotex tuff-R rigid polyurethane foam insulation board; foil faced both sides cut and mechanically fixed; aluminium foil self-adhesive taped joints; board thickness:**										
P103060A	12 mm	m²	0.23	3.90	–	6.25	10.15	4.29	–	6.88	11.17
P103060B	20 mm	m²	0.25	4.25	–	8.06	12.31	4.68	–	8.87	13.54
P103060C	25 mm	m²	0.26	4.41	–	9.23	13.64	4.85	–	10.15	15.00
P103060D	30 mm	m²	0.31	5.27	–	10.17	15.44	5.80	–	11.19	16.98
P103060E	35 mm	m²	0.36	6.12	–	11.18	17.30	6.73	–	12.30	19.03
P103060F	40 mm	m²	0.40	6.80	–	12.06	18.86	7.48	–	13.27	20.75
P103060G	45 mm	m²	0.45	7.64	–	13.42	21.06	8.40	–	14.76	23.17
P103060H	50 mm	m²	0.48	8.15	–	14.44	22.59	8.97	–	15.88	24.85
P103060I	55 mm	m²	0.52	8.83	–	15.83	24.66	9.71	–	17.41	27.13
P103060J	60 mm	m²	0.58	9.85	–	17.22	27.07	10.84	–	18.94	29.78
P103060K	65 mm	m²	0.62	10.52	–	18.60	29.12	11.57	–	20.46	32.03
P103060L	70 mm	m²	0.65	11.04	–	19.96	31.00	12.14	–	21.96	34.10
P103060M	80 mm	m²	0.68	11.54	–	22.64	34.18	12.69	–	24.90	37.60
P103060N	90 mm	m²	0.71	12.06	–	24.99	37.05	13.27	–	27.49	40.76
P103070	**Kingspan Kooltherm K7 Pitched Roof Board; foil faced both sides; cut and mechanically fixed over, between or under rafters; aluminium foil self adhesive taped joints; thickness:**										
P103070A	20 mm	m²	0.25	4.24	–	5.23	9.47	4.66	–	5.75	10.42
P103070B	25 mm	m²	0.26	4.41	–	5.79	10.20	4.85	–	6.37	11.22
P103070C	30 mm	m²	0.31	5.27	–	6.35	11.62	5.80	–	6.99	12.78
P103070D	35 mm	m²	0.36	6.11	–	6.94	13.05	6.72	–	7.63	14.36
P103070E	40 mm	m²	0.40	6.80	–	7.43	14.23	7.48	–	8.17	15.65
P103070F	50 mm	m²	0.48	8.15	–	8.87	17.02	8.97	–	9.76	18.72
P103070G	60 mm	m²	0.58	9.85	–	10.35	20.20	10.84	–	11.39	22.22
P103070H	70 mm	m²	0.65	11.04	–	11.93	22.97	12.14	–	13.12	25.27
P103073	**Kingspan Thermapitch TP10 rigid urethane insulation board; foil faced both sides secured with Helifix In-Skew fixings over, between or under rafters; aluminium foil self-adhesive taped joints; thickness:**										
P103073A	17 mm	m²	0.23	3.91	–	6.76	10.67	4.30	–	7.44	11.74
P103073B	20 mm	m²	0.25	4.24	–	7.29	11.53	4.66	–	8.02	12.68
P103073C	25 mm	m²	0.26	4.41	–	8.14	12.55	4.85	–	8.95	13.81
P103073D	30 mm	m²	0.31	5.26	–	8.75	14.01	5.79	–	9.63	15.41
P103073E	35 mm	m²	0.36	6.11	–	9.43	15.54	6.72	–	10.37	17.09
P103073F	40 mm	m²	0.40	6.79	–	9.95	16.74	7.47	–	10.95	18.41
P103073G	45 mm	m²	0.44	7.47	–	10.69	18.16	8.22	–	11.76	19.98
P103073H	50 mm	m²	0.48	8.15	–	11.44	19.59	8.97	–	12.58	21.55
P103073I	60 mm	m²	0.57	9.68	–	13.26	22.94	10.65	–	14.59	25.23
P103073J	70 mm	m²	0.63	10.70	–	14.96	25.66	11.77	–	16.46	28.23
P103073K	75 mm	m²	0.66	11.21	–	15.74	26.95	12.33	–	17.31	29.65
P103073L	80 mm	m²	0.72	12.22	–	16.73	28.95	13.44	–	18.40	31.85
P103073M	90 mm	m²	0.78	13.25	–	18.29	31.54	14.58	–	20.12	34.69
P103073N	100 mm	m²	0.85	14.43	–	19.88	34.31	15.87	–	21.87	37.74

Major Works 2009		Unit	Labour Hours	Labour Net	Plant Net	Materials Net	Unit Net	Labour Gross	Plant Gross	Materials Gross	Unit Price
				£	£	£	£	£	£	£	£
								(Gross rates include 10% profit)			
P10	**P10: SUNDRY INSULATION, PROOFING WORK AND FIRE STOPS**										
P1030	**Insulation boards**										
P103075	**Kingspan Thermawall TW50 rigid urethane insulation board; foil faced both sides partial cavity fill; cutting and fitting around wall ties and retaining disks; thickness:**										
P103075A	17 mm	m²	0.15	2.55	–	4.39	6.94	2.81	–	4.83	7.63
P103075B	20 mm	m²	0.15	2.54	–	4.78	7.32	2.79	–	5.26	8.05
P103075C	25 mm	m²	0.15	2.55	–	5.45	8.00	2.81	–	6.00	8.80
P103075D	30 mm	m²	0.16	2.72	–	6.11	8.83	2.99	–	6.72	9.71
P103075E	35 mm	m²	0.16	2.71	–	6.65	9.36	2.98	–	7.32	10.30
P103075F	40 mm	m²	0.17	2.89	–	7.67	10.56	3.18	–	8.44	11.62
P103075G	50 mm	m²	0.18	3.06	–	9.25	12.31	3.37	–	10.18	13.54
P103075H	60 mm	m²	0.19	3.22	–	11.05	14.27	3.54	–	12.16	15.70
P103075I	75 mm	m²	0.20	3.40	–	13.65	17.05	3.74	–	15.02	18.76
P1040	**Insulation loose fill**										
P104010	**Vermiculite bead insulation; loose fill poured between joists at 400 mm centres thickness:**										
P104010A	50 mm thick	m²	0.14	2.38	–	5.80	8.18	2.62	–	6.38	9.00
P104010B	75 mm thick	m²	0.20	3.40	–	8.64	12.04	3.74	–	9.50	13.24
P104010C	100 mm thick	m²	0.27	4.58	–	11.49	16.07	5.04	–	12.64	17.68
P104010D	150 mm thick	m²	0.35	5.94	–	17.29	23.23	6.53	–	19.02	25.55
P1060	**Fire barriers**										
P106010	**Rockwool fire barrier; plain faced roll thickness:**										
P106010A	60 mm thick	m²	0.17	2.88	–	6.68	9.56	3.17	–	7.35	10.52
P106015	**Rockwool fire barrier; foil faced one side; thickness:**										
P106015A	60 mm thick	m²	0.20	3.39	–	9.16	12.55	3.73	–	10.08	13.81
P1080	**Fire stops**										
P108010	**Rockwool fire stops; fitted between top of masonry wall and underside of concrete soffit; size of void:**										
P108010A	30 mm deep × 100 mm wide	m	0.06	1.02	–	4.42	5.44	1.12	–	4.86	5.98
P108010B	50 mm deep × 100 mm wide	m	0.07	1.19	–	5.82	7.01	1.31	–	6.40	7.71
P108010C	100 mm deep × 100 mm wide	m	0.09	1.53	–	9.28	10.81	1.68	–	10.21	11.89
P108010D	30 mm deep × 150 mm wide	m	0.07	1.19	–	6.68	7.87	1.31	–	7.35	8.66
P108010E	50 mm deep × 150 mm wide	m	0.08	1.36	–	8.68	10.04	1.50	–	9.55	11.04
P108010F	100 mm deep × 150 mm wide	m	0.10	1.70	–	13.86	15.56	1.87	–	15.25	17.12
P108010G	30 mm deep × 200 mm wide	m	0.08	1.35	–	8.95	10.30	1.49	–	9.85	11.33
P108010H	50 mm deep × 200 mm wide	m	0.10	1.69	–	11.69	13.38	1.86	–	12.86	14.72
P108010I	100 mm deep × 200 mm wide	m	0.12	2.04	–	18.44	20.48	2.24	–	20.28	22.53

Building Fabric Sundries

Major Works 2009		Unit	Labour Hours	Labour Net	Plant Net	Materials Net	Unit Net	Labour Gross	Plant Gross	Materials Gross	Unit Price
								(Gross rates include 10% profit)			
				£	£	£	£	£	£	£	£
P11	**P11: FOAMED, FIBRE AND BEAD CAVITY WALL INSULATION**										
P1101	**Blown fibre cavity insulation**										
P110101	**Granulated mineral fibre; drilling walls internally or externally and making good on completion; width of cavity:**										
P110101A	50 mm	m²	–	–	–	4.29	4.29	–	–	4.72	4.72
P110101B	75 mm	m²	–	–	–	4.58	4.58	–	–	5.04	5.04
P110101C	100 mm	m²	–	–	–	4.87	4.88	–	–	5.36	5.37
P20	**P20: UNFRAMED ISOLATED TRIMS, SKIRTINGS AND SUNDRY ITEMS**										
P2011	**Architraves, skirtings, picture rails or the like; wrought softwood; basic sizes**										
P201101	**Architraves; bullnosed or chamfered and rounded:**										
P201101A	19 × 50 mm	m	0.08	1.36	–	0.72	2.08	1.50	–	0.79	2.29
P201101B	19 × 75 mm	m	0.08	1.36	–	1.05	2.41	1.50	–	1.16	2.65
P201101C	19 × 100 mm	m	0.08	1.36	–	1.38	2.74	1.50	–	1.52	3.01
P201101D	25 × 50 mm	m	0.08	1.36	–	0.92	2.28	1.50	–	1.01	2.51
P201101E	25 × 75 mm	m	0.08	1.36	–	1.37	2.73	1.50	–	1.51	3.00
P201101F	25 × 100 mm	m	0.08	1.35	–	1.82	3.17	1.49	–	2.00	3.49
P201105	**Architraves; moulded:**										
P201105G	19 × 50 mm	m	0.10	1.70	–	0.87	2.57	1.87	–	0.96	2.83
P201105H	19 × 75 mm	m	0.10	1.70	–	1.27	2.97	1.87	–	1.40	3.27
P201105I	19 × 100 mm	m	0.10	1.70	–	1.70	3.40	1.87	–	1.87	3.74
P201105J	25 × 50 mm	m	0.12	2.03	–	1.21	3.24	2.23	–	1.33	3.56
P201105K	25 × 75 mm	m	0.12	2.04	–	1.80	3.84	2.24	–	1.98	4.22
P201105L	25 × 100 mm	m	0.12	2.03	–	2.70	4.73	2.23	–	2.97	5.20
P201105M	25 × 125 mm	m	0.14	2.38	–	3.38	5.76	2.62	–	3.72	6.34
P201105N	25 × 150 mm	m	0.14	2.38	–	3.56	5.94	2.62	–	3.92	6.53
P201105O	25 × 175 mm	m	0.14	2.38	–	4.22	6.60	2.62	–	4.64	7.26
P201116	**Skirtings; bullnosed or chamfered and rounded:**										
P201116A	19 × 75 mm	m	0.08	1.36	–	1.05	2.41	1.50	–	1.16	2.65
P201116B	19 × 100 mm	m	0.08	1.36	–	1.37	2.73	1.50	–	1.51	3.00
P201117	**Skirtings; dual purpose:**										
P201117C	19 × 100 mm	m	0.08	1.36	–	1.70	3.06	1.50	–	1.87	3.37
P201118	**Skirtings; pencil rounded:**										
P201118D	25 × 75 mm	m	0.08	1.36	–	1.37	2.73	1.50	–	1.51	3.00
P201118E	25 × 100 mm	m	0.08	1.35	–	1.82	3.17	1.49	–	2.00	3.49
P201118F	25 × 150 mm	m	0.10	1.69	–	2.69	4.38	1.86	–	2.96	4.82
P201119	**Skirtings; moulded:**										
P201119G	19 × 125 mm	m	0.12	2.04	–	2.10	4.14	2.24	–	2.31	4.55
P201119H	19 × 175 mm	m	0.14	2.38	–	2.96	5.34	2.62	–	3.26	5.87
P201119I	25 × 100 mm	m	0.12	2.03	–	2.70	4.73	2.23	–	2.97	5.20
P201119J	25 × 125 mm	m	0.14	2.38	–	3.38	5.76	2.62	–	3.72	6.34
P201119K	25 × 150 mm	m	0.14	2.38	–	3.56	5.94	2.62	–	3.92	6.53
P201119L	25 × 175 mm	m	0.14	2.38	–	4.22	6.60	2.62	–	4.64	7.26
P201126	**Picture rails; moulded:**										
P201126A	19 × 50 mm	m	0.10	1.70	–	0.87	2.57	1.87	–	0.96	2.83
P201126B	25 × 50 mm	m	0.10	1.70	–	1.13	2.83	1.87	–	1.24	3.11
P201126C	25 × 75 mm	m	0.12	2.03	–	1.43	3.46	2.23	–	1.57	3.81
P201126D	32 × 75 mm	m	0.12	2.03	–	1.82	3.85	2.23	–	2.00	4.24
P201136	**Dado rails; moulded:**										
P201136A	13 × 25 mm	m	0.10	1.70	–	0.48	2.18	1.87	–	0.53	2.40
P201136B	19 × 38 mm	m	0.10	1.70	–	0.71	2.41	1.87	–	0.78	2.65
P201136C	25 × 50 mm	m	0.12	2.03	–	1.20	3.23	2.23	–	1.32	3.55
P201136D	25 × 63 mm	m	0.12	2.04	–	1.53	3.57	2.24	–	1.68	3.93

Major Works 2009		Unit	Labour Hours	Labour Net	Plant Net	Materials Net	Unit Net	Labour Gross	Plant Gross	Materials Gross	Unit Price
								(Gross rates include 10% profit)			
				£	£	£	£	£	£	£	£
P20	**P20: UNFRAMED ISOLATED TRIMS, SKIRTINGS AND SUNDRY ITEMS**										
P2016	**Architraves, skirtings or the like; MDF mouldings; basic sizes**										
P201601	**Architraves:**										
P201601A	18 × 75 mm Torus	m	0.10	1.69	–	2.63	4.32	1.86	–	2.89	4.75
P201601B	18 × 63 mm Torus	m	0.10	1.70	–	2.25	3.95	1.87	–	2.48	4.35
P201601C	18 × 75 mm Ogee	m	0.10	1.70	–	2.62	4.32	1.87	–	2.88	4.75
P201601D	18 × 63 mm Ogee	m	0.10	1.70	–	2.25	3.95	1.87	–	2.48	4.35
P201601E	14.5 × 50 mm chamfered and rounded	m	0.08	1.36	–	1.57	2.93	1.50	–	1.73	3.22
P201601F	14.5 × 50 mm pencil rounded	m	0.08	1.36	–	1.57	2.93	1.50	–	1.73	3.22
P201602	**Skirtings:**										
P201602A	18 × 175 mm Torus	m	0.14	2.37	–	5.62	7.99	2.61	–	6.18	8.79
P201602B	18 × 150 mm Torus	m	0.14	2.38	–	4.85	7.23	2.62	–	5.34	7.95
P201602C	18 × 125 mm Torus	m	0.14	2.38	–	4.10	6.48	2.62	–	4.51	7.13
P201602D	18 × 150 mm Ogee	m	0.14	2.38	–	4.85	7.23	2.62	–	5.34	7.95
P201602E	18 × 125 mm Ogee	m	0.14	2.38	–	4.10	6.48	2.62	–	4.51	7.13
P201602F	14.5 × 100 mm chamfered and rounded	m	0.08	1.35	–	3.00	4.35	1.49	–	3.30	4.79
P201602G	14.5 × 75 mm chamfered and rounded	m	0.08	1.36	–	2.27	3.63	1.50	–	2.50	3.99
P201602H	14.5 × 100 mm pencil rounded	m	0.08	1.36	–	3.36	4.72	1.50	–	3.70	5.19
P201602I	14.5 × 75 mm pencil rounded	m	0.08	1.36	–	2.55	3.91	1.50	–	2.81	4.30
P2021	**Cover fillets, trims or the like; wrought softwood; basic sizes**										
P202104	**Cover fillets:**										
P202104A	13 × 25 mm	m	0.05	0.85	–	0.55	1.40	0.94	–	0.61	1.54
P202104B	13 × 50 mm	m	0.05	0.85	–	1.03	1.88	0.94	–	1.13	2.07
P202104C	13 × 75 mm	m	0.05	0.85	–	1.38	2.23	0.94	–	1.52	2.45
P2022	**Beads, stops or the like; wrought softwood; basic sizes**										
P202216	**Beads:**										
P202216A	6 × 13 mm	m	0.05	0.85	–	0.21	1.06	0.94	–	0.23	1.17
P202216B	6 × 19 mm	m	0.05	0.85	–	0.31	1.16	0.94	–	0.34	1.28
P202216C	6 × 25 mm	m	0.05	0.85	–	0.42	1.27	0.94	–	0.46	1.40
P202216D	13 × 13 mm	m	0.08	1.36	–	0.31	1.67	1.50	–	0.34	1.84
P202216E	13 × 19 mm	m	0.08	1.36	–	0.42	1.78	1.50	–	0.46	1.96
P202216F	13 × 25 mm	m	0.08	1.36	–	0.55	1.91	1.50	–	0.61	2.10
P202216G	13 × 32 mm	m	0.08	1.35	–	0.69	2.04	1.49	–	0.76	2.24
P202216H	19 × 19 mm	m	0.10	1.70	–	0.55	2.25	1.87	–	0.61	2.48
P202216I	19 × 25 mm	m	0.10	1.70	–	0.73	2.43	1.87	–	0.80	2.67
P202216J	19 × 32 mm	m	0.10	1.70	–	0.83	2.53	1.87	–	0.91	2.78
P202217	**Stops:**										
P202217A	13 × 25 mm	m	0.05	0.85	–	0.55	1.40	0.94	–	0.61	1.54
P202217B	13 × 38 mm	m	0.05	0.85	–	0.78	1.63	0.94	–	0.86	1.79
P202217C	13 × 50 mm	m	0.05	0.85	–	1.03	1.88	0.94	–	1.13	2.07
P202217D	19 × 25 mm	m	0.08	1.36	–	0.72	2.08	1.50	–	0.79	2.29
P202217E	19 × 38 mm	m	0.08	1.36	–	0.91	2.27	1.50	–	1.00	2.50
P202217F	19 × 50 mm	m	0.08	1.36	–	1.16	2.52	1.50	–	1.28	2.77
P202217G	25 × 25 mm	m	0.10	1.70	–	1.02	2.72	1.87	–	1.12	2.99
P202217H	25 × 38 mm	m	0.10	1.70	–	1.17	2.87	1.87	–	1.29	3.16
P202217I	25 × 50 mm	m	0.10	1.70	–	1.26	2.96	1.87	–	1.39	3.26

Building Fabric Sundries

Major Works 2009		Unit	Labour Hours	Labour Net	Plant Net	Materials Net	Unit Net	Labour Gross	Plant Gross	Materials Gross	Unit Price
								(Gross rates include 10% profit)			
				£	£	£	£	£	£	£	£
P20	**P20: UNFRAMED ISOLATED TRIMS, SKIRTINGS AND SUNDRY ITEMS**										
P2024	**Edgings, nosings or the like; wrought softwood; basic sizes**										
P202423	**Edgings:**										
P202423A	13 mm quadrant	m	0.08	1.36	–	0.29	1.65	1.50	–	0.32	1.82
P202423B	19 mm quadrant	m	0.08	1.36	–	0.56	1.92	1.50	–	0.62	2.11
P202423C	25 mm quadrant	m	0.08	1.36	–	1.05	2.41	1.50	–	1.16	2.65
P202423D	32 mm quadrant	m	0.08	1.36	–	1.19	2.55	1.50	–	1.31	2.81
P202423E	19 mm half round	m	0.08	1.36	–	0.56	1.92	1.50	–	0.62	2.11
P202423F	25 mm half round	m	0.08	1.36	–	1.05	2.41	1.50	–	1.16	2.65
P202423G	38 mm half round	m	0.08	1.36	–	1.36	2.72	1.50	–	1.50	2.99
P202423H	19 mm rebated half round . .	m	0.10	1.70	–	0.83	2.53	1.87	–	0.91	2.78
P202423I	25 × 25 mm scotia	m	0.10	1.70	–	1.25	2.95	1.87	–	1.38	3.25
P202423J	38 × 38 mm scotia	m	0.12	2.04	–	1.57	3.61	2.24	–	1.73	3.97
P202423K	50 × 50 mm scotia	m	0.12	2.04	–	2.35	4.39	2.24	–	2.59	4.83
P202425	**Nosings:**										
P202425A	25 × 50 mm; nosed	m	0.15	2.55	–	1.53	4.08	2.81	–	1.68	4.49
P202425B	32 × 50 mm; nosed	m	0.15	2.54	–	1.65	4.19	2.79	–	1.82	4.61
P202425C	32 × 50 mm; nosed scotia	m	0.15	2.55	–	1.90	4.45	2.81	–	2.09	4.90
P2025	**1.5 mm laminated plastic covering; fixing with adhesive**										
P202531	**Edgings:**										
P202531A	9 mm wide	m	0.20	3.39	–	0.59	3.98	3.73	–	0.65	4.38
P202531B	12 mm wide	m	0.20	3.40	–	0.74	4.14	3.74	–	0.81	4.55
P202531C	15 mm wide	m	0.20	3.40	–	1.01	4.41	3.74	–	1.11	4.85
P202531D	18 mm wide	m	0.22	3.74	–	1.19	4.93	4.11	–	1.31	5.42
P202531E	22 mm wide	m	0.22	3.74	–	1.39	5.13	4.11	–	1.53	5.64
P202531F	25 mm wide	m	0.22	3.73	–	1.69	5.42	4.10	–	1.86	5.96
P2030	**Shelving; MDF; medium density fibreboard**										
P203001	**Solid shelving; 15 mm thick:**										
P203001A	not exceeding 150 mm wide	m	0.21	3.57	–	0.75	4.32	3.93	–	0.83	4.75
P203001B	150-300 mm wide	m	0.24	4.08	–	1.46	5.54	4.49	–	1.61	6.09
P203001C	over 300 mm wide	m²	0.83	14.10	–	4.71	18.81	15.51	–	5.18	20.69
P203002	**Solid shelving; 18 mm thick:**										
P203002A	not exceeding 150 mm wide	m	0.22	3.73	–	1.03	4.76	4.10	–	1.13	5.24
P203002B	150-300 mm wide	m	0.25	4.25	–	2.01	6.26	4.68	–	2.21	6.89
P203002C	over 300 mm wide	m²	0.85	14.43	–	6.51	20.94	15.87	–	7.16	23.03
P203003	**Solid shelving; 25 mm thick:**										
P203003D	not exceeding 150 mm wide	m	0.23	3.90	–	1.48	5.38	4.29	–	1.63	5.92
P203003E	150-300 mm wide	m	0.26	4.42	–	2.91	7.33	4.86	–	3.20	8.06
P203003F	over 300 mm wide	m²	0.88	14.94	–	9.46	24.40	16.43	–	10.41	26.84

Major Works 2009		Unit	Labour Hours	Labour Net	Plant Net	Materials Net	Unit Net	Labour Gross	Plant Gross	Materials Gross	Unit Price
				£	£	£	£	(Gross rates include 10% profit)			
								£	£	£	£
P20	**P20: UNFRAMED ISOLATED TRIMS, SKIRTINGS AND SUNDRY ITEMS**										
P2031	**Shelving; wrought softwood; basic sizes**										
P203162	**Cross-tongued solid shelving:**										
P203162A	19 mm thick; not exceeding 150 mm wide	m	0.22	3.73	–	2.41	6.14	4.10	–	2.65	6.75
P203162B	19 mm thick; 150-300 mm wide	m	0.25	4.24	–	4.78	9.02	4.66	–	5.26	9.92
P203162C	19 mm thick; over 300 mm wide	m²	0.85	14.43	–	15.58	30.01	15.87	–	17.14	33.01
P203162D	25 mm thick; not exceeding 150 mm wide	m	0.23	3.91	–	2.84	6.75	4.30	–	3.12	7.43
P203162E	25 mm thick; 150-300 mm wide	m	0.26	4.42	–	5.64	10.06	4.86	–	6.20	11.07
P203162F	25 mm thick; over 300 mm wide	m²	0.88	14.94	–	18.43	33.37	16.43	–	20.27	36.71
P203163	**Slatted shelving:**										
P203163A	19 × 38 mm at 50 mm centres.	m²	1.30	22.08	–	18.28	40.36	24.29	–	20.11	44.40
P203163B	25 × 50 mm at 75 mm centres.	m²	0.95	16.13	–	16.81	32.94	17.74	–	18.49	36.23
P203163C	25 × 75 mm at 100 mm centres.	m²	0.70	11.88	–	17.67	29.55	13.07	–	19.44	32.51
P203164	**Removable slatted shelving:**										
P203164A	19 × 38 mm at 50 mm centres; 19 × 38 mm cross-bearers.	m²	1.50	25.47	–	20.94	46.41	28.02	–	23.03	51.05
P203164B	25 × 50 mm at 75 mm centres; 25 × 50 mm cross-bearers.	m²	1.10	18.68	–	20.50	39.18	20.55	–	22.55	43.10
P203164C	25 × 75 mm at 100 mm centres; 25 × 50 mm cross-bearers.	m²	0.90	15.28	–	17.33	32.61	16.81	–	19.06	35.87
P2032	**Shelving; birch faced SI grade BR bonding blockboard, BS 3444**										
P203201	**Solid shelving; 18 mm thick:**										
P203201A	not exceeding 150 mm wide	m	0.22	3.73	–	2.36	6.09	4.10	–	2.60	6.70
P203201B	150-300 mm wide	m	0.25	4.24	–	4.68	8.92	4.66	–	5.15	9.81
P203201C	over 300 mm wide	m²	0.85	14.43	–	15.26	29.69	15.87	–	16.79	32.66
P203202	**Solid shelving; 25 mm thick:**										
P203202D	not exceeding 150 mm wide	m	0.23	3.90	–	3.20	7.10	4.29	–	3.52	7.81
P203202E	150-300 mm wide	m	0.26	4.42	–	6.35	10.77	4.86	–	6.99	11.85
P203202F	over 300 mm wide	m²	0.88	14.94	–	20.76	35.70	16.43	–	22.84	39.27
P2033	**Chipboard; faced all sides with 1.5 mm Class 1 laminated plastic covering**										
P203372	**Solid shelving; 15 mm thick:**										
P203372A	not exceeding 150 mm wide	m	0.28	4.75	–	0.75	5.50	5.23	–	0.83	6.05
P203372B	150-300 mm wide	m	0.32	5.44	–	1.42	6.86	5.98	–	1.56	7.55
P203372C	over 300 mm wide	m²	1.10	18.68	–	4.48	23.16	20.55	–	4.93	25.48
P2034	**Laminated plastic covering; Class 1; fixing with adhesive**										
P203474	**To shelving; 1.5 mm thick:**										
P203474A	not exceeding 150 mm wide	m	0.45	7.64	–	4.21	11.85	8.40	–	4.63	13.04
P203474B	150-300 mm wide	m	0.65	11.04	–	8.41	19.45	12.14	–	9.25	21.40
P203474C	over 300 mm wide	m²	1.20	20.38	–	27.49	47.87	22.42	–	30.24	52.66

Building Fabric Sundries

		Unit	Labour Hours	Labour Net	Plant Net	Materials Net	Unit Net	Labour Gross	Plant Gross	Materials Gross	Unit Price
								(Gross rates include 10% profit)			
				£	£	£	£	£	£	£	£
P20	**P20: UNFRAMED ISOLATED TRIMS, SKIRTINGS AND SUNDRY ITEMS**										
P2038	**Fittings; worktops, seats or the like**										
P203809	**MDF; medium density fibreboard; 15 mm thick:**										
P203809F	15 × 450 mm...........	m	0.24	4.07	–	2.22	6.29	4.48	–	2.44	6.92
P203809G	15 × 500 mm...........	m	0.26	4.42	–	2.48	6.90	4.86	–	2.73	7.59
P203809H	15 × 600 mm...........	m	0.29	4.93	–	2.97	7.90	5.42	–	3.27	8.69
P203809I	15 × 750 mm...........	m	0.31	5.26	–	3.69	8.95	5.79	–	4.06	9.85
P203809J	15 × 900 mm...........	m	0.33	5.60	–	4.40	10.00	6.16	–	4.84	11.00
P203810	**MDF; medium density fibreboard; 18 mm thick:**										
P203810A	18 × 450 mm...........	m	0.25	4.24	–	3.04	7.28	4.66	–	3.34	8.01
P203810B	18 × 500 mm...........	m	0.27	4.58	–	3.41	7.99	5.04	–	3.75	8.79
P203810C	18 × 600 mm...........	m	0.30	5.09	–	4.09	9.18	5.60	–	4.50	10.10
P203810D	18 × 750 mm...........	m	0.32	5.43	–	5.07	10.50	5.97	–	5.58	11.55
P203810E	18 × 900 mm...........	m	0.34	5.77	–	6.06	11.83	6.35	–	6.67	13.01
P203812	**MDF; medium density fibreboard; 25 mm thick:**										
P203812F	25 × 450 mm...........	m	0.25	4.24	–	4.39	8.63	4.66	–	4.83	9.49
P203812G	25 × 500 mm...........	m	0.27	4.59	–	4.93	9.52	5.05	–	5.42	10.47
P203812H	25 × 600 mm...........	m	0.30	5.10	–	5.91	11.01	5.61	–	6.50	12.11
P203812I	25 × 750 mm...........	m	0.32	5.43	–	7.35	12.78	5.97	–	8.09	14.06
P203812J	25 × 900 mm...........	m	0.34	5.78	–	8.78	14.56	6.36	–	9.66	16.02
P203822	**Wrought softwood cross-tongued boarding; 19 mm thick:**										
P203822A	19 × 450 mm...........	m	0.25	4.24	–	7.19	11.43	4.66	–	7.91	12.57
P203822B	19 × 500 mm...........	m	0.27	4.59	–	8.07	12.66	5.05	–	8.88	13.93
P203822C	19 × 600 mm...........	m	0.30	5.10	–	9.70	14.80	5.61	–	10.67	16.28
P203822D	19 × 750 mm...........	m	0.32	5.43	–	12.07	17.50	5.97	–	13.28	19.25
P203822E	19 × 900 mm...........	m	0.34	5.77	–	14.44	20.21	6.35	–	15.88	22.23
P203823	**Wrought softwood cross-tongued boarding; 25 mm thick:**										
P203823F	25 × 450 mm...........	m	0.25	4.24	–	8.49	12.73	4.66	–	9.34	14.00
P203823G	25 × 500 mm...........	m	0.27	4.58	–	9.54	14.12	5.04	–	10.49	15.53
P203823H	25 × 600 mm...........	m	0.30	5.10	–	11.46	16.56	5.61	–	12.61	18.22
P203823I	25 × 750 mm...........	m	0.32	5.44	–	14.26	19.70	5.98	–	15.69	21.67
P203823J	25 × 900 mm...........	m	0.34	5.77	–	17.07	22.84	6.35	–	18.78	25.12
P203843	**Birch faced SI grade, BR bonding blockboard boarding; BS 3444; 18 mm thick:**										
P203843A	18 × 450 mm...........	m	0.25	4.24	–	7.04	11.28	4.66	–	7.74	12.41
P203843B	18 × 500 mm...........	m	0.27	4.58	–	7.91	12.49	5.04	–	8.70	13.74
P203843C	18 × 600 mm...........	m	0.30	5.09	–	9.50	14.59	5.60	–	10.45	16.05
P203843D	18 × 750 mm...........	m	0.32	5.43	–	11.82	17.25	5.97	–	13.00	18.98
P203843E	18 × 900 mm...........	m	0.34	5.77	–	14.14	19.91	6.35	–	15.55	21.90

Major Works 2009		Unit	Labour Hours	Labour Net	Plant Net	Materials Net	Unit Net	Labour Gross	Plant Gross	Materials Gross	Unit Price
								(Gross rates include 10% profit)			
				£	£	£	£	£	£	£	£
P20	**P20: UNFRAMED ISOLATED TRIMS, SKIRTINGS AND SUNDRY ITEMS**										
P2038	**Fittings; worktops, seats or the like**										
P203844	**Birch faced SI grade, BR bonding blockboard boarding; BS 3444; 25 mm thick:**										
P203844F	25 × 450 mm...........	m	0.25	4.25	–	9.55	13.80	4.68	–	10.51	15.18
P203844G	25 × 500 mm...........	m	0.27	4.58	–	10.74	15.32	5.04	–	11.81	16.85
P203844H	25 × 600 mm...........	m	0.30	5.09	–	12.91	18.00	5.60	–	14.20	19.80
P203844I	25 × 750 mm...........	m	0.32	5.44	–	16.06	21.50	5.98	–	17.67	23.65
P203844J	25 × 900 mm...........	m	0.34	5.77	–	19.22	24.99	6.35	–	21.14	27.49
P203864	**Birch faced grade BB interior quality plywood boarding; BS 1455; 15 mm thick:**										
P203864A	15 × 450 mm...........	m	0.22	3.74	–	6.92	10.66	4.11	–	7.61	11.73
P203864B	15 × 500 mm...........	m	0.24	4.07	–	7.78	11.85	4.48	–	8.56	13.04
P203864C	15 × 600 mm...........	m	0.26	4.42	–	9.34	13.76	4.86	–	10.27	15.14
P203864D	15 × 750 mm...........	m	0.28	4.76	–	11.62	16.38	5.24	–	12.78	18.02
P203864E	15 × 900 mm...........	m	0.30	5.10	–	13.90	19.00	5.61	–	15.29	20.90
P203865	**Birch faced grade BB interior quality plywood boarding; BS 1455; 18 mm thick:**										
P203865F	18 × 450 mm...........	m	0.22	3.73	–	8.36	12.09	4.10	–	9.20	13.30
P203865G	18 × 500 mm...........	m	0.24	4.08	–	9.39	13.47	4.49	–	10.33	14.82
P203865H	18 × 600 mm...........	m	0.26	4.41	–	11.29	15.70	4.85	–	12.42	17.27
P203865I	18 × 750 mm...........	m	0.28	4.75	–	14.05	18.80	5.23	–	15.46	20.68
P203865J	18 × 900 mm...........	m	0.30	5.10	–	16.80	21.90	5.61	–	18.48	24.09
P203866	**Birch faced grade BB interior quality plywood boarding; BS 1455; 25 mm thick:**										
P203866K	25 × 450 mm...........	m	0.25	4.25	–	11.00	15.25	4.68	–	12.10	16.78
P203866L	25 × 500 mm...........	m	0.27	4.58	–	12.37	16.95	5.04	–	13.61	18.65
P203866M	25 × 600 mm...........	m	0.30	5.09	–	14.87	19.96	5.60	–	16.36	21.96
P203866N	25 × 750 mm...........	m	0.32	5.43	–	18.51	23.94	5.97	–	20.36	26.33
P203866O	25 × 900 mm...........	m	0.34	5.77	–	22.15	27.92	6.35	–	24.37	30.71
P2041	**Window boards or the like; wrought softwood; basic sizes**										
P204124	**Window boards; nosed and tongued:**										
P204124A	25 × 150 mm...........	m	0.40	6.79	–	5.18	11.97	7.47	–	5.70	13.17
P204124B	25 × 175 mm...........	m	0.40	6.79	–	5.79	12.58	7.47	–	6.37	13.84
P204124C	25 × 200 mm...........	m	0.42	7.13	–	6.37	13.50	7.84	–	7.01	14.85
P204124D	25 × 225 mm...........	m	0.42	7.14	–	6.94	14.08	7.85	–	7.63	15.49
P204124E	25 × 250 mm...........	m	0.44	7.47	–	7.50	14.97	8.22	–	8.25	16.47
P2043	**Window boards or the like; MDF mouldings; basic sizes**										
P204301	**Window boards:**										
P204301A	25 × 175 mm...........	m	0.40	6.79	–	7.01	13.80	7.47	–	7.71	15.18
P204301B	25 × 200 mm...........	m	0.42	7.13	–	8.14	15.27	7.84	–	8.95	16.80
P204301C	25 × 225 mm...........	m	0.43	7.30	–	8.81	16.11	8.03	–	9.69	17.72
P204301D	25 × 250 mm...........	m	0.44	7.47	–	9.76	17.23	8.22	–	10.74	18.95
P204301E	25 × 275 mm...........	m	0.45	7.64	–	10.89	18.53	8.40	–	11.98	20.38

Building Fabric Sundries

Major Works 2009		Unit	Labour Hours	Labour Net	Plant Net	Materials Net	Unit Net	Labour Gross	Plant Gross	Materials Gross	Unit Price
								(Gross rates include 10% profit)			
				£	£	£	£	£	£	£	£
P20	**P20: UNFRAMED ISOLATED TRIMS, SKIRTINGS AND SUNDRY ITEMS**										
P2071	**Handrails or balustrades; wrought softwood; basic sizes**										
P207101	**Handrails; mopstick:**										
P207101A	50 mm dia	m	0.40	6.79	–	2.95	9.74	7.47	–	3.25	10.71
P207152	**Handrails; moulded:**										
P207152B	50 × 75 mm; moulded ...	m	0.40	6.79	–	4.09	10.88	7.47	–	4.50	11.97
P207152C	50 × 100 mm; moulded ..	m	0.45	7.64	–	6.16	13.80	8.40	–	6.78	15.18
P207152D	63 × 100 mm; moulded ..	m	0.45	7.64	–	7.43	15.07	8.40	–	8.17	16.58
P207152E	75 × 100 mm; moulded ..	m	0.50	8.49	–	9.14	17.63	9.34	–	10.05	19.39
P207153	**Balustrades; 25 × 25 mm balusters housed at 100 mm centres; 50 × 75 mm moulded handrail; 25 × 75 mm string capping:**										
P207153A	900 mm high; horizontal ...	m	2.80	47.54	–	36.42	83.96	52.29	–	40.06	92.36
P207153B	1000 mm high; horizontal ..	m	2.80	47.54	–	39.38	86.92	52.29	–	43.32	95.61
P207153C	900 mm high; raking	m	3.60	61.12	–	36.42	97.54	67.23	–	40.06	107.29
P207153D	1000 mm high; raking	m	3.60	61.12	–	39.38	100.50	67.23	–	43.32	110.55
P207154	**Newels:**										
P207154A	75 × 75 mm............	m	0.30	5.09	–	37.89	42.98	5.60	–	41.68	47.28
P207154B	100 × 100 mm..........	m	0.30	5.09	–	45.41	50.50	5.60	–	49.95	55.55

Major Works 2009		Unit	Labour Hours	Labour Net	Plant Net	Materials Net	Unit Net	Labour Gross	Plant Gross	Materials Gross	Unit Price
								(Gross rates include 10% profit)			
				£	£	£	£	£	£	£	£
P21	**P21: IRONMONGERY**										
P2101	**General ironmongery**										
P210101	**Supply and fit ironmongery to woodwork backgrounds; hinges:**										
P210101A	75 mm pressed steel butts .	Pr	0.15	2.55	–	0.61	3.16	2.81	–	0.67	3.48
P210101B	100 mm pressed steel butts	Pr	0.17	2.89	–	1.06	3.95	3.18	–	1.17	4.35
P210101C	125 mm pressed steel butts	Pr	0.19	3.23	–	1.37	4.60	3.55	–	1.51	5.06
P210101D	75 mm rising butts........	Pr	0.25	4.25	–	3.27	7.52	4.68	–	3.60	8.27
P210101E	100 mm rising butts.......	Pr	0.27	4.58	–	4.62	9.20	5.04	–	5.08	10.12
P210101F	125 mm rising butts.......	Pr	0.29	4.92	–	5.96	10.88	5.41	–	6.56	11.97
P210101G	75 mm lift off butts.......	Pr	0.25	4.25	–	4.99	9.24	4.68	–	5.49	10.16
P210101H	100 mm lift off butts......	Pr	0.27	4.58	–	6.92	11.50	5.04	–	7.61	12.65
P210101I	125 mm lift off butts.......	Pr	0.29	4.92	–	8.83	13.75	5.41	–	9.71	15.13
P210101J	100 mm Parliament hinges .	Pr	0.50	8.49	–	12.48	20.97	9.34	–	13.73	23.07
P210101K	300 mm tee hinges........	Pr	0.30	5.09	–	2.67	7.76	5.60	–	2.94	8.54
P210101L	400 mm tee hinges........	Pr	0.40	6.79	–	5.28	12.07	7.47	–	5.81	13.28
P210101M	500 mm tee hinges........	Pr	0.50	8.49	–	6.15	14.64	9.34	–	6.77	16.10
P210101N	450 mm hook and band hinges	Pr	0.75	12.74	–	16.33	29.07	14.01	–	17.96	31.98
P210101O	600 mm hook and band hinges	Pr	0.90	15.28	–	24.00	39.28	16.81	–	26.40	43.21
P210101P	750 mm hook and band hinges	Pr	1.05	17.83	–	35.52	53.35	19.61	–	39.07	58.69
P210101Q	900 mm hook and band hinges	Pr	1.20	20.38	–	46.08	66.46	22.42	–	50.69	73.11
P210103	**Supply and fit ironmongery to woodwork backgrounds; locks and latches:**										
P210103A	rebated mortice lock	Nr	0.70	11.89	–	20.15	32.04	13.08	–	22.17	35.24
P210103B	deadlocking cylinder night latch	Nr	0.75	12.74	–	34.57	47.31	14.01	–	38.03	52.04
P210103C	escutcheon	Nr	0.05	0.85	–	0.37	1.22	0.94	–	0.41	1.34
P210103R	rim latch	Nr	0.80	13.58	–	8.63	22.21	14.94	–	9.49	24.43
P210103S	mortice latch............	Nr	0.55	9.34	–	11.05	20.39	10.27	–	12.16	22.43
P210103T	rebated mortice latch......	Nr	0.70	11.89	–	12.98	24.87	13.08	–	14.28	27.36
P210103U	locking mortice latch	Nr	0.65	11.04	–	11.52	22.56	12.14	–	12.67	24.82
P210103V	Norfolk/Suffolk latch	Nr	0.75	12.74	–	5.19	17.93	14.01	–	5.71	19.72
P210103W	automatic gate latch.......	Nr	0.60	10.19	–	5.96	16.15	11.21	–	6.56	17.77
P210103X	ball catch	Nr	0.30	5.09	–	4.81	9.90	5.60	–	5.29	10.89
P210103Y	rim lock	Nr	0.80	13.58	–	12.48	26.06	14.94	–	13.73	28.67
P210103Z	mortice lock	Nr	0.55	9.34	–	11.52	20.86	10.27	–	12.67	22.95

Building Fabric Sundries

Major Works 2009		Unit	Labour Hours	Labour Net	Plant Net	Materials Net	Unit Net	Labour Gross	Plant Gross	Materials Gross	Unit Price
								(Gross rates include 10% profit)			
				£	£	£	£	£	£	£	£
P21	**P21: IRONMONGERY**										
P2101	**General ironmongery**										
P210105	**Supply and fit ironmongery to woodwork backgrounds; door closers:**										
P210105D	overhead door closer single action..................	Nr	0.90	15.28	–	115.21	130.49	16.81	–	126.73	143.54
P210105E	overhead door closer double action..................	Nr	1.10	18.68	–	130.55	149.23	20.55	–	143.61	164.15
P210105F	Perko door closer........	Nr	0.60	10.19	–	14.88	25.07	11.21	–	16.37	27.58
P210106	**Supply and fit ironmongery to woodwork backgrounds; door bolts:**										
P210106G	100 mm barrel bolt.......	Nr	0.25	4.25	–	3.26	7.51	4.68	–	3.59	8.26
P210106H	150 mm barrel bolt.......	Nr	0.30	5.09	–	4.19	9.28	5.60	–	4.61	10.21
P210106I	225 mm barrel bolt.......	Nr	0.35	5.94	–	5.11	11.05	6.53	–	5.62	12.16
P210106J	300 mm barrel bolt.......	Nr	0.40	6.79	–	6.51	13.30	7.47	–	7.16	14.63
P210106K	450 mm barrel bolt.......	Nr	0.50	8.49	–	8.84	17.33	9.34	–	9.72	19.06
P210106L	450 mm monkey tail bolts..	Nr	0.60	10.19	–	22.78	32.97	11.21	–	25.06	36.27
P210106M	600 mm monkey tail bolts..	Nr	0.75	12.74	–	27.43	40.17	14.01	–	30.17	44.19
P210106N	750 mm monkey tail bolts..	Nr	1.00	16.98	–	53.47	70.45	18.68	–	58.82	77.50
P210106O	100 mm flush bolts	Nr	0.50	8.49	–	11.16	19.65	9.34	–	12.28	21.62
P210106P	150 mm flush bolts	Nr	0.60	10.19	–	15.82	26.01	11.21	–	17.40	28.61
P210106Q	225 mm flush bolts	Nr	0.70	11.89	–	18.58	30.47	13.08	–	20.44	33.52
P210106R	300 mm flush bolts	Nr	0.80	13.58	–	26.03	39.61	14.94	–	28.63	43.57
P210106S	WC indicator bolt	Nr	0.50	8.49	–	12.45	20.94	9.34	–	13.70	23.03
P210106T	single door panic bolt	Nr	0.90	15.28	–	122.72	138.00	16.81	–	134.99	151.80
P210106U	double door panic bolt.....	Nr	1.40	23.77	–	145.05	168.82	26.15	–	159.56	185.70

Major Works 2009		Unit	Labour Hours	Labour Net	Plant Net	Materials Net	Unit Net	Labour Gross	Plant Gross	Materials Gross	Unit Price
				£	£	£	£	___ (Gross rates include 10% profit) ___			
								£	£	£	£
P21	**P21: IRONMONGERY**										
P2101	**General ironmongery**										
P210109	**Supply and fit ironmongery to woodwork backgrounds; door furniture:**										
P210109A	lever furniture	Set	0.25	4.25	–	14.06	18.31	4.68	–	15.47	20.14
P210109B	knob furniture	Set	0.30	5.09	–	21.77	26.86	5.60	–	23.95	29.55
P210109C	cupboard knobs	Nr	0.20	3.40	–	8.80	12.20	3.74	–	9.68	13.42
P210109Z	escutcheon	Nr	0.05	0.85	–	0.37	1.22	0.94	–	0.41	1.34
P210110	**Supply and fit ironmongery to woodwork backgrounds; handles and plates:**										
P210110D	150 mm pull handles	Nr	0.20	3.40	–	5.09	8.49	3.74	–	5.60	9.34
P210110E	225 mm pull handles	Nr	0.25	4.25	–	6.96	11.21	4.68	–	7.66	12.33
P210110F	300 mm pull handles	Nr	0.30	5.09	–	8.80	13.89	5.60	–	9.68	15.28
P210110G	450 mm pull handles	Nr	0.35	5.94	–	10.66	16.60	6.53	–	11.73	18.26
P210110H	600 mm pull handles	Nr	0.40	6.79	–	12.52	19.31	7.47	–	13.77	21.24
P210110I	200 mm push plates.	Nr	0.15	2.55	–	6.67	9.22	2.81	–	7.34	10.14
P210110J	300 mm push plates.	Nr	0.20	3.40	–	7.03	10.43	3.74	–	7.73	11.47
P210110K	600 mm push plates.	Nr	0.25	4.25	–	7.89	12.14	4.68	–	8.68	13.35
P210110L	600 × 225 mm kick plates	Nr	0.35	5.94	–	10.70	16.64	6.53	–	11.77	18.30
P210110M	750 × 225 mm kick plates	Nr	0.40	6.79	–	12.57	19.36	7.47	–	13.83	21.30
P210110N	900 × 225 mm kick plates	Nr	0.45	7.64	–	14.41	22.05	8.40	–	15.85	24.26
P210111	**Supply and fit ironmongery to woodwork backgrounds; window furniture:**										
P210111O	250 mm casement stay	Nr	0.25	4.25	–	5.01	9.26	4.68	–	5.51	10.19
P210111P	450 mm casement stay	Nr	0.30	5.09	–	8.90	13.99	5.60	–	9.79	15.39
P210111Q	casement fastener	Nr	0.15	2.55	–	4.81	7.36	2.81	–	5.29	8.10
P210111R	sash cockspur fastener	Nr	0.15	2.55	–	4.26	6.81	2.81	–	4.69	7.49
P210111S	sash lift	Nr	0.15	2.55	–	3.53	6.08	2.81	–	3.88	6.69
P210111T	sash pulley and cord	Nr	0.75	12.74	–	22.22	34.96	14.01	–	24.44	38.46
P210112	**Supply and fit ironmongery to woodwork backgrounds; door gear sets:**										
P210112A	single door sliding door set.	Nr	0.90	15.28	–	18.99	34.27	16.81	–	20.89	37.70
P210112B	double door sliding door set	Nr	1.40	23.77	–	26.86	50.63	26.15	–	29.55	55.69
P210112C	triple door sliding door set .	Nr	1.90	32.26	–	45.39	77.65	35.49	–	49.93	85.42
P210112D	double door Bi-Fold gear set	Nr	1.50	25.47	–	26.86	52.33	28.02	–	29.55	57.56
P210112E	triple door Bi-Fold gear set .	Nr	1.90	32.26	–	45.39	77.65	35.49	–	49.93	85.42
P210112F	quadruple door Bi-Fold gear set	Nr	2.40	40.75	–	49.55	90.30	44.83	–	54.51	99.33
P210114	**Supply and fit ironmongery to woodwork backgrounds; general items:**										
P210114A	towel rail	Nr	0.40	6.79	–	7.22	14.01	7.47	–	7.94	15.41
P210114B	letter plate including hole in door	Nr	0.75	12.74	–	7.59	20.33	14.01	–	8.35	22.36
P210114C	toilet roll holder.	Nr	0.25	4.25	–	11.52	15.77	4.68	–	12.67	17.35
P210114D	hat and coat hook.	Nr	0.10	1.70	–	3.07	4.77	1.87	–	3.38	5.25
P210114E	padlock hasp and staple . . .	Nr	0.25	4.25	–	4.03	8.28	4.68	–	4.43	9.11
P210114F	rubber door stop	Nr	0.10	1.70	–	1.72	3.42	1.87	–	1.89	3.76
P210114G	curtain track	m	0.40	6.80	–	17.05	23.85	7.48	–	18.76	26.24
P210114H	hanging rail.	m	0.45	7.64	–	2.30	9.94	8.40	–	2.53	10.93
P210114I	hanging rail end socket	Nr	0.15	2.55	–	1.26	3.81	2.81	–	1.39	4.19
P210114J	hanging rail centre bracket .	Nr	0.15	2.55	–	2.11	4.66	2.81	–	2.32	5.13

Building Fabric Sundries

Major Works 2009	Unit	Labour Hours	Labour Net	Plant Net	Materials Net	Unit Net	Labour Gross	Plant Gross	Materials Gross	Unit Price
P21	**P21: IRONMONGERY**									
P2101	**General ironmongery**									
P210125	**Supply and fit ironmongery to concrete; drilling, plugging and screwing; floor springs:**									
P210125A	single action floor springs..	Nr	1.75	29.72	–	325.68	355.40	32.69	–	358.25	390.94
P210125B	double action floor springs .	Nr	2.00	33.96	–	372.22	406.18	37.36	–	409.44	446.80
P210125C	rubber door stop	Nr	0.30	5.09	–	1.72	6.81	5.60	–	1.89	7.49
P210136	**Supply and fit ironmongery to masonry; drilling, plugging and screwing; general items:**									
P210136A	towel rail	Nr	0.50	8.49	–	7.22	15.71	9.34	–	7.94	17.28
P210136B	toilet roll holder..........	Nr	0.35	5.94	–	11.52	17.46	6.53	–	12.67	19.21
P210136C	hat and coat hook........	Nr	0.20	3.40	–	3.07	6.47	3.74	–	3.38	7.12
P210136D	rubber door stop	Nr	0.20	3.40	–	1.72	5.12	3.74	–	1.89	5.63
P210136E	shelf bracket	Nr	0.25	4.25	–	0.68	4.93	4.68	–	0.75	5.42
P210136F	padlock hasp and staple ...	Nr	0.35	5.94	–	4.03	9.97	6.53	–	4.43	10.97
P210136G	curtain track	m	0.50	8.50	–	17.05	25.55	9.35	–	18.76	28.11
P210136H	hanging rail..............	m	0.45	7.64	–	2.30	9.94	8.40	–	2.53	10.93
P210136I	hanging rail end socket	Nr	0.25	4.25	–	1.26	5.51	4.68	–	1.39	6.06
P210136J	hanging rail centre bracket .	Nr	0.25	4.25	–	2.11	6.36	4.68	–	2.32	7.00
P210191	**Boulton and Paul ironmongery sets; fixing to woodwork backgrounds:**									
P210191A	GENTPAK5L	Set	1.20	20.38	–	44.49	64.87	22.42	–	48.94	71.36
P210191B	VENTPAK5L	Set	1.20	20.38	–	44.49	64.87	22.42	–	48.94	71.36
P210191C	LOCPAK5L..............	Set	1.20	20.38	–	29.55	49.93	22.42	–	32.51	54.92
P210191D	GFPAK	Set	1.50	25.47	–	49.57	75.04	28.02	–	54.53	82.54
P210191E	VENTPAK...............	Set	1.50	25.47	–	49.50	74.97	28.02	–	54.45	82.47
P210191F	ENTPAK................	Set	1.50	25.47	–	30.44	55.91	28.02	–	33.48	61.50
P210191G	GENTPAK	Set	1.20	20.38	–	30.12	50.50	22.42	–	33.13	55.55
P210191H	VBPAK.................	Set	1.20	20.38	–	29.37	49.75	22.42	–	32.31	54.73
P210191I	LOCPAK................	Set	1.20	20.38	–	16.46	36.84	22.42	–	18.11	40.52
P210191J	REBPAKG	Set	1.80	30.56	–	67.31	97.87	33.62	–	74.04	107.66
P210191K	REBPAKV...............	Set	1.80	30.56	–	66.59	97.15	33.62	–	73.25	106.87
P210191L	REBPAK................	Set	1.80	30.56	–	54.63	85.19	33.62	–	60.09	93.71
P210191M	GINTPAK	Set	1.00	16.98	–	17.88	34.86	18.68	–	19.67	38.35
P210191N	VINTPAK	Set	1.00	16.98	–	15.47	32.45	18.68	–	17.02	35.70
P210191O	LATPAK	Set	1.00	16.98	–	9.06	26.04	18.68	–	9.97	28.64
P210191P	GILPAK	Set	1.20	20.38	–	30.65	51.03	22.42	–	33.72	56.13
P210191Q	VILPAK	Set	1.20	20.38	–	25.73	46.11	22.42	–	28.30	50.72
P210191R	BATPAK................	Set	1.00	16.98	–	14.92	31.90	18.68	–	16.41	35.09

Major Works 2009		Unit	Labour Hours	Labour Net	Plant Net	Materials Net	Unit Net	Labour Gross	Plant Gross	Materials Gross	Unit Price
								(Gross rates include 10% profit)			
				£	£	£	£	£	£	£	£
P21	**P21: IRONMONGERY**										
P2101	**General ironmongery**										
P210192	**Boulton and Paul ironmongery packs; fixing to woodwork backgrounds:**										
P210192A	DFMS5L................	Nr	0.90	15.28	–	33.59	48.87	16.81	–	36.95	53.76
P210192B	DFLPG; including hole through door............	Nr	0.75	12.74	–	12.78	25.52	14.01	–	14.06	28.07
P210192C	DFLPV; including hole through door............	Nr	0.75	12.74	–	13.18	25.92	14.01	–	14.50	28.51
P210192D	DFLPA; including hole through door............	Nr	0.75	12.74	–	6.05	18.79	14.01	–	6.66	20.67
P210192E	DFKG	Nr	0.25	4.25	–	10.41	14.66	4.68	–	11.45	16.13
P210192F	DFKV	Nr	0.25	4.25	–	9.82	14.07	4.68	–	10.80	15.48
P210192G	DFBG	Nr	0.15	2.55	–	5.30	7.85	2.81	–	5.83	8.64
P210192H	DFBV	Nr	0.15	2.55	–	5.23	7.78	2.81	–	5.75	8.56
P210192I	DFSB8	Nr	0.38	6.45	–	10.48	16.93	7.10	–	11.53	18.62
P210192J	DFSB6	Nr	0.35	5.94	–	7.54	13.48	6.53	–	8.29	14.83
P210192K	DFCB	Nr	0.40	6.79	–	2.16	8.95	7.47	–	2.38	9.85
P210192L	DFCC	Nr	0.40	6.79	–	2.44	9.23	7.47	–	2.68	10.15
P210192M	DFBBB4	Nr	0.25	4.25	–	2.12	6.37	4.68	–	2.33	7.01
P210192N	DFNBB4	Nr	0.28	4.67	–	2.03	6.70	5.14	–	2.23	7.37
P210192O	DFNBA4	Nr	0.28	4.67	–	2.08	6.75	5.14	–	2.29	7.43
P210192P	DFBBA4	Nr	0.25	4.25	–	1.96	6.21	4.68	–	2.16	6.83
P210192Q	DFHGB4	Set	0.30	5.09	–	10.98	16.07	5.60	–	12.08	17.68
P210192R	DFHGS4	Set	0.30	5.09	–	3.57	8.66	5.60	–	3.93	9.53
P210192S	DFHGB3	Set	0.15	2.55	–	6.59	9.14	2.81	–	7.25	10.05
P210192T	DFHGS3	Set	0.15	2.55	–	1.59	4.14	2.81	–	1.75	4.55
P210192U	DFDCS	Nr	0.90	15.28	–	47.30	62.58	16.81	–	52.03	68.84
P210192V	ceramic mortice knob sets .	Set	0.80	13.58	–	33.34	46.92	14.94	–	36.67	51.61
P210192W	ceramic privacy adaptors ..	Nr	0.25	4.25	–	22.22	26.47	4.68	–	24.44	29.12
P210192X	ceramic finger plates	Set	0.25	4.25	–	15.56	19.81	4.68	–	17.12	21.79
P2105	**Security fittings**										
P210513	**Supply and fit security ironmongery to woodwork backgrounds:**										
P210513A	door chain..............	Nr	0.40	6.79	–	8.84	15.63	7.47	–	9.72	17.19
P210513B	door viewer	Nr	0.60	10.19	–	7.22	17.41	11.21	–	7.94	19.15
P210513C	window locks	Nr	0.45	7.64	–	11.52	19.16	8.40	–	12.67	21.08
P2106	**Seals and excluders**										
P210601	**Supply and fit fire resisting intumescent strip to woodwork backgrounds:**										
P210601A	Palusol; White...........	m	0.15	2.54	–	4.15	6.69	2.79	–	4.57	7.36
P210601B	Palusol; Copper	m	0.15	2.54	–	4.15	6.69	2.79	–	4.57	7.36
P210601C	Palusol; White Smoke	m	0.15	2.55	–	8.47	11.02	2.81	–	9.32	12.12
P210601D	Palusol; Copper Smoke	m	0.15	2.55	–	8.47	11.02	2.81	–	9.32	12.12
P210615	**Supply and fit draught excluder seal to woodwork backgrounds:**										
P210615A	compression excluder aluminium................	m	0.15	2.55	–	15.36	17.91	2.81	–	16.90	19.70
P210615B	brush excluder aluminium .	m	0.15	2.55	–	6.15	8.70	2.81	–	6.77	9.57
P210615C	self adhesive rubber.......	m	0.10	1.70	–	5.35	7.05	1.87	–	5.89	7.76

Building Fabric Sundries

Major Works 2009		Unit	Labour Hours	Labour Net	Plant Net	Materials Net	Unit Net	Labour Gross	Plant Gross	Materials Gross	Unit Price
								——— (Gross rates include 10% profit) ———			
				£	£	£	£	£	£	£	£
P30	**P30: TRENCHES, PIPEWAYS AND PITS FOR BURIED ENGINEERING SERVICES**										
P3010	**Excavation of trenches by machine for service pipes, cables and the like including filling and on-site disposal**										
P301001	**Trenches to suit pipes not exceeding 200 mm diameter; average depth:**										
P301001A	0.50 m	m	0.12	1.52	1.93	–	3.45	1.67	2.12	–	3.80
P301001B	0.75 m	m	0.15	1.90	2.59	–	4.49	2.09	2.85	–	4.94
P301001C	1.00 m	m	0.22	2.79	3.36	–	6.15	3.07	3.70	–	6.77
P3011	**Excavation of trenches by machine for service pipes, cables or the like including filling and off-site disposal**										
P301113	**Trenches to suit pipes not exceeding 200 mm diameter; average depth:**										
P301113A	0.50 m	m	0.12	1.52	4.03	–	5.55	1.67	4.43	–	6.11
P301113B	0.75 m	m	0.15	1.91	5.71	–	7.62	2.10	6.28	–	8.38
P301113C	1.00 m	m	0.22	2.80	7.55	–	10.35	3.08	8.31	–	11.39
P3015	**Excavation of trenches by hand for service pipes, cables or the like, including disposal and filling**										
P301501	**Trenches to suit pipes not exceeding 200 mm diameter; average depth:**										
P301501A	0.50 m	m	1.32	16.77	0.17	–	16.94	18.45	0.19	–	18.63
P301501B	0.75 m	m	1.78	22.61	0.17	–	22.78	24.87	0.19	–	25.06
P301501C	1.00 m	m	2.23	28.33	0.29	–	28.62	31.16	0.32	–	31.48
P301542	**Trenches to suit pipes exceeding 200 mm diameter; average depth:**										
P301542A	0.50 m	m	1.76	22.35	0.23	–	22.58	24.59	0.25	–	24.84
P301542B	0.75 m	m	2.37	30.10	0.23	–	30.33	33.11	0.25	–	33.36
P301542C	1.00 m	m	2.97	37.72	0.38	–	38.10	41.49	0.42	–	41.91
P3040	**Beds for service pipes, ducts, cables and the like**										
P304001	**50 mm sand bed to pipes:**										
P304001A	not exceeding 200 mm diameter	m	0.06	0.76	0.07	0.53	1.36	0.84	0.08	0.58	1.50
P3041	**Beds for service pipes, ducts, cables and the like**										
P304131	**100 mm sand bed to pipes:**										
P304131A	not exceeding 200 mm diameter	m	0.09	1.09	0.11	1.00	2.20	1.20	0.12	1.10	2.42

Major Works 2009		Unit	Labour Hours	Labour Net	Plant Net	Materials Net	Unit Net	Labour Gross	Plant Gross	Materials Gross	Unit Price
								(Gross rates include 10% profit)			
				£	£	£	£	£	£	£	£
P30	**P30: TRENCHES, PIPEWAYS AND PITS FOR BURIED ENGINEERING SERVICES**										
P3042	**Beds and coverings for service pipes, ducts, cables or the like**										
P304232	**150 mm bed and 150 mm covering of pea shingle to pipes:**										
P304232A	not exceeding 200 mm diameter	m	0.20	2.56	0.94	6.51	10.01	2.82	1.03	7.16	11.01
P304233	**150 mm bed and 150 mm covering of C10P concrete to pipes:**										
P304233A	not exceeding 200 mm diameter	m	0.25	3.16	0.98	21.96	26.10	3.48	1.08	24.16	28.71
P3050	**Duct pipework**										
P305001	**Vitrified clay pipes; Hepworth Building Products; HepDuct:**										
P305001A	90 mm HepDuct	m	0.18	2.28	–	6.27	8.55	2.51	–	6.90	9.41
P305001B	100 mm HepDuct	m	0.20	2.54	–	6.96	9.50	2.79	–	7.66	10.45
P305001C	125 mm HepDuct	m	0.22	2.79	–	10.67	13.46	3.07	–	11.74	14.81
P305001D	150 mm HepDuct	m	0.23	2.92	–	15.15	18.07	3.21	–	16.67	19.88
P305001E	225 mm HepDuct	m	0.29	3.68	–	36.56	40.24	4.05	–	40.22	44.26
P305016	**Vitrified clay pipes; Hepworth Building Products; SuperSleve:**										
P305016A	100 mm SuperSleve	m	0.20	2.54	–	4.78	7.32	2.79	–	5.26	8.05
P305016B	150 mm SuperSleve	m	0.23	2.92	–	9.66	12.58	3.21	–	10.63	13.84
P305016C	225 mm SuperSleve	m	0.29	3.69	–	24.66	28.35	4.06	–	27.13	31.19
P305024	**Vitrified clay pipes; Hepworth Building Products; HepSeal:**										
P305024A	100 mm HepSeal	m	0.22	2.79	–	4.78	7.57	3.07	–	5.26	8.33
P305024B	150 mm HepSeal	m	0.27	3.43	–	9.66	13.09	3.77	–	10.63	14.40
P305024C	225 mm HepSeal	m	0.37	4.70	–	24.66	29.36	5.17	–	27.13	32.30
P305046	**Vitrified clay pipes; Hepworth Building Products; HepLine:**										
P305046A	150 mm HepLine	m	0.23	2.92	–	14.55	17.47	3.21	–	16.01	19.22
P305046B	225 mm HepLine	m	0.29	3.68	–	29.34	33.02	4.05	–	32.27	36.32
P305046C	300 mm HepLine	m	0.34	4.32	–	57.13	61.45	4.75	–	62.84	67.60
P305061	**UPVC pipes; OsmaDrain:**										
P305061A	82 mm	m	0.18	2.28	–	9.59	11.87	2.51	–	10.55	13.06
P305061B	110 mm	m	0.20	2.54	–	5.86	8.40	2.79	–	6.45	9.24
P305061C	160 mm	m	0.25	3.18	–	13.48	16.66	3.50	–	14.83	18.33
P305076	**Concrete pipes; BS 5911 Pt 1; Class L:**										
P305076A	150 mm	m	0.55	6.98	–	6.07	13.05	7.68	–	6.68	14.36
P305076B	225 mm	m	0.65	8.26	–	9.09	17.35	9.09	–	10.00	19.09
P305076C	300 mm	m	0.70	8.89	7.68	12.13	28.70	9.78	8.45	13.34	31.57
P305091	**Cast iron pipes; Timesaver; bolted joints:**										
P305091A	100 mm	m	0.45	15.29	–	35.56	50.85	16.82	–	39.12	55.94
P305091B	150 mm	m	0.65	22.09	–	65.84	87.93	24.30	–	72.42	96.72

Building Fabric Sundries

Major Works 2009		Unit	Labour Hours	Labour Net	Plant Net	Materials Net	Unit Net	Labour Gross	Plant Gross	Materials Gross	Unit Price
								—— (Gross rates include 10% profit) ——			
				£	£	£	£	£	£	£	£
P30	**P30: TRENCHES, PIPEWAYS AND PITS FOR BURIED ENGINEERING SERVICES**										
P3055	**Duct pipework fittings**										
P305501	**Vitrified clay fittings; Hepworth Building Products; HepDuct:**										
P305501A	90 mm bends	Nr	0.18	2.28	–	6.27	8.55	2.51	–	6.90	9.41
P305501B	100 mm bends	Nr	0.20	2.54	–	6.96	9.50	2.79	–	7.66	10.45
P305501C	125 mm bends	Nr	0.22	2.80	–	17.67	20.47	3.08	–	19.44	22.52
P305501D	150 mm bends	Nr	0.23	2.92	–	15.15	18.07	3.21	–	16.67	19.88
P305501E	225 mm bends	Nr	0.29	3.68	–	36.56	40.24	4.05	–	40.22	44.26
P305516	**Vitrified clay fittings; Hepworth Building Products; SuperSleve:**										
P305516A	100 mm bends	Nr	0.20	2.54	–	9.94	12.48	2.79	–	10.93	13.73
P305516B	100 mm rest bends	Nr	0.22	2.79	–	14.92	17.71	3.07	–	16.41	19.48
P305516C	100 × 100 mm junctions .	Nr	0.25	3.17	–	28.30	31.47	3.49	–	31.13	34.62
P305516D	150 mm bends	Nr	0.20	2.54	–	13.28	15.82	2.79	–	14.61	17.40
P305516E	150 mm rest bends	Nr	0.22	2.80	–	17.06	19.86	3.08	–	18.77	21.85
P305516F	150 × 100 mm junctions .	Nr	0.25	3.17	–	17.77	20.94	3.49	–	19.55	23.03
P305516G	150 × 150 mm junctions .	Nr	0.25	3.17	–	19.50	22.67	3.49	–	21.45	24.94
P305524	**Vitrified clay fittings; Hepworth Building Products; HepSleve:**										
P305524A	225 mm bends	Nr	0.20	2.54	–	67.71	70.25	2.79	–	74.48	77.28
P305524B	225 mm rest bends	Nr	0.22	2.79	–	74.05	76.84	3.07	–	81.46	84.52
P305524C	225 × 100 mm junctions .	Nr	0.25	3.18	–	94.52	97.70	3.50	–	103.97	107.47
P305524D	225 × 150 mm junctions .	Nr	0.25	3.18	–	94.52	97.70	3.50	–	103.97	107.47
P305531	**Vitrified clay fittings; Hepworth Building Products; HepSeal:**										
P305531A	100 mm bends	Nr	0.20	2.54	–	21.18	23.72	2.79	–	23.30	26.09
P305531B	100 mm rest bends	Nr	0.22	2.79	–	14.92	17.71	3.07	–	16.41	19.48
P305531C	100 × 100 mm junctions .	Nr	0.25	3.17	–	20.96	24.13	3.49	–	23.06	26.54
P305531D	150 mm bends	Nr	0.20	2.54	–	31.77	34.31	2.79	–	34.95	37.74
P305531E	150 mm rest bends	Nr	0.22	2.80	–	17.06	19.86	3.08	–	18.77	21.85
P305531F	150 × 100 mm junctions .	Nr	0.25	3.18	–	36.78	39.96	3.50	–	40.46	43.96
P305531G	150 × 150 mm junctions .	Nr	0.25	3.17	–	41.54	44.71	3.49	–	45.69	49.18
P305531H	225 mm bends	Nr	0.22	2.79	–	74.47	77.26	3.07	–	81.92	84.99
P305531I	225 mm rest bends	Nr	0.25	3.18	–	90.96	94.14	3.50	–	100.06	103.55
P305531J	225 × 100 mm junctions .	Nr	0.27	3.43	–	103.94	107.37	3.77	–	114.33	118.11
P305531K	225 × 150 mm junctions .	Nr	0.27	3.43	–	103.94	107.37	3.77	–	114.33	118.11
P305531L	300 mm bends	Nr	0.35	4.45	–	128.59	133.04	4.90	–	141.45	146.34
P305531M	300 mm rest bends	Nr	0.38	4.83	–	195.72	200.55	5.31	–	215.29	220.61
P305531N	300 × 100 mm junctions .	Nr	0.40	5.08	–	202.39	207.47	5.59	–	222.63	228.22
P305531O	300 × 150 mm junctions .	Nr	0.40	5.08	–	202.39	207.47	5.59	–	222.63	228.22
P305546	**Vitrified clay fittings; Hepworth Building Products; HepLine:**										
P305546A	100 mm bends	Nr	0.20	2.54	–	9.94	12.48	2.79	–	10.93	13.73
P305546B	100 × 100 mm junctions .	Nr	0.25	3.17	–	20.96	24.13	3.49	–	23.06	26.54
P305546C	150 mm bends	Nr	0.20	2.54	–	13.28	15.82	2.79	–	14.61	17.40
P305546D	150 × 100 mm junctions .	Nr	0.25	3.18	–	36.78	39.96	3.50	–	40.46	43.96
P305546E	150 × 150 mm junctions .	Nr	0.25	3.17	–	41.54	44.71	3.49	–	45.69	49.18
P305546F	225 mm bends	Nr	0.22	2.80	–	90.96	93.76	3.08	–	100.06	103.14
P305546G	225 × 100 mm junctions .	Nr	0.27	3.43	–	103.94	107.37	3.77	–	114.33	118.11
P305546H	225 × 150 mm junctions .	Nr	0.27	3.43	–	103.94	107.37	3.77	–	114.33	118.11
P305546I	300 mm bends	Nr	0.35	4.45	–	128.59	133.04	4.90	–	141.45	146.34
P305546J	300 × 100 mm junctions .	Nr	0.40	5.08	–	202.39	207.47	5.59	–	222.63	228.22
P305546K	300 × 150 mm junctions .	Nr	0.40	5.08	–	202.39	207.47	5.59	–	222.63	228.22

Major Works 2009		Unit	Labour Hours	Labour Net	Plant Net	Materials Net	Unit Net	Labour Gross	Plant Gross	Materials Gross	Unit Price
				£	£	£	£	£	£	£	£
								(Gross rates include 10% profit)			
P30	P30: TRENCHES, PIPEWAYS AND PITS FOR BURIED ENGINEERING SERVICES										
P3055	Duct pipework fittings										
P305561	UPVC fittings; OsmaDrain:										
P305561A	82 mm bends	Nr	0.10	1.28	–	16.28	17.56	1.41	–	17.91	19.32
P305561B	82 × 82 mm junctions	Nr	0.15	1.90	–	25.19	27.09	2.09	–	27.71	29.80
P305561C	110 mm bends	Nr	0.13	1.65	–	15.46	17.11	1.82	–	17.01	18.82
P305561D	110 mm rest bends	Nr	0.15	1.91	–	29.62	31.53	2.10	–	32.58	34.68
P305561E	110 × 110 mm junctions	Nr	0.18	2.29	–	21.83	24.12	2.52	–	24.01	26.53
P305561F	160 mm bends	Nr	0.20	2.54	–	39.45	41.99	2.79	–	43.40	46.19
P305561G	160 × 110 mm junctions	Nr	0.25	3.17	–	54.93	58.10	3.49	–	60.42	63.91
P305561H	160 × 160 mm junctions	Nr	0.25	3.18	–	71.25	74.43	3.50	–	78.38	81.87
P305569	UPVC fittings; UltraRib:										
P305569A	150 mm bends	Nr	0.28	3.55	–	17.60	21.15	3.91	–	19.36	23.27
P305569B	150 × 150 mm junctions	Nr	0.30	3.81	–	42.58	46.39	4.19	–	46.84	51.03
P305569C	225 mm bends	Nr	0.32	4.07	–	75.05	79.12	4.48	–	82.56	87.03
P305569D	225 × 110 mm junctions	Nr	0.35	4.45	–	98.70	103.15	4.90	–	108.57	113.47
P305569E	225 × 150 mm junctions	Nr	0.35	4.45	–	101.67	106.12	4.90	–	111.84	116.73
P305569F	225 × 225 mm junctions	Nr	0.35	4.44	–	141.29	145.73	4.88	–	155.42	160.30
P305569G	300 mm bends	Nr	0.34	4.32	–	149.91	154.23	4.75	–	164.90	169.65
P305569H	300 × 150 mm junctions	Nr	0.37	4.70	–	201.75	206.45	5.17	–	221.93	227.10
P305569I	300 × 225 mm junctions	Nr	0.37	4.70	–	310.77	315.47	5.17	–	341.85	347.02
P305576	Concrete fittings, BS 5911 Part 1, Class L:										
P305576A	150 mm bends	Nr	0.40	5.08	–	60.64	65.72	5.59	–	66.70	72.29
P305576B	150 × 150 mm junctions	Nr	0.50	6.35	–	42.45	48.80	6.99	–	46.70	53.68
P305576C	225 mm bends	Nr	0.45	5.72	–	90.96	96.68	6.29	–	100.06	106.35
P305576D	225 × 150 mm junctions	Nr	0.55	6.99	–	63.67	70.66	7.69	–	70.04	77.73
P305576E	300 mm bends	Nr	0.60	7.63	4.39	121.28	133.30	8.39	4.83	133.41	146.63
P305576F	300 × 150 mm junctions	Nr	0.70	8.89	4.39	84.89	98.17	9.78	4.83	93.38	107.99
P305591	Cast iron fittings; Timesaver bolted joints:										
P305591A	100 mm bends	Nr	0.50	16.98	–	30.16	47.14	18.68	–	33.18	51.85
P305591B	100 × 100 mm junction	Nr	0.65	22.08	–	40.02	62.10	24.29	–	44.02	68.31
P305591C	150 mm bends	Nr	0.75	25.48	–	69.39	94.87	28.03	–	76.33	104.36
P305591D	150 × 100 mm junction	Nr	0.85	28.87	–	90.44	119.31	31.76	–	99.48	131.24
P305591E	150 × 150 mm junction	Nr	0.85	28.88	–	98.73	127.61	31.77	–	108.60	140.37
P3080	Stop cock pits, valve chambers and the like										
P308010	Excavating stop cock pit; half brick wall; 100 mm C20 concrete base; hinged cast iron cove and frame bedded in cement mortar (1:3); nominal internal size:										
P308010A	100 × 100 × 750 mm deep	Nr	2.66	46.95	16.48	31.99	95.42	51.65	18.13	35.19	104.96
P308010B	225 × 225 × 750 mm deep	Nr	4.16	73.67	6.68	38.85	119.20	81.04	7.35	42.74	131.12
P308010C	450 × 450 × 750 mm deep	Nr	6.24	114.07	9.34	148.24	271.65	125.48	10.27	163.06	298.82
P308010G	600 × 450 × 1000 mm deep	Nr	9.14	168.67	27.53	111.04	307.24	185.54	30.28	122.14	337.96

Building Fabric Sundries

Major Works 2009		Unit	Labour Hours	Labour Net	Plant Net	Materials Net	Unit Net	Labour Gross	Plant Gross	Materials Gross	Unit Price
								(Gross rates include 10% profit)			
				£	£	£	£	£	£	£	£
P31	**P31: HOLES, CHASES, COVERS AND SUPPORTS FOR SERVICES**										
P3119	**Builder's work; cutting away for and making good after electrical works including mortices, notches, holes, sinkings and chases in structure and finishes**										
P311910	**Concealed installation works:**										
P311910A	lighting points............	Nr	0.36	4.57	–	–	4.57	5.03	–	–	5.03
P311910B	socket outlet points	Nr	0.60	7.62	–	–	7.62	8.38	–	–	8.38
P311910C	equipment and control gear points..................	Nr	0.65	8.26	–	–	8.26	9.09	–	–	9.09
P311910D	fitting points	Nr	0.85	10.80	–	–	10.80	11.88	–	–	11.88
P311920	**Exposed installation works:**										
P311920A	lighting points............	Nr	0.27	3.43	–	–	3.43	3.77	–	–	3.77
P311920B	socket outlet points	Nr	0.42	5.33	–	–	5.33	5.86	–	–	5.86
P311920C	equipment and control gear points..................	Nr	0.61	7.75	–	–	7.75	8.53	–	–	8.53
P311920D	fitting points	Nr	0.42	5.33	–	–	5.33	5.86	–	–	5.86
P3125	**Builder's work; cutting away for and making good after services installation including mortices, notches, holes, sinkings and chases in structure and finishes**										
P312510	**Cutting chases in brickwork for service pipework; vertical; nominal pipe diameter:**										
P312510A	not exceeding 55 mm......	m	0.35	4.45	–	–	4.45	4.90	–	–	4.90
P312510B	55-110 mm	m	0.65	8.26	–	–	8.26	9.09	–	–	9.09
P312515	**Cutting chases in blockwork for service pipework; vertical; nominal pipe diameter:**										
P312515A	not exceeding 55 mm......	m	0.22	2.79	–	–	2.79	3.07	–	–	3.07
P312515B	55-110 mm	m	0.40	5.08	–	–	5.08	5.59	–	–	5.59
P312520	**Cutting holes in structure for pipes or the like; not exceeding 55 mm nominal diameter:**										
P312520A	half brick wall	Nr	0.30	3.81	–	–	3.81	4.19	–	–	4.19
P312520B	one brick wall	Nr	0.58	7.37	–	–	7.37	8.11	–	–	8.11
P312520C	one and a half brick wall ...	Nr	0.85	10.80	–	–	10.80	11.88	–	–	11.88
P312520D	100 mm blockwork	Nr	0.24	3.05	–	–	3.05	3.36	–	–	3.36
P312520E	125 mm blockwork	Nr	0.28	3.56	–	–	3.56	3.92	–	–	3.92
P312520F	150 mm blockwork	Nr	0.32	4.06	–	–	4.06	4.47	–	–	4.47
P312520G	200 mm blockwork	Nr	0.39	4.95	–	–	4.95	5.45	–	–	5.45
P312525	**Cutting holes in structure for pipes or the like; 55-110 mm nominal diameter:**										
P312525A	half brick wall	Nr	0.36	4.57	–	–	4.57	5.03	–	–	5.03
P312525B	one brick wall	Nr	0.70	8.89	–	–	8.89	9.78	–	–	9.78
P312525C	one and a half brick wall ...	Nr	1.02	12.95	–	–	12.95	14.25	–	–	14.25
P312525D	100 mm blockwork	Nr	0.29	3.68	–	–	3.68	4.05	–	–	4.05
P312525E	125 mm blockwork	Nr	0.34	4.32	–	–	4.32	4.75	–	–	4.75
P312525F	150 mm blockwork	Nr	0.38	4.83	–	–	4.83	5.31	–	–	5.31
P312525G	200 mm blockwork	Nr	0.47	5.97	–	–	5.97	6.57	–	–	6.57

Major Works 2009		Unit	Labour Hours	Labour Net	Plant Net	Materials Net	Unit Net	Labour Gross	Plant Gross	Materials Gross	Unit Price
				£	£	£	£	£	£	£	£
								—— (Gross rates include 10% profit) ——			
P31	P31: HOLES, CHASES, COVERS AND SUPPORTS FOR SERVICES										
P3125	Builder's work; cutting away for and making good after services installation including mortices, notches, holes, sinkings and chases in structure and finishes										
P312550	Mortices in brickwork; grouting up with cement mortar (1:3); size:										
P312550A	50 × 50 × 100 mm deep	Nr	0.25	3.17	–	0.22	3.39	3.49	–	0.24	3.73
P312550B	75 × 75 × 100 mm deep	Nr	0.30	3.81	–	0.54	4.35	4.19	–	0.59	4.79
P312550C	75 × 75 × 150 mm deep	Nr	0.38	4.82	–	0.54	5.36	5.30	–	0.59	5.90
P312550D	75 × 75 × 200 mm deep	Nr	0.45	5.71	–	0.65	6.36	6.28	–	0.72	7.00
P312555	Mortices in brickwork for bars, bolts and the like:										
P312555A	M10 expansion bolt	Nr	0.16	2.03	–	–	2.03	2.23	–	–	2.23
P312555B	M20 bolt; 75 mm deep.....	Nr	0.15	1.91	–	–	1.91	2.10	–	–	2.10
P312555C	M20 bolt; 125 mm deep....	Nr	0.18	2.29	–	–	2.29	2.52	–	–	2.52
P312575	Holes in softwood for cables, small pipes and the like; timber thickness:										
P312575A	12 mm	Nr	0.03	0.38	–	–	0.38	0.42	–	–	0.42
P312575B	25 mm	Nr	0.05	0.64	–	–	0.64	0.70	–	–	0.70
P312575C	50 mm	Nr	0.08	1.02	–	–	1.02	1.12	–	–	1.12
P312575D	75 mm	Nr	0.12	1.52	–	–	1.52	1.67	–	–	1.67
P312575E	100 mm	Nr	0.15	1.91	–	–	1.91	2.10	–	–	2.10

 **Construction Accounting
Solutions
for Small, Medium and Large Enterprises**

Operational and Estimating Systems for the Construction Industry
Summit the Award Wining Solution from RedSky IT

Integrated Solution

RedSky IT's Summit system is the only truly integrated, construction specific, enterprise solution on the UK market. Summit covers the complete process within a single product:

Estimating	Planning	Budgeting	Requisitions
Procurement	Plant	Valuations	CVR
Financials	Payroll	Housebuilding	Service Management

Scalability

Whether you are a small growing subcontractor or a top 100 construction business there is a Summit solution to suit you, and as you grow you can simply upgrade to the next level of software keeping all your existing data.

Choice

Summit gives you freedom of choice to choose the appropriate technology for your business:
Microsoft SQL or Oracle Database
Windows or Linux
Scalable thin client windows or web interface.

Pedigree

Over 1300 clients from your industry have chosen RedSky IT. These secure partnerships drive an unrivalled depth of functionality into our solutions, making RedSky IT the FD's choice of financial software provider for large implementations in the CBI/Real Finance survey 2006 and enabling us to win Product of the Year at the 2007 Construction Computing Awards.

Customer Driven Solutions

As authors of our solutions and not resellers of a 3rd party product, RedSky IT and our customers make the critical decisions regarding product direction and development.

Winner of Most Successful IT
return On Investment

For more information on the Summit Solution contact RedSky IT: 020 3002 8600
or visit www.redskyit.com

PAVING, PLANTING, FENCING AND SITE FURNITURE

Major Works 2009	Unit	Labour Hours	Labour Net	Plant Net	Materials Net	Unit Net	Labour Gross	Plant Gross	Materials Gross	Unit Price
								(Gross rates include 10% profit)		
			£	£	£	£	£	£	£	£
Q10	**Q10: KERBS, EDGINGS, CHANNELS AND PAVING ACCESSORIES**									
Q1011	**Kerbs and edgings; Marley concrete block paviors**									
Q101151	**Splayed edging units; 100 mm wide; bed and point in cement mortar (1:3); haunching with 10 N/mm^2 concrete:**									
Q101151A	65 mm thick	m	0.25	3.18	–	24.17	27.35	3.50	–	26.59	30.09
Q101151B	65 mm thick; curved work . .	m	0.35	4.44	–	25.34	29.78	4.88	–	27.87	32.76
Q101151C	80 mm thick	m	0.25	3.18	–	25.68	28.86	3.50	–	28.25	31.75
Q101151D	80 mm thick; curved work . .	m	0.35	4.45	–	26.91	31.36	4.90	–	29.60	34.50
Q1015	**Kerbs and edgings; facing bricks**									
Q101561	**Kerbs, edgings or the like; bedding and pointing in cement mortar (1:3); haunching with 10 N/mm^2 concrete; brick on flat:**									
Q101561A	half brick wide	m	0.25	3.17	–	1.95	5.12	3.49	–	2.15	5.63
Q101561B	half brick wide; curved work	m	0.35	4.44	–	1.95	6.39	4.88	–	2.15	7.03
Q101562	**Kerbs, edgings or the like; bedding and pointing in cement mortar (1:3); haunching with 10 N/mm^2 concrete; brick on edge:**									
Q101562C	one brick wide	m	0.70	8.89	–	5.27	14.16	9.78	–	5.80	15.58
Q101562D	one brick wide; curved work	m	0.80	10.16	–	5.57	15.73	11.18	–	6.13	17.30
Q1021	**Kerbs or the like; precast concrete, BS 340**									
Q102101	**Kerbs; 125 × 255 mm; bedding and pointing in cement mortar (1:3); haunching with 20 N/mm^2 concrete:**									
Q102101A	Fig 2, 5, 7, 8	m	0.37	4.70	0.55	5.58	10.83	5.17	0.61	6.14	11.91
Q102101B	Fig 2, 5, 7, 8; curved work . .	m	0.45	5.71	0.55	5.69	11.95	6.28	0.61	6.26	13.15
Q102101E	Fig 2a, 7a, 8, 9	m	0.37	4.70	0.55	9.79	15.04	5.17	0.61	10.77	16.54
Q102101F	Fig 2a, 7a, 8, 9; curved work	m	0.45	5.71	0.55	10.11	16.37	6.28	0.61	11.12	18.01
Q102143	**Kerbs; 150 × 305 mm; bedding and pointing in cement mortar (1:3); haunching with 20 N/mm^2 concrete:**									
Q102143C	Fig. 1, 4, 6, 8	m	0.39	4.95	0.55	10.18	15.68	5.45	0.61	11.20	17.25
Q102143D	Fig. 1, 4, 6, 8; curved work .	m	0.47	5.97	0.55	10.45	16.97	6.57	0.61	11.50	18.67
Q102144	**Extra for:**									
Q102144A	droppers; Fig 16; 255 to 155 mm high 125 mm wide.	Nr	–	–	–	3.71	3.71	–	–	4.08	4.08
Q102144B	droppers; Fig 16; 305 to 205 mm high 150 mm wide.	Nr	–	–	–	11.56	11.56	–	–	12.72	12.72
Q102144C	quadrants; Fig 14; 450 × 450 × 250 m	Nr	–	–	–	9.08	9.08	–	–	9.99	9.99

Paving, Planting, Fencing and Site Furniture

Major Works 2009		Unit	Labour Hours	Labour Net	Plant Net	Materials Net	Unit Net	Labour Gross	Plant Gross	Materials Gross	Unit Price
									(Gross rates include 10% profit)		
				£	£	£	£	£	£	£	£
Q10	**Q10: KERBS, EDGINGS, CHANNELS AND PAVING ACCESSORIES**										
Q1031	**Edgings or the like; precast concrete, BS 340**										
Q103101	**Edgings; 50 × 150 mm; bedding and pointing in cement mortar (1:3); haunching with 10 N/mm^2 concrete:**										
Q103101A	Fig 11, 12, 13	m	0.20	2.54	0.55	2.10	5.19	2.79	0.61	2.31	5.71
Q103101B	Fig 11, 12, 13; curved work.	m	0.25	3.17	0.55	2.14	5.86	3.49	0.61	2.35	6.45
Q103102	**Edgings; 50 × 200 mm; bedding and pointing in cement mortar (1:3); haunching with 10 N/mm^2 concrete:**										
Q103102C	Fig 11, 13	m	0.20	2.54	0.55	3.36	6.45	2.79	0.61	3.70	7.10
Q103102D	Fig 11, 13; curved work	m	0.25	3.18	0.55	3.42	7.15	3.50	0.61	3.76	7.87
Q103145	**Edgings; 50 × 250 mm; bedding and pointing in cement mortar (1:3); haunching with 10 N/mm^2 concrete:**										
Q103145E	Fig 11, 12	m	0.22	2.79	0.55	4.67	8.01	3.07	0.61	5.14	8.81
Q103145F	Fig 11, 12; curved work	m	0.27	3.43	0.55	4.74	8.72	3.77	0.61	5.21	9.59
Q1041	**Channels or the like; precast concrete, BS 340**										
Q104101	**Channels; 125 × 255 mm; bedding and pointing in cement mortar (1:3); haunching with 10 N/mm^2 concrete:**										
Q104101A	Fig 2, 8	m	0.33	4.19	0.55	3.39	8.13	4.61	0.61	3.73	8.94
Q104101B	Fig 2, 8; curved work	m	0.42	5.33	0.55	3.49	9.37	5.86	0.61	3.84	10.31
Q104102	**Channels; 150 × 305 mm; bedding and pointing in cement mortar (1:3); haunching with 10 N/mm^2 concrete:**										
Q104102C	Fig 1, 8	m	0.35	4.44	0.55	11.30	16.29	4.88	0.61	12.43	17.92
Q104102D	Fig 1, 8; curved work	m	0.44	5.59	0.55	11.78	17.92	6.15	0.61	12.96	19.71
Q104142	**Channels; 125 × 150 mm; bedding and pointing in cement mortar (1:3); haunching with 10 N/mm^2 concrete:**										
Q104142E	Fig 2a, 8a	m	0.34	4.31	0.55	2.87	7.73	4.74	0.61	3.16	8.50
Q104142F	Fig 2a, 8a; curved work	m	0.43	5.46	0.55	2.96	8.97	6.01	0.61	3.26	9.87

Major Works 2009		Unit	Labour Hours	Labour Net	Plant Net	Materials Net	Unit Net	Labour Gross	Plant Gross	Materials Gross	Unit Price
								(Gross rates include 10% profit)			
				£	£	£	£	£	£	£	£
Q10	**Q10: KERBS, EDGINGS, CHANNELS AND PAVING ACCESSORIES**										
Q1043	**Drainage kerbs; precast concrete; Charcon Building Products**										
Q104301	**Safeticurb surface water drainage kerbs; 165 × 165 mm Junior Block; bedding and pointing in cement mortar (1:3); haunching with 10 N/mm² concrete:**										
Q104301A	76 mm bore.............	m	0.45	5.72	–	25.08	30.80	6.29	–	27.59	33.88
Q104301B	76 mm bore; curved work..	m	0.60	7.62	–	26.23	33.85	8.38	–	28.85	37.24
Q104302	**Safeticurb surface water drainage kerbs; 248 × 248 mm DBA/1; bedding and pointing in cement mortar (1:3); haunching with 10 N/mm² concrete:**										
Q104302E	127 mm bore.............	m	0.58	7.37	–	25.46	32.83	8.11	–	28.01	36.11
Q104302F	127 mm bore; curved work.	m	0.70	8.89	–	26.54	35.43	9.78	–	29.19	38.97
Q104302I	silt box..................	Nr	1.80	22.86	–	147.30	170.16	25.15	–	162.03	187.18
Q104302J	inspection unit	Nr	0.65	8.25	–	61.22	69.47	9.08	–	67.34	76.42
Q104303	**Safeticurb surface water drainage kerbs; 248 × 321 or 349 mm DBK; bedding and pointing in cement mortar (1:3); haunching with 10 N/mm² concrete:**										
Q104303K	248 × 321 or 349 mm DBK 127 mm bore...........	m	0.65	8.26	–	38.27	46.53	9.09	–	42.10	51.18
Q104303L	248 × 321 or 349 mm DBK 127 mm bore; curved work.	m	0.78	9.91	–	39.88	49.79	10.90	–	43.87	54.77
Q104303M	DBK to DBA transition unit .	Nr	0.45	5.71	–	40.32	46.03	6.28	–	44.35	50.63
Q104347	**Safeticurb surface water drainage kerbs; 305 × 305 mm Jumbo DBJ/2; bedding and pointing in cement mortar (1:3); haunching with 10 N/mm² concrete:**										
Q104347N	159 mm bore.............	m	0.85	10.80	–	47.79	58.59	11.88	–	52.57	64.45
Q104347O	159 mm bore; curved work.	m	1.00	12.70	–	49.89	62.59	13.97	–	54.88	68.85
Q104347R	silt box..................	Nr	2.20	27.94	–	270.17	298.11	30.73	–	297.19	327.92
Q104347S	inspection unit	Nr	0.85	10.79	–	85.12	95.91	11.87	–	93.63	105.50

Paving, Planting, Fencing and Site Furniture

Major Works 2009		Unit	Labour Hours	Labour Net	Plant Net	Materials Net	Unit Net	Labour Gross	Plant Gross	Materials Gross	Unit Price
								(Gross rates include 10% profit)			
				£	£	£	£	£	£	£	£
Q20	**Q20: GRANULAR SUB-BASES TO ROADS AND PAVINGS**										
Q2021	**Aggregate base fill**										
Q202101	**Filled into excavation; by hand; compacting in layers:**										
Q202101A	sand	m³	0.80	10.16	0.86	22.21	33.23	11.18	0.95	24.43	36.55
Q202101B	hardcore	m³	1.65	20.95	1.00	27.78	49.73	23.05	1.10	30.56	54.70
Q202101C	hoggin	m³	0.90	11.43	0.86	24.45	36.74	12.57	0.95	26.90	40.41
Q202101D	DTp type 1	m³	1.63	20.70	0.94	29.43	51.07	22.77	1.03	32.37	56.18
Q202101E	DTp type 2	m³	1.63	20.71	0.94	27.01	48.66	22.78	1.03	29.71	53.53
Q202101F	stone rejects	m³	1.65	20.95	1.00	28.00	49.95	23.05	1.10	30.80	54.95
Q202101G	granite scalpings	m³	1.65	20.96	0.94	25.14	47.04	23.06	1.03	27.65	51.74
Q202102	**Filled into excavation; by machine; compacting in layers:**										
Q202102A	sand	m³	0.30	3.81	5.25	22.21	31.27	4.19	5.78	24.43	34.40
Q202102B	hardcore	m³	0.35	4.45	8.68	27.78	40.91	4.90	9.55	30.56	45.00
Q202102C	hoggin	m³	0.30	3.81	7.44	24.45	35.70	4.19	8.18	26.90	39.27
Q202102D	DTp type 1	m³	0.33	4.19	8.62	29.43	42.24	4.61	9.48	32.37	46.46
Q202102E	DTp type 2	m³	0.33	4.19	8.62	27.01	39.82	4.61	9.48	29.71	43.80
Q202102F	stone rejects	m³	0.35	4.44	8.68	28.00	41.12	4.88	9.55	30.80	45.23
Q202102G	granite scalpings	m³	0.33	4.19	8.62	25.14	37.95	4.61	9.48	27.65	41.75
Q202103	**Filled in making up levels; by hand; compacting in layers:**										
Q202103A	sand	m³	0.83	10.55	1.07	22.21	33.83	11.61	1.18	24.43	37.21
Q202103B	hardcore	m³	1.46	18.54	1.07	27.78	47.39	20.39	1.18	30.56	52.13
Q202103C	hoggin	m³	0.93	11.81	1.07	24.45	37.33	12.99	1.18	26.90	41.06
Q202103D	DTp type 1	m³	1.40	17.78	1.07	29.43	48.28	19.56	1.18	32.37	53.11
Q202103E	DTp type 2	m³	1.40	17.78	1.07	27.01	45.86	19.56	1.18	29.71	50.45
Q202103F	stone rejects	m³	1.46	18.54	1.07	28.00	47.61	20.39	1.18	30.80	52.37
Q202103G	granite scalpings	m³	1.46	18.54	1.07	25.14	44.75	20.39	1.18	27.65	49.23
Q202104	**Filled in making up levels; by machine; compacting in layers:**										
Q202104A	sand	m³	0.13	1.65	2.17	22.21	26.03	1.82	2.39	24.43	28.63
Q202104B	hardcore	m³	0.13	1.65	3.27	27.78	32.70	1.82	3.60	30.56	35.97
Q202104C	hoggin	m³	0.13	1.65	2.83	24.45	28.93	1.82	3.11	26.90	31.82
Q202104D	DTp type 1	m³	0.13	1.65	2.83	29.43	33.91	1.82	3.11	32.37	37.30
Q202104E	DTp type 2	m³	0.13	1.65	2.83	27.01	31.49	1.82	3.11	29.71	34.64
Q202104F	stone rejects	m³	0.13	1.65	3.27	28.00	32.92	1.82	3.60	30.80	36.21
Q202104G	granite scalpings	m³	0.13	1.65	3.27	25.14	30.06	1.82	3.60	27.65	33.07

Major Works 2009		Unit	Labour Hours	Labour Net	Plant Net	Materials Net	Unit Net	Labour Gross	Plant Gross	Materials Gross	Unit Price
								(Gross rates include 10% profit)			
				£	£	£	£	£	£	£	£
Q20	**Q20: GRANULAR SUB-BASES TO ROADS AND PAVINGS**										
Q2021	**Aggregate base fill**										
Q202105	**Filled into oversite; by hand; compacting in layers; average 150 mm thick:**										
Q202105A	sand	m³	1.03	13.09	1.40	22.21	36.70	14.40	1.54	24.43	40.37
Q202105B	hardcore	m³	1.66	21.08	1.40	27.78	50.26	23.19	1.54	30.56	55.29
Q202105C	hoggin	m³	1.13	14.35	1.40	24.45	40.20	15.79	1.54	26.90	44.22
Q202105D	DTp type 1	m³	1.60	20.32	1.40	29.43	51.15	22.35	1.54	32.37	56.27
Q202105E	DTp type 2	m³	1.60	20.32	1.40	27.01	48.73	22.35	1.54	29.71	53.60
Q202105F	stone rejects	m³	1.66	21.08	1.40	28.00	50.48	23.19	1.54	30.80	55.53
Q202105G	granite scalpings	m³	1.66	21.08	1.40	25.14	47.62	23.19	1.54	27.65	52.38
Q202106	**Filled into oversite; by machine; compacting in layers; average 150 mm thick:**										
Q202106A	sand	m³	0.17	2.16	3.60	22.21	27.97	2.38	3.96	24.43	30.77
Q202106B	hardcore	m³	0.17	2.16	4.70	27.78	34.64	2.38	5.17	30.56	38.10
Q202106C	hoggin	m³	0.17	2.16	4.26	24.45	30.87	2.38	4.69	26.90	33.96
Q202106D	DTp type 1	m³	0.17	2.16	4.26	29.43	35.85	2.38	4.69	32.37	39.44
Q202106E	DTp type 2	m³	0.17	2.16	4.26	27.01	33.43	2.38	4.69	29.71	36.77
Q202106F	stone rejects	m³	0.17	2.16	4.70	28.00	34.86	2.38	5.17	30.80	38.35
Q202106G	granite scalpings	m³	0.17	2.16	4.70	25.14	32.00	2.38	5.17	27.65	35.20
Q2091	**Contour grading**										
Q209107	**Grading filled oversite to contours, embankments or the like; by hand:**										
Q209107A	to falls	m²	0.10	1.27	–	–	1.27	1.40	–	–	1.40
Q209107B	to falls and cross-falls	m²	0.17	2.16	–	–	2.16	2.38	–	–	2.38
Q209107C	to slopes	m²	0.09	1.14	–	–	1.14	1.25	–	–	1.25
Q209108	**Grading filled oversite to contours, embankments or the like; by machine:**										
Q209108A	to falls	m²	0.03	0.38	0.66	–	1.04	0.42	0.73	–	1.14
Q209108B	to falls and cross-falls	m²	0.05	0.63	1.10	–	1.73	0.69	1.21	–	1.90
Q209108C	to slopes	m²	0.02	0.25	0.44	–	0.69	0.28	0.48	–	0.76
Q2093	**Blinding surfaces**										
Q209309	**Blinding to hardcore:**										
Q209309A	25 mm sand	m²	0.04	0.51	–	0.50	1.01	0.56	–	0.55	1.11
Q209309B	50 mm sand	m²	0.06	0.70	–	0.98	1.68	0.77	–	1.08	1.85

Paving, Planting, Fencing and Site Furniture

Major Works 2009		Unit	Labour Hours	Labour Net	Plant Net	Materials Net	Unit Net	Labour Gross	Plant Gross	Materials Gross	Unit Price
								(Gross rates include 10% profit)			
				£	£	£	£	£	£	£	£
Q21	**Q21: IN SITU CONCRETE ROADS AND PAVINGS**										
Q2111	**Plain concrete; mix C20P**										
Q211102	**Foundations; combined and isolated bases:**										
Q211102A	not exceeding 150 mm thick	m³	1.20	15.24	–	101.60	116.84	16.76	–	111.76	128.52
Q211102B	150-300 mm thick	m³	0.90	11.43	–	101.60	113.03	12.57	–	111.76	124.33
Q211102C	over 300 mm thick	m³	0.70	8.89	–	101.60	110.49	9.78	–	111.76	121.54
Q211104	**Blinding:**										
Q211104A	not exceeding 150 mm thick	m³	0.90	11.43	–	96.98	108.41	12.57	–	106.68	119.25
Q211104B	150-300 mm thick	m³	0.55	6.98	–	96.98	103.96	7.68	–	106.68	114.36
Q211104C	over 300 mm thick	m³	0.40	5.08	–	96.98	102.06	5.59	–	106.68	112.27
Q211105	**Beds, roads and footpaths:**										
Q211105A	not exceeding 150 mm thick	m³	1.05	13.33	–	96.98	110.31	14.66	–	106.68	121.34
Q211105B	150-300 mm thick	m³	0.70	8.89	–	96.98	105.87	9.78	–	106.68	116.46
Q211105C	over 300 mm thick	m³	0.50	6.35	–	96.98	103.33	6.99	–	106.68	113.66
Q2115	**Reinforced concrete; mix C30P**										
Q211516	**Beds, roads and footpaths:**										
Q211516A	not exceeding 150 mm thick	m³	1.40	17.79	5.56	101.75	125.10	19.57	6.12	111.93	137.61
Q211516B	150-300 mm thick	m³	1.00	12.70	3.89	101.75	118.34	13.97	4.28	111.93	130.17
Q211516C	over 300 mm thick	m³	0.70	8.90	2.78	101.75	113.43	9.79	3.06	111.93	124.77
Q2121	**Formwork to general finish**										
Q212107	**Sloping upper surfaces over 15 degrees from horizontal:**										
Q212107A	over 300 mm wide	m²	1.86	31.64	–	21.98	53.62	34.80	–	24.18	58.98
Q212108	**Sides of foundations, bases and ground beams:**										
Q212108A	not exceeding 250 mm high	m	0.76	12.91	–	50.57	63.48	14.20	–	55.63	69.83
Q212108B	250-500 mm high.	m	1.15	19.45	–	100.38	119.83	21.40	–	110.42	131.81
Q212108C	500-1000 mm high	m	2.04	34.56	–	200.02	234.58	38.02	–	220.02	258.04
Q212108D	over 1000 mm high	m²	1.86	31.49	–	183.23	214.72	34.64	–	201.55	236.19
Q212119	**Vertical edges of slabs, faces of kerbs, upstands, breaks in upper surfaces or the like:**										
Q212119A	not exceeding 250 mm wide	m	0.71	11.97	–	5.82	17.79	13.17	–	6.40	19.57
Q212119B	250-500 mm wide	m	0.90	15.29	–	8.96	24.25	16.82	–	9.86	26.68
Q212119C	500-1000 mm wide	m	1.60	27.15	0.63	15.10	42.88	29.87	0.69	16.61	47.17
Q212119D	over 1000 mm wide	m²	1.46	24.76	1.25	15.96	41.97	27.24	1.38	17.56	46.17
Q212120	**Grooves, throats, rebates, chamfers or the like; sectional area:**										
Q212120A	2500-5000 mm²	m	0.26	4.46	–	3.92	8.38	4.91	–	4.31	9.22
Q212120B	5000-10000 mm²	m	0.69	11.68	–	7.73	19.41	12.85	–	8.50	21.35
Q212120C	10000-20000 mm²	m	0.83	14.01	–	13.65	27.66	15.41	–	15.02	30.43

Major Works 2009		Unit	Labour Hours	Labour Net	Plant Net	Materials Net	Unit Net	Labour Gross	Plant Gross	Materials Gross	Unit Price
								(Gross rates include 10% profit)			
				£	£	£	£	£	£	£	£
Q21	**Q21: IN SITU CONCRETE ROADS AND PAVINGS**										
Q2133	**Steel fabric reinforcement, BS 4483; delivered to site in standard sheets**										
Q213301	**Fabric reinforcement, laid horizontally, ref:**										
Q213301A	A98....................	m²	0.02	0.30	–	1.95	2.25	0.33	–	2.15	2.48
Q213301B	A142....................	m²	0.03	0.46	–	2.49	2.95	0.51	–	2.74	3.25
Q213301C	A193....................	m²	0.03	0.44	–	3.32	3.76	0.48	–	3.65	4.14
Q213301D	A252....................	m²	0.03	0.45	–	4.30	4.75	0.50	–	4.73	5.23
Q213301E	A393....................	m²	0.05	0.74	–	6.76	7.50	0.81	–	7.44	8.25
Q213301F	B196....................	m²	0.03	0.45	–	3.52	3.97	0.50	–	3.87	4.37
Q213301G	B283....................	m²	0.03	0.45	–	4.13	4.58	0.50	–	4.54	5.04
Q213301H	B385....................	m²	0.04	0.62	–	4.94	5.56	0.68	–	5.43	6.12
Q213301I	B503....................	m²	0.05	0.75	–	6.31	7.06	0.83	–	6.94	7.77
Q213301J	B785....................	m²	0.05	0.74	–	8.05	8.79	0.81	–	8.86	9.67
Q213301K	B1131....................	m²	0.07	1.04	–	10.72	11.76	1.14	–	11.79	12.94
Q213301L	C283....................	m²	0.03	0.45	–	3.11	3.56	0.50	–	3.42	3.92
Q213301M	C385....................	m²	0.03	0.45	–	3.94	4.39	0.50	–	4.33	4.83
Q213301N	C503....................	m²	0.04	0.62	–	4.88	5.50	0.68	–	5.37	6.05
Q213301O	C636....................	m²	0.04	0.60	–	6.18	6.78	0.66	–	6.80	7.46
Q213301P	C785....................	m²	0.05	0.74	–	6.82	7.56	0.81	–	7.50	8.32
Q213303	**Fabric reinforcement, fixed vertically, ref:**										
Q213303A	A98....................	m²	0.08	1.18	–	1.89	3.07	1.30	–	2.08	3.38
Q213303B	A142....................	m²	0.09	1.33	–	2.43	3.76	1.46	–	2.67	4.14
Q213303C	A193....................	m²	0.09	1.33	–	3.26	4.59	1.46	–	3.59	5.05
Q213303D	A252....................	m²	0.09	1.33	–	4.24	5.57	1.46	–	4.66	6.13
Q213303E	A393....................	m²	0.02	0.23	–	6.70	6.93	0.25	–	7.37	7.62
Q213303F	B196....................	m²	0.09	1.33	–	3.46	4.79	1.46	–	3.81	5.27
Q213303G	B283....................	m²	0.10	1.48	–	4.07	5.55	1.63	–	4.48	6.11
Q213303H	B385....................	m²	0.12	1.78	–	4.87	6.65	1.96	–	5.36	7.32
Q213303I	B503....................	m²	0.16	2.37	–	6.24	8.61	2.61	–	6.86	9.47
Q213303J	B785....................	m²	0.20	2.96	–	7.99	10.95	3.26	–	8.79	12.05
Q213303K	B1131....................	m²	0.22	3.25	–	10.66	13.91	3.58	–	11.73	15.30
Q213303L	C283....................	m²	0.08	1.19	–	3.05	4.24	1.31	–	3.36	4.66
Q213303M	C385....................	m²	0.09	1.33	–	3.88	5.21	1.46	–	4.27	5.73
Q213303N	C503....................	m²	0.12	1.78	–	4.81	6.59	1.96	–	5.29	7.25
Q213303O	C636....................	m²	0.15	2.22	–	6.12	8.34	2.44	–	6.73	9.17
Q213303P	C785....................	m²	0.16	2.36	–	6.76	9.12	2.60	–	7.44	10.03
Q2143	**Movement joints**										
Q214329	**Horizontal joints; 25 mm steel dowel bars 600 mm long, debonded for half length, dowel caps with compressible filler, notching shuttering for dowels 300 mm centres; including formwork:**										
Q214329A	100 mm high.............	m	0.92	15.62	–	15.36	30.98	17.18	–	16.90	34.08
Q214329B	150 mm high.............	m	1.09	18.51	–	18.33	36.84	20.36	–	20.16	40.52
Q214329C	200 mm high.............	m	1.11	18.85	–	21.30	40.15	20.74	–	23.43	44.17
Q214329D	250 mm high.............	m	1.13	19.18	–	37.08	56.26	21.10	–	40.79	61.89
Q214329E	300 mm high.............	m	1.19	20.21	–	40.73	60.94	22.23	–	44.80	67.03

Paving, Planting, Fencing and Site Furniture

Major Works 2009		Unit	Labour Hours	Labour Net	Plant Net	Materials Net	Unit Net	Labour Gross	Plant Gross	Materials Gross	Unit Price
								(Gross rates include 10% profit)			
				£	£	£	£	£	£	£	£
Q21	**Q21: IN SITU CONCRETE ROADS AND PAVINGS**										
Q2146	**Expansion materials**										
Q214611	**Flexcell fibreboard compressible joint filler; 10 mm thick:**										
Q214611A	not exceeding 150 mm wide	m	0.10	1.70	–	1.76	3.46	1.87	–	1.94	3.81
Q214611B	150–300 mm wide	m	0.18	2.97	–	3.51	6.48	3.27	–	3.86	7.13
Q214611C	300–450 mm wide	m	0.22	3.74	–	5.26	9.00	4.11	–	5.79	9.90
Q214612	**Flexcell fibreboard compressible joint filler; 13 mm thick:**										
Q214612A	not exceeding 150 mm wide	m	0.11	1.79	–	1.57	3.36	1.97	–	1.73	3.70
Q214612B	150–300 mm wide	m	0.18	3.06	–	3.13	6.19	3.37	–	3.44	6.81
Q214612C	300–450 mm wide	m	0.23	3.82	–	4.71	8.53	4.20	–	5.18	9.38
Q214613	**Flexcell fibreboard compressible joint filler; 19 mm thick:**										
Q214613A	not exceeding 150 mm wide	m	0.12	1.96	–	2.88	4.84	2.16	–	3.17	5.32
Q214613B	150–300 mm wide	m	0.20	3.31	–	5.75	9.06	3.64	–	6.33	9.97
Q214613C	300–450 mm wide	m	0.23	3.91	–	8.63	12.54	4.30	–	9.49	13.79
Q214614	**Flexcell fibreboard compressible joint filler; 25 mm thick:**										
Q214614A	not exceeding 150 mm wide	m	0.13	2.13	–	2.83	4.96	2.34	–	3.11	5.46
Q214614B	150–300 mm wide	m	0.20	3.31	–	5.65	8.96	3.64	–	6.22	9.86
Q214614C	300–450 mm wide	m	0.24	4.08	–	8.48	12.56	4.49	–	9.33	13.82
Q2148	**Joint sealants**										
Q214834	**Hot poured bituminous rubber compound:**										
Q214834A	10 × 25 mm............	m	0.03	0.42	0.21	1.77	2.40	0.46	0.23	1.95	2.64
Q214834B	13 × 25 mm............	m	0.03	0.51	0.24	2.10	2.85	0.56	0.26	2.31	3.14
Q214834C	19 × 25 mm............	m	0.04	0.68	0.26	3.32	4.26	0.75	0.29	3.65	4.69
Q214834D	25 × 25 mm............	m	0.06	1.01	0.30	4.58	5.89	1.11	0.33	5.04	6.48
Q214835	**Cold poured polysulphide rubber compound:**										
Q214835A	10 × 25 mm............	m	0.03	0.52	–	3.89	4.41	0.57	–	4.28	4.85
Q214835B	13 × 25 mm............	m	0.03	0.51	–	5.07	5.58	0.56	–	5.58	6.14
Q214835C	19 × 25 mm............	m	0.04	0.70	–	7.41	8.11	0.77	–	8.15	8.92
Q214835D	25 × 25 mm............	m	0.06	1.02	–	9.71	10.73	1.12	–	10.68	11.80
Q214836	**Cold poured polysulphide epoxy based compound:**										
Q214836A	10 × 25 mm............	m	0.03	0.52	–	0.64	1.16	0.57	–	0.70	1.28
Q214836B	13 × 25 mm............	m	0.03	0.51	–	0.84	1.35	0.56	–	0.92	1.49
Q214836C	19 × 25 mm............	m	0.04	0.70	–	1.21	1.91	0.77	–	1.33	2.10
Q214836D	25 × 25 mm............	m	0.06	1.02	–	1.98	3.00	1.12	–	2.18	3.30
Q214837	**Gun grade polysulphide rubber compound:**										
Q214837A	10 × 10 mm............	m	0.04	0.68	–	0.49	1.17	0.75	–	0.54	1.29
Q214837B	13 × 13 mm............	m	0.06	1.02	–	0.83	1.85	1.12	–	0.91	2.04
Q214837C	19 × 19 mm............	m	0.13	2.21	–	1.75	3.96	2.43	–	1.93	4.36
Q214837D	25 × 25 mm............	m	0.23	3.90	–	3.00	6.90	4.29	–	3.30	7.59

Major Works 2009		Unit	Labour Hours	Labour Net	Plant Net	Materials Net	Unit Net	Labour Gross	Plant Gross	Materials Gross	Unit Price
								(Gross rates include 10% profit)			
				£	£	£	£	£	£	£	£
Q21	**Q21: IN SITU CONCRETE ROADS AND PAVINGS**										
Q2151	**Surface finishes**										
Q215102	**Trowelling surfaces of concrete:**										
Q215102A	to levels	m²	0.16	2.03	–	–	2.03	2.23	–	–	2.23
Q215102B	to falls and crossfalls	m²	0.25	3.18	–	–	3.18	3.50	–	–	3.50
Q215103	**Power floating and trowelling concrete surfaces:**										
Q215103A	to levels	m²	0.15	1.91	0.59	–	2.50	2.10	0.65	–	2.75
Q215103B	to falls and crossfalls	m²	0.18	2.29	0.70	–	2.99	2.52	0.77	–	3.29
Q215104	**Lithurin surface hardener; brush applied to surfaces in accordance with manufacturer's instructions; two coats:**										
Q215104A	general surfaces of floors . .	m²	0.16	2.03	–	2.27	4.30	2.23	–	2.50	4.73
Q2153	**Form sinkings, channels or the like in face of concrete**										
Q215353	**Horizontally; including formwork:**										
Q215353A	not exceeding 150 mm girth	m	0.42	7.19	–	5.23	12.42	7.91	–	5.75	13.66
Q215353B	150-300 mm girth	m	0.85	14.36	–	8.26	22.62	15.80	–	9.09	24.88
Q215353C	over 300 mm girth	m²	1.46	24.76	–	15.83	40.59	27.24	–	17.41	44.65

Major Works 2009		Unit	Labour Hours	Labour Net	Plant Net	Materials Net	Unit Net	Labour Gross	Plant Gross	Materials Gross	Unit Price
								(Gross rates include 10% profit)			
				£	£	£	£	£	£	£	£
Q22	**Q22: COATED MACADAM AND ASPHALT ROADS AND PAVINGS**										
Q2201	**Coated macadam BS 4987**										
Q220124	**Hand laid surfacing:**										
Q220124B	60 mm thickness of 20 mm aggregate dense base course, 30 mm thickness o 10 mm aggregate close graded wearing course	m²	–	–	–	15.02	15.02	–	–	16.52	16.52
Q220124C	50 mm thickness of 20 mm aggregate open graded base course and 20 mm thickness of 6 mm aggregate medium graded wearing course	m²	–	–	–	13.32	13.32	–	–	14.65	14.65
Q220124D	50 mm thickness of 20 mm aggregate dense base course, 20 mm thickness of 6 mm aggregate dense wearing course...........	m²	–	–	–	12.32	12.32	–	–	13.55	13.55
Q220124E	45 mm thickness of 20 mm aggregate open graded base course, 15 mm thickness of fine graded wearing course.	m²	–	–	–	10.64	10.64	–	–	11.70	11.70
Q220125	**Machine laid surfacing:**										
Q220125A	50 mm thickness of 20 mm aggregate dense base course	m²	–	–	–	7.88	7.89	–	–	8.67	8.68
Q220125B	100 mm thickness of 40 mm aggregate dense base course	m²	–	–	–	12.95	12.95	–	–	14.25	14.25
Q220125C	80 mm thickness of 28 mm aggregate dense base course, 40 mm thickness of 14 mm aggregate close graded wearing course	m²	–	–	–	16.95	16.95	–	–	18.65	18.65
Q220125D	60 mm thickness of 20 mm aggregate dense base course, 30 mm thickness of 10 mm aggregate close graded wearing course	m²	–	–	–	14.03	14.03	–	–	15.43	15.43
Q220125E	45 mm thickness of 20 mm aggregate dense base course, 20 mm thickness of 6 mm aggregate dense wearing course...........	m²	–	–	–	12.48	12.48	–	–	13.73	13.73
Q220125F	surface dress with cut-back bitumen K1-70 emulsion and 10 mm aggregate single dressing................	m²	–	–	–	2.23	2.23	–	–	2.45	2.45
Q220125G	surface dress with cut-back bitumen K1-70 emulsion and 10 mm aggregate double dressing................	m²	–	–	–	3.21	3.21	–	–	3.53	3.53
Q220125H	surface dress with cut-back bitumen K1-70 emulsion and 6 mm aggregate single dressing................	m²	–	–	–	2.55	2.55	–	–	2.81	2.81
Q220125I	surface dress with cut-back bitumen K1-70 emulsion and 6 mm aggregate double dressing................	m²	–	–	–	3.57	3.57	–	–	3.93	3.93

Major Works 2009		Unit	Labour Hours	Labour Net	Plant Net	Materials Net	Unit Net	Labour Gross	Plant Gross	Materials Gross	Unit Price
								(Gross rates include 10% profit)			
				£	£	£	£	£	£	£	£
Q23	**Q23: GRAVEL, HOGGIN AND WOODCHIP ROADS AND PAVINGS**										
Q2301	**Aggregate base fill**										
Q230105	**Filled into oversite to level; by hand; compacting; 100 mm thick:**										
Q230105B	hardcore	m²	0.34	4.32	1.40	2.78	8.50	4.75	1.54	3.06	9.35
Q230105C	hoggin	m²	0.29	3.68	1.40	2.45	7.53	4.05	1.54	2.70	8.28
Q230105D	DTp type 1	m²	0.33	4.19	1.40	2.94	8.53	4.61	1.54	3.23	9.38
Q230105E	DTp type 2	m²	0.33	4.19	1.40	2.70	8.29	4.61	1.54	2.97	9.12
Q230105F	stone rejects	m²	0.34	4.32	1.40	2.80	8.52	4.75	1.54	3.08	9.37
Q230105G	granite scalpings	m²	0.34	4.31	1.40	2.51	8.22	4.74	1.54	2.76	9.04
Q230107	**Filled into oversite to level; by hand; compacting; 150 mm thick:**										
Q230107B	hardcore	m²	0.40	5.08	1.40	4.17	10.65	5.59	1.54	4.59	11.72
Q230107C	hoggin	m²	0.36	4.57	1.40	3.67	9.64	5.03	1.54	4.04	10.60
Q230107D	DTp type 1	m²	0.41	5.20	1.40	4.43	11.03	5.72	1.54	4.87	12.13
Q230107E	DTp type 2	m²	0.41	5.21	1.40	4.06	10.67	5.73	1.54	4.47	11.74
Q230107F	stone rejects	m²	0.43	5.46	1.40	4.21	11.07	6.01	1.54	4.63	12.18
Q230107G	granite scalpings	m²	0.41	5.21	1.40	3.77	10.38	5.73	1.54	4.15	11.42
Q230116	**Filled into oversite to levels; by machine; compacting; 100 mm thick:**										
Q230116B	hardcore	m²	0.17	2.16	1.84	2.78	6.78	2.38	2.02	3.06	7.46
Q230116C	hoggin	m²	0.17	2.16	1.84	2.45	6.45	2.38	2.02	2.70	7.10
Q230116D	DTp type 1	m²	0.17	2.16	1.84	2.94	6.94	2.38	2.02	3.23	7.63
Q230116E	DTp type 2	m²	0.17	2.16	1.84	2.70	6.70	2.38	2.02	2.97	7.37
Q230116F	stone rejects	m²	0.17	2.16	1.84	2.80	6.80	2.38	2.02	3.08	7.48
Q230116G	granite scalpings	m²	0.17	2.15	1.84	2.51	6.50	2.37	2.02	2.76	7.15
Q230118	**Filled into oversite to levels; by machine; compacting; 150 mm thick:**										
Q230118B	hardcore	m²	0.17	2.16	2.06	4.17	8.39	2.38	2.27	4.59	9.23
Q230118C	hoggin	m²	0.17	2.16	2.06	3.67	7.89	2.38	2.27	4.04	8.68
Q230118D	DTp type 1	m²	0.17	2.16	2.06	4.43	8.65	2.38	2.27	4.87	9.52
Q230118E	DTp type 2	m²	0.17	2.16	2.06	4.06	8.28	2.38	2.27	4.47	9.11
Q230118F	stone rejects	m²	0.17	2.16	2.06	4.21	8.43	2.38	2.27	4.63	9.27
Q230118G	granite scalpings	m²	0.17	2.16	2.06	3.77	7.99	2.38	2.27	4.15	8.79
Q2311	**Grading bases**										
Q231137	**Grading bases to slopes, falls and cross-falls; by hand:**										
Q231137A	to falls	m²	0.10	1.27	–	–	1.27	1.40	–	–	1.40
Q231137B	to falls and cross-falls	m²	0.17	2.16	–	–	2.16	2.38	–	–	2.38
Q231137C	to slopes	m²	0.09	1.14	–	–	1.14	1.25	–	–	1.25
Q231138	**Grading bases to slopes, falls and cross-falls; by machine:**										
Q231138A	to falls	m²	0.03	0.38	0.66	–	1.04	0.42	0.73	–	1.14
Q231138B	to falls and cross-falls	m²	0.05	0.63	1.10	–	1.73	0.69	1.21	–	1.90
Q231138C	to slopes	m²	0.02	0.25	0.44	–	0.69	0.28	0.48	–	0.76

Paving, Planting, Fencing and Site Furniture

Major Works 2009		Unit	Labour Hours	Labour Net	Plant Net	Materials Net	Unit Net	Labour Gross	Plant Gross	Materials Gross	Unit Price
								(Gross rates include 10% profit)			
				£	£	£	£	£	£	£	£
Q23	Q23: GRAVEL, HOGGIN AND WOODCHIP ROADS AND PAVINGS										
Q2318	Blinding										
Q231849	Blinding to hardcore base:										
Q231849A	25 mm sand	m²	0.04	0.51	–	0.50	1.01	0.56	–	0.55	1.11
Q231849B	50 mm sand	m²	0.06	0.70	–	0.98	1.68	0.77	–	1.08	1.85
Q2321	Pea shingle dressing										
Q232122	Roads, paths and driveways:										
Q232122A	25 mm thick	m²	0.10	1.27	0.14	0.85	2.26	1.40	0.15	0.94	2.49
Q232122B	50 mm thick	m²	0.12	1.52	0.28	1.70	3.50	1.67	0.31	1.87	3.85
Q2331	Treated sawn softwood edging										
Q233171	Road and path edging; 50 × 50 mm pegs at 1.00 m centres:										
Q233171A	25 × 150 mm	m	0.10	1.27	–	1.07	2.34	1.40	–	1.18	2.57
Q233171C	25 × 200 mm	m	0.12	1.52	–	1.55	3.07	1.67	–	1.71	3.38

Major Works 2009		Unit	Labour Hours	Labour Net	Plant Net	Materials Net	Unit Net	Labour Gross	Plant Gross	Materials Gross	Unit Price
								(Gross rates include 10% profit)			
				£	£	£	£	£	£	£	£
Q25	**Q25: SLAB, BRICK, BLOCK, SETT AND COBBLE PAVINGS**										
Q2521	**Precast concrete flag paving, BS 368**										
Q252111	**Pavings; bed in cement mortar (1:3), point in lime mortar (1:1:6):**										
Q252111M	600 × 450 × 50 mm thick	m²	0.51	6.48	–	17.73	24.21	7.13	–	19.50	26.63
Q252111N	600 × 600 × 50 mm thick	m²	0.43	5.46	–	14.12	19.58	6.01	–	15.53	21.54
Q252111O	600 × 750 × 50 mm thick	m²	0.39	4.95	–	14.51	19.46	5.45	–	15.96	21.41
Q252111P	600 × 900 × 50 mm thick	m²	0.35	4.44	–	12.94	17.38	4.88	–	14.23	19.12
Q252111Q	600 × 450 × 63 mm thick	m²	0.52	6.61	–	21.09	27.70	7.27	–	23.20	30.47
Q252111R	600 × 600 × 63 mm thick	m²	0.44	5.59	–	16.44	22.03	6.15	–	18.08	24.23
Q252111S	600 × 750 × 63 mm thick	m²	0.40	5.08	–	16.92	22.00	5.59	–	18.61	24.20
Q252111T	600 × 900 × 63 mm thick	m²	0.36	4.58	–	15.08	19.66	5.04	–	16.59	21.63
Q2522	**Brick paving**										
Q252215	**Pavings; bed and point in cement mortar (1:3): ·**										
Q252215A	brick on flat; half bond or 90 degree herringbone	m²	1.07	18.17	–	18.29	36.46	19.99	–	20.12	40.11
Q252215B	brick on flat; parquet bond or 45 degree herringbone	m²	1.12	19.02	0.22	19.19	38.43	20.92	0.24	21.11	42.27
Q252215C	brick on edge; half bond or 90 degree herringbone	m²	1.39	23.60	–	25.41	49.01	25.96	–	27.95	53.91
Q252215D	brick on edge; parquet bond or 90 degree herringbone . .	m²	1.44	24.45	0.22	26.31	50.98	26.90	0.24	28.94	56.08
Q2523	**Marley concrete block paving**										
Q252313	**200 × 100 mm chamfered blocks; laid and vibrator compacted on 50 mm sand bed:**										
Q252313A	65 mm thick; half bond or 90 degree herringbone	m²	1.11	18.85	0.23	11.60	30.68	20.74	0.25	12.76	33.75
Q252313B	65 mm thick; parquet bond or 45 degree herringbone . .	m²	1.21	20.55	0.44	12.11	33.10	22.61	0.48	13.32	36.41
Q252313C	80 mm thick; half bond or 90 degree herringbone	m²	1.11	18.85	0.23	14.00	33.08	20.74	0.25	15.40	36.39
Q252313D	80 mm thick; parquet bond or 45 degree herringbone . .	m²	1.21	20.54	0.44	14.62	35.60	22.59	0.48	16.08	39.16
Q2531	**Granite sett paving**										
Q253101	**Granite setts; bedding in cement mortar (1:3) on concrete base (measured separately); laid:**										
Q253101A	100 mm thick; level and to falls.	m²	1.75	43.96	–	78.82	122.78	48.36	–	86.70	135.06
Q2545	**Cobble paving**										
Q254501	**Cobbles; set and butted on concrete base (measured separately); dry grouted in cement and sand (1:3); wetted and brushed:**										
Q254501A	level and to falls; random . .	m²	1.95	48.98	–	70.32	119.30	53.88	–	77.35	131.23
Q254501B	level and to falls; to pattern .	m²	2.13	53.38	–	71.68	125.06	58.72	–	78.85	137.57

Paving, Planting, Fencing and Site Furniture

Major Works 2009		Unit	Labour Hours	Labour Net	Plant Net	Materials Net	Unit Net	Labour Gross	Plant Gross	Materials Gross	Unit Price
								(Gross rates include 10% profit)			
				£	£	£	£	£	£	£	£
Q25	**Q25: SLAB, BRICK, BLOCK, SETT AND COBBLE PAVINGS**										
Q2590	**Expansion materials**										
Q259011	**Flexcell fibreboard compressible joint filler; 10 mm thick:**										
Q259011A	not exceeding 150 mm wide	m	0.10	1.70	–	1.76	3.46	1.87	–	1.94	3.81
Q259011B	150-300 mm wide	m	0.18	2.97	–	3.51	6.48	3.27	–	3.86	7.13
Q259011C	300-450 mm wide	m	0.22	3.74	–	5.26	9.00	4.11	–	5.79	9.90
Q259012	**Flexcell fibreboard compressible joint filler; 13 mm thick:**										
Q259012A	not exceeding 150 mm wide	m	0.11	1.79	–	1.57	3.36	1.97	–	1.73	3.70
Q259012B	150-300 mm wide	m	0.18	3.06	–	3.13	6.19	3.37	–	3.44	6.81
Q259012C	300-450 mm wide	m	0.23	3.82	–	4.71	8.53	4.20	–	5.18	9.38
Q259013	**Flexcell fibreboard compressible joint filler; 19 mm thick:**										
Q259013A	not exceeding 150 mm wide	m	0.12	1.96	–	2.88	4.84	2.16	–	3.17	5.32
Q259013B	150-300 mm wide	m	0.20	3.31	–	5.75	9.06	3.64	–	6.33	9.97
Q259013C	300-450 mm wide	m	0.23	3.91	–	8.63	12.54	4.30	–	9.49	13.79
Q259014	**Flexcell fibreboard compressible joint filler; 25 mm thick:**										
Q259014A	not exceeding 150 mm wide	m	0.13	2.13	–	2.83	4.96	2.34	–	3.11	5.46
Q259014B	150-300 mm wide	m	0.20	3.31	–	5.65	8.96	3.64	–	6.22	9.86
Q259014C	300-450 mm wide	m	0.24	4.08	–	8.48	12.56	4.49	–	9.33	13.82
Q2592	**Joint sealants**										
Q259234	**Hot poured bituminous rubber compound:**										
Q259234A	10 × 25 mm	m	0.03	0.42	0.21	1.77	2.40	0.46	0.23	1.95	2.64
Q259234B	13 × 25 mm	m	0.03	0.51	0.24	2.10	2.85	0.56	0.26	2.31	3.14
Q259234C	19 × 25 mm	m	0.04	0.68	0.26	3.32	4.26	0.75	0.29	3.65	4.69
Q259234D	25 × 25 mm	m	0.06	1.01	0.30	4.58	5.89	1.11	0.33	5.04	6.48
Q259235	**Cold poured polysulphide rubber compound:**										
Q259235A	10 × 25 mm	m	0.03	0.52	–	3.89	4.41	0.57	–	4.28	4.85
Q259235B	13 × 25 mm	m	0.03	0.51	–	5.07	5.58	0.56	–	5.58	6.14
Q259235C	19 × 25 mm	m	0.04	0.70	–	7.41	8.11	0.77	–	8.15	8.92
Q259235D	25 × 25 mm	m	0.06	1.02	–	9.71	10.73	1.12	–	10.68	11.80
Q259236	**Cold poured polysulphide epoxy based compound:**										
Q259236A	10 × 25 mm	m	0.03	0.52	–	0.64	1.16	0.57	–	0.70	1.28
Q259236B	13 × 25 mm	m	0.03	0.51	–	0.84	1.35	0.56	–	0.92	1.49
Q259236C	19 × 25 mm	m	0.04	0.70	–	1.21	1.91	0.77	–	1.33	2.10
Q259236D	25 × 25 mm	m	0.06	1.02	–	1.98	3.00	1.12	–	2.18	3.30
Q259237	**Gun grade polysulphide rubber compound:**										
Q259237A	10 × 10 mm	m	0.04	0.68	–	0.49	1.17	0.75	–	0.54	1.29
Q259237B	13 × 13 mm	m	0.06	1.02	–	0.83	1.85	1.12	–	0.91	2.04
Q259237C	19 × 19 mm	m	0.13	2.21	–	1.75	3.96	2.43	–	1.93	4.36
Q259237D	25 × 25 mm	m	0.23	3.90	–	3.00	6.90	4.29	–	3.30	7.59

Major Works 2009		Unit	Labour Hours	Labour Net	Plant Net	Materials Net	Unit Net	Labour Gross	Plant Gross	Materials Gross	Unit Price
								(Gross rates include 10% profit)			
				£	£	£	£	£	£	£	£
Q30	**Q30: SEEDING AND TURFING**										
Q3010	**Cultivating**										
Q301002	**Cultivating; removing weeds, stones and the like:**										
Q301002A	hand excavation	m²	0.25	3.18	–	–	3.18	3.50	–	–	3.50
Q301002B	rotovating	m²	0.15	1.91	0.52	–	2.43	2.10	0.57	–	2.67
Q3015	**Soiling**										
Q301521	**Soiling with topsoil excavated from temporary spoil heaps on site; transporting not exceeding 100 m:**										
Q301521A	150 mm thick	m²	0.19	2.41	0.28	–	2.69	2.65	0.31	–	2.96
Q301521B	225 mm thick	m²	0.28	3.56	0.41	–	3.97	3.92	0.45	–	4.37
Q301521C	300 mm thick	m²	0.38	4.83	0.55	–	5.38	5.31	0.61	–	5.92
Q301522	**Soiling with imported topsoil:**										
Q301522A	150 mm thick	m²	0.13	1.65	–	1.70	3.35	1.82	–	1.87	3.69
Q301522B	225 mm thick	m²	0.19	2.41	–	2.61	5.02	2.65	–	2.87	5.52
Q301522C	300 mm thick	m²	0.25	3.17	–	3.51	6.68	3.49	–	3.86	7.35
Q3020	**Surface applications**										
Q302003	**Fertiliser; spreading by hand:**										
Q302003A	0.04 Kg per m²	m²	0.05	0.63	–	0.02	0.65	0.69	–	0.02	0.72
Q302003B	0.06 Kg per m²	m²	0.05	0.63	–	0.03	0.66	0.69	–	0.03	0.73
Q302005	**Weedkiller; by spreader:**										
Q302005A	0.03 Kg per m²	m²	0.10	1.27	–	0.11	1.38	1.40	–	0.12	1.52
Q3030	**Seeding**										
Q303001	**Seeding, weeding, watering, re-seeding and cutting until established; utility grass seed:**										
Q303001A	0.04 Kg per m²	m²	0.10	1.27	0.08	0.08	1.43	1.40	0.09	0.09	1.57
Q303001B	0.06 Kg per m²	m²	0.10	1.27	0.08	0.12	1.47	1.40	0.09	0.13	1.62
Q303003	**Seeding, weeding, watering, re-seeding and cutting until established; no rye grass seed:**										
Q303003A	0.04 Kg per m²	m²	0.10	1.27	0.08	0.11	1.46	1.40	0.09	0.12	1.61
Q303003B	0.06 Kg per m²	m²	0.10	1.27	0.08	0.17	1.52	1.40	0.09	0.19	1.67
Q303005	**Seeding, weeding, watering, re-seeding and cutting until established; low maintenance grass seed:**										
Q303005A	0.04 Kg per m²	m²	0.10	1.27	0.08	0.17	1.52	1.40	0.09	0.19	1.67
Q303005B	0.06 Kg per m²	m²	0.10	1.27	0.08	0.25	1.60	1.40	0.09	0.28	1.76
Q3040	**Turfing**										
Q304024	**Turfing, weeding, watering, rolling, re-turfing and cutting until established; turf:**										
Q304024A	meadow quality	m²	0.26	3.30	–	2.36	5.66	3.63	–	2.60	6.23

Paving, Planting, Fencing and Site Furniture

Major Works 2009		Unit	Labour Hours	Labour Net	Plant Net	Materials Net	Unit Net	Labour Gross	Plant Gross	Materials Gross	Unit Price
								(Gross rates include 10% profit)			
				£	£	£	£	£	£	£	£
Q31	**Q31: PLANTING**										
Q3104	**Provide trees and shrubs; excavation, disposal and backfilling; maintain until established**										
Q310442	**Trees including 50 × 50 mm treated softwood stakes, PVC ties and rabbit guards:**										
Q310442A	whip....................	Nr	0.25	3.17	–	5.79	8.96	3.49	–	6.37	9.86
Q310442B	feathered................	Nr	0.40	5.08	–	16.95	22.03	5.59	–	18.65	24.23
Q310442C	standard	Nr	0.65	8.26	–	36.18	44.44	9.09	–	39.80	48.88
Q310442D	semi-mature rootballed....	Nr	1.00	12.70	2.27	135.69	150.66	13.97	2.50	149.26	165.73
Q310443	**Shrubs:**										
Q310443A	small	Nr	0.15	1.90	–	4.18	6.08	2.09	–	4.60	6.69
Q310443B	medium................	Nr	0.25	3.18	–	14.50	17.68	3.50	–	15.95	19.45
Q310443C	large..................	Nr	0.40	5.08	–	40.99	46.07	5.59	–	45.09	50.68
Q3106	**Provide two year plants; excavation, disposal and backfilling; maintain until established**										
Q310632	**Privet; single row:**										
Q310632A	300 mm centres	m	0.18	2.29	–	12.11	14.40	2.52	–	13.32	15.84
Q310632B	450 mm centres	m	0.12	1.52	–	7.96	9.48	1.67	–	8.76	10.43
Q310632C	600 mm centres	m	0.09	1.15	–	6.06	7.21	1.27	–	6.67	7.93
Q310633	**Beech; double row, staggered:**										
Q310633A	300 mm centres	m	0.37	4.70	–	7.42	12.12	5.17	–	8.16	13.33
Q310633B	450 mm centres	m	0.24	3.04	–	4.88	7.92	3.34	–	5.37	8.71
Q310633C	600 mm centres	m	0.18	2.29	–	3.71	6.00	2.52	–	4.08	6.60

Major Works 2009		Unit		Specialist Net	Unit Net		Specialist Gross	Unit Price
							(Gross rates include 10% profit)	
			£	£	£	£	£	£	£	£

Q40   **Q40: FENCING**

Q4010   **Strained wire; BS 1722 Part 3**

Q401002   **Concrete posts at 3.0 m centres; excavation, disposal and filling:**

Code	Description	Unit				Specialist Net	Unit Net			Specialist Gross	Unit Price
Q401002A	0.85 m high 3 wire fence ...	m	–	–	–	15.17	15.17	–	–	16.69	16.69
Q401002B	end post	Nr	–	–	–	64.23	64.23	–	–	70.65	70.65
Q401002C	corner post	Nr	–	–	–	72.96	72.96	–	–	80.26	80.26
Q401002D	1.00 m high 6 wire fence ...	m	–	–	–	17.56	17.56	–	–	19.32	19.32
Q401002E	end post	Nr	–	–	–	70.08	70.08	–	–	77.09	77.09
Q401002F	corner post	Nr	–	–	–	78.74	78.74	–	–	86.61	86.61
Q401002G	1.40 m high 8 wire fence ...	m	–	–	–	20.08	20.08	–	–	22.09	22.09
Q401002H	end post	Nr	–	–	–	75.86	75.86	–	–	83.45	83.45
Q401002I	corner post	Nr	–	–	–	84.68	84.68	–	–	93.15	93.15

Q401003   **Treated softwood posts at 3.0 m centres; driven:**

Code	Description	Unit				Specialist Net	Unit Net			Specialist Gross	Unit Price
Q401003A	0.85 m high 3 wire fence ...	m	–	–	–	10.26	10.26	–	–	11.29	11.29
Q401003B	end post	Nr	–	–	–	30.71	30.71	–	–	33.78	33.78
Q401003C	corner post	Nr	–	–	–	35.04	35.04	–	–	38.54	38.54
Q401003D	1.00 m high 6 wire fence ...	m	–	–	–	12.58	12.58	–	–	13.84	13.84
Q401003E	end post	Nr	–	–	–	32.15	32.15	–	–	35.37	35.37
Q401003F	corner post	Nr	–	–	–	36.49	36.49	–	–	40.14	40.14
Q401003G	1.40 m high 8 wire fence ...	m	–	–	–	13.66	13.66	–	–	15.03	15.03
Q401003H	end post	Nr	–	–	–	33.60	33.60	–	–	36.96	36.96
Q401003I	corner post	Nr	–	–	–	37.93	37.93	–	–	41.72	41.72

Q4011   **Chain link; BS 1722 Part 1; 4 mm PVC coated mesh**

Q401105   **Concrete posts at 3.0 m centres; excavation, disposal and filling:**

Code	Description	Unit				Specialist Net	Unit Net			Specialist Gross	Unit Price
Q401105A	0.90 m high fence	m	–	–	–	19.36	19.36	–	–	21.30	21.30
Q401105B	end post	Nr	–	–	–	64.23	64.23	–	–	70.65	70.65
Q401105C	corner post	Nr	–	–	–	72.96	72.96	–	–	80.26	80.26
Q401105D	gate post	Nr	–	–	–	75.87	75.87	–	–	83.46	83.46
Q401105E	1.20 m high fence	m	–	–	–	22.25	22.25	–	–	24.48	24.48
Q401105F	end post	Nr	–	–	–	70.08	70.08	–	–	77.09	77.09
Q401105G	corner post	Nr	–	–	–	78.82	78.82	–	–	86.70	86.70
Q401105H	gate post	Nr	–	–	–	81.71	81.71	–	–	89.88	89.88
Q401105I	1.80 m high fence	m	–	–	–	28.11	28.11	–	–	30.92	30.92
Q401105J	end post	Nr	–	–	–	96.30	96.30	–	–	105.93	105.93
Q401105K	corner post	Nr	–	–	–	99.27	99.27	–	–	109.20	109.20
Q401105L	gate post	Nr	–	–	–	102.17	102.18	–	–	112.39	112.40

Q401106   **Galvanised steel posts at 3.0 m centres; excavation, disposal and filling:**

Code	Description	Unit				Specialist Net	Unit Net			Specialist Gross	Unit Price
Q401106A	0.90 m high fence	m	–	–	–	18.64	18.64	–	–	20.50	20.50
Q401106B	end post	Nr	–	–	–	59.81	59.81	–	–	65.79	65.79
Q401106C	corner post	Nr	–	–	–	68.64	68.64	–	–	75.50	75.50
Q401106D	gate post	Nr	–	–	–	71.53	71.53	–	–	78.68	78.68
Q401106E	1.20 m high fence	m	–	–	–	21.53	21.54	–	–	23.68	23.69
Q401106F	end post	Nr	–	–	–	65.67	65.67	–	–	72.24	72.24
Q401106G	corner post	Nr	–	–	–	74.42	74.42	–	–	81.86	81.86
Q401106H	gate post	Nr	–	–	–	77.36	77.36	–	–	85.10	85.10
Q401106I	1.80 m high fence	m	–	–	–	27.38	27.38	–	–	30.12	30.12
Q401106J	end post	Nr	–	–	–	91.97	91.97	–	–	101.17	101.17
Q401106K	corner post	Nr	–	–	–	94.86	94.86	–	–	104.35	104.35
Q401106L	gate post	Nr	–	–	–	97.76	97.77	–	–	107.54	107.55

Paving, Planting, Fencing and Site Furniture

Major Works 2009		Unit				Specialist Net	Unit Net			Specialist Gross	Unit Price
									(Gross rates include 10% profit)		
			£	£	£	£	£	£	£	£	£
Q40	**Q40: FENCING**										
Q4012	**Chain link BS 1722 Part 1; galvanised mesh; three rows barbed wire at top**										
Q401208	**Concrete posts with steel extension arms at 3.0 m centres; excavation, disposal and filling:**										
Q401208A	1.80 m high fence.........	m	–	–	–	30.63	30.63	–	–	33.69	33.69
Q401208B	end post.................	Nr	–	–	–	108.00	108.00	–	–	118.80	118.80
Q401208C	corner post	Nr	–	–	–	140.15	140.15	–	–	154.17	154.17
Q401208D	gate post	Nr	–	–	–	144.49	144.49	–	–	158.94	158.94
Q401208E	2.10 m high fence.........	m	–	–	–	33.60	33.60	–	–	36.96	36.96
Q401208F	end post.................	Nr	–	–	–	113.86	113.86	–	–	125.25	125.25
Q401208G	corner post	Nr	–	–	–	145.94	145.94	–	–	160.53	160.53
Q401208H	gate post	Nr	–	–	–	150.35	150.35	–	–	165.39	165.39
Q401209	**Concrete post with cranked tops at 3.0 m centres; excavation, disposal and filling:**										
Q401209A	1.80 m high fence.........	m	–	–	–	32.15	32.15	–	–	35.37	35.37
Q401209B	end post.................	Nr	–	–	–	108.73	108.73	–	–	119.60	119.60
Q401209C	corner post	Nr	–	–	–	141.24	141.24	–	–	155.36	155.36
Q401209D	gate post	Nr	–	–	–	143.77	143.77	–	–	158.15	158.15
Q401209E	2.10 m high fence.........	m	–	–	–	35.40	35.40	–	–	38.94	38.94
Q401209F	end post.................	Nr	–	–	–	114.58	114.58	–	–	126.04	126.04
Q401209G	corner post	Nr	–	–	–	147.38	147.38	–	–	162.12	162.12
Q401209H	gate post	Nr	–	–	–	151.07	151.07	–	–	166.18	166.18
Q401210	**Galvanised steel posts with cranked tops at 3.0 m centres; excavation, disposal and filling:**										
Q401210A	1.80 m high fence.........	m	–	–	–	26.30	26.30	–	–	28.93	28.93
Q401210B	end post.................	Nr	–	–	–	90.52	90.52	–	–	99.57	99.57
Q401210C	corner post	Nr	–	–	–	93.41	93.41	–	–	102.75	102.75
Q401210D	gate post	Nr	–	–	–	96.30	96.30	–	–	105.93	105.93
Q401210E	2.10 m high fence.........	m	–	–	–	29.18	29.18	–	–	32.10	32.10
Q401210F	end post.................	Nr	–	–	–	91.97	91.97	–	–	101.17	101.17
Q401210G	corner post	Nr	–	–	–	94.86	94.86	–	–	104.35	104.35
Q401210H	gate post	Nr	–	–	–	97.76	97.77	–	–	107.54	107.55
Q4013	**Chain link for tennis courts; BS 1722 Part 13; PVC coated**										
Q401312	**Galvanised steel posts at 3.0 m centres; excavation, disposal and filling:**										
Q401312A	2.75 m high fence.........	m	–	–	–	46.74	46.74	–	–	51.41	51.41
Q401312B	end post.................	Nr	–	–	–	151.79	151.79	–	–	166.97	166.97
Q401312C	corner post	Nr	–	–	–	163.49	163.50	–	–	179.84	179.85
Q401312D	gate post	Nr	–	–	–	169.27	169.27	–	–	186.20	186.20

Major Works 2009		Unit			Specialist Net	Unit Net			Specialist Gross	Unit Price
							(Gross rates include 10% profit)			
			£	£	£	£	£	£	£	£
Q40	**Q40: FENCING**									
Q4014	**Wooden post and rail; BS 1722 Part 7; sawn mortice**									
Q401421	**Treated softwood posts and rails; posts at 3.0 m centres; driven:**									
Q401421A	1.10 m high 3 rail fence	m	–	–	–	20.45	20.45	–	–	22.50	22.50
Q401421B	end post.................	Nr	–	–	–	17.56	17.56	–	–	19.32	19.32
Q401421C	corner post	Nr	–	–	–	21.89	21.89	–	–	24.08	24.08
Q401421D	intersection post..........	Nr	–	–	–	17.56	17.56	–	–	19.32	19.32
Q401421E	gate post	Nr	–	–	–	21.89	21.89	–	–	24.08	24.08
Q401421F	1.30 m high 4 rail fence	m	–	–	–	23.34	23.34	–	–	25.67	25.67
Q401421G	end post.................	Nr	–	–	–	18.99	18.99	–	–	20.89	20.89
Q401421H	corner post	Nr	–	–	–	23.34	23.34	–	–	25.67	25.67
Q401421I	intersection post..........	Nr	–	–	–	18.99	18.99	–	–	20.89	20.89
Q401421J	gate post	Nr	–	–	–	23.34	23.34	–	–	25.67	25.67
Q401422	**Untreated oak posts and rails; posts at 3.0 m centres; driven:**									
Q401422A	1.10 m high 3 rail fence	m	–	–	–	23.34	23.34	–	–	25.67	25.67
Q401422B	end post.................	Nr	–	–	–	20.45	20.45	–	–	22.50	22.50
Q401422C	corner post	Nr	–	–	–	23.34	23.34	–	–	25.67	25.67
Q401422D	intersection post..........	Nr	–	–	–	20.45	20.45	–	–	22.50	22.50
Q401422E	gate post	Nr	–	–	–	23.34	23.34	–	–	25.67	25.67
Q401422F	1.30 m high 4 rail fence	m	–	–	–	30.63	30.63	–	–	33.69	33.69
Q401422G	end post.................	Nr	–	–	–	21.89	21.89	–	–	24.08	24.08
Q401422H	corner post	Nr	–	–	–	26.30	26.30	–	–	28.93	28.93
Q401422I	intersection post..........	Nr	–	–	–	21.89	21.89	–	–	24.08	24.08
Q401422J	gate post	Nr	–	–	–	26.30	26.30	–	–	28.93	28.93
Q4015	**Wooden post and rail; BS 1722, Part 7; nailed**									
Q401524	**Treated softwood posts and rails; posts at 1.8 m centres; driven:**									
Q401524A	1.10 m high 3 rail fence	m	–	–	–	14.58	14.58	–	–	16.04	16.04
Q401524B	end post.................	Nr	–	–	–	17.56	17.56	–	–	19.32	19.32
Q401524C	corner post	Nr	–	–	–	21.89	21.89	–	–	24.08	24.08
Q401524D	intersection post..........	Nr	–	–	–	17.56	17.56	–	–	19.32	19.32
Q401524E	gate post	Nr	–	–	–	21.89	21.89	–	–	24.08	24.08
Q401524F	1.30 m high 4 rail fence	m	–	–	–	17.56	17.56	–	–	19.32	19.32
Q401524G	end post.................	Nr	–	–	–	18.99	18.99	–	–	20.89	20.89
Q401524H	corner post	Nr	–	–	–	23.34	23.34	–	–	25.67	25.67
Q401524I	intersection post..........	Nr	–	–	–	18.99	18.99	–	–	20.89	20.89
Q401524J	gate post	Nr	–	–	–	23.34	23.34	–	–	25.67	25.67

Major Works 2009		Unit			Specialist Net	Unit Net			Specialist Gross	Unit Price
								(Gross rates include 10% profit)		
			£	£	£	£	£	£	£	£
Q40	**Q40: FENCING**									
Q4016	**Wooden palisade; BS 1722 Part 6; nailed**									
Q401631	**Treated softwood posts and rails; posts at 3.0 m centres; excavation, disposal and filling:**									
Q401631A	1.00 m high 3 rail fence	m	–	–	–	35.04	35.04	–	–	38.54	38.54
Q401631B	end post.................	Nr	–	–	–	17.56	17.56	–	–	19.32	19.32
Q401631C	corner post	Nr	–	–	–	21.89	21.89	–	–	24.08	24.08
Q401631D	gate post	Nr	–	–	–	21.89	21.89	–	–	24.08	24.08
Q401631E	1.40 m high 4 rail fence	m	–	–	–	40.89	40.89	–	–	44.98	44.98
Q401631F	end post.................	Nr	–	–	–	18.99	18.99	–	–	20.89	20.89
Q401631G	corner post	Nr	–	–	–	23.34	23.34	–	–	25.67	25.67
Q401631H	gate post	Nr	–	–	–	23.34	23.34	–	–	25.67	25.67
Q401631I	1.80 m high 6 rail fence	m	–	–	–	46.74	46.74	–	–	51.41	51.41
Q401631J	end post.................	Nr	–	–	–	20.45	20.45	–	–	22.50	22.50
Q401631K	corner post	Nr	–	–	–	24.85	24.85	–	–	27.34	27.34
Q401631L	gate post	Nr	–	–	–	24.85	24.85	–	–	27.34	27.34
Q4017	**Chestnut paling; BS 1722 Part 4**									
Q401733	**Treated softwood posts at 3.0 m centres; driven:**									
Q401733A	0.90 m high fence.........	m	–	–	–	8.75	8.75	–	–	9.63	9.63
Q401733B	end post.................	Nr	–	–	–	11.70	11.70	–	–	12.87	12.87
Q401733C	corner post	Nr	–	–	–	17.56	17.56	–	–	19.32	19.32
Q401733D	1.05 m high fence.........	m	–	–	–	10.26	10.26	–	–	11.29	11.29
Q401733E	end post.................	Nr	–	–	–	11.70	11.70	–	–	12.87	12.87
Q401733F	corner post	Nr	–	–	–	17.56	17.56	–	–	19.32	19.32
Q401733G	1.20 m high fence.........	m	–	–	–	10.98	10.98	–	–	12.08	12.08
Q401733H	end post.................	Nr	–	–	–	11.70	11.70	–	–	12.87	12.87
Q401733I	corner post	Nr	–	–	–	17.56	17.56	–	–	19.32	19.32
Q401733J	1.35 m high fence.........	m	–	–	–	12.06	12.06	–	–	13.27	13.27
Q401733K	end post.................	Nr	–	–	–	13.15	13.15	–	–	14.47	14.47
Q401733L	corner post	Nr	–	–	–	18.99	18.99	–	–	20.89	20.89
Q401733M	1.80 m high fence.........	m	–	–	–	13.15	13.15	–	–	14.47	14.47
Q401733N	end post.................	Nr	–	–	–	14.58	14.58	–	–	16.04	16.04
Q401733O	corner post	Nr	–	–	–	20.45	20.45	–	–	22.50	22.50

Major Works 2009		Unit				Specialist Net	Unit Net			Specialist Gross	Unit Price
								——— (Gross rates include 10% profit) ———			
			£	£	£	£	£	£	£	£	£
Q40	**Q40: FENCING**										
Q4018	**Treated softwood close boarded; BS 1722 Part 5**										
Q401841	**Morticed concrete posts at 3.0 m centres; excavation, disposal and filling:**										
Q401841A	1.00 m high fence.........	m	–	–	–	33.60	33.60	–	–	36.96	36.96
Q401841B	end post.................	Nr	–	–	–	14.58	14.58	–	–	16.04	16.04
Q401841C	corner post	Nr	–	–	–	16.04	16.04	–	–	17.64	17.64
Q401841D	gate post	Nr	–	–	–	16.04	16.04	–	–	17.64	17.64
Q401841E	1.20 m high fence.........	m	–	–	–	37.93	37.93	–	–	41.72	41.72
Q401841F	end post.................	Nr	–	–	–	16.04	16.04	–	–	17.64	17.64
Q401841G	corner post	Nr	–	–	–	17.56	17.56	–	–	19.32	19.32
Q401841H	gate post	Nr	–	–	–	17.56	17.56	–	–	19.32	19.32
Q401841I	1.50 m high fence.........	m	–	–	–	42.33	42.33	–	–	46.56	46.56
Q401841J	end post.................	Nr	–	–	–	17.56	17.56	–	–	19.32	19.32
Q401841K	corner post	Nr	–	–	–	18.99	18.99	–	–	20.89	20.89
Q401841L	gate post	Nr	–	–	–	18.99	18.99	–	–	20.89	20.89
Q401841M	1.80 m high fence.........	m	–	–	–	46.74	46.74	–	–	51.41	51.41
Q401841N	end post.................	Nr	–	–	–	18.99	18.99	–	–	20.89	20.89
Q401841O	corner post	Nr	–	–	–	20.45	20.45	–	–	22.50	22.50
Q401841P	gate post	Nr	–	–	–	20.45	20.45	–	–	22.50	22.50
Q401842	**Treated sawn softwood posts at 3.0 m centres; excavation, disposal and filling:**										
Q401842A	1.00 m high fence.........	m	–	–	–	30.63	30.63	–	–	33.69	33.69
Q401842B	end post.................	Nr	–	–	–	11.70	11.70	–	–	12.87	12.87
Q401842C	corner post	Nr	–	–	–	13.15	13.15	–	–	14.47	14.47
Q401842D	gate post	Nr	–	–	–	13.15	13.15	–	–	14.47	14.47
Q401842E	1.20 m high fence.........	m	–	–	–	35.04	35.04	–	–	38.54	38.54
Q401842F	gate post	Nr	–	–	–	13.15	13.15	–	–	14.47	14.47
Q401842G	corner post	Nr	–	–	–	14.58	14.58	–	–	16.04	16.04
Q401842H	gate post	Nr	–	–	–	14.58	14.58	–	–	16.04	16.04
Q401842I	1.50 m high fence.........	m	–	–	–	39.39	39.39	–	–	43.33	43.33
Q401842J	end post.................	Nr	–	–	–	14.58	14.58	–	–	16.04	16.04
Q401842K	corner post	Nr	–	–	–	16.04	16.04	–	–	17.64	17.64
Q401842L	gate post	Nr	–	–	–	16.04	16.04	–	–	17.64	17.64
Q401842M	1.80 m high fence.........	m	–	–	–	43.79	43.79	–	–	48.17	48.17
Q401842N	end post.................	Nr	–	–	–	16.04	16.04	–	–	17.64	17.64
Q401842O	corner post	Nr	–	–	–	17.56	17.56	–	–	19.32	19.32
Q401842P	gate post	Nr	–	–	–	17.56	17.56	–	–	19.32	19.32

Paving, Planting, Fencing and Site Furniture

Major Works 2009		Unit			Specialist Net	Unit Net			Specialist Gross	Unit Price
							(Gross rates include 10% profit)			
			£	£	£	£	£	£	£	£
Q40	**Q40: FENCING**									
Q4019	**Treated softwood woven panels; BS 1722 Part 11**									
Q401951	**Concrete posts at 1.8 m centres; excavation, disposal and filling:**									
Q401951A	0.60 m high fence	m	–	–	–	30.63	30.63	–	–	33.69	33.69
Q401951B	end post	Nr	–	–	–	26.30	26.30	–	–	28.93	28.93
Q401951C	corner post	Nr	–	–	–	30.63	30.63	–	–	33.69	33.69
Q401951D	gate post	Nr	–	–	–	26.30	26.30	–	–	28.93	28.93
Q401951E	0.90 m high fence	m	–	–	–	36.49	36.49	–	–	40.14	40.14
Q401951F	end post	Nr	–	–	–	32.15	32.15	–	–	35.37	35.37
Q401951G	corner post	Nr	–	–	–	36.49	36.49	–	–	40.14	40.14
Q401951H	gate post	Nr	–	–	–	32.15	32.15	–	–	35.37	35.37
Q401951I	1.20 m high fence	m	–	–	–	42.34	42.34	–	–	46.57	46.57
Q401951J	end post	Nr	–	–	–	37.93	37.93	–	–	41.72	41.72
Q401951K	corner post	Nr	–	–	–	42.34	42.34	–	–	46.57	46.57
Q401951L	gate post	Nr	–	–	–	37.93	37.93	–	–	41.72	41.72
Q401951M	1.50 m high fence	m	–	–	–	48.18	48.18	–	–	53.00	53.00
Q401951N	end post	Nr	–	–	–	43.79	43.79	–	–	48.17	48.17
Q401951O	corner post	Nr	–	–	–	48.18	48.18	–	–	53.00	53.00
Q401951P	gate post	Nr	–	–	–	43.79	43.79	–	–	48.17	48.17
Q401951Q	1.80 m high fence	m	–	–	–	54.04	54.04	–	–	59.44	59.44
Q401951R	end post	Nr	–	–	–	49.63	49.63	–	–	54.59	54.59
Q401951S	corner post	Nr	–	–	–	53.97	53.97	–	–	59.37	59.37
Q401951T	gate post	Nr	–	–	–	49.63	49.63	–	–	54.59	54.59
Q401952	**Treated softwood posts at 1.8 m centres; excavation, disposal and filling:**									
Q401952A	0.60 m high fence	m	–	–	–	21.88	21.88	–	–	24.07	24.07
Q401952B	end post	Nr	–	–	–	17.56	17.56	–	–	19.32	19.32
Q401952C	corner post	Nr	–	–	–	21.88	21.88	–	–	24.07	24.07
Q401952D	gate post	Nr	–	–	–	17.56	17.56	–	–	19.32	19.32
Q401952E	0.90 m high fence	m	–	–	–	27.74	27.74	–	–	30.51	30.51
Q401952F	end post	Nr	–	–	–	23.34	23.34	–	–	25.67	25.67
Q401952G	corner post	Nr	–	–	–	27.74	27.74	–	–	30.51	30.51
Q401952H	gate post	Nr	–	–	–	23.34	23.34	–	–	25.67	25.67
Q401952I	1.20 m high fence	m	–	–	–	35.04	35.04	–	–	38.54	38.54
Q401952J	end post	Nr	–	–	–	30.63	30.63	–	–	33.69	33.69
Q401952K	corner post	Nr	–	–	–	35.04	35.04	–	–	38.54	38.54
Q401952L	gate post	Nr	–	–	–	30.63	30.63	–	–	33.69	33.69
Q401952M	1.50 m high fence	m	–	–	–	40.90	40.90	–	–	44.99	44.99
Q401952N	end post	Nr	–	–	–	36.49	36.49	–	–	40.14	40.14
Q401952O	corner post	Nr	–	–	–	40.90	40.90	–	–	44.99	44.99
Q401952P	gate post	Nr	–	–	–	36.49	36.49	–	–	40.14	40.14
Q401952Q	1.80 m high fence	m	–	–	–	46.74	46.74	–	–	51.41	51.41
Q401952R	end post	Nr	–	–	–	42.34	42.34	–	–	46.57	46.57
Q401952S	corner post	Nr	–	–	–	46.74	46.74	–	–	51.41	51.41
Q401952T	gate post	Nr	–	–	–	42.34	42.34	–	–	46.57	46.57

Major Works 2009		Unit				Specialist Net	Unit Net			Specialist Gross	Unit Price
									(Gross rates include 10% profit)		
				£	£	£	£	£	£	£	£
Q40	**Q40: FENCING**										
Q4050	**Field gates; BS 3470 Table 1**										
Q405062	**Treated softwood:**										
Q405062A	2.40 × 1.10 m high	Nr	–	–	–	169.27	169.27	–	–	186.20	186.20
Q405062B	2.70 × 1.10 m high	Nr	–	–	–	180.98	180.98	–	–	199.08	199.08
Q405062C	3.00 × 1.10 m high	Nr	–	–	–	192.68	192.69	–	–	211.95	211.96
Q405062D	3.30 × 1.10 m high	Nr	–	–	–	204.30	204.30	–	–	224.73	224.73
Q405062E	3.60 × 1.10 m high	Nr	–	–	–	216.02	216.02	–	–	237.62	237.62
Q405062F	3.90 × 1.10 m high	Nr	–	–	–	227.71	227.71	–	–	250.48	250.48
Q405062G	4.20 × 1.10 m high	Nr	–	–	–	239.35	239.35	–	–	263.29	263.29
Q405063	**Untreated hardwood:**										
Q405063A	2.40 × 1.10 m high	Nr	–	–	–	216.02	216.02	–	–	237.62	237.62
Q405063B	2.70 × 1.10 m high	Nr	–	–	–	227.71	227.71	–	–	250.48	250.48
Q405063C	3.00 × 1.10 m high	Nr	–	–	–	239.35	239.35	–	–	263.29	263.29
Q405063D	3.30 × 1.10 m high	Nr	–	–	–	251.06	251.07	–	–	276.17	276.18
Q405063E	3.60 × 1.10 m high	Nr	–	–	–	262.68	262.68	–	–	288.95	288.95
Q405063F	3.90 × 1.10 m high	Nr	–	–	–	274.39	274.39	–	–	301.83	301.83
Q405063H	4.20 × 1.10 m high	Nr	–	–	–	286.09	286.09	–	–	314.70	314.70
Q4051	**Domestic entrance gates; BS 4092 Part 2**										
Q405165	**Treated softwood:**										
Q405165A	0.81 × 0.90 m high	Nr	–	–	–	160.53	160.53	–	–	176.58	176.58
Q405165B	1.02 × 0.90 m high	Nr	–	–	–	183.87	183.87	–	–	202.26	202.26
Q405165C	2.13 × 0.90 m high	Nr	–	–	–	207.27	207.27	–	–	228.00	228.00
Q405165D	2.64 × 0.09 m high	Nr	–	–	–	230.61	230.61	–	–	253.67	253.67

Paving, Planting, Fencing and Site Furniture

Major Works 2009		Unit	Labour Hours	Labour Net	Plant Net	Materials Net	Unit Net	Labour Gross	Plant Gross	Materials Gross	Unit Price
								(Gross rates include 10% profit)			
				£	£	£	£	£	£	£	£
Q40	Q40: FENCING										
Q4052	Standard softwood gates										
Q405223	Boulton and Paul softwood preservative treated gates:										
Q405223H	GTE 30GTE; 914 × 1041 mm................	Nr	0.60	10.19	–	65.36	75.55	11.21	–	71.90	83.11
Q405223I	GTE 36GTE; 1067 × 1041 mm................	Nr	0.75	12.74	–	74.03	86.77	14.01	–	81.43	95.45
Q405223K	3060GS; 914 × 1981 mm; arch top gate.............	Nr	0.85	14.43	–	123.20	137.63	15.87	–	135.52	151.39

DISPOSAL SYSTEMS

Major Works 2009		Unit	Labour Hours	Labour Net	Plant Net	Materials Net	Unit Net	Labour Gross	Plant Gross	Materials Gross	Unit Price
				£	£	£	£	£	£	£	£
								(Gross rates include 10% profit)			
R10	**R10: RAINWATER PIPEWORK AND GUTTERS**										
R1011	**UPVC rainwater pipes and fittings; BS 4576**										
R101103	**Pipes; fixing with standard clips to masonry backgrounds:**										
R101103A	50 mm diameter	m	0.30	11.70	–	4.17	15.87	12.87	–	4.59	17.46
R101103B	68 mm diameter	m	0.31	12.09	–	4.99	17.08	13.30	–	5.49	18.79
R101103C	110 mm diameter	m	0.33	12.87	–	10.23	23.10	14.16	–	11.25	25.41
R101104	**Fittings:**										
R101104A	50 mm shoes	Nr	0.30	11.70	–	2.94	14.64	12.87	–	3.23	16.10
R101104B	50 mm bends	Nr	0.30	11.70	–	3.97	15.67	12.87	–	4.37	17.24
R101104C	50 mm offsets; 150 mm projection	Nr	0.35	13.65	–	8.92	22.57	15.02	–	9.81	24.83
R101104D	50 mm offsets; 300 mm projection	Nr	0.38	14.81	–	9.45	24.26	16.29	–	10.40	26.69
R101104E	50 mm branches..........	Nr	0.60	23.39	–	17.73	41.12	25.73	–	19.50	45.23
R101104F	68 mm shoes	Nr	0.32	12.48	–	3.20	15.68	13.73	–	3.52	17.25
R101104G	68 mm bends	Nr	0.32	12.48	–	3.04	15.52	13.73	–	3.34	17.07
R101104H	68 mm offsets; 150 mm projection	Nr	0.36	14.04	–	6.36	20.40	15.44	–	7.00	22.44
R101104I	68 mm offsets; 300 mm projection	Nr	0.40	15.59	–	6.93	22.52	17.15	–	7.62	24.77
R101104J	68 mm branches..........	Nr	0.32	12.48	–	9.67	22.15	13.73	–	10.64	24.37
R101104K	110 mm shoes	Nr	0.34	13.26	–	20.26	33.52	14.59	–	22.29	36.87
R101104L	110 mm bends	Nr	0.34	13.26	–	14.46	27.72	14.59	–	15.91	30.49
R101104M	110 mm offsets; 150 mm projection	Nr	0.39	15.21	–	27.77	42.98	16.73	–	30.55	47.28
R101104N	110 mm offsets; 300 mm projection	Nr	0.43	16.76	–	29.13	45.89	18.44	–	32.04	50.48
R101104O	110 mm branches	Nr	0.34	13.26	–	20.00	33.26	14.59	–	22.00	36.59
R1051	**UPVC rainwater gutters and fittings; BS 4576**										
R105106	**Gutters; fixing with standard clips to woodwork backgrounds:**										
R105106A	76 mm diameter	m	0.25	9.75	–	4.17	13.92	10.73	–	4.59	15.31
R105106B	112 mm diameter	m	0.27	10.53	–	5.53	16.06	11.58	–	6.08	17.67
R105106C	150 mm diameter	m	0.29	11.30	–	17.13	28.43	12.43	–	18.84	31.27
R105107	**Fittings:**										
R105107A	76 mm stop ends	Nr	0.16	6.24	–	3.77	10.01	6.86	–	4.15	11.01
R105107B	76 mm stop end outlets....	Nr	0.22	8.58	–	4.82	13.40	9.44	–	5.30	14.74
R105107C	76 mm running outlets	Nr	0.22	8.58	–	4.90	13.48	9.44	–	5.39	14.83
R105107D	76 mm angles...........	Nr	0.22	8.58	–	4.82	13.40	9.44	–	5.30	14.74
R105107E	112 mm stop ends	Nr	0.16	6.24	–	2.12	8.36	6.86	–	2.33	9.20
R105107F	112 mm stop end outlets...	Nr	0.22	8.58	–	7.83	16.41	9.44	–	8.61	18.05
R105107G	112 mm running outlets ...	Nr	0.22	8.58	–	6.49	15.07	9.44	–	7.14	16.58
R105107H	112 mm angles...........	Nr	0.22	8.58	–	6.17	14.75	9.44	–	6.79	16.23
R105107I	150 mm stop ends	Nr	0.16	6.24	–	7.93	14.17	6.86	–	8.72	15.59
R105107J	150 mm stop end outlets...	Nr	0.22	8.58	–	22.68	31.26	9.44	–	24.95	34.39
R105107K	150 mm running outlets ...	Nr	0.22	8.58	–	20.16	28.74	9.44	–	22.18	31.61
R105107L	150 mm angles...........	Nr	0.22	8.58	–	22.13	30.71	9.44	–	24.34	33.78

Disposal Systems

Major Works 2009		Unit	Labour Hours	Labour Net	Plant Net	Materials Net	Unit Net	Labour Gross	Plant Gross	Materials Gross	Unit Price
								(Gross rates include 10% profit)			
				£	£	£	£	£	£	£	£
R11	**R11: FOUL DRAINAGE ABOVE GROUND**										
R1111	**UPVC soil and vent pipes; BS 4514**										
R111122	**Pipes; fixing with standard clips to masonry backgrounds:**										
R111122A	82 mm diameter	m	0.40	15.60	–	12.58	28.18	17.16	–	13.84	31.00
R111122B	110 mm diameter	m	0.42	16.38	–	11.93	28.31	18.02	–	13.12	31.14
R111122C	160 mm diameter	m	0.46	17.94	–	31.33	49.27	19.73	–	34.46	54.20
R1113	**ABS waste pipes; BS 5255**										
R111325	**Pipes including fittings; fixing with standard clips to masonry backgrounds:**										
R111325A	32 mm diameter	m	0.26	10.14	–	2.22	12.36	11.15	–	2.44	13.60
R111325B	40 mm diameter	m	0.28	10.92	–	2.62	13.54	12.01	–	2.88	14.89
R111325C	50 mm diameter	m	0.30	11.70	–	4.77	16.47	12.87	–	5.25	18.12
R1115	**UPVC overflow pipes**										
R111527	**Pipes including fittings; fixing with standard clips to masonry backgrounds:**										
R111527A	19 mm diameter	m	0.18	7.02	–	1.50	8.52	7.72	–	1.65	9.37
R1120	**UPVC soil and vent pipe fittings; BS 4514**										
R112023	**Fittings:**										
R112023A	82 mm WC connectors	Nr	0.30	11.70	–	6.42	18.12	12.87	–	7.06	19.93
R112023B	82 mm bends	Nr	0.36	14.04	–	16.83	30.87	15.44	–	18.51	33.96
R112023C	82 mm branches.	Nr	0.45	17.55	–	22.92	40.47	19.31	–	25.21	44.52
R112023D	82 mm double branches . . .	Nr	0.85	33.14	–	45.84	78.98	36.45	–	50.42	86.88
R112023E	82 mm boss connectors . . .	Nr	0.45	17.55	–	12.87	30.42	19.31	–	14.16	33.46
R112023F	82 mm access doors	Nr	0.52	20.27	–	26.19	46.46	22.30	–	28.81	51.11
R112023G	82 mm bird guards.	Nr	0.20	7.80	–	3.65	11.45	8.58	–	4.02	12.60
R112023H	110 mm WC connectors . . .	Nr	0.32	12.48	–	6.42	18.90	13.73	–	7.06	20.79
R112023I	110 mm bends	Nr	0.39	15.21	–	17.41	32.62	16.73	–	19.15	35.88
R112023J	110 mm branches	Nr	0.50	19.50	–	23.31	42.81	21.45	–	25.64	47.09
R112023K	110 mm double branches . .	Nr	0.60	23.39	–	50.00	73.39	25.73	–	55.00	80.73
R112023L	110 mm boss connectors . .	Nr	0.50	19.50	–	14.42	33.92	21.45	–	15.86	37.31
R112023M	110 mm access doors	Nr	0.87	33.92	–	11.04	44.96	37.31	–	12.14	49.46
R112023N	110 mm bird guards.	Nr	0.20	7.80	–	3.17	10.97	8.58	–	3.49	12.07
R112023O	160 mm WC connectors . . .	Nr	0.34	13.26	–	24.92	38.18	14.59	–	27.41	42.00
R112023P	160 mm bends	Nr	0.41	15.99	–	76.98	92.97	17.59	–	84.68	102.27
R112023Q	160 mm branches	Nr	0.54	21.05	–	89.53	110.58	23.16	–	98.48	121.64
R112023R	160 mm double branches . .	Nr	0.65	25.34	–	133.26	158.60	27.87	–	146.59	174.46
R112023S	160 mm boss connectors . .	Nr	0.54	21.05	–	68.63	89.68	23.16	–	75.49	98.65
R112023T	160 mm access doors	Nr	0.90	35.09	–	90.03	125.12	38.60	–	99.03	137.67
R112023U	160 mm bird guards.	Nr	0.21	8.19	–	10.46	18.65	9.01	–	11.51	20.52

Major Works 2009		Unit	Labour Hours	Labour Net	Plant Net	Materials Net	Unit Net	Labour Gross	Plant Gross	Materials Gross	Unit Price
								—— (Gross rates include 10% profit) ——			
				£	£	£	£	£	£	£	£
R11	**R11: FOUL DRAINAGE ABOVE GROUND**										
R1121	**Polypropylene accessories; BS 5254**										
R112132	**Valves:**										
R112132A	110 mm air admittance valve	Nr	0.45	17.55	–	54.02	71.57	19.31	–	59.42	78.73
R112133	**Traps:**										
R112133A	32 mm bottle trap, 38 mm seal....................	Nr	0.22	8.58	–	4.68	13.26	9.44	–	5.15	14.59
R112133B	32 mm bottle trap, 76 mm seal, anti-syphon	Nr	0.42	16.38	–	31.44	47.82	18.02	–	34.58	52.60
R112133C	32 mm tubular S trap, 76 mm seal....................	Nr	0.22	8.58	–	5.41	13.99	9.44	–	5.95	15.39
R112133D	40 mm bottle P trap, 38 mm seal....................	Nr	0.24	9.36	–	5.73	15.09	10.30	–	6.30	16.60
R112133E	40 mm bottle P trap, 76 mm seal, anti-syphon	Nr	0.45	17.55	–	32.96	50.51	19.31	–	36.26	55.56
R112133F	40 mm tubular S trap, 76 mm seal....................	Nr	0.24	9.36	–	7.28	16.64	10.30	–	8.01	18.30
R112134	**Expansion compensators:**										
R112134A	32 mm	Nr	0.16	6.24	–	1.85	8.09	6.86	–	2.04	8.90
R112134B	40 mm	Nr	0.17	6.63	–	1.89	8.52	7.29	–	2.08	9.37
R112134C	50 mm	Nr	0.19	7.41	–	3.48	10.89	8.15	–	3.83	11.98

Disposal Systems

								(Gross rates include 10% profit)			
				£	£	£	£	£	£	£	£
R12	**R12: DRAINAGE BELOW GROUND**										
R1201	**Excavation of trenches; by machine; for drainage pipes or the like, including disposal and filling**										
R120113	**Trenches to suit pipes not exceeding 200 mm diameter; average depth:**										
R120113A	0.50 m	m	0.12	1.52	1.93	–	3.45	1.67	2.12	–	3.80
R120113B	0.75 m	m	0.15	1.90	2.59	–	4.49	2.09	2.85	–	4.94
R120113C	1.00 m	m	0.22	2.79	3.36	–	6.15	3.07	3.70	–	6.77
R120113D	1.25 m	m	0.29	3.69	4.51	–	8.20	4.06	4.96	–	9.02
R120113E	1.50 m	m	0.36	4.58	5.29	–	9.87	5.04	5.82	–	10.86
R120113F	1.75 m	m	0.42	5.33	6.22	–	11.55	5.86	6.84	–	12.71
R120113G	2.00 m	m	0.49	6.23	6.99	–	13.22	6.85	7.69	–	14.54
R120113H	2.25 m	m	0.57	7.24	8.59	–	15.83	7.96	9.45	–	17.41
R120113I	2.50 m	m	0.65	8.25	9.58	–	17.83	9.08	10.54	–	19.61
R120113J	2.75 m	m	0.73	9.27	10.57	–	19.84	10.20	11.63	–	21.82
R120113K	3.00 m	m	0.82	10.42	11.78	–	22.20	11.46	12.96	–	24.42
R120113L	3.25 m	m	0.91	11.56	12.99	–	24.55	12.72	14.29	–	27.01
R120113M	3.50 m	m	1.00	12.70	14.20	–	26.90	13.97	15.62	–	29.59
R120114	**Trenches to suit 225 mm diameter pipes; average depth:**										
R120114A	0.50 m	m	0.15	1.91	2.39	–	4.30	2.10	2.63	–	4.73
R120114B	0.75 m	m	0.19	2.42	3.27	–	5.69	2.66	3.60	–	6.26
R120114C	1.00 m	m	0.30	3.81	4.73	–	8.54	4.19	5.20	–	9.39
R120114D	1.25 m	m	0.37	4.70	5.89	–	10.59	5.17	6.48	–	11.65
R120114E	1.50 m	m	0.46	5.84	6.91	–	12.75	6.42	7.60	–	14.03
R120114F	1.75 m	m	0.53	6.73	8.06	–	14.79	7.40	8.87	–	16.27
R120114G	2.00 m	m	0.61	7.75	9.05	–	16.80	8.53	9.96	–	18.48
R120114H	2.25 m	m	0.73	9.28	11.33	–	20.61	10.21	12.46	–	22.67
R120114I	2.50 m	m	0.81	10.28	12.52	–	22.80	11.31	13.77	–	25.08
R120114J	2.75 m	m	0.89	11.30	13.51	–	24.81	12.43	14.86	–	27.29
R120114K	3.00 m	m	0.98	12.45	14.72	–	27.17	13.70	16.19	–	29.89
R120114L	3.25 m	m	1.07	13.59	15.93	–	29.52	14.95	17.52	–	32.47
R120114M	3.50 m	m	1.16	14.74	17.14	–	31.88	16.21	18.85	–	35.07
R120115	**Trenches to suit 300 mm diameter pipes; average depth:**										
R120115A	0.50 m	m	0.18	2.29	2.86	–	5.15	2.52	3.15	–	5.67
R120115B	0.75 m	m	0.23	2.92	3.96	–	6.88	3.21	4.36	–	7.57
R120115C	1.00 m	m	0.36	4.57	5.86	–	10.43	5.03	6.45	–	11.47
R120115D	1.25 m	m	0.43	5.46	7.01	–	12.47	6.01	7.71	–	13.72
R120115E	1.50 m	m	0.55	6.99	8.50	–	15.49	7.69	9.35	–	17.04
R120115F	1.75 m	m	0.62	7.88	9.66	–	17.54	8.67	10.63	–	19.29
R120115G	2.00 m	m	0.72	9.14	11.09	–	20.23	10.05	12.20	–	22.25
R120115H	2.25 m	m	0.87	11.05	13.83	–	24.88	12.16	15.21	–	27.37
R120115I	2.50 m	m	0.96	12.19	15.24	–	27.43	13.41	16.76	–	30.17
R120115J	2.75 m	m	1.06	13.46	16.67	–	30.13	14.81	18.34	–	33.14
R120115K	3.00 m	m	1.16	14.73	17.66	–	32.39	16.20	19.43	–	35.63
R120115L	3.25 m	m	1.25	15.88	18.65	–	34.53	17.47	20.52	–	37.98
R120115M	3.50 m	m	1.34	17.02	19.64	–	36.66	18.72	21.60	–	40.33

Major Works 2009		Unit	Labour Hours	Labour Net	Plant Net	Materials Net	Unit Net	Labour Gross	Plant Gross	Materials Gross	Unit Price
								(Gross rates include 10% profit)			
				£	£	£	£	£	£	£	£
R12	R12: DRAINAGE BELOW GROUND										
R1201	Excavation of trenches; by machine; for drainage pipes or the like, including disposal and filling										
R120116	Trenches to suit 400 mm diameter pipes; average depth:										
R120116A	0.50 m	m	0.21	2.67	3.55	–	6.22	2.94	3.91	–	6.84
R120116B	0.75 m	m	0.27	3.43	4.87	–	8.30	3.77	5.36	–	9.13
R120116C	1.00 m	m	0.39	4.96	6.55	–	11.51	5.46	7.21	–	12.66
R120116D	1.25 m	m	0.50	6.35	8.80	–	15.15	6.99	9.68	–	16.67
R120116E	1.50 m	m	0.64	8.13	10.53	–	18.66	8.94	11.58	–	20.53
R120116F	1.75 m	m	0.72	9.14	11.91	–	21.05	10.05	13.10	–	23.16
R120116G	2.00 m	m	0.83	10.54	13.56	–	24.10	11.59	14.92	–	26.51
R120116H	2.25 m	m	1.01	12.83	16.99	–	29.82	14.11	18.69	–	32.80
R120116I	2.50 m	m	1.11	14.10	18.61	–	32.71	15.51	20.47	–	35.98
R120116J	2.75 m	m	1.23	15.63	20.48	–	36.11	17.19	22.53	–	39.72
R120116K	3.00 m	m	1.34	17.02	22.14	–	39.16	18.72	24.35	–	43.08
R120116L	3.25 m	m	1.43	18.16	23.54	–	41.70	19.98	25.89	–	45.87
R120116M	3.50 m	m	1.52	19.30	24.72	–	44.02	21.23	27.19	–	48.42
R120117	Trenches to suit 450 mm diameter pipes; average depth:										
R120117A	0.50 m	m	0.24	3.04	4.02	–	7.06	3.34	4.42	–	7.77
R120117B	0.75 m	m	0.30	3.81	5.33	–	9.14	4.19	5.86	–	10.05
R120117C	1.00 m	m	0.42	5.34	7.01	–	12.35	5.87	7.71	–	13.59
R120117D	1.25 m	m	0.56	7.12	9.92	–	17.04	7.83	10.91	–	18.74
R120117E	1.50 m	m	0.72	9.14	11.91	–	21.05	10.05	13.10	–	23.16
R120117F	1.75 m	m	0.82	10.41	13.72	–	24.13	11.45	15.09	–	26.54
R120117G	2.00 m	m	0.94	11.94	15.59	–	27.53	13.13	17.15	–	30.28
R120117H	2.25 m	m	1.15	14.61	19.27	–	33.88	16.07	21.20	–	37.27
R120117I	2.50 m	m	1.28	16.26	21.33	–	37.59	17.89	23.46	–	41.35
R120117J	2.75 m	m	1.39	17.66	23.42	–	41.08	19.43	25.76	–	45.19
R120117K	3.00 m	m	1.52	19.31	25.51	–	44.82	21.24	28.06	–	49.30
R120117L	3.25 m	m	1.64	20.83	27.38	–	48.21	22.91	30.12	–	53.03
R120117M	3.50 m	m	1.76	22.36	29.25	–	51.61	24.60	32.18	–	56.77
R120118	Trenches to suit 525 mm diameter pipes; average depth:										
R120118A	0.50 m	m	0.27	3.43	4.70	–	8.13	3.77	5.17	–	8.94
R120118B	0.75 m	m	0.34	4.32	6.24	–	10.56	4.75	6.86	–	11.62
R120118C	1.00 m	m	0.47	5.97	8.14	–	14.11	6.57	8.95	–	15.52
R120118D	1.25 m	m	0.63	8.00	11.49	–	19.49	8.80	12.64	–	21.44
R120118E	1.50 m	m	0.81	10.29	13.72	–	24.01	11.32	15.09	–	26.41
R120118F	1.75 m	m	0.92	11.69	15.75	–	27.44	12.86	17.33	–	30.18
R120118G	2.00 m	m	1.06	13.46	17.87	–	31.33	14.81	19.66	–	34.46
R120118H	2.25 m	m	1.29	16.39	21.99	–	38.38	18.03	24.19	–	42.22
R120118I	2.50 m	m	1.42	18.04	24.27	–	42.31	19.84	26.70	–	46.54
R120118J	2.75 m	m	1.56	19.81	26.58	–	46.39	21.79	29.24	–	51.03
R120118K	3.00 m	m	1.70	21.59	28.89	–	50.48	23.75	31.78	–	55.53
R120118L	3.25 m	m	1.84	23.37	31.20	–	54.57	25.71	34.32	–	60.03
R120118M	3.50 m	m	1.98	25.15	33.51	–	58.66	27.67	36.86	–	64.53
R120119	Trenches to suit 600 mm diameter pipes; average depth:										
R120119A	1.00 m	m	0.53	6.73	9.29	–	16.02	7.40	10.22	–	17.62
R120119B	1.25 m	m	0.71	9.02	12.86	–	21.88	9.92	14.15	–	24.07
R120119C	1.50 m	m	0.90	11.43	15.31	–	26.74	12.57	16.84	–	29.41
R120119D	1.75 m	m	1.03	13.09	17.59	–	30.68	14.40	19.35	–	33.75
R120119E	2.00 m	m	1.18	14.99	19.93	–	34.92	16.49	21.92	–	38.41
R120119F	2.25 m	m	1.43	18.16	24.71	–	42.87	19.98	27.18	–	47.16
R120119G	2.50 m	m	1.57	19.94	27.21	–	47.15	21.93	29.93	–	51.87
R120119H	2.75 m	m	1.74	22.10	29.55	–	51.65	24.31	32.51	–	56.82
R120119I	3.00 m	m	1.89	24.00	32.08	–	56.08	26.40	35.29	–	61.69
R120119L	3.25 m	m	2.04	25.90	34.61	–	60.51	28.49	38.07	–	66.56
R120119M	3.50 m	m	2.19	27.82	37.14	–	64.96	30.60	40.85	–	71.46

Disposal Systems

Major Works 2009		Unit	Labour Hours	Labour Net	Plant Net	Materials Net	Unit Net	Labour Gross	Plant Gross	Materials Gross	Unit Price
								(Gross rates include 10% profit)			
				£	£	£	£	£	£	£	£
R12	**R12: DRAINAGE BELOW GROUND**										
R1201	**Excavation of trenches; by machine; for drainage pipes or the like, including disposal and filling**										
R120120	**Trenches to suit 700 mm diameter pipes; average depth:**										
R120120A	1.00 m	m	0.58	7.36	10.01	–	17.37	8.10	11.01	–	19.11
R120120B	1.25 m	m	0.76	9.65	13.58	–	23.23	10.62	14.94	–	25.55
R120120C	1.50 m	m	0.96	12.19	16.47	–	28.66	13.41	18.12	–	31.53
R120120D	1.75 m	m	1.11	14.09	19.00	–	33.09	15.50	20.90	–	36.40
R120120E	2.00 m	m	1.27	16.13	21.55	–	37.68	17.74	23.71	–	41.45
R120120F	2.25 m	m	1.54	19.56	26.33	–	45.89	21.52	28.96	–	50.48
R120120G	2.50 m	m	1.70	21.59	29.30	–	50.89	23.75	32.23	–	55.98
R120120H	2.75 m	m	1.87	23.75	32.08	–	55.83	26.13	35.29	–	61.41
R120120I	3.00 m	m	2.03	25.78	35.05	–	60.83	28.36	38.56	–	66.91
R120121	**Trenches to suit 800 mm diameter pipes; average depth:**										
R120121A	1.00 m	m	0.64	8.13	11.16	–	19.29	8.94	12.28	–	21.22
R120121B	1.25 m	m	0.85	10.79	15.20	–	25.99	11.87	16.72	–	28.59
R120121C	1.50 m	m	1.06	13.46	18.09	–	31.55	14.81	19.90	–	34.71
R120121D	1.75 m	m	1.23	15.62	20.87	–	36.49	17.18	22.96	–	40.14
R120121E	2.00 m	m	1.40	17.78	23.64	–	41.42	19.56	26.00	–	45.56
R120121F	2.25 m	m	1.70	21.59	29.11	–	50.70	23.75	32.02	–	55.77
R120121G	2.50 m	m	1.87	23.75	32.08	–	55.83	26.13	35.29	–	61.41
R120121H	2.75 m	m	2.06	26.16	35.32	–	61.48	28.78	38.85	–	67.63
R120121I	3.00 m	m	2.23	28.32	38.29	–	66.61	31.15	42.12	–	73.27

Major Works 2009		Unit	Labour Hours	Labour Net	Plant Net	Materials Net	Unit Net	Labour Gross	Plant Gross	Materials Gross	Unit Price
									(Gross rates include 10% profit)		
				£	£	£	£	£	£	£	£
R12	**R12: DRAINAGE BELOW GROUND**										
R1202	**Excavation of trenches; by hand; for drainage pipes or the like, including disposal and filling**										
R120242	**Trenches to suit pipes not exceeding 200 mm diameter; average depth:**										
R120242A	0.50 m	m	1.32	16.77	0.17	–	16.94	18.45	0.19	–	18.63
R120242B	0.75 m	m	1.78	22.61	0.17	–	22.78	24.87	0.19	–	25.06
R120242C	1.00 m	m	2.23	28.33	0.29	–	28.62	31.16	0.32	–	31.48
R120242D	1.25 m	m	2.94	37.34	0.34	–	37.68	41.07	0.37	–	41.45
R120242E	1.50 m	m	3.45	43.81	0.46	–	44.27	48.19	0.51	–	48.70
R120242F	1.75 m	m	3.96	50.30	0.51	–	50.81	55.33	0.56	–	55.89
R120242G	2.00 m	m	4.46	56.64	0.63	–	57.27	62.30	0.69	–	63.00
R120242H	2.25 m	m	5.48	69.60	0.68	–	70.28	76.56	0.75	–	77.31
R120242I	2.50 m	m	6.04	76.71	0.80	–	77.51	84.38	0.88	–	85.26
R120242J	2.75 m	m	6.60	83.82	0.91	–	84.73	92.20	1.00	–	93.20
R120242K	3.00 m	m	7.16	90.93	1.03	–	91.96	100.02	1.13	–	101.16
R120243	**Trenches to suit pipes not exceeding 225 mm diameter; average depth:**										
R120243A	0.50 m	m	1.76	22.35	0.20	–	22.55	24.59	0.22	–	24.81
R120243B	0.75 m	m	2.36	29.97	0.20	–	30.17	32.97	0.22	–	33.19
R120243C	1.00 m	m	2.97	37.72	0.34	–	38.06	41.49	0.37	–	41.87
R120243D	1.25 m	m	3.92	49.78	0.40	–	50.18	54.76	0.44	–	55.20
R120243E	1.50 m	m	4.59	58.29	0.54	–	58.83	64.12	0.59	–	64.71
R120243F	1.75 m	m	5.27	66.93	0.60	–	67.53	73.62	0.66	–	74.28
R120243G	2.00 m	m	5.94	75.44	0.71	–	76.15	82.98	0.78	–	83.77
R120243H	2.25 m	m	7.29	92.58	0.80	–	93.38	101.84	0.88	–	102.72
R120243I	2.50 m	m	8.04	102.11	0.88	–	102.99	112.32	0.97	–	113.29
R120243J	2.75 m	m	8.79	111.63	1.00	–	112.63	122.79	1.10	–	123.89
R120243K	3.00 m	m	9.54	121.16	1.11	–	122.27	133.28	1.22	–	134.50
R120244	**Trenches to suit pipes not exceeding 300 mm diameter; average depth:**										
R120244A	0.50 m	m	2.20	27.94	0.23	–	28.17	30.73	0.25	–	30.99
R120244B	0.75 m	m	2.96	37.59	0.23	–	37.82	41.35	0.25	–	41.60
R120244C	1.00 m	m	3.72	47.24	0.37	–	47.61	51.96	0.41	–	52.37
R120244D	1.25 m	m	4.90	62.23	0.43	–	62.66	68.45	0.47	–	68.93
R120244E	1.50 m	m	5.74	72.90	0.60	–	73.50	80.19	0.66	–	80.85
R120244F	1.75 m	m	6.59	83.69	0.66	–	84.35	92.06	0.73	–	92.79
R120244G	2.00 m	m	7.43	94.36	0.77	–	95.13	103.80	0.85	–	104.64
R120244H	2.25 m	m	9.12	115.83	0.88	–	116.71	127.41	0.97	–	128.38
R120244I	2.50 m	m	10.06	127.76	0.97	–	128.73	140.54	1.07	–	141.60
R120244J	2.75 m	m	10.99	139.58	1.08	–	140.66	153.54	1.19	–	154.73
R120244K	3.00 m	m	11.93	151.51	1.20	–	152.71	166.66	1.32	–	167.98
R120245	**Trenches to suit pipes not exceeding 400 mm diameter; average depth:**										
R120245A	0.50 m	m	3.24	41.14	0.26	–	41.40	45.25	0.29	–	45.54
R120245B	0.75 m	m	3.88	49.27	0.26	–	49.53	54.20	0.29	–	54.48
R120245C	1.00 m	m	4.80	60.96	0.40	–	61.36	67.06	0.44	–	67.50
R120245D	1.25 m	m	6.21	78.86	0.46	–	79.32	86.75	0.51	–	87.25
R120245E	1.50 m	m	7.33	93.09	0.66	–	93.75	102.40	0.73	–	103.13
R120245F	1.75 m	m	8.24	104.65	0.71	–	105.36	115.12	0.78	–	115.90
R120245G	2.00 m	m	9.25	117.47	0.83	–	118.30	129.22	0.91	–	130.13
R120245H	2.25 m	m	11.28	143.26	0.97	–	144.23	157.59	1.07	–	158.65
R120245I	2.50 m	m	12.40	157.48	1.05	–	158.53	173.23	1.16	–	174.38
R120245J	2.75 m	m	13.53	171.83	1.17	–	173.00	189.01	1.29	–	190.30
R120245K	3.00 m	m	14.65	186.06	1.28	–	187.34	204.67	1.41	–	206.07

Disposal Systems

		Unit	Labour Hours	Labour Net	Plant Net	Materials Net	Unit Net	Labour Gross	Plant Gross	Materials Gross	Unit Price
									(Gross rates include 10% profit)		
				£	£	£	£	£	£	£	£
R12	**R12: DRAINAGE BELOW GROUND**										
R1202	**Excavation of trenches; by hand; for drainage pipes or the like, including disposal and filling**										
R120246	**Trenches to suit pipes not exceeding 450 mm diameter; average depth:**										
R120246A	0.50 m	m	3.73	47.38	0.29	–	47.67	52.12	0.32	–	52.44
R120246B	0.75 m	m	4.47	56.77	0.29	–	57.06	62.45	0.32	–	62.77
R120246C	1.00 m	m	5.44	69.09	0.43	–	69.52	76.00	0.47	–	76.47
R120246D	1.25 m	m	7.05	89.54	0.48	–	90.02	98.49	0.53	–	99.02
R120246E	1.50 m	m	8.19	104.02	0.71	–	104.73	114.42	0.78	–	115.20
R120246F	1.75 m	m	9.32	118.36	0.77	–	119.13	130.20	0.85	–	131.04
R120246G	2.00 m	m	10.46	132.85	0.88	–	133.73	146.14	0.97	–	147.10
R120246H	2.25 m	m	12.78	162.31	1.05	–	163.36	178.54	1.16	–	179.70
R120246I	2.50 m	m	14.05	178.44	1.14	–	179.58	196.28	1.25	–	197.54
R120246J	2.75 m	m	15.31	194.44	1.25	–	195.69	213.88	1.38	–	215.26
R120246K	3.00 m	m	16.58	210.56	1.37	–	211.93	231.62	1.51	–	233.12
R120247	**Trenches to suit pipes not exceeding 525 mm diameter; average depth:**										
R120247A	0.50 m	m	5.58	70.87	0.31	–	71.18	77.96	0.34	–	78.30
R120247B	0.75 m	m	6.44	81.79	0.31	–	82.10	89.97	0.34	–	90.31
R120247C	1.00 m	m	7.29	92.58	0.46	–	93.04	101.84	0.51	–	102.34
R120247D	1.25 m	m	9.18	116.59	0.51	–	117.10	128.25	0.56	–	128.81
R120247E	1.50 m	m	10.53	133.73	0.77	–	134.50	147.10	0.85	–	147.95
R120247F	1.75 m	m	11.88	150.87	0.83	–	151.70	165.96	0.91	–	166.87
R120247G	2.00 m	m	13.23	168.02	0.97	–	168.99	184.82	1.07	–	185.89
R120247H	2.25 m	m	15.93	202.31	1.14	–	203.45	222.54	1.25	–	223.80
R120247I	2.50 m	m	17.43	221.36	1.23	–	222.59	243.50	1.35	–	244.85
R120247J	2.75 m	m	18.93	240.41	1.34	–	241.75	264.45	1.47	–	265.93
R120247K	3.00 m	m	20.43	259.46	1.45	–	260.91	285.41	1.60	–	287.00
R120248	**Trenches to suit pipes not exceeding 600 mm diameter; average depth:**										
R120248A	1.00 m	m	8.91	113.16	0.51	–	113.67	124.48	0.56	–	125.04
R120248B	1.25 m	m	10.63	135.00	0.57	–	135.57	148.50	0.63	–	149.13
R120248C	1.50 m	m	12.15	154.30	0.83	–	155.13	169.73	0.91	–	170.64
R120248D	1.75 m	m	13.67	173.61	0.91	–	174.52	190.97	1.00	–	191.97
R120248E	2.00 m	m	15.19	192.92	1.05	–	193.97	212.21	1.16	–	213.37
R120248F	2.25 m	m	18.22	231.39	1.23	–	232.62	254.53	1.35	–	255.88
R120248G	2.50 m	m	19.92	252.99	1.31	–	254.30	278.29	1.44	–	279.73
R120248H	2.75 m	m	21.60	274.32	1.45	–	275.77	301.75	1.60	–	303.35
R120248I	3.00 m	m	23.29	295.78	1.57	–	297.35	325.36	1.73	–	327.09
R120249	**Trenches to suit pipes not exceeding 700 mm diameter; average depth:**										
R120249A	1.00 m	m	10.36	131.57	0.57	–	132.14	144.73	0.63	–	145.35
R120249B	1.25 m	m	12.27	155.83	0.63	–	156.46	171.41	0.69	–	172.11
R120249C	1.50 m	m	13.96	177.30	0.88	–	178.18	195.03	0.97	–	196.00
R120249D	1.75 m	m	15.64	198.63	1.00	–	199.63	218.49	1.10	–	219.59
R120249E	2.00 m	m	17.33	220.09	1.14	–	221.23	242.10	1.25	–	243.35
R120249F	2.25 m	m	20.71	263.02	1.31	–	264.33	289.32	1.44	–	290.76
R120249G	2.50 m	m	22.58	286.77	1.43	–	288.20	315.45	1.57	–	317.02
R120249H	2.75 m	m	24.46	310.64	1.57	–	312.21	341.70	1.73	–	343.43
R120249I	3.00 m	m	26.33	334.39	1.68	–	336.07	367.83	1.85	–	369.68

Major Works 2009		Unit	Labour Hours	Labour Net	Plant Net	Materials Net	Unit Net	Labour Gross	Plant Gross	Materials Gross	Unit Price
								(Gross rates include 10% profit)			
				£	£	£	£	£	£	£	£
R12	**R12: DRAINAGE BELOW GROUND**										
R1202	**Excavation of trenches; by hand; for drainage pipes or the like, including disposal and filling**										
R120250	**Trenches to suit pipes not exceeding 800 mm diameter; average depth:**										
R120250A	1.00 m	m	11.88	150.87	0.63	–	151.50	165.96	0.69	–	166.65
R120250B	1.25 m	m	13.99	177.68	0.71	–	178.39	195.45	0.78	–	196.23
R120250C	1.50 m	m	15.35	194.94	0.97	–	195.91	214.43	1.07	–	215.50
R120250D	1.75 m	m	17.21	218.57	1.11	–	219.68	240.43	1.22	–	241.65
R120250E	2.00 m	m	19.06	242.07	1.25	–	243.32	266.28	1.38	–	267.65
R120250F	2.25 m	m	22.78	289.31	1.45	–	290.76	318.24	1.60	–	319.84
R120250G	2.50 m	m	24.84	315.47	1.57	–	317.04	347.02	1.73	–	348.74
R120250H	2.75 m	m	26.90	341.63	1.74	–	343.37	375.79	1.91	–	377.71
R120250I	3.00 m	m	28.96	367.79	1.85	–	369.64	404.57	2.04	–	406.60
R1221	**Breaking up obstructions with machine driven hammer**										
R122142	**Extra over excavation for breaking out:**										
R122142A	soft rock or brickwork	m³	–	–	8.28	–	8.28	–	9.11	–	9.11
R122142B	hard rock	m³	–	–	13.01	–	13.01	–	14.31	–	14.31
R122142C	plain concrete	m³	–	–	10.64	–	10.64	–	11.70	–	11.70
R122142D	reinforced concrete	m³	–	–	15.37	–	15.37	–	16.91	–	16.91
R1223	**Breaking up obstructions with hand held mechanical tools**										
R122344	**Extra over excavation for breaking out:**										
R122344A	soft rock or brickwork	m³	3.60	45.72	46.76	–	92.48	50.29	51.44	–	101.73
R122344B	hard rock	m³	6.40	81.28	83.14	–	164.42	89.41	91.45	–	180.86
R122344C	plain concrete	m³	5.00	63.50	64.95	–	128.45	69.85	71.45	–	141.30
R122344D	reinforced concrete	m³	7.20	91.44	93.53	–	184.97	100.58	102.88	–	203.47
R1225	**Breaking out pavings with machine driven hammer**										
R122533	**Excavation in tarmac paving:**										
R122533A	not exceeding 150 mm thick	m²	–	–	0.71	–	0.71	–	0.78	–	0.78
R122533B	150-300 mm thick	m²	–	–	1.18	–	1.18	–	1.30	–	1.30
R122533C	300-450 mm thick	m²	–	–	1.89	–	1.89	–	2.08	–	2.08
R122534	**Excavation in plain concrete paving:**										
R122534A	not exceeding 150 mm thick	m²	–	–	1.42	–	1.42	–	1.56	–	1.56
R122534B	150-300 mm thick	m²	–	0.01	2.37	–	2.38	0.01	2.61	–	2.62
R122534C	300-450 mm thick	m²	–	–	3.78	–	3.78	–	4.16	–	4.16
R122535	**Excavation in reinforced concrete paving:**										
R122535A	not exceeding 150 mm thick	m²	0.08	1.02	2.59	–	3.61	1.12	2.85	–	3.97
R122535B	150-300 mm thick	m²	0.08	1.01	3.77	–	4.78	1.11	4.15	–	5.26
R122535C	300-450 mm thick	m²	0.08	1.02	4.95	–	5.97	1.12	5.45	–	6.57

Disposal Systems

		Unit	Labour Hours	Labour Net	Plant Net	Materials Net	Unit Net	Labour Gross	Plant Gross	Materials Gross	Unit Price
								(Gross rates include 10% profit)			
				£	£	£	£	£	£	£	£
R12	**R12: DRAINAGE BELOW GROUND**										
R1227	**Breaking out pavings with hand held compressor tools**										
R122737	**Excavation in tarmac paving:**										
R122737A	not exceeding 150 mm thick	m²	0.40	5.08	2.60	–	7.68	5.59	2.86	–	8.45
R122737B	150-300 mm thick	m²	0.70	8.89	5.20	–	14.09	9.78	5.72	–	15.50
R122737C	300-450 mm thick	m²	1.00	12.70	7.79	–	20.49	13.97	8.57	–	22.54
R122738	**Excavation in plain concrete paving:**										
R122738A	not exceeding 150 mm thick	m²	0.60	7.62	5.20	–	12.82	8.38	5.72	–	14.10
R122738B	150-300 mm thick	m²	0.90	11.43	7.79	–	19.22	12.57	8.57	–	21.14
R122738C	300-450 mm thick	m²	0.12	1.53	10.39	–	11.92	1.68	11.43	–	13.11
R122739	**Excavation in reinforced concrete paving:**										
R122739A	not exceeding 150 mm thick	m²	0.80	10.16	8.21	–	18.37	11.18	9.03	–	20.21
R122739B	150-300 mm thick	m²	1.30	16.51	13.40	–	29.91	18.16	14.74	–	32.90
R122739C	300-450 mm thick	m²	2.00	25.40	21.20	–	46.60	27.94	23.32	–	51.26
R1244	**Beds for drainage pipes**										
R124431	**50 mm sand bed to pipes:**										
R124431A	not exceeding 200 mm diameter	m	0.06	0.82	0.10	0.50	1.42	0.90	0.11	0.55	1.56
R124431B	225 mm diameter	m	0.07	0.94	0.13	0.68	1.75	1.03	0.14	0.75	1.93
R124431C	300 mm diameter	m	0.08	1.07	0.17	0.84	2.08	1.18	0.19	0.92	2.29
R124431D	400 mm diameter	m	0.09	1.18	0.19	1.00	2.37	1.30	0.21	1.10	2.61
R124431E	450 mm diameter	m	0.11	1.37	0.23	1.17	2.77	1.51	0.25	1.29	3.05
R124431F	525 mm diameter	m	0.13	1.63	0.26	1.33	3.22	1.79	0.29	1.46	3.54
R124431G	600 mm diameter	m	0.14	1.74	0.29	1.49	3.52	1.91	0.32	1.64	3.87
R124431H	700 mm diameter	m	0.15	1.86	0.32	1.62	3.80	2.05	0.35	1.78	4.18
R124431I	800 mm diameter	m	0.15	1.96	0.34	1.72	4.02	2.16	0.37	1.89	4.42
R1246	**Beds and coverings for drainage pipes**										
R124632	**150 mm bed and 150 mm covering of pea shingle to pipes:**										
R124632A	not exceeding 200 mm diameter	m	0.20	2.56	0.94	6.51	10.01	2.82	1.03	7.16	11.01
R124632B	225 mm diameter	m	0.29	3.65	1.34	9.27	14.26	4.02	1.47	10.20	15.69
R124632C	300 mm diameter	m	0.40	5.02	1.84	12.76	19.62	5.52	2.02	14.04	21.58
R124632D	400 mm diameter	m	0.53	6.67	2.45	16.98	26.10	7.34	2.70	18.68	28.71
R124632E	450 mm diameter	m	0.65	8.30	3.05	21.14	32.49	9.13	3.36	23.25	35.74
R124632F	525 mm diameter	m	0.81	10.22	3.75	26.03	40.00	11.24	4.13	28.63	44.00
R124632G	600 mm diameter	m	0.97	12.32	4.51	31.36	48.19	13.55	4.96	34.50	53.01
R124632H	700 mm diameter	m	1.11	14.08	5.16	35.85	55.09	15.49	5.68	39.44	60.60
R124632I	800 mm diameter	m	1.25	15.90	5.83	40.49	62.22	17.49	6.41	44.54	68.44
R124633	**150 mm bed and 150 mm covering of C10P concrete to pipes:**										
R124633A	not exceeding 200 mm diameter	m	0.25	3.16	0.98	21.96	26.10	3.48	1.08	24.16	28.71
R124633B	225 mm diameter	m	0.35	4.49	1.39	23.72	29.60	4.94	1.53	26.09	32.56
R124633C	300 mm diameter	m	0.49	6.18	1.92	30.74	38.84	6.80	2.11	33.81	42.72
R124633D	400 mm diameter	m	0.65	8.23	2.55	38.65	49.43	9.05	2.81	42.52	54.37
R124633E	450 mm diameter	m	0.81	10.25	3.18	42.16	55.59	11.28	3.50	46.38	61.15
R124633F	525 mm diameter	m	0.99	12.61	3.91	50.95	67.47	13.87	4.30	56.05	74.22
R124633G	600 mm diameter	m	1.20	15.18	4.71	55.34	75.23	16.70	5.18	60.87	82.75
R124633H	700 mm diameter	m	1.37	17.37	5.38	64.12	86.87	19.11	5.92	70.53	95.56
R124633I	800 mm diameter	m	1.54	19.61	6.08	72.91	98.60	21.57	6.69	80.20	108.46

Major Works 2009		Unit	Labour Hours	Labour Net	Plant Net	Materials Net	Unit Net	Labour Gross	Plant Gross	Materials Gross	Unit Price
								(Gross rates include 10% profit)			
				£	£	£	£	£	£	£	£
R12	**R12: DRAINAGE BELOW GROUND**										
R1261	**Drainage pipes**										
R126102	**Vitrified clay pipes; Hepworth Building Products:**										
R126102A	100 mm SuperSleve.......	m	0.20	2.54	–	4.78	7.32	2.79	–	5.26	8.05
R126102B	150 mm SuperSleve.......	m	0.23	2.92	–	9.66	12.58	3.21	–	10.63	13.84
R126102C	225 mm SuperSleve.......	m	0.29	3.69	–	24.66	28.35	4.06	–	27.13	31.19
R126102E	150 mm SuperSeal........	m	0.27	3.43	–	9.66	13.09	3.77	–	10.63	14.40
R126102F	225 mm SuperSeal........	m	0.37	4.70	–	24.66	29.36	5.17	–	27.13	32.30
R126102G	300 mm HepSeal	m	0.52	6.60	–	52.62	59.22	7.26	–	57.88	65.14
R126102H	400 mm HepSeal	m	0.72	9.14	–	123.26	132.40	10.05	–	135.59	145.64
R126102I	450 mm HepSeal	m	0.80	10.16	8.78	160.10	179.04	11.18	9.66	176.11	196.94
R126102J	500 mm HepSeal	m	0.88	11.18	9.66	178.44	199.28	12.30	10.63	196.28	219.21
R126102K	600 mm HepSeal	m	0.95	12.06	10.54	284.13	306.73	13.27	11.59	312.54	337.40
R126102N	100 mm HepLine	m	0.20	2.54	–	8.01	10.55	2.79	–	8.81	11.61
R126102O	150 mm HepLine	m	0.23	2.92	–	14.55	17.47	3.21	–	16.01	19.22
R126102P	225 mm HepLine	m	0.29	3.68	–	29.34	33.02	4.05	–	32.27	36.32
R126102Q	300 mm HepLine	m	0.34	4.32	–	57.13	61.45	4.75	–	62.84	67.60
R126103	**Concrete pipes, BS 5911 Part 1, Class L:**										
R126103A	150 mm	m	0.55	6.98	–	6.07	13.05	7.68	–	6.68	14.36
R126103B	225 mm	m	0.65	8.26	–	9.09	17.35	9.09	–	10.00	19.09
R126103C	300 mm	m	0.70	8.89	7.68	12.13	28.70	9.78	8.45	13.34	31.57
R126103D	375 mm	m	0.85	10.80	9.44	14.96	35.20	11.88	10.38	16.46	38.72
R126103E	450 mm	m	1.05	13.34	11.63	18.04	43.01	14.67	12.79	19.84	47.31
R126103F	525 mm	m	1.35	17.15	14.93	23.00	55.08	18.87	16.42	25.30	60.59
R126103G	600 mm	m	1.65	20.95	18.22	29.14	68.31	23.05	20.04	32.05	75.14
R126104	**Cast iron pipes; Timesaver bolted joints:**										
R126104A	100 mm	m	0.22	7.47	–	45.73	53.20	8.22	–	50.30	58.52
R126104B	150 mm	m	0.27	9.00	–	89.22	98.22	9.90	–	98.14	108.04
R126105	**UPVC pipes; OsmaDrain:**										
R126105A	82 mm	m	0.18	2.28	–	9.59	11.87	2.51	–	10.55	13.06
R126105B	110 mm	m	0.20	2.54	–	5.86	8.40	2.79	–	6.45	9.24
R126105C	160 mm	m	0.25	3.18	–	13.48	16.66	3.50	–	14.83	18.33
R126105D	200 mm	m	0.24	3.05	–	7.14	10.19	3.36	–	7.85	11.21
R126105E	225 mm	m	0.28	3.56	–	17.69	21.25	3.92	–	19.46	23.38
R126105F	300 mm	m	0.32	4.06	–	27.25	31.31	4.47	–	29.98	34.44
R126105G	110 mm perforated	m	0.20	2.54	–	3.50	6.04	2.79	–	3.85	6.64
R126105H	160 mm perforated	m	0.25	3.17	–	4.54	7.71	3.49	–	4.99	8.48

Disposal Systems

Major Works 2009		Unit	Labour Hours	Labour Net	Plant Net	Materials Net	Unit Net	Labour Gross	Plant Gross	Materials Gross	Unit Price
								——— (Gross rates include 10% profit) ———			
				£	£	£	£	£	£	£	£
R12	**R12: DRAINAGE BELOW GROUND**										
R1264	**Drainage fittings**										
R126411	**Vitrified clay fittings; Hepworth Buidling Products; SuperSleve:**										
R126411A	100 mm bends	Nr	0.20	2.54	–	9.94	12.48	2.79	–	10.93	13.73
R126411B	100 mm rest bends	Nr	0.22	2.79	–	14.92	17.71	3.07	–	16.41	19.48
R126411C	100 × 100 mm junctions .	Nr	0.25	3.17	–	28.30	31.47	3.49	–	31.13	34.62
R126411D	150 mm bends	Nr	0.20	2.54	–	13.28	15.82	2.79	–	14.61	17.40
R126411E	150 mm rest bends	Nr	0.22	2.80	–	17.06	19.86	3.08	–	18.77	21.85
R126411F	150 × 100 mm junctions .	Nr	0.25	3.17	–	17.77	20.94	3.49	–	19.55	23.03
R126411G	150 × 150 mm junctions .	Nr	0.25	3.17	–	19.50	22.67	3.49	–	21.45	24.94
R126412	**Vitrified clay fittings; Hepworth Building Products; HepSleve:**										
R126412A	225 mm bends	Nr	0.20	2.54	–	67.71	70.25	2.79	–	74.48	77.28
R126412B	225 mm rest bends	Nr	0.22	2.79	–	74.05	76.84	3.07	–	81.46	84.52
R126412C	225 × 100 mm junctions .	Nr	0.25	3.18	–	94.52	97.70	3.50	–	103.97	107.47
R126412D	225 × 150 mm junctions .	Nr	0.25	3.18	–	94.52	97.70	3.50	–	103.97	107.47
R126413	**Vitrified clay fittings; Hepworth Building Products; HepSeal:**										
R126413A	100 mm bends	Nr	0.20	2.54	–	21.18	23.72	2.79	–	23.30	26.09
R126413B	100 mm rest bends	Nr	0.22	2.79	–	14.92	17.71	3.07	–	16.41	19.48
R126413C	100 × 100 mm junctions .	Nr	0.25	3.17	–	20.96	24.13	3.49	–	23.06	26.54
R126413D	150 mm bends	Nr	0.20	2.54	–	31.77	34.31	2.79	–	34.95	37.74
R126413E	150 mm rest bends	Nr	0.22	2.80	–	17.06	19.86	3.08	–	18.77	21.85
R126413F	150 × 100 mm junctions .	Nr	0.25	3.18	–	36.78	39.96	3.50	–	40.46	43.96
R126413G	150 × 150 mm junctions .	Nr	0.25	3.17	–	41.54	44.71	3.49	–	45.69	49.18
R126413H	225 mm bends	Nr	0.22	2.79	–	74.47	77.26	3.07	–	81.92	84.99
R126413I	225 mm rest bends	Nr	0.25	3.18	–	90.96	94.14	3.50	–	100.06	103.55
R126413J	225 × 100 mm junctions .	Nr	0.27	3.43	–	103.94	107.37	3.77	–	114.33	118.11
R126413K	225 × 150 mm junctions .	Nr	0.27	3.43	–	103.94	107.37	3.77	–	114.33	118.11
R126413L	300 mm bends	Nr	0.35	4.45	–	128.59	133.04	4.90	–	141.45	146.34
R126413M	300 mm rest bends	Nr	0.38	4.83	–	195.72	200.55	5.31	–	215.29	220.61
R126413N	300 × 100 mm junctions .	Nr	0.40	5.08	–	202.39	207.47	5.59	–	222.63	228.22
R126413O	300 × 150 mm junctions .	Nr	0.40	5.08	–	202.39	207.47	5.59	–	222.63	228.22
R126413P	400 mm bends	Nr	0.45	5.72	–	330.83	336.55	6.29	–	363.91	370.21
R126413R	400 × 100 mm junctions .	Nr	0.50	6.35	–	434.00	440.35	6.99	–	477.40	484.39
R126413S	400 × 150 mm junctions .	Nr	0.50	6.35	–	434.00	440.35	6.99	–	477.40	484.39
R126413T	450 mm bends	Nr	0.55	6.99	4.39	435.65	447.03	7.69	4.83	479.22	491.73
R126413V	450 × 100 mm junctions .	Nr	0.60	7.62	4.39	434.00	446.01	8.38	4.83	477.40	490.61
R126413W	450 × 150 mm junctions .	Nr	0.60	7.62	4.39	519.17	531.18	8.38	4.83	571.09	584.30
R126414	**Vitrified clay fittings; Hepworth Building Products; HepSeal:**										
R126414A	500 mm bends; 90 degree. .	Nr	0.60	7.62	4.39	757.11	769.12	8.38	4.83	832.82	846.03
R126414C	500 mm bends; 45 degree. .	Nr	0.60	7.62	4.39	540.81	552.82	8.38	4.83	594.89	608.10
R126414D	500 × 150 mm junctions .	Nr	0.68	8.63	4.39	652.43	665.45	9.49	4.83	717.67	732.00
R126414E	600 mm bends; 90 degree. .	Nr	0.70	8.89	4.39	1595.64	1608.92	9.78	4.83	1755.20	1769.81
R126414G	600 mm bends; 45 degree. .	Nr	0.78	9.91	4.39	390.59	404.89	10.90	4.83	429.65	445.38
R126414H	600 × 150 mm junctions .	Nr	0.78	9.91	4.39	467.26	481.56	10.90	4.83	513.99	529.72

Major Works 2009		Unit	Labour Hours	Labour Net	Plant Net	Materials Net	Unit Net	Labour Gross	Plant Gross	Materials Gross	Unit Price
								(Gross rates include 10% profit)			
				£	£	£	£	£	£	£	£
R12	**R12: DRAINAGE BELOW GROUND**										
R1264	**Drainage fittings**										
R126415	**Vitrified clay fittings; Hepworth Building Products; HepLine:**										
R126415A	100 mm bends	Nr	0.20	2.54	–	9.94	12.48	2.79	–	10.93	13.73
R126415B	100 × 100 mm junctions .	Nr	0.25	3.17	–	20.96	24.13	3.49	–	23.06	26.54
R126415C	150 mm bends	Nr	0.20	2.54	–	13.28	15.82	2.79	–	14.61	17.40
R126415D	150 × 100 mm junctions .	Nr	0.25	3.18	–	36.78	39.96	3.50	–	40.46	43.96
R126415E	150 × 150 mm junctions .	Nr	0.25	3.17	–	41.54	44.71	3.49	–	45.69	49.18
R126415F	225 mm bends	Nr	0.22	2.80	–	90.96	93.76	3.08	–	100.06	103.14
R126415G	225 × 100 mm junctions .	Nr	0.27	3.43	–	103.94	107.37	3.77	–	114.33	118.11
R126415H	225 × 150 mm junctions .	Nr	0.27	3.43	–	103.94	107.37	3.77	–	114.33	118.11
R126415I	300 mm bends	Nr	0.35	4.45	–	128.59	133.04	4.90	–	141.45	146.34
R126415J	300 × 100 mm junctions .	Nr	0.40	5.08	–	202.39	207.47	5.59	–	222.63	228.22
R126415K	300 × 150 mm junctions .	Nr	0.40	5.08	–	202.39	207.47	5.59	–	222.63	228.22
R126416	**Concrete fittings, BS 5911 Part 1, Class L:**										
R126416A	150 mm bends	Nr	0.40	5.08	–	60.64	65.72	5.59	–	66.70	72.29
R126416B	150 × 150 mm junctions .	Nr	0.50	6.35	–	42.45	48.80	6.99	–	46.70	53.68
R126416C	225 mm bends	Nr	0.45	5.72	–	90.96	96.68	6.29	–	100.06	106.35
R126416D	225 × 150 mm junctions .	Nr	0.55	6.99	–	63.67	70.66	7.69	–	70.04	77.73
R126416E	300 mm bends	Nr	0.60	7.63	4.39	121.28	133.30	8.39	4.83	133.41	146.63
R126416F	300 × 150 mm junctions .	Nr	0.70	8.89	4.39	84.89	98.17	9.78	4.83	93.38	107.99
R126416G	375 mm bends	Nr	0.75	9.53	4.39	149.63	163.55	10.48	4.83	164.59	179.91
R126416H	375 × 150 mm junctions .	Nr	0.80	10.16	4.39	104.74	119.29	11.18	4.83	115.21	131.22
R126416I	450 mm bends	Nr	0.85	10.79	4.39	180.34	195.52	11.87	4.83	198.37	215.07
R126416J	450 × 150 mm junctions .	Nr	0.90	11.43	4.39	126.24	142.06	12.57	4.83	138.86	156.27
R126416K	525 mm bends	Nr	1.00	12.70	5.49	229.95	248.14	13.97	6.04	252.95	272.95
R126416L	525 × 150 mm junctions .	Nr	1.10	13.97	5.49	160.97	180.43	15.37	6.04	177.07	198.47
R126416M	600 mm bends	Nr	1.20	15.24	6.15	291.38	312.77	16.76	6.77	320.52	344.05
R126416N	600 × 150 mm junctions .	Nr	1.30	16.51	6.15	203.96	226.62	18.16	6.77	224.36	249.28
R126417	**Cast iron fittings; Timesaver bolted joints:**										
R126417A	100 mm bends	Nr	0.26	8.97	–	62.20	71.17	9.87	–	68.42	78.29
R126417B	100 × 100 mm junction ..	Nr	0.37	12.70	–	104.11	116.81	13.97	–	114.52	128.49
R126417C	150 mm bends	Nr	0.31	10.49	–	143.13	153.62	11.54	–	157.44	168.98
R126417D	150 × 100 mm junction ..	Nr	0.37	12.71	–	196.21	208.92	13.98	–	215.83	229.81
R126417E	150 × 150 mm junction ..	Nr	0.37	12.71	–	246.19	258.90	13.98	–	270.81	284.79
R126418	**UPVC fittings; OsmaDrain:**										
R126418A	82 mm bends	Nr	0.10	1.28	–	16.28	17.56	1.41	–	17.91	19.32
R126418B	82 × 82 mm junctions ...	Nr	0.15	1.90	–	25.19	27.09	2.09	–	27.71	29.80
R126418C	110 mm bends	Nr	0.13	1.65	–	15.46	17.11	1.82	–	17.01	18.82
R126418D	110 mm rest bends	Nr	0.15	1.91	–	29.62	31.53	2.10	–	32.58	34.68
R126418E	110 × 110 mm junctions .	Nr	0.18	2.29	–	21.83	24.12	2.52	–	24.01	26.53
R126418F	160 mm bends	Nr	0.20	2.54	–	39.45	41.99	2.79	–	43.40	46.19
R126418G	160 × 110 mm junctions .	Nr	0.25	3.17	–	54.93	58.10	3.49	–	60.42	63.91
R126418H	160 × 160 mm junctions .	Nr	0.25	3.18	–	71.25	74.43	3.50	–	78.38	81.87
R126419	**UPVC fittings; UltraRib:**										
R126419A	150 mm bends	Nr	0.28	3.55	–	17.60	21.15	3.91	–	19.36	23.27
R126419B	150 × 110 mm junctions .	Nr	0.30	3.81	–	36.25	40.06	4.19	–	39.88	44.07
R126419C	150 × 150 mm junctions .	Nr	0.30	3.81	–	42.58	46.39	4.19	–	46.84	51.03
R126419D	225 mm bends	Nr	0.32	4.07	–	75.05	79.12	4.48	–	82.56	87.03
R126419E	225 × 110 mm junctions .	Nr	0.35	4.45	–	98.70	103.15	4.90	–	108.57	113.47
R126419F	225 × 150 mm junctions .	Nr	0.35	4.45	–	101.67	106.12	4.90	–	111.84	116.73
R126419G	225 × 160 mm junctions .	Nr	0.35	4.45	–	101.67	106.12	4.90	–	111.84	116.73
R126419H	225 × 225 mm junctions .	Nr	0.35	4.44	–	141.29	145.73	4.88	–	155.42	160.30
R126419I	300 mm bends	Nr	0.34	4.32	–	149.91	154.23	4.75	–	164.90	169.65
R126419J	300 × 150 mm junctions .	Nr	0.37	4.70	–	201.75	206.45	5.17	–	221.93	227.10
R126419K	300 × 160 mm junctions .	Nr	0.37	4.70	–	215.20	219.90	5.17	–	236.72	241.89
R126419L	300 × 225 mm junctions .	Nr	0.37	4.70	–	310.77	315.47	5.17	–	341.85	347.02
R126419M	300 × 300 mm junctions .	Nr	0.37	4.70	–	272.99	277.69	5.17	–	300.29	305.46

Disposal Systems

Major Works 2009		Unit	Labour Hours	Labour Net	Plant Net	Materials Net	Unit Net	Labour Gross	Plant Gross	Materials Gross	Unit Price
								(Gross rates include 10% profit)			
				£	£	£	£	£	£	£	£
R12	**R12: DRAINAGE BELOW GROUND**										
R1267	**Drainage accessories including concrete surrounds and additional excavation**										
R126721	**Vitrified clay accessories; Hepworth Building Products; SuperSleve:**										
R126721A	100 mm rodding eye and plate.....................	Nr	0.40	5.08	–	32.36	37.44	5.59	–	35.60	41.18
R126721B	100 mm rodding eye with airtight sea..............	Nr	0.40	5.08	–	40.46	45.54	5.59	–	44.51	50.09
R126721C	150 mm rodding eye and plate.....................	Nr	0.45	5.72	–	50.01	55.73	6.29	–	55.01	61.30
R126721D	100 mm polypropylene adaptor to soil waste or rainwater pipe............	Nr	0.05	0.63	–	10.64	11.27	0.69	–	11.70	12.40
R126721E	100 mm one piece gulley and grid....................	Nr	0.60	7.62	–	45.65	53.27	8.38	–	50.22	58.60
R126721F	100 mm two piece back inlet gully an grid	Nr	0.95	12.06	–	38.22	50.28	13.27	–	42.04	55.31
R126721G	150 mm two piece back inlet gully an grid	Nr	1.05	13.34	–	64.52	77.86	14.67	–	70.97	85.65
R126721H	100 mm access gully and grid....................	Nr	0.60	7.62	–	45.12	52.74	8.38	–	49.63	58.01
R126721I	polypropylene trapped road gully; 510 mm diameter × 840 mm deep with 150 mm outlet, grating and frame...	Nr	3.50	44.45	–	276.83	321.28	48.90	–	304.51	353.41

Major Works 2009		Unit	Labour Hours	Labour Net	Plant Net	Materials Net	Unit Net	Labour Gross	Plant Gross	Materials Gross	Unit Price
								(Gross rates include 10% profit)			
				£	£	£	£	£	£	£	£
R12	**R12: DRAINAGE BELOW GROUND**										
R1267	**Drainage accessories including concrete surrounds and additional excavation**										
R126722	**Vitrified clay accessories; Hepworth Buidling Products; HepSleve:**										
R126722A	garage gully and bucket; Deans type; 100 mm outlet .	Nr	2.50	31.75	–	86.69	118.44	34.93	–	95.36	130.28
R126722B	mud gully and bucket; Deans type; 100 mm outlet	Nr	2.80	35.56	–	86.69	122.25	39.12	–	95.36	134.48
R126722C	garage gully and bucket; Deans type; 150 mm outlet .	Nr	2.50	31.75	–	105.11	136.86	34.93	–	115.62	150.55
R126722D	mud gully and bucket; Deans type; 150 mm outlet	Nr	2.80	35.56	–	105.11	140.67	39.12	–	115.62	154.74
R126722E	road gully; RGR1/2; 300 mm diameter 600 mm deep; 100 or 150 mm outlet	Nr	2.50	31.75	–	114.49	146.24	34.93	–	125.94	160.86
R126722F	road gully; RGR3; 400 mm diameter × 750 mm deep; 150 mm outlet.	Nr	2.90	36.83	–	135.06	171.89	40.51	–	148.57	189.08
R126722G	road gully; RGR4; 450 mm diameter × 900 mm deep; 150 mm outlet.	Nr	3.30	41.91	–	180.93	222.84	46.10	–	199.02	245.12
R126722H	universal grease trap; 375 × 375 × 70 mm deep; 100 mm inlet and outlet. . . .	Nr	2.50	31.76	–	818.78	850.54	34.94	–	900.66	935.59
R126723	**Concrete accessories; BS 5911 Part 1, Class L:**										
R126723A	road gully; 375 mm diameter × 900 mm deep; with rodding eye and 150 mm outlet	Nr	3.50	44.45	6.59	197.74	248.78	48.90	7.25	217.51	273.66
R126724	**Cast iron accessories; Timesaver bolted joints:**										
R126724A	trap with 100 mm inlet and outlet	Nr	0.75	25.48	–	48.80	74.28	28.03	–	53.68	81.71
R126725	**UPVC accessories; OsmaDrain:**										
R126725A	110 mm rodding eye with airtight sea.	Nr	0.40	5.08	–	51.30	56.38	5.59	–	56.43	62.02
R126725B	110 mm one piece bottle gully	Nr	0.60	7.62	–	28.89	36.51	8.38	–	31.78	40.16
R126725C	110 mm two piece bottle gully	Nr	0.80	10.16	–	35.34	45.50	11.18	–	38.87	50.05

Disposal Systems

		Unit	Labour Hours	Labour Net	Plant Net	Materials Net	Unit Net	Labour Gross	Plant Gross	Materials Gross	Unit Price
								(Gross rates include 10% profit)			
				£	£	£	£	£	£	£	£
R12	**R12: DRAINAGE BELOW GROUND**										
R1271	**Inspection chambers or the like**										
R127110	**Excavation by machine for manholes, inspection chambers, septic tanks and soakaways; in firm ground; depth not exceeding:**										
R127110B	1.00 m	m³	0.31	3.94	6.80	–	10.74	4.33	7.48	–	11.81
R127110C	2.00 m	m³	0.35	4.45	7.68	–	12.13	4.90	8.45	–	13.34
R127110D	4.00 m	m³	0.40	5.08	8.78	–	13.86	5.59	9.66	–	15.25
R127110E	6.00 m	m³	0.44	5.59	9.66	–	15.25	6.15	10.63	–	16.78
R127120	**Disposal of excavated material; off sit to tip; including lower rate Landfill Tax (rocks and soil); distance to tip:**										
R127120A	10 km	m³	–	–	20.14	3.29	23.43	–	22.15	3.62	25.77
R127120B	20 km	m³	–	–	34.09	3.29	37.38	–	37.50	3.62	41.12
R127125	**Disposal of excavated material; on site depositing in spoil heaps; distance:**										
R127125A	50 m	m³	0.07	0.89	1.54	–	2.43	0.98	1.69	–	2.67
R127127	**Filling to excavations with materials arising from earthworks; compacting in 250 mm layers:**										
R127127A	generally	m³	0.30	3.81	6.34	–	10.15	4.19	6.97	–	11.17
R127129	**Filling to excavations with imported materials; compacting in 250 mm layers:**										
R127129A	sand	m³	0.30	3.81	5.25	22.21	31.27	4.19	5.78	24.43	34.40
R127129B	hardcore	m³	0.35	4.45	8.68	27.78	40.91	4.90	9.55	30.56	45.00
R127129C	hoggin	m³	0.30	3.81	7.44	24.45	35.70	4.19	8.18	26.90	39.27
R127129D	DTp type 1	m³	0.33	4.19	8.62	29.43	42.24	4.61	9.48	32.37	46.46
R127129E	DTp type 2	m³	0.33	4.19	8.62	27.01	39.82	4.61	9.48	29.71	43.80
R127130	**Timber earthwork support in firm ground to sides of excavation not exceeding 2.00 m apart; open boarded; depth not exceeding:**										
R127130A	1.00 m	m²	0.30	3.81	–	0.73	4.54	4.19	–	0.80	4.99
R127130B	2.00 m	m²	0.36	4.57	–	0.97	5.54	5.03	–	1.07	6.09
R127130C	4.00 m	m²	0.48	6.09	–	1.45	7.54	6.70	–	1.60	8.29
R127130D	6.00 m	m²	0.72	9.15	–	1.93	11.08	10.07	–	2.12	12.19
R127131	**Timber earthwork support in firm ground to sides of excavation 2.00-4.00 m apart; open boarded; depth not exceeding:**										
R127131A	1.00 m	m²	0.42	5.34	–	1.20	6.54	5.87	–	1.32	7.19
R127131B	2.00 m	m²	0.48	6.09	–	1.45	7.54	6.70	–	1.60	8.29
R127131C	4.00 m	m²	0.60	7.62	–	1.93	9.55	8.38	–	2.12	10.51
R127131D	6.00 m	m²	0.84	10.67	–	2.42	13.09	11.74	–	2.66	14.40

Major Works 2009		Unit	Labour Hours	Labour Net	Plant Net	Materials Net	Unit Net	Labour Gross	Plant Gross	Materials Gross	Unit Price
								(Gross rates include 10% profit)			
				£	£	£	£	£	£	£	£
R12	**R12: DRAINAGE BELOW GROUND**										
R1271	**Inspection chambers or the like**										
R127132	**Timber earthwork support in firm ground to sides of excavation over 4.00 m apart; open boarded; depth not exceeding:**										
R127132A	1.00 m	m²	0.36	4.57	–	0.73	5.30	5.03	–	0.80	5.83
R127132B	2.00 m	m²	0.60	7.62	–	1.45	9.07	8.38	–	1.60	9.98
R127132C	4.00 m	m²	0.72	9.15	–	2.41	11.56	10.07	–	2.65	12.72
R127132D	6.00 m	m²	0.96	12.19	–	3.38	15.57	13.41	–	3.72	17.13
R127133	**Plain in situ concrete C10; 14 mm aggregate; in bases and surrounds:**										
R127133A	in bases and benchings	m³	1.90	24.13	–	92.23	116.36	26.54	–	101.45	128.00
R127133B	in surrounds	m³	1.95	24.76	–	94.43	119.19	27.24	–	103.87	131.11
R127134	**Plain in situ concrete C20; 20 mm aggregate; not exceeding 150 mm thick:**										
R127134A	in bases and benchings	m³	1.90	24.13	–	96.98	121.11	26.54	–	106.68	133.22
R127134B	in surrounds	m³	1.95	24.76	–	99.29	124.05	27.24	–	109.22	136.46
R127135	**Plain in situ concrete C25; 20 mm aggregate; in bases and benchings:**										
R127135A	not exceeding 150 mm thick	m³	2.10	26.67	8.34	96.98	131.99	29.34	9.17	106.68	145.19
R127135B	150-450 mm thick	m³	1.55	19.69	6.12	96.98	122.79	21.66	6.73	106.68	135.07
R127135C	exceeding 450 mm thick ...	m³	1.05	13.33	4.17	96.98	114.48	14.66	4.59	106.68	125.93
R127136	**Reinforced in situ concrete C25; 20 mm aggregate; in suspended slabs:**										
R127136A	not exceeding 150 mm thick	m³	2.10	26.67	8.34	99.03	134.04	29.34	9.17	108.93	147.44
R127136B	150-450 mm thick	m³	1.55	19.69	6.12	99.03	124.84	21.66	6.73	108.93	137.32
R127137	**Reinforcement bar; BS 4483; hot rolled high yield plain round steel; bent; nominal diameter:**										
R127137A	8 mm	Tonne	54.00	799.20	–	1073.24	1872.44	879.12	–	1180.56	2059.68
R127137B	10 mm	Tonne	44.00	651.20	–	1004.79	1655.99	716.32	–	1105.27	1821.59
R127137C	12 mm	Tonne	38.00	562.40	–	958.98	1521.38	618.64	–	1054.88	1673.52
R127137D	16 mm	Tonne	30.00	444.00	–	894.29	1338.29	488.40	–	983.72	1472.12
R127137E	20 mm	Tonne	26.00	384.80	–	878.96	1263.76	423.28	–	966.86	1390.14
R127137F	25 mm	Tonne	23.00	340.40	–	853.94	1194.34	374.44	–	939.33	1313.77
R127138	**Reinforcement fabric; BS 4483; steel; cut, lapped and tied; laid horizontally over 300 mm wide; reference:**										
R127138A	A98; 1.54 kg/m²	m²	0.02	0.30	–	1.95	2.25	0.33	–	2.15	2.48
R127138B	A142; 2.22 kg/m²	m²	0.03	0.46	–	2.49	2.95	0.51	–	2.74	3.25
R127138C	A193; 3.02 kg/m²	m²	0.03	0.44	–	3.32	3.76	0.48	–	3.65	4.14
R127139	**Formwork for in situ concrete; soffits of isolated slabs; slab thickness not exceeding 200 mm; height from base to soffit:**										
R127139A	not exceeding 1.50 m......	m²	1.16	17.21	0.52	21.16	38.89	18.93	0.57	23.28	42.78
R127139B	1.50-3.0 m.	m²	1.40	20.26	0.52	21.16	41.94	22.29	0.57	23.28	46.13

Disposal Systems

Major Works 2009		Unit	Labour Hours	Labour Net	Plant Net	Materials Net	Unit Net	Labour Gross	Plant Gross	Materials Gross	Unit Price
								(Gross rates include 10% profit)			
				£	£	£	£	£	£	£	£
R12	**R12: DRAINAGE BELOW GROUND**										
R1271	**Inspection chambers or the like**										
R127140	**Formwork for in situ concrete; isolated surrounds and casings; vertical:**										
R127140A	in flat plane	m²	1.56	23.16	1.53	13.40	38.09	25.48	1.68	14.74	41.90
R127140B	in curved plane	m²	1.94	27.98	1.53	14.59	44.10	30.78	1.68	16.05	48.51
R127141	**Vitrified clay inspection chambers; surrounding in concrete; Hepworth Iron Co; 100 mm SuperSleve:**										
R127141A	225 mm diameter base, raising piece, cover and frame; straight through	Nr	1.20	15.24	–	143.64	158.88	16.76	–	158.00	174.77
R127141B	225 mm diameter base, raising piece, cover and frame; one branch	Nr	1.30	16.51	–	165.23	181.74	18.16	–	181.75	199.91
R127141C	225 mm diameter base, raising piece, cover and frame; two branches	Nr	1.40	17.78	–	188.04	205.82	19.56	–	206.84	226.40
R127142	**Polypropylene inspection chambers; granular bed and surround; Hepworth Iron Co; 100 mm SuperSleve:**										
R127142A	475 mm diameter base, raising piece, cover and frame; 585 mm deep	Nr	1.75	22.23	–	140.19	162.42	24.45	–	154.21	178.66
R127142B	475 mm diameter base, raising piece, cover and frame; 930 mm deep	Nr	1.80	22.86	–	207.68	230.54	25.15	–	228.45	253.59
R127143	**Construct manhole complete; excavation; disposal; earthwork support; 150 mm thick plain concrete bed; one brick thick class B engineering brick walls; cover and frame; depth to invert:**										
R127143A	not exceeding 1.00 m	Nr	10.62	196.04	29.75	250.84	476.63	215.64	32.73	275.92	524.29
R127143B	1.00-1.25 m	Nr	13.91	251.73	36.62	307.55	595.90	276.90	40.28	338.31	655.49
R127143C	1.25-1.50 m	Nr	16.36	297.01	44.82	362.50	704.33	326.71	49.30	398.75	774.76
R127143D	1.50-1.75 m	Nr	18.75	341.52	51.70	416.50	809.72	375.67	56.87	458.15	890.69
R127143E	1.75-2.00 m	Nr	21.16	386.28	56.99	471.43	914.70	424.91	62.69	518.57	1006.17
R127144	**Construct manhole complete; excavation; disposal; earthwork support; 150 mm thick plain concrete bed; 1050 mm diameter precast concrete chamber rings with step irons; concrete cover slab; cover and frame; depth to invert:**										
R127144A	1.50-2.00 m	Nr	18.32	245.46	112.64	369.13	727.23	270.01	123.90	406.04	799.95
R127144B	2.00-2.50 m	Nr	25.91	329.06	148.20	447.33	924.59	361.97	163.02	492.06	1017.05
R127144C	2.50-3.00 m	Nr	31.20	411.02	168.65	496.36	1076.03	452.12	185.52	546.00	1183.63
R127144D	3.00-3.50 m	Nr	36.14	474.75	200.48	564.86	1240.09	522.23	220.53	621.35	1364.10
R127144E	3.50-4.00 m	Nr	40.32	528.83	220.93	614.79	1364.55	581.71	243.02	676.27	1501.01

Major Works 2009		Unit	Labour Hours	Labour Net	Plant Net	Materials Net	Unit Net	Labour Gross	Plant Gross	Materials Gross	Unit Price
								(Gross rates include 10% profit)			
				£	£	£	£	£	£	£	£
R12	**R12: DRAINAGE BELOW GROUND**										
R1271	**Inspection chambers or the like**										
R127145	**Construct manhole complete; excavation; disposal; earthwork support; 150 mm thick plain concrete bed; 1200 mm diameter precast concrete chamber rings with step irons; concrete cover slab; cover and frame; depth to invert:**										
R127145A	1.50-2.00 m	Nr	20.22	269.59	133.05	421.48	824.12	296.55	146.36	463.63	906.53
R127145B	2.00-2.50 m	Nr	29.87	393.13	173.75	511.48	1078.36	432.44	191.13	562.63	1186.20
R127145C	2.50-3.00 m	Nr	34.60	454.20	199.52	567.82	1221.54	499.62	219.47	624.60	1343.69
R127145D	3.00-3.50 m	Nr	40.01	523.90	235.87	647.10	1406.87	576.29	259.46	711.81	1547.56
R127145E	3.50-4.00 m	Nr	44.68	584.21	261.23	702.52	1547.96	642.63	287.35	772.77	1702.76
R127146	**Construct soakaway complete; excavation; disposal; earthwork support; 150 mm thick plain concrete bed; 1500 mm diameter precast concrete perforated rings; cover slab; cover and frame; depth to invert:**										
R127146A	not exceeding 1.00 m	Nr	9.84	133.78	99.89	288.30	521.97	147.16	109.88	317.13	574.17
R127146B	1.00-1.50 m	Nr	15.35	203.77	150.39	624.85	979.01	224.15	165.43	687.34	1076.91
R127146C	1.50-2.00 m	Nr	19.47	256.09	187.58	414.49	858.16	281.70	206.34	455.94	943.98
R127146D	2.00-2.50 m	Nr	29.93	388.93	243.35	762.65	1394.93	427.82	267.69	838.92	1534.42
R127146E	2.50-3.00 m	Nr	35.22	456.11	281.60	554.76	1292.47	501.72	309.76	610.24	1421.72
R127147	**Extra over inspection chambers or the like for the following:**										
R127147A	heavy duty cast iron cover and frame 600 × 450 mm	Nr	–	–	–	139.37	139.37	–	–	153.31	153.31
R127147B	medium duty cast iron cover and frame; 500 mm diameter	Nr	–	–	–	115.04	115.04	–	–	126.54	126.54
R127147C	heavy duty cast iron cover and frame 500 mm diameter	Nr	–	–	–	236.51	236.51	–	–	260.16	260.16
R127147D	150 mm diameter half round straight channel	m	–	–	–	3.78	3.78	–	–	4.16	4.16
R127147E	225 mm diameter half round straight channel	m	–	–	–	15.50	15.50	–	–	17.05	17.05
R127147F	100 mm diameter half round curved channel	m	–	–	–	2.85	2.85	–	–	3.14	3.14
R127147G	150 mm diameter half round curved channel	m	–	–	–	9.03	9.03	–	–	9.93	9.93
R127147H	225 mm diameter half round curved channel	m	–	–	–	51.23	51.23	–	–	56.35	56.35
R127147I	150 mm diameter three quarter section branches. . .	Nr	–	–	–	9.31	9.31	–	–	10.24	10.24
R127147J	225 mm diameter three quarter section branches. . .	Nr	–	–	–	64.43	64.43	–	–	70.87	70.87
R127155	**Manhole cover and frame; grey iron light duty single seal solid; BS EN124 Class A15 42 mm deep; clear opening size:**										
R127155A	450 × 450 mm; MHC-5140	Nr	1.50	19.05	–	49.82	68.87	20.96	–	54.80	75.76
R127155B	600 × 450 mm; MHC-5145	Nr	1.55	19.68	–	49.88	69.56	21.65	–	54.87	76.52
R127155C	600 mm dia; MHC-5150 . . .	Nr	1.60	20.32	–	99.32	119.64	22.35	–	109.25	131.60
R127155D	600 × 600 mm; MHC-5155	Nr	1.60	20.32	–	76.93	97.25	22.35	–	84.62	106.98
R127155E	750 × 600 mm; MHC-5165	Nr	1.65	20.96	–	150.78	171.74	23.06	–	165.86	188.91
R127155F	900 × 600 mm; MHC-5175	Nr	1.70	21.59	–	165.24	186.83	23.75	–	181.76	205.51

Disposal Systems

Major Works 2009		Unit	Labour Hours	Labour Net	Plant Net	Materials Net	Unit Net	Labour Gross	Plant Gross	Materials Gross	Unit Price
								(Gross rates include 10% profit)			
				£	£	£	£	£	£	£	£
R12	**R12: DRAINAGE BELOW GROUND**										
R1271	**Inspection chambers or the like**										
R127156	**Manhole cover and frame; grey iron light duty double seal solid; BS EN124 Class A15 42 mm deep; clear opening size:**										
R127156A	600 × 450 mm; MHC-5146	Nr	1.70	21.59	–	65.66	87.25	23.75	–	72.23	95.98
R127156B	600 × 600 mm; MHC-5156	Nr	1.80	22.86	–	94.15	117.01	25.15	–	103.57	128.71
R127157	**Manhole cover and frame; grey iron light duty single seal recessed; BS EN124 Class A15 65 mm deep; clear opening size:**										
R127157A	600 × 450 mm; MHC-5147	Nr	1.70	21.59	–	54.78	76.37	23.75	–	60.26	84.01
R127157B	600 × 600 mm; MHC-5157	Nr	1.80	22.86	–	81.08	103.94	25.15	–	89.19	114.33
R127158	**Manhole cover and frame; grey iron light duty double seal recessed; BS EN124 Class A15 65 mm deep; clear opening size:**										
R127158A	600 × 450 mm; MHC-5148	Nr	1.70	21.59	–	73.12	94.71	23.75	–	80.43	104.18
R127158B	600 × 600 mm; MHC-5158	Nr	1.80	22.86	–	113.65	136.51	25.15	–	125.02	150.16
R127159	**Manhole cover and frame; ductile iron medium duty single seal solid top; BS EN124 Class BA125 45 mm deep; clear opening size:**										
R127159A	450 × 450 mm; MHC-5240	Nr	1.65	20.96	–	81.71	102.67	23.06	–	89.88	112.94
R127159B	600 × 450 mm; MHC-5245	Nr	1.70	21.59	–	81.77	103.36	23.75	–	89.95	113.70
R127159C	600 × 600 mm; MHC-5255	Nr	1.75	22.23	–	101.48	123.71	24.45	–	111.63	136.08
R127159D	750 × 600 mm; MHC-5265	Nr	1.80	22.86	–	174.45	197.31	25.15	–	191.90	217.04
R127159E	900 × 600 mm; MHC-5275	Nr	2.00	25.40	–	198.71	224.11	27.94	–	218.58	246.52
R127160	**Manhole cover and frame; ductile iron medium duty single seal solid top; BS EN124 Class B125 75 mm deep; clear opening size:**										
R127160A	450 × 450 mm; MHC-5241	Nr	1.65	20.96	–	122.42	143.38	23.06	–	134.66	157.72
R127160B	600 × 450 mm; MHC-5246	Nr	1.70	21.59	–	122.48	144.07	23.75	–	134.73	158.48
R127160C	600 × 600 mm; MHC-5256	Nr	1.75	22.23	–	152.05	174.28	24.45	–	167.26	191.71
R127160D	750 × 600 mm; MHC-5266	Nr	1.80	22.86	–	209.42	232.28	25.15	–	230.36	255.51
R127160E	900 × 600 mm; MHC-5276	Nr	2.00	25.40	–	255.34	280.74	27.94	–	280.87	308.81
R127175	**Precast concrete manhole rings; BS 5911-200; bedding, jointing and pointing in cement and sand mortar (1:3); 900 mm nominal internal diameter shaft rings; unit height:**										
R127175A	250 mm	Nr	2.00	25.40	6.59	17.48	49.47	27.94	7.25	19.23	54.42
R127175B	500 mm	Nr	2.20	27.94	6.59	25.93	60.46	30.73	7.25	28.52	66.51
R127175C	750 mm	Nr	2.40	30.48	6.59	25.93	63.00	33.53	7.25	28.52	69.30
R127175D	1000 mm	Nr	2.60	33.02	6.59	34.38	73.99	36.32	7.25	37.82	81.39

Major Works 2009		Unit	Labour Hours	Labour Net	Plant Net	Materials Net	Unit Net	Labour Gross	Plant Gross	Materials Gross	Unit Price
								——— (Gross rates include 10% profit) ———			
				£	£	£	£	£	£	£	£
R12	**R12: DRAINAGE BELOW GROUND**										
R1271	**Inspection chambers or the like**										
R127176	**Precast concrete manhole rings; BS 5911-200; bedding, jointing and pointing in cement and sand mortar (1:3); 1050 mm nominal internal diameter shaft rings; unit height:**										
R127176A	250 mm	Nr	2.10	26.67	7.02	18.54	52.23	29.34	7.72	20.39	57.45
R127176B	500 mm	Nr	2.25	28.57	7.02	27.55	63.14	31.43	7.72	30.31	69.45
R127176C	750 mm	Nr	2.50	31.75	7.02	27.55	66.32	34.93	7.72	30.31	72.95
R127176D	1000 mm	Nr	2.70	34.29	7.02	36.48	77.79	37.72	7.72	40.13	85.57
R127177	**Precast concrete manhole rings; BS 5911-200; bedding, jointing and pointing in cement and sand mortar (1:3); 1200 mm nominal internal diameter shaft rings; unit height:**										
R127177A	250 mm	Nr	2.20	27.94	7.24	22.92	58.10	30.73	7.96	25.21	63.91
R127177B	500 mm	Nr	2.44	30.99	7.24	33.86	72.09	34.09	7.96	37.25	79.30
R127177C	750 mm	Nr	2.70	34.29	7.24	33.86	75.39	37.72	7.96	37.25	82.93
R127177D	1000 mm	Nr	3.00	38.10	7.24	44.80	90.14	41.91	7.96	49.28	99.15
R127178	**Precast concrete manhole rings; BS 5911-200; bedding, jointing and pointing in cement and sand mortar (1:3); 1350 mm nominal internal diameter shaft rings; unit height:**										
R127178B	500 mm	Nr	2.50	31.75	7.68	49.84	89.27	34.93	8.45	54.82	98.20
R127178C	750 mm	Nr	2.80	35.56	7.68	49.84	93.08	39.12	8.45	54.82	102.39
R127178D	1000 mm	Nr	3.10	39.37	7.68	66.02	113.07	43.31	8.45	72.62	124.38
R127179	**Precast concrete manhole rings; BS 5911-200; bedding, jointing and pointing in cement and sand mortar (1:3); 1500 mm nominal internal diameter shaft rings; unit height:**										
R127179B	500 mm	Nr	2.70	34.29	8.34	62.85	105.48	37.72	9.17	69.14	116.03
R127179C	750 mm	Nr	3.00	38.10	8.34	62.85	109.29	41.91	9.17	69.14	120.22
R127179D	1000 mm	Nr	3.30	41.91	8.34	83.31	133.56	46.10	9.17	91.64	146.92
R127180	**Precast concrete manhole rings; BS 5911-200; bedding, jointing and pointing in cement and sand mortar (1:3); 1800 mm nominal internal diameter shaft rings; unit height:**										
R127180B	500 mm	Nr	3.00	38.10	8.78	78.46	125.34	41.91	9.66	86.31	137.87
R127180C	750 mm	Nr	3.40	43.18	8.78	78.46	130.42	47.50	9.66	86.31	143.46
R127180D	1000 mm	Nr	3.80	48.26	8.78	103.93	160.97	53.09	9.66	114.32	177.07
R127181	**Precast concrete manhole rings; BS 5911-200; bedding, jointing and pointing in cement and sand mortar (1:3); 2100 mm nominal internal diameter shaft rings; unit height:**										
R127181B	500 mm	Nr	3.20	40.64	10.54	152.59	203.77	44.70	11.59	167.85	224.15
R127181C	750 mm	Nr	3.60	45.72	10.54	152.59	208.85	50.29	11.59	167.85	229.74
R127181D	1000 mm	Nr	4.00	50.80	10.54	202.59	263.93	55.88	11.59	222.85	290.32

Disposal Systems

Major Works 2009		Unit	Labour Hours	Labour Net	Plant Net	Materials Net	Unit Net	Labour Gross	Plant Gross	Materials Gross	Unit Price
								(Gross rates include 10% profit)			
				£	£	£	£	£	£	£	£
R12	R12: DRAINAGE BELOW GROUND										
R1271	Inspection chambers or the like										
R127182	Precast concrete manhole rings; BS 5911-200; bedding, jointing and pointing in cement and sand mortar (1:3); 2400 mm nominal internal diameter shaft rings; unit height:										
R127182B	500 mm	Nr	3.60	45.72	10.98	196.31	253.01	50.29	12.08	215.94	278.31
R127182C	750 mm	Nr	4.00	50.80	10.98	196.31	258.09	55.88	12.08	215.94	283.90
R127182D	1000 mm	Nr	4.50	57.15	10.98	260.67	328.80	62.87	12.08	286.74	361.68
R127183	Precast concrete manhole rings; BS 5911-200; bedding, jointing and pointing in cement and sand mortar (1:3); 2700 mm nominal internal diameter shaft rings; unit height:										
R127183B	500 mm	Nr	4.10	52.07	12.07	228.66	292.80	57.28	13.28	251.53	322.08
R127183C	750 mm	Nr	4.50	57.15	12.07	228.66	297.88	62.87	13.28	251.53	327.67
R127183D	1000 mm	Nr	4.80	60.96	12.07	303.66	376.69	67.06	13.28	334.03	414.36
R127184	Precast concrete manhole cover slabs; B 5911-200; bedding, jointing and pointing in cement and sand mortar (1:3); heavy duty; to suit shaft ring nominal internal diameter:										
R127184A	900 mm	Nr	2.40	30.48	6.59	35.75	72.82	33.53	7.25	39.33	80.10
R127184B	1050 mm	Nr	2.60	33.02	7.02	38.43	78.47	36.32	7.72	42.27	86.32
R127184C	1200 mm	Nr	2.80	35.56	7.24	47.88	90.68	39.12	7.96	52.67	99.75
R127184D	1350 mm	Nr	3.00	38.10	7.68	70.06	115.84	41.91	8.45	77.07	127.42
R127184E	1500 mm	Nr	3.20	40.64	8.34	85.33	134.31	44.70	9.17	93.86	147.74
R127184F	1800 mm	Nr	3.50	44.45	8.78	117.93	171.16	48.90	9.66	129.72	188.28
R127184G	2100 mm	Nr	3.80	48.26	10.54	248.95	307.75	53.09	11.59	273.85	338.53
R127184H	2400 mm	Nr	4.10	52.07	10.98	340.14	403.19	57.28	12.08	374.15	443.51
R127184I	2700 mm	Nr	4.50	57.15	12.07	522.85	592.07	62.87	13.28	575.14	651.28

Major Works 2009		Unit	Labour Hours	Labour Net	Plant Net	Materials Net	Unit Net	Labour Gross	Plant Gross	Materials Gross	Unit Price
				£	£	£	£	£	£	£	£
								(Gross rates include 10% profit)			
R12	R12: DRAINAGE BELOW GROUND										
R1271	Inspection chambers or the like										
R127190	Class B engineering bricks in cement and sand mortar (1:3) in manhole walls and raising courses; flush pointing:										
R127190A	half brick thick	m²	2.06	51.74	–	28.17	79.91	56.91	–	30.99	87.90
R127190B	one brick thick	m²	3.50	87.92	–	56.44	144.36	96.71	–	62.08	158.80
R127190C	one and a half brick thick...	m²	5.15	129.37	–	84.66	214.03	142.31	–	93.13	235.43
R127192	Step irons; galvanised general purpose pattern; built into brickwork:										
R127192A	short tail	Nr	–	–	–	5.53	5.53	–	–	6.08	6.08
R127192B	long tail	Nr	–	–	–	6.08	6.08	–	–	6.69	6.69
R127193	Manhole step rungs; cast into pc concrete manhole rings; galvanised mild steel; patterned finish:										
R127193A	single	Nr	–	–	–	5.53	5.53	–	–	6.08	6.08
R127193B	double	Nr	–	–	–	6.08	6.08	–	–	6.69	6.69
R127195	Benching to manholes; concrete (1:3:6) to slopes to channels and branches; finished with 13 mm thick cement mortar (1:3) trowelled smooth; average thickness:										
R127195A	225 mm	m²	2.65	33.66	–	23.64	57.30	37.03	–	26.00	63.03
R127195B	300 mm	m²	3.31	42.04	–	31.01	73.05	46.24	–	34.11	80.36
R127196	In situ finishings; cement and sand (1:3); steel trowelled; to brickwork; 13 mm thick in one coat:										
R127196A	over 300 mm wide	m²	0.25	4.25	–	1.42	5.67	4.68	–	1.56	6.24

Disposal Systems

Major Works 2009		Unit	Labour Hours	Labour Net	Plant Net	Materials Net	Unit Net	Labour Gross	Plant Gross	Materials Gross	Unit Price
				£	£	£	£	£ (Gross rates include 10% profit)	£	£	£
R12	R12: DRAINAGE BELOW GROUND										
R1271	Inspection chambers or the like										
R127197	Vitrified clay half round; bedding and pointing in cement sand mortar (1:3); to manholes and chambers:										
R127197A	100 mm dia straight channel; 300 mm	Nr	0.32	4.06	–	3.98	8.04	4.47	–	4.38	8.84
R127197B	100 mm dia straight channel; 600 mm	Nr	0.33	4.19	–	3.98	8.17	4.61	–	4.38	8.99
R127197C	100 mm dia straight channel; 1000 mm	Nr	0.35	4.45	–	5.63	10.08	4.90	–	6.19	11.09
R127197D	150 mm dia straight channel; 300 mm	Nr	0.36	4.57	–	6.70	11.27	5.03	–	7.37	12.40
R127197E	150 mm dia straight channel; 600 mm	Nr	0.37	4.70	–	6.70	11.40	5.17	–	7.37	12.54
R127197F	150 mm dia straight channel; 1000 mm	Nr	0.39	4.95	–	9.41	14.36	5.45	–	10.35	15.80
R127197G	225 mm dia straight channel; 300 mm	Nr	0.40	5.08	–	19.31	24.39	5.59	–	21.24	26.83
R127197H	225 mm dia straight channel; 600 mm	Nr	0.42	5.33	–	19.31	24.64	5.86	–	21.24	27.10
R127197I	225 mm dia straight channel; 1000 mm	Nr	0.44	5.59	–	21.13	26.72	6.15	–	23.24	29.39
R127197J	300 mm dia straight channel; 300 mm	m	0.44	5.59	–	39.17	44.76	6.15	–	43.09	49.24
R127197K	300 mm dia straight channel; 600 mm	m	0.46	5.84	–	39.17	45.01	6.42	–	43.09	49.51
R127197L	300 mm dia straight channel; 1000 mm	m	0.49	6.22	–	43.38	49.60	6.84	–	47.72	54.56
R127197M	100 mm dia half round channel bend	Nr	0.30	3.81	–	5.08	8.89	4.19	–	5.59	9.78
R127197N	150 mm dia half round channel bend	Nr	0.36	4.57	–	8.78	13.35	5.03	–	9.66	14.69
R127197O	225 mm dia half section channel bend	Nr	0.40	5.08	–	34.05	39.13	5.59	–	37.46	43.04
R127197P	300 mm dia half section channel bend	Nr	0.44	5.59	–	69.42	75.01	6.15	–	76.36	82.51
R127197Q	100 mm dia half section branch channel bend	Nr	0.32	4.06	–	12.43	16.49	4.47	–	13.67	18.14
R127197R	150 mm dia half section branch channel bend	Nr	0.36	4.57	–	20.38	24.95	5.03	–	22.42	27.45
R127197S	225 mm dia half section branch channel bend	Nr	0.40	5.08	–	68.27	73.35	5.59	–	75.10	80.69
R127197T	100 mm dia three quarter section branch channel bend	Nr	0.34	4.32	–	13.71	18.03	4.75	–	15.08	19.83
R127197U	150 mm dia three quarter section branch channel bend		0.40	5.08	–	23.02	28.10	5.59	–	25.32	30.91
R127197V	225 mm dia three quarter section branch channel bend	Nr	0.44	5.59	–	78.14	83.73	6.15	–	85.95	92.10
R127198	Building in ends of pipes into manhole walls; pipe diameter:										
R127198A	100 mm	Nr	0.09	1.53	–	0.32	1.85	1.68	–	0.35	2.04
R127198B	150 mm	Nr	0.12	2.04	–	0.54	2.58	2.24	–	0.59	2.84
R127198C	225 mm	Nr	0.16	2.72	–	0.97	3.69	2.99	–	1.07	4.06
R127198D	300 mm	Nr	0.22	3.74	–	1.29	5.03	4.11	–	1.42	5.53

Major Works 2009		Unit	Labour Hours	Labour Net	Plant Net	Materials Net	Unit Net	Labour Gross	Plant Gross	Materials Gross	Unit Price
									(Gross rates include 10% profit)		
				£	£	£	£	£	£	£	£
R12	**R12: DRAINAGE BELOW GROUND**										
R1273	**Soakaways**										
R127310	**Soakaways; excavation; disposal off site; DTp type 1 fill; geotextile cover; topsoil return; capacity below pipe invert level:**										
R127310A	1.20 m³	Nr	1.26	16.05	56.25	48.61	120.91	17.66	61.88	53.47	133.00
R127310B	2.50 m³	Nr	2.40	30.45	110.58	96.37	237.40	33.50	121.64	106.01	261.14
R127310C	3.75 m³	Nr	3.56	45.16	164.75	143.72	353.63	49.68	181.23	158.09	388.99
R127310D	5.00 m³	Nr	5.19	65.91	232.28	200.98	499.17	72.50	255.51	221.08	549.09
R127310E	7.50 m³	Nr	6.89	87.50	323.39	282.77	693.66	96.25	355.73	311.05	763.03
R1275	**Septic tank installation**										
R127561	**Klargester standard grade septic tank installation complete; excavation; disposal; earthwork support; 150 mm thick concrete bed; fibreglass tank; granular surround; cover and frame; capacity:**										
R127561A	2720 Litres	Nr	51.65	655.96	457.71	1242.13	2355.80	721.56	503.48	1366.34	2591.38
R127561B	3750 Litres	Nr	60.85	772.79	549.93	1584.42	2907.14	850.07	604.92	1742.86	3197.85
R127562	**Klargester heavy duty septic tank installation complete; excavation; disposal; earthwork support; 150 mm thick plain concrete; fibreglass tank; concrete cover slab; cover and frame; capacity:**										
R127562A	6000 Litres	Nr	101.40	1287.78	1097.29	2744.02	5129.09	1416.56	1207.02	3018.42	5642.00
R127562B	7500 Litres	Nr	106.30	1350.01	1212.20	3562.33	6124.54	1485.01	1333.42	3918.56	6736.99

Disposal Systems

		Unit	Labour Hours	Labour Net	Plant Net	Materials Net	Unit Net	Labour Gross	Plant Gross	Materials Gross	Unit Price
									(Gross rates include 10% profit)		
				£	£	£	£	£	£	£	£
R12	**R12: DRAINAGE BELOW GROUND**										
R1286	**Connections to existing drains**										
R128651	**Break into existing live sewer; make new connection and make good; excavation; backfilling; reinstatement (excluding statutory authority fees):**										
R128651A	100 mm vitrified clay sewer; 100 × 100 mm junction; in garden; 1.00 m deep	Nr	10.50	133.35	5.08	34.11	172.54	146.69	5.59	37.52	189.79
R128651B	150 mm vitrified clay sewer; 150 × 100 mm junction; in footpath; 1.50 m deep	Nr	18.20	231.14	10.90	63.28	305.32	254.25	11.99	69.61	335.85
R128651C	225 mm vitrified clay sewer; 225 × 150 mm junction; in road; 2.00 m deep.........	Nr	24.86	315.72	11.82	176.03	503.57	347.29	13.00	193.63	553.93
R128651D	300 mm vitrified clay sewer; 300 × 150 mm junction; in road; 3.00 m deep.........	Nr	41.89	532.01	18.01	297.85	847.87	585.21	19.81	327.64	932.66
R128652	**Break into existing live manhole; build in end of new pipe and make good walls and benching; excavation; backfilling; reinstatement (excluding statutory authority fees):**										
R128652A	one brick thick engineering brick walls; 100 mm pipe; 225 mm concrete benching; in garden; 1.00 m deep	Nr	10.00	144.08	7.03	7.50	158.61	158.49	7.73	8.25	174.47
R128652B	one brick thick engineering brick walls: 150 mm pipe; 225 mm concrete benching; in footpath; 1.50 m deep ...	Nr	15.95	219.65	12.84	45.75	278.24	241.62	14.12	50.33	306.06
R128652C	one brick thick engineering brick walls; 150 mm pipe; 225 mm concrete benching; in road; 2.00 m deep	Nr	22.14	298.26	17.73	76.76	392.75	328.09	19.50	84.44	432.03
R128652D	precast concrete chamber rings with 150 mm concrete surround; 150 mm backdrop pipe; in road 1.50 m deep ..	Nr	18.72	237.75	18.96	153.52	410.23	261.53	20.86	168.87	451.25
R128652E	precast concrete chamber rings with 150 mm concrete surround; 225 mm backdrop pipe; in road 2.00 m deep ..	Nr	24.25	307.98	19.39	400.65	728.02	338.78	21.33	440.72	800.82

PIPED SUPPLY SYSTEMS

Major Works 2009		Unit	Labour Hours	Labour Net	Plant Net	Materials Net	Unit Net	Labour Gross	Plant Gross	Materials Gross	Unit Price
								(Gross rates include 10% profit)			
				£	£	£	£	£	£	£	£
S12	**S12: HOT AND COLD WATER (SMALL SCALE)**										
S1210	**Copper pipework and fittings**										
S121001	**Copper pipework; capillary joints; BS 2871 Part 1, Table X; fixing with standard clips to masonry backgrounds; pipe diameter:**										
S121001A	8 mm	m	0.20	7.80	–	1.61	9.41	8.58	–	1.77	10.35
S121001B	10 mm	m	0.21	8.19	–	2.14	10.33	9.01	–	2.35	11.36
S121001C	12 mm	m	0.23	8.97	–	2.34	11.31	9.87	–	2.57	12.44
S121001D	15 mm	m	0.24	9.36	–	2.39	11.75	10.30	–	2.63	12.93
S121001E	22 mm	m	0.27	10.52	–	4.59	15.11	11.57	–	5.05	16.62
S121001F	28 mm	m	0.31	12.09	–	7.67	19.76	13.30	–	8.44	21.74
S121001G	35 mm	m	0.36	14.03	–	13.98	28.01	15.43	–	15.38	30.81
S121031	**Copper pipe fittings; capillary joints; BS 2871 Part 1, Table X; elbows; to suit pipe diameter:**										
S121031A	8 mm	Nr	0.16	6.23	–	1.40	7.63	6.85	–	1.54	8.39
S121031B	10 mm	Nr	0.18	7.02	–	1.33	8.35	7.72	–	1.46	9.19
S121031C	12 mm	Nr	0.19	7.41	–	1.44	8.85	8.15	–	1.58	9.74
S121031D	15 mm	Nr	0.20	7.80	–	0.48	8.28	8.58	–	0.53	9.11
S121031E	22 mm	Nr	0.22	8.58	–	1.11	9.69	9.44	–	1.22	10.66
S121031F	28 mm	Nr	0.25	9.75	–	2.28	12.03	10.73	–	2.51	13.23
S121031G	35 mm	Nr	0.30	11.70	–	7.16	18.86	12.87	–	7.88	20.75
S121051	**Copper pipe fittings; capillary joints; BS 2871 Part 1, Table X; equal tees; to suit pipe diameter:**										
S121051A	8 mm	Nr	0.24	9.35	–	2.66	12.01	10.29	–	2.93	13.21
S121051B	10 mm	Nr	0.27	10.53	–	2.40	12.93	11.58	–	2.64	14.22
S121051C	12 mm	Nr	0.29	11.31	–	2.37	13.68	12.44	–	2.61	15.05
S121051D	15 mm	Nr	0.30	11.70	–	0.84	12.54	12.87	–	0.92	13.79
S121051E	22 mm	Nr	0.33	12.87	–	1.93	14.80	14.16	–	2.12	16.28
S121051F	28 mm	Nr	0.38	14.82	–	4.71	19.53	16.30	–	5.18	21.48
S121051G	35 mm	Nr	0.45	17.55	–	12.40	29.95	19.31	–	13.64	32.95
S121071	**Copper pipe fittings; capillary joints; BS 2871 Part 1, Table X; unequal tees; size:**										
S121071A	15 × 15 × 8 mm	Nr	0.30	11.69	–	4.36	16.05	12.86	–	4.80	17.66
S121071B	15 × 15 × 10 mm	Nr	0.30	11.69	–	4.34	16.03	12.86	–	4.77	17.63
S121071C	15 × 15 × 12 mm	Nr	0.30	11.69	–	2.44	14.13	12.86	–	2.68	15.54
S121071D	22 × 22 × 8 mm	Nr	0.33	12.87	–	6.39	19.26	14.16	–	7.03	21.19
S121071E	22 × 22 × 10 mm	Nr	0.33	12.86	–	5.59	18.45	14.15	–	6.15	20.30
S121071F	22 × 22 × 12 mm	Nr	0.33	12.87	–	5.71	18.58	14.16	–	6.28	20.44
S121071G	22 × 22 × 15 mm	Nr	0.33	12.86	–	1.85	14.71	14.15	–	2.04	16.18
S121071H	28 × 28 × 15 mm	Nr	0.38	14.82	–	6.31	21.13	16.30	–	6.94	23.24
S121071I	28 × 28 × 22 mm	Nr	0.38	14.82	–	6.71	21.53	16.30	–	7.38	23.68
S121071J	35 × 35 × 15 mm	Nr	0.45	17.54	–	13.61	31.15	19.29	–	14.97	34.27
S121071K	35 × 35 × 22 mm	Nr	0.45	17.55	–	13.76	31.31	19.31	–	15.14	34.44
S121071L	35 × 35 × 28 mm	Nr	0.45	17.55	–	13.71	31.26	19.31	–	15.08	34.39

Piped Supply Systems

Major Works 2009		Unit	Labour Hours	Labour Net	Plant Net	Materials Net	Unit Net	Labour Gross	Plant Gross	Materials Gross	Unit Price
								(Gross rates include 10% profit)			
				£	£	£	£	£	£	£	£
S12	**S12: HOT AND COLD WATER (SMALL SCALE)**										
S1215	**Polythene pipework and fittings**										
S121501	**Polyethylene pipework; blue 12 bar medium duty; compression couplings; laying in trench; diameter:**										
S121501A	20 mm	m	0.15	5.84	–	1.56	7.40	6.42	–	1.72	8.14
S121501B	25 mm	m	0.17	6.62	–	2.16	8.78	7.28	–	2.38	9.66
S121501C	32 mm	m	0.18	7.02	–	3.57	10.59	7.72	–	3.93	11.65
S121501D	50 mm	m	0.21	8.19	–	5.43	13.62	9.01	–	5.97	14.98
S1220	**Gunmetal and brass accessories**										
S122001	**Stopcock valves; BS 1010; jointing to copper pipe; size:**										
S122001A	15 mm	Nr	0.18	7.02	–	5.24	12.26	7.72	–	5.76	13.49
S122001B	22 mm	Nr	0.20	7.80	–	12.52	20.32	8.58	–	13.77	22.35
S122011	**Gate valves; BS 5154; jointing to copper pipe; size:**										
S122011A	15 mm	Nr	0.18	7.02	–	6.70	13.72	7.72	–	7.37	15.09
S122011B	22 mm	Nr	0.20	7.80	–	11.16	18.96	8.58	–	12.28	20.86
S122011C	28 mm	Nr	0.22	8.58	–	26.25	34.83	9.44	–	28.88	38.31
S122021	**Isolating valves for central heating pumps; self colour; size:**										
S122021A	22 mm	Nr	0.25	9.75	–	4.36	14.11	10.73	–	4.80	15.52
S122021B	28 mm	Nr	0.28	10.92	–	5.18	16.10	12.01	–	5.70	17.71
S122031	**Ball valves with plastic floats; drilling and fixing to tanks; size:**										
S122031A	15 mm piston type	Nr	0.20	7.80	–	10.74	18.54	8.58	–	11.81	20.39
S122031B	22 mm piston type	Nr	0.22	8.58	–	16.94	25.52	9.44	–	18.63	28.07

Major Works 2009		Unit	Labour Hours	Labour Net	Plant Net	Materials Net	Unit Net	Labour Gross	Plant Gross	Materials Gross	Unit Price
				£	£	£	£	£	£	£	£
S12	**S12: HOT AND COLD WATER (SMALL SCALE)**										
S1222	**Water storage tanks and cylinders**										
S122201	**Plastic water storage cisterns with lids and insulation; BS 4213; capacity:**										
S122201A	25 litre	Nr	0.75	29.24	–	18.31	47.55	32.16	–	20.14	52.31
S122201B	227 litre	Nr	1.25	48.74	–	78.50	127.24	53.61	–	86.35	139.96
S122221	**Copper hot water cylinders; BS 699; Grade 3 direct; insulation jacket; capacity:**										
S122221A	120 litre	Nr	0.60	23.39	–	156.93	180.32	25.73	–	172.62	198.35
S122221B	210 litre	Nr	0.85	33.14	–	236.89	270.03	36.45	–	260.58	297.03
S122231	**Copper hot water cylinders; BS 1566; Grade 3 indirect; insulation jacket; capacity:**										
S122231A	114 litre	Nr	1.00	38.99	–	182.41	221.40	42.89	–	200.65	243.54
S122231B	120 litre	Nr	1.00	38.99	–	242.80	281.79	42.89	–	267.08	309.97
S122251	**Copper hot water cylinders; BS 1566; indirect; Economy 7; ready lagged; capacity:**										
S122251A	116 litre	Nr	0.95	37.04	–	141.94	178.98	40.74	–	156.13	196.88
S122251B	227 litre	Nr	1.15	44.84	–	251.87	296.71	49.32	–	277.06	326.38
S122271	**Copper combination hot water storage and cold water header tanks; BS 3198; with lids; direct; capacity:**										
S122271A	115 litre hot, 45 litre cold	Nr	1.15	44.84	–	441.69	486.53	49.32	–	485.86	535.18
S122271B	115 litre hot, 115 litre cold	Nr	1.30	50.69	–	469.14	519.83	55.76	–	516.05	571.81
S122281	**Copper combination hot water storage and cold water header tanks; BS 3198; with lids; indirect; capacity:**										
S122281A	115 litre hot, 45 litre cold	Nr	1.15	44.84	–	503.74	548.58	49.32	–	554.11	603.44
S122281B	115 litre hot, 115 litre cold	Nr	1.30	50.69	–	522.32	573.01	55.76	–	574.55	630.31
S1224	**Oil fuel storage tanks**										
S122401	**Mild steel tanks; BS 799; capacity:**										
S122401A	1130 litre	Nr	0.75	29.24	–	214.50	243.74	32.16	–	235.95	268.11
S122401B	1360 litre	Nr	0.85	33.14	–	246.46	279.60	36.45	–	271.11	307.56
S122401C	2730 litre	Nr	0.95	37.04	–	351.42	388.46	40.74	–	386.56	427.31
S122401D	4550 litre	Nr	1.20	46.79	–	643.50	690.29	51.47	–	707.85	759.32

Header note: —— (Gross rates include 10% profit) ——

Piped Supply Systems

Major Works 2009		Unit	Labour Hours	Labour Net	Plant Net	Materials Net	Unit Net	Labour Gross	Plant Gross	Materials Gross	Unit Price
								——— (Gross rates include 10% profit) ———			
				£	£	£	£	£	£	£	£
S12	S12: HOT AND COLD WATER (SMALL SCALE)										
S1250	Thermal insulation										
S125001	Rigid foam insulation to pipework; Armaflex or equal and approved; 9 mm wall thickness; fixing to pipes with tape: pipe diameter:										
S125001A	15 mm	m	0.15	5.85	–	2.16	8.01	6.44	–	2.38	8.81
S125001B	22 mm	m	0.17	6.63	–	2.78	9.41	7.29	–	3.06	10.35
S125001C	28 mm	m	0.20	7.80	–	3.00	10.80	8.58	–	3.30	11.88
S125002	Crown pipe insulation for steel pipes; with aluminium foil facing; reinforced; 25 mm wall thickness; pipe diameter:										
S125002A	32 mm	m	0.20	7.80	–	1.67	9.47	8.58	–	1.84	10.42
S125002B	50 mm	m	0.22	8.57	–	2.22	10.79	9.43	–	2.44	11.87
S125002C	100 mm	m	0.24	9.36	–	3.81	13.17	10.30	–	4.19	14.49
S125003	Crown pipe insulation for copper pipes; with aluminium foil facing; reinforced; 25 mm wall thickness; pipe diameter:										
S125003A	50 mm	m	0.22	8.58	–	1.91	10.49	9.44	–	2.10	11.54
S125003B	65 mm	m	0.23	8.96	–	2.46	11.42	9.86	–	2.71	12.56
S125003C	100 mm	m	0.25	9.74	–	3.71	13.45	10.71	–	4.08	14.80

ELECTRICAL SUPPLY, POWER AND LIGHTING SYSTEMS

Major Works 2009	Unit	Labour Hours	Labour Net	Plant Net	Materials Net	Unit Net	Labour Gross	Plant Gross	Materials Gross	Unit Price
			£	£	£	£	(Gross rates include 10% profit)			
							£	£	£	£
V90 **V90: ELECTRICAL INSTALLATION (SMALL SCALE)**										
V9001 **Two storey housing installations**										
V900101 Consumer unit, standard metal enclosure with 100A main switch, surface mounted to outside wall:										
V900101A 8 ways with miniature circuit breakers: 4 × 32A for power ring mains, 2 × 6A for lighting circuits, 1 × 40A cooker circuit, 1 × 16A immersion heater circuit ...	Nr	0.75	15.92	–	148.17	164.09	17.51	–	162.99	180.50
V900111 Socket outlets, switched, flush mounted including associated concealed wiring and mounting box:										
V900111A 2 gang	Nr	0.83	17.50	–	30.48	47.98	19.25	–	33.53	52.78
V900111B 1 gang	Nr	0.76	15.01	–	27.17	42.18	16.51	–	29.89	46.40
V900111C 1 gang with RCD protection	Nr	0.80	15.84	–	112.45	128.29	17.42	–	123.70	141.12
V900112 Socket outlets, unswitched, flush mounted including associated concealed wiring and mounting box:										
V900112A Shaver socket, dual voltage with neon indicator	Nr	0.80	15.84	–	64.63	80.47	17.42	–	71.09	88.52
V900121 Fused connection unit only, switched, for domestic equipment, flush mounted, including associated concealed wiring and mounting box:										
V900121A 13A	Nr	0.74	14.57	–	29.77	44.34	16.03	–	32.75	48.77
V900131 Fused connection unit only, switched, for domestic equipment, flush mounted, with neon indicator, including associated concealed wiring and mounting box:										
V900131A 15A	Nr	3.51	68.56	–	106.11	174.67	75.42	–	116.72	192.14
V900141 Cooker power units:										
V900141A 45A DP with integral 13A SP switched socket outlet and neon indicator, for domestic kitchen. Surface mounted, including associated concealed wiring and mounting box	Nr	1.95	38.35	–	136.41	174.76	42.19	–	150.05	192.24
V900151 Lighting points, ceiling mounted, including associated concealed cabling and mounting boxes:										
V900151A 1-way switch control	Nr	1.35	26.93	–	20.69	47.62	29.62	–	22.76	52.38
V900151B 2 switches in 2-way switch control	Nr	2.76	55.32	–	66.43	121.75	60.85	–	73.07	133.93
V900151C 3 switches in intermediate switch control	Nr	4.48	89.83	–	67.57	157.40	98.81	–	74.33	173.14

Electrical Supply/Power Lighting Systems

Major Works 2009		Unit	Labour Hours	Labour Net	Plant Net	Materials Net	Unit Net	Labour Gross	Plant Gross	Materials Gross	Unit Price
								(Gross rates include 10% profit)			
				£	£	£	£	£	£	£	£
V90	**V90: ELECTRICAL INSTALLATION (SMALL SCALE)**										
V9001	**Two storey housing installations**										
V900152	**External lighting units:**										
V900152A	Bulkhead light fitting for exterior of domestic premises, single 100W, surface mounted, including all associated concealed wiring and mounting boxes. 1-way switch control	Nr	1.52	29.77	–	30.65	60.42	32.75	–	33.72	66.46
V900161	**Extractor fan, domestic 3KW, for air intake and/or extraction, with fan controller, connection unit, fixing to structure and associated concealed wiring and mounting boxes. (Associated vent trunking measured separately):**										
V900161A	For WC/bathroom, manual pull cord, flush mounted in ceiling	Nr	1.59	30.29	–	204.38	234.67	33.32	–	224.82	258.14
V900161B	For WC/bathroom, automatic delay timer flush mounted in ceiling	Nr	1.62	30.01	–	178.10	208.11	33.01	–	195.91	228.92
V900161C	General purpose, manual 30W, flush mounted in wall.	Nr	2.34	40.39	–	247.55	287.94	44.43	–	272.31	316.73
V900161D	General purpose, automatic delay timer 60W, flush mounted in wall	Nr	1.62	30.75	–	457.68	488.43	33.83	–	503.45	537.27
V900171	**Immersion water heater, 3KW domestic, with thermostat, controller, connection unit, fixing to structure and associate concealed wiring and mounting boxes. (Associated plumbing installations, pipework, lagging etc measured separately):**										
V900171A	Standard 27, with 24 hour timeswitch	Nr	4.09	80.82	–	175.97	256.79	88.90	–	193.57	282.47
V900171B	Aqualoy 27, with 24 hour timeswitch	Nr	4.04	79.81	–	182.38	262.19	87.79	–	200.62	288.41
V900171C	Standard 27, with Newlec Economy 7 quartz timeswitch	Nr	4.14	81.82	–	202.12	283.94	90.00	–	222.33	312.33

Major Works 2009		Unit	Labour Hours	Labour Net	Plant Net	Materials Net	Unit Net	Labour Gross	Plant Gross	Materials Gross	Unit Price
								(Gross rates include 10% profit)			
				£	£	£	£	£	£	£	£
V90	**V90: ELECTRICAL INSTALLATION (SMALL SCALE)**										
V9001	**Two storey housing installations**										
V900181	**Fire detection and alarm systems, domestic, surface mounted and fixed to structure, including associated fire resistant wiring and accessories:**										
V900181A	Fire alarm panel, self contained, 2 zone, Gent Ltd., complete with batteries and charger, mounted on wall in hallway..................	Nr	1.91	38.10	–	302.31	340.41	41.91	–	332.54	374.45
V900181B	Smoke detector head, Ionisation type surface mounted to ceiling	Nr	1.58	30.65	–	125.11	155.76	33.72	–	137.62	171.34
V900181C	Manual call point, surface mounted to wall	Nr	0.41	7.88	–	25.47	33.35	8.67	–	28.02	36.69
V900181D	Alarm sounder, indoor type, electronic, 24v polarised ...	Nr	1.54	30.18	–	69.67	99.85	33.20	–	76.64	109.84
V900181E	Alarm sounder, weatherproof, electronic, 24v polarised	Nr	1.52	29.63	–	99.07	128.70	32.59	–	108.98	141.57
V9010	**Domestic garage/outbuilding installation**										
V901001	**Lighting points, ceiling mounted, including associated concealed wiring and mounting boxes:**										
V901001A	Heavy duty pendant, 1 way switch control	Nr	0.95	19.70	–	28.84	48.54	21.67	–	31.72	53.39
V901002	**External lighting units:**										
V901002A	Bulkhead light fittings, rectangular 100W surface mounted, including associated concealed wiring, 1 way switch control	Nr	1.01	20.48	–	37.27	57.75	22.53	–	41.00	63.53
V901003	**Socket outlet, switched, surface mounted metalclad, including associated part concealed wiring and part wiring in PVC conduit with mounting box:**										
V901003A	2 gang	Nr	1.42	28.62	–	55.43	84.05	31.48	–	60.97	92.46
V901003B	1 gang	Nr	1.38	27.80	–	44.65	72.45	30.58	–	49.12	79.70

TRANSPORT SYSTEMS

Major Works 2009		Unit	£	£	Specialist Net £	Unit Net £	£	£	Specialist Gross £	Unit Price £
							(Gross rates include 10% profit)			
X10	**LIFTS**									
X1010	**Passenger lifts; hydraulic; standard finish; single opening; internal fireman's control; in-car telephone; controls; suitable for disabled people**									
X101010	**Wall mounted 6 person; 450 kg; size 850 × 1400 × 2200 mm; serving:**									
X101010A	2 floors	Nr	–	–	–	33990.19	33990.19	–	–	37389.21	37389.21
X101010B	3 floors	Nr	–	–	–	37361.74	37361.74	–	–	41097.91	41097.91
X101010C	4 floors	Nr	–	–	–	40733.30	40733.30	–	–	44806.63	44806.63
X101015	**Wall mounted 8 person; 630 kg; size 110 × 1400 × 2200 mm; serving:**									
X101015A	2 floors	Nr	–	–	–	35959.36	35959.36	–	–	39555.30	39555.30
X101015B	3 floors	Nr	–	–	–	39524.91	39524.91	–	–	43477.40	43477.40
X101015C	4 floors	Nr	–	–	–	43091.63	43091.63	–	–	47400.79	47400.79
X101020	**Wall mounted 10 person; 800 kg; size 1300 × 1400 × 2200 mm; serving:**									
X101020A	2 floors	Nr	–	–	–	37371.09	37371.09	–	–	41108.20	41108.20
X101020B	3 floors	Nr	–	–	–	40733.30	40733.30	–	–	44806.63	44806.63
X101020C	4 floors	Nr	–	–	–	44104.85	44104.85	–	–	48515.34	48515.34
X101025	**Wall mounted 13 person; 1000 kg; size 1100 × 2100 × 2200 mm; serving:**									
X101025A	2 floors	Nr	–	–	–	41901.95	41901.95	–	–	46092.15	46092.15
X101025B	3 floors	Nr	–	–	–	46757.69	46757.69	–	–	51433.46	51433.46
X101025C	4 floors	Nr	–	–	–	49030.72	49030.72	–	–	53933.79	53933.79
X1020	**Goods lifts; hydraulic; twin opening; heavy duty finish with shutter gates; internal lighting**									
X102010	**Wall mounted lift; 1000 kg; car size 1400 × 1800 × 2000 mm; serving:**									
X102010A	2 floors	Nr	–	–	–	42351.88	42351.88	–	–	46587.07	46587.07
X102010B	3 floors	Nr	–	–	–	46582.39	46582.39	–	–	51240.63	51240.63
X102010C	4 floors	Nr	–	–	–	50818.75	50818.75	–	–	55900.63	55900.63
X102015	**Wall mounted lift; 1500 kg; car size 1700 × 2000 × 2300 mm; serving:**									
X102015A	2 floors	Nr	–	–	–	52939.85	52939.86	–	–	58233.84	58233.85
X102015B	3 floors	Nr	–	–	–	57170.36	57170.36	–	–	62887.40	62887.40
X102015C	4 floors	Nr	–	–	–	61406.72	61406.72	–	–	67547.39	67547.39
X102020	**Wall mounted lift; 3000 kg; car size 2000 × 3000 × 2300 mm; serving:**									
X102020A	2 floors	Nr	–	–	–	84697.90	84697.90	–	–	93167.69	93167.69
X102020B	3 floors	Nr	–	–	–	88934.27	88934.27	–	–	97827.70	97827.70
X102020C	4 floors	Nr	–	–	–	93170.63	93170.63	–	–	102487.69	102487.69

APPROXIMATE ESTIMATING RATES

Major Works 2009		Unit	Labour Hours	Labour Net	Plant Net	Materials Net	Unit Net	Labour Gross	Plant Gross	Materials Gross	Unit Price
								(Gross rates include 10% profit)			
				£	£	£	£	£	£	£	£
Z10	**SUBSTRUCTURE: IN SITU CONCRETE BEDS**										
Z1010	**Plain in situ concrete bed**										
Z101001	Excavation, disposal; compaction, hardcore bed; sand blinding; 1200 gauge polythene dpm; plain in situ concrete C25-20mm aggregate; power float finish; bed thickness:										
Z101001C	150 mm	m²	0.32	6.03	2.62	16.75	25.40	6.63	2.88	18.43	27.94
Z101010	Excavation average 150 mm deep; off site disposal; compact surface; 150 mm compacted hardcore bed; 25 mm sand blinding; 1200g polythene d.p.m.; 100 mm C20 concrete bed, tamped finish; sand cement screed (1:4); thickness:										
Z101010A	38 mm	m²	0.59	9.85	4.05	19.69	33.59	10.84	4.46	21.66	36.95
Z101010B	50 mm	m²	0.61	10.33	4.05	21.50	35.88	11.36	4.46	23.65	39.47
Z101010C	75 mm	m²	0.66	11.50	4.05	23.32	38.87	12.65	4.46	25.65	42.76
Z101010D	50 mm on 25 mm Floormate insulation.	m²	0.78	12.97	4.05	31.32	48.34	14.27	4.46	34.45	53.17
Z101010E	50 mm on 50 mm Floormate insulation.	m²	0.74	12.53	4.05	31.96	48.54	13.78	4.46	35.16	53.39
Z101010F	75 mm on 50 mm Floormate insulation.	m²	0.84	14.30	4.05	38.16	56.51	15.73	4.46	41.98	62.16
Z101011	Excavation average 225 mm deep; off site disposal; compact surface; 225 mm compacted hardcore bed; 25 mm sand blinding; 1200g polythene d.p.m.; 100 mm C20 concrete bed, tamped finish; sand cement screed (1:4); thickness:										
Z101011A	38 mm	m²	0.59	9.86	5.76	21.72	37.34	10.85	6.34	23.89	41.07
Z101011B	50 mm	m²	0.61	10.32	5.76	23.54	39.62	11.35	6.34	25.89	43.58
Z101011C	75 mm	m²	0.66	11.49	5.76	25.36	42.61	12.64	6.34	27.90	46.87
Z101011D	50 mm on 25 mm Floormate insulation.	m²	0.73	12.36	5.76	28.97	47.09	13.60	6.34	31.87	51.80
Z101011E	50 mm on 50 mm Floormate insulation.	m²	0.74	12.53	5.76	34.00	52.29	13.78	6.34	37.40	57.52
Z101011F	75 mm on 50 mm Floormate insulation.	m²	0.79	13.71	5.76	35.81	55.28	15.08	6.34	39.39	60.81

Approximate Estimating Rates

Major Works 2009		Unit	Labour Hours	Labour Net	Plant Net	Materials Net	Unit Net	Labour Gross	Plant Gross	Materials Gross	Unit Price
								(Gross rates include 10% profit)			
				£	£	£	£	£	£	£	£
Z10	**SUBSTRUCTURE: IN SITU CONCRETE BEDS**										
Z1010	**Plain in situ concrete bed**										
Z101012	**Excavation average 300 mm deep; off site disposal; compact surface; 300 mm compacted hardcore bed; 25 mm sand blinding; 1200g polythene d.p.m.; 100 mm C20 concrete bed, tamped finish; sand cement screed (1:4); thickness:**										
Z101012A	38 mm	m²	0.59	9.86	7.50	23.76	41.12	10.85	8.25	26.14	45.23
Z101012B	50 mm	m²	0.61	10.32	7.50	25.58	43.40	11.35	8.25	28.14	47.74
Z101012C	75 mm	m²	0.66	11.50	7.50	27.39	46.39	12.65	8.25	30.13	51.03
Z101012D	50 mm on 25 mm Floormate insulation.	m²	0.73	12.36	7.50	31.00	50.86	13.60	8.25	34.10	55.95
Z101012E	50 mm on 50 mm Floormate insulation.	m²	0.74	12.54	7.50	36.03	56.07	13.79	8.25	39.63	61.68
Z101012F	75 mm on 50 mm Floormate insulation.	m²	0.79	13.71	7.50	37.85	59.06	15.08	8.25	41.64	64.97
Z101020	**Excavation average 150 mm deep; off site disposal; compact surface; 150 mm compacted hardcore bed; 25 mm sand blinding; 100 mm C20 concrete bed, tamped finish; two coats liquid d.p.m.; sand cement screed (1:4); thickness:**										
Z101020A	38 mm	m²	0.64	10.49	4.05	24.76	39.30	11.54	4.46	27.24	43.23
Z101020B	50 mm	m²	0.66	10.96	4.05	26.58	41.59	12.06	4.46	29.24	45.75
Z101020C	75 mm	m²	0.71	12.13	4.05	28.39	44.57	13.34	4.46	31.23	49.03
Z101020D	50 mm on 25 mm Floormate insulation.	m²	0.78	13.00	4.05	32.01	49.06	14.30	4.46	35.21	53.97
Z101020E	50 mm on 50 mm Floormate insulation.	m²	0.79	13.16	4.05	37.03	54.24	14.48	4.46	40.73	59.66
Z101020F	75 mm on 50 mm Floormate insulation.	m²	0.84	14.34	4.05	38.85	57.24	15.77	4.46	42.74	62.96
Z101021	**Excavation average 225 mm deep; off site disposal; compact surface; 225 mm compacted hardcore bed; 25 mm sand blinding; 100 mm C20 concrete bed, tamped finish; two coat liquid d.p.m.; sand cement screed (1:4); thickness:**										
Z101021A	38 mm	m²	0.64	10.49	5.76	26.80	43.05	11.54	6.34	29.48	47.36
Z101021B	50 mm	m²	0.66	10.96	5.76	28.61	45.33	12.06	6.34	31.47	49.86
Z101021C	75 mm	m²	0.71	12.13	5.76	30.43	48.32	13.34	6.34	33.47	53.15
Z101021D	50 mm on 25 mm Floormate insulation.	m²	0.78	13.00	5.76	34.04	52.80	14.30	6.34	37.44	58.08
Z101021E	50 mm on 50 mm Floormate insulation.	m²	0.79	13.17	5.76	39.07	58.00	14.49	6.34	42.98	63.80
Z101021F	75 mm on 50 mm Floormate insulation.	m²	0.84	14.34	5.76	40.89	60.99	15.77	6.34	44.98	67.09

Major Works 2009		Unit	Labour Hours	Labour Net	Plant Net	Materials Net	Unit Net	Labour Gross	Plant Gross	Materials Gross	Unit Price
								(Gross rates include 10% profit)			
				£	£	£	£	£	£	£	£
Z10	**SUBSTRUCTURE: IN SITU CONCRETE BEDS**										
Z1010	**Plain in situ concrete bed**										
Z101022	**Excavation average 300 mm deep; off site disposal; compact surface; 300 mm compacted hardcore bed; 25 mm sand blinding; 100 mm C20 concrete bed, tamped finish; two coat liquid d.p.m.; sand cement screed (1:4); thickness:**										
Z101022A	38 mm	m²	0.64	10.49	7.50	28.83	46.82	11.54	8.25	31.71	51.50
Z101022B	50 mm	m²	0.66	10.96	7.50	30.65	49.11	12.06	8.25	33.72	54.02
Z101022C	75 mm	m²	0.71	12.13	7.50	32.47	52.10	13.34	8.25	35.72	57.31
Z101022D	50 mm on 25 mm Floormate insulation.	m²	0.78	13.00	7.50	36.08	56.58	14.30	8.25	39.69	62.24
Z101022E	50 mm on 50 mm Floormate insulation.	m²	0.79	13.17	7.50	41.11	61.78	14.49	8.25	45.22	67.96
Z101022F	75 mm on 50 mm Floormate insulation.	m²	0.84	14.34	7.50	42.93	64.77	15.77	8.25	47.22	71.25
Z101030	**Excavation average 150 mm deep; off site disposal; compact surface; 150 mm compacted hardcore bed; 25 mm sand blinding; 1200g polythene d.p.m.; 150 m C20 concrete bed, tamped finish; sand cement screed (1:4); thickness:**										
Z101030A	38 mm	m²	0.52	8.94	3.72	22.87	35.53	9.83	4.09	25.16	39.08
Z101030B	50 mm	m²	0.54	9.40	4.00	25.25	38.65	10.34	4.40	27.78	42.52
Z101030C	75 mm	m²	0.59	10.57	4.00	27.71	42.28	11.63	4.40	30.48	46.51
Z101030D	50 mm on 25 mm Floormate insulation.	m²	0.66	11.44	4.00	31.21	46.65	12.58	4.40	34.33	51.32
Z101030E	50 mm on 50 mm Floormate insulation.	m²	0.67	11.62	3.72	35.71	51.05	12.78	4.09	39.28	56.16
Z101030F	75 mm on 50 mm Floormate insulation.	m²	0.72	12.78	3.72	38.16	54.66	14.06	4.09	41.98	60.13
Z101031	**Excavation average 225 mm deep; off site disposal; compact surface; 225 mm compacted hardcore bed; 25 mm sand blinding; 1200g polythene d.p.m.; 150 m C20 concrete bed, tamped finish; sand cement screed (1:4); thickness:**										
Z101031A	38 mm	m²	0.52	8.93	5.29	24.07	38.29	9.82	5.82	26.48	42.12
Z101031B	50 mm	m²	0.54	9.40	5.29	25.25	39.94	10.34	5.82	27.78	43.93
Z101031C	75 mm	m²	0.59	10.57	5.29	27.61	43.47	11.63	5.82	30.37	47.82
Z101031D	50 mm on 25 mm Floormate insulation.	m²	0.66	11.44	5.29	31.21	47.94	12.58	5.82	34.33	52.73
Z101031E	50 mm on 50 mm Floormate insulation.	m²	0.67	11.62	5.29	35.71	52.62	12.78	5.82	39.28	57.88
Z101031F	75 mm on 50 mm Floormate insulation.	m²	0.72	12.78	5.29	38.07	56.14	14.06	5.82	41.88	61.75

Approximate Estimating Rates

Major Works 2009		Unit	Labour Hours	Labour Net	Plant Net	Materials Net	Unit Net	Labour Gross	Plant Gross	Materials Gross	Unit Price
								(Gross rates include 10% profit)			
				£	£	£	£	£	£	£	£
Z10	**SUBSTRUCTURE: IN SITU CONCRETE BEDS**										
Z1010	**Plain in situ concrete bed**										
Z101032	**Excavation average 300 mm deep; off site disposal; compact surface; 300 mm compacted hardcore bed; 25 mm sand blinding; 1200g polythene d.p.m.; 150 m C20 concrete bed, tamped finish; sand cement screed (1:4); thickness:**										
Z101032A	38 mm	m²	0.52	8.94	6.97	25.92	41.83	9.83	7.67	28.51	46.01
Z101032B	50 mm	m²	0.64	10.67	6.97	27.10	44.74	11.74	7.67	29.81	49.21
Z101032C	75 mm	m²	0.59	10.58	6.97	29.47	47.02	11.64	7.67	32.42	51.72
Z101032D	50 mm on 25 mm Floormate insulation.	m²	0.66	11.44	6.97	33.07	51.48	12.58	7.67	36.38	56.63
Z101032E	50 mm on 50 mm Floormate insulation.	m²	0.67	11.61	6.97	37.56	56.14	12.77	7.67	41.32	61.75
Z101032F	75 mm on 50 mm Floormate insulation.	m²	0.72	12.78	6.97	39.92	59.67	14.06	7.67	43.91	65.64
Z101040	**Excavation average 150 mm deep; off site disposal; compact surface; 150 mm compacted hardcore bed; 25 mm sand blinding; Synthaprufe d.p.m.; 150 mm C20 concrete bed, tamped finish; sand cement screed (1:4); thickness:**										
Z101040A	38 mm	m²	0.41	7.57	3.72	27.77	39.06	8.33	4.09	30.55	42.97
Z101040B	50 mm	m²	0.54	9.41	4.00	30.15	43.56	10.35	4.40	33.17	47.92
Z101040C	75 mm	m²	0.59	10.58	4.00	32.60	47.18	11.64	4.40	35.86	51.90
Z101040D	50 mm on 25 mm Floormate insulation.	m²	0.66	11.45	4.00	36.11	51.56	12.60	4.40	39.72	56.72
Z101040E	50 mm on 50 mm Floormate insulation.	m²	0.67	11.61	3.72	40.61	55.94	12.77	4.09	44.67	61.53
Z101040F	75 mm on 50 mm Floormate insulation.	m²	0.72	12.78	6.97	44.82	64.57	14.06	7.67	49.30	71.03

Major Works 2009		Unit	Labour Hours	Labour Net	Plant Net	Materials Net	Unit Net	Labour Gross	Plant Gross	Materials Gross	Unit Price
								——— (Gross rates include 10% profit) ———			
				£	£	£	£	£	£	£	£
Z10	**SUBSTRUCTURE: IN SITU CONCRETE BEDS**										
Z1010	**Plain in situ concrete bed**										
Z101041	**Excavation average 225 mm deep; off site disposal; compact surface; 150 mm compacted hardcore bed; 25 mm sand blinding; Synthaprufe d.p.m.; 150 mm C20 concrete bed, tamped finish; sand cement screed (1:4); thickness:**										
Z101041A	38 mm	m²	0.52	8.94	5.29	28.97	43.20	9.83	5.82	31.87	47.52
Z101041B	50 mm	m²	0.54	9.41	5.29	30.15	44.85	10.35	5.82	33.17	49.34
Z101041C	75 mm	m²	0.59	10.57	5.29	32.51	48.37	11.63	5.82	35.76	53.21
Z101041D	50 mm on 25 mm Floormate insulation	m²	0.66	11.44	5.29	36.11	52.84	12.58	5.82	39.72	58.12
Z101041E	50 mm on 50 mm Floormate insulation	m²	0.67	11.61	5.29	40.61	57.51	12.77	5.82	44.67	63.26
Z101041F	75 mm on 50 mm Floormate insulation	m²	0.72	12.79	5.29	42.97	61.05	14.07	5.82	47.27	67.16
Z101042	**Excavation average 300 mm deep; off site disposal; compact surface; 150 mm compacted hardcore bed; 25 mm sand blinding; Synthaprufe d.p.m.; 150 mm C20 concrete bed, tamped finish; sand cement screed (1:4); thickness:**										
Z101042A	38 mm	m²	0.52	8.93	6.97	30.82	46.72	9.82	7.67	33.90	51.39
Z101042B	50 mm	m²	0.64	10.67	6.97	32.00	49.64	11.74	7.67	35.20	54.60
Z101042C	75 mm	m²	0.59	10.58	6.97	34.36	51.91	11.64	7.67	37.80	57.10
Z101042D	50 mm on 25 mm Floormate insulation	m²	0.66	11.44	6.97	37.96	56.37	12.58	7.67	41.76	62.01
Z101042E	50 mm on 50 mm Floormate insulation	m²	0.67	11.61	6.97	42.46	61.04	12.77	7.67	46.71	67.14
Z101042F	75 mm on 50 mm Floormate insulation	m²	0.72	12.78	6.97	44.82	64.57	14.06	7.67	49.30	71.03

Approximate Estimating Rates

Major Works 2009		Unit	Labour Hours	Labour Net	Plant Net	Materials Net	Unit Net	Labour Gross	Plant Gross	Materials Gross	Unit Price
								(Gross rates include 10% profit)			
				£	£	£	£	£	£	£	£
Z10	**SUBSTRUCTURE: IN SITU CONCRETE BEDS**										
Z1020	**Reinforced in situ concrete bed**										
Z102001	**C25 concrete bed; A252 fabric reinforcement; power float finish; thickness:**										
Z102001A	200 mm	m²	0.31	6.59	0.97	19.90	27.46	7.25	1.07	21.89	30.21
Z102002	**C25 concrete bed; waterproof admixture; A252 fabric reinforcement; power float finish;**										
Z102002A	Reinforced concrete slab; 200mm thick; C25 mix; waterproofed	m²	0.31	6.59	0.97	22.58	30.14	7.25	1.07	24.84	33.15
Z102003	**Excavation, disposal; compaction, hardcore bed; sand blinding; 1200 gauge polythene dpm; plain in situ concrete C25-20mm aggregate; A193 fabric reinforcement; power float finish; bed thickness:**										
Z102003C	150 mm	m²	0.35	6.48	2.62	19.73	28.83	7.13	2.88	21.70	31.71
Z102004	**Excavation, disposal; compaction, hardcore bed; sand blinding; 1200 gauge polythene dpm; plain in situ concrete C25-20mm aggregate; A252 fabric reinforcement; power float finish; bed thickness:**										
Z102004D	200 mm	m²	0.35	7.21	2.69	24.54	34.44	7.93	2.96	26.99	37.88
Z102005	**Excavation, disposal; compaction, hardcore bed; sand blinding; 1200 gauge polythene dpm; plain in situ concrete C25-20mm aggregate; A393 fabric reinforcement; power float finish; bed thickness:**										
Z102005E	250 mm	m²	0.37	8.19	2.71	30.68	41.58	9.01	2.98	33.75	45.74

Major Works 2009		Unit	Labour Hours	Labour Net	Plant Net	Materials Net	Unit Net	Labour Gross	Plant Gross	Materials Gross	Unit Price
								(Gross rates include 10% profit)			
				£	£	£	£	£	£	£	£
Z10	**SUBSTRUCTURE: IN SITU CONCRETE BEDS**										
Z1020	**Reinforced in situ concrete bed**										
Z102010	**Excavation average 150 mm deep; off site disposal; compact surface; 150 mm hardcore; 25 mm sand blinding; 1200g polythene d.p.m.; 100 mm C20 concrete bed; one layer A142 mesh reinforcement; sand cement screed (1:4); thickness:**										
Z102010A	38 mm	m²	0.65	10.68	4.61	22.18	37.47	11.75	5.07	24.40	41.22
Z102010B	50 mm	m²	0.67	11.15	4.61	23.99	39.75	12.27	5.07	26.39	43.73
Z102010C	75 mm	m²	0.72	12.32	4.61	25.81	42.74	13.55	5.07	28.39	47.01
Z102010D	50 mm on 25 mm Floormate insulation	m²	0.79	13.19	4.61	29.42	47.22	14.51	5.07	32.36	51.94
Z102010E	50 mm on 50 mm Floormate insulation	m²	0.80	13.36	4.61	34.45	52.42	14.70	5.07	37.90	57.66
Z102010F	75 mm on 50 mm Floormate insulation	m²	0.85	14.53	4.61	36.27	55.41	15.98	5.07	39.90	60.95
Z102011	**Excavation average 225 mm deep; off site disposal; compact surface; 225 mm hardcore; 25 mm sand blinding; 1200g polythene d.p.m.; 100 mm C20 concrete bed; one layer A142 mesh reinforcement; sand cement screed (1:4); thickness:**										
Z102011A	38 mm	m²	0.65	10.68	6.32	24.22	41.22	11.75	6.95	26.64	45.34
Z102011B	50 mm	m²	0.67	11.15	6.32	26.03	43.50	12.27	6.95	28.63	47.85
Z102011C	75 mm	m²	0.72	12.33	6.32	27.85	46.50	13.56	6.95	30.64	51.15
Z102011D	50 mm on 25 mm Floormate insulation	m²	0.79	13.18	6.32	31.46	50.96	14.50	6.95	34.61	56.06
Z102011E	50 mm on 50 mm Floormate insulation	m²	0.80	13.35	6.32	36.49	56.16	14.69	6.95	40.14	61.78
Z102011F	75 mm on 50 mm Floormate insulation	m²	0.85	14.53	6.32	38.31	59.16	15.98	6.95	42.14	65.08
Z102012	**Excavation average 300 mm deep; off site disposal; compact surface; 300 mm hardcore; 25 mm sand blinding; 1200g polythene d.p.m.; 100 mm C20 concrete bed; one layer A142 mesh reinforcement; sand cement screed (1:4); thickness:**										
Z102012A	38 mm	m²	0.65	10.68	8.06	26.25	44.99	11.75	8.87	28.88	49.49
Z102012B	50 mm	m²	0.67	11.15	8.06	28.07	47.28	12.27	8.87	30.88	52.01
Z102012C	75 mm	m²	0.72	12.32	8.06	29.89	50.27	13.55	8.87	32.88	55.30
Z102012D	50 mm on 25 mm Floormate insulation	m²	0.79	13.19	8.06	33.50	54.75	14.51	8.87	36.85	60.23
Z102012E	50 mm on 50 mm Floormate insulation	m²	0.80	13.36	8.06	38.53	59.95	14.70	8.87	42.38	65.95
Z102012F	75 mm on 50 mm Floormate insulation	m²	0.85	14.53	8.06	40.34	62.93	15.98	8.87	44.37	69.22

Approximate Estimating Rates

Major Works 2009		Unit	Labour Hours	Labour Net	Plant Net	Materials Net	Unit Net	Labour Gross	Plant Gross	Materials Gross	Unit Price
								(Gross rates include 10% profit)			
				£	£	£	£	£	£	£	£
Z10	**SUBSTRUCTURE: IN SITU CONCRETE BEDS**										
Z1020	**Reinforced in situ concrete bed**										
Z102020	**Excavation average 150 mm deep; off site disposal; compact surface; 150 mm hardcore; 25 mm sand blinding; 100 mm C20 concrete bed; two coats liquid d.p.m.; layer A142 mesh reinforcement; sand cement screed (1:4); thickness:**										
Z102020A	38 mm	m²	0.70	11.32	4.61	27.25	43.18	12.45	5.07	29.98	47.50
Z102020B	50 mm	m²	0.72	11.78	4.61	29.07	45.46	12.96	5.07	31.98	50.01
Z102020C	75 mm	m²	0.77	12.96	4.61	30.89	48.46	14.26	5.07	33.98	53.31
Z102020D	50 mm on 25 mm Floormate insulation	m²	0.84	13.82	4.61	34.50	52.93	15.20	5.07	37.95	58.22
Z102020E	50 mm on 50 mm Floormate insulation	m²	0.85	13.99	4.61	39.53	58.13	15.39	5.07	43.48	63.94
Z102020F	75 mm on 50 mm Floormate insulation	m²	0.90	15.17	4.61	41.34	61.12	16.69	5.07	45.47	67.23
Z102021	**Excavation average 225 mm deep; off site disposal; compact surface; 225 mm hardcore; 25 mm sand blinding; 100 mm C20 concrete bed; two coat liquid d.p.m.; layer A142 mesh reinforcement; sand cement screed (1:4); thickness:**										
Z102021A	38 mm	m²	0.70	11.31	6.32	29.29	46.92	12.44	6.95	32.22	51.61
Z102021B	50 mm	m²	0.72	11.79	6.32	31.11	49.22	12.97	6.95	34.22	54.14
Z102021C	75 mm	m²	0.77	12.96	6.32	32.92	52.20	14.26	6.95	36.21	57.42
Z102021D	50 mm on 25 mm Floormate insulation	m²	0.84	13.82	6.32	36.54	56.68	15.20	6.95	40.19	62.35
Z102021E	50 mm on 50 mm Floormate insulation	m²	0.85	13.99	6.32	41.57	61.88	15.39	6.95	45.73	68.07
Z102021F	75 mm on 50 mm Floormate insulation	m²	0.90	15.16	6.32	43.38	64.86	16.68	6.95	47.72	71.35
Z102022	**Excavation average 300 mm deep; off site disposal; compact surface; 300 mm hardcore; 25 mm sand blinding; 100 mm C20 concrete bed; two coat liquid d.p.m.; layer A142 mesh reinforcement; sand cement screed (1:4); thickness:**										
Z102022A	38 mm	m²	0.70	11.32	8.06	31.33	50.71	12.45	8.87	34.46	55.78
Z102022B	50 mm	m²	0.72	11.79	8.06	33.14	52.99	12.97	8.87	36.45	58.29
Z102022C	75 mm	m²	0.77	12.95	8.06	34.96	55.97	14.25	8.87	38.46	61.57
Z102022D	50 mm on 25 mm Floormate insulation	m²	0.84	13.82	8.06	38.57	60.45	15.20	8.87	42.43	66.50
Z102022E	50 mm on 50 mm Floormate insulation	m²	0.85	13.99	8.06	43.60	65.65	15.39	8.87	47.96	72.22
Z102022F	75 mm on 50 mm Floormate insulation	m²	0.90	15.16	8.06	45.42	68.64	16.68	8.87	49.96	75.50

Major Works 2009		Unit	Labour Hours	Labour Net	Plant Net	Materials Net	Unit Net	Labour Gross	Plant Gross	Materials Gross	Unit Price
								(Gross rates include 10% profit)			
				£	£	£	£	£	£	£	£
Z10	**SUBSTRUCTURE: IN SITU CONCRETE BEDS**										
Z1020	**Reinforced in situ concrete bed**										
Z102030	**Excavation average 150 mm deep; off site disposal; compact surface; 225 mm hardcore; 25 mm sand blinding; 1200g polythene d.p.m.; 150 mm C20 concrete bed; one layer A393 mesh reinforcement; sand cement screed (1:4); thickness:**										
Z102030A	38 mm	m²	0.65	10.68	4.61	22.18	37.47	11.75	5.07	24.40	41.22
Z102030B	50 mm	m²	0.67	11.15	4.61	23.99	39.75	12.27	5.07	26.39	43.73
Z102030C	75 mm	m²	0.72	12.32	4.61	25.81	42.74	13.55	5.07	28.39	47.01
Z102030D	50 mm on 25 mm Floormate insulation................	m²	0.79	13.19	4.61	29.42	47.22	14.51	5.07	32.36	51.94
Z102030E	50 mm on 50 mm Floormate insulation................	m²	0.80	13.36	4.61	34.45	52.42	14.70	5.07	37.90	57.66
Z102030F	75 mm on 50 mm Floormate insulation................	m²	0.85	14.53	4.61	36.27	55.41	15.98	5.07	39.90	60.95
Z102031	**Excavation average 225 mm deep; off site disposal; compact surface; 225 mm hardcore; 25 mm sand blinding; 1200g polythene d.p.m.; 150 mm C20 concrete bed; one layer A393 mesh reinforcement; sand cement screed (1:4); thickness:**										
Z102031A	38 mm	m²	0.73	11.72	6.32	32.87	50.91	12.89	6.95	36.16	56.00
Z102031B	50 mm	m²	0.75	12.18	6.32	34.69	53.19	13.40	6.95	38.16	58.51
Z102031C	75 mm	m²	0.80	13.36	6.32	36.51	56.19	14.70	6.95	40.16	61.81
Z102031D	50 mm on 25 mm Floormate insulation................	m²	0.87	14.22	6.32	40.12	60.66	15.64	6.95	44.13	66.73
Z102031E	50 mm on 50 mm Floormate insulation................	m²	0.88	14.40	6.32	45.15	65.87	15.84	6.95	49.67	72.46
Z102031F	75 mm on 50 mm Floormate insulation................	m²	0.93	15.57	6.32	46.97	68.86	17.13	6.95	51.67	75.75

Approximate Estimating Rates

Major Works 2009		Unit	Labour Hours	Labour Net	Plant Net	Materials Net	Unit Net	Labour Gross	Plant Gross	Materials Gross	Unit Price
								(Gross rates include 10% profit)			
				£	£	£	£	£	£	£	£
Z10	**SUBSTRUCTURE: IN SITU CONCRETE BEDS**										
Z1020	**Reinforced in situ concrete bed**										
Z102032	**Excavation average 300 mm deep; off site disposal; compact surface; 225 mm hardcore; 25 mm sand blinding; 1200g polythene d.p.m.; 150 mm C20 concrete bed; one layer A393 mesh reinforcement; sand cement screed (1:4); thickness:**										
Z102032A	38 mm	m²	0.65	10.68	8.06	26.25	44.99	11.75	8.87	28.88	49.49
Z102032B	50 mm	m²	0.67	11.15	8.06	28.07	47.28	12.27	8.87	30.88	52.01
Z102032C	75 mm	m²	0.72	12.32	8.06	29.89	50.27	13.55	8.87	32.88	55.30
Z102032D	50 mm on 25 mm Floormate insulation	m²	0.79	13.19	8.06	33.50	54.75	14.51	8.87	36.85	60.23
Z102032E	50 mm on 50 mm Floormate insulation	m²	0.80	13.36	8.06	38.53	59.95	14.70	8.87	42.38	65.95
Z102032F	75 mm on 50 mm Floormate insulation	m²	0.85	14.53	8.06	40.34	62.93	15.98	8.87	44.37	69.22
Z102040	**Excavation average 150 mm deep; off site disposal; compact surface; 225 mm hardcore; 25 mm sand blinding; two coat Synthaprufe d.p.m.; 150 mm C20 concrete bed; one layer A393 mesh reinforcement; sand cement screed (1:4); thickness:**										
Z102040A	38 mm	m²	0.70	11.32	4.61	27.25	43.18	12.45	5.07	29.98	47.50
Z102040B	50 mm	m²	0.67	11.15	4.61	28.89	44.65	12.27	5.07	31.78	49.12
Z102040C	75 mm	m²	0.72	12.32	4.61	30.71	47.64	13.55	5.07	33.78	52.40
Z102040D	50 mm on 25 mm Floormate insulation	m²	0.79	13.19	4.61	34.32	52.12	14.51	5.07	37.75	57.33
Z102040E	50 mm on 50 mm Floormate insulation	m²	0.80	13.36	4.61	39.35	57.32	14.70	5.07	43.29	63.05
Z102040F	75 mm on 50 mm Floormate insulation	m²	0.85	14.53	4.61	41.17	60.31	15.98	5.07	45.29	66.34

Major Works 2009		Unit	Labour Hours	Labour Net	Plant Net	Materials Net	Unit Net	Labour Gross	Plant Gross	Materials Gross	Unit Price
								(Gross rates include 10% profit)			
				£	£	£	£	£	£	£	£
Z10	**SUBSTRUCTURE: IN SITU CONCRETE BEDS**										
Z1020	**Reinforced in situ concrete bed**										
Z102041	**Excavation average 225 mm deep; off site disposal; compact surface; 225 mm hardcore; 25 mm sand blinding; two coat Synthaprufe d.p.m.; 150 mm C20 concrete bed; one layer A393 mesh reinforcement; sand cement screed (1:4); thickness:**										
Z102041A	38 mm	m²	0.73	11.72	6.32	37.77	55.81	12.89	6.95	41.55	61.39
Z102041B	50 mm	m²	0.75	12.19	6.32	39.59	58.10	13.41	6.95	43.55	63.91
Z102041C	75 mm	m²	0.80	13.36	6.32	41.40	61.08	14.70	6.95	45.54	67.19
Z102041D	50 mm on 25 mm Floormate insulation................	m²	0.87	14.23	6.32	45.02	65.57	15.65	6.95	49.52	72.13
Z102041E	50 mm on 50 mm Floormate insulation................	m²	0.88	14.40	6.32	50.05	70.77	15.84	6.95	55.06	77.85
Z102041F	75 mm on 50 mm Floormate insulation................	m²	0.93	15.56	6.32	51.86	73.74	17.12	6.95	57.05	81.11
Z102042	**Excavation average 300 mm deep; off site disposal; compact surface; 225 mm hardcore; 25 mm sand blinding; two coat Synthaprufe d.p.m.; 150 mm C20 concrete bed; one layer A393 mesh reinforcement; sand cement screed (1:4); thickness:**										
Z102042A	38 mm	m²	0.65	10.68	8.06	31.15	49.89	11.75	8.87	34.27	54.88
Z102042B	50 mm	m²	0.67	11.15	8.06	32.97	52.18	12.27	8.87	36.27	57.40
Z102042C	75 mm	m²	0.72	12.32	8.06	34.78	55.16	13.55	8.87	38.26	60.68
Z102042D	50 mm on 25 mm Floormate insulation................	m²	0.79	13.19	8.06	38.40	59.65	14.51	8.87	42.24	65.62
Z102042E	50 mm on 50 mm Floormate insulation................	m²	0.80	13.36	8.06	43.42	64.84	14.70	8.87	47.76	71.32
Z102042F	75 mm on 50 mm Floormate insulation................	m²	0.85	14.53	8.06	45.24	67.83	15.98	8.87	49.76	74.61

Approximate Estimating Rates

Major Works 2009		Unit	Labour Hours	Labour Net	Plant Net	Materials Net	Unit Net	Labour Gross	Plant Gross	Materials Gross	Unit Price
									(Gross rates include 10% profit)		
				£	£	£	£	£	£	£	£
Z12	SUBSTRUCTURE: SUSPENDED PRECAST CONCRETE										
Z1210	Precast concrete flooring system										
Z121010	Beam and block flooring system; excavate oversite 150 mm deep; off site disposal; weedkiller treated; concrete beams at 600 mm centres; concrete block infill; cement slurry grout; 1200g polythene d.p.m.; screed thickness:										
Z121010A	38 mm	m²	0.79	17.73	3.23	31.40	52.36	19.50	3.55	34.54	57.60
Z121010B	50 mm	m²	0.81	18.21	3.23	33.21	54.65	20.03	3.55	36.53	60.12
Z121010C	75 mm	m²	0.86	19.38	3.23	35.03	57.64	21.32	3.55	38.53	63.40
Z121010D	50 mm on 25 mm Floormate insulation	m²	0.93	20.24	3.23	38.64	62.11	22.26	3.55	42.50	68.32
Z121010E	50 mm on 50 mm Floormate insulation	m²	0.94	20.41	3.23	43.67	67.31	22.45	3.55	48.04	74.04
Z121010F	75 mm on 50 mm Floormate insulation	m²	0.99	21.58	3.23	45.49	70.30	23.74	3.55	50.04	77.33
Z121015	Beam and block flooring system; excavate 150 mm deep; disposal; weedkiller treated; 100 mm concrete blinding; beams at 600 mm centres; concrete block infill; cement slurry grout; 1200g d.p.m.; screed thickness:										
Z121015A	38 mm	m²	0.90	19.13	3.23	41.06	63.42	21.04	3.55	45.17	69.76
Z121015B	50 mm	m²	0.92	19.61	3.23	42.88	65.72	21.57	3.55	47.17	72.29
Z121015C	75 mm	m²	0.97	20.77	3.23	44.69	68.69	22.85	3.55	49.16	75.56
Z121015D	50 mm on 25 mm Floormate insulation	m²	1.04	21.64	3.23	48.30	73.17	23.80	3.55	53.13	80.49
Z121015E	50 mm on 50 mm Floormate insulation	m²	1.16	24.38	3.23	56.06	83.67	26.82	3.55	61.67	92.04
Z121015F	75 mm on 50 mm Floormate insulation	m²	1.34	28.49	3.23	60.14	91.86	31.34	3.55	66.15	101.05
Z121020	Beam and block flooring system; excavate oversite 150 mm deep; off site disposal; weedkiller treated; concrete beams at 600 mm centres; concrete block infill; slurry grout; 1200g d.p.m.; V313 T&G flooring chipboard; thickness:										
Z121020A	18 mm on 25 mm Floormate insulation	m²	1.09	21.41	3.23	38.92	63.56	23.55	3.55	42.81	69.92
Z121020B	18 mm on 50 mm Floormate insulation	m²	1.10	21.58	3.23	43.95	68.76	23.74	3.55	48.35	75.64
Z121020C	22 mm on 25 mm Floormate insulation	m²	1.09	21.41	3.23	40.00	64.64	23.55	3.55	44.00	71.10
Z121020D	22 mm on 50 mm Floormate insulation	m²	0.80	16.02	3.23	53.33	72.58	17.62	3.55	58.66	79.84

Major Works 2009		Unit	Labour Hours	Labour Net	Plant Net	Materials Net	Unit Net	Labour Gross	Plant Gross	Materials Gross	Unit Price
								——— (Gross rates include 10% profit) ———			
				£	£	£	£	£	£	£	£
Z12	**SUBSTRUCTURE: SUSPENDED PRECAST CONCRETE**										
Z1210	**Precast concrete flooring system**										
Z121025	**Beam and block flooring system; excavate 150 mm; disposal; weedkiller treated; 100 mm concrete blinding; beams at 600 mm centres; concrete block infill; slurry grout; 1200g d.p.m.; V313 T&G flooring chipboard; thickness:**										
Z121025A	18 mm on 25 mm Floormate insulation..............	m²	1.20	22.80	3.23	48.58	74.61	25.08	3.55	53.44	82.07
Z121025B	18 mm on 50 mm Floormate insulation..............	m²	1.21	22.97	3.23	53.61	79.81	25.27	3.55	58.97	87.79
Z121025C	22 mm on 25 mm Floormate insulation..............	m²	1.20	22.80	3.23	49.66	75.69	25.08	3.55	54.63	83.26
Z121025D	22 mm on 50 mm Floormate insulation..............	m²	1.21	22.97	3.23	54.69	80.89	25.27	3.55	60.16	88.98
Z13	**SUBSTRUCTURE: IN SITU CONCRETE PAD FOUNDATIONS**										
Z1305	**Plain in situ concrete base**										
Z130510	**Excavation including working space; earthwork support; disposal off site; part return fill and ram; construct formwork; in situ concrete C25 N/mm²; 1.00 m excavation depth; pad size:**										
Z130510D	600 × 600 × 300 mm ..	nr	7.02	104.04	44.43	33.62	182.09	114.44	48.87	36.98	200.30
Z130515	**Excavation including working space; earthwork support; disposal off site; part return, fill and ram; construct formwork; in situ concrete C25 N/mm²; 1.25 m excavation depth; pad size:**										
Z130515F	900 × 900 × 450 mm ..	nr	10.76	164.73	78.47	66.02	309.22	181.20	86.32	72.62	340.14
Z130520	**Excavation including working space; earthwork support; disposal off site; part return, fill and ram; construct formwork; in situ concrete C25 N/mm²; 1.50 m excavation depth; pad size:**										
Z130520H	1500 × 1500 × 600 mm	nr	18.82	308.06	166.59	181.93	656.58	338.87	183.25	200.12	722.24
Z130520M	2700 × 2700 × 1000 mm	nr	41.11	819.86	425.46	739.90	1985.22	901.85	468.01	813.89	2183.74

Approximate Estimating Rates

Major Works 2009		Unit	Labour Hours	Labour Net	Plant Net	Materials Net	Unit Net	Labour Gross	Plant Gross	Materials Gross	Unit Price
								(Gross rates include 10% profit)			
				£	£	£	£	£	£	£	£
Z13	**SUBSTRUCTURE: IN SITU CONCRETE PAD FOUNDATIONS**										
Z1310	**Plain in situ concrete base**										
Z131010	**Excavate; earthwork support; disposal off site; construct formwork; in situ concrete C30 N/mm²; pad size:**										
Z131010A	900 × 900 × 600 mm thick	Nr	11.38	175.86	30.74	771.48	978.08	193.45	33.81	848.63	1075.89
Z131010B	1050 × 1050 × 600 mm thick	Nr	13.48	207.77	38.31	909.50	1155.58	228.55	42.14	1000.45	1271.14
Z131010C	1200 × 1200 × 600 mm thick	Nr	15.64	240.40	46.56	1050.09	1337.05	264.44	51.22	1155.10	1470.76
Z131010D	900 × 900 × 750 mm thick	Nr	12.39	188.74	38.43	784.38	1011.55	207.61	42.27	862.82	1112.71
Z131010E	1050 × 1050 × 750 mm thick	Nr	14.71	223.42	47.88	926.79	1198.09	245.76	52.67	1019.47	1317.90
Z131010F	1200 × 1200 × 750 mm thick	Nr	17.11	259.04	58.20	1072.58	1389.82	284.94	64.02	1179.84	1528.80
Z131010G	1500 × 1500 × 750 mm thick	Nr	22.11	333.07	81.49	1374.28	1788.84	366.38	89.64	1511.71	1967.72
Z131010H	1050 × 1050 × 900 mm thick	Nr	15.94	239.07	57.44	944.09	1240.60	262.98	63.18	1038.50	1364.66
Z131010I	1200 × 1200 × 900 mm thick	Nr	18.57	277.67	69.85	1095.07	1442.59	305.44	76.84	1204.58	1586.85
Z131010J	1500 × 1500 × 900 mm thick	Nr	24.09	358.20	97.78	1409.05	1865.03	394.02	107.56	1549.96	2051.53
Z131010K	1200 × 1200 × 1050 mm thick	Nr	22.65	327.61	81.49	1088.19	1497.29	360.37	89.64	1197.01	1647.02
Z131010L	1500 × 1500 × 1050 mm thick	Nr	29.33	422.47	114.08	1407.19	1943.74	464.72	125.49	1547.91	2138.11
Z131010M	1800 × 1800 × 1050 mm thick	Nr	36.42	522.51	151.54	1744.87	2418.92	574.76	166.69	1919.36	2660.81
Z131010N	1200 × 1200 × 1200 mm thick	Nr	25.88	374.40	93.13	1243.64	1711.17	411.84	102.44	1368.00	1882.29
Z131010O	1500 × 1500 × 1200 mm thick	Nr	33.52	482.82	130.37	1608.17	2221.36	531.10	143.41	1768.99	2443.50
Z131010P	1800 × 1800 × 1200 mm thick	Nr	41.62	597.15	173.19	1994.14	2764.48	656.87	190.51	2193.55	3040.93

Major Works 2009		Unit	Labour Hours	Labour Net	Plant Net	Materials Net	Unit Net	Labour Gross	Plant Gross	Materials Gross	Unit Price
								(Gross rates include 10% profit)			
				£	£	£	£	£	£	£	£
Z13	SUBSTRUCTURE: IN SITU CONCRETE PAD FOUNDATIONS										
Z1320	Reinforced in situ concrete base										
Z132001	Excavation including working space; earthwork support; disposal off site; part return, fill and ram; construct formwork; reinforced in situ concrete C25 N/mm²; reinforcement at 50 kg/m³; 1.00 m excavation depth; pad size:										
Z132001C	600 × 600 × 300 mm	nr	7.23	107.14	44.43	37.42	188.99	117.85	48.87	41.16	207.89
Z132002	Excavation including working space; earthwork support; disposal off site; part return, fill and ram; construct formwork; reinforced in situ concrete C25 N/mm²; reinforcement at 50 kg/m³; 1.25 m excavation depth; pad size:										
Z132002F	900 × 900 × 450 mm	nr	11.47	175.26	78.47	75.48	329.21	192.79	86.32	83.03	362.13
Z132003	Excavation including working space; earthwork support; disposal off site; part return, fill and ram; construct formwork; reinforced in situ concrete C25 N/mm²; reinforcement at 50 kg/m³; 1.50 m excavation depth; pad size:										
Z132003H	1500 × 1500 × 600 mm	nr	21.46	347.11	166.59	216.44	730.14	381.82	183.25	238.08	803.15
Z132003M	2700 × 2700 × 1000 mm	nr	55.34	1030.47	425.46	817.22	2273.15	1133.52	468.01	898.94	2500.47
Z132004	Excavation including working space; earthwork support; disposal off site; part return, fill and ram; construct formwork; reinforced in situ concrete C25 N/mm²; reinforcement at 75 kg/m³; 1.00 m excavation depth; pad size:										
Z132004C	600 × 600 × 300 mm	nr	7.34	108.70	44.43	38.85	191.98	119.57	48.87	42.74	211.18

Approximate Estimating Rates

Major Works 2009		Unit	Labour Hours	Labour Net	Plant Net	Materials Net	Unit Net	Labour Gross	Plant Gross	Materials Gross	Unit Price
								(Gross rates include 10% profit)			
				£	£	£	£	£	£	£	£
Z13	**SUBSTRUCTURE: IN SITU CONCRETE PAD FOUNDATIONS**										
Z1320	**Reinforced in situ concrete base**										
Z132005	Excavation including working space; earthwork support; disposal off site; part return, fill and ram; construct formwork; reinforced in situ concrete C25 N/mm^2; reinforcement at 75 kg/m^3; 1.25m excavation depth; pad size:										
Z132005F	900 × 900 × 450 mm ..	nr	11.33	173.23	78.47	79.93	331.63	190.55	86.32	87.92	364.79
Z132006	Excavation including working space; earthwork support; disposal off site; part return, fill and ram; construct formwork; reinforced in situ concrete C25 N/mm^2; reinforcement at 75 kg/m^3; 1.50m excavation depth; pad size:										
Z132006H	1500 × 1500 × 600 mm	nr	22.77	366.63	166.59	233.47	766.69	403.29	183.25	256.82	843.36
Z132006M	2700 × 2700 × 1000 mm	nr	62.46	1135.76	425.46	1016.10	2577.32	1249.34	468.01	1117.71	2835.05
Z132007	Excavation including working space; earthwork support; disposal off site; part return, fill and ram; construct formwork; reinforced in situ concrete C25 N/mm^2; reinforcement at 100 kg/m^3; 1.00m excavation depth; pad size:										
Z132007C	600 × 600 × 300 mm ..	nr	7.44	110.25	44.43	39.81	194.49	121.28	48.87	43.79	213.94
Z132008	Excavation including working space; earthwork support; disposal off site; part return, fill and ram; construct formwork; reinforced in situ concrete C25 N/mm^2; reinforcement at 100 kg/m^3; 1.25m excavation depth; pad size:										
Z132008F	900 × 900 × 450 mm...	nr	12.18	185.81	78.47	85.78	350.06	204.39	86.32	94.36	385.07
Z132009	Excavation including working space; earthwork support; disposal off site; part return, fill and ram; construct formwork; reinforced in situ concrete C25 N/mm^2; reinforcement at 100 kg/m^3; 1.50m excavation depth; pad size:										
Z132009H	1500 × 1500 × 600 mm	nr	24.09	386.13	166.59	250.09	802.81	424.74	183.25	275.10	883.09
Z132009M	2700 × 2700 × 1000 mm	nr	69.57	1241.06	425.46	1107.69	2774.21	1365.17	468.01	1218.46	3051.63

Major Works 2009		Unit	Labour Hours	Labour Net	Plant Net	Materials Net	Unit Net	Labour Gross	Plant Gross	Materials Gross	Unit Price
								(Gross rates include 10% profit)			
				£	£	£	£	£	£	£	£
Z13	SUBSTRUCTURE: IN SITU CONCRETE PAD FOUNDATIONS										
Z1320	Reinforced in situ concrete base										
Z132010	Excavate; earthwork support; disposal off site; construct formwork; in situ concrete C30 N/mm²; steel bar reinforcement; pad size:										
Z132010A	900 × 900 × 600 mm thick	Nr	13.71	210.08	39.69	855.27	1105.04	231.09	43.66	940.80	1215.54
Z132010B	1050 × 1050 × 600 mm thick	Nr	16.66	254.47	50.50	1023.86	1328.83	279.92	55.55	1126.25	1461.71
Z132010C	1200 × 1200 × 600 mm thick	Nr	19.79	301.36	62.47	1199.28	1563.11	331.50	68.72	1319.21	1719.42
Z132010D	900 × 900 × 750 mm thick	Nr	15.30	231.52	49.63	889.07	1170.22	254.67	54.59	977.98	1287.24
Z132010E	1050 × 1050 × 750 mm thick	Nr	18.67	281.53	63.11	1069.03	1413.67	309.68	69.42	1175.93	1555.04
Z132010F	1200 × 1200 × 750 mm thick	Nr	22.27	334.97	78.09	1258.46	1671.52	368.47	85.90	1384.31	1838.67
Z132010G	1500 × 1500 × 750 mm thick	Nr	30.19	451.79	112.58	1664.95	2229.32	496.97	123.84	1831.45	2452.25
Z132010H	1050 × 1050 × 900 mm thick	Nr	20.70	308.93	75.71	1115.16	1499.80	339.82	83.28	1226.68	1649.78
Z132010I	1200 × 1200 × 900 mm thick	Nr	24.78	368.93	93.71	1318.48	1781.12	405.82	103.08	1450.33	1959.23
Z132010J	1500 × 1500 × 900 mm thick	Nr	33.80	500.79	135.06	1758.16	2394.01	550.87	148.57	1933.98	2633.41
Z132010K	1200 × 1200 × 1050 mm thick	Nr	29.90	434.18	109.33	1349.14	1892.65	477.60	120.26	1484.05	2081.92
Z132010L	1500 × 1500 × 1050 mm thick	Nr	40.66	588.94	157.60	1814.74	2561.28	647.83	173.36	1996.21	2817.41
Z132010M	1800 × 1800 × 1050 mm thick	Nr	52.72	762.06	214.18	2331.32	3307.56	838.27	235.60	2564.45	3638.32
Z132010N	1200 × 1200 × 1200 mm thick	Nr	34.16	495.96	124.95	1541.28	2162.19	545.56	137.45	1695.41	2378.41
Z132010O	1500 × 1500 × 1200 mm thick	Nr	46.45	672.82	180.08	2073.39	2926.29	740.10	198.09	2280.73	3218.92
Z132010P	1800 × 1800 × 1200 mm thick	Nr	60.26	870.93	244.78	2664.38	3780.09	958.02	269.26	2930.82	4158.10

Approximate Estimating Rates

Major Works 2009		Unit	Labour Hours	Labour Net	Plant Net	Materials Net	Unit Net	Labour Gross	Plant Gross	Materials Gross	Unit Price
								(Gross rates include 10% profit)			
				£	£	£	£	£	£	£	£
Z13	SUBSTRUCTURE: IN SITU CONCRETE PAD FOUNDATIONS										
Z1350	Reinforced in situ concrete cap										
Z135001	Excavation including working space; earthwork support; disposal; part return, fill and ram, cut off pile head and prepare reinforcement; formwork; in situ concrete C25-20mm aggregate; 50kg/m³ reinforcement; pile cap size:										
Z135001C	up to 900 × 900mm × 1.00m; single pile	Nr	21.65	318.88	134.09	136.61	589.58	350.77	147.50	150.27	648.54
Z135001F	up to 2100 × 2100mm × 1.00m; two piles	Nr	49.53	813.15	370.72	528.09	1711.96	894.47	407.79	580.90	1883.16
Z135001H	up to 2400 × 2400mm × 1.25m; three piles	Nr	70.00	1180.82	520.19	854.31	2555.32	1298.90	572.21	939.74	2810.85
Z135001L	up to 2700 × 2700mm × 1.50m; four piles	Nr	93.78	1624.58	705.87	1264.67	3595.12	1787.04	776.46	1391.14	3954.63
Z135002	Excavation including working space; earthwork support; disposal; part return, fill and ram, cut off pile head and prepare reinforcement; formwork; in situ concrete C25-20mm aggregate; 75kg/m³ reinforcement; pile cap size:										
Z135002C	up to 900 × 900mm × 1.00m; single pile	Nr	22.39	329.77	134.09	145.30	609.16	362.75	147.50	159.83	670.08
Z135002F	up to 2100 × 2100mm × 1.00m; two piles	Nr	53.64	873.97	370.69	591.79	1836.45	961.37	407.76	650.97	2020.10
Z135002H	up to 2400 × 2400mm × 1.25m; three piles	Nr	76.70	1279.96	520.19	928.58	2728.73	1407.96	572.21	1021.44	3001.60
Z135002L	up to 2700 × 2700mm × 1.50m; four piles	Nr	103.95	1775.17	705.87	1382.64	3863.68	1952.69	776.46	1520.90	4250.05
Z135003	Excavation including working space; earthwork support; disposal; part return, fill and ram, cut off pile head and prepare reinforcement; formwork; in situ concrete C25-20mm aggregate; 100kg/m³ reinforcement; pile cap size:										
Z135003C	up to 900 × 900mm × 1.00m; single pile	Nr	23.13	340.84	134.09	154.54	629.47	374.92	147.50	169.99	692.42
Z135003F	up to 2100 × 2100mm × 1.00m; two piles	Nr	57.76	934.90	370.69	639.70	1945.29	1028.39	407.76	703.67	2139.82
Z135003H	up to 2400 × 2400mm × 1.25m; three piles	Nr	83.39	1379.06	520.19	1005.13	2904.38	1516.97	572.21	1105.64	3194.82
Z135003L	up to 2700 × 2700mm × 1.50m; four piles	Nr	114.13	1925.75	705.87	1501.00	4132.62	2118.33	776.46	1651.10	4545.88

Major Works 2009		Unit	Labour Hours	Labour Net	Plant Net	Materials Net	Unit Net	Labour Gross	Plant Gross	Materials Gross	Unit Price
								(Gross rates include 10% profit)			
				£	£	£	£	£	£	£	£
Z13	**SUBSTRUCTURE: IN SITU CONCRETE PAD FOUNDATIONS**										
Z1350	**Reinforced in situ concrete cap**										
Z135004	**Excavation including working space; earthwork support; disposal; part return, fill and ram, cut off pile head and prepare reinforcement; formwork; in situ concrete C30-20mm aggregate; 50kg/m^3**										
Z135004C	up to 900 × 900mm × 1.00m; single pile	Nr	21.65	318.88	134.09	137.67	590.64	350.77	147.50	151.44	649.70
Z135004F	up to 2100 × 2100mm × 1.00m; two piles	Nr	49.52	813.02	370.69	549.55	1733.26	894.32	407.76	604.51	1906.59
Z135004H	up to 2400 × 2400mm × 1.25m; three piles	Nr	70.00	1180.82	520.11	863.68	2564.61	1298.90	572.12	950.05	2821.07
Z135004L	up to 2700 × 2700mm × 1.50m; four piles	Nr	93.78	1624.58	705.87	1278.90	3609.35	1787.04	776.46	1406.79	3970.29
Z135005	**Excavation including working space; earthwork support; disposal; part return, fill and ram, cut off pile head and prepare reinforcement; formwork; in situ concrete C30-20mm aggregate; 75kg/m^3 reinforcement; pile cap size:**										
Z135005C	up to 900 × 900mm × 1.00m; single pile	Nr	22.39	329.78	134.09	146.36	610.23	362.76	147.50	161.00	671.25
Z135005F	up to 2100 × 2100mm × 1.00m; two piles	Nr	53.64	873.97	370.69	597.53	1842.19	961.37	407.76	657.28	2026.41
Z135005H	up to 2400 × 2400mm × 1.25m; three piles	Nr	76.70	1279.95	520.19	937.01	2737.15	1407.95	572.21	1030.71	3010.87
Z135005L	up to 2700 × 2700mm × 1.50m; four piles	Nr	103.95	1775.17	705.87	1396.87	3877.91	1952.69	776.46	1536.56	4265.70
Z135006	**Excavation including working space; earthwork support; disposal; part return, fill and ram, cut off pile head and prepare reinforcement; formwork; in situ concrete C30-20mm aggregate; 100kg/m^3 reinforcement; pile cap size:**										
Z135006C	up to 900 × 900mm × 1.00m; single pile	Nr	23.13	340.85	134.09	155.60	630.54	374.94	147.50	171.16	693.59
Z135006F	up to 2100 × 2100mm × 1.00m; two piles	Nr	57.76	934.90	370.69	645.44	1951.03	1028.39	407.76	709.98	2146.13
Z135006H	up to 2400 × 2400mm × 1.25m; three piles	Nr	83.39	1379.07	520.19	1014.51	2913.77	1516.98	572.21	1115.96	3205.15
Z135006L	up to 2700 × 2700mm × 1.50m; four piles	Nr	114.13	1925.75	705.87	1515.23	4146.85	2118.33	776.46	1666.75	4561.54

Approximate Estimating Rates

Major Works 2009		Unit	Labour Hours	Labour Net	Plant Net	Materials Net	Unit Net	Labour Gross	Plant Gross	Materials Gross	Unit Price
								(Gross rates include 10% profit)			
				£	£	£	£	£	£	£	£
Z13	**SUBSTRUCTURE: IN SITU CONCRETE PAD FOUNDATIONS**										
Z1350	**Reinforced in situ concrete cap**										
Z135007	**Excavation including working space; earthwork support; disposal; part return, fill and ram, cut off pile head and prepare reinforcement; formwork; in situ concrete C40-20mm aggregate; 50kg/m³ reinforcement; pile cap size:**										
Z135007C	up to 900 × 900mm × 1.00m; single pile	Nr	21.65	318.89	134.09	140.34	593.32	350.78	147.50	154.37	652.65
Z135007F	up to 2100 × 2100mm × 1.00m; two piles	Nr	49.52	813.02	370.69	564.09	1747.80	894.32	407.76	620.50	1922.58
Z135007H	up to 2400 × 2400mm × 1.25m; three piles	Nr	72.00	1206.22	520.19	887.42	2613.83	1326.84	572.21	976.16	2875.21
Z135007L	up to 2700 × 2700mm × 1.50m; four piles	Nr	93.78	1624.58	705.87	1314.95	3645.40	1787.04	776.46	1446.45	4009.94
Z135008	**Excavation including working space; earthwork support; disposal; part return, fill and ram, cut off pile head and prepare reinforcement; formwork; in situ concrete C40-20mm aggregate; 75kg/m³ reinforcement; pile cap size:**										
Z135008C	up to 900 × 900mm × 1.00m; single pile	Nr	22.39	329.78	134.09	149.03	612.90	362.76	147.50	163.93	674.19
Z135008F	up to 2100 × 2100mm × 1.00m; two piles	Nr	53.64	873.97	370.69	612.07	1856.73	961.37	407.76	673.28	2042.40
Z135008H	up to 2400 × 2400mm × 1.25m; three piles	Nr	76.70	1279.95	520.19	961.69	2761.83	1407.95	572.21	1057.86	3038.01
Z135008L	up to 2700 × 2700mm × 1.50m; four piles	Nr	103.95	1775.17	705.87	1432.92	3913.96	1952.69	776.46	1576.21	4305.36
Z135009	**Excavation including working space; earthwork support; disposal; part return, fill and ram, cut off pile head and prepare reinforcement; formwork; in situ concrete C40-20mm aggregate; 100kg/m³ reinforcement; pile cap size:**										
Z135009C	up to 900 × 900mm × 1.00m; single pile	Nr	23.13	340.85	134.09	158.27	633.21	374.94	147.50	174.10	696.53
Z135009F	up to 2100 × 2100mm × 1.00m; two piles	Nr	57.76	934.90	370.69	659.98	1965.57	1028.39	407.76	725.98	2162.13
Z135009H	up to 2400 × 2400mm × 1.25m; three piles	Nr	83.39	1379.07	520.19	1038.24	2937.50	1516.98	572.21	1142.06	3231.25
Z135009L	up to 2700 × 2700mm × 1.50m; four piles	Nr	114.13	1925.75	705.87	1551.28	4182.90	2118.33	776.46	1706.41	4601.19

Major Works 2009		Unit	Labour Hours	Labour Net	Plant Net	Materials Net	Unit Net	Labour Gross	Plant Gross	Materials Gross	Unit Price
								(Gross rates include 10% profit)			
				£	£	£	£	£	£	£	£
Z13	SUBSTRUCTURE: IN SITU CONCRETE PAD FOUNDATIONS										
Z1350	Reinforced in situ concrete cap										
Z135010	Excavation; earthwork support; disposal off site; cut off pile head and prepare reinforcement; construct formwork; in situ concrete C30 N/mm^2; steel bar reinforcement; single pile; pile cap size:										
Z135010A	900 × 900 × 900 mm thick	Nr	23.65	360.27	29.75	918.16	1308.18	396.30	32.73	1009.98	1439.00
Z135010B	1050 × 1050 × 900 mm thick	Nr	29.14	437.62	39.95	1109.67	1587.24	481.38	43.95	1220.64	1745.96
Z135010C	1200 × 1200 × 900 mm thick	Nr	35.09	521.32	51.66	1312.21	1885.19	573.45	56.83	1443.43	2073.71
Z135010D	1500 × 1500 × 900 mm thick	Nr	49.01	715.50	79.57	1750.31	2545.38	787.05	87.53	1925.34	2799.92
Z135010E	900 × 900 × 1050 mm thick	Nr	25.97	389.54	34.73	923.68	1347.95	428.49	38.20	1016.05	1482.75
Z135010F	1050 × 1050 × 1050 mm thick	Nr	32.12	475.56	46.63	1122.90	1645.09	523.12	51.29	1235.19	1809.60
Z135010G	1200 × 1200 × 1050 mm thick	Nr	41.78	612.34	60.89	1466.46	2139.69	673.57	66.98	1613.11	2353.66
Z135010H	1500 × 1500 × 1050 mm thick	Nr	53.81	777.50	92.85	1796.49	2666.84	855.25	102.14	1976.14	2933.52
Z135010I	900 × 900 × 1200 mm thick	Nr	29.60	441.07	39.67	1055.63	1536.37	485.18	43.64	1161.19	1690.01
Z135010J	1050 × 1050 × 1200 mm thick	Nr	36.61	539.15	53.28	1282.59	1875.02	593.07	58.61	1410.85	2062.52
Z135010K	1200 × 1200 × 1200 mm thick	Nr	44.25	645.76	68.88	1524.59	2239.23	710.34	75.77	1677.05	2463.15
Z135010L	1500 × 1500 × 1200 mm thick	Nr	61.40	884.21	106.09	2052.53	3042.83	972.63	116.70	2257.78	3347.11
Z135010M	1800 × 1800 × 1200 mm thick	Nr	81.01	1156.08	151.30	2638.50	3945.88	1271.69	166.43	2902.35	4340.47
Z135010N	2100 × 2100 × 1200 mm thick	Nr	103.13	1461.70	204.50	3283.55	4949.75	1607.87	224.95	3611.91	5444.73
Z1350100	2400 × 2400 × 1200 mm thick	Nr	121.10	1711.29	244.37	3830.84	5786.50	1882.42	268.81	4213.92	6365.15
Z135010P	2700 × 2700 × 1200 mm thick	Nr	154.81	2173.89	334.88	4749.64	7258.41	2391.28	368.37	5224.60	7984.25
Z135010Q	3000 × 3000 × 1200 mm thick	Nr	184.38	2580.44	412.06	5570.70	8563.20	2838.48	453.27	6127.77	9419.52

Approximate Estimating Rates

Major Works 2009		Unit	Labour Hours	Labour Net	Plant Net	Materials Net	Unit Net	Labour Gross	Plant Gross	Materials Gross	Unit Price
								(Gross rates include 10% profit)			
				£	£	£	£	£	£	£	£
Z14	**SUBSTRUCTURE: IN SITU CONCRETE STRIP FOUNDATIONS**										
Z1410	**Traditional concrete strip foundation**										
Z141010	**Excavation; earthwork support; partial backfill; partial disposal off site; C20 concrete foundation 700 × 225 mm; two skins 100 mm concrete blocks 7N in cement mortar (1:3); three course facing brickwork (300:00/ 1000) in gauged mortar (1:1:6) where exposed as facework; 50 m cavity with lean mix concrete C7.5; Hyload d.p.c.; footing depth:**										
Z141010A	0.75 mm	m	2.88	49.84	10.55	48.40	108.79	54.82	11.61	53.24	119.67
Z141010B	1.00 mm	m	2.50	48.40	12.08	58.06	118.54	53.24	13.29	63.87	130.39
Z141010C	1.25 mm	m	3.35	63.28	16.87	67.59	147.74	69.61	18.56	74.35	162.51
Z141010D	1.50 mm	m	3.87	72.49	19.89	76.89	169.27	79.74	21.88	84.58	186.20
Z141015	**Excavation; earthwork support; partial backfill; partial disposal off site; C20 concrete foundation 700 × 225 mm; two skins 105 mm common brickwork in cement mortar; three course facing brick work (300:00/1000) in gauged mortar where exposed as facework; 50 mm cavity with lean mix concrete C7.5 fill; Hyload d.p.c.; footing depth:**										
Z141015A	0.75 m	m	2.03	39.69	12.02	53.21	104.92	43.66	13.22	58.53	115.41
Z141015B	1.00 m	m	2.78	55.42	12.08	66.14	133.64	60.96	13.29	72.75	147.00
Z141015C	1.25 m	m	3.58	69.07	16.87	76.92	162.86	75.98	18.56	84.61	179.15
Z141015D	1.50 m	m	4.22	81.79	19.01	89.73	190.53	89.97	20.91	98.70	209.58
Z141020	**Excavation; earthwork support; partial backfill; partial disposal off site; C20 concrete foundation 700 × 225 mm; two skins 105 mm Class B engineering brickwork in cement mortar; three course facing brickwork (300:00/ 1000) in gauged mortar where exposed as facework; 50 mm cavity with lean mix concrete C7.5 fill; Hyload d.p.c.; footing depth:**										
Z141020A	0.75 m	m	2.06	40.45	12.02	65.77	118.24	44.50	13.22	72.35	130.06
Z141020B	1.00 m	m	2.72	53.92	12.08	84.08	150.08	59.31	13.29	92.49	165.09
Z141020C	1.25 m	m	3.64	70.57	16.87	102.06	189.50	77.63	18.56	112.27	208.45
Z141020D	1.50 m	m	4.29	83.55	19.01	121.15	223.71	91.91	20.91	133.27	246.08

Major Works 2009		Unit	Labour Hours	Labour Net	Plant Net	Materials Net	Unit Net	Labour Gross	Plant Gross	Materials Gross	Unit Price
								— (Gross rates include 10% profit) —			
				£	£	£	£	£	£	£	£
Z14	**SUBSTRUCTURE: IN SITU CONCRETE STRIP FOUNDATIONS**										
Z1410	**Traditional concrete strip foundation**										
Z141025	**Excavation; earthwork support; partial backfill; partial disposal off site; C20 concrete foundation 600 × 225 mm; 255 mm wall of trench blocks in cement mortar; cavity with galvanised ties and lean mix fill; Hyload d.p.c.; depth of trench:**										
Z141025A	0.75 m	m	1.52	27.62	10.16	45.76	83.54	30.38	11.18	50.34	91.89
Z141025B	1.00 m	m	1.96	35.45	12.95	55.25	103.65	39.00	14.25	60.78	114.02
Z141025C	1.25 m	m	2.57	45.31	16.87	65.39	127.57	49.84	18.56	71.93	140.33
Z141025D	1.50 m	m	3.01	52.88	19.89	75.05	147.82	58.17	21.88	82.56	162.60
Z141030	**Excavation; earthwork support; partial backfill; partial disposal off site; C20 concrete foundation 450 × 225 mm; 215 mm wall of common bricks in cement mortar; Hyload d.p.c.; depth of trench:**										
Z141030A	0.75 m	m	1.63	32.62	7.74	42.62	82.98	35.88	8.51	46.88	91.28
Z141030B	1.00 m	m	2.17	43.71	10.16	56.14	110.01	48.08	11.18	61.75	121.01
Z141030C	1.25 m	m	2.89	57.07	12.80	66.58	136.45	62.78	14.08	73.24	150.10
Z141030D	1.50 m	m	3.45	68.41	15.41	77.74	161.56	75.25	16.95	85.51	177.72
Z141035	**Excavation; earthwork support; partial backfill; partial disposal off site; C20 concrete foundation 450 × 225 mm; 200 mm wall of concrete blocks in cement mortar; Hyload d.p.c.; depth of trench:**										
Z141035A	0.75 m	m	1.21	21.95	7.55	37.79	67.29	24.15	8.31	41.57	74.02
Z141035B	1.00 m	m	1.59	29.01	9.97	46.13	85.11	31.91	10.97	50.74	93.62
Z141035C	1.25 m	m	2.15	38.23	12.80	54.65	105.68	42.05	14.08	60.12	116.25
Z141035D	1.50 m	m	2.56	45.68	15.23	63.40	124.31	50.25	16.75	69.74	136.74

Approximate Estimating Rates

Major Works 2009		Unit	Labour Hours	Labour Net	Plant Net	Materials Net	Unit Net	Labour Gross	Plant Gross	Materials Gross	Unit Price
								(Gross rates include 10% profit)			
				£	£	£	£	£	£	£	£
Z14	**SUBSTRUCTURE: IN SITU CONCRETE STRIP FOUNDATIONS**										
Z1410	**Traditional concrete strip foundation**										
Z141040	**Excavation; earthwork support; partial backfill; partial disposal off site; C20 concrete foundation 450 × 225 mm; 150 mm wall of concrete blocks in cement mortar; Hyload d.p.c.; depth of trench:**										
Z141040A	0.75 m	m	1.17	20.57	7.36	31.29	59.22	22.63	8.10	34.42	65.14
Z141040B	1.00 m	m	1.54	27.14	9.41	38.29	74.84	29.85	10.35	42.12	82.32
Z141040C	1.25 m	m	2.10	36.23	12.30	45.12	93.65	39.85	13.53	49.63	103.02
Z141040D	1.50 m	m	2.51	43.43	14.32	52.11	109.86	47.77	15.75	57.32	120.85
Z141045	**Excavation; earthwork support; partial backfill; partial disposal off site; C20 concrete foundation 450 × 225 mm; 100 mm wall of concrete blocks in cement mortar; Hyload d.p.c.; depth of trench:**										
Z141045A	0.75 m	m	1.17	20.08	7.24	27.67	54.99	22.09	7.96	30.44	60.49
Z141045B	1.00 m	m	1.55	26.64	9.07	33.21	68.92	29.30	9.98	36.53	75.81
Z141045C	1.25 m	m	2.10	35.36	11.77	38.94	86.07	38.90	12.95	42.83	94.68
Z141045D	1.50 m	m	2.51	42.31	13.82	44.60	100.73	46.54	15.20	49.06	110.80
Z141050	**Excavation; earthwork support; partial backfill; partial disposal off site; C20 concrete foundation 450 × 225 mm; 105 mm wall of common bricks in cement mortar; Hyload d.p.c.; depth of trench:**										
Z141050A	0.75 m	m	1.24	21.83	7.24	30.06	59.13	24.01	7.96	33.07	65.04
Z141050B	1.00 m	m	1.58	28.27	9.07	38.33	75.67	31.10	9.98	42.16	83.24
Z141050C	1.25 m	m	2.23	38.63	11.77	43.51	93.91	42.49	12.95	47.86	103.30
Z141050D	1.50 m	m	2.71	47.34	13.82	69.72	130.88	52.07	15.20	76.69	143.97

Major Works 2009		Unit	Labour Hours	Labour Net	Plant Net	Materials Net	Unit Net	Labour Gross	Plant Gross	Materials Gross	Unit Price
								(Gross rates include 10% profit)			
				£	£	£	£	£	£	£	£
Z14	SUBSTRUCTURE: IN SITU CONCRETE STRIP FOUNDATIONS										
Z1410	Traditional concrete strip foundation										
Z141055	Excavation; earthwork support; partial backfill; partial disposal off site; C20 concrete foundation 450 × 225 mm; 105 mm wall of Class B engineering bricks in cement mortar; Hyload d.p.c.; depth of trench:										
Z141055A	0.75 m	m	1.26	22.33	7.24	37.54	67.11	24.56	7.96	41.29	73.82
Z141055B	1.00 m	m	1.60	28.77	9.07	50.90	88.74	31.65	9.98	55.99	97.61
Z141055C	1.25 m	m	2.26	39.38	11.77	57.27	108.42	43.32	12.95	63.00	119.26
Z141055D	1.50 m	m	2.71	47.34	13.82	69.72	130.88	52.07	15.20	76.69	143.97
Z141060	Excavation; earthwork support; partial backfill; partial disposal off site; C20 concrete foundation 600 × 225 mm; cavity wall construction; 100 mm concrete blockwork outer leaf in gauged mortar; three course brickwork in gauged mortar where exposed as facework; 75 mm cavity with lean mix concrete C7.5 fill; 125 mm concrete block inner leaf; Hyload d.p.c.; 0.975 m footing depth; exposed external face:										
Z141060A	3 course high common bricks	m	2.39	94.67	15.81	45.69	156.17	104.14	17.39	50.26	171.79
Z141060C	3 course high facing bricks PC £350.00/1000	m	2.41	95.23	15.81	47.28	158.32	104.75	17.39	52.01	174.15
Z141060E	3 course high facing bricks PC £475.00/1000	m	2.41	95.23	15.81	49.03	160.07	104.75	17.39	53.93	176.08
Z141065	Excavation; earthwork support; partial backfill; partial disposal off site; C20 concrete foundation 600 × 225 mm; cavity wall construction; 100 mm concrete blockwork outer leaf in gauged mortar; three course brickwork in gauged mortar where exposed as facework; 75 mm cavity with lean mix concrete C7.5 fill; 125 mm concrete block inner leaf; Hyload d.p.c.; 1.425 m footing depth; exposed external face:										
Z141065A	3 course high common bricks	m	3.55	119.19	23.15	64.19	206.53	131.11	25.47	70.61	227.18
Z141065C	3 course high facing bricks PC £350.00/1000	m	3.64	120.63	23.15	65.79	209.57	132.69	25.47	72.37	230.53
Z141065E	3 course high facing bricks PC £475.00/1000	m	3.57	119.74	23.33	67.54	210.61	131.71	25.66	74.29	231.67

Approximate Estimating Rates

Major Works 2009		Unit	Labour Hours	Labour Net	Plant Net	Materials Net	Unit Net	Labour Gross	Plant Gross	Materials Gross	Unit Price
								— (Gross rates include 10% profit) —			
				£	£	£	£	£	£	£	£
Z14	**SUBSTRUCTURE: IN SITU CONCRETE STRIP FOUNDATIONS**										
Z1420	**Trench fill foundation**										
Z142010	Excavation; disposal off site; C10 concrete trench fill foundation 600 mm wide; three courses facing brickwork externally (PC £250:00/1000) on single course blockwork; two courses block inner skin; cavity with lean mix fill; depth of trench:										
Z142010A	0.75 m	m	1.61	29.38	10.82	50.82	91.02	32.32	11.90	55.90	100.12
Z142010B	1.00 m	m	1.87	32.69	14.71	66.84	114.24	35.96	16.18	73.52	125.66
Z142010C	1.25 m	m	2.31	38.28	19.25	82.96	140.49	42.11	21.18	91.26	154.54
Z142010D	1.50 m	m	2.60	41.96	23.14	98.98	164.08	46.16	25.45	108.88	180.49
Z142015	Excavation; disposal off site; C20 concrete trench fill foundation 600 mm wide; two skins of common bricks six courses high in cement mortar; cavity with lean mix fill; Hyload d.p.c.; depth of trench:										
Z142015A	0.75 m	m	1.65	30.39	10.82	55.53	96.74	33.43	11.90	61.08	106.41
Z142015B	1.00 m	m	1.91	33.69	14.71	69.86	118.26	37.06	16.18	76.85	130.09
Z142015C	1.25 m	m	2.35	39.28	19.25	85.98	144.51	43.21	21.18	94.58	158.96
Z142015D	1.50 m	m	2.64	42.97	23.14	102.00	168.11	47.27	25.45	112.20	184.92
Z142020	Excavation; earthwork support; disposal off site; C20 concrete foundation 600 mm wide; 215 mm wall of common bricks six courses high in cement mortar; Hyload d.p.c.; depth of trench:										
Z142020A	0.75 m	m	1.52	27.50	10.63	52.88	91.01	30.25	11.69	58.17	100.11
Z142020B	1.00 m	m	1.78	30.81	14.52	68.90	114.23	33.89	15.97	75.79	125.65
Z142020C	1.25 m	m	2.22	36.40	19.07	85.02	140.49	40.04	20.98	93.52	154.54
Z142020D	1.50 m	m	2.51	40.08	22.95	101.04	164.07	44.09	25.25	111.14	180.48
Z142025	Excavation; earthwork support; disposal off site; C20 concrete foundation 600 m wide; 105 mm wall of common bricks six courses high in cement mortar; Hyload d.p.c.; depth of trench:										
Z142025A	0.75 m	m	1.24	19.97	10.66	42.31	72.94	21.97	11.73	46.54	80.23
Z142025B	1.00 m	m	1.50	23.27	14.55	58.33	96.15	25.60	16.01	64.16	105.77
Z142025C	1.25 m	m	1.94	28.86	19.09	74.45	122.40	31.75	21.00	81.90	134.64
Z142025D	1.50 m	m	2.23	32.55	22.98	90.47	146.00	35.81	25.28	99.52	160.60
Z142030	Excavation; earthwork support; disposal off site; C20 concrete foundation 450 mm wide; three course facings on single course of blockwork outer leaf; block inner leaf; cavity with lean mix fill; Hyload d.p.c.; depth of trench:										
Z142030A	0.75 m	m	1.41	26.85	8.24	43.94	79.03	29.54	9.06	48.33	86.93
Z142030B	1.00 m	m	1.64	29.77	11.16	56.36	97.29	32.75	12.28	62.00	107.02
Z142030C	1.25 m	m	2.04	34.85	14.52	68.78	118.15	38.34	15.97	75.66	129.97
Z142030D	1.50 m	m	2.28	37.90	17.63	81.20	136.73	41.69	19.39	89.32	150.40

Major Works 2009		Unit	Labour Hours	Labour Net	Plant Net	Materials Net	Unit Net	Labour Gross	Plant Gross	Materials Gross	Unit Price
								(Gross rates include 10% profit)			
				£	£	£	£	£	£	£	£
Z14	**SUBSTRUCTURE: IN SITU CONCRETE STRIP FOUNDATIONS**										
Z1420	**Trench fill foundation**										
Z142035	**Excavation; earthwork support; disposal off site; C20 concrete foundation 450 m wide; two skins 105 mm common bricks six courses high in cement mortar; cavity with lean mix fill; Hyload d.p.c.; depth of trench:**										
Z142035A	0.75 m	m	1.47	28.11	8.24	46.91	83.26	30.92	9.06	51.60	91.59
Z142035B	1.00 m	m	1.68	30.78	11.16	59.33	101.27	33.86	12.28	65.26	111.40
Z142035C	1.25 m	m	2.08	35.85	14.52	71.75	122.12	39.44	15.97	78.93	134.33
Z142035D	1.50 m	m	2.32	38.90	17.63	84.17	140.70	42.79	19.39	92.59	154.77
Z142040	**Excavation; earthwork support; disposal off site; C20 concrete foundation 450 mm wide; 215 mm wall of common bricks six courses high in cement mortar; Hyload d.p.c.; depth of trench:**										
Z142040A	0.75 m	m	1.35	25.35	8.05	45.95	79.35	27.89	8.86	50.55	87.29
Z142040B	1.00 m	m	1.56	28.00	11.16	58.37	97.53	30.80	12.28	64.21	107.28
Z142040C	1.25 m	m	1.96	33.09	14.52	70.79	118.40	36.40	15.97	77.87	130.24
Z142040D	1.50 m	m	2.20	36.14	17.45	83.22	136.81	39.75	19.20	91.54	150.49
Z142045	**Excavation; earthwork support; disposal off site; C20 concrete foundation 450 mm wide; 105 mm wall of common bricks six courses high in cement mortar; Hyload d.p.c.; depth of trench:**										
Z142045A	0.75 m	m	1.07	17.81	7.89	35.20	60.90	19.59	8.68	38.72	66.99
Z142045B	1.00 m	m	1.28	20.48	10.82	47.62	78.92	22.53	11.90	52.38	86.81
Z142045C	1.25 m	m	1.68	25.56	14.18	60.04	99.78	28.12	15.60	66.04	109.76
Z142045D	1.50 m	m	1.92	28.60	16.89	72.46	117.95	31.46	18.58	79.71	129.75
Z142050	**Excavation; earthwork support; disposal off site; C20 concrete foundation 450 m wide; 100 mm wall of concrete blocks 450 mm high in cement mortar; Hyload d.p.c.; depth of trench:**										
Z142050A	0.75 m	m	1.26	23.45	7.89	40.79	72.13	25.80	8.68	44.87	79.34
Z142050B	1.00 m	m	1.47	26.13	10.82	53.21	90.16	28.74	11.90	58.53	99.18
Z142050C	1.25 m	m	1.94	32.09	14.18	64.72	110.99	35.30	15.60	71.19	122.09
Z142050D	1.50 m	m	2.11	34.25	16.89	78.05	129.19	37.68	18.58	85.86	142.11

Approximate Estimating Rates

Major Works 2009		Unit	Labour Hours	Labour Net	Plant Net	Materials Net	Unit Net	Labour Gross	Plant Gross	Materials Gross	Unit Price
								(Gross rates include 10% profit)			
				£	£	£	£	£	£	£	£
Z14	**SUBSTRUCTURE: IN SITU CONCRETE STRIP FOUNDATIONS**										
Z1420	**Trench fill foundation**										
Z142060	Excavation; earthwork support; partial backfill; partial disposal off site; C20 concrete trench fill foundation 600 mm wide; cavity wall construction; 100 mm concrete blockwork outer leaf in gauged mortar; three course brickwork in gauged mortar where exposed as facework; 75 mm cavity with lean mix concrete C7.5 fill; 125 mm concrete block inner leaf; Hyload d.p.c.; 0.975 m footing depth; exposed external face:										
Z142060A	3 course high common bricks	m	0.80	156.85	16.28	48.33	221.46	172.54	17.91	53.16	243.61
Z142060C	3 course high facing bricks PC £350.00/1000	m	0.82	157.39	16.28	49.92	223.59	173.13	17.91	54.91	245.95
Z142060E	3 course high facing bricks PC £475.00/1000	m	0.82	157.39	16.28	51.67	225.34	173.13	17.91	56.84	247.87
Z142065	Excavation; earthwork support; partial backfill; partial disposal off site; C20 concrete trench fill foundation 600 mm wide; cavity wall construction; 100 mm concrete blockwork outer leaf in gauged mortar; three course brickwork in gauged mortar where exposed as facework; 75 mm cavity with lean mix concrete C7.5 fill; 125 mm concrete block inner leaf; Hyload d.p.c.; 1.425 m footing depth; exposed external face:										
Z142065A	3 course high common bricks	m	0.87	249.82	24.06	70.07	343.95	274.80	26.47	77.08	378.35
Z142065C	3 course high facing bricks PC £350.00/1000	m	0.82	249.49	16.28	71.67	337.44	274.44	17.91	78.84	371.18
Z142065E	3 course high facing bricks PC £475.00/1000	m	0.82	249.49	16.28	73.42	339.19	274.44	17.91	80.76	373.11

Major Works 2009		Unit	Labour Hours	Labour Net	Plant Net	Materials Net	Unit Net	Labour Gross	Plant Gross	Materials Gross	Unit Price
								(Gross rates include 10% profit)			
				£	£	£	£	£	£	£	£
Z15	**SUBSTRUCTURE: IN SITU CONCRETE GROUND BEAMS**										
Z1510	**Reinforced concrete ground beams**										
Z151010	**Excavate; earthwork support; disposal off site; construct formwork; in situ concrete C30 N/mm^2; steel bar reinforcement; ground beam size:**										
Z151010A	900 × 600 mm thick	m	9.46	142.78	33.21	197.75	373.74	157.06	36.53	217.53	411.11
Z151010B	1050 × 600 mm thick	m	10.10	151.67	37.19	222.45	411.31	166.84	40.91	244.70	452.44
Z151010C	1200 × 600 mm thick	m	10.73	160.55	41.17	247.06	448.78	176.61	45.29	271.77	493.66
Z151010D	900 × 750 mm thick	m	10.82	161.29	41.51	235.19	437.99	177.42	45.66	258.71	481.79
Z151010E	1050 × 750 mm thick	m	11.60	172.24	46.51	265.57	484.32	189.46	51.16	292.13	532.75
Z151010F	1200 × 750 mm thick	m	12.37	183.15	51.47	295.95	530.57	201.47	56.62	325.55	583.63
Z151010G	1500 × 750 mm thick	m	13.92	204.96	61.34	356.41	622.71	225.46	67.47	392.05	684.98
Z151010H	1050 × 900 mm thick	m	13.10	192.77	55.79	308.69	557.25	212.05	61.37	339.56	612.98
Z151010I	1200 × 900 mm thick	m	14.04	206.10	61.76	345.60	613.46	226.71	67.94	380.16	674.81
Z151010J	1500 × 900 mm thick	m	15.94	232.75	73.71	419.52	725.98	256.03	81.08	461.47	798.58
Z151010K	1200 × 1050 mm thick . . .	m	15.96	231.42	72.05	396.27	699.74	254.56	79.26	435.90	769.71
Z151010L	1500 × 1050 mm thick . . .	m	18.17	262.50	86.00	482.49	830.99	288.75	94.60	530.74	914.09
Z151010M	1800 × 1050 mm thick . . .	m	20.37	293.59	99.94	568.81	962.34	322.95	109.93	625.69	1058.57
Z151010N	1200 × 1200 mm thick . . .	m	18.24	264.57	82.35	453.15	800.07	291.03	90.59	498.47	880.08
Z151010O	1500 × 1200 mm thick . . .	m	20.77	300.10	98.28	551.67	950.05	330.11	108.11	606.84	1045.06
Z151010P	1800 × 1200 mm thick . . .	m	23.29	335.63	114.21	650.29	1100.13	369.19	125.63	715.32	1210.14

Approximate Estimating Rates

Major Works 2009		Unit	Labour Hours	Labour Net	Plant Net	Materials Net	Unit Net	Labour Gross	Plant Gross	Materials Gross	Unit Price
								(Gross rates include 10% profit)			
				£	£	£	£	£	£	£	£
Z20	**SUPERSTRUCTURE: FRAME**										
Z2010	**Concrete frame**										
Z201010	**Reinforced concrete column; in situ concrete C20; 80 kg/m³ high yield steel bar reinforcement; formwork to fair finish; column size:**										
Z201010E	250 × 250mm	m	2.66	43.83	3.05	32.23	79.11	48.21	3.36	35.45	87.02
Z201015	**Reinforced concrete columns; in situ concrete C25-20mm aggregate; 120kg/m³ high yield steel bar reinforcement; formwork to fair finish; column size:**										
Z201015F	500 × 300mm	m	4.19	75.37	4.14	63.26	142.77	82.91	4.55	69.59	157.05
Z201015H	600 × 300mm	m	4.90	88.20	4.86	72.49	165.55	97.02	5.35	79.74	182.11
Z201015K	900 × 300mm	m	6.68	121.09	7.01	100.09	228.19	133.20	7.71	110.10	251.01
Z201017	**Reinforced concrete columns; in situ concrete C25-20mm aggregate; 180kg/m³ high yield steel bar reinforcement; formwork to fair finish; column size:**										
Z201017F	500 × 300mm	m	4.52	80.31	4.14	67.02	151.47	88.34	4.55	73.72	166.62
Z201017H	600 × 300mm	m	5.30	94.14	4.86	77.11	176.11	103.55	5.35	84.82	193.72
Z201017K	900 × 300mm	m	7.29	130.01	7.01	107.60	244.62	143.01	7.71	118.36	269.08
Z201018	**Reinforced concrete columns; in situ concrete C25-20mm aggregate; 240kg/m³ high yield steel bar reinforcement; formwork to fair finish; column size:**										
Z201018F	500 × 300mm	m	4.86	85.28	4.14	71.16	160.58	93.81	4.55	78.28	176.64
Z201018H	600 × 300mm	m	5.70	100.09	4.86	82.11	187.06	110.10	5.35	90.32	205.77
Z201018K	900 × 300mm	m	7.89	138.93	7.01	114.65	260.59	152.82	7.71	126.12	286.65
Z201020	**Reinforced concrete column; in situ concrete C20; 120 kg/m³ high yield steel bar reinforcement; formwork to fair finish; column size:**										
Z201020D	350 × 300mm	m	3.66	59.57	4.78	49.74	114.09	65.53	5.26	54.71	125.50
Z201020G	500 × 300mm	m	4.66	75.38	6.59	65.47	147.44	82.92	7.25	72.02	162.18
Z201020H	550 × 300mm	m	5.12	82.77	7.19	70.76	160.72	91.05	7.91	77.84	176.79
Z201020I	600 × 300mm	m	5.47	88.29	7.80	76.01	172.10	97.12	8.58	83.61	189.31
Z201020L	900 × 300mm	m	7.53	121.16	11.42	107.57	240.15	133.28	12.56	118.33	264.17
Z201022	**Plain concrete casing to steel column; in situ concrete C25-20mm aggregate; formwork to fair finish; column size:**										
Z201022F	500 × 300mm	m	3.52	65.45	4.14	53.95	123.54	72.00	4.55	59.35	135.89
Z201022H	600 × 300mm	m	4.09	76.31	4.86	61.53	142.70	83.94	5.35	67.68	156.97
Z201022K	900 × 300mm	m	5.48	103.25	7.01	84.52	194.78	113.58	7.71	92.97	214.26

Major Works 2009		Unit	Labour Hours	Labour Net	Plant Net	Materials Net	Unit Net	Labour Gross	Plant Gross	Materials Gross	Unit Price
								(Gross rates include 10% profit)			
				£	£	£	£	£	£	£	£
Z20	**SUPERSTRUCTURE: FRAME**										
Z2010	**Concrete frame**										
Z201025	**Reinforced attached concrete beams; in situ concrete C25-20mm aggregate; 200kg/m³ high yield steel bar reinforcement; formwork to fair finish; beam size:**										
Z201025C	225 × 450mm	m	2.73	48.61	2.63	41.83	93.07	53.47	2.89	46.01	102.38
Z201025E	300 × 600mm	m	4.05	72.59	4.31	63.11	140.01	79.85	4.74	69.42	154.01
Z201025G	450 × 600mm	m	5.38	97.12	6.19	86.19	189.50	106.83	6.81	94.81	208.45
Z201025K	600 × 600mm	m	6.84	123.88	8.07	109.72	241.67	136.27	8.88	120.69	265.84
Z201027	**Reinforced attached concrete beams; in situ concrete C25-20mm aggregate; 240kg/m³ high yield steel bar reinforcement; formwork to fair finish; beam size:**										
Z201027C	225 × 450mm	m	2.88	50.83	2.63	43.94	97.40	55.91	2.89	48.33	107.14
Z201027E	300 × 600mm	m	4.31	76.56	4.31	66.48	147.35	84.22	4.74	73.13	162.09
Z201027G	450 × 600mm	m	5.78	103.07	6.19	91.20	200.46	113.38	6.81	100.32	220.51
Z201027K	600 × 600mm	m	7.37	131.82	8.07	116.93	256.82	145.00	8.88	128.62	282.50
Z201029	**In situ concrete casing to steel beams; concrete C25-20mm aggregate; formwork to fair finish; beam size:**										
Z201029C	225 × 450mm	m	1.98	37.45	2.63	31.73	71.81	41.20	2.89	34.90	78.99
Z201029E	300 × 600mm	m	2.71	52.77	4.31	45.90	102.98	58.05	4.74	50.49	113.28
Z201029G	450 × 600mm	m	3.37	67.38	6.19	61.07	134.64	74.12	6.81	67.18	148.10
Z201029K	600 × 600mm	m	4.16	84.25	8.07	76.24	168.56	92.68	8.88	83.86	185.42
Z2050	**Steel frame**										
Z205010	**Structural steel framing; columns; universal columns; grade S355 JR; shot blasted and primed at works; size**										
Z205010F	356 × 368mm × 202kg/m	Tonne	22.00	537.46	230.00	933.04	1700.50	591.21	253.00	1026.34	1870.55
Z205010H	356 × 406mm × 235kg/m	Tonne	21.00	513.03	230.00	933.04	1676.07	564.33	253.00	1026.34	1843.68
Z205020	**Structural steel framing; columns; rectangular hollow sections; grade S355 JR; shot blasted and primed at works; size**										
Z205020D	300 × 200mm × 12.5mm × 92.6kg/m	Tonne	28.00	684.04	316.25	1021.90	2022.19	752.44	347.88	1124.09	2224.41
Z205020F	400 × 200mm × 16.0mm × 142kg/m	Tonne	26.00	635.18	287.50	1055.95	1978.63	698.70	316.25	1161.55	2176.49
Z205020H	450 × 250mm × 16.0mm × 167kg/m	Tonne	24.00	586.32	258.75	1055.95	1901.02	644.95	284.63	1161.55	2091.12

Approximate Estimating Rates

Major Works 2009		Unit	Labour Hours	Labour Net	Plant Net	Materials Net	Unit Net	Labour Gross	Plant Gross	Materials Gross	Unit Price
								(Gross rates include 10% profit)			
				£	£	£	£	£	£	£	£
Z21	SUPERSTRUCTURE: UPPER FLOOR										
Z2130	Timber suspended floors										
Z213010	22 mm s.w. T&G floor boarding; 12.5 mm plasterboard and skim coat plaster soffit; two coat emulsion; preservative treated s.w. SC3 joists at 400 mm centres with mid span herringbone strutting; joist size:										
Z213010A	38 × 175 mm	m²	1.68	30.66	–	31.59	62.25	33.73	–	34.75	68.48
Z213010B	38 × 200 mm	m²	1.72	31.33	–	32.43	63.76	34.46	–	35.67	70.14
Z213010C	38 × 225 mm	m²	1.70	31.00	–	33.17	64.17	34.10	–	36.49	70.59
Z213010D	47 × 175 mm	m²	1.70	31.00	–	33.26	64.26	34.10	–	36.59	70.69
Z213010E	47 × 200 mm	m²	1.72	31.34	–	34.17	65.51	34.47	–	37.59	72.06
Z213010F	47 × 225 mm	m²	1.73	31.51	–	35.13	66.64	34.66	–	38.64	73.30
Z213012	Joisted floor; plasterboard and skim ceiling; emulsion; 22 mm t&g chipboard flooring; vinyl floor finish; sw skirtings, decorated; joist size:										
Z213012A	50 × 200 mm at 400 cs	m²	2.27	40.66	–	50.57	91.23	44.73	–	55.63	100.35
Z213015	22 mm V313 chipboard flooring; 12.5 mm plasterboard and skim coat plaster soffit; two coat emulsion; preservative treated s.w. SC3 joists at 400 mm centres with mid span herringbone strutting; joist size:										
Z213015A	38 × 175 mm	m²	1.43	26.41	–	17.95	44.36	29.05	–	19.75	48.80
Z213015B	38 × 200 mm	m²	1.47	27.09	–	18.78	45.87	29.80	–	20.66	50.46
Z213015C	38 × 225 mm	m²	1.45	26.75	–	19.53	46.28	29.43	–	21.48	50.91
Z213015D	47 × 175 mm	m²	1.45	26.76	–	19.61	46.37	29.44	–	21.57	51.01
Z213015E	47 × 200 mm	m²	1.47	27.10	–	20.52	47.62	29.81	–	22.57	52.38
Z213015F	47 × 225 mm	m²	1.48	27.27	–	21.48	48.75	30.00	–	23.63	53.63

Major Works 2009		Unit	Labour Hours	Labour Net	Plant Net	Materials Net	Unit Net	Labour Gross	Plant Gross	Materials Gross	Unit Price
				£	£	£	£	£	£	£	£
								(Gross rates include 10% profit)			
Z22	**SUPERSTRUCTURE: ROOF**										
Z2210	**Pitched roof structures and coverings**										
Z221002	**Roof tiling; coverings including battens and underfelt; proportion of eaves and ventilation unit, verge and ridge to typical roofing layout; measured on slope**										
Z221002A	Sandtoft Old English clay pantiles	m²	0.94	15.96	–	31.24	47.20	17.56	–	34.36	51.92
Z221002C	Redland clay pantiles	m²	0.94	15.96	–	27.84	43.80	17.56	–	30.62	48.18
Z221002G	Clay plain tile coverings	m²	2.36	40.07	–	47.35	87.42	44.08	–	52.09	96.16
Z221002L	Eternit 2000 slate coverings	m²	0.86	14.53	–	28.50	43.03	15.98	–	31.35	47.33
Z221002N	Welsh slate coverings	m²	0.85	14.36	–	74.52	88.88	15.80	–	81.97	97.77
Z221002P	Spanish slate coverings	m²	1.38	23.36	–	29.74	53.10	25.70	–	32.71	58.41
Z221002S	Westerland man-made slate coverings	m²	0.87	14.79	–	21.68	36.47	16.27	–	23.85	40.12
Z221002U	Reconstituted interlocking slate coverings	m²	0.74	12.53	–	53.76	66.29	13.78	–	59.14	72.92
Z221010	**Redland concrete tiles; felt; battens; gangnail roof trusses 600 mm centres; bracing; plates; straps; ridges; eaves ventilation; 150 mm glassfibre roof insulation; 12.5 mm plasterboard skim coated soffit; emulsion paint; pitch:**										
Z221010A	30 degrees.	m²	2.11	37.70	–	55.81	93.51	41.47	–	61.39	102.86
Z221010B	35 degrees.	m²	2.14	38.21	–	56.76	94.97	42.03	–	62.44	104.47
Z221010C	40 degrees.	m²	2.18	38.89	–	58.57	97.46	42.78	–	64.43	107.21
Z221010D	45 degrees.	m²	2.26	40.25	–	59.42	99.67	44.28	–	65.36	109.64
Z221015	**Sandtoft clay tiles; felt; battens; gangnail roof trusses 600 mm centres; bracing; plates; straps; ridges; eaves ventilation; 150 mm glassfibre roof insulation; 12.5 mm plasterboard skim coated soffit; emulsion paint; pitch:**										
Z221015A	30 degrees.	m²	2.25	40.08	–	96.83	136.91	44.09	–	106.51	150.60
Z221015B	35 degrees.	m²	2.29	40.76	–	97.48	138.24	44.84	–	107.23	152.06
Z221015C	40 degrees.	m²	2.36	41.94	–	98.41	140.35	46.13	–	108.25	154.39
Z221015D	45 degrees.	m²	2.44	43.31	–	110.50	153.81	47.64	–	121.55	169.19
Z221050	**Welsh slate; felt; battens; gangnail roof trusses 600 mm centres; bracing; plates; straps; ridges; eaves ventilation; 150 mm glassfibre roof insulation; 12.5 mm plasterboard skim coated soffit; emulsion paint; pitch:**										
Z221050A	30 degrees.	m²	2.50	44.32	–	178.23	222.55	48.75	–	196.05	244.81
Z221050B	35 degrees.	m²	2.57	45.52	–	178.98	224.50	50.07	–	196.88	246.95
Z221050C	40 degrees.	m²	2.64	46.70	–	207.73	254.43	51.37	–	228.50	279.87
Z221050D	45 degrees.	m²	2.75	48.57	–	208.62	257.19	53.43	–	229.48	282.91

Approximate Estimating Rates

Major Works 2009		Unit	Labour Hours	Labour Net	Plant Net	Materials Net	Unit Net	Labour Gross	Plant Gross	Materials Gross	Unit Price
								(Gross rates include 10% profit)			
				£	£	£	£	£	£	£	£
Z22	**SUPERSTRUCTURE: ROOF**										
Z2210	**Pitched roof structures and coverings**										
Z221055	**Artificial slate; felt; battens; gangnail roof trusses 600 mm centres; bracing; plates; straps; ridges; eaves ventilation; 150 mm glassfibre roof insulation; 12.5 mm plasterboard skim coated soffit; emulsion paint; pitch:**										
Z221055A	30 degrees...............	m²	2.46	43.65	–	85.83	129.48	48.02	–	94.41	142.43
Z221055B	35 degrees...............	m²	2.52	44.67	–	96.17	140.84	49.14	–	105.79	154.92
Z221055C	40 degrees...............	m²	2.59	45.85	–	97.06	142.91	50.44	–	106.77	157.20
Z221055D	45 degrees...............	m²	2.69	47.55	–	98.11	145.66	52.31	–	107.92	160.23
Z221070	**Plastic coated galvanised profiled sheet cladding; fixed with drive screws; eaves filler and closure; bargeboards and two piece ridge capping; proportion of eaves, verge and capping**										
Z221070A	Profile 6 plastic coated steel corrugated profile sheets at 20 deg pitch	m²	0.33	11.20	–	21.95	33.15	12.32	–	24.15	36.47
Z221075	**Fibre cement profiled sheet cladding; fixed with drive screws; eaves filler and closure; bargeboards and two piece ridge capping; proportion of eaves, verge and capping**										
Z221075A	150 mm corrugated profile sheets at 20 deg pitch	m²	0.33	11.36	–	24.04	35.40	12.50	–	26.44	38.94

Major Works 2009		Unit	Labour Hours	Labour Net	Plant Net	Materials Net	Unit Net	Labour Gross	Plant Gross	Materials Gross	Unit Price
								(Gross rates include 10% profit)			
				£	£	£	£	£	£	£	£
Z22	**SUPERSTRUCTURE: ROOF**										
Z2210	**Pitched roof structures and coverings**										
Z221080	**Pitched roof structure; 40 deg roof trusses at 600mm centres; insulation; roof coverings; 20 × 150mm sw fascia; oil paint decorations; uPVC rainwater goods; plasterboard and skim; emulsion paint; measured on slope**										
Z221080A	concrete interlocking tiles ..	m²	1.57	28.12	–	43.21	71.33	30.93	–	47.53	78.46
Z221080C	Clay pantile coverings	m²	1.77	31.64	–	49.65	81.29	34.80	–	54.62	89.42
Z221080G	Clay plain tile coverings....	m²	3.19	55.76	–	65.78	121.54	61.34	–	72.36	133.69
Z221080L	Natural slate coverings	m²	1.68	30.04	–	99.72	129.76	33.04	–	109.69	142.74
Z221080N	Eternit 2000 slate coverings	m²	1.64	29.41	–	49.33	78.74	32.35	–	54.26	86.61
Z221080P	Reconstituted interlocking slate coverings	m²	1.61	28.93	–	85.84	114.77	31.82	–	94.42	126.25
Z221082	**Pitched roof structure; 40 deg roof trusses at 600mm centres; insulation; roof coverings; 20 × 150mm sw fascia; oil paint decorations; uPVC rainwater goods; plasterboard and skim; emulsion paint; measured on plan**										
Z221082A	Concrete interlocking tiles..	m²	2.02	36.18	–	56.03	92.21	39.80	–	61.63	101.43
Z221082C	Clay pantile coverings	m²	2.28	40.69	–	63.59	104.28	44.76	–	69.95	114.71
Z221082G	Clay plain tile coverings....	m²	4.11	71.69	–	84.04	155.73	78.86	–	92.44	171.30
Z221082L	Natural slate coverings	m²	2.16	38.62	–	123.35	161.97	42.48	–	135.69	178.17
Z221082N	Eternit 2000 slate coverings	m²	2.18	38.88	–	65.02	103.90	42.77	–	71.52	114.29
Z221082P	Reconstituted interlocking slate coverings	m²	2.08	37.18	–	103.63	140.81	40.90	–	113.99	154.89

Approximate Estimating Rates

Major Works 2009		Unit	Labour Hours	Labour Net	Plant Net	Materials Net	Unit Net	Labour Gross	Plant Gross	Materials Gross	Unit Price
								(Gross rates include 10% profit)			
				£	£	£	£	£	£	£	£
Z22	**SUPERSTRUCTURE: ROOF**										
Z2210	**Pitched roof structures and coverings**										
Z221084	**Pitched roof structure; 40 deg roof trusses at 600mm centres; insulation; roof coverings; 20 × 150mm sw fascia; oil paint decorations; uPVC rainwater goods; plasterboard and skim; emulsion paint; measured on GFA**										
Z221084A	Concrete interlocking tiles..	m²	2.66	47.72	–	71.99	119.71	52.49	–	79.19	131.68
Z221084C	Clay pantile coverings	m²	2.96	52.72	–	81.67	134.39	57.99	–	89.84	147.83
Z221084G	Clay Plain tile coverings....	m²	5.40	95.76	–	108.86	204.62	105.34	–	119.75	225.08
Z221084L	Natural slate coverings	m²	2.80	50.07	–	161.13	211.20	55.08	–	177.24	232.32
Z221084N	Eternit 2000 slate coverings	m²	2.75	49.18	–	83.32	132.50	54.10	–	91.65	145.75
Z221084P	Reconstituted interlocking slate coverings	m²	2.76	51.04	–	129.86	180.90	56.14	–	142.85	198.99
Z221090	**Standard trussed rafters; preservative treated and stress graded softwood; standard fink trusses; 450mm overhang at eaves**										
Z221090A	40 degree pitch; 7.00m span overall plates; plan area measure.................	m²	0.34	5.70	–	14.93	20.63	6.27	–	16.42	22.69
Z221090C	40 degree pitch; 7.00m span overall plates; GFA measure	m²	0.40	6.77	–	17.99	24.76	7.45	–	19.79	27.24
Z2215	**Flat roof structures and coverings**										
Z221502	**Reinforced concrete C35; in suspended slab; temporary formwork; no finishes:**										
Z221502A	150 mm thick; single layer A252 fabric	m²	3.97	60.75	6.64	40.15	107.54	66.83	7.30	44.17	118.29
Z221502D	200 mm thick; single layer A252 fabric	m²	3.97	60.74	6.64	44.94	112.32	66.81	7.30	49.43	123.55
Z221502F	250 mm thick; single layer B503 fabric	m²	3.97	60.75	6.64	48.46	115.85	66.83	7.30	53.31	127.44
Z221502H	300 mm thick; two layers B503 fabric	m²	3.97	60.75	6.64	52.39	119.78	66.83	7.30	57.63	131.76
Z221504	**Reinforced concrete C35; in suspended slab; Holorib permanent formwork weighing 14.3 Kg/m²; no finishes:**										
Z221504A	150 mm thick; single layer A252 fabric	m²	2.49	35.54	6.37	102.70	144.61	39.09	7.01	112.97	159.07
Z221504D	200 mm thick; single layer A252 fabric	m²	2.49	35.55	6.37	103.67	145.59	39.11	7.01	114.04	160.15
Z221504F	250 mm thick; single layer B503 fabric	m²	2.49	35.55	6.37	105.94	147.86	39.11	7.01	116.53	162.65
Z221504H	300 mm thick; two layers B503 fabric	m²	2.49	35.54	6.37	106.04	147.95	39.09	7.01	116.64	162.75

Major Works 2009		Unit	Labour Hours	Labour Net	Plant Net	Materials Net	Unit Net	Labour Gross	Plant Gross	Materials Gross	Unit Price
								(Gross rates include 10% profit)			
				£	£	£	£	£	£	£	£
Z22	**SUPERSTRUCTURE: ROOF**										
Z2215	**Flat roof structures and coverings**										
Z221510	**Three layer glassfibre based felt; chippings; 25 mm s.w. T&G boarding and firrings; joists at 400 mm centres; solid strutting; plates; straps; 150 mm insulation; d.p.m.; 12.5 mm foil backed skimmed plasterboard; joist size:**										
Z221510A	38 × 150 mm	m²	2.97	56.44	0.77	71.48	128.69	62.08	0.85	78.63	141.56
Z221510B	38 × 175 mm	m²	2.99	56.77	0.77	72.19	129.73	62.45	0.85	79.41	142.70
Z221510C	38 × 200 mm	m²	3.00	56.94	0.77	72.98	130.69	62.63	0.85	80.28	143.76
Z221510D	50 × 150 mm	m²	3.00	56.95	0.77	72.89	130.61	62.65	0.85	80.18	143.67
Z221510E	50 × 175 mm	m²	3.01	57.11	0.77	73.83	131.71	62.82	0.85	81.21	144.88
Z221510F	50 × 200 mm	m²	3.02	57.28	0.77	74.83	132.88	63.01	0.85	82.31	146.17
Z221515	**Three layer glassfibre based felt; chippings; 25 mm WBP ply boarding and firrings; joists at 400 mm centres; solid strutting; plates; straps; 150 mm insulation; d.p.m.; 12.5 mm foil backed skimmed plasterboard; joist size:**										
Z221515A	38 × 150 mm	m²	2.71	52.02	0.77	69.19	121.98	57.22	0.85	76.11	134.18
Z221515B	38 × 175 mm	m²	2.73	52.37	0.77	69.90	123.04	57.61	0.85	76.89	135.34
Z221515C	38 × 200 mm	m²	2.74	52.54	0.77	70.68	123.99	57.79	0.85	77.75	136.39
Z221515D	50 × 150 mm	m²	2.74	52.53	0.77	70.60	123.90	57.78	0.85	77.66	136.29
Z221515E	50 × 175 mm	m²	2.75	52.71	0.77	71.53	125.01	57.98	0.85	78.68	137.51
Z221515F	50 × 200 mm	m²	2.76	52.88	0.77	72.53	126.18	58.17	0.85	79.78	138.80
Z221520	**Three layer glassfibre based felt; chippings; 22 mm V313 T&G boarding and firrings; joists at 400 mm centres; solid strutting; plates; straps; 150 mm insulation; d.p.m.; 12.5 mm foil backed skimmed plasterboard; joist size:**										
Z221520A	38 × 150 mm	m²	2.76	52.88	0.77	57.00	110.65	58.17	0.85	62.70	121.72
Z221520B	38 × 175 mm	m²	2.78	53.21	0.77	57.71	111.69	58.53	0.85	63.48	122.86
Z221520C	38 × 200 mm	m²	2.79	53.38	0.77	58.50	112.65	58.72	0.85	64.35	123.92
Z221520D	50 × 150 mm	m²	2.79	53.39	0.77	58.41	112.57	58.73	0.85	64.25	123.83
Z221520E	50 × 175 mm	m²	2.80	53.55	0.77	59.34	113.66	58.91	0.85	65.27	125.03
Z221520F	50 × 200 mm	m²	2.81	53.72	0.77	60.34	114.83	59.09	0.85	66.37	126.31

Approximate Estimating Rates

Major Works 2009		Unit	Labour Hours	Labour Net	Plant Net	Materials Net	Unit Net	Labour Gross	Plant Gross	Materials Gross	Unit Price
								(Gross rates include 10% profit)			
				£	£	£	£	£	£	£	£
Z22	SUPERSTRUCTURE: ROOF										
Z2215	Flat roof structures and coverings										
Z221550	Steel roof decking; 0.70 mm thick; 100 mm Kingspan Thermaroof TR20 insulation:										
Z221550A	Three layer built up felt roofing; chippings	m²	1.02	23.52	–	50.69	74.21	25.87	–	55.76	81.63
Z221552	Aluminium roof decking; 0.90 mm thick; 100 mm Kingspan Thermaroof TR20 insulation:										
Z221552A	Three layer built up felt roofing; vapour control membrane...............	m²	1.06	24.13	–	57.14	81.27	26.54	–	62.85	89.40
Z221560	Single layer roofing; polymer roofing membrane; 50mm Kingspan Thermaroof TR31 insulation board; vapour barrier:										
Z221560A	Sarnafil G410-EL	m²	1.18	25.87	–	45.62	71.49	28.46	–	50.18	78.64
Z221561	Single layer roofing; polymer roofing membrane; 50mm Rockwool tapered insulation board; vapour barrier:										
Z221561A	Sarnafil G410-EL	m²	1.20	26.21	–	54.11	80.32	28.83	–	59.52	88.35

Major Works 2009	Unit	Labour Hours	Labour Net	Plant Net	Materials Net	Unit Net	Labour Gross	Plant Gross	Materials Gross	Unit Price
			£	£	£	£	£ (Gross rates include 10% profit)	£	£	£
Z22	**SUPERSTRUCTURE: ROOF**									
Z2220	**Fascias, soffits, rainwater goods**									
Z222005	**Eaves to sloping roof; 25 × 150mm grooved softwood fascia; 225 × 6mm Masterboard; decorations:**									
Z222005A	112mm uPVC gutter	m	1.17	26.63	–	14.50	41.13	29.29	–	15.95	45.24
Z222005D	150mm uPVC gutter	m	1.19	27.40	–	28.17	55.57	30.14	–	30.99	61.13
Z222005G	100mm cast iron gutter; decorated	m	1.48	34.01	–	24.77	58.78	37.41	–	27.25	64.66
Z222005J	150mm cast iron gutter; decorated	m	1.60	38.69	–	41.03	79.72	42.56	–	45.13	87.69
Z222010	**25 × 150 mm grooved softwood fascia; 9 mm thick Supalux soffit 250 mm wide; 25 × 38 mm softwood batten to masonry; gutter and fittings:**									
Z222010A	112 mm diameter half round uPVC	m	1.24	28.76	–	17.60	46.36	31.64	–	19.36	51.00
Z222010B	100 mm Squareline uPVC ..	m	1.24	28.76	–	18.32	47.08	31.64	–	20.15	51.79
Z222012	**25 × 175 mm grooved softwood fascia; 9 mm thick Supalux soffit 250 mm wide; 25 × 38 mm softwood batten to masonry; gutter and fittings:**									
Z222012A	112 mm diameter half round uPVC	m	1.25	28.93	–	18.13	47.06	31.82	–	19.94	51.77
Z222012B	100 mm Squareline uPVC ..	m	1.25	28.93	–	18.67	47.60	31.82	–	20.54	52.36
Z222014	**25 × 200 mm grooved softwood fascia; 9 mm thick Supalux soffit 250 mm wide; 25 × 38 mm softwood batten to masonry; gutter and fittings:**									
Z222014A	112 mm diameter half round uPVC	m	1.26	29.10	–	18.52	47.62	32.01	–	20.37	52.38
Z222014B	100 mm Squareline uPVC ..	m	1.26	29.10	–	19.24	48.34	32.01	–	21.16	53.17
Z222025	**Edges to felt flat roofs:**									
Z222025A	Softwood angle fillet; 25 × 225mm softwood fascia; decorated in oil paint; aluminium edge trim	m	0.77	12.99	–	17.73	30.72	14.29	–	19.50	33.79
Z222025D	Softwood fascia 25 × 225mm; decorated in oil paint; 110mm uPVC gutter .	m	0.80	13.58	–	18.12	31.70	14.94	–	19.93	34.87
Z222025G	Softwood fascia 25 × 225mm; decorated in oil paint; 100mm cast iron gutter; decorated in oil paint	m	1.21	31.86	–	32.79	64.65	35.05	–	36.07	71.12

Approximate Estimating Rates

Major Works 2009		Unit	Labour Hours	Labour Net	Plant Net	Materials Net	Unit Net	Labour Gross	Plant Gross	Materials Gross	Unit Price
								(Gross rates include 10% profit)			
				£	£	£	£	£	£	£	£
Z22	SUPERSTRUCTURE: ROOF										
Z2230	Rainwater gutter and downpipe systems										
Z223085	Rainwater gutters and downpipes complete with all fittings; average single storey structure:										
Z223085A	112 mm Osma RoofLine uPVC gutter..............	m	0.46	18.00	–	8.73	26.73	19.80	–	9.60	29.40
Z223085B	100 mm Osma SquareLine uPVC gutter..............	m	0.51	19.20	–	10.57	29.77	21.12	–	11.63	32.75
Z223086	Rainwater gutters and downpipes complete with all fittings; average two storey structure:										
Z223086A	112 mm Osma RoofLine uPVC gutter..............	m	0.53	20.65	–	9.83	30.48	22.72	–	10.81	33.53
Z223086B	100 mm Osma SquareLine uPVC gutter..............	m	0.57	21.86	–	11.70	33.56	24.05	–	12.87	36.92
Z223090	Rainwater pipes; fixed to masonry backgrounds; including offsets and shoes:										
Z223090A	UPVC; 68 mm dia; single storey.................	m	0.59	22.88	–	9.81	32.69	25.17	–	10.79	35.96
Z223090B	UPVC; 68 mm dia; two storey	m	0.45	17.43	–	7.38	24.81	19.17	–	8.12	27.29
Z223090E	UPVC; 110 mm dia; single storey.................	m	0.60	23.35	–	30.38	53.73	25.69	–	33.42	59.10
Z223090F	UPVC; 110 mm dia; two storey.................	m	0.48	18.60	–	20.22	38.82	20.46	–	22.24	42.70
Z223090J	Cast iron; 75 mm dia; single storey.................	m	0.86	28.62	–	57.13	85.75	31.48	–	62.84	94.33
Z223090K	Cast iron; 75 mm dia; two storey.................	m	0.72	23.17	–	33.99	57.16	25.49	–	37.39	62.88
Z223090P	Cast iron; 100 mm dia; single storey.................	m	0.93	31.35	–	62.75	94.10	34.49	–	69.03	103.51
Z223090Q	Cast iron; 100 mm dia; two storey.................	m	0.78	25.51	–	48.61	74.12	28.06	–	53.47	81.53

Major Works 2009		Unit	Labour Hours	Labour Net	Plant Net	Materials Net	Unit Net	Labour Gross	Plant Gross	Materials Gross	Unit Price
								(Gross rates include 10% profit)			
				£	£	£	£	£	£	£	£
Z22	**SUPERSTRUCTURE: ROOF**										
Z2260	**Rooflights, patent glazing and glazed roofs**										
Z226010	**Velux rooflights type GGL 3073; complete with tile flashing; shaft construction and finishings; rooflight ref:**										
Z226010D	M04: 780 × 980mm	Nr	4.39	79.25	–	347.19	426.44	87.18	–	381.91	469.08
Z226050	**Room dome; triple skin polycarbonate; complete with matching upstand; fixing in position; size:**										
Z226050C	950 × 950mm	Nr	3.00	50.94	–	617.61	668.55	56.03	–	679.37	735.41
Z226050F	1250 × 1250mm	Nr	4.00	67.92	–	1062.63	1130.55	74.71	–	1168.89	1243.61
Z226050K	1600 × 1600mm	Nr	5.50	93.39	–	1691.77	1785.16	102.73	–	1860.95	1963.68
Z23	**SUPERSTRUCTURE: STAIRS**										
Z2310	**Proprietary softwood staircases**										
Z231010	**Standard pattern staircase: 2600 mm rise; handrail; balusters; newels; apron lining; trimming joists; 855 mm width; style:**										
Z231010A	straight flight unit; ref M ...	Nr	48.37	821.32	–	1054.58	1875.90	903.45	–	1160.04	2063.49
Z231010B	straight flight unit; ref WM .	Nr	49.81	851.78	–	926.69	1778.47	936.96	–	1019.36	1956.32
Z231010C	winder unit; ref W4DBTW whitewood................	Nr	59.00	1003.37	–	1843.63	2847.00	1103.71	–	2027.99	3131.70
Z231010D	winder unit; ref W4DBTP parana pine	Nr	58.87	1000.39	–	1952.30	2952.69	1100.43	–	2147.53	3247.96

Approximate Estimating Rates

Major Works 2009		Unit	Labour Hours	Labour Net	Plant Net	Materials Net	Unit Net	Labour Gross	Plant Gross	Materials Gross	Unit Price
								(Gross rates include 10% profit)			
				£	£	£	£	£	£	£	£
Z24	**SUPERSTRUCTURE: EXTERNAL WALLS**										
Z2410	**Cavity walls; insulated**										
Z241010	**Facings externally (PC 250:00/ 1000) 105 mm skin; cavity with stainless steel ties; 50 mm Dritherm cavity insulation; 100 mm blockwork inner skin finished:**										
Z241010A	fair to receive finishes	m²	1.66	41.70	–	35.35	77.05	45.87	–	38.89	84.76
Z241010B	with gypsum plaster and emulsion	m²	2.12	51.29	–	39.63	90.92	56.42	–	43.59	100.01
Z241010C	with drylining and emulsion	m²	2.04	49.41	–	42.07	91.48	54.35	–	46.28	100.63
Z241015	**Facings externally (PC 250:00/ 1000) 105 mm skin; cavity with stainless steel ties; 75 mm Dritherm cavity insulation; 100 mm blockwork inner skin finished:**										
Z241015A	fair to receive finishes	m²	1.68	42.20	–	35.85	78.05	46.42	–	39.44	85.86
Z241015B	with gypsum plaster and emulsion	m²	2.14	51.79	–	40.13	91.92	56.97	–	44.14	101.11
Z241015C	with drylining and emulsion	m²	2.06	49.91	–	42.56	92.47	54.90	–	46.82	101.72
Z241018	**Facing brickwork outer skin; 100mm thermal block inner leaf; 100mm insulation; plaster base coat; skim coat plaster; emulsion paint finish**										
Z241018A	Facing bricks PC £350.00 per 1000..................	m²	2.15	51.80	–	48.79	100.59	56.98	–	53.67	110.65
Z241018C	Facing bricks PC £475.00 per 1000..................	m²	2.15	51.80	–	56.20	108.00	56.98	–	61.82	118.80
Z241020	**100 mm blockwork externally; rendered with Tyrolean finish; cavity with stainless steel ties; 50 mm Dritherm cavity insulation; 100 mm blockwork inner skin finished:**										
Z241020A	fair to receive finishes	m²	1.71	42.28	0.19	26.68	69.15	46.51	0.21	29.35	76.07
Z241020B	with gypsum plaster and emulsion	m²	2.17	51.87	0.19	33.19	85.25	57.06	0.21	36.51	93.78
Z241020C	with drylining and emulsion	m²	2.10	50.23	0.19	34.14	84.56	55.25	0.21	37.55	93.02
Z241025	**100 mm blockwork externally; rendered with Tyrolean finish; cavity with stainless steel ties; 75 mm Dritherm cavity insulation; 100 mm blockwork inner skin finished:**										
Z241025A	fair to receive finishes	m²	1.73	42.79	0.19	28.97	71.95	47.07	0.21	31.87	79.15
Z241025B	with gypsum plaster and emulsion	m²	2.19	52.37	0.19	33.68	86.24	57.61	0.21	37.05	94.86
Z241025C	with drylining and emulsion	m²	2.12	50.73	0.19	34.64	85.56	55.80	0.21	38.10	94.12
Z241030	**100mm blockwork externally; rendered finish; 100mm thermal block inner leaf; 100mm insulation; render base coat; skim coat plaster; emulsion paint finish internally:**										
Z241030A	Sandtex finish externally ...	m²	2.33	54.33	–	39.47	93.80	59.76	–	43.42	103.18

Major Works 2009		Unit	Labour Hours	Labour Net	Plant Net	Materials Net	Unit Net	Labour Gross	Plant Gross	Materials Gross	Unit Price
								— (Gross rates include 10% profit) —			
				£	£	£	£	£	£	£	£
Z24	**SUPERSTRUCTURE: EXTERNAL WALLS**										
Z2415	**Cavity wall; left clear**										
Z241505	**Facings externally (PC £250:00/1000) 105 mm skin; cavity with stainless steel ties; 100 mm blockwork inner skin finished:**										
Z241505A	fair to receive finishes	m²	1.50	37.68	–	33.27	70.95	41.45	–	36.60	78.05
Z241505B	with gypsum plaster and emulsion	m²	1.96	47.27	–	37.73	85.00	52.00	–	41.50	93.50
Z241505C	with drylining and emulsion	m²	1.91	46.10	–	39.47	85.57	50.71	–	43.42	94.13
Z241508	**Facings externally (PC 250:00/ 1000) 105 mm skin; cavity with stainless steel ties; 125 mm blockwork inner skin finished:**										
Z241508A	fair to receive finishes	m²	1.52	38.19	–	35.41	73.60	42.01	–	38.95	80.96
Z241508B	with gypsum plaster and emulsion	m²	1.98	47.77	–	39.87	87.64	52.55	–	43.86	96.40
Z241508C	with drylining and emulsion	m²	1.93	46.60	–	41.61	88.21	51.26	–	45.77	97.03
Z241510	**Facings externally (PC 250:00/ 1000) 105 mm skin; cavity with stainless steel ties; 150 mm blockwork inner skin finished:**										
Z241510A	fair to receive finishes	m²	1.54	38.68	–	38.44	77.12	42.55	–	42.28	84.83
Z241510B	with gypsum plaster and emulsion	m²	2.00	48.27	–	42.90	91.17	53.10	–	47.19	100.29
Z241510C	with drylining and emulsion	m²	1.95	47.10	–	44.64	91.74	51.81	–	49.10	100.91
Z241520	**100 mm blockwork externally; rendered and Tyrolean finish; cavity with stainless steel ties; 150 mm blockwork inner skin finished:**										
Z241520A	fair to receive finishes	m²	1.59	39.26	0.19	31.23	70.68	43.19	0.21	34.35	77.75
Z241520B	with gypsum plaster and emulsion	m²	2.05	48.86	0.19	35.69	84.74	53.75	0.21	39.26	93.21
Z241520C	with drylining and emulsion	m²	2.00	47.68	0.19	37.43	85.30	52.45	0.21	41.17	93.83
Z241522	**125 mm blockwork externally; rendered and Tyrolean finish; cavity with stainless steel ties; 150 mm blockwork inner skin finished:**										
Z241522A	fair to receive finishes	m²	1.61	39.77	0.19	33.38	73.34	43.75	0.21	36.72	80.67
Z241522B	with gypsum plaster and emulsion	m²	2.07	49.35	0.19	37.83	87.37	54.29	0.21	41.61	96.11
Z241522C	with drylining and emulsion	m²	2.02	48.18	0.19	39.58	87.95	53.00	0.21	43.54	96.75
Z241524	**150 mm blockwork externally; rendered and Tyrolean finish; cavity with stainless steel ties; 150 mm blockwork inner skin finished:**										
Z241524A	fair to receive finishes	m²	1.63	40.28	0.19	36.40	76.87	44.31	0.21	40.04	84.56
Z241524B	with gypsum plaster and emulsion	m²	2.09	49.86	0.19	40.86	90.91	54.85	0.21	44.95	100.00
Z241524C	with drylining and emulsion	m²	2.04	48.69	0.19	42.60	91.48	53.56	0.21	46.86	100.63

Approximate Estimating Rates

Major Works 2009		Unit	Labour Hours	Labour Net	Plant Net	Materials Net	Unit Net	Labour Gross	Plant Gross	Materials Gross	Unit Price
								(Gross rates include 10% profit)			
				£	£	£	£	£	£	£	£
Z24	**SUPERSTRUCTURE: EXTERNAL WALLS**										
Z2420	**Solid brick walls**										
Z242002	**Common bricks; in gauged mortar (1:2:9):**										
Z242002A	Half brick thick	m²	0.68	17.08	–	16.64	33.72	18.79	–	18.30	37.09
Z242002B	One brick thick	m²	1.36	34.17	–	33.48	67.65	37.59	–	36.83	74.42
Z242002C	One and a half brick thick ..	m²	2.04	51.25	–	50.12	101.37	56.38	–	55.13	111.51
Z242004	**Engineering bricks; Class B; in gauged mortar (1:2:9):**										
Z242004A	Half brick thick	m²	0.73	18.34	–	21.47	39.81	20.17	–	23.62	43.79
Z242004B	One brick thick	m²	1.47	36.93	–	43.14	80.07	40.62	–	47.45	88.08
Z242006	**Facing bricks; PC 300.00 per 1000; in gauged mortar (1:2:9); flush pointing both sides:**										
Z242006A	Half brick thick	m²	1.01	25.37	–	20.74	46.11	27.91	–	22.81	50.72
Z242006B	One brick thick	m²	1.80	45.22	–	41.67	86.89	49.74	–	45.84	95.58
Z242010	**Common bricks; plaster and emulsion paint one side; thickness:**										
Z242010A	102.5 mm	m²	1.22	28.68	–	21.29	49.97	31.55	–	23.42	54.97
Z242010B	215 mm	m²	1.90	45.76	–	38.83	84.59	50.34	–	42.71	93.05
Z242010C	322 mm	m²	2.57	62.59	–	57.17	119.76	68.85	–	62.89	131.74
Z2425	**Solid block walls**										
Z242505	**Thermalite Shield blocks in gauged mortar; unfinished; thickness:**										
Z242505B	100mm	m²	0.57	14.32	–	11.59	25.91	15.75	–	12.75	28.50
Z242505D	150mm	m²	0.63	15.82	–	17.32	33.14	17.40	–	19.05	36.45
Z242505F	200mm	m²	0.71	17.83	–	18.24	36.07	19.61	–	20.06	39.68
Z242510	**Lightweight blocks; plaster and emulsion paint one side; fair face other side; thickness:**										
Z242510A	100 mm thick	m²	0.98	22.64	–	16.56	39.20	24.90	–	18.22	43.12
Z242510B	125 mm thick	m²	1.00	23.15	–	18.97	42.12	25.47	–	20.87	46.33
Z242510C	150 mm thick	m²	1.02	23.65	–	21.46	45.11	26.02	–	23.61	49.62
Z242510D	200 mm thick	m²	1.09	25.41	–	26.47	51.88	27.95	–	29.12	57.07
Z242540	**Dense aggregate concrete blocks; 3.5N/mm²; in gauged mortar; unfinished; thickness:**										
Z242540A	100mm	m²	0.65	16.33	–	12.74	29.07	17.96	–	14.01	31.98
Z242540D	140mm	m²	0.72	18.08	–	17.89	35.97	19.89	–	19.68	39.57
Z242545	**Dense aggregate concrete blocks; 7N/mm²; in gauged mortar; unfinished; thickness:**										
Z242545B	100mm	m²	0.69	17.34	–	12.92	30.26	19.07	–	14.21	33.29
Z242545D	140mm	m²	0.75	18.84	–	18.22	37.06	20.72	–	20.04	40.77
Z242550	**Forticrete concrete blocks; coloured; in gauged mortar; unfinished; thickness:**										
Z242550C	90mm	m²	0.98	24.62	–	26.56	51.18	27.08	–	29.22	56.30
Z242550E	140mm	m²	1.06	26.63	–	34.83	61.46	29.29	–	38.31	67.61
Z242550G	190mm	m²	1.14	28.64	–	43.08	71.72	31.50	–	47.39	78.89
Z242550H	215mm	m²	1.19	29.90	–	45.79	75.69	32.89	–	50.37	83.26

Major Works 2009		Unit	Labour Hours	Labour Net	Plant Net	Materials Net	Unit Net	Labour Gross	Plant Gross	Materials Gross	Unit Price
								(Gross rates include 10% profit)			
				£	£	£	£	£	£	£	£
Z24	**SUPERSTRUCTURE: EXTERNAL WALLS**										
Z2450	**Composite walls**										
Z245010	**Half brick outer leaf; 75mm clear cavity; vapour barrier and 6.5mm plywood sheathing; 50 × 100mm studs at 400mm cs; plasterboard and skim finish internally; emulsion paint decorations; 100mm glass fibre insulation quilt between studs; framing secured to brickwork with ties; outer leaf in**										
Z245010A	Facing bricks PC £350.00 per 1000	m²	2.68	55.07	–	50.65	105.72	60.58	–	55.72	116.29
Z245010C	Facing bricks PC £475.00 per 1000	m²	2.68	55.06	–	58.07	113.13	60.57	–	63.88	124.44
Z2485	**External cladding**										
Z248510	**Softwood boarding; tanalised; fixing with nails to 25 × 38mm treated softwood batten grounds at 450mm centres screw fixed to substrate; finished with Sadolin Classic**										
Z248510A	25mm tongued and grooved section	m²	1.36	23.09	–	21.19	44.28	25.40	–	23.31	48.71
Z248510D	25mm shiplap section	m²	1.36	23.09	–	29.35	52.44	25.40	–	32.29	57.68
Z248510H	19mm feather edge section	m²	1.36	23.09	–	15.14	38.23	25.40	–	16.65	42.05

Approximate Estimating Rates

Major Works 2009		Unit	Labour Hours	Labour Net	Plant Net	Materials Net	Unit Net	Labour Gross	Plant Gross	Materials Gross	Unit Price
								—— (Gross rates include 10% profit) ——			
				£	£	£	£	£	£	£	£
Z25	**SUPERSTRUCTURE: WINDOWS AND EXTERNAL DOORS**										
Z2510	**Hardwood windows**										
Z251010	**Standard hardwood casement; hermetically sealed double glazing; two coat stain externally and three coat oil paint internally; steel cavity wall lintel; Thermabate cavity closer; window size:**										
Z251010A	630 × 900 mm high	Nr	2.84	52.14	–	337.18	389.32	57.35	–	370.90	428.25
Z251010B	630 × 1200 mm high	Nr	3.62	66.23	–	312.32	378.55	72.85	–	343.55	416.41
Z251010C	915 × 1050 mm high	Nr	4.19	76.15	–	370.35	446.50	83.77	–	407.39	491.15
Z251010D	915 × 1200 mm high	Nr	5.00	90.47	–	413.57	504.04	99.52	–	454.93	554.44
Z251010E	1200 × 1050 mm high	Nr	5.03	90.86	–	432.86	523.72	99.95	–	476.15	576.09
Z251010F	1200 × 1500 mm high	Nr	6.60	118.81	–	496.08	614.89	130.69	–	545.69	676.38
Z251010G	1770 × 1050 mm high	Nr	6.96	124.55	–	643.47	768.02	137.01	–	707.82	844.82
Z251010H	1770 × 1350 mm high	Nr	8.64	153.77	–	729.50	883.27	169.15	–	802.45	971.60
Z251010I	2339 × 1200 mm high	Nr	10.25	181.90	–	981.78	1163.68	200.09	–	1079.96	1280.05
Z251010J	2339 × 1350 mm high	Nr	11.38	201.58	–	1022.91	1224.49	221.74	–	1125.20	1346.94
Z251015	**Standard hardwood horizontal bar; hermetically sealed double glazing units; two coat stain externally; three coat oil paint internally; Thermabate cavity closer; steel wall lintel; window size:**										
Z251015A	630 × 900 mm high	Nr	3.24	59.02	–	309.81	368.83	64.92	–	340.79	405.71
Z251015B	630 × 1200 mm high	Nr	4.14	76.77	–	329.70	406.47	84.45	–	362.67	447.12
Z251015C	630 × 1350 mm high	Nr	4.63	85.58	–	355.78	441.36	94.14	–	391.36	485.50
Z251015D	915 × 1050 mm high	Nr	5.36	96.83	–	458.53	555.36	106.51	–	504.38	610.90
Z251015E	915 × 1200 mm high	Nr	5.86	106.99	–	488.52	595.51	117.69	–	537.37	655.06
Z251015F	1200 × 1050 mm high	Nr	6.35	114.90	–	486.98	601.88	126.39	–	535.68	662.07
Z251015G	1200 × 1350 mm high	Nr	8.02	144.60	–	547.03	691.63	159.06	–	601.73	760.79
Z251015H	1770 × 1050 mm high	Nr	8.87	158.61	–	731.93	890.54	174.47	–	805.12	979.59
Z251015I	1770 × 1350 mm high	Nr	11.16	198.42	–	816.91	1015.33	218.26	–	898.60	1116.86
Z251015J	2339 × 1200 mm high	Nr	13.64	242.07	–	1064.15	1306.22	266.28	–	1170.57	1436.84
Z2530	**UPVC windows**										
Z253010	**Standard uPVC casements; hermetically sealed double glazing units; steel cavity wall lintel; Thermabate cavity closer; window size:**										
Z253010A	900 × 1000 mm high	Nr	2.04	39.52	–	185.28	224.80	43.47	–	203.81	247.28
Z253010B	900 × 1200 mm high	Nr	2.39	46.03	–	197.02	243.05	50.63	–	216.72	267.36
Z253010C	900 × 1500 mm high	Nr	2.79	53.67	–	216.95	270.62	59.04	–	238.65	297.68
Z253010D	1200 × 1000 mm high	Nr	2.29	44.21	–	213.69	257.90	48.63	–	235.06	283.69
Z253010E	1200 × 1200 mm high	Nr	2.64	50.72	–	226.35	277.07	55.79	–	248.99	304.78
Z253010F	1200 × 1500 mm high	Nr	3.04	58.36	–	243.08	301.44	64.20	–	267.39	331.58
Z253010G	1800 × 1000 mm high	Nr	3.09	58.68	–	283.58	342.26	64.55	–	311.94	376.49
Z253010H	1800 × 1200 mm high	Nr	3.34	63.49	–	296.44	359.93	69.84	–	326.08	395.92
Z253010I	1800 × 1500 mm high	Nr	3.49	66.88	–	321.97	388.85	73.57	–	354.17	427.74
Z253010J	2400 × 1000 mm high	Nr	4.12	77.70	–	430.55	508.25	85.47	–	473.61	559.08
Z253010K	2400 × 1500 mm high	Nr	4.53	86.16	–	503.97	590.13	94.78	–	554.37	649.14

Major Works 2009		Unit	Labour Hours	Labour Net	Plant Net	Materials Net	Unit Net	Labour Gross	Plant Gross	Materials Gross	Unit Price
								(Gross rates include 10% profit)			
				£	£	£	£	£	£	£	£
Z25	**SUPERSTRUCTURE: WINDOWS AND EXTERNAL DOORS**										
Z2550	**Hardwood external doors and frames**										
Z255010	**External door set: door and frame with ironmongery; steel cavity wall lintel; Thermabate cavity closer; two coat stain finish external; three coat oil paint internal; 6.4 mm laminated glass as required; door size and reference:**										
Z255010A	838 × 1981 mm: Chatton 29CHA	Nr	14.37	252.00	–	732.46	984.46	277.20	–	805.71	1082.91
Z255010B	838 × 1981 mm: Felton 29FEL	Nr	14.37	252.00	–	773.54	1025.54	277.20	–	850.89	1128.09
Z255010C	838 × 1981 mm: Coleridge 29CRG	Nr	13.22	232.47	–	683.25	915.72	255.72	–	751.58	1007.29
Z2560	**Softwood external doors and frames**										
Z256010	**Henderson u/o garage door; ironmongery; softwood frame; steel wall lintel; Thermabate cavity closer; three coat oil paint finish internal and external; door size and reference:**										
Z256010A	2134 × 2134 mm: Henderson Regent 707	Nr	10.45	192.11	–	686.75	878.86	211.32	–	755.43	966.75
Z256010B	2134 × 2134 mm: Henderson Doric 7070.	Nr	10.45	192.11	–	768.35	960.46	211.32	–	845.19	1056.51
Z256010C	2135 × 2134 mm: Henderson Merlin 707	Nr	10.45	192.11	–	656.35	848.46	211.32	–	721.99	933.31
Z256010D	2136 × 2134 mm: Henderson Merlin Chevron 7070.	Nr	10.45	192.11	–	704.35	896.46	211.32	–	774.79	986.11
Z256010E	4270 × 2134 mm: Henderson Regent Chevron 1470.	Nr	16.65	302.40	–	1574.58	1876.98	332.64	–	1732.04	2064.68
Z256010F	4270 × 2134 mm: Henderson Doric 1470.	Nr	16.65	302.40	–	1722.58	2024.98	332.64	–	1894.84	2227.48

Approximate Estimating Rates

Major Works 2009		Unit				Specialist Net	Unit Net			Specialist Gross	Unit Price
										(Gross rates include 10% profit)	
				£	£	£	£	£	£	£	£
Z25	**SUPERSTRUCTURE: WINDOWS AND EXTERNAL DOORS**										
Z2595	**Brise-soleil**										
Z259510	**Brise-soleil; extruded aluminium blades fixed horizontally on brackets; to frame (measured separately); size:**										
Z259510A	2.5 × 1.0 m	Nr	–	–	–	788.84	788.84	–	–	867.72	867.72
Z259510B	5.0 × 1.5 m	Nr	–	–	–	2267.77	2267.77	–	–	2494.55	2494.55
Z259510C	7.5 × 2.0 m	Nr	–	–	–	4338.61	4338.61	–	–	4772.47	4772.47
Z259510D	10.0 × 2.5 m	Nr	–	–	–	6900.88	6900.88	–	–	7590.97	7590.97

Major Works 2009		Unit	Labour Hours	Labour Net	Plant Net	Materials Net	Unit Net	Labour Gross	Plant Gross	Materials Gross	Unit Price
								(Gross rates include 10% profit)			
				£	£	£	£	£	£	£	£
Z28	**SUPERSTRUCTURE: INTERNAL WALLS AND PARTITIONS**										
Z2810	**Solid brick walls**										
Z281010	**Common bricks; plaster and emulsion paint both sides; thickness:**										
Z281010A	102.5 mm	m²	1.64	37.26	–	25.04	62.30	40.99	–	27.54	68.53
Z281010B	215 mm	m²	2.32	54.34	–	42.84	97.18	59.77	–	47.12	106.90
Z281010C	322 mm	m²	2.99	71.17	–	61.17	132.34	78.29	–	67.29	145.57
Z2820	**Solid block walls**										
Z282010	**Lightweight blocks; plaster and emulsion paint one side; fair face other side; thickness:**										
Z282010A	100 mm thick	m²	0.98	22.64	–	16.56	39.20	24.90	–	18.22	43.12
Z282010B	125 mm thick	m²	1.00	23.15	–	18.97	42.12	25.47	–	20.87	46.33
Z282010C	150 mm thick	m²	1.02	23.65	–	21.46	45.11	26.02	–	23.61	49.62
Z282010D	200 mm thick	m²	1.09	25.41	–	26.47	51.88	27.95	–	29.12	57.07
Z2830	**Timber framed walls**										
Z283010	**50 × 100 mm SC3 treated softwood studwork at 400 mm centres vertically; sole and head plates; strutting; 100 mm glassfibre insulation; clad both sides with 12.5 mm plasterboard; finished:**										
Z283010A	to receive direct decoration.	m²	1.24	23.90	–	17.26	41.16	26.29	–	18.99	45.28
Z283010B	with two coats emulsion ...	m²	1.60	30.01	–	21.38	51.39	33.01	–	23.52	56.53
Z283010C	skim coat plaster and emulsion	m²	1.87	36.34	–	21.18	57.52	39.97	–	23.30	63.27

Approximate Estimating Rates

Major Works 2009		Unit	Labour Hours	Labour Net	Plant Net	Materials Net	Unit Net	Labour Gross	Plant Gross	Materials Gross	Unit Price
								(Gross rates include 10% profit)			
				£	£	£	£	£	£	£	£
Z29	**SUPERSTRUCTURE: INTERNAL DOORS**										
Z2910	**Hardwood internal doors**										
Z291010	**Internal panel door set: door, softwood lining and architraves with three coat oil paint finish; steel internal wall lintel; hardwood door size and reference:**										
Z291010A	686 × 1981 mm: 23HISA .	Nr	5.73	98.27	–	227.66	325.93	108.10	–	250.43	358.52
Z291010B	762 × 1981 mm: 26HISA .	Nr	5.73	98.27	–	228.36	326.63	108.10	–	251.20	359.29
Z291010C	1168 × 1981 mm: 310HISA (pair)	Nr	6.09	105.03	–	390.26	495.29	115.53	–	429.29	544.82
Z2920	**Softwood internal doors**										
Z292010	**Internal panel door set; door, linings and architrave; ironmongery; steel wall lintel; three coat oil paint finish; 6.4 mm laminated glazing as required; softwood door size and reference:**										
Z292010A	686 × 1981 mm: 23ISA ..	Nr	9.44	161.27	–	300.38	461.65	177.40	–	330.42	507.82
Z292010B	762 × 1981 mm: 26ISA ..	Nr	9.79	167.22	–	315.08	482.30	183.94	–	346.59	530.53
Z292010C	838 × 1981 mm: 29ISA ..	Nr	10.10	172.47	–	332.81	505.28	189.72	–	366.09	555.81
Z292015	**Internal flush door set; door, linings and architrave; ironmongery; steel wall lintel; three coat oil paint finish to linings and architrave; veneer finish; door size and reference:**										
Z292015A	686 × 1981 mm: 23SDL Sapele	Nr	5.27	90.46	–	131.35	221.81	99.51	–	144.49	243.99
Z292015B	762 × 1981 mm: 26SDL Sapele	Nr	5.43	93.17	–	131.86	225.03	102.49	–	145.05	247.53
Z292015C	838 × 1981 mm: 29SDL Sapele	Nr	5.52	94.71	–	137.26	231.97	104.18	–	150.99	255.17

Major Works 2009		Unit	Labour Hours	Labour Net	Plant Net	Materials Net	Unit Net	Labour Gross	Plant Gross	Materials Gross	Unit Price
								(Gross rates include 10% profit)			
				£	£	£	£	£	£	£	£
Z32	**FINISHES: INTERNAL WALL FINISHES**										
Z3210	**Wall lining finishes**										
Z321010	**Gyproc linings; 12.5 mm wallboard; to woodwork backgrounds; taped joints; 2 mm skim coat of plaster; finished:**										
Z321010A	mist, two full coats emulsion paint	m²	0.48	9.99	–	6.20	16.19	10.99	–	6.82	17.81
Z321010B	undercoat, two coats eggshell paint	m²	0.66	13.05	–	6.09	19.14	14.36	–	6.70	21.05
Z321010C	plain lining paper; mist coat and two full coats emulsion paint	m²	0.74	14.41	–	6.68	21.09	15.85	–	7.35	23.20
Z321010D	plain lining paper; undercoat and two full coats eggshell paint	m²	0.92	17.46	–	6.57	24.03	19.21	–	7.23	26.43
Z321010E	decorative wallpaper at 6.50 per roll	m²	0.60	12.03	–	6.43	18.46	13.23	–	7.07	20.31
Z321010F	decorative wallpaper at 9.00 per roll	m²	0.60	12.02	–	6.32	18.34	13.22	–	6.95	20.17
Z321015	**Gyproc linings; 12.5 mm; to masonry or concrete walls; fixing by Thistlebond system; joints flush filled and taped; finished:**										
Z321015A	mist, two full coats emulsion paint	m²	0.43	8.91	–	6.43	15.34	9.80	–	7.07	16.87
Z321015B	undercoat, two coats eggshell paint	m²	0.61	11.98	–	6.31	18.29	13.18	–	6.94	20.12
Z321015C	plain lining paper; mist coat and two full coats emulsion paint	m²	0.69	13.34	–	6.90	20.24	14.67	–	7.59	22.26
Z321015D	plain lining paper; undercoat and two full coats eggshell paint	m²	0.87	16.39	–	6.79	23.18	18.03	–	7.47	25.50
Z321015E	decorative wallpaper at 6.50 per roll	m²	0.55	10.95	–	6.66	17.61	12.05	–	7.33	19.37
Z321015F	decorative wallpaper at 9.00 per roll	m²	0.55	10.95	–	6.54	17.49	12.05	–	7.19	19.24
Z321020	**Gyproc linings; 12.5 mm Fireline board; to masonry or concrete walls; fixing by Thistlebond system; joints flush filled and taped; finished:**										
Z321020A	mist, two full coats emulsion paint	m²	0.46	9.62	–	11.98	21.60	10.58	–	13.18	23.76
Z321020B	undercoat, two coats eggshell paint	m²	0.61	11.98	–	7.97	19.95	13.18	–	8.77	21.95
Z321020C	plain lining paper; mist coat and two full coats emulsion paint	m²	0.70	13.42	–	8.73	22.15	14.76	–	9.60	24.37
Z321020D	plain lining paper; undercoat and two full coats eggshell paint	m²	0.88	16.56	–	8.45	25.01	18.22	–	9.30	27.51
Z321020E	decorative wallpaper at 6.50 per roll	m²	0.55	10.95	–	8.32	19.27	12.05	–	9.15	21.20
Z321020F	decorative wallpaper at 9.00 per roll	m²	0.55	10.95	–	8.20	19.15	12.05	–	9.02	21.07

Approximate Estimating Rates

Major Works 2009		Unit	Labour Hours	Labour Net	Plant Net	Materials Net	Unit Net	Labour Gross	Plant Gross	Materials Gross	Unit Price
								(Gross rates include 10% profit)			
				£	£	£	£	£	£	£	£
Z32	**FINISHES: INTERNAL WALL FINISHES**										
Z3220	**Applied wall finishes**										
Z322010	**Cement and sand (1:3) floated finish; two coat work 18 mm thick; to masonry backgrounds; 2 mm Thistle finishing plaster; finished:**										
Z322010A	mist, two full coats emulsion paint....................	m²	0.55	11.73	–	4.25	15.98	12.90	–	4.68	17.58
Z322010B	undercoat, two coats eggshell paint	m²	0.73	14.79	–	4.14	18.93	16.27	–	4.55	20.82
Z322010C	plain lining paper; mist coat and two full coats emulsion paint....................	m²	0.82	16.23	–	4.90	21.13	17.85	–	5.39	23.24
Z322010D	plain lining paper; undercoat and two full coats eggshell paint....................	m²	1.00	19.37	–	4.62	23.99	21.31	–	5.08	26.39
Z322010E	decorative wallpaper at 6.50 per roll	m²	0.67	13.77	–	4.48	18.25	15.15	–	4.93	20.08
Z322010F	decorative wallpaper at 9.00 per roll	m²	0.67	13.77	–	4.36	18.13	15.15	–	4.80	19.94
Z322020	**Carlite lightweight plaster; 13 mm thick two coat work; to masonry backgrounds; browning backing and 2 mm top coat; finished:**										
Z322020A	mist, two full coats emulsion paint....................	m²	0.48	10.09	–	4.17	14.26	11.10	–	4.59	15.69
Z322020B	undercoat, two coats eggshell paint	m²	0.66	13.15	–	4.06	17.21	14.47	–	4.47	18.93
Z322020C	plain lining paper; mist coat and two full coats emulsion paint....................	m²	0.75	14.59	–	4.82	19.41	16.05	–	5.30	21.35
Z322020D	plain lining paper; undercoat and two full coats eggshell paint....................	m²	0.93	17.73	–	4.54	22.27	19.50	–	4.99	24.50
Z322020E	decorative wallpaper at 6.50 per roll	m²	0.60	12.13	–	4.40	16.53	13.34	–	4.84	18.18
Z322020F	decorative wallpaper at 9.00 per roll	m²	0.60	12.12	–	4.29	16.41	13.33	–	4.72	18.05

Major Works 2009		Unit	Labour Hours	Labour Net	Plant Net	Materials Net	Unit Net	Labour Gross	Plant Gross	Materials Gross	Unit Price
								——— (Gross rates include 10% profit) ———			
				£	£	£	£	£	£	£	£
Z34	**FINISHES: INTERNAL FLOOR FINISHES**										
Z3410	**Sheet and tile flooring**										
Z341010	**Vinyl sheet flooring; Marleyflor Plus; welded seams; fixing with adhesive; to sand and cement base**										
Z341010A	2.00mm thick; over 300mm wide	m²	0.37	6.28	–	6.46	12.74	6.91	–	7.11	14.01
Z341012	**Vinyl tile flooring; Marleyflor Plus; fixing with adhesive; to sand and cement base**										
Z341012A	610 × 610 × 2.00mm thick; over 300mm wide . . .	m²	0.42	7.13	–	6.46	13.59	7.84	–	7.11	14.95
Z341014	**Thermoplastic tile flooring; Marleyflex; fixing with adhesive; to sand and cement base**										
Z341014A	300 × 300 × 2.50mm thick; series 4; over 300mm wide	m²	0.45	7.65	–	5.98	13.63	8.42	–	6.58	14.99
Z341016	**Linoleum flooring; Forbo-Nairn Marmoleum; welded seams; fixing with adhesive; to sand and cement base**										
Z341016A	2.50mm thick; over 300mm wide	m²	0.46	7.81	–	27.35	35.16	8.59	–	30.09	38.68
Z341018	**Rubber tile flooring**										
Z341018A	Rubber floor tiles; heavy duty raised studded pattern; fixing with adhesive	m²	0.42	7.14	–	25.53	32.67	7.85	–	28.08	35.94
Z341020	**Carpet flooring**										
Z341020A	Axminster Regal Twist carpet; tack fixed felt underlay; tackless gripper on timber base	m²	0.34	5.78	–	31.78	37.56	6.36	–	34.96	41.32
Z341022	**Carpet floor tiles**										
Z341022A	Heuga Horizons; 500 × 500mm; tufted plain level loop; fixing with adhesive . .	m²	0.30	5.10	–	15.09	20.19	5.61	–	16.60	22.21
Z341025	**Ceramic floor tiling**										
Z341025A	Vitrified ceramic floor tiles; 150 × 150 × 12mm; bedded, jointed and pointed in cement mortar (1:3)	m²	0.98	16.64	–	35.38	52.02	18.30	–	38.92	57.22

Approximate Estimating Rates

Major Works 2009		Unit	Labour Hours	Labour Net	Plant Net	Materials Net	Unit Net	Labour Gross	Plant Gross	Materials Gross	Unit Price
								(Gross rates include 10% profit)			
				£	£	£	£	£	£	£	£
Z36	**FINISHES: CEILING FINISHES**										
Z3610	**Ceiling boarded finishes**										
Z361010	**Gyproc linings to ceilings; 12.5 mm; to woodwork backgrounds; joints taped; skin coat of plaster; surface finish:**										
Z361010A	mist, two full coats emulsion paint....................	m²	0.55	11.49	–	6.20	17.69	12.64	–	6.82	19.46
Z361010B	undercoat, two coats eggshell paint............	m²	0.75	15.01	–	6.09	21.10	16.51	–	6.70	23.21
Z361010C	plain lining paper; mist coat and two full coats emulsion paint....................	m²	0.85	16.70	–	6.68	23.38	18.37	–	7.35	25.72
Z361010D	plain lining paper; undercoat and two full coats eggshell paint....................	m²	1.05	20.08	–	6.57	26.65	22.09	–	7.23	29.32
Z361015	**Gyproc linings; 12.5 mm; to concrete ceilings; shot fired fixing to timber battens; joints flush filled and taped; surface finish:**										
Z361015A	mist, two full coats emulsion paint....................	m²	0.90	16.85	–	8.02	24.87	18.54	–	8.82	27.36
Z361015B	undercoat, two coats eggshell paint............	m²	1.08	19.90	–	7.91	27.81	21.89	–	8.70	30.59
Z361015C	plain lining paper; mist coat and two full coats emulsion paint....................	m²	1.16	21.26	–	8.50	29.76	23.39	–	9.35	32.74
Z361015D	plain lining paper; undercoat and two full coats eggshell paint....................	m²	1.34	24.31	–	8.39	32.70	26.74	–	9.23	35.97
Z50	**SERVICES: SANITARY FITTINGS**										
Z5010	**Sanitaryware installations**										
Z501010	**Complete bathroom suite comprising; bath; pedestal basin; low level WC suite; bath panelling; taps; waste; overflows; builder's work; fixed into position:**										
Z501010A	standard white suite (PC 150)....................	Nr	7.25	282.68	–	170.10	452.78	310.95	–	187.11	498.06
Z501010B	standard coloured suite (PC 350)....................	Nr	7.25	282.68	–	396.90	679.58	310.95	–	436.59	747.54
Z501015	**Complete cloakroom suite comprising; wall hung basin; low level WC suite; taps; waste; overflows; builder's work; fixed into position:**										
Z501015A	standard white suite (PC 100)....................	Nr	4.25	165.71	–	113.40	279.11	182.28	–	124.74	307.02
Z501015B	standard coloured suite (PC 250)....................	Nr	4.25	165.71	–	283.50	449.21	182.28	–	311.85	494.13

Major Works 2009		Unit	Labour Hours	Labour Net	Plant Net	Materials Net	Unit Net	Labour Gross	Plant Gross	Materials Gross	Unit Price
								(Gross rates include 10% profit)			
				£	£	£	£	£	£	£	£
Z52	**SERVICES: INSTALLATIONS**										
Z5211	**Soil and waste pipe installations**										
Z521110	**UPVC pipework and fittings; builder's work; testing on completion; single storey dwelling:**										
Z521110A	Kitchen; Bathroom	Nr	7.20	280.73	–	184.22	464.95	308.80	–	202.64	511.45
Z521110B	Kitchen; Bathroom; Cloakroom.	Nr	8.59	334.93	–	191.67	526.60	368.42	–	210.84	579.26
Z521110C	Kitchen; 2 Bathrooms	Nr	10.39	405.11	–	250.38	655.49	445.62	–	275.42	721.04
Z521110D	Kitchen; 2 Bathrooms; Cloakroom.	Nr	12.44	485.04	–	298.00	783.04	533.54	–	327.80	861.34
Z521115	**UPVC pipework and fittings; builder's work; testing on completion; two storey dwelling:**										
Z521115A	Kitchen; Bathroom	Nr	10.79	420.71	–	294.62	715.33	462.78	–	324.08	786.86
Z521115B	Kitchen; Bathroom; Cloakroom.	Nr	12.21	476.07	–	329.55	805.62	523.68	–	362.51	886.18
Z521115C	Kitchen; 2 Bathrooms	Nr	13.68	533.39	–	418.27	951.66	586.73	–	460.10	1046.83
Z521115D	Kitchen; 2 Bathrooms; Cloakroom.	Nr	15.28	595.77	–	449.85	1045.62	655.35	–	494.84	1150.18
Z5221	**Hot and cold water installations**										
Z522110	**Copper service pipework and fittings; plastic storage cistern; copper direct cylinder; pipe and equipment insulation builder's work; testing on completion; single storey dwelling:**										
Z522110A	Kitchen; Bathroom	Nr	64.00	2422.60	–	659.11	3081.71	2664.86	–	725.02	3389.88
Z522110B	Kitchen; Bathroom; Cloakroom.	Nr	69.00	2617.55	–	684.62	3302.17	2879.31	–	753.08	3632.39
Z522110C	Kitchen; 2 Bathrooms	Nr	74.00	2812.50	–	783.64	3596.14	3093.75	–	862.00	3955.75
Z522110D	Kitchen; 2 Bathrooms; Cloakroom.	Nr	84.00	3202.41	–	813.00	4015.41	3522.65	–	894.30	4416.95
Z522115	**Copper service pipework and fittings; plastic storage cistern; copper direct cylinder; pipe and equipment insulation builder's work; testing on completion; two storey dwelling:**										
Z522115A	Kitchen; Bathroom	Nr	70.00	2656.54	–	729.88	3386.42	2922.19	–	802.87	3725.06
Z522115B	Kitchen; Bathroom; Cloakroom.	Nr	75.00	2851.49	–	749.78	3601.27	3136.64	–	824.76	3961.40
Z522115C	Kitchen; 2 Bathrooms	Nr	80.00	3046.44	–	843.39	3889.83	3351.08	–	927.73	4278.81
Z522115D	Kitchen; 2 Bathrooms; Cloakroom.	Nr	90.00	3436.34	–	878.15	4314.49	3779.97	–	965.97	4745.94

Approximate Estimating Rates

Major Works 2009		Unit	Labour Hours	Labour Net	Plant Net	Materials Net	Unit Net	Labour Gross	Plant Gross	Materials Gross	Unit Price
								(Gross rates include 10% profit)			
				£	£	£	£	£	£	£	£
Z52	**SERVICES: INSTALLATIONS**										
Z5231	**Domestic wiring installations**										
Z523110	**Complete electrical installation comprising: power circuits; lighting circuits; outlets; switches; consumer unit; immersion heater; cooker point; extract ventilation; builder's work; testing:**										
Z523110A	single storey dwelling; 1 Bedroom	Nr	93.10	1682.35	–	1235.73	2918.08	1850.59	–	1359.30	3209.89
Z523110B	single storey dwelling; 2 Bedroom	Nr	100.00	1802.03	–	1334.94	3136.97	1982.23	–	1468.43	3450.67
Z523110C	single storey dwelling; 3 Bedroom	Nr	105.40	1902.66	–	1403.57	3306.23	2092.93	–	1543.93	3636.85
Z523110D	two storey dwelling; 2 Bedroom	Nr	109.70	1982.91	–	1588.47	3571.38	2181.20	–	1747.32	3928.52
Z523110E	two storey dwelling; 3 Bedroom	Nr	115.60	2083.48	–	1650.49	3733.97	2291.83	–	1815.54	4107.37
Z523110F	two storey dwelling; 4 Bedroom	Nr	124.30	2232.43	–	1731.09	3963.52	2455.67	–	1904.20	4359.87
Z53	**SERVICES: M&E INSTALLATIONS**										
Z5321	**Central heating installations**										
Z532110	**Gas fired wet system:**										
Z532110A	single storey unit; 6 radiators	Nr	82.05	3134.13	–	2924.32	6058.45	3447.54	–	3216.75	6664.30
Z532110B	single storey unit; 8 radiators	Nr	86.09	3279.77	–	3430.16	6709.93	3607.75	–	3773.18	7380.92
Z532110C	two storey unit; 8 radiators .	Nr	88.52	3370.56	–	3556.56	6927.12	3707.62	–	3912.22	7619.83
Z532110D	two storey unit; 10 radiators	Nr	92.58	3518.73	–	4436.96	7955.69	3870.60	–	4880.66	8751.26
Z532115	**Oil fired wet system:**										
Z532115A	single storey unit; 6 radiators	Nr	86.91	3222.74	7.63	3331.34	6561.71	3545.01	8.39	3664.47	7217.88
Z532115B	single storey unit; 8 radiators	Nr	90.95	3368.38	7.63	3596.52	6972.53	3705.22	8.39	3956.17	7669.78
Z532115C	two storey unit; 8 radiators .	Nr	93.38	3459.16	7.63	3827.61	7294.40	3805.08	8.39	4210.37	8023.84
Z532115D	two storey unit; 10 radiators	Nr	97.44	3607.33	7.63	4416.12	8031.08	3968.06	8.39	4857.73	8834.19
Z532120	**Solid fuel wet system:**										
Z532120A	single storey unit; 6 radiators	Nr	79.55	3036.66	–	2808.71	5845.37	3340.33	–	3089.58	6429.91
Z532120B	single storey unit; 8 radiators	Nr	83.59	3182.30	–	3145.80	6328.10	3500.53	–	3460.38	6960.91
Z532120C	two storey unit; 8 radiators .	Nr	86.02	3273.08	–	3272.20	6545.28	3600.39	–	3599.42	7199.81
Z532120D	two storey unit; 10 radiators	Nr	90.08	3421.26	–	3626.07	7047.33	3763.39	–	3988.68	7752.06

Major Works 2009		Unit				Specialist Net	Unit Net			Specialist Gross	Unit Price
								——— (Gross rates include 10% profit) ———			
				£	£	£	£	£	£	£	£
Z53	SERVICES: M&E INSTALLATIONS										
Z5365	Lift and conveyor installations										
Z536510	Passenger lifts; traction; machine room less; standard finish; 630 kg; 8 person 1.0 m/s; serving:										
Z536510A	2 floors	Nr	–	–	–	35959.36	35959.36	–	–	39555.30	39555.30
Z536510B	3 floors	Nr	–	–	–	40733.30	40733.30	–	–	44806.63	44806.63
Z536510C	4 floors	Nr	–	–	–	44104.85	44104.85	–	–	48515.34	48515.34
Z536512	Passenger lifts; traction; machine room less; standard finish; 1,000 kg; 13 person; 1.0 m/s; serving:										
Z536512A	2 floors	Nr	–	–	–	37361.74	37361.74	–	–	41097.91	41097.91
Z536512B	3 floors	Nr	–	–	–	40733.30	40733.30	–	–	44806.63	44806.63
Z536512C	4 floors	Nr	–	–	–	44104.41	44104.41	–	–	48514.85	48514.85
Z536512D	5 floors	Nr	–	–	–	48516.51	48516.51	–	–	53368.16	53368.16
Z536514	Passenger lifts; traction; machine room less; standard finish; 1,250 kg; 16 person; 1.0 m/s; serving:										
Z536514A	2 floors	Nr	–	–	–	41903.12	41903.12	–	–	46093.43	46093.43
Z536514B	3 floors	Nr	–	–	–	46761.19	46761.19	–	–	51437.31	51437.31
Z536514C	4 floors	Nr	–	–	–	49034.21	49034.21	–	–	53937.63	53937.63

Approximate Estimating Rates

Major Works 2009		Unit	Labour Hours	Labour Net	Plant Net	Materials Net	Unit Net	Labour Gross	Plant Gross	Materials Gross	Unit Price
								(Gross rates include 10% profit)			
				£	£	£	£	£	£	£	£
Z58	**SERVICES: BWIC**										
Z5810	**Builder's work in connection with services**										
Z581010	**Gas services:**										
Z581010A	100 mm duct in trench 0.75 m deep	m	0.43	5.46	2.94	8.22	16.62	6.01	3.23	9.04	18.28
Z581010B	external consumer meter cupboard...............	Nr	0.50	12.56	–	10.94	23.50	13.82	–	12.03	25.85
Z581015	**Water services:**										
Z581015A	19 mm MDPE pipe in trench 0.75 m deep	m	0.38	4.83	3.43	1.58	9.84	5.31	3.77	1.74	10.82
Z581015B	external consumer meter pit	Nr	1.20	15.24	1.12	23.75	40.11	16.76	1.23	26.13	44.12
Z581020	**Electricity services:**										
Z581020A	100 mm duct in trench 0.75 m deep	m	0.43	5.46	2.65	8.22	16.33	6.01	2.92	9.04	17.96
Z581020B	external consumer meter cupboard...............	Nr	0.50	12.56	–	10.94	23.50	13.82	–	12.03	25.85
Z581025	**Telecom and Cable TV services:**										
Z581025A	90 mm duct in trench 0.50 m deep...................	m	0.38	4.83	2.00	7.46	14.29	5.31	2.20	8.21	15.72

Major Works 2009		Unit	Labour Hours	Labour Net	Plant Net	Materials Net	Unit Net	Labour Gross	Plant Gross	Materials Gross	Unit Price
								(Gross rates include 10% profit)			
				£	£	£	£	£	£	£	£
Z60	**SITE EXTERNAL WORKS**										
Z6030	**Paving**										
Z603010	**Block paviors; 150 mm blinded hardcore; excavation; disposal off site; laid to herringbone pattern; matching margins bedded in concrete; precast concrete pavior thickness:**										
Z603010A	65 mm	m²	1.08	17.44	11.60	40.00	69.04	19.18	12.76	44.00	75.94
Z603010B	80 mm	m²	1.08	17.44	11.60	42.41	71.45	19.18	12.76	46.65	78.60
Z603010C	65 mm; herringbone pattern	m²	1.32	21.52	11.60	40.00	73.12	23.67	12.76	44.00	80.43
Z603010D	80 mm; herringbone pattern	m²	1.32	21.52	11.60	42.41	75.53	23.67	12.76	46.65	83.08
Z603030	**Plain in situ concrete, C20; 150 mm blinded hardcore; excavation; disposal off site; tamped finish; trowelled margins; formwork to edge of slab; concrete thickness:**										
Z603030A	100 mm	m²	0.76	11.45	6.77	18.70	36.92	12.60	7.45	20.57	40.61
Z603030B	150 mm	m²	0.95	13.86	11.93	46.84	72.63	15.25	13.12	51.52	79.89
Z603035	**Reinforced in situ concrete, C20; 150 m blinded hardcore; excavation; disposal off site; tamped finish; trowelled margins; formwork to edge of slab; layer A193 steel fabric; concrete thickness:**										
Z603035A	100 mm	m²	0.82	12.28	7.33	22.02	41.63	13.51	8.06	24.22	45.79
Z603035B	150 mm	m²	1.03	14.94	12.76	50.16	77.86	16.43	14.04	55.18	85.65
Z603040	**Precast concrete slab paving; 50 mm; 150 mm blinded hardcore; excavation; disposal off site; slabs bedded and pointed in cement mortar; slab size:**										
Z603040A	450 × 450 mm	m²	0.86	10.92	10.07	47.48	68.47	12.01	11.08	52.23	75.32
Z603040B	450 × 600 mm	m²	0.72	9.14	10.07	46.28	65.49	10.05	11.08	50.91	72.04
Z603040C	600 × 600 mm	m²	0.64	8.12	10.07	42.67	60.86	8.93	11.08	46.94	66.95
Z603040D	600 × 900 mm	m²	0.56	7.11	10.07	41.60	58.78	7.82	11.08	45.76	64.66
Z603050	**Natural Yorkstone slab paving; 50 mm; 150 mm blinded hardcore; excavation; disposal off site; slabs bedded and pointed in Yorkstone mortar; pattern:**										
Z603050A	random	m²	1.11	14.10	10.07	140.54	164.71	15.51	11.08	154.59	181.18
Z603050B	to design layout	m²	1.21	15.37	10.07	160.04	185.48	16.91	11.08	176.04	204.03

Approximate Estimating Rates

Major Works 2009		Unit	Labour Hours	Labour Net	Plant Net	Materials Net	Unit Net	Labour Gross	Plant Gross	Materials Gross	Unit Price
								(Gross rates include 10% profit)			
				£	£	£	£	£	£	£	£
Z60	**SITE EXTERNAL WORKS**										
Z6050	**Landscaping**										
Z605010	**Rotovating; preparing for planting:**										
Z605010A	150 mm deep	m²	0.15	1.91	0.52	–	2.43	2.10	0.57	–	2.67
Z605010B	225 mm deep	m²	0.20	2.54	0.70	–	3.24	2.79	0.77	–	3.56
Z605010C	300 mm deep	m²	0.25	3.18	0.87	–	4.05	3.50	0.96	–	4.46
Z605020	**Grass seeding to prepared ground; maintaining; first cut; reseeding if required:**										
Z605020A	rye mixture; fertiliser	m²	0.15	1.91	0.08	0.10	2.09	2.10	0.09	0.11	2.30
Z605020B	non-rye mixture; fertiliser . .	m²	0.15	1.90	0.08	0.13	2.11	2.09	0.09	0.14	2.32
Z605030	**Turfing to prepared ground; maintaining first cut; returfing if required:**										
Z605030A	meadow quality	m²	0.26	3.30	–	2.36	5.66	3.63	–	2.60	6.23
Z605030B	first grade lawn quality	m²	0.26	3.30	–	3.10	6.40	3.63	–	3.41	7.04
Z605030C	golf tee quality	m²	0.26	3.30	–	4.66	7.96	3.63	–	5.13	8.76
Z6070	**Enclosures**										
Z607070	**Close boarded softwood fencing; oak posts; treated with two coats timber preservative; excavation and concrete surround to posts; height of fence:**										
Z607070A	1.20 m	m	2.70	40.19	–	54.69	94.88	44.21	–	60.16	104.37
Z607070B	1.50 m	m	3.01	44.56	–	64.07	108.63	49.02	–	70.48	119.49
Z607070C	1.80 m	m	3.31	48.80	–	73.37	122.17	53.68	–	80.71	134.39
Z607075	**Interwoven softwood panel fencing; oak posts; treated with two coats timber preservative; excavation and concrete surround to posts; height of fence:**										
Z607075A	1.20 m	m	2.21	30.76	–	60.83	91.59	33.84	–	66.91	100.75
Z607075B	1.50 m	m	2.49	34.53	–	69.17	103.70	37.98	–	76.09	114.07
Z607075C	1.80 m	m	2.76	38.18	–	77.43	115.61	42.00	–	85.17	127.17

Major Works 2009		Unit	Labour Hours	Labour Net	Plant Net	Materials Net	Unit Net	Labour Gross	Plant Gross	Materials Gross	Unit Price
								(Gross rates include 10% profit)			
				£	£	£	£	£	£	£	£
Z61	**DRAINAGE**										
Z6110	**Drainage; pipework**										
Z611005	**Machine excavation; trench support; lay and joint pipes and fittings; bed and haunch/cover; vitrified clayware pipes and fittings; socketed with push-fit flexible joints; laid straight; nominal size: 100 mm; average depth of pipe invert:**										
Z611005A	0.50 m	m	0.82	10.43	2.86	12.01	25.30	11.47	3.15	13.21	27.83
Z611005B	0.75 m	m	1.00	12.71	3.52	12.37	28.60	13.98	3.87	13.61	31.46
Z611005C	1.00 m	m	1.22	15.51	4.30	12.74	32.55	17.06	4.73	14.01	35.81
Z611005D	1.25 m	m	1.59	20.20	5.45	13.70	39.35	22.22	6.00	15.07	43.29
Z611005E	1.50 m	m	1.84	23.38	6.22	14.18	43.78	25.72	6.84	15.60	48.16
Z611005F	1.75 m	m	2.08	26.43	7.16	14.66	48.25	29.07	7.88	16.13	53.08
Z611005G	2.00 m	m	2.33	29.60	7.93	15.15	52.68	32.56	8.72	16.67	57.95
Z611010	**Machine excavation; trench support; lay and joint pipes and fittings; bed and haunch/cover; vitrified clayware pipes and fittings; socketed with push-fit flexible joints; laid straight; nominal size: 150 mm; average depth of pipe invert:**										
Z611010C	1.00 m	m	1.25	15.89	4.30	17.62	37.81	17.48	4.73	19.38	41.59
Z611010D	1.25 m	m	1.62	20.59	5.45	18.58	44.62	22.65	6.00	20.44	49.08
Z611010E	1.50 m	m	1.87	23.76	6.22	19.06	49.04	26.14	6.84	20.97	53.94
Z611010F	1.75 m	m	2.11	26.81	7.16	19.55	53.52	29.49	7.88	21.51	58.87
Z611010G	2.00 m	m	2.36	29.98	7.93	20.03	57.94	32.98	8.72	22.03	63.73
Z611010H	2.25 m	m	2.62	33.28	9.52	20.51	63.31	36.61	10.47	22.56	69.64
Z611010I	2.50 m	m	3.48	44.21	10.52	23.41	78.14	48.63	11.57	25.75	85.95
Z611010J	2.75 m	m	3.80	48.27	11.51	24.13	83.91	53.10	12.66	26.54	92.30
Z611010K	3.00 m	m	4.13	52.46	12.72	24.86	90.04	57.71	13.99	27.35	99.04
Z611010L	3.25 m	m	4.46	56.66	13.93	25.58	96.17	62.33	15.32	28.14	105.79
Z611010M	3.50 m	m	4.79	60.84	15.14	26.31	102.29	66.92	16.65	28.94	112.52
Z611015	**Machine excavation; trench support; lay and joint pipes and fittings; bed and haunch/cover; vitrified clayware pipes and fittings; socketed with push-fit flexible joints; laid straight; nominal size: 225 mm; average depth of pipe invert:**										
Z611015E	1.50 m	m	2.12	26.89	8.24	36.84	71.97	29.58	9.06	40.52	79.17
Z611015F	1.75 m	m	2.37	30.06	9.40	37.32	76.78	33.07	10.34	41.05	84.46
Z611015G	2.00 m	m	2.63	33.36	10.39	37.80	81.55	36.70	11.43	41.58	89.71
Z611015H	2.25 m	m	3.47	44.03	12.67	40.46	97.16	48.43	13.94	44.51	106.88
Z611015I	2.50 m	m	3.79	48.10	13.85	41.18	103.13	52.91	15.24	45.30	113.44
Z611015J	2.75 m	m	4.11	52.16	14.85	41.91	108.92	57.38	16.34	46.10	119.81
Z611015K	3.00 m	m	4.44	56.35	16.06	42.63	115.04	61.99	17.67	46.89	126.54
Z611015L	3.25 m	m	4.77	60.54	17.27	43.35	121.16	66.59	19.00	47.69	133.28
Z611015M	3.50 m	m	5.10	64.73	18.48	44.08	127.29	71.20	20.33	48.49	140.02

Approximate Estimating Rates

Major Works 2009		Unit	Labour Hours	Labour Net	Plant Net	Materials Net	Unit Net	Labour Gross	Plant Gross	Materials Gross	Unit Price
								(Gross rates include 10% profit)			
				£	£	£	£	£	£	£	£
Z61	**DRAINAGE**										
Z6110	**Drainage; pipework**										
Z611020	**Machine excavation; trench support; lay and joint pipes and fittings; bed and haunch/cover; vitrified clayware pipes and fittings; socketed with push-fit flexible joints; laid straight; nominal size: 300 mm; average depth of pipe invert:**										
Z611020E	1.50 m	m	2.62	33.21	11.49	68.28	112.98	36.53	12.64	75.11	124.28
Z611020F	1.75 m	m	2.80	35.50	11.49	68.76	115.75	39.05	12.64	75.64	127.33
Z611020G	2.00 m	m	3.08	39.05	12.93	69.24	121.22	42.96	14.22	76.16	133.34
Z611020H	2.25 m	m	3.95	50.10	15.67	71.90	137.67	55.11	17.24	79.09	151.44
Z611020I	2.50 m	m	4.28	54.29	17.08	72.62	143.99	59.72	18.79	79.88	158.39
Z611020J	2.75 m	m	4.62	58.61	18.51	73.35	150.47	64.47	20.36	80.69	165.52
Z611020K	3.00 m	m	4.96	62.93	19.50	74.07	156.50	69.22	21.45	81.48	172.15
Z611020L	3.25 m	m	5.29	67.12	20.49	74.80	162.41	73.83	22.54	82.28	178.65
Z611020M	3.50 m	m	5.62	71.31	21.48	75.52	168.31	78.44	23.63	83.07	185.14
Z611025	**Machine excavation; trench support; lay and joint pipes and fittings; bed and haunch/cover; vitrified clayware pipes and fittings; socketed with push-fit flexible joints; laid straight; nominal size: 400 mm; average depth of pipe invert:**										
Z611025E	1.50 m	m	2.97	37.66	12.98	143.13	193.77	41.43	14.28	157.44	213.15
Z611025F	1.75 m	m	3.23	40.96	14.35	143.62	198.93	45.06	15.79	157.98	218.82
Z611025G	2.00 m	m	3.52	44.64	16.00	144.10	204.74	49.10	17.60	158.51	225.21
Z611025H	2.25 m	m	4.42	56.07	19.44	146.76	222.27	61.68	21.38	161.44	244.50
Z611025I	2.50 m	m	4.76	60.39	21.06	147.48	228.93	66.43	23.17	162.23	251.82
Z611025J	2.75 m	m	5.12	64.96	22.93	148.20	236.09	71.46	25.22	163.02	259.70
Z611025K	3.00 m	m	5.47	69.40	24.58	148.93	242.91	76.34	27.04	163.82	267.20
Z611025L	3.25 m	m	5.60	71.05	25.98	149.65	246.68	78.16	28.58	164.62	271.35
Z611025M	3.50 m	m	6.13	77.79	27.17	150.38	255.34	85.57	29.89	165.42	280.87
Z611030	**Machine excavation; trench support; lay and joint pipes and fittings; bed and haunch/cover; vitrified clayware pipes and fittings; socketed with push-fit flexible joints; laid straight; nominal size: 450 mm; average depth of pipe invert:**										
Z611030E	1.50 m	m	3.25	41.33	23.73	184.14	249.20	45.46	26.10	202.55	274.12
Z611030F	1.75 m	m	3.53	44.88	25.55	184.62	255.05	49.37	28.11	203.08	280.56
Z611030G	2.00 m	m	3.83	48.69	27.42	185.11	261.22	53.56	30.16	203.62	287.34
Z611030H	2.25 m	m	4.76	60.50	31.10	187.76	279.36	66.55	34.21	206.54	307.30
Z611030I	2.50 m	m	5.13	65.20	33.16	188.49	286.85	71.72	36.48	207.34	315.54
Z611030J	2.75 m	m	5.48	69.65	35.25	189.21	294.11	76.62	38.78	208.13	323.52
Z611030K	3.00 m	m	5.85	74.35	37.34	189.94	301.63	81.79	41.07	208.93	331.79
Z611030L	3.25 m	m	6.21	78.92	39.21	190.66	308.79	86.81	43.13	209.73	339.67
Z611030M	3.50 m	m	6.57	83.49	41.08	191.38	315.95	91.84	45.19	210.52	347.55

Major Works 2009		Unit	Labour Hours	Labour Net	Plant Net	Materials Net	Unit Net	Labour Gross	Plant Gross	Materials Gross	Unit Price
								(Gross rates include 10% profit)			
				£	£	£	£	£	£	£	£
Z61	**DRAINAGE**										
Z6110	**Drainage; pipework**										
Z611033	**100 mm SuperSleve: machine excavation; disposal of excess; earthwork support; granular bedding; pipework; backfill; testing; average depth of trench:**										
Z611033A	0.75 m	m	2.06	26.17	3.55	13.44	43.16	28.79	3.91	14.78	47.48
Z611033B	1.00 m	m	2.63	33.40	4.32	14.17	51.89	36.74	4.75	15.59	57.08
Z611033C	1.25 m	m	3.70	46.99	5.48	16.09	68.56	51.69	6.03	17.70	75.42
Z611033D	1.50 m	m	4.37	55.50	6.25	17.05	78.80	61.05	6.88	18.76	86.68
Z611033E	1.75 m	m	5.03	63.88	7.18	18.02	89.08	70.27	7.90	19.82	97.99
Z611033F	2.00 m	m	5.70	72.39	7.96	18.98	99.33	79.63	8.76	20.88	109.26
Z611034	**150 mm SuperSleve: machine excavation; disposal of excess; earthwork support; granular bedding; pipework; backfill; testing; average depth of trench:**										
Z611034A	0.75 m	m	2.09	26.54	3.55	18.33	48.42	29.19	3.91	20.16	53.26
Z611034B	1.00 m	m	2.66	33.78	4.32	19.05	57.15	37.16	4.75	20.96	62.87
Z611034C	1.25 m	m	3.73	47.37	5.48	20.97	73.82	52.11	6.03	23.07	81.20
Z611034D	1.50 m	m	4.40	55.88	6.25	21.94	84.07	61.47	6.88	24.13	92.48
Z611034E	1.75 m	m	5.06	64.26	7.18	22.90	94.34	70.69	7.90	25.19	103.77
Z611034F	2.00 m	m	5.73	72.78	7.96	23.87	104.61	80.06	8.76	26.26	115.07
Z611040	**110 mm uPVC: machine excavation; disposal of excess; earthwork support; granular bedding; pipework; backfill; testing; average depth of trench:**										
Z611040A	0.75 m	m	2.06	26.17	3.55	14.52	44.24	28.79	3.91	15.97	48.66
Z611040B	1.00 m	m	2.63	33.40	4.32	15.25	52.97	36.74	4.75	16.78	58.27
Z611040C	1.25 m	m	3.70	46.99	5.48	17.17	69.64	51.69	6.03	18.89	76.60
Z611040D	1.50 m	m	4.37	55.50	6.25	18.14	79.89	61.05	6.88	19.95	87.88
Z611040E	1.75 m	m	5.03	63.88	7.18	19.10	90.16	70.27	7.90	21.01	99.18
Z611040F	2.00 m	m	5.70	72.39	7.96	20.07	100.42	79.63	8.76	22.08	110.46
Z611041	**160 mm uPVC: machine excavation; disposal of excess; earthwork support; granular bedding; pipework; backfill; testing; average depth of trench:**										
Z611041A	0.75 m	m	2.11	26.79	3.55	22.15	52.49	29.47	3.91	24.37	57.74
Z611041B	1.00 m	m	2.68	34.04	4.32	22.87	61.23	37.44	4.75	25.16	67.35
Z611041C	1.25 m	m	3.75	47.62	5.48	24.79	77.89	52.38	6.03	27.27	85.68
Z611041D	1.50 m	m	4.42	56.13	6.25	25.76	88.14	61.74	6.88	28.34	96.95
Z611041E	1.75 m	m	5.08	64.51	7.18	26.72	98.41	70.96	7.90	29.39	108.25
Z611041F	2.00 m	m	5.75	73.02	7.96	27.69	108.67	80.32	8.76	30.46	119.54

Approximate Estimating Rates

Major Works 2009		Unit	Labour Hours	Labour Net	Plant Net	Materials Net	Unit Net	Labour Gross	Plant Gross	Materials Gross	Unit Price
								(Gross rates include 10% profit)			
				£	£	£	£	£	£	£	£
Z61	**DRAINAGE**										
Z6110	**Drainage; pipework**										
Z611050	**Machine excavation; trench support; lay and joint pipes and fittings; bed and cover; spun concrete pipes Class L; socketed with push-fit flexible joints laid straight; nominal size: 450 mm; average depth of pipe invert:**										
Z611050C	1.00 m	m	3.14	39.93	24.98	46.07	110.98	43.92	27.48	50.68	122.08
Z611050D	1.25 m	m	4.23	53.72	35.59	84.05	173.36	59.09	39.15	92.46	190.70
Z611050E	1.50 m	m	3.50	44.50	26.59	42.08	113.17	48.95	29.25	46.29	124.49
Z611050F	1.75 m	m	3.78	48.06	28.40	42.56	119.02	52.87	31.24	46.82	130.92
Z611050G	2.00 m	m	4.08	51.87	30.27	43.04	125.18	57.06	33.30	47.34	137.70
Z611050H	2.25 m	m	5.01	63.68	33.95	45.70	143.33	70.05	37.35	50.27	157.66
Z611050I	2.50 m	m	5.38	68.37	36.01	46.42	150.80	75.21	39.61	51.06	165.88
Z611050J	2.75 m	m	5.73	72.82	38.10	47.15	158.07	80.10	41.91	51.87	173.88
Z611050K	3.00 m	m	6.10	77.52	40.19	47.87	165.58	85.27	44.21	52.66	182.14
Z611050L	3.25 m	m	6.46	82.09	42.06	48.60	172.75	90.30	46.27	53.46	190.03
Z611050M	3.50 m	m	6.82	86.67	43.93	49.32	179.92	95.34	48.32	54.25	197.91
Z611052	**Machine excavation; trench support; lay and joint pipes and fittings; bed and cover; spun concrete pipes Class L; socketed with push-fit flexible joints laid straight; nominal size: 525 mm; average depth of pipe invert:**										
Z611052C	1.00 m	m	4.05	51.44	35.59	62.43	149.46	56.58	39.15	68.67	164.41
Z611052D	1.25 m	m	3.87	49.09	32.39	51.44	132.92	54.00	35.63	56.58	146.21
Z611052E	1.50 m	m	4.05	51.37	32.39	51.92	135.68	56.51	35.63	57.11	149.25
Z611052F	1.75 m	m	4.34	55.05	34.43	52.40	141.88	60.56	37.87	57.64	156.07
Z611052G	2.00 m	m	4.66	59.12	36.54	52.88	148.54	65.03	40.19	58.17	163.39
Z611052H	2.25 m	m	5.61	71.18	40.67	55.54	167.39	78.30	44.74	61.09	184.13
Z611052I	2.50 m	m	5.98	75.88	42.95	56.26	175.09	83.47	47.25	61.89	192.60
Z611052J	2.75 m	m	6.36	80.70	45.26	56.99	182.95	88.77	49.79	62.69	201.25
Z611052K	3.00 m	m	6.74	85.53	47.57	57.71	190.81	94.08	52.33	63.48	209.89
Z611052L	3.25 m	m	7.12	90.36	49.87	58.44	198.67	99.40	54.86	64.28	218.54
Z611052M	3.50 m	m	7.50	95.19	52.18	59.16	206.53	104.71	57.40	65.08	227.18
Z611054	**Machine excavation; trench support; lay and joint pipes and fittings; bed and cover; spun concrete pipes Class L; socketed with push-fit flexible joints laid straight; nominal size: 600 mm; average depth of pipe invert:**										
Z611054C	1.00 m	m	3.87	49.14	32.02	62.43	143.59	54.05	35.22	68.67	157.95
Z611054D	1.25 m	m	4.23	53.72	35.59	62.91	152.22	59.09	39.15	69.20	167.44
Z611054E	1.50 m	m	4.60	58.42	38.04	63.40	159.86	64.26	41.84	69.74	175.85
Z611054F	1.75 m	m	4.91	62.36	40.33	63.88	166.57	68.60	44.36	70.27	183.23
Z611054G	2.00 m	m	5.24	66.54	42.66	64.36	173.56	73.19	46.93	70.80	190.92
Z611054H	2.25 m	m	6.21	78.87	47.44	67.02	193.33	86.76	52.18	73.72	212.66
Z611054I	2.50 m	m	6.59	83.69	49.94	67.74	201.37	92.06	54.93	74.51	221.51
Z611054J	2.75 m	m	7.00	88.90	52.28	68.47	209.65	97.79	57.51	75.32	230.62
Z611054K	3.00 m	m	7.39	93.85	54.81	69.19	217.85	103.24	60.29	76.11	239.64
Z611054L	3.25 m	m	7.78	98.81	57.34	69.92	226.07	108.69	63.07	76.91	248.68
Z611054M	3.50 m	m	8.17	103.75	59.87	70.64	234.26	114.13	65.86	77.70	257.69

Major Works 2009		Unit	Labour Hours	Labour Net	Plant Net	Materials Net	Unit Net	Labour Gross	Plant Gross	Materials Gross	Unit Price
								(Gross rates include 10% profit)			
				£	£	£	£	£	£	£	£
Z61	**DRAINAGE**										
Z6120	**Manholes and inspection chambers; concrete ring construction**										
Z612010	Excavation in firm ground; disposal off site; earthwork support; concrete ST4 t base and benching; 13 mm render coat cut to channel and branches in mortar (1:3) precast concrete ring and cover slab construction; 150 mm concrete surround; 600 × 600 mm cast iron manhole cover and frame bedded and set on 225 mm Class B engineering brickwork; DTp type 1 backfill; step rungs; 900 mm nominal internal diameter; depth to invert:										
Z612010B	1.00 m	Nr	24.25	384.71	104.73	506.66	996.10	423.18	115.20	557.33	1095.71
Z612010C	1.25 m	Nr	27.71	437.27	127.13	559.60	1124.00	481.00	139.84	615.56	1236.40
Z612010D	1.50 m	Nr	30.75	484.71	147.12	603.37	1235.20	533.18	161.83	663.71	1358.72
Z612012	Excavation in firm ground; disposal off site; earthwork support; concrete ST4 t base and benching; 13 mm render coat cut to channel and branches in mortar (1:3) precast concrete ring and cover slab construction; 150 mm concrete surround; 600 × 600 mm cast iron manhole cover and frame bedded and set on 225 mm Class B engineering brickwork; DTp type 1 backfill; step rungs; 1050 mm nominal internal diameter; depth to invert:										
Z612012D	1.50 m	Nr	32.00	500.70	174.86	635.70	1311.26	550.77	192.35	699.27	1442.39
Z612012E	1.75 m	Nr	35.46	553.47	198.63	686.82	1438.92	608.82	218.49	755.50	1582.81
Z612012F	2.00 m	Nr	40.81	630.02	229.40	759.56	1618.98	693.02	252.34	835.52	1780.88
Z612014	Excavation in firm ground; disposal off site; earthwork support; concrete ST4 t base and benching; 13 mm render coat cut to channel and branches in mortar (1:3) precast concrete ring and cover slab construction; 150 mm concrete surround; 600 × 600 mm cast iron manhole cover and frame bedded and set on 225 mm Class B engineering brickwork; DTp type 1 backfill; step rungs; 1200 mm nominal internal diameter; depth to invert:										
Z612014D	1.50 m	Nr	37.73	582.44	232.18	775.59	1590.21	640.68	255.40	853.15	1749.23
Z612014E	1.75 m	Nr	43.27	661.53	267.31	850.58	1779.42	727.68	294.04	935.64	1957.36
Z612014F	2.00 m	Nr	43.27	661.53	267.31	850.58	1779.42	727.68	294.04	935.64	1957.36

Approximate Estimating Rates

Major Works 2009		Unit	Labour Hours	Labour Net	Plant Net	Materials Net	Unit Net	Labour Gross	Plant Gross	Materials Gross	Unit Price
								(Gross rates include 10% profit)			
				£	£	£	£	£	£	£	£
Z61	**DRAINAGE**										
Z6120	**Manholes and inspection chambers; concrete ring construction**										
Z612016	**Excavation in firm ground; disposal off site; earthwork support; concrete ST4 t base and benching; 13 mm render coat cut to channel and branches in mortar (1:3) precast concrete ring and cover slab construction; 150 mm concrete surround; 600 × 600 mm cast iron manhole cover and frame bedded and set on 225 mm Class B engineering brickwork; DTp type 1 backfill; step rungs; 1350 mm nominal internal diameter; depth to invert:**										
Z612016D	1.50 m	Nr	36.29	555.61	236.89	821.64	1614.14	611.17	260.58	903.80	1775.55
Z612016E	1.75 m	Nr	39.70	607.73	269.11	877.63	1754.47	668.50	296.02	965.39	1929.92
Z612016F	2.00 m	Nr	51.74	778.24	391.30	1119.25	2288.79	856.06	430.43	1231.18	2517.67
Z612016G	2.25 m	Nr	49.08	744.28	341.13	1038.69	2124.10	818.71	375.24	1142.56	2336.51
Z612016H	2.50 m	Nr	52.82	800.52	373.34	1094.44	2268.30	880.57	410.67	1203.88	2495.13
Z612018	**Excavation in firm ground; disposal off site; earthwork support; concrete ST4 t base and benching; 13 mm render coat cut to channel and branches in mortar (1:3) precast concrete ring and cover slab construction; 150 mm concrete surround; 600 × 600 mm cast iron manhole cover and frame bedded and set on 225 mm Class B engineering brickwork; DTp type 1 backfill; step rungs; 1500 mm nominal internal diameter; depth to invert:**										
Z612018F	2.00 m	Nr	47.89	720.69	354.49	1059.78	2134.96	792.76	389.94	1165.76	2348.46
Z612018G	2.25 m	Nr	51.74	778.24	391.30	1119.25	2288.79	856.06	430.43	1231.18	2517.67
Z612018H	2.50 m	Nr	55.58	835.83	428.40	1199.23	2463.46	919.41	471.24	1319.15	2709.81
Z612018I	2.75 m	Nr	59.43	893.38	465.21	1279.15	2637.74	982.72	511.73	1407.07	2901.51
Z612018J	3.00 m	Nr	65.38	977.64	510.46	1381.32	2869.42	1075.40	561.51	1519.45	3156.36
Z612018K	3.25 m	Nr	69.22	1035.18	547.27	1461.25	3043.70	1138.70	602.00	1607.38	3348.07
Z612018L	3.50 m	Nr	73.07	1092.78	584.37	1520.76	3197.91	1202.06	642.81	1672.84	3517.70
Z612018M	3.75 m	Nr	76.92	1150.36	599.27	1600.97	3350.60	1265.40	659.20	1761.07	3685.66
Z612018N	4.00 m	Nr	82.88	1234.92	644.44	1702.99	3582.35	1358.41	708.88	1873.29	3940.59

Major Works 2009		Unit	Labour Hours	Labour Net	Plant Net	Materials Net	Unit Net	Labour Gross	Plant Gross	Materials Gross	Unit Price
								(Gross rates include 10% profit)			
				£	£	£	£	£	£	£	£
Z61	**DRAINAGE**										
Z6125	**Manholes and inspection chambers; brick chamber construction**										
Z612510	Excavation; disposal; backfilling; concrete base; Class B engineering brickwork 215 mm thick; 100 mm channels set in benching; cast iron cover and frame; 600 × 450 mm internal size; depth to invert:										
Z612510A	0.75 m	Nr	12.27	198.43	29.51	251.87	479.81	218.27	32.46	277.06	527.79
Z612510B	1.00 m	Nr	15.06	248.27	37.19	305.86	591.32	273.10	40.91	336.45	650.45
Z612510C	1.25 m	Nr	19.37	317.66	46.66	368.62	732.94	349.43	51.33	405.48	806.23
Z612510D	1.50 m	Nr	22.44	371.18	55.00	424.12	850.30	408.30	60.50	466.53	935.33
Z612510E	1.75 m	Nr	25.50	424.57	62.90	479.62	967.09	467.03	69.19	527.58	1063.80
Z612515	Excavation; disposal; backfilling; concrete base; Class B engineering brickwork 215 mm thick; 100 mm channels set in benching; cast iron cover and frame; 900 × 600 mm internal size; depth to invert:										
Z612515A	0.75 m	Nr	15.77	255.18	42.36	337.38	634.92	280.70	46.60	371.12	698.41
Z612515B	1.00 m	Nr	19.20	317.37	53.21	406.87	777.45	349.11	58.53	447.56	855.20
Z612515C	1.25 m	Nr	24.45	402.67	67.32	480.39	950.38	442.94	74.05	528.43	1045.42
Z612515D	1.50 m	Nr	28.21	469.05	78.83	555.06	1102.94	515.96	86.71	610.57	1213.23
Z612515E	1.75 m	Nr	31.96	535.31	90.37	625.27	1250.95	588.84	99.41	687.80	1376.05
Z6130	**Manholes and inspection chambers; uPVC construction**										
Z613010	UPVC chamber; 250 mm diameter; shallow chamber; bed on granular fill; granular surround; cover and frame with concrete support collar; depth to invert:										
Z613010A	0.60 m	Nr	1.38	17.52	–	117.19	134.71	19.27	–	128.91	148.18
Z613015	UPVC chamber; 300 mm diameter; shallow chamber; bed on granular fill; granular surround; cover and frame with concrete support collar; depth to invert:										
Z613015A	0.75 m	Nr	2.92	39.09	–	189.20	228.29	43.00	–	208.12	251.12
Z613020	UPVC chamber; 450 mm diameter; shallow chamber; bed on granular fill; granular surround; cover and frame with concrete support collar; depth to invert:										
Z613020A	0.75 m	Nr	7.21	94.10	7.07	258.69	359.86	103.51	7.78	284.56	395.85
Z613020B	1.00 m	Nr	8.75	113.65	9.11	291.87	414.63	125.02	10.02	321.06	456.09

Approximate Estimating Rates

Major Works 2009		Unit	Labour Hours	Labour Net	Plant Net	Materials Net	Unit Net	Labour Gross	Plant Gross	Materials Gross	Unit Price
								—— (Gross rates include 10% profit) ——			
				£	£	£	£	£	£	£	£
Z61	**DRAINAGE**										
Z6140	**Soakaways; precast concrete; perforated rings; complete**										
Z614010	**Excavation; disposal off site; concrete foundation; concrete ring construction; cover slab; hardcore backfill; brick access shaft; c.i. cover and frame; 1050 mm dia; depth below pipe invert:**										
Z614010A	0.75 m	Nr	19.98	270.21	93.06	262.22	625.49	297.23	102.37	288.44	688.04
Z614010B	1.00 m	Nr	25.42	339.30	98.29	258.17	695.76	373.23	108.12	283.99	765.34
Z614010C	1.25 m	Nr	27.66	367.75	115.98	274.04	757.77	404.53	127.58	301.44	833.55
Z614010D	1.50 m	Nr	30.44	403.05	146.65	320.20	869.90	443.36	161.32	352.22	956.89
Z614010E	1.75 m	Nr	32.48	428.96	159.91	336.69	925.56	471.86	175.90	370.36	1018.12
Z614015	**Excavation; disposal off site; concrete foundation; concrete ring construction; cover slab; hardcore backfill; brick access shaft; c.i. cover and frame; 1200 mm dia; depth below pipe invert:**										
Z614015A	0.75 m	Nr	18.48	252.19	110.35	295.48	658.02	277.41	121.39	325.03	723.82
Z614015B	1.00 m	Nr	20.97	283.81	136.72	324.61	745.14	312.19	150.39	357.07	819.65
Z614015C	1.25 m	Nr	27.75	369.92	156.94	354.46	881.32	406.91	172.63	389.91	969.45
Z614015D	1.50 m	Nr	30.02	398.75	172.97	362.92	934.64	438.63	190.27	399.21	1028.10
Z614015E	1.75 m	Nr	32.30	427.70	189.02	382.34	999.06	470.47	207.92	420.57	1098.97
Z6145	**Soakaways; rubble filled; complete**										
Z614510	**Excavation; disposal off site; rubble fill; geotextile membrane cover; topsoil cover; capacity:**										
Z614510A	0.75 m³	Nr	1.61	20.39	38.41	26.47	85.27	22.43	42.25	29.12	93.80
Z614510B	1.50 m³	Nr	2.16	27.44	71.13	49.49	148.06	30.18	78.24	54.44	162.87
Z614510C	2.00 m³	Nr	3.21	40.77	102.64	70.12	213.53	44.85	112.90	77.13	234.88
Z614510D	2.50 m³	Nr	2.40	30.45	110.58	96.37	237.40	33.50	121.64	106.01	261.14
Z614510E	3.75 m³	Nr	3.56	45.16	164.75	143.72	353.63	49.68	181.23	158.09	388.99
Z614510F	5.00 m³	Nr	5.19	65.91	232.28	200.98	499.17	72.50	255.51	221.08	549.09
Z614510G	7.50 m³	Nr	6.89	87.50	323.39	282.77	693.66	96.25	355.73	311.05	763.03
Z6170	**Gullies; complete**										
Z617010	**Clay back inlet gully; excavation; concrete surround; grating; bucket; outlet:**										
Z617010A	100 mm	Nr	1.53	19.43	2.05	63.26	84.74	21.37	2.26	69.59	93.21
Z617010B	150 mm	Nr	2.84	36.06	2.79	95.04	133.89	39.67	3.07	104.54	147.28
Z617015	**Clay yard gully; excavation; concrete surround; grating; bucket; outlet:**										
Z617015A	100 mm	Nr	4.42	56.13	2.23	96.36	154.72	61.74	2.45	106.00	170.19
Z617015B	150 mm	Nr	4.79	60.84	2.79	116.53	180.16	66.92	3.07	128.18	198.18
Z617020	**Clay surface water gully; excavation; concrete surround; grating; bucket; outlet:**										
Z617020A	100 mm	Nr	1.15	14.61	2.05	50.92	67.58	16.07	2.26	56.01	74.34
Z617020B	150 mm	Nr	3.04	38.61	2.79	37.52	78.92	42.47	3.07	41.27	86.81

Major Works 2009		Unit	Labour Hours	Labour Net	Plant Net	Materials Net	Unit Net	Labour Gross	Plant Gross	Materials Gross	Unit Price
								(Gross rates include 10% profit)			
				£	£	£	£	£	£	£	£
Z66	**WORK TO EXISTING BUILDINGS**										
Z6602	**Forming openings in cavity walls**										
Z660210	**Form door opening; close cavity; make good reveals; build in lintel; make good plaster and emulsion paint one side; opening size:**										
Z660210A	900 × 2100 mm.........	Nr	11.83	256.85	25.99	107.65	390.49	282.54	28.59	118.42	429.54
Z660210B	1200 × 2100 mm	Nr	14.62	308.89	34.58	122.90	466.37	339.78	38.04	135.19	513.01
Z660210C	1800 × 2100 mm	Nr	18.84	371.78	55.83	162.44	590.05	408.96	61.41	178.68	649.06
Z660210D	2400 × 2100 mm	Nr	23.11	437.45	74.25	267.91	779.61	481.20	81.68	294.70	857.57
Z660250	**Form window opening; close cavity; make good reveals; build in lintel; make good plaster and emulsion paint one side; opening size:**										
Z660250A	630 × 750 mm.........	Nr	3.67	80.85	6.34	68.69	155.88	88.94	6.97	75.56	171.47
Z660250B	630 × 1050 mm.........	Nr	5.01	108.15	9.86	73.15	191.16	118.97	10.85	80.47	210.28
Z660250C	915 × 1050 mm.........	Nr	5.96	121.27	14.17	87.47	222.91	133.40	15.59	96.22	245.20
Z660250D	915 × 1350 mm.........	Nr	7.39	149.66	18.23	92.33	260.22	164.63	20.05	101.56	286.24
Z660250E	1200 × 1050 mm	Nr	7.06	138.11	18.45	100.07	256.63	151.92	20.30	110.08	282.29
Z660250F	1200 × 1350 mm	Nr	8.73	169.55	24.01	104.92	298.48	186.51	26.41	115.41	328.33
Z660250G	1770 × 1050 mm	Nr	9.19	169.70	27.52	138.63	335.85	186.67	30.27	152.49	369.44
Z660250H	1770 × 1350 mm	Nr	11.25	206.14	34.82	145.71	386.67	226.75	38.30	160.28	425.34
Z6604	**Forming openings in solid brick walls**										
Z660410	**Form door opening in half brick wall; make good reveals; build in lintel; make good finishes both sides; opening size:**										
Z660410A	900 × 2100 mm.........	Nr	7.93	142.24	21.25	60.89	224.38	156.46	23.38	66.98	246.82
Z660410B	1200 × 2100 mm	Nr	9.65	167.21	28.15	68.24	263.60	183.93	30.97	75.06	289.96
Z660410C	1800 × 2100 mm	Nr	13.01	214.88	42.19	95.59	352.66	236.37	46.41	105.15	387.93
Z660410D	2400 × 2100 mm	Nr	16.80	268.64	58.27	223.24	550.15	295.50	64.10	245.56	605.17
Z660415	**Form door opening in one brick wall; make good reveals; build in lintels; make good finishes both sides; opening size:**										
Z660415A	900 × 2100 mm.........	Nr	10.01	183.71	28.36	102.24	314.31	202.08	31.20	112.46	345.74
Z660415B	1200 × 2100 mm	Nr	10.50	193.32	32.95	124.23	350.50	212.65	36.25	136.65	385.55
Z660415C	1800 × 2100 mm	Nr	12.95	230.16	46.82	159.73	436.71	253.18	51.50	175.70	480.38
Z660415D	2400 × 2100 mm	Nr	20.55	332.87	78.11	322.62	733.60	366.16	85.92	354.88	806.96
Z660420	**Form door opening in one and a half brick wall; make good reveals; build in lintels; make good finishes both sides; opening size:**										
Z660420A	900 × 2100 mm.........	Nr	13.21	248.73	38.01	150.83	437.57	273.60	41.81	165.91	481.33
Z660420B	1200 × 2100 mm	Nr	15.95	288.95	50.57	177.60	517.12	317.85	55.63	195.36	568.83
Z660420C	1800 × 2100 mm	Nr	21.28	365.36	75.73	232.14	673.23	401.90	83.30	255.35	740.55
Z660420D	2400 × 2100 mm	Nr	27.25	450.35	104.34	529.27	1083.96	495.39	114.77	582.20	1192.36

Approximate Estimating Rates

Major Works 2009		Unit	Labour Hours	Labour Net	Plant Net	Materials Net	Unit Net	Labour Gross	Plant Gross	Materials Gross	Unit Price
								(Gross rates include 10% profit)			
				£	£	£	£	£	£	£	£
Z66	**WORK TO EXISTING BUILDINGS**										
Z6604	**Forming openings in solid brick walls**										
Z660425	**Form window opening in half brick wall; make good reveals; build in lintel; make good finishes both sides; opening size:**										
Z660425A	630 × 750 mm..........	Nr	2.76	59.05	4.37	37.85	101.27	64.96	4.81	41.64	111.40
Z660425B	630 × 1050 mm........	Nr	3.70	77.21	6.71	41.80	125.72	84.93	7.38	45.98	138.29
Z660425C	915 × 1050 mm........	Nr	4.45	87.74	9.96	59.91	157.61	96.51	10.96	65.90	173.37
Z660425D	915 × 1350 mm........	Nr	5.43	106.32	12.59	52.17	171.08	116.95	13.85	57.39	188.19
Z660425E	1200 × 1050 mm	Nr	5.33	101.79	12.98	60.77	175.54	111.97	14.28	66.85	193.09
Z660425F	1200 × 1350 mm	Nr	6.50	122.78	16.65	61.67	201.10	135.06	18.32	67.84	221.21
Z660425G	1770 × 1050 mm	Nr	7.02	127.79	19.02	87.06	233.87	140.57	20.92	95.77	257.26
Z660425H	1770 × 1350 mm	Nr	8.49	152.64	24.16	90.18	266.98	167.90	26.58	99.20	293.68
Z660450	**Form window opening in one brick wall; make good reveals; build in lintel; make good finishes both sides; opening size:**										
Z660450A	630 × 750 mm..........	Nr	3.68	82.84	5.59	62.56	150.99	91.12	6.15	68.82	166.09
Z660450B	630 × 1050 mm........	Nr	4.94	109.12	8.57	66.51	184.20	120.03	9.43	73.16	202.62
Z660450C	915 × 1050 mm........	Nr	5.80	121.09	12.50	81.11	214.70	133.20	13.75	89.22	236.17
Z660450D	915 × 1350 mm........	Nr	7.15	148.47	16.24	85.06	249.77	163.32	17.86	93.57	274.75
Z660450E	1200 × 1050 mm	Nr	6.81	136.80	16.42	100.84	254.06	150.48	18.06	110.92	279.47
Z660450F	1200 × 1350 mm	Nr	8.36	166.71	21.30	104.79	292.80	183.38	23.43	115.27	322.08
Z660450G	1770 × 1050 mm	Nr	8.74	165.84	24.28	135.02	325.14	182.42	26.71	148.52	357.65
Z660450H	1770 × 1350 mm	Nr	10.65	200.38	30.96	141.19	372.53	220.42	34.06	155.31	409.78
Z660455	**Form window opening in one and a half brick wall; make good reveals; build in lintel; make good finishes both sides; opening size:**										
Z660455A	630 × 750 mm..........	Nr	4.15	88.08	7.70	98.54	194.32	96.89	8.47	108.39	213.75
Z660455B	630 × 1050 mm........	Nr	5.10	101.20	12.21	99.43	212.84	111.32	13.43	109.37	234.12
Z660455C	915 × 1050 mm........	Nr	6.92	135.75	17.52	124.16	277.43	149.33	19.27	136.58	305.17
Z660455D	915 × 1350 mm........	Nr	8.38	161.96	22.83	128.33	313.12	178.16	25.11	141.16	344.43
Z660455E	1200 × 1050 mm	Nr	8.46	161.29	23.08	148.67	333.04	177.42	25.39	163.54	366.34
Z660455F	1200 × 1350 mm	Nr	10.19	190.93	29.67	152.84	373.44	210.02	32.64	168.12	410.78
Z660455G	1770 × 1050 mm	Nr	11.19	203.61	33.90	208.28	445.79	223.97	37.29	229.11	490.37
Z660455H	1770 × 1350 mm	Nr	13.41	239.51	43.15	214.66	497.32	263.46	47.47	236.13	547.05

Major Works 2009		Unit	Labour Hours	Labour Net	Plant Net	Materials Net	Unit Net	Labour Gross	Plant Gross	Materials Gross	Unit Price
								(Gross rates include 10% profit)			
				£	£	£	£	£	£	£	£
Z66	**WORK TO EXISTING BUILDINGS**										
Z6606	**Forming openings in solid block walls**										
Z660610	**Form door opening in 100 mm block wall; make good reveals; build in lintel; make good finishes both sides; opening size:**										
Z660610A	900 × 2100 mm.........	Nr	7.11	128.23	20.22	58.24	206.69	141.05	22.24	64.06	227.36
Z660610B	1200 × 2100 mm	Nr	8.63	150.67	26.79	65.37	242.83	165.74	29.47	71.91	267.11
Z660610C	1800 × 2100 mm	Nr	11.59	193.25	40.20	92.73	326.18	212.58	44.22	102.00	358.80
Z660610D	2400 × 2100 mm	Nr	14.81	238.37	55.48	220.38	514.23	262.21	61.03	242.42	565.65
Z660615	**Form door opening in 150 mm block wall; make good reveals; build in lintel; make good finishes both sides; opening size:**										
Z660615A	900 × 2100 mm.........	Nr	8.47	158.36	22.85	71.93	253.14	174.20	25.14	79.12	278.45
Z660615B	1200 × 2100 mm	Nr	10.12	182.87	30.31	86.12	299.30	201.16	33.34	94.73	329.23
Z660615C	1800 × 2100 mm	Nr	13.31	228.42	45.45	117.39	391.26	251.26	50.00	129.13	430.39
Z660615D	2400 × 2100 mm	Nr	16.82	277.78	62.79	221.81	562.38	305.56	69.07	243.99	618.62
Z660620	**Form door opening in 200 mm block wall; make good reveals; build in lintel; make good finishes both sides; opening size:**										
Z660620A	900 × 2100 mm.........	Nr	9.82	183.03	28.18	75.31	286.52	201.33	31.00	82.84	315.17
Z660620B	1200 × 2100 mm	Nr	11.77	211.18	37.55	88.59	337.32	232.30	41.31	97.45	371.05
Z660620C	1800 × 2100 mm	Nr	15.60	265.37	56.33	120.77	442.47	291.91	61.96	132.85	486.72
Z660620D	2400 × 2100 mm	Nr	19.08	314.51	74.95	225.19	614.65	345.96	82.45	247.71	676.12
Z660650	**Form window opening in 100 mm block wall; make good reveals; build in lintel; make good finishes both sides; opening size:**										
Z660650A	630 × 750 mm..........	Nr	2.96	59.10	4.20	65.81	129.11	65.01	4.62	72.39	142.02
Z660650B	630 × 1050 mm.........	Nr	3.82	74.26	6.51	71.45	152.22	81.69	7.16	78.60	167.44
Z660650C	915 × 1050 mm.........	Nr	4.66	87.11	9.41	80.50	177.02	95.82	10.35	88.55	194.72
Z660650D	915 × 1350 mm.........	Nr	5.58	102.99	12.15	86.58	201.72	113.29	13.37	95.24	221.89
Z660650E	1200 × 1050 mm.........	Nr	6.26	111.44	14.59	90.67	216.70	122.58	16.05	99.74	238.37
Z660650F	1200 × 1350 mm	Nr	6.71	121.30	15.86	94.63	231.79	133.43	17.45	104.09	254.97
Z660650G	1770 × 1050 mm	Nr	7.52	134.11	18.17	125.42	277.70	147.52	19.99	137.96	305.47
Z660650H	1770 × 1350 mm	Nr	8.87	155.49	20.93	134.57	310.99	171.04	23.02	148.03	342.09

Approximate Estimating Rates

Major Works 2009		Unit	Labour Hours	Labour Net	Plant Net	Materials Net	Unit Net	Labour Gross	Plant Gross	Materials Gross	Unit Price
								(Gross rates include 10% profit)			
				£	£	£	£	£	£	£	£
Z66	**WORK TO EXISTING BUILDINGS**										
Z6606	**Forming openings in solid block walls**										
Z660655	**Form window opening in 150 mm block wall; make good reveals; build in lintel; make good finishes both sides; opening size:**										
Z660655A	630 × 750 mm..........	Nr	3.26	66.83	4.80	64.77	136.40	73.51	5.28	71.25	150.04
Z660655B	630 × 1050 mm........	Nr	4.23	84.92	7.37	70.75	163.04	93.41	8.11	77.83	179.34
Z660655C	915 × 1050 mm........	Nr	5.34	104.81	10.81	84.79	200.41	115.29	11.89	93.27	220.45
Z660655D	915 × 1350 mm........	Nr	6.17	117.49	13.92	90.18	221.59	129.24	15.31	99.20	243.75
Z660655E	1200 × 1050 mm	Nr	6.16	115.63	14.06	99.30	228.99	127.19	15.47	109.23	251.89
Z660655F	1200 × 1350 mm	Nr	7.37	136.69	18.17	105.29	260.15	150.36	19.99	115.82	286.17
Z660655G	1770 × 1050 mm	Nr	8.13	147.33	21.01	137.76	306.10	162.06	23.11	151.54	336.71
Z660655H	1770 × 1350 mm	Nr	9.63	172.15	23.53	147.25	342.93	189.37	25.88	161.98	377.22
Z660660	**Form window opening in 200 mm block wall; make good reveals; build in lintel; make good finishes both sides; opening size:**										
Z660660A	630 × 750 mm..........	Nr	3.26	66.83	4.80	64.77	136.40	73.51	5.28	71.25	150.04
Z660660B	630 × 1050 mm........	Nr	4.23	84.92	7.37	70.75	163.04	93.41	8.11	77.83	179.34
Z660660C	915 × 1050 mm........	Nr	5.34	104.81	10.81	84.79	200.41	115.29	11.89	93.27	220.45
Z660660D	915 × 1350 mm........	Nr	6.17	117.49	13.92	90.18	221.59	129.24	15.31	99.20	243.75
Z660660E	1200 × 1050 mm	Nr	6.16	115.63	14.06	99.30	228.99	127.19	15.47	109.23	251.89
Z660660F	1200 × 1350 mm	Nr	7.37	136.69	18.17	105.29	260.15	150.36	19.99	115.82	286.17
Z660660G	1770 × 1050 mm	Nr	8.13	147.33	21.01	137.76	306.10	162.06	23.11	151.54	336.71
Z660660H	1770 × 1350 mm	Nr	9.63	172.15	23.53	147.25	342.93	189.37	25.88	161.98	377.22

Major Works 2009		Unit	Labour Hours	Labour Net	Plant Net	Materials Net	Unit Net	Labour Gross	Plant Gross	Materials Gross	Unit Price
									(Gross rates include 10% profit)		
				£	£	£	£	£	£	£	£
Z66	**WORK TO EXISTING BUILDINGS**										
Z6610	**Blocking up openings in cavity walls**										
Z661010	**Block up opening in cavity wall; 105 mm facing brick outer leaf, 50 mm fully insulated cavity and 100 mm blockwork inner leaf; face point externally; plaster with emulsion paint finish internally; opening size:**										
Z661010A	630 × 900 mm	Nr	3.79	110.75	–	36.75	147.50	121.83	–	40.43	162.25
Z661010B	915 × 1050 mm	Nr	5.43	158.55	–	53.20	211.75	174.41	–	58.52	232.93
Z661010C	1200 × 1200 mm	Nr	7.62	221.40	–	72.09	293.49	243.54	–	79.30	322.84
Z661010D	1770 × 1350 mm	Nr	11.46	332.15	–	109.87	442.02	365.37	–	120.86	486.22
Z661010E	900 × 2100 mm	Nr	10.97	319.45	–	98.36	417.81	351.40	–	108.20	459.59
Z661010F	1200 × 2100 mm	Nr	13.33	387.34	–	121.46	508.80	426.07	–	133.61	559.68
Z661010G	1800 × 2100 mm	Nr	18.07	523.64	–	168.85	692.49	576.00	–	185.74	761.74
Z661010H	2400 × 2100 mm	Nr	22.81	659.90	–	220.82	880.72	725.89	–	242.90	968.79
Z661015	**Block up opening in cavity wall; 105 mm facing brick outer leaf, 50 mm fully insulated cavity and 125 mm blockwork inner leaf; face point externally; plaster with emulsion paint finish internally; opening size:**										
Z661015A	630 × 900 mm	Nr	3.86	112.83	–	39.58	152.41	124.11	–	43.54	167.65
Z661015B	915 × 1050 mm	Nr	5.55	162.12	–	57.36	219.48	178.33	–	63.10	241.43
Z661015C	1200 × 1200 mm	Nr	7.76	225.57	–	77.86	303.43	248.13	–	85.65	333.77
Z661015D	1770 × 1350 mm	Nr	11.67	338.39	–	118.64	457.03	372.23	–	130.50	502.73
Z661015E	900 × 2100 mm	Nr	11.19	326.00	–	106.60	432.60	358.60	–	117.26	475.86
Z661015F	1200 × 2100 mm	Nr	13.59	395.08	–	132.66	527.74	434.59	–	145.93	580.51
Z661015G	1800 × 2100 mm	Nr	18.38	532.87	–	182.69	715.56	586.16	–	200.96	787.12
Z661015H	2400 × 2100 mm	Nr	23.19	671.22	–	238.39	909.61	738.34	–	262.23	1000.57
Z661020	**Block up opening in cavity wall; 100 mm blockwork outer leaf, 50 mm insulated cavity and 100 mm blockwork inner leaf; render and masonry paint externally; plaster with emulsion paint finish internally; opening size:**										
Z661020A	630 × 900 mm	Nr	3.38	96.06	–	33.54	129.60	105.67	–	36.89	142.56
Z661020B	915 × 1050 mm	Nr	4.99	141.20	–	45.47	186.67	155.32	–	50.02	205.34
Z661020C	1200 × 1200 mm	Nr	7.19	202.14	–	62.83	264.97	222.35	–	69.11	291.47
Z661020D	1770 × 1350 mm	Nr	11.09	310.41	–	94.42	404.83	341.45	–	103.86	445.31
Z661020E	900 × 2100 mm	Nr	10.14	285.79	–	87.78	373.57	314.37	–	96.56	410.93
Z661020F	1200 × 2100 mm	Nr	12.60	353.79	–	106.59	460.38	389.17	–	117.25	506.42
Z661020G	1800 × 2100 mm	Nr	17.58	491.30	–	150.69	641.99	540.43	–	165.76	706.19
Z661020H	2400 × 2100 mm	Nr	22.55	628.42	–	195.93	824.35	691.26	–	215.52	906.79
Z661025	**Block up opening in cavity wall; 100 mm blockwork outer leaf, 50 mm insulated cavity and 125 mm blockwork inner leaf; render and masonry paint externally; plaster with emulsion paint finish internally; opening size:**										
Z661025A	630 × 900 mm	Nr	3.45	98.15	–	36.37	134.52	107.97	–	40.01	147.97
Z661025B	915 × 1050 mm	Nr	5.11	144.77	–	49.63	194.40	159.25	–	54.59	213.84
Z661025C	1200 × 1200 mm	Nr	7.33	206.31	–	68.60	274.91	226.94	–	75.46	302.40
Z661025D	1770 × 1350 mm	Nr	11.30	316.67	–	103.19	419.86	348.34	–	113.51	461.85
Z661025E	900 × 2100 mm	Nr	10.36	292.35	–	96.01	388.36	321.59	–	105.61	427.20
Z661025F	1200 × 2100 mm	Nr	12.86	361.53	–	117.79	479.32	397.68	–	129.57	527.25
Z661025G	1800 × 2100 mm	Nr	17.89	500.54	–	164.53	665.07	550.59	–	180.98	731.58
Z661025H	2400 × 2100 mm	Nr	22.93	639.73	–	213.51	853.24	703.70	–	234.86	938.56

Approximate Estimating Rates

Major Works 2009		Unit	Labour Hours	Labour Net	Plant Net	Materials Net	Unit Net	Labour Gross	Plant Gross	Materials Gross	Unit Price
								(Gross rates include 10% profit)			
				£	£	£	£	£	£	£	£
Z66	**WORK TO EXISTING BUILDINGS**										
Z6612	**Blocking up openings in solid brick walls**										
Z661210	**Block up opening in half brick wall; facing bricks; pointed externally; plaster with emulsion paint finish internally; opening size:**										
Z661210A	630 × 900 mm	Nr	2.63	76.90	–	23.11	100.01	84.59	–	25.42	110.01
Z661210B	915 × 1050 mm	Nr	3.89	113.39	–	34.39	147.78	124.73	–	37.83	162.56
Z661210C	1200 × 1200 mm	Nr	5.38	156.51	–	45.67	202.18	172.16	–	50.24	222.40
Z661210D	1770 × 1350 mm	Nr	8.17	237.15	–	70.10	307.25	260.87	–	77.11	337.98
Z661210E	900 × 2100 mm	Nr	7.70	224.44	–	61.88	286.32	246.88	–	68.07	314.95
Z661210F	1200 × 2100 mm	Nr	9.42	274.07	–	76.55	350.62	301.48	–	84.21	385.68
Z661210G	1800 × 2100 mm	Nr	12.87	373.54	–	106.16	479.70	410.89	–	116.78	527.67
Z661210H	2400 × 2100 mm	Nr	16.32	473.01	–	140.17	613.18	520.31	–	154.19	674.50
Z661215	**Block up opening in one brick wall; facing bricks; pointed externally; plaster with emulsion paint finish internally; opening size:**										
Z661215A	630 × 900 mm	Nr	3.54	103.95	–	40.56	144.51	114.35	–	44.62	158.96
Z661215B	915 × 1050 mm	Nr	5.19	152.10	–	59.04	211.14	167.31	–	64.94	232.25
Z661215C	1200 × 1200 mm	Nr	7.14	208.88	–	84.71	293.59	229.77	–	93.18	322.95
Z661215D	1770 × 1350 mm	Nr	10.76	314.23	–	129.65	443.88	345.65	–	142.62	488.27
Z661215E	900 × 2100 mm	Nr	7.70	224.44	–	61.88	286.32	246.88	–	68.07	314.95
Z661215F	1200 × 2100 mm	Nr	12.50	365.74	–	141.15	506.89	402.31	–	155.27	557.58
Z661215G	1800 × 2100 mm	Nr	16.95	495.00	–	203.51	698.51	544.50	–	223.86	768.36
Z661215H	2400 × 2100 mm	Nr	21.42	624.80	–	265.22	890.02	687.28	–	291.74	979.02
Z661220	**Block up opening in one and a half brick wall; facing bricks; pointed externally; plaster with emulsion paint finish internally; opening size:**										
Z661220A	630 × 900 mm	Nr	4.73	139.40	–	54.36	193.76	153.34	–	59.80	213.14
Z661220B	915 × 1050 mm	Nr	6.79	199.75	–	81.02	280.77	219.73	–	89.12	308.85
Z661220C	1200 × 1200 mm	Nr	9.23	271.13	–	114.27	385.40	298.24	–	125.70	423.94
Z661220D	1770 × 1350 mm	Nr	13.68	401.19	–	177.25	578.44	441.31	–	194.98	636.28
Z661220E	900 × 2100 mm	Nr	13.45	395.63	–	154.78	550.41	435.19	–	170.26	605.45
Z661220F	1200 × 2100 mm	Nr	16.15	474.44	–	194.38	668.82	521.88	–	213.82	735.70
Z661220G	1800 × 2100 mm	Nr	21.55	631.98	–	276.56	908.54	695.18	–	304.22	999.39
Z661220H	2400 × 2100 mm	Nr	26.96	789.77	–	360.44	1150.21	868.75	–	396.48	1265.23
Z661230	**Block up opening in half brick wall; common bricks; plaster with emulsion paint finish both sides; opening size:**										
Z661230A	630 × 900 mm	Nr	3.09	89.46	–	20.12	109.58	98.41	–	22.13	120.54
Z661230B	915 × 1050 mm	Nr	4.83	139.36	–	32.23	171.59	153.30	–	35.45	188.75
Z661230C	1200 × 1200 mm	Nr	6.93	199.72	–	43.22	242.94	219.69	–	47.54	267.23
Z661230D	1770 × 1350 mm	Nr	10.95	315.08	–	68.13	383.21	346.59	–	74.94	421.53
Z661230E	900 × 2100 mm	Nr	9.53	275.10	–	58.94	334.04	302.61	–	64.83	367.44
Z661230F	1200 × 2100 mm	Nr	12.12	349.29	–	75.79	425.08	384.22	–	83.37	467.59
Z661230G	1800 × 2100 mm	Nr	17.30	497.79	–	105.19	602.98	547.57	–	115.71	663.28
Z661230H	2400 × 2100 mm	Nr	22.47	645.99	–	138.64	784.63	710.59	–	152.50	863.09

Major Works 2009		Unit	Labour Hours	Labour Net	Plant Net	Materials Net	Unit Net	Labour Gross	Plant Gross	Materials Gross	Unit Price
								(Gross rates include 10% profit)			
				£	£	£	£	£	£	£	£
Z66	**WORK TO EXISTING BUILDINGS**										
Z6612	**Blocking up openings in solid brick walls**										
Z661235	**Block up opening in one brick wall; common bricks; plaster with emulsion paint finish both sides; opening size:**										
Z661235A	630 × 900 mm	Nr	3.87	112.69	–	35.02	147.71	123.96	–	38.52	162.48
Z661235B	915 × 1050 mm	Nr	5.97	173.31	–	54.04	227.35	190.64	–	59.44	250.09
Z661235C	1200 × 1200 mm	Nr	8.49	246.18	–	75.57	321.75	270.80	–	83.13	353.93
Z661235D	1770 × 1350 mm	Nr	13.29	384.77	–	117.93	502.70	423.25	–	129.72	552.97
Z661235E	900 × 2100 mm	Nr	11.79	342.40	–	100.38	442.78	376.64	–	110.42	487.06
Z661235F	1200 × 2100 mm	Nr	14.85	430.58	–	129.96	560.54	473.64	–	142.96	616.59
Z661235G	1800 × 2100 mm	Nr	20.97	607.08	–	186.08	793.16	667.79	–	204.69	872.48
Z661235H	2400 × 2100 mm	Nr	27.09	783.57	–	242.79	1026.36	861.93	–	267.07	1129.00
Z661240	**Block up opening in one and a half brick wall; common bricks; plaster with emulsion paint finish both sides; opening size:**										
Z661240A	630 × 900 mm	Nr	4.66	136.22	–	49.92	186.14	149.84	–	54.91	204.75
Z661240B	915 × 1050 mm	Nr	7.11	207.25	–	76.03	283.28	227.98	–	83.63	311.61
Z661240C	1200 × 1200 mm	Nr	10.05	292.63	–	103.37	396.00	321.89	–	113.71	435.60
Z661240D	1770 × 1350 mm	Nr	15.62	454.16	–	166.44	620.60	499.58	–	183.08	682.66
Z661240E	900 × 2100 mm	Nr	14.04	409.40	–	143.08	552.48	450.34	–	157.39	607.73
Z661240F	1200 × 2100 mm	Nr	17.58	511.89	–	183.19	695.08	563.08	–	201.51	764.59
Z661240G	1800 × 2100 mm	Nr	24.65	716.67	–	261.48	978.15	788.34	–	287.63	1075.97
Z661240H	2400 × 2100 mm	Nr	31.71	921.16	–	338.00	1259.16	1013.28	–	371.80	1385.08
Z661245	**Block up opening in half brick wall; common bricks; render and masonry paint finish externally; plaster with emulsion paint finish internally; opening size:**										
Z661245A	630 × 900 mm	Nr	2.40	67.57	–	21.84	89.41	74.33	–	24.02	98.35
Z661245B	915 × 1050 mm	Nr	3.66	102.29	–	32.13	134.42	112.52	–	35.34	147.86
Z661245C	1200 × 1200 mm	Nr	5.19	144.40	–	45.52	189.92	158.84	–	50.07	208.91
Z661245D	1770 × 1350 mm	Nr	8.07	223.46	–	69.66	293.12	245.81	–	76.63	322.43
Z661245E	900 × 2100 mm	Nr	7.29	203.30	–	63.26	266.56	223.63	–	69.59	293.22
Z661245F	1200 × 2100 mm	Nr	9.11	253.02	–	77.68	330.70	278.32	–	85.45	363.77
Z661245G	1800 × 2100 mm	Nr	12.80	353.71	–	109.68	463.39	389.08	–	120.65	509.73
Z661245H	2400 × 2100 mm	Nr	16.48	454.04	–	145.01	599.05	499.44	–	159.51	658.96
Z661250	**Block up opening in one brick wall; common bricks; render and masonry paint finish externally; plaster with emulsion paint finish internally; opening size:**										
Z661250A	630 × 900 mm	Nr	3.18	90.80	–	36.74	127.54	99.88	–	40.41	140.29
Z661250B	915 × 1050 mm	Nr	4.80	136.23	–	53.95	190.18	149.85	–	59.35	209.20
Z661250C	1200 × 1200 mm	Nr	6.75	190.86	–	77.87	268.73	209.95	–	85.66	295.60
Z661250D	1770 × 1350 mm	Nr	10.41	293.14	–	119.46	412.60	322.45	–	131.41	453.86
Z661250E	900 × 2100 mm	Nr	9.55	270.59	–	104.70	375.29	297.65	–	115.17	412.82
Z661250F	1200 × 2100 mm	Nr	11.84	334.32	–	131.84	466.16	367.75	–	145.02	512.78
Z661250G	1800 × 2100 mm	Nr	16.47	463.00	–	190.57	653.57	509.30	–	209.63	718.93
Z661250H	2400 × 2100 mm	Nr	21.10	591.62	–	249.16	840.78	650.78	–	274.08	924.86

Approximate Estimating Rates

Major Works 2009		Unit	Labour Hours	Labour Net	Plant Net	Materials Net	Unit Net	Labour Gross	Plant Gross	Materials Gross	Unit Price
								— (Gross rates include 10% profit) —			
				£	£	£	£	£	£	£	£
Z66	**WORK TO EXISTING BUILDINGS**										
Z6612	**Blocking up openings in solid brick walls**										
Z661255	**Block up opening in one and a half brick wall; common bricks; render and masonry paint finish externally; plaster with emulsion paint finish internally; opening size:**										
Z661255A	630 × 900 mm..........	Nr	3.97	114.33	–	51.64	165.97	125.76	–	56.80	182.57
Z661255B	915 × 1050 mm........	Nr	5.94	170.18	–	75.93	246.11	187.20	–	83.52	270.72
Z661255C	1200 × 1200 mm	Nr	8.31	237.31	–	105.67	342.98	261.04	–	116.24	377.28
Z661255D	1770 × 1350 mm	Nr	12.74	362.53	–	167.98	530.51	398.78	–	184.78	583.56
Z661255E	900 × 2100 mm.........	Nr	11.80	337.61	–	147.39	485.00	371.37	–	162.13	533.50
Z661255F	1200 × 2100 mm	Nr	14.57	415.62	–	185.08	600.70	457.18	–	203.59	660.77
Z661255G	1800 × 2100 mm	Nr	20.15	572.59	–	265.97	838.56	629.85	–	292.57	922.42
Z661255H	2400 × 2100 mm	Nr	25.72	729.20	–	344.38	1073.58	802.12	–	378.82	1180.94
Z6620	**Blocking up openings in solid block walls**										
Z662010	**Block up opening in solid block wall; 100 mm thick; plaster with emulsion paint finish both sides; opening size:**										
Z662010A	630 × 900 mm..........	Nr	2.91	84.10	–	18.19	102.29	92.51	–	20.01	112.52
Z662010B	915 × 1050 mm........	Nr	4.62	133.11	–	26.76	159.87	146.42	–	29.44	175.86
Z662010C	1200 × 1200 mm	Nr	6.69	192.58	–	34.10	226.68	211.84	–	37.51	249.35
Z662010D	1770 × 1350 mm	Nr	10.68	307.04	–	53.13	360.17	337.74	–	58.44	396.19
Z662010E	900 × 2100 mm.........	Nr	9.11	262.59	–	46.97	309.56	288.85	–	51.67	340.52
Z662010F	1200 × 2100 mm	Nr	11.70	336.78	–	59.80	396.58	370.46	–	65.78	436.24
Z662010G	1800 × 2100 mm	Nr	16.88	485.28	–	83.51	568.79	533.81	–	91.86	625.67
Z662010H	2400 × 2100 mm	Nr	22.05	633.48	–	108.92	742.40	696.83	–	119.81	816.64
Z662015	**Block up opening in solid block wall; 150 mm thick; plaster with emulsion paint finish both sides; opening size:**										
Z662015A	630 × 900 mm..........	Nr	3.10	89.76	–	23.11	112.87	98.74	–	25.42	124.16
Z662015B	915 × 1050 mm........	Nr	4.89	141.14	–	34.00	175.14	155.25	–	37.40	192.65
Z662015C	1200 × 1200 mm	Nr	7.02	202.40	–	44.14	246.54	222.64	–	48.55	271.19
Z662015D	1770 × 1350 mm	Nr	11.14	320.74	–	69.47	390.21	352.81	–	76.42	429.23
Z662015E	900 × 2100 mm.........	Nr	9.64	278.38	–	62.38	340.76	306.22	–	68.62	374.84
Z662015F	1200 × 2100 mm	Nr	12.29	354.35	–	78.46	432.81	389.79	–	86.31	476.09
Z662015G	1800 × 2100 mm	Nr	17.59	506.42	–	108.67	615.09	557.06	–	119.54	676.60
Z662015H	2400 × 2100 mm	Nr	22.89	658.50	–	140.56	799.06	724.35	–	154.62	878.97

Approximate Estimating Rates

Major Works 2009		Unit	Labour Hours	Labour Net	Plant Net	Materials Net	Unit Net	Labour Gross	Plant Gross	Materials Gross	Unit Price
								(Gross rates include 10% profit)			
				£	£	£	£	£	£	£	£
Z66	**WORK TO EXISTING BUILDINGS**										
Z6620	**Blocking up openings in solid block walls**										
Z662020	**Block up opening in solid block wall; 215 mm thick; plaster with emulsion paint finish both sides; opening size:**										
Z662020A	630 × 900 mm..........	Nr	3.51	101.97	–	30.17	132.14	112.17	–	33.19	145.35
Z662020B	915 × 1050 mm.........	Nr	5.45	157.82	–	44.37	202.19	173.60	–	48.81	222.41
Z662020C	1200 × 1200 mm	Nr	7.74	223.84	–	59.64	283.48	246.22	–	65.60	311.83
Z662020D	1770 × 1350 mm	Nr	12.15	350.81	–	92.46	443.27	385.89	–	101.71	487.60
Z662020E	900 × 2100 mm.........	Nr	10.74	311.14	–	84.02	395.16	342.25	–	92.42	434.68
Z662020F	1200 × 2100 mm	Nr	13.55	391.87	–	104.76	496.63	431.06	–	115.24	546.29
Z662020G	1800 × 2100 mm	Nr	19.17	553.48	–	145.38	698.86	608.83	–	159.92	768.75
Z662020H	2400 × 2100 mm	Nr	22.89	658.50	–	140.56	799.06	724.35	–	154.62	878.97
Z662025	**Block up opening in solid block wall; 215 mm thick; render coat with masonry paint finish externally; plaster with emulsion paint internally; opening size:**										
Z662025A	630 × 900 mm..........	Nr	2.82	80.09	–	30.19	110.28	88.10	–	33.21	121.31
Z662025B	915 × 1050 mm.........	Nr	4.28	120.75	–	44.27	165.02	132.83	–	48.70	181.52
Z662025C	1200 × 1200 mm	Nr	6.00	168.53	–	61.94	230.47	185.38	–	68.13	253.52
Z662025D	1770 × 1350 mm	Nr	9.27	259.19	–	93.99	353.18	285.11	–	103.39	388.50
Z662025E	900 × 2100 mm.........	Nr	8.50	239.33	–	88.34	327.67	263.26	–	97.17	360.44
Z662025F	1200 × 2100 mm	Nr	10.54	295.60	–	106.65	402.25	325.16	–	117.32	442.48
Z662025G	1800 × 2100 mm	Nr	14.67	409.40	–	149.87	559.27	450.34	–	164.86	615.20
Z662025H	2400 × 2100 mm	Nr	11.23	297.69	–	194.07	491.76	327.46	–	213.48	540.94

LANSDOWNE ROAD STADIUM, DUBLIN

OPTIMUM SOLUTIONS

At Franklin Sports Business we provide timely, accurate and professional
cost consultancy advice to the sport and leisure industry – but what makes
us different is that we do this in the context of the overall business equation.
We guide our clients to invest in an efficient manner so that the end product
represents a sustainable optimum solution.

We have worked on some of the world's highest-profile projects including
England's new Wembley Stadium, the Lansdowne Road Stadium in Ireland
and the new National Indoor Sports Arena and Velodrome in Scotland. We
have worked with local, national and international sporting organisations
including Fulham FC (UK), FC Internazionale (Italy), Galatasaray FC
(Turkey) and the City of Warsaw for a new Polish national stadium.

For more information please contact Barry Winterton:
T +44 (0)20 7803 4501
E sport&leisure@franklinandrews.com

Franklin Sports Business is a member of the Mott MacDonald Group

www.franklinandrews.com

FRANKLIN
SPORTS
BUSINESS

HUTCHINS
MAJOR WORKS INDEX

Major Works Index

Major Works Index

Major Works Index

Elemental Analyses

Through the analysis of a large number of existing projects Elemental Benchmark Costs have been produced for the following 46 facility types.

Prices are all current at second quarter 2008 levels based on a UK average.

When using any of the following information the reader should be aware of the need to take into account specific cost drivers applicable to the proposed project.

National factors and indicative International factors are supplied in the appendices section of the book to enable the reader to make adjustments to suit any given location.

The following figures are provided as a guide only and a proper appraisal should be carried out during the preparation of any feasibility study.

Railway Stations	Public Houses
Multi-Storey Car Parks	Restaurants
Petrol Stations	Theatres
Airport Terminal Buildings	Community Centres
Chemical Factories	Covered Swimming Pools
Electronics Factories	Gymnasia
Factories	Sports Centres
Advanced Factories	Sports Centres incl pool
Warehouses	Sports Halls
Town Halls	Sports Stadia
Law Courts	Crematoria
Offices	Primary Schools
Offices with Shops	Middle Schools
Banks / Building Societies	High Schools
Shops	Sixth Form Colleges
Super / Hypermarkets	Universities
Department Stores	Laboratory Blocks
Shopping Centres	Research Facilities
Retail Warehouses	Detached Housing
General Hospitals	Semi-Detached Housing
Mixed Facility Hospitals	Estate Housing
Homes for Elderly	Hotels
Veterinary Surgeries	Halls of Residence

Elemental Analyses

Element		Railway Stations		Multi-Storey Car Parks		Petrol Stations		Airport Terminal Buildings	
		Cost/m^2	%	Cost/m^2	%	Cost/m^2	%	Cost/m^2	%
1	SUBSTRUCTURE	89.44	5.51%	64.49	17.27%	232.61	4.12%	116.67	2.79%
2A	Frame	166.90	10.28%	34.15	9.14%	39.00	0.69%	512.60	12.27%
2B	Upper floors	42.29	2.60%	72.64	19.45%	0.00	0.00%	112.96	2.70%
2C	Roof	70.96	4.37%	13.99	3.75%	194.27	3.44%	89.18	2.14%
2D	Stairs	8.10	0.50%	4.37	1.17%	0.00	0.00%	14.84	0.36%
2E	External walls	45.57	2.81%	29.02	7.77%	266.98	4.73%	330.98	7.92%
2F	Windows and external doors	88.28	5.44%	5.16	1.38%	224.54	3.98%	8.29	0.20%
2G	Internal walls and partitions	79.24	4.88%	1.77	0.47%	38.99	0.69%	58.62	1.40%
2H	Internal doors	21.46	1.32%	1.63	0.44%	54.61	0.97%	44.80	1.07%
2	SUPERSTRUCTURE	522.80	32.20%	162.73	43.57%	818.39	14.49%	1,172.25	28.07%
3A	Wall finishes	52.25	3.22%	1.62	0.43%	53.38	0.95%	158.83	3.80%
3B	Floor finishes	39.13	2.41%	8.72	2.34%	82.27	1.46%	91.16	2.18%
3C	Ceiling finishes	17.78	1.10%	4.17	1.12%	52.39	0.93%	77.69	1.86%
3	INTERNAL FINISHES	109.16	6.72%	14.52	3.89%	188.04	3.33%	327.67	7.85%
4	FITTINGS AND FURNISHINGS	36.54	2.25%	5.96	1.59%	200.84	3.56%	236.48	5.66%
5A	Sanitary appliances	11.60	0.71%	0.36	0.10%	7.01	0.12%	15.78	0.38%
5B	Services equipment	2.99	0.18%	0.27	0.07%	0.00	0.00%	74.74	1.79%
5C	Disposal installations	10.57	0.65%	2.11	0.57%	28.97	0.51%	30.00	0.72%
5D	Water installations	0.00	0.00%	0.92	0.25%	9.64	0.17%	27.20	0.65%
5E	Heat source	92.28	5.68%	0.00	0.00%	0.00	0.00%	24.77	0.59%
5F	Space heating and air treatment	0.00	0.00%	0.03	0.01%	22.76	0.40%	263.32	6.30%
5G	Ventilating systems	0.00	0.00%	0.00	0.00%	54.24	0.96%	21.86	0.52%
5H	Electrical installations	70.18	4.32%	12.69	3.40%	369.85	6.55%	266.00	6.37%
5I	Gas installations	0.00	0.00%	0.00	0.00%	0.00	0.00%	2.16	0.05%
5J	Lift and conveyor installations	58.18	3.58%	4.76	1.28%	0.00	0.00%	61.99	1.48%
5K	Protective installations	0.00	0.00%	3.49	0.94%	1.19	0.02%	68.80	1.65%
5L	Communication installations	0.00	0.00%	4.69	1.26%	20.69	0.37%	89.19	2.14%
5M	Special Installations	0.00	0.00%	0.00	0.00%	33.10	0.59%	393.10	9.41%
5N	Builder's work in connection	28.84	1.78%	1.19	0.32%	34.50	0.61%	39.96	0.96%
5O	Builder's profit and attendance	6.82	0.42%	0.00	0.00%	0.42	0.01%	160.25	3.84%
5	SERVICES	281.47	17.33%	30.51	8.17%	582.36	10.31%	1,539.13	36.85%
	Building sub-total	1,039.41	64.01%	278.21	74.48%	2,022.25	35.81%	3,392.19	81.22%
6A	Site works	179.78	11.07%	38.37	10.27%	1,557.36	27.58%	462.94	11.08%
6B	Drainage	74.46	4.59%	8.27	2.22%	349.52	6.19%	13.90	0.33%
6C	External services	32.45	2.00%	2.48	0.66%	65.67	1.16%	59.97	1.44%
6D	Minor building works	88.40	5.44%	22.57	6.04%	1,111.87	19.69%	72.44	1.73%
6	EXTERNAL WORKS	375.09	23.10%	71.70	19.20%	3,084.42	54.62%	609.26	14.59%
7	PRELIMINARIES	209.26	12.89%	23.61	6.32%	540.53	9.57%	175.22	4.20%
	FACILITY CONSTRUCTION COST	1,623.76	100.00%	373.51	100.00%	5,647.19	100.00%	4,176.67	100.00%

Element		Chemical Factories		Electronics Factories		Factories		Advanced Factories	
		Cost/m^2	%	Cost/m^2	%	Cost/m^2	%	Cost/m^2	%
1	**SUBSTRUCTURE**	**95.89**	**10.22%**	**115.54**	**8.45%**	**96.72**	**13.45%**	**117.89**	**12.45%**
2A	Frame	137.17	14.62%	109.69	8.02%	66.81	9.29%	140.51	14.83%
2B	Upper floors	4.31	0.46%	12.02	0.88%	2.37	0.33%	0.00	0.00%
2C	Roof	97.78	10.42%	81.13	5.93%	64.61	8.98%	56.00	5.91%
2D	Stairs	2.13	0.23%	11.65	0.85%	3.68	0.51%	0.00	0.00%
2E	External walls	48.96	5.22%	116.91	8.55%	78.84	10.96%	58.60	6.19%
2F	Windows and external doors	21.88	2.33%	31.13	2.28%	35.56	4.94%	36.38	3.84%
2G	Internal walls and partitions	18.67	1.99%	42.75	3.13%	17.44	2.43%	23.09	2.44%
2H	Internal doors	8.33	0.89%	26.27	1.92%	6.96	0.97%	9.21	0.97%
2	**SUPERSTRUCTURE**	**339.21**	**36.14%**	**431.56**	**31.56%**	**276.27**	**38.41%**	**323.79**	**34.18%**
3A	Wall finishes	29.61	3.15%	17.39	1.27%	11.06	1.54%	21.26	2.24%
3B	Floor finishes	8.16	0.87%	45.17	3.30%	2.43	0.34%	3.66	0.39%
3C	Ceiling finishes	7.54	0.80%	15.35	1.12%	3.90	0.54%	2.62	0.28%
3	**INTERNAL FINISHES**	**45.30**	**4.83%**	**77.90**	**5.70%**	**17.40**	**2.42%**	**27.54**	**2.91%**
4	**FITTINGS AND FURNISHINGS**	**18.18**	**1.94%**	**14.91**	**1.09%**	**2.90**	**0.40%**	**1.77**	**0.19%**
5A	Sanitary appliances	1.72	0.18%	1.28	0.09%	5.96	0.83%	7.40	0.78%
5B	Services equipment	0.00	0.00%	3.38	0.25%	0.03	0.00%	0.00	0.00%
5C	Disposal installations	0.86	0.09%	1.43	0.10%	5.71	0.79%	3.57	0.38%
5D	Water installations	3.65	0.39%	24.27	1.77%	6.12	0.85%	11.19	1.18%
5E	Heat source	0.42	0.04%	2.07	0.15%	0.00	0.00%	2.43	0.26%
5F	Space heating and air treatment	37.86	4.03%	129.72	9.49%	8.63	1.20%	36.05	3.81%
5G	Ventilating systems	12.53	1.34%	43.78	3.20%	4.10	0.57%	2.32	0.24%
5H	Electrical installations	121.38	12.93%	126.67	9.26%	23.20	3.23%	93.97	9.92%
5I	Gas installations	0.00	0.00%	0.00	0.00%	0.58	0.08%	3.44	0.36%
5J	Lift and conveyor installations	2.78	0.30%	5.94	0.43%	0.00	0.00%	0.00	0.00%
5K	Protective installations	13.21	1.41%	23.28	1.70%	2.33	0.32%	3.72	0.39%
5L	Communication installations	0.00	0.00%	8.64	0.63%	0.00	0.00%	5.23	0.55%
5M	Special Installations	33.03	3.52%	1.09	0.08%	0.00	0.00%	11.96	1.26%
5N	Builder's work in connection	4.23	0.45%	20.20	1.48%	2.63	0.37%	8.30	0.88%
5O	Builder's profit and attendance	0.00	0.00%	0.28	0.02%	1.21	0.17%	0.89	0.09%
5	**SERVICES**	**231.68**	**24.69%**	**392.05**	**28.67%**	**60.51**	**8.41%**	**190.47**	**20.11%**
	Building sub-total	**730.26**	**77.81%**	**1,031.97**	**75.46%**	**453.80**	**63.10%**	**661.46**	**69.83%**
6A	Site works	98.77	10.52%	227.21	16.61%	94.90	13.19%	137.09	14.47%
6B	Drainage	40.58	4.32%	41.33	3.02%	55.75	7.75%	33.71	3.56%
6C	External services	6.78	0.72%	6.40	0.47%	44.32	6.16%	38.13	4.03%
6D	Minor building works	24.24	2.58%	10.30	0.75%	0.00	0.00%	11.35	1.20%
6	**EXTERNAL WORKS**	**170.38**	**18.15%**	**285.25**	**20.86%**	**194.96**	**27.11%**	**220.28**	**23.25%**
7	**PRELIMINARIES**	**37.86**	**4.03%**	**50.39**	**3.68%**	**70.45**	**9.80%**	**65.51**	**6.92%**
	FACILITY CONSTRUCTION COST	**938.51**	**100.00%**	**1,367.60**	**100.00%**	**719.21**	**100.00%**	**947.25**	**100.00%**

Elemental Analyses

Element		Warehouses		Law Courts		Town Halls		Offices	
		Cost/m^2	%	Cost/m^2	%	Cost/m^2	%	Cost/m^2	%
1	**SUBSTRUCTURE**	**95.04**	**14.65%**	**96.01**	**4.68%**	**99.61**	**7.20%**	**97.19**	**7.28%**
2A	Frame	91.93	14.17%	105.80	5.16%	54.45	3.93%	51.99	3.90%
2B	Upper floors	6.57	1.01%	41.98	2.05%	53.23	3.85%	30.47	2.28%
2C	Roof	81.47	12.56%	119.87	5.84%	102.80	7.43%	92.17	6.91%
2D	Stairs	12.47	1.92%	39.44	1.92%	8.50	0.61%	13.62	1.02%
2E	External walls	39.48	6.09%	194.49	9.48%	76.15	5.50%	137.15	10.28%
2F	Windows and external doors	37.21	5.74%	78.18	3.81%	47.24	3.41%	58.34	4.37%
2G	Internal walls and partitions	15.22	2.35%	100.62	4.90%	26.42	1.91%	95.57	7.16%
2H	Internal doors	14.98	2.31%	80.04	3.90%	36.26	2.62%	49.65	3.72%
2	**SUPERSTRUCTURE**	**299.33**	**46.15%**	**760.42**	**37.06%**	**405.06**	**29.27%**	**528.95**	**39.64%**
3A	Wall finishes	26.97	4.16%	68.22	3.32%	10.43	0.75%	23.16	1.74%
3B	Floor finishes	8.63	1.33%	57.11	2.78%	59.71	4.31%	37.12	2.78%
3C	Ceiling finishes	7.93	1.22%	41.31	2.01%	54.91	3.97%	26.18	1.96%
3	**INTERNAL FINISHES**	**43.53**	**6.71%**	**166.63**	**8.12%**	**125.05**	**9.04%**	**86.46**	**6.48%**
4	**FITTINGS AND FURNISHINGS**	**3.38**	**0.52%**	**98.73**	**4.81%**	**60.42**	**4.37%**	**20.11**	**1.51%**
5A	Sanitary appliances	4.65	0.72%	16.13	0.79%	3.71	0.27%	9.46	0.71%
5B	Services equipment	0.00	0.00%	0.00	0.00%	10.02	0.72%	0.00	0.00%
5C	Disposal installations	0.00	0.00%	5.13	0.25%	1.07	0.08%	6.30	0.47%
5D	Water installations	0.00	0.00%	3.49	0.17%	4.61	0.33%	6.51	0.49%
5E	Heat source	0.00	0.00%	6.99	0.34%	16.92	1.22%	5.20	0.39%
5F	Space heating and air treatment	57.04	8.79%	213.10	10.39%	79.27	5.73%	77.11	5.78%
5G	Ventilating systems	0.00	0.00%	18.96	0.92%	66.93	4.84%	9.89	0.74%
5H	Electrical installations	32.52	5.01%	203.63	9.92%	107.01	7.73%	125.44	9.40%
5I	Gas installations	0.00	0.00%	45.74	2.23%	2.50	0.18%	0.74	0.06%
5J	Lift and conveyor installations	0.00	0.00%	34.04	1.66%	12.98	0.94%	21.50	1.61%
5K	Protective installations	0.00	0.00%	1.74	0.08%	2.33	0.17%	8.28	0.62%
5L	Communication installations	0.00	0.00%	7.37	0.36%	0.00	0.00%	7.67	0.58%
5M	Special Installations	0.00	0.00%	7.86	0.38%	4.24	0.31%	4.51	0.34%
5N	Builder's work in connection	0.00	0.00%	31.05	1.51%	20.93	1.51%	14.19	1.06%
5O	Builder's profit and attendance	0.00	0.00%	8.61	0.42%	6.91	0.50%	3.85	0.29%
5	**SERVICES**	**94.21**	**14.52%**	**603.84**	**29.43%**	**339.43**	**24.53%**	**300.65**	**22.53%**
	Building sub-total	**535.49**	**82.56%**	**1,725.64**	**84.10%**	**1,029.57**	**74.40%**	**1,033.36**	**77.45%**
6A	Site works	77.37	11.93%	101.51	4.95%	130.93	9.46%	101.38	7.60%
6B	Drainage	12.32	1.90%	21.78	1.06%	18.40	1.33%	51.39	3.85%
6C	External services	7.37	1.14%	5.40	0.26%	5.80	0.42%	37.77	2.83%
6D	Minor building works	0.00	0.00%	14.16	0.69%	30.68	2.22%	3.36	0.25%
6	**EXTERNAL WORKS**	**97.07**	**14.97%**	**142.86**	**6.96%**	**185.81**	**13.43%**	**193.90**	**14.53%**
7	**PRELIMINARIES**	**16.05**	**2.47%**	**183.49**	**8.94%**	**168.49**	**12.18%**	**107.02**	**8.02%**
	FACILITY CONSTRUCTION COST	**648.61**	**100.00%**	**2,051.98**	**100.00%**	**1,383.87**	**100.00%**	**1,334.29**	**100.00%**

Element		Offices with Shops		Banks/Building Societies		Shops		Super / Hypermarkets	
		Cost/m^2	%	Cost/m^2	%	Cost/m^2	%	Cost/m^2	%
1	**SUBSTRUCTURE**	**82.75**	**7.22%**	**229.16**	**9.84%**	**124.50**	**17.49%**	**110.10**	**9.76%**
2A	Frame	67.79	5.92%	96.12	4.13%	45.62	6.41%	99.75	8.84%
2B	Upper floors	30.46	2.66%	18.11	0.78%	47.50	6.67%	3.50	0.31%
2C	Roof	81.99	7.16%	188.02	8.07%	94.32	13.25%	87.07	7.72%
2D	Stairs	26.69	2.33%	11.44	0.49%	20.71	2.91%	2.38	0.21%
2E	External walls	132.46	11.56%	118.58	5.09%	100.35	14.10%	52.50	4.65%
2F	Windows and external doors	70.83	6.18%	143.70	6.17%	25.73	3.62%	28.31	2.51%
2G	Internal walls and partitions	17.23	1.50%	60.72	2.61%	12.75	1.79%	13.26	1.17%
2H	Internal doors	45.32	3.96%	63.55	2.73%	20.83	2.93%	10.41	0.92%
2	**SUPERSTRUCTURE**	**472.77**	**41.27%**	**700.25**	**30.06%**	**367.81**	**51.69%**	**297.19**	**26.34%**
3A	Wall finishes	26.05	2.27%	38.66	1.66%	9.87	1.39%	14.47	1.28%
3B	Floor finishes	49.62	4.33%	70.92	3.04%	11.82	1.66%	31.53	2.79%
3C	Ceiling finishes	22.30	1.95%	32.78	1.41%	15.22	2.14%	17.71	1.57%
3	**INTERNAL FINISHES**	**97.97**	**8.55%**	**142.36**	**6.11%**	**36.90**	**5.19%**	**63.72**	**5.65%**
4	**FITTINGS AND FURNISHINGS**	**20.17**	**1.76%**	**206.21**	**8.85%**	**12.21**	**1.72%**	**13.43**	**1.19%**
5A	Sanitary appliances	6.61	0.58%	9.87	0.42%	2.76	0.39%	11.56	1.02%
5B	Services equipment	0.00	0.00%	0.00	0.00%	0.00	0.00%	0.00	0.00%
5C	Disposal installations	1.78	0.16%	16.98	0.73%	2.10	0.30%	0.96	0.08%
5D	Water installations	1.86	0.16%	7.29	0.31%	2.29	0.32%	2.59	0.23%
5E	Heat source	0.00	0.00%	0.00	0.00%	0.00	0.00%	14.16	1.26%
5F	Space heating and air treatment	100.38	8.76%	90.74	3.89%	8.81	1.24%	42.69	3.78%
5G	Ventilating systems	0.73	0.06%	39.65	1.70%	0.00	0.00%	1.56	0.14%
5H	Electrical installations	94.57	8.25%	312.35	13.41%	9.54	1.34%	57.08	5.06%
5I	Gas installations	0.17	0.02%	0.00	0.00%	0.00	0.00%	0.24	0.02%
5J	Lift and conveyor installations	17.95	1.57%	0.00	0.00%	0.00	0.00%	4.77	0.42%
5K	Protective installations	0.38	0.03%	0.00	0.00%	0.00	0.00%	17.95	1.59%
5L	Communication installations	0.05	0.00%	37.20	1.60%	0.00	0.00%	7.14	0.63%
5M	Special Installations	0.00	0.00%	0.00	0.00%	0.00	0.00%	75.77	6.71%
5N	Builder's work in connection	7.80	0.68%	21.38	0.92%	1.92	0.27%	14.71	1.30%
5O	Builder's profit and attendance	0.00	0.00%	0.00	0.00%	0.00	0.00%	0.54	0.05%
5	**SERVICES**	**232.29**	**20.28%**	**535.46**	**22.98%**	**27.41**	**3.85%**	**251.71**	**22.31%**
	Building sub-total	**905.95**	**79.08%**	**1,813.43**	**77.84%**	**568.83**	**79.93%**	**736.15**	**65.23%**
6A	Site works	33.60	2.93%	91.88	3.94%	45.66	6.42%	201.57	17.86%
6B	Drainage	16.70	1.46%	86.41	3.71%	19.30	2.71%	39.32	3.48%
6C	External services	16.16	1.41%	34.89	1.50%	11.23	1.58%	36.86	3.27%
6D	Minor building works	0.00	0.00%	84.89	3.64%	0.00	0.00%	4.12	0.37%
6	**EXTERNAL WORKS**	**66.46**	**5.80%**	**298.08**	**12.79%**	**76.18**	**10.71%**	**281.87**	**24.98%**
7	**PRELIMINARIES**	**173.27**	**15.12%**	**218.32**	**9.37%**	**66.61**	**9.36%**	**110.46**	**9.79%**
	FACILITY CONSTRUCTION COST	**1,145.69**	**100.00%**	**2,329.83**	**100.00%**	**711.62**	**100.00%**	**1,128.48**	**100.00%**

Elemental Analyses

Element		Department Stores		Shopping Centres		Retail Warehouses		General Hospitals	
		Cost/m^2	%	Cost/m^2	%	Cost/m^2	%	Cost/m^2	%
1	**SUBSTRUCTURE**	**73.54**	**10.95%**	**80.70**	**10.45%**	**94.37**	**15.85%**	**85.38**	**4.36%**
2A	Frame	110.10	16.39%	57.62	7.46%	92.22	15.49%	25.75	1.32%
2B	Upper floors	27.91	4.15%	32.89	4.26%	5.26	0.88%	57.44	2.93%
2C	Roof	62.69	9.33%	109.39	14.17%	41.91	7.04%	165.07	8.43%
2D	Stairs	5.49	0.82%	9.67	1.25%	1.83	0.31%	9.17	0.47%
2E	External walls	58.53	8.71%	59.11	7.66%	37.88	6.36%	76.46	3.91%
2F	Windows and external doors	13.69	2.04%	34.39	4.45%	20.44	3.43%	71.09	3.63%
2G	Internal walls and partitions	13.11	1.95%	30.70	3.98%	11.08	1.86%	53.19	2.72%
2H	Internal doors	4.64	0.69%	5.94	0.77%	3.58	0.60%	77.81	3.97%
2	**SUPERSTRUCTURE**	**296.14**	**44.08%**	**339.70**	**43.99%**	**214.20**	**35.99%**	**535.98**	**27.38%**
3A	Wall finishes	10.24	1.52%	29.96	3.88%	4.54	0.76%	45.90	2.34%
3B	Floor finishes	15.13	2.25%	22.81	2.95%	4.87	0.82%	51.39	2.63%
3C	Ceiling finishes	11.57	1.72%	13.22	1.71%	7.41	1.24%	34.27	1.75%
3	**INTERNAL FINISHES**	**36.94**	**5.50%**	**65.99**	**8.55%**	**16.82**	**2.83%**	**131.56**	**6.72%**
4	**FITTINGS AND FURNISHINGS**	**0.58**	**0.09%**	**4.92**	**0.64%**	**1.17**	**0.20%**	**80.64**	**4.12%**
5A	Sanitary appliances	0.75	0.11%	1.50	0.19%	1.26	0.21%	50.81	2.60%
5B	Services equipment	0.00	0.00%	0.00	0.00%	0.00	0.00%	0.85	0.04%
5C	Disposal installations	3.10	0.46%	9.36	1.21%	0.25	0.04%	19.07	0.97%
5D	Water installations	0.00	0.00%	3.12	0.40%	0.07	0.01%	75.10	3.84%
5E	Heat source	23.18	3.45%	0.00	0.00%	0.00	0.00%	3.24	0.17%
5F	Space heating and air treatment	0.00	0.00%	20.07	2.60%	12.88	2.16%	204.22	10.43%
5G	Ventilating systems	0.00	0.00%	3.05	0.39%	1.88	0.32%	56.96	2.91%
5H	Electrical installations	37.35	5.56%	27.17	3.52%	23.53	3.95%	173.00	8.84%
5I	Gas installations	0.00	0.00%	0.00	0.00%	0.00	0.00%	7.35	0.38%
5J	Lift and conveyor installations	29.19	4.34%	27.00	3.50%	4.84	0.81%	21.69	1.11%
5K	Protective installations	15.77	2.35%	11.25	1.46%	1.07	0.18%	7.79	0.40%
5L	Communication installations	0.00	0.00%	3.16	0.41%	0.02	0.00%	72.25	3.69%
5M	Special Installations	0.00	0.00%	2.41	0.31%	0.00	0.00%	42.55	2.17%
5N	Builder's work in connection	4.97	0.74%	2.56	0.33%	1.73	0.29%	30.05	1.53%
5O	Builder's profit and attendance	6.98	1.04%	3.71	0.48%	0.00	0.00%	0.00	0.00%
5	**SERVICES**	**121.28**	**18.05%**	**114.35**	**14.81%**	**47.54**	**7.99%**	**764.91**	**39.07%**
	Building sub-total	**528.49**	**78.66%**	**605.67**	**78.44%**	**374.10**	**62.85%**	**1,598.46**	**81.65%**
6A	Site works	51.98	7.74%	37.58	4.87%	139.47	23.43%	65.96	3.37%
6B	Drainage	16.94	2.52%	14.20	1.84%	28.61	4.81%	33.17	1.69%
6C	External services	3.43	0.51%	16.76	2.17%	9.63	1.62%	22.10	1.13%
6D	Minor building works	0.00	0.00%	3.20	0.41%	1.60	0.27%	41.61	2.13%
6	**EXTERNAL WORKS**	**72.35**	**10.77%**	**71.75**	**9.29%**	**179.30**	**30.12%**	**162.84**	**8.32%**
7	**PRELIMINARIES**	**71.05**	**10.57%**	**94.75**	**12.27%**	**41.81**	**7.02%**	**196.31**	**10.03%**
	FACILITY CONSTRUCTION COST	**671.89**	**100.00%**	**772.16**	**100.00%**	**595.21**	**100.00%**	**1,957.61**	**100.00%**

Elemental Analyses

Element		Mixed Facility Hospitals		Homes for Elderly		Veterinary Surgeries		Public Houses	
		Cost/m²	%	Cost/m²	%	Cost/m²	%	Cost/m²	%
1	SUBSTRUCTURE	103.53	6.01%	58.08	3.97%	242.23	12.45%	141.65	6.68%
2A	Frame	82.80	4.81%	11.74	0.80%	0.00	0.00%	35.29	1.66%
2B	Upper floors	56.23	3.27%	41.92	2.87%	0.00	0.00%	18.10	0.85%
2C	Roof	69.87	4.06%	60.06	4.11%	141.94	7.30%	159.02	7.49%
2D	Stairs	8.65	0.50%	4.63	0.32%	0.00	0.00%	10.07	0.47%
2E	External walls	70.63	4.10%	89.91	6.15%	80.63	4.15%	102.22	4.82%
2F	Windows and external doors	61.45	3.57%	118.21	8.09%	145.20	7.46%	90.40	4.26%
2G	Internal walls and partitions	65.21	3.79%	57.84	3.96%	28.55	1.47%	52.85	2.49%
2H	Internal doors	58.21	3.38%	70.93	4.85%	0.00	0.00%	43.50	2.05%
2	SUPERSTRUCTURE	473.04	27.47%	455.24	31.15%	396.33	20.37%	511.45	24.10%
3A	Wall finishes	31.66	1.84%	50.00	3.42%	154.75	7.96%	64.35	3.03%
3B	Floor finishes	43.39	2.52%	50.98	3.49%	0.00	0.00%	78.88	3.72%
3C	Ceiling finishes	27.08	1.57%	47.75	3.27%	0.00	0.00%	46.60	2.20%
3	INTERNAL FINISHES	102.13	5.93%	148.73	10.18%	154.75	7.96%	189.83	8.95%
4	FITTINGS AND FURNISHINGS	54.42	3.16%	100.23	6.86%	132.83	6.83%	275.31	12.98%
5A	Sanitary appliances	25.70	1.49%	42.80	2.93%	45.72	2.35%	39.52	1.86%
5B	Services equipment	5.61	0.33%	10.69	0.73%	0.00	0.00%	58.97	2.78%
5C	Disposal installations	25.82	1.50%	8.49	0.58%	0.00	0.00%	3.49	0.16%
5D	Water installations	19.95	1.16%	0.00	0.00%	0.00	0.00%	0.00	0.00%
5E	Heat source	32.79	1.90%	0.00	0.00%	0.00	0.00%	0.00	0.00%
5F	Space heating and air treatment	294.93	17.13%	182.51	12.49%	252.36	12.97%	172.39	8.12%
5G	Ventilating systems	35.72	2.07%	0.00	0.00%	0.00	0.00%	13.57	0.64%
5H	Electrical installations	179.59	10.43%	195.44	13.37%	229.18	11.78%	137.79	6.49%
5I	Gas installations	4.56	0.27%	0.00	0.00%	0.00	0.00%	0.00	0.00%
5J	Lift and conveyor installations	20.42	1.19%	24.30	1.66%	0.00	0.00%	0.00	0.00%
5K	Protective installations	6.39	0.37%	0.00	0.00%	0.00	0.00%	3.15	0.15%
5L	Communication installations	18.03	1.05%	0.00	0.00%	0.00	0.00%	11.77	0.55%
5M	Special Installations	7.73	0.45%	0.00	0.00%	1.36	0.07%	6.70	0.32%
5N	Builder's work in connection	28.12	1.63%	13.58	0.93%	11.52	0.59%	19.50	0.92%
5O	Builder's profit and attendance	2.80	0.16%	0.00	0.00%	0.00	0.00%	0.00	0.00%
5	SERVICES	708.17	41.13%	477.81	32.69%	540.13	27.77%	466.86	22.00%
	Building sub-total	1,441.29	83.70%	1,240.10	84.84%	1,466.27	75.37%	1,585.10	74.70%
6A	Site works	74.03	4.30%	55.16	3.77%	177.38	9.12%	242.74	11.44%
6B	Drainage	36.11	2.10%	14.31	0.98%	61.25	3.15%	90.37	4.26%
6C	External services	22.14	1.29%	14.98	1.03%	0.00	0.00%	38.28	1.80%
6D	Minor building works	22.58	1.31%	0.00	0.00%	0.00	0.00%	12.86	0.61%
6	EXTERNAL WORKS	154.85	8.99%	84.45	5.78%	238.63	12.27%	384.24	18.11%
7	PRELIMINARIES	125.78	7.30%	137.14	9.38%	240.41	12.36%	152.50	7.19%
	FACILITY CONSTRUCTION COST	1,721.92	100.00%	1,461.68	100.00%	1,945.32	100.00%	2,121.84	100.00%

Elemental Analyses

Element		Restaurants		Theatres		Community Centres		Covered Swimming Pools	
		Cost/m^2	%	Cost/m^2	%	Cost/m^2	%	Cost/m^2	%
1	SUBSTRUCTURE	73.99	5.09%	114.80	6.68%	143.47	9.98%	205.99	8.51%
2A	Frame	55.24	3.80%	167.28	9.74%	12.08	0.84%	171.50	7.08%
2B	Upper floors	10.92	0.75%	55.68	3.24%	3.72	0.26%	54.93	2.27%
2C	Roof	123.10	8.47%	107.35	6.25%	165.05	11.48%	158.82	6.56%
2D	Stairs	21.41	1.47%	20.86	1.21%	1.22	0.08%	37.65	1.55%
2E	External walls	93.61	6.44%	101.07	5.88%	79.55	5.53%	147.60	6.09%
2F	Windows and external doors	126.46	8.70%	48.57	2.83%	99.45	6.92%	54.04	2.23%
2G	Internal walls and partitions	41.00	2.82%	38.80	2.26%	32.45	2.26%	65.27	2.69%
2H	Internal doors	37.88	2.61%	31.47	1.83%	51.18	3.56%	23.77	0.98%
2	SUPERSTRUCTURE	509.64	35.06%	571.09	33.24%	444.70	30.93%	713.59	29.46%
3A	Wall finishes	31.57	2.17%	20.27	1.18%	32.43	2.26%	76.48	3.16%
3B	Floor finishes	42.47	2.92%	43.83	2.55%	51.56	3.59%	89.00	3.67%
3C	Ceiling finishes	21.37	1.47%	18.08	1.05%	21.76	1.51%	19.63	0.81%
3	INTERNAL FINISHES	95.41	6.56%	82.19	4.78%	105.75	7.36%	185.10	7.64%
4	FITTINGS AND FURNISHINGS	171.86	11.82%	191.55	11.15%	32.12	2.23%	167.56	6.92%
5A	Sanitary appliances	19.84	1.37%	8.76	0.51%	19.38	1.35%	10.87	0.45%
5B	Services equipment	54.95	3.78%	23.98	1.40%	0.00	0.00%	0.90	0.04%
5C	Disposal installations	8.07	0.55%	6.85	0.40%	4.42	0.31%	4.04	0.17%
5D	Water installations	164.81	11.34%	21.18	1.23%	7.31	0.51%	29.76	1.23%
5E	Heat source	18.99	1.31%	8.15	0.47%	3.91	0.27%	21.70	0.90%
5F	Space heating and air treatment	4.74	0.33%	159.49	9.28%	131.76	9.16%	132.25	5.46%
5G	Ventilating systems	7.11	0.49%	21.51	1.25%	0.00	0.00%	111.49	4.60%
5H	Electrical installations	116.18	7.99%	135.55	7.89%	104.46	7.27%	139.63	5.77%
5I	Gas installations	2.37	0.16%	0.30	0.02%	1.08	0.08%	3.77	0.16%
5J	Lift and conveyor installations	0.00	0.00%	6.24	0.36%	0.00	0.00%	4.13	0.17%
5K	Protective installations	2.37	0.16%	6.12	0.36%	2.19	0.15%	14.45	0.60%
5L	Communication installations	2.37	0.16%	16.00	0.93%	2.98	0.21%	3.88	0.16%
5M	Special Installations	4.74	0.33%	0.00	0.00%	0.00	0.00%	226.45	9.35%
5N	Builder's work in connection	14.70	1.01%	24.26	1.41%	12.28	0.85%	23.31	0.96%
5O	Builder's profit and attendance	0.00	0.00%	0.46	0.03%	0.00	0.00%	0.00	0.00%
5	SERVICES	421.24	28.98%	438.85	25.55%	289.77	20.15%	726.63	30.00%
	Building sub-total	1,272.15	87.53%	1,398.47	81.41%	1,015.81	70.65%	1,998.88	82.53%
6A	Site works	31.52	2.17%	50.56	2.94%	158.72	11.04%	110.84	4.58%
6B	Drainage	48.67	3.35%	21.34	1.24%	51.50	3.58%	47.04	1.94%
6C	External services	6.58	0.45%	24.89	1.45%	30.23	2.10%	15.89	0.66%
6D	Minor building works	0.00	0.00%	11.29	0.66%	0.00	0.00%	2.23	0.09%
6	EXTERNAL WORKS	86.77	5.97%	108.08	6.29%	240.46	16.72%	175.99	7.27%
7	PRELIMINARIES	94.54	6.50%	211.34	12.30%	181.45	12.62%	247.10	10.20%
	FACILITY CONSTRUCTION COST	1,453.45	100.00%	1,717.90	100.00%	1,437.72	100.00%	2,421.97	100.00%

Element		Gymnasia		Sports Centres		Sports Centres incl. Pool		Sports Halls	
		Cost/m²	%	Cost/m²	%	Cost/m²	%	Cost/m²	%
1	**SUBSTRUCTURE**	**117.54**	**6.62%**	**107.26**	**7.78%**	**151.96**	**7.51%**	**114.07**	**9.19%**
2A	Frame	161.74	9.11%	85.91	6.23%	132.93	6.57%	96.34	7.76%
2B	Upper floors	11.36	0.64%	19.71	1.43%	11.70	0.58%	7.64	0.62%
2C	Roof	117.53	6.62%	102.13	7.41%	154.15	7.62%	103.10	8.31%
2D	Stairs	10.49	0.59%	20.96	1.52%	15.82	0.78%	3.00	0.24%
2E	External walls	256.53	14.45%	98.46	7.14%	131.69	6.51%	96.51	7.77%
2F	Windows and external doors	37.77	2.13%	36.17	2.62%	46.82	2.31%	45.24	3.64%
2G	Internal walls and partitions	81.67	4.60%	19.22	1.39%	64.90	3.21%	32.15	2.59%
2H	Internal doors	22.16	1.25%	39.59	2.87%	24.79	1.22%	116.81	9.41%
2	**SUPERSTRUCTURE**	**699.26**	**39.38%**	**422.14**	**30.62%**	**582.80**	**28.79%**	**500.80**	**40.34%**
3A	Wall finishes	23.69	1.33%	32.69	2.37%	41.30	2.04%	38.71	3.12%
3B	Floor finishes	41.71	2.35%	71.13	5.16%	78.66	3.89%	47.38	3.82%
3C	Ceiling finishes	9.88	0.56%	21.39	1.55%	22.69	1.12%	19.37	1.56%
3	**INTERNAL FINISHES**	**75.27**	**4.24%**	**125.21**	**9.08%**	**142.65**	**7.05%**	**105.46**	**8.50%**
4	**FITTINGS AND FURNISHINGS**	**87.70**	**4.94%**	**61.31**	**4.45%**	**92.05**	**4.55%**	**38.50**	**3.10%**
5A	Sanitary appliances	14.82	0.83%	11.30	0.82%	12.67	0.63%	10.63	0.86%
5B	Services equipment	0.00	0.00%	1.18	0.09%	0.00	0.00%	0.00	0.00%
5C	Disposal installations	6.49	0.37%	6.72	0.49%	6.11	0.30%	7.53	0.61%
5D	Water installations	2.32	0.13%	7.80	0.57%	26.29	1.30%	5.13	0.41%
5E	Heat source	0.00	0.00%	0.00	0.00%	0.74	0.04%	22.14	1.78%
5F	Space heating and air treatment	162.31	9.14%	153.98	11.17%	290.95	14.37%	75.40	6.07%
5G	Ventilating systems	41.95	2.36%	11.68	0.85%	18.98	0.94%	26.71	2.15%
5H	Electrical installations	103.26	5.82%	105.97	7.69%	91.06	4.50%	93.10	7.50%
5I	Gas installations	0.00	0.00%	0.00	0.00%	0.00	0.00%	6.32	0.51%
5J	Lift and conveyor installations	12.48	0.70%	12.31	0.89%	10.92	0.54%	3.25	0.26%
5K	Protective installations	2.57	0.15%	2.21	0.16%	4.81	0.24%	0.28	0.02%
5L	Communication installations	14.23	0.80%	4.17	0.30%	13.45	0.66%	4.99	0.40%
5M	Special Installations	0.00	0.00%	41.60	3.02%	89.27	4.41%	0.00	0.00%
5N	Builder's work in connection	7.60	0.43%	11.01	0.80%	18.81	0.93%	7.64	0.62%
5O	Builder's profit and attendance	0.00	0.00%	0.00	0.00%	0.00	0.00%	0.00	0.00%
5	**SERVICES**	**368.03**	**20.73%**	**369.94**	**26.83%**	**584.06**	**28.86%**	**263.10**	**21.19%**
	Building sub-total	**1,347.80**	**75.91%**	**1,085.86**	**78.76%**	**1,553.53**	**76.75%**	**1,021.94**	**82.32%**
6A	Site works	137.34	7.74%	84.84	6.15%	127.08	6.28%	57.14	4.60%
6B	Drainage	46.43	2.62%	33.38	2.42%	60.98	3.01%	24.95	2.01%
6C	External services	10.27	0.58%	10.82	0.78%	32.56	1.61%	8.93	0.72%
6D	Minor building works	4.29	0.24%	10.05	0.73%	5.77	0.29%	2.13	0.17%
6	**EXTERNAL WORKS**	**198.33**	**11.17%**	**139.08**	**10.09%**	**226.38**	**11.18%**	**93.14**	**7.50%**
7	**PRELIMINARIES**	**229.31**	**12.92%**	**153.83**	**11.16%**	**244.21**	**12.07%**	**126.35**	**10.18%**
	FACILITY CONSTRUCTION COST	**1,775.44**	**100.00%**	**1,378.78**	**100.00%**	**2,024.12**	**100.00%**	**1,241.44**	**100.00%**

Elemental Analyses

Element		Sports Stadia		Crematoria		Primary Schools		Middle Schools	
		Cost/m^2	%	Cost/m^2	%	Cost/m^2	%	Cost/m^2	%
1	**SUBSTRUCTURE**	**99.43**	**10.34%**	**97.79**	**4.15%**	**156.93**	**10.34%**	**70.49**	**6.51%**
2A	Frame	85.11	8.85%	0.00	0.00%	32.09	2.12%	65.11	6.01%
2B	Upper floors	81.73	8.50%	0.00	0.00%	1.25	0.08%	7.83	0.72%
2C	Roof	48.09	5.00%	216.57	9.18%	152.48	10.05%	102.39	9.46%
2D	Stairs	13.09	1.36%	0.00	0.00%	0.21	0.01%	5.19	0.48%
2E	External walls	100.03	10.40%	226.20	9.59%	68.26	4.50%	81.14	7.49%
2F	Windows and external doors	22.50	2.34%	91.50	3.88%	92.63	6.10%	61.00	5.63%
2G	Internal walls and partitions	24.69	2.57%	48.08	2.04%	53.20	3.51%	41.55	3.84%
2H	Internal doors	15.55	1.62%	54.39	2.31%	34.36	2.26%	29.14	2.69%
2	**SUPERSTRUCTURE**	**390.80**	**40.64%**	**636.75**	**26.99%**	**434.47**	**28.63%**	**393.36**	**36.32%**
3A	Wall finishes	11.95	1.24%	19.20	0.81%	21.74	1.43%	18.26	1.69%
3B	Floor finishes	24.97	2.60%	35.13	1.49%	46.88	3.09%	44.80	4.14%
3C	Ceiling finishes	7.44	0.77%	57.97	2.46%	30.74	2.03%	35.87	3.31%
3	**INTERNAL FINISHES**	**44.36**	**4.61%**	**112.29**	**4.76%**	**99.35**	**6.55%**	**98.93**	**9.14%**
4	**FITTINGS AND FURNISHINGS**	**27.27**	**2.84%**	**52.78**	**2.24%**	**49.59**	**3.27%**	**46.89**	**4.33%**
5A	Sanitary appliances	10.39	1.08%	11.38	0.48%	20.64	1.36%	7.51	0.69%
5B	Services equipment	0.00	0.00%	0.00	0.00%	4.96	0.33%	3.00	0.28%
5C	Disposal installations	2.68	0.28%	8.07	0.34%	8.72	0.57%	3.21	0.30%
5D	Water installations	3.69	0.38%	0.00	0.00%	15.76	1.04%	12.71	1.17%
5E	Heat source	5.18	0.54%	0.00	0.00%	9.52	0.63%	24.39	2.25%
5F	Space heating and air treatment	61.54	6.40%	62.63	2.65%	130.07	8.57%	56.99	5.26%
5G	Ventilating systems	11.02	1.15%	0.00	0.00%	15.47	1.02%	6.37	0.59%
5H	Electrical installations	50.83	5.29%	124.93	5.30%	118.05	7.78%	56.26	5.20%
5I	Gas installations	0.44	0.05%	0.00	0.00%	1.10	0.07%	0.81	0.07%
5J	Lift and conveyor installations	2.32	0.24%	0.00	0.00%	0.00	0.00%	0.00	0.00%
5K	Protective installations	3.59	0.37%	0.00	0.00%	2.73	0.18%	1.61	0.15%
5L	Communication installations	4.88	0.51%	0.00	0.00%	20.02	1.32%	4.41	0.41%
5M	Special Installations	17.32	1.80%	353.06	14.97%	7.40	0.49%	1.71	0.16%
5N	Builder's work in connection	4.36	0.45%	14.22	0.60%	13.24	0.87%	6.92	0.64%
5O	Builder's profit and attendance	1.42	0.15%	0.00	0.00%	1.64	0.11%	1.49	0.14%
5	**SERVICES**	**179.66**	**18.68%**	**574.29**	**24.35%**	**369.32**	**24.34%**	**187.40**	**17.30%**
	Building sub-total	**741.54**	**77.11%**	**1,473.90**	**62.49%**	**1,109.66**	**73.13%**	**797.06**	**73.60%**
6A	Site works	80.01	8.32%	503.22	21.33%	152.74	10.07%	116.69	10.78%
6B	Drainage	34.51	3.59%	84.76	3.59%	53.35	3.52%	49.41	4.56%
6C	External services	18.90	1.96%	86.88	3.68%	24.12	1.59%	5.56	0.51%
6D	Minor building works	6.18	0.64%	29.08	1.23%	58.29	3.84%	14.14	1.31%
6	**EXTERNAL WORKS**	**139.59**	**14.52%**	**703.94**	**29.84%**	**288.50**	**19.01%**	**185.80**	**17.16%**
7	**PRELIMINARIES**	**80.50**	**8.37%**	**180.94**	**7.67%**	**119.17**	**7.85%**	**100.07**	**9.24%**
	FACILITY CONSTRUCTION COST	**961.62**	**100.00%**	**2,358.78**	**100.00%**	**1,517.33**	**100.00%**	**1,082.93**	**100.00%**

Element		High Schools		Sixth Form Colleges		Universities		Laboratory Blocks	
		Cost/m^2	%	Cost/m^2	%	Cost/m^2	%	Cost/m^2	%
1	**SUBSTRUCTURE**	**98.36**	**8.21%**	**107.55**	**9.09%**	**129.34**	**6.51%**	**116.95**	**3.31%**
2A	Frame	62.58	5.22%	68.60	5.80%	42.57	2.14%	61.48	1.74%
2B	Upper floors	11.10	0.93%	30.04	2.54%	56.65	2.85%	48.24	1.36%
2C	Roof	116.97	9.76%	83.80	7.08%	134.44	6.76%	148.04	4.19%
2D	Stairs	15.47	1.29%	10.76	0.91%	43.83	2.21%	14.48	0.41%
2E	External walls	67.63	5.64%	51.00	4.31%	453.93	22.84%	125.66	3.55%
2F	Windows and external doors	69.96	5.84%	140.69	11.89%	87.25	4.39%	46.56	1.32%
2G	Internal walls and partitions	42.49	3.54%	51.66	4.36%	39.68	2.00%	69.75	1.97%
2H	Internal doors	41.82	3.49%	34.23	2.89%	37.06	1.86%	33.11	0.94%
2	**SUPERSTRUCTURE**	**428.02**	**35.71%**	**470.79**	**39.78%**	**895.40**	**45.05%**	**547.32**	**15.48%**
3A	Wall finishes	21.29	1.78%	16.99	1.44%	35.85	1.80%	27.58	0.78%
3B	Floor finishes	41.26	3.44%	34.71	2.93%	53.64	2.70%	56.59	1.60%
3C	Ceiling finishes	15.88	1.32%	16.40	1.39%	52.03	2.62%	44.32	1.25%
3	**INTERNAL FINISHES**	**78.43**	**6.54%**	**68.09**	**5.75%**	**141.52**	**7.12%**	**128.49**	**3.63%**
4	**FITTINGS AND FURNISHINGS**	**41.43**	**3.46%**	**40.32**	**3.41%**	**87.46**	**4.40%**	**87.47**	**2.47%**
5A	Sanitary appliances	8.11	0.68%	34.18	2.89%	8.36	0.42%	16.55	0.47%
5B	Services equipment	0.00	0.00%	0.80	0.07%	3.40	0.17%	11.57	0.33%
5C	Disposal installations	3.66	0.30%	6.58	0.56%	16.31	0.82%	1.83	0.05%
5D	Water installations	0.00	0.00%	5.21	0.44%	8.10	0.41%	43.02	1.22%
5E	Heat source	0.00	0.00%	11.79	1.00%	7.52	0.38%	0.00	0.00%
5F	Space heating and air treatment	116.74	9.74%	68.21	5.76%	109.38	5.50%	163.25	4.62%
5G	Ventilating systems	0.00	0.00%	6.69	0.57%	16.65	0.84%	83.90	2.37%
5H	Electrical installations	108.37	9.04%	95.10	8.03%	107.71	5.42%	198.54	5.61%
5I	Gas installations	0.00	0.00%	0.00	0.00%	0.27	0.01%	8.33	0.24%
5J	Lift and conveyor installations	0.00	0.00%	3.72	0.31%	28.64	1.44%	11.56	0.33%
5K	Protective installations	0.30	0.03%	1.34	0.11%	3.53	0.18%	0.83	0.02%
5L	Communication installations	3.68	0.31%	2.75	0.23%	5.70	0.29%	38.13	1.08%
5M	Special Installations	2.10	0.18%	0.48	0.04%	0.00	0.00%	184.67	5.22%
5N	Builder's work in connection	15.00	1.25%	16.01	1.35%	19.26	0.97%	25.00	0.71%
5O	Builder's profit and attendance	0.00	0.00%	5.78	0.49%	0.80	0.04%	4.81	0.14%
5	**SERVICES**	**257.95**	**21.52%**	**258.63**	**21.85%**	**335.66**	**16.89%**	**791.99**	**22.40%**
	Building sub-total	**904.18**	**75.44%**	**945.38**	**79.87%**	**1,589.38**	**79.97%**	**1,672.21**	**47.29%**
6A	Site works	88.50	7.38%	81.67	6.90%	73.29	3.69%	84.90	2.40%
6B	Drainage	31.23	2.61%	23.60	1.99%	30.27	1.52%	30.44	0.86%
6C	External services	25.07	2.09%	18.91	1.60%	17.57	0.88%	24.84	0.70%
6D	Minor building works	11.24	0.94%	36.52	3.09%	35.57	1.79%	1,466.73	41.48%
6	**EXTERNAL WORKS**	**156.04**	**13.02%**	**160.70**	**13.58%**	**156.71**	**7.88%**	**1,606.92**	**45.44%**
7	**PRELIMINARIES**	**138.38**	**11.55%**	**77.53**	**6.55%**	**241.48**	**12.15%**	**257.15**	**7.27%**
	FACILITY CONSTRUCTION COST	**1,198.60**	**100.00%**	**1,183.61**	**100.00%**	**1,987.57**	**100.00%**	**3,536.28**	**100.00%**

Elemental Analyses

Element		Research Facilities		Detached Housing		Semi-detached Housing		Estate Housing	
		Cost/m^2	%	Cost/m^2	%	Cost/m^2	%	Cost/m^2	%
1	**SUBSTRUCTURE**	**167.55**	**8.71%**	**88.52**	**5.97%**	**101.19**	**8.88%**	**88.58**	**8.07%**
2A	Frame	192.47	10.01%	26.57	1.79%	0.00	0.00%	0.09	0.01%
2B	Upper floors	45.25	2.35%	32.10	2.17%	11.13	0.98%	15.53	1.42%
2C	Roof	81.62	4.24%	156.00	10.52%	127.56	11.20%	87.96	8.02%
2D	Stairs	35.23	1.83%	19.44	1.31%	6.89	0.60%	10.07	0.92%
2E	External walls	92.24	4.80%	98.80	6.67%	143.57	12.60%	125.04	11.40%
2F	Windows and external doors	79.31	4.12%	132.26	8.92%	93.82	8.23%	61.11	5.57%
2G	Internal walls and partitions	51.34	2.67%	29.85	2.01%	60.75	5.33%	29.10	2.65%
2H	Internal doors	25.88	1.35%	52.16	3.52%	42.46	3.73%	32.51	2.96%
2	**SUPERSTRUCTURE**	**603.33**	**31.37%**	**547.18**	**36.92%**	**486.19**	**42.67%**	**361.41**	**32.94%**
3A	Wall finishes	18.32	0.95%	51.64	3.48%	32.50	2.85%	48.17	4.39%
3B	Floor finishes	36.54	1.90%	33.35	2.25%	33.92	2.98%	31.93	2.91%
3C	Ceiling finishes	18.11	0.94%	34.04	2.30%	18.08	1.59%	18.34	1.67%
3	**INTERNAL FINISHES**	**72.97**	**3.79%**	**119.03**	**8.03%**	**84.50**	**7.42%**	**98.44**	**8.97%**
4	**FITTINGS AND FURNISHINGS**	**14.54**	**0.76%**	**88.86**	**6.00%**	**22.08**	**1.94%**	**21.07**	**1.92%**
5A	Sanitary appliances	4.90	0.25%	22.20	1.50%	38.46	3.38%	15.51	1.41%
5B	Services equipment	435.97	22.66%	0.00	0.00%	0.00	0.00%	0.00	0.00%
5C	Disposal installations	15.77	0.82%	17.30	1.17%	8.15	0.71%	4.92	0.45%
5D	Water installations	22.02	1.14%	6.01	0.41%	16.85	1.48%	6.20	0.57%
5E	Heat source	0.00	0.00%	13.22	0.89%	9.27	0.81%	0.00	0.00%
5F	Space heating and air treatment	110.35	5.74%	80.80	5.45%	34.83	3.06%	52.92	4.82%
5G	Ventilating systems	3.12	0.16%	0.00	0.00%	0.00	0.00%	0.77	0.07%
5H	Electrical installations	145.09	7.54%	55.81	3.77%	22.24	1.95%	30.06	2.74%
5I	Gas installations	1.00	0.05%	0.00	0.00%	0.59	0.05%	0.87	0.08%
5J	Lift and conveyor installations	15.54	0.81%	4.95	0.33%	0.00	0.00%	0.00	0.00%
5K	Protective installations	13.23	0.69%	0.00	0.00%	0.00	0.00%	0.36	0.03%
5L	Communication installations	12.70	0.66%	0.55	0.04%	0.00	0.00%	1.52	0.14%
5M	Special Installations	4.59	0.24%	27.10	1.83%	0.00	0.00%	0.36	0.03%
5N	Builder's work in connection	25.81	1.34%	6.50	0.44%	7.65	0.67%	9.87	0.90%
5O	Builder's profit and attendance	0.00	0.00%	1.49	0.10%	6.70	0.59%	0.22	0.02%
5	**SERVICES**	**810.10**	**42.11%**	**235.95**	**15.92%**	**144.74**	**12.70%**	**123.56**	**11.26%**
	Building sub-total	**1,668.50**	**86.74%**	**1,079.53**	**72.83%**	**838.69**	**73.61%**	**693.07**	**63.17%**
6A	Site works	88.35	4.59%	158.45	10.69%	165.01	14.48%	199.85	18.22%
6B	Drainage	20.43	1.06%	42.17	2.85%	50.56	4.44%	55.58	5.07%
6C	External services	2.50	0.13%	62.31	4.20%	48.02	4.21%	47.07	4.29%
6D	Minor building works	0.00	0.00%	8.06	0.54%	0.00	0.00%	2.81	0.26%
6	**EXTERNAL WORKS**	**111.29**	**5.79%**	**270.99**	**18.28%**	**263.60**	**23.13%**	**305.30**	**27.83%**
7	**PRELIMINARIES**	**143.80**	**7.48%**	**131.67**	**8.88%**	**37.13**	**3.26%**	**98.69**	**9.00%**
	FACILITY CONSTRUCTION COST	**1,923.59**	**100.00%**	**1,482.20**	**100.00%**	**1,139.42**	**100.00%**	**1,097.06**	**100.00%**

Element		Hotels		Halls of Residence	
		Cost/m^2	%	Cost/m^2	%
1	**SUBSTRUCTURE**	**66.75**	**5.25%**	**71.87**	**5.10%**
2A	Frame	25.18	1.98%	40.14	2.85%
2B	Upper floors	62.50	4.92%	29.01	2.06%
2C	Roof	80.39	6.33%	81.84	5.81%
2D	Stairs	11.47	0.90%	27.16	1.93%
2E	External walls	61.58	4.85%	88.69	6.30%
2F	Windows and external doors	69.13	5.44%	77.48	5.50%
2G	Internal walls and partitions	59.56	4.69%	32.92	2.34%
2H	Internal doors	31.99	2.52%	76.95	5.47%
2	**SUPERSTRUCTURE**	**401.80**	**31.63%**	**454.20**	**32.26%**
3A	Wall finishes	49.54	3.90%	47.52	3.37%
3B	Floor finishes	43.49	3.42%	47.58	3.38%
3C	Ceiling finishes	29.17	2.30%	21.56	1.53%
3	**INTERNAL FINISHES**	**122.20**	**9.62%**	**116.66**	**8.29%**
4	**FITTINGS AND FURNISHINGS**	**59.57**	**4.69%**	**86.08**	**6.11%**
5A	Sanitary appliances	13.96	1.10%	110.26	7.83%
5B	Services equipment	0.28	0.02%	4.02	0.29%
5C	Disposal installations	0.00	0.00%	19.68	1.40%
5D	Water installations	0.00	0.00%	30.51	2.17%
5E	Heat source	41.58	3.27%	0.00	0.00%
5F	Space heating and air treatment	159.58	12.56%	98.69	7.01%
5G	Ventilating systems	0.00	0.00%	0.12	0.01%
5H	Electrical installations	117.28	9.23%	155.93	11.07%
5I	Gas installations	0.00	0.00%	0.52	0.04%
5J	Lift and conveyor installations	18.72	1.47%	1.08	0.08%
5K	Protective installations	0.00	0.00%	0.56	0.04%
5L	Communication installations	0.49	0.04%	19.27	1.37%
5M	Special Installations	18.76	1.48%	5.09	0.36%
5N	Builder's work in connection	11.09	0.87%	36.47	2.59%
5O	Builder's profit and attendance	0.00	0.00%	0.24	0.02%
5	**SERVICES**	**381.74**	**30.05%**	**482.43**	**34.27%**
	Building sub-total	**1,032.06**	**81.24%**	**1,211.25**	**86.03%**
6A	Site works	74.90	5.90%	49.28	3.50%
6B	Drainage	22.78	1.79%	22.19	1.58%
6C	External services	8.11	0.64%	20.16	1.43%
6D	Minor building works	12.40	0.98%	5.90	0.42%
6	**EXTERNAL WORKS**	**118.19**	**9.30%**	**97.52**	**6.93%**
7	**PRELIMINARIES**	**120.14**	**9.46%**	**99.16**	**7.04%**
	FACILITY CONSTRUCTION COST	**1,270.39**	**100.00%**	**1,407.93**	**100.00%**

REDROW'S CELESTIA DEVELOPMENT, CARDIFF

FROM ASPIRATION TO REALITY

Franklin + Andrews is recognised as one of the world's leading construction economists. We work with many leading organisations world-wide and take great pride in delivering added value to their businesses.

Driven by our core skill of quantity surveying, we operate in sectors such as government, utilities, transport, property and energy. We provide a comprehensive range of commercial management services and tailored business solutions throughout the whole project lifecycle.

Our dedicated team produces industry recognised construction cost and economic data including project specific inflation forecasting, performance and cost benchmarking and economic modelling. We also offer whole life costing services, enabling you to make strategic decisions with confidence.

For more information please contact Lisa Page:
T +44 (0)20 7633 9966
E enquiries@franklinandrews.com

Franklin + Andrews is part of the Mott MacDonald Group

www.franklinandrews.com

FRANKLIN ANDREWS
CONSTRUCTION ECONOMISTS

Facility Benchmark Costs

Facility Benchmark Costs

The following facility rates and ranges are taken from high level analyses of a large number of projects.

As construction projects are homogenous in their nature we advise caution in the use of the figures without a fuller appraisal of the project and any likely cost drivers.

The costs are for a completed project at second quarter 2008 levels based on a UK average location but do not include VAT, fees or any site acquisition costs.

Although the figures are taken from a large number of existing projects it is possible for construction costs to fall outside the given range.

Facility Type	Benchmark Cost £/m^2 GFA	Low	High
Railway Stations	2,460	608	4,437
Railway Signal Boxes	1,258	822	1,687
Multi-storey Car Parks	373	197	615
Petrol Stations	2,165	806	4,978
Airport Terminal Buildings	2,137	950	4,166
Air Traffic Control Buildings	4,645	1,535	10,635
Recording Studios	1,543	770	3,050
Sorting Offices	988	328	2,154
Refuse Depots	599	325	929
Stables and the like	962	589	1,360
Chemicals Factories	1,053	444	2,391
Electronics Factories	1,170	733	1,899
Factories	669	208	2,737
Advanced Factories	583	274	2,191
Purpose Built Factories	839	257	2,737
Purpose Built Factories/Offices Mixed	783	333	1,898
Warehouses	621	172	2,338
Town Halls	1,472	1,042	2,705
Law Courts	1,793	784	2,605
Offices	1,412	399	3,657
Offices with Shops	1,485	353	3,492
Offices - Purpose Built	1,657	1,119	2,975
Offices - Speculative	1,741	1,045	2,438
Offices - Traditional	1,286	505	2,591
Banks / Building Societies	1,817	788	3,632
Retail Warehouses	587	224	2,097
Shopping Centres	916	359	1,796
Department Stores	1,119	386	2,127
Hypermarkets / Supermarkets	1,093	202	2,131
Shops	852	286	2,289
Cold Stores	991	279	1,886
Other Shops	954	459	2,398
Fire Stations	1,625	673	3,092
Police Stations	1,698	985	2,752
Closed Prisons	1,897	972	2,593
Gynaecological Hospital Facilities	1,708	1,165	3,070
Paediatric Units	1,434	807	2,389
Ward Blocks	1,468	832	2,113
Outpatients / Casualty Units	1,768	1,191	2,533
Day Hospital	1,802	1,112	2,485
Intensive Care / Acute Wards	1,748	1,047	3,242
Health Centres	1,200	461	2,562

Facility Benchmark Costs

Facility Benchmark Costs (cont'd)

Facility Type	Benchmark Cost £/m² GFA	Low	High
Nursing Homes	1,307	640	2,699
Homes for Mentally Handicapped	1,254	639	2,427
Homes for the Elderly	1,166	602	2,258
Day Centres	1,406	696	2,333
Veterinary Hospitals	1,545	1,313	1,854
Restaurants	1,785	834	3,900
Public Houses	1,419	757	2,563
Theatres	1,970	1,177	3,212
Cinemas	1,513	1,018	2,570
Community Centres	1,220	519	2,715
Clubs	1,170	623	1,774
Covered Swimming Pools	2,193	594	5,131
Sports Centres excl. Pools	1,140	473	2,542
Sports Centres incl. Pools	1,746	512	3,840
Sports Halls	1,050	343	2,107
Gymnasia	1,568	677	2,682
Squash Courts	1,119	792	2,253
Indoor Tennis Courts	462	276	730
Indoor Bowling Greens	587	329	1,042
Stadia	1,307	444	2,637
Golf Driving Ranges	845	416	1,464
Covered Ice Rinks	1,228	657	1,675
Pavilions / Sports Club Houses	1,240	329	4,710
Churches	1,474	628	2,957
Mission Halls	1,543	916	3,622
Crematoria	2,058	1,261	3,025
Schools	1,274	516	3,659
Nursey Schools	1,509	538	3,013
Primary Schools	1,240	517	2,635
Middle Schools	1,073	664	1,641
High Schools	1,152	579	3,659
Sixth Form Colleges	1,246	571	2,105
Special Schools	1,251	728	2,178
Universities	1,512	837	4,482
University Specialist Teaching Block	1,244	586	2,590
Colleges	1,330	594	2,588
Research Facilities	1,774	852	5,052
Laboratories	1,767	603	3,393
Exhibition Buildings	1,896	1,212	4,322
Public Libraries	1,409	808	2,757
Estate Housing	822	363	1,966
Estate Housing - Detached	885	508	1,525
Estate Housing - Semi-detached	837	451	1,966
Estate Housing - Terraced	762	400	1,583
Flats	955	386	2,795
Housing - Detached	1,372	441	4,859
Housing - Semi-detached	961	625	1,442
Sheltered Housing	977	477	2,200
Hotels	1,358	803	2,585
Halls of Residence	1,360	771	2,808

Whole Life Costs

Whole Life Costs

The initial capital expenditure costs (Capex) of a construction type is only the beginning in the financial aspect relating to the overall costs of a building. A significant financial outflow will come into effect once the basic construction programme is complete and the building effectively comes on line to serve the function of its designed use. These are the running costs or, more precisely, the operating expenditure costs (Opex) and these will need to be carefully managed during the whole term of a building s useful life.

This cost liability can have a considerable impact on the full financial picture and any knowledge of operating costs, or costs in use, for structures of a similar specification can be extremely useful to the potential building owner if relative costs for such structures are available. A more rational and accurate appraisal of the cost implications for a particular building design specification can be assessed through access to actual running cost data in respect of actual buildings. It should be appreciated that cost data that is now available is based on historic projects and as advances are made in technology these costs may not fully reflect current financial situations. With knowledge of the operating costs for various total schemes or the individual elements of a scheme decisions concerning appropriate and cost effective specification can be made during the design phase and before the building process takes place. The research currently being undertaken into Life Cycle Costing or Whole Life Costs provides a valuable resource for use in such decision making.

Typical Life Cycle Costs ($£/m^2$) for various construction types have been collated and are reproduced here to enable the building owner, together with the professional advisors involved, to make any necessary adjustments to the building specification in order that control may be taken of any operating costs. This once highly speculative process can now be more accurately managed and cost predictions for the operating costs for a specific building facility more precisely calculated.

Prices are all current at second quarter 2008 levels based on a UK average location.

Whole Life Costs

Element	Colleges	Schools	Estate Housing	Hotels	Community Centres	Offices	Super-markets	Shopping Centres	Factories	Ware-houses
Asset Acquisition										
Fees	188.40	192.26	124.37	205.61	183.75	211.61	166.73	139.46	101.35	94.00
Construction Cost (less capital allowances)	1,569.97	1,602.21	1,036.44	1,713.43	1,531.28	1,763.39	1,389.44	1,162.16	844.62	783.37
Subtotal	**1,758.36**	**1,794.47**	**1,160.81**	**1,919.04**	**1,715.04**	**1,975.00**	**1,556.17**	**1,301.62**	**945.98**	**877.38**
Total Building Cost	**1,758.36**	**1,794.47**	**1,160.81**	**1,919.04**	**1,715.04**	**1,975.00**	**1,556.17**	**1,301.62**	**945.98**	**877.38**
Occupancy Costs for 25 years										
M&E and Lifts Maintenance	413.18	350.58	206.59	469.52	319.28	488.30	469.52	244.15	206.59	206.59
Fabric	434.12	460.43	256.53	493.32	355.19	414.39	394.66	286.13	217.06	217.06
Cleaning	342.09	390.10	54.01	612.16	450.12	396.11	630.17	288.08	288.08	180.05
Waste	5.66	3.56	5.34	8.80	6.60	9.12	19.49	3.14	4.40	3.46
Electricity	177.85	111.98	156.96	276.65	207.49	286.53	612.58	98.80	138.32	108.68
Gas installations	10.48	6.60	9.15	16.31	12.23	16.89	36.11	5.82	8.15	6.41
Water	11.70	7.36	11.05	18.19	13.64	18.84	40.28	6.50	9.10	7.15
Communications	177.22	111.58	167.37	275.67	206.75	285.52	610.42	98.45	137.84	108.30
Post Room	13.74	14.39	6.87	12.76	8.83	25.52	12.27	16.68	10.31	7.85
Porterage	29.12	30.51	14.56	27.04	18.72	54.08	26.00	35.36	21.84	16.64
Internal moves	354.91	371.81	177.46	329.56	228.16	659.12	316.89	430.96	266.18	202.81
Security	113.99	119.42	57.00	105.85	73.28	211.70	101.78	138.42	85.50	65.14
Management	74.13	77.66	37.07	68.84	47.66	137.67	66.19	90.02	55.60	42.36
Subtotal	**2,158.19**	**2,056.00**	**1,159.95**	**2,714.68**	**1,947.95**	**3,003.79**	**3,336.36**	**1,742.53**	**1,448.96**	**1,172.49**
Whole-life cost over 25 years	**3,916.56**	**3,850.47**	**2,320.76**	**4,633.72**	**3,662.99**	**4,978.79**	**4,892.53**	**3,044.15**	**2,394.94**	**2,049.87**

Note: The indicated costs exclude the following:-
Land acquisition, finance costs, rental, external land, internal planting, reception, catering, asset disposal and Value Added Tax

Appendices

Indices

The following all-in tender price, building cost and mechanical + electrical cost indices are calculated through the analysis of a large number of projects and construction data. The costs of construction materials, plant and labour are regularly monitored and tracked to calculate the cost indices.

Building Cost Indices

The Building Cost Index measures changes in contractors costs. It is constructed using a calculated weighting of wage rates, material costs and plant and overhead charges. The weighting represents the levels of resources used in a typical building project. Please note that variances in inflationary levels are likely to be recorded depending on the type and resource weighting of the building being adjusted.

Mechanical + Electrical Cost Indices

Mechanical and Electrical (M+E) Cost Index measures changes in the M+E contractors costs. It is constructed using a calculated weighting of wage rates, material costs and plant and overhead charges. The weighting represents the levels of resources used in a typical building project. Please note that variances in inflationary levels are likely to be recorded depending on the type and resource weighting of the building being adjusted.

All-in Tender Price Indices

The All-in Tender Price Index measures the trend of contractors' pricing levels in accepted tenders, i.e. what the client has to pay for the building. It therefore takes into account building costs, but it also makes an allowance for market conditions and profit.

Franklin + Andrews' Indices

The following table reflects the change in tender prices, building costs and M+E costs in the UK construction market since 2000.

Base 2000 = 100

Quarter	Building Cost Index	M+E Cost Index	All-in Tender Price Index
1Q00	98	99	97
2Q00	99	100	99
3Q00	101	100	101
4Q00	102	102	103
1Q01	103	104	105
2Q01	103	104	105
3Q01	104	104	109
4Q01	104	105	110
1Q02	105	106	112
2Q02	106	107	116
3Q02	109	107	119
4Q02	110	110	119
1Q03	111	111	121
2Q03	112	112	122
3Q03	114	112	124
4Q03	115	113	125
1Q04	116	116	129
2Q04	118	117	131
3Q04	122	118	132
4Q04	124	121	134
1Q05	125	123	137
2Q05	126	123	139
3Q05	129	124	140
4Q05	129	126	142
1Q06	131	128	144
2Q06	133	130	145
3Q06	136	132	147
4Q06	137	133	148
1Q07	138	135	150
2Q07	140	136	152
3Q07	142	137	154
4Q07	143	138	155
1Q08	144	140	157
2Q08	145	141	159

Location Factors

UK Location Factors

Inner London	1.18
Outer London	1.15
Scotland	0.99
South East (excl London)	1.04
Northern	1.01
Yorkshire and Humberside	1.00
East Anglia	0.99
North West	0.94
West Midlands	0.96
South West	0.98
East Midlands	0.94
Northern Ireland	0.90
Wales	0.91

Indicative International Location Factors

By the analysis of similar projects throughout various locations around the world the following indicative international location factors have been calculated.

Care should be exercised when applying an international factor to another country's project. Procurement, technology, availability of materials, labour and plant may be different within any individual country, sometimes resulting in a project being factored that cannot actually be built in another part of the world.

These factors are presented as a guide only, a full study should be undertaken to obtain an accurate feasibility report in respect of any proposed project.

(Note: UK = 1.00)

	Mean	Low	High		Mean	Low	High
ARGENTINA	0.70	0.38	1.26	**CANADA**	0.92	0.36	1.58
				Edmonton	0.81		
AUSTRALIA	1.06	0.63	1.87	Calgary	0.85		
Adelaide	0.93			Halifax	0.97		
Brisbane	0.90			Montreal	0.83		
Darwin	1.21			Ottowa	0.90		
Hobart	1.07			Quebec	0.83		
Perth	0.92			Toronto	0.92		
Sydney	1.06			St. Johns	1.04		
Melbourne	1.00			Vancouver	0.87		
Queensland Islands	1.19			Winnipeg	0.81		
AUSTRIA	0.93	0.41	1.31	**CHILE**	0.77	0.30	1.34
BAHRAIN	0.84	0.41	1.46	**CHINA**	0.40	0.12	1.05
				Shenzen	0.40		
BANGLADESH	0.76	0.22	1.53	Beijing	0.42		
				Shanghai	0.43		
BELGIUM	0.86	0.45	1.21	Macao	0.45		
BOLIVIA	0.63	0.33	1.59	**COLOMBIA**	0.72	0.35	1.98
BRAZIL	0.76	0.34	1.44	**COTE D'IVOIRE**	0.88	0.39	1.75
Rio de Janeiro	0.76						
Sao Paulo	0.78			**CYPRUS**	0.87	0.47	1.60
Curitiba	0.78						
Salvador	0.80			**CZECH REP**	0.70	0.22	1.20
				Prague	0.70		
BULGARIA	0.60	0.27	1.20	Brno	0.67		
				Liberec	0.65		

Indicative Location Factors

	Location Factor				Location Factor		
	Mean	Low	High		Mean	Low	High
DENMARK	1.26	0.65	2.10	**HONG KONG**	0.75	0.24	0.96
Copenhagen	1.26						
Odense	1.35			**HUNGARY**	0.68	0.24	1.04
Arhus	1.39			Budapest	0.68		
EGYPT	0.66	0.28	1.26	**INDIA**	0.52	0.14	0.99
Alexandria	0.61						
Cairo	0.66			**INDONESIA**	0.46	0.14	0.71
Port Said	0.61			Bandung	0.43		
Suez	0.61			Jakarta	0.46		
Other Areas	0.56			Medan	0.43		
				Surabaya	0.41		
EL SALVADOR	0.59	0.27	1.39	Other Areas	0.37		
FINLAND	0.99	0.43	1.63	**IRELAND**	1.08	0.66	1.68
				Central Dublin	1.11		
FRANCE	0.94	0.53	1.39	Greater Dublin	1.08		
Paris	0.94			Shannon	1.00		
Ardenne	0.91			Cork	1.03		
Picardie	0.90			South West	0.98		
Haute-Normandie	0.87			South East	1.00		
Centre	0.92			Midlands East	1.00		
Basse Normandie	0.93			West	0.99		
Bourgogne	0.95			North West	0.97		
Nord-Pas-de-Calais	0.90						
Lorraine	0.93			**ITALY**	0.92	0.43	1.59
Alsace	0.94			Bari	0.83		
Franche Comte	0.92			Bologna	0.90		
				Cagliari	0.79		
GERMANY	0.90	0.47	1.36	Florence	0.93		
Baden - Stuttgart	0.95			Genoa	0.91		
Bavaria, Munich	0.95			Milan	0.92		
Berlin	1.08			Naples	0.83		
Bremen	0.87			Rome	0.87		
Hamburg	0.87			Palermo	0.79		
Hannover	0.86			Turin	0.93		
Frankfurt	0.90			Venice	0.93		
Pomerania	0.86						
Cologne	0.92						
Ludwigshaven	0.93						
Saarbrucken	0.96						
GHANA	0.87	0.38	1.71				
GREECE	0.74	0.31	1.21				

	Location Factor				**Location Factor**		
	Mean	**Low**	**High**		**Mean**	**Low**	**High**
JAPAN	**1.06**	**0.34**	**1.70**	**NETHERLANDS**	**0.97**	**0.55**	**1.42**
Fukuoka	0.93			Arnhem	0.92		
Kitakyusha	0.93			Amsterdam	0.97		
Hiroshima	0.99			Apeldorn	0.92		
Kawasaki	1.02			Einhoven	0.90		
Yokohama	1.02			Enschede	0.89		
Kobe / Kyoto	1.17			Groningen	0.88		
Nagoya	1.04			Rotterdam	0.98		
Osaka	1.11			The Hague	0.99		
Sapporo	1.03			Utrecht	0.97		
Tokyo	1.06						
				NEW ZEALAND	**0.96**	**0.50**	**1.40**
KENYA	**0.52**	**0.14**	**1.07**				
				NIGERIA	**0.75**	**0.35**	**1.56**
KOREA, SOUTH	**0.64**	**0.33**	**1.46**	Abuja	0.71		
Incheon	0.63			Lagos	0.75		
Pusan	0.63			Port Harcourt	0.71		
Seoul	0.64						
Taegu	0.62			**NORWAY**	**0.99**	**0.46**	**2.21**
				Bergen	0.96		
KUWAIT	**0.82**	**0.39**	**2.08**	Kristiansand	0.98		
Kuwait	0.82			Oslo	0.99		
Al Jahrah	0.88			Stavanger	0.97		
Ad Dawhah	0.93			Trondheim	1.01		
Ash Shuaybah	1.02						
				OMAN	**0.80**	**0.32**	**1.41**
LIBYA	**0.69**	**0.36**	**0.99**				
				PAKISTAN	**0.68**	**0.35**	**1.54**
MALAWI	**0.70**	**0.32**	**1.41**				
				PERU	**0.61**	**0.27**	**1.18**
MALAYSIA	**0.53**	**0.14**	**0.86**				
Kuala Lumpur	0.53			**PHILIPPINES**	**0.45**	**0.09**	**0.87**
Johor Baharu	0.58						
MEXICO	**0.70**	**0.28**	**1.26**	**POLAND**	**0.70**	**0.24**	**1.58**
Ciudad Juarez	0.81			Lodz	0.67		
Guadalajara	0.65			Krakow	0.68		
Merida	0.61			Poznan	0.67		
Mexico City	0.70			Warsaw	0.70		
Monterrey	0.67			Other Areas	0.63		
Puebla	0.67						

Indicative Location Factors

	Location Factor				Location Factor		
	Mean	**Low**	**High**		**Mean**	**Low**	**High**
PORTUGAL	**0.75**	**0.38**	**1.68**	**SWEDEN**	**1.19**	**0.29**	**1.96**
Lisbon	0.75			Gothenburg	1.15		
Setubal	0.74			Malmo	1.18		
Coimbra	0.71			Norrkoping	1.18		
Braga	0.68			Orebro	1.17		
Faro	0.86			Stockholm	1.19		
				Uppsala	1.17		
ROMANIA	**0.68**	**0.33**	**1.28**				
				SWITZERLAND	**1.30**	**0.72**	**2.21**
RUSSIAN FED.	**1.08**	**0.59**	**1.94**				
				TAIWAN	**0.77**	**0.52**	**2.36**
SAUDI ARABIA	**0.77**	**0.35**	**1.93**				
Dammam / Dhahran	0.81			**THAILAND**	**0.49**	**0.19**	**0.78**
Jeddah	0.73						
Mecca	0.73			**TURKEY**	**0.75**	**0.25**	**1.30**
Riyadh	0.77			Istanbul	0.77		
Other Areas	0.69			Ankara	0.74		
				Other Areas	0.64		
SINGAPORE	**0.63**	**0.23**	**1.04**				
				UGANDA	**0.72**	**0.33**	**1.45**
SLOVENIA	**0.66**	**0.25**	**1.09**				
				UKRAINE	**0.77**	**0.35**	**1.54**
SOUTH AFRICA	**0.75**	**0.25**	**1.25**				
Cape Town	0.72			**UNITED ARAB**			
Durban	0.73			**EMIRATES**	**0.85**	**0.31**	**1.26**
Johannesburg	0.75						
Pretoria	0.74			**UNITED KINGDOM**	**1.00**	**0.45**	**2.00**
Port Elizabeth	0.74						
				USA	**0.98**	**0.56**	**2.26**
SPAIN	**0.75**	**0.35**	**1.16**	Atlanta	0.86		
Barcelona	0.77			Boston	1.06		
Bilbao	0.73			Chicago	1.05	0.60	2.42
Las Palmas de				Dallas	0.87		
Gran Canaria	0.71			Los Angeles	1.09	0.62	2.51
Malaga	0.73			New York City	1.20	0.68	2.76
Madrid	0.75			San Francisco	1.18		
Palma	0.74			Seattle	0.91		
Valencia	0.74			Washington D.C	0.98		
Seville	0.76						
				VENEZUELA	**0.76**	**0.38**	**1.71**
SRI LANKA	**0.76**	**0.31**	**1.38**				
				VIETNAM	**0.64**	**0.29**	**1.28**
St. KITTS (Caribbean)	**1.25**	**0.49**	**1.54**				
				WEST INDIES	**1.03**	**0.46**	**2.05**
				ZIMBABWE	**0.69**	**0.37**	**1.64**

Sustainability

Sustainability

Sustainability is an environmental concept which embraces social and economic issues. In theory it is a way of configuring human activity so that society can meet its needs whilst preserving biodiversity and ecosystems for future generations, coupled with providing a comfortable, energy-saving and human-friendly environment

Sustainability is increasingly accepted as a guideline for improvement and innovation in future development within the global construction sector. It is also becoming a more important issue as consumers become more ethical along with the requirement to meet increasingly stringent building legislation.

There are a number of solutions which are currently being implemented and researched, and this section of the book provides budget costs for a host of solutions which are being adopted in society today.

The costs provided below are based on a domestic facility occupying 4 people. All costs exclude grants and maintenance.

Prices are all current at second quarter 2008 levels based on a UK average location.

Forms of Renewable Energy

There are various ways of generating renewable electricity, this section focuses on costs for heat pump installations and wind turbines. Photovoltaic (PV) panels are also considered and are listed later, under 'Roofing Systems'.

Ground Source Heat Pumps (GSHPs) include the cost for the unit and all associated pipework. Air Source Heat Pumps (ASHPs) include the cost for the unit and controller. GSHPs are approximately 60% more efficient than ASHPs at present, however ASHPs do not require piping and are an emerging solution as they are further developed. Roof mounted wind turbines are significantly cheaper than standalone wind turbines, however they have a longer payback period as they are considerably less productive. The life expectancy of the systems below range between 25–30 years.

Cost	Unit	
GSHP – 8KW	£8,500 – £11,000	Per System
GSHP – 23KW	£14,000 – £17,500	Per System
ASHP – 8KW	£5,750 – £8,000	Per System
ASHP – 148KW	£6,800 – £9,000	Per System
Roof Mounted Wind Turbine – 1.0KW	£1,550 – £3,000	Per System
Standalone Wind Turbine – 1.2KW	£10,500 – £12,000	Per System
Standalone Wind Turbine – 2.5KW	£12,000 – £14,500	Per System
Standalone Wind Turbine – 6.0KW	£19,000 – £23,000	Per System
Standalone Wind Turbine – 15.0KW	£41,000 – £44,500	Per System

Wall Construction

A number of sustainable methods for constructing walls to provide high insulation standards have been in existence for hundreds of years. These sustainable methods are continually being developed but are still a relatively rare solution, only tending to appeal to ethical-minded consumers.

Stabilised Rammed Earth (SRE) is formed by compressing a damp mixture of earth with quantities of sand, gravel and clay into formwork. Cob is formed in the same way as SRE but has a slightly different composition, utilising clay, sand, straw, water and earth. The straw bale wall cost includes three coats of lime render on both sides of the wall. The timber wall cost includes structural insulated panel (SIPs) and joists.

	Cost	Unit
Straw bale (450mm)	£100 – £150	£/m^2
Timber (450mm)	£200 – £300	£/m^2
Cob Blocks (450mm)	£150 – £200	£/m^2
Cob (450mm)	£125 – £175	£/m^2
Stabilised Rammed Earth – SRE (300mm) – Without encapsulated insulation used for internal partition walls or garden walls	£100 – £150	£/m^2
Stabilised Rammed Earth – SRE (450mm) – Solid cavity walls with sufficient insulation to meet Building Regulations	£125 – £175	£/m^2

Roofing Systems

Photovoltaic (PV) Panels

PV panels are another form of providing renewable energy and exploit light created by the sun. Monocrystalline systems typically last approximately 30 years and tend to be slightly more efficient than polycrystalline systems. Polycrystalline are significantly lighter than the Monocrystalline systems being approximately half the thickness and typically last 25 years.

	Cost	Unit
Monocrystalline Silicon-based System	£895 – £1050	£/m^2
Polycrystalline Silicon-based System	£895 – £1050	£/m^2

Solar Hot water system options

Solar hot water systems facilitate the process of heating water, reducing the requirement for water heating. Solar hot water systems utilise the sun and are therefore better suited to sunnier climates. There are two main types of system employed in the United Kingdom; evacuated tube solar collectors and flat plate solar collectors. Flat plate solar collectors tend to comprise a thin absorber sheet backed by tubes containing water or antifreeze and are enclosed in an insulated shell, faced with glass. Evacuated tube solar collectors consist of a number of modular transparent glass tubes containing absorber tubes and are mounted in rows parallel to each other. Sunlight passes through the glass tubing and heats the absorber tube encased within them. For both systems the liquid within the tube is circulated and transported to a device which utilises the heated fluid, such as an insulated water tank or heat exchanger.

Sustainability

Evacuated tube collectors are more efficient, lighter and typically last around 25–30 years. Flat plate solar collectors panels are generally larger and last around 20–25 years.

Evacuated Tube Solar Collectors

	Cost	Unit
20 tube twin coil system (1050mm x 450mm) Sufficient for 144 litres	£3,370 – £3,600	£/unit
30 tube twin coil system (1800mm x 400mm) Sufficient for 210 litres	£3,700 – £3,900	£/unit

Flat Plate Solar Collectors

	Cost	Unit
2400mm x 1300mm, Sufficient for 210 litres	£3,450 – £3,700	£/unit

Landscaped roofs

Landscaped roofs, also known as green roofs, can be classified into three main categories; intensive, semi-intensive and extensive. Each category is classified by the amount of maintenance required and the depth of the soils. Intensive green roofs require a reasonable depth of soil to facilitate the growth of large plants and are labour-intensive. Extensive green roofs, by contrast, are designed to be virtually self-sustaining and require minimum maintenance. Semi-intensive green roofs fall in between extensive and intensive green roof systems. Some advantages associated with green roofs are; they utilise space and provide an amenity place for building users, they can reduce storm water run off, they advocate the habitat of wildlife and they can also reduce heating requirements because the high insulation standards they achieve.

	Cost	Unit
Intensive	£175 – £210	£/m^2
Semi-Intensive	£165 – £190	£/m^2
Extensive	£140 – £180	£/m^2

Roof Lights

Rooflights are an effective means of reducing the requirement of artificial lighting as they exploit the use of natural light from by the sun. The drawback associated with rooflights is they tend to have poorer insulation standards than the roof they occupy. The costs for the rooflights take into consideration the cost associated with cutting a hole in the roof and installing them.

	Cost	Unit
Stardome double skin polycarbonate dome with a PVC kerb – 600mm x 600mm	£395 – £450	£/Unit
– 1200mm x 1200mm	£790 – £900	£/Unit
– 1800mm x 1800mm	£1,350 – £1,600	£/Unit

Sunpipes

Sunpipes are another effective means of reducing the requirement of artificial lighting as they exploit the use of natural light created by the sun. Sunpipes can pipe natural daylight where daylight from windows cannot reach. A minor drawback associated with sunpipes is that they tend to have poorer insulation standards than the roof they occupy, but due to the size of the sunpipe the effect they have is minimal. The costs for the sunpipes take into consideration installation costs including forming the roof aperture to accommodate the unit.

		Cost	Unit
Pitched Roof Sunpipe	– 230mm	£415 – £550	£/Unit
	– 300mm	£475 – £700	£/Unit
	– 450mm	£565 – £800	£/Unit
	– 530mm	£615 – £950	£/Unit
Flat Roof Sunpipe	– 230mm	£450 – £550	£/Unit
	– 300mm	£525 – £600	£/Unit
	– 450mm	£655 – £750	£/Unit
	– 530mm	£732 – £800	£/Unit

Domestic Rainwater Recycling

Domestic rainwater recycling, also referred to as rainwater harvesting, is an effective way of reducing the requirement of mains water. Rainwater is collected from the roof of the house and drained into a storage tank. This water can be used for a range of systems and, if treated correctly, can be potable. In the instance below we have considered systems which only use the water for partial main water use, such as for flushing toilets and washing laundry. The costs for the rainwater recycling systems take into consideration installation costs along with the cost for supplying a full working system.

Glass Reinforced Plastic (GRP) Tank

	Cost	Unit
3000-litre – underground tank, partial mains water use	£3,250 – £3,600	£/unit
3000-litre – above-ground tank, partial mains water use	£3,500 – £3,900	£/unit

Sustainability

Concrete Tank

	Cost	Unit
3000-litre – underground tank, partial mains water use	£3,450 – £3,800	£/unit
3000-litre – above-ground tank, partial mains water use	£3,750 – £4,300	£/unit

Compost Toilet

Toilets traditionally account for approximately a quarter of water use within residential facilities. Compost toilets do not use water and therefore save on its use. Composting toilets provide an environment for waste to decompose naturally. Materials such as sawdust and straw are used to help absorb excess liquid and when the container is filled, the waste is removed. The costs for the compost toilet take into consideration the cost for supply and installation.

	Cost	Unit
Compost Toilet	£3,950 – £4,800	£/unit

Memoranda

EXCAVATION

Excavated material bulking

Material	Bulking per m^3
Loose sand	1.05
Loose gravel	1.10
Compacted sand	1.20
Compacted gravel	1.25
Soft clay	1.25
Firm clay	1.25
Loamy soil	1.25
Vegetable soil	1.25
Subsoil	1.25
Stiff clay	1.40
Hard boulder clay	1.50
Weathered rock	1.60
Solid chalk	1.75
Unweathered rock	1.75

CONCRETE WORK

Material quantities per 1 m^3 of concrete

Nominal concrete mix (by volume)	Cement (m^3)	Moist sand (m^3)	Coarse aggregate (m^3)
1:1.5:3	0.273	0.545	0.818
1:2:4	0.214	0.572	0.857
1:3:6	0.150	0.600	0.900

Nominal concrete mix (by weight)	Cement (tonnes)	Moist sand (tonnes)	Coarse aggregate (tonnes)
1:1.5:3	0.393	0.687	1.227
1:2:4	0.308	0.721	1.286
1:3:6	0.216	0.756	1.350

REINFORCEMENT

Steel bar reinforcement

Bar diameter	Nominal weight (kg/m)	Length (m/tonne)	Sectional area (mm^2)
6 mm	0.222	4505	28.27
8 mm	0.395	2532	50.27
10 mm	0.616	1623	78.54
12 mm	0.888	1126	113.10
16 mm	1.579	633	201.06
20 mm	2.466	406	314.16
25 mm	3.854	259	452.39
32 mm	6.313	158	804.25
40 mm	9.864	101	1256.64
50 mm	15.413	65	1963.50

Steel fabric reinforcement

BS 4483 reference	Nominal weight (kg/m^2)	Mesh dimensions Main (mm)	Cross (mm)	Wire diameters Main (mm)	Cross (mm)
A 98	1.54	200	200	5	5
A 142	2.22	200	200	6	6
A 193	3.02	200	200	7	7
A 252	3.95	200	200	8	8
A 393	6.16	200	200	10	10
B 196	3.05	100	200	5	7
B 283	3.73	100	200	6	7
B 385	4.53	100	200	7	7
B 503	5.93	100	200	8	8
B 785	8.14	100	200	10	8
B 1131	10.90	100	200	12	8
C 283	2.61	100	400	6	5
C 385	3.41	100	400	7	5
C 503	4.34	100	400	8	5
C 636	5.55	80-130	400	8-10	6
C 785	6.72	100	400	10	6
D 49	0.77	100	100	2.5	2.5
D 98	1.54	200	200	5	5

BRICKWORK AND BLOCKWORK

Quantities of bricks and mortar per m² (excluding waste)

Basis: 215 x 102.5 x 65 mm size bricks

10 mm mortar joints, 4 courses = 300 mm
One snapped header per facing brick
Net quantities, no allowance for waste

	Common bricks Nr/m²	Facing bricks Nr/mm²	Mortar for brick types	
			Solid mm³/mm²	Single frog mm³/mm²
Unfaced walls				
102.5 mm	59.26	–	0.018	0.022
215 mm	118.52	–	0.045	0.054
327.5 mm	177.78	–	0.073	0.086
Faced walls				
102.5 mm in stretcher bond	–	59.3	0.018	0.022
102.5 mm in English bond with snapped headers	–	88.9	0.020	0.025
102.5 mm in Flemish bond with snapped headers	–	79.0	0.019	0.024
Walls in English bond				
215 mm – faced one side	29.6	88.9	0.045	0.054
327.5 mm – faced one side	88.9	88.9	0.073	0.086
Walls in English bond				
215 mm – faced both sides	–	118.5	0.045	0.054
327.5 mm – faced both sides	–	177.8	0.074	0.086
Walls in Flemish bond				
215 mm – faced one side	39.5	79.0	0.045	0.054
327.5 mm – faced one side	98.8	79.0	0.074	0.086
Walls in Flemish bond				
215 mm – faced both sides	-	118.5	0.045	0.054
327.5 mm – faced both sides	19.8	158.0	0.074	0.086

Quantities of blocks and mortar per m² (excluding waste)
Basis: 440 x 215mm x nominated thickness work size blocks
10 mm mortar joints
Net quantities, no allowance for waste

Wall thickness	Blocks (Nr/m²)	Mortar (m³/m²)
60 mm	9.9	0.004
75 mm	9.9	0.005
90 mm	9.9	0.006
100 mm	9.9	0.007
140 mm	9.9	0.009
190 mm	9.9	0.013
215 mm	9.9	0.104
215 mm–100 mm blocks laid flat	20.2	0.024
215 mm–140 mm blocks laid flat	14.8	0.019

Mortar mixes
Basis: Cement 1440 kg/m³
Hydrated lime 500 kg/m³
Sand: 1260 kg/m³ moist
Net quantities, no allowance for waste
By volume (per m³ of mortar):

Mix	Cement m³	Lime m³	Sand (moist) m³
1:1	0.725	-	0.967
1:2	0.467	-	1.244
1:3	0.338	-	1.349
1:4	0.260	-	1.387
1:6	0.179	-	1.428
1:1:5	0.196	0.196	1.311
1:1:6	0.169	0.169	1.349
1:2:9	0.113	0.225	1.349

Mortar mixes
By weight (per m³ of mortar):

Mix	Cement kg	Lime kg	Sand (moist) kg
1:1	1044	–	1218
1:2	672	–	1567
1:3	487	–	1700
1:4	374	–	1748
1:6	258	–	1799
1:1:5	282	98	1652
1:1:6	243	85	1700
1:2:9	163	113	1700

Memoranda

STEELWORK

Structural steel sections

Size mm	Weight kg/m	Size mm	Weight kg/m	Size mm	Weight kg/m
Universal beams - BS 4: Part 1: 1993		457 × 191	98.3	152 × 89	16.0
1016 × 305	487.0		89.3	127 × 76	13.0
	438.0		82.0		
	393.0		74.3	**Universal columns - BS**	
	349.0	457 × 152	67.1	**EN10025 1993 Grade 275 JR**	
	314.0		82.1		
	272.0		74.2	356 × 406	633.9
	249.0		67.2		551.0
	222.0		59.8		467.0
914 × 419	388.0		52.3		393.0
	343.3	406 × 178	74.2		339.9
914 × 305	289.1		67.1		287.1
	253.4		60.1		235.1
	224.2		54.1		
	200.9	406 × 140	46.0	356 × 368	201.9
838 × 292	226.5		39.0		177.0
	193.8	356 × 171	67.1		152.9
	175.9		57.0		129.0
762 × 267	196.8		51.0		
	173.0		45.0	305 × 305	282.9
	146.9	356 × 127	39.1		240.0
	133.9		33.1		198.1
686 × 254	170.2	305 × 165	54.0		158.1
	152.4		46.1		136.9
	140.1		40.3		117.9
	125.2	305 × 127	48.1		96.9
610 × 305	238.1		41.9		
	179.0		37.0	254 × 254	167.1
	149.1	305 × 102	32.8		132.0
610 X 229	139.9		28.2		107.1
	125.1		24.8		88.9
	113.0	254 × 146	43.0		73.1
	101.2		37.0		
533 × 210	122.0		31.1	203 × 203	86.1
	109.0	254 × 102	28.3		71.0
	101.0		25.2		60.0
	92.1		22.0		52.0
	82.2	203 × 133	30.0		46.1
			25.1		
		203 × 102	23.1		
		178 × 102	19.0		

Structural steel sections (contd)

Size mm	Weight kg/m	Size mm	Weight kg/m	Size mm	Weight kg/m
152 × 152	37.0	**Equal angles**		40 × 40 × 6	3.52
	30.0			40 × 40 × 5	2.97
	23.0	200 × 200 × 24	71.1	40 × 40 × 4	2.42
		200 × 200 × 20	59.9	40 × 40 × 3	1.84
Joists		200 × 200 × 18	54.2	30 × 30 × 5	2.18
		200 × 200 × 16	48.5	30 × 30 × 4	1.78
254 × 203	82.0	150 × 150 × 18	40.1	30 × 30 × 3	1.36
203 × 152	53.3	150 × 150 × 15	33.8	25 × 25 × 5	1.77
152 × 127	37.3	150 × 150 × 12	27.3	25 × 25 × 4	1.45
127 × 114	29.3	150 × 150 × 10	23.0	25 × 25 × 3	1.11
127 × 114	27.1	120 × 120 × 15	26.6		
102 × 102	23.0	120 × 120 × 12	21.6	**Unequal angles**	
102 × 44	7.5	120 × 120 × 10	18.2		
89 × 89	19.5	120 × 120 × 8	14.7	200 × 150 × 18	47.1
76 × 76	12.8	100 × 100 × 15	21.9	200 × 150 × 15	39.6
		100 × 100 × 12	17.8	200 × 150 × 12	32.0
Channels		100 × 100 × 10	15.0	200 × 100 × 15	33.7
		100 × 100 × 8	12.2	200 × 100 × 12	27.3
430 × 100	64.4	90 × 90 × 12	15.9	200 × 100 × 10	23.0
		90 × 90 × 10	13.4		
380 × 100	54.0	90 × 90 × 8	10.9	150 × 90 × 15	26.6
300 × 100	45.5	90 × 90 × 7	9.61	150 × 90 × 12	21.6
300 × 90	41.4	90 × 90 × 6	8.30	150 × 90 × 10	18.2
				150 × 75 × 15	24.8
260 × 90	34.8	80 × 80 × 10	11.9	150 × 75 × 12	20.2
260 × 75	27.6	80 × 80 × 8	9.63	150 × 75 × 10	17.0
230 × 90	32.2	80 × 80 × 6	7.34	125 × 75 × 12	17.8
230xX 75	25.7	70 × 70 × 10	10.3	125 × 75 × 10	15.0
200 × 90	29.7	70 × 70 × 8	8.36	125 × 75 × 8	12.2
200 × 75	23.4	70 × 70 × 6	6.38	100 × 75 × 12	15.4
		60 × 60 × 10	8.69	100 × 75 × 10	13.0
180 × 90	26.1	60 × 60 × 8	7.09	100 × 75 × 8	10.6
180 × 75	20.3	60 × 60 × 6	5.42	100 × 65 × 10	12.3
150 × 90	23.9	60 × 60 × 5	4.57	100 × 65 × 8	9.94
150 × 75	17.9	50 × 50 × 8	5.82	100 × 65 × 7	8.77
125 × 65	14.8	50 × 50 × 6	4.47		
100 × 50	10.2	50 × 50 × 5	3.77	80 × 60 × 8	8.34
		50 × 50 × 4	3.06	80 × 60 × 7	7.36
		50 × 50 × 3	2.33	80 × 60 × 6	6.37
		45 × 45 × 6	4.00	75 × 50 × 8	7.39
		45 × 45 × 5	3.38	75 × 50 × 6	5.65
		45 × 45 × 4	2.74	65 × 50 × 8	6.75
		45 × 45 × 3	2.09	65 × 50 × 6	5.16

Structural steel sections (contd)

Size mm	Weight kg/m	Size mm	Weight kg/m	Size mm	Weight kg/m
65 × 50 × 5	4.35	244.5 × 20	111	48.3 × 5	5.34
60 × 30 × 6	3.99	244.5 × 16	90.2	48.3 × 4	4.37
60 × 30 × 5	3.37	244.5 × 12.5	71.5	48.3 × 3.2	3.56
40 × 25 × 4	1.93	244.5 × 10	57.8	42.4 × 4	3.79
		244.5 × 8	46.7	42.4 × 3.2	3.09
Circular hollow sections – EN 10210		244.5 × 6.3	37.0	42.4 × 2.5	2.46
		219.1 × 20	98.2	33.7 × 4	2.93
		219.1 × 16	80.1	33.7 × 3.2	2.41
457 × 40	411	219.1 × 12.5	63.7	33.7 × 2.5	1.92
457 × 32	335	219.1 × 10	51.6	26.9 × 3.2	1.87
457 × 25	266	219.1 × 8	41.6	21.3 × 3.2	1.43
457 × 20	216	219.1 × 6.3	33.1		
457 × 16	174			**Rectangular hollow sections**	
457 × 12.5	137	193.7 × 16	70.1		
457 × 10	110	193.7 × 12.5	55.9		
406.4 × 32	295	193.7 × 10	45.3	450 × 250 × 16	166
406.4 × 25	235	193.7 × 8	36.6	450 × 250 × 12.5	131
406.4 × 20	191	193.7 × 6.3	29.1	450 × 250 × 10	106
406.4 × 16	154	193.7 × 5.0	23.3	400 × 200 x16	141
406.4 × 12.5	121			400 × 200 × 12.5	112
406.4 × 10	97.8			400 × 200 × 10	90.2
		168.3 × 10	39.0		
355.6 × 25	204	168.3 × 8	31.6	300 × 200 × 16	115
355.6 × 20	166	168.3 × 6.3	25.2	300 × 200 × 12.5	91.9
355.6 × 16	134	168.3 × 5	20.1	300 × 200 × 10	74.5
355.6 × 12.5	106	139.7 × 10	32.0	300 × 200 × 8	60.3
355.6 × 10	85.2	139.7 × 8	26.0	300 × 200 × 6.5	47.9
355.6 × 8	68.6	139.7 × 6.3	20.7		
323.9 × 25	184	139.7 × 5	16.6	250 × 150 × 16	90.3
323.9 × 20	150	114.3 × 6.3	16.8	250 × 150 × 12.5	72.3
323.9 × 16	121	114.3 × 5	13.5	250 × 150 × 10	58.8
323.9 × 12.5	96.0	114.3 × 3.6	9.83	250 × 150 × 8	47.7
323.9 × 10	77.4			250 × 150 × 6.3	38.0
323.9 × 8	62.3	88.9 × 5	10.3	200 × 100 × 16	65.2
		88.9 × 4	8.38	200 × 100 × 12.5	52.7
273 × 25	153	88.9 × 3.2	6.76	200 × 100 × 10	43.1
273 × 20	125	76.1 × 5	8.77	200 × 100 × 8	35.1
273 × 16	101	76.1 × 4	7.11	200 × 100 × 6.3	28.1
273 × 12.5	80.3	76.1 × 3.2	5.75	200 × 100 × 5	22.6
273 × 10	64.9	60.3 × 5	6.82		
273 × 8	52.3	60.3 × 4	5.55	160 × 80 × 10	33.7
273 × 6.3	41.4	60.3 × 3.2	4.51	160 × 80 × 8	27.6

Structural steel sections (contd)

Size mm	Weight kg/m	Size mm	Weight kg/m	Size mm	Weight kg/m
160 × 80 × 6.3	22.2	350 × 350 × 16	166	100 × 100 × 8	22.6
160 × 80 × 5	17.8	350 × 350 × 12.5	131	100 × 100 × 6.3	18.2
150 × 100 × 10	35.3	350 × 350 × 10	106	100 × 100 × 5	14.7
150 × 100 × 8	28.9	300 × 300 × 16	141	100 × 100 × 4	11.9
150 × 100 × 6.3	23.1	300 × 300 × 12.5	112		
150 × 100 × 5	18.6	300 × 300 × 10	90.2	90 × 90 × 6.3	16.2
120 × 80 × 10	27.4			90 × 90 × 5	13.1
120 × 80 × 8	22.6	250 × 250 × 16	115	90 × 90 × 3.6	9.66
120 × 80 × 6.3	18.2	250 × 250 × 12.5	91.9	80 × 80 × 6.3	14.2
120 × 80 × 5	14.7	250 × 250 × 10	74.5	80 × 80 × 5	11.6
120 × 60 × 6.3	16.2	250 × 250 × 8	60.3	80 × 80 × 3.6	8.53
120 × 60 × 5	13.1	250 × 250 × 6.3	47.9	70 × 70 × 5	9.99
120 × 60 × 3.6	9.72	200 × 200 × 16	90.3	70 × 70 × 3.6	7.40
100 × 60 × 6.3	14.2	200 × 200 × 12.5	72.3	60 × 60 × 5	8.42
100 × 60 × 5	11.6	200 × 200 × 10	58.8	60 × 60 × 4	6.90
100 × 60 × 3.6	8.53	200 × 200 × 8	47.7	60 × 60 × 3.2	5.62
100 × 50 × 5	10.8	200 × 200 × 6.3	38.0	50 × 50 × 5	6.85
100 × 50 × 4	8.78			50 × 50 × 4	5.64
100 × 50 × 3.2	7.13	180 × 180 × 16	80.2	50 × 50 × 3.2	4.62
		180 × 180 × 12.5	64.4	40 × 40 × 4	4.39
90 × 50 × 5	9.99	180 × 180 × 10	52.5	40 × 40 × 3.2	3.61
90 × 50 × 3.6	7.40	180 × 180 × 8	42.7	40 × 40 × 2.6	2.89
80 × 40 × 4	6.90	180 × 180 × 6.3	34.0	30 × 30 × 3.2	2.65
80 × 40 × 3.2	5.62	150 × 150 × 16	65.2	30 × 30 × 2.6	2.21
60 × 40 × 4	5.64	150 × 150 × 12.5	52.7	20 × 20 × 2.6	1.39
60 × 40 × 3.2	4.62	150 × 150 × 10	43.1	20 × 20 × 2	1.12
50 × 30 × 3.2	3.61	150 × 150 × 8	35.1		
50 × 30 × 2.5	2.89	150 × 150 × 6.3	28.1		
		150 × 150 × 5	22.6		
Square hollow sections - EN 10210		120 × 120 × 10	33.7		
		120 × 120 × 8	27.6		
		120 × 120 × 6.3	22.2		
400 × 400 × 12.5	151	120 × 120 × 5	17.8		
400 × 400 × 10	122	100 × 100 × 10	27.4		

ROOFING

Slating and tiling quantities per m²

Basis: Lap is length of cover of one tile/slate over unit under
Gauge is tiling/slating batten centres and length of tile/slate exposed

Centre nailed slates

Slate size mm	Lap mm	Gauge mm	Slates Nr/m²	Battens m/m²
610 × 305	76	267	12.3	3.7
610 × 305	100	255	12.9	3.9
600 × 300	76	262	12.7	3.8
600 × 300	100	250	13.3	4.0
510 × 255	76	217	18.1	4.6
510 × 255	100	205	19.1	4.9
500 × 250	76	212	18.9	4.7
500 × 250	100	200	20.0	5.0
405 × 205	75	165	29.6	6.1
405 × 205	95	155	31.5	6.5
400 × 200	70	165	30.3	6.1
400 × 200	90	155	32.3	6.5

Plain tiles

Tile size mm	Lap mm	Gauge mm	Tiles Nr/m²	Battens m/m²
265 × 165	38	114	53.2	8.8
265 × 165	65	100	60.6	10.0

Single lap tiles

Tile size mm	Cover width mm	Lap mm	Gauge mm	Tiles Nr/m²	Battens m/m²
430 × 380	343	75	355	8.2	2.8
430 × 380	343	100	330	8.8	3.0
420 × 332	300	75	345	9.7	2.9
420 × 332	300	100	320	10.4	3.1
413 × 330	292	75	338	10.1	3.0
413 × 330	292	100	313	10.9	3.2
380 × 230	200	75	305	16.4	3.3
380 × 230	200	100	280	17.9	3.6

Nail quantities per kilogramme

Round lost head nails

Aluminium		Copper		Steel	
Length × shank mm	Nr/kg	Length × shank mm	Nr/kg	Length × shank mm	Nr/kg
75 × 3.75	448	65 × 3.75	178	75 × 3.75	160
65 × 3.35	672	65 × 3.35	194	65 × 3.35	240
60 × 3.35	756	50 × 3.35	292	65 × 3.00	270
50 × 3.35	860	50 × 3.00	308	60 × 3.35	270
50 × 3.00	1008	40 × 2.65	474	60 × 3.00	330
40 × 2.65	1390	40 × 2.36	554	50 × 3.00	360
40 × 2.36	2128			50 × 2.65	420
				40 × 2.36	760

Extra large head felt nails

Aluminium		Copper		Steel	
Length × shank mm	Nr/kg	Length × shank mm	Nr/kg	Length × shank mm	Nr/kg
25 × 3.35	1296	25 × 3.35	440	40 × 3.00	350
25 × 3.00	1636	25 × 3.00	517	30 × 3.00	420
20 × 3.35	1848	20 × 3.35	544	25 × 3.00	485
20 × 3.00	2130	20 × 3.00	627	20 × 3.00	580
15 × 3.35	1840	15 × 3.00	691	15 × 3.00	650
15 × 3.00	2283	13 × 3.00	880	13 × 3.00	780

Memoranda

Clout, slate or tile nails

Aluminium		Copper		Steel	
Length × shank mm	Nr/kg	Length × shank mm	Nr/kg	Length × shank mm	Nr/kg
65 × 3.75	504	65 × 3.75	170	100 × 4.50	75
60 × 3.75	550	65 × 3.35	195	90 × 4.50	85
60 × 3.35	680	50 × 3.35	241	75 × 3.75	150
50 × 3.75	644	50 × 3.00	276	65 × 3.75	180
50 × 3.35	812	50 × 2.65	327	50 × 3.75	230
50 × 3.00	952	45 × 3.35	308	50 × 3.35	290
45 × 3.35	924	45 × 3.00	366	50 × 3.00	340
45 × 3.00	1060	45 × 2.65	456	50 × 2.65	430
40 × 3.35	980	40 × 3.35	335	45 × 3.35	330
40 × 3.00	1200	40 × 3.00	398	45 × 2.65	460
40 × 2.65	1596	40 × 2.65	460	40 × 3.35	350
40 × 2.36	1960	40 × 2.36	553	40 × 2.65	570
30 × 3.00	1512	30 × 3.35	448	40 × 2.36	700
30 × 2.65	1848	30 × 3.00	550	30 × 3.00	540
30 × 2.36	2324	30 × 2.65	621	30 × 2.65	660
30 × 2.00	3000	30 × 2.36	748	30 × 2.36	830
25 × 3.35	1540	25 × 2.65	740	25 × 2.65	815
25 × 3.00	1750	20 × 2.65	920	20 × 2.65	1035
25 × 2.65	2282			15 × 2.36	1540
25 × 2.00	3800			15 × 2.00	2380
20 × 3.00	2300				
20 × 2.65	2898				

Sheet metal information

Sheet lead

Thickness mm	BS Code	Colour Code
1.32	3	Green
1.80	4	Blue
2.24	5	Red
2.65	6	Black
3.15	7	White
3.55	8	Orange

Sheet zinc

Thickness mm	ZG
0.45	9
0.65	12
0.80	14

Sheet copper

Thickness mm	SWG
0.45	26
0.55	24
0.70	22

Sheet aluminium

Thickness mm	SWG
0.60	23
0.80	21

Sawn timber lengths per m^3

Basis: No allowance for saw cut waste

Timber section size mm × mm

x	16	19	22	25	32	44	50	63	75	100	125	150	175	200	225	250	275	300
16	3906	3289	2841	2500	1953	1420	1250	992	833	625	500	417	357	313	278	250	227	208
19	3289	2770	2392	2105	1645	1196	1053	835	702	526	421	351	301	263	234	211	191	175
22	2841	2392	2066	1818	1420	1033	909	722	606	455	364	303	260	227	202	182	165	152
25	2500	2105	1818	1600	1250	909	800	635	533	400	320	267	229	200	178	160	145	133
32	1953	1645	1420	1250	977	710	625	496	417	313	250	208	179	156	139	125	114	104
44	1420	1196	1033	909	710	517	455	361	303	227	182	152	130	114	101	91	83	76
50	1250	1053	909	800	625	455	400	317	267	200	160	133	114	100	89	80	73	67
63	992	835	722	635	496	361	317	252	212	159	127	106	91	79	71	63	58	53
75	833	702	606	533	417	303	267	212	178	133	107	89	76	67	59	53	48	44
100	625	526	455	400	313	227	200	159	133	100	80	67	57	50	44	40	36	33
125	500	421	364	320	250	182	160	127	107	80	64	53	46	40	36	32	29	27
150	417	351	303	267	208	152	133	106	89	67	53	44	38	33	30	27	24	22
175	357	301	260	229	179	130	114	91	76	57	46	38	33	29	25	23	21	19
200	313	263	227	200	156	114	100	79	67	50	40	33	29	25	22	20	18	17
225	278	234	202	178	139	101	89	71	59	44	36	30	25	22	20	18	16	15
250	250	211	182	160	125	91	80	63	53	40	32	27	23	20	18	16	15	13
275	227	191	165	145	114	83	73	58	48	36	29	24	21	18	16	15	13	12
300	208	175	152	133	104	76	67	53	44	33	27	22	19	17	15	13	12	11

WOODWORK

Standard sawn softwood lengths

1.8 m			
2.1 m	2.4 m	2.7 m	
3.0 m	3.3 m	3.6 m	3.9 m
4.2 m	4.5 m	4.8 m	
5.1 m	5.4 m	5.7 m	
6.0 m	6.3 m	6.6 m	6.9 m
7.2 m			

Timber boarding quantities per m^2

Basis: No allowance for waste

Cover width mm	Length m/m^2
75	13.33
100	10.00
125	8.00
150	6.67
175	5.71
200	5.00

FINISHES

Plaster coverage per tonne

Basis: No allowance for waste

Type	Thickness of coating				
	2 mm m²/tonne	3 mm m²/tonne	5 mm m²/tonne	8 mm m²/tonne	11 mm m²/tonne
Thistle plaster					
Undercoat	–	–	–	160	115
Finish	400	260	165	–	–
Carlite plaster					
Browning	–	–	–	–	140
Metal lathing	–	–	–	–	65
Bonding coat	–	–	–	135	90
Finish coat	450	–	–	–	–

Render coverings per m³

Basis: No allowance for waste

	Thickness of coating				
	6 mm m²/m³	10 mm m²/m³	13 mm m²/m³	16 mm m²/m³	20 mm m²/m³
Background					
Blockwork (non-grooved or keyless faces)	109	72	58	48	40
Brickwork (grooved face or raked joints)	87	62	51	43	36
Rubble substrate	72	54	46	40	33

PAINTING & DECORATING

Coverage of decorating materials

	Surface finish					
	Plaster m^2/litre	Render m^2/litre	Concrete m^2/litre	Brickwork m^2/litre	Blockwork m^2/litre	Joinery m^2/litre
Water thinned primer as primer	13–15	–	–	–	–	10–14
Water thinned primer as u/coat	–	–	–	–	–	12–15
Oil wood primer	–	–	–	–	–	8–11
Emulsion – contract	10–12	7–11	10–12	7–10	5–9	10–12
Emulsion – standard	12–15	8–12	11–14	8–12	6–10	10–12
Plaster primer	9–11	8–12	9–11	7–9	5–7	–
Alkali resistant primer	7–11	6–8	7–11	6–8	5–7	–
External wall primer sealer	6–8	6–7	6–8	5–7	4–6	–
Undercoat	11–14	7–9	7–9	6–8	6–8	11–14
Gloss top coat	11–14	8–10	8–10	7–9	6–8	11–14
Eggshell (oil based)	11–14	9–11	11–14	8–10	7–9	11–14
Masonry paint	5–7	4–6	5–7	4–6	3–5	–
	m^2/kg	m^2/kg	m^2/kg	m^2/kg	m^2/kg	
Cement based paint	-	4–6	6–7	3–6	3–6	–
Oil bound water paint	7–9	4–6	7–9	4–6	5–7	

DRAINAGE

Pipe bedding and coverings per m length

Basis: No allowance for waste

Pipe internal diameter	100 mm	150 mm	225 mm	300 mm
Width of bed	450 mm	525 mm	600 mm	750 mm
Material requirements (m^3/m):				
50 mm bed	0.023	0.026	0.030	0.038
100 mm bed	0.045	0.053	0.060	0.075
150 mm bed	0.068	0.079	0.090	0.113
100 mm bed and haunching	0.070	0.089	0.113	0.158
150 mm bed and haunching	0.093	0.116	0.143	0.196
100 mm bed and surround	0.140	0.179	0.225	0.316
150 mm bed and surround	0.185	0.231	0.285	0.391